W9-CLN-172

Introduction to Computer Science with C++

SECOND EDITION

Introduction to Computer Science with C++

Kenneth A. Lambert
Washington and Lee University

Douglas W. Nance
Central Michigan University

Thomas L. Naps
Lawrence University

Australia • Canada • Mexico • Singapore • Spain • United Kingdom • United States

Sponsoring Editor: *Kallie Swanson*
Marketing Team: *Nathan Wilbur, Christina De Veto, Samantha Cabaluna*
Editorial Assistant: *Grace Fujimoto*
Production Coordinator: *Kelsey McGee*
Project Management: *Carlisle Publishers Services/Larry Goldberg*
Manuscript Editor: *Frank Hubert*
Permissions Editor: *Mary Kay Hancharick*
Interior Design: *John Edeen*
Cover Design: *Laurie Albrecht*
Typesetting: *Carlisle Communications, Ltd.*
Cover Printing: *Phoenix Color Corporation*
Printing and Binding: *World Color Corporation/Versailles*

For more information, contact:
BROOKS/COLE
511 Forest Lodge Road
Pacific Grove, CA 93950 USA
www.brookscole.com

Printed in the United States of America

10 9 8 7 6 5 4 3 2

Library of Congress Cataloging-in-Publication Data

Lambert, Kenneth Alfred, 1951–
Introduction to computer science with C++/Kenneth A. Lambert, Douglas W. Nance, Thomas L. Naps.—2nd ed.
p. cm.
ISBN 0-534-36893-X
1. Computer science. 2. C++ (Computer program language) I. Nance, Douglas W. II. Naps, Thomas L. III. Title.
QA76.L26 2000
005.13'3—dc21 99-026729

To Ken's children: Sara, Jason, Caleb, Catherine, Savannah, and Nathaniel

Contents

5 Selection Statements 153

6 Repetition Statements 225

Preface

In many introductory science and math courses, one textbook is used over two or three semesters. This spiral approach allows, at each stage of the course sequence, an integration of recurring themes as well as a gradual increase in the complexity and abstraction of the concepts presented. Although a student's introductory experience in computer science has matured into a two-semester sequence (typically labeled CS1 and CS2 following the guidelines of the ACM's Curriculum Committee), we still find that there is a dearth of texts designed to span such a sequence. Too often, we find that CS1 is taught using a text that does not go much beyond learning to write programs in a particular language. Then, in the CS2 course, students are asked to switch gears and adapt to a much more rigorous style of presentation.

A related problem has arisen concerning students' knowledge of a programming language when they begin the CS2 course. This was not a major problem when CS1 and CS2 used Pascal because most instructors assumed that most students had covered most of the language in CS1. However, the enormous size of C++ has made it possible to cover widely varying subsets of the language in the CS1 course, so students may come to CS2 with widely different competencies in the language.

Our goal in developing *Introduction to Computer Science with C++* is to provide a text that views CS1 and CS2 as a unified whole. In particular, this text is designed with the following objectives in mind:

1. To provide students with a fundamental understanding of how to solve problems in C++. Such knowledge of C++ is viewed as one of the foundational blocks that allows students to explore the ideas and techniques of computer science.
2. To present C++ in a context that emphasizes a structured, top-down approach to problem solving. Students should realize that computer science is primarily problem solving, not programming.
3. To demonstrate the application of software engineering principles in designing, coding, and testing large programs.
4. To introduce students to essential data structures such as linked lists, stacks, queues, trees, and (optionally) graphs. This introduction emphasizes the specification of each structure as an abstract data type (ADT) before discussing implementations and applications of that structure.
5. To make students aware of the importance of object-oriented methods in developing software, particularly in the design and implementation of abstract data types.
6. To provide a systematic approach to the study of algorithms that focuses first on understanding the action of the algorithm and then on analyzing the algorithm from a space/time perspective. In particular, searching, sorting, and recursive algorithms are covered in detail.
7. To give students an overview of what lies ahead in computer science.

Overview and Organization

Chapters 1 through 9 constitute the core of a CS1 course. The material in Chapters 1 through 6 covers the basics of problem solving and algorithm development using the standard control structures of expression evaluation, sequencing, selection, iteration, and procedural abstraction. This material is presented at a deliberate pace. If students in the class have already had some programming experience, these chapters may be covered rapidly. However, students must be able to solve problems with top-down design and stepwise refinement. If this is overlooked, they will have difficulty designing solutions to more complex problems later.

Subprograms are presented fairly early in the text. User-defined functions with input and output parameters are presented in Chapter 4 before either selection statements (Chapter 5) or iteration statements (Chapter 6). This facilitates good problem-solving habits in that a completely modular approach can be emphasized early in the course.

We have made a large effort to acknowledge the increasing importance of object-oriented methods in the computer science community. In the first six chapters, this effort takes the form of allusions to and brief discussions of object-oriented design when appropriate. We also introduce the use of objects for strings, so students become familiar with the basic idea of sending a message to an object to receive a service. However, we have deliberately avoided presenting the implementation of user-defined classes in the first six chapters. We believe that students can best learn the fundamentals of algorithm development if they are provided with a small subset of C++ syntax and a model of computation that focuses on algorithms and the use of objects from the perspective of client programs that view objects as pure abstractions. The syntax required for implementation of user-defined classes is not simple; it is best introduced only when needed, primarily to develop data structures in the second half of a first course in computer science and to continue this development in the second course.

The material in Chapters 7 through 9 covers the use of basic data structures such as files, strings, records, and arrays. Careful attention is paid to the specification and implementation of all data structures as abstract data types. The focus in this part of the text shifts from the procedural approach used in developing algorithms to an object-oriented approach used in developing abstract data types.

Chapter 7 introduces file stream processing. It focuses on the use of file stream operations, primarily in conjunction with numeric, character, and string data. Because of its simple approach, this chapter could be used earlier or later in the first course if desired.

Chapter 8 explores object-oriented design in depth, using examples from data processing (a bank account management system) and mathematics (rational numbers). Appropriate examples of some useful features of object-oriented design, such as operator overloading, inheritance, and software reuse, are discussed and developed in these examples. We introduce a standard method of discussing user requirements, specifying attributes and behavior, and declaring and implementing a class, and then we use this method in the remaining chapters.

Chapter 9 discusses array operations in detail. After presenting a complete treatment of standard C++ arrays, we develop three important classes using arrays: a string class, a vector class, and a matrix class. These classes were developed for the Advanced Placement (AP) course in computer science and are similar to those in the C++ Standard Template Library.

Chapters 10 through 17 contain material for what might typically be called a CS2 course. Chapters 10 and 11 present more detailed treatment of the software engineering principles introduced in earlier chapters. Chapter 10 introduces big-O analysis as the essential tool used by the computer scientist in evaluating alternative strategies from a time/space perspective. Simple sorting and searching algorithms are used as examples for the application of big-O analysis. By reviewing some of the algorithms already presented in Chapter 9, we allow the student to concentrate on the intricacies of big-O analysis without having to worry about unraveling new and complex algorithms.

Chapter 11 continues and amplifies the formalism used to present abstract data types introduced in Chapters 8 and 9. This formalism consists of specifying an ADT's attributes and operations as a set of language-independent preconditions and post-conditions before moving to a C++ class declaration as an interface for the ADT. Rules for using and implementing ADTs are developed. Ordered collections, sorted collections, one-key tables, and two-key tables are presented as examples of ADTs. Because these ADTs lend themselves naturally to the use of keys and elements of different data types, the notions of generic ADTs and parameterized types can be introduced in this chapter and can be implemented with C++ class templates. Because students have studied big-O analysis in the preceding chapter, they are well equipped to compare and contrast the efficiencies of various implementations of these ADTs. These four ADTs and the use of class templates recur in the remainder of the text as we explore more advanced techniques for implementing other ADTs.

Chapter 11 also pulls together and expands on the software engineering issues introduced in earlier chapters. The chapter presents a detailed treatment of the analysis, design, implementation, testing, and maintenance stages of the software system life cycle. This treatment has been completely revised from the previous edition to emphasize a more object-oriented perspective on software engineering.

Chapters 12 through 15 cover the use of essential data structures and recursion in advanced problem-solving techniques. Each data structure is first defined as an abstract data type and then declared as a C++ class. Various implementations are discussed and compared using the big-O terminology of Chapter 10. This provides a convincing demonstration of the utility of big-O analysis.

Chapter 12, devoted to dynamic memory management, pointers, and linked lists, discusses how linked lists might be used as an alternative implementation of the ADTs introduced in Chapters 9 and 11. Chapter 13 covers stacks and queues, discussing parsing and simulation as applications of these ADTs. Chapter 14 explores recursion in depth. A graduated series of examples is presented, culminating with the use of trial-and-error backtracking as a problem-solving technique. Chapter 15 provides examples of the utility of recursion by using it as the primary technique for processing data in binary trees, general trees, and graphs. The importance of binary search trees as an alternative way of representing keyed tables is also discussed, with comparisons drawn to the array and linked list implementations previously covered in Chapters 11 and 12. The material on general trees, graphs, and networks in the final two sections of Chapter 15 can be omitted without affecting a student's understanding of the chapters that follow.

The background in software engineering and data structures found in Chapters 10 through 15 prepares the student for the more complex sorting and searching algorithms of Chapters 16 and 17. In Chapter 16, sorting methods that break the $O(n^2)$ barrier are investigated. These methods include the shell sort, quick sort, heap sort, and merge sort. Chapter 17 scrutinizes search techniques such as hashing, indexing, indexed sequential search, B-trees, and tries.

Throughout the text, we have attempted to explain and develop concepts carefully. These are illustrated by frequent examples and diagrams. New concepts are then used in complete programs to show how they aid in solving problems. We place an early and consistent emphasis on good writing habits and neat, readable documentation. We frequently offer communication and style tips where appropriate.

New in the Second Edition

As a result of extensive feedback from many users, we have made the following major changes for this edition:

1. We introduce the use of classes earlier, but we delay the discussion of how classes are implemented a bit longer. A string class appears for use in Chapter 3, but its implementation is not discussed until Chapter 9. Simple user-defined classes are first introduced in Chapter 8.
2. Material on structs has been inserted before the discussion of user-defined classes in Chapter 8.
3. Files are presented earlier, in Chapter 7.
4. The AP classes for strings, vectors, and matrices are discussed and thoroughly developed in the first nine chapters. Thereafter, these classes are frequently referred to; however, the vector and matrix classes are not used exclusively at the expense of avoiding all mention of standard C++ arrays. Hence, although the text is certainly appropriate for an AP course, it is also designed for instructors who want their students to acquire familiarity with C++ arrays beyond the classes developed for the AP curriculum.
5. The material on ADTs and software engineering in the second part of the book has been streamlined and consolidated into one chapter.
6. Linked lists (Chapter 12) are developed in a top-down manner, with a discussion of abstract operations preceding the implementation details of pointers.
7. Many Notes of Interest, Case Studies, and Programming Problems and Projects have been altered or replaced.

Features

This text has a number of noteworthy pedagogical features.

Chapter Outlines: Lists of the important topics covered are given at the beginning of each chapter.

Objectives: Each section starts with a concise list of learning objectives.

Communication and Style Tips: These suggestions for programming style are intended to enhance readability. The ACM has recently encouraged the development of communication skills to enhance the portability of programs.

Exercises: Short-answer questions intended to build analytical skills appear at the end of each section.

Programming Problems and Projects: Starting with Chapter 2, lengthy lists of suggestions for complete programs and projects are given at the end of each chapter. These cover different problem areas in computer science, such as data processing and mathematics. Some problems and projects run from chapter to chapter, providing students with a sense of problem solving as a cumulative enterprise that often requires programming in the large. Several assignments focus explicitly on improving students' communication skills in refining designs and writing documentation.

Module Specifications: Specifications are given for many program modules.

Structure Charts: We provide charts that reflect modular development and include the use of data flow arrows to emphasize transmission of data to and/or from each module. These charts set the stage for understanding the use of value and reference parameters when functions are introduced.

Notes of Interest: These are tidbits of information intended to create awareness of and interest in various aspects of computer science, including its historical context. Special attention is paid to issues of computer ethics and security.

Suggestions for Test Programs: Ideas included in the exercises are intended to encourage students to use the computer to determine answers to questions and to see how to implement concepts in short programs.

Case Studies: With the exceptions of Chapters 1 and 2 and a few of the later chapters, a complete program is listed at the end of the chapter that illustrates utilization of the concepts developed within the chapter. This section includes the complete development of a project from user requirements to specifications to pseudocode design to implementation and testing.

Running, Testing, and Debugging Hints: These hints will be useful to students as they work on the end-of-chapter programming problems.

Reading References: When appropriate, pointers are given to excellent sources for further reading on topics introduced in the text.

Key Terms: Important terms are italicized when introduced and listed at the end of each chapter.

There is a complete glossary, as well as appendices on reserved words, useful library functions, syntax diagrams, character sets, and the AP classes. The final section of the book provides answers to selected exercises.

This book covers only that portion of C++ necessary for the first two courses in computer science. Students wanting to learn more about the language are referred to the excellent source given in Appendix A.

Ancillaries

It is our belief that a broad-based teaching support package is essential for an introductory course using C++. Thus, the following ancillary materials are available from Brooks/Cole Publishing Company:

1. *Programs:* Programs from the text can be accessed via the publisher's Web site. The programs are written in platform-independent C++, which can be run immediately on most implementations.
2. *Instructor's Manual:* This manual contains, for each chapter, the chapter outline, teaching test questions, chapter test questions, answers to test questions, and solutions to even-numbered exercises and selected programming problems.
3. *Transparency Masters:* More than 100 transparency masters are available on-line to adopters of the text. The set of masters includes figures, tables, and selected other material from the text.

Each program segment in the text has been compiled and run. Hence, original versions were all working. Unfortunately, the publication process does allow errors in code to occur after a program has been run. Every effort has been made to produce an error-free text, although this cannot be guaranteed. We assume full responsibility for all errors and omissions. If you detect any, please be tolerant and notify us at *klambert@wlu.edu* so they can be corrected in subsequent printings and editions.

Acknowledgments

We would like to take this opportunity to thank those who in some way contributed to the completion of this text. Several reviewers contributed significant constructive comments during various phases of manuscript development. They include Hisham Al-Haddad, Marshall University; Charles Burris, Seattle Pacific University; Richard Genung, Meadville (Pennsylvania) Area Senior High School; Bryant Julstrom, St. Cloud State University; Ray Nanney, Furman University; William Hooper, Belmont University; Tadeusz Strzemecki, Fordham University at Lincoln Center; Renbing Xiong, Edinboro University of Pennsylvania; Brent Wilson, George Fox University; Erik Sand, Jamestown College; Riad Hammoudeh, Passaic County Community College; Jim Clark, University of Tennessee at Martin; and Michael Bolton, Northeastern State University.

Several other people deserve special mention because, without their expertise, this book would not exist:

Frank Hubert, copyeditor. Frank has a wonderful sense of where to apply Occam's razor to a sentence or paragraph and made many useful suggestions for improving not only style, but content as well.

Kelsey McGee, production coordinator. Kelsey has done a great job of coordinating work on several texts simultaneously. She keeps things running smoothly, and it is a pleasure working with her.

Larry Goldberg, production editor (Carlisle Publishers Services). Larry shepherded the manuscript through the editing and production phases and is responsible for the much improved look of the book.

Nathan Wibur, marketing manager. Nathan worked hard to highlight the features of the text that will make it known to the computer science community and has done a fine job.

Marlene Thom, media editor. Marlene assisted in putting together several of the ancillary materials.

Kallie Swanson, editor, and Suzanne Jeans, project developmental editor. Kallie and Suzanne lined up great reviewers and provided them with all of the relevant questions. They then digested the reviews into analyses that focused our attention immediately on the improvements that needed to be made at each phase of the development process.

Kenneth A. Lambert
Douglas W. Nance
Thomas L. Naps

Introduction to Computer Science with C++

1

Computer Science, Computer Architecture, and Computer Languages

Chapter Outline

A jet airplane crash-lands near a large American city. Although the plane catches fire on impact, all of the passengers and crew miraculously survive. Investigators find no clues from the crew or the flight recorders that point to the cause of the crash. However, using reports of observers on the ground about the behavior of the plane, they construct a computer simulation of the plane's behavior in the air. From this simulation, they hypothesize that a flaw in the plane's rudder might have caused it to go into a tailspin. They examine the parts of the rudder found at the crash site and confirm their hypothesis. The results of their investigation will be used to correct the flaw in the rudders of several hundred airplanes.

The investigators who constructed this simulation solved a problem by designing a program and running it on a computer. They may not have been trained as computer scientists, but they used techniques that have come to be associated with this exciting field.

This chapter provides a quick introduction to computer science, computer architecture, and computer languages. Section 1.1 provides a preview of the study of computer science. Section 1.2 examines the structure and parts of a computer and introduces the idea of computer software. Section 1.3 analyzes how computer languages are used to make a computer run.

As you read this chapter, do not be overly concerned about the introduction and early use of technical terminology. All terms will be subsequently developed. A good approach to an introductory chapter such as this is to reread it periodically. This will help you maintain a good perspective on how new concepts and techniques fit in the broader picture of using computers. Finally, remember that learning a language that will make a computer work can be exciting; being able to control such a machine can lead to quite a sense of accomplishment.

1.1 Computer Science: A Preview

Objectives

To understand that computer science is

a. mathematics and logic
b. science
c. engineering
d. communication
e. interdisciplinary

Computer science is a very young discipline. Electronic computers were initially developed in the 1940s. Those who worked with computers in the 1940s and 1950s often did so by teaching themselves about computers; most schools did not offer any instruction in computer science at that time. However, as these early pioneers in computers learned more about the machines they were using, a collection of principles began to evolve into the discipline we now call computer science. Because it emerged from the efforts of people using computers in a variety of disciplines, the influence of these disciplines can often be seen in computer science. With that in mind, in the next sections we will briefly describe what computer science is.

Computer Science as Computer Literacy

At the end of the 20th century, computer-literate people know how to use a variety of computer software to make their professional and domestic lives more productive and easier. This software includes, for instance, word processors for writing and data management systems for storing every conceivable form of information (from address lists to recipes).

The computer-literate person who wants to acquire an understanding of computer science is in much the same position as the driver of a car who wants to learn how to change its spark plugs. For the driver, this curiosity can lead to a study of how automobile engines function generally. For the literate user of computer software, this curiosity can lead from the software's instruction manual to designing and writing a program with that software and then to a deep understanding of a computer as a general-purpose problem-solving tool. The computer-literate person will come to understand that the collection of problems that computer science encompasses and the techniques used to solve those problems are the real substance of this rapidly expanding discipline.

Computer Science as Mathematics and Logic

The problem-solving emphasis of computer science borrows heavily from the areas of mathematics and logic. Faced with a problem, computer scientists must first formulate a solution. This method of solution, or *algorithm* as it is often called in computer science, must be thoroughly understood before the computer scientists make any attempt to implement the solution on the computer. Thus, at the early stages of problem solution, computer scientists work solely with their minds and do not rely on the machine (except, perhaps, as a word processor for making notes).

Once the solution is understood, computer scientists must then state the solution to this problem in a formal language called a *programming language.* This parallels the fashion in which mathematicians or logicians must develop a proof or argument in the formal language of mathematics. This formal solution as stated in a programming language must then be evaluated in terms of its correctness, style, and efficiency. Part of this evaluation process involves entering the formally stated algorithm as a programmed series of steps for the computer to follow.

Another part of the evaluation process is distinctly separate from a consideration of whether or not the computer produces the "right answer" when the program is executed. Indeed, one of the main areas of emphasis throughout this book is in developing well-designed solutions to problems and in recognizing the difference between such solutions and ones that work, but are not elegant. True computer scientists seek not just solutions to problems, but the best possible solutions.

Computer Science as Science

Perhaps nothing is as intrinsic to the scientific method as the formulation of hypotheses to explain phenomena and the careful testing of these hypotheses to prove them right or wrong. This same process plays an integral role in the way computer scientists work.

When confronted with a problem, such as a long list of names that needs to be arranged in alphabetical order, computer scientists formulate a hypothesis in the form of an algorithm that they believe will effectively solve the problem. Using mathematical techniques, they can make predictions about how such a proposed algorithm will solve the problem. But because the problems facing computer scientists arise from the world of real applications, predictive techniques relying solely on mathematical theory are not sufficient to prove an algorithm correct. Ultimately, computer scientists must implement their solutions on computers and test them in the complex situations that originally gave rise to the problems. Only after such thorough testing can the hypothetical solutions be declared right or wrong.

Moreover, just as many scientific principles are not 100% right or wrong, the hypothetical solutions posed by computer scientists are often subject to limitations. An understanding of those limitations—of when the method is appropriate and when it is not—is a crucial part of the knowledge that computer scientists must have. This is analogous to the way in which any scientist must be aware of the particular limitations of a scientific theory in explaining a given set of phenomena.

Do not forget the experimental nature of computer science as you study this book. You must participate in computer science to truly learn it. Although a good book can help, you must solve the problems, implement those solutions on the computer, and then test the results. View each of the problems you are assigned as an experiment for which you are to propose a solution and then verify the correctness of your solution by testing it on the computer. If the solution does not work exactly as you hypothesized, do not become discouraged. Instead, ask yourself why it did not work; by doing so, you will acquire a deeper understanding of the problem and your solution. In this sense, the computer represents the experimental tool of the computer scientist. Do not be afraid to use it for exploration.

Computer Science as Engineering

Whatever the area of specialization, an engineer must neatly combine a firm grasp of scientific principles with implementation techniques. Without knowledge of the principles, the engineer's ability to design creative models for a problem's solution is severely limited. Such model building is crucial to the engineering design process. The ultimate design of a bridge, for instance, is the result of an engineer considering many possible models of the bridge and then selecting the best one. The transformation of abstract ideas into models of a problem's solution is thus central to the engineering design process. The ability to generate a variety of models that can be explored is the hallmark of creative engineering.

Similarly, the computer scientist is a model builder. Faced with a problem, the computer scientist must construct models for its solution. Such models take the form of an information structure to hold the data pertinent to the problem and the algorithmic method to manipulate that information structure to solve the problem. Just as an engineer must have an in-depth understanding of scientific principles to build a model, so must a computer scientist. With these principles, the computer scientist can conceive of models that are elegant, efficient, and appropriate to the problem at hand.

An understanding of principles alone is not sufficient for either the engineer or the computer scientist. Experience with the actual implementation of hypothetical models is also necessary. Without such experience, you can have only very limited intuition about what is feasible and how a large-scale project should be organized to reach a successful conclusion. Ultimately, computers are used to solve problems in the real world. In the real world, you need to design programs that come in on time, that are within (if not under) the budget, and that solve all aspects of the original problem. The experience you acquire in designing problem solutions and then implementing them is vital to your being a complete computer scientist. Hence, remember that you cannot study computer science without actively doing it. To merely read about computer science techniques will leave you with an unrealistic perspective of what is possible.

Computer Science as Communication

As the discipline of computer science continues to evolve, communication is assuming a more significant role in the undergraduate curriculum. The Association for Computing Machinery (ACM), Inc., curriculum guidelines for 1991 state, "undergraduate programs should prepare students to . . . define a problem clearly; . . . document that solution; . . . and to communicate that solution to colleagues, professionals in other fields, and the general public" (p. 7).

It is no longer sufficient to be content with a program that runs correctly. Extra attention should be devoted to the communication aspects associated with such a program. For instance, you might be asked to submit a written proposal prior to designing a solution, to document a program carefully and completely as it is being designed, or to write a follow-up report after a program has been completed. These are some ways in which communication can be emphasized as an integral part of computer science. Several opportunities will be provided in the exercises and problem lists of this text for you to focus on the communication aspects associated with computer science.

Computer Science as an Interdisciplinary Field

The problems solved by computer scientists come from a variety of disciplines—mathematics, physics, chemistry, biology, geology, economics, business, engineering, linguistics, and psychology, to name but a few. As a computer scientist working on a problem in one of these areas, you must be a quasi-expert in that discipline as well as in computer science. For instance, you cannot write a program to manage a bank's checking account system unless you thoroughly understand how banks work and how that bank runs its checking accounts. At a minimum, you must be literate enough in other disciplines to converse with the people for whom you are writing programs and to learn precisely what it is they want the computer to do for them. Because such people may be naive about the computer and its capabilities, you will have to possess considerable communication skills as well as a knowledge of that other discipline.

Are you beginning to think that a computer scientist must be knowledgeable about much more than just the computer? If so, you are correct. Too often, computer scientists are viewed as technicians, tucked away in their own little worlds and not thinking or caring about anything other than computers. Nothing could be further from the truth. The successful computer scientist must be able to communicate, to learn new ideas quickly, and to adapt to ever-changing conditions. Computer science is emerging from its early dark ages into a rapidly maturing field, one that we hope you will find rewarding and exciting. In studying computer science, you will develop many talents; this text can get you started on the road to that development process.

A NOTE OF INTEREST

Ethics and Computer Science

The Association for Computing Machinery is the flagship organization for computing professionals. The ACM supports publications of research results and new trends in computer science, sponsors conferences and professional meetings, and provides standards for computer scientists as professionals. The standards concerning the conduct and professional responsibility of computer scientists have been published in the ACM Code of Ethics. The code is intended as a basis for ethical decision making and for judging the merits of complaints about violations of professional ethical standards.

The code lists several general moral imperatives for computer professionals:

- Contribute to society and human well-being.
- Avoid harm to others.
- Be honest and trustworthy.
- Be fair and take action not to discriminate.
- Honor property rights, including copyrights and patents.
- Give proper credit for intellectual property.
- Respect the privacy of others.
- Honor confidentiality.

The code also lists several more specific professional responsibilities:

- Strive to achieve the highest quality, effectiveness, and dignity in both the process and products of professional work.
- Acquire and maintain professional competence.
- Know and respect existing laws pertaining to professional work.
- Accept and provide appropriate professional review.
- Give comprehensive and thorough evaluations of computer systems and their impacts, including analysis of possible risks.
- Honor contracts, agreements, and assigned responsibilities.
- Improve public understanding of computing and its consequences.
- Access computing and communication resources only when authorized to do so.

In addition to these principles, the code offers a set of guidelines to provide professionals with explanations of various issues contained in the principles. The complete text of the ACM Code of Ethics is available at the ACM's World Wide Web site, http://www.acm.org.

You will see further Notes of Interest on this area of critical concern later in this book.

1.2 Computer Architecture

Objectives

a. to understand the historical development of computers

b. to know what constitutes computer hardware

c. to know what constitutes computer software

This section is intended to provide you with a brief overview of what computers are and how they are used. Although there are various sizes, makes, and models of computers, you will see that they all operate in basically the same straightforward manner. Whether you work on a personal computer that costs a few hundred dollars or on a mainframe that costs in the millions, the principles of making the machine work are essentially the same.

Modern Computers

The search for aids to perform calculations is almost as old as number systems. Early devices included the abacus, Napier's bones, the slide rule, and mechanical adding machines. More recently, calculators have changed the nature of personal computing as a result of their availability, low cost, and high speed. The development of computers over time is highlighted in Figure 1.1. (For more complete information, see *A History of Modern Computing* by Paul E. Ceruzzi, MIT Press, 1998.) Since the mid-1980s, the most significant change in computing machines in the world's history has resulted in improvements that have led to modern computers. As recently as the 1960s, a computer required several rooms because of its size. However, the advent of silicon chips has reduced the size and increased the availability of computers so that

Figure 1.1 Development of computers

Era	Early Computing Devices		Mechanical Computers	Electro-mechanical Computers
Year	1000 B.C.	A.D. 1614	1650 — 1900	1900 — 1945
Development	Abacus	Napier's bones	Adding machine Slide rule Difference engine Analytic engine	Cogged wheels Instruction register Operation code Address Plug board Harvard Mark I Tabulating machine

parents are able to purchase personal computers as presents for their children. These smaller computers are also more powerful than the early behemoths.

What is a computer? According to *Webster's New World Dictionary of the American Language* (2nd College Edition), a computer is "an electronic machine which, by means of stored instructions and information, performs rapid, often complex calculations or compiles, correlates, and selects data." Basically, a computer can be thought of as a machine that manipulates information in the form of numbers and characters. This information is referred to as *data*. What makes computers remarkable is the extreme speed and precision with which they can store, retrieve, and manipulate data.

Several types of computers currently are available. An oversimplification is to categorize computers as mainframes, minicomputers, or microcomputers. In this grouping, *mainframe* computers are the large machines used by major companies, government agencies, and universities. They have the capability of being used by as many as 100 or more people at the same time and can cost millions of dollars. *Minicomputers,* in a sense, are smaller versions of large computers. They can be used by several people at once but have less storage capacity and cost far less. *Microcomputers* are frequently referred to as personal computers. They have limited storage capacity (in a relative sense), are generally used by one person at a time, and can be purchased for as little as a few hundred dollars. *Workstations* have a larger storage capacity and faster processing speeds than microcomputers, but can still fit on a desktop and rely on similar microprocessing technology.

Most modern computers in organizations such as companies and universities are linked in a network. A *network* allows users of different computers to communicate and share resources. For example, the user of a microcomputer might receive electronic mail from a colleague in another office, send a file to a departmental laser printer, or connect to a cluster of workstations to perform tasks that require intensive processing.

Networked computers make use of a *client/server relationship.* One can think of clients as users requiring services and servers as agents that perform services. For example, a single workstation might be an electronic mail server for 100 personal computers (the clients) in an organization.

Figure 1.1 Continued

Noncommercial Electronic Computers	Batch Processing	Time-Sharing Systems	Personal Computers
1945 — 1950	1950 — 1965	1965 — 1975	1975 — Present
First-generation computers Vacuum tubes Machine language programming ENIAC	Second-generation computers Transistors Magnetic core memory Assemblers Compilers UNIVAC I IBM 704	Third-generation computers Integrated circuit technology Operating system software Teleprocessing	Fourth-generation computers Fifth-generation computers (supercomputers) Microprocessors Workstations

As you begin your work with computers, you will hear people talking about *hardware* and *software*. Hardware refers to the actual machine and its support devices. Software refers to programs that make the machine do something. Many software packages exist for today's computers. They include word processing, database programs, spreadsheets, games, operating systems, and compilers. You can (and will!) learn to create your own software. In fact, that is what this book is all about.

A *program* is a set of instructions that tells the machine what to do. When you have written a program, the computer will behave exactly as you have instructed it. It will do no more or no less than what is contained in your specific instructions. For example, the following listing is a C++ program that allows three scores to be entered from a keyboard, computes their average, and then prints the result:

```
// Program file: average.cpp
// This program reads three scores and displays their average.

#include <iostream.h>
#include <iomanip.h>

int main()
{
   // Data for the program
   int score1, score2, score3;
   double average;

   // Get the input scores from the user
   cout << "Enter the first score and press <Enter>: ";
   cin >> score1;
   cout << "Enter the second score and press <Enter>: ";
   cin >> score2;
   cout << "Enter the third score and press <Enter>: ";
   cin >> score3;
```

continued

```
    // Compute the average score
    average = double(score1 + score2 + score3) / 3;

    // Output the average score
    cout << setiosflags(ios::fixed | ios::showpoint) << setprecision(2);
    cout << The average score is  << average << endl;

    return 0;
}
```

Do not be concerned about specific parts of this program. It is intended only to illustrate the idea of a set of instructions. Very soon, you will be able to write significantly more sophisticated programs.

Learning to write programs requires two skills.

1. You need to use specific terminology and punctuation that can be understood by the machine; that is, you need to learn a programming language.
2. You need to develop a plan for solving a particular problem. This plan—or algorithm—is a sequence of steps that, when followed, will lead to a solution of the problem.

Initially, you may think that learning a language is the more difficult task because your problems will have relatively easy solutions. Nothing could be further from the truth! **The single most important thing you can do as a student of computer science is to develop the skill to solve problems.** Once you have this skill, you can learn to write programs in several different languages.

Computer Hardware

Let's take another look at the question: What is a computer? Our previous answer indicated it is a machine. Although there are several forms, names, and brands of computers, each consists of a *main unit* that is subsequently connected to peripheral devices. The main unit of a computer consists of a *central processing unit (CPU)* and *main (primary) memory*. The CPU is the "brain" of the computer. It contains an *arithmetic/logic unit (ALU),* which is capable of performing arithmetic operations and evaluating expressions to see if they are true or false, and the *control unit,* which controls the action of the remaining components so your program can be followed step by step, or *executed.*

Main memory can be thought of as mailboxes in a post office. It is a sequence of locations where information representing instructions, numbers, characters, and so on can be stored. Main memory is usable while the computer is turned on. It is where the program being executed is stored along with data it is manipulating.

As you develop a greater appreciation of how the computer works, you might wonder: How are data stored in memory? Each memory location has an address and is capable of holding a sequence of *binary digits* (0 or 1), which are commonly referred to as *bits.* Instructions, symbols, letters, numbers, and so on are translated into an appropriate pattern of binary digits and then stored in various memory locations. These are retrieved, used, and changed according to instructions in your program. In fact, the program itself is similarly translated and stored in part of main memory. Main memory can be envisioned as in Figure 1.2, and the main unit can be envisioned as in Figure 1.3.

Peripherals can be divided into three categories: *input devices, output devices,* and *secondary (auxiliary) memory devices.* Input devices are necessary to give infor-

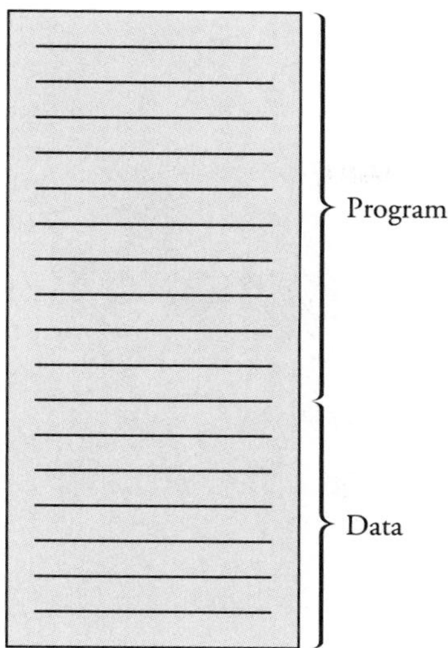

Figure 1.2
Main memory

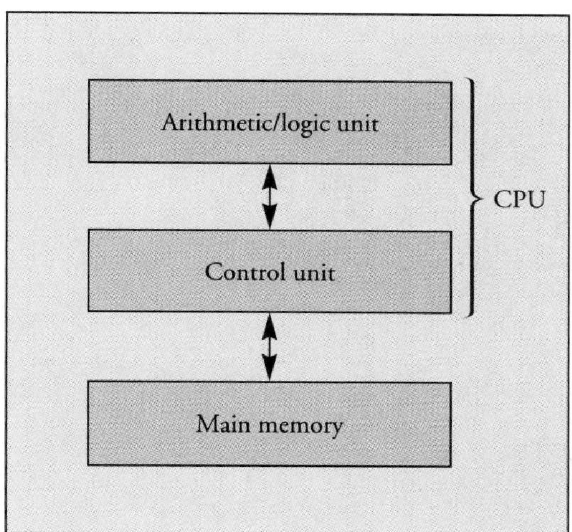

Figure 1.3
Main unit

mation to a computer. Programs are entered through an input device and then program statements are translated and stored as previously indicated. One input device (a typical keyboard) is shown in Figure 1.4.

Output devices are necessary to show the results of a program. These are normally in the form of a screen, line printer, impact printer, or laser printer (Figure 1.5). Input and output devices are frequently referred to as *I/O devices.*

Secondary (auxiliary) memory devices are used if additional memory is needed. On small computers, these secondary memory devices could be floppy disks or hard disks (Figure 1.6), CD-ROM disks, or magnetic tapes. Programs and data waiting to be executed are kept "waiting in the wings" in secondary memory.

Communication between components of a computer is frequently organized around a group of wires called a *bus.* The relationship between a bus and various computer components can be envisioned as in Figure 1.7. A photograph of a bus is shown in Figure 1.8. What appear to be lines between the slots are actually wires imprinted on the underlying board. Boards with wires connected to peripheral devices can be inserted into the slots.

Figure 1.4
Keyboard

Figure 1.5 (a) Screen, (b) line printer (mainframe), (c) impact printer (microcomputer), and (d) laser printer

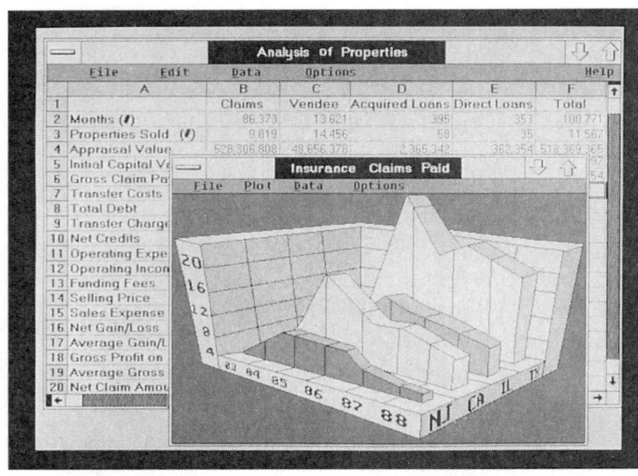

(a)

(b)

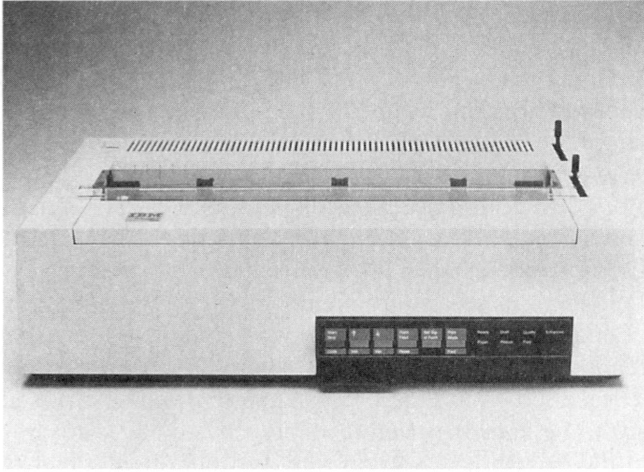

(c)

(d)

Figure 1.6 (a) Disk drive and (b) microcomputer with hard disk

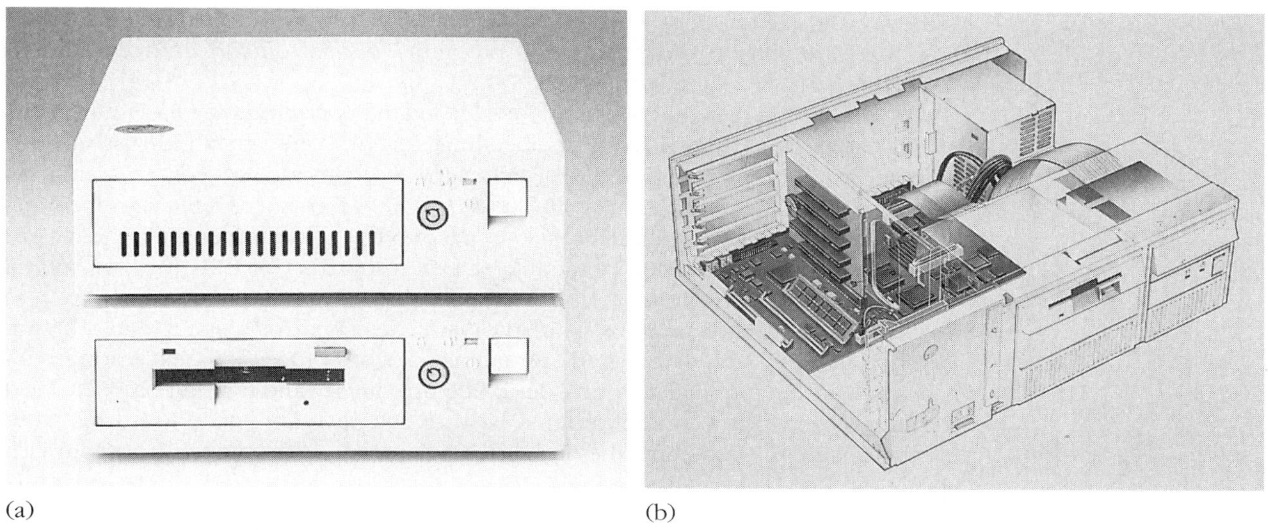

Figure 1.7 Illustration of a bus

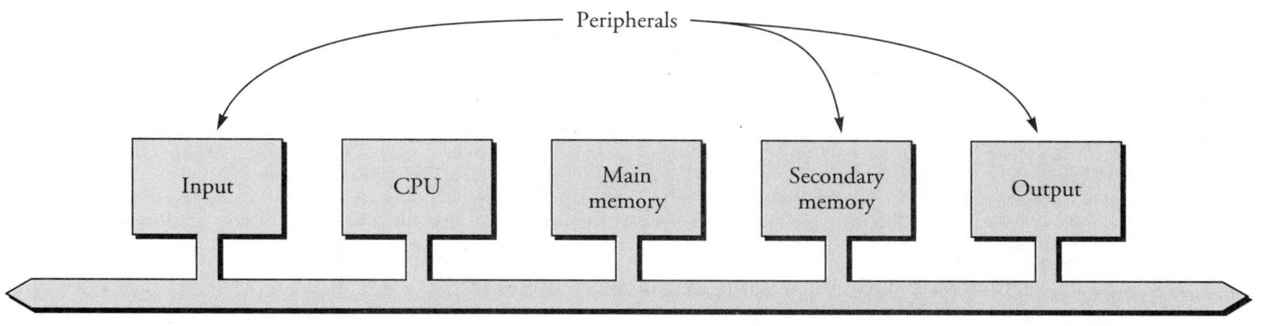

Figure 1.8
Bus

Computer Software

As previously stated, software refers to programs that make the machine do something. Software consists of two kinds of programs: *system software* and *applications software*.

System software includes what is often called the *operating system*. (For instance, the ubiquitous DOS stands for disk operating system.) The operating system for a computer is a large program and is usually supplied with a computer. This program allows the user to communicate with the hardware. More specifically, an operating system might control computer access (via passwords), allocate peripheral resources (perhaps with a printer queue), schedule shared resources (for CPU use), or control execution of other programs.

Applications software consists of programs designed for a specific use. Examples of applications software include programs for word processing, text editing, simulating spreadsheets, playing games, designing machinery, and figuring payrolls. Most computer users work with applications software and have little need to learn a computer language; the programs they require have already been written to accomplish their tasks.

1.3 Computer Languages

Objectives

a. to understand what a computer language is
b. to understand the difference between a low-level language and a high-level language
c. to understand the difference between a source program and an object program

What is a computer language? All data transmission, manipulation, storage, and retrieval is done by the machine using electrical pulses representing sequences of binary digits. If eight-digit binary codes are used, there are 256 numbered instructions from 00000000 to 11111111. Instructions for adding two numbers would consist of a sequence of these eight-digit codes.

Instructions written in this form are referred to as *machine language*. It is possible to write an entire program in machine language. However, this is very time consuming and difficult to read and understand.

Therefore, the next level of computer language allows words and symbols to be used in an unsophisticated manner to accomplish simple tasks. For example, the machine code for adding two integers might be

```
010000110011101000111010100000100101011010000010
```

This is replaced by

```
LOAD A
ADD B
STORE C
```

This causes the number in A to be added to the number in B, and the result is stored for later use in C. This computer language is an *assembly language*, which is generally referred to as a *low-level language*. What happens is that words and symbols are translated into appropriate binary digits and the machine uses the translated form.

Although assembly language is an improvement on machine language for readability and program development, it is still a bit cumbersome. Consequently, many *high-level languages* have been developed; these include Pascal, PL/I, FORTRAN, BASIC, COBOL, C, Ada, Modula-2, Logo, and others. These languages simplify even further the terminology and symbolism necessary for directing the machine to perform various manipulations of data. For example, in these languages, the task of adding two integers would be written as

A NOTE OF INTEREST

Why Learn C++?

C++ is a superset of C, which is a programming language developed at AT&T Bell Laboratories by Dennis Ritchie in 1972. Ritchie originally intended C to be used to write the UNIX operating system and to write tools to be used with that system. Over the years, however, C has achieved widespread popularity for writing various systems' programs in industry and is now the language of choice in most graduate schools of computer science.

According to Richard P. Gabriel ("The End of History and the Last Programming Language," *Journal of Object-Oriented Programming,* Jul.–Aug. 1993), C and C++ are among the few programming languages that are not either dead or moribund. There are several reasons for this. C is available on a wide range of computers and requires minimal computer resources to design, implement, and run programs. C represents a simple machine model that closely corresponds to the structure of actual computers. This property supports the development of very efficient programs. C is also similar to several different popular programming languages, such as Pascal, FORTRAN, and assembly language. Finally, C requires almost no mathematical sophistication to learn.

Critics claim that C is a dangerous language in three respects. First, C encourages professional programmers to write large systems that lack structure and are difficult to read and maintain. Second, C encourages beginning programmers to learn bad habits, such as writing small programs that lack structure and are difficult to read and maintain. Third, C lacks many of the fail-safe features of modern programming languages, such as thorough compile-time type checking.

Responding to this challenge, Bjarne Stroustrup, also of AT&T Bell Laboratories, developed C++ in the 1980s. C++ incorporates all of the desirable and undesirable features of C just enumerated. However, some additional features, if used properly, make C++ a safer language and support the design and implementation of well-structured, easily maintained programs for both beginners and professionals. For example, C++ has strong support for data types and type checking and also features that support the discipline of *object-oriented programming.* Object-oriented programming is a method of developing and maintaining large software systems that we will introduce and discuss in later chapters in this text.

Critics claim that C++ introduces its own costs: The language is enormous, the machine model that it represents is more complex than that of C, and programmers must have more mathematical sophistication to make use of its improved features. However, if Gabriel is right, students will do well to learn this language because it will be used in industry for many years to come.

Our approach in this text will be to focus on those features of C++ that support the design and implementation of well-structured programs that are easy to read and maintain. C++ is a powerful tool that should be wielded carefully.

`C := A + B;`	(Pascal, Modula-2, Ada)
`C = A + B;`	(PL/I, C++)
`C = A + B`	(FORTRAN, BASIC)
`ADD A, B GIVING C`	(COBOL)
`MAKE "C :A + :B`	(Logo)

A high-level language makes it easier to read, write, and understand a program. This book develops the concepts, symbolism, and terminology necessary for using C++ as a programming language for solving problems. After you have become proficient in using C++, you should find it relatively easy to learn the nuances of other high-level languages.

For a moment, let's consider how an instruction such as

```
C = A + B;
```

gets translated into machine code. The actual bit pattern for this code varies according to the machine and software version, but it could be as previously indicated. For the translation to happen, a special program called a *compiler* "reads" the high-level instructions and translates them into machine code. This compiled version is then run using some appropriate data, and the results are presented through some form of output device. The special programs that activate the compiler, run the machine-code version, and cause output to be printed are examples of system programs (software). The written program is a *source program,* and the machine-code version generated by the compiler is an *object program* (also referred to as *object code*).

As you will soon see, the compiler does more than just translate instructions into machine code. It also detects certain errors in your source program and prints appropriate messages. For example, if you write the instruction

```
C = (A + B;
```

in which a parenthesis is missing, when the compiler attempts to translate this line into machine code, it will detect that ")" is needed to close the parenthetical expression. It will then give you an error message such as

```
Error: ')' expected
```

You will then need to correct the error (and any others) and recompile your source program before running it with the data.

You are now ready to begin a detailed study of C++. You will undoubtedly spend much time and encounter some frustration during the course of your work. We hope your efforts result in an exciting and rewarding learning experience. Good luck.

Summary

Key Terms

algorithm
applications software
arithmetic/logic unit (ALU)
assembly language
binary digits
bits
bus
central processing unit (CPU)
client/server relationship
compiler
control unit
data
hardware
high-level language
input device
I/O devices
low-level language
machine language
main (primary) memory
main unit
mainframe
microcomputer
minicomputer
network
object code
object program
operating system
output device
program
programming language
secondary (auxiliary) memory devices
software
source program
system software
workstation

2

Problem-Solving Fundamentals: Data Types and Output

Chapter Outline

Chapter 1 presented an overview of computers and computer languages. We are now ready to examine problems that computers can solve. First, we need to know how to solve a problem and then we need to learn how to use a programming language to implement our solution on the computer. Section 2.1 lays the foundation for what many consider the most important aspect of entry-level courses in computer science—program development. The problem-solving theme in this section is continued throughout the text.

Before looking at problem solving and writing programs for the computer, we should consider some psychological aspects of working in computer science. Studying computer science can cause a significant amount of frustration for these reasons:

1. Planning is a critical issue. First, you must plan to develop instructions to solve your problem and then you should plan to translate those instructions into code before you sit down at the keyboard. You should not attempt to type in code "off the top of your head."
2. Time is a major problem. You cannot expect to complete a programming assignment by staying up late the night before it is due. You must begin early and expect to make several revisions before your final version is ready.
3. Successful problem solving and programming require extreme precision. Generally, concepts in computer science are not difficult; however, implementation of these concepts allows no room for error. For example, one misplaced word in a 1000-line program could prevent the program from working.

In other words, you must be prepared to plan well, start early, be patient, handle frustration, and work hard to succeed in software development. If you cannot do this, you will probably not enjoy software development or be successful at it.

2.1 Program Development: Top-Down Design

Objectives

a. to understand what an algorithm is
b. to understand what top-down design is
c. to understand what stepwise refinement is
d. to understand what modularity is
e. to develop algorithms

The key to writing a successful program is planning. Good programs do not just happen; they are the result of careful design and patience. Just as an artist commissioned to paint a portrait does not start out by shading in the lips and eyes, a good computer programmer does not attack a problem by immediately trying to write code for a program to solve the problem. Writing a program is like writing an essay: An overall theme is envisioned, an outline of major ideas is developed, each major idea is subdivided into several parts, and each part is developed using individual sentences.

Six Steps to Good Programming Habits

In developing a program to solve a problem, six steps should be followed: analyze the problem, develop an algorithm, document the program, write code for the program, run the program, and test the results. These steps will help develop good problem-solving habits and, in turn, solve programming problems correctly. A brief discussion of each of these steps follows.

Step 1: Analyze the Problem

This is not a trivial task. Before you can do anything, you must know exactly what it is you are to do. You must formulate a clear and precise statement of what is to be done. You should understand completely what data are available and what may be assumed. You should also know exactly what output is desired and the form it should take. When analyzing a complex problem, it helps to divide the problem into subproblems whose solutions can be developed and tested independently before they are combined into a complete solution.

Step 2: Develop an Algorithm

An algorithm is a finite sequence of effective statements that, when applied to the problem, will solve it. An *effective statement* is a clear, unambiguous instruction that can be carried out. Each algorithm you develop should have a specific beginning. By the completion of one step, the next step should be uniquely determined. And it should have an ending that is reached in a reasonable amount of time.

Step 3: Document the Program

It is very important to completely document a program. The writer knows how the program works; if others are to modify it, they must know the logic used. Moreover, users will need to know the details of how to use the program effectively. Documentation can come directly out of steps 1 and 2 before you write any code.

Step 4: Write Code for the Program

When the algorithm correctly solves the problem, you can think about translating your algorithm into a high-level language. An effective algorithm will significantly reduce the time you need to complete this step.

Step 5: Run the Program

After writing the code, you are ready to run the program. This means that, using an editor, you type the program code into the computer, compile the program, and run it. At compile time, you may discover syntax errors, which are mistakes in the way you have formed sentences in the program. Once these errors have been corrected, you may discover other errors at run time. Some of these mistakes may be as simple as an attempt to divide by zero. Other errors, called logic errors, may be more subtle and cause the program to produce mysterious results. They may require a reevaluation of all or parts of your algorithm. The probability of having to make some corrections or changes is quite high.

Step 6: Test the Results

After your program has run, you need to be sure that the results are correct, that they are in a form you like, and that your program produces the correct solution in all cases. To be sure the results are correct, you must look at them and compare them with what you expect. In the case of a program that uses arithmetic operations, this means checking some results with pencil and paper. With complex programs, you will need to test the program thoroughly by running it many times using data that you have carefully selected. Often you will need to make revisions by returning to one of the previous steps.

You should bear in mind that programs of any significant size (more than 100 lines of code) are never constructed all at once. The six steps just described are used to build programs incrementally. That is, a program is created out of small pieces that are designed, coded, tested, and documented to solve small problems. These pieces are then glued together to solve the problem set for the overall program.

Developing Algorithms

Algorithms for solving a problem can be developed by stating the problem and then subdividing the problem into major subtasks. Each subtask can then be subdivided into smaller tasks. This process is repeated until each remaining task is one that is easily solved. This process is known as *top-down design,* and each successive subdivision is referred to as a *stepwise refinement*. Tasks identified at each stage of this process are called *modules*. The relationship between modules can be shown graphically in a *structure chart* (see Figure 2.1).

To illustrate developing an algorithm, we will use the problem of updating a checkbook after a transaction has been made. A first-level refinement is shown in Figure 2.2. An arrow pointing into a module means information is needed before the task can be performed. An arrow pointing out of a module means the module task has

Figure 2.1 Structure chart illustrating top-down design

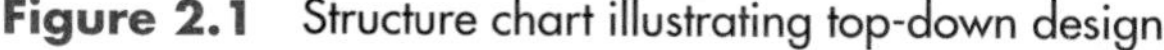

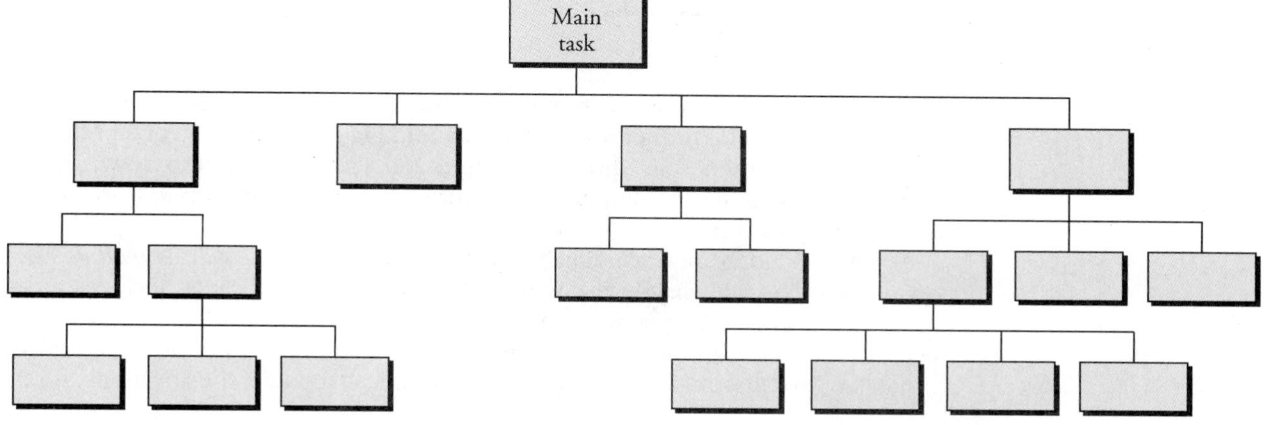

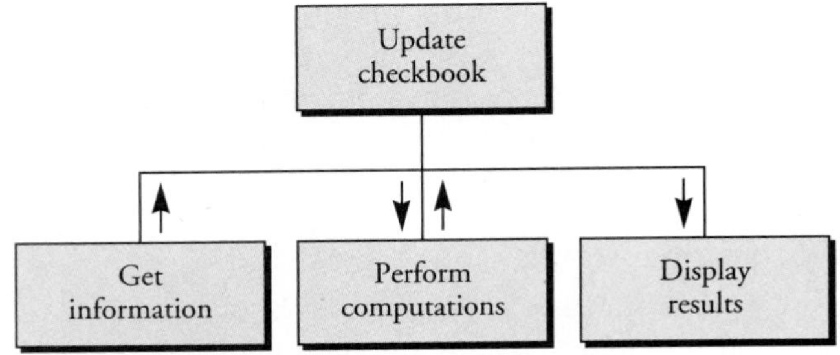

Figure 2.2
First-level refinement

Figure 2.3 Second-level refinement

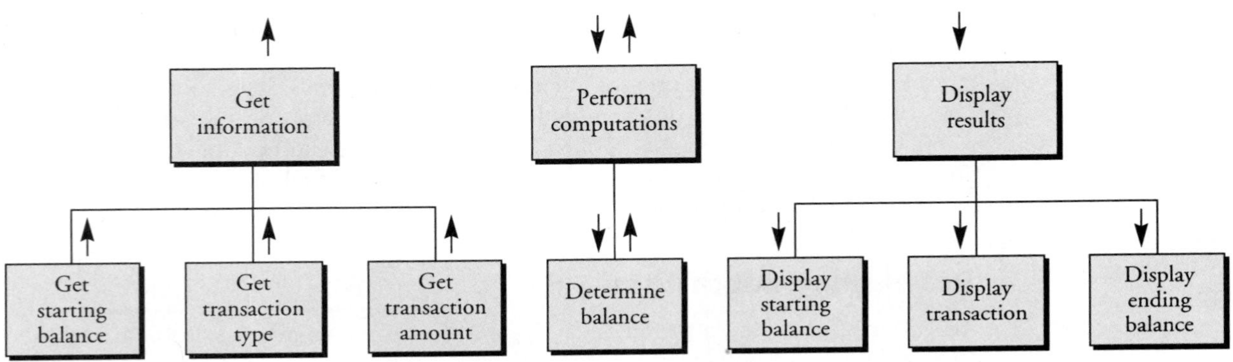

Figure 2.4
Third-level refinement

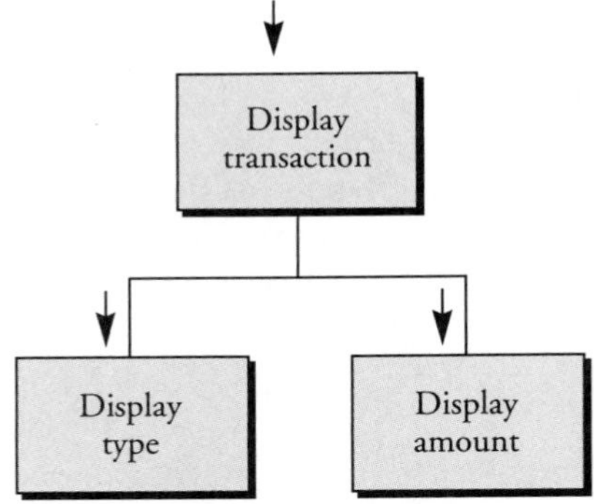

been completed and information required for subsequent work is available. Each of these modules could be further refined as shown in Figure 2.3. Finally, one of the last modules could be refined as shown in Figure 2.4. The complete top-down design could then be envisioned as illustrated in Figure 2.5. Notice that each remaining task can be accomplished in a very direct manner.

As a further aid to understanding how data are transmitted, we will list *module specifications* for each main (first-level) module. Each module specification includes a description of inputs or data received, outputs or information returned, and the task performed by the module. In cases where there are no inputs or outputs, none are specified.

For the checkbook-balancing problem, complete module specifications are as follows:

Figure 2.5 Structure chart for top-down design

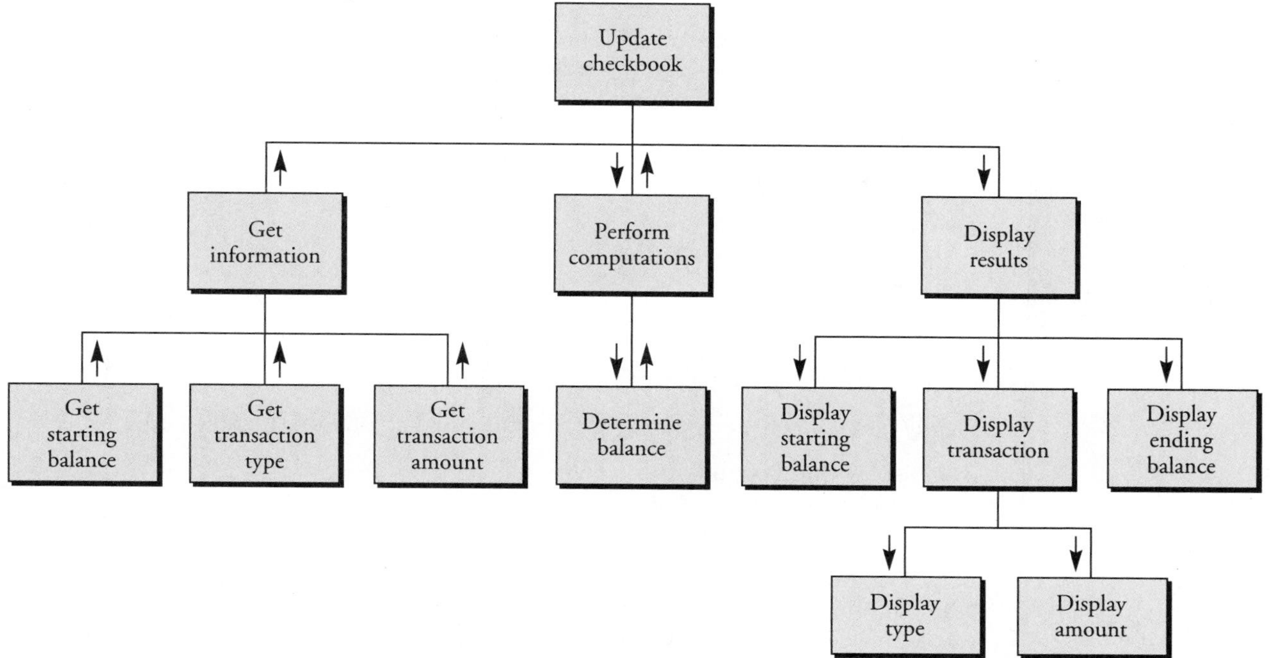

Module: Get information
Task: Have the user enter information from the keyboard
Outputs: starting balance, transaction type, transaction amount

Module: Perform computations
Task: If transaction is a deposit, add it to the starting balance; otherwise, subtract it
Inputs: starting balance, transaction type, transaction amount
Output: ending balance

Module: Display results
Task: Display the results in readable form
Inputs: starting balance, transaction type, transaction amount, ending balance

At least two comments should be made about top-down design. First, different people can (and probably will) have different designs for the solution of a problem. However, each good design will have well-defined modules with functional subtasks. Second, the graphic method just used helps to formulate general logic for solving a problem but is somewhat awkward for translating to code. Thus, we will use a stylized, half-English, half-code method called *pseudocode* to illustrate stepwise refinement in such a design. Pseudocode is written in English, but the sentence structure and indentations will suggest C++ code. Major tasks will be numbered with whole numbers and subtasks with decimal numbers. After you become used to the pseudocode notation, the numbering of lines will be omitted. First-level pseudocode for the checkbook-balancing problem is

1. Get information
2. Perform computations
3. Display results

A second-level pseudocode development produces

1. Get information
  1.1 get starting balance
  1.2 get transaction type
  1.3 get transaction amount
2. Perform computations
  2.1 if deposit then
      add to balance
    else
      subtract from balance
3. Display results
  3.1 display starting balance
  3.2 display transaction
  3.3 display ending balance

Finally, step 3.2 of the pseudocode is subdivided as previously indicated into

3.2 display transaction
  3.2.1 display transaction type
  3.2.2 display transaction amount

Two final comments are in order. First, each module developed should be tested with data for that module. Once you are sure each module does what you want, the whole program should work when the modules are used together. Second, the process of dividing a task into subtasks is especially suitable for writing programs in C++. As you will see, the language supports development of subprograms for specific subtasks.

A C++ program for the checkbook-balancing problem follows:

```
// Program file: chbook.cpp
// This program updates a checkbook.

#include <iostream.h>
#include <iomanip.h>

int main ()
{
   double startingBalance, endingBalance, transAmount;
   char transType;

   // Module for getting the data.

   cout << "Enter the starting balance and press <Enter>: ";
   cin >> startingBalance;
   cout << "Enter the transaction type (D) deposit or (W) withdrawal ";
   cout << "and press <Enter>: ";
   cin >> transType;
   cout << "Enter the transaction amount and press <Enter>: ";
   cin >> transAmount;

   // Module for performing computations.

   if (transType == 'D')
      endingBalance = startingBalance + transAmount;
```

```
   else
      endingBalance = startingBalance - transAmount;

   // Module for displaying results.

   cout << setiosflags(ios::fixed | ios::showpoint | ios::right)
        << setprecision(2);
   cout << endl;
   cout << "Starting balance    $" << setw(8) << startingBalance << endl;
   cout << "Transaction         $" << setw(8) << transAmount << setw(2)
        << transType << endl;
   cout << setw(27) << "--------" << endl ;
   cout << "Ending balance      $" << setw(8) << endingBalance << endl;

   return 0;

}
```

Notice how sections of the program correspond to module specifications. Sample runs of the program produce this output:

```
Enter the starting balance and press <Enter> 235.16
Enter the transaction type (D) deposit or (W) withdrawal and press <Enter>: D
Enter the transaction amount and press <Enter>: 75.00
Starting Balance  $  235.16

Transaction       $   75.00 D
                    --------
Ending Balance    $  310.16

Enter the starting balance and press <Enter>: 310.16
Enter the transaction type (D) deposit or (W) withdrawal and press <Enter>: W
Enter the transaction amount and press <Enter>: 65.75

Starting Balance  $  310.16

Transaction       $   65.75 W
                    --------
Ending Balance    $  244.41
```

You probably would not use the power of a computer for something as simple as this program. You could just press a few calculator keys instead. However, as you will see, the language supports development of subprograms for specific subtasks. You will, for example, soon be able to enhance this program to check for overdrafts, save the new balance for later use, and repeat the process for several transactions. Learning to think in terms of modular development now will aid you not just in creating algorithms to solve problems, but in writing programs to solve problems.

Software Engineering

The phrase *software engineering* is used roughly to refer to the process of developing and maintaining very large software systems. Before becoming engrossed in the specifics of solving problems and writing relatively small programs, it is instructive to consider the broader picture faced by those who develop software for "real-world" use.

It is not unusual for software systems to be programs that, if written in this size type, would require between 100 and 150 pages of text. These systems must be reliable, economical, and subject to use by a diverse audience. Because of these requirements, software developers must be aware of and practice certain techniques.

As you might imagine, such large programs are not the work of a single individual but are developed by teams of programmers. Issues such as communication, writing style, and technique become as important as the development of algorithms to solve particular parts of the problem. Management, coordination, and design are major considerations that need resolution very early in the process. Although you will not face these larger organizational issues in this course, you will see how some of what you learn has implications for larger design issues.

Software engineering has been so titled because techniques and principles from the more established engineering disciplines are used to guide the large-scale development required in major software. To illustrate, consider the problems faced by an engineer who is to design and supervise construction of a bridge. This analysis was presented by Alfred Spector and David Gifford in an article entitled "A Computer Science Perspective on Bridge Design" published in *Communications of the ACM,* Apr. 1986.

Engineers designing a bridge view it first as a hierarchy of substructures. This decomposition process continues on the substructures themselves until a level of very fundamental objects (such as beams and plates) ultimately is reached. This decomposition technique is similar to the stepwise refinement technique used by software designers, who break a complex problem down into a hierarchy of subproblems each of which ultimately can be solved by a relatively simple algorithm.

Engineers build conceptual models before actually constructing a bridge. This model-building allows them to evaluate various design alternatives in a way which eventually leads to the best possible design for the application being considered. This process is analogous to the way in which a skilled software designer builds models of a software system using structure charts and first-level pseudocode descriptions of modules. The designer then studies these conceptual models and eventually chooses the most elegant and efficient model for the application.

By the fashion in which engineers initially break down the bridge design, they insure that different aspects of the design can be addressed by different subordinate groups of design engineers working in a relatively independent fashion. This is similar to the goal of a software designer who oversees a program development team. The design of the software system must insure that individual components may be developed simultaneously by separate groups whose work will not have harmful side effects when the components are finally pulled together.

This overview is presented to give you a better perspective on how developments in this text are part of a greater whole. As you progress through your study of C++, you will see specific illustrations of how concepts and techniques can be viewed as part of the software engineering process.

Software System Life Cycle

Software engineering is the activity of producing large software systems. As you might imagine, these systems need to be maintained and modified; ultimately, they are replaced with other systems. This entire process parallels that of an organism. That is, there is a development, maintenance, and subsequent demise. Thus, this process is referred to as the *software system life cycle*. Specifically, a system life cycle can be viewed in the following phases:

1. Analysis
2. Design

A NOTE OF INTEREST

Software Verification

Located approximately 44 miles (70 kilometers) east of Toronto on the shore of Lake Ontario, the Darlington Nuclear Generating Station looks much like any other large nuclear power plant of the Canadian variety. But behind its ordinary exterior lies an unusual design feature.

Darlington is the first Canadian nuclear station to use computers to operate the two emergency shutdown systems that safeguard each of its four reactors. In both shutdown systems, a computer program replaces an array of electrically operated mechanical devices—switches and relays—designed to respond to sensors that are monitoring conditions critical to a reactor's safe operation, such as water levels in boilers.

Darlington's four reactors supply enough electricity to serve a city of 2 million people. Its Toronto-based builder, Ontario Hydro, opted for sophisticated software rather than old-fashioned hardware in the belief that a computer-operated shutdown system would be more economical, flexible, reliable, and safe than one under mechanical control.

This new approach, however, turned out to have unanticipated costs. To satisfy regulators that the shutdown software would function as advertised, Ontario Hydro engineers had to go through a frustrating but essential checking process that required nearly 3 years of extra effort. "There are lots of examples where software has gone wrong with serious consequences," says engineer Glenn H. Archinoff of Ontario Hydro. "If you want a shutdown system to work when you need it, you have to have a high level of assurance."

The Darlington experience demonstrates the tremendous effort involved in establishing the correctness of even relatively short and straightforward computer programs. The 10,000 "lines" of instructions, or code, required for each shutdown system pale in comparison with the 100,000 lines that constitute a typical word-processing program or the millions of lines needed to operate a long-distance telephone network or a space shuttle.

3. Coding
4. Testing/verification
5. Maintenance
6. Obsolescence

It probably comes as a surprise that computer scientists view this process as having a phase that precedes the design phase. However, it is extremely critical that a problem be completely understood before any attempt is made to design a solution. The analysis phase is complicated by the fact that potential users may not supply enough information when describing their intended use of a system. Analysis requires careful attention to items such as

- The exact form of input
- The exact form of output
- How data entry errors (there will be some) should be handled
- How large the databases will become
- How much training in the use of the system will be provided
- What possible modifications might be required as the intended audience increases/decreases

Clearly, the analysis phase requires an experienced communicator.

The design phase is what much of this book is about. This is where the solution is developed using a modular approach. Attention must be paid to techniques that include communication, algorithm development, writing style, teamwork, and so on. The key product of this phase is a detailed specification of the intended software product.

Coding closely follows design. Unfortunately, many beginning students want to write code too quickly. This can be a painful lesson if you have to scrap several days' worth of work because your original design was not sufficient. You are encouraged to make sure your designs are complete before writing any code. In the real world, teams of designers work long hours before programmers ever get a chance to start writing code.

The testing phase of a large system is a significant undertaking. Early testing is done on individual modules to get them running properly. Larger data sets must then be run on the entire program to make sure the modules interact properly with the main program. When the system appears ready to the designers, it is usually field tested by selected users. Each of these testing levels is likely to require changes in the design and coding of the system.

Finally, the system is released to the public and the maintenance phase begins. This phase lasts throughout the remainder of the program's useful life. During this phase, we are concerned with repairing problems that arise after the system has been put into use. These problems are not necessarily bugs introduced during the coding phases. More often they are the result of user needs that change over time. For instance, annual changes in the tax laws necessitate changes in even the best payroll programs. Or problems may arise as a result of misinterpretation of user needs during the early analysis phase. Whatever the reason, we must expect that a program will have to undergo numerous changes during its lifetime. During the maintenance phase, the time spent documenting the original program will be repaid many times over. One of the worst tasks imaginable in software development is to be asked to maintain an undocumented program. Undocumented code can quickly become virtually unintelligible, even to the program's original author. Indeed, one of the measures of a good program is how well it stands up to the maintenance phase.

Of course, no matter how good a program is, it will eventually become obsolete. At that time, the system life cycle starts all over again with the development of a new system to replace the obsolete one. Hence, the system life cycle is never ending, being itself part of a larger repetitive pattern that continues to evolve with changing user needs and more powerful technology.

Object-Oriented Design

Since the early 1980s, a methodology has emerged that promises to make the task of maintaining large software systems easier. According to this method, large software systems should be constructed from smaller software components called objects. Software objects are a bit like building blocks in that they can be pulled out of a box and put together in different ways to construct different applications. Objects can also be customized; that is, they can be adapted if they do not quite fit the task at hand. It is claimed that the use of software objects results in several benefits:

1. Because software objects can represent the behavior of the "real" objects that a software system is created to model, the differences between the analysis, design, and coding phases of the software life cycle tend to collapse.
2. Instead of changing existing code or writing new code, software maintenance involves plugging objects into a system or unplugging them from a system.
3. Systems can be more easily developed in increments, starting with a rough prototype whose detailed functions are eventually filled in until they are complete.

Although object-oriented design holds much promise for the development of solutions to complex problems, it is not necessarily the easiest and most straightforward way to learn to solve problems with a computer. In particular, the need for objects will not become apparent until we begin to define and use our own data structures for solving problems in Chapters 8 and 9. After we have explored some other typical problem-solving techniques, we will introduce object-oriented problem solving and programming with C++ in Chapter 8.

Exercises 2.1

1. Which of the following can be considered effective statements; that is, which are clear, unambiguous instructions that can be carried out? For each statement, explain why it is effective or why it is not.
   a. Pay the cashier $9.15.
   b. Water the plants a day before they die.
   c. Determine all positive prime numbers less than 1,000,000.
   d. Choose *X* to be the smallest positive fraction.
   e. Invest your money in a stock that will increase in value.

2. What additional information must be obtained to understand each of the following problems?
   a. Find the largest number of a set of numbers.
   b. Alphabetize a list of names.
   c. Compute charges for a telephone bill.

3. Outline the main tasks for solving each of the following problems:
   a. Write a good term paper.
   b. Take a vacation.
   c. Choose a college.
   d. Get a summer job.
   e. Compute the semester average for a student in a computer science course and print all pertinent data.

4. Refine the main tasks in each part of Exercise 3 into a sufficient number of levels so that the problem can be solved in a well-defined manner.

5. Use pseudocode to write a solution for each of the following problems. Indicate each stage of your development.
   a. Compute the wages for two employees of a company. The input information will consist of the hourly wage and the number of hours worked in 1 week. The output should contain a list of all deductions, gross pay, and net pay. For this problem, assume deductions are made for federal withholding taxes, state withholding taxes, social security, and union dues.
   b. Compute the average test score for five students in a class. Input for this problem will consist of five scores. Output should include each score and the average of these scores.

6. Develop an algorithm to find the total, average, and largest number in a given list of 25 numbers.

7. Develop an algorithm to find the greatest common divisor (gcd) of two positive integers.

8. Develop an algorithm for solving the following system of equations:
   $ax + by = c$
   $dx + ey = f$

9. Draw a structure chart and write module specifications for each of the following exercises:
   a. Exercise 5a.
   b. Exercise 5b.
   c. Exercise 6.

10. Discuss how the top-down design principles of software engineering are similar to the design problems faced by a construction engineer for a building. Be sure to include anticipated work with all subcontractors.
11. Using the construction analogy of Exercise 10, give an example of some specific communication required between electricians and the masons who finish the interior walls. Discuss why this information flow should be coordinated by a construction engineer.
12. State the phases of the software system life cycle.
13. Contact some company or major user of a software system to see what kinds of modifications might be required in a system after it has been released to the public. (Your own computer center might be sufficient.)

2.2 Writing Programs

Objectives

a. to recognize reserved words and standard library identifiers
b. to recognize and declare valid identifiers
c. to know the basic components of a program
d. to understand the basic structure of a C++ program

The Vocabulary of C++

Consider the following complete C++ program.

```
// Program file: reswords.cpp
// This program illustrates the use of reserved words.

#include <iostream.h>
#include <iomanip.h>

const int LOOP_LIMIT = 10;

int main ()
{
   int j, number, sum;
   double average;

   sum = 0;
   for (j = 1; j <= LOOP_LIMIT; ++j)
   {
      cout << "Enter a number and press <Enter>: ";
      cin >> number;
      sum = sum + number;
   }
   average = double(sum) / LOOP_LIMIT;
   cout << setiosflags (ios::fixed | ios::showpoint | ios::right)
        << setprecision(2);
   cout << endl;
   cout << setw(10) << "The average is"
        << setw(8) << average << endl;
   cout << endl;
   cout << setw(10) << "The number of scores is "
        << setw(3) << LOOP_LIMIT << endl;
   return 0;
}
```

The vocabulary of C++ consists of several kinds of words. Words with a predefined meaning that cannot be changed are called *reserved words*. Some other predefined words (*library identifiers*) can have their meanings changed if the programmer has strong reasons for doing so. Other words (*programmer-supplied identifiers*) must be created according to a well-defined set of rules but can have any meaning subject to those rules.

Case Sensitivity

C++ is case sensitive. This means that the word `while` will have a different meaning to the compiler than the word `While`, even though the two words might appear to mean the same thing to a human being. All reserved words and many library identifiers in C++ must be typed in lowercase letters only. Constant identifiers in C++ are typed in uppercase by convention. Identifiers that you create for your own purposes may be typed in any case you like, as long as you remember that the same words written in different cases will mean different things.

Case Conventions

All reserved words in C++ use lowercase letters. By convention, most C++ programmers use two conventions for identifiers, which we follow in this book:

1. Names of constants, like `DOUBLE_MAX`, use uppercase letters and underscores to indicate separate words in the names.
2. All other names, such as `pricePerSquareInch`, use lowercase letters. The capital letters indicate the presence of one or more words after the first one in this kind of identifier.

Reserved Words

In C++, reserved words are predefined and cannot be used in a program for anything other than the purpose for which they are reserved. Some examples are `for`, `if`, `while`, `do`, `switch`, and `int`. As you continue in C++, you will learn where and how these words are used. The C++ reserved words are listed in Table 2.1.

Library Identifiers

A second set of predefined words, library identifiers, can have their meanings changed by the programmer. For example, if you could develop a better algorithm for the trigonometric function `sin`, you could then substitute it in the program. However, these words should not be used for anything other than their intended use. This list will vary somewhat from compiler to compiler, so you should obtain a list of library identifiers used in your local implementation of C++. Some library identifiers are listed in Table 2.2 and in Appendix B. The term *keywords* is used to refer to both reserved words and library identifiers in subsequent discussions.

Table 2.1
Reserved Words in C++

asm	continue	float	new	signed	try
auto	default	for	operator	sizeof	typedef
break	delete	friend	private	static	union
case	do	goto	protected	struct	unsigned
catch	double	if	public	switch	virtual
char	else	inline	register	template	void
class	enum	int	return	this	volatile
const	extern	long	short	throw	while

Table 2.2
Some Library Identifiers

```
cin
cout
pow
setprecision
setw
sin
sqrt
string
```

Syntax

Syntax refers to the rules governing construction of valid statements. This includes the order in which words and statements occur, together with appropriate punctuation. We use two methods of expressing syntax rules in this book. In the body of the text, the form of most new expressions in the language will be written using an angle bracket notation. In this notation, words that appear directly in the expression, such as `if` and `==`, will be written as is. Other components of the expression requiring further definition, such as type names or parameter lists, will be described by enclosing a term, such as type name or parameter list, within angle brackets (< and >). Thus, the rule for function call expressions looks like this:

<function name> (<actual parameter list>)

This rule means that a function call expression is a function name, followed by a left parenthesis, followed by a list of actual parameters if the function expects any, followed by a right parenthesis.

Another method of expressing a syntax rule uses a diagram. A list of syntax diagrams covering the portion of C++ used in this text appears in Appendix C.

Identifiers

Reserved words and library identifiers are restricted in their use. Most C++ programs require programmer-supplied identifiers; the more complicated the program, the more identifiers are needed. **A valid identifier must start with a letter of the alphabet or an underscore (_) and must consist of only letters, digits, and underscores.** A syntax diagram for forming identifiers appears in Appendix C. Table 2.3 gives some valid and invalid identifiers along with the reasons for those that are invalid. A valid identifier can be of any length. However, some versions of C++ recognize only the first part of a long identifier, for example, the first eight or the first ten characters. Therefore, identifiers such as `mathTestScore1` and `mathTestScore2` might be the same identifier to a computer and could not be used as different identifiers in a program. Thus, you should learn what restrictions are imposed by your compiler.

The most common use of identifiers is to name the variables to be used in a program. Other uses for identifiers include symbolic constants, new data types, and subprogram names, all of which are discussed later. Even though single-letter identifiers are permitted, you should always use descriptive names for identifiers because, as you'll see, descriptive names are easier to follow in a program.

A NOTE OF INTEREST

Program Libraries

When computer scientist John Backus developed the programming language FORTRAN in 1954, he decided to place the code for frequently used mathematical functions in compiled libraries. Programmers writing applications in FORTRAN had merely to link their own programs with the libraries to use these functions. Soon they began to construct and share libraries of their own functions. The practice of borrowing software tools "off the shelf" from libraries became a standard way of constructing large software systems quickly and safely. A library enhanced program safety because its tools were already debugged or shown to work correctly. A library enhanced system maintenance because changes to the importing application or to the exporting library could be made independently. Finally, a library enhanced the portability of a software system from one hardware installation to another because low-level, machine-dependent tasks could be packaged in the library and thereby insulated from the rest of the system.

One of the reasons C++ is so popular is that there are so many program libraries that enhance the safety, maintenance, and portability of systems written in the language.

Table 2.3
Valid and Invalid Identifiers

Identifier	Valid	If Invalid, Reason
`Sum`	Yes	
`X+Y`	No	"+" is not allowed
`Average`	Yes	
`Text1`	Yes	
`1stNum`	No	Must start with a letter or "_"
`X30`	Yes	
`K mart`	No	Spaces are not allowed
`thisIsALongOne`	Yes	

Basic Program Components

A large, well-structured C++ program normally consists of many small *modules* whose text appears in different files. A small, simple program such as many of those used in this text appears in a single file. For now, a simple program in C++ consists of five components: an optional set of *preprocessor directives,* an optional *constant and type definition section,* a *main function heading,* an optional *declaration section,* and a *statement section.* These five components are illustrated in the program shown in Figure 2.6. Figure 2.7 illustrates the program components of the sample program that started this section; appropriate program parts are indicated.

The preprocessor directives are usually the first part of any C++ program. Preprocessor directives are preceded by the symbol `#`. One of them, `#include`, should be used if you wish to use certain library identifiers in your program. `#include` directs the preprocessor to include the contents of the designated library file with your source program for compilation. `#include` should be followed by the name of a library file. For now, the name of the library file should be enclosed in angle brackets. In later chapters of this text, we will see some library file names enclosed in double quotation marks.

The constant and type definition section contains the definitions of symbolic constants and names of data types used in the rest of the program.

Figure 2.6
Components of a simple C++ program

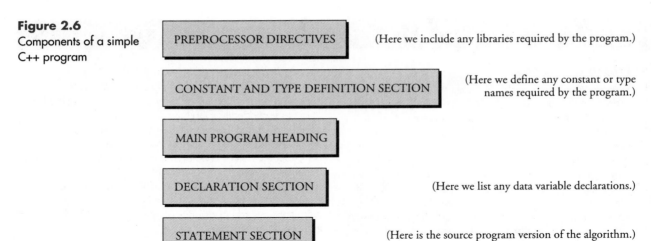

PREPROCESSOR DIRECTIVES	(Here we include any libraries required by the program.)
CONSTANT AND TYPE DEFINITION SECTION	(Here we define any constant or type names required by the program.)
MAIN PROGRAM HEADING	
DECLARATION SECTION	(Here we list any data variable declarations.)
STATEMENT SECTION	(Here is the source program version of the algorithm.)

Figure 2.7 Components of example program

```
// Program file: reswords.cpp
// This program illustrates the use of reserved words.

#include <iostream.h>                    ← Preprocessor directives
#include <iomanip.h>

const int LOOP_LIMIT = 10;               ← Constant definition section

int main ()                              ← Main program heading
{
   int j, number, sum;                   ← Declaration section
   double average;

   sum = 0;                              ← Statement section
   for (j = 1; j <= LOOP_LIMIT; ++j)
   {
      cout << "Enter a number and press <Enter>: ";
      cin >> number;
      sum  = sum + number;
   }
   average = double (sum) / LOOP_LIMIT
   cout << setiosflags (ios::fixed | ios::showpoint | ios::right)
        << setprecision(2);
   cout <<endl;
   cout << setw(10) << "The average is"
        << setw(8) << average << endl;
   cout << endl;
   cout << setw(10) << "The number of scores is "
        << setw(3) << LOOP_LIMIT << endl;
   return 0;
}
```

Constants name values that cannot change in a program. The form for defining a constant is

const <type identifier> <identifier> = <value>;

An example of a *constant definition* is

```
const int LOOP_LIMIT = 10;
```

If a constant is used that has not been declared, an error will occur when the program is compiled. Values of constant identifiers cannot be changed during program execution.

If a value is of type `char`, it must be enclosed in single quotation marks.

Any number of constants can be defined in this section. A typical constant definition portion of the declaration section could be

```
const int CLASS_SIZE = 35;
const int SPEED_LIMIT = 65;
const double CM_TO_INCHES = 0.3937;
```

We will discuss the mechanism for defining new data types in Chapters 5 and 8. The main function heading is required in any C++ program. It consists of the word `int`, followed by the word `main`, followed by a set of parentheses. The main function heading indicates the starting point of execution at run time.

The remainder of the program is sometimes referred to as the *main block.* A main block must begin with a left curly brace (`{`) and end with a right curly brace (`}`). The major parts of a main block are a declaration section and a statement section. The declaration section is used to declare (name) variables that are necessary to the program. If a variable is used that has not been declared, an error will occur when the program is compiled. For now, we assume all data used in a C++ program must be one of three *simple types:* `int`, `double`, or `char`. Types `int`, `double`, and `char` are discussed in Section 2.3.

Variables name values that can change in a program. The form required for declaring variables is somewhat different from that used for defining constants. One form simply omits the reserved word `const`:

<type identifier> <identifier> = <value>;

```
int sum = 0;
char ch = 'a';
```

When you need to declare more than one variable of the same type, it is convenient to list the variable names after the type on one line.

```
int length, width, area;
```

In general, it is considered good, defensive programming practice to provide variables with initial values when they are declared. Failure to do so can be the cause of mysterious program errors at execution time.

The fifth basic component of a simple C++ program is the statement section. This section contains the statements that cause the computer to do something.

Writing Code in C++

We are now ready to examine the use of the statement section of a program. In C++, a basic unit of grammar is an *executable statement,* which consists of library identifiers, programmer-defined identifiers, reserved words, numbers, and/or characters together with appropriate punctuation.

One of the main rules for writing code in C++ is that a semicolon almost always terminates executable statements. For example, if the expression

```
cout << setw(20) << "The results are" << setw(8) << sum << "and" << setw(6)
     << aver
```

is used in a program, it will not be treated as a statement unless it is followed by a semicolon. Thus, it should be

```
cout << setw(20) << "The results are" << setw(8) << sum << "and" << setw(6)
     << aver;
```

There is one typical instance where a semicolon is not needed. Occasionally, you will wish to enclose a series of statements within curly braces so that they can be treated as a statement unit (the main program block is a good example). In this case, a semicolon is not needed after the right curly brace. You can visualize the statement section as shown in Figure 2.8. C++ does not require each statement to be on a separate line. Actually, you could write a program as one long line (which may wrap around to fit the screen) if you wish; however, it would be difficult to read. Compare, for example, the readability of the following two programs.

```
// program file: format.cpp // This program illustrates the use of formatting.
#include <iostream.h> #include <iomanip.h> const int AGE = 26; int main () { int j,
sum; sum = 0; for (j = 1; j <= 10; ++j) {sum = sum + j;} cout << setw(28)
<< "My name is George" << endl; cout << setw(27) << "My age is " << AGE
<< endl; cout << endl; cout << setw(28) << "The sum is " << sum << endl; return 0;}
```

```
// Program file: format.cpp
// This program illustrates the use of formatting.

#include <iostream.h>
#include <iomanip.h>

const int AGE = 26;

int main ()
{
   int j, sum;

   sum = 0;
   for (j = 1; j <= 10; ++j)
   {
      sum = sum + j;
   }
   cout << setw(28) << "My name is George" << endl;
   cout << setw(27) << "My age is " << AGE << endl;
   cout << endl;
   cout << setw(28) << "The sum is " << sum << endl;
   return 0;
}
```

Figure 2.8
Executable section

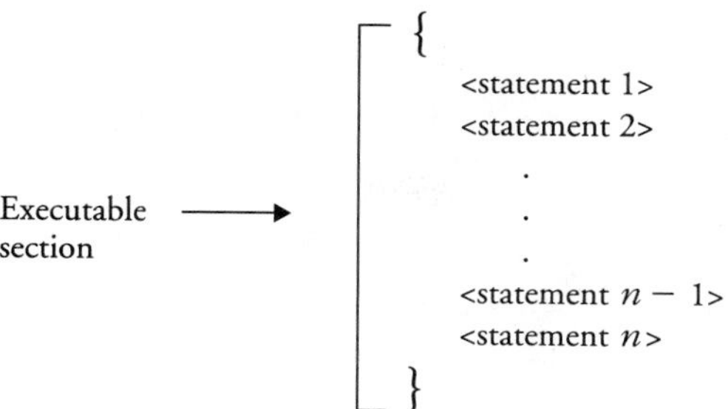

You are not expected to know exactly what some of these statements mean at this point, but it should be obvious that the second program is much more readable than the first. In addition, it is easier to change if corrections are necessary. Note, however, that these programs would be executed similarly because C++ ignores extra spaces and line boundaries.

We will discuss many kinds of statements in the following chapters. In every program in this text, you will see the statement

```
return 0;
```

at the end. When it occurs in the main program, this statement tells the computer that the program is finished running.

Program Comments

Programming languages typically include some provision for putting *comments* in a program. These comments are nonexecutable and are used to document and explain various parts of the program. In C++, programmers commonly use an *end-of-line comment,* which begins with two slash characters (//) and runs for just one line. For multiline comments, we just place the slash characters at the beginning of each line.

Exercises 2.2

1. List the rules for forming valid identifiers.

2. Which of the following are valid identifiers? Give an explanation for those that are invalid.

a. `7Up`
b. `payroll`
c. `room222`
d. `Name List`
e. `A`
f. `A1`
g. `1A`
h. `Time&Place`
i. `const`
j. `X*Y`
k. `listOfEmployees`
l. `Lima,Ohio`

3. Which of the following are valid main function headings? Give an explanation for those that are invalid.

a. `int main()`
b. `PROGRAM GettingBetter (output);`

c. `main(input, output)`
d. `MAIN();`

4. Name the five main sections of a simple C++ program.
5. Write constant definition statements for the following:
   a. your gender
   b. your age
   c. pi
6. Find all errors in the following definitions and declarations:
   a. `const char ch a;`
      `double salary;`
   b. `int const;`
   c. `int 32;`
   d. `area int;`
   e. `char int;`
7. Discuss the significance of a semicolon in writing C++ statements. Include an explanation of when semicolons are not required in a program.

2.3 Data Types and Output

Objectives

a. to understand and use the data types `int`, `double`, and `char`
b. to understand the difference between the floating-point form and the fixed-point form of decimal numbers
c. to understand the syntax for and use of output statements
d. to format output

Type `int`

C++ requires that all variables used in a program be given a *data type*. Since numbers in some form will be used in computer programs, we will first look at numbers of type `int`. Values of this type are used to represent integers or whole numbers. Some rules that must be observed when using integers are:

1. Plus (+) signs do not have to be written before a positive integer, although they may be.
2. Minus (–) signs must be written when using a negative number.
3. Decimal points cannot be used when writing integers. Although 14 and 14.0 have the same value, 14.0 is not of type `int`.
4. Commas cannot be used when writing integers; hence, 271,362 is not allowed; it must be written as 271362.
5. Leading zeros should be avoided. If you use leading zeros, the compiler will interpret the number as an octal (base 8) number.

There is a limit on the largest and the smallest integer constants. The way you determine this limit is discussed in Chapter 3. Different machines have different values for these constants; you should check your C++ implementation to see what they are. Operations with integers and integer variables are examined in Chapter 3.

C++ also supports the data types `short int` and `long int`, which represent, respectively, a smaller and a larger range of integer values than `int`. Adding the prefix `unsigned` to any of these types means that you wish to represent nonnegative integers only. For example, the declaration

```
unsigned short int x, y;
```

reserves memory for representing two relatively small nonnegative integers.

Type `double`

Values of type `double` are used to represent real numbers. Plus (+) and minus (–) signs for data of type `double` are treated exactly as with integers. When working with real numbers, however, trailing zeros are ignored. As with integers, leading zeros should be avoided. Thus, +23.45, 23.45, and 23.450 have the same value, but 023.45 may be interpreted by some C++ compilers as an octal number followed by a decimal point, which is a syntax error.

All real numbers seen thus far have been in *fixed-point* form. The computer will also accept real numbers in *floating-point* or exponential form. Floating-point form is an equivalent method for writing numbers in scientific notation to accommodate numbers that may have very large or very small values. The difference is that, instead of writing the base decimal times some power of 10, the base decimal is followed by E and the appropriate power of 10. For example, 231.6 in scientific notation would be 2.316×10^2 and in floating-point form would be 2.316E2. Table 2.4 sets forth several fixed-point decimal numbers with the equivalent scientific notation and floating-point form.

Floating-point form for real numbers does not require exactly one digit on the left of the decimal point. In fact, it can be used with no decimal points written. To illustrate, 4.16E1, 41.6, 416.0E-1, and 416E-1 have the same value and all are permissible. However, it is not a good habit to use floating-point form for decimal numbers unless exactly one nonzero digit appears on the left of the decimal. In most other cases, fixed-point form is preferable. Also, `double` is the data type of any numeric literal that is expressed in fixed-point notation in a program.

In addition to `double`, C++ supports the types `float` and `long double`. `float` supports a less precise representation of real numbers but uses less memory than `double`. `long double` supports a more precise representation of real numbers, at the cost of more computer memory. However, to avoid confusion, we will use the term "real number" or double to characterize fixed-point numeric literals in this text.

When using real numbers in a program, you may use either fixed-point or floating-point form. But the computer prints out real numbers in floating-point form unless you specify otherwise. Formatting of output is discussed later in this section.

Type `char`

Another data type available in C++ is `char`, which is used to represent character data. In standard C++, data of type `char` can be only a single character (which could be a blank space). These characters come from an available character set that differs somewhat from computer to computer, but always includes the letters of the alphabet (uppercase and lowercase); the digits 0, 1, 2, 3, 4, 5, 6, 7, 8, and 9; and special symbols such as #, &, !, +, –, *, /, and so on. A common character set is given in Appendix D. Character constants of type `char` must be enclosed in single quotation

Table 2.4
Forms for Equivalent Numbers

Fixed-Point Form	Scientific Notation	Floating-Point Form
46.345	4.6345×10^1	4.6345E1
59214.3	5.92143×10^4	5.92143E4
0.00042	4.2×10^{-4}	4.2E–4
36000000000.0	3.6×10^{10}	3.6E10
0.000000005	5.0×10^{-9}	5.0E–9
–341000.0	-3.41×10^5	–3.41E5

marks when used in a program. Otherwise, they are treated as variables and subsequent use may cause a compilation error. Thus, to use the letter `A` as a constant, you would type `'A'`. The use of digits and standard operation symbols as characters is also permitted; for example, `'7'` would be considered a character, but `7` is an integer.

Several nonprintable characters, such as the backspace, the horizontal tab, the newline, and the bell, are represented by using the backslash (`'\'`) in an escape sequence. For example, to use the backspace character, one would type `'\b'` in a C++ program. Some commonly used escape sequences are listed in Table 2.5.

Strings

Strings are used in programs to represent textual information, such as the names of people and companies. In C++, a *string constant* must be enclosed in double quotation marks. The following are examples of strings:

1. `"Hello world!"`
2. `"125"`
3. `""`
4. `"\n"`
5. `"\t"`
6. `"the word \"hello\""`

Note the difference between the second string, `"125"`, and the integer value 125. They are different data types in C++. The third string, `""`, is the empty string because it contains no characters.

The fourth string contains a backslash (\) or escape character. This character tells the compiler to treat the following character, `n`, not as a literal character, but as a special code that represents a special character, in this case, a newline character. Thus, the string `"\n"` really contains just one character, the newline character. The fifth string represents a horizontal tab character. The last string uses two backslash characters to wrap double quotes around the word `"hello"`. Note that when you wish the double quotes to appear literally in a string, they must be escaped with the backslash character. In general, to mention any special character in a string, including the backslash character itself, you prefix it with a backslash character. Consult your local implementation for a list of these special characters.

String variables can be declared and manipulated with several functions. Programs that use these must include the C++ library header file `apstring.h`:

```
#include "apstring.h"
```

Table 2.5
Escape Sequences

Escape Sequence	Character Value
`'\b'`	blank space
`'\n'`	newline
`'\t'`	tab
`'\\'`	backslash
`'\''`	apostrophe
`'\"'`	double quote

Note that the `apstring` library is not standard in C++, but is provided on the disk that comes with this book. The use of string variables and string operations is discussed in detail in Chapter 3.

Output

The goal of most programs is to output something. What gets printed (either on paper, on a screen, or in a file) is referred to as output. The simplest way to produce screen output in C++ is to direct a value to the *standard output stream*. This stream is made available to a program by including the C++ library file `iostream.h`:

```
#include <iostream.h>
```

The name of this stream is `cout`, and the operator used to direct output to this stream is <<. Output values are usually character strings, numbers, numerical expressions, or variable names. The general form of an output statement is

`cout<<` <expression 1> << <expression 2> << `...` << <expression *n*>`;`

You can think of `cout` as the name of an intelligent agent. This agent receives a message from you that you wish to display a value on the terminal screen and it then performs the desired action. The agent may also understand messages to format the output in a special way. We will discuss the methods for creating our own intelligent agents when we introduce object-oriented programming in Chapter 8. Normally, the output statement causes subsequent output to be on the same line. If you wish subsequent output to begin on the next line, you must direct an end-of-line character to the standard output stream. When output is to a monitor, the following two lines each cause the cursor to move to the next line for the next I/O operation:

```
cout << "\n";
cout << endl;
```

The following are examples of single-line and multiline output:

```
cout << "This is a test.";
cout << "How many lines are printed?" << endl;
```

causes the output

```
This is a test.How many lines are printed?
```

whereas

```
cout << "This is a test." << endl;
cout << "How many lines are printed?" << endl;
```

causes the output

```
This is a test.
How many lines are printed?
```

Character strings can be printed by enclosing the string in double quotation marks. Numerical data can be printed by typing the desired number or numbers. Thus,

```
cout << 100;
```

produces

```
100
```

Example 2.1 Let's write a complete C++ program to print the following address:

1403 South Drive
Apartment 3B
Pittsburgh, PA 15238

A complete program to print this is

```
// Program file: printaddr.cpp
// This program prints an address

#include <iostream.h>

int main()
{
   cout << "1403 South Drive" << endl;

   cout << "Apartment 3B" << '\n';

   cout << "Pittsburgh, PA 15238" << "\n";

   return 0;
}
```

Note the different ways of instructing the computer to output a newline to the terminal screen.

Formatting Integers

Output of integers can be controlled with *format manipulators*. First, you must include the library header file `iomanip.h` (short for "input/output manipulators") to gain access to the format manipulators:

```
#include <iomanip.h>
```

Second, you instruct the computer to right justify the output by running the statement

```
cout << setiosflags(ios::right);
```

Third, you specify the field width for the next output operation by using the `setw` manipulator with the size of the number of columns to be filled. Then, on the next output operation, the value of an integer, identifier, or integer expression will be printed on the right side of the specified field. Thus,

```
cout << setw(10) << 100 << setw(10) << 50 << setw(10) << 25;
```

produces

```
*******100********50********25
```

where each "*" indicates a blank. Some illustrations for formatting integer output are given in Table 2.6.

The output of end of lines at the beginning and end of the executable section will separate desired output from other messages or directions. Thus, the previous program for printing an address could have been

```
int main()
{
   cout << endl << endl;
   cout << "1403 South Drive" << endl;
   cout << "Apartment 3B" << endl;
   cout << "Pittsburgh, PA, 15238" << endl;
   return 0;
}
```

Formatting Real Numbers

Output of real numbers can also be controlled by formatting. First, you must include the `iomanip.h` library to have access to the formatting functions. As with integers, you use `setw` to specify the total field width of each real number. However, if you wish real numbers to be displayed in decimal form, you must specify a fixed-point format with the number of positions to the right of the decimal. The following output statement does this for a desired precision of two places to the right of the decimal:

```
cout << setiosflags (ios::fixed | ios::showpoint | ios::right)
     << setprecision(2);
```

Then,

```
cout << setw(8) << 736.23;
```

Table 2.6
Formatting Integer Output

Program Statement	Output
`cout << setw(6) << 123;`	`***123`
`cout << 15 << setw(5) << 10;`	`15***10`
`cout << setw(7) << -263 << setw(3) << 21;`	`***-263*21`
`cout << setw(6) << +5062;`	`**5062`
`cout << setw(3) << 65221;`	`65221`

Table 2.7
Useful Flags

Flag Name	Meaning
`ios::showpoint`	Display decimal point with trailing zeros
`ios::fixed`	Display real numbers in fixed-point notation
`ios::scientific`	Display real numbers in floating-point notation
`ios::right`	Display values right justified

produces

```
736.23
```

The expression

```
setiosflags(ios::fixed | ios::showpoint | ios::right)
```

instructs the output stream to display real numbers in fixed-point format using a decimal point. The general form for using `setiosflags` is

`setiosflags` (<flag1> | <flag2> | . . . | <flag$_n$>)

Some useful flags are listed in Table 2.7.

The function `setprecision` specifies the number of digits to the right of the decimal point to be displayed. A precision of 2 will remain in effect for all subsequent outputs of real numbers until the programmer specifies a change with another `setprecision` function.

Formatting real numbers causes the following to happen:

1. The decimal point uses one position in the specified field width.
2. Trailing zeros are printed to the specified number of positions to the right of the decimal.
3. Leading plus (+) signs are omitted.
4. Leading minus (–) signs are printed and use one position of the specified field.
5. Digits appearing to the right of the decimal have been rounded rather than truncated.

As with integers, if a specified field width is too small, most versions of C++ will default to the minimum width required to present all digits to the left of the decimal as well as the specified digits to the right of the decimal. Real numbers in floating-point form can also be used in a formatted output statement. Table 2.8 illustrates how output using data of type double can be formatted. The asterisk (*) indicates a blank space in the output.

Formatting Strings

Strings and string constants can be formatted by using `setw` to specify field width. The string will be right justified in the field. Unlike real numbers, strings are truncated when necessary. Thus,

```
cout << "field" << setw(10) << "width" << setw(15) << "check" << endl;
```

produces

Table 2.8
Formatting Fixed-Point Output

Program Statement	Output
`cout << setprecision(3) << setw(10) << 765.432;`	`***765.432`
`cout << setprecision(2) << setw(10) << 023.14;`	`*****23.14`
`cout << setprecision(2) << setw(10) << 65.50`	`*****65.50`
`cout << setprecision(2) << setw(10) << +341.2;`	`****341.20`
`cout << setprecision(2) << setw(10) << -341.2;`	`***-341.20`
`cout << setprecision(2) << setw(10) <<16.458;`	`*****16.46`
`cout << setprecision(4) << setw(10) << 0.00456;`	`****0.0046`
`cout << setprecision(2) << setw(6) << 136.51;`	`136.51`

```
field   width   check
```

and

```
cout << setw(4) << "check" << endl;
```

produces

```
chec
```

Test Programs

Programmers should develop the habit of using test programs to improve their knowledge and programming skills. Test programs should be relatively short and written to provide an answer to a specific question. They allow you to play with the computer. You can answer "What if . . . " questions by adopting a "try it and see" attitude. This is an excellent way to become comfortable with your computer and the programming language you are using.

Exercises 2.3

1. Which of the following are valid `int` constants? Explain why the others are invalid.
   a. 521
   b. –32.0
   c. 5,621
   d. +00784
   e. +65
   f. 6521492183
   g. –0

2. Which of the following are valid `double` constants? Explain why the others are invalid.
   a. 26.3
   b. +181.0
   c. –.14
   d. 492.
   e. +017.400
   f. 43E2
   g. –0.2E–3

h. 43,162.3E5
i. –176.52E+1
j. 1.43000E+2

3. Change the following fixed-point decimals to floating-point decimals with exactly one nonzero digit to the left of the decimal.
a. 173.0
b. 743927000000.0
c. –0.000000023
d. +014.768
e. –5.2

4. Change the following floating-point decimals to fixed-point decimals.
a. –1.0046E+3
b. 4.2E–8
c. 9.020E10
d. –4.615230E3
e. –8.02E–3

5. Indicate the data type for each of the following:
a. –720
b. –720.0
c. 150E3
d. 150
e. 150
f. 23.4E2
g. 23.4E–2

6. Write and run test programs for each of the following:
a. Examine the output for a decimal number without field width specified; for example,

```
cout << 2.31;
```

b. Try to print a message without using quotation marks for a character string; for example,

```
cout << Hello;
```

7. For each of the following, write a program that produces the indicated output.

```
a. Score                                 b. Price
86                                         $19.94
82                                        $100.00
79                                         $58.95
```

where "S" is in column 10. where "P" is in column 50.

8. Assume the hourly wages of five students are $6.65, $8.10, $4.89, $10.00, and $8.50. Write a program that produces the following output, where the `E` of `Employee` is in column 20.

```
Employee      Hourly Wage
1               $  6.65
2               $  8.10
3               $  4.89
4               $ 10.00
5               $  8.50
```

9. What is the output from the following segment of code on your printer or terminal?

```
cout << "My test average is" << 87.5;
cout << setw(20) << "My test average is"
     << setw(10) << 87.5;
cout << setw(25) << "My test average is"
     << setprecision(2) << setw(10) << 87.5;
cout << setw(25) << "My test average is"
     << setprecision(2) << setw(6) << 87.5;
```

10. Write a program that produces the following output. Start `Student` in column 20 and `Test` in column 40.

```
Student Name                Test Score
Adams, Mike                   73
Conley, Theresa               86
Samson, Ron                   92
O'Malley, Colleen             81
```

11. The Great Lakes Shipping Company is going to use a computer program to generate billing statements for its customers. The heading of each bill is

```
  GREAT LAKES SHIPPING COMPANY
  SAULT STE. MARIE, MICHIGAN
Thank you for doing business with our company. The information listed below
was used to determine your total cargo fee. We hope you were satisfied with
our service.
            CARGO        TONNAGE        RATE/TON        TOTAL DUE
```

Write a complete C++ program that produces this heading.

12. What output is produced by each of the following statements or sequences of statements when executed by the computer?

a.
```
cout << 1234 << setw(8) << 1234 << setw(6) << 1234;
```

b.
```
cout << setw(4) <<12 << setw(4) << -21 << setw(4) << 120;
```

c.
```
cout << "FIGURE AREA PERIMETER";
cout << "";
cout << endl;
cout << "SQUARE" << setw(5) << 16 << setw(12) <<16;
cout << endl;
cout << "RECT"  << setw(5) << 24 << setw(12) << 20;
```

13. Write a complete program that produces the following table:

```
WIDTH       LENGTH       AREA
 4          2              8
21          5            105
```

14. What output is produced when each of the following is executed?

a.
```
cout << setprecision(2) << setw(15) << 2.134;
```

b.
```
cout << setprecision(2) << setw(5) << 423.73;
```

c.
```
cout << setprecision(3) << setw(8) << -42.1;
```

d.
```
cout << setprecision(2) << setw(2) << -4.21E3;
```

e.
```
cout << 10.25;
```

f.
```
cout << 1.25 << setprecision(2) << setw(6) << 1.25 << setprecision(1)
     << setw(2) << 1.25;
```

15. Write a complete program that produces the following output:

```
Hourly Wage          Hours Worked         Total
     5.0                  20.0            100.00
     7.50                 15.25           114.375
```

16. What type of data would be used to print each of the following?
a. your age
b. your grade-point average
c. your name
d. a test score
e. the average test score
f. your grade

Summary

Key Terms

comments
constant definition
data type
declaration section
effective statement
end-of-line comment
executable statement
fixed point
floating point
format manipulator
formatting
keyword
library identifier
main function heading
module
module specifications
object-oriented design
preprocessor directories
programmer-supplied identifiers
pseudocode
reserved words
software engineering
software system life cycle
statement section
stepwise refinement
string
string constant
structure chart
syntax
top-down design

Keywords

char
const
double
int
long
short
unsigned

Key Concepts

- Six steps in problem solving include the following: analyze the problem, develop an algorithm, document the program, write code for the program, run the program, and test the results against answers manually computed with paper and pencil.
- Top-down design is a process of dividing tasks into subtasks until each subtask can be readily accomplished.
- Stepwise refinement refers to refinements of tasks into subtasks.
- A structure chart is a graphic representation of the relationship between modules.
- Software engineering is the process of developing and maintaining large software systems.
- The software system life cycle consists of the following phases: analysis, design, coding, testing/verification, maintenance, and obsolescence.
- Valid identifiers must begin with a letter or underscore and they can contain only letters, digits, and underscores.
- The five components of a simple C++ program are preprocessor directives, constant and type definitions, program heading, declaration section, and executable statement section.
- Semicolons are used to terminate most executable statements.
- Extra spaces and blank lines are ignored in C++.
- Output is generated by using `cout` and <<.
- Strings are formatted using the function `setw` with a positive integer that specifies the total field width, for example,

```
cout << setw(30) << "This is a string";
```

- The following table summarizes the use of the data types `int`, `double`, and `char`.

Data Type	Permissible Data	Formatting
`int`	numeric	`setw` (an integer); for example `cout << setw(6) << 25;`

`double`	numeric	`setiosflags(ios::fixed |ios::showpoint)`, `setprecision` (an integer), and `setw` (an integer);
		
		for example
		`cout << setiosflags(ios::fixed |`
		`ios::showpoint)`
		`<< setprecision(2)`
		`<< setw(8) << 1234.5;`

`char`	character	`setw` (integer); for example `cout << setw(6) << 'A';`

Programming Problems and Projects

1. Write and run a short program to print your initials in block letters. Your output could look like

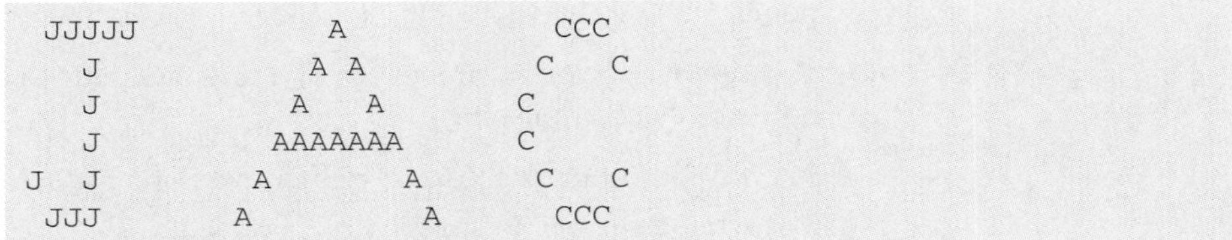

```
 JJJJJ          A           CCC
   J           A A         C   C
   J          A   A       C
   J         AAAAAAA      C
J  J        A       A      C   C
 JJJ       A         A      CCC
```

2. Design a simple picture and print it using output statements. If you plan the picture on a sheet of graph paper, keeping track of spacing will be easier.
3. Write and run a program to print your mailing address.
4. Our Lady of Mercy Hospital prints billing statements for patients when they are ready to leave the hospital. Write a program that prints a heading for each statement as follows:

```
//////////////////////////////////////////////////
/                                                /
/                                                /
/         Our Lady of Mercy Hospital             /
/                                                /
/                                                /
/                                                /
/                                                /
/            1306 Central City                   /
/                                                /
/                                                /
/            Phone (416) 333-5555                /
/                                                /
/                                                /
/                                                /
/                                                /
/                                                /
//////////////////////////////////////////////////
```

5. Your computer science instructor wants course and program information included as part of every assignment. Write a program that can be used to print this information. Sample output should look like this:

```
*****************************************
*                                       *
*      Author:          Mary Smith      *
*      Course:          CPS-150         *
*      Assignment:      Program #3      *
*                                       *
*      Due Date:        September 18    *
*      Instructor:      Mr. Samson      *
*                                       *
*****************************************
```

6. As part of a programming project that will compute and print grades for each student in your class, you have been asked to write a program that produces a heading for each student report. The columns in which the various headings should be are as follows:

The border for the class name starts in column 30.
Student Name starts in column 20.
Test Average starts in column 40.
Grade starts in column 55.

Write a program to print the heading as follows:

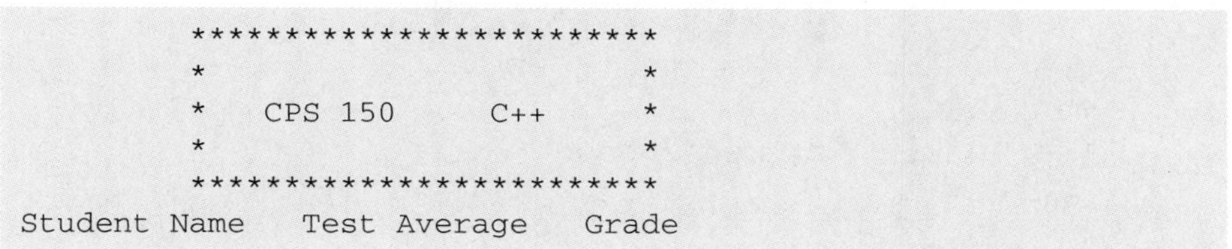

```
         **************************
         *                        *
         *   CPS 150      C++     *
         *                        *
         **************************
Student Name   Test Average    Grade
```

7. Mr. Fixit's bill for the repair of a leaking roof looks like this:

```
   Fixit Roof Repair Service
Date: July 20, 1998

Cost of labor:         $150.00
Cost of materials:       53.00
Tax:                      7.21
                       -------
Total cost:            $210.21
```

Write a program that produces this output. Be sure to use the C++ format manipulators `setprecision` and `setw` in your program.

3

More Problem-Solving Fundamentals: Calculation and Input

Chapter Outline

Pocket calculators provide a set of built-in arithmetic functions. Many also provide built-in constants, such as `PI`, and users can program them to perform a series of functions that share data with variables. In this chapter, we will discuss all of these concepts, including arithmetic operations, using data in a program, obtaining input, and using constants and variables. We will also discuss the use of functions to perform standard operations such as finding a square root or raising a number to a given power.

3.1 Arithmetic in C++

Basic Operations for Integers

Integer arithmetic in C++ allows the operations of addition, subtraction, multiplication, division, and modulus to be performed. The notation for these operations is shown in Table 3.1. In a standard integer division problem, there is a quotient and a remainder. In C++, the slash (/) produces the quotient and % produces the remainder when the first operand is positive. For example, in the problem 17 divided by 3, `17 / 3` produces 5, and `17 % 3` produces 2. Avoid using `/ 0` (zero) and `% 0`. Division by zero will cause a run-time error. Note that % in C++ means modulus or remainder, not percent.

Several integer expressions and their values are shown in Table 3.2. Notice that when 3 is multiplied by −2, the expression is written as `3 * (-2)` rather than `3 * -2`. The parentheses make the expression more readable but are not required.

Table 3.1
Integer Arithmetic Operations

Symbol	Operation	Example	Value
+	Addition	3 + 5	8
-	Subtraction	43 – 25	18
*	Multiplication	4 * 7	28
/	Division	9 / 2	4
%	Modulus	9 % 2	1

Table 3.2
Values of Integer Expressions

Expression	Value
`-3 + 2`	–1
`2 - 3`	–1
`-3 * 2`	–6
`3 * (-2)`	–6
`-3 * (-2)`	6
`17 / 3`	5
`17 % 3`	2
`17 / (-3)`	–5
`-17 / 3`	–5
`-17 % 7`	3
`-17 / (-3)`	5

Objectives

a. to understand what an expression is in C++
b. to evaluate arithmetic expressions using data of type `int`
c. to evaluate arithmetic expressions using data of type `double`
d. to understand the order of operations for evaluating expressions
e. to identify mixed-mode expressions
f. to distinguish between valid and invalid mixed-mode expressions
g. to evaluate mixed-mode expressions

Table 3.3
Integer Arithmetic Priority

Expression or Operation	Priority
`( )`	1. Evaluate from inside out
`*, %, /`	2. Evaluate from left to right
`+, -`	3. Evaluate from left to right

Order of Operations for Integers

Expressions involving more than one operation are frequently used when writing programs. When this happens, it is important to know the order in which these operations are performed. The order of operations is referred to as the *precedence rule*. The priorities for these are as follows:

1. All expressions within a set of parentheses are evaluated first. If there are parentheses within parentheses (the parentheses are nested), the innermost expressions are evaluated first.
2. The operations `*`, `%`, and `/` are evaluated next in order from left to right.
3. The operations `+` and `-` are evaluated last from left to right.

These operations are similar to algebraic operations; they are summarized in Table 3.3. To illustrate how expressions are evaluated, consider the values of the expressions listed

Table 3.4
Priority of Operations

Expression	Value
`3 - 4 * 5`	–17
`3 - (4 * 5)`	–17
`(3 - 4) * 5`	–5
`3 * 4 - 5`	7
`3 * (4 - 5)`	–3
`17 - 10 - 3`	4
`17 - (10 - 3)`	10
`(17 - 10) - 3`	4
`-42 + 50 % 17`	–26

in Table 3.4. As expressions get more elaborate, it can be helpful to list partial evaluations in a manner similar to the order in which the computer performs the evaluations. For example, suppose the expression

```
(3 - 4) + 18 / 5 + 2
```

is to be evaluated. If we consider the order in which subexpressions are evaluated, we get

```
(3 - 4) + 18 / 5 + 2
-1 + 18 / 5 + 2
-1 + 3 + 2
2 + 2
4
```

Using Modulus and Division

Modulus and division can be used when it is necessary to perform conversions within arithmetic operations. For example, consider the problem of adding two weights given in units of pounds and ounces. This problem can be solved by converting both weights to ounces, adding the ounces, and then converting the total ounces to pounds and ounces. The conversion from ounces to pounds can be accomplished by using modulus and division. If the total number of ounces is 243, then `243 / 16` yields the number of pounds (15), and `243 % 16` yields the number of ounces (3).

Representation of Integers

Computer representation of integers is different from what we see when we work with integers. Integers are stored in *binary notation,* and the operations performed on them are those of *binary arithmetic*. Thus, the integer 19, which can be written as

$$\begin{aligned} 19 &= 16 + 0 + 0 + 2 + 1 \\ &= 1 * 2^4 + 0 * 2^3 + 0 * 2^2 + 1 * 2^1 + 1 * 2^0 \end{aligned}$$

is stored as 1 0 0 1 1. This binary number is actually stored in a *word* in memory, which consists of several individual locations called bits, as mentioned in Chapter 1.

The number of bits used to store an integer is machine dependent. If you use a 16-bit machine, then 19 is

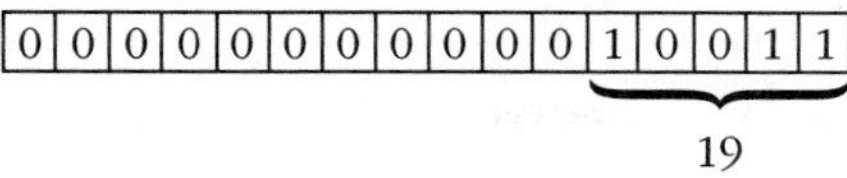

In this representation, the leftmost bit is reserved for the sign of the integer (1 meaning negative, 0 meaning positive).

We can make two observations regarding the storage and mechanics of the operations on integers. First, integers produce exact answers; numbers are stored exactly (up to the limits of the machine). Second, a maximum and a minimum number can be represented. In a 16-bit machine, these numbers are

0	1	1	1	1	1	1	1	1	1	1	1	1	1	1	1

where the leftmost 0 represents a positive number equaling 32,767, and

1	0	0	0	0	0	0	0	0	0	0	0	0	0	0	0

where the leftmost 1 represents a negative number equaling –32,768. To find out the minimum and maximum integer values for your particular system, you can use the C++ library constants discussed in Section 3.5.

If a program contains an integer operation that produces a number outside of your machine's range, this is referred to as *integer overflow,* which means that the number is too large or too small to be stored. Ideally, an error message is printed when such a situation arises. However, many systems merely store an unpredictable value and continue with the program. In Section 5.3, we will discuss how to protect a program against this problem.

Basic Operations for Real Numbers

The operations of addition, subtraction, and multiplication are the same for data of type `double` as for integers. Additionally, real division is now permitted. The modulus operator `(%)` is restricted to data of type `int`. The symbol for division of data of type `double` is the slash `(/)`. The *real arithmetic operations* are shown on Table 3.5.

Division is given the same priority as multiplication when arithmetic expressions are evaluated by the computer. The rules for order of operation are the same as those for evaluating integer arithmetic expressions. A summary of these operations is shown in Table 3.6. Some example calculations using data of type `double` are shown in

Table 3.5
Real Arithmetic Operations

Symbol	Operation	Example	Value
+	Addition	`4.2 + 19.36`	23.56
–	Subtraction	`19.36 - 4.2`	15.16
*	Multiplication	`3.1 * 2.0`	6.2
/	Division	`54.6 / 2.0`	27.3

Table 3.6
Real Arithmetic Priority

Expression or Operation	Priority
( )	1. Evaluate from inside out
*, /	2. Evaluate from left to right
+, -	3. Evaluate from left to right

Table 3.7
Type `double` Calculations

Expression	Value
–1.0 + 3.5 + 2.0	4.5
–1.0 + 3.5 * 2.0	6.0
2.0 * (1.2 – 4.3)	–6.2
2.0 * 1.2 – 4.3	–1.9
–12.6 / 3.0 + 3.0	–1.2
–12.6 / (3.0 + 3.0)	–2.1

Table 3.7. As expressions get a bit more complicated, it is again helpful to write out the expression and evaluate it step by step. For example,

```
18.2 + (-4.3) * (10.1 + (72.3 / 3.0 - 4.5))
18.2 + (-4.3) * (10.1 + (24.1 - 4.5))
18.2 + (-4.3) * (10.1 + 19.6)
18.2 + (-4.3) * 29.7
18.2 +  -127.71

-109.51
```

Representation of Real Numbers

As with integers, real numbers are stored and operations are performed using binary notation. Unlike integers, however, the storage and representation of real numbers frequently produce answers that are not exact. For example, an operation such as

```
1 / 3.0
```

produces the repeating decimal .3333 . . . . At some point, this decimal must be truncated or rounded so that it can be stored. Such conversions produce *round-off errors*.

Now let us consider some errors that occur when working with real numbers. A value very close to zero may be stored as 0. Thus, you may think you are working with

```
1.23 * 10-20 = .0000000000000000000123
```

but in fact, this value may have been stored as a zero. This condition is referred to as *underflow*. Generally, this would not be a problem because replacing numbers very close to zero with 0 does not affect the accuracy of most answers. However, sometimes this replacement can make a difference; therefore, you should be aware of the limitations of the system on which you are working.

Because operations with real numbers are not stored exactly, errors referred to as *representational errors* can be introduced. To illustrate, suppose we are using a machine that only yields three digits of accuracy (most machines exhibit much greater accuracy) and we want to add the three numbers 45.6, −45.5, and .215. The order in which we add these numbers makes a difference in the result we obtain. For example, −45.5 + 45.6 yields .1. Then, .1 + .215 yields .315. Thus, we have

```
(-45.5 + 45.6) + .215 = .315
```

However, if we consider 45.6 + .215 first, then the arithmetic result is 45.815. Since our hypothetical computer only yields three digits of accuracy, this result will be stored as 45.8. Then, −45.5 + 45.8 yields .3. Thus, we have

```
-45.5 + (45.6 + .215) = .3
```

This operation produces a representational error. Another form of representational error occurs when numbers of substantially different size are used in an operation. For example, consider the expression 2 + .0005. We would expect this value to be 2.0005, but stored to only three digits of accuracy, the result is 2.00. In effect, the smaller of the two numbers disappears or is cancelled from the expression. This form of error is called a *cancellation error.*

Although representational and cancellation errors cannot be avoided, their effects can be minimized. Operations should be grouped in such a way that numbers of approximately the same magnitude are used together before the resulting operand is used with another number. For example, all very small numbers should be summed before adding them to a large number.

Attempting to store very large real numbers can result in *real overflow*. In principle, real numbers are stored with locations reserved for the exponents. An oversimplified illustration using base-10 digits is

1	2	3	+	0	8

for the number $123 * 10^8$. Different computers place different limits on the size of the exponent that can be stored. An attempt to use numbers outside the defined range causes overflow in much the same way that integer overflow occurs, with results that depend on the particular run-time system.

Mixed-Mode Expressions

Arithmetic expressions using data of two or more types are called *mixed-mode expressions.* In a mixed-mode expression involving both `int` and `double` data types, the value will be of type `double`. When formatting output of mixed-mode expressions, always format for real numbers. *Note:* Avoid using `%` with mixed-mode expressions. The way in which C++ deals with mixed-mode expressions in general is fairly complex and is discussed in detail in Section 3.7. You may wish to avoid using mixed-mode expressions until you read that section.

Exercises 3.1

1. Find the value of each of the following expressions:

a. `17 - 3 * 2`

b. `-15 * 3 - 4`

c. `123 % 5`
d. `123 / 5`
e. `5 * 123 / 5 - 123 % 5`
f. `-21 * 3 * (-1)`
g. `14 * (3 - 18 / 4) - 50`
h. `100 - (4 * (3 - 2)) * (-2)`
i. `-56 % 3`
j. `14 * 8 % 5 - 23 / (-4)`

2. Find the value of each of the following expressions:
a. `3.21 - - 5.02 - 6.1`
b. `6.0 / 2.0 * 3.0`
c. `6.0 / (2.0 + 3.0)`
d. `-20.5 * (2.1 + 2.0)`
e. `-2.0 * ((56.8 / 4.0 + 0.8) + 5.0)`
f. `1.04E2 * 0.02E3`
g. `800.0E-2 / 4.0 - 15.3`

3. Which of the following are valid expressions? For those that are valid, indicate whether they are of type `int` or `double`.
a. `18 - (5 * 2)`
b. `(18 - 5) * 2`
c. `18 - 5 * 2.0`
d. `25 * (14 % 7.0)`
e. `1.4E3 * 5`
f. `28 / 7`
g. `28.0 / 4`
h. `10.5 + 14 / 3`
i. `24 / 6 / 3`
j. `24 / (6 / 3)`

4. Evaluate each of the valid expressions in Exercise 3.

5. What is the output produced by the following program?

```
#include <iostream.h>
#include <iomanip.h>

int main ()
{
   cout << setiosflags(ios::showpoint | ios::fixed)
        << setprecision(3);
   cout << endl << "Expression Value" << endl;
   cout << "----------------" << endl << endl;
   cout << " 10 / 5" << setw(12) << 10/5 << endl;
   cout << " 2.0+7*(-1)" << 2.0 + 7 * (-1) << endl << endl;
   return 0;
}
```

3.2 Using Variables

Memory Locations

It is frequently necessary to store values for later use. This is done by putting the value into a *memory location* and using a symbolic name to refer to this location. If the contents of the location are to be changed during a program, the symbolic name is referred to as a *variable;* if the contents are not to be changed, it is referred to as a *constant.*

Objectives

a. to understand the utilization of memory for storing data
b. to distinguish between the name of a memory location and the value stored in a memory location
c. to use variables in assignment statements, expressions, and output statements

A graphic way to think about memory locations is to envision them as boxes; each box is named and a value is stored inside. For example, suppose a program is written to add a sequence of numbers. If we name the memory location to be used sum, initially we have

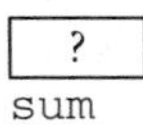

sum

which depicts a memory location that has been reserved and can be accessed by a reference to sum. If we then add the integers 10, 20, and 30 and store them in sum, we have

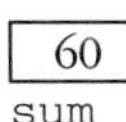

sum

It is important to distinguish between the name of a memory location (sum) and the value or contents of a memory location (60). The name does not change during a program, but the contents can be changed as often as necessary. (Contents of memory locations that are referred to by constants cannot be changed.) If 30 were added to the contents in the previous example, the new value stored in sum could be depicted as

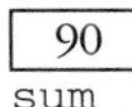

sum

Those symbolic names representing memory locations whose values will be changing must be declared before they are used (as indicated in Section 2.4); for example,

```
int sum;
```

Those that represent memory locations whose values will not be changing must also be defined before they are used.

Assignment Statements

Now we will examine how the contents of variables are manipulated. When variables are declared in a C++ program, they contain values. However, a programmer does not know what these values are. Henceforth, we shall denote these system-supplied values with a question mark (?). The programmer may put a value into a memory location with an *assignment statement* in the form of

```
<variable name>=<value>;
```

or

```
<variable name>=<expression>;
```

where <variable name> is the name of the memory location. For example, if sum has an unknown value, then

```
sum = 30;
```

A NOTE OF INTEREST

Herman Hollerith

Herman Hollerith (1860–1929) was hired by the U.S. Census Bureau in 1879 at the age of 19. Since the 1880 census was predicted to take a long time to complete (it actually took until 1887), Hollerith was assigned the task of developing a mechanical method of tabulating census data. He introduced his census machine in 1887. It consisted of four parts:

1. A punched paper card that represented data using a special code (Hollerith code)
2. A card punch apparatus
3. A tabulator that read the punched cards
4. A sorting machine with 24 compartments.

The punched cards used by Hollerith were the same size as cards still in use until recently.

Using Hollerith's techniques and equipment, the 1890 census tabulation was completed in one-third the time required for the previous census tabulation. This included working with data for 12 million additional people.

Hollerith proceeded to form the Tabulating Machine Company (1896), which supplied equipment to census bureaus in the United States, Canada, and western Europe. After a disagreement with the census director, Hollerith began marketing his equipment in other commercial areas. Hollerith sold his company in 1911. It was later combined with 12 others to form the Computing-Tabulating-Recording Company, a direct ancestor of International Business Machines Corporation.

In the meantime, Hollerith's successor at the census bureau, James Powers, redesigned the census machine. He then formed his own company, which subsequently became Remington Rand, then Sperry Univac, and finally Unisys.

changes

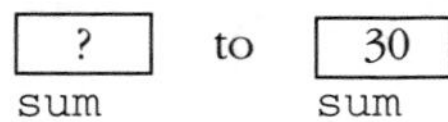

Some important rules follow concerning assignment statements:

1. The assignment is always made from right to left (←).
2. Constants cannot be on the left side of the assignment symbol.
3. The expression can be a constant, a constant expression, a variable that has previously been assigned a value, or a combination of variables and constants.
4. Normally, values on the right side of the assignment symbol are not changed by the assignment.
5. The variable and expression must be of compatible data types.
6. Only one value can be stored in a variable at a time, so the previous value of a variable is thrown away.

One common error that beginners make is trying to assign from left to right.

Repeated assignments can be made. For example, if `sum` is an integer variable, the statements

```
sum = 50;

sum = 70;

sum = 100;
```

produce first 50, then 70, and finally 100 as shown:

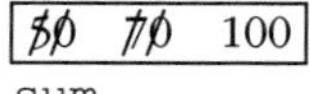

In this sense, memory is destructible in that it retains only the last value assigned.

C++ variables are symbolic addresses that can hold values. When a variable is declared, the type of values it will store must be specified (*declared*). Storing a value of the wrong type in a variable leads to a program error. This means that data types must be compatible when using assignment statements. For now, consider all of the basic data types—`char`, `int`, and `double`—as compatible with each other. This means that assignments of values to variables are allowed for any possible combination of these types on both sides of an assignment statement. Type compatibility and type conversion are discussed in Section 3.7.

Assignments of character constants to a character variable require that the constant be enclosed in single quotation marks. For example, if `letter` is of type `char` and you want to store the letter C in `letter`, use the assignment statement

```
letter = 'C';
```

This could be pictured as

C
`letter`

Furthermore, only one character can be assigned or stored in a character variable at a time.

Expressions

The use of variables in a program is usually more elaborate than what we have just seen. Variables may be used in any manner that does not violate their type declarations. This includes both arithmetic operations and assignment statements. For example, if `score1`, `score2`, `score3`, and `average` are `double` variables,

```
score1 = 72.3;

score2 = 89.4;

score3 = 95.6;

average = (score1 + score2 + score3) / 3.0;
```

is a valid fragment of code.

Now consider the problem of accumulating a total. Assuming `newScore` and `total` are integer variables, the following code is valid:

```
total = 0;
newScore = 5;
total = total + newScore;
newScore = 7;
total = total + newScore;
```

As this code is executed, the values of memory locations for `total` and `newScore` could be depicted as

	total	newScore
`total = 0;`	0	?
`newScore = 5;`	0	5
`total = total + newScore;`	5	5
`newScore = 7;`	5	7
`total = total + newScore;`	12	7

Compound Assignment

Consider the expression `x = x + y`. This expression

1. adds the value of `x` and the value of `y` and then
2. stores the sum in `x`.

This kind of expression occurs so often in programs that C++ provides a shorthand form of it called *compound assignment.* Using this form, the expression

```
x = x + y
```

can be rewritten as

```
x += y
```

Although these two expressions look different, they mean exactly the same thing. The clue for interpreting this compound expression is that the + sign comes before the = sign in the operator +=. This means that the values of `x` and `y` are added before the result is stored in `x`.

As Table 3.8 shows, C++ supports compound assignment operators for each of the standard arithmetic operations. For readability, we will continue to use the longer form of these expressions throughout this text.

Output

Variables and variable expressions can be used when creating output. When used in an output statement, they perform the same function as a constant. For example, if the assignment statement

```
age = 5;
```

Table 3.8
The Compound Assignment Operators

Operator	Form for Use	Equivalent Longer Form
+=	`x += y`	`x = x + y`
-=	`x -= y`	`x = x - y`
*=	`x *= y`	`x = x * y`
/=	`x /= y`	`x = x / y`
%=	`x %= y`	`x = x % y`

has been made, these two statements

```
cout << 5;
cout << age;
```

produce the same output. If `age1`, `age2`, `age3`, and `sum` are integer variables and the assignments

```
age1 = 21;
age2 = 30;
age3 = 12;
sum = age1 + age2 + age3;
```

are made, then

```
cout << "The sum is " << 21 + 30 + 12;
cout << "The sum is " << age1 + age2 + age3;
cout << "The sum is " << sum;
```

all produce the same output.

Formatting variables and variable expressions in output statements follows the same rules that were presented in Chapter 2 for formatting constants. The statements needed to write the sum of the problem we just saw in a field width of four are

```
cout << "The sum is " << setw(4) << 21 + 30 + 12;
cout << "The sum is " << setw(4) << age1 + age2 + age3;
cout << "The sum is " << setw(4) << sum;
```

Example 3.1 Suppose you want a program to print data about the cost of three textbooks and the average price of the books. The variable declaration section could include:

```
double mathText, bioText, compSciText, total, average;
```

A portion of the program could be

```
mathText = 53.95;

bioText = 57.50;

compSciText = 49.95;

total = mathText + bioText + compSciText;

average = total / 3;
```

The output could be created by

```
cout << setiosflags(ios::fixed | ios::showpoint | ios::right)

cout << setprecision(2) << endl;
cout << "Text                    Price" << endl;
```

continued

```
cout << "----                          -----" << endl;
cout << endl;
cout << "Math" << setw(18) << mathText << endl;
cout << "Biology" << setw(15) << bioText << endl;
cout << "CompSci" << setw(15) << compSciText << endl;
cout << endl;
cout << "Total" << setw(17) << total << endl;
cout << endl;
cout << "The average price is" << setw(7) << average << endl;
```

The output would be

```
Text                 Price
----                 -----

Math                 53.95

Biology              57.50

CompSci              49.95

Total               161.40

The average price is    53.80
```

Software Engineering

The communication aspect of software engineering can be simplified by judicious choices of meaningful identifiers. Systems programmers must be aware that over time many others will need to read and analyze the code. Some extra time spent thinking about and using descriptive identifiers provides great time savings during the testing and maintenance phases. Code that is written using descriptive identifiers is referred to as *self-documenting code.*

Exercises 3.2

1. Assume the variable declaration section of a program is

```
int age, IQ;
double income;
```

Indicate which of the following are valid assignment statements. If a statement is invalid, give the reason why.

a. `age = 21;`
b. `IQ = age + 100;`
c. `IQ = 120.5;`
d. `age + IQ = 150;`
e. `income = 22000;`
f. `income = 100 * (age + IQ);`
g. `age = IQ / 3;`
h. `IQ = 3 * age;`

2. Write and run a test program to illustrate what happens when values of one data type are assigned to variables of another type.

3. Suppose a, b, and temp have been declared as integer variables. Indicate the contents of a and b at the end of each sequence of statements.

a.
```
a = 5;
b = -2;
a = a + b;
b = b - a;
```
b.
```
a = 31;
b = 26;
temp = a;
a = b;
b = temp;
```
c.
```
a = 0;
b = 7;
a = a + b % 2 * (-3);
b = b + 4 * a;
```
d.
```
a = -8;
b = 3;
temp = a + b;
a = 3 * b;
b = a;
temp = temp + a + b;
```

4. Suppose x and y are real variables and the assignments

```
x = 121.3;
y = 98.6;
```

have been made. What output statements would cause the following output?

a.
```
The value of x is 121.3
```

b.
```
The sum of x and y is 219.9
```

c.
```
x =     121.3
y =      98.6
      -------
Total = 219.9
```

5. Assume the variable declaration section of a program is

```
int age, height;
double weight;
char gender;
```

What output would be created by the following program fragment?

```
age = 23;
height = 73;
weight = 186.5;
gender = 'M';
cout << setprecision(1);
cout << "Gender" << setw(10) << gender << endl;
cout << "Age" << setw(14) << age << endl;
cout << "Height" << setw(11) << height << " inches" << endl;
cout << "Weight" << setw(14) << weight << " lbs" << endl;
```

6. Write a complete program that allows you to add five integers and then print
   a. The integers.
   b. Their sum.
   c. Their average.

7. Assume `ch` and `age` have been appropriately declared. What output is produced by the following?

```
ch = 'M';

age = 21;
cout  << setw(40) << "******************************" << endl;
cout  << setw(11) << "*" << setw(29) << "*" << endl;
cout  << setw(11) << "*" << setw(7) << "Name" << setw(9) << "Age";
cout  << setw(6) << "Gender" << setw(4) << "*" << endl;
cout  << setw(11) << "*" setw(7) << "----" << setw(9) << "----" << setw(9)
      << "----" << setw(4) << "*" << endl;
cout  << endl;
cout  << setw(11) << "*" << setw(8) << "Jones" << setw(8) << age
      << setw(9) << ch << setw(4) << "*" << endl;
cout  << endl;
cout  << setw(11) << "*" << setw(29) << "*" << endl;
cout  << setw(40) << "******************************" << endl;
```

8. Assume the variable declaration section of a program is

```
int weight1, weight2;
double averageWeight;
```

and the following assignment statements have been made:

```
weight1 = 165;
weight2 = 174;
averageWeight = (weight1 + weight2) / 2;
```

a. What output would be produced by the following section of code?

```
cout << "Weight" << endl;
cout << "------" << endl;
cout << endl;
cout << weight1 << endl;
cout << weight2 << endl;
cout << endl;
cout << "The average weight is" << (weight1 + weight2) / 2 << endl;
```

b. Write a segment of code to produce the following output (use `averageWeight`).

```
            Weight
            ------
              165
              174
              ---
Total         339

The average weight is 169.5 pounds.
```

9. Assume the variable declaration section of a program is `char letter;` and the following assignment has been made: `letter = 'A';`. What output is produced from the following segment of code?

```
cout << setw(40) << "This reviews string formatting" << endl;
cout << "When a letter" << letter << "is used" << endl;
cout << setw(14) << "Oops!" << setw(20) << "I forgot to format."
     << endl;
cout << setw(22) << "When a letter" << setw(2) << letter
     << setw(9) << "is used" << endl;
cout << setw(38) << "it is a string of length one." << endl;
```

10. Explain why it is a good idea to assign a value to a variable as soon as it is declared.

3.3 Input

Objectives

a. to use the standard input stream and its operator to get data for a program
b. to design a program that supports interactive input of data

Earlier, "running a program" was subdivided into the three general categories of getting the data, manipulating it appropriately, and printing the results. Our work thus far has centered on creating output and manipulating data. We are now going to focus on how to get data for a program.

Input Statements

Data for a program are usually obtained from an input device, which can be a keyboard or disk. When such data are obtained from the keyboard, the standard input stream, `cin`, normally is associated with one of these input devices.

The standard input stream, `cin`, is used in a way similar to the standard output stream, `cout`. `cin` behaves like an intelligent agent that knows how to take input from the keyboard and pass it back to a program. To make `cin` available to a program, you must include the C++ library header file `iostream.h`:

```
#include <iostream.h>
```

To obtain input from the standard input stream, you direct it into a variable with the *extractor* operator `>>` (note that the arrows point in the opposite direction from the *inserter* operator, `<<`). For example, assume that `length` is a variable of type `int`. Then the following statement takes input from the keyboard and stores it in `length`:

```
cin >> length;
```

When an input statement is used to get data, the value of the data item is stored in the indicated memory location. Data read into a program must match the type of variable specified. To illustrate, if variable declarations are

```
int age;
double wage;
```

and the data items are

```
21        5.25
```

then

```
cin >> age >> wage;
```

results in

21	5.25
age	wage

Interactive Input

Interactive input refers to entering values from the keyboard while the program is running. An input statement causes the program to halt and wait for data items to be typed. For example, if you want to enter three scores at some point in a program, you can use

```
cin >> score1 >> score2 >> score3;
```

as program statements. At this point, you must enter at least three integers, separated by at least one blank space, and press `<Enter>`. The remaining part of the program is then executed. To illustrate, the following program reads in three integers and prints the integers and their average as output.

```
//Program file: input.cpp
//This program illustrates the use of input statements.

#include <iostream.h>
#include <iomanip.h>
int main ()
{

   int score1, score2, score3;
   double average;

   cin >> score1 >> score2 >> score3;
   average = (score1 + score2 + score3) / 3.0;
   cout << setiosflags (ios::fixed | ios::showpoint | ios::right);
   cout << endl;
   cout << setw(10) << "The numbers are" << setw(4)
        << score1 << setw(4) << score2 << setw(4) << score3
        << endl;
   cout << endl;
   cout << setprecision(2);
   cout << "Their average is"
        << average << endl;
   return 0;

}
```

When the program runs, if you type in

```
89  90  91
```

and press `<Enter>`, output is

```
The numbers are  89  90  91

Their average is 90.00
```

Interactive programs should have a prompting message that tells the user what to do when the program pauses for input. For example, the program in the previous example can be modified by the line

```
cout >> "Please enter 3 scores separated by spaces, ";
cout >> "and then press <Enter>. ";
```

before the line

```
cin >> score1 >> score2 >> score3;
```

The screen will display the message

```
Please enter 3 scores separated by spaces, and then press <Enter>.
```

when the program is run. Another method for getting the three inputs mentioned above is to prompt the user for each one on a separate line. Clearly stated screen messages to the person running a program are what make a program *user-friendly*.

Example 3.2 Pythagorean triples are sets of three integers that satisfy the Pythagorean theorem. That is, integers *a, b,* and *c* such that $a^2 + b^2 = c^2$. The integers 3, 4, and 5 make up such a triple because $3^2 + 4^2 = 5^2$. Formulas for generating Pythagorean triples are $a = m^2 - n^2$, $b = 2mn$, and $c = m^2 + n^2$ where m and n are positive integers such that $m > n$. The following interactive program allows the user to enter values for m and n and then have the Pythagorean triple printed:

```
// Program file: triples.cpp
// This program illustrates Pythagorean triples.

#include <iostream.h>
#include <iomanip.h>

int main ()
{
   int m, n, a, b, c;

   cout << "Enter a positive integer and press <Enter>. ";
   cin >> n;
   cout << "Enter a positive integer greater than " << n;
   cout << " and press <Enter>. ";
   cin >> m;
   a = (m * m) - (n * n);
```

```
    b = 2 * m * n;
    c = (m * m) + (n * n);
    cout << endl;
    cout << "For M = " << m << " and N = " << n;
    cout << " the Pythagorean triple is ";
    cout << setw(5) << a << setw(5) << b << setw(5) << c << endl;
    return 0;

}
```

Sample runs of this program, using data (1,2) and (2,5), produce the following:

```
Enter a positive integer and press <Enter>. 1
Enter a positive integer greater than 1 and press <Enter>. 2

For M = 2 and N = 1 the Pythagorean triple is 3 4 5

Enter a positive integer and press <Enter>. 2
Enter a positive integer greater than 2 and press <Enter>. 5

For M = 5 and N = 2 the Pythagorean triple is 21 20 29
```

Reading Numeric Data

Reading numeric data into a program is reasonably straightforward. At least one character of white space must be used to separate numbers. White space characters are typed by hitting the space bar, the `<Tab>` key, or the `<Enter>` key.

Character Sets

Before we look at reading character data, we need to examine the way in which character data are stored. In the `char` data type, each character is associated with an integer. Thus, the sequence of characters is associated with a sequence of integers. The particular sequence used by a machine for this purpose is referred to as the *collating sequence* for that *character set*. The principal sequence currently in use is the American Standard Code for Information Interchange (ASCII).

Each collating sequence contains an ordering of the characters in a character set and is listed in Appendix D. For programs in this text, we use the ASCII code. As shown in Table 3.9, 52 of these characters are letters, 10 are digits, and the rest are punctuation marks and other special characters. The table included here shows the ordering of the ASCII character set. The printable characters range from ASCII 33 to ASCII 126. The values from ASCII 0 to ASCII 32 and ASCII 127 are associated with white space characters, such as the horizontal tab (HT), or nonprinting control characters, such as the escape key (ESC). The digits in the left column represent the leftmost digits of the ASCII code, and the digits in the top row are the rightmost digits in the ASCII code. Thus, the ASCII code of the character R at row 8, column 2, is 82.

Reading Character Data

Reading characters from the standard input stream using >> is much the same as reading numeric data. If you want to read in a student's initials followed by three test scores, the following code will do that:

Table 3.9
The ASCII Character Set

	0	1	2	3	4	5	6	7	8	9
0	NUL	SOH	STX	ETX	EOT	ENQ	ACK	BEL	BS	HT
1	LF	VT	FF	CR	SO	SI	DLE	DC1	DC2	DC3
2	DC4	NAK	SYN	ETB	CAN	EM	SUB	ESC	FS	GS
3	RS	US	SP	!	"	#	$	%	&	'
4	(	)	*	+	,	-	.	/	0	1
5	2	3	4	5	6	7	8	9	:	;
6	<	=	>	?	@	A	B	C	D	E
7	F	G	H	I	J	K	L	M	N	O
8	P	Q	R	S	T	U	V	W	X	Y
9	Z	[	\	]	^	_	`	a	b	c
10	d	e	f	g	h	i	j	k	l	m
11	n	o	p	q	r	s	t	u	v	w
12	x	y	z	{	|	}	~	DEL		

```
char firstInitial, middleInitial, lastInitial;
int score1, score2, score3;

cin >> firstInitial >> middleInitial >> lastInitial >> score1
    >> score2 >> score3;
```

When program execution is halted, you would type in something like

```
J D K 89 90 91
```

and press <Enter>.

Debugging Output Statements

A frequently used technique for debugging programs is to insert an output statement to print the values of variables. Once you have determined that the desired values are obtained, you can delete the output statements. For example, if your program segment is to read in three scores and three initials, you could write

```
cin >> score1 >> score2 >> score3;
// for debugging
cout << score1 << " " << score2 << " " << score3;

cin >> firstInitial >> middleInitial >> lastInitial;
// for debugging
cout << firstInitial << " " << middleInitial << " " << lastInitial;
```

These debugging lines might be left in until the program has been sufficiently tested for input.

Exercises 3.3

1. Discuss the difference between `cin` and `cout`.
2. Assume a variable declaration section is

```
int num1, num2;

double num3;

char ch;
```

and you wish to enter the data

```
15 65.3 -20
```

Note that a single space separates these data. Explain what results from each statement. Also indicate what values are assigned to appropriate variables.

a. `cin >> num1 >> num3 >> num2;`
b. `cin >> num1 >> num2 >> num3;`
c. `cin >> num1 >> num2 >> ch >> num3;`
d. `cin >> num2 >> num3 >> ch >> num2;`
e. `cin >> num2 >> num3 >> ch >> ch >> num2;`
f. `cin >> num3 >> num2;`
g. `cin >> num1 >> num3;`
h. `cin >> num1 >> ch >> num3;`

3. Write a program statement to be used to print a message to the screen directing the user to enter data in the form used for Exercise 2. Write an appropriate program statement (or statements) to produce a screen message and write an appropriate input statement for each of the following.

a. Desired input is number of hours worked and hourly pay rate.
b. Desired input is three positive integers followed by –999.
c. Desired input is price of an automobile and the state sales tax rate.
d. Desired input is the game statistics for one basketball player (check with a coach to see what must be entered).
e. Desired input is a student's initials, age, height, weight, and gender.

4. Assume variables are declared as in Exercise 2. If an input statement is

```
cin >> num1 >> num2 >> ch >> num3;
```

indicate which lines of the following data do not result in an error message. For those that do not, indicate the values of the variables. For those that produce an error, explain what the error is.

a. `83 95 100`
b. `83 95.0 100`
c. `83-72 93.5`
d. `83 72 93.5`
e. `83.5`
f. `70 73-80.5`
g. `91 92 93 94`
h. `-76-81-16.5`

5. Why is it a good idea to print values of variables that have been read into a program?

6. Write a complete program that will read your initials and five test scores. Your program should then compute your test average and print all information in a reasonable form with suitable messages.

3.4 String Variables

Objectives

a. to learn how to declare and use string variables
b. to learn how to input a string one word at a time or one line at a time
c. to learn how strings are represented in computer memory
d. to learn how to concatenate strings

The `apstring` data type is defined in the C++ `apstring` library. `apstring` is a nonstandard library, the code for which is on the disk that comes with this book. This data type can be used to declare string variables. Before declaring a string variable, you must include the library header file, `apstring.h`, at the beginning of the program. The following program fragment declares a string variable, assigns it a value, and outputs it on the screen:

```
#include "apstring.h"

apstring name;

name = "John Doe";
cout << name;
```

String Input with >>

A string variable can also receive input from the standard input stream, as in the following example:

```
#include "apstring.h"

apstring name;

cout << "Enter your last name: ";
cin >> name;
```

As with numbers, the >> operator ignores leading white space characters (a space, a tab, or a carriage return) and then reads nonblank characters up to the next white space character. The user is allowed to erase any input characters with the backspace or delete key until the trailing white space key is struck. When the user strikes the trailing white space key, the computer allocates memory for the string and stores the nonblank input characters in this memory.

String Input with `getline`

The >> operator cannot be used to enter a string containing spaces. Thus, the string "John Doe" cannot be input into a string variable with the >> operator. To solve this problem, the `apstring` library provides the function `getline`. As the name implies, this function reads characters, including the tab and space characters, from an input stream into a string variable, until a newline (`'\n'`) character is detected. The newline character is not stored in the string variable.

```
getline(<input stream>,<string variable>)
```

Recall that `cin` is the name of the standard input stream for reading characters from the keyboard. Thus, the following code segment could obtain the string "John Doe" from the keyboard:

```
#include "apstring.h"

apstring name;

cout << "Enter your full name: ";
getline(cin, name);
```

Because `getline` does not ignore leading white space characters, you should take special care when using it in conjunction with >>. Consider the following example:

```
#include "apstring.h"

apstring name;
int age;

cout << "Enter your age: ";
cin >> age;
cout << "Enter your full name: ";
getline(cin, name);
cout << name ", you are " << age << endl;
```

This program segment will allow the user to enter the age. It then prompts for the name but displays the results immediately without pausing for the input of the name. The reason is that >> reads and stores characters up to the newline character in `age`. `getline` then detects this newline character as the first character "in" the input of the name, so it returns with an empty string before the user can enter any characters.

Here are two ways to avoid this problem:

1. Reverse the order of the inputs, with `getline` being called before >>. In general, if you adopt this method, a call to `getline` can come after another call to `getline`, but never after a call to >>. Thus, a correct code segment is

```
#include "apstring.h"

apstring name;
int age;

cout << "Enter your full name: ";
getline(cin, name);
cout << "Enter your age: ";
cin >> age;
cout << name ", you are " << age << endl;
```

2. In cases where at least one call of >> must come before a call of `getline`, you must "consume" the trailing newline character first. A simple way to do this is to declare a dummy string variable and run `getline` with it after the >> operation. This has the effect of "throwing away" the extra newline character before the next call to `getline`. A correct code segment that uses this method is

```
#include "apstring.h"

apstring name, dummy;
int age;
```

A NOTE OF INTEREST

Computer Ethics: Copyright, Intellectual Property, and Digital Information

For hundreds of years, copyright law has existed to regulate the use of intellectual property. At stake are the rights of authors and publishers to a return on their investment in works of the intellect, which include printed matter (books, articles, etc.), recorded music, film, and video. More recently, copyright law has been extended to include software and other forms of digital information. For example, the software on the disk bundled with this book is protected by copyright law. This prohibits the purchaser from reproducing the software for sale or free distribution to others. If the software is stolen or "pirated" in this way, the perpetrator can be prosecuted and punished by law. However, copyright law also allows for "fair use"—the purchaser may make backup copies of the software for personal use. When the purchaser sells the software to another user, the seller thereby relinquishes the right to use it and the new purchaser acquires this right.

When they design copyright legislation, governments try to balance the rights of authors and publishers to a return on their work against the rights of the public to fair use. In the case of printed matter and other works that have a physical embodiment, the meaning of fair use is fairly clear. Without fair use, borrowing a book from a library or playing a CD at a high school dance would be unlawful.

With the rapid rise of digital information and its easy transmission on networks, different interest groups—authors, publishers, users, and computer professionals—are beginning to question the traditional balance of ownership rights and fair use. For example, is browsing a copyrighted manuscript on a network service an instance of fair use? Or does it involve a reproduction of the manuscript that violates the rights of the author or publisher? Is the manuscript a physical piece of intellectual property when browsed or just a temporary pattern of bits in a computer's memory? Users and technical experts tend to favor free access to any information placed on a network. Publishers and, to a lesser extent, authors tend to worry that their work, when placed on a network, will be resold for profit.

Legislators struggling with the adjustment of copyright law to a digital environment face many of these questions and concerns. Providers and users of digital information should also be aware of the issues. For a detailed discussion, see Pamela Samuelson, "Regulation of Technologies to Protect Copyrighted Works," *Communications of the ACM,* Vol. 39, No. 7, Jul. 1996, pp. 17–22, and "Good News and Bad News on the Intellectual Property Front," *Communications of the ACM,* Vol. 42, No. 3, Mar. 1999, pp. 19–24.

```
cout << "Enter your age: ";
cin >> age;
getline(cin, dummy);                  // Consume the trailing newline
cout << "Enter your full name: ";
getline(cin, name);
cout << name ", you are " << age << endl;
```

To summarize, we use `>>` when we want to read a single word into a string variable, and we use `getline` when we want to read an entire line of words into a string variable.

Example 3.3 Faculty members at the local college are categorized by name, rank, and number of years of service. The following complete program uses string variables to take this information as input and display it as output.

```
//Program faculty.cpp
//This program echoes the name, rank, and number of years of
//service of a college professor.

#include <iostream.h>
#include "apstring.h"
```

continued

```
int main ()
{
   apstring name, rank;
   char middleInitial;
   int yearsOfService;

   cout << "Enter the full name: ";
   getline(cin, name);
   cout << "Enter the rank (Assistant, Associate, or Full): ";
   cin >> rank;
   cout << "Enter the number of years of service: ";
   cin >> yearsOfService;
   cout << endl << endl;
   cout << "Name: " << name << endl;
   cout << "Rank: " << rank << " Professor" << endl;
   cout << "Years of service: " << yearsOfService << endl;
   return 0;
}
```

A sample interaction with this program is

```
Enter the name: Albert H. Einstein
Enter the rank (Assistant, Associate, or Full): Full
Enter the number of years of service: 25


Name: Albert H. Einstein
Rank: Full Professor
Years of service: 25
```

Memory for String Variables

The computer manages memory for string variables and numeric variables differently. Memory for a numeric variable is always of a fixed size, although the actual size varies with the numeric type. When a string variable is declared, no memory for the string's character data is initially provided. During an assignment statement or an input statement, the computer automatically adjusts the memory for a string variable to accommodate the number of characters to be stored there. For example, suppose that the following code segment has just run:

```
int num1, num2;
apstring word1, word2;

num1 = 10;
num2 = 100;
word1 = "Hi there";
word2 = "Hello";
```

The memory allocated for these variables can be visualized in this way:

10

num1

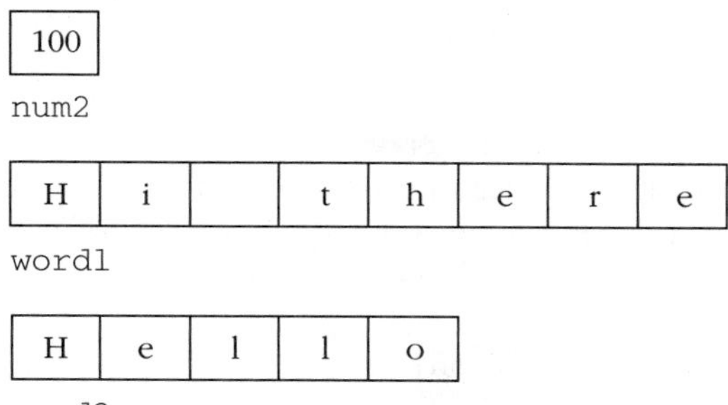

Note that the memory cells for the two integers are the same size, even though the integer values stored there are of different sizes. But the memory cells for the two strings are of different sizes to accommodate string values containing different numbers of characters.

The `length` function returns the number of characters currently stored in a string variable. The form for calling `length` is different from that of ordinary function calls and will take some getting used to:

```
<string variable>.length()
```

Thus, the following code segment

```
cout << "Length of " << word1 << " = " << word1.length() << endl;
cout << "Length of " << word2 << " = " << word2.length() << endl;
```

produces the output

```
Length of Hi there = 8
Length of Hello = 5
```

The `apstring` library limits the number of characters in a string to 1023. However, most strings that you encounter will be considerably smaller than this.

The Empty String

Although no memory is allocated for character data when a string variable is declared, the computer considers the variable to contain the empty string. The empty string is represented in C++ as the literal "" (two consecutive double quotation marks). Thus, the memory allocated for the string variable in the following code segment does not change:

```
apstring word;

cout << word.length() << endl;
word = "";
cout << word.length() << endl;
```

The output produced by this code segment is

```
0
0
```

String Concatenation

An important operation on strings is *concatenation.* Concatenation puts two objects together in such a way that the second one follows the first one in a new object. One version of this operation copies the characters in two strings to a third string. The following code segment concatenates the strings "Hi" and "there" to form the string "Hi there" and then displays this string on the screen:

```
apstring first, second, third;

first = "Hi";
second = " there";
third = first + second;
cout << third;
```

The concatentation operator for strings is +. Note that when used with numbers, + means "add," but when used with strings, + means "concatenate."

The + operator can also be used to append a character to the end of a string. For example, the following code segment displays the string "fishes" on the screen:

```
string singular;

singular = "fish";
cout << (singular + 'e' + 's') << endl;
```

Note the following points about this code:

1. The concatenation operations in this example are performed from left to right. The first operation builds the string "fishe" from "fish" and 'e'. The second operation builds the string "fishes" from "fishe" and 's'.
2. The concatenation operator does not change the contents of its operands. It builds a new string with the contents of its operands and returns this string as a value.
3. The sequence of concatenations is enclosed within parentheses. We do this to guarantee that the program will perform these operations before the output operation.

Compound Assignment with Strings

Another form of string concatenation occurs when the compound assignment operator `+=` is used. Recall from Section 3.2 that in the context of numbers, the expression `x += y` means the same thing as `x = x + y`. In the context of strings, where `x` is a string and `y` is a string, the two expressions are equivalent also, but + now means concatentation. For example, the following code segment

```
apstring x, y;

x = "Hi ";
y = "there.";
x += y;
cout << x << endl;
```

would display the string

```
Hi there.
```

Note that the expression `x + y` builds and returns a new string but does not change `x` and `y`. However, the expression `x += y` builds a new string from `x` and `y` and then stores this string in the variable `x`.

The compound assignment operator can also be used to concatenate a character value to the left operand as follows:

```
apstring x;
char y;

x = "rose";
y = 's';
x += y;
```

However, the expression `y += x` is invalid because the resulting string cannot be stored in the character variable `y`.

For readability, we will continue to use the long form, `x = x + y`, for assignment with string concatenation in this text.

Exercises 3.4

1. Assume the user has entered the strings "The" and "rain" into the string variables `first` and `second`, respectively. Write program statements that use these variables to perform the following tasks:
   a. output the string "The rain"
   b. store the string "The rain" in a new string variable, `third`
   c. reset the value of each variable to an empty string
   d. prompt the user for new strings to be entered into the variables and input them
2. Explain why the `>>` operator can only read one word at a time from an input stream.
3. Suppose the user types the string "567 is a small number" at the keyboard followed by a carriage return. `word1` and `word2` are string variables and `number` is an `int`. Describe the contents of the variables when the following statements are run to receive this input:
   a. `cin >> word1;`
   b. `getline(cin, word1);`
   c. `cin >> number;`
   d. `cin >> number >> word1;`
   e. `cin >> number;`
      `getline(cin, word1);`
   f. `cin >> number;`
      `getline(cin, word1);`
      `getline(cin, word2);`
4. Draw a picture that shows how the character data for the string "Computer Science" might be stored in a string variable named `department`. Then draw another picture that shows what might happen to this memory when the variable `department` is reset to "French."
5. Indicate which of the following expressions are valid. If an expression is valid, describe the value returned. If an expression is invalid, explain why.
   a. `"Hi" + "there"`
   b. `"Hi" + 's'`
   c. `"Hi" + 4`
   d. `'H' + 'i' + 's'`
   e. `"H" + 'i' + 's'`

6. Write an expression that concatenates the character values 'H', 'i', and 's' to form the string "His". (*Hint:* You must use a special string value in the expression.)
7. Write a complete interactive program that inputs your name, address, and telephone number into string variables and displays them on the screen. Be sure to issue the appropriate prompts for the input information.
8. Explain why the + operator is used for addition of numbers and concatenation of strings.

3.5 Using Constants

Objectives

a. to be aware of the appropriate use of constants
b. to use constants in programs
c. to format constants

The word *constant* has several interpretations. In this section, we distinguish between a symbolic constant, such as PI, and a literal constant, such as 3.14. Symbolic constants are defined by giving them the values of literal constants. Recall that a C++ program as we know it thus far consists of preprocessor directives, an optional constant and type definition section, a program heading, an optional variable declaration section, and an executable section. We will now examine uses for constants defined in the constant subsection.

Rationale for Uses

There are many reasons to use constants in a program. If a number is to be used frequently, the programmer may wish to give it a descriptive name in the constant definition subsection and then use the descriptive name in the executable section, thus making the program easier to read. For example, if a program included a segment that computed a person's state income tax, and the state tax rate was 6.25% of taxable income, the constant section might include:

```
const double STATE_TAX_RATE = 0.0625;
```

This defines both the value and type for `STATE_TAX_RATE`. In the executable portion of the program, the statement

```
stateTax = income * STATE_TAX_RATE;
```

computes the state tax owed. Or suppose you wanted a program to compute areas of circles. Depending on the accuracy you desire, you could define π as

```
const double PI = 3.14159;
```

You could then have a statement in the executable section such as

```
area = PI * radius * radius;
```

where `area` and `radius` are appropriately declared variables.

Perhaps the most important use of constants is for currently fixed values that are subject to change for subsequent updates of the program. If these are defined in the constant section, they can be used throughout the program. If the value changes later, only one change needs to be made to keep the program current. This prevents the need to locate all uses of a constant in a program. Some examples might be

```
const double MINIMUM_WAGE = 4.25;
const int SPEED_LIMIT = 65;
const double PRICE = 0.75;
const double STATE_TAX_RATE = 0.0625;
```

Be careful to specify the type of the constant you are declaring. If you omit the type, the result can be quite unexpected. For example, the declaration

```
const PI = 3.14;
```

gives `PI` the integer value 3 because numeric constants without a type default to type `int`!

Software Engineering

The appropriate use of constants is consistent with principles of software engineering. Communication between teams of programmers is enhanced when program constants have been agreed on. Each team should have a list of these constants for use as they work on their part of the system.

The maintenance phase of the software system life cycle is also aided by the use of defined constants. Clearly, a large payroll system depends on performing computations that include deductions for federal tax, state tax, FICA, Medicare, health insurance, retirement options, and so on. If appropriate constants are defined for these deductions, system changes are easily made as necessary. For example, the current salary limit for deducting FICA taxes is $62,500. Since this amount changes regularly, one could define

```
const double FICA_LIMIT = 62500.00;
```

Program maintenance is then simplified by changing the value of this constant as the law changes.

Library Constants

Some constants are provided in C++ libraries. For example, it is often necessary to determine the range of integer values allowed by a particular computer system, the range of real number values, or the number of digits of precision supported by the system. The C++ library header files `limits.h` and `double.h` define constants for each of these important values for your particular system. When you include these files at the beginning of your source program, each of the constants appearing in Table 3.10 will be available for use.

Table 3.10
Library Constants for Maximum Numeric Values

Library Constant	Meaning
INT_MAX	The maximum allowable positive integer value
INT_MIN	The maximum allowable negative integer value
DBL_MAX	The maximum allowable positive double value
DBL_MIN	The maximum allowable negative double value
DBL_DIG	The maximum number of digits of precision

A NOTE OF INTEREST

Defined Constants and Space Shuttle Computing

An excellent illustration of the utilization of defined constants in a program was given by J. F. ("Jack") Clemons, former manager of avionics flight software development and verification for the space shuttle on-board computers. In an interview with David Gifford, editor for *Communications of the ACM,* Clemons was asked: "Have you tried to restructure the software so that it can be changed easily?"

His response was, "By changing certain data constants, we can change relatively large portions of the software on a mission-to-mission basis. For example, we've designed the software so that characteristics like atmospheric conditions on launch day or different lift-off weights can be loaded as initial constants into the code. This is important when there are postponements or last-minute payload changes that invalidate the original inputs."

Formatting Constants

Formatting symbolic constants is identical to formatting real and integer values as discussed in Section 2.3.

Exercises 3.5

1. Write a short program that includes the `limits` and `float` libraries and displays the values of the constants listed in Table 3.10.
2. Why is the use of symbolic constants preferable to literal constants?
3. Write C++ code to define the following symbolic constants:
   a. `PI`
   b. The number of degrees to be added to a Celsius temperature to produce a Fahrenheit temperature.
   c. The number of degrees in a right angle.
   d. The last letters (upper- and lowercase) in the alphabet.

3.6 Library Functions

Objectives

a. to understand the reasons for having library functions
b. to use library functions in a program
c. to use appropriate data types for the arguments of library functions

Some standard operations required by programmers are squaring numbers and finding square roots of numbers. Because these operations are so basic, C++ provides *library functions* for them. Different versions of C++ and other programming languages have differing library functions available, so you should always check which functions can be used. Appendix B sets forth some of those available in most versions of C++.

A function can be used in a program if it appears in the following form:

```
<function name>(<argument list>)
```

where *argument* is a value or variable with an assigned value. When a function appears in this manner, it is said to be *called* or *invoked.* A function is invoked by using it in a program statement. After the function performs its work, it may *return a value.* If, for example, you want to raise 3 to the fourth power, you include the `math.h` library header file and then

```
cout << pow(3, 4) << endl;
```

produces the desired result and returns it as a value to the caller.

Table 3.11
Some Math Library Functions

Function Declaration	Action of Function
`double fmod(double x, double y);`	returns floating-point remainder of `x / y`
`double log(double x);`	returns natural logarithm of `x`
`double pow(double x, double y);`	returns `x` raised to power of `y`
`double sqrt(double x);`	returns square root of `x`
`double cos(double x);`	returns cosine of `x`

Table 3.12
Values of Function Expressions

Expression	Value
`pow(2, 4)`	16
`pow(2.0, 4)`	16.0
`pow(-3, 2)`	9
`fmod(5.3, 2.1)`	1.1
`sqrt(25.0)`	5.0
`sqrt(25)`	5
`sqrt(0.0)`	0.0
`sqrt(-2.0)`	Not permissible

Many functions operate on numbers, starting with a given number and returning some associated value. Table 3.11 shows five math library functions, each with its argument type, data type of return, and an explanation of the value returned. A more complete list of library functions can be found in Appendix B. Several examples of specific function expressions together with the value returned by each expression are depicted in Table 3.12.

Using Functions

When a function is invoked, it produces a value in much the same way that 3 + 3 produces 6. Thus, the use of a function should be treated similarly to the use of constants or values of an expression. Typical uses are in assignment statements,

```
x = sqrt(16.0);
```

output statements,

```
cout << setw(20) << pow(2, 5);
```

or arithmetic expressions

```
hypotenuse = sqrt(pow(base, 2) + pow(height, 2));
```

Arguments of functions can be expressions, variables, or constants.

Member Functions

Some library functions are associated with C++ data types called *classes*. The `apstring` data type is one of these classes. The functions defined for strings are called *member functions*. A member function behaves just like a standard C++ function but is invoked with a different syntax. As you have seen, the `string` member function `length` examines a string and returns the number of characters currently stored in it.

```
apstring word;

cout << word.length();
word = "Hello";
cout << word.length();
```

Note that the syntax used to call this function is different from that of other more conventional function calls that you have seen. Instead of the form

<conventional function name>(<variable name>)

we have

<variable name>.<member function name>()

In either case, the important point is not the syntax, but what the function does. Table 3.13 lists some commonly used `apstring` member functions. A complete list of the `apstring` functions appears in Appendix E.

Table 3.13
Some `apstring` Member Functions

`apstring` Member Function	What It Does	Example of Use

`int length()`	Returns the number of characters in the string.	`apstring s = "Hello there";`
		`cout << s.length();`
		`// Displays 11`

`int find(<a string>)`	Returns the starting position of the first occurrence of a string or –1 if the string does not exist.	`apstring s = "Hello there";`
		`cout << s.find("there");`
		`// Displays 6`

`int find(<a character>)`	Returns the starting position of the first occurrence of a character or –1 if the character does not exist.	`apstring s = "Hello there";`
		`cout << s.find('H');`
		`// Displays 0`

`apstring substr(<position>, <length>)`	Returns a substring of `length` characters starting at `position`.	`apstring s = "Hello there";`
		`cout << s.substr(3, 2);`
		`// Displays "lo"`

Random Numbers

Many applications require the use of random numbers. For example, a computerized game of backgammon requires the roll of two dice on each move. The results can be computed by selecting two random numbers between 1 and 6. C++ provides a library function, `rand`, that returns an integer between 0 and the compiler-dependent constant `RAND_MAX`, inclusive. Both the function and the constant are declared in the library header file `stdlib.h`. Unfortunately, the numbers generated by `rand` are not as random as we would like. The reason is the number returned by `rand` depends on an initial value, called a *seed*, that is the same for each run of a program. Thus, the sequence of random numbers generated by a program that uses this method will be exactly the same on each run of the program.

To help solve this problem, another function, `srand(seed)`, also declared in `stdlib.h`, allows an application to specify the initial value used by `rand` at program start-up. Using this method, two runs of a program that use different values for `seed` will thus receive different sequences of random numbers. The problem then becomes one of providing an arbitrary seed value. Rather than force a user to enter this value interactively, most applications obtain it by reading the current time from the computer's internal clock. The C++ data type `time_t` and the function `time`, both declared in the `time.h` library header file, can be used to obtain the current time on the computer's clock. When converted to an unsigned integer, the current time can serve as a fairly arbitrary seed for a random number generator in most programs.

To summarize the discussion so far, the following program would display three random numbers between 0 and `RAND_MAX`, depending on the current time on the computer's clock at program start-up:

```
// Program file: randtest.cpp

// Displays three random numbers

#include <iostream.h>
#include <stdlib.h>
#include <time.h>

int main()
{
   time_t seconds;

   time(&seconds);
   srand((unsigned int) seconds);
   cout << rand() << endl;
   cout << rand() << endl;
   cout << rand() << endl;
   return 0;
}
```

Users of a random number generator might desire a narrower or a wider range of numbers than `rand` provides. Ideally, a user would specify the range with integer values representing the lower and upper bounds. To see how we might use `rand` to accomplish this, first consider how to generate a number between 0 and an arbitrary upper bound, `high`, inclusive. For any two integers, a and b, $a \% b$ is between 0 and b–1, inclusive. Thus, the expression `rand() % high + 1` would generate a random number between 1 and `high`, inclusive, where `high` is less than or equal to RAND_MAX. To place a lower bound other than 1 on the result, we can generate a random number between 0 and `high - low` and then add `low` to the result. Thus, the complete expression for computing a random number between a lower bound and an upper bound is `rand() % (high - low + 1) + low`.

Example 3.4 The following complete program uses constants and random numbers to display the results of two rolls of dice:

```
// Program file: dice.cpp
// This program displays the results of two rolls of dice.

#include <iostream.h>
#include <stdlib.h>
#include <time.h>

const int LOW = 1;
const int HIGH = 6;

int main ()
{
   int firstDie, secondDie;
   time_t seconds;

   time(&seconds);
   srand((unsigned int) seconds);
   firstDie = rand() % (HIGH - LOW + 1) + LOW;
   secondDie = rand() % (HIGH - LOW + 1) + LOW;
   cout << "Your roll is (" <<firstDie <<", "
        << secondDie << ")" << endl << endl;
   firstDie = rand() % (HIGH - LOW + 1) + LOW;
   secondDie = rand() % (HIGH - LOW + 1) + LOW;
   cout << "My roll is (" << firstDie << ", "
        << secondDie << ")" << endl << endl;
   return 0;
}
```

A sample run might produce the following output:

```
Your roll is (1, 4)
My roll is (6, 6)
```

Note that the use of constants and the complete expressions for computing random numbers are not really necessary for this program. We could have used the expression `rand() % 6 + 1` for simplicity.

Exercises 3.6

1. Write a short program that displays the square root of an input number. Test the program with input values whose square roots are whole numbers and whose square roots are not whole numbers.
2. Test the program from Exercise 1 with a negative input value. How does your computer respond?
3. Explain the facts that a programmer must know about a function to use it properly.

4. Suppose that a programmer wants to generate a random real number between 0 and 1. Suggest an algorithm for accomplishing this.

5. Write a program to test your suggestion in Exercise 4.

3.7 Type Compatibility and Type Conversion

Objectives

a. to understand how different data types are related to each other

b. to understand how one data type can be converted to another

We mentioned in Section 3.2 that the operands of arithmetic expressions and assignment statements must be of compatible data types. For example, we saw that we could not only add an integer to an integer, but also add an integer to a real number. In the latter case, the computer performs an *implicit type conversion* of the integer operand before performing the addition and then returns a real number as the sum. This kind of type conversion is also referred to as *type promotion* because the value of a less inclusive type, `int`, is elevated to a value of a more inclusive type, `double`.

Implicit type conversion also occurs when an integer value is assigned to a variable of type `double`. In this case, a copy of the integer value is placed in the real number's storage location and then promoted by adding to it a fractional part of zero. For example, assuming that `realNumber` is of type `double`, the following two lines of code would produce an output of 3.00:

```
realNumber = 3;
cout << setiosflags(ios::showpoint | ios::fixed)
cout << setprecision(2) << realNumber << endl;
```

Conversely, when you assign a real number to a variable of type `int`, the system drops or truncates a copy of the real number's value before placing it in the integer's storage location. Thus, the following two lines of code would display the value 5, assuming that `wholeNumber` is an `int`:

```
wholeNumber = 5.76;
cout << wholeNumber << endl;
```

The Character Set Once Again

It turns out that characters and integers are also compatible types in C++. This means that character values can be assigned to integer variables, integer values can be assigned to character variables, and integers can be added to characters. Moreover, each of these operations involves an implicit type conversion. To make sense of this apparently strange phenomenon, we must consider the character set once more.

Ordering a character set requires association of an integer with each character. Data types ordered in some association with the integers are known as *ordinal data types*. Each integer is the ordinal of its associated value. Character sets are considered to be an ordinal data type, as shown in Table 3.9. In each case, the ordinal of the character appears to the left of the character. Using ASCII, as shown in Table 3.9, the ordinal of a capital a (A) is 65, the ordinal of the character representing the Arabic number one (1) is 49, the ordinal of a blank is 32, and the ordinal of a lowercase a (a) is 97. Once we realize that characters are really represented as integers in a computer, we can begin to see how we can perform mixed-mode operations on these two data types. When a character value is assigned to an integer variable, the run-time system copies the character's ordinal into the integer's storage location. Thus, assuming an

ASCII representation and our `wholeNumber` variable of type `int`, the following two lines of code display the number 65:

```
wholeNumber = 'A';
cout << wholeNumber << endl;
```

Conversely, assuming that `letter` is of type `char`, the following two lines of code display the letter A:

```
letter = 65;
cout << letter << endl;
```

When arithmetic operations are performed on characters (either two character values or one character and one integer), each character value is first promoted to a more inclusive type, namely, an integer. Then the system performs the operation, and the result returned is an integer. For example, the following two lines of code display the value 66:

```
wholeNumber = 'A' + 1;
cout << wholeNumber << endl;
```

It turns out that since the decimal digits are in the collating sequence from 0 to 9 in the character set, the integer value of a given digit can be computed quite easily with *character arithmetic*. For example, assuming that `digit` is of type `int`, the following two lines of code compute and display the integer value of the digit 5:

```
digit = '5' - '0';
cout << digit << endl;
```

In the next example, we show how to use character arithmetic to convert an uppercase letter to lowercase.

Example 3.3 On computer systems that use the ASCII ordering of characters, we can use character arithmetic to convert an uppercase letter to lowercase. Let us assume that our task is to convert the letter 'H' to the letter 'h'. We first subtract 'A' from 'H' to obtain

```
'H' - 'A'
```

which is

```
72 - 65 = 7
```

We now add 'a' to get

```
'H' - 'A' + 'a'
```

which yields

```
72 - 65 + 97 = 104
```

This is the ordinal of 'h'. It can be converted to the letter by assigning it to a variable of type `char`. Thus,

```
letter = 'H' - 'A' + 'a';
```

places the letter 'h' in the variable letter, where letter is of type char.

In general, the following is sufficient for converting from uppercase to lowercase, where the two names are of type char:

```
lowerCase = upperCase - 'A' + 'a';
```

Note that if you always use the same ASCII ordering,

```
-'A' + 'a'
```

could be replaced by the constant 32. If you choose to do this, 32 should be given a name. A typical definition is

```
const int UPPER_TO_LOWER_SHIFT = 32;
```

You would then write the lowercase conversion as

```
lowerCase = upperCase + UPPER_TO_LOWER_SHIFT;
```

The C++ library ctype defines several functions that can be used to process individual characters. See Appendix B for a list of these functions.

Type Casts

Occasionally, we would like to force the conversion of a value from one type to another without resorting to an assignment statement. For example, the expression wholeNumber % realNumber will generate an error because the modulus operator is not defined on real numbers. We would like to convert the real number to an integer within the expression rather than complicate matters by declaring an extra integer variable, assigning the real number to it, and then using the integer variable.

C++ provides a set of operators called *type casts* for performing *explicit type conversions* of this sort. You can think of a type cast as a function whose name is the name of the type to which you wish to convert a value. The argument of this function is the value to be converted, and the value returned by the function is the converted value. For example, the following line of code uses the type cast for integers to display the integer value 3:

```
cout << int(3.14) << endl;
```

Our method of converting an uppercase letter to lowercase can make good use of the type cast for characters:

```
cout << char(upperCase - UPPER_TO_LOWER_SHIFT) << endl;
```

The form of a type cast that we will use in this text is

<type name> (<expression>)

where <type name> is the name of the target type and <expression> evaluates to a type of value that the cast is capable of converting. In some rare cases, such as a conversion to type long int, the following form of type cast should be used:

```
(<type name>) <expression>
```

For example, the following statement converts an integer value to a `long int` for output:

```
cout << (long int) anInteger;
```

Exercises 3.7

1. Find the value of each of the following expressions:
   a. `sqrt(15.51)`
   b. `pow(-14.2, 3)`
   c. `4 * 11 % sqrt(16)`
   d. `pow(17 / 5 * 2, 2)`
   e. `-5.0 + sqrt(5 * 5 - 4 * 6) / 2.0`
2. Write a test program that illustrates what happens when an inappropriate argument is used with a function. Be sure to include something like `sqrt(-1)`.
3. Two standard algebraic problems come from the Pythagorean theorem and the quadratic formula. Assume variables *a*, *b*, and *c* have been declared in a program. Write C++ expressions that allow you to evaluate the following:
   a. The length of the hypotenuse of a right triangle: $\sqrt{a^2 + b^2}$
   b. Both solutions to the quadratic formula: $\dfrac{-b \pm \sqrt{b^2 - 4ac}}{2a}$
4. Indicate whether the following are valid or invalid expressions. Find the value of those that are valid; explain why the others are invalid.
   a. `-6 % (sqrt(16))`
   b. `8 / sqrt(65)`
   c. `sqrt(63 % (2))`
   d. `-sqrt(pow(3, 2) - 7)`
   e. `sqrt(16 / (-3))`
   f. `sqrt(pow(-4, 2))`
5. Using ASCII, find the values of each of the following expressions:
   a. 13 + 4 % 3
   b. 'E'
   c. 'E' + 1
   d. 5
   e. '5'
   f. '+'
   g. 40
6. Assume the variable declaration section of a program is

```
double x;
int a;
char ch;
```

   What output is produced by each of the following program fragments?
   a.
```
x = -4.3;
cout << setprecision(2) << setw(6) << x << int(x) << endl;
```
   b.
```
x = -4.3;
a = x;
cout << a << int('a');
```

c. `ch = char(76);`
   `cout << setw(5) << ch << setw(5) << char(ch - 1);`

7. Write a complete program to print each uppercase letter of the alphabet and its ordinal in the collating sequence used by your machine's version of C++. (*Hint:* The first output statement might be `cout << 'A' << int('A') << endl;`.)

8. Using ASCII, show how each of the following conversions can be made:
   a. A lowercase letter converted into its uppercase equivalent.
   b. A digit entered as a char value into its indicated numeric value.

Writing styles and suggestions are gathered for quick reference in the following style tip summary. These tips are intended to stimulate rather than terminate your imagination.

Communication and Style Tips

1. Use descriptive identifiers. Words—`sum`, `score`, `average`—are easier to understand than letters—`a`, `b`, `c` or `x`, `y`, `z`.

2. The decimal points in the output of a column of reals should be aligned:

```
 14.32
181.50
 93.63
```

3. Output can be made more attractive by using columns, left or right justification, underlining, and blank lines.

4. Extra output statements at the beginning and end of the executable section will separate desired output from other messages.

```
cout << endl;
      .
      .(program body here)
      .
cout << endl;
```

Case Study: Computing the Cost of Pizza

Beginning in this chapter, a case study develops a complete program to illustrate concepts. In each case, we follow the software life cycle phases of analysis, design, and implementation. A typical problem is stated and a trace of the input and output is displayed. A solution is developed in pseudocode and illustrated with a structure chart. Module specifications are written for appropriate modules. Now, on to the problem for this chapter.

User Request

Write a complete program to find the unit price for a pizza.

Analysis

In analysis, we describe what the program will do without going into how the program does it. The focus is on the user's view of the behavior of the program. This behavior can be described in terms of the program's inputs and outputs. Input for the program consists of the price (a real number) and size (an integer) of the pizza. Size is the diameter of the pizza ordered. Output consists of the price per square inch in dollars and cents. Here is a trace of a typical input and output during execution:

```
Enter the pizza price and press <Enter>. 10.50
Enter the pizza size and press <Enter>. 16
The price per square inch is $0.05
```

Design

In design, we describe how the program performs its tasks. A first-level design for the pizza program is

1. Get the data
2. Perform the computations
3. Print the results

A structure chart for this problem is given in Figure 3.1. Module specifications for the main modules are

Module: Get data
Task: Get cost and size of pizza from the user at the keyboard
Outputs: cost and size

Module: Compute price per square inch
Task: Compute the price per square inch of pizza
Input: cost and size of pizza
Output: price per square inch

Module: Print results
Task: Print the price per square inch
Input: price per square inch

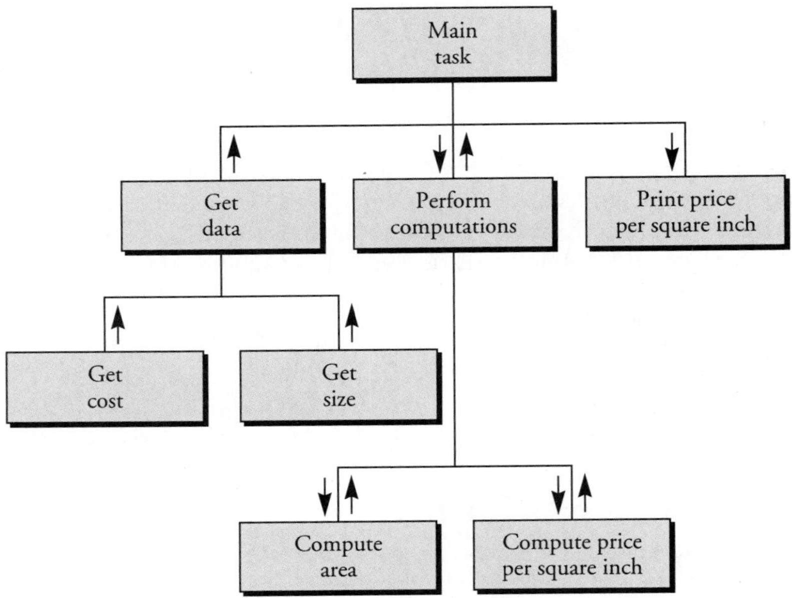

Figure 3.1
Structure chart for the pizza problem

A further refinement of the pseudocode produces

1. Get the data
   1.1 get price
   1.2 get size
2. Perform the computations
   2.1 compute area
   2.2 calculate unit price

Step 3 of the pseudocode, "Print the results," only requires printing the price per square inch, so no further development is required.

Implementation

In implementation, we translate the design description into a program in C++. A complete listing of the program in C++ follows:

```
// Program file: pizza.cpp

#include <iostream.h>
#include <iomanip.h>
#include <math.h>

const double PI = 3.14

int main ()
{

   double size, radius, cost, area, pricePerSquareInch;

   //This module gets the data.

   cout << "Enter the pizza price and press <Enter>. ";
   cin >> cost;
   cout << "Enter the pizza size and press <Enter>. ";
   cin >> size;

   // This module computes the unit price.

   radius = size / 2;
   area = PI * pow(radius, 2);
   pricePerSquareInch = cost / area;

   //This module prints the results.

   cout << setiosflags(ios::fixed | ios::showpoint | ios::right)
        << setprecision(2) << endl;
   cout << "The price per square inch is $" << setw(4)
        << pricePerSquareInch << endl;
   return 0;

}
```

Summary

Key Terms

argument
assignment statement
binary arithmetic
binary notation
cancellation error
character arithmetic
character set
collating sequence
compound assignment
concatenation
constant
extractor
implicit type conversion
inserter
integer arithmetic operations: +, –, *, /, %
integer overflow
interactive input
invoke (call)
library (built-in) function
member function
memory location
mixed-mode expression
ordinal data type
precedence rule
real arithmetic operations: +, –, *, /
real overflow
representational error
round-off errors
self-documenting code
type promotion
underflow
user-friendly
variable
word

Key Concepts

- Operations and priorities for data of type `int` and `double` are summarized:

Data Type	Operations	Priority
int	*, %, /	1. Evaluate in order from left to right.
	+, –	2. Evaluate in order from left to right.
double	*, /	1. Evaluate in order from left to right.
	+, –	2. Evaluate in order from left to right.

- Mixed-mode expressions involving `int` and `double` values return values of type `double`.
- Priority for order of operations on mixed-mode expressions is
  1. *, /: in order from left to right.
  2. +,–: in order from left to right.
- Overflow is caused by a value too large for computing on a particular machine.
- Underflow is caused by a value too small (close to zero) for computing. These numbers are automatically replaced by zero.
- A memory location can have a name that can be used to refer to the contents of the location.
- The name of a memory location is different from the contents of the memory location.
- Self-documenting code is code that is written using descriptive identifiers.
- Assignment statements are used to assign values to memory locations, for example,

```
sum = 30 + 60;
```

- Variables and variable expressions can be used in output statements.
- `cin` is used to get data; the correct form is

```
cin >> variable1 >> variable2 . . . >> variablen;
```

- `cin >> <variable>;` causes a value to be transferred to the variable location.
- Interactive input expects data items to be entered from the keyboard at appropriate times during execution of the program.
- Data types for variables in an input statement should match data items read as input.
- Appropriate uses for constants in the declaration section include frequently used numbers; current values subject to change over time, for example,

```
const double MINIMUM_WAGE = 6.25
```

- Five math library functions available in C++ are `pow`, `sqrt`, `sin`, `cos`, and `tan`.
- Functions can be used in assignment statements, for example,

```
x = sqrt(16.0);
```

in output statements

```
cout << pow(-8, 2);
```

and in arithmetic expressions

```
x = sqrt(3.78) + pow(5, 5);
```

- Member functions are used in conjunction with objects, such as strings. The notation for calling a member function is

```
<object>.<member function name>(<parameters>)
```

Examples of the use of member functions are

```
apstring str = "Hi there!";                       // Define a string object
cout << str.length() << str.find('H') << endl;  // Print 90
```

- Type casts can be used to convert one type of value to another type, for example, `int(3.14)`.

Programming Problems and Projects

Write a complete C++ program for each of the following problems. When a program requires input from the user, each input statement should be preceded by an appropriate prompting message.

1. Susan purchases a computer for $985. The sales tax on the purchase is 5.5%. Compute and print the total purchase price.
2. Find and print the area and perimeter of a rectangle that is 4.5 feet long and 2.3 feet wide. Print both rounded to the nearest tenth of a foot.
3. Compute and print the number of minutes in a year.
4. Light travels as $3 * 10^8$ meters per second. Compute and print the distance a light beam would travel in 1 year. (This is called a light year.)

5. The 1927 New York Yankees won 110 games and lost 44. Compute their winning percentage and print it rounded to three decimal places.
6. A 10-kilogram object is traveling at 12 meters per second. Compute and print its momentum (momentum is mass times velocity).
7. Convert 98.0 degrees Fahrenheit to degrees Celsius.
8. Given a positive number, print its square and square root.
9. The Golden Sales Company pays its salespeople $0.27 for each item they sell. Given the number of items sold by a salesperson, print the amount of pay due.
10. Given the length and width of a rectangle, print its area and perimeter.
11. The kinetic energy of a moving object is given by the formula $KE = (1/2)mv^2$. Given the mass (m) and the speed (v) of an object, find its kinetic energy.
12. The arithmetic mean of two numbers is the result of dividing their sum by 2. The geometric mean of two numbers is the square root of their product. The harmonic mean of two numbers is the arithmetic mean of their reciprocals. Write a program that takes two floating-point numbers as inputs and displays these three means.
13. A supermarket wants to install a computerized weighing system in its produce department. Input to this system will consist of a single-letter identifier for the type of produce, the weight of the produce purchase (in pounds), and the cost per pound of the produce. A typical input screen is

```
Enter each of the following:

Description <Enter> A
Weight <Enter> 2.0
Price/lb. <Enter> 1.98
```

Print a label showing the input information along with the total cost of the purchase. The label should appear as follows:

```
%%%%%%%%%%%%%%%%%%%%%%%%%%%%%%%%%%%%%%%%%%%%%%
         Penny Spender Supermarket
            Produce Department

ITEM        WEIGHT        COST/lb        COST

A           2.0 lb        $1.98          $3.96

                 Thank You!

%%%%%%%%%%%%%%%%%%%%%%%%%%%%%%%%%%%%%%%%%%%%%%
```

14. The New Wave Computer Company sells its product, the NW-PC, for $675. In addition, they sell memory expansion cards for $69.95, disk drives for $198.50, and software for $34.98 each. Given the number of memory cards, disk drives, and software packages desired by a customer purchasing an NW-PC, print out a bill of sale that appears as follows:

```
****************************
   New Wave Computers

     ITEM                   COST
1 NW-PC                  $675.00
2 Memory card             139.90
```

```
1 Disk drive                     198.50
4 Software                       139.92

              TOTAL            $1153.32
```

15. Write a test program that allows you to see a character contained within the character set of your computer. Given a positive integer, you can use the `char` type cast to determine the corresponding character. On most computers, only integers less than 256 are valid for this. Also, remember that most character sets contain some unprintable characters such as ASCII values less than 32. Print your output in the form:

```
Character number nnn is x.
```

16. Mr. Vigneault, a coach at Shepherd High School, is working on a program that can be used to assist cross-country runners in analyzing their times. As part of the program, a coach enters elapsed times for each runner given in units of minutes, seconds, and hundredths. In a 5000-meter (5K) race, elapsed times are entered at the 1-mile and 2-mile marks. These elapsed times are then used to compute "splits" for each part of the race; that is, how long it takes a runner to run each of the three race segments. Write a complete program that will accept as input three times given in units of minutes, seconds, and hundredths and then produce output that includes the split for each segment. Typical input is:

```
Runner number                  234

Mile times:         1        5:34.22

                    2       11:21.67

Finish time:                17:46.85
```

Typical output is:

```
 Runner number                 234

 Split one                   5:34.22

 Split two                   5:47.45

 Split three                 6:25.18

 Finish time                17:46.85
```

4

Subprograms: Functions for Problem Solving

Chapter Outline

Recall from Section 2.3 the process of solving a problem by top-down design and stepwise refinement of tasks into subtasks. The structure of a top-down design can be reflected in a C++ program that uses *subprograms.*

The concept of a subprogram is not difficult to understand. It is a program within a program and is provided by most programming languages. Each subprogram should complete some task, the nature of which can range from simple to complex. You could have a subprogram that prints only a line of data, or you could rewrite an entire program as a subprogram. To extend the metaphor of the programmable pocket calculator introduced in Chapter 3, we create a subprogram by giving a name to a sequence of program statements. We then specify the data that this sequence will take as inputs and return as outputs. Next, we store this name with the built-in functions in the calculator. Finally, we use the name as if it were a built-in function wherever it is appropriate in any program.

■ 4.1 Program Design

Objectives

a. to understand the concepts of modularity and bottom-up testing
b. to be aware of the use of structured programming

Modularity

We have previously discussed and illustrated the process of solving a problem by top-down design. Using this method, we divide the main task into major subtasks and then continue to divide the subtasks (stepwise refinement) into smaller subtasks until all subtasks can be easily performed. Once an algorithm for solving a problem has been developed using top-down design, the programmer then writes code to translate the general solution into a C++ program.

As you have seen, code written to perform one well-defined subtask can be referred to as a *module.* One should be able to design, code, and test each module in a program independently from the rest of the program. In this sense, a module is a subprogram containing all definitions and declarations needed to perform the indicated subtask. Everything required for the subtask (but not needed in other parts of the program) can be created in the subprogram. Consequently, the definitions and declarations have meaning only when the module is being used.

At the lowest level in a programming language such as C++, a module is a single function. However, at a higher level in a design, one can also think of a module as consisting of several functions and related data. One important kind of higher level module of this sort is known as an *abstract data type.* The design and construction of abstract data type modules are discussed in some detail in Chapters 8 through 17. You have already been using some standard abstract data type modules whenever you have used the operations on integers, real numbers, and characters in your C++ programs.

A program that has been created using modules to perform various tasks is said to possess *modularity.* In general, modular programs are easier to test, debug, and correct than programs that are not modular because each independent module can be tested by running it from a test driver. Then, once the modules are running correctly, they can become part of a longer program. This independent testing of modules is referred to as *bottom-up testing.* A modular program is also easier to maintain than a nonmodular program because we can replace one module without modifying the other modules at all. For example, a new version of the C++ compiler might provide faster operations for floating-point arithmetic in the module that defines these operations. All you have to do to maintain your system is recompile your program.

Structured Programming and Design

Structured programming is the process of developing a program where emphasis is placed on the flow of control between independent modules. *Structured design* is the process of organizing communication between modules. Connections between these modules are specified in parameter lists and are usually controlled by the main function. Structured programming and design are especially suitable to large programs being worked on by teams. By carefully designing the modules and specifying what information is to be received by and returned from the module, a team of programmers can independently develop a module and then connect it to the complete program.

The remainder of this chapter is devoted to seeing how subprograms can be written to accomplish specific tasks. Subprograms in C++ are called *functions.* We discussed library functions in Section 3.5. We will now learn how to write our own functions.

4.2 User-Defined Functions

Objectives

a. to understand the need for user-defined functions
b. to use correct syntax when declaring and implementing a function
c. to use stubs and drivers to test functions

User-defined functions resemble the library functions `sqrt` and `pow` that were introduced in Section 3.5. To review briefly, note the following concepts when using these functions:

1. An argument is required for each; thus, `sqrt(y)` and `pow(2, 5)` are appropriate.
2. Functions can be used in expressions; for example,

```
x = sqrt(y) + sqrt(z);
```

3. Functions can be used in output statements; for example,

```
cout << setw(8) << setprecision(2) << sqrt(3);
```

Need for User-Defined Functions

It is relatively easy to envision the need for functions that are not on the list of library functions available in C++. For example, if you must frequently cube numbers, it would be convenient to have a function named `cube` that would allow you to make an assignment such as

```
x = cube(y);
```

Other examples from mathematics include computing a factorial ($n!$), computing a discriminant ($b^2 - 4ac$), and finding roots of a quadratic equation:

$$\frac{-b \pm \sqrt{b^2 - 4ac}}{2a}$$

In business, a motel might like to have available a function to determine a customer's bill given the number in the party, the length of stay, and any telephone charges. Similarly, a hospital might need a function to compute the room charge for a patient given the type of room (private, ward, and so on) and various other options, including telephone (yes or no) and television (yes or no). Functions such as these are not library functions. However, in C++, we can create *user-defined functions* to perform these tasks. The following code segment illustrates the components of a simple C++ program that has one user-defined function:

```
#include <iostream.h>

// Function: cube
// Computes the cube of an integer
//
// Input: an integer value
// Output: an integer representing the cube of the input

int cube (int x);

int main()
{
   int number;

   cout << "enter a number followed by <Enter>."
   cin >> number;
   cout << "The cube of " << number << " is "
        << cube(number) << endl;
   return 0;
}

int cube (int x)
{
   return x * x * x;
}
```

Function Declarations

In Chapters 2 and 3 of this text, you learned how to import library functions from library files with the `#include` directive and then invoke or call these functions in your application program. An important point to remember is that you do not know

A NOTE OF INTEREST

Structured Programming

From 1950 to the early 1970s, programs were designed and written on a linear basis. Programs written and designed on such a basis can be called unstructured programs. These programs consist of long linear sequences of statements. Control flows from each statement in the sequence to the next statement, unless it is transferred by means of a GOTO statement. Structured programming, on the other hand, organizes a program around separate semi-independent modules that are linked by a single sequence of simple commands, including structured control statements for selection and iteration (see Chapters 5 and 6).

In 1964, mathematicians Corrado Bohm and Guiseppe Jacopini proved that any program logic, regardless of complexity, can be expressed by using the control structures of sequencing, selection, and iteration. This result is termed the *structure theorem*. This theorem, combined with the efforts of Edger W. Dijkstra, led to a significant move toward structured programming and away from the use of GOTO statements.

In fact, in a letter to the editor of *Communications of the ACM*, Vol. 11, Mar. 1968, Dijkstra stated that the GOTO statement "should be abolished from all 'higher level' programming languages. . . . [The GOTO statement] is just too primitive; it is too much an invitation to make a mess of one's program."

Structured programming concepts were applied to a large-scale data processing application for the first time in IBM Corporation's "New York Times Project," which ran from 1969 to 1971. Using these techniques, programmers posted productivity figures from four to six times higher than those of the average programmer. In addition, the error rate was a phenomenally low 0.0004 per line of coding.

anything about how these functions are written or *implemented*. All you know is the *declaration* of a function. A function's declaration consists of its name, the number and kind of arguments it expects when you invoke it, and the type of value, if any, that it returns when its job is done. A function's declaration gives you all the information needed to know how to use the function, and no more. For example, the declaration of the library function `pow` might be written as follows:

```
double pow(double base, double exponent);
```

The first word in this expression, `double`, tells us the type of value returned by the function. The second word, `pow`, is the name of the function. The words enclosed in the parentheses and separated by commas denote the types of arguments expected when the function is invoked, that is, two arguments of type `double`. Note that the names used for these arguments, `base` and `exponent`, also serve to document the role that they play in the function.

The general form for a function declaration is

```
<return type> <function name> ( <list of argument specifiers> );
```

to which the following comments apply:

1. `<function name>` is any valid identifier.
2. The function name should be descriptive.
3. `<return type>` declares the data type for the function name. This indicates what type of value, if any, will be returned to the caller.

It is good programming practice to supply with a declaration some comments that describe the inputs or data received by the function (its *arguments*) and the output or information returned (its *value* or *result*). In addition, we might specify any assumptions about the function's arguments that must be satisfied so that the function can perform its task correctly. For example, the function `sqrt` assumes that its argument is not just any `double`, but a nonnegative `double`. Therefore, we supply a comment about the function's arguments and value:

```
// Function: sqrt
// Compute the square root of a double-precision floating-point number
//
// Input: a nonnegative double-precision floating-point number
// Output: a nonnegative double-precision floating-point number
// representing the square root of the data received

double sqrt (double x);
```

Note that we have given no information about *how* the function performs its task. Nonetheless, the reader has enough information to invoke or use the function. This is the kind of function declaration and comment that we will use in examples of user-defined functions throughout this text. Hereafter, when we say declaration, we mean a C++ function declaration and any supporting comments. Writing out all of your function declarations in this way will encourage you to think in terms of the uses of your functions before you become immersed in their implementation details

Declaring Functions in a Program

Before you can use functions that you write yourself, you must provide declarations for them. All function declarations, if there are any, should appear in the region of your source program file between the global data declarations and the main function heading:

```
preprocessor directives

global data declarations

function declaration 1
.
.
.
function declaration n

int main()
{
   main function data declarations

   statements

}

function implementation 1
.
.
.
function implementation n
```

Implementing Functions in a Program

After you have decided how your functions will be used and what their declarations will be, and even after you have written a main function that will call them, you can turn to the job of implementing or writing them. A function *implementation* describes in detail how the function performs its task. Simply put, a function implementation is a complete, brief program that produces some effects if certain assumptions about the arguments to the function are satisfied. For example, let's assume that the data value `x` is a number. Then the following expression produces the square of the number:

```
x * x
```

We can use this expression to implement a function `sqr(x)`, where `x` is any number, as follows:

```
double sqr(double x)
{
    return x * x;
}
```

You will note that the first line of the implementation, called the *function heading*, looks almost like a function declaration. The only difference is that the semicolon following the right parenthesis is omitted. The rest of the implementation after the heading is a little program block. Like the main function block, this block contains optional data declarations and at least one executable statement. The single statement in our example says that the block will return (as the value of the function) the result of multiplying `x` (the argument of the function) by itself. The form for a function implementation is

<function heading>
{
<optional data declarations>
<executable statements>
}

Function Headings

A function heading in a C++ program must match up with a corresponding function declaration. A return type and a function name must be the same in a heading as they are in a declaration, and the types of the arguments must match and be in the same positions. In addition, each type in the argument list of a function heading must be followed by an argument name, usually called a *formal parameter*. The formal parameter list must match the number of the arguments (usually called *actual parameters*) used when the function is called. Thus, if you are writing a function to compute the area of a rectangle and you want to call the function from the main function by

```
rectArea = area(width, length);
```

the function implementation might have

```
int area (int w, int l)
```

as a heading. The two formal parameters, `w` and `l`, correspond to the actual parameters, `width` and `length`. You should make sure the formal parameter list and actual parameter list match up as indicated:

```
(int w, int l)
(width, length)
```

In general, the formal parameters and actual parameters must match in number, type, and position.

A function to compute the cube of an integer could use the following as a heading:

```
int cube(int x)
```

The general form for a function heading is

<return type> <function name> (<list of formal parameters>)

Using this general form, we note the following:

1. `<function name>` is any valid identifier.
   a. The function name should be descriptive.
   b. If it is expected, some value should be returned in the executable section of the function.
2. `<return type>` declares the data type for the function name. This indicates what type of value will be returned to the caller, if expected.
3. The list of formal parameters consists of a series of pairs of names, where the first name in the pair is the name of a data type, and the second name in the pair is the name of a formal parameter. The pairs in the list must be separated by commas.

Hereafter in this chapter, when we say *heading,* we mean a C++ function heading.

The formal parameters in a function heading must also match the types of the arguments used when the function is called. The compiler uses the same type checking rules for matching the types of formal and actual parameters as it does for matching the operands of an assignment statement. When an actual parameter passed to a function is not exactly the same type as the formal parameter in its position, the compiler checks to see whether or not the actual parameter's type can be converted by an implicit type cast to the type of the formal parameter. For example, an integer value passed to a function that expects a `double` would be converted to a `double` before being processed in the function. Conversely, a `double` that is passed to a function expecting an `int` would be implicitly truncated to an `int`.

Data and Executable Statements in a Function Implementation

As in the main function, a function does not require a declaration section, but when there is one, only constants and variables needed in the function should be declared. Further, the section is usually not very elaborate because the purpose of a function is normally a small single task.

The executable statement section of a function's implementation has the same form as the executable statement section of the main function. Remember that at least one statement, of the form `return <expression>`, should return the value of the function if a returned value is expected.

We will now illustrate user-defined functions with several examples.

Example 4.1 Implement a function to compute the cube of an integer. First, consider what a typical call to this function from the main function will look like:

```
a = cube(5);
```

Then decide what the assumptions about the arguments are, what the effects of the function will be, and write down a function declaration:

```
// Function: cube
// Computes the cube of an integer
//
// Input: an integer value
// Output: an integer representing the cube of the input

int cube (int x);
```

Because the actual parameter from the caller will be of `int` type, we have as an implementation

```
int cube (int x)
{
    return x * x * x;
}
```

Example 4.2 Let us write a function to perform the task of computing unit cost for pizza. Data sent to the function are size and cost. The function returns the unit cost. Formal parameters are cost and size. Using the function name `pricePerSquareInch`, the function could be invoked in a main function as follows:

```
unitCost = pricePerSquareInch(cost, price);
```

Therefore, we write the declaration

```
// Function: pricePerSquareInch
// Computes the price per square inch of pizza
//
// Input: two positive real numbers representing the cost in dollars and
// cents and the diameter in inches of a pizza
// Output: a real number representing the price, in dollars and cents, per
// square inch of pizza

double pricePerSquareInch(double cost, double size);
```

The implementation then is

```
double pricePerSquareInch(double cost, double size)
{
     double radius, area;

     radius = size / 2.0;
     area = PI * sqr(radius);
     return cost / area;
}
```

You should note that this function has some *locally declared data*. The variables `radius` and `area` are declared within the local block of the function because they are needed only for computing the area of a pizza. In general, data that are not needed elsewhere in a program should be declared locally within functions. You should also note that there are two important, unstated assumptions made by this implementation: First, the constant `PI` must be defined, and second, the function `sqr` must be declared. These names can be defined or declared in the area above the main function. The function `sqr` must then also be implemented, along with the function `pricePerSquareInch`, after the main function.

Example 4.3 We want to implement a function that converts digits to integer values. Our version of the function, called `charToInt`, has the following declaration:

```
// Function: charToInt
// Computes the integer value of a digit
//
// Input: a digit
// Output: the integer value represented by the digit

int charToInt(char ch);
```

The implementation uses the method we developed in Chapter 3:

```
int charToInt(char ch)
{
   return ch - '0';
}
```

Use in a Program

Now that you have seen several examples of user-defined functions, let us consider their use in a program. Once they are written, they can be used in the same manner as library functions. This usually means in one of the following forms.

1. Assignment statements:

```
a = 5;
b = cube(a);
```

2. Arithmetic expressions:

```
a = 5;
a = 3 * cube(a) + 2;
```

3. Output statements:

```
a = 5;
cout << setw(17) << cube(a) << endl;
```

Using Stubs

As programs get longer and incorporate more subprograms, a technique frequently used to get the program running is *stub programming*. A stub program is a no-frills, simple version of what will be a final program. It does not contain details of output and full algorithm development. It does contain declarations and rough implementations of each subprogram. When the stub version runs, you know your logic is correct and values are appropriately being passed to and from subprograms. Then you can fill in the necessary details to get a complete program.

Using Drivers

The main function is sometimes referred to as the *main driver.* When subprograms are used in a program, this driver can be modified to check subprograms in a sequential fashion. For example, you can start with a main driver that gets some input data:

```
// Program file: driver.cpp

#include<iostream.h>

int main()
{
   int data;

   cout << "Enter an integer: ";
   cin >> data;
   return 0;
}
```

You can think of this driver as a "function factory" for building and testing functions. First, you add a function declaration and then add a rough implementation of the function that simply returns a value that is usually the value of one of the arguments of the function. You test this function stub by placing a call to the function, with an input value, inside of an output statement in the main driver. If you were building the `sqr` function, your next version of the program would look like this:

```
// Program file: driver.cpp

#include <iostream.h>

// Function: sqr
// Computes the square of a number
//
// Input: a double-precision floating-point number
// Output: a double-precision floating-point number representing the square
// of the input
double sqr(double x);

int main()
{
   int data;

   cout << "Enter an integer: ";
   cin >> data;
   cout << "The square is " << sqr(data) << endl;
   return 0;
}

double sqr(double x)
{
   return x;
}
```

Once you are sure that a subprogram is running and that data are being transmitted properly to it, you can proceed to fill in the rest of the details of its implementation. In the case of the `sqr` function, you merely substitute `x * x` for `x` in the `return` statement and test the driver again. As you complete the implementation, you can be more confident that the function will return the values expected.

Functions Without Returned Values (`void` Functions)

Some functions require data to do their work, but return no values to their callers. For example, displaying several values with their labels to the terminal screen is such a task. This function might be called as follows:

```
displayResults(result1, result2, result3);
```

The implementation of this function would probably send the parameter values and the appropriate string labels to the standard output stream. Note that the function call appears by itself in a complete C++ statement. That is, a value is not assigned to a variable or passed on as an intermediate value within a more complex expression. Functions of this sort are called *void functions* because they return no values. The example function is declared as follows:

```
void displayResults(int result1, int result2, int result3);
```

The reserved word `void` indicates that the function is not meant to return a value. When a void function is implemented, it need not end with a return statement:

```
void displayResults(int result1, int result2, int result3)
{
   cout << "The first result is  " << result1 << endl;
   cout << "The second result is " << result2 << endl;
   cout << "The third result is  " << result3 << endl;
}
```

The declarations of `void functions have the following form:`

```
void <function name> ( <list of argument specifiers> );
```

Functions Without Parameters

Occasionally, a function is needed to do some work without receiving any data from the caller. It may or may not return a value as well. An example of such a function is one whose task is that of displaying a chunk of text as a header for a table of output data. One might invoke this function as follows:

```
displayHeader();
```

This function takes no data from parameters and returns no value to the caller. Its sole purpose is to display some text on the terminal screen. Its declaration is

```
void displayHeader();
```

Its implementation might display a header for a table of names and grades:

```
void displayHeader()
{
    cout << "GRADES FOR COMPUTER SCIENCE 110" << endl;
    cout << endl;
    cout << "Student Name                 Grade" << endl;
    cout << "------------                 -----" << endl;
}
```

Another example of this kind of function would display a sign-on or greeting at the start of a program.

An example of a function that takes no parameters, but still returns a result to the caller, would be a function that controls interactive input. The function prompts the user for input, reads the input value, and then returns it to the caller. The function might be used as follows:

```
data = getInteger();
```

Note that because this function returns a value, the value is intended for the use of the caller. In this example, the value is stored in a variable with an assignment statement. A declaration for the function is

```
int getInteger();
```

Its implementation prompts the user for an integer value, reads it in from the standard input stream, and then returns it as the value of the function. Because a place is needed to store the value during input, we declare a local variable for this purpose within the function:

```
int getInteger()
{
   int number;

   cout << "Enter an integer value, followed by <Enter>. ";
   cin >> number;
   return number;
}
```

Functions with Strings

Often it is useful to write functions that take strings as parameters. For example, we could rewrite the `getInteger` function so that the prompt could be passed as a string parameter. The following code segment shows how this version of `getInteger` could be called to present the user with two different prompts:

```
int length, width;

length = getInteger("Enter the length: ");
width = getInteger("Enter the width: ");
```

The caller provides the exact form of the prompt to be displayed, and the function takes care of displaying it and reading the data. The declaration of this function is

```
int getInteger(apstring prompt);
```

The implementation displays the string parameter with an output statement.

```
int getInteger(apstring prompt)
{
   int data;

   cout << prompt;
   cin >> data;
   return data;
}
```

Note that the use of parameters makes this version of `getInteger` more general than the first version of `getInteger`. In the first version, the programmer specifies a particular prompt in the body of the function. The use of other prompts would require other function definitions. By making the prompt a parameter of the function in the second version, the same function can be defined once and invoked with many different particular prompts.

A similar function could be developed to obtain a string as input and return it as a value.

```
apstring getString(apstring prompt)
{
   apstring data;

   cout << prompt;
   cin >> data;
   return data;
}
```

Communication and Style Tips

It is considered good programming practice to design a function to be as *general* as possible. General functions solve a *class* of problems rather than a particular problem. For example, separate functions to prompt for and input the length and the width solve particular problems, whereas a single function to get any integer value solves both of these particular problems as well as others. You should strive to make your functions as general as those you find in the C++ libraries. Designing general functions from scratch is not an easy thing to do. Frequently, you will not spot the need for a general function until you have written several more specialized functions that reveal a common or redundant pattern of code. When that happens, you can take two steps to design a more general function. First, write a single function that contains the common pattern of code that you see in the more specialized functions. Second, add parameters that will allow the callers of the new function to use it for their more specialized purposes.

Exercises 4.2

1. Indicate which of the following are valid function declarations. Explain what is wrong with those that are invalid.
   a. `roundTenth(double x);`
   b. `double makeChange(X, Y);`

c. `int max(int x, int y, int z);`
d. `char sign(double x);`

2. Find all errors in each of the following functions:

a.
```
int average (int n1, int n2);
{
    return N1 + N2 / 2;
}
```

b.
```
int total (int n1, int n2)
{
    int sum;
    return 0;
    sum = n1 + n2;
}
```

3. Write a function for each of the following:
a. Round a real number to the nearest tenth.
b. Round a real number to the nearest hundredth.
c. Convert degrees Fahrenheit to degrees Celsius.
d. Compute the charge for cars at a parking lot; the rate is 75 cents per hour or fraction thereof.

4. Write a program that uses the function you wrote for Exercise 3d to print a ticket for a customer who parks in the lot. Assume the input is in minutes.

5. Use the functions `sqr` and `cube` to write a program to print a chart of the integers 1 to 5 together with their squares and cubes. Output from this program should be

```
Number       Number Squared      Number Cubed
------       --------------      ------------
1                  1                   1

2                  4                   8

3                  9                  27

4                 16                  64

5                 25                 125
```

6. Write a program that contains a function that allows the user to enter a base (a) and exponent (x) and then have the program print the value of a^x.

4.3 Parameters

Value Parameters

We have seen that parameters are used so that data values can be transmitted, or passed, from the caller to a function. If values are to be passed *only* from the caller to a function, the parameters are called *value parameters*. The following program demonstrates the use of value parameters:

Objectives

a. to understand the need for and appropriate use of parameters in functions
b. to understand the difference between value and reference parameters

```
// Program file: area.cpp

#include <iostream.h>

// Function: area
// Computes the area of a rectangle
//
// Inputs: two integers representing the length and the
// width of the rectangle
// Outputs: an integer representing the area of the
// rectangle

int area(int length, int width);

int main()
{
   int thisLength, thisWidth;

   cout << "Enter the length: ";
   cin >> thisLength;
   cout << "Enter the width: ";
   cin >> thisWidth;
   cout << "The area is " << area(thisLength, thisWidth) << endl;
   return 0;
}

int area(int length, int width)
{
   return length * width;
}
```

In this program, the formal parameters `length` and `width` are used for one-way transmission of values to the function `area`. When the function is called, the values of the actual parameters, `thisLength` and `thisWidth`, are copied into separate memory locations for the formal parameters `length` and `width`. The fact that there are separate memory locations for the formal and actual parameters guarantees that any changes to the formal parameters will leave the actual parameters unchanged.

Suppose that the user enters 8 for `thisLength` and 7 for `thisWidth`. The state of the machine is now

8

`thisLength`

7

`thisWidth`

Note that the only memory locations visible to the program are those for the variables `thisLength` and `thisWidth`. The function is then called to compute the area. The system *allocates* memory locations for the formal parameters `length` and `width`. These names and their memory locations now become visible to the block of statements within the function. The system then places copies of the values 8 and 7 into the memory locations for `length` and `width`. This is why value parameters are said to be *passed by value*. The state of the machine is now

```
 8
thisLength

 7
thisWidth

 8
length

 7
width
```

When the function returns from its call, the computer *deallocates* the memory locations for `length` and `width`. Also, because the function is no longer active, its formal parameters are no longer visible to the program. The values of `thisLength` and `thisWidth`, which are still visible, have not changed. A value parameter always indicates a *local copy* of the value transmitted to the function.

Reference Parameters

You will frequently want a function to return more than one value to a caller. A good example of a task that calls for more than one value to be returned is the interaction with the user for two input values in the program that computes the area of a rectangle. The C++ code for this task reads integer values from the keyboard into two variables:

```
cout << "Enter the length: ";
cin >> thisLength;
cout << "Enter the width: ";
cin >> thisWidth;
```

We could document this task as follows:

```
// Prompts the user for two input integers representing the length and
// width of a rectangle
```

We can represent information to be returned with *reference parameters* in the parameter list of a C++ function. In a function declaration, reference parameters are declared by using the symbol `&` before the appropriate formal parameters. The form of a reference parameter declaration in a function declaration is

<type name> &<formal parameter name>

The C++ declaration for a function `getData` to perform this task can be added to the documentation:

```
// Function: getData
// Prompts the user for two input integers representing the length and width
// of a rectangle
//
// Outputs: two integers representing the length and width of a rectangle

void getData(int &length, int &width);
```

Note that the parameter and type names look the same as they would in declarations of functions that would use the parameters to receive data. However, in this function, they will be used to return information to the caller, as is indicated by the `&` symbols.

The form of a reference parameter declaration in the heading of a function implementation is

<type name> &<formal parameter name>

Our `getData` function can now be implemented as follows:

```
void getData(int &length, int &width)
{

   cout << "Enter the length: ";
   cin >> length;
   cout << "Enter the width: ";
   cin >> width;
}
```

When reference parameters are declared, values appear to be sent from the function to the caller. Actually, when reference parameters are used, values are not transmitted at all. Reference parameters in the function heading are merely *aliases* for actual variables used by the caller. Thus, variables are said to be *passed by reference* rather than by value. When reference parameters are used, any change of values in the function produces a corresponding change of values in the caller's block.

The notion of aliasing can be seen during a run of the program where the user enters the values 8 and 7 as inputs. Just before the function `getData` returns, the state of the machine is as follows:

```
[ 8 ]
thisLength
length

[ 7 ]
thisWidth
width
```

Note that there are only two memory locations for data in the program thus far. However, each location has two different names associated with it, which means that an assignment to either of the two names, say, `thisWidth` or `width`, will change the value stored in the corresponding memory location.

Technically, `length` and `width` do not exist as variables. They contain pointers to the same memory locations as `thisLength` and `thisWidth`, respectively. Thus, a statement in the function such as

```
length = 5;
```

causes the memory location reserved for `length` to receive the value 5. That is, it causes the net action

```
thisLength = 5;
```

Thus, constants cannot be used when calling a function with reference parameters. For example,

```
getData(8, 7);
```

produces a compile-time error because 8 and 7 are passed in the positions of reference parameters.

An error would also occur if we tried to pass the value of an expression in the position of a reference parameter. For example, the following call would generate an error for the second parameter:

```
getData(thisLength, thisWidth + 1);
```

In general, the only legitimate actual parameter to pass by reference is a variable or the name of another function's parameter because only names of this sort can refer to memory locations capable of being aliased by a reference parameter.

The next example also shows a useful function that requires reference parameters.

Example 4.4 Many problems call for a function that will exchange the values of data in two variables. For any two variables `a` and `b`, the effect of calling the function `swap(a, b)` will be to replace the value of `a` with the value of `b` and to replace the value of `b` with the value of `a`. Clearly, a function that returns a single value cannot accomplish this task. We will assume that the values to be swapped are real numbers. Two parameters will be used both to receive data from the caller and to return information as well. Thus, the function's declaration can be written as follows:

```
// Function: swap
// Exchanges the values of the two input variables
//
// Inputs: two real numbers
// Outputs: the two real numbers in reversed order

void swap(double &a, double &b);
```

The function's implementation will use a temporary variable to save one of the input values during the exchange:

```
void swap(double &a, double &b)
{
   double temp;

   temp = a;
   a = b;
   b = temp;
}
```

Note that this function itself returns no value to the caller. This is not unusual for functions that have reference parameters.

A NOTE OF INTEREST

The History of Parameter Passing

The use of parameters to communicate information among subprograms is almost as old as the use of subprograms. As soon as subprograms became available in high-level programming languages, programmers realized that subprograms would be virtually useless without parameters. The inclusion of parameters in programming languages allowed programmers to design better code in two respects. First, the use of parameters made code more readable. The parameters of a subprogram module gave it a manifest interface for receiving information from and sending it to other modules. Second, the use of parameters made subprograms more general. Before parameters became available, each subprogram's operations were restricted to a particular problem involving particular data. The addition of parameters allowed programmers to generalize their solutions to manipulate whole classes of data.

The design of different parameter passing mechanisms has been an important chapter in the history of programming languages. Each major step in this process has reflected both the vision of computer scientists about what they consider important in a programming context and the limitations of the available hardware and software technology.

When the use of parameters first appeared in the mid-1950s in the programming language FORTRAN, the focus of programmers was on efficiency. FORTRAN was used primarily to perform mathematical and scientific computations (FORmula TRANslation language). This kind of application demanded a high processing speed and large amounts of memory. But early processors were slow, and memory was expensive. With these resources at a premium, John Backus, the designer of FORTRAN, decided that all parameters in the language would be passed by reference. Pass by reference is less expensive than pass by value because no extra memory needs to be allocated for a local copy of the actual parameter and no extra processing time is needed to copy it. Because FORTRAN subprograms always manipulated the actual arguments passed to them by reference, the subprograms ran very quickly even when large data structures were passed. The use of a single-parameter passing mode also made the language easy to learn and its compiler easy to write.

Needless to say, the early FORTRAN programs were not safe. Programmers discovered this to be true especially for large programs that passed many parameters among subprograms. Unintended side effects were numerous. Because of the way that constant symbols were represented, even constants could be changed if they were passed as parameters to FORTRAN subprograms!

After a few years of experience with FORTRAN, John McCarthy, a mathematician at the Massachusetts Institute of Technology, designed LISP (LISt Processing language). LISP was intended for processing lists of symbols and was based on a theory of computation known as the recursive lambda calculus. According to this theory, programs should consist of functions that receive zero or more arguments and return a single value. In the process, these functions should not change the arguments themselves. To enforce this requirement, McCarthy designed a pass by value mechanism for parameters. In cases where an actual argument was a simple data type, such as a number, functions worked on a local copy of the actual argument so that no side effects were possible. Efficiency was not important because LISP was a highly interactive and interpreted language. Thus, the time taken to allocate the extra memory for a formal parameter and copy the value of the actual parameter to it was insignificant compared to the time taken to interpret LISP expressions generally. In cases where an actual argument was a structured data type, such as a string or a list of numbers, a copy of a pointer to the argument was passed for reasons of efficiency. The parameter passing mechanism of LISP thus reflected concerns of both safety and efficiency.

The primary teaching language in computer science from 1984 to 1994 was Pascal. Named after the French mathematician, Pascal was designed by Niklaus Wirth. Pascal has two parameter passing modes. Pass by value worked like pass by value in LISP. However, Wirth extended pass by value to structured data values as well, making this mode expensive to use at run time. Pass by reference worked as in FORTRAN, except that constants and expressions were disallowed as actual reference parameters. Pascal also allows subprograms to be passed as parameters. This is an important development in our story because subprograms can be generalized still further by being parameterized for more specific subprograms. The following example of a general summation function in Pascal illustrates this point:

```
function sum(low, high : integer;
             function f(x : integer) :
             integer) : integer;
   var
      i, accum : integer;
   begin
   accum := 0;
   for i := low to high do
      accum := accum + f(i);
   sum := accum;
   end;

begin
writeln(sum(1, 10, square));
end.
```

A NOTE OF INTEREST (continued)

The syntax of Pascal is fairly close to that of C++. Assuming that the function `square` had been defined elsewhere, the `sum` function would return the summation of the squares of all of the integers between 1 and 10 in this example. The name `square` substitutes for `f` inside of the function at run time. The summation function will work with any function parameter of one integer argument that returns an integer value. As you can see, passing functions as parameters is a powerful way to generalize functions and reduce the redundancy of code in programs. C++ allows functions to be passed as parameters, as discussed in Chapter 13.

Constant Reference Parameters

Recall from Section 3.4 that a string variable requires a chunk of computer memory large enough to accommodate all of the characters in the string. When a string variable is passed by value to a function, all of the characters in the variable must be copied to temporary memory locations for the parameter. This process can be costly in time (to copy the characters) and memory (to store them) for large strings. To cut these costs, one might decide to pass all string parameters by reference. However, this move is unsafe because unintended changes to the original string variables might occur.

As a solution to this problem, C++ provides a third parameter passing mode called *constant reference*. A constant reference parameter is passed by reference, so it has the efficiency of reference parameters. However, the C++ compiler disallows all assignments to a constant reference parameter within the body of the function where it is declared. Thus, a constant reference parameter is also as safe as a value parameter.

The form of a constant reference parameter declaration is just like a reference parameter declaration, except that it is prefixed by the reserved word `const`:

```
const <type name> &<parameter name>
```

The `getString` function developed in Section 4.2 is a good candidate for the use of a constant reference parameter. Its new declaration would be

```
apstring getString(const apstring &prompt);
```

Except for the change in the heading, the implementation of the function is the same as that of the earlier version.

Communication and Style Tips

Choosing the appropriate mode when declaring a parameter for a function takes practice. Here are some rules of thumb to keep in mind:

1. When the value of the original variable (the actual parameter) must be changed by the function, declare the formal parameter as a reference parameter.
2. When the value of the original variable should not be changed by the function and the size of the data is relatively small (an `int`, a `double`, or a short string), declare the formal parameter as a value parameter.
3. When the value of the original variable should not be changed by the function and the size of the data is relatively large (a long string), declare the formal parameter as a constant reference parameter.

Exercises 4.3

1. Find the errors in the following function declarations:

a.
```
// Function: getData
// Prompts user for two integer input values
//
// Outputs: two integers

void getData(int length, int width);
```

b.
```
// Function: area
// Computes the area of a rectangle
//
// Inputs: two integers representing the length
// and the width of the rectangle
// Outputs: an integer representing the area
// of the rectangle

int area(int length, int &width);
```

c.
```
// Function: circleAttributes
// Computes the diameter and area of a circle
//
// Input: a real number representing the radius
// of the circle
// Outputs: two real numbers representing
// the diameter and area of the circle

void circleAttributes(double &radius, double &diameter,
      double &area);
```

2. Write and test a function `intDivide` that receives two integer values and two integer variables from the caller. When the function completes execution, the values in these variables should be the quotient and the remainder produced by dividing the second value by the first value. Be sure to name your parameters descriptively to aid the reader of the function.
3. Explain the differences between value parameters, reference parameters, and constant reference parameters.

4.4 Functions As Subprograms

Objectives

a. to understand how functions can be used to design programs
b. to use functions to get data for programs
c. to use functions to perform required tasks in programs
d. to use functions for output

Functions can be used as subprograms for a number of purposes. Two significant uses are to facilitate the top-down design philosophy of problem solving and to avoid having to write repeated segments of code.

Functions facilitate problem solving. Recall the Case Study problem in Chapter 3. In that problem, you were asked to compute the unit cost for a pizza. The main modules were

1. Get the data
2. Perform the computations
3. Print the results

A function can be written for each of these tasks, and the program can then call each function as needed. Thus, the statement portion of the program has the form

```
data = getData();
results = performComputations(data);
printResults(results);
```

This makes it easy to see and understand the main tasks of the program.

Once you develop the ability to write and use subprograms, you will usually write the main function first. Your main function should be written so a programmer can easily read it but still contain enough structure to enable a programmer to know what to do if asked to write code for the tasks. In this sense, it is not necessary for a person reading the main function to understand *how* a subprogram accomplishes its task; it need only be apparent *what* the subprogram does.

When you design subprograms, you should also consider the problem of data flow. The most difficult aspect of learning to use subprograms is handling transmission of data. Recall from the structure charts shown earlier that arrows were used to indicate whether data were received by and/or sent from a module. Also, each module specification indicated if the module received data and if information was sent from it. Since a subprogram will be written to accomplish the task of each module, we must be able to transmit data as indicated. Once you have developed this ability, using functions becomes routine.

Using Subprograms

Use of subprograms facilitates writing programs for problems whose solutions have been developed using top-down design. A function can be written for each main task.

How complex should a function be? In general, functions should be relatively short and perform a specific task. Some programmers prefer to limit functions to no more than one full screen of text. If longer than a page or screen, the task might need to be subdivided into smaller functions.

Cohesive Subprograms

The cohesion of a subprogram is the degree to which the subprogram performs a single task. A subprogram that is developed in such a way is called a *cohesive subprogram*. As you use subprograms to implement a design based on modular development, you should always try to write cohesive subprograms.

The property of cohesion is not well defined. Subtask complexity varies in the minds of different programmers. In general, if the task is unclear, the corresponding subprogram will not be cohesive. When this happens, you should subdivide the task until a subsequent development allows cohesive subprograms.

To illustrate briefly the concept of cohesion, consider the first-level design of a problem to compute grades for a class. Step 3 of this design could be

3. Process grades for each student

Clearly, this is not a well-defined task. Thus, if you were to write a subprogram for this task, the subprogram would not be cohesive. Consider the subsequent development:

3. Process grades for each student
while not end of input
3.1 get a line of data
3.2 compute average
3.3 compute letter grade

3.4 print data
3.5 compute totals

Here we see that functions to accomplish subtasks 3.1, 3.2, 3.3, and 3.4 are cohesive because each subtask consists of a single task. The final subtask, compute totals, may or may not result in a cohesive subprogram. More information is needed before you can decide what is to be done at this step.

Functional Abstraction

The purpose of using functions is to simplify reasoning. During the design stage, as a problem is subdivided into tasks, the problem solver (you) should have to consider only what a function is to do and not be concerned about details of the function. Instead, the function name and comments at the beginning of the function should be sufficient to inform the user as to what the function does. Developing functions in this manner is referred to as *functional abstraction* (this notion is also called *procedural abstraction* because some languages support subprograms known as *procedures* that are similar to functions).

Functional abstraction is the first step in designing and writing a function. The list of parameters and comments about the action of the function should precede development of the body of the function. This forces clarity of thought and aids design. Use of this method might cause you to discover that your design is not sufficient to solve the task and a redesign is necessary. Therefore, you could reduce design errors and save time when writing code.

Functional abstraction becomes especially important when teams work on a project. Each member of the writing team should understand the purpose and use of functions written by other team members without having to analyze the body of each function. This is analogous to the situation in which you use a predefined function without really understanding how the function works.

Functional abstraction is perhaps best formalized in terms of preconditions and postconditions. A *precondition* is a comment that states precisely what is true before a certain action is taken. A *postcondition* states what is true after the action has been taken. Carefully written preconditions and postconditions used with functions enhance the concept of functional abstraction. (Additional uses of preconditions and postconditions are discussed in Sections 5.6 and 6.5.)

In summary, functional abstraction means that, when writing or using functions, you should think of them as single, clearly understood units, each of which accomplishes a specific task.

Information Hiding

Information hiding can be thought of as the process of hiding the implementation details of a subprogram. This is just what we do when we use a top-down design to solve a problem. We decide which tasks and subtasks are necessary to solve a problem without worrying about how the specific subtasks will be accomplished. In the sense of software engineering, information hiding is what allows teams to work on a large system: It is only necessary to know what another team is doing, not how they are doing it.

Interface and Documentation

Independent subprograms need to communicate with the main function and other subprograms. A formal statement of how such communication occurs is called the *interface* of the subprogram. This usually consists of comments at the beginning of a subprogram and includes all the documentation the reader will need to use the sub-

A NOTE OF INTEREST

Computer Ethics: Hacking and Other Intrusions

A famous sequence of computer intrusions has been detailed by Clifford Stoll. The prime intruder came to Stoll's attention in August 1986, when an intruder attempted to penetrate a computer at Lawrence Berkeley Laboratory (LBL). Instead of denying the intruder access, management at LBL went along with Stoll's recommendation that they attempt to unmask the intruder, even though the risk was substantial because the intruder had gained system-manager privileges.

The intruder, Markus H., a member of a small group of West Germans, was unusually persistent, but no computer wizard. He made use of known deficiencies in the half-dozen or so operating systems, including UNIX, VMS, VM-TSO, and EMBOS, with which he was familiar, but he did not invent any new modes of entry. He penetrated 30 of the 450 computers then on the network system at LBL.

After Markus H. was successfully traced, efforts were instituted to make LBL's computers less vulnerable. To ensure high security, it would have been necessary to change all passwords overnight and recertify each user. This and other demanding measures were deemed impractical. Instead, deletion of all expired passwords was instituted; shared accounts were eliminated; monitoring of incoming traffic was extended, with alarms set in key places; and education of users was attempted.

The episode was summed up by Stoll as a powerful learning experience for those involved in the detection process and for all those concerned about computer security. That the intruder was caught at all is testimony to the ability of a large number of concerned professionals to keep the tracing effort secret.

In a later incident, an intruder left the following embarrassing message in a computer file assigned to Clifford Stoll: "The cuckoo has egg on his face." The reference was to Stoll's book, *The Cuckoo's Egg,* which tracked the intrusions of the West German hacker just described. The embarrassment was heightened by the fact that the computer, owned by Harvard University with which astronomer Stoll is now associated, was on the Internet network. The intruder, or intruders, who goes by the name of Dave, also attempted to break into dozens of other computers on the same network—and succeeded.

The *nom de guerre* of "Dave" was used by one or more of three Australians recently arrested by the federal police Down Under. The three, who at the time of their arrest were respectively 18, 20, and 21 years of age, successfully penetrated computers in both Australia and the United States.

The three Australians went beyond browsing to damage data in computers in their own nation and the United States. At the time they began their intrusions in 1988 (when the youngest was only 16), there was no law in Australia under which they could be prosecuted. It was not until legislation making such intrusions prosecutable was passed that the police began to take action.

program. We have seen examples of subprogram interfaces in the function declarations and headings that have appeared in this chapter.

Software Engineering

Perhaps the greatest difference between beginning students in computer science and "real-world" programmers is how they perceive the need for documentation. Typically, beginning students want to make a program run; they view anything that delays this process as an impediment. Thus, some students consider using descriptive identifiers, writing variable dictionaries, describing a problem as part of program documentation, and using appropriate comments throughout a program as a nuisance. In contrast, system designers and programmers who write code for a living often spend up to 50% of their time and effort on documentation. There are at least three reasons for this difference in perspective.

First, real programmers work on large, complex systems with highly developed logical paths. Without proper documentation, even the person who developed an algorithm will have difficulty following its logic 6 months later. Second, communication among teams is required as systems are developed. Complete, clear statements about what the problems are and how they are being solved are essential. Third, programmers know they can develop algorithms and write the necessary code. They are trained so

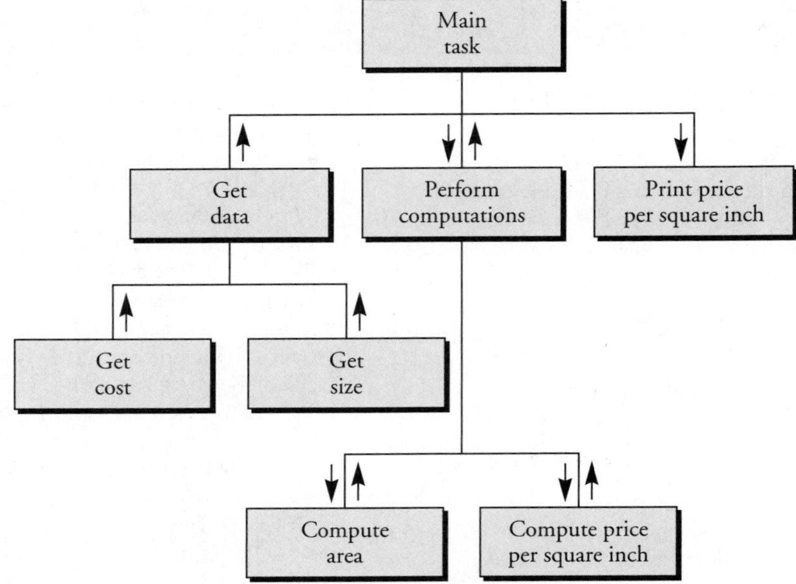

Figure 4.1
Structure chart for the pizza problem

that problems of searching, sorting, and file manipulation are routine. Knowing that they can solve a problem thus allows them to devote more time and energy to documenting how the solution has been achieved.

We close this section with a revision of the program from Chapter 3 that found the unit cost for a pizza. The original program was designed using module specifications but implemented in C++ as a long sequence of statements in the main function section. The revision will implement each module of the design as a C++ function to be called from the main function section. The structure chart is shown in Figure 4.1. The module specifications are

Module: Get data
Task: Get cost and size of pizza from the user at the keyboard
Outputs: cost and size

Module: Compute price per square inch
Task: Compute the price per square inch of pizza
Input: Cost and size of pizza
Output: price per square inch

Module: Print results
Task: Print the price per square inch
Input: price per square inch

The module for getting the data receives no data but returns two data values to the caller. The C++ function declaration specifies a function named `getData` and two reference parameters, `cost` and `size`, in which the input data are returned to the caller:

```
// Function: getData
// Gets cost and size of pizza from the user
// at the keyboard
//
// Outputs: The cost and size

void getData(double &cost, int &size);
```

The C++ function implementation prompts the user for the cost and then for the size of the pizza and returns the two input values in the reference parameters:

```
void getData(double &cost, int &size)
{
    cout << "Enter the pizza price and press < <Enter>. ";
    cin >> cost;
    cout << "Enter the pizza size and press <Enter>. ";
    cin >> size;
}
```

We next write a function for performing the desired computations. This function receives the cost and size and then returns the price per square inch. Thus, cost and size are parameters and the price per square inch is the returned value of the function. If we name the function `pricePerSquareInch`, we can write its declaration as follows:

```
// Function: pricePerSquareInch
// Compute the price per square inch of pizza
//
// Input: cost and size of pizza
// Output: price per square inch

double pricePerSquareInch(double cost, int size);
```

The implementation of this function also requires variables `radius` and `area` to be declared in the data declaration section of the function. Assuming `PI` has been defined as a constant and `sqr` has been defined as a function, the function's implementation is

```
double pricePerSquareInch(double pizzaCost, int pizzaSize)
{
   double radius, area;
   radius = pizzaSize / 2;
   area = PI * sqr(radius);
   return pizzaCost / area;
}
```

A function to print the results receives the unit cost. A declaration for the function is

```
// Function: printResults
// Print the price per square inch
//
// Input: price per square inch

void printResults(double pricePerSqInch);
```

The function's implementation is:

```
void printResults(double pricePerSqInch)
{
   cout << setiosflags(ios::fixed | ios::showpoint)
        << setprecision(2) << endl;
   cout << "The price per square inch is $";
   cout << setw(6) << pricePerSqInch << endl;
}
```

The complete program for this problem is as follows:

```
// Program file: pizza.cpp

#include <iostream.h>
#include <iomanip.h>

const double PI = 3.14159;

// Function: getData
// Gets cost and size of pizza from the user at the keyboard
//
// Outputs: The cost and size

void getData(double &cost, int &size);

// Function: pricePerSquareInch
// Compute the price per square inch of pizza
//
// Input: cost and size of pizza
// Output: price per square inch

double pricePerSquareInch(double cost, int size);

// Function: printResults
// Print the price per square inch
//
// Input: price per square inch

void printResults(double pricePerSqInch);

// Function: sqr
// Computes the square of a number
//
// Input: a real number
// Output: a real number representing the square of the input

double sqr(double x);

int main()
{
   int size;
   double cost, price;

   getData(cost, size);
   price = pricePerSquareInch(cost, size);
   printResults(price);
   return 0;
}

void getData(double &cost, int &size)
{
   cout << "Enter the pizza price and press <Enter>. ";
   cin >> cost;
   cout << "Enter the pizza size and press <Enter>. ";
   cin >> size;
}
```

```
double pricePerSquareInch(double cost, int size)
{
   double radius, area;
   radius = size / 2;
   area = PI * sqr(radius);
   return cost / area;
}

void printResults(double pricePerSqInch)
{
   cout << setiosflags(ios::fixed | ios::showpoint)
        << setprecision(2) << endl;
   cout << "The price per square inch is $";
   cout << setw(6) << pricePerSqInch << endl;
}

double sqr(double x)
{
   return x * x;
}
```

Note how the use of subprograms has simplified the structure of the main function compared with the original version in Chapter 3.

Sample runs of this program produce the following output:

```
Enter the pizza price and press <Enter>. 10.50
Enter the pizza size and press <Enter>. 16

The price per square inch is $ 0.05

Enter the pizza price and press <Enter>. 8.75
Enter the pizza size and press <Enter>. 14

The price per square inch is $ 0.06
```

Exercises 4.4

1. Draw a structure chart for a program that prompts the user for an integer, computes its square root, and displays this result with an informative label on the terminal screen. Your chart should contain three modules: one for getting the data, one for computing the result, and one for printing the result. Be sure to label the data flow between the modules with arrows.
2. Construct a main function module in C++ and add to it the declarations of three functions that will carry out the tasks of the modules from Exercise 1.
3. Implement and test each of the functions from Exercise 2. You will have to declare at least one integer variable to pass the data from module to module.

4.5 Scope of Identifiers

Global and Local Identifiers

Identifiers used to declare variables in the declaration section of a program can be used throughout the entire program. For purposes of this section, we will think of the global text of the program file as a *block* and the main function and each subprogram

Objectives

a. to understand what is meant by local identifiers
b. to understand what is meant by global identifiers
c. to understand the scope of an identifier
d. to recognize the appropriate and inappropriate uses of global identifiers
e. to understand and control side effects in programs
f. to use appropriate names for identifiers

as a *subblock* for the main function or subprogram. Each subblock may contain a parameter list, a local declaration section, and the body of the block. A program file block can be envisioned as shown in Figure 4.2. Furthermore, if `X1` is a variable in the main function block, we will indicate this as shown in Figure 4.3, where an area in memory has been set aside for `X1`. When a program contains a subprogram, a separate memory area within the memory area for the program is set aside for the subprogram to use while it executes. Thus, if the program file contains a function named `subprog1`, we can envision this as shown in Figure 4.4. If `subprog1` contains the variable `X2`, we have the program shown in Figure 4.5. This could be indicated in the program by

```
const double PI = 3.14;

double subprog1 (double x2);

int main;
{
   double x1;

   subprog1(x1);
   .
   .
   .
```

The *scope of an identifier* refers to the area of the program text in which it can be used. When subprograms are used, each identifier is available to the block in which it is declared and any nested blocks. Identifiers are not available outside their blocks.

Identifiers that are declared before the main block are called *global identifiers;* identifiers that are restricted to use within the main block or a subblock are called *local identifiers*. Constant `PI` in Figure 4.5 can be used throughout the main function

Figure 4.2
Program file block

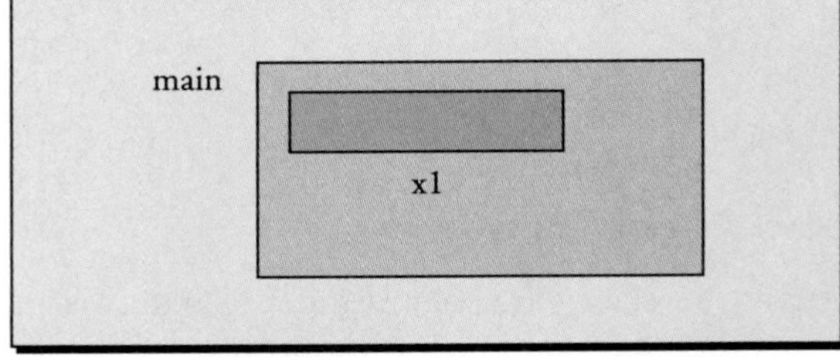

Figure 4.3
Variable location in main block

and in the function `subprog1`; therefore, it is a global identifier. Variable `X1` can be used in the main function but not in the function `subprog1`; it is a local identifier. Variable `X2` can only be used within the function where it is declared; it is a local identifier. Any attempt to reference `X2` outside the function will result in an error. Lastly, function `subprog1` can be used either in the main function block, within another function's block, or within its own block. This last use is a recursive one, which we will discuss in Chapter 14.

As a matter of C++ syntax, function names must be declared as global identifiers. Constant, variable, and type names can be declared either globally or locally. However, as a matter of good programming style, constant and type names are usually declared globally, and variable names are declared locally.

Let us now examine an illustration of local and global identifiers. Consider the program and function declaration

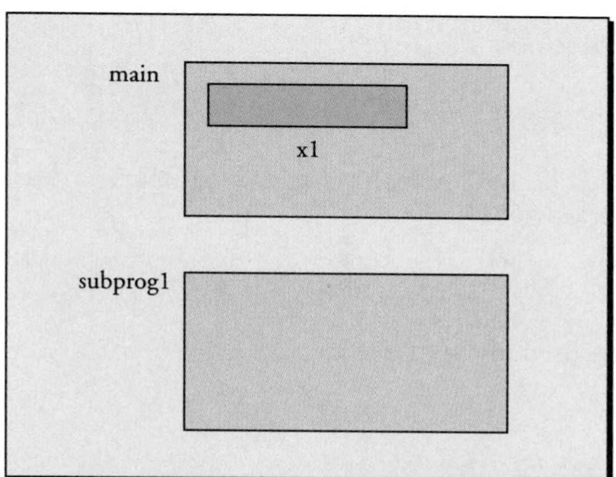

Figure 4.4
Illustration of a subblock

Figure 4.5
Variable location within a subblock

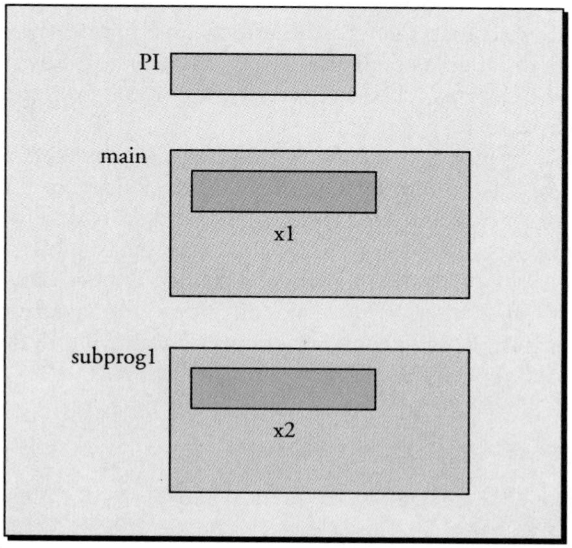

```
const int A = 10;

int subprog(int a1);

int main()
{
   int x, y;
   .
   .
}

int subprog (int a1)
{
   double x;
   .
   .
```

Blocks for this program can be envisioned as shown in Figure 4.6. Because `A` is global, the statement

```
cout << A << a1 << x << endl;
```

could be used in the function `subprog`, although `A` has not been specifically declared there. However,

```
cout << A << a1 << x << endl;
```

could not be used in the main function because `a1` and `x` are local to the function `subprog`.

Using Global Identifiers

In general, it is not good practice to refer to global variables within functions. A *side effect* is a change in a nonlocal variable that is the result of some action taken in a program. The use of locally defined variables in functions and in the main function block helps avoid unexpected side effects and protects your programs. In addition, locally defined variables facilitate debugging and top-down design and enhance the portability of functions. This is especially important if different people are working on different functions for a program.

The use of global constants is different. Because the values cannot be changed by a function, it is preferred that constants be defined in the data declaration section before the main function block and then be used whenever needed by any subprogram. This is especially important if the constant is subject to change over time, for example, `STATE_TAX_RATE`. When a change is necessary, one change in the main function is all that is needed to make all subprograms current. If a constant is used in only one function, some programmers prefer to have it defined near the point of use. Thus, they define it in the subprogram in which it is used.

Side Effects and Parameters

Unintentional side effects are frequently caused by the misuse of reference parameters. Since any change in a reference parameter causes a change in the corresponding actual parameter in the calling program or function, you should use reference pa-

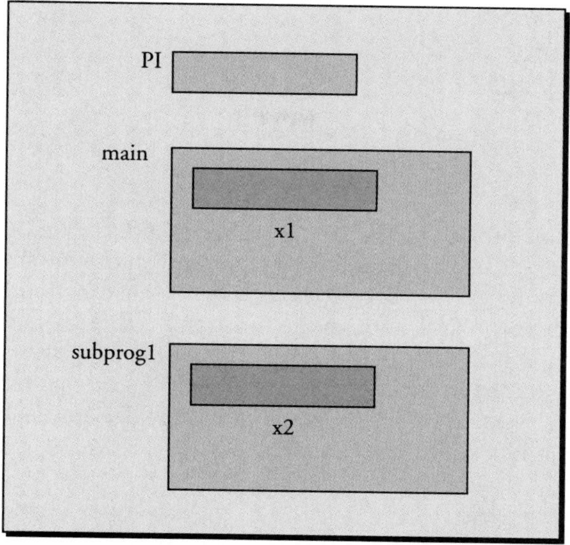

Figure 4.6
Scope of identifiers

rameters only when your intent is to produce such changes. In all other cases, use value parameters. For example, the following program would produce a syntax error because a function attempts to access a variable declared in the main block:

```
void badSquare();

int main()
{
   int mainData = 2;

   badSquare();
   return 0;

}

void badSquare();
{
   mainData = mainData * mainData;
}
```

If we move the declaration of `mainData` outside of the main block, we can extend its scope into the local block of the function, unless the name is redeclared within the function as a parameter or local variable:

```
int mainData = 2;

void badsquare();

int main()
{

   badSquare();
   return 0;
```

continued

```
}

void badSquare();
{
   mainData = mainData * mainData;
}
```

We have named the function `badSquare` to indicate that the assignment that occurs in the function is bad programming practice, even though the result might be intended by the programmer. Not only does the use of this function result in a serious side effect, but there is no indication in the function's declaration or in the function's call that the function will modify the global variable. Keeping the declarations of these variables inside the main function block will help guard against this problem.

A better version of this program moves the declaration of the global variable back into the main block and passes the variable as a reference parameter to the function:

```
void betterSquare(int &x);

int main()
{
   int mainData = 2;

   betterSquare(mainData);
   return 0;
}

void betterSquare (int &x)
{
   x = x * x;
}
```

The function `betterSquare` improves on `badSquare` in two respects. First, the function now has a *manifest interface.* A function has a manifest interface if we can see, just from looking at the function's declaration and the function's call, exactly what data the function is manipulating and that it will be subject to change within the function. In other words, we are given clear notice that a side effect will occur in the function and a clear indication of what that side effect will be. Second, the function can be used to take the square of any variable passed to it as an actual parameter. We have indicated this by using `x` to name the formal parameter of the function. Thus, `betterSquare` is more general than `badSquare`, which could take the square of just one variable.

While `betterSquare` is an improvement on `badSquare`, we can write a still better version of this function:

```
int bestSquare(int x);

int main()
{
   int mainData = 2;
   mainData = bestSquare(mainData);
   return 0;
}
```

```
int bestSquare(int x)
{
   return x * x;
}
```

This version of the function is best for two reasons. First, it has a manifest interface. The caller knows exactly what data will be used by the function. Second, the function produces no side effects. The caller passes the function a value to be squared, and the square of this value is returned to the caller. In particular, if the caller passes a variable to this function, the caller can be sure that the function will not change the variable. If the caller wants to set a variable to the value returned by the function, then this assignment must be explicitly done by the caller after the function returns its value.

All three versions of the function in this example are technically correct in that they accomplish the task intended by the programmer. However, as the example demonstrates, whenever possible, it is best to write functions that have manifest interfaces and that produce no side effects.

Names of Identifiers

Because separate areas in memory are set aside when subprograms are used, it is possible to have identifiers with the same name in both the main function and a subprogram. Thus

```
int main()
{
   int age;
   .
   .
}
int subprog (int age)
```

can be envisioned as shown in Figure 4.7. When the same name is used in this manner, any reference to this name results in action being taken as locally as possible. Thus, the assignment statement

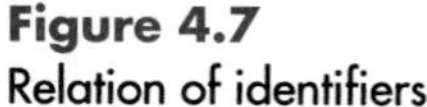
Figure 4.7
Relation of identifiers

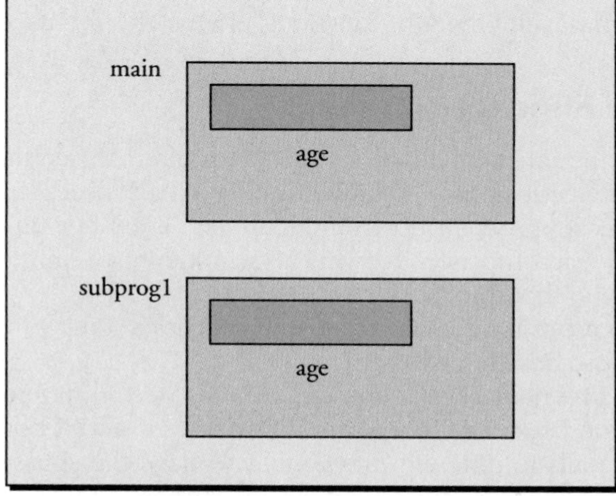

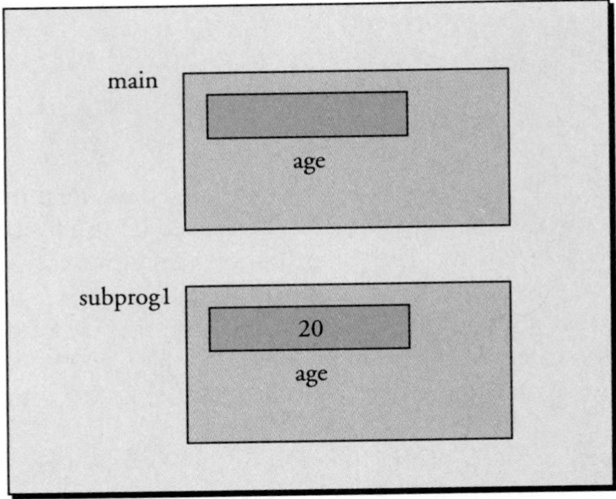

Figure 4.8 Assigning values in subprograms

```
age = 20;
```

made in the function subprog assigns 20 to age{r} in the function but not in the main function (see Figure 4.8).

Now that you know you can use the same name for an identifier in a subprogram and the main function, the question is: Should you? There are two schools of thought regarding this issue. If you use the same name in the functions, it facilitates matching parameter lists and independent development of functions. However, this practice can be confusing when you first start working with subprograms. Thus, some instructors prefer using different, but related, identifiers. For example,

```
displayData (score1, score2);
```

in the main function could have a function heading of

```
void displayData (int sc1, int sc2);
```

In this case, the use of sc1 and sc2 is obvious. Although this may facilitate better understanding in early work with subprograms, it is less conducive to portability and independent development of functions. Both styles are used in this text.

Multiple Functions

More than one function can be used in a program. When this occurs, all of the previous uses and restrictions of identifiers apply to each function. Blocks for multiple functions can be depicted as shown in Figure 4.9. Identifiers in the main function can be accessed by each function. However, local identifiers in the functions cannot be accessed outside their blocks.

When a program contains several functions, they can be called from the main part of the program in any order.

The same names for identifiers can be used in different functions. Thus, if the main function uses variables wage and hours and if both of these are used as arguments in calls to different functions, you have the situation shown in Figure 4.10. Using the same names for identifiers in different functions makes it easier to keep

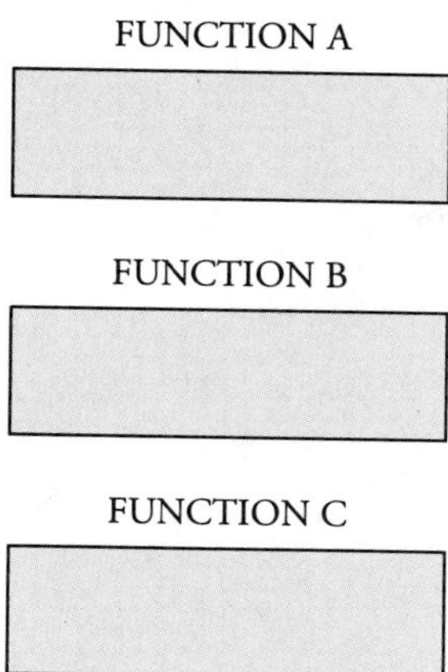

Figure 4.9
Blocks for multiple functions

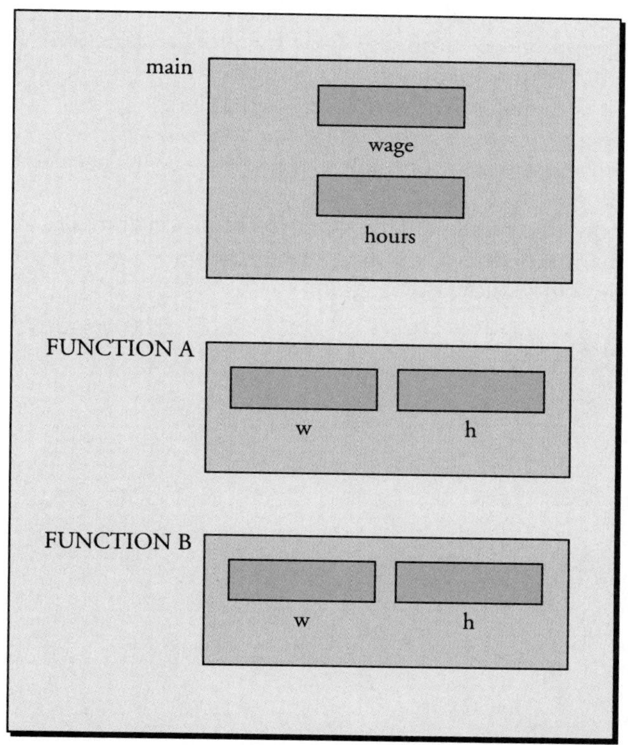

Figure 4.10
Identifiers in multiple subprograms

track of the relationship between variables in the main function and their associated parameters in each subprogram.

Communication and Style Tips

1. Adopt a convention of listing all of the value parameters in a function declaration and heading before you list any of the reference parameters. This will aid in reading the function. For example, the following declaration has six parameters, three of which are value parameters and three of which are reference parameters:

```
void processData(double a, double b, int x,
                 double &c, double &d, int &y);
```

2. In most cases where a function returns a single value to the caller, you should use value parameters only. You should use reference parameters only where you wish to return more than one value to the caller.
3. Most functions that use reference parameters should be `void` functions. This will avoid confusion about how many values are returned.
4. To help minimize side effects, declare all variables used by the main program within the main program block.

Exercises 4.5

1. Explain the difference between local and global identifiers.
2. State the advantages of using local identifiers.
3. Discuss some appropriate uses for global identifiers. List several constants that would be appropriate global definitions.
4. What is meant by the scope of an identifier?
5. Write a test program that will enable you to see
   a. what happens when an attempt is made to access an identifier outside of its scope
   b. how the values change as a result of assignments in the subprogram and the main function when the same identifier is used in both
6. Review the following program:

```
int main()
{
    int a, b;
    double x;
    char ch;
      .
      .
}
int sub1(int a1)
{
    int b1;
      .
      .
}

int sub2(int a1, int b1)
{
    double x1;
    char ch1;
      .
      .
}
```

   a. List all global variables.
   b. List all local variables.
   c. Indicate the scope of each identifier.
7. Provide a schematic representation of the program and all subprograms and variables in Exercise 6.

A NOTE OF INTEREST

John Backus

You have read about John Backus, the inventor of FORTRAN, in A Note of Interest on program libraries in Chapter 2, and we also mentioned him earlier in this chapter. Backus has had a long and distinguished career as a computer scientist with IBM. During the late 1950s, he sat on a committee that developed ALGOL, the first *block-structured* programming language. The block structure of ALGOL represented a significant advance over FORTRAN. A block in ALGOL is a set of related data declarations and executable statements. The data declared in a block are visible only within it. This greatly enhances program security, readability, and maintenance. Most modern programming languages developed after ALGOL, including C++, have been block structured.

In 1977, Backus was given the Turing Award for his contributions to computer science at the annual meeting of the Association for Computing Machinery. Each recipient of this annual award presents a lecture. Backus discussed a new discipline called *function-oriented programming* in his talk. This style of programming was developed to address concerns about the reliability and maintainability of large software systems. One of the principal causes of errors in large programs is the presence of side effects and unintentional modifications of variables. These modifications can occur anywhere in a program with assignment statements whose targets are global variables. Backus proposed that function-oriented programming could eliminate side effects by eliminating the assignment statement and keeping global variables to a minimum. Function-oriented programs consist of sets of function declarations and *function applications*. A function application simply evaluates the arguments to a function, applies the function to these values, and returns a result to the caller. No assignment statements to global variables are allowed within a function. No side effects occur.

The philosophy of function-oriented programming has motivated the design of function-oriented languages. These languages do not allow the programmer to perform assignments to global variables within functions. Although C++ allows programmers to declare and use functions, the language does not forbid this kind of side effect. However, by exercising some discipline, C++ programmers can still emulate a function-oriented style to prevent side effects from occurring in their programs.

8. Using the program with variables and subprograms as depicted in Figure 4.11, state the scope of each identifier.

9. What is the output from the following program?

```
#include <iostream.h>

void sub1 (int a);

int main()
{
   int a;
   a = 10;

   cout << a << endl;
   sub1 (a);
   cout << a << endl;
   return 0;
}

void sub1 (int a)
{
   a = 20;
   cout << a << endl;
}
```

10. Write appropriate headings and declaration sections for the program and subprograms illustrated in Figure 4.12.

Figure 4.11

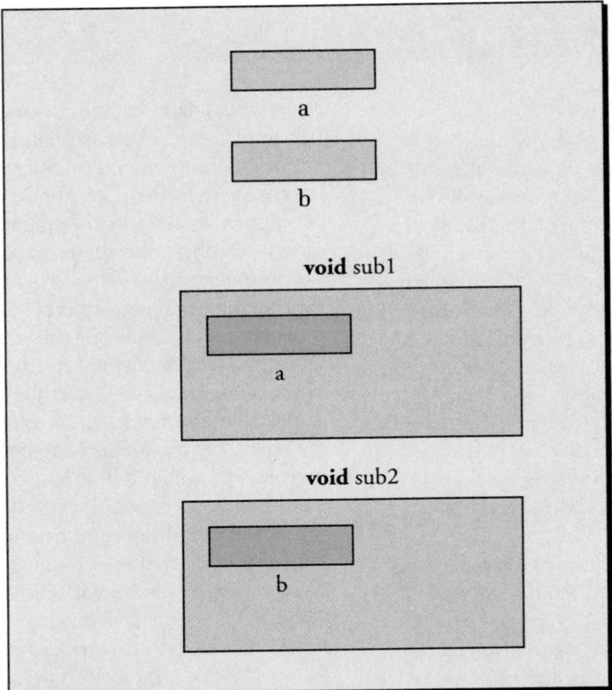

Figure 4.12

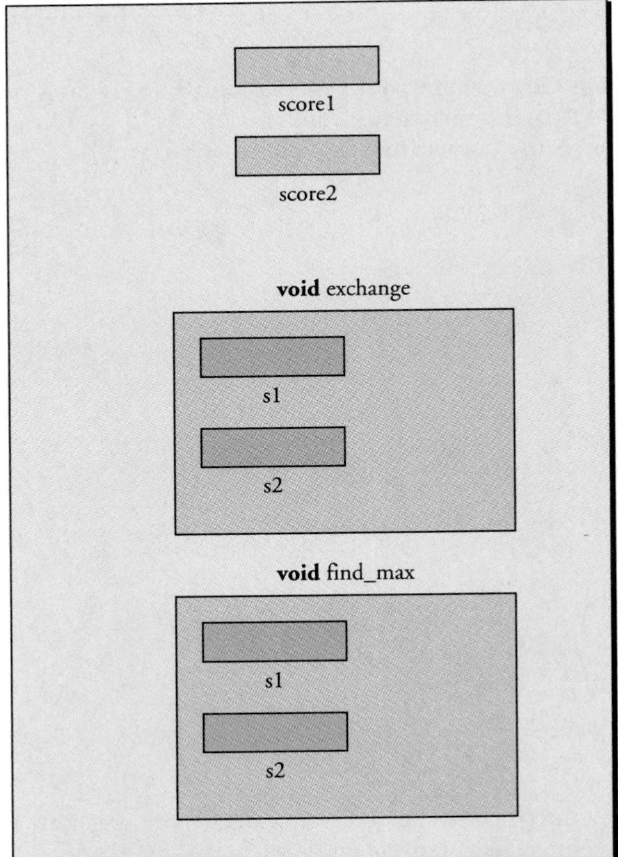

11. Find all errors in the following program.

```
int main()
{
   double x, y;
   x = 10;
   y = 2 * x;
   cout << x << y << endl;
   sub1(x);
   cout << x1 << x << y << endl;
   return 0;
}

void sub1 (int x1)
{
    cout << x1 << x << y << endl;
}
```

12. Discuss the advantages and disadvantages of using the same names for identifiers in a subprogram and the main function.

4.6 Programmer-Defined Libraries

Objectives

a. to define libraries
b. to distinguish between library header files and library implementation files

As you develop functions, you will find that some of them are useful in a wide range of programs. It is convenient to create your own libraries of functions so that you can include them in any program where they are needed. There are two steps for creating a library:

1. Declare the functions and save this code in a *library header file*. The name of this file should have a `.h` extension and will be included by any program needing these functions.
2. Implement the same functions and save this code in a *library implementation file*. For many C++ compilers, the name of this file should have a `.cpp` extension.

An Example Library Header File

Let us create a library of interactive input functions. The two functions, `getInteger` and `getString`, were discussed in Section 4.2, although we use here the updated versions with constant reference parameters. The declarations of the functions go in a header file named `myinput.h`. The text of this file follows:

```
// Library header file: myinput.h

#ifndef MY_INPUT
#define MY_INPUT

#include "apstring.h"

// Function: getInteger
// Prompts user for an integer, inputs it, and returns it
//
// Input: A string representing the prompt
// Output: The integer input by the user
```

continued

```
int getInteger(const apstring &prompt);

// Function: getString
// Prompts user for a string, inputs it, and returns it
//
// Input: A string representing the prompt
// Output: The string input by the user

apstring getString(const apstring &prompt);

#endif
```

Note that comments documenting the functions go with the declarations in the header file. The header file serves as the communication link between the implementers of the library and its users. Thus, it is very important to maintain adequate documentation of the library functions in this file.

Note also the use of the preprocessor directives `#ifndef`, `#define`, and `#endif`. These directives are used to prevent the preprocessor from including a library file more than once in an application at compile time. For example, the header file `apstring.h` is included in this file so that the identifier `apstring` will have a definition. But the same header file would also be included in the main program, which would use it to declare string variables. The new directives work to prevent multiple inclusions from occurring as follows:

1. The first directive, `#ifndef`, asks if a file identifier has been defined. If it has, the library file has already been preprocessed, so the preprocessor skips the current inclusion by jumping to `#endif` at the end of the file.
2. If the file identifier has not been defined, the preprocessor will reach the `#define` directive. This directive then makes visible a global file identifier so that the next inclusion after this one will behave as in step 1.

In general, every library header file should use these directives to avoid compilation errors. The basic form of a header file is

```
#ifndef <file identifier>
#define <file identifier>
<function declarations>
#endif
```

An Example Library Implementation File

The implementation file for the `myinput` library contains the function implementations and is named `myinput.cpp`.

```
// Library implementation file: myinput.cpp

#include "myinput.h"

int getInteger(const apstring &prompt)
{
   int data;

   cout << prompt;
   cin >> data;
```

```
    return data;
}
apstring getString(const apstring &prompt)
{
    apstring data;

    cout << prompt;
    cin >> data;
    return data;
}
```

The implementation file includes the header file before defining the functions. This order is necessary for the compiler to check that the function declarations in the header file match the headings in the implementation file. Note that the file name used with the `#include` directive is enclosed in double quotes rather than angle brackets. You have already seen this notation used with the `apstring` library, and it is typical for programmer-defined libraries.

Example Use of a Programmer-Defined Library

The following driver program tests the functions defined in the `myinput` library:

```
// Program file: testmyin.cpp

#include <iostream.h>
#include "apstring.h"
#include "myinput.h"

int main()
{
    int age;
    apstring name;

    name = getString("Enter your first name: ");
    age = getInteger("Enter your age: ");
    cout << "Name = " << name << endl;
    cout << "Age = " << age << endl;
    return 0;
}
```

Note the use of double quotes to enclose the file name rather than angle brackets. In general, names of programmer-defined libraries will appear this way when they are included in example programs in this text. Names of standard libraries will continue to appear in angle brackets.

Exercises 4.6

1. Why is it a good idea to put commonly used functions in a program library?
2. Discuss the difference between a library header file and a library implementation file. What are the roles and responsibilities of each file?
3. Discuss how C++ processes code in library files before compilation. Be sure to address the role of the directives `#include`, `#ifndef`, `#define`, and `#endif` in this process.
4. Create a program library named `mymath`. This library should define functions for computing the areas of rectangles, circles, and triangles.

Case Study: Subsidized Parking

To encourage people to shop downtown, the Downtown Businesses Association partially subsidizes parking. Participating lots charge customers $0.75 for each full hour of parking. There is no charge for part of an hour. Thus, if someone has used the lot for less than an hour, there would be no charge.

Each parking lot must be open from 9:00 A.M. until 11:00 P.M. When a vehicle enters, the driver is given a ticket with the entry time printed in military style. Thus, if a car entered the lot at 9:30 A.M., the ticket would read 930. If a vehicle entered at 1:20 P.M., the ticket would read 1320. When the vehicle leaves, the driver presents the ticket to the attendant and the amount due is computed.

User Request

Write a program to assist the attendant.

Analysis

Input consists of

- The name of the parking lot
- The parking lot's address
- The customer's starting time
- The customer's ending time.

Output should be a statement to the customer indicating the input information, the total amount due, a heading, and a closing message. Sample output for the data 1050 (10:50 A.M.) and 1500 (3:00 P.M.) is

```
Please enter the lot's name and press <Enter>. E - Z Parking
Please enter the lot's address and press <Enter>. 51 State Street
Please enter the time in (24 hour notation) and press <Enter>. 1050
Please enter the time out and press <Enter>. 1500

          E - Z Parking
        51 State Street

 Time in: 1050 Time out: 1500

 Amount due      $ 3.00

Thank you for using E - Z Parking

           BUCKLE UP
         and DRIVE SAFELY
```

A sample run using the data 930 as entry time and 1320 as exit time produces

```
Please enter the lot's name and press <Enter>. E - Z Parking
Please enter the lot's address and press <Enter>. 51 State Street
Please enter the time in (24 hour notation) and press <Enter>. 930
Please enter the time out and press <Enter>. 1320

          E - Z Parking
        51 State Street

 Time in: 930 Time out: 1320
```

```
 Amount due      $ 2.25
Thank you for using E - Z Parking

          BUCKLE UP
        and DRIVE SAFELY
```

Design

A first-level design for this problem is

1. Get the data
2. Compute amount
3. Print results

A structure chart for this problem is given in Figure 4.13. (Recall that an arrow pointing into a module indicates data are being received, whereas an arrow pointing out indicates data are being sent from the module.) Module specifications for the three main modules are

Module: Get data
Task: Prompts user for and inputs name and address of parking lot and entry time and exit time of customer
Outputs: integers representing entry time and exit time and strings representing name and address of parking lot

Module: Compute amount
Task: Compute the amount due in dollars and cents
Inputs: integers representing entry time and exit time
Output: a real number representing the amount due

Module: Print results
Task: Print heading, entry and exit times, amount due, and closing message
Inputs: integers representing entry time and exit time and a real number representing the amount due, and strings representing name and address of parking lot

Figure 4.13 Structure chart for the parking lot program

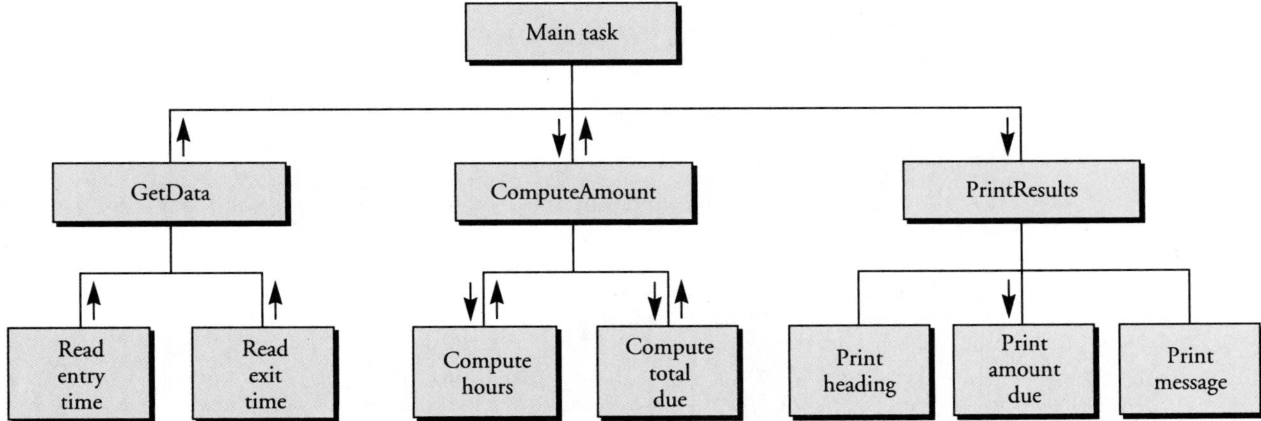

Module: Print heading
Task: Print heading with name and address of parking lot
Inputs: strings representing name and address of parking lot

Module: Print message
Task: Print closing message with name of parking lot
Input: string representing name of parking lot

By examining the module specifications, we see that `getData` needs four parameters, `computeAmount` needs two parameters, and `printResults` needs five parameters.

A second-level pseudocode development is

1. Get the data
  1.1 prompt user for name of lot
  1.2 read name entered
  1.3 prompt user for address of lot
  1.4 read address entered
  1.5 prompt user for time entered
  1.6 read time entered
  1.7 prompt user for time exited
  1.8 read time exited
2. Compute amount
  2.1 compute number of hours
  2.2 compute amount due
3. Print results
  3.1 print a heading with name and address of lot
  3.2 print amount due
  3.3 print a closing message with name of lot

Implementation

Here is a complete listing of the code for the program:

```
// This program prints statements for customers of a subsidized
// parking lot. Interactive input consists of the lot's name
// and address and the customer's entry time and exit time
// from the lot. Output consists of a customer statement.
// Emphasis is placed on using functions to develop the program.

// Program file: parking.cpp

#include <iostream.h>
#include <iomanip.h>
#include "apstring.h"

const double HOURLY_RATE = 0.75;

// Function: getData
// Prompts user for and inputs lot name, lot address,
// entry time, and exit time

// Outputs: integers representing entry time and exit time
//          strings representing lot name and lot address

void getData(int &entryTime, int &exitTime,
             apstring &name, apstring &address);
```

```
// Function: computeAmount
// Computes the amount due in dollars and cents
//
// Inputs: integers representing entry time and exit time
// Output: a real number representing the amount due

double computeAmount(int entryTime, int exitTime);

// Function:  printResults
// Prints heading, entry and exit times, amount due,
// and closing message
//
// Inputs: integers representing entry time and exit time,
//         and a real number representing the amount due
//         strings representing lot name and address

void printResults(int entryTime, int exitTime, double amountDue,
                  const apstring &name, const apstring &address);

// Function: printHeading
// Print a heading for the ticket
//
// Inputs: strings representing lot name and address

void printHeading(const apstring &name, const apstring &address);

// Function: printMessage
// Print a closing message for the ticket
//
// Input: string representing lot name

void printMessage(const apstring &name);

int main()
{
   int entryTime;      // Time of entry into parking lot
   int exitTime;       // Time of exit from parking lot
   double amountDue;   //  Cost of parking in lot
   apstring name, address;

   getData(entryTime, exitTime, name, address);
   amountDue = computeAmount(entryTime, exitTime);
   printResults (entryTime, exitTime, amountDue, name, address);
   return 0;
}

void getData(int &entryTime, int &exitTime,
             apstring &name, apstring &address)
{
   cout << "Please enter the lot's name and press <Enter>. ";
   getline(cin, name);
   cout << "Please enter the lot's address and press <Enter>. ";
   getline(cin, address);
   cout << "Please enter the time in (24 hour notation) "
        << "and press <Enter>. ";
   cin >> entryTime;
```

continued

```
   cout << "Please enter the time out and press <Enter>. ";
   cin >> exitTime;
}

double computeAmount (int entryTime, int exitTime)
{
   int numberOfHours;

   numberOfHours = (exitTime - entryTime) / 100;
   return numberOfHours * HOURLY_RATE;
}

void printHeading(const apstring &name, const apstring &address)
{
   cout << endl;
   cout << setw(25) << name << endl;
   cout << setw(25) << address << endl;
   cout << endl;
}

void printMessage(const apstring &name)
{
   cout << endl;
   cout << setw(4)
        << ("Thank you for using " + name) << endl;
   cout << endl;
   cout << setw(21) << "BUCKLE UP" << endl;
   cout << setw(25) << "and DRIVE SAFELY";
   cout << endl;
}

void printResults(int entryTime, int exitTime, double amountDue,
                  const apstring &name, const apstring &address)
{
   cout << setiosflags(ios::fixed | ios::showpoint | ios::right)
        << setprecision(2);
   printHeading(name, address);
   cout << setw(13) << "Time in:"
        << setw(5) << entryTime;
   cout << "Time out:"
        << setw(5) << exitTime << endl;
   cout << endl;
   cout << setw(17) << "Amount due $"
        << setw(6) << amountDue << endl;
   printMessage(name);
}
```

Running, Testing, and Debugging Hints

1. Each subprogram can be tested separately to see if it is producing the desired result. This is accomplished by a main function that calls and tests only the subprogram in question.
2. You can use related or identical variable names in the parameter lists. For example,

```
double compute (int n1, int n2);
```

or

```
double compute (int number1, int number2);
```

could be called by

```
compute (number1, number2);
```

3. Be sure the type, order, and purpose of actual parameters and formal parameters agree. You can do this by listing them one below the other. For example,

```
void displayData (char init1, char init2, int sc);
```

could be called by

```
displayData (a, b, 9);
```

4. Be sure that you really need to use a reference parameter in a function before you declare it. If a function returns only one value to the caller, use no reference parameters.
5. If a function does not seem to return a value to the caller as expected, perhaps a parameter has not been declared as a reference parameter. Check the function's heading and declaration to be sure that the symbol `&` is associated with the desired output parameter.

Summary

Key Terms

actual parameter
alias
block
bottom-up testing
cohesive subprogram
formal parameter
functional abstraction
global identifier
information hiding
interface
local copy
local identifier
main driver
manifest interface
modularity
module
pass by reference
pass by value
postcondition
precondition
procedural abstraction
reference parameter
scope of an identifier
side effect
structured design
structured programming
stub programming
subblock
subprogram
user-defined function
value parameter

Keywords

`return` `void`

Key Concepts

- A subprogram is a program within a program; functions are subprograms.
- Subprograms can be utilized to perform specific tasks in a program. Functions are often used to initialize variables, get data, print headings (no parameters needed), perform computations, and print data.
- The general form for a function declaration is

```
<type identifier> <name> (<parameter list>);
```

- A typical parameter list is

```
void displayData (int n1, int n2, double x, double y);
```

- A formal parameter is one listed in the subprogram heading; it is like a blank waiting to receive a value from the calling program.
- An actual parameter is a variable listed in the subprogram call in the calling program.
- The formal parameter list in the subprogram heading must match the number and types of actual parameters used in the main function when the subprogram is called.

```
void arithmetic (char sym, int n1, int n2);
arithmetic (symbol, num1, num2);
```

- The type of an actual parameter being passed to a function must be compatible with the type of the formal parameter in its position in a function heading; implicit type conversions are made whenever possible.
- If the symbol `&` appears in a formal parameter declaration, then the formal parameter is a reference parameter; otherwise, the formal parameter is a value parameter.
- For value parameters, a copy of the actual parameter's value is passed to a function when it is called.
- Pass by value is safe; the value of the actual parameter does not change during the call of the function.
- For reference parameters, the address of the actual parameter is passed to the function when it is called.
- Pass by reference is not safe; it should be used with caution and only when side effects are intended.
- Global identifiers can be used by the main function and all subprograms.
- Local identifiers are available only to the main function block or the subprogram block in which they are declared.
- Each identifier is available to the block in which it is declared.
- Identifiers are not available outside their blocks.
- The scope of an identifier refers to the area of text in which the identifier is available.
- Understanding the scope of identifiers is aided by graphic illustration of blocks in a program; thus, the following program can be visualized as shown in Figure 4.14. A user-defined function is a subprogram that performs a specific task.

```
const double PI = 3.14;

double sub1(double);
double sub2(double);

int main()
```

Figure 4.14

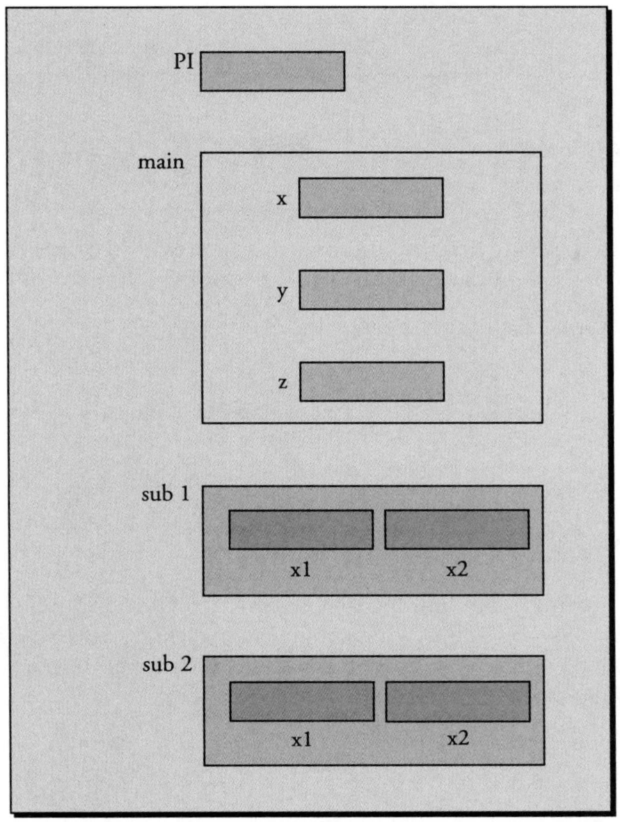


```
{
   double x, y, z;
   .
   .
   .
}

double sub1(double x1)
{
   double x2;
   .
   .
   .
}

double sub2(double x1)
{
   double z2;
   .
   .
   .
}
```

- The form for a user-defined function is

```
<type identifier> <function name> (<parameter list>)
{
<data declarations>
<executable statements>
}
```

- A programmer-defined library is a useful way to organize the definitions of related functions. A library consists of a header file and an implementation file.
- The form of a library header file is

```
#ifndef <file identifier>
<function declarations>
#define <file identifier>
#endif
```

Programming Problems and Projects

The following programming problems will be run on a very limited set of data. In later chapters, as you build your programming skills, you will run these problems with larger databases and subprograms for various parts. *Be sure to package coherent tasks in functions wherever possible.*

1. Write a program to get the coefficients of a quadratic equation

$$ax^2 + bx + c = 0$$

from the keyboard and then print the value of the discriminant $b^2 - 4ac$. A sample display for getting input is

```
Enter coefficients a, b, and c for the quadratic equation
```

$$ax^2 + bx + c = 0$$

a = ?
b = ?
c = ?

Run this program at least three times using test data that result in $b^2 - 4ac = 0$, $b^2 - 4ac > 0$, and $b^2 - 4ac < 0$.

2. Write a program to compute the cost for carpeting a room. Input should consist of the room length, room width, and carpet price per square yard. Use constants for the pad charge and installation charge. Include a heading as part of the output. A typical input screen is:

```
What is the room length in feet? <Enter> ?
What is the room width in feet? <Enter> ?
What is the carpet price/square yard? <Enter> ?
```

Output for a sample run of this program (without a heading) could be

```
Dimensions of the room (in feet) are 17 x 22.
The area to be carpeted is 41.6 square yards.
The carpet price is $11.95 per yard.
```

```
Room dimensions                17 x 22

Carpet required                41.6 square yards

Carpet price/yard             $11.95

Pad price/yard                 $2.95

Installation price/yard        $ .95

Total price/yard              $15.85

Total price                  $659.36
```

3. Williamson's Paint and Papering store wants a computer program to help them determine how much paint is needed to paint a room. Assuming a room is to have four walls and the ceiling painted, input for the program should be the length, width, and height of the room. Use a constant for the wall height (usually 8 feet). One gallon of paint should cover 250 square feet. Cost of paint for the walls and ceiling should be entered by the user. Output should be the amount and cost for each kind of paint and the total cost.
4. The Fairfield College faculty recently signed a 3-year contract that included salary increments of 7, 6, and 5%, respectively, for the next 3 years. Write a program that allows a user to enter the current salary and then prints the compounded salary for each of the next 3 years.
5. Several instructors use various weights (percentage of the final grade) for test scores. Write a program that allows the user to enter three test scores and the weight for each score. Output should consist of the input data, the weighted score for each test, and the total score (sum of the weighted scores).
6. The Roll-Em Lanes bowling team would like to have a computer program to print the team results for one series of games. The team consists of four members whose names are Weber, Fazio, Martin, and Patterson. Each person on the team bowls three games during the series; thus, the input will contain three lines, each with four integer scores. Your output should include all input data, individual series totals, game average for each member, team series, and team average. Sample output is

```
NAME          GAME 1      GAME 2      GAME 3     TOTAL      AVERAGE

Weber         212         220         190        622        207.3

Fazio         195         235         210        640        213.3

Martin        178         190         206        574        191.3

Patterson     195         215         210        620        206.7

   Team Total:  2456

   Team Average:  818.7
```

7. The Natural Pine Furniture Company has recently hired you to help them convert their antiquated payroll system to a computer-based model. They know you are still learning, so all they want right now is a program that will print a 1-week payroll

report for three employees. You should use the constant definition section for the following:

a. Federal withholding tax rate, 18%
b. State withholding tax rate, 4.5%
c. Hospitalization, $26.65
d. Union dues, $7.85

Each line of input will contain the employee's initials, the number of hours worked, and the employee's hourly rate. Your output should include a report for each employee and a summary report for the company files. A sample employee form follows:

```
Employee:                          KAL
Hours Worked:                    40.00
Hourly Rate:                      9.75
Total Wages:                    390.00

   Deductions:
   Federal Withholding          70.20
   State Withholding            17.55
   Hospitalization              26.65
   Union Dues                    7.85
   Total Deductions            122.25
   Net Pay                    $267.75
```

Output labels for a summary report could be

```
      Natural Pine Furniture Company

                Weekly Summary

Gross Wages:

Deductions:
   Federal Withholding
   State Withholding
   Hospitalization
   Union Dues
         Total Deductions

Net Wages
```

8. The Child-Growth Encyclopedia Company wants a computer program that will print a monthly sales chart. Products produced by the company, prices, and sales commissions for each are

a. Basic encyclopedia, $325.00; 22%
b. Child educational supplement, $127.50; 15%
c. Annual update book, $18.95; 20%

Monthly sales data for one region consist of a two-letter region identifier (such as MI) and three integers representing the number of units sold for each product listed above. A typical input screen would be:

```
What is your sales region? MI
How many Basic Encyclopedias were sold? 150
How many Child Supplements were sold? 120
How many Annual Updates were sold? 105
```

Write a program that will get the monthly sales data for two sales regions and produce the desired company chart. The prices may vary from month to month and should be defined in the constant definition section. The commissions are not subject to change. Typical output could be:

```
                    MONTHLY SALES CHART

                     Basic              Child          Annual
   Region            Encyclopedia       Supplement     Update

Units sold MI             150              120             105

(by region) TX            225              200             150

Total units sold          375              320             255

Price/unit                $325.00          $127.50         $18.95

Gross sales               $121875.00       $40800.00       $4832.25

Commission rate           22%              15%             20%

Commissions paid          $26812.50        $6120.00        $966.45
```

9. The Village Variety Store is having its annual Christmas sale. They would like you to write a program to produce a daily report for the store. Each item sold is identified by a code consisting of one letter followed by one digit. Your report should include data for three items. Each of the three lines of data will include item code, number of items sold, original item price, and reduction percentage. Your report should include a chart with the input data, sale price per item, and total amount of sales per item. You should also print a daily summary. Sample input is

```
A1  13  5.95  15

A2  24  7.95  20

A3  80  3.95  50
```

Typical output form could be:

```
Item Code  # Sold  Original Price  Reductions  Sale Price  Income

   A1         13          $5.95          15%        $5.06     $65.78

Daily Summary

   Gross Income:
```

10. The Holiday-Out Motel Company, Inc., wants a program that will print a statement for each overnight customer. Each line of input will contain room number (integer), number of nights (integer), room rate (real), telephone charges (real), and restaurant charges (real). You should use the constant definition section for the date and current tax rate. Each customer statement should include all input data, the date, tax rate and amount, total due, appropriate heading, and appropriate closing message. Test your program by running it for two customers. The tax rate applies only to the room cost. A typical input screen is

```
Room number? 135
Room rate? 39.95
Number of nights? 3
Telephone charges? 3.75
Meals? 57.50
```

A customer statement form is

```
         Holiday-Out Motel Company, Inc.

Date:                 XX-XX-XX
Room #                135
Room Rate:            $39.95
Number of Nights: 3
Room Cost:           $119.85
Tax: XXX%               4.79
    Subtotal:        $124.64

Telephone:              3.75
Meals:                 57.50

    TOTAL DUE        $185.89
Thank you for staying at Holiday-Out
            Drive safely
          Please come again
```

11. As a part-time job this semester, you are working for the Family Budget Assistance Center. Your boss has asked you to write and execute a program that will analyze data for a family. Input for each family will consist of

```
Family ID number (int)
Number in family (int)
Income (double)
Total debts (double)
```

Your program should output the following:

a. An appropriate header.
b. The family's identification number, number in family, income, and total debts.
c. Predicted family living expenses ($3000 times the number in family).
d. The monthly payment necessary to pay off the debt in 1 year.
e. The amount the family should save [the family size times 2% of the income minus debt: `famSize * 0.02 * (income - debt)`].
f. Your service fee (0.5% of the income).

Run your program for the following two families:

Identification Number	Size Income	Debt
51	18,000.00	4800.00
4	26,000.00	3200.00

Output for the first family could be:

```
      Family Budget Assistance Center
           March 1999
      Telephone: (800)555-1234

Identification number           51
Family size                     4
Annual income                   $ 18000.00
Total debt                      $ 2000.00
Expected living expenses        $ 12000.00
Monthly payment                 $ 166.67
Savings                         $ 1280.00
Service fee                     $ 90.00
```

12. The Caswell Catering and Convention Service has asked you to write a computer program to produce customers' bills. The program should read in the following data.

a. The number of adults to be served.
b. The number of children to be served.
c. The cost per adult's meal.
d. The cost per child's meal (60% of the cost of the adult's meal).
e. The cost for dessert (same for adults and children).
f. The room fee (no room fee if catered at the person's home).
g. A percentage for tip and tax (not applied to the room fee).
h. Any deposit should be deducted from the bill.

Write a program and test it using data sets 2, 3, and 4 from the following table:

Set	Child Count	Adult Count	Adult Cost	Dessert Cost	Room Cost	Tip/Tax Rate	Deposit
1	7	23	12.75	1.00	45.00	18%	50.00
2	3	54	13.50	1.25	65.00	19%	40.00
3	15	24	12.00	0.00	45.00	18%	75.00
4	2	71	11.15	1.50	0.00	6%	0.00

Note that data set 1 was used to produce the following sample output.

```
     Caswell Catering and Convention Service
                 Final Bill

Number of adults: 23
Number of children: 7
Cost per adult without dessert:           $     12.75
Cost per child without dessert:           $      7.65
Cost per dessert:                         $      1.00
Room fee:                                 $     45.00
Tip and tax rate:                                0.18

Total cost for adult meals:               $    293.25
Total cost for child meals:               $     53.55
Total cost for dessert:                   $     30.00
Total food cost:                          $    376.80
Plus tip and tax:                         $     67.82
Plus room fee:                            $     45.00
Less deposit:                             $     50.00

Balance due:                              $    439.62
```

13. The Maripot Carpet Store has asked you to write a computer program to calculate the amount a customer should be charged. The president of the company has given you the following information to help in writing the program.

a. The carpet charge is equal to the number of square yards purchased times the carpet cost per square yard.
b. The labor cost is equal to the number of square yards purchased times the labor cost per square yard. A fixed fee for floor preparation is added to some customers' bills.
c. Large-volume customers are given a percentage discount, but the discount applies only to the carpet charge, not the labor costs.
d. All customers are charged 4% sales tax on the carpet; there is no sales tax on the labor cost.

Write the program and test it for customers 2, 3, and 4.

Customer	Sq. yd.	Cost per sq. yd.	Labor per sq. yd.	Prep. Cost	Discount
1	17	18.50	3.50	38.50	0.02
2	40	24.95	2.95	0.00	0.14
3	23	16.80	3.25	57.95	0.00
4	26	21.25	0.00	80.00	0.00

Note that the data for customer 1 were used to produce the following sample output.

```
Square yards purchased:                  17
   Cost per square yard:     $        18.50
  Labor per square yard:     $         3.50
  Floor preparation cost:    $        38.50

       Cost for carpet:      $       314.50
       Cost for labor:       $        98.00
  Discount on carpet:        $         6.29
       Tax on carpet:        $        12.33
  Charge to customer:        $       418.54
```

14. The manager of the Croswell Carpet Store has asked you to write a program to print customers' bills. The manager has given you the following information.

- The store expresses the length and width of a room in terms of feet and tenths of a foot. For example, the length might be reported as 16.7 feet.
- The amount of carpet purchased is expressed as square yards. It is found by dividing the area of the room (in square feet) by 9.
- The store does not sell a fraction of a square yard. Thus, square yards must always be rounded up.
- The carpet charge is equal to the number of square yards purchased times the carpet cost per square yard. Sales tax equal to 4% of the carpet cost must be added to the bill.
- All customers are sold a carpet pad at $2.25 per square yard. Sales tax equal to 4% of the pad cost must be added to the bill.
- The labor cost is equal to the number of square yards purchased times $2.40, which is the labor cost per square yard. No tax is charged on labor.
- Large-volume customers may be given a discount. The discount may apply only to the carpet cost (before sales tax is added), only to the pad cost (before sales tax is added), only to the labor cost, or to any combination of the three charges.

- Each customer is identified by a five-digit number, and that number should appear on the bill. The sample output follows:

```
  Croswell Carpet Store

        Invoice

Customer number:                26817

         Carpet :              574.20
            Pad :               81.00
          Labor :               86.40

       Subtotal :              741.60
  Less discount :               65.52

       Subtotal :              676.08
       Plus tax :               23.59
          Total :              699.67
```

Write the program and test it for the following three customers.

a. Mr. Wilson (customer 81429) ordered carpet for his family room, which measures 25 feet long and 18 feet wide. The carpet sells for $12.95 per square yard and the manager agreed to give him a discount of 8% on the carpet and 6% on the labor.

b. Mr. and Mrs. Adams (customer 04246) ordered carpet for their bedroom, which measures 16.5 by 15.4 feet. The carpet sells for $18.90 per square yard and the manager granted a discount of 12% on everything.

c. Ms. Logan (customer 39050) ordered carpet that cost $8.95 per square yard for her daughter's bedroom. The room measures 13.1 by 12.5 feet. No discounts were given.

15. Each week Abduhl's Flying Carpets pays its salespeople a base salary plus a bonus for each carpet they sell. In addition, they pay a commission of 10% of the total sales made by each salesperson. Write a program to compute a salesperson's salary for the month by inputting base, bonus, quantity, and sales, and making the necessary calculations. Use the following test data:

Salesperson	Base	Bonus	Quantity	Commission	Sales
1	250.00	15.00	20	10%	1543.69
2	280.00	19.50	36	10%	2375.90

The commission figure is 10%. Be sure you can change this easily if necessary. Sample output follows:

```
   Salesperson     :      1
          Base     :    250.00
         Bonus     :     15.00
      Quantity     :     20
   Total Bonus     :    300.00
    Commission     :     10%
         Sales     :   1543.69
Total Commission :      154.37
           Pay :        704.37
```

16. Write a program to help people convert their height and weight from inches and pounds to centimeters and kilograms. The program should take keyboard input of a person's height (in feet and inches) and weight (rounded to the nearest pound). Output should consist of the height and weight in metric units.

17. Discuss the issue of documenting subprograms with instructors of computer science, upper level students majoring in computer science, and some of your classmates. Prepare a report for the class on this issue. Your report should contain information about different forms of documentation, the perceived need for documentation by various groups, the significance of documenting data transmission, and so forth. If possible, use specific examples to illustrate good versus poor documentation of subprograms.

18. Reread the material in Section 4.4 concerning functional abstraction. Then, from Problems 5, 7, 8, and 11, select one that you have not yet worked. Develop a structure chart and write module specifications for each module required for the problem you have chosen. Also, write a main driver for your program and write complete documentation for each subprogram, including comments about all parameters.

5

Selection Statements

Chapter Outline

Objectives

a. to understand the need for a Boolean data type
b. to use relational operators
c. to understand the hierarchy for evaluating simple Boolean expressions
d. to use the logical operators that express and, or, and not
e. to use compound Boolean expressions
f. to understand the short-circuit evaluation of compound Boolean expressions

The previous chapters set the stage for using computers to solve problems. You have seen how programs in C++ can be used to get data, perform computations, and print results. You should be able to write complete, short programs, so it is now time to examine other aspects of problem solving.

Let us review the metaphor of the programmable pocket calculator that we have been using in the last two chapters. Our calculator allows us to solve some simple and complex problems by using built-in functions or by creating and using functions of our own. However, the calculator is limited in that it can only take input, calculate results, and display them as output. We would like a more flexible calculator that can respond in different ways to different inputs or changes in its environment.

A major feature of a full-fledged computer, as opposed to our calculator, is the ability to make decisions. For example, a condition is examined and a decision is made as to which program statement is executed next. Statements that permit a computer to make decisions are called *selection statements*. Selection statements are examples of control structures because they allow the programmer to control the flow of execution of program statements.

■ 5.1 Boolean Expressions

Before looking at decision making, we need to examine the logical constructs in C++, which include a new data type called Boolean. This data type allows you to represent something as true or false. Although this sounds relatively simple (and it is), this is a very significant feature of computers.

Defining Boolean Constants and a Boolean Data Type

Thus far, we have used only the three data types `int`, `double`, and `char`. In any C++ program, the value 0 means *false*, and any other value means *true*. Instead of having to remember these associations, it would be convenient to use the names `true` and `false` to denote the Boolean constants, as well as to use the name `bool` when we wish to refer to the data type itself. For example, we might like to declare a variable `b` of type `bool` and assign it an initial value of `true`:

```
bool b = true;
```

As with other data types, if two variables are of type `bool`, the value of one variable can be assigned to another variable as

```
bool b = true;
bool a = b;
```

and can be envisioned as

true

a

true

b

Many C++ compilers already provide the names `bool`, `true`, and `false` for use with Boolean expressions. If your compiler does not, you can follow these steps. So that C++ programs can use these names properly, we define the constants `false` and `true` to have the values 0 and 1, respectively:

```
const int false = 0;
const int true = 1;
```

To create a new type name, `bool`, for declaring variables, function parameters, and function returns of these values, we use a C++ type definition:

```
typedef int bool;
```

`typedef` is a reserved word in C++. The general form of a *type definition* is

`typedef` <data type> <new type name>;

where `<data type>` is any C++ data type. All that our `typedef` example does is create a synonym, `bool`, for a built-in type name, `int`.

Some systems may have already defined the words `true` and `false`. In that case, you can override these definitions by using the preprocessor directive `#undef` as follows:

```
#undef false
#undef true
const int false = 0;
```

```
const int true = 1;
typedef int bool;
```

The Boolean values `true` and `false` and the type name `bool` will be mentioned in many applications. Entering the same five lines of code by hand to define these names in every new source program will be an annoying task. Instead, we can place the definitions in a library header file to be included at the top of every program that uses them. The file is named `bool.h` and contains these definitions:

```
// Library file: bool.h

// Defines Boolean constants and a type name for any application.

#ifndef BOOL_H
#define BOOL_H
#undef false
#undef true

const int false = 0;
const int true = 1;

typedef int bool;

#endif
```

This file can then be included in any source program by means of the following line of code:

```
#include "bool.h"
```

Placing the definitions of a new type in a library file is another example of information hiding. Programmers who use the `bool.h` library need not be concerned with the representation of Boolean values as integers any more than they have already been concerned with the representation of integers as bit patterns. All that we need to know about Boolean values, aside from their names, is how they can be used to make decisions in programs.

Relational Operators and Simple Boolean Expressions

In arithmetic, integers and reals can be compared for the relationships of equality, inequality, less than, and greater than. C++ also provides for the comparison of numbers or values of variables. The operators used for comparison are called *relational operators* and there are six of them. Their arithmetic notation, C++ notation, and meaning are given in Table 5.1.

When two numbers or variable values are compared using a single relational operator, the expression is referred to as a *simple Boolean expression*. Each simple Boolean expression has the Boolean value `true` or `false` according to the arithmetic validity of the expression. In general, data of most of the built-in types can be compared. For example, when a character value is compared to an integer, the ASCII value of the character is used. When comparing reals, however, the computer representation of a real number might not be the exact real number intended.

Table 5.1
Relational Operators

Arithmetic Operation	Relational Operator	Meaning
=	==	Is equal to
<	<	Is less than
>	>	Is greater than
≤	<=	Is less than or equal to
≥	>=	Is greater than or equal to
≠	!=	Is not equal to

Table 5.2
Values of Simple Boolean Expressions

Simple Boolean Expression	Boolean Value
`7 == 7`	`true`
`-3.0 == 0.0`	`false`
`4.2 > 3.7`	`true`
`-18 < -15`	`true`
`13 < 0.013`	`false`
`-17.32 != -17.32`	`false`
`a == a`	`true`

Table 5.2 sets forth several Boolean expressions and their respective Boolean values, assuming the assignment statements `a = 3` and `b = 3` have been made.

Arithmetic expressions can also be used in simple Boolean expressions. Thus,

```
4 < (3 + 2)
```

has the value `true`. When the computer evaluates this expression, the parentheses dictate that `(3 + 2)` is evaluated first and then the relational operator. Sequentially, this becomes

```
4 < (3 + 2)
4 < 5
true
```

What if the parentheses had not been used? Could the expression be evaluated? This type of expression assumes a priority level for the relational operators and the arithmetic operators. A summary for the priority of these operations follows:

Expression	Priority
`( )`	1
`*, /, %`	2
`+, -`	3
`==, <, >, <=, >=, !=`	4

Thus, we see that the relational operators are evaluated last. As with arithmetic operators, these are evaluated in order from left to right. Thus, the expression

```
4 < 3 + 2
```

could be evaluated without parentheses and would have the same Boolean value.

The following example illustrates the evaluation of a somewhat more complex Boolean expression.

Example 5.1 Indicate the successive steps in the evaluation of the following Boolean expression:

```
10 % 4 * 3 - 8 <= 18 + 30 / 4 - 20
```

The steps in this evaluation are

```
10 % 4 * 3 - 8 <= 18 + 30 / 4 - 20

2 * 3 - 8 <= 18 + 30 / 4 - 20

6 - 8 <= 18 + 30 / 4 - 20

- 2 <= 18 + 30 / 4 - 20

- 2 <= 18 + 7 - 20

- 2 <= 25 - 20

- 2 <= 5

true
```

As shown here, even though parentheses are not required when using arithmetic expressions with relational operators, it is usually a good idea to use them to enhance the readability of the expression and to avoid using an incorrect expression.

Comparing Strings

When a programmer includes the `apstring.h` header file, all of the comparison operators in Table 5.1 can be used with strings. For example, a string variable can be compared with a string literal as follows:

```
#include "apstring.h"

apstring fruit;

cout << "Enter the name of a fruit: ";
cin >> fruit;
cout << (fruit == "apple") << endl;
```

If the user enters “apple” as input, the output is 1 (indicating `true`); otherwise, the output is 0 (indicating `false`).

In general, each string has some lexicographic relationship to any other string as defined by the collating sequence of characters within the strings. For example, the strings “hi”, “there”, and “Jane” are in the lexicographic relationship “Jane” < “hi” <“there” (note that “J” precedes “h” because the ASCII value of any capital letter is less than that of any lowercase letter).

A special case occurs when one string is shorter than the other string, but every character in the two strings is the same up to the end of the shorter string. In this case, the shorter string is considered less than the longer string. For example, the following program segment outputs the value 1:

```
#include "apstring.h"

apstring string1, string2;

string1 = "William";
string2 = "Williams";
cout << (string1 <  string2) << endl;
```

Confusing = and ==

Note that the equality operator in C++ is ==, not =. As you know, = means assignment in C++. The equality operator does not change the values of its operands, whereas the assignment operator changes the value of its left operand. Unfortunately, the assignment operator also returns a value and can be used in a C++ program wherever the == operator is used. This can be the source of some frustrating errors. Consider the following code segment:

```
int x = 1;
int y = 0;

cout << "x equals " << x << endl;
cout << "y equals " << y << endl;
cout << "Boolean for x equals y: "
     << (x = y) << endl;
cout << "Boolean for x not equal to y: "
     << (x != y) << endl;
cout << "x equals " << x << endl;
cout << "y equals " << y << endl;
```

The output of this code is:

```
x equals 1
y equals 0
Boolean for x equals y: 0
Boolean for x not equal to y: 0
x equals 0
y equals 0
```

After displaying the values of x and y, this code outputs the Boolean results of comparing x and y for equality and inequality. The Boolean values should be 0 and 1, but they are both 0. Here is what really happens:

1. The programmer has omitted the second = of the equality operator.
2. The computer interprets the single = as an assignment operator.
3. As a result, the value of y is stored in x.
4. This value, 0, is returned from the assignment operation.
5. The output statement displays the 0, so we think that x and y are not equal.
6. The next output statement also displays a 0, so we think that x and y are equal.
7. The second output of x shows a change from the previous output of x.

To make a long story short, the omission of the second = from the equality operator has caused an unwelcome side effect on a variable.

In general, the value returned by an assignment operation is the value of the expression on its right side. If this value is zero, it will be considered false in a Boolean expression. If this value is any value other than zero, it will be considered true in a Boolean expression. The C++ compiler will not protect you from this kind of mistake. Thus, be careful not to use = in C++ when you mean "equals."

Boolean Functions

Suppose we wish to have a function called even that takes an integer as an argument and returns the value true if the integer is even and false otherwise. We compare the remainder of dividing the argument by 2 to 0. We then return this result:

```
bool even(int x)
{
   return x % 2 == 0;
}
```

Logical Operators and Compound Boolean Expressions

Boolean values can also be generated by using *logical operators* with simple Boolean expressions. The logical operators used by C++ are && (meaning *and*), || (meaning *or*), and ! (meaning *not*). Operators && and || are used to connect two Boolean expressions, and ! is used to negate the Boolean value of an expression; hence, it is sometimes referred to as *negation*. When one of these connectives or negation is used to generate Boolean values, the complete expression is referred to as a *compound Boolean expression*.

If && is used to join two simple Boolean expressions, the resulting compound expression is true only when both simple expressions are true. If || is used, the result is true if either or both of the expressions are true. This is summarized in the *truth table* on the following page.

Expression 1 (E1)	Expression 2 (E2)	E1 && E2	E1 || E2
true	true	true	true
true	false	false	true
false	true	false	true
false	false	false	false

As previously indicated, ! merely produces the logical complement of an expression as follows:

Expression (E)	! E
true	false
false	true

Illustrations of the Boolean values generated using logical operators are given in Table 5.3.

Complex Boolean expressions can be generated by using several logical operators in an expression. The priority for evaluating these operators is

Operator	Priority
!	1
&&	2
||	3

When complex expressions are being evaluated, the logical operators, arithmetic expressions, and relational operators are evaluated during successive passes through the expression. The priority list is as follows:

Expression or Operation	Priority
( )	Evaluate from inside out
!	Evaluate from left to right
*, /, %	Evaluate from left to right
+, -	Evaluate from left to right
<, <=, >, >=, ==, !=	Evaluate from left to right
&&	Evaluate from left to right
||	Evaluate from left to right

Table 5.3
Values of Compound Boolean Expressions

Expression	Boolean Value
(4.2 >= 5.0) && (8 == (3 + 5))	false
(4.2 >= 5.0) || (8 == (3 + 5))	true
(-2 < 0) && (18 >= 10)	true
(-2 < 0) || (18 >= 0)	true
(3 > 5) && (14.1 == 0.0)	false
(3 > 5) || (14.1 == 0.0)	false
! (18 == (10 + 8))	false
! (- 4 > 0)	true

As a matter of style, it is useful to parenthesize any comparison that is used as an operand for a logical operator. The following examples illustrate evaluation of some complex Boolean expressions.

Example 5.2

```
(3 < 5) || (21 < 18) && (-81 > 0)
(3 < 5) || false && (-81 > 0) (parentheses first, then &&)
(3 < 5) || false && false
(3 < 5) || false
true || false
true
```

Example 5.3

```
! ((-5.0 == -6.2) || ((7 < 3) && (6 == (3 + 3))))
        ↓                  ↓                ↓
! (    false       || ( false   &&    (6 == 6)))
                                        ↓
! (    false       || ( false   &&      true))
                                ↓
! (    false       ||           false)
                   ↓
!                 false
    ↓
    true
```

Short-Circuit Evaluation of Boolean Expressions

Whenever two Boolean expressions are separated by a logical operator in C++, either `&&` or `||`, the computer uses *short-circuit evaluation*. The rules for this kind of evaluation are as follows:

1. In compound Boolean expressions connected by `||`, stop and return `true` at the first Boolean expression that returns `true`. Evaluate the next Boolean expression only if the current one returns `false`. This rule captures the notion that a disjunction is `true` only if at least one of the disjuncts is `true` and `false` only if all of the disjuncts are false.
2. In compound Boolean expressions connected by `&&`, stop and return `false` at the first Boolean expression that returns `false`. Evaluate the next Boolean expression only if the current one returns `true`. This rule captures the notion that a conjunction is `false` only if at least one of the conjuncts is `false` and `true` only if all of the conjuncts are `true`.

Short-circuit evaluation can enhance the efficiency of programs. For example, C++ evaluates the expression in Example 5.2 in three lines rather than six:

```
(3 < 5) || (21 < 18) && (-81 > 0)
                ↓
(3 < 5) ||    false
  ↓
true
```

Short-circuit evaluation can also be used to make some simple decisions. For example, one might guard against division by zero as follows:

A NOTE OF INTEREST

George Boole

George Boole was born in 1815 in Lincoln, England. He was the son of a small shopkeeper and his family belonged to the lowest social class. In an attempt to rise above his station, Boole spent his early years teaching himself Latin and Greek. During this period, he also received elementary instruction in mathematics from his father.

At the age of 16, Boole worked as a teacher in an elementary school. He used most of his wages to help support his parents. At the age of 20 (after a brief, unsuccessful attempt to study for the clergy), he opened his own school. As part of his preparation for running his school, he had to learn more mathematics. This activity led to the development of some of the most significant mathematics of the 19th century.

Boole's major contributions were in the field of logic. An indication of his genius is given by the fact that his early work included the discovery of invariants. The mathematical significance of this is perhaps best explained by noting that the theory of relativity developed by Albert Einstein would not have been possible without the previous work on invariants.

Boole's first published contribution was *The Mathematical Analysis of Logic,* which appeared in 1848 while he was still working as an elementary school teacher and the sole support for his parents. In 1849, he was appointed professor of mathematics at Queen's College in Cork, Ireland. The relative freedom from financial worry and time constraints the college appointment provided allowed him to pursue his work in mathematics. His masterpiece, *An Investigation of the Laws of Thought, on Which Are Founded the Mathematical Theories of Logic and Probabilities,* was published in 1854. Boole was then 39, relatively old for such original work. According to Bertrand Russell, pure mathematics was discovered by Boole in this work.

The brilliance of Boole's work laid the foundation for what is currently studied as formal logic. The data type Boolean is named in honor of Boole because of his contribution to the development of logic as part of mathematics. Boole died in 1864. His early death resulted from pneumonia contracted by keeping a lecture engagement when he was soaked to the skin.

```
(y != 0) && (x / y == 2)
```

Note that if `y` equals zero, the second expression, which divides a number by `y`, will not be evaluated in C++.

Exercises 5.1

1. Assume the variable declaration section of a program is

```
bool flag1, flag2;
```

What output is produced by the following segment of code?

```
flag1 = true;
flag2 = false;
cout << flag1 <<  << true <<  << flag2 << endl;
flag1 = flag2;
cout << flag2 << endl;
```

2. Assume the variable declaration section of a program is

```
char ch;
bool flag;
```

For each of the following assignment statements, indicate whether it is valid or invalid.

a. `flag = "true";`
b. `flag = T;`
c. `flag = true;`
d. `ch = flag;`
e. `ch = true;`
f. `ch = T;`

3. Evaluate each of the following expressions:

a. `(3 < 7) && (2 < 0) || (6 == 3 + 3)`
b. `((3 < 7) && (2 < 0)) || (6 == 3 + 3)`
c. `(3 < 7) && ((2 < 0) || (6 == 3 + 3))`
d. `! ((-4.2 < 3.0) && (10 < 20))`
e. `(! (-4.2 < 3.0)) || (! (10 < 20))`

4. For each of the following simple Boolean expressions, indicate whether it is `true`, `false`, or invalid.

a. `-3.01 <= -3.001`
b. `-3.0 == -3`
c. `25 - 10 < 3 * 5`
d. `42 % 5 < 42 / 5`
e. `-5 * (3 + 2) >= 2 * (-10)`
f. `10 / 5 < 1 + 1`
g. `3 + 8 % 5 == 6 - 12 % 2`

5. For each of the following expressions, indicate whether it is valid or invalid. Evaluate those that are valid.

a. `3 < 4 || 5 < 6`
b. `! 3.0 == 6 / 2`
c. `! (true || false)`
d. `! true || false`
e. `! true || ! false`
f. `! (18 < 25) && || (-3 < 0)`
g. `8 * 3 < 20 + 10`

6. Assume the variable declaration section of a program is

```
int int1, int2;
double fl1, fl2;
bool flag1, flag2;
```

and the values of the variables are

0	8	–15.2	–20.0	false	true
`int1`	`int2`	`fl1`	`fl2`	`flag1`	`flag2`

Evaluate each of the following expressions:

a. `(int1 <= int2) || ! (fl2 == fl1)`
b. `! (flag1) || ! (flag2)`
c. `! (flag1 && flag2)`
d. `((fl1-fl2) < 100/int2) && ((int1 < 1) && ! (flag2))`
e. `! ((int2 - 16 / 2) == int1) && flag1`

7. DeMorgan's laws state the following:

a. ! (A || B) is equivalent to (! A) && (! B)
b. ! (A && B) is equivalent to (! A) || (! B)

Write a test program that demonstrates the validity of each of these equivalent statements.

5.2 `if` Statements

Objectives

a. to learn the syntax of the `if` statement
b. to understand the flow of control when using an `if` statement
c. to use an `if` statement in a program
d. to understand why compound statements are needed
e. to use correct syntax in writing a compound statement
f. to design programs using `if` statements

The first decision-making statement we will examine is the `if` statement. An `if` statement is used to make a program do something only when certain conditions are used. The form and syntax for an `if` statement are

```
if (<Boolean expression>)
   <statement>
```

where `<statement>` represents any C++ statement. Note that the parentheses enclosing the Boolean expression are required.

The Boolean expression can be any valid expression that is either `true` or `false at` the time of evaluation. If it is `true`, the statement following the Boolean expression is executed. If it is `false`, control is transferred to the first program statement following the complete `if` statement. In general, code has the form

```
<statement 1>
if (<Boolean expression>)
   <statement2>
<statement 3>
```

as illustrated in Figure 5.1. As a further illustration of how an `if` statement works, consider the program fragment

```
sum = 0.0;
cin >> num;
if (num > 0.0)
   sum = sum + num;
cout << setiosflags(ios::fixed | ios::showpoint) << setprecision(2)
     << setw(10) << sum << endl;
```

Figure 5.1
`if` flow diagram

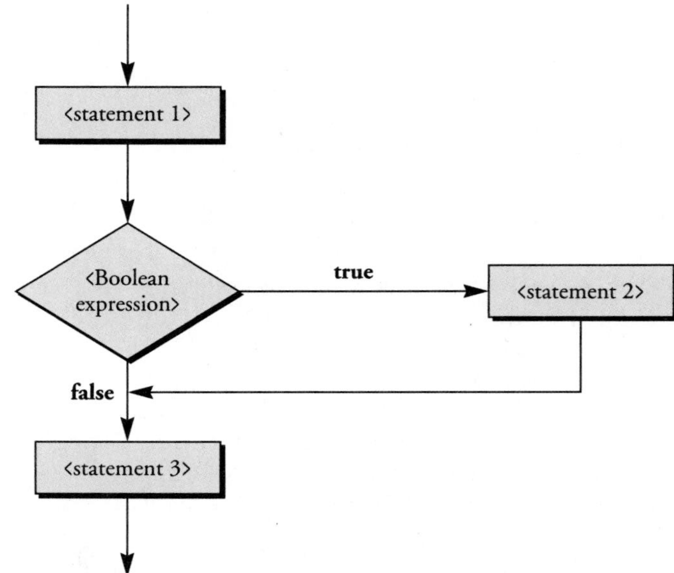

If the value read is 75.85, prior to execution of the `if` statement, the contents of `num` and `sum` are

75.85	0.0
num	sum

The Boolean expression `num > 0.0` is now evaluated and, since it is `true`, the statement

```
sum = sum + num;
```

is executed and we have

75.85	75.85
num	sum

The next program statement is executed and produces the output

```
75.85
```

However, if the value read is –25.5, the variable values are

–25.5	0.0
num	sum

The Boolean expression `num > 0.0` is `false` and control is transferred to the line

```
cout << setiosflags(ios::fixed | ios::showpoint) << setprecision(2)
     << setw(10) << sum << endl;
```

Thus, the output is

```
0.00
```

Now, let's suppose you want a program in which one objective is to count the number of zeros in the input. Assuming suitable initialization and declaration, a program fragment for this task could be

```
cin >> num;
if (num == 0)
   zeroCount = zeroCount + 1;
```

One writing style for using an `if` statement calls for indenting the program statement to be executed if the Boolean expression is true. This, of course, is not required. The following code

```
if (num == 0)
   zeroCount = zeroCount + 1;
```

could be written

```
if (num == 0) zeroCount = zeroCount + 1;
```

However, the indenting style for simple `if` statements is consistent with the style used with more elaborate conditional statements.

Compound Statements

The last concept needed before looking further at selection in C++ is that of a *compound statement*. In a C++ program, simple statements end with a semicolon. Thus,

```
cin >> a >> b;
a = 3 * b;
cout << b;
```

are three simple statements.

In some instances, it is necessary to perform several simple statements when some condition is true. For example, you may want the program to do certain things if a condition is true. In this situation, several simple statements that can be written as a single compound statement would be helpful. In general, there are several C++ constructs that require compound statements. A compound statement is created by using the symbols `{` and `}` at the beginning and end, respectively, of a sequence of simple statements. Correct syntax for a compound statement is

```
{
 <statement 1>
 <statement 2>
  .
  .
  .
 <statement n>
}
```

Simple statements within a compound statement end with semicolons. The end of the compound statement is not followed by a semicolon.

When a compound statement is executed within a program, the entire segment of code between `{` and `}` is treated as a single action. This is referred to as a *statement block*. In addition to statements, data declarations can appear within a block. The scope of names declared within a block is the area of program text below their declarations, terminating with the enclosing `}` symbol. These so-called "block variables" behave like local variables in a function because they are invisible outside the block.

It is important to develop a consistent, acceptable style for writing compound statements. What you use will vary according to your instructor's wishes and your personal preferences. Examples in this text will align each statement within the compound statement with the enclosing symbols. Thus,

```
{
    int a, b;
    cin >> a >> b;
    a = 3 * b;
    cout << b;
}
```

is a compound statement in a program; what it does is easily identified.

Using Compound Statements

As you might expect, compound statements can be (and frequently are) used as part of an `if` statement. The form and syntax for this are

```
if (<Boolean expression>)
{
  <statement 1>
   .
   .
   .
  <statement n>
}
```

Program control is exactly as before depending on the value of the Boolean expression. For example, suppose you are writing a function to keep track of and compute fees for vehicles in a parking lot where separate records are kept for senior citizens. A segment of code in the function could be

```
if (customer == 'S')
{
   seniorCount = seniorCount + 1;
   amountDue = seniorCitizenRate;
}
```

Confusing == and = Again

In Section 5.1, we discussed the errors caused by using `=` instead of `==` in a Boolean expression. When a Boolean expression is used to control an `if` statement, these errors can be even more harmful to a program. For example, consider what would happen if `==` were replaced by `=` in the code segment just given:

```
if (customer = 'S')
{
   seniorCount = seniorCount + 1;
   amountDue = seniorCitizenRate;
}
```

The use of the assignment operator causes two unfortunate things to happen:

1. The value of `customer` is changed to `'S'`, a side effect.
2. The statements inside the `if` statement execute even if `customer` did not have the value `'S'` to begin with. The reason is that `=` returns the value just assigned to `customer`, namely, `'S'`, which is nonzero and thus the same as `true`.

As you can see, you must take great care to use `==` where you mean equality in C++.

`if` Statements with Functions

The next example designs a program to solve a problem using an `if` statement with a function.

Example 5.4 Let us write a program that reads two integers and prints them in the order of larger first, smaller second. The first-level pseudocode solution is

1. Read numbers
2. Determine the larger
3. Print results

A structure chart for this is given in Figure 5.2. Reading the numbers and printing the results require no further discussion of their design or implementation. Our strategy for determining the larger of the two numbers will be to maintain three variables, `min`, `max`, and `temp`. Step 2 assumes that the numbers have been read in to variables `min` and `max`. We will compare the values, and if `min` is greater than `max`, we will use the variable `temp` to help swap the values of `min` and `max`. Thus, step 2 will have the effect of placing the larger value in `max` and the smaller value in `min`. The pseudocode for step 2 is

```
if min > max
   assign min to temp
   assign max to min
   assign temp to max
```

This algorithm translates to the following C++ function:

```
// Function: determineLarger
// Enforces the ordering relation min <= max between two integer variables
//
// Inputs: two integer variables in random order
// Outputs: min will contain the smaller of the two inputs,
//          and max the larger

void determineLarger(int &min, int &max)
{
   int temp;

   if (min > max)
   {
      temp = min;
      min = max;
      max = temp;
   }
}
```

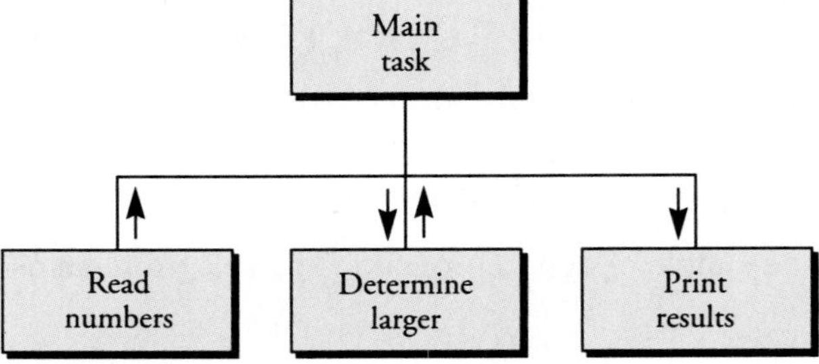

Figure 5.2
Structure chart for ordering two numbers

A complete program for this follows:

```
// Program file: minmax.cpp

#include <iostream.h>
#include <iomanip.h>

// Function: getData
// Prompts for and obtains two integers from user
//
// Outputs: two integers

void getData(int &first, int &second);

// Function: determineLarger
// Enforces the ordering relation min <= max between two integer variables
//
// Inputs: two integer variables in random order
// Outputs: min will contain the smaller of the two inputs,
//          and max the larger

void determineLarger(int &min, int &max);

// Function: printResults
// Displays results on screen
//
// Inputs: two integers, the smaller in min, the larger in max

void printResults(int min, int max);

int main()
{
   int min, max;

   getData(min, max);
   determineLarger(min, max);
   printResults(min, max);
   return 0;
}

void getData(int &first, int &second)
{
   cout << "Enter the first number and press <Enter>. ";
   cin >> first;
   cout << "Enter the second number and press <Enter>. ";
   cin >> second;
}

void determineLarger(int &min, int &max)
{
   int temp;

   if (min > max)
   {
      temp = min;
```

continued

```
      min = max;
      max = temp;
   }
}

void printResults(int min, int max)
{
   cout << setiosflags(ios::right) << endl;
   cout << setw(19) << "Larger number"
        << setw(15) << "Smaller number" << endl;
   cout << setw(19) << "-------------"
        << setw(15) << "--------------" << endl;
   cout << endl;
   cout << setw(15) << max << setw(15) << min << endl;
}
```

Sample runs of this program produce

```
Enter the first number and press <Enter>. 35
Enter the second number and press <Enter>. 115

                    Larger number           Smaller number
                    -------------           --------------

                          115                     35

Enter the first number and press <Enter>. 85
Enter the second number and press <Enter>. 26

                      Larger number         Smaller number
                      -------------         --------------

                            85                    26
```

Note that two runs of this program are required to test the logic of the `if` statement.

Exercises 5.2

1. What is the output from each of the following program fragments? Assume the following assignment statements precede each fragment:

```
a = 10;
b = 5;
```

a.
```
if (a <= b)
    b = a;
cout << a << endl << b << endl;
```

b.
```
if (a <= b)
{
    b = a;
    cout << a << endl << b << endl;
}
```

c.
```
if (a < b)
    temp = a;
a = b;
b = temp;
cout << a << endl << b endl;
```

d.
```
if (a < b)
{
    temp = a;
    a = b;
    b = temp;
}
cout << a << endl << b << endl;
```
e.
```
if ((a < b) || (b - a < 0))
{
    a = a + b;
    b = b - 1;
    cout << a << endl << b << endl;
}
cout << a << endl << b << endl;
```
f.
```
if ((a < b) && (b - a < 0))
{
    a = a + b;
    b = b - 1;
    cout << a << endl << b << endl;
}
cout << a << endl << b << endl;
```

2. Write a test program to illustrate what happens when a semicolon is inadvertently inserted after a Boolean expression in an `if` statement. For example,

```
if (a > 0);

    sum = sum + a;
```

3. Find and explain the errors in each of the following program fragments. Assume all variables have been suitably declared.

a.
```
if (a == 10)
    cout << a << endl;
```
b.
```
x = 7;
if (3 < x <  10)
{
    x = x + 1;
    cout << x << endl;
}
```
c.
```
count = 0;
sum = 0;
a = 50;
if (a > 0)
    count = count + 1;
sum = sum + a;
```
d.
```
cin >> ch;
if (ch = a || b)
    cout << ch << endl;
```

4. What is the output from each of the following program fragments? Assume all variables have been suitably declared.

a.
```
j = 18;
if (j % 5 == 0)
    cout << j << endl;
```

b.
```
a = 5;
b = 90;
b = b / a - 5;
if (b > a)
   b = a * 30;
cout << a << endl << b << endl;
```

5. Can a simple statement be written using a `{. . .}` block? Write a short program that allows you to verify your answer.
6. Discuss the differences in the following programs. Predict the output for each program using sample values for `num`.

a.

```
int main()
{
   int num;
   cout << "Enter an integer and press <Enter>.";
   cin >> num;
   if (num > 0)
      cout << endl;
   cout << setw(22) << "The number is" << setw(6) << num << endl;
   cout << endl;
   cout << setw(30) << "The number squared is" << setw(6) << num * num
        << endl;
   cout << setw(28) << "The number cubed is" << setw(6) << num * num * num
        << endl;
   cout << endl;
   return 0;
}
```

b.

```
int main()
{
   int num;
   cout << "Enter an integer and press <Enter>. ";
   cin >> num;
   if (num > 0)
   {
      cout << endl;
      cout << setw(22) << "The number is" << setw(6) << num << endl;
      cout << endl;
      cout << setw(30) << "The number squared is" << setw(6) << num * num
           << endl;
      cout << setw(28) << "The number cubed is" << setw(6) << num * num * num
           << endl;
      cout << endl;
   }
   return 0;
}
```

7. Discuss writing style and readability of compound statements.
8. Find all errors in the following compound statements.

a.
```
{
cin >> a
cout << a << endl
}
```

b.
```
{
sum = sum + num
};
```
c.
```
{
cin >> size1 >> size2;
cout << setw(8) << size1 << setw(8) << size2 << endl
}
```
d.
```
{
cin << age << weight;
totalage = totalage + age;
totalweight = totalweight + weight;
cout << setw(8) << age << weight << endl;
```

9. Write a single compound statement that will do the following:
   a. Read three integers from the keyboard.
   b. Add them to a previous total.
   c. Print the numbers on one line.
   d. Skip a line (output).
   e. Print the new total.
10. Write a program fragment that reads three reals, counts the number of positive reals, and accumulates the sum of positive reals.
11. Write a program fragment that reads three characters and then prints them only if the letters have been read in alphabetical order (for example, print "boy" but do not print "dog").
12. Given two integers, `A` and `B`, `A` is a divisor of `B` if `B % A == 0`. Write a complete program that reads two positive integers `A` and `B` and then, if `A` is a divisor of `B`,
    a. Print `A`.
    b. Print `B`.
    c. Print the result of `B` divided by `A`.

    For example, the output could be

```
A is 14
B is 42
B divided by A is 3
```

5.3 `if...else` Statements

Objectives

a. to learn the syntax of `if...else` statements

b. to understand the flow of control when using `if...else` statements

c. to use an `if...else` statement in a program

d. to design programs using `if...else` statements

Form and Syntax

The previous section discussed the one-way selection statement `if`. We will now examine the two-way selection statement `if...else`. The correct form and syntax for `if...else` are

```
if (<Boolean expression>)
<statement>
else
<statement>
```

Flow of control when using an `if...else` statement is as follows:

1. The Boolean expression is evaluated.
2. If the Boolean expression is `true`, the statement following the expression is executed and control is transferred to the first program statement following the complete `if...else` statement.

3. If the Boolean expression is `false`, the statement following `else` is executed and control is transferred to the first program statement following the `if...else` statement.

A flow diagram is given in Figure 5.3. A few points follow that you should remember concerning `if...else` statements:

1. The Boolean expression can be any valid expression having a value of `true` or `false` at the time it is evaluated.
2. The complete `if...else` statement is one program statement and is separated from other complete statements by a semicolon whenever appropriate.
3. Writing style should include indenting within the `else` option in a manner consistent with indenting in the `if` option.

Example 5.5 Let us write a program fragment to keep separate counts of negative and nonnegative numbers entered as data. Assuming all variables have been suitably declared and initialized, an `if...else` statement could be used as follows:

```
cout << "Please enter a number and press <Enter>.";
cin >> num;
if (num < 0)
    negCount = negCount + 1;
else
    nonNegCount = nonNegCount + 1;
```

Using Compound Statements

Program statements in both the `if` option and the `else` option can be compound statements. When using compound statements in these options, you should use a consistent, readable indenting style; remember to use `{...}` for each compound statement, and do not put a semicolon after `}`.

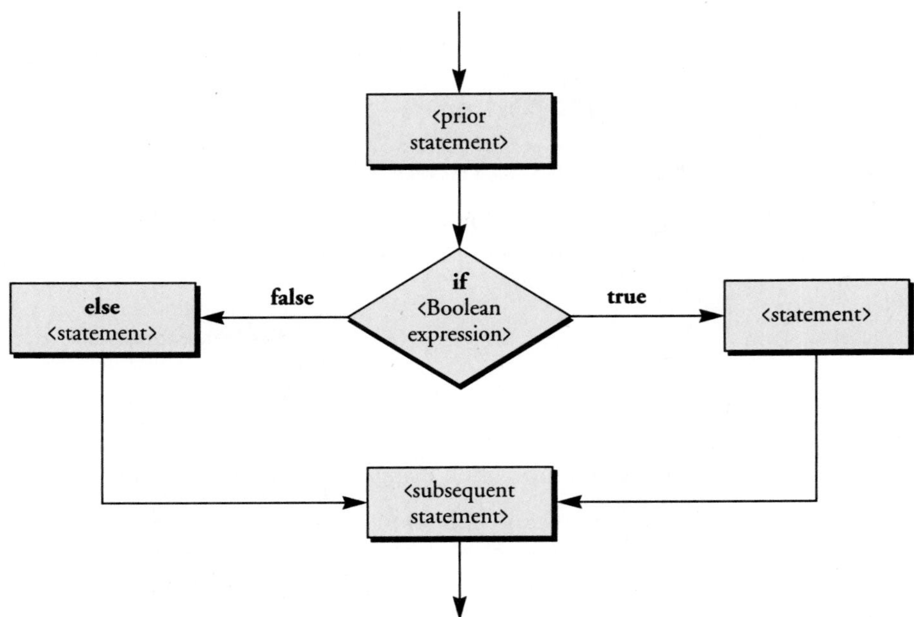

Figure 5.3
`if...else` flow diagram

Example 5.6 Suppose you want a program to read a number, count it as negative or nonnegative, and print it in either a column of nonnegative numbers or a column of negative numbers. Assuming all variables have been suitably declared and initialized, the fragment might be

```
cout << "Please enter a number and press <Enter>.";
cin >> num;
if (num < 0)
{
   negCount = negCount + 1;
   cout << setw(15) << num << endl;
}                                               // end of if option
else
{
   nonNegCount = nonNegCount + 1;
   cout << setw(30) << num << endl;
}                                               // end of else option
```

We next consider an example of a program fragment that requires the use of compound statements within an `if...else` statement.

Example 5.7 We want to write a function that computes gross wages for an employee of the Florida OJ Canning Company. Input includes hours worked and the hourly rate. Overtime (more than 40 hours) pay is computed as time and a half. A function would be

```
const double WEEKLY_HOURS = 40.0;
const double TIME_AND_A_HALF = 1.5;

double computeWages (double hours, double payRate)
{
   double overtime;
   if (hours <= WEEKLY_HOURS )
      return hours * payRate;
   else
   {
      overtime = TIME_AND_A_HALF * (hours - WEEKLY_HOURS) * payRate;
      return WEEKLY_HOURS * payRate + overtime;
   }
}
```

Robust Programs

If a program is completely protected against all possible crashes from bad data and unexpected values, it is said to be *robust*. The preceding examples have all assumed that desired data would be accurately entered from the keyboard. In actual practice, this is seldom the case. The `if...else` statements can be used to guard against bad data entries. For example, if a program is designed to use positive numbers, you could guard against negatives and zero by

```
cout << "Enter a positive number and press <Enter>. ";
cin >> number;
```

continued

A NOTE OF INTEREST

Artificial Intelligence

Artificial intelligence (AI) research seeks to understand the principles of human intelligence and apply those principles to the creation of smarter computer programs. The original goal of AI research was to create programs with humanlike intelligence and capabilities, yet after many years of research, little progress has been made toward this goal.

Since the late 1980s, however, AI researchers have pursued much more modest goals with much greater success. Programs based on AI techniques are playing increasingly important roles in such down-to-earth areas as medicine, education, recreation, business, and industry. Such programs come nowhere near achieving human levels of intelligence, but they often have capabilities that are not easily achieved with non-AI programs.

The main principles of AI can be summarized as follows:

Search: A method whereby the computer solves a problem by searching through all logically possible solutions.

Rules: Knowledge about what actions to take in particular circumstances is stored as rules. Each rule has the form: if situation, then action or conclusion.

Reasoning: Programs can use reasoning to draw conclusions from the facts and rules available to the program.

Planning: The control program plans the actions that must be taken to accomplish a particular goal, and then modifies the plan if unexpected obstacles are encountered; this is most widely used in robot control.

Pattern recognition: Important for rule-based systems, the if part of a rule specifies a particular pattern of facts; the rule is to be applied when that pattern is recognized in the facts known to the program.

Knowledge bases: Storage of the facts and rules that govern the operation of an AI program.

```
if (number <= 0)
   cout << "You entered a nonpositive number." << endl;
else
   .
   . <code for expected action here>
   .
```

This program protection can be used anywhere in a program. For example, if you are finding square roots of numbers, you could avoid a program crash by using this code:

```
if (num < 0)
   cout << "The number << num << is negative" << endl;
else
   .
   . <compute the square root of num here>
   .
```

In actual practice, students need to balance robustness against amount of code and efficiency. An overemphasis on making a program robust can detract from time spent learning new programming concepts. You should discuss this with your instructor and decide what is best for your situation. Generally, there should be an agreement between the programmer and the customer regarding the level of robustness required. For most programs and examples in this text, it is assumed that valid data are entered when requested.

Example 5.8 Callers of functions that take input would like to be signaled that it is within a given lower and upper bound. For example, a function that inputs the age of an employee might check to see that the integer value entered by the user is greater than 17 and less than 70 (assuming these are conventional age limits for employable persons). In this example, the function would return `true` if the age is greater than 17 and also less than 70 or `false` otherwise. The caller of the function takes care of prompting the user for information, and of error recovery, such as an error message and a loop for more input. The function, named `getValidData`, is passed the values of the lower and the upper bounds, and variables for the data and a Boolean flag indicating a valid input value. One might invoke the function as follows:

```
bool ageOk;
int age;

cout << "Enter the employee's age: ";
getValidData(17, 70, age, ageOk);
if (! ageOk)
   cout << "Age must be greater than 17 and less than 70" << endl;
else
   <process the age, etc.>
```

A declaration of the function is therefore

```
// Function: getValidData
// Takes an input integer from the user and checks it for validity
//
// Inputs: two integers representing the lower and upper bounds
//         of valid input
// Outputs: an integer representing the input and a Boolean value
//          representing its validity

void getValidData(int low, int high, int &data, bool &dataOk);
```

The function does not prompt the user, but simply reads data. The function then compares the data to the limits. If the data are within the limits, the flag is set to `true`; if not, the flag is set to `false`.

```
void getValidData(int low, int high, int &data, bool &dataOk)
{
   cin >> data;
   if ((data > low) && (data < high))
      dataOk = true;
   else
      dataOk = false;
}
```

Guarding Against Overflow

As we discussed in Chapter 3, integer overflow occurs when the absolute value of an integer exceeds a maximum, and real overflow occurs when a value is obtained that is too large to be stored in a memory location. Both of these values vary according to the compiler being used. The maximum value of an integer is named by the constant `INT_MAX`, and the maximum value of a real number is named by the constant `DBL_MAX`. Both constants become available to a C++ program by including the library files `limits.h` and `double. h`.

One method used to guard against integer overflow is based on the principle of checking a number against some function of `INT_MAX`. Thus, if you want to multiply a number by 10, you first compare it to `INT_MAX / 10`. A typical segment of code could be

```
if (num > INT_MAX / 10)
   (overflow message)
else
{
   num = num * 10;
   (rest of action)
}
```

We can now use this same idea with a Boolean-valued function. For example, consider the function

```
bool nearOverflow (int num)
{
   return num > INT_MAX / 10;
}
```

This could be used in the following manner:

```
if (nearOverflow(num))
   (overflow message)
else
{
   num = num * 10;
   <rest of action>
}
```

Exercises 5.3

1. What output is produced from each of the following program fragments? Assume all variables have been suitably declared.

a.
```
a = -14;
b = 0;
if (a < b)
   cout << a << endl;
else
   cout << a * b << endl;
```

b.
```
a = 50;
b = 25;
count = 0;
sum = 0;
if (a == b)
   cout << a << b << endl;
else
{
   count = count + 1;
   sum = sum + a + b;
   cout << a << b << endl;
```

```
   }
   cout << count << sum << endl;
c. temp = 0;
   a = 10;
   b = 5;
   if (a > b)
      cout << a << b << endl;
   else
      temp = a;
   a = b;
   b = temp;
   cout << a << b << endl;
```

2. Find all errors in the following program fragments.

```
a. if (ch < .)
      charCount = charCount + 1;
      cout << ch << endl;
   else
      periodCount = periodCount + 1;
b. if (age < 20)
   {
      youngCount = youngCount + 1;
      youngAge = youngAge + age;
   };
   else
   {
      oldCount = oldCount + 1;
      oldAge = oldAge + age;
   };
c. if (age < 20)
   {
      youngCount = youngCount + 1;
      youngAge = youngAge + age
   }
   else
      oldCount = oldCount + 1;
   oldAge = oldAge + age;
```

5.4 Nested and Extended if Statements

Objectives

a. to learn the syntax of nested if statements
b. to know when to use nested if statements
c. to use extended if statements
d. to trace the logic of nested if statements
e. to develop a consistent writing style when using nested if statements

Multiway Selection

Sections 5.2 and 5.3 examined one-way (if) and two-way (if...else) selection. Because each of these is a single C++ statement, either can be used as part of a selection statement to achieve multiple selection. In this case, the multiple selection statement is referred to as a *nested if statement*. These nested statements can be any combination of if or if...else statements.

To illustrate, let us write a program fragment to issue interim progress reports for students in a class. If a student's score is below 50, the student is failing. If the score is between 50 and 69 inclusive, the progress is unsatisfactory. If the score is 70 or above, the progress is satisfactory. The first decision to be made is based on whether the score is below 50 or not; the design is

```
if (score >= 50)

    .
    . <progress report here>
    .

else
   cout << setw(34) << "You are currently failing." << endl;
```

We now use a nested `if...else` statement for the progress report for students who are not failing. The complete fragment is

```
if (score >= 50)
   if (score > 69)
      cout << setw(38) << "Your progress is satisfactory." << endl;
   else
      cout << setw(40) << "Your progress is unsatisfactory." << endl;
else
   cout << setw(34) << "You are currently failing." << endl;
```

One particular instance of nesting selection statements requires special development. When additional `if...else` statements are used in the `else` option, we call this an *extended if statement* and use the following form:

```
if (<condition 1>)
.
. <action 1 here>
.
else if (<condition 2>)
.
.<action 2 here>
.
else if (<condition 3>)
.
.<action 3 here>
.
else
.
.<action 4 here>
.
```

Using this form, we could redesign the previous fragment that printed progress reports as follows:

```
if (score > 69)
   cout << setw(38) << "Your progress is satisfactory." << endl;
else if (score >= 50)
   cout << setw(40) << "Your progress is unsatisfactory." << endl;
else
   cout << setw(34) << "You are currently failing." << endl;
```

If you trace through both fragments with scores of 40, 60, and 80, you will see they produce identical output.

Another method of writing the nested fragment is to use sequential selection statements as follows:

```
if (score > 69)
   cout << setw(38) << "Your progress is satisfactory." << endl;
if ((score <= 69) && (score >= 50))
   cout << setw(40) << "Your progress is unsatisfactory." << endl;
if (score < 50)
   cout << setw(34) << "You are currently failing." << endl;
```

However, there are two reasons why this is not considered good programming practice. First, this is less efficient because the condition of each `if` statement is evaluated each time through the program. Second, only one of the three conditions can be true; they are said to be *mutually exclusive.* In general, mutually exclusive conditions are most accurately represented with extended `if...else` statements. You should generally avoid using sequential `if` statements if an extended `if` statement can be used.

Tracing the flow of logic through nested or extended `if` statements can be tedious. However, it is essential that you develop this ability. For practice, let us trace through the following example.

Example 5.9 Consider the statement

```
if (a > 0)
   if (a % 2 == 0)
      sum1 = sum1 + a;
   else
      sum2 = sum2 + a;
else if (a == 0)
   cout << setw(18) << "a is zero" << endl;
else
   negSum = negSum + a;
cout << setw(17) << "All done" << endl;
```

We will trace through this statement and discover what action is taken when `a` is assigned 20, 15, 0, and –30, respectively. For `a == 20`, the expression `a > 0` is `true`; hence

```
a % 2 == 0
```

is evaluated. This is `true`, so

```
sum1 = sum1 + a;
```

is executed and control is transferred to

```
cout << setw(17) << "All done" << endl;
```

For `a == 15, a > 0` is `true` and

```
a % 2 == 0
```

is evaluated. This is `false`, so

```
sum2 = sum2 + a;
```

is executed and control is again transferred out of the nested statement to

```
cout << setw(17) << "All done" << endl;
```

For `a == 0`, `a > 0` is `false`, thus

```
a == 0
```

is evaluated. Since this is `true`, the statement

```
cout << setw(18) << "a is zero" << endl;
```

is executed and control is transferred to

```
cout << setw(17) << "All done" << endl;
```

Finally, for `a == -30`, `a > 0` is `false`, thus

```
a == 0
```

is evaluated. This is `false`, so

```
negSum = negSum + a;
```

is executed and control is transferred to

```
cout << setw(17) << "All done" << endl;
```

Note that this example traces through all possibilities involved in the statement. This is essential to guarantee your statement is properly constructed.

Designing solutions to problems that require multiway selection can be difficult. A few guidelines can help. If a decision has two courses of action and one is complex and the other is fairly simple, nest the complex part in the `if` option and the simple part in the `else` option. This method is frequently used to check for bad data. An example of the program design for this could be:

```
   .
   . <get the data>
   .
if (dataOk)
   .
   . <complex action here>
   .
else
   <message about bad data>
```

This method could also be used to guard against dividing by zero in computation. For instance, we could have

```
divisor = <value>;
if (divisor != 0)
```

```
    .
    . (proceed with action)
    .
else
   cout << "ERROR: division by zero" << endl;
```

When there are several courses of action that can be considered sequentially, an extended `if...else` should be used. To illustrate, consider the program fragment of Example 5.10.

Example 5.10 Let us write a program fragment that allows you to assign letter grades based on students' semester averages. Grades are assigned according to the following scale:

```
100 >= X >= 90    A
90 > X >= 80      B
80 > X >= 70      C
70 > X >= 55      D
55 > X            F
```

Extended `if` statements can be used to accomplish this as follows:

```
if (average >= 90)
   grade = 'A';
else if (average >= 80)
   grade = 'B';
else if (average >= 70)
   grade = 'C';
else if (average >= 55)
   grade = 'D';
else
   grade = 'F';
```

Because any average of more than 100 or less than zero is a sign of some data or program error, this example could be protected with a statement as follows:

```
if ((average <= 100) && (average >= 0))
   .
   . <compute letter grade>
   .
else
   cout << setw(38) << "There is an error. Average is" << setw(8)
        << average << endl;
```

Protecting parts of a program in this manner will help you avoid unexpected results or program crashes. It also allows you to identify the source of an error.

Form and Syntax

The rule for matching `else` in nested selection statements is:

When an `else` *is encountered, it is matched with the most recent* `if` *that has not yet been matched.*

The matching of `ifs` with `elses` is a common source of errors. When designing programs, you should be very careful to match them correctly. For example, consider the following situation, which can lead to an error:

```
if (<condition 1>)
    .
    . <action 1>
    .
else
    .
    . <action 2>
    .
```

where action 1 consists of an `if` statement. Specifically, suppose you want a fragment of code to read a list of positive integers and print those that are perfect squares. A method of protecting against negative integers and zero could be:

```
cin >> num;
if (num > 0)
    .
    . (action 1 here)
    .
else
   cout << num << " is not positive." << endl;
```

If we now develop action 1 so that it prints only those positive integers that are perfect squares, it is

```
if (sqrt(num) == int(sqrt(num)))
   cout << num << endl;
```

Nesting this selection statement in our design, we have

```
cin >> num;
if (num > 0)
   if (sqrt(num) == int(sqrt(num))
      cout << num << endl;
else
   cout << num << " is not positive." << endl;
```

If you now use this segment with input of 20 for `num`, the output is

```
20 is not positive.
```

Thus, this fragment does not correctly solve the problem. The indenting is consistent with our intent, but the actual execution of the fragment treated the code as

```
cin >> num;
if (num > 0)
   if (sqrt(num) == int(sqrt(num)))
        cout << num << endl;
   else
        cout << num << " is not positive." << endl;
```

because the `else` is matched with the most recent `if`. This problem can be resolved by redesigning the fragment as follows:

```
cin >> num;
if (num <= 0)
   cout << num << " is not positive." << endl;
else if (sqrt(num) == int(sqrt(num)))
   cout << num << endl;
```

Example 5.11 Write a program that computes the gross pay for an employee of the Clean Products Corporation of America. The corporation produces three products: A, B, and C. Supervisors earn a commission of 7% of sales and representatives earn 5%. Bonuses of $100 are paid to supervisors whose monthly commission exceeds $300 and to representatives whose commission exceeds $200. Input is in the form

```
S 18 15 10
```

where the first position contains an S or R for supervisor or representative, respectively. The next three integers include the number of units of each of the products sold. Because product prices may vary over time, the constant definition section will be used to indicate the current prices. The constants for this problem will be

```
const double SUPER_RATE = 0.07;
const double REP_RATE = 0.05;
const double A_PRICE = 13.95;
const double B_PRICE = 17.95;
const double C_PRICE = 29.95;
```

A first-level pseudocode development for this problem is

1. Get the data
2. Compute commission and bonus
3. Print heading
4. Print results

The structure chart for this is given in Figure 5.4. Module specifications for each of the main modules follow:

Module: Get the data
Task: Read input data from the keyboard
Outputs: employee classification and sales of products A, B, and C

Module: Compute commission and bonus
Task: if a supervisor
    compute total commission
    compute bonus
  else
    compute total commission
    compute bonus
Inputs: classification, aSales, bSales, cSales
Outputs: aCommission, bCommission, cCommission, totalCommission, bonus

Module: Print heading
Task: Print a heading for the report

Figure 5.4
Structure chart for Example 5.11

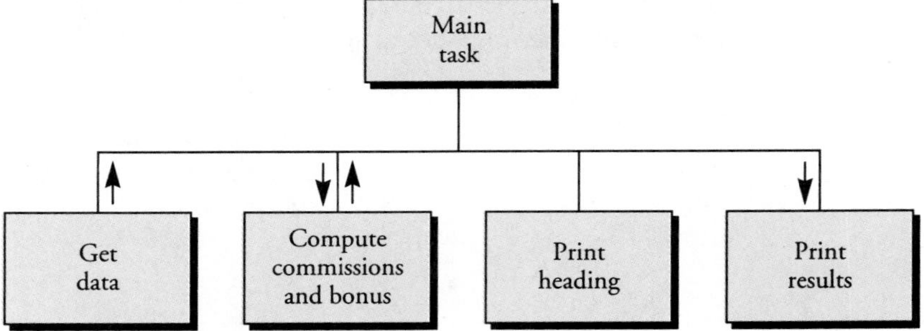

Module: Print results
Task: Print the employee's report
Inputs: classification
aSales
bSales
cSales
aCommission
bCommission
cCommission
totalCommission
bonus

Modules for get the data, print heading, and print results are similar to those previously developed. The module compute commission and bonus requires some development. Step 2 of the pseudocode becomes

2. Compute commission and bonus
2.1 if employee is supervisor
compute supervisor's earnings
else
compute representative's earnings

where "compute supervisor's earnings" is refined to

2.1.1 compute commission from sales of A
2.1.2 compute commission from sales of B
2.1.3 compute commission from sales of C
2.1.4 compute total commission
2.1.5 compute supervisor's bonus
2.1.5.1 if total commission > 300
bonus is 100.00
else
bonus is 0.00

A similar development follows for computing a representative's earnings. Step 3 will be an appropriate function to print a heading. Step 4 will contain whatever you feel is appropriate for output. It should include at least the number of sales, amount of sales, commissions, bonuses, and total compensation.

The main function for this problem is

```
int main()
{
   int aSales, bSales, cSales;          // Sales of Products A, B, C
   double aComm, bComm, cComm;          // Commission on sales of A, B, C
```

```
    double bonus;                          // Bonus, if earned
    double totalCommission;                // Commission on all products
    char classification;                   // S-Supervisor or R-Representative

    getdata(classification, aSales, bSales, cSales);
    computecommissionandbonus(classification, aSales,
                              bSales, cSales, aComm, bComm,
                              cComm, totalCommission, bonus);
    printheading(classification);
    printresults(classification, aSales, bSales, cSales, aComm, bComm,
                 cComm, totalCommission, bonus);
    return 0;
}
```

A complete program for this is

```
// This program computes gross pay for an employee.
// Note the use of constants and selection.

// Program file: sales.cpp

#include <iostream.h>
#include <iomanip.h>

const double SUPER_RATE = 0.07;
const double REP_RATE = 0.05;
const double A_PRICE = 13.95;
const double B_PRICE = 17.95;
const double C_PRICE = 29.95;

// Function: getData
// gets input data from the user
//
// Outputs: employee classification and sales
// of products A, B, and C

void getData(char &classification, int &aSales,
   int &bSales, int &cSales);

// Function: computeCommissionAndBonus
// If a supervisor
//       compute total commission
//       compute bonus
// else
//       compute total commission
//       compute bonus
// Inputs: classification, aSales, bSales, cSales
// Outputs: aCommission, bCommission, cCommission,
//  totalCommission, bonus

void computeCommissionAndBonus (char classification, int aSales,
   int bSales, int cSales, double &aCommission, double& bCommission,
   double &cCommission, double &totalCommission, double &bonus);

// Function: printResults
```

continued

```
// Prints employee's report
//
// Inputs:
//        aSales
//        bSales
//        cSales
//        aCommission
//        bCommission
//        cCommission
//        totalCommission
//        bonus

void printResults(int aSales, int bSales,
   int cSales, double aComm, double bComm, double cComm,
   double totalCommission, double bonus);

// Function: printHeading
// Print heading for results
//
// Input: classification

void printHeading(char classification);

int main()
{
   int aSales, bSales, cSales;
// Sales of Products A, B, C
   double aComm, bComm, cComm;
// Commission on sales of A, B, C
   double bonus;
// bonus, if earned
   double totalCommission;
// Commission on all products
   char classification;
// S-Supervisor or R-Representative

   getData(classification, aSales, bSales, cSales);
   computeCommissionAndBonus(classification, aSales,
                             bSales, cSales,  aComm,  bComm,
                             cComm, totalCommission, bonus);
   printHeading(classification);
   printResults(aSales, bSales,
                cSales, aComm, bComm, cComm,
                totalCommission, bonus);
   return 0;
 }

void getData(char &classification, int &aSales,
   int &bSales, int &cSales)
{
   cout << "Enter S or R for classification: ";
   cin >> classification;
   cout << "Enter aSales, bSales, cSales: ";
   cin >> aSales >> bSales >>cSales;
}

void computeCommissionAndBonus(char classification, int aSales,
```

```
   int bSales, int cSales, double &aCommission, double& bCommission,
   double &cCommission, double &totalCommission, double &bonus)
{
   if (classification == 'S')
   // Supervisor
   {
      aCommission = aSales * A_PRICE * SUPER_RATE;
      bCommission = bSales * B_PRICE * SUPER_RATE;
      cCommission = cSales * C_PRICE * SUPER_RATE;
      totalCommission = aCommission + bCommission
                        + cCommission;
      if (totalCommission > 300.0)
         bonus = 100.0;
      else
         bonus = 0.0 ;
   }
   else
   // Representative
   {
      aCommission = aSales * A_PRICE * REP_RATE;
      bCommission = bSales * B_PRICE * REP_RATE;
      cCommission = cSales * C_PRICE * REP_RATE;
      totalCommission = aCommission + bCommission
                        + cCommission;
      if (totalCommission > 200.0)
         bonus = 100.0;
      else
         bonus = 0.0;
   }
}

void printHeading(char classification)
{
   cout << setiosflags(ios::fixed | ios::showpoint | ios::right);
   cout << endl;
   cout << setw(29)
        << "Clean Products Corporation of America" << endl;
   cout << endl;
   cout << setw(29) << "Sales Report for" << setw(11)
           << "June" << endl;
   cout << endl;
   cout << setw(27) << "classification";
   if (classification == 'S')
     cout << setw(18) << "Supervisor" << endl;
   else
     cout  << setw(18) << "Representative" << endl;
   cout << endl;
   cout << setw(44)
        << "Product    Sales       Commission" << endl;
   cout << setw(44)
        << "-------    -----       ----------" << endl;
   cout << endl;
}

void printResults(int aSales, int bSales,
                  int cSales, double aComm, double bComm, double cComm,
```

continued

```
                   double totalCommission, double bonus)
{
   cout << setprecision(2);
   cout << setw(15) << "A" << setw(13) << aSales
        << setw(14) << aComm << endl;
   cout << setw(15) << "B" << setw(13) <<  bSales
        << setw(14) << bComm << endl;
   cout << setw(15) << "C" << setw(13) << cSales
        << setw(14) << cComm << endl;
   cout << endl;
   cout << setw(31) << "Subtotal"<< setw(3) << "$" << setw(9)
        << totalCommission << endl;
   cout << endl;
   cout << setw(31) << "Your bonus is:" << setw(3) << "$"
        << setw(9) << bonus << endl;
   cout << endl;
   cout << setw(31) << "Total Due" << setw(3) << "$"
        << setw(9) << (totalCommission + bonus) << endl;
}
```

A sample run produces the following output:

```
Enter R or S for classification: S
Enter aSales, bSales, cSales: 1100 990 510

         Clean Products Corporation of America

         Sales Report for         June

         classification           Supervisor

         Product     Sales        Commission
         -------     -----        ----------

         A           1100         1074.15

         B             990        1243.93

         C             510        1069.21

                Subtotal         $3387.29

                Your bonus is:    $100.00

                Total Due        $3487.30
```

Communication and Style Tips It is very important to use a consistent, readable writing style when using nested or extended `if` statements. The style used here for nested `if` statements is to indent each nested statement a single tab stop. Also, each `else` of an `if . . . else` statement is in the same column as the `if` of that statement. This allows you to see at a glance where the `else`s match with the `if`s. For example,

```
if
   if
```

```
   else
else
```

An extended `if` statement has all the `else`s on the same indented level as the first `if`. This reinforces the concept of extended `if`. For example,

```
if
else if
else if
else
```

Program Testing

In actual practice, a great deal of time is spent testing programs in an attempt to make them run properly when they are installed for some specific purpose. Formal program verification is discussed in Section 5.6 and is developed more fully in subsequent coursework. However, examining the issue of which data are minimally necessary for program testing is appropriate when working with selection statements.

As you might expect, test data should include information that tests every logical branch in a program. Whenever a program contains an `if...else` statement of the form

```
if (<condition>)
   <action 1 here>
else
   <action 2 here>
```

the test data should guarantee that both the `if` and the `else` options are executed.

Nesting and the use of extended `if` statements require a bit more care when selecting test data. In general, a single `if...else` statement requires at least two data items for testing. If an `if...else` statement is nested within the `if` option, at least two more data items are required to test the nested selection statement.

For purposes of illustration, let us reexamine the compute commission and bonus module from Example 5.11. This module contains the logic

```
if (classification == 'S')
   .
   .
   .
   if (totalCommission > 300.00)
      .
      .
      .
   else
      .
      .
      .
else
   .
   .
   .
```

continued

```
if (totalCommission > 200.00)
    .
    .
    .
else
    .
    .
    .
```

To see what data should minimally be used to test this function, consider the following table:

Classification	Total Commission
S	400.00
S	250.00
R	250.00
R	150.00

It is a good idea to also include boundary conditions in the test data. Thus, the previous table could also have listed 300.00 as the total commission for `S` and 200.00 as the total commission for `R`.

In summary, you should always make sure every logical branch is executed when running the program with test data.

Exercises 5.4

1. Consider the program fragment

```
if (x >= 0.0)
    if x < 1000.00
    {
        y = 2 * x;
        if (x <= 500)
            x = x / 10;
    }
    else
        y = 3 * x;
else
    y = abs(x);
```

The function `abs` is user-defined and returns the absolute value of its argument. Indicate the values of `x` and `y` after this fragment is executed for each of the following initial values of `x`:

a. `x = 381.5;`
b. `x = -21.0;`
c. `x = 600.0;`
d. `x = 3000.0;`

2. Write and run a test program that illustrates the checking of all branches of nested `if...else` statements.

3. Rewrite each of the following fragments using nested or extended `if` statements without compound conditions:

a.
```
if ((ch == 'M') && (sum > 1000))
    x = x + 1;
if ((ch == 'M') && (sum <= 1000))
```

```
   x = x + 2;
if ((ch == 'F') && (sum > 1000))
   x = x + 3;
if ((ch == 'F') && (sum <= 1000))
   x = x + 5;
```

b.
```
cin >> num;
if ((num > 0) && (num <= 10000))
{
   count = count + 1;
   sum = sum + num;
}
else
   cout << setw(27) << Value out of range << endl;
```

c.
```
if ((a > 0) && (b > 0))
   cout << setw(22) << Both positive << endl;
else
   cout << setw(22) << Some negative << endl;
```

d.
```
if (((a > 0) && (b > 0)) || (c > 0))
   cout << setw(19) << Option one << endl;
else
   cout <<setw(19) << Option two << endl;
```

4. Consider each of the following program fragments:

a.
```
if (a < 0)
   if (b < 0)
      a = b;
   else
      a = b + 10;
cout << a << b << endl;
```

b.
```
if (a < 0)
{
   if (b < 0)
      a = b;
}
else
   a = b + 10;
cout << a << b << endl;
```

c.
```
if (a == 0)
   a = b + 10;
else if (b < 0)
   a = b;
cout << a << b << endl;
```

d.
```
if (a >= 0)
   a = b + 10;
if (b < 0)
   a = b;
cout << a << b << endl;
```

Indicate the output of each fragment for each of the following assignment statements:

i.
```
a = -5;
b = 5;
```

ii.
```
a = -5;
b = -3;
```

iii.
```
a = 10;
b = 8;
```

iv.
```
a = 10;
b = -4;
```

5. Look back to Example 5.10, in which we assigned grades to students, and rewrite the grade assignment fragment using a different nesting. Could you rewrite it without using any nesting? Should you?
6. Many nationally based tests report scores and indicate in which quartile the score lies. Assume the following quartile designation:

Score	Quartile
100–75	1
74–50	2
49–25	3
24–0	4

Write a program to read a score from the keyboard and report in which quartile the score lies.
7. What are the values of a, b, and c after the following program fragment is executed?

```
a = -8; b = 21;
c = a + b;
if (a > b)
{
    a = b;
    c = a * b;
}
else if (a < 0)
{
    a = abs(a);
    b = b - a;
    c = a * b;
}
else
    c = 0;
```

8. Create minimal sets of test data for each part of Exercise 4 and for Exercise 7. Explain why each piece of test data has been included.
9. Discuss a technique that could be used as a debugging aid to guarantee that all possible logical paths of a program have been used.

5.5 switch Statements

Objectives

a. to learn the syntax of the `switch` statement
b. to understand how `switch` statements can be used as an alternate method for multiway selection
c. to use `switch` statements in designing programs

Thus far, this chapter has examined one-way selection, two-way selection, and multiway selection. Section 5.4 illustrated how multiple selection can be achieved using nested and extended `if` statements. Because multiple selection can sometimes be difficult to follow, C++ provides an alternative method of handling this concept, the `switch` statement.

Form and Syntax

C++ switch statements are often used when several options depend on the value of a single variable or expression. The general structure for a switch statement follows:

```
switch (<selector>)
{
        case <label 1> :        <statements 1>
                                break;
        case <label 2> :        <statements 2>
                                break;
                  .
                  .
                  .
        case <label n> :        <statements n>
                                break;
        default:                <statements>
}
```

This structure is shown graphically in Figure 5.5. The words `switch`, `case`, `break`, and `default` are reserved. The selector can be any variable or expression whose value is any data type we have studied previously except for `double` and

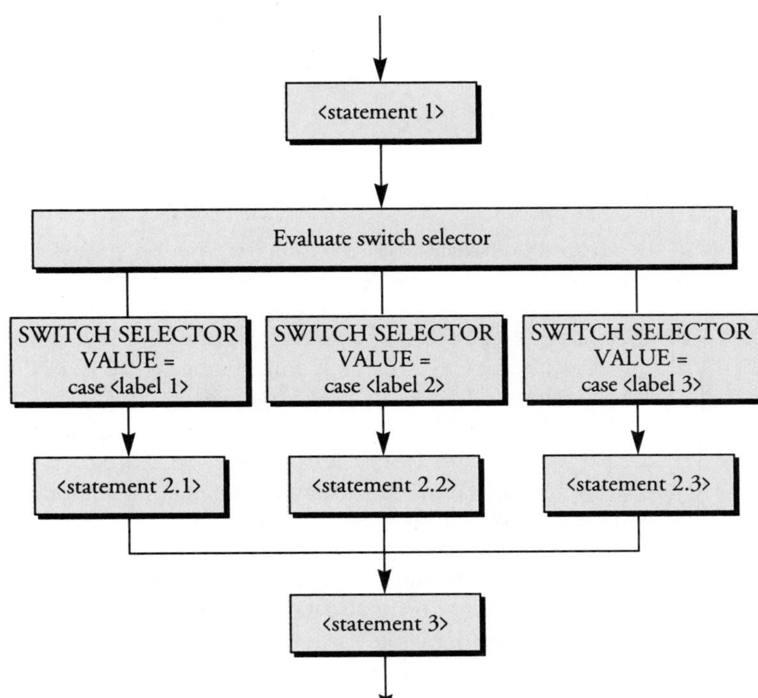

Figure 5.5
The `switch` statement flow diagram

apstring (only ordinal data types can be used). Values of the selector constitute the labels. Thus, if age is an integer variable whose values might be 18, 19, and 20, we could have

```
switch (age)
{
   case 18 :        <statement 1>
                    break;
   case 19 :        <statement 2>
                    break;
   case 20 :        <statement 3>
                    break;
   default:         <default statement>
}
```

When this program statement is executed, the value of age will determine to which statement control is transferred. More specifically, the program fragment

```
age = 19;
switch (age)
{
   case 18 :     cout << "I just became a legal voter." << endl;
                 break;
   case 19 :     cout << "This is my second year to vote." << endl;
                 break;
   case 20 :     cout << "I am almost twenty-one." << endl;
                 break;
   default:      if (age > 20)
                    cout << "I have all of the privileges of adulthood."
                         << endl;
                 else
                    cout << "I have no privileges at all." << endl;
}
```

produces the output

```
This is my second year to vote.
```

Before considering more examples, several comments are in order. The flow of logic within a switch statement is as follows:

1. The value of the selector is determined.
2. The first instance of a value is found among the labels.
3. The statements following this value are executed.
4. break statements are optional. If a break statement occurs within these statements, then control is transferred to the first program statement following the entire switch statement; otherwise, execution continues. In general, you should end every case with a break statement.

The selector can have a value of any type previously studied except double and apstring. Only ordinal data types may be used.

Several cases may be associated with an alternative action. For example, if <statement 1> should be run when age has the integer value of 10 or 100, the switch statement could appear as

```
switch (age)
{
   case 10:
   case 100 :    <statement 1>
                 break;
   case 19 :     <statement 2>
                 break;
   case 20 :     <statement 3>
                 break;
   default :     <default statement>
}
```

All possible values of the switch selector do not have to be listed. However, if an unlisted value is used, subtle logic errors can occur. Consequently, it is preferable to use a *default option*. If certain values require no action, the program will finish executing the switch statement by running the default as the last option; for example,

```
switch (age)
{
   case 10:
   case 100 :    <statement 1>
                 break;
   case 19 :     <statement 2>
                 break;
   case 20 :     <statement 3>
                 break;
   default:      cout << "There is no case for " << age << endl;
}
```

Like the break statement, the default statement is optional.

At this stage, we will consider several examples that illustrate various uses of switch statements. Because our purpose is for illustration, the examples are somewhat contrived. Later examples will serve to illustrate how these statements are used in solving problems.

Communication and Style Tips

Writing style for a switch statement should be consistent with your previously developed style. The lines containing options should be indented. Thus, a typical switch statement is

```
switch (score)
{
   case 10:
   case 9:
   case 8:    cout << "Excellent" << endl;
              break;
   case 7:
   case 6:
   case 5:    cout << "Fair" << endl;
              break;
   case 4:
   case 3:
   case 2:
   case 1:
```

continued

```
    case 0:    cout << "Failing" << endl;
               break;
    default:   cout << "Error in switch statement " << score << endl;
}
```

Example 5.12 The selector can have a value of type `char`, and the ordinal of the character determines the option. Thus, the label list must contain the appropriate characters in single quotation marks. If `grade` has values 'A', 'B', 'C', 'D', or 'F', a `switch` statement could be

```
switch (grade)
{
   case 'A' :         points = 4.0;
                      break;
   case 'B' :         points = 3.0;
                      break;
   case 'C' :         points = 2.0;
                      break;
   case 'D' :         points = 1.0;
                      break;
   case 'F' :         points = 0.0;
}
```

Example 5.13 Let us rewrite the following program fragment using a `switch` statement.

```
if ((score == 10) || (score == 9))
   grade = 'A';
else if ((score == 8) || (score == 7))
   grade = 'B';
else if ((score == 6) || (score == 5))
   grade = 'C';
else
   grade = 'F';
```

If we assume `score` is an integer variable with values 0, 1, 2, . . . , 10, we could use a `switch` statement as follows:

```
switch (score)
{
    case 10:
    case 9:        grade = 'A';
                   break;
    case 8:
    case 7:        grade = 'B';
                   break;
    case 6:
    case 5:        grade = 'C';
                   break;
    default:       grade = 'F';
}
```

A NOTE OF INTEREST

A Software Glitch

The software glitch that disrupted AT&T's long-distance telephone service for 9 hours in January 1990 dramatically demonstrates what can go wrong even in the most reliable and scrupulously tested systems. Of the roughly 100 million telephone calls placed with AT&T during that period, only about half got through. The breakdown cost the company more than $60 million in lost revenues and caused considerable inconvenience and irritation for telephone-dependent customers.

The trouble began at a "switch"—one of 114 interconnected, computer-operated electronic switching systems scattered across the United States. These sophisticated systems, each a maze of electronic equipment housed in a large room, form the backbone of the AT&T long-distance telephone network.

When a local exchange delivers a telephone call to the network, it arrives at one of these switching centers, which can handle up to 700,000 calls an hour. The switch immediately springs into action. It scans a list of 14 different routes it can use to complete the call, and at the same time hands off the telephone number to a parallel signaling network, invisible to any caller. This private data network allows computers to scout the possible routes and determine whether the switch at the other end can deliver the call to the local company it serves.

If the answer is no, the call is stopped at the original switch to keep it from tying up a line, and the caller gets a busy signal. If the answer is yes, a signaling-network computer makes a reservation at the destination switch and orders the original switch to pass along the waiting call—after that switch makes a final check to ensure that the chosen line is functioning properly. The whole process of passing a call down the network takes 4 to 6 seconds. Because the switches must keep in constant touch with the signaling network and its computers, each switch has a computer program that handles all the necessary communications between the switch and the signaling network.

AT&T's first indication that something might be amiss appeared on a giant video display at the company's network control center in Bedminster, New Jersey. At 2:25 P.M. on Monday, January 15, 1990, network managers saw an alarming increase in the number of red warning signals appearing on many of the 75 video screens showing the status of various parts of AT&T's worldwide network. The warnings signaled a serious collapse in the network's ability to complete calls within the United States.

To bring the network back up to speed, AT&T engineers first tried a number of standard procedures that had worked in the past. But this time, the methods failed. The engineers realized they had a problem they'd never seen before. Nonetheless, within a few hours, they managed to stabilize the network by temporarily cutting back on the number of messages moving through the signaling network. They cleared the last defective link at 11:30 that night.

Meanwhile, a team of more than 100 telephone technicians tried frantically to track down the fault. Because the problem involved the signaling network and seemed to bounce from one switch to another, they zeroed in on the software that permitted each switch to communicate with the signaling-network computers.

The day after the slowdown, AT&T personnel removed the apparently faulty software from each switch, temporarily replacing it with an earlier version of the communications program. A close examination of the flawed software turned up a single error in one line of the program. Just 1 month earlier, network technicians had changed the software to speed the processing of certain messages, and the change had inadvertently introduced a flaw into the system. From that finding, AT&T could reconstruct what had happened.

Use in Problems

The `switch` statements should not be used for relational tests involving large ranges of values. For example, if one wanted to examine a range from 0–100 to determine test scores, nested selection would be better than a `switch` statement. We close this section with some examples that illustrate how `switch` statements can be used in solving problems.

Example 5.14 Suppose you are writing a program for a gasoline station owner who sells four grades of gasoline: regular, plus, super, and diesel. Your program reads a character (R, P, S, D) that designates which kind of gasoline was purchased and then takes subsequent action. The outline for this fragment is

```
cin >> gastype;
switch (gastype)
{
   case 'R' :    <action for regular>;
                 break;
   case 'P' :    <action for plus>;
                 break;
   case 'S' :    <action for super>;
                 break;
   case 'D' :    <action for diesel>;
                 break;
}
```

Equivalent of Extended `if` Statements

As previously indicated, `switch` statements can sometimes (when ordinal data types are involved) be used instead of extended `if` statements when multiple selection is required for solving a problem. The following example illustrates this use.

Example 5.15 An alternative method of assigning letter grades based on integer scores between 0 and 100 inclusive is to divide the score by 10 and assign grades according to some scale. This idea could be used in conjunction with a `switch` statement as follows:

```
newScore = score / 10;
switch (newScore)
{
   case 10:
   case 9:       grade = 'A';
                 break;
   case 8:       grade = 'B';
                 break;
   case 7:       grade = 'C';
                 break;
   case 6:
   case 5:       grade = 'D';
                 break;
   case 4:
   case 3:
   case 2:
   case 1:
   case 0:       grade = 'F';
}
```

Exercises 5.5

1. Discuss the need for program protection when using a `switch` statement.
2. Show how the following `switch` statement could be protected against unexpected values.

```
switch (age / 10)
{
   case 10:
   case 9:
   case 8:
```

```
    case 7:      cout << setw(40) << "These are retirement years" << endl;
                 break;
    case 6:
    case 5:
    case 4:      cout << setw(40) << "These are middle age years" << endl;
                 break;
    case 3:
    case 2:      cout << setw(40) << "These are mobile years" << endl;
                 break;
    case 1:      cout << setw(40) << "These are school years" << endl;
}
```

3. Find all errors in the following statements:

a.
```
switch (a)
case 1        :
                break;
case 2        : a = 2 * a
                break;
case 3        ; a = 3 * a;
                break;
case 4; 5; 6 : a = 4 * a;
}
```

b.
```
switch (num)
{
   case 5:               num = num + 5;
                         break;
   case 6:
   case 7:      ;        num = num + 6;
                         break;
   case 7, 8, 9, 10 : num = num + 10;
}
```

c.
```
switch (age)
{
  15, 16, 17  : ycount = ycount + 1;
                cout << age << ycount << endl;
    case 18:
    case 19:
    case 20:      mcount = mcount + 1;
    case 21:      cout << age endl;
}
```

d.
```
switch (ch)
{
    a :     points =      4.0;
            break;
    b :     points =      3.0;
            break;
    c :     points =      2.0;
            break;
    d :     points =      1.0;
            break;
    e :     points =      0.0
}
```

e.
```
switch (score)
{
    case 5 :    grade = A;
                break;
    case 4 :    grade = B;
                break;
    case 3 :    grade = C;
                break;
    case 2 :
    case 1:,
    case 0:    grade = E;
}
```

f.
```
switch (num / 10)
{
    case 1 :    num = num + 1;
                break;
    case 2 :    num = num + 2;
                break;
    case 3 :    num = num + 3;
}
```

4. What is the output from each of the following program fragments?

a.
```
a = 5;
power = 3;
switch (power)
{
    case 0:       b = 1;
                  break;
    case 1:       b = a;
                  break;
    case 2:       b = a * a;
                  break;
    case 3:       b = a * a * a;
}
cout << a << power << b << endl;
```

b.
```
gastype = 'S';
cout << You have purchased ;
switch (gastype)
{
    case 'R':    cout << Regular;
                 break;
    case 'P':    cout << Premium;
                 break;
    case 'U':    cout << Unleaded;
                 break;
    case 'S':    cout << Super Unleaded;
}
cout << gasoline << endl;
```

c.
```
a = 6;
b = -3;
switch (a)
```

```
{
    case 10:
    case 9:
    case 8:       switch b
                  {
                      case -3:
                      case -4:
                      case -5:      a = a * b;
                                    break;
                      case 0:
                      case -1:
                      case -2:      a = a + b;
                  }
                  break;
    case 7:
    case 6:
    case 5:       switch (b)
                  {
                      case -5:
                      case -4:      a = a * b;
                                    break;
                      case -3:
                      case -2:      a = a + b;
                                    break;
                      case -1:
                      case 0:       a = a - b;
                  }
}
cout << a << b << endl;
```

d.

```
symbol = '-';
a = 5;
b = 10;
switch (symbol)
{
    case '+' :    num = a + b;
    case '-' :    num = a - b;
    case '*' :    num = a * b;
}
cout << a << b << num << endl;
```

5. Rewrite each of the following program fragments using a `switch` statement.

a.

```
if (power == 1)
   num = a;
if (power == 2)
   num = a * a;
if (power == 3)
   num = a * a * a;
```

b. Assume `score` is an integer between 0 and 10.

```
if (score > 9)
     grade = 'A'
```

continued

```
else if (score > 8)
     grade = 'B'
else if (score > 7)
     grade = 'C'
else if (score > 5)
     grade = 'D'
else
     grade = 'F';
```

c. Assume measurement is either `M` or `N`.

```
if (measurement == 'M')
{
     cout << setw(37) << "This is a metric measurement." << endl;
     cout << setw(42) << "It will be converted to nonmetric." << endl;
     length = num * CM_TO_INCHES;
}
else
{
     cout << setw(40) << "This is a nonmetric measurement." << endl;
     cout << setw(39) << "It will be converted to metric." << endl;
     length = num * INCHES_TO_CM;
}
```

6. Show how a `switch` statement can be used in a program to compute college tuition fees. Assume there are different fee rates for each of undergraduates (U), graduates (G), non-U.S. students (F), and special students (S).

7. Use nested `switch` statements to design a program fragment to compute postage for domestic (noninternational) mail. The design should include four weight categories for both letters and packages. Each can be sent first, second, third, or fourth class.

5.6 Assertions

Objectives

a. to know how to use assertions as preconditions
b. to know how to use assertions as postconditions

An *assertion* is a statement about what we expect to be true at the point in the program where the assertion is placed. For example, if you wish to compute a test average by dividing the `sumOfScores` by `numberOfStudents`, you could state your intent that `numberOfStudents` is not equal to zero with a comment:

```
// assert that (numberOfStudents != 0)
classAverage = sumOfScores / numberOfStudents;
```

Assertions are usually Boolean-valued expressions and typically concern program action. In the preceding example, the assertion that appears in a comment reminds the programmer that a certain condition must be true before an action is taken. Modern programming languages such as C++ provide a way of executing an assertion at run time. The computer verifies that the assertion is true, and if it is false, the computer halts program execution with an error message. To use this kind of feature in C++, you must include the `assert.h` library file:

```
#include <assert.h>
```

Then you can state your assertion by calling the function `assert` with the Boolean expression as a parameter. The previous example might now look like this:

```
assert(numberOfStudents != 0);
classAverage = sumOfScores / numberOfStudents;
```

At execution time, this program would halt with an error message before an attempt to divide by zero.

Assertions frequently come in pairs: one preceding program action and one following the action. In this format, the first assertion is a precondition and the second is a postcondition. To illustrate preconditions and postconditions, consider the following segment of code:

```
if (num1 < num2)
{
   temp = num1;
   num1 = num2;
   num2 = temp;
}
```

The intent of this code is to have `num1` be greater than or equal to `num2`. If we intend for both `num1` and `num2` to be positive, we can write

```
assert((num1 >= 0) && (num2 >= 0));          // Precondition
if (num1 < num2)
{
   temp = num1;
   num1 = num2;
   num2 = temp;
}
assert((num1 >= num2) && (num2 >= 0));       // Postcondition
```

As a second example, consider a `switch` statement used to assign grades based on quiz scores.

```
switch (score)
{
   case 10:      grade = 'A';
                 break;
   case 9:
   case 8:       grade = 'B';
                 break;
   case 7:
   case 6:       grade = 'C';
                 break;
   case 5:
   case 4:       grade = 'D';
                 break;
   case 3:
   case 2:
   case 1:
   case 0:       grade = 'F';
}
```

Assertions can be used as preconditions and postconditions in the following manner.

```
assert((score >= 0) && (score <= 10));                 // Precondition
switch (score)
```

continued

```
{
   case 10:      grade = 'A';
                 break;
   case 9:
   case 8:       grade = 'B';
                 break;
   case 7:
   case 6:       grade = 'C';
                 break;
   case 5:
   case 4:       grade = 'D';
                 break;
   case 3:
   case 2:
   case 1:
   case 0:       grade = 'F';
}
assert(((score == 10) && (grade == 'A')) ||          // Postcondition
       ((score == 9) && (grade == 'B')) ||
       ((score == 8) && (grade == 'B')) ||
       ((score == 7) && (grade == 'C')) ||
       ((score == 6) && (grade == 'C')) ||
       ((score == 5) && (grade == 'D')) ||
       ((score == 4) && (grade == 'D')) ||
       (((score >= 0) && (score <= 3)) && (grade == 'F')));
```

Assertions can be used in *program proofs.* Simply put, a program proof is an analysis of a program that attempts to verify the correctness of program results. A detailed study of program proofs is beyond the scope of this text. If, however, you use assertions as preconditions and postconditions now, you will better understand them in subsequent courses. They are especially useful for making a program safer, even if you cannot be sure that their use will guarantee that the program is correct. If you do choose to use assertions in this manner, be aware that the postcondition of one action is the precondition of the next action.

Case Study: The Gas-N-Clean Service Station

The Gas-N-Clean Service Station sells gasoline and has a car wash. Fees for the car wash are $1.25 with a gasoline purchase of $10.00 or more and $3.00 otherwise. Three kinds of gasoline are available: regular at $1.149, plus at $1.199, and super at $1.289 per gallon.

User Request

Write a program that prints a statement for a customer.

Analysis

Input consists of number of gallons purchased, kind of gasoline purchased (R, P, S, or, for no purchase, N), and car wash desired (Y or N). Gasoline prices should be program-defined constants. Your output should include appropriate messages. Sample output for these data is

```
Enter number of gallons and press <Enter>. 9.7
Enter gas type (R, P, S, or N) and press <Enter>. R
Enter Y or N for car wash and press <Enter>. Y
```

```
************************************
*                                  *
*     Gas-N-Clean Service Station  *
*                                  *
*           July 25, 1995          *
*                                  *
************************************

Amount of gasoline purchased       9.700 Gallons

Price per gallon               $   1.149

Total gasoline cost            $  11.15

Car wash cost                  $   1.25

Total due                      $  12.40

            Thank you for stopping

            Please come again

      Remember to buckle up and drive safely
```

Design

A first-level pseudocode development is

1. Get data
2. Compute charges
3. Print results

A structure chart for this problem is given in Figure 5.6. Module specifications for the main modules follow:

Module: Get the data
Task: Get information interactively from the keyboard
Outputs: number of gallons purchased, type of gasoline, a choice as to whether or not a car wash is desired

Module: Compute the charges
Task: Compute the gas cost, wash cost, and total cost
Inputs: number of gallons, gas type, wash option
Outputs: gas cost, wash cost, total cost

Module: Print the results
Task: Print the results
Inputs: number of gallons purchased, type of gasoline, gas cost, wash cost, total cost

Further refinement of the pseudocode produces

1. Get data
   1.1 read number of gallons
   1.2 read kind of gas purchased
   1.3 read car wash option

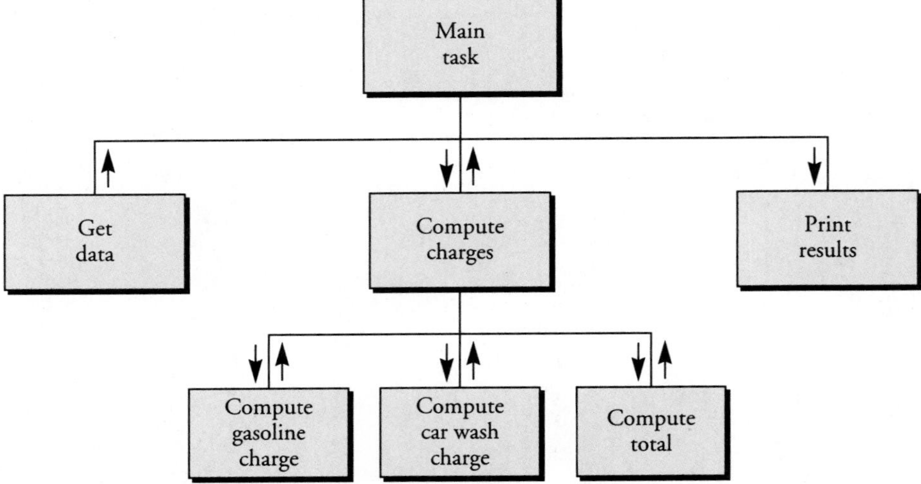

Figure 5.6 Structure chart for the Gas-N-Clean Service Station problem

2. Compute charges
  2.1 compute gasoline charge
  2.2 compute car wash charge
  2.3 compute total
3. Print results
  3.1 print heading
  3.2 print information in transaction
  3.3 print closing message

Module 2 consists of three subtasks. A refined pseudocode development of this step is

```
2. Compute charges
   2.1 compute gasoline charge
       2.1.1 switch gasType
             'R'
             'P'
             'S'
             'N'
   2.2 compute car wash charge
       2.2.1 if washOption is yes
               compute charge
             else
               charge is 0.0
   2.3 compute total
       2.3.1 total is gasCost plus washCost
```

Implementation

A C++ program for this problem follows.

```
// This program is used to compute the amount due from a
// customer of the Gas-N-Clean Service Station. Constants
// are used for gasoline prices. Note the use of nested
// selection to compute cost of the car wash.
```

```
//Program file: gas.cpp

#include <iostream.h>
#include <iomanip.h>

const double REGULAR_PRICE = 1.149;
const double PLUS_PRICE = 1.199;
const double SUPER_PRICE = 1.289;

// Function: printHeading
// Prints a signon message for program

void printHeading();

// Function: getData
// Get information interactively from the keyboard.
// Outputs: number of gallons purchased, type of gasoline,
// a choice as to whether or not a car wash is desired

void getData(double &numGallons, char &gasType,
             char &washOption);

// Function: computeCharges
// Computes the gas cost, wash cost, and total cost
// Inputs: number of gallons, gas type, wash option
// Outputs: gas cost, wash cost, total cost

void computeCharges(double numGallons, char gasType,
                    char washOption, double &gasCost,
                    double &washCost, double &totalCost);

// Function: printMessage
// Prints a signoff message for program

void printMessage();

// Function: printResults
// Print the results
//
// Inputs: number of gallons purchased, type of gasoline,
// gas cost, wash cost, total cost

void printResults (double numGallons, char gasType,
                   double gasCost, double washCost,
                   double totalCost);

int main()
{
   char gasType;            //    Type of gasoline purchased (R,P,S,N)
   char washOption;         //    Character designating option (Y,N)
   double numGallons;       //    Number of gallons purchased
   double gasCost;          //    Computed cost for gasoline
   double washCost;         //    Car wash cost
   double totalCost;        //    Total amount due

   getData(numGallons, gasType, washOption);
```

continued

```
   computeCharges(numGallons, gasType, washOption,
                  gasCost, washCost, totalCost);
   printResults(numGallons, gasType,
                gasCost, washCost, totalCost);
   return 0;
}

void printHeading()
{
   cout << setiosflags(ios::right) << endl;
   cout << setw(55)
        << "****************************************"
        << endl;
   cout << setw(55)
        << "*                                      *"
        << endl;
   cout << setw(55)
        << "* Gas-N-Clean Service Station          *"
        << endl;
   cout << setw(55)
        << "*                                      *"
        << endl;
   cout << setw(55)
        << "*         July 25, 1997                *"
        << endl;
   cout << setw(55)
        << "*                                      *"
        << endl;
   cout << setw(55)
        << "****************************************"
        << endl;
   cout << endl;
}
void getData(double &numGallons, char &gasType,
              char &washOption)
{
   cout << "Enter number of gallons and press <Enter>. ";
   cin >> numGallons;
   cout << "Enter gas type (R, P, S, or N) and press <Enter>. ";
   cin >> gasType;
   cout << "Enter Y or N for car wash and press <Enter>. ";
   cin >> washOption;
}

void computeCharges(double numGallons, char gasType,
                     char washOption, double &gasCost,
                     double &washCost, double &totalCost)
{
   switch (gasType)
   {
      case 'R':  gasCost = numGallons * REGULAR_PRICE;
                 break;
      case 'P':  gasCost = numGallons * PLUS_PRICE;
                 break;
      case 'S':  gasCost = numGallons * SUPER_PRICE;
                 break;
```

```
      case 'N':  gasCost = 0.0;
   }
   // Compute car wash cost
   if (washOption == 'Y')
      if (gasCost >= 10.0)
         washCost = 1.25;
      else
         washCost = 3.0;
   else
      washCost = 0.0;
   totalCost = gasCost + washCost;
}

void printMessage()
{
   cout << endl;
   cout << setw(48) << "Thank you for stopping" << endl;
   cout << endl;
   cout << setw(43) << "Please come again" << endl;
   cout << endl;
   cout << setw(55)
        << "Remember to buckle up and drive safely"
        << endl;
   cout << endl;
}

void printResults(double numGallons, char gasType,
                  double gasCost, double washCost,
                  double totalCost)
{
   printHeading();
   cout << setiosflags(ios::fixed | ios::showpoint);
   cout << setw(43) << "Amount of gasoline purchased"
        << setw(12) << setw(6) << setprecision(3)
        << numGallons << " Gallons" << endl;
   cout << setw(31) << "Price per gallon"
        << setw(22) << "$";
   switch (gasType)
   {
      case 'R': cout << setw(7) << REGULAR_PRICE << endl;
                break;
      case 'P': cout << setw(7) << PLUS_PRICE << endl;
                break;
      case 'S': cout << setw(7) << SUPER_PRICE
                     << endl;
                break;
      case 'N': cout << setw(7) << 0.0 << endl;
  }
  cout << setw(34) << "Total gasoline cost"
       << setw(19) << "$"
       << setw(6) << setprecision(2) << gasCost
       << endl;
  if (washCost > 0)
     cout << setw(28) << "Car wash cost"
          << setw(25) << "$"
```

continued

```
        << setw(6) << washCost << endl;
    cout << setw(31) << "Total due"
        << setw(22) << "$" << setw(6)
        << totalCost << endl;
    printMessage();
}
```

Running, Testing, and Debugging Hints

1. `if . . . else` is a single statement in C++.
2. A misplaced semicolon used with an `if` statement can be a problem. For example,

   Incorrect

   ```
   if (a > 0) ;
      cout << a << endl;
   ```

   Correct

   ```
   if (a > 0)
      cout << a << endl;
   ```

3. Be careful with compound statements as options in an `if . . . else` statement. They must be in a `{ . . . }` block, and a trailing `}` must not be followed by a semicolon.

   Incorrect

   ```
   if (a >= 0)
      cout << a << endl;
      a = a + 10;
   else
      cout << a << " is negative" << endl;
   ```

   Correct

   ```
   if (a >= 0)
   {
       cout << a << endl;
       a = a + 10;
   }
   else
       cout << a << " is negative" << endl;
   ```

4. Your test data should include values that will check both options of an `if . . . else` statement.
5. The `if . . . else` statement can be used to check for other program errors. In particular,

   a. Check for bad data by

   ```
   cin >> <data>;
   if (<bad data>)

          .
          . <error message>
          .
   ```

```
else
    .
    . <proceed with program>
    .
```

b. Check for reasonable computed values by

```
if (<unreasonable values>)
    .
    . <error message>
    .

else
    .
    . <proceed with program>
    .
```

For example, if you were computing a student's test average, you could have

```
if ((testaverage > 100) || (testaverage < 0))
    .
    . <error message>
    .

else
    .
    . <proceed with program>
    .
```

6. Be careful with Boolean expressions. You should always keep expressions reasonably simple, use parentheses, and minimize the use of `!` .

7. Be careful to properly match `else`s with `if`s in nested `if...else` statements. Indented levels for writing code are very helpful.

```
if (<condition 1>)
   if (<condition 2>)
      .
      . <action here>
      .
   else
      .
      . <action here>
      .
else
   .
   . <action here>
   .
```

8. The form for using extended `if` statements is

```
if (<condition 1>)
   .
   . <action 1 here>
   .
else if (<condition 2>)
```

continued

```
        .
        . <action 2 here>
        .
else
        .
        . <final option here>
        .
```

9. Be sure to include `break` statements and a default option where necessary in a `switch` statement.

Summary

Key Terms

{ . . . } block
compound Boolean expression
compound statement
extended `if` statement
logical operators: `&&`, `||`, `!`
negation
nested `if` statement
relational operator
robust
selection statement
short-circuit evaluation
simple Boolean expression
type definition

Key Terms (Optional)

assertion
program proof

Keywords

`break`
`case`
`default`
`if`
`else`
`switch`
`typedef`

Key Concepts

- Boolean constants have the values `1 = true` and `0 = false`. To make these values obvious in programs, one can define them as symbolic constants. Because some C++ compilers use the symbols `true` and `false` for other purposes, one can "undefine" them with the preprocessor directive `#undef` before reusing them as follows:

```
#undef true
#undef false
const int true = 1;
const int false = 0;
```

- Data types can be given more descriptive names by using a `typedef`. For example, a data type for Boolean variables can be defined with

```
typedef int bool;
```

and variables can then be declared with

```
bool done = false;
```

- Frequently used data definitions, such as those for the Boolean type, can be placed in a program library and included in application programs. For example, the library file `bool.h` can be included with

```
#include bool.h
```

- Relational operators are `==`, `>`, `<`, `>=`, `<=`, `!=`.
- Logical operators `&&`, `||`, and `!` are used as operators on Boolean expressions.
- Boolean expressions will be interpreted during execution as having the values 1 (meaning `true`) or 0 (meaning `false`).
- A complete priority listing of arithmetic operators, relational operators, and logical operators is

Expression or Operation	Priority
`( )`	Evaluate from inside out
`!`	Evaluate from left to right
`* , / , %`	Evaluate from left to right
`+ , -`	Evaluate from left to right
`< , <= , > , >= , == , !=`	Evaluate from left to right
`&&`	Evaluate from left to right
`||`	Evaluate from left to right

- The values of compound Boolean expressions connected by `||` or `&&` are computed by using short-circuit evaluation.
- A selection statement is a program statement that transfers control to various branches of the program.
- A compound statement is sometimes referred to as a `{...}` block; when it is executed, the entire segment of code between the `{` and `}` is treated like a single statement.
- `if...else` is a two-way selection statement.
- If the Boolean expression in an `if...else` statement is `true`, the command following `if` is executed; if the expression is `false`, the command following `else` is executed.
- Multiple selections can be achieved by using decision statements within decision statements; this is termed multiway selection.
- An extended `if` statement is a statement of the form

```
if (<condition 1>)
    .
    . <action 1 here>
    .

else if (<condition 2>)
```

continued

```
    .
    . <action 2 here>
    .
else if (<condition 3>)
    .
    . <action 3 here>
    .
else
    .
    . <action 4 here>
    .
```

- Program protection can be achieved by using selection statements to guard against unexpected results.
- `switch` statements can sometimes be used as alternatives to multiple selection.
- `default`, a reserved word in C++, can be used to handle values not listed in the `switch` statement.

Programming Problems and Projects

The first 13 problems listed here are relatively short, but to complete them you must use concepts presented in this chapter.

Some of the remaining programming problems are used as the basis for writing programs for subsequent chapters as well as for this chapter. In this chapter, each program is run on a very limited set of data. Material in later chapters permits us to run the programs on larger databases.

1. A 3-minute telephone call to Scio, New York, costs $1.15. Each additional minute costs $0.26. Given the total length of a call in minutes, calculate and print the cost.
2. When you first learned to divide, you expressed answers using a quotient and a remainder rather than a fraction or decimal quotient. For example, if you divided 7 by 2, your answer would have been given as 3 r. 1. Given two integers, divide the larger by the smaller and print the answer in this form. Do not assume that the numbers are entered in any order.
3. Revise Problem 2 so that, if there is no remainder, you print only the quotient without a remainder or the letter r.
4. Given the coordinates of two points on a graph, find and print the slope of a line passing through them. Remember that the slope of a line can be undefined.
5. Dr. Lae Z. Programmer wishes to computerize his grading system. He gives five tests and then averages only the four highest scores. An average of 90 or better earns a grade of A; 80–89, a grade of B; and so on. Write a program that accepts five test scores and prints the average and grade according to this method.
6. Given the lengths of three sides of a triangle, print whether the triangle is scalene, isosceles, or equilateral.
7. Given the lengths of three sides of a triangle, determine whether or not the triangle is a right triangle using the Pythagorean theorem. Do not assume that the sides are entered in any order.

8. Given three integers, print only the largest.

9. The island nation of Babbage charges its citizens an income tax each year. The tax rate is based on the following table:

Income	Tax Rate
$ 0–5,000	0
5,001–10,000	3%
10,001–20,000	5.5%
20,001–40,000	10.8%
over $40,000	23.7%

Write a program that, when given a person's income, prints the tax owed rounded to the nearest dollar.

10. Many states base the cost of car registration on the weight of the vehicle. Suppose the fees are as follows:

Weight	Cost
0–1500 pounds	$23.75
1501–2500 pounds	$27.95
2501–3000 pounds	$30.25
over 3000 pounds	$37.00

Given the weight of a car, find and print the cost of registration.

11. The Mapes Railroad Corporation pays an annual bonus as a part of its profit sharing plan. This year all employees who have been with the company for 10 years or more receive a bonus of 12% of their annual salary, and those who have worked at Mapes from 5 through 9 years receive a bonus of 5.75%. Those who have been with the company fewer than 5 years receive no bonus.

Given the initials of an employee, the employee's annual salary, and the number of years employed with the company, find and print the bonus. All bonuses are rounded to the nearest dollar. Output should be in the following form:

```
     MAPES RAILROAD CORP.

Employee: xxx
Years of service: nn
Bonus earned: $ yyyy
```

12. A substance floats in water if its density (mass/volume) is less than 1 g/cm^3. It sinks if it is 1 or more. Given the mass and volume of an object, calculate and print whether it will sink or double.

13. Mr. Arthur Einstein, your high school physics teacher, wants a program for English-to-metric conversions. You are given a letter indicating whether the measurement is in pounds (P), feet (F), or miles (M). Such measures are to be converted to newtons, meters, and kilometers, respectively. (There are 4.9 newtons in a pound, 3.28 feet in a meter, and 1.61 kilometers in a mile.) Given an appropriate identifying letter and the size of the measurement, convert it to metric units. Print the answer in the following form:

```
3.0 miles = 4.83 kilometers.
```

14. The Caswell Catering and Convention Service (Chapter 4, Problem 12) has decided to revise its billing practices and is in need of a new program to prepare bills. The changes Caswell wishes to make are:

a. For adults, deluxe meals will cost $15.80 per person and standard meals will cost $11.75 per person, dessert included. Children's meals will cost 60% of adult meals. Everyone within a given party must be served the same meal type.

b. There are five banquet halls. Room A rents for $55.00, room B rents for $75.00, room C rents for $85.00, room D rents for $100.00, and room E rents for $130.00. The Caswells are considering increasing the room fees in about 6 months, and this should be taken into account.

c. A surcharge, currently 7%, is added to the total bill if the catering is done on a weekend (Friday, Saturday, or Sunday).

d. All customers will be charged the same rate for tip and tax, currently 18%. It is applied only to the cost of food.

e. To induce customers to pay promptly, a discount is offered if payment is made within 10 days. This discount depends on the amount of the total bill. If the bill is less than $100.00, the discount is 0.5%; if the bill is at least $100.00 but less than $200.00, the discount is 1.5%; if the bill is at least $200.00 but less than $400.00, the discount is 3%; if the bill is at least $400.00 but less than $800.00, the discount is 4%; and if the bill is at least $800.00, the discount is 5%.

Test your program on each of the following three customers.

Customer A: This customer is using room C on Tuesday night. The party includes 80 adults and 6 children. The standard meal is being served. The customer paid a $60.00 deposit.

Customer B: This customer is using room A on Saturday night. Deluxe meals are being served to 15 adults. A deposit of $50.00 was paid.

Customer C: This customer is using room D on Sunday afternoon. The party includes 30 children and 2 adults, all of whom are being served the standard meal.

Output should be in the same form as that for Problem 12, Chapter 4.

15. State University charges $90.00 for each semester hour of credit, $200.00 per semester for a regular room, $250.00 per semester for an air-conditioned room, and $400.00 per semester for food. All students are charged a $30.00 matriculation fee. Graduating students must also pay a $35.00 diploma fee. Write a program to compute the fees that must be paid by a student. Your program should include an appropriate warning message if a student is taking more than 21 credit hours or fewer than 12 credit hours. A typical line of data for one student would include student number (in four digits), room type (R or A), credit hours, and graduation status (T or F).

16. Write a program to determine the day of the week a person was born given his or her birth date. Following are the steps you should use to find the day of the week corresponding to any date in the 20th century.

a. Divide the last two digits of the birth year by 4. Put the quotient (ignoring the remainder) in total. For example, if the person was born in 1983, divide 83 by 4 and store 20 in total.

b. Add the last two digits of the birth year to total.

c. Add the last two digits of the birth date to total.

d. Using the following table, find the "month number" and add it to total.

January = 1
February = 4
March = 4
April = 0
May = 2
June = 5

July = 0
August = 3
September = 6
October = 1
November = 4
December = 6

e. If the year is a leap year and if the month you are working with is either January or February, then subtract 1 from the total.
f. Find the remainder when total is divided by 7. Look up the remainder in the following table to determine the day of the week the person was born. Note that you should not use this procedure if the person's year of birth is earlier than 1900.
1 = Sunday
2 = Monday
3 = Tuesday
4 = Wednesday
5 = Thursday
6 = Friday
0 = Saturday
Typical input is
5-15 78

where the first entry (5-15) represents the birth date (May 15) and the second entry (78) represents the birth year. An appropriate error message should be printed if a person's year of birth is before 1900. For an added challenge, make sure the program works for birthdates in the 21st century as well.

17. Community Hospital needs a program to compute and print a statement for each patient. Charges for each day are as follows:
a. room charges: private room, \$125.00; semiprivate room, \$95.00; or ward, \$75.00
b. telephone charge: \$1.75
c. television charge: \$3.50

Write a program to get a line of data from the keyboard, compute the patient's bill, and print an appropriate statement. Typical input is

```
5PNY
```

where 5 indicates the number of days spent in the hospital, P represents the room type (P, S, or W), N represents the telephone option (Y or N), and Y represents the television option (Y or N). A statement for the data given follows:

```
         Community Hospital

      Patient Billing Statement

Number of days in hospital: 5

Type of room: Private

Room charge                     $ 625.00

Telephone charge                $   0.00

Television charge               $  17.50

    TOTAL DUE            $ 642.50
```

18. Write a program that converts degrees Fahrenheit to degrees Celsius and degrees Celsius to degrees Fahrenheit. In the input, the temperature is followed by a designator (F or C) indicating whether the given temperature is Fahrenheit or Celsius.

19. The city of Mt. Pleasant bills its residents for sewage, water, and sanitation every 3 months. The sewer and water charge is figured according to how much water is used by the resident. The scale is

Amount (gallons)	Rate (per gallon)
Less than 1000	$0.03
1000 to 1999	$30 + $0.02 for each gallon over 1000
2000 or more	$50 + $0.015 for each gallon over 2000

The sanitation charge is $7.50 per month.

Write a program to read the number of months for which a resident is being billed (1, 2, or 3) and how much water was used; then print a statement with appropriate charges and messages. Use the constant definition section for all rates and include an error check for incorrect number of months. Typical input is

```
3 2175
```

20. Al Derrick, owner of the Lucky Wildcat Well Corporation, wants a program to help him decide whether or not a well is making money. Data for a well will consist of one or two lines. The first line contains a single character (D for a dry well, O for oil found, and G for gas found) followed by a real number for the cost of the well. If an "O" or "G" is detected, the cost will be followed by an integer indicating the volume of oil or gas found. In this case, there will also be a second line containing an "N" or "S" indicating whether or not sulfur is present. If there is sulfur, the "S" will be followed by the percentage of sulfur present in the oil or gas. Unit prices are $5.50 for oil and $2.20 for gas. These should be defined as constants. Your program should compute the total revenue for a well (reduce output for sulfur present) and print all pertinent information with an appropriate message to Mr. Derrick. A gusher is defined as a well with profit in excess of $50,000. Typical input is

```
G 8000.00 20000 S 0.15
```

21. The Mathematical Association of America hosts an annual summer meeting. Each state sends one official delegate to the section officer's meeting at this summer session. The national organization reimburses the official state delegates according to the following scale:

Round-trip Mileage	Rate
Up to 500 miles	15 cents per mile
501 to 1000 miles	$75.00 plus 12 cents for each mile over 500
1001 to 1500 miles	$135.00 plus 10 cents for each mile over 1000
1501 to 2000 miles	$185.00 plus 8 cents for each mile over 1500
2001 to 3000 miles	$225.00 plus 6 cents for each mile over 2000
3001 or more miles	$285.00 plus 5 cents for each mile over 3000

Write a program that will accept as input the number of round-trip miles for a delegate and compute the amount of reimbursement.

22. Dr. Lae Z. Programmer (Problem 5) wants you to write a program to compute and print the grade for a student in his class. The grade is based on three examinations (worth a possible 100 points each), five quizzes (10 points each), and a 200-point final examination. Your output should include all scores, the percentage grade, and the letter grade. The grading scale is

90 <= average <= 100	A
80 <= average < 90	B
70 <= average < 80	C
60 <= average < 70	D
0 <= average < 60	F

Typical input is

```
80 93 85 (examination scores)
9 10 8 7 10 (quiz scores)
175 (final examination)
```

23. Dr. Lae Z. Programmer now wants you to modify Problem 22 by adding a check for bad data. Any time an unexpected score occurs, you are to print an appropriate error message and terminate the program.

24. A quadratic equation is one of the form

$$ax^2 + bx + c = 0$$

where $a \neq 0$. Real number solutions to this equation are given by

$$x = \frac{-b \pm \sqrt{b^2 - 4ac}}{2a}$$

where the quantity $(b^2 - 4ac)$ is referred to as the discriminant of the equation. Write a program to read three integers as the respective coefficients (a, b, and c), compute the discriminant, and print the solutions. Use the following rules:

a. discriminant = 0 -> single root
b. discriminant < 0 -> no real number solution
c. discriminant > 0 -> two distinct real solutions

25. Write a program that gets as input the lengths of three sides of a triangle. Output should first identify the triangle as scalene, isosceles, or equilateral. The program should use the Pythagorean theorem to determine whether or not scalene or isosceles triangles are right triangles. An appropriate message should be part of the output.

26. The sign on the attendant's booth at the Pentagon parking lot is

```
PENTAGON VISITOR PARKING
Cars:
First 2 hours     Free
Next 3 hours     0.50/hour
Next 10 hours     0.25/hour
Trucks:
First 1 hour     Free
Next 2 hours     1.00/hour
Next 12 hours     0.75/hour
Senior Citizens:     No charge
```

Write a program that will accept as input a one-character designator (C, T, or S) followed by the number of minutes a vehicle has been in the lot. The program should then compute the appropriate charge and print a ticket for the customer. Any part of an hour is counted as a full hour.

27. Milt Walker, the chief of advertising for the Isabella Potato Industry, wants you to write a program to compute an itemized bill and total cost of his "This Spud's for You!" ad campaign. The standard black-and-white full-page ads have base prices as follows:

Drillers' News (code N) $ 400
Playperson (code P) $2000
Outdoors (code O) $ 900
Independent News (code I) $1200

Each ad is allowed 15 lines of print with a rate of $20.00 for each line in excess of 15 lines. Each ad is either black and white (code B) and subject to the base prices or is in color (code C) and subject to the following rates: three colors (code T), 40% increase over base; full color (code F), 60% increase over base.

Write a program to input Milt's choice of magazine (N, P, O, or I), the number of lines of print (integer), and either black and white (B) or color (C) with a choice of three colors (T) or full color (F). Output should include an appropriate title, all the information and costs used to compute the price of an ad, the total price of the ad, and finally, the total price of all ads.

28. Write a program that will add, subtract, multiply, and divide fractions. Input will consist of a single line representing a fraction arithmetic problem as follows: integer/integer operation integer/integer. For example, a line of input might be

```
2/3 + 1/2
```

Your program should do the following:

a. Check for division by zero.
b. Check for proper operation symbols.
c. Print the problem in its original form.
d. Print the answer.
e. Print all fractions in horizontal form.

Your answer need not be in lowest terms. For the sample input

```
2/3 + 1/2
```

sample output is

```
2      1      7
-- +  -- =  --
3      2      6
```

29. Write an interactive program that permits the user to print various recipes. Write a procedure for each recipe. After the user enters a one-letter identifier for the desired recipe, a switch statement should be used to call the appropriate function. Part of the code could be

```
cin >> selection;
switch (selection)
{
```

```
        case 'J':        jambalaya();
                         break;
        case 'S':        spaghetti();
                         break;
        case 'T':        tacos();
    }
```

30. The force of gravity is different for each of the nine planets in our solar system. For example, on Mercury it is only 0.38 times as strong as on Earth. Thus, if you weigh 100 pounds (on Earth), you would weigh only 38 pounds on Mercury. Write an interactive program that allows you to enter your Earth weight and your choice of planet to which you would like your weight converted. Output should be your weight on the desired planet together with the planet name. The screen message for input should include a menu for planet choice. Use a `switch` statement in the program for computation and output. The relative forces of gravity are
Earth 1.00
Jupiter 2.65
Mars 0.39
Mercury 0.38
Neptune 1.23
Pluto 0.05
Saturn 1.17
Uranus 1.05
Venus 0.78

31. Cramer's rule is a method for solving a system of linear equations. If you have two equations with variables x and y written as

$$ax + by = c$$
$$dx + ey = f$$

then the solution for x and y can be given as

$$x = \frac{\begin{vmatrix} cb \\ fe \end{vmatrix}}{\begin{vmatrix} ab \\ de \end{vmatrix}}$$

$$y = \frac{\begin{vmatrix} ac \\ df \end{vmatrix}}{\begin{vmatrix} ab \\ de \end{vmatrix}}$$

Using this notation,

$$\begin{vmatrix} ab \\ de \end{vmatrix}$$

is the determinant of the matrix
and is equal to $ae–bd$.

Write a complete program that will solve a system of two equations using Cramer's rule. Input will be all coefficients and constants in the system. Output will be the solution to the system. Typical output is

```
For the system of equations

x + 2y = 5
2x - y = 0

we have the solution

x = 1
y = 2
```

Use an `if...else` statement to guard against division by zero.

32. Contact a programmer and discuss the concept of robustness in a program. Prepare a report of your conversation for class. Your report should include a list of specific instances of how programmers make programs robust.

33. Conduct an unscientific survey of at least two people from each of the following groups: students in upper level computer science courses, instructors of computer science, and programmers working in industry. Your survey should attempt to ascertain the importance of and use of robustness at each level. Discuss the similarities and differences of your findings with those of other class members.

34. Selecting appropriate test data for a program that uses nested selection is a nontrivial task. Create diagrams that allow you to trace the flow of logic when nested selection is used. Use your diagrams to draw conclusions about minimal test data required to test all branches of a program that uses nested selection to various levels.

Repetition Statements

Chapter Outline

The previous chapter on selection introduced you to a control structure that takes advantage of a computer's ability to make choices. A second major control structure takes advantage of a computer's ability to repeat the same task many times. The control structures for selection and repetition allow us to specify any algorithm we need to solve a problem with a computer.

This chapter examines the different methods C++ permits for performing a process repeatedly. For example, as yet we cannot conveniently write a program that solves the simple problem of adding the integers from 1 to 100 or processing the grades of 30 students in a class. By the end of this chapter, you will be able to solve these problems three different ways. The three forms of repetition (loops) are

1. `for` <a definite number of times> <do an action>
2. `while` <condition is true> <do an action>
3. `do` <action> `while` <condition is true>

Each of these three loops contains the basic constructs necessary for repetition: A variable is assigned some value, the variable value changes at some point in the loop, and repetition continues until the value reaches some predetermined value. When the predetermined value (or Boolean condition) is reached, repetition is terminated and program control moves to the next executable statement.

■ 6.1 Classifying Loops

Pretest and Posttest Loops

A loop that uses a condition to control whether or not the body of the loop is executed before going through the loop is a *pretest* or *entrance-controlled loop*. The testing condition is the *pretest condition*. If the condition is `true`, the body of the loop is executed. If the condition is `false`, the program skips to the first line of code following the loop. The `for` loop and the `while` loop are pretest loops.

Objectives

a. to understand the difference between a pretest loop and a posttest loop
b. to understand what a fixed repetition loop is
c. to understand when to use a fixed repetition loop
d. to understand what a variable condition loop is

A loop that examines a Boolean expression after the loop body is executed is a *posttest* or *exit-controlled loop*. This is the `do...while` loop.

Fixed Repetition Versus Variable Condition Loops

Fixed repetition (iterated) loops are used when it can be determined in advance how often a segment of code needs to be repeated. For instance, you might know that you need a predetermined number of repetitions of a segment of code for a program that adds the integers from 1 to 100 or for a program that uses a fixed number of data lines, for example, game statistics for a team of 12 basketball players. The number of repetitions need not be constant. For example, a user might enter information during execution of a program that would determine how often a segment should be repeated. In this chapter, we will introduce a class of `for` loops that are fixed repetition loops.

Variable condition loops are needed to solve problems for which conditions change within the body of the loop. These conditions involve sentinel values, Boolean flags, arithmetic expressions, or end-of-line and end-of-file markers (see Chapter 7). A variable condition loop provides more power than a fixed repetition loop. The `while` and `do...while` loops are variable condition loops.

6.2 `for` Loops

Objectives

a. to understand how the loop control variable is used in a loop
b. to understand the flow of control when using a fixed repetition loop in a program
c. to use a `for` loop in a program
d. to use a `for` loop that counts down in a program

The `for` loop is a pretest loop. Although one can write variable condition `for` loops in C++, we will discuss only fixed repetition `for` loops. The typical form of a `for` loop is

```
for (<initialization expression>; <termination condition>;
   <update expression>) <statement>
```

In the following example, a `for` loop displays all of the numbers between 1 and 10:

```
for (i = 1; i <= 10; i = i + 1)
   cout << i << endl;
```

A `for` loop is considered a single executable statement. The information contained within the parentheses is referred to as the *heading* of the loop. The actions performed in the loop are referred to as the *body* of the loop.

The heading of a `for` loop consists of three parts:

1. *Initialization expression:* In fixed repetition `for` loops, this part sets a *control variable* to an initial value. This variable will control the number of times that the body of the loop is executed.
2. *Termination condition:* This part normally consists of a comparison of the control variable to a value. The body of the loop will execute while this condition is `true`.
3. *Update expression:* This part normally consists of a statement that makes the value of the control variable approach the value specified in the termination condition. In `for` loops that count up, this part increments the control variable by some value; in `for` loops that count down, this part decrements the control variable by some value.

The internal logic of a `for` loop that counts up is as follows:

1. The *control variable* is assigned an initial value in the initialization expression.
2. The termination condition is evaluated.

3. If the termination condition is `true`, then (a) the body of the loop is executed and (b) the update expression is evaluated.
4. If the termination condition is `false`, then control of the program is transferred to the first statement following the loop.

As you can see, a `for` loop proceeds by *counting up* from a *lower bound* to an *upper bound*. A flow diagram for this example is given in Figure 6.1.

We have discussed only a typical form of the `for` loop, one that counts up. We will see variations on this form, such as `for` loops that count from an upper bound down to a lower bound or count by some factor other than 1, in later sections of this chapter.

The Increment and Decrement Operators

C++ has a pair of operators that increment or decrement variables. These operators are very concise and handy to use in loops. The increment operator, ++, precedes or follows a variable in a complete C++ statement. For example, the statement

```
++x;
```

would increment (add 1 to) the variable `x`. It has the same effect as the assignment statement

```
x = x + 1;
```

Thus, the example `for` statement could be rewritten more concisely as

```
for (i = 1; i <= 10; ++i)
   cout << i << endl;
```

Figure 6.1

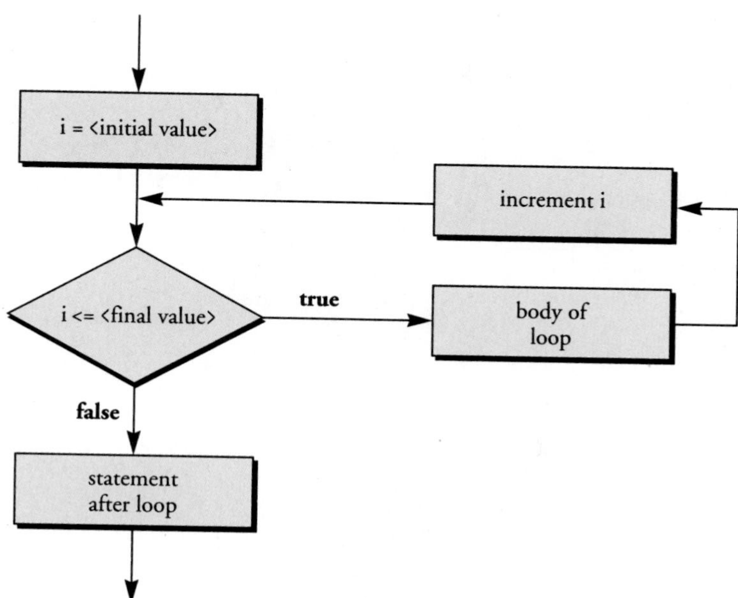

The decrement operator, `--`, precedes or follows a variable in a complete C++ statement. The operator has the effect of subtracting 1 from the variable and storing the result in it.

When these operators precede a variable, they are called *prefix operators;* when they follow a variable, they are called *postfix operators*. We use the prefix form in the examples in this book.

Accumulators

The problem of adding the integers from 1 to 100 needs only one statement in the body of the loop. This problem can be solved by code that constructs an *accumulator.* An accumulator merely sums values of some variable. In the following code, the loop control variable, `lcv`, successively assumes the values 1, 2, 3, . . . , 100.

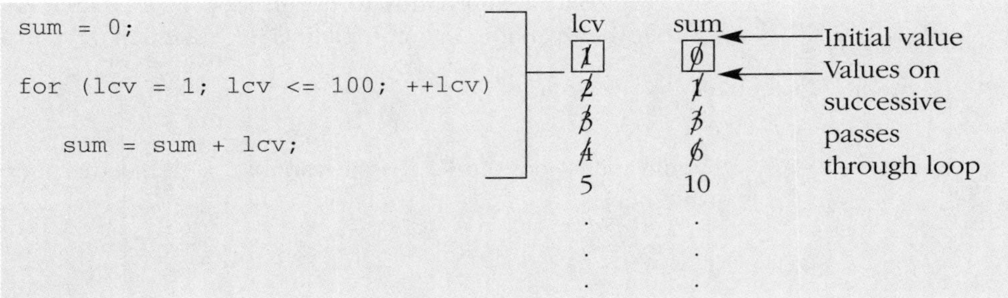

This program segment contains an example of graphic documentation. Throughout the text, these insets will be used to help illustrate what the code is actually doing. The insets are not part of the program; they merely show what some specific code is trying to accomplish.

To see how `sum` accumulates these values, let us trace through the code for several values of `lcv`. Initially, `sum` is set to zero by

```
sum = 0;
```

When `lcv` is assigned the value 1,

```
sum = sum + lcv;
```

produces

1	∅ 1
lcv	sum

For `lcv = 2`, we get

2	1̸ 3
lcv	sum

`lcv = 3` yields

3	3̸ 6
lcv	sum

Note that `sum` has been assigned a value equal to 1 + 2 + 3. The final value for `lcv` is 100. Once this value has been added to `sum`, the value of `sum` will be 5050, which is the sum of 1 + 2 + 3 + . . . + 100. Accumulators are frequently used in loops. The general form for this use is

```
accumulator = 0;
for (lcv = <initial value>; lcv <= <final value>; ++lcv)
   accumulator = accumulator + lcv;
```

Scope of a Loop Control Variable

In general, the loop control variable of a `for` loop must be declared before it is used in the loop. In accordance with the scope rules of C++, the scope of this variable will be the program block within which it is declared. However, on many occasions, a loop control variable will only be used within a loop. In these cases, using a variable whose scope extends beyond a loop opens the program to serious side effects. To minimize these, the loop control variable can be declared when it is initialized within the loop. The visibility of the variable will be restricted to the body of the loop. For example, the following loop performs the equivalent task of our first example, but its loop control variable cannot be accessed outside the body of the loop:

```
// References to i are not allowed here
// (i has not been declared yet).

for (int i = 1; i <= 10; ++i)
   cout << i << endl;

// References to i are not allowed here, either.
```

In general, it is safe programming practice to restrict the scope of variables to only those areas of a program in which it is necessary to access them.

Some comments concerning the syntax and form of `for` loops are now necessary:

1. The loop control variable must be declared as a variable. We will usually declare this variable as part of the loop heading.
2. The loop control variable can be any valid identifier.
3. The loop control variable can be used within the loop just as any other variable except that the value of the variable should not be changed by the statements in the body of the loop.
4. The initial and final values can be constants or variable expressions with appropriate values.
5. The loop will be repeated for each value of the loop control variable in the range indicated by the initial and final values.

At this point, you might try writing some test programs to see what happens if you do not follow these rules. Then consider the following examples, which illustrate the features of `for` loops.

Example 6.1 Write a segment of code to list the integers from 1 to 10 together with their squares and cubes. This can be done by

```
for (int j = 1; j <= 10; ++j)
   cout << j << setw(10) << j * j << setw(8) << j * j * j << endl;
```

This segment produces

```
1              1       1
2              4       8
3              9      27
4             16      64
5             25     125
6             36     216
7             49     343
8             64     512
9             81     729
10           100    1000
```

Example 6.2 Write a `for` loop to produce the following design:

```
    **
   *  *
  *    *
 *      *
*        *
```

Assuming the first asterisk is in column 20, the following loop will produce the desired result. Note carefully how the output is formatted.

```
for (int j = 1; j <= 5; ++j)
   cout << setw(21 - j) << '*' << setw(2 * j - 1) << '*' << endl;
```

Example 6.3 When computing compound interest, it is necessary to evaluate the quantity $(1 + r)^n$ where r is the interest rate for one time period and n is the number of time periods. A `for` loop can be used to perform this computation. If we declare a variable `base`, this can be solved by

```
base = 1;

for (int j = 1; j <= n; ++j)


   base = base * (1 + r);
```

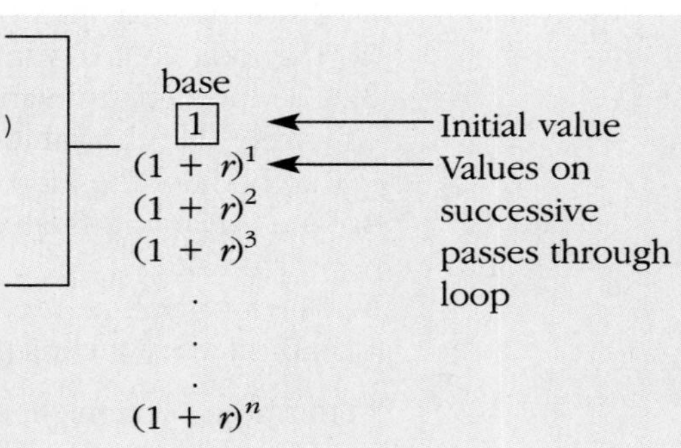

base

1 ← Initial value

$(1 + r)^1$ ← Values on successive passes through loop

$(1 + r)^2$

$(1 + r)^3$

.

.

.

$(1 + r)^n$

`for` Loops That Count Down

A second kind of pretest, fixed repetition loop is a `for` loop that counts down. This loop does exactly what you expect; it is identical to a `for` loop that counts up, except the loop control variable is decreased by 1 instead of increased by 1 each time through the loop. This is referred to as a *decrement*. The test is loop control value >= final value. The loop terminates when the loop control value is less than the final value. The decrement operator is used to adjust the loop control variable on each pass through the loop. Proper form and syntax for a loop of this type are the same as that of `for` loops that count up; however, the contents of the statements within the loop heading will be the opposite of those `for` loops that count up:

1. The initialization part sets the control variable to an upper bound rather than a lower bound.
2. The termination part consists of a comparison to see whether the control variable is greater than or equal to a value that is the lower bound of the loop.
3. The update part decrements rather than increments the control variable by some value.

We will now consider an example of a `for` loop that counts down.

Example 6.4 Illustrate the control values of a `for` loop that counts down by writing the control value during each pass through the loop. The segment of code for this could be

```
for (int k = 20; k >= 15; --k)
   cout << "K =" << setw(4) << k << endl;
```

and the output is

```
K =   20
K =   19
K =   18
K =   17
K =   16
K =   15
```

Loops That Count by Factors Other Than 1

Thus far, we have examined `for` loops that count up or count down. They do this by incrementing or decrementing a loop control variable by 1. There are some occasions when we would like to count by a factor of 2 or more. One example is the problem of adding all of the even numbers between a lower and an upper bound. For this problem, the loop should count up or down by twos. The following example solves this problem for the numbers 2 through 10 by incrementing the loop control variable by 2 in an assignment expression:

```
sum = 0;
for (int j = 2; j <= 10; j = j + 2)
   sum = sum + j;
cout << sum << endl;
```

Writing Style for Loops

As you can see, writing style is an important consideration when writing code using loops. There are three features to consider. First, the body of the loop should be indented. Compare the following two pieces of code:

```
for (int j = 1; j <= 10; ++j)
{
   cin >> num >> amt;
   total1 = total1 + amt;
   total2 = total2 + num;
   cout << "The number is" << setw(6) << num << endl;
}
cout << "The total amount is"
     << setiosflags(ios::fixed | ios::showpoint)
     << setw(8) << setprecision(2) << total1 << endl;
average = total2 / 10.0;

for (int j = 1; j <= 10; ++j)
{
cin >> num >> amt;
total1 = total1 + amt;
total2 = total2 + num;
cout << "The number is" << setw(6) << num << endl;
}
cout << "The total amount is"
     << setiosflags(ios::fixed | ios::showpoint)
     << setw(8) << setprecision(2) << total1 << endl;
average = total2 / 10.0;
```

The indenting in the first segment makes it easier to determine what is contained in the body of the loop than it is in the second segment, without any indenting.

Second, blank lines can be used before and after a loop for better readability. Compare the following:

```
cin >> x >> y;
cout << setiosflags(ios::fixed | ios::showpoint);
cout << setw(6) << setprecision(2) << x << setw(6) << y << endl;
cout << endl;

for  (int j = -3; j <= 5; ++j)
   cout << setw(3) << j << setw(5) << "*" << endl;

sum = sum + x;
cout << setw(10) << setprecision(2) << sum << endl;

cin >> x >> y;
cout << setiosflags(ios::fixed | ios::showpoint);
cout << setw(6) << setprecision(2) << x << setw(6) << y << endl;
cout << endl;
for  (int j = -3; j <= 5; ++j)
     cout << setw(3) << j << setw(5) << "*" << endl;
sum = sum + x;
cout << setw(10) << setprecision(2) << sum << endl;
```

Again, the first segment is a bit clearer because it emphasizes that the entire loop is a single executable statement and makes it easy to locate the loop.

Third, comments used within loops make them more readable. In particular, a comment could accompany the end of a compound statement that is the body of a loop. The general form for this is

```
// Get a test score
for (int j = 1; j <= 50; ++j)
{
    .
    . (body of the loop)
    .
} // end of for loop
```

We close this section with an example that uses a `for` loop to solve a problem.

Example 6.5 Suppose you have been asked to write a segment of code to compute the test average for each of 30 students in a class and the overall class average. Data for each student consist of the student's initials and four test scores.

A first-level pseudocode development is

1. Print a heading
2. Initialize total
3. Process data for each of 30 students
4. Compute class average
5. Print a summary

A `for` loop could be used to implement step 3. The step could first be refined to

3. Process data for each of 30 students
   3.1 get data for a student
   3.2 compute average
   3.3 add to total
   3.4 print student data

The code for this step is

```
for (int lcv = 1; lcv <= CLASS_SIZE; ++lcv)
{
   cout << "Enter three initials and press <Enter>. ";
   cin >> init1 >> init2 >> init3;
   cout << "Enter four test scores and press <Enter>. ";
   cin >> score1 >> score2 >> score3 >> score4;
   average = (score1 + score2 + score3 + score4) / 4.0;
   total = total + average;
   cout << endl;
   cout << setw(4) << init1 << init2 << init3;
   cout << setw(6) <<score1 << setw(6) << score2
        << setw(6) << score3 << setw(6) <<score4;
   cout << setprecision(2) << setw(10) << average
        << endl;
}
```

`for` Loops with Strings

A `for` loop can be used to examine or modify individual characters in a string. The programmer can access a character at a given position by using the operator `[]`, as in the following example code segment:

A NOTE OF INTEREST

Charles Babbage

The first person to propose the concept of the modern computer was Charles Babbage (1791–1871), a man truly ahead of his time. Babbage was a professor of mathematics at Cambridge University, as well as an inventor. As a mathematician, he realized the time-consuming and boring nature of constructing mathematical tables (squares, logarithms, sines, cosines, and so on). Because the calculators developed by Pascal and Leibniz could not provide the calculations required for these more complex tables, Babbage proposed the idea of building a machine that could compute the various properties of numbers, accurate to 20 digits.

With a grant from the British government, he designed and partially built a simple model of the difference engine. However, the lack of technology in the 1800s prevented him from making a working model. Discouraged by his inability to materialize his ideas, Babbage imagined a better version, which would be a general-purpose, problem-solving machine—the analytical engine.

The similarities between the analytical engine and the modern computer are amazing. Babbage's analytical engine, which was intended to be a steam-powered device, had four components:

1. A "mill" that manipulated and computed the data
2. A "store" that held the data
3. An "operator" of the system that carried out instructions
4. A separate device that entered data and received processed information via punched cards.

After spending many years sketching variations and improvements for this new model, Babbage received some assistance in 1842 from Ada Augusta Byron (see the next Note of Interest).

```
apstring str = "Hello there";
cout << str[0];                    // Outputs 'H' from position 0
cout << str[str.length() - 1];     // Outputs 'e' from the last position
str[1] = 'a';                      // Changes 'e' to 'a' at position 1
cout << str;                       // Outputs "Hallo there"
```

Note that the positions in a string are numbered from 0 to the length of the string minus 1. Now, suppose we wanted to convert the letters in a string to uppercase. To do this, we would write a `for` loop that would visit each character in the string and convert it to uppercase, using the `ctype` library function `toupper`. The next code segment shows the use of this loop:

```
#include <ctype.h>

apstring str = "Hello there";
for (int i = 0; i < str.length(); ++i)
   str[i] = toupper(str[i]);
cout << str;                              // Outputs "HELLO THERE"
```

Note that the value of `i` for the first pass of the loop is 0, the first position in the string. The value of `i` for the final pass of the loop is the length of the string minus 1, the last position in the string.

Exercises 6.2

1. What is the output from each of the following segments of code?

a.
```
for (k = 3; k <= 8; ++k)
   cout << setw(k) << * << endl;
```
b.
```
for (j = 1; j <= 10; ++j)
   cout << setw(4) << j << ":" << setw(5)  << (10 - j)
        << endl;
```
c.
```
a = 2;
for (j = (3 * 2 - 4); j <= 10 * a; ++j)
   cout << setw(4) << j << endl;
```
d.
```
for (j = 50; j >= 30; --j)
   cout << setw(5) << (51 - j) << endl;
```

2. Write a test program for each of the following:

a. Illustrate what happens when the loop control variable is assigned a value inside the loop.

b. Demonstrate how an accumulator works. For this test program, sum the integers from 1 to 10. Your output should show each partial sum as it is assigned to the accumulator.

3. Write segments of code using a loop that counts up and a loop that counts down to produce the following designs. Start each design in column 2.

a.
```
 *
 *
 *
 *
```

b.
```
 ***
  ***
   ***
    ***
     ***
      ***
       ***
        ***
```

c.
```
     *
    * *
   *   *
  *     *
 ***   ***
   *   *
   *   *
   *****
```

d.

```
*********
 *******
  *****
   ***
    *
```

4. Which of the following segments of code do you think accomplishes its intended task? For those that do not, what changes would you suggest?

a.

```
for (k = 1; k <= 5; ++k);
   cout << k << endl;
```

b.

```
sum = 0;
for (j = 1; j <= 10; ++j)
   cin >>a;
sum = sum + a;
cout << setw(15) << sum << endl;
```

c.

```
sum = 0;
for (j = -3; j <= 3; ++j)
   sum = sum + j;
```

d.

```
a = 0;
for (k = 1; k <= 10; ++k)
{
   a = a + k;
   cout << setw(5) << k << setw(5) << a << setw(5) << (a + k) << endl;
}
cout << setw(5) << k << setw(5) << a << setw(5) << (a + k) << endl;
```

5. Produce each of the following outputs using a loop that counts up and a loop that counts down.

a.

```
1 2 3 4 5
```

b.

```
*
 *
  *
   *
    *
```

6. Rewrite the following segment of code using a loop that counts down to produce the same result.

```
sum = 0;
for (k = 1; k <= 4; ++k)
{
   cout << setw(21 + k) << endl;
   sum = sum + k;
}
```

7. Rewrite the following segment of code using a loop that counts up to produce the same result.

```
for (j = 10; j >= 2; --j)
    cout << setw(j) << j << endl;
```

8. Write a complete program that produces a table showing the temperature equivalents in degrees Fahrenheit and degrees Celsius. Let the user enter the starting and ending values. Use the formula

```
celsTemp = 5.0/9.0 (farenTemp - 32.0)
```

9. Write a complete program to produce a chart consisting of the multiples of 5 from –50 to 50 together with the squares and cubes of these numbers. Use a function to print a suitable heading and user-defined functions for square and cube.
10. The formula $A = P(1 + R)^N$ can be used to compute the amount due (A) when a principal (P) has been borrowed at a monthly rate (R) for a period of N months. Write a complete program that will read in the principal, annual interest rate (divide by 12 for monthly rate), and number of months and then produce a chart that shows how much will be due at the end of each month.
11. Write a function that converts a given string parameter to uppercase.

6.3 while Loops

Objectives

a. to understand when variable repetition should be used in a program
b. to understand why `while` is a variable repetition loop
c. to understand the flow of control when using a `while` loop
d. to use a counter in a `while` loop
e. to use a `while` loop in a program

In Section 6.2, we studied `for` loops in which the body of the loop is repeated a fixed number of times. For some problems, this kind of loop is inappropriate because a segment of code may need to be repeated an unknown number of times. The condition controlling the loop must be variable rather than constant. C++ provides two repetition statements that are especially well suited to handle variable control conditions, one with a pretest condition and one with a posttest condition.

A useful pretest loop with variable conditions in C++ is the `while` loop. The condition controlling the loop is a Boolean expression written between parentheses. The correct form and syntax for such a loop are

```
while ( <Boolean expression> )
    <statement>
```

Note that the parentheses enclosing the Boolean expression are required. The flow diagram for a `while` loop is given in Figure 6.2. Program control, when using a `while` loop, is in order as follows:

1. The loop condition is examined.
2. If the loop condition is `true`, the entire body of the loop is executed before another check is made.
3. If the loop condition is `false`, control is transferred to the first statement following the loop. For example,

```
a = 1;
while (a < 0)
```

continued

```
{
   num = 5;
   cout << num << endl;
   a = a + 10;
}
cout << a << endl;
```

produces the single line of output

```
1
```

Before analyzing the components of the `while` statement, we should consider a short example.

Figure 6.2

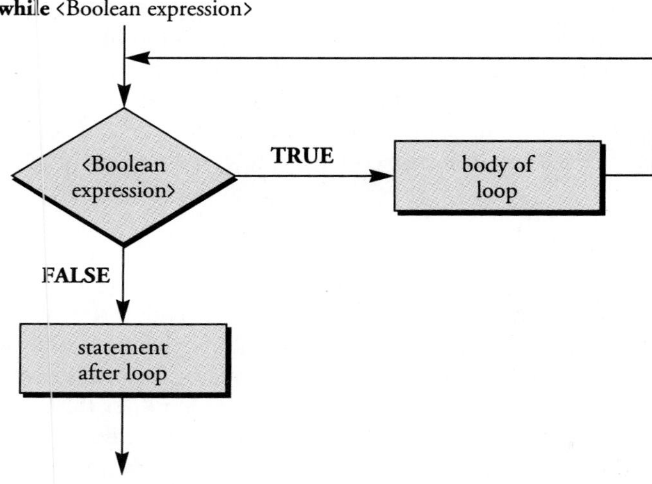

Example 6.6 This example prints some powers of 2.

```
power2 = 1;

while (power2 < 100)

{

   cout << setw(2) << power2 << endl;

   power2 = power2 * 2;

}
```

power2
1 ← Initial value
2^1 ← Value on successive passes through loop
2^2
2^3 .
2^4 .
2^5 .
2^6
2^7 ← `while` condition no longer `TRUE`

The output from this segment of code is

```
1
2
4
```

```
 8
16
32
64
```

With this example in mind, let us examine the general form for using a `while` loop.

1. The condition can be any expression that has a Boolean value. Standard examples include relational operators and Boolean variables; thus, each of the following would be appropriate:

```
while (j < 10)
while (a < b)
while (! done)
```

2. The Boolean expression must have a value prior to entering the loop.
3. The body of the loop can be a simple statement or a compound statement.
4. Provision must be made for appropriately changing the loop control condition in the body of the loop. If no such changes are made, the following could happen:
   a. If the loop condition is `true` and no changes are made, a condition called an *infinite loop* is caused. For example,

```
a = 1;
while (a > 0)
{
    num = 5;
    cout<< num << endl;
}
cout << a << endl;
```

   The condition `a > 0` is `true`, the body is executed, and the condition is retested. However, because the condition is not changed within the loop body, it will always be `true` and will cause an infinite loop. It will not produce a compilation error, but when you run the program, the output will be a column of fives.

   b. If the loop condition is `true` and changes are made, but the condition never becomes `false`, you again have an infinite loop. An example of this is

```
power3 = 1;
while (power3 != 100)
{
    cout << power3 << endl;
    power3 = power3 * 3
}
```

   Since the variable `power3` never is assigned the value 100, the condition `power3 != 100` is always `true`. At run time, the computer will continue to multiply `power3` by 3 until an integer overflow error occurs. In general, it is best to avoid the use of `!=` in the Boolean expression of a count-controlled loop.

Sentinel Values

The Boolean expression of a variable control loop is frequently controlled by a *sentinel value.* For example, a program might require the user to enter numeric data. When there are no more data, the user will be instructed to enter a special (sentinel) value. This then signifies the end of the process. Example 6.7 illustrates the use of such a sentinel.

Example 6.7 Here we write a segment of code that allows the user to enter a set of test scores and then print the average score.

```
numScores = 0;
sum = 0;
cout << "Enter a score and press <Enter>, -999 to quit. ";
cin >> score;
while (score != -999)
{
   numScores = numScores + 1;
   sum = sum + score;
   cout << "Enter a score and press <Enter>, -999 to quit. ";
   cin >> score;
}
if (numScores > 0)
{
   average = sum / double(numScores);
   cout << endl;
   cout << "The average of" << setw(4) << numScores << " scores is"
        << setiosflags(ios::fixed | ios::showpoint)
        << setw(6) << setprecision(2) << average << endl;
}
else
    cout << "No scores were entered" << endl;
```

Writing Style

Writing style for `while` loops should be similar to that adopted for `for` loops; that is, indenting, skipped lines, and comments should all be used to enhance readability.

Using Counters

Because `while` loops can be repeated a variable number of times, it is a common practice to count the number of times the loop body is executed. This is accomplished by declaring an appropriately named integer variable, initializing it to zero before the loop, and then incrementing it by 1 each time through the loop. For example, if you use `count` for your variable name, Example 6.6 (in which we printed some powers of 2) could be modified to

```
count = 0;
power2 = 1;
while (power2 < 100)
{
   cout << setw(2) << power2 << endl;
```

```
    power2 = power2 * 2;
    count = count + 1;
}

cout << "There are" << setw(4) << count << " powers of 2 less than 100."
     << endl;
```

The output from this segment of code is

```
  1
  2
  4
  8
 16
 32
 64

There are 7 powers of 2 less than 100.
```

Although the process is tedious, it is instructive to trace the values of variables through a loop where a *counter* is used. Therefore, let us consider the segment of code we have just seen. Before the loop is entered, we have

0	1
`count`	`power2`

The loop control is `power2 < 100` (`1 < 100`). Since this is `true`, the loop body is executed and the new values become

1	2
`count`	`power2`

Prior to each successive time through the loop, the condition `power2 < 100` is checked. Thus, the loop produces the following sequence of values:

count	power2
1	2
2	4
3	8
4	16
5	32
6	64
7	128

Although `power2` is 128, the remainder of the loop is executed before checking the loop condition. Once a loop is entered, it is executed completely before the loop control condition is reexamined. Because `128 < 100` is `false`, control is transferred to the statement following the loop.

Compound Conditions

All previous examples and illustrations of `while` loops have used simple Boolean expressions. However, because any Boolean expression can be used as a loop control condition, compound Boolean expressions can also be used. For example,

```
cin >> a >> b;
while ((a > 0) && (b > 0))
{
   cout << a << " " << b << endl;
   a = a - 5;
   b = b - 3;
}
```

will go through the body of the loop only when the Boolean expression `(a > 0) && (b > 0)` is `true`. Thus, if the values of `a` and `b` obtained from the keyboard are

```
17  8
```

the output from this segment of code is

```
17 8
12 5
7 2
```

Compound Boolean expressions can be as complex as you wish to make them. However, if several conditions are involved, the program can become difficult to read and debug; therefore, you may wish to redesign your solution to avoid this problem.

Exercises 6.3

1. Compare and contrast `for` loops with `while` loops.
2. Write a test program that illustrates what happens when you have an infinite loop.
3. What is the output from each of the following segments of code?

a.
```
k = 1;
while (k <= 10)
{
   cout << k << endl;
   k = k + 1;
}
```

b.
```
a = 1;
while (17 % a < 5)
{
   cout << a << 17 % a << endl;
   a = a + 1;
}
```

c.
```
a = 2;
b = 50;
while (a < b)
   a = a * 3;
cout << a << b << endl;
```

d.
```
count = 0;
sum = 0;
while (count < 5)
{
   count = count + 1;
```

A NOTE OF INTEREST

Ada Augusta Byron

Ada Augusta Byron, Countess of Lovelace (1815–1852), became interested in Charles Babbage's efforts when she was translating a paper on the analytical engine from French to English. Upon meeting Babbage, she began the task of writing an original paper. Through the process, she documented Babbage's ideas and made it possible to understand Babbage's original intentions. Over time, she became a full collaborator on the project, correcting some errors and suggesting the use of the binary system of storage rather than the decimal.

Lady Lovelace's most important contribution was her concept of a loop. She observed that a repetition of a sequence of instructions often was necessary to perform a single calculation. Thus, she discovered that by using a single set of cards and a conditional jump facility, the calculation could be performed with a fraction of the effort. This idea has earned her the distinction of being the first programmer. In honor of her role as the first computer programmer, the U.S. Department of Defense named its computer language Ada.

```
  sum = sum + count;
  cout << "The partial sum is" << setw(4) << sum << endl;
}
cout << "The count is" << setw(4) << count << endl;
```

e.

```
x = 3.0;
y = 2.0;
while (x * y < 100)
   x = x * y;
cout << setprecision(2) << setw(10) << x << setw(10) << y << endl;
```

4. Indicate which of the following are infinite loops and explain why they are infinite.

a.
```
j = 1;
while (j < 10)
   cout << j;
   j = j + 1;
```

b.
```
a = 2;
while (a < 20)
{
   cout << a << endl;
   a = a * 2;
}
```

c.
```
a = 2;
while (a != 20)
{
   cout << a << endl;
   a = a * 2;
}
```

d.
```
b = 15;
while (b / 3 == 5)
{
   cout << b << b / 5 << endl;
   b = b - 1;
}
```

5. Write a `while` loop for each of the following tasks:
   a. Print a positive real number, `num`, and then print successive values where each value is 0.5 less than the previous value. The list should continue as long as values to be printed are positive.
   b. Print a list of squares of positive integers as long as the difference between consecutive squares is less than 50.
6. Write a segment of code that reads a positive integer and prints a list of powers of the integer that are less than 10,000.

6.4 `do...while` Loops

Objectives

a. to understand that a `do...while` loop is a posttest loop
b. to understand the flow of control using a `do...while` loop
c. to use a `do...while` loop in a program
d. to use `do...while` loops with multiple conditions

The previous two sections discussed two kinds of repetition. We looked at fixed repetition using `for` loops and variable repetition using `while` loops. C++ provides a second form of variable repetition, a `do...while` loop, which is a *posttest* or *exit-controlled loop*. The basic form and syntax for a `do...while` loop are

```
do
{
   <statement>
} while (<Boolean expression>);
```

A flow diagram for a `do...while` loop is given in Figure 6.3. Prior to examining this form, let us consider the following fragment of code:

```
count = 0;
do
{
   count = count + 1;
   cout << count << endl;
} while (count < 5);
cout << setw(10) <<"All done" << endl;
```

The output for this fragment is

```
1
2
3
4
5
All done
```

With this example in mind, the following comments concerning the use of a `do...while` loop are in order.

1. The Boolean expression must have a value before it is used at the end of the loop.
2. The loop must be entered at least once because the Boolean expression is not evaluated until after the loop body has been executed.

Figure 6.3

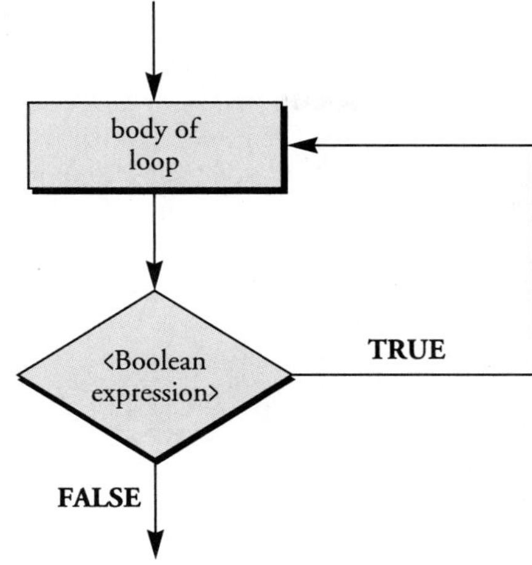

3. When the Boolean expression is evaluated, if it is `true`, control is transferred back to the top of the loop; if it is `false`, control is transferred to the next program statement.
4. Provision must be made for changing values inside the loop so that the Boolean expression used to control the loop will eventually be `false`. If this is not done, you will have an infinite loop, as shown here:

```
j = 0;
do
{
   j = j + 2;
   cout << j << endl;
} while (j != 5);
```

5. Writing style for using `do...while` loops should be consistent with your style for other loop structures.

There is one important difference between `while` and `do...while` loops. A `do...while` loop must be executed at least once, but a `while` loop can be skipped if the initial value of the Boolean expression is `false`. Because of this, `do...while` loops are generally used less frequently than `while` loops.

Example 6.8 An early method of approximating square roots was the Newton-Raphson method. This method consisted of starting with an approximation and then getting successively better approximations until the desired degree of accuracy was achieved.

Writing code for this method, each `newGuess` is defined to be

```
newGuess = 1.0/2.0 * (oldGuess + number / oldGuess)
```

Thus, if the number entered was 34 and the first approximation was 5, the second approximation would be

```
1/2 * (5 + 34 / 5)  (5.9)
```

and the third approximation would be

```
1/2 * (5.9 + 34 / 5.9)   (5.83135593)
```

Let's see how a `do...while` loop can be used to obtain successively better approximations until a desired degree of accuracy is reached. Assume `number` contains the number whose square root we wish to approximate, `oldGuess` contains a first approximation, and `DESIRED_ACCURACY` is a defined constant. A loop used in the solution of this problem is

```
cout << setprecision(8) << setw(12) << newGuess << endl;
do
{
   oldGuess = newGuess;
   newGuess = 1/2 * (oldGuess + number / oldGuess);
   cout << setw(12) << newGuess << endl << endl;
} while (abs(newGuess - oldGuess) >= DESIRED_ACCURACY);
```

If `DESIRED_ACCURACY` is 0.0001, number is 34, and `newGuess` is originally 5, the output from this segment is

```
5.00000000

5.90000000

5.83135593

5.83095191

5.83095189
```

Example 6.9 Interactive programming frequently requires the use of a menu to give the user a choice of options. For example, suppose you want a menu like this one:

```
Which of the following recipes do you wish to see?

(T)acos
(J)ambalaya
(G)umbo
(Q)uit

Enter the first letter and press <Enter>.
```

This screen message could be written as a function `menu`, and the main function could use a `do . . . while` loop as follows:

```
char selection;
do
{
   menu();
   cin >> selection;
   switch (selection)
   {
      case 'T' :  tacos();
```

```
                    break;
        case 'J' :  jambalaya();
                    break;
        case 'G' :  gumbo();
                    break;
        case 'Q' :  goodbyeMessage();
    }
} while (selection != 'Q');
```

where `tacos`, `jambalaya`, `gumbo`, and `goodbyeMessage` are each separate functions with appropriate messages.

Compound Conditions

The Boolean expression used with a `do...while` loop can be as complex as you choose to make it. However, as with while loops, if the expression gets too complicated, you might enhance program readability and design by redesigning the algorithm to use simpler expressions.

Choosing the Correct Loop

"Which type of loop should I use?" is a question often faced by programmers. A partial answer is easy. If a loop is to be repeated a predetermined number of times during execution, a `for` loop is preferable. If the number of repetitions is not known, one of the variable control loops is preferable.

The more difficult part of the answer is deciding which variable control loop is appropriate. Simply stated, if a control check is needed before the loop is executed, use a `while` loop. If the check is needed at the end of the loop, use a `do...while` loop. Remember, however, that a `do...while` loop must always be executed at least once. Therefore, if there is a possibility that the loop will never be executed, a `while` loop must be used. For example, when reading data (especially from files, see Chapter 7), if there is a possibility of no data, a `while` loop must be used with a prompting input statement or other control check prior to the loop. Thus, you could have

```
int score;
cout <<"Enter a score, -999 to quit. ";
cin << score;
while (score != -999)
{
    .
    . <process data>
    .
  cout << "Enter a score, -999 to quit. ";
  cin << score;
}
```

In the event either variable control loop can be used, the problem itself might help with the decision. Does the process need to be repeated until something happens, or does the process continue as long as (while) some condition is true? If either of these is apparent, use the code that most accurately reflects the solution to the problem.

Data Validation

Variable condition loops can be used to make programs more robust. In particular, suppose you are writing an interactive program that expects positive integers entered from the keyboard, with a sentinel value of –999 entered when you wish to quit. You can guard against bad data by using the following:

```
int num;
do
{
   cout << "Enter a positive integer; <-999> to quit. ";
   cin >> num;
} while ((num > 0) && (num != -999));
```

This process of examining data prior to its use in a program is referred to as *data validation,* and loops are useful for such validation. A second example of using a loop for this purpose follows.

Example 6.10 One problem associated with interactive programs is guarding against typing errors. This example illustrates how a `do...while` loop can be used to avoid having something entered other than the anticipated responses. Specifically, suppose users of an interactive program are asked to indicate whether or not they wish to continue by entering either a "Y" or "N". The screen message could be

```
Do you wish to continue? <Y or N>
```

You wish to allow any of 'Y', 'y', 'N', or 'n' to be used as an appropriate response. Any other entry is considered an error. This can be accomplished by the following:

```
bool goodResponse;
char response;
do
{
   cout << "Do you wish to continue? <Y or N> ";
   cin >> response;
   goodResponse = (response == 'Y') || (response == 'y') ||
                  (response == 'N') || (response == 'n');
} while (! goodResponse);
```

Any response other than those permitted as good data ('Y', 'y', 'N', 'n') results in `goodResponse` being `false` and the loop being executed again.

Exercises 6.4

1. Explain the difference between a pretest loop and a posttest loop.
2. Indicate what the output will be from each of the following code fragments.

a.
```
a = 0;
b = 10;
do
{
   a = a + 1;
   b = b - 1;
   cout << a << b << endl;
} while (a <= b);
```

b.
```
power = 1;
do
{
   power = power * 2;
   cout << power << endl;
} while (power <= 100);
```

c.
```
j = 1;
do
{
   cout << j << endl;
   j = j + 1;
} while (j <= 10);
```

d.
```
a = 1;
do
{
   cout << a << 17 % a << endl;
   a = a + 1;
} while (17 % a != 5);
```

3. Indicate which of the following are infinite loops and explain why.

a.
```
j = 1;
do
{
   cout << j << endl;
} while (j <= 10);
j = j + 1;
```

b.
```
a = 2;
do
{
   cout << a << endl;
   a = a * 2;
} while (a <= 20);
```

c.
```
a = 2;
do
{
   cout << a << endl;
   a = a * 2;
} while (a != 20);
```

d.
```
b = 15;
do
{
   cout << b << b / 5 << endl;
   b = b - 1;
} while (b / 3 >= 5);
```

4. Write a `do...while` loop for each of the following tasks:

a. Print a positive real number, `num`, and then print successive values where each value is 0.5 less than the previous value. The list should continue as long as values to be printed are positive.

b. Print a list of squares of positive integers as long as the difference between consecutive squares is less than 50.

5. Discuss whether or not a priming input is needed before a `do...while` loop that is used to get data.
6. Give an example of a situation that would require a predetermined number of repetitions.
7. In mathematics and science, many applications require a certain level or degree of accuracy obtained by successive approximations. Explain how the process of reaching the desired level of accuracy relates to loops in C++.
8. Write a program that utilizes the algorithm for approximating a square root as shown in Example 6.8. Let the defined accuracy be 0.0001. Input should consist of a number whose square root is desired. Your program should guard against bad data entries (negatives and zero). Output should include a list of approximations and a check of your final approximation.
9. Compare and contrast the three repetition structures previously discussed in this chapter.

6.5 Loop Verification

Objectives

a. to understand how input assertions and output assertions can be used to verify loops
b. to understand how loop invariants and loop variants can be used to verify loops

Loop verification is the process of guaranteeing that a loop performs its intended task. Such verification is part of program testing and correctness to which we referred in Chapter 5. Some work has been done on constructing formal proofs to determine if loops are "correct." We now examine a modified version of loop verification; a complete treatment of the issue will be the topic of subsequent coursework.

Preconditions and Postconditions with Loops

Preconditions and postconditions can be used with loops. Loop preconditions are referred to as *input assertions*. They state what can be expected to be `true` before the loop is entered. Loop postconditions are referred to as *output assertions*. They state what can be expected to be `true` when the loop is exited.

To illustrate input and output assertions, we consider the mathematical problem of summing the proper divisors of a positive integer. For example, we have these integers:

Integer	Proper Divisors	Sum
6	1, 2, 3	6
9	1, 3	4
12	1, 2, 3, 4, 6	16

As part of a program that will have a positive integer as input and as output will have a determination of whether the integer is perfect (sum = integer), abundant (sum > integer), or deficient (sum < integer), it is necessary to sum the divisors. The following loop performs this task:

```
divisorSum = 0;
for (trialDivisor = 1; trialDivisor <= num / 2; ++trialDivisor)
   if (num % trialDivisor == 0)
      divisorSum = divisorSum + trialDivisor;
```

An input assertion for this loop is

```
Precondition:       1. num is a positive integer.
                    2. divisorSum = 0.
```

An output assertion is

```
Postcondition: divisorSum is the sum of all proper divisors of num.
```

When these are placed with the previous code, we have

```
divisorSum = 0;
assert((num > 0) && (divisorSum > 0));
for (trialDivisor = 1; trialDivisor <= num / 2; ++trialDivisor)
   if (num % trialDivisor == 0)
      divisorSum = divisorSum + trialDivisor;
// Postcondition: divisorSum is the sum of all proper divisors of num.
```

Note that we pass the precondition to the `assert` function of C++ so that the run-time system actually establishes the truth of that assertion. However, we cannot do this with the postcondition because the sum of all the proper divisors of a number is just what we are computing in the `for` loop!

Invariant and Variant Assertions

A *loop invariant* is an assertion that expresses a relationship between variables that remains constant throughout all iterations of the loop. In other words, it is a statement that is true both before the loop is entered and after each pass through the loop. An invariant assertion for the preceding code segment could be

```
DivisorSum is the sum of proper divisors of num that are less
than or equal to trialDivisor.
```

A *loop variant* is an assertion whose truth changes between the first and final execution of the loop. The loop variant expression should be stated in such a way that it guarantees the loop is exited. Thus, it contains some statement about the loop variable being incremented (or decremented) during execution of the loop. In the preceding code, we could have

```
trialDivisor is incremented by 1 each time through the loop.
It eventually exceeds the value num / 2, at which point
the loop is exited.
```

Variant and invariant assertions usually occur in pairs.

We now use four kinds of assertions—input, output, variant, and invariant—to produce the formally verified loop that follows:

```
divisorSum = 0;
// Precondition: 1. num is a positive integer.          (input assertion)
//               2. divisorSum = 0. assert((num > 0) && (divisorSum == 0));
```

continued

```
for (trialDivisor = 1; trialDivisor <= num / 2; ++trialDivisor)

// trialDivisor is incremented by 1 each time          (variant assertion)
// through the loop. It eventually exceeds the
// value (num / 2), at which point the loop is exited.

    if (num % trialDivisor == 0)
        divisorSum = divisorSum + trialDivisor;

// divisorSum is the sum of proper divisors of          (invariant assertion)
// num that are less than or equal to trialDivisor.

// Postcondition: divisorSum is the sum of              (output assertion)
// all proper divisors of num.
```

In general, code that is presented in this text does not include formal verification of the loops. This issue is similar to that of robustness. In an introductory course, a decision must be made on the trade-off between learning new concepts and writing robust programs with formal verification of loops. We encourage the practice, but space and time considerations make it inconvenient to include such documentation at this level. We close this discussion with another example illustrating loop verification.

Example 6.11 Consider the problem of finding the greatest common divisor (`gcd`) of two positive integers. To illustrate, we have this information:

num1	num2	gcd(num 1, num2)
8	12	4
20	10	10
15	32	1
70	40	10

A segment of code to produce the `gcd` of two positive integers after they have been ordered as `small, large` is

```
int trialGcd = small;
bool gcdFound = false;
while (! gcdFound)
   if ((large % trialGcd == 0) && (small % trialGcd == 0))
   {
      gcd = trialGcd;
      gcdFound = true;
   }
   else
      trialGcd = trialGcd - 1;
```

Using assertions as previously indicated, this code would appear as

```
int trialGcd = small;
bool gcdFound = false;

// Precondition:     1. small <= large
```

```
//                   2. trialGcd (small) is the first candidate for gcd
//                   3. gcdFound is false

assert((small <= large) && (small == trialGcd) && ! gcdFound);

while (! gcdFound)

// trialGcd assumes integer values ranging from small
// to 1. It is decremented by 1 each time through the
// loop. When trialGcd divides both small and large,
// the loop is exited. Exit is guaranteed since 1
// divides both small and large.

   if ((large % trialGcd == 0) && (small % trialGcd == 0))

// When trialGcd divides both large and small,
// then gcd is assigned that value.

   {
      assert((large % trialGcd == 0) && (small % trialGcd == 0));

      gcd = trialGcd;
      gcdFound = true;
   }
   else
      trialgcd = trialgcd - 1;

// Postcondition: gcd is the greatest common divisor of small and large.
```

Exercises 6.5

1. Write appropriate input assertions and output assertions for each of the following loops.

   a.
   ```
    cin >> score;
   while (score != -999)
   {
      numScores = numScores + 1;
      sum = sum + score;
   cout <<"Enter a score; -999 to quit. ";
   cin >> score;
   }
   ```

   b.
   ```
   count = 0;
   power2 = 1;
   while (power2 < 100)
   {
      cout << power2 << endl;
      power2 = power2 * 2;
      count = count + 1;
   }
   ```

   c. (From Example 6.8)

```
do
{
   oldGuess = newGuess;
   newGuess = 1/2 * (oldGuess + number / oldGuess);
   cout << setprecision(8) << setw(10) << newGuess << endl;
} while (abs(newGuess - oldGuess) < DESIRED_ACCURACY);
```

2. Write appropriate loop invariant and loop variant assertions for each of the loops in Exercise 1.
3. Consider the following loop. The user enters a number, `guess`, and the computer then displays a message indicating whether the `guess` is correct, too high, or too low. Add appropriate input assertions, output assertions, loop invariant assertions, and loop variant assertions to the following code.

```
correct = false;
count = 0;
while ((count < MAX_TRIES) && (! correct))
{
    count = count + 1;
    cout << "Enter choice number: " << count << endl;
    cin >> guess;
    if (guess == choice)
    {
       correct = true;
       cout << "Congratulations!" << endl;
    }
    else if (guess < choice)
       cout << "Your guess is too low" << end;
    else
       cout << "Your guess is too high" << endl;
}
```

6.6 Nested Loops

Objectives

a. to use nested loops
b. to understand the flow of control when using nested loops
c. to employ a consistent writing style when using nested loops

In this chapter, we have examined three loop structures. Each of them has been discussed with respect to syntax, semantics, form, writing style, and use in programs. But remember that each loop is treated as a single C++ statement. In this sense, it is possible to have a loop as one of the statements in the body of another loop. When this happens, the loops are said to be *nested.*

Loops can be nested to any depth; that is, a loop can be within a loop within a loop and so on. Also, any of the three types of loops can be nested within any loop. However, a programmer should be careful not to design a program with nesting that is too complex. If program logic becomes too difficult to follow, you might be better off redesigning the program, perhaps by splitting off the inner logic into a separate subprogram.

Flow of Control

As a first example of using a loop within a loop, consider

```
for (k = 1; k <= 5; ++k)
   for (j = 1; j <= 3; ++j)
      cout << (k + j) << endl;
```

When this fragment is executed, the following happens:

1. Variable k is assigned a value.
2. For each value of k, the following loop is executed.

```
for (j = 1; j <= 3; ++j)
    cout << (k + j) << endl;
```

Thus, for k = 1, the "inside" or nested loop produces the output

```
2
3
4
```

At this point, k = 2. The next portion of the output produced by the nested loop is

```
3
4
5
```

The complete output from these nested loops is

```
2
3 from k = 1
4
```

```
3
4 from k = 2
5
```

```
4
5 from k = 3
6
```

```
5
6 from k = 4
7
```

```
6
7 from k = 5
8
```

As you can see, for each value assigned to the index of the outside loop, the inside loop is executed completely. Suppose you want the output to be printed in the form of a chart as follows:

```
2    3    4

3    4    5
```

continued

```
4     5     6

5     6     7

6     7     8
```

The pseudocode design to produce this output is

1. for (k = 1; k <= 5; ++k)
   produce a line

A refinement of this is

1. for (k = 1; k <= 5; ++k)
   1.1 print on one line
   1.2 advance the printer

The C++ code for this development becomes

```
for (k = 1; k <= 5; ++k)
{
   for (j = 1; j <= 3; ++j)                // print on one line
       cout << setw(4) << (k + j);
   cout << endl;                           // advance the printer
}
```

Our next example shows how nested loops can be used to produce a design.

Example 6.12 Use nested `for` loops to produce the following output:

```
*
**
***
****
*****
```

The left asterisks are in column 10. The first-level pseudocode to solve this problem could be

1. for (k = 1; k <= 5; ++k)
   produce a line

A refinement of this could be

1. for (k = 1; k <= 5; ++k)
   1.1 print on one line
   1.2 advance the printer

Step 1.1 is not yet sufficiently refined, so our next level could be

1. for (k = 1; k <= 5; ++k)
   1.1 print on one line
      1.1.1 put a blank in column 9
      1.1.2 print k asterisks
   1.2 advance the printer

We can now write a program fragment to produce the desired output as follows:

```
for (k = 1; k <= 5; ++k)
{
    cout << setw(9) <<   ;
    for (j = 1; j <= k; ++j)
        cout << '*';
    cout << endl;
}
```

A significant feature has been added to this program fragment. Note that the upper bound for the inner loop is the loop control variable of the outer loop.

Thus far, nested loops have been used only with `for` loops, but any of the loop structures can be used in nesting. Our next example shows a `do...while` loop nested within a `while` loop.

Comunication and Style Tips

When working with nested loops, use line comments to indicate the effect of each loop control variable. For example,

```
// Each value produces a line
for (k = 1; k <= 5; ++k)
{
    // This moves across one line
    cout << setw(9) << ' ' ;
    for (j = 1; j <= k; ++j)
        cout << '*';
    cout << endl;
}
```

Example 6.13 Trace the flow of control and indicate the output for the following program fragment:

```
a = 10;
b = 0;
while (a > b)
{
    cout << setw(5) << a << endl;
    do
    {
        cout << setw(5) << a << setw(5) << b << setw(5) << (a + b) << endl;
        a = a - 2;
    } while (a > 6);
    b = b + 2;
}
cout << endl;
cout << setw(20) << "All done" << endl;
```

The assignment statements produce

10	0
a	b

and `a > b` is `true`; thus, the `while` loop is entered. The first time through this loop, the `do . . . while` loop is used. Output for the first pass is

```
10
10    0    10
```

and the values for `a` and `b` are

8	0
a	b

The Boolean expression `a > 6` is `true` and the `do...while` loop is executed again to produce the next line of output:

```
8       0       8
```

and the values for a and b become

6	0
a	b

At this point, `a > 6` is `false` and control transfers to the line of code

```
b = b + 2;
```

Thus, the variable values are

6	2
a	b

and the Boolean expression `a > b` is `true`. This means the `while` loop will be repeated. The output for the second time through this loop is

```
6
6       2       8
```

and the values for the variables are

4	4
a	b

Now `a > b` is `false` and control is transferred to the line following the `while` loop. Output for the complete fragment is

```
10
10       0       10
8        0        8
6
6        2        8

          All done
```

This example is a bit contrived and tracing the flow of control is somewhat tedious. However, it is important for you to follow the logic involved in using nested loops.

Writing Style

As usual, you should be aware of the significance of using a consistent, readable style of writing when using nested loops. There are at least three features you should consider.

1. *Indenting:* Each loop should have its own level of indenting. This makes it easier to identify the body of the loop. If the loop body consists of a compound statement, the `{` and `}` should start in the same column. Using our previous indenting style, a typical nesting might be

```
for (k = 1; k <= 10; ++k)
{
   while (a > 0)
   {
      do
      {
         .
         .
         .
      } while (<condition>);      // end of do . . . while loop
         <statement>
   }                              // end of while loop
   <statement>
}                                 // end of for loop
```

   If the body of a loop becomes very long, it is sometimes difficult to match the `{` with the proper `}`. In this case, you should either redesign the program (for example, write a separate subprogram) or be especially careful.

2. *Using comments:* Comments can precede a loop and explain what the loop will do, or they can be used with statements inside the loop to explain what the statement does. They should be used to indicate the end of a loop where the loop body is a compound statement.

3. *Skipping lines:* This is an effective way of isolating loops within a program and making nested loops easier to identify.

   A note of caution is in order with respect to writing style. Program documentation is important; however, excessive use of comments and skipped lines can detract from readability. You should develop a happy medium.

Statement Execution in Nested Loops

Using nested loops can significantly increase the number of times statements get executed in a program. To illustrate, suppose a program contains a `do...while` loop that gets executed six times before it is exited, as illustrated here:

```
           do
           .
6 times    . <action here>
           .
           while (<condition 1);
```

If one of the statements inside this loop is another loop, the inner loop will be executed six times. Suppose this inner loop is repeated five times whenever it is entered. This means that each statement within the inner loop will be executed $6 \times 5 = 30$ times when the program is run. This is illustrated by

```
        do
        {
              .
              .  <action here>
              .
6 times
              while (<condition 2>)
              {
                    <statement>          // reach end of     5 times
              }                          // while 30 times
              .
              .
              .
        } while (<condition 1>);
```

When a third level of nesting is used, the number of times a statement is executed can be determined by the product of three factors, $n_1 * n_2 * n_3$, where n_1 represents the number of repetitions of the outside loop, n_2 represents the number of repetitions for the first level of nesting, and n_3 represents the number of repetitions for the innermost loop.

We close this section with an example of a program that uses nested loops to print a multiplication table.

Example 6.14 This example presents a complete program whose output is the multiplication table from 1 × 1 to 10 × 10. A suitable heading is part of the output.

```
// Program file: multab.cpp

#include <iostream.h>
#include <iomanip.h>

// Function: printHeading
// Print a heading for multiplication table

void printHeading();

// Function: printTable
// Print multiplication table

void printTable();

int main()
{
   printHeading();
   printTable();
   return 0;
}

void printHeading()
{
   cout << setiosflags(ios::right) << endl;
```

```
   cout <<  setw(28)
        << "Multiplication Table" << endl;
   cout <<  setw(28)
        << "--------------------" << endl;
   cout << "(  Generated by nested for loops  )"
        << endl;
   cout << endl;
}

void printTable()
{
   int row, column;

   //Print the column heads

   cout << "    ";
   for (int i = 1; i <= 10; ++i)
      cout << setw(4) << i;
   cout << endl;
   cout << "---!----------------------------------------"
        << endl;

   // Now start the loop

   for (row = 1; row <= 10; ++row)
   {
      // print one row
      cout << setw(2) << row << " !";
      for (column = 1; column <= 10; ++column)
         cout << setw(4) << (row * column);
      cout << endl;
   }  // end of each row
   cout << endl;
}
```

The output from this program is

```
         Multiplication Table
         --------------------
(  Generated by nested for loops  )

       1   2   3   4   5   6   7   8   9  10
---!----------------------------------------
 1 !   1   2   3   4   5   6   7   8   9  10
 2 !   2   4   6   8  10  12  14  16  18  20
 3 !   3   6   9  12  15  18  21  24  27  30
 4 !   4   8  12  16  20  24  28  32  36  40
 5 !   5  10  15  20  25  30  35  40  45  50
 6 !   6  12  18  24  30  36  42  48  54  60
 7 !   7  14  21  28  35  42  49  56  63  70
 8 !   8  16  24  32  40  48  56  64  72  80
 9 !   9  18  27  36  45  54  63  72  81  90
10 !  10  20  30  40  50  60  70  80  90 100
```

A NOTE OF INTEREST

A Digital Matter of Life and Death

A radiation-therapy machine, the Therac 25 linear accelerator, was designed to send a penetrating x-ray or electron beam deep into a cancer patient's body to destroy embedded tumors without injuring skin tissue. But in three separate instances in 1985 and 1986, the machine failed. Instead of delivering a safe level of radiation, the Therac 25 administered a dose that was more than 100 times larger than the typical treatment dose. Two patients died and a third was severely burned.

The malfunction was caused by an error in the computer program controlling the machine. It was a subtle error that no one had picked up during the extensive testing the machine had undergone. The error surfaced only when a technician happened to use a specific, unusual combination of keystrokes to instruct the machine.

The Therac incidents and other cases of medical device failures caused by computer errors have focused attention on the increasingly important role played by computers in medical applications. Computers or machines with built-in microprocessors perform functions that range from keeping track of patients to diagnosing ailments and providing treatments.

"The impact of computers on medical care and the medical community is the most significant factor that we have to face," says Frank E. Samuel, Jr., president of the Health Industry Manufacturers Association (HIMA), based in Washington, D.C. "Health care will change more dramatically in the next 10 years because of software-driven products than for any other single cause." Samuel made his remarks at a HIMA-sponsored conference on the regulation of medical software.

At the same time, reports of medical devices with computer-related problems are appearing more and more frequently. In 1985, the Food and Drug Administration (FDA) reported that recalls of medical devices because of computer faults had roughly doubled over the previous 5 years. Since then, the number of such complaints has risen further.

The FDA, in its mandated role as guardian of public health and safety, is now preparing to regulate the software component of medical devices. The agency's effort has already raised questions about what kinds of products, software, and information systems should be regulated.

Exercises 6.6

1. Write a program fragment that uses nested loops to produce each of the following designs.

a.
```
*****
****
***
**
*
```

b.
```
*
***
*****
*******
*****
***
*
```

c.
```
***
***
***
***
******
******
******
```

2. What is the output from each of the following code fragments?

a.
```
for (k = 2; k <= 6; ++k)
{
   for (j = 5; j <= 10; ++j)
      cout << (k + j);
   cout << endl;
}
```

b.
```
for (k = 2; k <= 6; ++k)
{
   for (j = 5; j <= 10; ++j)
      cout << (k + j);
   cout << endl;
}
```

c.
```
sum = 0;
a = 7;
while (a < 10)
{
   for (k = a; k <= 10; ++k)
      sum = sum + k;
   a = a + 1;
}
cout << sum << endl;
```

d.
```
sum = 0;
for (k = 1; k <= 10; ++k)
   for (j = (10 * k - 9); j <= (10 * k); ++j)
      sum = sum + j;
cout << sum << endl;
```

3. What output is produced from the following segment of code?

```
a = 4;
b = 7;
do
{
   num = a;
   while (num <= b)
   {
      for (k = a; k <= b; ++k)
         cout << setw(4) << num;
      cout << endl;
      num = num + 1;
   } // end of while
   cout << endl;
   a = a + 1;
}
while (a != b); // end of do...while loop
```

4. Write a program fragment that uses nested loops to produce the following output.

```
2    4    6    8   10
3    6    9   12   15
4    8   12   16   20
5   10   15   20   25
```

6.7 Repetition and Selection

Selection Within Repetition (Loops)

In Chapter 5, we discussed the use of selection statements. In this chapter, we have discussed the use of three different types of loops. It is now time to see how they are used together. We will first examine selection statements contained within the body of a loop.

Example 6.15

Objectives

a. to use a selection statement within the body of a loop
b. to use a loop within an option of a selection statement

Write a program fragment that computes gross weekly wages for employees of the Florida OJ Canning Company. The data consist of three initials, the total hours worked, and the hourly rate; for example,

```
JHA 44.5 12.75
```

Overtime (more than 40 hours) is computed as time and a half. The output should include all input data and a column of gross wages.

A first-level pseudocode development for this program is

```
1. while moreEmployees
   1.1 process one employee
   1.2 print results
```

This could be refined to

```
1. while moreEmployees
   1.1 process one employee
       1.1.1 get data
       1.1.2 compute wage
   1.2 print results
```

Step 1.1.2 can be refined to

```
1.1.2 compute wage
      1.1.2.1 if hours <= 40.0
                   compute regular time
              else
                   compute time and a half
```

And the final algorithm for the fragment is

```
1. while moreEmployees
   1.1 process one employee
       1.1.1 get data
       1.1.2 compute wage
             1.1.2.1 if hours <= 40.0
                          compute regular time
                     else
                          compute time and a half
   1.2 print results
```

The code for this fragment follows:

```
cout <<  setiosflags(ios::fixed | ios::showpoint);
cout << "Any employees? <Y> or <N> ";
cin >> choice;
moreEmployees = (choice == 'Y') || (choice == 'y');
while (moreEmployees)
{
   cout << endl;
   cout << "Enter initials, hours, and payrate. ";
   cin >> init1 >> init2 >> init3 >> hours >> payRate;
   if (hours <= 40.0)
      totalWage = hours * payRate;
   else
   {
      overtime = 1.5 * (hours - 40.0) * payRate;
      totalWage = 40 * payRate + overtime;
   }
   cout << endl;
   cout << setw(5) << init1 << init2 << init3;
   cout << setprecision(2) << setw(10) << hours
        << setw(10) << payRate;
   cout << setw(10) << '$' << setw(7) << totalWage;
   cout << endl;
   cout << "Any more employees? <Y> or <N> ";
   cin >> choice;
   moreEmployees = (choice == 'Y') || (choice == 'y');
}
```

Repetition (Loops) Within Selection

The next example illustrates the use of a loop within an `if` statement.

Example 6.16 Write a program fragment that allows you to read an integer from the keyboard. If the integer is between 0 and 50, you are to print a chart containing all positive integers less than the integer, their squares, and their cubes. Thus, if 4 is read, the chart is

```
1   1   1

2   4   8

3   9  27
```

The design for this problem has a first-level pseudocode development of

1. input num
2. if (num > 0) && (num < 50)
   2.1 print the chart

Step 2.1 can be refined to

2.1 print the chart
   2.1.1 for (k = 1; k <= (num − 1); ++k)
      2.1.1.1 print each line

We can now write the code for this fragment as follows:

```
cin >> num;
if ((num > 0) && (num < 50))
    for (k = 1; k <= num - 1; ++k)
        cout << k << (k * k) << (k * k * k) << endl;
```

Exercises 6.7

1. Find and explain the errors in each of the following program fragments. Assume all variables have been suitably declared.

a.
```
a = 25;
flag = true;
while (flag == true)
    if (a >= 100)
    {
        cout << a << endl;
        flag = false;
    }
```

b.
```
for (k = 1; k <= 10; ++k)
    cout << k << (k * k) << endl;
if (k % 3 == 0)
{
    cout << k;
    cout <<  is a multiple of three << endl;
}
```

2. What is the output from each of the following program fragments? Assume all variables have been suitably declared.

a.
```
for (k = 1; k <= 100; ++k)
    if (k % 5 == 0)
        cout << k << endl;
```

b.
```
j = 20;
if (j % 5 == 0)
    for (k = 1: k <= 100; ++k)
        cout << k << endl;
```

c.
```
a = 5;
b = 90;
do
{
    b = b / a - 5;
    if (b > a)
        b = a + 30;
} while (b >= 0);
cout << a << b << endl;
```

d.
```
count = 0;
for (k = -5; k <= 5; ++k)
    if (k % 3 == 0)
```

```
{
    cout << "k = " << setw(4) << k <<  output ;
    while (count < 10)
    {
       count = count + 1;
       cout << setw(4) << count << endl;
    }
    count = 0;
    cout << endl;
}
```

e.
```
a = 5;
b = 2;
if (a < b)
   for (k = a; k <= b; ++k)
      cout << k << endl;
else
   for (k = a; k >= b; --k)
      cout << k << endl;
```

f.
```
for (k = -5; k <= 5; ++k)
{
   cout << "k = " << setw(4) << k << output ;
   a = k;
   if (k < 0)
      // k = -5, -4, -3, -2, -1
      do
      {
          cout << setw(5) << (-2 * a) << endl;
             a = a + 1;
      } while (a > 0);
   else // K = 0, 1, 2, 3, 4, 5
      while (a % 2 == 0)
      {
          cout << a << endl;
          a = a + 1;
      }
   cout << endl;
}
```

3. Write a program fragment that reads reals from the keyboard, counts the number of positive reals, and accumulates their sum.
4. Given two integers, `a` and `b`, `a` is a divisor of `b` if `b % a = 0`. Write a complete program that reads a positive integer `b` and then prints all the positive divisors of `b`.

Case Study 6.1: Prime Numbers

This case study illustrates the combined use of repetition and selection statements.

User Request

Write a program that allows the user to compute and display prime numbers.

Analysis

The user enters positive integers from the keyboard and, for each such entry, lists all primes less than or equal to the number. The program includes a check for bad data and use of a sentinel value to terminate the process. Typical output for the integer 17 is

```
Enter a positive integer; <-999> to quit. 17

          The number is 17. The prime numbers less than or equal
          to 17 are:

                          2
                          3
                          5
                          7
                         11
                         13
                         17

Enter a positive integer; <-999> to quit. -999
```

For purposes of this program, note the mathematical property that a number `k` is prime if it has no divisors (other than 1) less than its square root. For example, because 37 is not divisible by 2, 3, or 5, it is prime. Thus, when we check for divisors, it is only necessary to check up to `sqrt(k)`. Also note that 1 is not prime by definition.

Other sample runs of this program produce this output:

```
Enter a positive integer; <-999> to quit. 10

The number is 10. The prime numbers
less than or equal to 10 are:

                                  2
                                  3
                                  5
                                  7

Enter a positive integer; <-999> to quit. 17

The number is 17. The prime numbers
less than or equal to 17 are:

                                  2
                                  3
                                  5
                                  7
                                 11
                                 13
                                 17

Enter a positive integer; <-999> to quit. 1

1 is not prime by definition.

Enter a positive integer; <-999> to quit. 25
```

```
The number is 25. The prime numbers
less than or equal to 25 are:

                                   2
                                   3
                                   5
                                   7
                                  11
                                  13
                                  17
                                  19
                                  23

Enter a positive integer; <-999> to quit. -3

Enter a positive integer; <-999> to quit. 2

The number is 2. The prime numbers
less than or equal to 2 are:

                                   2

Enter a positive integer; <-999> to quit. -999
```

Design

A first-level pseudocode development for this problem is

1. Get a number
   while moreData
2. Examine the number
3. Get a number

A structure chart for this problem is shown in Figure 6.4. The module specifications for the main modules are

Module: Get a number
Task: Get an entry from the keyboard
Output: a number

Module: Examine the number
Task: If the number is 1
   Print a message
else
   Print a heading
   Print list of all primes less than or equal to the integer read
Input: the integer read

A second-level development is

1. Get a number
   1.1 Get entry from the keyboard
      while moreData
2. Examine the number
   if number is 1

Figure 6.4

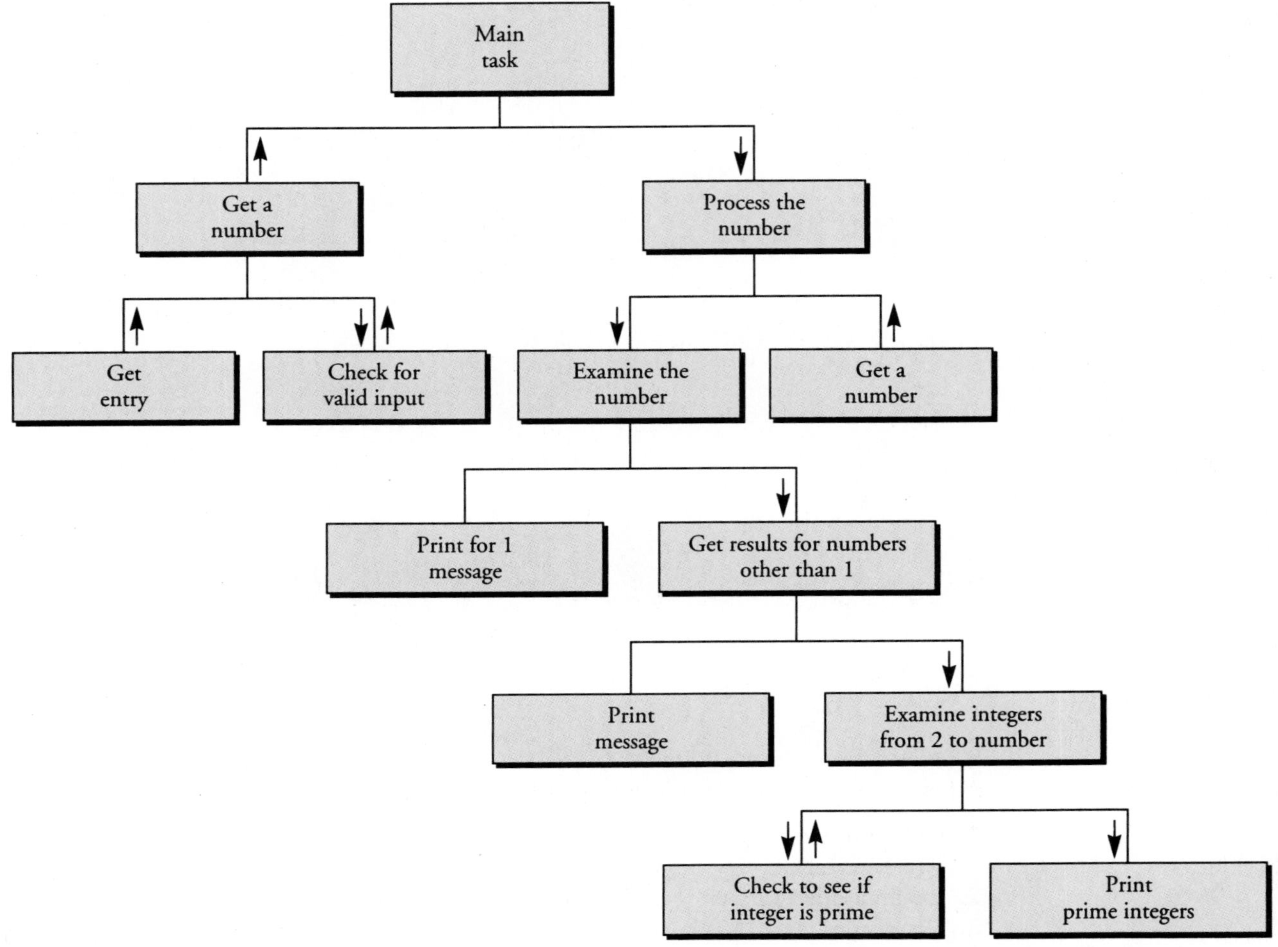

2.1 print a message for 1
    else
    list the primes
2.2 print a message
2.3 check for primes less than or equal to number

3. Get a number
   3.1 Get entry from the keyboard
   3.2 Check for valid entry

Step 2.3 can be refined to

2.3 check for primes less than or equal to number
    for (k = 2; k <= number; ++k)
    2.3.1 check to see if k is prime
    2.3.2 if k is prime
        print k in list of primes

Instead of maintaining `moreData` as a simple Boolean flag, we will write a function that takes the number as a parameter, determines whether or not the number is the sentinel value, and returns `true` or `false` depending on what it finds. The pseudocode for this function is

Make sure it is a valid entry or the sentinel value for terminating the process.
If it is the sentinel value, return `false;` otherwise, return `true.`

Thus, the complete pseudocode development is

1. Get a number
   1.1 Get entry from the keyboard
       while moreData
2. Examine the number
   if number is 1
   2.1 print a message for 1
       else
       list the primes
   2.2 print a message
   2.3 check for primes less than or equal to number
       for (k = 2; k <= number; ++k)
       2.3.1 check to see if k is prime
       2.3.2 if k is prime
             print k in list of primes
3. Get a number
   3.1 Get entry from the keyboard
   3.2 Check for valid entry

Implementation

With the pseudocode development mentioned in the design, the main program is:

```
num = getANumber();
while (moreData(num))
{
   examineTheNumber(num);
   num = getANumber();
}
```

The complete program for this problem follows:

```
// Program file: primes.cpp

#include <iostream.h>
#include <iomanip.h>
#include <math.h>

int getANumber();

// Function: printOneMessage
// Print a message for 1

void printOneMessage();

// Function: printMessage
// Print a heading for the output
//
// Input: the integer read

void printMessage(int number);
```

continued

```
// Function: listAllPrimes
// Print list of all primes less than or equal
// to the integer read
//
// Input: the integer read

void listAllPrimes(int number);

// Function: examineTheNumber
// If integer read is one,
// then print a message for one
// else
// Print list of all primes less than or equal
// to the integer read
//
// Input: the integer read

void examineTheNumber(int number);

// Function: moreData
// Determines whether number = -999
// (the sentinel for end of input)
// Input: the integer read
// Output: true, if the input is not
// the sentinel, false otherwise

bool moreData(int number);

int main()
{
   int number;

   cout << setiosflags(ios::right);
   number = getANumber ();
   while (moreData(number))
   {
      examineTheNumber (number);
      number = getANumber ();
   }
   return 0;
}

int getANumber()
{
   int number;
   bool done;

   do
   {
      cout << endl;
      cout << "Enter a positive integer; <-999> to quit.";
      cin >> number;
      done = (number == -999) || (number >= 0);
   } while (! done);          // assumes valid data
   return number;
}
```

```
void printOneMessage()
{
   cout << endl;
   cout << "1 is not prime by definition." << endl;
}

void printMessage(int number)
{
   cout << endl;
   cout << "The number is " << number
        << ". The prime numbers" << endl;
   cout << "less than or equal to "<< number
        << " are:" << endl;
   cout << endl;
}

void listAllPrimes(int number)
{
   bool prime;
   int candidate, divisor;
   double limitForCheck;

   for (candidate = 2; candidate <= number; ++candidate)
   {
      prime = true;
      divisor = 2;
      limitForCheck = sqrt(candidate);
      while ((divisor <= limitForCheck) && prime)
         if (candidate % divisor == 0)
            prime = false;
         // candidate has a divisor
         else
            divisor = divisor + 1;
      if (prime)
      //Print list of primes
         cout << setw(35) << candidate << endl;
   }
}

void examineTheNumber(int number)
{
   if (number == 1)
      printOneMessage();
   else
   {
      printMessage(number);
      listAllPrimes (number);
   }
}

bool moreData(int number)
{
   return number != -999;
}
```

More efficient algorithms than what we used here do exist. However, the purpose of this program was to see how loops can be used to solve a problem.

Case Study 6.2: A Sentence Analyzer

Good writing style traditionally has emphasized short- to medium-length words and sentences. An important part of text evaluation is obtaining statistics on word and sentence length. This kind of computation is now a standard tool provided with word processing packages.

User Request

Develop a small text analysis system that works on individual sentences entered at the keyboard.

Analysis

The program will proceed interactively as follows:

1. The user is prompted for a sentence, which is a series of words ending with a word that is terminated by a period ('.').
2. The system computes and displays statistics about the number of words in the sentence and the average length of a word. It also displays the longest word in the sentence.
3. The user is asked whether another input is desired with a yes/no prompt. If the answer is "Y," the program repeats steps 1 and 2, and if "N," the program terminates.

A sample session with this program follows:

```
Enter a sentence [terminating with a period ('.'): Hi there.

Number of words: 2
Number of characters: 8
Average length of a word: 4
Longest word: there.

Run once more? [Y/N]: y
Enter a sentence [terminating with a period ('.')]: This is a longer
sentence, going down to the next line.

Number of words: 11
Number of characters: 45
Average length of a word: 4
Longest word: sentence,

Run once more? [Y/N]: n
```

Design

The top-level module runs a simple query driver loop:

Module: main program
  do
    prompt for a sentence
    analyze a sentence

query for further input
while query does not equal 'N'

Here is a C++ main function that represents this main program module:

```
int main()
{
   char query;
   do
   {
      cout << "Enter a sentence [terminating with a period ('.')]: ";
      analyzeSentence();
      cout << "Run once more? [Y/N]: ";
      cin >> query;
   } while ((query == 'Y') || (query == 'y'));
   return 0;
}
```

The module to analyze a sentence is responsible for taking input from the keyboard, computing the statistics, and displaying them. This process can be described by a loop that reads individual words from the keyboard until a word terminated by a period is entered:

Module: Analyze a sentence
Task: Read words from keyboard and update statistics until word ending with `'.'` is reached

Initialize the data
Do
    Input a word
    Update the statistics
While the word does not end with `'.'`
Display the statistics

The statistics will consist of the number of words, the total number of characters in the words, the average length of a word, and the longest word in the sentence. Therefore, this module will need two integer variables and two string variables to maintain the data. The integer data are locally declared, initialized to 0, and simply passed to the other modules for further processing. That leaves us with the problem of detecting a period ('.') at the end of an input word. The `apstring` library provides an operator, `[]`, that can be used to access a character at a position in a string variable. The form for using this operator is

<string variable>[<position>]

where <position> is an integer value ranging from 0 to the length of the string minus 1. Thus, the expression `word [0]` would return the first character in the string, while the expression `word[word.length()-1]` would return the last character in the string, assuming that `word.length()` is greater than or equal to 1.

```
void analyzeSentence()
{
   apstring word, longestWord;
   int wordCount, charCount;
```

continued

```
   wordCount = 0;
   charCount = 0;
   do
   {
      cin >> word;
      updateStatistics(word, longestWord, wordCount, charCount);
   } while (word[word.length() - 1] != '.');
   displayStatistics(longestWord, wordCount, charCount);
}
```

The module for updating the statistics is responsible for increasing the count of characters and words and for changing the value of the longest word if necessary.

Module: Update statistics
Task: Adjust character count and word count and adjust longest word if necessary
Inputs: the current input word, the longest word so far, word count, character count
 If the length of current input word > length of longest word so far then
  Set longest word so far to current input word
 Increment the word count by 1
 Increment the character count by the length of the input word

Updating statistics compares the length of the current input word to the length of the longest word seen so far. If the new word is longer, it becomes the longest word.

```
void updateStatistics(apstring word, apstring &longestWord,
                      int &wordCount, int &charCount)
{
   int length = word.length();

   if (length > longestWord.length())
      longestWord = word;
   ++wordCount;
   charCount = charCount + length;
}
```

The display of statistics module computes the average length of a word as a function of the word count and the character count. Then it displays the labeled statistics on the terminal screen:

```
void displayStatistics(apstring longestWord, int wordCount,
                       int charCount)
{
   cout << endl << "Number of words: " << wordCount << endl;
   cout << "Number of characters: " << charCount << endl;
   cout << "Average length of a word: "
        << charCount / wordCount << endl;
   cout << "Longest word: " << longestWord << endl << endl;
}
```

Our program will use the `apstring` library. The main C++ program is

```
// Program file: stats.cpp

#include <iostream.h>
```

```
#include "apstring.h"

// <function declarations>

int main()
{
   char query;
   do
   {
      cout << "Enter a sentence [terminating with a period ('.')]: ";
      analyzeSentence();
      cout << "Run once more? [Y/N]: ";
      cin >> query;
   } while ((query == 'Y') || (query == 'y'));
   return 0;
}

// <function implementations discussed earlier>
```

Running, Debugging, and Testing Hints

1. Most errors involving loops are not compilation errors. Thus, you will not be able to detect most errors until you try to run the program.
2. An error that will not be detected by the compiler is an infinite loop. The fragment

```
b = 10;
while (b > 0)
{
   cin >> a;
   cout << a << endl;
}
```

will loop forever because `b` never becomes zero inside the loop.
3. Carefully check entry conditions for each loop.
4. Carefully check exit conditions for each loop. Make sure the loop is exited (not infinite) and that you have the correct number of repetitions.
5. Loop entry, execution, and exit can be checked by
   a. pencil and paper check on initial and final values
   b. count of the number of repetitions
   c. use of debugging output statements:
      i. Boolean condition prior to loop
      ii. variables inside loop
      iii. values of the counter in loop
      iv. Boolean values inside loop
      v. values after loop is exited

Summary

Key Terms

accumulator
counter
data validation
decrement
fixed repetition (iterated) loop
infinite loop
input assertion
loop invariant

loop variant
loop verification
nested loop
output assertion
posttest (exit-controlled) loop
pretest condition
pretest (entrance-controlled) loop
sentinel value
variable condition loop

Keywords

do
for
while

Key Concepts

- The following table provides a comparison summary of the three repetition structures discussed in this chapter.

Traits of Loops	`for` Loop	`while` Loop	`do...while` Loop
Pretest loop	yes	yes	no
Posttest loop	no	no	yes
`{...}` for compound statements	required	required	required
Repetition	fixed/variable	variable	variable

- A fixed repetition loop is to be used when you know exactly how many times something is to be repeated.
- The basic form of a `for` loop is

```
for (j = 1; j <= 5; ++j)
   <statement>
```

- A `while` loop is a pretest loop that can have a variable loop control; a typical loop is

```
score = 0;
sum = 0;
moreData = true;
while (moreData)
{
   sum = sum + score;
   cout << "Enter a score; -999 to quit. ";
   cin >> score;
   moreData = (score != -999);
}
```

- A counter is a variable that indicates how often the body of a loop is executed.
- An accumulator is a variable that sums values.
- An infinite `while` loop is caused by having a `true` loop control a condition that is never changed to `false`.
- A posttest loop has a Boolean condition checked after the loop body has been completed.

- A `do...while` loop is a posttest loop; a typical loop is

```
do
{
   cout << "Enter a positive integer; <-999> to quit. ";
   cin >> num;
} while ((num > 0) && (num != -999));
```

- `do...while` and `while` are variable control loops; `for` is usually a fixed control loop.
- `while` and `for` are pretest loops; `do...while` is a posttest loop.
- Any one of these loops can be nested within any other of the loops.
- Indenting each loop is important for program readability.
- Several levels of nesting make the logic of a program difficult to follow.
- Loops and conditionals are frequently used together. Careful program design will facilitate writing code in which these concepts are integrated; typical forms are

```
while (<condition1>) do
{
   .
   .
   .
   if (<condition2>)
      .
      .
      .
   else
      .
      .
      .
} // end of while
```

and

```
if <condition>
{
   .
   .
   .
   for (j = <value1>; j <= <valueN>; ++j)
   {
      .
      .
      .
   } // end of for loop...
}     // end of if...else
```

Programming Problems and Projects

1. The Caswell Catering and Convention Service (Problem 12, Chapter 4, and Problem 14, Chapter 5) wants you to upgrade their program so they can use it for all of their customers.

2. Modify your program for a service station owner (Focus on Program Design, Chapter 5) so that it can be used for an unknown number of customers. Your output should include the number of customers and all other pertinent items in a daily summary.
3. Modify the Community Hospital program (Problem 17, Chapter 5) so that it can be run for all patients leaving the hospital in one day. Include appropriate bad data checks and daily summary items.
4. The greatest common divisor (gcd) of two integers *a* and *b* is a positive integer *c* such that *c* divides *a*, *c* divides *b*, and for any other common divisor *d* of *a* and *b*, *d* is less than or equal to *c*. (For example, the gcd of 18 and 45 is 9.) One method of finding the gcd of two positive integers (*a*, *b*) is to begin with the smaller (*a*) and see if it is a divisor of the larger (*b*). If it is, then the smaller is the gcd. If not, find the next largest divisor of *a* and see if it is a divisor of *b*. Continue this process until you find a divisor of both *a* and *b*. This is the gcd of *a* and *b*.
   Write an interactive program that will accept two positive integers as input and then print out their gcd. Enhance your output by printing all divisors of *a* that do not divide *b*. A sample run could produce

```
Enter two positive integers. 42 72

The divisors of 42 that do not divide 72 are:

   42
   21
   14
    7

The gcd of 42 and 72 is 6.
```

5. The least common multiple (lcm) of two positive integers *a* and *b* is a positive integer *c* such that *c* is a multiple of both *a* and *b* and for any other multiple *m* of *a* and *b*, *c* is a divisor of *m*. (For example, the lcm of 12 and 8 is 24.) Write a program that allows the user to enter two positive integers and then print the lcm. The program should guard against bad data and allow the user the option of "trying another pair" or quitting.
6. A perfect number is a positive integer such that the sum of the proper divisors equals the number. Thus, 28 = 1 + 2 + 4 + 7 + 14 is a perfect number. If the sum of the divisors is less than the number, it is deficient. If the sum exceeds the number, it is abundant.
   a. Write a program that allows the user to enter a positive integer and then displays the result indicating whether the number entered is perfect, deficient, or abundant.
   b. Write another program that allows the user to enter a positive integer *N* and then displays all perfect numbers less than or equal to *N*.

   Your programs should guard against bad data and allow the user the option of entering another integer or quitting.
7. In these days of increased awareness of automobile mileage, more motorists are computing their miles per gallon (mpg) than ever before. Write a program that will perform these computations for a traveler. Data for the program will be entered as indicated by the following table:

Odometer Reading	Gallons of Fuel Purchased
18828	(start) —
19240	9.7
19616	10.2
19944	8.8
20329	10.1
20769	(finish) 10.3

The program should compute the mpg for each tank and the cumulative mpg each time the tank is filled. Your output should produce a chart with the following headings:

```
Odometer   Odometer   Fuel     Miles    Fuel     Miles    Mpg      Mpg
(begin)    (end)      (tank)   (tank)   (trip)   (trip)   (tank)   (trip)
```

8. Parkside's other triangle is generated from two positive integers, one for the size and one for the seed. For example,

Size 6, Seed 1	Size 5, Seed 3
1 2 4 7 2 7	3 4 6 9 4
3 5 8 3 8	5 7 1 5
6 9 4 9	8 2 6
1 5 1	3 7
6 2	8
3	

Size gives the number of columns. Seed specifies the starting value for column 1. Column n contains n values. The successive values are obtained by adding 1 to the previous value. When 9 is reached, the next value becomes 1.

Write a program that reads pairs of positive integers and produces Parkside's Other Triangle for each pair. The check for bad data should include checking for seeds between 1 and 9 inclusive.

9. Modify the sewage, water, and sanitation problem (Problem 19, Chapter 5) so that it can be used with data containing appropriate information for all residents of the community.

10. Modify the program for the Lucky Wildcat Well Corporation (Problem 20, Chapter 5) so that it can be run with data containing information about all of Al Derrick's wells.

11. Modify the program concerning the Mathematical Association of America (Problem 21, Chapter 5). There will be 50 official state delegates attending the next summer national meeting. The new data file will contain the two-letter state abbreviation for each delegate. Output should include one column with the state abbreviation and another with the amount reimbursed.

12. In Fibonacci's sequence, *0, 1, 1, 2, 3, 5, 8, 13, . . .*, the first two terms are 0 and 1, and each successive term is formed by adding the previous two terms. Write a program that will read positive integers and then print the number of terms indicated by each integer read. Be sure to test your program with data that includes the integers 1 and 2.

13. Dr. Lae Z. Programmer is at it again. Now that you have written a program to compute the grade for one student in his class (Problems 5, 22, and 23, Chapter 5), he

wants you to modify this program so it can be used for the entire class. He will help you by making the first entry be a positive integer representing the number of students in the class. Your new version should compute an overall class average and the number of students receiving each letter grade.

14. Modify the Pentagon parking lot problem (Problem 26, Chapter 5) so that it can be used for all customers in 1 day. In the new program, time should be entered in military style as a four-digit integer. The lot opens at 0600 (6:00 A.M.) and closes at 2200 (10:00 P.M.). Your program should include appropriate summary information.

15. The Natural Pine Furniture Company (Problem 7, Chapter 4) now wants you to refine your program so that it will print a 1 week pay report for each employee. You do not know how many employees there are, but you do know that all information for each employee is on a separate line. Each line of input will contain the employee's initials, the number of hours worked, and the hourly rate. You are to use the constant definition section for the following:

Federal withholding tax rate	18%
State withholding tax rate	4.5%
Hospitalization	\$26.65
Union dues	\$ 7.85

Your output should include a report for each employee and a summary report for the company files.

16. Orlando Tree Service, Incorporated, offers the following services and rates to its customers:

a. Tree removal \$500 per tree
b. Tree trimming \$80 per hour
c. Stump grinding \$25 plus \$2 per inch for each stump whose diameter exceeds 10 inches. The \$2 charge is only for the diameter inches in excess of 10.

Write a complete program to allow the manager, Mr. Sorwind, to provide an estimate when he bids on a job. Your output should include a listing of each separate charge and a total. A 10% discount is given for any job whose total exceeds \$1000. Typical data for one customer are

```
R 7
T 6.5
G 8
8 10  12  14  15  15  20  25
```

where R, T, and G are codes for removal, trimming, and grinding, respectively. The integer following G represents the number of stumps to be ground. The next line of integers represents the diameters of stumps to be ground.

17. A standard science experiment is to drop a ball and see how high it bounces. Once the "bounciness" of the ball has been determined, the ratio gives a bounciness index. For example, if a ball dropped from a height of 10 feet bounces 6 feet high, the index is 0.6 and the total distance traveled by the ball is 16 feet after one bounce. If the ball were to continue bouncing, the distance after two bounces would be 10 ft + 6 ft + 6 ft + 3.6 ft = 25.6 ft. Note that distance traveled for each successive bounce is the distance to the floor plus 0.6 of that distance as the ball comes back up.

Write a program that lets the user enter the initial height of the ball and the number of times the ball is allowed to continue bouncing. Output should be the total distance traveled by the ball. At some point in this process, the distance traveled by the ball becomes negligible. Use the constant section to define a "negligible" distance (for example, 0.00001 inches). Terminate the computing when the distance becomes negligible. When this stage is reached, include the number of bounces as part of the output.

18. Write a program that prints a calendar for 1 month. Input consists of an integer specifying the first day of the month (1 = Sunday) and an integer specifying how many days are in a month.

19. An amortization table shows the rate at which a loan is paid off. It contains monthly entries showing the interest paid that month, the principal paid, and the remaining balance. Given the amount of money borrowed (the principal), the annual interest rate, and the amount the person wishes to repay each month, print an amortization table. (Be certain that the payment desired is larger than the first month's interest.) Your table should stop when the loan is paid off, and it should be printed with the following heads.

```
MONTH NUMBER     INTEREST PAID     PRINCIPAL PAID     BALANCE
```

20. Computers work in the binary system, which is based on powers of 2. Write a program that prints out the first 15 powers of 2 beginning with 2 to the zero power. Print your output in headed columns.

21. Print a list of the positive integers less than 500 that are divisible by either 5 or 7. When the list is complete, print a count of the number of integers found.

22. Write a program that reads in 20 real numbers and then prints the average of the positive numbers and the average of the negative numbers.

23. In 1626, the Dutch settlers purchased Manhattan Island from the Native Americans. According to legend, the purchase price was $24. Suppose the Native Americans had invested this amount at 3% annual interest compounded quarterly. If the money had earned interest from the start of 1626 to the end of last year, how much money would they have in the bank today? (*Hint:* Use nested loops for the compounding.)

24. Write a program to print the sum of the odd integers from 1 to 99.

25. The theory of relativity holds that as an object moves, it gets smaller. The new length of the object can be determined from the formula:

$$\text{NewLength} = \text{Original Length} * \sqrt{1 - B^2}$$

where B^2 is the percentage of the speed of light at which the object is moving, entered in decimal form. Given the length of an object, print its new length for speeds ranging from 0 to 99% of the speed of light. Print the output in the following columns:

```
Percent of Light           Speed           Length
----------------           -----           ------
```

26. Mr. Christian uses a 90%, 80%, 70%, 60% grading scale on his tests. Given a list of test scores, print out the number of As, Bs, Cs, Ds, and Fs on the test. Terminate the list of scores with a sentinel value.

27. The mathematician Gottfried Leibniz determined a formula for estimating the value of π:

$$\pi/4 = 1 - 1/3 + 1/5 - 1/7 + 1/9 - 1/11 + \ldots$$

Evaluate the first 200 terms of this formula and print its approximation of π.

28. In a biology experiment, Carey finds that a sample population of an organism doubles every 12 hours. If she starts with 1000 organisms, in how many hours will she have 1 million?

29. C++ has a function that permits raising a number to a power. We can easily write a program to perform this function, however. Given an integer to represent the base number and a positive integer to represent the power desired, write a program that prints the number raised to that power.

30. Mr. Thomas has negotiated a salary schedule for his new job. He will be paid one cent ($0.01) the first day, with the daily rate doubling each day. Write a program that will find his total earnings for 30 days. Print your results in a table set up as follows:

```
Day Number        Daily Salary        Total Earned

  1                   .01                 .01

  2                   .02                 .03

  3                    .                   .

  .                    .                   .

  .                    .                   .

  30
```

31. Write a program to print the perimeter and area of rectangles using all combinations of lengths and widths running from 1 foot to 10 feet in increments of 1 foot. Print the output in headed columns.

32. Teachers in most school districts are paid on a salary schedule that provides a salary based on their number of years of teaching experience. Suppose that a beginning teacher in the Babbage School District is paid $26,000 the first year. For each year of experience after this up to 12 years, a 4% increase over the preceding value is received. Write a program that prints a salary schedule for teachers in this district. The output should appear as follows:

```
Years Experience            Salary

      0                     $26000.00

      1                     $27040.00

      2                     $28121.60

      3                     $29246.46

      .                         .

      .                         .

      .                         .

     12
```

(Actually, most teachers' salary schedules are more complex than this. As an additional problem, you might like to find out how the salary schedule is determined in your school district and write a program to print it.)

33. The Euclidean algorithm can be used to find the greatest common divisor (gcd) of two positive integers (n_1, n_2). For example, suppose $n_1 = 72$ and $n_2 = 42$; you can use this algorithm in the following manner:

(1) Divide the larger by the smaller:

72 = 42 * 1 + 30

(2) Divide the divisor (42) by the remainder (30):

42 = 30 * 1 + 12

(3) Repeat this process until you get a remainder of zero:

30 = 12 * 2 + 6

12 = 6 * 2 + 0

The last nonzero remainder is the gcd of n_1 and n_2.

Write a program that lets the user enter two integers and then prints each step in the process of using the Euclidean algorithm to find their gcd.

34. Cramer's rule for solving a system of equations was given in Problem 31, Chapter 5. Add an enhancement to your program by using a loop to guarantee that the coefficients and constants entered by the user are precisely those that were intended.

35. Gaussian elimination is another method used to solve systems of equations. To illustrate, if the system is

$$\begin{aligned} x - 2y &= 1 \\ 2x + y &= 7 \end{aligned}$$

Gaussian elimination would start with the augmented matrix

$$\begin{bmatrix} 1 & -2 & 1 \\ 2 & 1 & 7 \end{bmatrix}$$

and proceed to produce the identity matrix on the left side

$$\begin{bmatrix} 1 & 0 & 3 \\ 0 & 1 & 1 \end{bmatrix}$$

At this stage, the solution to the system is seen to be $x = 3$ and $y = 1$.

Write a program in which the user enters coefficients for a system of two equations containing two variables. The program should then solve the system and display the answer. Your program should include the following:

a. A check for bad data
b. A solvable system check
c. A display of partial results as the matrix operations are performed

36. A Pythagorean triple consists of three integers *A*, *B*, and *C* such that $A^2 + B^2 = C^2$. For example, 3, 4, 5 is such a triple because $3^2 + 4^2 = 5^2$. These triples can be generated by positive integers *m*, *n*, ($m > n$), where $a = m^2 - n^2$, $b = 2mn$, and $c = m^2 + n^2$. These triples will be primitive (no common factors) if *m* and *n* have no common factors and are not both odd. Write a program that allows the user to enter a value for *m* and then prints all possible primitive Pythagorean triples such that $m > n$. Use one function to find the greatest common factor of *m* and *n*, another to see if *m* and *n* are both odd, and another to guard against overflow. For the input value of $m = 5$, typical output would be

```
m   n   a   b   c   a²    b²    c²

2   1   3   4   5    9    16    25

3   2   5  12  13   25   144   169

4   1  15   8  17  225    64   289

4   3   7  24  25   49   576   625

5   2  21  20  29  441   400   841

5   4   9  40  41   81  1600  1681
```

37. Case Study 6.1 determined whether or not an integer was prime by checking for divisors less than or equal to the square root of the number. The check started with 2 and incremented trial divisors by 1 each time as seen by the code

```
prime = true;
divisor = 2;
limitForCheck = sqrt(candidate);
while ((divisor <= limitForCheck) && prime)
   if (candidate % divisor == 0)
      prime = false;
   else
      divisor = divisor + 1;
```

Other methods can be used to determine whether or not an integer N is prime. For example, you may

a. check divisors from 2 to $N-1$ incrementing by 1
b. check divisors from 2 to $(N-1)/2$ incrementing by 1
c. check divisor 2, 3, 5, . . . $(N-1)/2$ incrementing by 2
d. check divisor 2, 3, 5, . . . sqrt(N) incrementing by 2

Write a program that allows the user to choose between these options to compare the relative efficiency of different algorithms. Use a function for each option.

38. The prime factorization of a positive integer is the positive integer written as the product of primes. For example, the prime factorization of 72 is

```
72 = 2 * 3 * 3 * 4
```

Write a program that allows the user to enter a positive integer and then displays the prime factorization of the integer. A minimal main program is

```
num = getANumber ();
if (numberIsPrime(num))
   cout << num<< " is prime" << endl;
else
   printFactorization(num);
```

Enhancements to this program could include an error trap for bad data and a loop for repeated trials.

39. As you might expect, instructors of computer science do not agree on whether a `do...while` loop or a `while` loop is the preferred variable control loop in C++. Interview several computer science instructors at your institution to determine what preference (if any) they have regarding these two forms of repetition. Prepare a class report based on your interviews. Include advantages and disadvantages of each form of repetition.
40. Examine the repetition constructs of at least five other programming languages. Prepare a report that compares and contrasts repetition in each of the languages. Be sure to include information such as which languages provide for both fixed and variable repetition and which languages have more than one kind of variable repetition. Which language appears to have the most desirable form of repetition? Include your rationale for this decision in your report.
41. Examine some old computer science texts and talk to some computer science instructors who worked with the early languages to see how repetition was achieved in the "early days." Prepare a brief chronological chart for class display that depicts the various stages in developing repetition.

7

Files

Chapter Outline

Having now completed six chapters, you've made significant steps in the process of learning to use a programming language for the purpose of solving problems. Thus far, however, it has been impossible to work with large amounts of data. To write programs that solve problems using large databases, it is necessary to store, retrieve, and manage the data.

Consider the relatively simple problem of using a computer to compute and print water bills for a community of 30,000 customers. If the data needed consist of a customer name, address, and amount of water used, you can imagine that entering this information interactively every billing period would involve an enormous amount of time. In addition to saving that time, it is often desirable to save information between runs of a program for later use. For example, in large software systems, the information output by one program might be the input of another program.

To avoid these problems, we can store data in some secondary storage device, usually magnetic tapes or disks. Data can be created by one program, stored on these devices, and then accessed by other programs when necessary. It is also possible to modify and save this information for other runs of the same program or for running another program using these same data. In this chapter, we look at storage and retrieval of data in another data structure called a file.

■ 7.1 Streams and Stream Processing

Objectives

a. to understand the use of streams in obtaining input and output data
b. to understand how streams are used to access data in files
c. to use loops with file streams

Before you can work with files, you need to become acquainted with the notion of a *stream*. You can think of a stream as a channel or conduit on which data are passed from senders to receivers. Data can be sent out on a stream, in which case we are using an *output stream*. Or data can be received from a stream, in which case we are using an *input stream*. Streams are connected to *devices*. For example, at program start-up, the standard input stream, named by `cin`, is connected to the keyboard device, and the standard output stream, named by `cout`, is connected to the terminal screen. Thus, you can think of the keyboard as the *source* from which data are received from an input stream. The terminal screen is the *destination* to which data are sent on an output stream.

The essential characteristic of stream processing is that data elements must be sent to or received from a stream one at a time or in *serial* fashion. For example, if we have a collection of data elements to be printed on the terminal screen, they must be written one after the other, not all at once. When you think about the use of streams for interactive input and output, this restriction makes sense. For output, each character sent to the output stream must wait its turn to be displayed on a terminal screen. For input, the receiver in the program must wait for each character typed at the keyboard.

We can think of a stream as an abstract data type. Stream processing requires at least five abstract operations. First, the stream must be *opened* for use. If the stream has been opened for input, an operation is needed to *get* the next data item from the stream. In addition, an operation is needed to detect the *end of an input stream,* or the condition that there are no more data to be received from the stream. If the stream has been opened for output, an operation is needed to *put* the next data item into the stream. Finally, when the program is finished using a stream, an operation is necessary to *close* it.

The Standard Input and Output Streams

You are already familiar with the use of the standard input and output streams in C++. Let's take a look at how they work in more detail. These streams and the operations we perform on them become available to a program by including the `iostream.h` library. In the case of the standard input stream, a programmer obtains access to the variable `cin`, which names the stream, and the operator >>, which is used to receive or get the next data item from the stream. In the case of the standard output stream, a programmer obtains access to the variable `cout`, which names the stream, and the operator <<, which is used to send or put the next data item into the stream. The operations that open and close these streams are run automatically by the system when the program begins and finishes execution. Opening the streams simply connects each stream to its respective device, the keyboard or the terminal screen. Closing the streams disconnects them. The standard input and output streams and the devices to which they are connected are depicted in Figure 7.1.

File Streams

Files are data structures that are stored on a *disk device.* To work with a file, you must connect a stream to the file on a disk. The kind of stream used to receive input from a file is called an *input file stream.* The kind of stream used to send output to a file is called an *output file stream.* Input and output file streams and the devices to which they are connected are depicted in Figure 7.2. To create a file stream, you must first include the C++ library file `fstream.h`. After doing so, two new classes, `ofstream` (output file stream) and `ifstream` (input file stream), become available to a program.

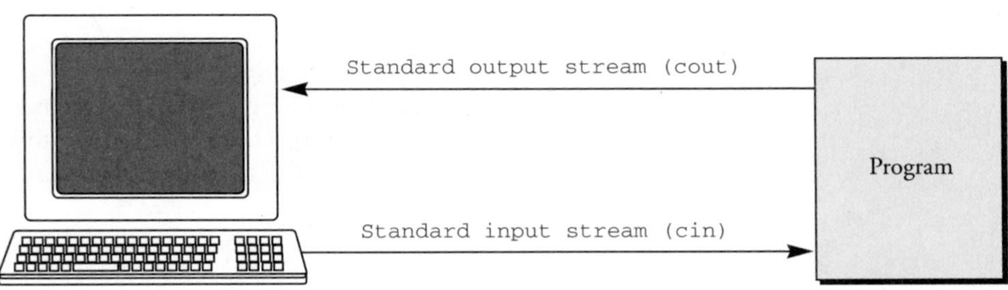

Figure 7.1
The standard input and output streams and their devices

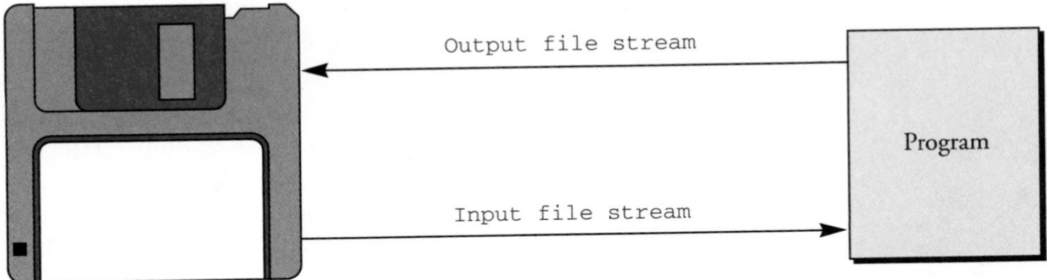

Figure 7.2
Input and output file streams and a disk device

Output File Streams

You can declare and open an output file stream as in the following example:

```
#include <fstream.h>
.
.
.
ofstream outfile;
.
.
.
outfile.open("myfile");
```

Syntactically, the second line of code is a C++ variable declaration. The class name, `ofstream`, appears on the left, followed by the variable name, `outfile`. The third line of code tells the system to connect the output file stream to a file on disk named `myfile`. The syntax of this statement is that used for expressing calls of member functions with objects introduced in Chapter 3. It consists of the name of the file stream, followed by a period ("."), followed by a call to the `open` function with a string parameter. When this statement is executed, the following steps take place:

1. If a file named `myfile` exists on disk, it is opened for output and connected to the output stream `outfile`. Any data in the file when it is opened are erased.
2. Otherwise, a file named `myfile` does not exist on disk. A new file with that name is created, opened for output, and connected to the output stream `outfile`.

The general form for creating an output file stream is

```
ofstream <stream variable name>;
<stream variable name>.open(<file name>);
```

The stream variable name can be any legitimate C++ identifier. The file name must be a string that is consistent with the way files can be named on your particular implementation. You should consult your local system manual for the rules governing the naming of files.

When a program is finished using a file stream, it should be closed. Most computer systems close any data files when a program terminates execution. However, the `close` function can be run with the file stream to do this under program control. If `outfile` is an output file stream, the following statement will close the stream:

```
outfile.close();
```

Note that the name of the file does not appear as a parameter to this function, as it does with `open`.

Detecting Errors Opening and Closing Files

Occasionally, an error occurs when a program attempts to open or close a stream on a file. For example, a disk may be full and no more room exists for new data when a new file is requested. To detect these errors, C++ provides a fail function, `fail()`, for use with streams. The following code shows how to detect and respond to these errors in opening and closing an output file stream:

```
#include <fstream.h>
#include <assert.h>
.
.
.
ofstream outfile;
.
.
.
outfile.open("myfile");
assert(! outfile.fail());
    <send data to file>
outfile.close();
assert(! outfile.fail());
```

Using Output File Streams

Once a file stream has been opened for output, all of the operations for terminal screen output that you are familiar with can be used for file output. For example, assuming that the variable `outfile` names an output file stream, the following statement will write a line of text to the file:

```
outfile << "This is a test." << endl;
```

Note that this statement has exactly the same format as a statement to write the same data to the terminal screen using the standard output stream:

```
cout << "This is a test." << endl;
```

The output of integers and real numbers works the same way:

```
outfile << "The number ten is " << 10 << " or " << 10.0 << endl;
```

If the C++ library for formatting output, `iomanip.h`, is included, you will be able to use familiar formatting commands with file output:

```
#include <iomanip.h>
.
.
.
outfile << setprecision(4);
outfile << setw(10) << 3.1416 << endl;
```

There are two important points to note here about output streams.

1. The operations on output streams are *abstract.* It does not matter whether the destination of the output is a file on disk or the terminal screen. All we need to know is the name of the stream and the form of the statement to send data to the stream. Moreover, the results of sending data to output streams are similar, even when the destinations are different devices. The data saved in a disk file should "look the same" as the data displayed on a terminal screen. You can verify this by running our sample statements and then examining the contents of your test file with a local text editor.
2. Programs that use output stream processing are *portable.* They can be written on one hardware system, transported to another hardware system, and then recompiled and run on the latter system without changes to the code. This will be true even though the representation of files on a disk and data on a terminal screen tend to vary greatly from system to system. If we had to make changes to a program every time we wanted to move it to a new hardware system, we would have an enormous maintenance headache. The use of conventional output streams insulates a program from these machine dependencies in areas where they are most likely to occur.

Loops with Output File Streams

Most of the examples of sending data to an output file stream that we have seen thus far are unrealistic because only one or two data values are written. Programs typically output large amounts of data to files. One typical form of data processing with files takes input data from the user at the keyboard, processes the data, and writes the results to a file. A pseudocode algorithm for this process is

```
Open the output file
Read data from the keyboard
While data do not equal a sentinel value do
   Process the data
   Write the result to the file, followed by an end of line
   Read data from the keyboard
Close the output file
```

Note that each data value sent to the file is followed by an end of line. It is essential that an end of line or a space character be used to separate the data values in the file. This will allow the data values to be recognized and read from the file subsequently.

Example 7.1 The following program uses a `while` loop to read integers from the keyboard and write them to a file until a sentinel is encountered.

```
// Program file: kbdfile.cpp

#include <iostream.h>
#include <fstream.h>

const int SENTINEL = -999;

int main()
{
   int data;
   ofstream outfile;
```

```
    outfile.open("myfile");
    cout << "Enter an integer (-999 to end input): ";
    cin >> data;
    while (data != SENTINEL)
    {
       outfile << data << endl;
       cout << "Enter an integer (-999 to end input): ";
       cin >> data;
    }
    outfile.close();
    return 0;
}
```

Input File Streams

You can create an input file stream as in the following example:

```
#include <fstream.h>
.
.
.
ifstream infile;
.
.
.
infile.open("myfile");
```

Syntactically, the first line of code is a C++ variable declaration. On the second line, the class name, `ifstream`, appears on the left, followed by the variable name, `infile`. The third line of code tells the system to connect the input file stream to a file on disk named `myfile`. The syntax of this statement is the same as that for output streams. When this statement is executed, the following steps take place:

1. If a file named `myfile` exists on disk, it is opened for input and connected to the input stream `infile`.
2. Otherwise, a file named `myfile` does not exist on disk. In some implementations of C++, a new file with that name is created, opened for input, and connected to the input stream `infile`.

The general form for creating an input file stream is

```
ifstream <stream variable name>;
<stream variable name>.open(<file name>);
```

The stream variable name can be any legitimate C++ identifier. The file name must be a string that is consistent with the way files can be named on your particular system.

Using Input File Streams

We have seen that programs can use the standard operator <<, called an *inserter,* to send data to the terminal screen or to an output file. Programs can also use the standard operator >>, called an *extractor,* to receive data from the keyboard or from an input file.

Let us review what happens when a program gets data from the keyboard or standard input stream.

1. The user types one or more characters at the keyboard, followed by a blank space or by a new line character.
2. The computer converts the characters to the data value that the characters represent. What the characters represent depends on the type of variable used for input. For example, the characters '1', '0', and '4' will be converted to the integer value 104 if the program's input statement is receiving the input data for an integer variable. Or the same characters will be placed into a string value "104" if the input statement is using a string variable.
3. The computer stores the data value from step 2 in the variable following the >> operator.

The success of an input operation from the keyboard thus depends on two things: the format of the data typed by the user and the data type of the variable appearing in the input statement. For example, the code

```
int intVar;
double doubleVar;
apstring stringVar;

cin >> intVar >> doubleVar >> stringVar;
```

will run successfully if the user types a string of digits, followed by one or more white space characters, followed by a string of digits that may or may not contain a decimal point, followed by one or more white space characters, followed by a string of characters, followed by optional white space characters, and ending with a new line character.

There are two important points to note about the standard input stream. First, at the source or keyboard, the data are individual characters. At the receiving end, however, these data are implicitly converted to a type that the program can use, such as integers, real numbers, or strings.

Once we are aware of these two conditions, we can proceed to use an input file stream in the same way as we use the keyboard. For example, assuming that the file `threevals` contains a line of characters representing an integer, a real number, and a string, the following program will successfully read these data from the file and display them on the terminal screen:

```
// Program file: filescr.cpp

#include <iostream.h>
#include <fstream.h>
#include <assert.h>
#include "apstring.h"

int main()
{
   int intVar;
   double doubleVar;
   apstring stringVar;
   ifstream infile;
   infile.open("threevals");
   assert(! infile.fail());
   infile >> intVar >> doubleVar >> stringVar;
```

```
    cout << intVar << endl << doubleVar << endl << stringVar << endl;
    infile.close();
    assert(! infile.fail());
    return 0;
}
```

Loops with Input File Streams

The contents of an input file are almost never as precisely determined as those you just saw in the last example. Usually, all we know is the general format of a file and the type of data used to receive the input. The number of these data values that are stored in the file is *indefinite*. There may be 2, 20, or 20,000 of them. Processing input file data will consist of reading each data value from the file stream, processing it, and halting when there are no more data to be read from the stream.

The C++ function `fail()` returns nonzero (meaning true) when there are no more data to be read from an input file stream and zero (meaning false) otherwise. The general form for using this function is

<input file stream>`.fail()`

If we assume that `data` is the variable into which each data element of a file will be read, `infile` is the input file stream, and `processData(data)` is the specification of a function that processes the data, then the following code can serve as a model of input file processing in many C++ programs:

```
infile >> data;
while (! infile.fail())
{
   processData(data);
   infile >> data;
}
```

There are several important points to make about this model:

1. An attempt to read an initial datum from the file stream must be made *before* the `fail` function is executed. If the file contains no data initially, then `fail` will return `true` after this initial input operation. This operation is sometimes called a *priming input statement.*
2. *Placing the fail* condition at the beginning of a `while` loop guards against processing data after the program has reached the end of the file stream.
3. Placing the next extraction operation at the bottom of the loop allows the loop to advance through the file to the end of the input data.
4. When this model is used, remember that `fail` is `true` when an attempt to read a value is made and there are no remaining values in the file.

Communication and Style Tips

1. Always test for the end-of-file condition before processing data read from an input file stream. This means:
   a. Use a priming input statement before the loop.
   b. Use an input statement at the bottom of the loop.
2. Use a `while` loop for getting data from an input file stream. (A `for` loop is desirable only when you know the exact number of data items in the file.)

Example 7.2 The following program reads integers from an input file and displays them in a column on the terminal screen. The program assumes that the integers in the file are separated by one or more white space characters. Thus, this program can be used to input the data from files produced by the program of Example 7.1.

```
// Program file: intfile.cpp

#include <iostream.h>
#include <fstream.h>

int main()
{
   int data;
   ifstream infile;
   infile.open("myfile");
   infile >> data;
   while (! infile.fail())
   {
      cout << data << endl;
      infile >> data;
   }
   infile.close();
   return 0;
}
```

There is a shorter form of a loop that can be used for file input in C++. This form is restricted to programs that use the >> operator and depends on the fact that >> returns 0 when there are no more data in the file. Here is the form of this input loop:

```
while (infile >> data)
   <process the data>
```

Note that the data are input within the Boolean expression at the top of the loop. Then the computer tests the result of >> for nonzero, and if that is true, the data are processed. Otherwise, there are no data remaining in the file, so the body of the loop is not entered. The advantage of this form of input loop is that it eliminates the need for a separate priming input statement. However, not all input loops can rely on this technique, as we will see shortly.

Exercises 7.1

1. Assume that an input file stream, `infile`, has been opened on a file containing two integers and that `number` is an integer variable. Describe what happens when each of the following pieces of code is run:

a.
```
infile >> number;
cout << number << endl;
infile >> number;
cout << number << endl;
infile >> number;
cout << number << endl;
```

b.
```
infile >> number;
while (! infile.fail())
```

```
{
   cout << number << endl;
   infile >> number;
}
```

c.
```
while (! infile.fail())
{
   infile >> number;
   cout << number << endl;
}
```

2. Write and test a program that allows you to input your name, address, and age from the keyboard (define a string type and variables for the first two inputs). Then save this information in an output file. Be sure to place separators, either spaces or new line characters, between the data values in the file. Examine the file with a text editor to make sure that the data have been saved.
3. Write and test a program to input the data from the output file of Exercise 2 and display it on the terminal screen.
4. Extend the program of Exercise 1 so that you can input many names, addresses, and ages from the keyboard and then save them in a file (halt keyboard input when name is "done").
5. Extend the program of Exercise 2 so that it reads all of the names, addresses, and ages from a file and displays them on the terminal screen.
6. Write a program that copies integers from an input file to an output file. You should assume that the data in the input file are separated by spaces or end-of-line characters. Test the program with files containing zero, one, and ten data values. You can create test files with a text editor.
7. Extend the program of Exercise 6 so that it echoes the input data to the terminal screen as they are processed.
8. Rewrite the program of Example 7.2 so that it uses the `>>` operator to terminate the loop.

7.2 Using Functions with Files

Objectives

a. to design functions for use with file streams
b. to use file streams in conjunction with strings
c. to understand the use of buffered input of data from file streams into strings

Now that you know how to create and use file streams, we will examine how to write functions that package some useful file handling operations. Consider the problem of opening a file. This process is seldom as simple as we have seen in our examples so far, where we have assumed that the only file being processed is named `myfile`. In many cases, the user will be asked for the name of the desired file to be opened for input or output. This task involves prompting the user for the file name, reading the name into a string variable, and passing the C format of this string to the `open` operation for the file stream. In addition, we might also check for a successful opening of the stream. We can hide these details in a pair of functions, `openInputFile` and `openOutputFile`, that can be called in any application as follows:

```
openInputFile(infile);
openOutputFile(outfile);
```

`infile` and `outfile` have been declared as input and output file streams, respectively.

Each function opens a stream on the file whose name the user specifies. The file stream is returned as a reference parameter. The declaration of `openInputFile` is

```
// Function: openInputFile
// Prompts user for a file name and opens
// input stream on the file
//
// Outputs: an input file stream

void openInputFile(ifstream &infile);
```

The implementation of `openInputFile` is

```
void openInputFile(ifstream &infile)
{
   apstring infileName;

   cout << Enter the input file name: ;
   cin >> infileName;
   infile.open(infileName.c_str());      // Convert to C format string
   assert(! infile.fail());
}
```

Note that the file stream is passed as a *reference parameter*. You should never try to pass a stream as a value parameter. This may be a syntax error in some implementations of C++. `openOutputFile` has a similar declaration and implementation.

Another useful function copies the contents of a file of integers to another file. The function assumes that the two files have been successfully opened, one for input and one for output. Its declaration declares just the file stream parameters:

```
// Function: copyIntegers
// Copies integers from one file to another
//
// Inputs: an opened input file wherein integers are separated by spaces
// and an opened output file
// Output: an output file containing the contents of the input file

void copyIntegers(ifstream &infile, ofstream &outfile);
```

The implementation uses a standard `while` loop structure for input file processing:

```
void copyIntegers(ifstream &infile, ofstream &outfile)
{
   int data;

   infile >> data;
   while (! infile.fail())
   {
      outfile << data << " ";
      infile >> data;
   }
}
```

Example 7.3 The following program uses the functions we have developed to copy integers from an input file to an output file.

```
// Program file: intfile.cpp

#include <iostream.h>
#include <fstream.h>
#include <assert.h>

int main()
{
   ifstream infile;
   ofstream outfile;

   openInputFile(infile);
   openOutputFile(outfile);
   copyIntegers(infile, outfile);
   infile.close();
   outfile.close();
   return 0;
}
```

Note that the `copyIntegers` function assumes that the application will be opening and closing its files. File processing functions can be more general if they are not responsible for these details.

Files and Strings

File and string processing form the backbone of many word processing and database applications. In the following examples, we will use the string class defined in the `apstring` library. Consider the problem of searching for a given word in a file. The user inputs the desired word and file name from the keyboard. The program searches for the first instance of the word in the file. If the word is found, the program displays the position of the word in the file and asks the user whether a search for the next instance is desired. If the word is not found, the program terminates with a message. An algorithm describing the top-level process is

```
Set position to 0
Open input file
Get word from user
Do
   Search file for next instance of word
   If word is found then
      Display position of word in file
      Ask user whether another search is desired
   Else
      Display message that word was not found
While word was found and another search is desired
Close input file
```

The main loop can be controlled by two Boolean flags, which are `wordFound` and `anotherSearch`. The process of searching a file for the next instance of a given word can be handled by a function, `searchForWord`. The function has four parameters: an opened input file stream, the desired word, the `wordFound` flag, and the position of the word in the file. We can use the `openInputFile` function developed earlier in the chapter to open the file and detect an error. We can now translate the main algorithm to a main function in C++:

```
int main()
{
   apstring desiredWord;
   bool wordFound, anotherSearch;
   char query;
   ifstream infile;
   int position = 0;

   openInputFile(infile);
   cout << "Enter the word you would like to find: ";
   cin >> desiredWord;
   do
   {
      searchForWord(infile, desiredWord, position, wordFound);
      if (wordFound)
      {
         cout << "The word is at position " << position << endl;
         cout << "Search for the next instance? [Y/N]: ";
         cin >> query;
         anotherSearch = (query == 'Y') || (query == 'y');
      }
      else
         cout << "The word was not found." << endl;
   } while (wordFound && anotherSearch);
   infile.close();
   return 0;
}
```

The declaration of the function that performs the search is

```
// Function: searchForWord
// Searches for the next instance of a given word in a file
//
// Inputs: an opened input file stream, a word, and a position
// Outputs: the file stream and a Boolean flag that will be true
// if the next instance of the word was found, or false otherwise.
// If the word was found, its position in the file will be returned.
// If the word was not found, the file stream will be at its end

void searchForWord(ifstream &infile, apstring desiredWord,
                   int &position, bool &wordFound);
```

On each call, the function advances through the file stream until the next instance of the desired word is found or the `fail` condition is reached. The function increments the position parameter after reading each word. If the function finds the word in the file, it sets the flag to `true` and returns the word's position; otherwise, it sets the flag to `false`. An algorithm describing the search process is

```
Read a word from the file
Increment the position
While not end of file and the input word does not equal the desired word do
```

```
   Read a word from the file
   Increment the position
Set wordFound to not end of file
```

Note that the loop stops when we hit the end of file (there are no more words to consider) or when we have found the next instance of the desired word. The loop describes a standard process called *sequential search*. In a sequential search, we begin at the first available data item, examine it, and continue until a match is found or we run out of items to consider. If the search terminates with no more items to consider, then we have not found a match, as the assignment to the flag at the end of the algorithm indicates. The translation of the algorithm into the C++ function is

```
void searchForWord(ifstream &infile, apstring desiredWord,
                   int &position, bool &wordFound)
{
   apstring inputWord;

   infile >> inputWord;
   ++position;
   while (! infile.fail() && (inputWord != desiredWord))
   {
         infile >> inputWord;
         ++position;
   }
   wordFound = ! infile.fail();
}
```

Note that the fail condition is tested before the strings are compared in the `while` loop condition. The order of these two subexpressions within the Boolean expression is critical. If the end-of-file condition is `true`, the next subexpression will be skipped over, and the Boolean expression will return `false`. This kind of process, known as short-circuit evaluation, was introduced in Chapter 5 and guards against errors such as comparing two strings when the data for one are not defined. In our example, if the two strings were compared before the end of file was tested and end of file happened to be `true`, the program might produce mysterious and erroneous results.

The complete C++ program for searching for a word in a file is left as an exercise.

Buffered File Input

We frequently wish to take account of the line-by-line format of text in file processing. For example, we might want to count the number of lines in a file or copy the contents of one file to another with the same format. Unfortunately, the techniques we have seen thus far are inadequate for this purpose. The standard >> operator for file input treats the end-of-line character in a file as a separator between words, not lines.

The `apstring` library provides a function, `getline`, that will allow us to input lines of text from files. The form of a call to `getline` for reading a line of text is

```
getline(<input stream>, <string variable>);
```

`getline` reads characters from the input stream and stores them in the string variable until the number of characters read equals a library-specified value or the end-of-line character is reached in the stream. The end-of-line character is not stored in the variable. However, the null character is stored in the variable.

For example, suppose we declared a string variable called `line` and we wished to read a line of text from a file stream called `infile` into the variable. The following code declares the variable and inputs the text:

```
apstring line;
ifstream infile;

// Code for opening the file stream would go here

getline(infile, line);
```

The maximum number of characters that can be read with `getline` is 1024. This is not normally relevant during keyboard input, but a file might have longer lines of text.

`getline` supports a process called *buffered file input*. This process utilizes a block of computer memory, called a *buffer,* into which the data from a file are placed for transmission to a program. The main advantage of buffered file input is efficiency: Because the system reserves a block of memory of definite size for input data, the process can run very quickly.

Example 7.4 In this example, we copy the contents of one text file to another, maintaining the line-by-line format. We assume that the maximum length of a line of text in the source file is 100 characters.

```
// Program file: buffcopy.cpp

#include <iostream.h>
#include <fstream.h>
#include <assert.h>
#include "apstring.h"

// Function: openInputFile
// Prompts user for a file name and opens input stream on the file
//
// Outputs: an input file stream

void openInputFile(ifstream &infile);

// Function: openOutputFile
// Prompts user for a file name and opens output
// stream on the file
//
// Outputs: an output file stream

void openOutputFile(ofstream &outfile);

// Function: copyFile
// Copies contents of one text file to another
//
// Inputs: opened input and output file streams

void copyFile(ifstream &infile, ofstream &outfile);
```

```
int main()
{
   ifstream infile;
   ofstream outfile;

   openInputFile(infile);
   openOutputFile(outfile);
   copyFile(infile, outfile);
   infile.close();
   outfile.close();
   return 0;
}

void openInputFile(ifstream &infile)
{
   apstring infileName;

   cout << "Enter the input file name: ";
   cin >> infileName;
   infile.open(infileName.c_str());
   assert(! infile.fail());
}
void openOutputFile(ofstream &outfile)
{
   apstring outfileName;

   cout << "Enter the output file name: ";
   cin >> outfileName;
   outfile.open(outfileName.c_str());
   assert(! outfile.fail());
}

void copyFile(ifstream &infile, ofstream &outfile)
{
   apstring line;

   while (! infile.fail())
   {
      getline(infile, line);
      outfile << line << endl;
   }
}
```

Note that loop in the function `copyFile` tests for the end-of-file condition before the first input of text with `getline`. This order is different from a loop with the `>>` operator because of the difference in the way that the two operations scan the input.

Exercises 7.2

1. Write a function that counts and displays on the screen the number of words in an input file. The program assumes that words in the file are separated by blank spaces or end of lines. Test the program with files containing no words, one word, and several words.
2. Write a function that determines what the longest word in a file is. The function should display the longest word and its length on the terminal screen.
3. Write a function that finds and displays the average length of the words in a file.

A NOTE OF INTEREST

Computer Ethics: Viruses

A *virus* is a computer program that can replicate itself and move from computer to computer. Some programmers of viruses intend no harm; they just want to demonstrate their prowess by creating viruses that go undetected. Other programmers of viruses intend harm by causing system crashes, corruption of data, or hardware failures. Viruses migrate by attaching themselves to normal programs and then become active again when these programs are launched. Early viruses were easily detected if one had detection software. This software examined portions of each program on the suspect computer and could repair infected programs.

However, viruses and virus detectors have coevolved through the years, and both kinds of software have become very sophisticated. Viruses now hide themselves better than they used to; virus detectors can no longer just examine pieces of data stored in memory to reveal the presence or absence of a virus. Researchers have recently developed a method of running a program that might contain a virus to see whether or not the virus becomes active. The suspect program runs in a "safe" environment that protects the computer from any potential harm. As you can imagine, this process takes time and costs money. For an overview of the history of viruses and the new detection technology, see Carey Nachenberg, "Computer Virus–Antivirus Coevolution," *Communications of the ACM*, Vol. 40, No. 1, Jan. 1997, pp. 46–51.

4. Write a function that prompts the user for a word from the keyboard. Write a second function that counts the number of times this word appears in a file. The program that uses this function should display the word count on the terminal screen.

7.3 Character Input and Output

Objectives

a. to obtain character data from input and output file streams
b. to distinguish character-level input and output from the input and output of other data types

Many problems call for the input and output of individual characters with file streams. Consider the problems of counting the total number of characters in a file and counting the total number of lines of text in a file. If these data include individual space or new line characters, we cannot rely on formatting conventions and the use of the >> operator for input. Recall that the >> operator treats space or new line characters as separators between data values in an input stream. Therefore, the >> operator cannot be used to input white space characters as data values in their own right. C++ provides two lower level operators, `get` and `put`, for handling character-level operations on streams.

Character Output with `put`

Character output with `put` is not much different than character output with <<. Assuming that `outfile` is an output file stream, the following three statements will have exactly the same effect on the file:

```
// Output a string with <<

outfile << "abcd";

// Output 4 characters with <<

for (char ch = 'a'; ch <= 'd'; ++ch)
   outfile << ch;
```

```
// Output 4 characters with put

for (char ch = 'a'; ch <= 'd'; ++ch)
   outfile.put(ch);
```

The form of a statement that uses `put` is

<output file stream>`.put(`<character value>`);`

`put` is called as a function with a character value as its parameter. The function call is associated with the output stream by placing a period (".") between the name of the stream and the name of the function.

In general, `put` is defined such that it can work with any output stream. The loop

```
for (int j = 0; j < name.length(); j ++)
   cout.put(name [j]);
```

will print the contents of the string on the terminal screen.

Character Input with `get`

Character input with `get` works in much the same way as character input with >>. One difference is that blank space and new line characters will be treated as character values in their own right. The form of a statement that uses `get` is

<input stream>`.get(`<character variable>`);`

The following statement would get the first character in a file and place it in the character variable `ch`:

```
infile.get(ch);
```

Detecting the End of File at the Character Level

A special character value is reserved to mark the end of a file of characters. In the case of an empty file, this character is the only character present in the file. It is important to detect this character during input so that further input is not attempted. It turns out that after the end-of-file character has been read with `get`, the `fail` function will return `true`. Otherwise, it will return `false`.

`<file stream>.fail()` can be used to control a `while` loop for processing an entire stream of characters. A standard form of a loop for processing character-level input from a file stream is

```
<input stream name>.get(<character variable>);
while (! <input stream name>.fail())
{
   processData(<character variable>);
   <input stream name>.get(<character variable>);
}
```

Note the order of the operations in this process. We get a character first, since there will be at least one character in the file. Then the condition in the `while` loop protects the program from attempting to get or process any more characters when the end-of-file condition becomes `true`. The first step in the body of the loop is to process the character just read (either the initial one or the one from the previous pass through the loop). The second step in the loop is to get the next character, which eventually will be the end-of-file character.

The next three examples illustrate algorithms for counting the number of characters in a file, counting the number of lines in a file, and copying the contents of one file to another file.

Example 7.5

```
// This program counts and displays the number of characters in a file.
// We don't count the end-of-file character as one of these.

// Program file: charcnt.cpp

#include <iostream.h>
#include <fstream.h>

int main()
{
   ifstream infile;
   char ch;
   int count;

   infile.open("myfile");
   count = 0;
   infile.get(ch);
   while (! infile.fail())
   {
      ++count ;
      infile.get(ch);
   }
   cout << "The total number of characters in myfile is " << count << endl;
   infile.close();
   return 0;
}
```

Example 7.6 To count the number of lines of text in a file, we can count the number of instances of the new line character denoted by `'\n'` in C++.

```
// This program counts and displays the number of lines in a file.

// Program file: linecnt.cpp

#include <iostream.h>
#include <fstream.h>

int main()
{
```

```
   ifstream infile;
   char ch;
   int count;

   infile.open("myfile");
   count = 0;
   infile.get(ch);
   while (! infile.fail())
   {
      if (ch == '\n')
         ++count;
      infile.get(ch);
   }
   infile.close();
   cout << "The total number of lines in myfile is " << count << endl;
   return 0;
}
```

Example 7.7

```
// This program copies the contents of one file to another file.

// Program file: copyfile.cpp

#include <iostream.h>
#include <fstream.h>

int main()
{
   ifstream infile;
   ofstream outfile;
   char ch;

   infile.open("myfile");
   outfile.open("newfile");
   infile.get(ch);
   while (! infile.fail())
   {
         outfile.put(ch);
         infile.get(ch);
   }
   infile.close();
   outfile.close();
   return 0;
}
```

The last example calls for some comment. We copy every character from the input file to the output file, except for the input file's end-of-file character. This might lead you to think that the output file has no end-of-file character. However, the computer takes care of appending an end-of-file character to an output file whenever it is closed. Therefore, we were right to ignore the input file's end-of-file character. If we had copied it to the output file, this file would have contained two end-of-file characters and would not have reflected the contents of the input file accurately.

A NOTE OF INTEREST

Digital Video Disks

Technology is changing so rapidly that it is almost futile to comment on the current state of events. Nevertheless, we do so for two reasons. The first reason is to make you aware of rapidly changing technology; the second is that it is always interesting to mark a point in time from a historical perspective. Thus, we offer an observation about the current status of computer memory.

It is predicted that computer memory is about to undergo a tremendous revolution. Digital video disks (DVDs) are the latest disks in the ever-changing world of data storage. They are marketed as 4.75-inch disks, the same as current CDs. When recorded on two sides, they hold up to 18 gigabytes (giga means billion). The basic entry-level DVD with only one side recorded holds 4.7 gigabytes. That is as much as 7.5 ordinary CDs or 3450 3.5-inch high-density floppy disks. Potential computer applications are enormous. In a business worth more than $20 billion a year, 120 million DVDs are currently being marketed.

In its read-only format, a DVD creates memory able to hold not only encyclopedias but entire libraries. In rewritable configurations, a DVD allows a personal computer to map the heavens or project accurate star maps from any perspective in the sky. DVD technology reduces mainframe computer storage systems from rooms of disk drives to a few DVD players on a bookshelf. The potential for entertainment is immense. A single disk is able to hold one movie of over 2 hours on a side with three audio tracks. Interactive players allow a viewer to choose camera angles such as pan, scan, widescreen, and closeup for as many as nine camera angles. DVD technology, high-definition television, and high-end audio equipment could create a multiple playback system that had been confined to recording studios until now.

Exercises 7.3

1. Assume that an input file stream, `infile`, has been opened on a file and that `ch` is a character variable. Describe what happens when each of the following pieces of code is run:

a.
```
infile.get(ch);
cout.put(ch);
infile.get(ch);
cout.put(ch);
infile.get(ch);
cout.put(ch);
```

b.
```
infile.get(ch);
while (! infile.fail())
{
   cout.put(ch);
   infile.get(ch);
}
```

c.
```
while (! infile.fail())
{
   infile.get(ch);
   cout.put(ch);
}
```

2. Write a program that deletes all blanks from a file. Your program should save the revised file for later use. (*Hint:* Copy the contents of the input file to another file, omitting the blanks.)
3. Write a program using a `switch` statement to scramble a file by replacing all blanks with an asterisk (*) and interchanging all As with U's and E's with I's. Your program should print out the scrambled file and save it for subsequent use.

4. Write a program to update a file by numbering the lines consecutively as 1, 2, 3, ... The input file should not be modified.
5. Write a program to count the number of uppercase characters in a file.
6. Write a program to count the number of words in a text file. Assume that each word is followed by a blank or a period. The program should use `get` rather than `>>` to receive the input from the file.
7. Write a program to find the longest word in a file. Output should include the word and its length. The program should use `get` rather than `>>` to receive the input from the file.
8. Write a program to compute the average length of words in a file. The program should use `get` rather than `>>` to receive the input from the file.
9. Write a program that performs a search-and-replace operation on a file. The program will prompt the user for the word to search and the word to use as a replacement. The program should replace all of the instances of the target word with the replacement word.

Case Study: Analyzing a File of Sentences

The case study program for this chapter analyzes sentences in a file of text. It builds on Case Study 6.2, in which we analyzed single sentences entered from the keyboard. That program displayed statistics about the number of characters and words in the sentence and printed the longest word in the sentence as well. We used strings to represent words and string functions to handle the tasks of input, output, comparison, and determining word length.

User Request

Write a program that analyzes sentences in a text file.

Analysis

The current program will prompt the user for a file name and open the file. If no error occurs, the program will compute and display statistics for

1. The total number of sentences in the file
2. The total number of words in the file
3. The average length of a sentence in the file
4. The length of the longest sentence in the file.

The program will recognize several kinds of sentences: those ending in a period ('.'), a question mark ('?'), and an exclamation point ('!'). Normally, a word ending with one of these characters will be treated as the last word in a sentence. As a special case, if one of these characters does not end the last word in the file, then that word is also treated as the last word in a sentence.

After the statistics are displayed, the program will ask the user if the analysis of another file is desired. If the answer is "Yes," the program will repeat the process; otherwise, the program will terminate execution.

Design

A reasonable top-level module is

```
Do
    Open input file
```

continued

```
    If there was no error opening the file then
       Initialize data
       Analyze sentences in file
       Close input file
       Display statistics
    Else
       Display error message
    Query user for another analysis
While answer to query is Yes
```

Before we can examine the submodules within this module, we must make explicit the data that are transmitted among them. The modules for opening and closing a file, and for analyzing sentences in the file, require a file stream. The modules for initializing data, analyzing sentences, and displaying statistics all require three integers, which represent the total number of sentences, the total number of words, and the length of the longest sentence. Average sentence length can be computed locally in the display statistics module as a function of the other data. This data flow is shown in the structure chart in Figure 7.3.

The main module translates to the following C++ main function:

```
int main()
{
   char query;
   ifstream infile;
   int wordCount, sentenceCount, longestSentenceLength;

   do
   {
      openInputFile(infile);
      initializeData(wordCount, sentenceCount,
                     longestSentenceLength);
      analyzeSentences(infile, wordCount, sentenceCount,
                       longestSentenceLength);
      infile.close();
      displayStatistics(wordCount, sentenceCount,
                        longestSentenceLength);
```

Figure 7.3
A structure chart for analyzing sentences

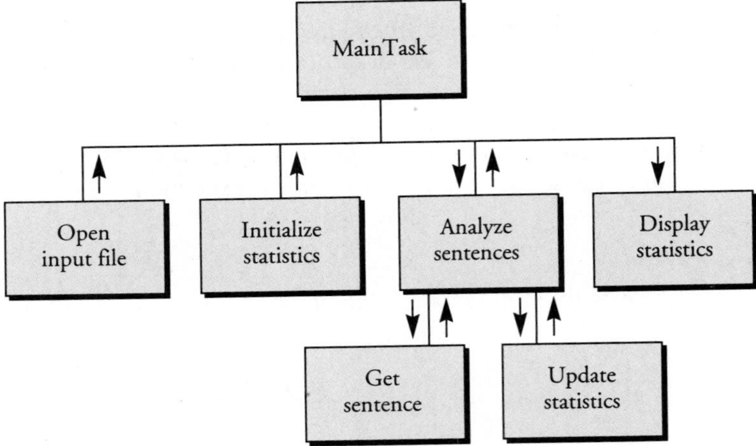

```
      cout << "Analyze another file? [Y/N] ";
      cin >> query;
   } while ((query == 'Y') || (query == 'y'));
   return 0;
}
```

The module to initialize the data sets all of the integers to zero.

Module: Initialize data
Task: Set all integers to zero
Outputs: integers representing the total number of sentences, the total number of words, and the length of the longest sentence

```
Set sentence count to 0
Set word count to 0
Set longest sentence length to 0
```

The C++ implementation is

```
void initializeData(int &wordCount, int &sentenceCount,
                     int &longestSentenceLength)
{
   wordCount = 0;
   sentenceCount = 0;
   longestSentenceLength = 0;
}
```

The module to analyze sentences must repeatedly invoke a process we developed in the program in Chapter 6 to analyze a single sentence. The difference here is that we read a sentence from a file and return just a word count. This value is then passed with the other data to a submodule that updates the statistics. The subprocesses are structured within a standard input file process.

Module: Analyze sentences
Task: Read sentences from a file and compute statistics
Inputs: a file stream and integers representing the total number of sentences, the total number of words, and the length of the longest sentence
Outputs: the integers updated

```
Do
   Get a word count on an input sentence
   If the word count > 0 then
      Update statistics
While not end of file
```

Note that a sentence may have a word count of zero. This occurs only in the special case where the input file is empty. The C++ implementation maintains the word count of the current input sentence as a local variable, `currentCount`:

```
void analyzeSentences(ifstream &infile,
                      int &wordCount,
                      int &sentenceCount,
                      int &longestSentenceLength)
```

continued

```
{
   int currentCount;

   do
   {
      getSentence(infile, currentCount);
      if (currentCount > 0)
         updateStatistics(currentCount, wordCount, sentenceCount,
                          longestSentenceLength);
   } while (! infile.fail());
}
```

The module to display statistics computes the average length of a sentence and displays the four integer values with descriptive labels. Here is the C++ implementation:

```
void displayStatistics(int wordCount, int sentenceCount,
                       int longestSentenceLength)
{
   cout << endl << "Statistics for the current file. " << endl << endl;
   cout << "The number of words is " << wordCount << "." << endl;
   cout << "The number of sentences is " << sentenceCount << "." << endl;
   cout << "The average length of a sentence is "
        << wordCount / sentenceCount << "." << endl;
   cout << "The longest sentence had " << longestSentenceLength
        << " words." << endl << endl;
}
```

The get sentence module reads words from the file and maintains a count of them. This is an iterative process with two possible termination conditions: Either the end of file has been reached, or the last input word contains a sentence termination character ('.', '?', or '!') at the end.

Module: Get sentence
Task: Read words from a sentence and maintain a count of words
Input: an input file stream
Output: the count of words in the sentence; 0 words means no sentence at all

```
Set count to 0
Read a word from the file
If not end of file then
  Increment count by one
  While not end of file and word not at end of sentence do
     Read a word from the file
     Increment count by one
```

The initial test for an end of file guards against the case where the file is empty. The C++ implementation is

```
void getSentence(ifstream &infile, int &count)
{
   apstring word;

   count = 0;
   infile >> word;
```

```
   if (! infile.fail())
   {
      ++count;
      while (! infile.fail() && ! endOfSentence(word))
      {
         infile >> word;
         ++count;
      }
   }
}
```

The update statistics module increments the word count and the sentence count and adjusts the length of the longest sentence if necessary.

Module: Update statistics
Task: Increment word and sentence counts and adjust length of longest sentence if necessary
Inputs: integers representing the number of words in the current sentence, the total number of sentences, the total number of words, and the length of the longest sentence
Outputs: the last three input integers updated

```
Increment the word count by the number of words in the current sentence
Increment the sentence count by one
If number of words in the current sentence > length of the longest sentence
   Set length of the longest sentence to number of words
   in the current sentence
```

The C++ implementation is

```
void updateStatistics(int currentCount,
                      int &wordCount,
                      int &sentenceCount,
                      int &longestSentenceLength)
{
   wordCount = wordCount + currentCount;
   ++sentenceCount;
   if (currentCount > longestSentenceLength)
      longestSentenceLength = currentCount;
}
```

At the lowest level of our design, the end-of-sentence module tests a word to see whether it marks the end of a sentence.

Module: End of sentence
Task: Determine whether a word marks the end of a sentence
Input: a word
Output: true if the word ends with '.', '?', or '!', and false otherwise

Here is the C++ implementation of the module:

```
bool endOfSentence(apstring word)
{
   char lastCh = word[word.length() - 1];

   return(lastCh == '.') || (lastCh == '?') || (lastCh == '!');
}
```

Running, Debugging, and Testing Hints

1. `>>` treats an end-of-line marker and a blank space as input separators.
2. `get` treats an end-of-line marker and a blank space as character data.
3. Always test for the end-of-file condition after getting a character from an input file. If the condition is true, do not attempt to process the most recently read character or to read more characters from the file.

Summary

Key Terms

buffer
destination device
end-of-input stream
input file stream
output file stream
serial processing
source device
stream

Key Concepts

- Files can be used to store data between runs of a program.
- Access to file stream operations can be obtained by

```
#include <fstream.h>
```

- An input file stream can be declared by

```
ifstream <stream name>;
```

- An output file stream can be declared by

```
ofstream <stream name>;
```

- File streams must be opened before they can be written to or read from.
- A file stream can be opened by

```
<stream name>.open(<file name>);
```

- A file stream can be closed by

```
<stream name>.close();
```

- An error in connecting a stream to a file can be detected by

```
<stream name>.fail();
```

- For input data of most types, reading from a file stream can be accomplished by

```
<input file stream name> >> <variable name> . . . >> <variable name>;
```

- For output data of most types, writing to a file stream can be accomplished by

```
<output file stream name> << <expression> . . . << <expression>;
```

- When reading data from a file stream with >>, the absence of more data in an input stream can be detected by reading a datum and then running

```
<input stream name>.fail()
```

- Alternatively, to detect the end of file, an input operation with >> can be placed in a loop control condition, such as

```
while (<input stream name> >> data)
```

- This condition will be `true` if there are more data to be read and `false` otherwise.
- When reading character-level input, the absence of more data in an input stream can be detected by reading a character and then running

```
<input stream name>.fail()
```

- A line of text can be read from an input stream by using the buffered input `apstring` function `getline` as follows:

```
getline(<input stream name>, <string variable);
```

- Character data can be read from an input stream by

```
<input stream name>.get(<character variable>);
```

- Character data can be written to an output stream by

```
<output stream name>.put(<character value>);
```

- A file exists outside the program block in secondary storage.

Programming Problems and Projects

1. Write a program to print the contents of a text file omitting any occurrences of the letter 'e' from the output.
2. A text file contains a list of integers in order from lowest to highest. Write a program to read and print the text file with all duplications eliminated.
3. Mr. John Napier, professor at Lancaster Community College, wants a program to compute grade-point averages. Each line of a text file contains three initials followed by an unknown number of letter grades. These grades are A, B, C, D, or E. Write a program that reads the file and prints a list of the students' initials and their grade-point averages. (Assume an A is 4 points, a B is 3 points, and so on.) Print an asterisk next to any grade-point average that is greater than 3.75.
4. An amortization table (Problem 19, Chapter 6) shows the rate at which a loan is paid off. It contains monthly entries showing the interest paid that month, the principal

paid, and the remaining balance. Given the amount of money borrowed (the principal), the annual interest rate, and the amount the person wishes to repay each month, save an amortization table to an output file. (The payment desired must be larger than the first month's interest.) Your table should stop when the loan is paid off and should be printed with the following heads:

```
MONTH NUMBER    INTEREST PAID    PRINCIPAL PAID    BALANCE
```

Require the loan to be paid back within 60 months.

5. Mr. Christian (Problem 26, Chapter 6) uses a 90%, 80%, 70%, 60% grading scale on his tests. Given a list of test scores, save the number of As, Bs, Cs, Ds, and Fs on the test to an output file. Terminate the list of scores with a sentinel value.
6. Write a program to print the perimeter and area of rectangles using all combinations of lengths and widths running from 1 foot to 10 feet in increments of 1 foot. Print the output in headed columns.
7. Using a team of three or four students, contact businesses and offices that use computers for data storage. Find exactly how they enter, store, and retrieve data. Discuss with them methods by which they use their databases and how large the databases are. Discuss what they like and dislike about data entry and retrieval. Ask if they have suggestions for modifying any aspect of working with their databases. Prepare a report for class that summarizes your team's findings.
8. Read in a list of 50 integers from the data file `numberlist`. Place the even numbers into an output file called `even`, the odd numbers into an output file called `odd`, and the negatives into an output file called `negative`. Print all three files after all numbers have been read.
9. Assume that a data file named `testfile` contains real numbers separated by spaces or end of lines. Write a program that inputs these data and displays the largest value, the smallest value, the average value, and the sum of all of the values in the terminal window.
10. The data file `instructorlist` contains a list of the instructors in your school along with the room number to which each is assigned. Write a program that, given the name of the instructor, does a search to find and print the room to which the instructor is assigned.

8

Building Structured Data: Structs and Classes

Chapter Outline

Thus far in this text, you have been designing algorithms to solve problems and coding your solutions in C++ using the major control structures of sequencing, selection, iteration, and functional abstraction. In the last chapter, we began a shift in focus that will guide us through the rest of the text. We considered how to solve problems by structuring the data of a program appropriately with files. In the present chapter, we continue this approach. We begin by examining a new kind of data structure called a *record* in some programming languages and a *struct* in C++. Unlike a file or a string, which organizes data elements that are all of the same type, a struct organizes data elements that are of different types. We then explore the development of some simple data structures using C++ *classes*. Classes are useful for building models of real-world objects. In the process, we begin the transition from a *procedural programming* style to an *object-oriented programming* style.

8.1 The Struct Data Type

Basic Idea and Notation

Consider the problem of maintaining information for an employee of a company. This information might include a name, an address (street, city, state, and zip code), an age, and a salary. We could declare separate variables to store all of this information as follows:

```
apstring name, street, city, state, zipCode;
int age;
double salary;
```

However, there are several problems with this way of representing the information:

1. We will have to repeat all of these declarations, using different variable names, for each employee used by an application.

Objectives

a. to understand the idea of a struct as a structured data type
b. to declare and use structs to represent and process information
c. to use functions with structs
d. to use structs to build more complex data structures
e. to understand the benefits of data abstraction
f. to define abstract data types in libraries

2. If we want to add other kinds of information about an employee, such as length of service and job classification, we will have to add new variables for every employee in the application.
3. It might be useful to consider the information for an employee as one unit containing several items. For example, we might want to store several such units in a file of these units or pass the unit as an argument to a function.

In C++, a convenient way to represent a collection of different data items as a unit is to use a *struct*. To return to our example of an employee's information, we could declare two struct variables, `employee1` and `employee2`, each of which contains the data elements for an employee as follows:

```
struct
{
   apstring name, street, city, state, zipCode;
   int age;
   double salary;
} employee1, employee2;
```

When these struct variables are declared, the computer allocates memory for all of the components in both structs. These components are called *fields* or *members* of the struct. The form of a struct variable declaration is

```
struct
{
       <data type><member name 1>;
       .
       .
       <data type><member name n>;
} <list of struct variable names>;
```

Note the following points:

1. The word `struct` is reserved.
2. The members of a struct can be of any data type, including user-defined types.
3. There can be any number of members in a struct, but usually there are at least two.
4. The struct type created with this form is *anonymous*. We show how to create named struct types shortly.

The members of a struct are accessed by using a *selector*. A selector is formed by placing a period (`.`) between a struct variable and the name of a member. For example, the following code segment initializes the members of the `employee1` variable to default values:

```
employee1.name = "John Doe";
employee1.street = "102 Maple Lane";
employee1.city = "York";
employee1.state = "PA";
employee1.zipCode = "12309";
employee1.age = 21;
employee1.salary = 10000.00;
```

The form for accessing a member of a struct variable is

```
<struct variable>.<member name>
```

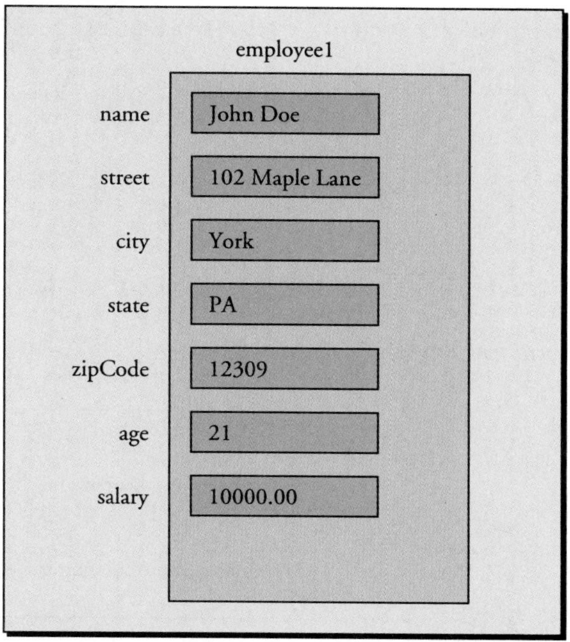

Figure 8.1
Visualization of a struct variable

After the statements in this code segment have executed, the memory for the `employee1` variable could be visualized as shown in Figure 8.1.

The important thing to note about a struct variable is that its name serves as a label for an entire group of data items, whereas each member name serves as a label for a data item contained in the struct variable.

One manipulation of a struct variable as a unit is assignment. For example, the following statement copies all of the members of `employee1` to `employee2`:

```
employee2 = employee1;
```

This statement has the same effect as a series of assignments of all of the members.

```
employee2.name = employee1.name;
employee2.street = employee1.street;
employee2.city = employee1.city;
employee2.state = employee1.state;
employee2.zipCode = employee1.zipCode;
employee2.age = employee1.age;
employee2.salary = employee1.salary;
```

Note that the assignment of one struct variable to another struct variable has the desired effect of copying all of the data elements.

As with Booleans, it is often convenient to define a type name for a struct and use this name to declare struct variable names and struct function parameters. For example, the following code defines a struct type name, `employeeType`, and declares two variables of that type:

```
struct employeeType
{
```

continued

```
    apstring name, street, city, state, zipCode;
    int age;
    double salary;
};

.
.
.

employeeType employee1, employee2;
```

The form for defining a struct type is

```
struct <new type name>
{
        <data type><member name 1>;
        .
        .
        <data type><member name n>;
};
```

Note that a semicolon (`;`) must immediately follow the right curly brace (`}`) at the end of the definition.

One advantage of this way of structuring the information is that an application has one place, the type definition, where the attributes of all employees are specified as members of a struct. Each variable of this type will then have its own memory allocated for its particular member values.

A struct can be used to build more complex data structures. For example, it might be convenient to treat the address of each employee as a single unit consisting of a street, a city, and a zip code. The following code segment defines a type name, `addressType`, to represent this information and then uses this name to simplify the definition of the struct for an employee.

```
struct addressType
{
    apstring street, city, zipCode;
};

struct employeeType
{
    apstring name;
    addressType address;
    int age;
    double salary;
};

employeeType employee1, employee2;
```

The parts of an employee's address are now accessed by using more than one selector. For example, the expression

```
cout << << "City: " << employee1.address.city << endl;
```

outputs the `city` member (a string) contained in the `address` member (a struct) of the `employee1` variable (a struct). For now, however, we continue to use the previous definition of `employeeType` in our examples.

Communication and Style Tips

1. When working with complex information, try to simplify the way it is represented by grouping related data together and treating them as a unit.
2. When the related data are of different types and it is useful to access them by specifying names, use a struct to group them.
3. Like algorithms, data structures can be developed in a top-down fashion using stepwise refinement. Begin by defining the top-level data structure, such as an employee structure. Then work your way down (up in the program's text) to lower levels of data structures, such as the structure of an employee's address. This refinement will eventually lead you to a complete definition of the data structures necessary for an application.

Using Structs with Functions

One purpose of a function is to enable an application to treat a complex set of operations on the elements of a data structure as a single operation on a single data structure. This simplicity is evident in the following sequence of statements:

```
apstring str = "Hi there";
cin >> str;
cout << str;
```

Functions can be used with structs in a similar way. Different functions might initialize a struct, input data into it, and display it. We assume that someone has provided functions named `initEmployee`, `readEmployee`, and `printEmployee`. The first two functions return a value of type `employeeType`. The third function expects a parameter of type `employeeType`.

```
// Declare the employee

employeeType employee;

// Initialize the employee

employee = initEmployee();

// Input the employee

employee = readEmployee();

// Output the employee

printEmployee(employee);
```

Note that the reader of this application can see what tasks are accomplished for an employee without having to read and understand how they are accomplished.

The use of types names for structs simplifies the declarations of functions that process them. The declarations of `initEmployee` and `readEmployee` expect no parameters and return a value of type `employeeType` (a struct).

```
// Function: initEmployee
// Initializes the components of
// the structure of an employee
// to their default values
//
// Output: an employee structure

employeeType initEmployee();

// Function: readEmployee
// Prompts for and inputs the components
// of an employee structure
//
// Output: an employee structure

employeeType readEmployee();
```

The implementations of these functions hide the details of setting the members of the employee's struct to the appropriate values.

```
employeeType initEmployee()
{
   employeeType employee;

   employee.name = "John Doe";
   employee.street = "102 Maple Lane";
   employee.city = "York";
   employee.state = "PA";
   employee.zipCode = "12309";
   employee.age = 21;
   employee.salary = 10000.00;
   return employee;
}
```

```
employeeType readEmployee()
{
   employeeType employee;

   cout << "Enter the name: ";
   getline(cin, employee.name);
   cout << "Enter the street: ";
   getline(cin, employee.street);
   cout << "Enter the city: ";
   getline(cin, employee.city);
   cout << "Enter the state: ";
   cin >> employee.state;
   cout << "Enter the zip code: ";
   cin >> employee.zipCode;
   cout << "Enter the age: ";
   cin >> employee.age;
```

```
    cout << "Enter the salary: $";
    cin >> employee.salary;
    return employee;
}
```

Note that each of these functions declares a local `employeeType` variable. This variable is used to store the values of the employee's attributes and is then returned as the value of the function.

The declaration of `printEmployee` specifies a parameter of type `employeeType`.

```
// Function: printEmployee
// Displays the components of the
// structure of an employee
//
// Input: an employee structure

void printEmployee(const employeeType &employee);
```

Note that the `employee` parameter is declared as a constant reference parameter. Recall that constant reference parameters were discussed in Chapter 4. In C++, structs may be passed as value parameters, reference parameters, or constant reference parameters. When passed by value, all of the components of a struct are copied into temporary storage locations. Therefore, to economize on memory, constant reference is the preferred parameter passing mode for structs when they have several members.

The implementation of `printEmployee` follows:

```
void printEmployee(const employeeType &employee)
{
    cout << "Name:     " << employee.name << endl;
    cout << "Address: " << employee.street << endl;
    cout << "          " << employee.city
         << " " << employee.state << "  "
         << employee.zipCode << endl;
    cout << "Age:      " << employee.age << endl;
    cout << "Salary:   $" << employee.salary << endl;
}
```

Data Abstraction and Abstract Data Types

The separation of functions, whereby we associate a set of functions with each kind of data structure, is known as *data abstraction*. As you learned in Chapter 4, a function is an abstraction in that it simplifies a complex task for its users. To simplify complex data for users, we need to provide two components:

1. A data structure, such as a string or a struct, preferably labeled with a type name
2. A set of functions that perform the operations on the data structure

Data types that provide operations in this way are known as *abstract data types* or ADTs. The primary benefits of an abstract data type are simplicity and ease of use. For example, the types `int`, `double`, and `apstring` are easy to understand and use because they are abstract—they come with sets of operations that literally say what they do without divulging the complex details of how they do it. We now provide a more formal definition of an abstract data type:

An abstract data type (ADT) consists of a set of values, a defined set of properties of these values, and a set of operations for processing the values.

Note that the definition of an ADT makes no mention of how it is implemented or even of the uses to which it may be put in a program.

Many ADTs in C++ are already defined in libraries. The library header file contains the type definitions for the data structures and the declarations of the functions for the ADT. The library implementation file contains the implementations of the functions. Thus, a programmer might provide some ADTs for other programmers by creating the appropriate library files.

As an example, an application that uses employees would benefit by having a library file for the `employeeType` ADT. A very simple version of this ADT might support just the operations for initializing, reading, and printing values that we explored earlier in this section.

Example 8.1 The header file for the `employeeType` ADT contains the definition of `employeeType` and the declarations of the functions `initEmployee`, `readEmployee`, and `printEmployee`. The file depends on the definition of the `apstring` ADT, so the `apstring.h` library header file is included.

```
// Library header file: employee.h

#ifndef EMPLOYEE_H
#define EMPLOYEE_H

#include "apstring.h"

struct employeeType
{
   apstring name, street, city, state, zipCode;
   int age;
   double salary;
};

// Function: initEmployee
// Initializes the components of
// the structure of an employee
// to their default values
//
// Output: an employee structure

employeeType initEmployee();

// Function: readEmployee
// Prompts for and inputs the components
// of an employee structure
//
// Output: an employee structure

employeeType readEmployee();

// Function: printEmployee
// Displays the components of the
// structure of an employee
```

```
//
// Input: an employee structure

void printEmployee(const employeeType &employee);

#endif
```

Communication and Style Tips

1. When designing a new data structure to solve a problem, begin by describing the operations that manipulate this structure. Declare these as C++ functions with the appropriate documentation.
2. Place the type definition of a new data structure and the function declarations for its operations in a library header file.
3. Implement the functions for a new data structure in a library implementation file.
4. Maintain a separate library for each new data structure that you develop.

Exercises 8.1

1. Explain the differences between strings and structs as structured data types.
2. Use a `struct` to define a new type called `teamMember`. This type should contain the components for a name, age, weight, height, and scoring average.
3. Use a `struct` to define a new type called `book`. This type should contain the components for a title, author, publication date, and price.
4. Use a `struct` to define a new type called `student`. This type should contain the components for a name, social security number, four test scores, and the average of these scores.

   For Exercises 5 and 6, draw a diagram of the memory allocated for the variables of the indicated types.

5.
```
struct
{
   apstring name, ssn;
   int numOfDep;
   double wage;
} employee;
```

6.
```
struct
{
   apstring location;
   int age, numRooms, numBaths;
   double taxes, price;
} houseInfo;
```

7. Assume that a new type has been defined as

```
struct student
{
   apstring name;
   int totalPoints;
   char letterGrade;
};
```

Write a function that computes a student's letter grade (A, B, C, or F) based on the cutoff levels of 90%, 80%, 70%, and 60%. Show how this function can be used in a program to set the appropriate member of a student structure.

8. Write a function named `equals` that takes two parameters of type `employeeType` as defined in this section. The function should return a Boolean value indicating whether or not the `name` members in the two employee structures are the same.
9. Compare the two ways of structuring the data in Example 8.6, assessing their relative advantages and disadvantages.
10. Why is it a good idea to define a set of functions for each new data structure?

8.2 Introduction to User-Defined Classes

Objectives

a. to understand problems with data security that arise during the development of abstract data types
b. to learn about implementing abstract data types as classes that guarantee data security
c. to examine the implementation and use of an ADT as a class

Abstract Data Types and Data Security

Viewed as an abstract data type, the `employeeType` developed in the preceding section consists of a set of high-level operations, such as copying, comparisons, input, and output. Viewed as a C++ implementation, the `employeeType` consists of a `struct` type and several C++ function definitions. Although this implementation of the `employeeType` ADT is quite useful, it is not ideal. The primary problem is that the data in the implementation are not secure. There are too many ways in which users' modules can access the data and cause side effects. For example, the age in a given employee's structure should change only as a result of running certain employee processing functions as follows:

```
initEmployee(employee); // Initialize all attributes

readEmployee(employee); // Input all attributes

incrementAge(employee); // Update the age attribute on the
                        // employee's birthday
```

However, given the scope rules of C++, nothing prevents the user of the `employee` variable from running statements such as

```
employee.age = employee.age - 5;    // Makes employee younger
```

This statement is allowed by the language, but it violates the intent of the programmers who provide the `employeeType` module. Errors due to side effects in large software systems are usually more subtle than this one. But the problem is quite general. What we would like to do is develop a way of defining a data type that restricts the access that users have to the internal structure of the data to just those operations or functions provided by the data type. Program comments, warnings, and self-imposed restraint are not enough: These restrictions must be imposed by the compiler of the programming language. In other words, statements such as the last one should be prohibited outside of the module that implements the data type.

Data Encapsulation, Classes, and Objects

An ADT should give users just a *logical view* of the data in terms of the operations on it so that users need not be concerned with the details of how the data are *represented*. For example, a string ADT might have operations for assignment, output, input, and comparisons. Ideally, the user of an individual string should not be able to access its component parts except by invoking these operations. If this is the case, the data are said to be *encapsulated*.

C++ allows programmers to define ADTs as *classes*. By defining an ADT as a class, we can restrict the access that users have to the data of any *objects* or *instances* of that class. An object is like an intelligent agent that takes a request for a service from a user and processes its own internal data to carry out the request.

We now show how to define and implement a class to represent bank accounts. Since this is our first opportunity to define and implement a C++ class, do not expect to master all of the details right away. However, we are not going to hide anything from you. We will develop other ADTs as classes in later chapters.

User Requirements for a Bank Account Class

The first step in developing a new class to solve a problem is to draw up a list of user requirements. These state the *attributes* and *operations* that users expect the class to have. A minimal set of attributes for a bank account might be:

1. A password (a string)
2. A balance (a real number)

The operations that users expect to perform on bank accounts follow:

1. Create a new account with default password and balance
2. Create a new account with user-specified password and balance
3. Change the password
4. Deposit money
5. Withdraw money
6. Observe the balance

These lists of attributes and operations can be visualized as shown in Figure 8.2.

Users expect the balance in an account to be secure. They do not want Smith's deposit going into Jones's account, unless it is a joint account. Access to an account's attributes cannot occur without knowledge of the owner's password. Thus, the owner's password must be passed as a parameter to the operations that observe or

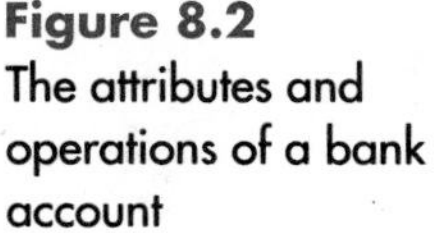
Figure 8.2
The attributes and operations of a bank account

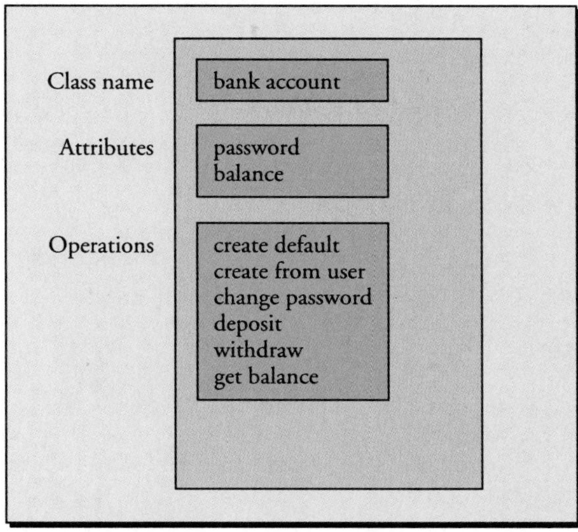

modify any of the attributes. Each of these operations will verify the validity of the password. If access is denied, each operation will return –1. Otherwise, some other value will be returned, such as the amount of the current balance. The withdrawal operation will return –2 if the user has insufficient funds.

Example 8.2 Assume that a class called `account` has been defined in a library file. The following driver program shows how to create and access a bank account object:

```
// Program file: bankdriv.cpp

#include <iostream.h>
#include <iomanip.h>

#include "account.h"

int main()
{
   // Create two accounts and a dummy target

   account judy("honeybee", 50.00);
   account jim("spider", 100.00);
   account target;

   cout << setiosflags(ios::fixed | ios::showpoint)
        << setprecision(2);

   // Look up balances

   cout << "Judy's balance = $"
        << judy.getBalance("honeybee") << endl;

   cout << "Jim's balance = $"
        << jim.getBalance("spider") << endl;

   // An invalid password

   cout << "Result of invalid password = "
           << jim.getBalance("rosebud") << endl;

   // Make a deposit

   cout << "Depositing $20.00 to Jim, new balance = $"
        << jim.deposit("spider", 20.00) << endl;

   // An attempted overdraft

   cout << "Result of overdraft from Judy ($51.00) = "
        << judy.withdraw("honeybee", 51.00) << endl;

   // Copy to dummy target

   target = judy;
   cout << "Target's balance = $"
        << target.getBalance("honeybee") << endl;
   return 0;
}
```

The output that this program produces is

```
Judy's balance = $50.00
Jim's balance = $100.00
Result of invalid password = -1.00
Depositing $20.00 to Jim, new balance = $120.00
Result of overdraft from Judy ($51.00) = -2.00
Target's balance = $50.00
```

Note the following points about this example:

1. The header file for the `account` class, `account.h`, is included like any other library header file.
2. Account objects are created by declaring them in much the same way as C++ variables. However, the parameters following the variable names in these declarations allow the programmer to set the values of the attributes of the objects when they are created. The form for this special kind of declaration is

   <class name><variable name>(<parameter list>)

3. The operations on account objects use the syntax of member function calls that you learned in Section 3.6 and used with file streams in Chapter 7. Recall that the form of a member function call is

   <object name>.<function name>(<parameter list>)

and that member functions can expect parameters and return values like any other functions in C++.

Specifying the Operations

Once we have outlined the user requirements of a class, we can provide *formal specifications* for it. A formal specification describes the inputs, outputs, and any other assumptions about the data or the effects of an operation. We use preconditions and postconditions, as introduced in Chapter 5.

The names of the attributes of a bank account object are `myPassword` and `myBalance`. The formal specifications of the bank account operations follow:

Create Operation (Default Values)

Preconditions:	The account object is in an unpredictable state.
Postconditions:	`myBalance` is set to 0.00, and `myPassword` is set to an empty string in the account object.

Create Operation (Initial Values Specified)

Preconditions:	The account object is in an unpredictable state, the parameter `password` is a string representing the password, and the parameter `balance` is a real number representing the initial amount to be deposited into the account.
Postconditions:	`myPassword` is set to `password` and `myBalance` is set to `balance` in the account object.

Set Password Operation

Preconditions:	The account object is appropriately initialized, the parameter `password` is a string representing the password, and `newPassword` is a string representing the new password.

Postconditions:	If `password` and `myPassword` are the same, `myPassword` is set to `newPassword`, and 1 is returned; otherwise, –1 is returned.
Deposit Operation	
Preconditions:	The account object is appropriately initialized, the parameter `password` is a string representing the password, and `amount` is the amount (a real number) to be deposited.
Postconditions:	If the password is valid, then `myBalance` is increased by `amount`, and its value is returned; otherwise, –1 is returned.
Withdrawal Operation	
Preconditions:	The account object is appropriately initialized, the parameter `password` is a string representing the password, and `amount` is the amount (a real number) to be withdrawn.
Postconditions:	If the password is valid, then if there are sufficient funds, `myBalance` is decreased by `amount`, and its value is returned. If the password is invalid, –1 is returned. If there are insufficient funds, then –2 is returned.
Get Balance Operation	
Preconditions:	The account object is appropriately initialized and the parameter `password` is a string representing the password.
Postconditions:	If the password is valid, then the value of `myBalance` is returned; otherwise, –1 is returned.
Assignment Operation	
Preconditions:	The target and source accounts are appropriately initialized.
Postconditions:	The attributes of the source account have been copied into the target account and a reference to the target account is returned.

As you can see, these specifications give users a precise idea of the assumptions that they must satisfy for the operations to run correctly. They also serve as a blueprint for declaring the operations as member functions of a C++ class.

Declaring a Bank Account Class

A description of an individual class in C++ consists of two parts, a *class declaration section* and a *class implementation section,* which are usually placed in separate files. This arrangement resembles the one we have used thus far for constructing a new library. The first file for our account class, called `account.h`, contains the declaration section of the class. Its text appears as follows:

```
// Class declaration file: account.h

#ifndef ACCOUNT_H
#define ACCOUNT_H

#include "apstring.h"

class account
{
   public:

   // Constructors

   account();
   account(const apstring &password, double balance);
   account(const account &a);
```

```
    // Accessor

    double getBalance(const apstring &password) const;

    // Modifiers

    int setPassword(const apstring &password,
                    const apstring newPassword);
    double deposit(const apstring &password,
                   double amount);
    double withdraw(const apstring &password,
                    double amount);

    // Assignment

    const account& operator = (const account &a);

    private:

    // Data members

    apstring myPassword;
    double myBalance;
};

#endif
```

The general form for writing a simple class declaration section in C++ is

```
<preprocessor directives>
<constant definitions>
class <class name>
{
    public:
    <public data declarations>
    <public function declarations>
    private:
    <private data declarations>
    <private function declarations>
};
```

Several items call for comment:

1. The data and the functions belonging to a class are called its *members*. The data are called *data members*, and the functions are called *member functions*.
2. *Public members* can be referenced by any module that includes the class library. They should be restricted to the minimum necessary to serve users of the class.
3. *Private members* cannot be referenced directly by users of the class. Private member functions may be invoked indirectly by invoking public member functions, and private data members may be accessed indirectly by invoking public member functions.
4. The declarations of the member functions look exactly like the declarations of other functions in C++.
5. A semicolon must follow the right curly brace at the end of the class declaration.

6. The member functions belong to several categories, including
   a. *constructors,* which create objects of the class
   b. *accessors,* which return the values of attributes
   c. *modifiers,* which modify the values of attributes
7. The operation to copy the attributes of one account to another account uses the assignment operator (=).

Using a Class and Using a Struct

A good way to clarify what we have done in developing an account class is to compare its use with the use of a bank account represented as a struct. We could define a type for bank accounts with a struct as follows:

```
struct accountType
{
   apstring myPassword;
   double myBalance;
};
```

Using this definition in the same program as the `account` class, we could run the following segment of code:

```
account first;                          // Create an object
accountType second;                     // Create a struct

first.setPassword("rosebud");           // Set members
first.deposit(50.00);                   // of object

second.myPassword = "shazzam";          // Set members
second.myBalance = 75.00;               // of struct
```

The state of the memory reserved for these variables after the code segment is run appears in Figure 8.3. Note that the memory for the two variables seems to be represented in exactly the same way. However, the code for modifying the contents of the variables is quite different. `account` member functions must be used with the `account` object to modify its data members. Selectors can be used with the

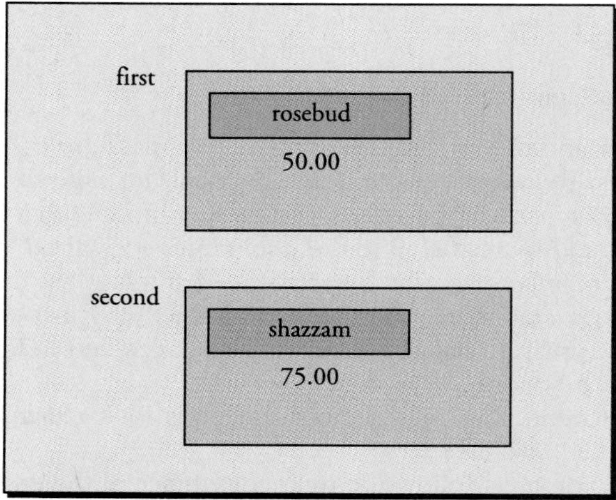

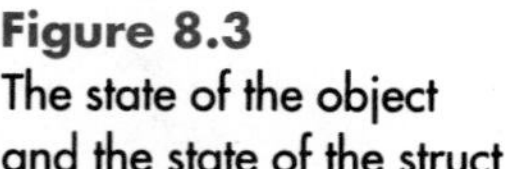
Figure 8.3
The state of the object and the state of the struct

accountType (struct) variable to modify its members. Program statements of the following kind,

```
first.myPassword = "rosebud";
first.myBalance = 50.00;
```

which use selectors to modify the data members of an account object, are illegal unless the data members myPassword and myBalance have been declared public in the account class.

Implementing a Bank Account Class

The account class implementation file will have the form

```
// Class implementation file: account.cpp
<member function implementation 1>
.
.
<member function implementation n>
```

The headings of the function implementations must have the form

```
<return type><class name>::<function name> (<optional parameter list>)
```

This form enables the compiler to resolve conflicts with the names of other globally defined functions. Otherwise, data declarations and function implementations have the same syntax as those you have already seen in C++.

Creating Instances of a Bank Account Class with Constructors

Instances of a class, or objects, can be created in C++ in several ways. We can declare one or more instances as variables. If no constructors are provided in the class declaration, the computer creates the named instances and leaves their data members in an unpredictable state, just as with ordinary C++ variable declarations. To guarantee that new instances of a class always have their data members initialized, you should declare constructors for that purpose.

Default Constructors

Our account class declaration specifies three class constructors. The first constructor, account(), is run when a program declares account variables as in the following code:

```
account first, second;
```

This kind of constructor is called a *default constructor.* It should provide reasonable initial values for the attributes of an object when the user does not specify them. The implementation of the default constructor for an account sets the password to an empty string and the balance to zero.

```
account::account()
{
   myPassword = "";
   myBalance = 0.00;
}
```

Note that the implementation references the data members for the account object even though they are not declared as parameters. The use of the prefix `account::` in a function heading allows the data members and other member functions of the `account` class to be visible in the function implementation. Note also that the constructor has no return type.

Constructors for Specifying Initial Values

The second constructor,

```
account(const apstring &password, double balance);
```

is run when users wish to declare an account variable with specified attributes, as in the code

```
account judy("honeybee", 100.00);
```

The user appears to pass two values as parameters to the variable `judy`. In this example, what really happens is that the computer runs the second constructor. The implementation of this constructor assigns the values of the parameters to the corresponding data members of the account object.

```
account::account(const apstring &password,
                 double balance)
{
   myPassword = password;
   myBalance = balance;
}
```

Copy Constructors

The third constructor is called the *copy constructor* for the `account` class. This function is run whenever an account object is passed by value as a parameter to a function. Recall that when C++ passes data by value in a parameter, the data value is copied to a temporary memory location for the use of the function. If a class does not specify its own copy constructor, the computer performs what is known as a *shallow copy* of the object when it is passed by value. In a shallow copy, not all of the object's data members are necessarily copied into temporary memory locations. To guarantee a complete copy in all situations, we define a copy constructor that takes another account object as a parameter:

```
account::account(const account &a)
{
   myPassword = a.myPassword;
   myBalance = a.myBalance;
}
```

Note that the parameter, an account object, is passed by constant reference. The data members of the new account object, called the *receiver object*, are referenced by name. The data members of the account object to be copied, called the *parameter object*, are accessed by the selector notation used with C++ structs. In general, any of the data members of a parameter such as this one can be accessed within a member function in the class implementation by using the form

<parameter name>.<data member name>

Accessors and Modifiers

The role of accessor functions is to allow users to observe the attributes of an object without changing them. To guarantee that no changes occur, we can declare an accessor function as a *const function*, using the form

<return type><function name>(<formal parameter declarations>) `const;`

The implementation of the accessor function for account objects, `getBalance`, follows:

```
double account::getBalance(const apstring &password) const
{
   if (password == myPassword)
      return myBalance;
   else
      return -1;
}
```

The role of modifier functions is to set one or more of the attributes of an object to new values. We provide the implementation of the modifier function `withdraw` for account objects and leave the rest as exercises.

```
double account::withdraw(const apstring &password,
                         double amount)
{
   if (password == myPassword)
      if ((amount >= 0) && (amount <= myBalance))
      {
         myBalance = myBalance - amount;
         return myBalance;
      }
      else
         return -2;      // Invalid amount
   else
      return -1;         // Invalid password
}
```

Note the logic of the nested `if` statements in this function. Two conditions must be satisfied to update the balance and return its value. Otherwise, the function returns different negative values to indicate an invalid amount or an invalid password.

The Assignment Operator, Polymorphism, and Overloading

Many of the built-in operators in C++ are *polymorphic*, which means "many structures." For example, the operators +, ==, and >> are polymorphic for integers and real numbers. This means that the same operators designate the same general operations (arithmetic, comparisons, input/output), even though the actual operations performed may vary with the type or structure of the operands. (Think of the difference between scanning input characters and converting them to an integer and doing the same thing for a real number, even though the symbol >> is used for both.)

C++ allows a programmer to reuse any built-in operator (or function name) to designate an operation on new data types. This process is called *overloading an operation.* For example, rather than use the named function

```
copy(account1, account2)
```

programmers can use

```
account1 = account2
```

We begin by specifying the declaration of the member function to be overloaded:

```
const account& operator = (const account &a);
```

Note that `operator` is a reserved word in `C++`. The receiver object will be the left operand of the assignment, and the parameter object will serve as the right operand. The general form for specifying operators is

<return type>`operator`<standard operator symbol> `(`<parameter list>`);`

The implementation is written by placing a similar form in the function heading. If the target and the source objects are not the same object, the function copies the data members of the source object to the target object. The function returns a reference to the target object.

```
const account& account::operator = (const account &a)
{
    if (this != &a)
    {
        myPassword = a.myPassword;
        myBalance = a.myBalance;
    }
    return *this;
}
```

You probably will not fully understand this code until you have studied the use of pointers in Chapters 9 and 13. However, here is a brief explanation:

1. The reserved word `this` always refers to the address of the receiver object. The expression `&a` returns the address of the parameter object `a`. Thus, the expression `(this != &a)` returns `true` if the operands are addresses of different objects.
2. The assignment operator in C++ normally returns an *l-value.* An l-value is an object that can be the target of an assignment operation in C++. In the case of simple assignment statements such as `a = b;`, the l-value returned by the operation is not used. However, in the case of a *cascade* of assignments, such as `(a = b) = c;`, the expression `(a = b)` returns an l-value that can serve as the target of the value `c`. In this case, the value returned is `a` as an l-value.

3. For this mechanism to work correctly, the return type of an assignment operator should be a reference to the class of the target object. The return type for our assignment operator for accounts would therefore be specified as `account&`. However, in this book, we discourage the return of an l-value from an assignment. Instead, we return a constant reference, specified in this example as `const account&`. By returning a constant reference, we do not allow the programmer to assign to the same variable more than once in an assignment expression, so the compiler prohibits expressions of the form `(a = b) = c`. However, expressions of the form `a = b = c` are valid. Because assignment is right-associative, the value of `c` is first assigned to `b`. Then, the value of `b` is assigned to `a`. Thus, only one assignment is being made to each of the variables `b` and `a`.
4. The effect of the last line of code in our example is to return the receiver object. To gain access to the object itself, we apply the *dereference operator* (*) to `this`. The receiver object will be returned as a constant l-value because the return type is specified as a constant reference to a class.

Using a Class with Functions

There are many occasions for which we might want to include a class in a program and process its instances by means of functions. For example, consider the problem of interacting with the user for the input of the amount to withdraw from a bank account. A user interface function that performs this task is:

```
void makeWithdrawal(account &thisAccount)
{
   double amount, result;
   apstring password;

   cout << "Enter your password: ";
   cin >> password;
   cout << "Enter the amount to withdraw: ";
   cin >> amount;
   result = thisAccount.withdraw(password, amount);
   if (result >= 0)
      cout << "Thank you. Your new balance is "
           << result << endl;
   else if (result == -1)
      cout << "Sorry, invalid password." << endl;
   else
      cout << "Sorry, insufficient funds." << endl;
}
```

An alternative to this approach is to make this function a member of the `account` class. Then it could be invoked as

```
thisAccount.makeWithdrawal();
```

There are two problems with this second approach:

1. It makes more work for the developer, who must write new code for the `account` class rather than reuse existing code in the user interface module.
2. It makes application-specific components, such as the messages to the user in a particular context, part of a general class definition. This makes the `account` class less general and application independent than it should be.

As you can see, the processing of classes and their instances integrates very easily with the more conventional style of programming in C++. This feature enables developers to introduce objects and the object-oriented style into an existing software system without redesigning and rewriting the entire system.

Exercises 8.2

1. Describe the differences between a class and a data structure, such as an array or a struct. Pay particular attention to the concepts of an abstract data type and data encapsulation.
2. Discuss the roles played by user requirements, formal specifications, class declaration, and class implementation in developing a C++ class.
3. Describe the differences between a default constructor, a constructor with user-specified initial values, and a copy constructor.

   Exercises 4–7 ask you to add attributes or behavior to the bank account class we have just discussed.
4. Add a data member for representing an account user's name. Add behavior so that each account is given a user's name when it is created.
5. Update the member functions `getBalance`, `deposit`, and `withdraw` so that each takes a user name and password as parameters. Perform the expected operations only if the name and password sent by the user match the name and password data members of the account. Otherwise, do nothing.
6. Add a data member to maintain a record of the number of times a user has failed to enter the correct name and password. It should be set to zero when the account is created and whenever the user successfully makes a deposit, withdrawal, or balance check. It should be incremented whenever these operations are unsuccessful.
7. Add a `private` member function that is run when the number of failed transactions becomes greater than three. It should print a message that the user's ATM card is being confiscated.
8. Discuss the concept of overloading, which allows the assignment operator to be defined for the `account` class developed in this section.
9. Develop the user requirements and formal specifications for a new class, called `employee`, to represent the `employeeType` from Section 8.1.
10. Write a C++ class declaration file for the `employee` class of Exercise 9.
11. Write a code segment that illustrates the differences between the `employeeType` and the class `employee` from Exercises 9 and 10. Explain why the class would be better to use than the struct.

8.3 Object-Oriented Programming and Software Maintenance

You might be wondering why we went to all that trouble to define an `account` class in the previous section, when we could have coded an `account` type as a C++ struct. We have already stated one reason: data security. The members of a struct are public, or visible for access or modification to all parts of an application. The private data members of a class are available for access or modification only by means of specially designated member functions.

There are other reasons for developing classes and using object-oriented methods. Through the study and development of large and complex software systems over the years, computer scientists have come to the conclusion that the techniques and tools that we have discussed through Section 8.1 are far from adequate for dealing

Objectives

a. to understand the problems associated with software maintenance
b. to understand the way in which reuse of software enhances software maintenance
c. to become familiar with some basic terms of object-oriented programming

with the challenges of building these systems. In this section, we explain why object-oriented programming should be added to our arsenal of tools and techniques for problem solving.

The Problem of Software Maintenance

Perhaps the most serious problem posed by a large software system is that of maintaining it over a period of years. After the initial release of a commercial system, users send complaints about errors and requests for additional features or functions to the developers almost immediately. Before a new version with corrections and additional features or functions can be released, the developers must search the system to fix the errors and add or remove features or functions. They must do so in such a way as not to disturb other parts of the system that are working correctly. Moreover, the developers must divide up the maintenance tasks so they can work independently and efficiently. Finally, some of the developers who maintain the software may not have been on the original development team. All of these factors add time and cost to the maintenance of large software systems.

The tools and techniques of structured programming and modular design go part of the way toward easing the software maintenance task. For example, if an error occurs in a particular function of a system, a programmer might locate the error in a C++ function within a particular library file and fix the problem by changing a single line of code within the function. If an error occurs while the system is using a particular data structure such as a linked list, a programmer might find and correct the problem in the C++ library file where the list processing functions are implemented.

In Chapter 4, we saw that another kind of error, a side effect, is more difficult to track down. Many side effects are caused by allowing users too much access to the implementation of a module. We also saw that implementing a module as a class in C++ helps control this kind of side effect by encapsulating or denying users direct access to the data.

Reuse of Software

Another major factor that adds to the cost of software maintenance is the need to rewrite entire modules to add features or functions to a system. For example, suppose that a module already exists in a bank management system for processing checking accounts. Savings accounts resemble checking accounts to a certain extent, as do the functions for processing each kind of account. However, using conventional structured programming techniques, developers must add a completely new module with a different set of data type definitions and functions for savings accounts. Much of this code will not only be redundant but may also contain errors.

Developers should be able to *reuse* existing software modules to build new ones. In the example of savings and checking accounts, a developer could write a module for handling the structure and behavior that all accounts have in common. Other developers could then *specialize* this module, with extra data or functions, for more specific kinds of accounts. By reusing software components, developers can eliminate the redundancy and many of the errors that occur with more conventional methods. As we will see shortly, object-oriented programming provides a way of reusing software components in this manner.

The Client/Server Relationship

We can think of an object as a *server* to which a user makes requests as a *client*. None of the data belonging to a server is accessible to a client, unless the client invokes a

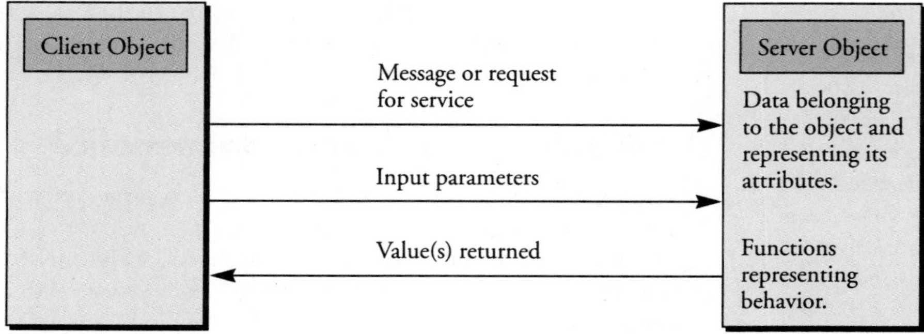

Figure 8.4
Anatomy of objects as clients and servers

server-defined request to use or modify those data. In other words, the data belonging to an object are fully encapsulated. Figure 8.4 illustrates these concepts.

Each object is an instance of a class that defines its data and behavior. The client of an object obtains its services by creating an instance of its class and then sending requests to this instance. The implementer of an object defines its services or behavior by defining the class to which the object belongs. An object that sends a request to another object is called the *sender* of the request; the object that receives the request is called the *receiver.*

Inheritance

The common behavior of several classes may be generalized by defining a *base class.* Each of the original, more specific classes can retain its own distinctive behavior as a *derived class.* Behavior can be added to a derived class to specialize it further, even if this behavior redefines the behavior already defined in the base class. The process of adding derived classes therefore allows developers to reuse existing software very easily.

Polymorphism and Overloading

The common behavior of several classes is also expressed by means of overloading the operations that define similar behavior. The operators that designate these operations are polymorphic, or have many forms. A polymorphic operator, such as <, really has one general meaning when used by clients: determine whether two objects are related by less than. But it can have more than one specific meaning when implemented by different server classes, such as integers and strings, which carry out different operations on different data representations to determine the relation.

8.4 A Rational Number Class

Our next example of the design of a class comes from pure mathematics, a different domain than that of finance and data processing. C++ has standard data types for representing real numbers and integers, but not rational numbers. In this section, we develop a new class, called `rational`, that allows applications to use rational numbers in much the same way as the other kinds of numbers are used.

User Requirements

A rational number has two attributes, a numerator and a denominator, both of which are integer values. One constructor operation for rational numbers should therefore

A NOTE OF INTEREST

The Origins of the Object-Oriented Philosophy

We saw in an earlier Note of Interest that a philosophy can serve as the underpinning of a new approach to problem solving and software design. Such was the case with function-oriented programming. This approach was the direct result of efforts by two computer scientists, John McCarthy and John Backus, to bring a certain formal theory of computation, the recursive lambda calculus, to bear on the design of complex software systems.

The object-oriented approach to problem solving and software design has a different kind of origin. In this case, there is no single theory of computation we can point to as the model for the approach. Object orientation in languages, programming style, and thinking has evolved over time and is the result of diverse sources and trends that eventually converged on a single body of ideas. However, there is one computer scientist in whose vision these sources and trends have been brought together. This scientist, Alan Kay, recounts the history of the development of the object-oriented philosophy in "The Early History of Smalltalk," *ACM SIGPLAN Notices,* Vol. 28, No. 3, Mar. 1993. Some of the important sources in the development of the object-oriented approach were:

- Ivan Sutherland's work on an interactive graphical programming environment called *Sketchpad.*
- The development of Simula, a language for representing classes of objects.
- Kay's work on Smalltalk, the first complete environment for object-oriented software development.
- The work of Douglas Engelbart, Daniel Ingalls, Kay, and others at Xerox on WIMP (window, icon, mouse, pull-down menu) user interfaces.

For an interesting attempt to derive a new theory of computing from object-oriented techniques, see Peter Wegner, "Why Interaction Is More Powerful Than Algorithms," *Communications of the ACM,* Vol. 40, No. 5, May 1997, pp. 80–91.

Objectives

a. to design a numeric class whose use and behavior are compatible with the use and behavior of built-in numeric data types
b. to understand the use of overloaded operations in designing a numeric class with standard behavior
c. to use overloaded operations to implement mixed-mode operations on new classes and built-in data types

take two integer parameters representing these attributes. For example, one might create the rational numbers 1/2 and 5/6 as follows:

```
rational oneHalf(1, 2);
rational fiveSixths(5, 6);
```

Because rational numbers are expressed in the form

```
numerator
---------
denominator
```

definitions of the form

```
rational <name>(<integer>, 0);
```

should not be allowed. Therefore, a precondition of the constructor is that the denominator can be any integer other than zero.

Access to the numerator and denominator is provided as in the following code segment:

```
rational sevenEighths(7, 8);
cout << "Numerator = " << sevenEighths.numerator() << endl;
cout << "Denominator = " << sevenEighths.denominator() << endl;
```

which produces the output

```
Numerator = 7
Denominator = 8
```

Users should be able to perform some standard arithmetic operations on rational numbers and output the resulting values. For example, the following statement outputs the sum of the two example numbers just defined to the screen:

```
cout << oneHalf + fiveSixths << endl;
```

The output of this statement would be

```
4/3
```

Note that the sum of the two numbers is expressed in lowest terms.

Keyboard input of rational numbers allows users to work with rational numbers interactively. To make the scanning of the input simple, we might require a definite format, such as

<integer>/<integer><enter key>

Assignment of one rational number to another should also be provided in the form

<rational number variable> = <rational number object>

where `<rational number object>` is the value returned by an expression. Finally, users of rational numbers would like to compare them for the standard relationships of equality, less than, and greater than. The following code is an example of the use of the equality operator with two rational numbers:

```
rational oneHalf(1, 2);
rational number;

cout << "Enter a rational number: ";
cin >> number;
if (number == oneHalf)
.
.
```

Note that we have provided a second class constructor that takes no initial values for the numerator and the denominator. This constructor is used to create rational number objects that will be targets of subsequent input or assignment operations. These numbers can be given a default initial value of 1/1.

Specifying the Operations

Now that clients' requirements have been discussed, we can present a formal specification of the desired operations for rational numbers. The attributes of a rational number are `myNumerator` and `myDenominator`.

Create Operation (Default Value)

Preconditions:	The rational number is in an unpredictable state.
Postconditions:	`myNumerator` is set to 1, and `myDenominator` is set to 1.

Create Operation (Initial Values Specified)

Preconditions:	The rational number is in an unpredictable state, `numerator` is an integer value, and `denominator` is an integer value other than 0.

Postconditions: `myNumerator` is set to `numerator`, and `myDenominator` is set to `denominator`. `myNumerator/myDenominator` is reduced to lowest terms.

Numerator Operation

Preconditions: The rational number is appropriately initialized.

Postconditions: An integer representing the numerator of the rational number is returned.

Denominator Operation

Preconditions: The rational number is appropriately initialized.

Postconditions: An integer representing the denominator of the rational number is returned.

Addition Operation

Preconditions: The parameter objects are rational numbers appropriately initialized.

Postconditions: A rational number representing the sum of the two rational numbers is returned.

Subtraction Operation

Preconditions: The parameter objects are rational numbers appropriately initialized.

Postconditions: A rational number representing the difference of the two rational numbers is returned.

Multiplication Operation

Preconditions: The parameter objects are rational numbers appropriately initialized.

Postconditions: A rational number representing the product of the two rational numbers is returned.

Division Operation

Preconditions: The parameter objects are rational numbers appropriately initialized, and the numerator of the parameter object does not equal 0.

Postconditions: A rational number representing the division of the two rational numbers is returned.

Equality Operation

Preconditions: The parameter objects are rational numbers appropriately initialized.

Postconditions: The Boolean value `true` is returned if the two rational numbers are equal, and `false` is returned otherwise.

Assignment Operation

Preconditions: Receiver and parameter objects are rational numbers appropriately initialized.

Postconditions: `myNumerator` and `myDenominator` of the parameter object are copied into the receiver object.

Input Operation

Preconditions: The receiver is an `istream` object appropriately initialized, and the parameter is a rational number appropriately initialized. The form of input to the stream should be `<integer>/<integer><enter key>`.

Postconditions: The numerator and the denominator in the rational number parameter are modified by the input values, the rational number parameter is reduced to lowest terms, and the `istream` object is returned.

Output Operation

Preconditions: The receiver is an `ostream` object appropriately initialized, and the parameter is a rational number appropriately initialized.

Postconditions: The rational number parameter is written to the stream in the form `<myNumerator>/<myDenominator>`, and the `ostream` object is returned.

Note that the specifications state that a rational number will not be created if the denominator is zero and that any new rational number will be reduced to lowest terms when it is created.

Declaring the Class

The class declaration module for rational numbers can now be presented:

```
// Class declaration file: rational.h

#ifndef RATIONAL_H
#define RATIONAL_H

#include <iostream.h>
#include "bool.h"

class rational
{
   public:

   // Constructors

   rational();
   rational(int numerator, int denominator);
   rational(const rational &r);

   // Accessors

   int numerator() const;
   int denominator() const;

   // Assignment

   const rational& operator = (const rational &rhs);

   private:

   // Data members

   int myNumerator, myDenominator;

   // Utility function

   void reduce();
};

// The following free (non-member) functions operate on
// rational numbers

// Arithmetic

rational operator + (const rational &lhs,
                     const rational &rhs);
rational operator - (const rational &lhs,
                     const rational &rhs);
rational operator * (const rational &lhs,
                     const rational &rhs);
rational operator / (const rational &lhs,
                     const rational &rhs);
```

```
// Comparison

bool operator == (const rational &lhs,
                  const rational &rhs);

// Input and output

istream& operator >> (istream &is, rational &r);
ostream& operator << (ostream &os, const rational &r);

#endif
```

Note two things about this class declaration module:

1. The module declares `reduce` as a `private` member function. This function will be run by the class implementation whenever a rational number object must be reduced to lowest terms.
2. Several *free functions* are declared. These are nonmember functions for manipulating rational numbers and consist of several standard operators.

Implementing the Class

The class implementation for rational numbers appears in the `rational.cpp` file. Here we present the portion of the file that defines the three class constructors:

```
// Class implementation file: rational.cpp

#include <assert.h>

#include "rational.h"
#include "gcd.h"

rational::rational()
{
   myNumerator = 1;
   myDenominator = 1;

}

rational::rational(int numerator, int denominator)
{
   assert(denominator != 0);
   myNumerator = numerator;
   myDenominator = denominator;
   reduce();
}

rational::rational(const rational &r)
{
   myNumerator = r.myNumerator;
   myDenominator = r.myDenominator;
}
```

Only the second constructor calls for comment. A precondition of the operation is that the `denominator` parameter must not be zero. Therefore, the implementation verifies this condition with the C++ `assert` function. A postcondition of the operation is that the new rational number has been reduced to lowest terms. To achieve this result, we compute the greatest common divisor of the two parameters and then reduce them by dividing by this factor. Here is the implementation of the `reduce` function:

```
void rational::reduce()
{
    int commonDivisor = gcd(myNumerator, myDenominator);
    myNumerator = myNumerator / commonDivisor;
    myDenominator = myDenominator / commonDivisor;
}
```

The implementation of the `gcd` function, which was used in an example in Section 6.5, appears in the `gcd` library and is left as an exercise.

The development of the arithmetic operations for rational numbers depends on our knowledge of the rules of rational number arithmetic. These rules are specified by the following relations:

$$\frac{n_1}{d_1} + \frac{n_2}{d_2} = \frac{n_1 d_2 + n_2 d_1}{d_1 d_2}$$

$$\frac{n_1}{d_1} + \frac{n_2}{d_2} = \frac{n_1 d_2 - n_2 d_1}{d_1 d_2}$$

$$\frac{n_1}{d_1} \times \frac{n_2}{d_2} = \frac{n_1 n_2}{d_1 d_2}$$

$$\frac{n_1/d_1}{n_2/d_2} = \frac{n_1 d_2}{d_1 n_2}$$

We present the implementation of the free function for the addition operation and leave the others as exercises:

```
rational operator + (const rational &lhs,
                     const rational &rhs)
{
    int numerator = lhs.numerator() * rhs. denominator()
                  + rhs. numerator() * lhs.denominator();
    int denominator = lhs.denominator() * rhs.denominator();
    rational sum(numerator, denominator);
    return sum;
}
```

The first two statements in this implementation use the rule for addition to compute the numerator and the denominator of the sum. Note the use of the member functions `numerator` and `denominator` to access the appropriate data members of the two rational numbers. Because `+` is a free function, we cannot access the data members of the rational numbers with the selector notation. The third statement uses these values to construct a new rational number expressed in lowest terms. The last line returns the new rational number to the caller of the function.

The free function for the output operation writes a rational number to an output stream in the form <numerator>/<denominator>:

```
ostream& operator << (ostream &os, const rational &r)
{
   os << r.numerator() << "/" << r.denominator();
   return os;
{
```

Note the following:

1. We use the ostream class to declare the type of the output stream parameter and the return type. The use of this class allows our definition of << to be used either with the standard output stream, cout, or with any output file stream.
2. We return a reference to an output stream. This allows output operations to one stream to be cascaded, as in the expression cout << r1 << r2 << r3 << endl.
3. We have been careful to write the data to the output stream in exactly the same form as they might appear for reading from an input stream. This technique allows correct processing of rational numbers with file streams.

The input operation expects data in the input stream to have the form <integer>/<integer>. Therefore, the implementation uses assert to enforce the use of this format:

```
istream& operator >> (istream &is, rational &r)
{
   char divisionSymbol;
   int numerator = 0, denominator = 0;

   is >> numerator >> divisionSymbol >> denominator;
   assert(divisionSymbol == '/');
   assert(denominator != 0);
   rational number(numerator, denominator);
   r = number;
   return is;
}
```

Note that the implementation also verifies that the denominator from the input stream is not zero. The implementations of the assignment and equality operations are left as exercises.

Example 8.3 This example is a program that prompts the user for three rational numbers and outputs the result of an expression of the form r1 + r2 * r3.

```
// Program file: ratdriv.cpp

#include <iostream.h>

#include "rational.h"

int main()
{
   rational r1, r2, r3;
```

continued

```
    cout << "Enter the first number (<integer>/<integer>): ";
    cin >> r1;
    cout << "Enter the second number (<integer>/<integer>): ";
    cin >> r2;
    cout << "Enter the third number (<integer>/<integer>): ";
    cin >> r3;
    cout << "The result of r1 + r2 * r3 is "
         << r1 + r2 * r3 << endl;
    return 0;
}
```

An example run of this program might produce the output

```
Enter the first number (<integer>/<integer>): 1/2
Enter the second number (<integer>/<integer>): 1/2
Enter the third number (<integer>/<integer>): 1/2
The result of r1 + r2 * r3 is 3/4
```

Note that the output is 3/4 rather than 1/2. This means that the standard operator precedence of multiplication over addition is also enforced for rational numbers.

Mixed-Mode Operations

In Chapter 3, you were introduced to the notion of a mixed-mode operation. This kind of operation has two operands of different types and performs a type conversion operation before computing a result value. For example, the addition operation promotes an integer operand to a real number before adding it to a real number operand. The result returned is then a real number.

When a rational number class is added to a software system, clients might be provided with a similar capability to perform mixed-mode operations on rational numbers and other kinds of numbers. For example, where the operands are an integer and a rational number, the integer would first be promoted to a rational number, and then rational number arithmetic would be performed. Where the operands are a real number and a rational number, the rational number would first be promoted to a real number, and then real number arithmetic would be performed. The following code and its output when executed illustrate some mixed-mode operations:

```
rational oneHalf(1, 2);
cout << setiosflags(ios::fixed | ios::showpoint);
cout << "Rational + integer = " << oneHalf + 2 << endl;
cout << "Rational + real = " << oneHalf + 3.4 << endl;
```

```
Rational + integer = 5/2
Rational + real = 3.9
```

Table 8.1 illustrates some operand and return types for addition.

We can provide mixed-mode operations for arithmetic with rational numbers by overloading. Let's consider just the case of addition and leave the other operations for exercises. For the cases where the first operand is a rational number, we add free functions to the class declaration module of the rational number class:

```
rational operator + (const rational &lhs, int rhs);
double operator + (const rational &lhs, double rhs);
```

Table 8.1
Types of Data for Mixed-Mode Addition

Operand 1 Type	Operand 2 Type	Result Type
`int`	`rational`	`rational`
`rational`	`int`	`rational`
`double`	`rational`	`double`
`rational`	`double`	`double`

Each of these operations adds a number (an `int` or a `double`) to the first parameter, a rational.

To add an `int` to a rational number, we must promote the `int` to a rational number. We use the `int` parameter to create a new rational number object and then add it (using the rational number operation named +) to the rational number parameter:

```
rational operator + (const rational &lhs, int rhs)
{
   rational newOperand(rhs, 1);
   return lhs + newOperand;
}
```

To add a `double` to a rational number, we must promote the rational number to a `double`. We cast the rational number's numerator as a `double`, divide the result by its denominator, and then add the result (using the real number operation +) to the `double` parameter:

```
double operator + (const rational &lhs, double rhs);
{
   return double(lhs.numerator()) / lhs.denominator() + rhs;
}
```

Exercises 8.4

1. Complete the implementation of the rational number class and test it with a simple driver program. (*Hint:* Two rational numbers are equal if and only if $n_1d_2 = n_2d_1$.)
2. What is the total number of mixed-mode operations (+, -, *, /) for the three data types `int`, `double`, and `rational`?
3. State a general formula for the total number of mixed-mode operations, where M is the number of operators and N is the number of data types.
4. The implementation of rational numbers presented in this section always reduces a rational number to lowest terms when it is created. Another method would be to wait until an output operation is executed to express a rational number in lowest terms. Assess the costs and benefits of these two strategies. (Be sure to take into account the speed of evaluating complex arithmetic operations and the possibility of integer overflow.)
5. Rational numbers such as 9/1 should be output as whole numbers and used as whole numbers in arithmetic and comparison operations. Decide where to do this in the system and implement the change.
6. A prefix increment operator for rational numbers would have the form ++ <rational number>. Overload this operator for the rational number class. (*Hint:* The

A NOTE OF INTEREST

Pure and Hybrid Object-Oriented Languages

It is possible to classify programming languages in terms of the degree to which they possess object-oriented features. Older languages such as FORTRAN, C, and standard Pascal have no object-oriented features at all. None of them supports classes, user-defined polymorphic operators, data encapsulation, or inheritance.

Smalltalk purports to be an object-oriented language in a "pure" sense. In this language, every data type is a class. All data values, including classes themselves, are objects. All subprograms and operators can be overloaded. Data can be fully encapsulated. Every operation on data comes about as a result of a request being sent to an object.

A third class of languages is a hybrid of object-oriented languages and older languages. Many of these are the older languages themselves, with object-oriented features grafted onto them. For example, C++ is an extension of C. Most current implementations of Pascal have object-oriented extensions. CLOS (Common LISP Object System) is an object-oriented extension that comes with almost every Common LISP package.

The difference between hybrid languages and the pure object-oriented languages is that it is possible to write programs in a hybrid language that omit the object-oriented features entirely. For example, one could write a large program, or even a large software system consisting of many library modules, in C++ that would be indistinguishable from a C program. This possibility has led to a debate in the computer science community concerning the desirability of hybrid languages.

Proponents of the pure object-oriented languages argue that the object-oriented approach has superseded more traditional styles of programming. Therefore, one should use a language that enforces the superior approach rather than a language that allows drift or slippage into inferior approaches. Moreover, proponents claim that the pure languages are better vehicles for training new computer scientists because they enforce object-oriented thinking from the very beginning.

Proponents of the hybrid languages offer several counters to these points. First, it is not clear that object orientation is the best or most natural way to approach all problems. For example, problems in numerical analysis may find more natural solutions in terms of systems of functions, calling for a function-oriented approach. The notion of sending a request to a number to add 1 to itself seems somewhat silly from this perspective. A hybrid language offers object orientation as one possible approach among others that can be chosen when it is the most natural alternative.

Second, although object orientation might be the best possible approach to the design and maintenance of large software systems, smaller programs may be more easily designed and written using traditional techniques of structured programming.

Finally, a pure object-oriented language may not be the best vehicle for teaching programming. Beginning programmers start with simple problems, but pure object-oriented languages do not rest on a simple model of computation. Beginning programmers need to learn about the structure and behavior of real computers, about concepts such as memory, the distinction between an address and a data value, branching, and subprogram calls. Pure object-oriented languages tend to insulate a programmer from these features of real machines.

We suggest that you study and try out several of these languages, if they are available, and make your own judgments about the relative virtues of pure object-oriented and hybrid programming languages.

operator is a member function that expects no parameters and returns a constant reference to the rational number object.)

7. Simon Seeplus claims that it would be easier to represent a rational number as a struct with associated library functions rather than as a class. Criticize the merits of this proposal.

■ 8.5 Derived Classes and Inheritance

One of the advantages of using classes and objects in a program is that they can be reused to develop new features. Consider the bank account example of Section 8.2. We defined a class to represent the kind of data and behavior that any account might possess, such as depositing into or withdrawing from a balance. Many more specialized kinds of bank accounts exist that have both this general sort of data and behavior and also other more specific data and behavior. For example, a savings account will

Objectives

a. to understand how the behavior and attributes of a class can be reused by developing a derived class that inherits them
b. to understand how to control access to data and behavior so that they are available to derived classes but protected from clients

need data and operations to compute the interest on the balance. A timed savings account will not allow withdrawals before a certain date from the time of the deposit.

Instead of reinventing the wheel and defining a whole new class for each of these types of bank accounts, we can make each new kind of account a derived class of our abstract `account` class. Each class derived from `account` then ***inherits*** all of the common, more abstract data and behavior from the `account` class. To each derived class we need only add the data and behavior necessary to define it as a special class of `account`.

C++ provides support for defining derived classes. A derived class declaration is quite similar to a top-level class declaration. For example, here is a declaration of a `savingsAccount` class, with specific data and behavior for representing the computation of interest:

```
// Class declaration file: savings.h

#ifndef SAVINGS_H
#define SAVINGS_H

#include "account.h"

class savingsAccount : public account
{
   public:

   // Constructors

   savingsAccount();
   savingsAccount(const apstring &password, double balance);
   savingsAccount(const savingsAccount &a);

   // Accessor

   double getInterest(const apstring &password) const;

   // Modifier

   void computeInterest(double rate);

   // Assignment

   const savingsAccount& operator = (const savingsAccount &a);

   private:

   // Data member

   double myInterest;
};

#endif
```

The only difference in form between a derived class declaration and a top-level class declaration lies in the text immediately following the reserved word `class`. As before, we have the name of the new class. Then we see a colon (:), followed by an *access specifier*, followed by the name of the class from which the new class is being derived. The form for this is

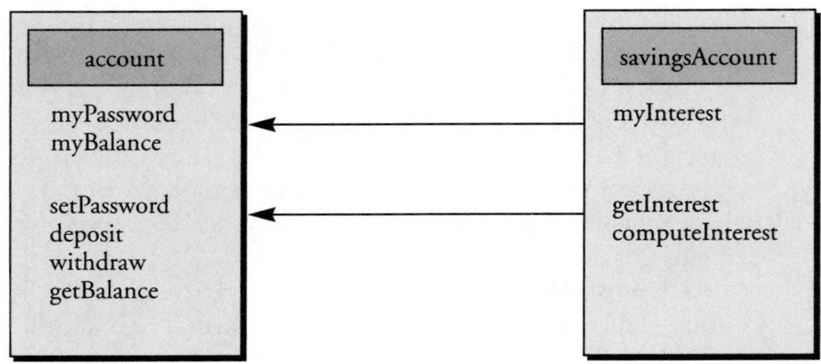

Figure 8.5
The account and savings account classes

```
class <new derived class name>:<access specifier><parent class name>
```

The access specifier in this example is the reserved word `public`. This means that the public members of the base class are also public in the derived class. If this specifier were the reserved word `private`, then the public members of the base class would become private members in the derived class.

Figure 8.5 is a *class hierarchy* diagram showing the relationship between the account class and the savings account class. Note that the member functions `setPassword`, `deposit`, `withdraw`, and `getBalance` are not declared in the savings account class. They are declared in the base class, `account`, but are still considered public members of the savings account class by inheritance. Note also that the assignment operation for savings accounts cannot be inherited from the base class. The reason is that the operation must copy an additional data member, `myInterest`, that is defined in `savingsAccount`.

The implementation file of the savings account class is

```
// Class implementation file: savings.cpp

#include "savings.h"

savingsAccount::savingsAccount()
    : account()
{
    myInterest = 0.00;
}

savingsAccount::savingsAccount(const apstring &password,
                               double balance)
    : account(password, balance)
{
    myInterest = 0.00;
}

savingsAccount::savingsAccount(const savingsAccount &a)
    : account(a)
{
   myInterest = a.myInterest;
}

const savingsAccount& savingsAccount::operator =
                      (const savingsAccount &a)
```

```
{
   if (this != &a)
   {
      myPassword = a.myPassword;
      myBalance = a.myBalance;
      myInterest = a.myInterest;
   }
   return *this;
}

double savingsAccount::getInterest(const apstring &password) const
{
   if (password == myPassword)
      return myInterest;
   else
      return -1;
}

void savingsAccount::computeInterest(double rate,
                                     const apstring &password)
{
   myInterest = getBalance(password) * rate;
}
```

The constructors for `savingsAccount` must first run the constructors for the base class, `account`, so that the data members belonging to the base class can be initialized. This is done by placing an expression of the form

: <base class constructor name> (<list of actual parameters>)

immediately after the heading of the constructor for the derived class. After this step, the data member `interest` belonging to the derived class is initialized.

Within the implementation of the member function `computeInterest`, we cannot refer directly to the savings account's balance because access to private data members cannot be inherited from a base class. Therefore, we must access the savings account's balance indirectly by invoking the base class public member function `getBalance`. As you might suppose, lack of direct access to the data members of a base class can make the implementation of derived classes inconvenient. We examine a way to remedy this problem shortly.

The following lines of code create and use a new instance of our savings account class:

```
savingsAccount myAccount("rosebud", 50.00);
myAccount.withdraw("rosebud", 20.00);
myAccount.computeInterest(.025, "rosebud");
cout << setiosflags(ios::fixed | ios::showpoint) << setprecision(2);;
cout << "Balance = $"
     << myAccount.getBalance("rosebud") << endl;
cout << "Interest = $"
     << myAccount.getInterest("rosebud") << endl;
```

The first line declares a new savings account called `myAccount`. The computer runs the class constructor for savings accounts. This, in turn, runs the constructor in the base class, which gives `myAccount` an initial balance of 50.00. The constructor in the derived class then sets the interest to a default value of 0.00.

The second line asks `myAccount` to withdraw 20.00. Since this member function is also not defined for savings accounts, the computer locates and runs the function as defined in the base class.

The third line asks `myAccount` to compute the interest, with a rate of .025. Because a member function is defined for this operation directly in the `savingsAccount` class, this function is invoked.

The last two lines of code ask `myAccount` for the values of the balance and interest so that they can be displayed to the user. The request for the balance has the effect of invoking a member function of the base class, whereas the request for the interest has the effect of invoking a member function of the derived class.

The rule that the computer uses for deciding which member function to run is fairly simple. If a member function exists in the defining class, then it is run. Otherwise, the computer searches for a member function in the base class, if one exists. This search continues until a member function is found in the next most immediate ancestor class, if one exists. If no member function is found, a syntax error occurs. The same search process occurs for `public` data member references as well.

As you can see, derived classes and inheritance provide powerful techniques for reusing software and eliminating redundant code.

Example 8.4 The following driver program tests the savings account class that we have just implemented:

```
// Program file: savedriv.cpp

#include <iostream.h>
#include <iomanip.h>
#include "savings.h"

int main()
{
   savingsAccount
          smith("narcissus", 0.00),
          jones("clio", 45.00);

   cout << setiosflags(ios::fixed | ios::showpoint)
        << setprecision(2);
   cout << "Smith's balance = $"
        << smith.getBalance("narcissus") << endl;
   cout << "Jones's balance = $"
        << jones.getBalance("clio") << endl;
   smith.deposit("narcissus", 50.00);
   cout << "Smith's balance = $"
        << smith.getBalance("narcissus") << endl;
   cout << "Jones's balance = $"
        << jones.getBalance("clio") << endl;
   smith.withdraw("narcissus", 20.00);
   cout << "Smith's balance = $"
        << smith.getBalance("narcissus") << endl;
   cout << "Jones's balance = $"
        << jones.getBalance("clio") << endl;
   smith.computeInterest(.025, "narcissus");
   cout << "Smith's interest = $"
        << smith.getInterest("narcissus") << endl;
   return 0;
}
```

The program produces the output

```
Smith's balance = $0.00
Jones's balance = $45.00
Smith's balance = $50.00
Jones's balance = $45.00
Smith's balance = $30.00
Jones's balance = $45.00
Smith's interest = $0.75
```

Inheritance and Protected Members

In the previous section, we mentioned that `private` data members of a base class cannot be directly referenced from a derived class. For example, the savings account class must invoke a `public` member function of the account class, such as `getBalance("clio")`, to access the value of the private data member `myBalance`. This kind of encapsulation is too restrictive. A derived class should be able to access frequently used and modified data members of a base class directly. A less restrictive type of encapsulation can be obtained by using the access specifier `protected` for certain data and member functions. A data or function member of a class is considered a *protected member* if it is visible to a derived class but not visible to any other part of a program. Thus, `protected` members behave like `public` members for derived classes but like `private` members for any other classes or modules in a software system.

The following code updates the account class by making the balance a `protected` data member rather than a `private` one:

```
// Class declaration file: account.h

#ifndef ACCOUNT_H
#define ACCOUNT_H

#include "apstring.h"

class account
{
   public:

   // Constructors

   account();
   account(const apstring &password, double balance);
   account(const account &a);

   // Accessor

   double getBalance(const apstring &password) const;

   // Modifiers

   int setPassword(const apstring &password,
                   const apstring newPassword);
   double deposit(const apstring &password, double amount);
   double withdraw(const apstring &password, double amount);
```

continued

```
    // Assignment

    const account& operator = (const account &a);

    protected:

    // Data members

    apstring myPassword;
    double myBalance;
};
#endif
```

We have replaced the reserved word `private` in the previous version with the reserved word `protected`. The implementation section of this module is the same as before. Once we have made this change in the account class declaration, we can refer to the data member `myBalance` in the savings account class implementation. For example, the member function `computeInterest` can be changed so that the balance is referenced directly:

```
void savingsAccount::computeInterest(double rate,
                                     const apstring &password)
{
   myInterest = myBalance * rate;
}
```

Communication and Style Tips

1. Data and function members that must be used by the entire system should be declared `public`. In general, there should be very few public data members of a class.
2. Data and function members that must be used by derived classes should be declared `protected`.
3. Data and function members that should be used only by the defining class should be declared `private`.

Exercises 8.5

1. Add members to the savings account class given in this section for maintaining a current interest rate.
2. A checking account is a special version of an account that requires data and behavior for maintaining the number of checks written. Write a derived class for an account called `checkingAccount` that captures this information.
3. Draw a diagram showing the hierarchy of classes used in a system that manages checking and savings accounts.
4. Some checking accounts bear interest. Propose a strategy for reusing the existing classes in a bank management system to support checking accounts with interest. Draw a diagram of the new class hierarchy.
5. Unlike the other kinds of accounts, timed savings accounts may not permit access via a password. Explain how you would fit timed savings accounts into a bank management system as a new class in such a way that the use of a password for these accounts would be disallowed. Draw a diagram of the new class hierarchy.

Case Study: An ATM Machine

Thus far in our case studies we have stated a problem, written out the top-level design of a solution as an algorithm, refined the design if necessary, and presented a complete program to solve the problem. In more recent chapters, we have focused on the use of the appropriate data structures for solving a problem as well. Now that we are using object-oriented techniques, our focus must shift somewhat further away from top-down design and refinement of algorithms. In this section, we present part of a complete program and leave the rest for the Programming Problems and Projects section. In fact, it would be in the object-oriented spirit if this project and those to follow were divided among students who form a team of programmers.

We begin as usual with analysis or a statement of the problem. But now we immediately consider how the behavior of certain classes of objects can help solve the problem. If these classes have already been written, we can use them right away. If they do not quite fit the problem at hand, perhaps we can reuse them by creating a derived class for the desired behavior. Some algorithm and data structure design will still be necessary at the level of implementing a new class, but in general, there will be less work to do because there is less code to write. Rather than thinking in terms of data structures and algorithms, we can think in terms of clients and servers, many of which already exist and simply need to be hooked together in the appropriate way.

Consider the problem of simulating at automated teller machine (ATM). An ATM is a server that allows users to enter a name (on the card) and password to gain access to different kinds of bank accounts. The user can then select among various functions, each of which may request other inputs. A successful transaction results in output to the user and may result in a change to an account. An unsuccessful transaction (using a bad password, for example) may lead to other outputs.

The ATM relies on other servers for support. Two of these are an `iostream` class and an account class. The role of the ATM is to serve as an interface handler that controls the communication between a user and his or her account. Put another way, you can think of an ATM class as both a model for an ATM machine and as an "application class" that drives the simulation.

To design an object-oriented system to solve this problem, we first take an inventory of existing classes to see how they can capture the desired behavior. Let's assume that we have an account class at our disposal. The account class has been extended to support user names and passwords.

Now that we know what we have, we can think about what we have to develop. The ATM can be represented as a new class. It will use, as servers, the `iostream` class and the account class. It will maintain the following data members:

1. Master name and password (used to start up or shut down the system)
2. Current account (the account currently being processed)

The ATM will serve users in two different modes:

1. **Master user mode.** This mode allows an authorized bank employee to start up the machine in customer mode, to perform service functions such as entering a new account, and to shut the machine down.
2. **Customer mode.** This mode allows an authorized customer to access an account to perform transactions.

Let's look at the abstract behavior that the ATM provides for each mode:

1. Master mode
   1.1 Enter a new account
   1.2 Start customer mode
   1.3 Shut machine down

2. Customer mode
  2.1 Get name and password
  2.2 If they belong to master mode then
  2.3 Run master mode
  2.4 Else if they belong to an account then
  2.5 Perform a transaction on the account
  2.6 Else handle user error

Many of the numbered items in both modes describe requests to which an ATM object can respond. Master mode really is a menu-driven command interpreter. Let's develop code for the algorithm. First, when the request `masterMode` is sent to an ATM object, a member function should enter a command loop. The loop should display the master mode menu and wait for the user to enter the number of a command. When this occurs, the ATM runs the corresponding member function. After the function returns, the loop is entered once more. The following code might be an implementation of the `masterMode` member function:

```
void ATM::masterMode()
{
   int command;

   do
   {
      printMasterMenu();
      command = getCommand(1, 3);
      switch (command)
      {
         case 1:        enterAccount();
                        break;
         case 2:        customerMode();
                        break;
         case 3:        shutDown();
      }
   } while (command != 3);
}
```

Note that the manager launches customer mode by entering command 2 and shuts the machine down by entering command 3.

The member function `customerMode` is

```
void ATM::customerMode()
{
   apstring name, password;
   bool masterOn = false;

   do
   {
      cout << "Enter your name: ";
      cin >> name;
      cout << "Enter your password: ";
      cin >> password;
      if (masterAccount(name, password))
         masterOn = true;
      else if (customerAccount(name, password))
         performTransaction(password);
```

```
        else
            cout << "Sorry, you entered an "
                 << "incorrect name or password."
                 << endl;
    } while (! masterOn);
}
```

masterAccount is a member function that returns true if the name and password match those of an authorized employee and false otherwise. The loop terminates when an authorized employee enters a name and password for master mode.

performTransaction displays a menu of transaction options to the user, takes a command number, and performs the corresponding command:

```
void ATM::performTransaction(const apstring &password)
{
    int command;

    printTransactionMenu();
    command = getCommand(1, 3);
    switch (command)
    {
        case 1:         getBalance(password);
                        break;
        case 2:         makeDeposit(password);
                        break;
        case 3:         makeWithdrawal(password);
    }
}
```

As you can see, the ATM class that we have developed thus far is a large body of code broken down into many small member functions (the use of classes does not free developers entirely from top-down design and algorithm development!). Most of these can be declared private for the internal use of the ATM class only. A single member function, masterMode, can be declared public. This function can be invoked from a main program in C++ right after an ATM instance is declared. It would run master mode and wait for commands. The main program is:

```
// Program file: atmdriv.cpp

#include <iostream.h>

#include "apstring.h"
#include "atm.h"

int main()
{
    apstring name, password;

    cout << "Enter your name: ";
    cin >> name;
    cout << "Enter your password: ";
    cin >> password;
    ATM teller(name, password);
    teller.masterMode();
    return 0;
}
```

Here is the header file for the ATM class:

```
// Class declaration file: atm.h

#ifndef ATM_H
#define ATM_H

#include "bool.h"
#include "apstring.h"
#include "account.h"

class ATM
{
   public:

   // Class constructors

   ATM(const apstring &n, const apstring &p);

   // Member functions

   void masterMode();

   private:

   // Data members

   // Used to start up or shut down the system

   apstring masterName, masterPassword;

   // The account currently being processed

   account currentAccount;

   // Member functions

   void customerMode();
   bool masterAccount(const apstring &n, const apstring &p);
   bool customerAccount(const apstring &n, const apstring &p);
   void performTransaction(const apstring &password);
   void getBalance(const apstring &password);
   void makeDeposit(const apstring &password);
   void makeWithdrawal(const apstring &password);
   int getCommand(int low, int high);
   void enterAccount();
   void shutDown();
   void printTransactionMenu();
   void printMasterMenu();
};

#endif
```

The complete implementation file is left as an exercise.

Running, Debugging, and Testing Hints

1. Before you write a definition of a new class, write a description of the data members and abstract behavior that the class should exhibit.
2. Write a simple driver program to test each member function of a class.

Summary

Key Terms

abstract data type
access specifier
accessor
anonymous type
attribute
base class
behavior
cascade
class
class constructor
class declaration section
class hierarchy
class implementation section
client
const function
constructor
copy constructor
data abstraction
data member
default constructor
dereference operator
derived class
encapsulation
formal specifications
free function
inheritance
instance
l-value
member
member function
modifier
object-oriented programming
overloading
parameter object
polymorphism
private member
procedural programming
protected member
public member
receiver
receiver object
selector
sender
server
shallow copy
struct

Keywords

- `class private protected public struct this`

Key Concepts

- A struct is a data structure that allows components of different types to be referenced by name. The form of a struct type definition is

```
struct <new type name>
{
        <data type> <member name 1>;
        .
        .
        <data type> <member name n>;
};
```

- The component parts of a struct are called members. They are accessed by the selector notation according to the following form:

```
<struct variable>.<member name>
```

- Data abstraction is the process of separating a conceptual definition of a data structure from its implementation details.

- An abstract data type (ADT) consists of a class of objects, a defined set of properties for the objects, and a set of operations for processing the objects.
- Libraries for abstract data types can be created by specifying a header file and an implementation file.
- A class defines the abstract behavior and attributes belonging to an object.
- Objects provide services by responding to the requests sent by clients.
- Objects can be used to model or simulate objects in the real world, such as bank accounts, or computational objects, such as rational numbers.
- A class declaration specifies the public and private data and function members for a class of objects.
- A class implementation provides the implementations of the member functions for a class of objects.
- Polymorphic operators have the same general meaning but can be used with data of different types or classes.
- Free (nonmember) functions are not declared within the scope of the class declaration.
- Classes can reuse data and behavior by inheriting them from a base class.
- Derived classes can specialize inherited behavior by extending it or overriding it.
- Data and operations can be hidden from all users by declaring them `private` within a class.
- Data and operations can be made available to all users by declaring them `public` within a class.
- Data and operations can be made available to derived classes but hidden from all other users by declaring them `protected` within a class.

Suggestions for Further Reading

Booch, Grady, *Object-Oriented Analysis and Design,* 2nd ed. Redwood City, CA: Benjamin/Cummings, 1994.

Coad, Peter, & Yourdon, Edward, *Object-Oriented Analysis,* 2nd ed. Englewood Cliffs, NJ: Yourdon Press, 1991.

Jacobson, I., Christerson, M., Jonsoon, P., & Overgaard, G., *Object-Oriented Software Engineering*. Reading, MA: Addison-Wesley, 1992.

Lambert, K., & Osborne, M., *Java: A Framework for Programming and Problem Solving*. Pacific Grove, CA: Brooks/Cole Publishing Company, 1999.

Rumbaugh, J., et al., *Object-Oriented Modeling and Design*. Upper Saddle River, NJ: Prentice Hall, 1991.

Wirfs-Brock, R., Wilkerson, B., & Wiener, L., *Designing Object-Oriented Software*. Upper Saddle River, NJ: Prentice Hall, 1990.

Programming Problems and Projects

1. Write a program to read data containing the name, address, telephone number, and class of a friend into an object and print its contents.

2. The Falcon Manufacturing Company wishes to keep computerized structures of its telephone-order customers. They want the name, street address, city, state, and zip code for each customer. They include either a "T" if the customer is a business or an "F" if the customer is an individual. A 30-character description of each business is also included. An individual's credit limit is in the structure.

Write a program to read the information for the customer from the keyboard and print the information on the screen.

3. Write a program to be used by the registrar of a university. The program should get information from the keyboard, and the data for each student should include student name, student number, classification (1 for freshman, 2 for sophomore, 3 for junior, 4 for senior, or 7 for special student), hours completed, hours taking, and grade point average. You should design a class to represent a student as an abstract data type.

4. Implement and extend the ATM class to handle user errors by confiscating a card after three unsuccessful attempts to gain access to an account.

5. Complex numbers are of the form $a + bi$ where a and b are real and i represents $\sqrt{-1}$. Complex number arithmetic is defined by

Sum	$(a + bi) + (c + di) = (a + c) + (b + d)i$
Difference	$(a + bi) - (c + di) = (a - c) + (b - d)i$
Product	$(a + bi)(c + di) = (ac - bd) + (ad + bc)i$
Quotient	$(a + bi)/(c + di) = \frac{ac + bd}{c^2 + d^2} + \frac{(bc - ad)i}{c^2 + d^2}$

Write a program that will perform these calculations on two complex numbers. Each line of data consists of a single character designator (S, D, P, or Q) followed by four reals representing two complex numbers. For example, $(2 + 3i) + (5 - 2i)$ is represented by

```
S2 3 5-2
```

An instance of a class should be used for each complex number. The arithmetic operators should be overloaded to carry out the operations. Input and output should be in the form $a + bi$ (overload the input and output operators as well).

6. The Readmore Public Library wants a program to keep track of the books checked out. Information for each book should be kept in an object, and the data members should include the author's name, a nonfiction designator (Boolean), the title, the library catalog number, and the copyright date. Each customer can check out at most ten books. Develop an abstract data type for representing a book as a C++ class. There should be public member functions for returning each attribute of a book, and input and output operations for initializing and printing them as well.

7. Write a program that uses objects to analyze poker hands. Each hand consists of five objects (cards). Each object should have one data member for the suit and one for the value. Rankings for the hands from high to low are

straight flush
four of a kind
full house
flush
straight
three of a kind
two pair
one pair
none of the above

Your program should read data for five cards from the keyboard, evaluate the hand, and print out the hand together with a message indicating its value.

8. Problem 7 can be modified in several ways. A first modification is to compare two different hands using only the ranking indicated. A second (more difficult) modification is to also compare hands that have the same ranking. For example, a pair of 8s is better than a pair of 7s. Extend Problem 7 to incorporate some of these modifications.
9. The university biology department has a Conservation Club that works with the state's Department of Natural Resources (DNR). Their project for the semester is to help capture and tag migratory birds. You have been asked to write a computer program to help them store information. In general, the program must have information for each bird tagged entered interactively in an object for subsequent use. For each bird tagged, you need a data member for the tag number, tagging site, sex, bird type, date, and name of the DNR officer doing the tagging. After all data have been entered, the program should print the contents of the object. (*Hint:* Save the bird objects to a file as they are input.)
10. Ms. Crown, your computer science instructor, wishes to keep track of the maintenance record of her computers and has turned to you for help. She wants to keep track of the type of machine, its serial number (up to ten characters), the year of purchase, and a Boolean variable indicating whether the machine is under service contract. Write a program that permits the entry of this information and prints a record for a machine.
11. Design and implement a `Dice` class. Each instance of this class should have as attributes the die's current side (number of dots), the total number of times it has been rolled, and the average of all the sides it has displayed. There should be observer functions for all of these attributes, as well as a `toString` function that returns a string representation of them. Two other functions, `roll` and `reset`, are the modifier methods. `roll` should use a random number to determine the current side of a die. Develop the class for dice by writing formal specifications and test it in a simple tester program.
12. In the game of craps, a player provides an initial bankroll and bets from this amount on each roll of the dice. On each roll, the sum of the faces is taken. The outcomes are as follows:

    - If 7 or 11 is rolled, the player wins.
    - If 2, 3, or 12 is rolled, the player loses.
    - Otherwise, the number rolled becomes the player's point. The player rolls the dice repeatedly until he or she wins by making the point (getting the same number as on the first roll) or loses by crapping out (getting a 7).

    Design and implement a machine that allows the user to play craps. This machine should be defined as a new class that uses the `Dice` class defined in Problem 11. The user interface accepts an amount of money representing an initial bankroll. Before each roll of the dice, the user must place a bet. At the end of the game, the program should display the amount of the user's current bankroll (after adding the gains and deducting the losses).

9

Arrays

Chapter Outline

Thus far in this text, we have been able to store large amounts of data in files, but we have been unable to manipulate them in a convenient way. For example, we can write a program that allows the user to enter a long list of bank accounts interactively and save the list in a file. However, the file structure does not efficiently support functions to process the accounts in the list, such as searching for an account, updating information in it, or computing statistics on all accounts. Other objects are difficult to represent at all with the data structures at our disposal. Consider the example of representing a student whose attributes are a name and a list of ten quiz grades. Representing these attributes as eleven separate named data members in a class definition is unwieldy.

Fortunately, C++ provides a structured data type called an *array* to facilitate solving problems that require working with large amounts of data. The use of arrays permits us to set aside a group of memory locations that we can then manipulate as a single entity or that gives us direct access to any component. Standard applications for arrays include implementing strings, creating tabular output (tables), alphabetizing a list of names, analyzing a list of test scores, and keeping an inventory.

In this chapter, we discuss the use of the array as a general data structuring mechanism. Then we develop two classes, `apvector` and `apmatrix`, that make array processing safe and convenient.

9.1 Arrays

Basic Idea and Notation

As previously mentioned, many instances arise in which several variables of the same data type are required. Let us work with a list of five integers: 18, 17, 21, 18, and 19. Prior to this chapter, we would have declared five variables—*A, B, C, D,* and *E*—and assigned them appropriate values or read them from the keyboard. This would have produced five values in memory, each accessed by a separate identifier.

Objectives

a. to understand the basic concept of an array
b. to use correct notation for arrays
c. to declare arrays with variable declarations and with type definitions
d. to use array components with appropriate arithmetic operations
e. to use array components with appropriate input and output statements

18	17	21	18	19
A	B	C	D	E

If the list were very long, this would be an inefficient way to work with these data; an alternative is to use an array. In C++, we declare a variable as an array variable using either of the following methods:

1. `int list[5];`
2. `typedef int listType[5];`
`listType list;`

With either of these declarations, we now have five integer variables with which to work. They are denoted by

list[0] list[1] list[2] list[3] list[4]

and each is referred to as a *component* (or *element*) *of the array*. A good way to visualize these variables is to assume that memory locations are aligned in a column on top of each other and the name of the column is `list`. If we then assign the five values of our list to these five variables, we have the following in memory:

list	
18	list [0]
17	list [1]
21	list [2]
18	list [3]
19	list [4]

The components of an array are referred to by their relative position in the array. This relative position is called the *index* or *subscript* of the component. In the array of our five values, the component `list[2]` has an index of 2 and a value of 21. Note that an array index is always numbered from 0 rather than 1. The index of the last component in an array is always N–1, where N is the number of elements in the array.

For the sake of convenience, you may choose to depict an array by listing only the index beside its appropriate component. Thus, `list` could be shown as

list	
	0
	1
	2
	3
	4

If you choose this method, remember that the array elements are referenced by the array name and the index, for example, `list[2]` for the third component. Whichever method you use, it is important to remember that each array component is a variable and can be treated exactly like any other declared variable of that base type in the program.

Declaring an Array

An earlier declaration of an array was

```
int list[5];
```

Let us now examine this declaration more closely. Several comments are in order.

1. The key word `int` indicates the data type for the components. This can, of course, be another data type such as `char`, as we have seen in our definition of a string type.
2. `[5]` is the syntax that indicates the array consists of five memory locations accessed by specifying each of the numbers, 0, 1, 2, 3, and 4. We frequently say the array is of length five. The information inside the brackets must be an integer constant or an expression whose value can be computed at compile time. This value must lie in the range from 1 to an upper bound defined for the particular system on which you are running your programs. (You can look this value up in the manual for your system.) The integer constant can be expressed either literally (`[5]`) or as a named constant (`[MAX_LIST_SIZE]`). The latter form is preferred for better program maintenance.
3. `list`, the name of the variable, can be any valid identifier. As always, it is good practice to use descriptive names to enhance readability.

The form for declaring an array variable is

<component type><variable name> [<integer value>] ;

where `<component type>` is any predefined or user-defined data type and `<variable name>` is any valid identifier.

The following example illustrates another declaration of an array variable.

Example 9.1 Suppose you want to create a list of ten integer variables for the hours worked by ten employees as follows:

Employee Number	Hours Worked
0	35
1	40
2	20
3	38
4	25
5	40
6	25
7	40
8	20
9	45

Declare an array that has ten components of type `int` and show how it can be visualized. A descriptive name for the variable could be `hours`. There are ten items, so we will define a constant, `MAX_LIST_SIZE = 10`, and use `[MAX_LIST_SIZE]` in the array variable declaration. Because the data consist of integers, the component type will be `int`. An appropriate definition and subsequent declaration could be

```
const int MAX_LIST_SIZE = 10;
int hours [MAX_LIST_SIZE];
```

At this stage, the components can be visualized as

hours	
	hours[0]
	hours[1]
	hours[2]
	hours[3]
	hours[4]
	hours[5]
	hours[6]
	hours[7]
	hours[8]
	hours[9]

After making appropriate assignment statements, `hours` can be visualized as

hours	
35	hours[0]
40	hours[1]
20	hours[2]
38	hours[3]
25	hours[4]
40	hours[5]
25	hours[6]
40	hours[7]
20	hours[8]
45	hours[9]

Other Element Types

The previous two arrays used element types that were integers. The following examples illustrate some array definitions with other element types.

Example 9.2 Declare an array that allows you to store the hourly price for a share of IBM stock. A descriptive name could be `stockPrices`. A price is quoted at each hour from 9:00 A.M. to 3:00 P.M., so we will use `MAX_LIST_SIZE = 7` in the declaration section. Because the data consist of real numbers, the data type must be `double`. A possible declaration could be

```
const int MAX_LIST_SIZE = 7;
double stockPrices[MAX_LIST_SIZE];
```

This would then allow us to store the 9:00 A.M. price in `stockPrices [0]`, the 1:00 P.M. price in `stockPrices [4]`, and so on.

Example 9.3 The declaration

```
const int MAX_LIST_SIZE = 6;
char alphas[MAX_LIST_SIZE];
```

will reserve six character components.

Example 9.4 The declaration

```
const int MAX_LIST_SIZE = 4;
bool flags[MAX_LIST_SIZE];
```

will produce an array whose components are Boolean values.

It is important to note that in each example the array components will have no predictable values assigned until the program specifically makes some kind of assignment. Declaring an array does not assign values to any of the components.

Assignment Statements

Suppose we have declared an array

```
const int MAX = 5;
int a [MAX];
```

and we want to put the values 1, 4, 9, 16, and 25 into the respective components. We can accomplish this with the assignment statements

```
a[0] = 1;
a[1] = 4;
a[2] = 9;
a[3] = 16;
a[4] = 25;
```

If variables `b` and `c` of type `int` are declared in the program, then the following are also appropriate assignment statements:

```
a[3] = b;
c = a[2];
a[2] = a[4];
```

If you want to interchange values of two components (for example, exchange `a[2]` with `a[3]`), you could use a third integer variable:

```
b = a[2];
a[2] = a[3];
a[3] = b;
```

This exchange is frequently used in sorting algorithms, so let us examine it more closely. Assume `b` contains no previously assigned value, and `a[2]` and `a[3]` contain 4 and 9, respectively.

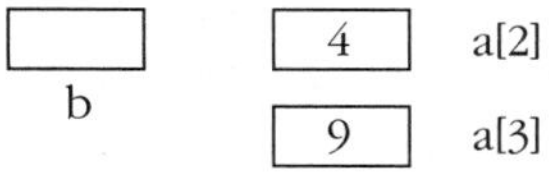

```
[   ]       [ 4 ]  a[2]
  b
            [ 9 ]  a[3]
```

The assignment statement `b = a[2]` produces

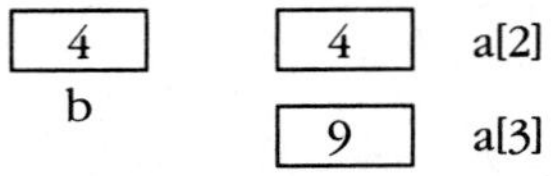

4		4	a[2]
b		9	a[3]

The assignment statement `a[2] = a[3]` produces

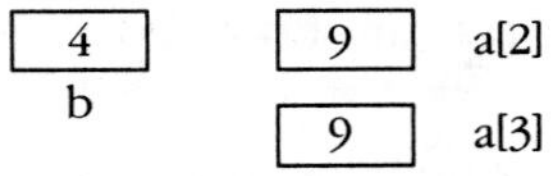

4		9	a[2]
b		9	a[3]

and finally, the assignment statement `a[3] = b` produces

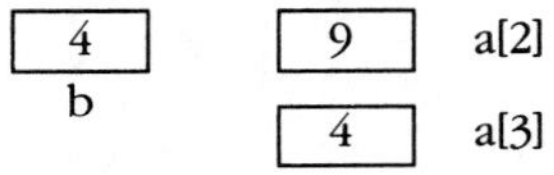

4		9	a[2]
b		4	a[3]

in which the original values of `a[2]` and `a[3]` have been interchanged.

Arithmetic

Components of an array can also be used in any appropriate arithmetic operation. For example, suppose `a` is the following array of integers

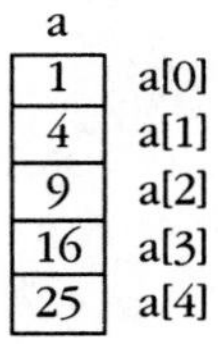

a	
1	a[0]
4	a[1]
9	a[2]
16	a[3]
25	a[4]

and that the values of the components of the array are to be added. This could be accomplished by the statement

```
sum = a[0] + a[1] + a[2] + a[3] + a[4];
```

Each of the following would also be a valid use of an array component:

```
b = 3 * a[1];
c = a[4] % 3;
d = a[1] * a[4];
```

For the array `a` given earlier, these assignment statements produce

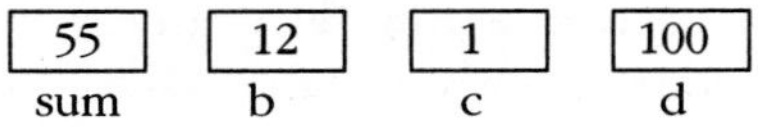

55	12	1	100
sum	b	c	d

Some invalid assignment statements and the reasons they are invalid follow:

```
a[6] = 7;
```

This statement will compile and run. However, because 6 is not a valid subscript for the array, the program may behave strangely.

```
a[2.0] = 3;
```

The statement will not compile because a subscript of type `double` is not allowed.

Reading and Writing

Because array components are names for variables, they can be used in input and output statements. For example, if `scores` is an array of five integers and you want to input the scores 65, 43, 98, 75, and 83 from the keyboard, you could use the code

```
cin >> scores[0] >> scores[1] >> scores[2] >> scores[3] >> scores[4];
```

This produces the array

scores	
65	scores[0]
43	scores[1]
98	scores[2]
75	scores[3]
83	scores[4]

If you want to print the scores above 80, you could use the code

```
cout << setw(10) << scores[2] << setw(10) << scores[4] << endl;
```

to produce

```
98    83
```

It is important to note that you cannot input or output values into or from an entire array by a reference to the array name. Statements such as `cout << a;` are legitimate, but they display the address of the array rather than its contents.

Out-of-Range Array References

You have seen that an array in C++ has index values in the range 0 . . . N–1, where N is the number of cells for storing data in the array. For example, the data declarations

```
const MAX_LIST_SIZE = 5;
int weekDays[MAX_LIST_SIZE];
```

cause the system to allocate five cells of memory for an array whose index ranges from 0 to 4. The index values used in array references should also range from 0 to 4. If a programmer uses an index value outside this range, a *range bound error* occurs. If the offending index is a variable, as in

```
int i = 5;
weekDays[i] = 10;
```

the error will occur at run time, although the computer will not halt program execution with an error message that this error has occurred.

Even if the offending index is a constant, as in

```
weekDays[5] = 10;
```

A NOTE OF INTEREST

Why Computer Scientists Number Things from 0 to *N*–1

In Chapter 1, we mentioned that C++ incorporates features of high-level programming languages that make programs easy to read, modify, and maintain and features of low-level programming languages that give programmers control over the structure and behavior of real computers. The numbering of array indices from 0 rather than 1 is one of the low-level features of the language that calls for further comment.

An array index is numbered from 0 in C++ because of the way in which the individual array cells are represented and accessed in the computer's memory. You can think of the computer's memory as a huge stack of cells or little boxes. Each cell has an address that allows the computer to locate it and either fetch data from it or store data in it. Now, suppose that five of these cells have to be allocated for a new array variable in a program. The computer locates the next available contiguous block of five cells and copies the address of the first cell into a sixth cell. This address will be the *base address* of the entire array. Suppose this base address is 276 in our example, and a programmer wishes to store data in the second cell of the array. The address of the second cell, or 277, can be computed by taking the base address of the array, or 276, from the sixth cell and adding 1 to it. The address of the third cell can be obtained by adding 2 to the base address, the address of the fourth cell by adding 3, and so on. In general, the address of the *N*th cell in an array can be computed by adding *N*–1 to the base address. The value *N*–1 is called the *offset* of the *N*th cell from the base address. The offset of the first cell in any array is 0, and the offset of the last cell is *N*–1, where *N* is the total number of cells in the array.

There is also a more important reason why an array index is numbered from 0. The address of the first cell in the entire memory of a computer typically is 0. The address of the last cell in memory is then *N*–1, where *N* is the total number of cells in memory. You might think that computer scientists are a weird bunch, having set up computer systems so that their internal components are numbered in a way that is consistently off by 1 from the way that ordinary folks would number them. However, there is a very good reason to number things from 0 to *N*–1 in computers. Each address must itself be capable of being stored in a memory cell in the computer. As you know, a memory cell can store a number of finite size. The size of the number represented depends on the number of bits available in the memory cell. In general, numbers ranging from 0 to 2^N–1 can be stored in a memory cell containing *N* bits. For example, numbers ranging from 0 index from 1 to *N* in a high-level programming language. This notation would be more intuitive and agree with common sense. Some languages, such as Pascal, allow the programmer to specify the lowest and highest index values when an array type is defined, and a Pascal programmer typically will define an index from 1 to *N*. The compiler then takes care of translating a reference such as `a[1]` to the underlying machine address a[0].

You might then ask why the designers of C++ still made array indexing a low-level feature of the language. The reason is that programmers can then manipulate arrays not only with standard indexing, but also with *pointer arithmetic*. Assume the reference `a[1]` in C++ adds 1 to the base address of the array `a`. Then the reference `a` by itself is to the base address of the array. Therefore, the reference `*(a + 1)` locates the same array cell in memory as the reference `a[1]`. Needless to say, pointer arithmetic is an even lower level feature of C++ than regular indexing and is not recommended for novices!

the error will not be caught at compile time. *C++ does not do range bound error checking*. This means that the program will compile and execute, and the reference will be to some area of memory other than the cells allocated for the array. In the case of an assignment to that location, a serious side effect will occur and may cause the program to behave in very mysterious ways.

Range bound errors in C++ programs are most often caused by failure to remember that the upper bound on the array index is *N*–1, where *N* is the number of cells in the array. One way to avoid range bound errors with arrays is to be careful always to use an index that satisfies the condition 0 <= index < *N*, where *N* is the integer constant used to define the array type. You may wish to use the C++ assertion facility to place this precondition on array references in spots in a program where range bound errors are likely to occur.

In Section 9.5, we will develop an array class that supports range bound checking.

Communication and Style Tips The use of descriptive constants is not necessary for creating arrays. However, programs that use this method are much easier to maintain than those that use declarations such as `int list[20];`. You will appreciate the use of symbolic constants and array type names better when you learn how to process arrays with loops and functions in the following sections of this chapter.

Exercises 9.1

1. Using descriptive names, define an array type and declare subsequent variables for each of the following:
   a. A list of 35 test scores
   b. The prices of 20 automobiles
   c. The answers to 50 true–false questions
   d. A list of letter grades for the classes you are taking this semester
2. Write a test program in which you declare an array of three components, read values into each component, sum the components, and print the sum and value of each component.
3. Assume the array list is declared as

```
int list[100];
```

   and that all other variables have been appropriately declared. Label the following as valid or invalid. Include an explanation for any that are invalid.
   a. `cin >> list[3];`
   b. `a = list[3] + list[4];`
   c. `cout << list;`
   d. `list[10] = 3.2;`
   e. `max = list[50];`
   f. `average = (list[0] + list[8]) / 2;`
   g. `cout << list[25, 50, 75];`
   h. `cout << list[10] + list[25];`
   i. `for (j = 0; j < 100; ++j)`
      `cin >> list;`
   j. `list[36] = list[100];`
   k. `listType[47] = 92;`
   l. `list[40] = list[41] / 2;`
4. Change each of the following so that a `typedef` is used to define the array type.
   a. `char letterList[26];`
   b. `char companyName[30];`
   c. `double scoreList[30];`
5. Consider the array declared by

```
int waistSizes[5]
```

   a. Sketch how the array should be envisioned in memory.
   b. After assignments

```
waistSizes [0] = 34;
waistSizes [1] = 36;
waistSizes [2] = 32;
waistSizes [3] = 2 * 15;
waistSizes [4] = (waistSizes [0] + waistSizes [2]) / 2;
```

   have been made, sketch the array and indicate the contents of each component.

6. Let the array money be declared by

```
double money[3];
```

Let temp, x, and y be double variables and assume money has the following values:

money	
19.26	money[0]
10.04	money[1]
17.32	money[2]

Assuming money contains the values indicated before each segment is executed, indicate what the array would contain after each section of code.

a.
```
temp = 173.21;
x = temp + money[1];
money[0] = x;
```

b.
```
if (money[1] < money[0])
{
   temp = money[2];
   money[1] = money[1];
   money[0] = temp;
}
```

c.
```
money[2] = 20.0 - money[2];
```

7. Let the array list be declared by

```
double list[10];
```

Write a program segment to initialize all components of list to 0.0.

9.2 Using Arrays

Loops for Input and Output

Objectives

a. to use loops to input data into an array
b. to use loops to output data from an array
c. to assign array values by component assignment

One advantage of using arrays is the small amount of code needed when for loops are used to manipulate array components. For example, suppose a list of 100 scores is to be used in a program. If an array is declared by

```
const int MAX_LIST_SIZE = 100;
int scores[MAX_LIST_SIZE];
```

the values can be read into the array using a for loop as follows:

```
for (j = 0; j <MAX_LIST_SIZE ; ++j)
{
   cout << "Enter a score: ";
   cin >> scores[j];
}
```

Note that the control variable is initialized to 0 and that the comparison in the termination condition is a simple less than operator (<). The reason is that the index positions in the array have been defined to range from 0 to 99, inclusive. Note also that the size of the array, `MAX_LIST_SIZE`, is used both in the array variable declaration and in the `for` loop. If we want to change the size of the array, we need only change the value 100 in the constant definition and not in the array variable declaration or in the loop. As always, the use of symbolic constants greatly enhances program maintenance. Note finally that a statement such as `cin >> score` will not have the desired effect. You may only read data elements into individual components of the array.

Loops can be similarly used to produce output of array components. For example, if the array of test scores just given is to be printed in a column,

```
for (j = 0; j < MAX_LIST_SIZE; ++j)
   cout << scores[j] << endl;
```

will accomplish this. If the components of scores contain the values

scores	
78	scores[0]
93	scores[1]
.	.
.	.
82	scores[99]

the loop for writing produces

```
78
93
.
.
.
82
```

Note that you cannot cause the array components to be printed by a statement such as `cout << scores`. You must refer to the individual components.

Loops for output are seldom this simple. Usually we are required to format the output in some manner. For example, suppose the array `scores` is as declared earlier and we wish to print ten scores to a line, each with a field width of five spaces. The following segment of code accomplishes this:

```
for (j = 0; j < MAX_LIST_SIZE; ++j)
{
   cout << setw(5) << scores[j];
   if (j % 10 == 0)
      cout << endl;
}
```

Loops for Assigning

Loops can also be used to assign values to array components. In certain instances, you might wish to have an array contain values that are not read from the keyboard. The following examples show how loops can be used to solve such instances.

Example 9.5 Recall array `a` in Section 9.1 in which we made the following assignments:

```
a[0] = 1;
a[1] = 4;
a[2] = 9;
a[3] = 16;
a[4] = 25;
```

These assignments could have been made with the loop

```
for (j = 0; j < 4; ++j)
   a[j] = (j + 1) * (j + 1);
```

Example 9.6 Suppose an array is needed whose components contain the letters of the alphabet in order from A to Z. Assuming you are using the ASCII character set, the desired array could be declared by

```
const int MAX_LIST_SIZE = 26;
char alphabet[MAX_LIST_SIZE];
```

The array `alphabet` could then be assigned the desired characters by the statement

```
for (j = 0; j < MAX_LIST_SIZE; ++j)
   alphabet[j] = char(j +'A');
```

If `j = 0;` we have

```
alphabet[0] = char('A');
```

Thus,

```
alphabet[0] = 'A';
```

Similarly, for `j = 1;` we have

```
alphabet[1] = char(1 + 'A');
```

Eventually, we obtain

alphabet	
'A'	alphabet[0]
'B'	alphabet[1]
'C'	alphabet[2]
.	.
.	.
.	.
'Z'	alphabet[25]

Assignment of values from components of one array to corresponding components of another array is a frequently encountered problem. For example, suppose the arrays a and b are declared as

```
const int MAX_LIST_SIZE = 50;
double a[MAX_LIST_SIZE];
double b[MAX_LIST_SIZE];
```

If b has been assigned values and you want to put the contents of b into a component by component, you must use the loop

```
for (j = 0; j < MAX_LIST_SIZE; ++j)
   a[j] = b[j];
```

Now suppose you tried a shortcut by assigning one whole array variable to another:

```
a = b;
```

This assignment does *not necessarily* cause 50 assignments to be made at the component level. In some implementations of C++, the assignment will cause the name a to be an alias for the array b. The reason is that references to array variables are really references to the addresses of the arrays. In other implementations of C++, the assignment is a syntax error. It would be a good practice to write a function that copies components from one array to another and use it in your various programs.

Processing with Loops

Loops are especially suitable for reading, writing, and assigning array components, and they can be used in conjunction with arrays to process data. The following examples illustrate additional uses of loops for processing data contained in array variables.

Example 9.7 Recall the problem earlier in this section in which we read 100 test scores into an array. Assume the scores have been read and you now wish to find the average score and the largest score. Assume variables sum, max, and average have been appropriately declared. The following segment will compute the average.

```
sum = 0;
for (j = 0; j < MAX_LIST_SIZE; ++j)
   sum = sum + scores[j];
average = sum / MAX_LIST_SIZE;
```

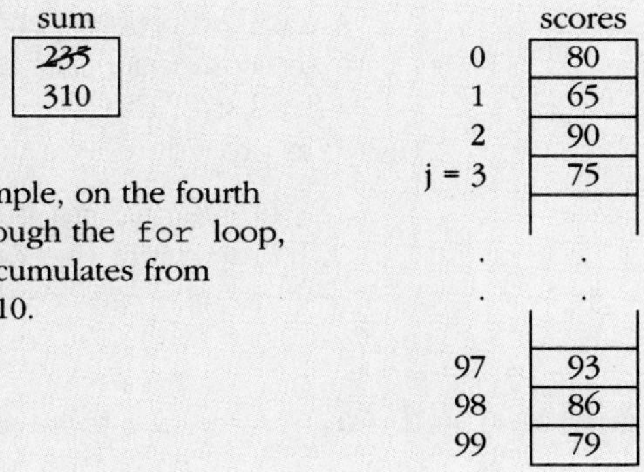

sum: ~~235~~ 310

	scores
0	80
1	65
2	90
j = 3	75
.	.
.	.
97	93
98	86
99	79

For example, on the fourth time through the for loop, sum accumulates from 235 to 310.

The maximum score can be found by using the following segment of code:

```
max = scores[0];
for (j = 1; j < MAX_LIST_SIZE; ++ j)
   if (scores[j] > max)
      max = scores [j];
```

max
~~80~~
90

For example, when j is 2, max would be updated from 80 to 90.

	scores
0	80
1	65
j = 2	90
3	75
.	.
.	.
97	93
98	86
99	79

Example 9.8 Write a segment of code to find the position of the smallest value in array a. Assume the variables have been declared as

```
const int MAX_LIST_SIZE = 100;
double a[MAX_LIST_SIZE];
double min;
int index;
```

and the values have been read into components of a. The following code will solve the problem:

```
index = 0;
for (j = 1; j < MAX_LIST_SIZE; ++ j)
   if (a[j] < a [index])
      index = j;
```

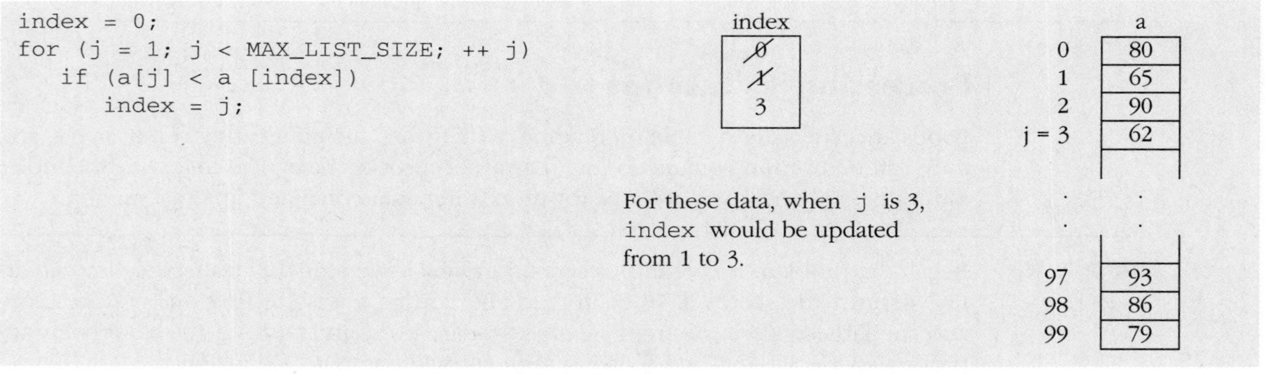

A standard problem encountered when working with arrays is not knowing exactly how many components of an array will be needed. In C++, the standard array data type has a fixed size. Thus, you must decide some upper limit for the length of the array. A standard procedure is to declare a reasonable limit, keeping two points in mind:

1. The length must be sufficient to store all the data.
2. The amount of storage space must not be excessive; do not set aside excessive amounts of space that will not be used.

Exercises 9.2

1. Assume the following array declarations:

```
typedef int numListType[5];
typedef bool answerListType[10];
typedef char nameListType[20];
```

```
numListType list, scores;
answerListType answers;
nameListType initials;
```

Indicate the contents of the arrays after each segment of code.

a.
```
for (j = 0; j < 5; ++j)
    list[j] = j / 3;
```

b.
```
for (j = 1; j < 6; ++j)
{
    list[j - 1] = j + 3;
    scores[j - 1] = list[j - 1] / 3;
}
```

c.
```
for (j = 0; j < 10; ++j)
    if (j % 2 == 0)
            answers[j] = true;
    else
            answers[j] = false;
```

d.
```
for (j = 0; j < 20; ++j)
    initials[j] = char(j + 64);
```

2. Write a test program to illustrate what happens when you try to use an index that is not in the defined range for an array; for example, try to use the loop

```
for (j = 0; j < 10; ++j)
   cin >> a[j];
```

when `a` has been declared as `int a[5];`

3. Let the array `best` be declared by

```
int best[30];
```

and assume that test scores have been read into `best`. What does the following section of code do?

```
count = 0;
for (j = 0; j < 30; ++j);
   if (best [j] > 90)
      ++count;
```

4. Declare an array and write a segment of code to do the following:
a. Read 20 integer test scores into the array.
b. Count the number of scores greater than or equal to 55.

5. Declare an array using a `typedef` and write a section of code to read a name of 20 characters from a line of input.

6. Let the array `list` be declared by `int list[7];` and assume the components have values of

list	
–2	list[0]
3	list[1]
0	list[2]
–8	list[3]
20	list[4]
14	list[5]
–121	list[6]

Show what the array components would be after the following program segment is executed:

```
for (j = 0; j < 7; ++j)
   if (list[j] < 0)
      list[j] = 0;
```

7. Assume array `a` is declared as

```
double a[100];
```

Write a segment of code that uses a loop to initialize all components to zero.

8. Let the array `n` be declared as `char n[21];` and assume the array components have been assigned the values

J	O	H	N		S	M	I	T	H
n[0]	n[1]	n[2]	n[3]	n[4]	n[5]	n[6]	n[7]	n[8]	n[9]

What output is produced by the following?

a.
```
for (j= 0; j < 10; ++j)
   cout << n[j];
cout << endl;
```

b.
```
for (j= 5; j < 10; ++j)
   cout << n[j];
cout << , ;
for (j= 0; j < 4; ++j)
   cout << n[j];
cout << endl;
```

c.
```
for (j = 9; j >= 0; --j)
   cout << n[j];
```

9. Assume an array has been declared as

```
int testScores[50];
```

Write a segment of code to print a suitable heading (assume this is a list of test scores) and then output a numbered list of the array components.

9.3 Array Parameters and Functions

Objectives

a. to use functions to process arrays
b. to pass arrays as parameters to functions
c. to understand the difference between array parameters and parameters of other data types

Functions can be used with array parameters to maintain a structured design. Consider the problem of computing the mean of a list of test scores. We can represent the list of scores as an array that can be passed to several functions for processing. A first-level pseudocode development of a solution to this problem is:

1. Get the scores (function `getData`)
2. Compute the average (function `calcMean`)
3. Print a header (function `printHeader`)
4. Print the results (function `printResults`)

The functions `getData`, `calcMean`, and `printResults` all take an array parameter and an integer parameter representing the number of data elements currently stored in the array. Here are the declarations of these functions:

```
// Function: getData
// Gets list of scores from the user at the keyboard
// until a sentinel is entered
//
// Inputs: length, representing the maximum physical size
// of the list
// Outputs: an array of integers representing the list
// and length, representing
// its logical size

void getData(int list[ ], int &length);

// Function: calcMean
// Computes the mean of the scores in the list
//
// Inputs: an array of integers and its length
// Output: a real number representing the mean of the
// integers in the array

double calcMean(int list[ ], int length);

// Function: printResults
// Displays the scores and the mean score
//
// Inputs: an array of integers and the mean on the
// screen

void printResults(int list[ ], int length, double ave);
```

There are several things to note about these declarations:

1. None of the arrays appears to be passed by reference to the functions, but they all are. In C++, the address of an actual parameter of an array is always passed to a function. In the case of actual parameters that are array variables, the corresponding formal parameters in the function will serve as aliases for the variables. Therefore, changes to the array cells referenced by a formal array parameter will also be changes to the array cells referenced by the actual parameter.

2. The maximum size of each array does not appear to be specified in the formal parameter declarations, where we see a pair of empty square brackets ([ ]). Because the arrays are all passed by reference, the computer does not have to know how large the actual array will be when a function is called. Leaving the physical size of the array unspecified in the formal parameter declaration will allow a function to be called with arrays of different physical sizes as long as the element type (in this case, int) is the same.
3. The length parameter for getData represents the *physical size* of the array parameter when the function is called, and it represents the *logical size,* or number of data elements input, when the function returns.
4. Although the form <element type> <parameter name> [ ] is most commonly used to declare array parameters, other forms may specify the physical size of the array or may precede the array parameter name with an array type name.

The implementation of getData is

```
void getData(int list[ ], int &length)
{
   int data, logicalLength;

   logicalLength = 0;
   cout <> "Enter an integer (" << INPUT_SENTINEL << " to end input): ";
   cin >> data;
   while ((logicalLength < length) && ! endOfInput(data))
   {
        list [logicalLength] = data;
        ++logicalLength;
        cout << "Enter an integer (" << INPUT_SENTINEL
             << " to end input): ";
        cin >> data;
   }
   length = logicalLength;
}
```

Using two different lists and their lengths, getData could be called by

```
const int MAX1 = 10;
const int MAX2 = 20;

int list1[MAX1];
int list2[MAX2];

int length1 = MAX1;
int length2 = MAX2;

getData(list1, length1);
getData(list2, length2);
```

The average score in a list could be computed by the function calcMean:

```
double calcMean (int list [ ], int length)
{
   int sum = 0;
```

```
    for (int j = 0; j < length; ++j)
       sum = sum + list[j];
    return double(sum) / length;
}
```

A function to print a heading is written in a manner similar to that we have used previously. If we want the output to be

```
Test Scores
-----------
    99
    98
    97
    96
    95

The average score on this test was 97.00.
```

The function for the heading could be

```
void printheader()
{
    cout << endl;
    cout << "Test Scores" << endl;
    cout << "-----------" << endl;
    cout << endl;
}
```

A function to print the results could be

```
void printResults (int list[ ], int length, double ave)
{
    for (int j = 0; j < length; ++j)
       cout << setw(5) << list[j] << endl;
    cout << endl << setiosflags(ios::fixed | ios::showpoint)
         << setprecision(2);
    cout << "The average score on this test was" << setw(6) << ave << endl;
}
```

This function could be called by

```
printResults(scores, length, ave);
```

where `ave` is found by

```
ave = calcMean(scores, length);
```

The important point to remember about array parameters is that they are treated very differently from parameters of other data types in C++. For reasons of efficiency, the address of a C++ array variable (which is identified by the array name and also is the address of the first data value in the array) is always passed to a function expecting an array parameter. The following rules of thumb will help in designing functions for processing arrays:

1. Never use the `&` symbol when specifying a formal array parameter in a function declaration or heading.
2. Specify a constant array formal parameter of the form `const <element type> <parameter name> [ ]` when you want to guarantee that no changes will be made to the array variable being passed to a function.

The special nature of array parameters in C++ can be a source of confusion for beginning programmers. In Section 9.6, we develop a new array class that allows array parameters to be treated like parameters of other data types in C++.

Exercises 9.3

1. Assume the following declarations have been made in a program:

```
typedef int rowType[10];
typedef double columnType[30];
typedef char string20Type[21];

rowType list1, list2;
columnType aray;
string20Type name1, name2;
int a[10];
int b[10];
```

Indicate which of the following are valid function declarations. Write an appropriate line of code that will use each valid declaration. Include an explanation for those that are invalid.

a. `void newList (rowType x, columnType y);`
b. `void newList (rowType &x, columnType &y);`
c. `void newList (int x[ ]);`
d. `void newList (rowType &x, rowType &y);`
e. `void newList (rowType &rowType);`
f. `void wordWeek (int days[7]);`
g. `void surname (name x);`
h. `void surnames (string20Type x, string20Type y);`
i. `void getData (int x, name &y);`
j. `void table (rowType &x, rowType &y);`

2. When possible, use the declarations of Exercise 1 to write function declarations so that each of the following statements in the main program is an appropriate call to a function. Explain any inappropriate calls.

a. `oldList (list1, aray);`
b. `changeList (list1, name1, b);`
c. `scores (a, b);`
d. `surname (string20Type);`

3. Write an appropriate function declaration and a line of code to call the function for each of the following:

a. A function to input 20 test scores into an array.
b. A function to count the number of occurrences of the letter 'A' in an array of 50 characters.

c. A function to input integer test scores from the keyboard, count the number of scores, count the number of scores greater than or equal to 90, and save this information for later use.

4. Assume the following declarations have been made:

```
typedef int columnType[10];
columnType list1, list2;
```

Indicate the contents of each array after the call to the corresponding function.

a.
```
void sample (columnType &list1, columnType list2)
{
    for (int j = 0; j < 10; ++j)
    {
        list1[j]= j *j;
        list2[j]= list1[j] % 2;
    }
}

for (int k = 0; k < 10; ++k)
{
    list1[k] = 0;
    list2[k] = 0;
}
sample (list1, list2);
```

b. Replace the function call with

```
sample (list2, list1);
```

c. Replace the function call with consecutive calls

```
sample (list1, list2);
sample (list2, list1);
```

5. Write a function to examine an array of integers and then return the maximum value, minimum value, and number of negative values to the main program.

6. Discuss some of the implementation details you need to read a list of names into an array.

9.4 Sorting and Searching an Array

Objectives

a. to sort an array using a selection sort

b. to search an array using a sequential search

Sorting an Array

Arrays often need to be sorted in either ascending or descending order. We will consider here one of the easier methods for doing this, the *selection sort,* and examine other sorting methods in Chapters 10 and 16.

Suppose we have an array `a` of five integers that we wish to sort from smallest to largest. The values currently in `a` are as depicted on the left; we wish to end up with values as on the right.

a		a	
6	a[0]	1	a[0]
4	a[1]	4	a[1]
8	a[2]	6	a[2]
10	a[3]	8	a[3]
1	a[4]	10	a[4]

The basic idea of a selection sort for each index position *I* is:

1. Find the smallest data value in the array from positions *I* through length–1, where length is the number of data values stored.
2. Exchange the smallest value with the value at position *I*.

The first pass through the loop produces

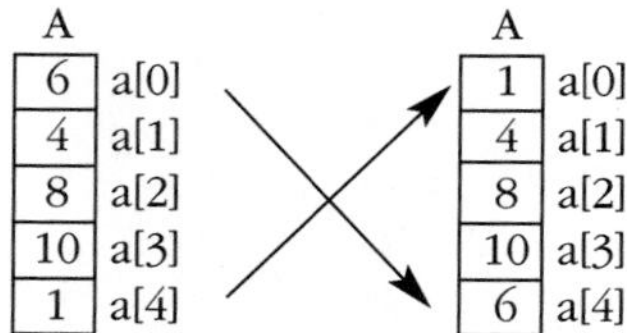

The second, third, and fourth passes produce

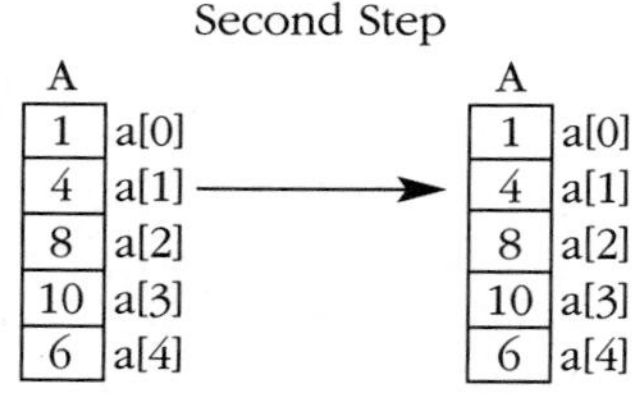

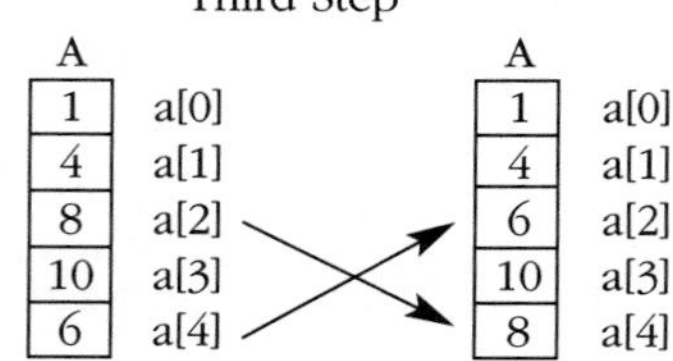

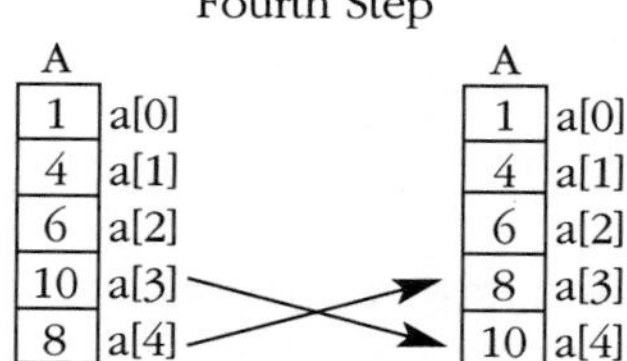

Notice that in the second pass, since the second smallest number was already in place, we need not exchange anything. Before writing the algorithm for this sorting procedure, note the following:

1. If the array is of length *n*, we need *n*–1 steps.
2. We must be able to find the smallest number.
3. We need to exchange appropriate array components.

When the code is written for this sort, note that strict inequality (<) rather than weak inequality (<=) is used when looking for the smallest remaining value. The algorithm to sort by selection is

```
For each j from 0 to n - 1 do
   Find the smallest value among a[j], a[j + 1], . . . a[n - 1]
       and store the index of the smallest value in index
   Exchange the values of a[j] and a[index], if necessary
```

In Section 9.2, Example 9.8, we saw a segment of code required to find the smallest value of array `a`. With suitable changes, we will incorporate this in the segment of code as a function, `findMinimum`, for the selection sort. We will also develop a function, `swap`, that exchanges the elements in an array when necessary.

Using these two functions, the implementation of a sort function is

```
void sort(int a[ ], int length)
{
   int minIndex = 0;

   for (int j = 0; j < length - 1; ++j)
   {
      minIndex = findMinimum(a, j, length);
      if (minIndex != j)
         swap(a[j], a[minIndex]);
   }
}
```

The function for finding the minimum value in an array takes three parameters: the array, the position to start the search, and the length or logical size of the array. The function returns the index position of the minimum element in the array. Its implementation uses a `for` loop:

```
int findMinimum(int a[ ], int first, int length)
{
   int minIndex = first;

   for (int k = first + 1; k < length; ++k)
      if (a[k] < a[minIndex])
         minIndex = k;
   return minIndex;
}
```

The `swap` function exchanges the values of two integer variables:

```
void swap(int &x, int &y)
{
   int temp = x;
   x = y;
   y = temp;
}
```

Let us now trace this sort for the five integers in the array we sorted at the beginning of this section.

a	
6	a[0]
4	a[1]
8	a[2]
10	a[3]
1	a[4]

For `j = 0, minIndex = 0` (in `findMinimum`), and this produces

0

minIndex

For the loop (in `findMinimum`) `for (k = 1; k < 5; ++k)`, we get successive assignments

k	minIndex
1	1
2	1
3	1
4	4

The statements (in `swap`)

```
temp = a[j];
a[j] = a[minIndex];
a[minIndex] = temp;
```

produce the partially sorted array:

a	
1	a[0]
4	a[1]
8	a[2]
10	a[3]
6	a[4]

Searching an Array

The need to search an array for a value is a common problem. For example, you might wish to replace a test score for a student, delete a name from a directory or mailing list, or upgrade the pay scale for certain employees. These and other problems require you to examine elements in some list until the desired value is located. When it is found, some action is taken. In this section, we assume all lists are nonempty.

The most common searching algorithm is a *sequential (linear) search*. This process is accomplished by examining the first element in some list and then proceeding to examine the elements in the order they appear until a match is found. Variations of this basic process include searching a sorted list for the first occurrence of a value, searching a sorted list for all occurrences of a value, and searching an unsorted list for the first occurrence of a value. We will look at another method, the binary search, in Chapter 10.

To illustrate a sequential search, suppose you have an array `list` of integers and you want to find the first occurrence of some particular target value. As you search the array, if the desired value is located, you want to return its position. If the value is not in the array, you return –1. The algorithm for such a search follows:

```
Set index to 0
Set found to false
While index < length and not found do
   If list[index] is equal to target then
      Set found to true
```

```
   Else
      Increment the index by 1
If found then
   Return index
Else
   Return -1
```

Note that the loop runs as long as the index can locate a value in the array and the target has not been found. A C++ sequential search function is

```
int search(int target, int list[ ], int length)
{
   int index = 0;
   bool found = false;
   while ((index < length) && ! found)
      if (list[index] == target)
         found = true;
      else
         ++index;
   if (found)
      return index;
   else
      return -1;
}
```

Let's now consider some variations of this problem. Our code works for both sorted and unsorted lists. However, if we are searching a sorted list, the algorithm can be improved. For example, if the array components are sorted from low to high, we need to continue the search only until the value in an array component exceeds the value of `target`. At that point, there is no need to examine the remaining components. The only change required in the loop for searching is to add a middle alternative to the `if` statement.

```
if (list[index] == target)
   found = true;
else if (list[index] > target)        // Target not in list.
   index = length;
else
   ++index;
```

Note that the loop now terminates when the target "falls between" two data values in the sorted list.

A relatively easy modification of the sequential search is to return the number of occurrences of some value. To illustrate, if `list` is an array of integers and `target` is an integer value, we can search a for the number of occurrences of `target` by

```
int occurrencesOf(int target, int list[ ], int length)
{
   count = 0;
   for (int index = 0; index < length; ++ index)
      if (list[index] == target)
         ++count;
   return count;
}
```

This code works for an unsorted list. A modification of the code for working with a sorted list is included as an exercise.

Exercises 9.4

1. Assume the array `column` is to be sorted from low to high using the selection sort.

column
–20
10
0
10
8
30
–2

   a. Sketch the contents of the array after each of the first two passes.
   b. How many exchanges are made during the sort?
2. Write a test program that prints the partially sorted arrays after each pass during a selection sort.
3. Change the code for the selection sort so it sorts an array from high to low.
4. Write a complete program that does the following:
   a. Read ten doubles into an array from the keyboard.
   b. If the first `double` is positive, sort the array from high to low; if it is negative, sort the array from low to high.
   c. Print a numbered column containing the sorted doubles with the format of ten columns of field width and two decimal places of precision.
5. Modify the selection sort by including a counter that counts the number of assignments of array elements made during a sort.
6. Using the modification in Exercise 5, sort lists of differing lengths that contain randomly generated numbers. Display the results of how many assignments were made for each sort on a graph. Use lists whose lengths are multiples of 10.
7. Suppose you have an array of student names and an array of these students' test scores. How would the array of names be affected if you sorted the test scores from high to low?
8. Modify the `occurrencesOf` function so that it works efficiently with a sorted array.

9.5 Two-Dimensional Arrays

Basic Idea and Notation

The arrays that we have been using thus far are *one-dimensional arrays* because we locate each data element in the array by specifying a single index position. However, suppose that we want to work with data that are best represented in tabular form. For example:

1. Box scores in baseball are reported with one player name listed for each row and one statistic listed for each column.
2. A teacher's grade book lists one name for each row and an exam or lab score for each column.

In each of these cases, a multiple reference is needed for each data item. Other common computer applications, such as spreadsheets and bitmaps for graphics, also use tabular data with multiple reference.

Objectives

a. to understand the need for representing the data for some problems as a two-dimensional grid
b. to represent this data structure as a two-dimensional array
c. to declare a two-dimensional array
d. to manipulate the components of a two-dimensional array
e. to use two-dimensional arrays with functions

In C++, multiple reference is accomplished with *two-dimensional arrays*. In these arrays, the row index precedes the column index. To illustrate, suppose we want to display the table

1	2	3	4
2	4	6	8
3	6	9	12

where we need to access both the row and column for a single data entry. The memory for this table could be produced by the following declaration:

```
int table[3] [4];
```

This memory can be visualized as three rows, each of which holds four integer variables. Thus, 12 memory cells have been reserved as shown.

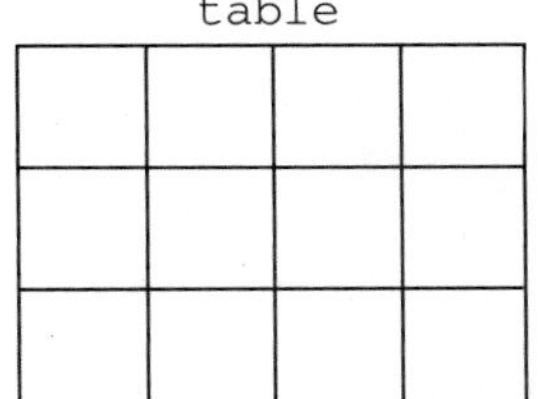

The form for declaring two-dimensional arrays is

<item type> <array variable>[<rows>][<columns>]

A more maintainable declaration of this data structure defines the number of the rows and columns as symbolic constants and uses a `typedef` to specify the type name for all tables.

```
// Define constants for bounds of tables

const int MAX_ROWS = 3;
const int MAX_COLS = 5;

// Define type for all tables

typedef int tableType[MAX_ROWS] [MAX_COLS];

// Declare two table variables

tableType table1, table2;
```

Now we have to consider how to access the data items in a two-dimensional array. As with one-dimensional arrays, C++ uses zero-based indexing to access data elements in a two-dimensional array. Thus, the first row is numbered 0, and the first column is numbered 0 also. Note that in the table

1	2	3	4
2	4	6	8
3	6	9	12

8 is in row 1, column 3. Therefore, to put 8 in this position, we could use assignment statements, such as

```
row = 1;
col = 3;
table[row] [col] = 8;
```

Next, we could assign the values to the appropriate cells in `table` using 12 assignments as follows:

```
table[0] [0] = 1;
table[0] [1] = 2;
table[0] [2] = 3;
table[0] [3] = 4;
table[1] [0] = 2;
table[1] [1] = 4;
table[1] [2] = 6;
table[1] [3] = 8;
table[2] [0] = 3;
table[2] [1] = 6;
table[2] [2] = 9;
table[2] [3] = 12;
```

As you can see, this is very tedious. Instead, we can note the relationship between the indices and the assigned values and use the variables `row` and `column` for the two indices. Each value to be assigned is then `(row + 1) * (column + 1)`, and we can use nested loops to perform the assignments.

```
for (int row = 0; row < MAX_ROWS; ++row)
    for (int col = 0; col < MAX_COLS; ++col)
       table[row] [col] = (row + 1) * (col + 1);
```

Because two-dimensional arrays frequently require working with nested loops, let us examine what this segment of code does. When `row` equals 0, the loop

```
for (int col = 0; col < MAX_COLS; ++col)
   table[0] [col] = 1 * (col + 1);
```

is executed. This performs the four assignments

```
table[0] [0] = 1;
table[0] [1] = 2;
table[0] [2] = 3;
table[0] [3] = 4;
```

and we have the memory

table

1	2	3	4

Similar results hold for `row` equals 1 and `row` equals 2, and we produce a two-dimensional array that can be visualized as

table

1	2	3	4
2	4	6	8
3	6	9	12

Example 9.9 Declare a two-dimensional array and write a segment of code to produce the memory area and contents depicted.

table

0	1	2	3	4	5	6
1	2	3	4	5	6	7
2	3	4	5	6	7	8
3	4	5	6	7	8	9

An appropriate declaration is

```
const int MAX_ROWS = 4;
const int MAX_COLS = 7;

int table[MAX_ROWS] [MAX_COLS];
```

A segment of code to produce the desired contents is

```
for (int row = 0; row < MAX_ROWS; ++row)
   for (int col = 0; col < MAX_COLS; ++col)
      table[row] [col] = row + col;
```

Reading and Writing

Input and output with two-dimensional arrays resemble the same operations with one-dimensional arrays. In general, the forms to use are

<input stream> >> <array variable>[<row>][<col>]
<output stream> << <array variable>[<row>][<col>]

For example, consider the input and output of baseball statistics. Two arrays are required to represent the data. The first is a one-dimensional array of strings for the players' last names. The second is two-dimensional array of real numbers. Each row in this array contains the statistics for an individual player. Each column in the array represents a statistic. A very simple set of statistics might include at bats, hits, and batting average. When displayed, the data in these arrays might look like this:

```
Player                AB      HITS     AVE

Alomar               521      192     .369
Brett                493      180     .365
Canseco              451      160     .354
Dribble              590      205     .347
Hubble               501      167     .333
Marachino            485      156     .321
Noguchi              562      180     .320
Perez                499      159     .318
Sokoloski            480      149     .310
Tanenbaum            490      150     .306
```

It is clear that the two-dimensional array of statistics will need three columns. It will also need a number of rows that can accommodate the statistics for the maximum number of players allowed in the array of strings. Thus, the appropriate data declarations for these structures are

```
const int MAX_PLAYERS = 20;
const in MAX_ROWS = MAX_PLAYERS;
const int MAX_COLS = 3;

apstring players[MAX_PLAYERS];

double stats[MAX_ROWS] [MAX_COLS];

int numPlayers = 0;
```

Note the use of constants for maintainability. If the maximum number of players must be changed, the maximum number of player names in the array of strings and the maximum number of rows in the table of statistics will be updated automatically when the program is recompiled. The variable `numPlayers` maintains the number of players currently stored in the `players` array, which always equals the number of rows of data currently stored in the `stats` array.

When the `players` and `stats` arrays are initialized with the data in the tables, they can be visualized as

players		0	1	2
Alomar	0	521	192	.369
Brett	1	493	180	.365
Canseco	2	451	160	.354
Dribble	3	590	205	.347
Hubble	4	501	167	.333
Marachino	5	485	156	.321
Noguchi	6	562	180	.320
Perez	7	499	159	.318
Sokoloski	8	480	149	.310
Tanenbaum	9	490	150	.306

players stats

To access a statistic for a player in the table, we use the index of the player in the `players` array as the row index and a number from 0 to 2 (0 = at bats, 1 = hits, 2 = average) as the column index. Thus, assuming that the index of Alomar is 0 and the column for average is 2, the average for Alomar can be looked up with the expression

```
stats[0] [2]
```

To output the contents of the arrays, we access the first array to display a player's name at the beginning of each line. We then loop through the corresponding row of numbers in the second array to display the player's statistics on the rest of the line. The code for this process is:

```
// Display header of table

cout << "Player                    AB      HITS      AVE" << endl;

// Loop through number of players in array

for (int row = 0; row < numPlayers; ++row)
{

   // Output player's name

   cout << players[row];

   // Loop through numbers in a row

   for (int col = 0; col < MAX_COLS; ++col)
      cout << setw(10) << stats[row] [col];

   // Output end of line for row

   cout << endl;
}
```

Note that the number of rows occupied by data in the `stats` array may vary (depending on the number of players), but each column in an occupied row always has data (every player has the same number of statistics).

The input process is slightly more complicated. We begin by prompting for a player's name. If the user enters a name containing just one character, this signals that the process is completed. Otherwise, we prompt for each statistic of the player, and enter the player's name into the `players` array and the statistics into their respective positions in the `stats` array. The code for this process follows:

```
numPlayers = 0;
cout << "Enter the player's name (or one letter to quit): ";
cin >> name;

// Halt process when name has 1 character or array is full

while ((name.length() > 1) && (numPlayers < MAX_ROWS))
{
   // Store the name in the players array

   players[numPlayers]= name;

   // Enter the row of statistics for the player

   for (int col = 0; col < MAX_COLS; ++col)
```

continued

```
    {
       switch (col)
       {
          case 0:        cout << "Enter at bats: ";
                         break;
          case 1:        cout << "Enter hits: ";
                         break;
          case 2:        cout << "Enter average: ";
       }
       cin >> stats[numPlayers] [col];
    }

    // Update the count of players and get the next name

    ++numPlayers;
    cout << "Enter the player's name (or one letter to quit): ";
    cin >> name;
}
```

Note the use of the switch statement to select the relevant prompt for a statistic.

We mentioned earlier that the maximum number of players allowed by this application can be changed easily. The number of statistics for each player is also fixed, and that too can be changed with a few modifications of our code segments. We first change the value of MAX_COLS in the constant definition section. Then, in the output process, we change the header to be displayed for the table to include the new names (such as HR for home runs). Note that no change is needed to output the new data values. Finally, we modify the switch statement in the input loop so that the prompts for the new statistics appear in the appropriate order.

Manipulating Components

Once data have been stored in a two-dimensional array, they can be manipulated in much the same way as when they are stored in a one-dimensional array. For example, one might want to compute the average test score from a table of scores for students. Each row in the table contains an individual student's scores, and the number of rows equals the number of students in the class. Assuming that table is the name of this array, numStudents names the current number of rows of data, and numScores names the current number of scores in the table for each and every student, the following code segment computes and outputs the average test score:

```
int sum = 0;
for (int row = 0; row < numStudents; ++row)
   for (int col = 0; col < numScores; ++col)
      sum = sum + table[row] [col];
cout << "The average score is "
     << sum / (numStudents * numScores) << endl;
```

As you can see, this process would move across each row in the table, adding the numbers in the row to the running total. When the additions are finished, the last line computes the total number of scores by multiplying the current number of rows by the current number of columns.

Another common manipulation of two-dimensional arrays involves placing the results of some computations in certain cells of the array. Spreadsheet applications are based on this idea. For example, in the case of a table of baseball statistics for players on one team, the cells in the last row of the table could be reserved for storing the totals of each column, except for the batting average column. In this last case, the average of all of the batting averages would be placed in the bottom cell. The table might be displayed as follows:

```
Player                  AB      HITS    AVE

Alomar                  521     192     .369
Brett                   493     180     .365
Canseco                 451     160     .354
Dribble                 590     205     .347
Hubble                  501     167     .333
Marachino               485     156     .321
Noguchi                 562     180     .320
Perez                   499     159     .318
Sokoloski               480     149     .310
Tanenbaum               490     150     .306

Totals                  5072    1698    .335
```

The algorithm for computing a result for each column must traverse the two-dimensional array in a different order than we have seen in the examples thus far. The process starts at the top of a column and moves down that column to the last row of data, going row by row. To accomplish this pattern of movement, the outer loop of the algorithm uses the column as its control variable, and the inner loop uses the row as its control variable. Assuming that `table` is the name of this array and that `numPlayers` names the current number of rows of data, the following code segment describes the desired process:

```
int sum = 0;
for (int col = 0; col < MAX_COLS; ++col)
{
   sum = 0;
   for (int row = 0; row < numPlayers; ++row)
      sum = sum + table[row] [col];
   if (col == MAX_COLS - 1)
      table[MAX_ROWS - 1] [col] = sum / numPlayers;
   else
      table[MAX_ROWS - 1] [col] = sum;
}
```

Note how the `if` statement inside the loop handles the alternatives of storing a sum or storing an average in the case of the column representing the batting averages.

In a real spreadsheet, not every result of every column needs to be recalculated when a change of data occurs. In the case of the baseball statistics, if one player gets a hit, then all of the results will have to be recalculated. If the player gets an at bat with no hit, then only the results for at bats and batting average need to be recalculated.

Use with Functions

Two-dimensional arrays are passed as parameters to functions in the same way as other arrays. For example, we could package the code for displaying the table of baseball statistics in a function named `displayStatistics` and invoke it as follows:

```
displayStatistics(players, table, numPlayers);
```

Note that the `players` and `table` arrays and the integer variable `numPlayers` are passed as arguments to this function. These data, and the global constants `MAX_ROWS` and `MAX_COLS`, represent all of the information that the function needs to perform its task. The function's declaration is:

```
void displayStatistics(apstring players [ ],
                       double table[ ] [MAX_COLS],
                       int numPlayers);
```

Note the two different array parameter declarations. Recall that C++ allows the programmer to omit the physical size of a one-dimensional array when declaring the type of a formal array parameter as follows:

```
void process1dArray(int a[ ]);
```

When declaring the type of a formal two-dimensional array parameter in C++, the programmer must specify the physical size of the second dimension of the array. Thus, only the second of the following two function declarations is valid:

```
void process2dArray(int a[ ] [ ]);

void process2dArray(int a[ ] [MAX_COLS]);
```

The implementation of `displayStatistics` displays the header for the table and then runs a nested loop to display the contents of each row:

```
void displayStatistics(apstring players[ ],
                       double table[ ] [MAX_COLS] ],
                       int numPlayers)
{
   // Display header of table

   cout << "Player                         AB     HITS    AVE" <<endl;

   // Loop through number of players in array

   for (int row = 0; row < numPlayers; ++row)
   {

      // Output player's name from the players array

      cout << players[row];

      // Loop through numbers in a row of the table array

      for (int col = 0; col < MAX_COLS; ++col)
         cout << setw(10) << stats[row] [col];

      // Output the end of line for the row

      cout << endl;
   }
}
```

Communication and Style Tips

1. Use descriptive identifiers when working with two-dimensional arrays. For example, `row` and `col` are appropriate identifiers for index variables, and `MAX_ROWS` and `MAX_COLS` are useful identifiers for specifying the upper bounds of an array type.
2. Remember that C++ does not report range bound errors with any arrays, so use care when indexing.

Exercises 9.5

For Exercises 1–3, declare a two-dimensional array for the tables described.

1. A table with real number entries that shows the prices for four different drugs charged by five different drugstores.
2. A table with character entries that shows the grades earned by 20 students in six courses.
3. A table with integer entries that shows the 12 quiz scores earned by 30 students in a class.
4. Write a test program to read integers into a 3 × 5 array and then display the array components together with each row sum and column sum.

For Exercises 5–8, sketch the area of memory reserved for the data. In each case, state how many variables are available to the programmer.

5.
```
double shippingCostTable[10]  [4];
int gradeBookTable[15]  [6];
```
6.
```
type int matrix[3]  [6];
matrix a, b;
```
7.
```
bool schedule[7, 3];
```
8.
```
const int QUESTIONS = 50;
const int ANSWERS = 5;
char table[QUESTIONS] [ANSWERS];
```

For Exercises 9-12, assume array `table` has been declared

```
int table3x5[3]  [5];
```

Indicate the array contents produced by each of the following:

9.
```
for (int j = 0; j < 3; ++j)
for (int k = 0; k < 5; ++k)
   table3x5[j] [k] = j - k;
```
10.
```
for (int j = 0; j < 3; ++j)
for (int k = 0; k < 5; ++k)
   table3x5[j] [k: = j]
```
11.
```
for (int k = 0; k < 5; ++k)
for (int j = 0; j < 3; ++j)
   table3x5[j] [k] = j;
```
12.
```
for (int j = 2; j >=0; --j)
for (int k = 0; k < 5; ++k)
   table3x5[j] [k] = j % k;
```

For Exercises 13–15, let the two-dimensional array `table3x6` be declared by

```
int table3x6[3]  [6];
```

Write nested loops to store the following values in `table3x6`.

13.

table 3x6

3	4	5	6	7	8
5	6	7	8	9	10
7	8	9	10	11	10

14.

table 3x6

0	0	0	0	0	0
0	0	0	0	0	0
0	0	0	0	0	0

15.

table 3x6

2	2	2	2	2	2
4	4	4	4	4	4
6	6	6	6	6	6

16. Suppose you want to work with a table that has three rows and eight columns of integers.
a. Declare an appropriate two-dimensional array for this table.
b. Write a function that replaces all negative numbers in a table with zero.
c. Show what is needed to call the function.

9.6 Safe Arrays: Vectors

The C++ array is a useful data structure, but some features can cause inconvenience or, even worse, errors in users' programs. Perhaps the most serious problem is the absence of built-in range checking. Recall that references to data locations within an array must be specified by an index value that is within the range from 0 (the first location) to `MAX_ARRAY_SIZE - 1` (the last location), where `MAX_ARRAY_SIZE` is the number of locations specified by the array variable declaration. Because range errors go undetected, they may cause undesirable behavior such as logic errors (unexpected output) or system crashes (side effects on the underlying operating system). Clearly, an array would be safer if it detected range errors and halted program execution with a message rather than cause logic errors or crashes.

Several other features of C++ arrays are inconvenient:

1. A user should be able to copy the contents of one array to another by means of an assignment statement (`a = b`), but this is prohibited or can lead to incorrect results in most implementations of C++.

Objectives

a. to understand the requirements for a safe array
b. to design and implement a new class that satisfies these requirements
c. to understand and implement range checking
d. to understand and implement a class template
e. to understand how a class template allows users to specify the element type of a safe array
f. to understand how dynamic storage allocation allows users to specify the size of a safe array and allows a safe array to adjust its size as needed

2. A user might want to copy the contents of one array into another of lesser or greater size. However, a standard C++ array cannot adjust its capacity to store data elements as needed.
3. Users might be confused about passing an array as a parameter to a function. They might prefer to see formal array parameters specified like other parameters, with the `&` symbol meaning pass by reference and the absence of this symbol meaning pass by value. However, C++ arrays are always passed by reference, even when the `&` symbol is omitted in the parameter declaration.

In this section, we develop a C++ class that solves these problems with the use of arrays.

User Requirements

The first step in developing a new class to solve the problems with C++ arrays is to draw up a list of user requirements. These state the features and behavior that users or clients expect the class to have. We have seen that C++ arrays are both unsafe and inconvenient. Users would like the new class to retain the desirable features of arrays and avoid the undesirable ones. The list of features for the new class, called *vector,* follows:

1. Like arrays, vectors should support the subscript or indexing operation. This operation uses an integer index value to access a data element in constant time.
2. Indexing should be safe; range errors should be detected at run time.
3. Like arrays, vectors can contain data elements of any type, as long as the data elements in a given vector are all of the same type. The user specifies the type of element when a vector variable is declared.
4. Like arrays, vectors should have a fixed size or number of allowable data elements. This size can be specified when the user declares a vector variable, or it can be a default value of zero. The user should be able to examine and change the storage capacity of a vector.
5. Users should be able to specify a *fill value* to initialize the data elements in a vector when it is declared.
6. Vectors should support the standard assignment operation.
7. Vectors should adjust their size as needed during assignment operations.

To summarize, the use of instances of the vector class should resemble the use of standard C++ arrays but be safer, cleaner, and more convenient. The following two examples compare the use of an array with the use of a vector to solve a problem.

Example 9.10 This program uses an array to obtain a user-specified number of integers as inputs. The program computes and displays the average of the integers in the array.

```
// Program file: arrayav.cpp

#include <iostream.h>

int const MAX_LIST_SIZE = 100;

int main()
{
   int list[MAX_LIST_SIZE];
   int count;
```

continued

```
  cout << "Enter the number of integers: ";
  cin >> count;
  if (count > MAX_LIST_SIZE)
     cout << "Sorry, not enough memory" << endl;
  else
  {
     int i, data;
     for (i = 0; i < count; ++i)
     {
        cout << "Enter the next integer: ";
        cin >> data;
        list[i] = data;
      }
      int sum = 0;
      for (i = 0; i < count; ++i)
         sum = sum + list[i];
      cout << "The average is "
             << sum / count;
   }
   return 0;
}
```

Note that the user is limited by the size of the array defined by the program. If the user's count is greater than this size, the program quits with an error message. Also, if one of the loops is off by 1, any range error will go undetected, possibly causing a system crash or a logic error.

Example 9.11 The program of Example 9.10 is modified to use a vector rather than an array to store the input data. The program assumes that the vector class is implemented in the library file `apvector.cpp`. A complete specification of the `apvector` class appears in Appendix E.

```
// Program file: vectorav.cpp

#include <iostream.h>

#include "apvector.h"

int main()
{
   int count;

   cout << "Enter the number of integers: ";
   cin >> count;

   apvector<int> list(count); // Create a vector of
                              // count integers
   int i, data;
   for (i = 0; i < count; ++i)
   {
      cout << "Enter the next integer: ";
      cin >> data;
      list[i] = data;
   }
```

```
    int sum = 0;
    for (i = 0; i < count; ++i)
        sum = sum + list[i];
    cout << "The average is "
         << sum / count;
    return 0;
}
```

The most obvious change from the previous example is that the program defines the size of the vector with the user's count (a variable). In other words, the computer automatically allocates just the right amount of memory to store the user's data. Another change, which is in the syntax of the vector's declaration, is the use of the angle bracket < > notation to specify the element type of the vector. The least obvious change is that range errors may still occur in the loops, but the computer will detect them and halt execution with appropriate error messages.

The most important difference between vectors and standard C++ arrays is that vectors know about their size. They can use this knowledge to perform their own run-time range checking and to increase or decrease their capacity to hold data elements as needed.

Specifying the Operations for Vectors

Recall from previous chapters that these specifications take the form of preconditions and postconditions on all of the allowable operations for the class. The attributes of a vector are

1. `mySize` (the vector's capacity)
2. `myList` (the vector's data elements)
3. `itemType` (the vector's element type)

A formal specification of the vector class is

Create Operation (Default Size)

Preconditions:	The vector is in an unpredictable state.
Postconditions:	`mySize` and `myList` are set to 0.

Create Operation (User-Specified Size)

Preconditions:	The vector is in an unpredictable state. `size` is an integer value >= 0. There is memory available for creating a vector capable of storing `size` data elements.
Postconditions:	Memory is reserved for a vector object capable of storing `size` data elements, and `mySize` is set to `size`.

Create Operation (User-Specified Size and Fill Value)

Preconditions:	The vector is in an unpredictable state. `size` is an integer value >= 0. `fillValue` is a data element of the element type of the vector. There is memory available for creating a vector capable of storing `size` data elements.
Postconditions:	Memory is reserved for a vector object capable of storing `size` data elements, `mySize` is set to `size`, and all of the cells in the vector are set to `fillValue`.

Destroy Operation

Preconditions:	The vector is appropriately initialized.
Postconditions:	The memory for the vector is made available to the computer for other applications.

Length Operation
Preconditions: The vector is appropriately initialized.
Postconditions: The value of `mySize` is returned.

Resize Operation
Preconditions: The vector is appropriately initialized. `newSize` is an integer specifying the desired capacity of the vector.
Postconditions: The capacity of the vector is adjusted to the desired size, if memory is available, and `mySize` is set to `newSize`. Any data elements stored in the vector are copied to the resized vector. Some data may be lost if the new size is less than the old size.

Subscript Operation (for Observation or Modification of a Data Element)
Preconditions: The vector is appropriately initialized. `index` is an integer value in the range `0 <= index < mySize`.
Postconditions: The location of a data element, which can be used either to observe or to store an object, is returned.

Subscript Operation (for Observation of a Data Element Only)
Preconditions: The vector is appropriately initialized. `index` is an integer value in the range `0 <= index < mySize`.
Postconditions: The object at the index position is returned.

Assignment Operation
Preconditions: The target vector is appropriately initialized. The source vector is appropriately initialized. There is memory available for making the capacity of the target object equal to the capacity of the source object.
Postconditions: The capacity of the target object is adjusted to the capacity of the source object, and the contents of the source object are copied into the target object.

Note that these specifications include a *destroy* operation. We discuss the need for this operation shortly.

Declaring the Vector Class

To maintain consistency with the conventional uses of arrays, we use the standard operators for subscripting and assignment in the class declaration and provide overloaded operations for them in the class implementation.

```
// Class declaration file: apvector.h

#ifndef _APVECTOR_H
#define _APVECTOR_H

template <class itemType> class apvector
{
   public:

   // constructors
   apvector();
   apvector(int size);
   apvector(int size, const itemType &fillValue);
   apvector(const apvector<itemType> &vec);

   // destructor

   ~apvector();
```

```
    // assignment

    const apvector<itemType>& operator =
           (const apvector<itemType> &rhs);

    // accessor

    int length() const;          // capacity of vector

    // indexing

    const itemType& operator [ ] (int index) const
    itemType& operator [ ] (int index);

    // modifier

    void resize(int newSize);

    private:

    // Data members

    int mySize;              // # elements in array
    itemType *myList;        // array used for storage
};

#include "apvector.cpp"

#endif
```

Note that we declare two different subscript (`[ ]`) operations. The first subscript is declared as a constant operator that returns the value at the specified index position. This operation will be used in cases where the vector's contents cannot be changed, such as within functions that receive a vector as a constant parameter. The second subscript returns a reference to a memory cell in the vector, allowing either access to or modifications of the cell's contents. Note also the notation `itemType *myList` used to declare the array representing the data elements in a vector. We discuss this notation shortly. Finally, note that the `.cpp` file is included at the end of the header file. The reason for this change from earlier practice will also be explained shortly.

Class Templates

A *class template* in C++ allows users to specify the component types in a class when instances of that class are created. In the case of the vector class, a user could create a vector of integers, a vector of real numbers, and a vector of strings using the angle bracket notation shown earlier:

```
apvector<int> intVector;
apvector<double> doubleVector;
apvector<apstring> stringVector;
```

The angle brackets appear again in the class declaration, this time surrounding information about the component type. We use the notations `template <class`

itemType> and apvector<itemType> to specify that the class can have any element type. The name itemType behaves like a formal type parameter in the class definition. It holds a place for any actual type parameter provided by the user, such as int, double, or apstring, when an instance of the class is created. Other than learning this new syntax and some special restrictions on included files (noted later), working with class templates should be about the same as working with ordinary C++ classes.

Pointers and Dynamic Memory

The data members for the apvector class are mySize, an integer, and myList, a pointer to an item type. We use a *pointer variable* in C++ when we cannot predict the size of a data structure. A pointer variable can hold the address of a chunk of *dynamic memory*. Dynamic memory is memory that the programmer can request when it is needed by an application. You do not need a complete understanding of these ideas to use them to implement vectors. We examine the form and behavior of pointers and dynamic memory in more detail in Chapter 13.

Constructing Vectors

The first member functions to be implemented are the creation operations or constructors. The default constructor sets the mySize data member to zero and the myList data member to zero:

```
template <class itemType>
apvector<itemType>::apvector()
   : mySize(0), myList(0)
{
}
```

Note the following:

1. The notation : mySize(0), myList(0) is equivalent to the following pair of assignment statements:

```
mySize = 0;
myList = 0;
```

2. The special pointer value 0 is used to indicate an empty pointer, or the fact that no dynamic memory has yet been allocated to store data in myList.
3. There are no statements within the { }.

The second constructor allows the user to specify the capacity of the vector with a parameter:

```
template <class itemType>
apvector<itemType>::apvector(int size)
{
   assert (size > 0);
   mySize = size;
   myList = new itemType[size];
   assert myList != 0;
}
```

This constructor asks for memory for the vector by running a statement of the form

<pointer variable> = `new` <item type> `[`<number of items>`];`

We use `new` in C++ to allocate memory for a data object dynamically, or as needed by a program. `new` is an operator that returns a pointer to a block of memory if memory is available. If memory is not available, `new` returns the pointer value 0. This block of memory, referenced by `myList` in a vector, behaves just like a standard C++ array. When working with `new` to allocate dynamic memory for arrays, remember these two important points:

1. The type and number of data elements should be specified.
2. You should verify that memory is available and has been allocated. We use the `assert` function for this throughout the class definition.

The difference between the two constructors can be illustrated as follows. Suppose that we have the declarations

```
apvector<int> v1;
apvector<int> v2(25);
```

Then the statements

```
cout << v1.length() << endl;
cout << v2.length() << endl;
```

will produce the output

```
0
25
```

If we then run the statement

```
v1.resize(25);
```

the vectors `v1` and `v2` will have the same size because `resize` allocates dynamic memory for `v1`.

The Destructor for Vectors

The programmer is responsible for returning dynamic memory to the computer system when it is no longer needed. To help automate this process, C++ will run a special function called a *destructor* if it is in the class definition. C++ runs this function whenever locally declared pointer variables go out of scope, as in the following situation:

```
void loseMemory()
{
   apvector<int> localVector(200);
}
```

This function appears to do nothing but declare a vector of 200 integers and return. However, unlike memory used for ordinary local variables, the dynamic memory allocated for the vector is not automatically returned to the system. If this function were called often enough, the program would run out of memory and crash.

If a destructor function is defined that returns the memory for the vector to the system, the computer will run the destructor automatically. The destructor for vectors follows:

```
template <class itemType >
apvector<itemType>::~apvector()
{
   delete [] myList;
}
```

The `delete` operator is the inverse of `new`. `delete` returns the memory pointed to by its operand to the system.

Remember that the destructor, `~vector`, is run automatically and does not have to be invoked by the programmer.

Copy Constructor and Assignment

The copy constructor attempts to allocate memory for a copy of the data member `myList` of the vector parameter and to verify allocation. Then it iterates through the elements in this data member, copying the value of each element into the corresponding location in the data member of the receiver object.

```
template <class itemType>
apvector<itemType>::apvector(const apvector<itemType> &vec)
{
   mySize = vec.length();
   myList = new itemType [mySize];
   assert(myList != 0);
   for (int j = 0; j < mySize; ++j)
      myList[j]= vec.myList[j];
}
```

The assignment operation involves a similar process of memory allocation and copying. However, memory for the target object is first returned to the system, and a constant reference to the target object is returned at the end of the function.

```
template <class itemType>
const apvector& apvector<itemType>::operator =
    (const apvector<itemType> &rhs)
{
   if (this != &rhs)
   {
      delete [] myList;
      mySize = rhs.length();
      myList = new itemType [mySize];
      assert(myList != 0);
      for(int k=0; k < mySize; ++k)
         myList[k] = rhs.myList[k];
   }
   return *this;
}
```

Note that both of these operations assume that an assignment operation exists for the element objects. Remember that complex objects (such as bank accounts, strings, and safe arrays) should implement their own assignment operations so that all of their data members are accurately copied.

Indexing

The indexing or subscript operations provide the primary benefit of a vector class: run-time range checking. The implementations use `assert` to enforce the preconditions governing the index value. If the value of the index parameter is out of range, the program will halt with an error message.

```
template <class itemType>
const itemType& apvector<itemType>::operator [ ] (int index) const
{
   assert((index >= 0) && (index < mySize));
   return myList[index];
}

template <class itemType>
itemType& apvector<itemType>::operator [ ] (int index)
{
   assert((index >= 0) && (index < mySize));
   return myList[index];
}
```

Example 9.12 The following program is a driver for testing many of the `apvector` operations:

```
// Program file: vectdriv.cpp

#include <iostream.h>

#include "apvector.h"

int main()
{
   apvector<int> a(10), b;
   int i;

// Test subscripts
   for (i = 0; i < a.length(); ++i)
      a[i] = i;

   cout<< "Values in vector a are: " << endl;
   for (i = 0; i < a.length(); ++i)
      cout << a[i] <<" ";
   cout << endl;

// Test assignment
   b = a;

   cout<< "Values in vector b are: " << endl;
   for (i = 0; i < b.length(); ++i)
      cout << b[i] << " ";
   cout << endl;
```

continued

```
// Test range error check
    cout << a[10]<< endl;
    return 0;
}
```

The program produces the following output (the error message generated by `assert` may vary on different implementations):

```
Values in vector a are:
0 1 2 3 4 5 6 7 8 9
Values in vector b are:
0 1 2 3 4 5 6 7 8 9
vector.cpp:80 (index >= 0) && (index < size) -- assertion failed
abort -- terminating
```

Including Libraries of Class Templates

We mentioned earlier that the class implementation file, `apvector.cpp`, is included in the header or declaration file, `apvector.h`. Moreover, the header file is not included in the implementation file. This unusual practice is required for the compiler to generate code for the templates when they are specialized for an element type in a module. You should make this inclusion order a rule of thumb when defining class templates in C++.

Exercises 9.6

1. Declare variables for the following data:
   a. A vector of 20 integers
   b. A vector of 100 characters, each initialized to 'a'
   c. A vector of 50 persons (assume that class `person` is already defined)
   d. A vector of 20 vectors of 20 integers (*Hint:* Your declaration will have nested angle brackets.)
2. Write and test a program that runs the following code with vectors and explain what happens:

```
apvector<int> a;

for (int i = 0; i <= 10; ++i)

    a[i] = i;
```

3. Describe the difference between the two indexing operations defined for vectors. What would happen if the constant indexing operation were not defined?
4. The assignment operation for vectors references every memory location in the source vector. Discuss any problems that might arise from these references. For example, predict what happens when you run the following pieces of code:

a.

```
apvector<int> a(100, 55);
for (int i = 0; i < 100; ++i)
    cout << a[i] << endl;
```

b.
```
apvector<int> a(100);
for (int i = 0; i < 100; ++i)
   cout << a[i] << endl;
```

c.
```
apvector<int> a, b(100);
a = b;
for (int i = 0; i < 100; ++i)
   cout << a[i] << endl;
```

5. The assignment operation for vectors deletes and reallocates memory for the target vector, even if it has the same capacity as the source vector. Modify this member function in the implementation so that this unnecessary process will not occur.

9.7 Strings

Objectives

a. to understand the requirements for a string
b. to design and implement a class that satisfies these requirements
c. to understand and implement range checking for strings
d. to understand the difference between the length of a string and the capacity of its underlying data structure

User Requirements

Throughout this text, we have been using a string class (`apstring`) to declare string variables and manipulate them with operations such as input (>>) and concatenation (+). As an abstract data type, the string class allows users to process strings without concern for the way in which the strings' data and operations are implemented. Viewed abstractly, a string is like a safe array, because individual characters within the string can be accessed with a subscript operation, as long as the index is within a certain range. For example, in the following code segment, the first subscript operation, which returns the character 'i', is valid, but the second one produces an error:

```
apstring myString;

myString = "Hi there!";
cout << myString[1] << endl;
cout << myString[myString.length()] << endl;
```

The valid index positions for this string are the integers 0 through 8. The length of the string, 9, is an invalid index position.

However, a string is unlike a safe array in that its length refers to the number of characters currently stored in the string rather than the capacity (number of memory cells) of the underlying data structure. Users of strings are not aware of this distinction, but it may (and does) play a role in the implementation of a string class, as we will see shortly.

In addition to the operations that we have seen thus far in this text, there are operations to search for given characters or *substrings* in a string and to access substrings at given positions.

Example 9.13 This program illustrates the use of the substring operations.

```
// Program file: substr.cpp

#include <iostream.h>
#include "apstring.h"
```

continued

```
int main()
{
   apstring myString;

   myString = "Hi there!";

   // Output the index position of 't' (3)

   cout << myString.find('t') << endl;

   // Output the starting index position
   // of "here" (4)

   cout << myString.find("here") << endl;

   // Output the substring starting at position 0
   // and having a length of 2 ("Hi")

   cout << myString.substr(0, 2) << endl;

   return 0;
}
```

Specifying the Operations for Strings

The attributes of a string are

1. `myCapacity` (the number of cells for storing characters)
2. `myLength` (the number of characters currently stored)
3. `myCString` (the string's characters)

We present formal specifications for only some of the string operations. A complete specification of the `apstring` class appears in Appendix E.

Create Operation (Default)
Preconditions: The string is in an unpredictable state.
Postconditions: `myCapacity` and `myLength` are set to 0.

Create Operation (with String Literal from User)
Preconditions: The string is in an unpredictable state. The parameter `s` is a string literal. There is memory available for creating a string capable of storing `s`.
Postconditions: Memory is reserved for storing the characters in `s`, including the null character, which are copied into `myCString`. `myCapacity` is set to the size of this memory, and `myLength` is set to `myCapacity - 1`.

Destroy Operation
Preconditions: The string is appropriately initialized.
Postconditions: The memory for the string is made available to the computer for other applications.

Length Operation
Preconditions: The string is appropriately initialized.
Postconditions: The value of `myLength` is returned.

Subscript Operation (for Observation of a Data Element Only)
Preconditions: The string is appropriately initialized. `index` is an integer value in the range `0 <= index < myLength`.
Postconditions: The object at the index position is returned.

Assignment Operation (Another String Object)

Preconditions: The target string is appropriately initialized. The source string is appropriately initialized. There is memory available for making the capacity of the target object equal to the capacity of the source object.

Postconditions: If the capacity of the source object exceeds that of the target object, the capacity of the target object is adjusted to the capacity of the source object. The length of the target object is set to the length of the source object, and the contents of the source object are copied into the target object.

Assignment Operation (a String Literal)

Preconditions: The target string is appropriately initialized. The source string is a string literal. There is memory available for making the capacity of the target object equal to the capacity of the source object.

Postconditions: The length of the target object is adjusted to the length of the source object, and the contents of the source object are copied into the target object.

Assignment Operation (a Character)

Preconditions: The target string is appropriately initialized. The source character is appropriately initialized. There is memory available for creating a target object whose capacity is 2.

Postconditions: The capacity of the target object is set to 2, its length is set to 1, and the source character is copied into `myCString` at the first position.

Find Operation (a Character)

Preconditions: The string is appropriately initialized. `ch` is the character to be found.

Postconditions: If the character is not in the string, –1 is returned. Otherwise, the index of the first instance of the character in the string is returned.

Find Operation (a Substring)

Preconditions: The string is appropriately initialized. `str` is the substring to be found.

Postconditions: If the substring is not in the string, –1 is returned. Otherwise, the starting index of the first instance of the substring in the string is returned.

Substring Operation

Preconditions: The string is appropriately initialized. `pos` is the index of the first character of the substring, `len` is the length of the substring, and `0 <= pos <= pos + len - 1 < myLength`.

Postconditions: Returns the substring of characters from position `pos` to position `pos + len - 1`.

C string Operation

Preconditions: The string is appropriately initialized.

Postconditions: Returns an equivalent string as represented by the C language (actually, the attribute `myCString`).

Concatenate Operation (Two String Objects)

Preconditions: The string parameters are appropriately initialized. There is memory to create a string whose length equals the sum of the lengths of the parameter strings.

Postconditions: Returns a new string representing the first parameter string followed by the second parameter string.

Note the following points:

1. Throughout the specifications, we distinguish between the capacity of a string and its length. A string's capacity is always at least 1 greater than its length. This allows for the storage of a null character (`'\0'`) at the end of the string. This character is used to mark the end of the string in the underlying data structure, but it is not considered part of the string data from the user's perspective.
2. There is a constructor for creating a string object from a string literal. This constructor is used when string literals are passed as parameters to functions that expect string objects.

3. There are three assignment operations, allowing for the assignment of string objects, string literals, or individual characters to string variables.

Declaring the String Class

The class declaration file for the `apstring` class is

```
//Class declaration file: apstring.h

#ifndef _APSTRING_H
#define _APSTRING_H

#include <iostream.h>
#include "bool.h"

class apstring
{
   public:

   // Constructors

   apstring();
   apstring(const char *s);
   apstring(const apstring &str );

   // Destructor

    ~apstring( );

    // Assignment

    const apstring& operator = (const apstring &str ); // assign str
    const apstring& operator = (const char *s );       // assign s
    const apstring& operator = (char ch);              // assign ch

    // Accessors

    // number of chars

    int length() const;

    // index of first occurrence of str

    int find(const apstring &str) const;

    // index of first occurrence of ch

    int find(char ch) const;

    // substring of len chars starting at pos

    apstring substr(int pos, int len) const;

    // Conversion to type of string literal
```

```
    const char* c_str() const;

    // Indexing

    char operator [ ](int index) const;
    char& operator [ ](int index);

    // Modifiers

    const apstring& operator += (const apstring &str);
    const apstring& operator += (char ch);

    private:

    // Data members

    int myLength;
    int myCapacity;
    char* myCstring;
};

// The following free (non-member)
// functions operate on strings

// I/O functions

ostream& operator << (ostream &os, const apstring &str);
istream& operator >> (istream &is, apstring &str);
istream& getline(istream &is, apstring &str);

// comparison operators:

bool operator == (const apstring &lhs, const apstring &rhs);
bool operator != (const apstring &lhs, const apstring &rhs);
bool operator < (const apstring &lhs, const apstring &rhs);
bool operator <= (const apstring &lhs, const apstring &rhs);
bool operator > (const apstring &lhs, const apstring &rhs);
bool operator >= (const apstring &lhs, const apstring &rhs);

// concatenation operator +

apstring operator + (const apstring &lhs, const apstring &rhs);
apstring operator + (char ch, const apstring &str);
apstring operator + (const apstring &str, char ch);

#endif
```

Constructing Strings

The data member `myCString` of the `apstring` class is declared as a pointer to a character. When a string object is created, memory is allocated for an array of characters, and `myCString` is set to this memory, as is done with a vector object. However, in the case of a string, a single character, the null character (`'\0'`), is stored in this array:

```
apstring::apstring()
{
   myLength = 0;
   myCapacity = 1;
   myCString = new char[myCapacity];
   myCString[0]= '\0';
}
```

We use a null character at the end of `myCString` because this is how strings are represented in the C language. This language, which is a subset of C++, has a `string` library that defines several functions used by the implementation of the `apstring` class to manipulate `myCString`. The null character serves as a sentinel value that allows these functions to detect the end of a string within an array. Two `string` library functions, `strcpy` and `strlen`, are used in the next `apstring` constructor:

```
apstring::apstring(const char *s)
{
   myLength = strlen(s);
   myCapacity = myLength + 1;
   myCString = new char[myCapacity];
   strcpy(myCstring, s);
}
```

This function expects a C-style string (a string literal, for example) as a parameter. It performs the following steps:

1. Sets the `myLength` data member to `strlen(s)`, which returns the length of the parameter `s`.
2. Sets `myCapacity`, the physical size of `myCString`, to 1 greater than `myLength`, leaving room for the null character.
3. Allocates memory for `myCString`.
4. Runs `strcpy(myCString, s)`, which copies all of the characters in `s`, including its null character, into `myCString`.

The implementation of the copy constructor is left as an exercise.

Conversion to a C-Style String

The use of a C-style string to represent the data within an `apstring` object is especially obvious in the implementation of the `c_str` function. This function returns the `myCString` data member, which is a C-style string:

```
const char* apstring::c_str() const
{
   return myCstring;
}
```

The `c_str` function serves as an accessor to the `myCstring` data member. However, because it is defined as a `const` function, the caller who receives the C-style string as a returned value will not be allowed to modify its contents.

Substrings

There are two `find` functions. The first one returns the position of the first instance of a given character in a string after a simple sequential search:

```
int apstring::find(char ch) const
{
    for(int k = 0; k < myLength; ++k)
        if (myCstring [k] == ch)
            return k;
    return -1;
}
```

The second `find` function returns the starting position of the first instance of a given substring in the string. It uses the `string` library function `strncmp`. This function expects three parameters:

1. the string to be scanned (a C-style string)
2. a potential substring (a C-style string)
3. *n*, the number of characters to be compared

`strncmp` compares the first *n* characters in the two strings and returns zero if they are equal; otherwise, the function returns nonzero.

The implementation of `find` first computes the value of the third parameter as the difference between the lengths of the two strings. It then enters a loop that calls `strncmp` to test for the presence of a substring. The loop advances by adding the value of the loop control variable, `k`, to the address of the enclosing string. This operation has the effect of stripping a character off the beginning of the scanned string on each pass through the loop.

```
int apstring::find(const apstring &str) const
{
    int len = str.length();
    int lastIndex = length() - len;
    for(int k = 0; k <= lastIndex; ++k)
        if (strncmp(myCstring + k, str.c_str(), len) == 0)
            return k;
    return -1;
}
```

The `substr` function returns a substring of a given length starting at a given index position. It begins by adjusting its parameters to fit the preconditions, if necessary. It then copies the characters in the given range from receiver object to a new string and returns this string.

```
apstring apstring::substr(int pos, int len) const
{
    // start at front when pos < 0

    if (pos < 0)
        pos = 0;

    if (pos >= myLength)
        return "";       // empty string

    // last char's index (to copy)
    // off end of string?

    int lastIndex = pos + len - 1;
    if (lastIndex >= myLength)
        lastIndex = myLength - 1;
```

continued

```
    apstring result(*this);

    int j, k;
    for(j = 0,k = pos; k <= lastIndex; ++j, ++k)
       result.myCstring[j]= myCstring[k];

    // properly terminate C-string

    result.myCstring[j] = '\0';

    // record length properly

    result.myLength = j;

    return result;
}
```

Assignment

The assignment operations must take into account the potential difference in length between the target string and the source string. If the target string is longer, then the characters from the source string, including its null character, are simply copied to the target's data member. Any extra memory in the target is retained as surplus capacity. If the source string is longer, then the target string's memory is deleted and new memory equal to the capacity of the source string is allocated for the target string before copying the characters.

```
const apstring& apstring::operator = (const apstring &rhs)
{
    if (this != &rhs)
    {
       // more memory needed?
       if (myCapacity < rhs.length() + 1)
       {
          delete[] myCstring;
          myCapacity = rhs.length() + 1;
          myCstring = new char[myCapacity];
       }
    myLength = rhs.length();
    strcpy(myCstring, rhs.myCstring);
    }
    return *this;
}
```

The implementations of the remaining assignment operations are left as exercises.

Concatenation

The concatenation operation for two string objects first builds a copy of the left operand with a local variable. It then uses the compound assignment operator for strings to concatenate the right operand to this value and finally returns this value as the result.

```
apstring operator + (const apstring &lhs,
    const apstring &rhs)
```

```
{
   apstring result(lhs);
   result += rhs;
   return result;
}
```

Compound Assignment

The += operator is used to concatenate the right operand string to the left operand string before assigning the result to the left operand string. Note the use of the function strcpy to copy the data from one C-style string to another.

```
const apstring& apstring::operator += (const apstring &str)
{
   // Create a copy to avoid aliasing

   apstring copystring(str);

   // self + added string

   int newLength = length() = str.length();

   // index of '\0'

   int lastLocation = length ();

   // check to see if local buffer not big enough

   if (newLength >= myCapacity)
   {
      myCapacity = newLength + 1;
      char * newBuffer = new char[myCapacity];
      strcpy(newBuffer, myCstring); // copy into new buffer
      delete [] myCstring;          // delete old string
      myLength = newLength;         // update information
      myCstring = newBuffer;
   }

   // now catenate str (copystring) to end of myCstring

   strcpy(myCstring + lastLocation, copystring.c_str());

   return *this;
}
```

Input and Output

The input and output operations use the operators >> and <<, as we did with rational numbers in Section 8.4. This technique of overloading can be seen very clearly in the output operation, which runs the same operator on the string object's C-style string.

```
ostream& operator <<(ostream &os, const apstring &str)
{
   return os << str.c_str();
}
```

The input operations make use of the string concatenation operator + to build a string from characters coming from the input stream. The first input operation, >>, behaves like the standard `iostream` extractor for numbers. It ignores leading whitespace characters and accepts a string of characters terminated by a whitespace character.

```
istream& operator >>(istream & is, apstring & str)
{
   char ch;
   str = "";     // empty string, will build one char at-a-time
   is >> ch;     // whitespace skipped, first non-white char in ch
   if (! is.fail())
   {
      do
      {
         str += ch;
         is.get(ch);
      } while (! is.fail() && ! isspace(ch));
      if (isspace(ch))        // put whitespace back on the stream
        is.putback(ch);
   }
   return is;
}
```

The second input operation is used to obtain a string of characters that might contain a whitespace. The input operation in this case is terminated by the detection of an end-of-line character (`'\n'`).

```
istream & getline(istream & is, apstring & str)
{
   char ch;
   str = "";      // empty string, will build one char at-a-time
   while (is.get(ch) && ch != '/n')
      str += ch;
   return is;
{
```

Note that both input operations place no limit on the size of a string obtained from the input source.

String Comparisons

The comparison operations for the `apstring` class depend on the use of the string library function `strcmp`. This function expects two C-style strings as parameters. It returns the following possible values:

1. zero if the two parameters are equal
2. a negative number if the left parameter is less than the right parameter
3. a positive number if the left parameter is greater than the right parameter

Only the `==` and `<` operations use the `strcmp` function directly. The other comparison operations can be defined in terms of `==` and `<`.

```
bool operator == (const apstring &lhs, const apstring &rhs)
{
   return strcmp(lhs.c_str(),
                 rhs.c_str()) == 0;
}
```

```
bool operator < (const apstring &lhs, const apstring &rhs)
{
   return strcmp(lhs.c_str(),
                 rhs.c_str()) < 0;
}
```

Exercises 9.7

1. Implement the remaining apstring class operations and test them with a driver program.
2. Describe the differences between a string object and a vector object.
3. What is the difference between a string object and a C-style string?
4. Simon Seeplus proposes that we represent the myCString data member of the apstring class as a vector. Discuss the merits of this proposal.
5. Write a free function, makeUppercase, that expects a string object as a parameter. The function should return a new string object that is a copy of the parameter with all of its letters in uppercase.

9.8 Safe Arrays: Matrices

User Requirements

Objectives

a. to understand the requirements for a safe two-dimensional array
b. to design and implement a new class that satisfies these requirements

In Section 9.5, we discussed the use of two-dimensional arrays in C++ programs. These arrays have all of the problems enumerated in Section 9.6. In addition, because two-dimensional arrays require two subscripts, the potential for range errors is twice as great as with one-dimensional arrays. A *matrix* class can solve these problems. Users can think of a matrix as a safe two-dimensional array. The capacity of a matrix is the product of the number of its rows and the number of its columns. The rows and columns can be specified, along with an initial fill value, when the matrix is created. A user can inspect the number of rows and the number of columns and resize a matrix by invoking the appropriate operations. Matrices can also be resized during assignment operations (with some data potentially being lost). Finally, a matrix supports two-dimensional indexing with range checking.

Example 9.14 The following driver program tests many of the user requirements for a matrix class. We assume that the class apmatrix has been defined in the implementation file apmatrix.cpp. A complete specification of the apmatrix class appears in Appendix E.

```
// Program file: matrdriv.cpp

#include <iostream.h>
#include "apmatrix.h"

int main()
{
   // Create a 4 X 4 matrix

   apmatrix<int> table(4, 4, 0);

   // Display number of rows and columns

   cout << "Rows = " << table.numrows() << endl;
   cout << "Columns = " << table.numcols() << endl;
```

continued

```
    // Set contents of each cell to row * column

    for (int row = 0; row < table.numrows(); ++row)
       for (int col = 0; col < table.numcols(); ++col)
          table[row] [col] = row * col;

    // Display positions and values

    for (int row = 0; row < table.numrows(); ++row)
       for (int col = 0; col < table.numcols(); ++col)
          cout << row << " "  << col << " "
                << table[row] [col] << endl;

    // Resize the matrix

    table.resize(8, 4);

    // Cause a range error

    table[8] [4] = 1;

    return 0;
}
```

This program produces the following output:

```
Rows = 4
Columns = 4
0 0 0
0 1 0
0 2 0
0 3 0
1 0 0
1 1 1
1 2 2
1 3 3
2 0 0
2 1 2
2 2 4
2 3 6
3 0 0
3 1 3
3 2 6
3 3 9
apmatrix.cpp:164 (k >= 0) && (k < myRows) -- assertion failed
abort -- terminating
```

Specifying the Operations for Matrices

The attributes of a matrix are

1. `myRows` (the number of rows)
2. `myCols` (the number of columns)
3. `myMatrix` (the data elements)
4. `itemType` (the matrix's element type)

The formal specifications of the operations for a matrix class are

Create Operation (Default Size)

Preconditions: The matrix is in an unpredictable state.

Postconditions: `myRows`, `myCols`, and `myMatrix` are set to 0.

Create Operation (User Specified Rows and Columns)

Preconditions: The matrix is in an unpredictable state. `rows` and `cols` are integer values >= 0. There is memory available for creating a matrix capable of storing `rows * cols` data elements.

Postconditions: Memory is reserved for a vector object capable of storing rows * cols data elements, `myRows` is set to `rows`, and `myCols` is set to `cols`.

Create Operation (User-Specified Rows, Columns, and Fill Value)

Preconditions: The matrix is in an unpredictable state. `rows` and `cols` are integer values >= 0. `fillValue` is a data element of the element type of the matrix. There is memory available for creating a vector capable of storing `size` data elements.

Postconditions: Memory is reserved for a matrix object capable of `rows * cols` data elements, `myRows` is set to `rows`, `myCols` is set to `cols`, and all of the cells in the matrix are set to `fillValue`.

Destroy Operation

Preconditions: The matrix is appropriately initialized.

Postconditions: The memory for the matrix is made available to the computer for other applications.

Numrows Operation

Preconditions: The matrix is appropriately initialized.

Postconditions: The value of `myRows` is returned.

Numcols Operation

Preconditions: The matrix is appropriately initialized.

Postconditions: The value of `myCols` is returned.

Resize Operation

Preconditions: The matrix is appropriately initialized. `newRows` and `newCols` are integers specifying the desired capacity of the matrix.

Postconditions: The capacity of the matrix is adjusted to the desired size if memory is available, `myRows` is set to `rows`, and `myCols` is set to `cols`. Any data elements stored in the matrix are copied to the resized matrix. Some data may be lost if the new size is less than the old size.

Subscript Operation (for Observation or Modification of a Data Element)

Preconditions: The matrix is appropriately initialized. `row` is an integer value in the range `0 <= row < myRows`. `col` is an integer value in the range `0 <= col < myCols`.

Postconditions: The location of a data element, which can be used either to observe or to store an object, is returned.

Subscript Operation (for Observation of a Data Element Only)

Preconditions: The matrix is appropriately initialized. `row` is an integer value in the range `0 <= row < myRows`. `col` is an integer value in the range `0 <= col < myCols`.

Postconditions: The object at the index position is returned.

Assignment Operation

Preconditions: The target matrix is appropriately initialized. The source matrix is appropriately initialized. There is memory available for making the capacity of the target object equal to the capacity of the source object.

Postconditions: The capacity of the target object is adjusted to the capacity of the source object, and the contents of the source object are copied into the target object.

Declaring the Matrix Class

The matrix class uses a vector of vectors to represent the data member for the two-dimensional array. Thus, the C++ declaration file must include the `apvector` library:

```
// Class declaration file: apmatrix.h

#ifndef _APMATRIX_H
#define _APMATRIX_H

#include "apvector.h"

template <class itemType> class apmatrix
{
   public:

   // Constructors

   apmatrix( );
   apmatrix(int rows, int cols);
   apmatrix(int rows, int cols, const itemType &fillValue);
   apmatrix(const apmatrix<itemType> &mat);

   // Destructor

   ~apmatrix( );

   // assignment

   const apmatrix& operator = (const apmatrix &rhs);

   // Accessors

   int numrows() const;
   int numcols() const;

   // Indexing

   const apvector<itemType>& operator [ ] (int row) const;
   apvector<itemType>& operator [ ] (int row);

   // Modifiers

   void resize(int newRows, int newCols);

   private:

   // Data members

   int myRows;
   int myCols;
   apvector<apvector<itemType> > myMatrix;
};

#include "apmatrix.cpp"

#endif
```

One unusual aspect of this code is the declaration

```
apvector<apvector<itemType> > myMatrix;
```

This code says that the data member `myMatrix` is a vector of vectors of type `itemType`. Note that two type parameters are nested within the angle brackets, and the two rightmost brackets are separated by a space. The space is merely a stylistic precaution to prevent the reader from mistaking this notation for the input operator >>.

Another point to note concerns the declarations of the indexing operations. They each specify a single `[ ]` operator, even though users invoke them with two consecutive `[ ]` operators. The computer executes the user's first `[ ]` operator as a matrix index operation. This operation returns a vector object (actually a row in the matrix). The computer then executes the user's second `[ ]` operator as a vector index operation. This operation returns the data or cell at the specified position in the vector.

Implementing the Matrix Class

The default constructor for the matrix class sets the data members for the rows and columns to zero. It then runs the constructor for vectors with the `myMatrix` data member, which creates a vector of size zero.

```
template <class itemType>
apmatrix<itemType>::apmatrix()
    : myRows(0),
    myCols(0),
    myMatrix(0)
{
}
```

The next constructor begins with a similar method, but with user-specified rows and columns. At the end of this portion of code, `myMatrix` is a vector of one or more empty vectors. The constructor then enters a `for` loop to resize each of these vectors to the size specified by the `cols` parameter. At the end of the entire process, `myMatrix` is a vector of `rows` vectors of `cols` cells of type `itemType`.

```
template <class itemType>
apmatrix<itemType>::apmatrix(int rows, int cols)
    : myRows(rows),
    myCols(cols),
    myMatrix(rows)
{
     for(int k = 0; k < rows; ++k)
          myMatrix[k].resize(cols);
}
```

To fill each cell of the matrix with an initial value, the next constructor extends the previous one with a nested `for` loop.

```
template <class itemType>
apmatrix<itemType>::apmatrix(int rows, int cols,
    const itemType & fillValue)
    : myRows(rows),
```

continued

```
    myCols(cols),
    myMatrix(rows)
{
    for(int j = 0; j < rows; ++j)
    {
      myMatrix[j].resize(cols);
      for(int k = 0; k < cols; ++k)
         myMatrix[j][k] = fillValue;
    }
}
```

The destructor for the matrix class appears to do nothing. However, the computer automatically invokes the destructor for the vector data member `myMatrix`. This call in turn results in further calls of this destructor for each of the vectors stored in `myMatrix`. In general, the destructor for any class that uses other classes with destructors can be written in this way.

```
template <class itemType>
apmatrix<itemType>::~apmatrix ()
{
// vector destructor frees everything
}
```

The index operations check the value of the row parameter against the range allowed by the vector `myMatrix`. They then invoke the `[ ]` operator with this vector, which does its own range checking for the second index value.

```
template <class itemType>
apvector<itemType>& apmatrix<itemType>::operator []
    (int row)
{
    assert((row >= 0) && (row < myRows));
    return myMatrix[row];
}
```

The implementations of the other matrix operations are left as exercises.

Exercises 9.8

1. Complete the implementations of the operations in the `apmatrix` class and test this class with the driver program of Example 9.14.
2. Explain why the destructor for the `apmatrix` class appears to do nothing.
3. The indexing operations for the `apmatrix` class run `assert` to check the validity of the first index value. If this statement is removed from the implementation, would both index values still be checked and, if so, where?
4. Why is the data member `myMatrix` in the `apmatrix` class represented as a vector rather than a two-dimensional C++ array?
5. Write a function `sum` that returns the sum of all of the values in a matrix of integers. You should assume that the entire matrix is occupied by data.

Case Study: Word Frequencies

As you saw in earlier chapters, much of word processing involves the use of strings to represent words or sentences. Many applications must maintain tables or dictionaries that are keyed by words that are associated with other information, such as salaries or phone numbers. We will examine how to set up a table that allows an application to count the frequencies of all the words in a file.

User Request

Write a program that displays the frequencies of the words in a file.

Analysis

The application will use the `apvector` class developed in Section 9.6. The input to the program will be a text file. The output will be two columns of data. In the first column will be an alphabetical listing of the words in the file. In the second column will be integers representing the frequency of each word in the file. Here is an example output from a run of the program:

```
There are some words in this
file but not many words

                     Word Frequency
                    There     1
                      are     1
                      but     1
                     file     1
                       in     1
                     many     1
                      not     1
                     some     1
                     this     1
                    words     2
```

To solve this problem, the program will need to represent a table of words and their frequencies. There are many ways to represent a table. Perhaps the simplest representation from our perspective is to use two parallel vectors. One vector contains the distinct words (strings) and the other vector contains the frequencies (integers). In this scheme, a word and its frequency have the same index position in their respective vectors. We assume that there are at most 50 unique words in a file.

Design

A top-level design of the program follows:

1. Open the input file and create the vectors.
2. As the words are input from the file, insert the distinct words and their frequencies into the vectors.
3. Close the input file.
4. Sort the vectors by order of words.
5. Display the contents of the vectors.

This design translates to a main function that consists of a series of function calls. The functions for steps 2, 4, and 5 each take the two vectors as parameters. Thus, we define global types for a vector of strings and for a vector of integers to assist in writing these functions:

```
const int MAX_WORDS = 50;

typedef apvector<apstring> stringVector;
typedef apvector<int> intVector;
```

The main function now looks like this:

```
int main()
{
   ifstream inputFile;
   stringVector words(MAX_WORDS);
   intVector frequencies(MAX_WORDS);
   int length = 0;

   openInputFile(inputFile);
   inputWords(inputFile, words, frequencies, length);
   sortTable(words, frequences, length);
   displayTable(words, frequencies, length);
   return 0;
}
```

The general idea for `inputWords` is to implement a loop that reads words from a file and inserts them into the table. The lower level function `insertWord` handles the insertions. Here is the code for `inputWords`:

```
void inputWords(ifstream &inputFile, apstringVector &words,
                 intVector &frequencies, int &length)
{
   while ((inputFile >> word) && (length < MAX_WORDS))
      insertWord(word, words, frequencies, length);

   assert(inputFile.fail());          // Signal error if not enough room in
}                                     // the vector for words
```

As each word is imput, the function `insertWord` searches the `words` vector for a matching word. If a matcing word is found, the function locates the corresponding position in the frequencies vector and increments the value there. If no match is found, the function adds the word to the logical end of the vector and sets the corresponding frequency in the `frequencies` vector to 1. Here is the code:

```
void insertWord(stringVector &words,
                 intVector &frequencies, int &length)
{
   int probe = 0;
   bool found = false;
   while (probe < length && ! found)
      if (word == words[probe]
         found = true;
      else
         ++probe;
   if (found)
      frequencies[probe] = frequencies[probe] + 1;
   else
   {
      words[length] = word;
      frequencies[length] = 1;
      ++length;
   }
}
```

The `sortTable` function uses the selection sort algorithm discussed in Section 9.4 to sort the vectors. The sort compares the words and reorders both them and their associated frequencies as necessary. We use a helper function `findMinimum` (left as an exercise) to locate the minimum word but omit the `swap` function. Here is the code:

```
void sortTable(stringVector &words,
               intVector &frequencies, int length)
{
   apstring tempWord;
   int tempFreq;
   int minIndex = 0;

   for (int j = 0; j < length - 1; ++j)
   {
      minIndex = findMinimum(words, j, length);
      if (minIndex != j)
      {
         tempWord = words[j];
         words[j] = words[minIndex];
         words[minIndex] = tempWord;
         tempFreq = frequencies[j];
         frequencies [j] = frequencies [minIndex];
         frequencies [minIndex] = tempFreq;
      }
   }
}
```

The `printTable` function displays a header and then loops through the two vectors, displaying the word and its frequency on a line:

```
void printTable(stringVector &words,
               intVector &frequencies, int length)
{
   cout << setw(25) << "Word" << setw(5) << "Frequency" << endl;

   for (int i = 0; i < length(); ++i)
      cout << setw(25) << words[i]
           << setw(5) << frequencies[i] << endl;
}
```

Summary Key Terms

base address
class template
component (element) of an array
destructor
dynamic memory
fill value
index (subscript)
logical size
matrix
offset
one-dimensional array
physical size
pointer variable
range bound error
row-major order
selection sort
sequential (linear) search
substring
two-dimensional array
vector

Key Concepts

- An array is a structured variable; a declaration of a single variable reserves several memory locations for data elements.
- It is good practice to use a symbolic constant to declare the size of array variables; for example,

```
const int MAX_ARRAY_SIZE = 10;
int list1[MAX_ARRAY_SIZE];
double list2 [MAX_ARRAY_SIZE];
```

- Arrays can be visualized as lists; thus, the preceding arrays could be envisioned as

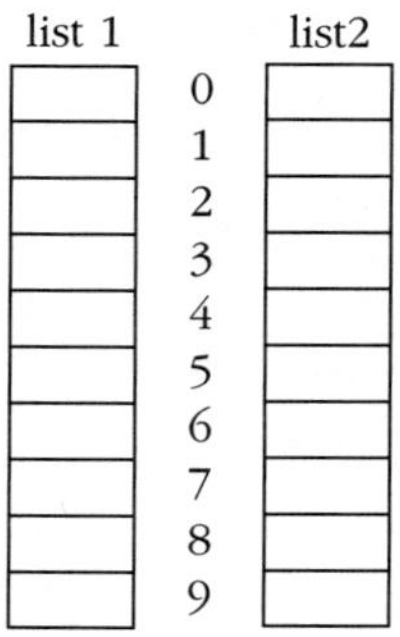

list 1		list2
	0	
	1	
	2	
	3	
	4	
	5	
	6	
	7	
	8	
	9	

- Each component of an array is a variable of the declared type and can be used in the same way as any other variable of that type.
- Loops can be used to read data into arrays; for example,

```
length = 0;
while ((infile >> data) &&(length < MAX_ARRAY_SIZE))
{
    a[length] = data;
    ++length;
}
```

- Loops can be used to print data from arrays; for example, if `scores` is an array of 20 test scores, the scores can be printed by

```
for (int j = 0; j < 20; ++j)
   cout << scores[j] << endl;
```

- Manipulating components of an array is generally accomplished by using the index as a loop variable; for example, assuming the preceding `scores` array, to find the smallest value in the array, we can use

```
small = scores[0];
for (int j = 1; j < 20; ++j)
   if (scores[j] < small)
      small = scores[j];
```

- A selection sort is one method of sorting elements in an array from high to low or low to high. This sort repeatedly finds the minimum element in the unsorted portion of the array and exchanges it with the first element in that portion.

- C++ array parameters are always passed by reference and should not be declared as reference parameters.
- A sequential search of a list consists of examining the first item in a list and then proceeding through the list in sequence until the desired value is found or the end of the list is reached.
- The logical size of an array is the number of data elements currently stored in it; this size may differ from the array's physical size.
- Two-dimensional arrays may be specified by declaring a variable that has upper bounds on two indices:

```
int table[20] [10];
```

- References to cells in two-dimensional arrays specify the index of the row first and the index of the column second:

```
table[row] [col] = 125;
```

- A vector allows users to work with an array that supports run-time range checking.
- A class template allows users to specify the element types contained in objects of that class.
- A pointer variable can contain the address of a chunk of memory. This memory is known as dynamic memory because it is allocated under program control. The form for declaring a pointer variable is

```
<element type>*<pointer variable name>
```

- A destructor is a special member function that the computer runs automatically to return dynamic memory allocated for an object to the system.
- The operator `new` allocates storage for an object from dynamic memory. The form for its use with arrays is

```
<pointer variable name> = new <element type> [<number of elements>]
```

- The operator `delete` is used to return dynamic memory from an object to the system. The form for its use with arrays is

```
delete [ ] <pointer variable>
```

- A matrix allows users to work with a two-dimensional array that supports run-time range checking on both dimensions.

Programming Problems and Projects

1. Write a program to read an unknown number of integer test scores from the keyboard (assume at most 150 scores). Print the original list of scores, the scores sorted from low to high, the scores sorted from high to low, the highest score, the lowest score, and the average score.
2. Write a program to help you balance your checkbook. The input consists of the beginning balance and then a sequence of transactions, each followed by a

transaction code. Deposits are followed by "D" and withdrawals are followed by "W." The output should consist of a list of transactions, a running balance, an ending balance, the number of withdrawals, and the number of deposits. Include an appropriate message for overdrawn accounts. Your program should represent the attributes and behavior of a transaction as a class.

3. One of the problems faced by designers of word processors is that of printing text without separating a word at the end of a line (that is, without hyphenating). Write a program to read several lines of text as input. Then print the message with each line starting in column 10 and no line exceeding column 70. No word should be separated at the end of a line.
4. Your local state university has to raise funds for an art center. As a first step, they are going to approach five previously identified donors and ask for additional donations. Because the donors wish to remain anonymous, only the respective totals of their previous donations are available for input. After they are contacted, the additional donations are listed at the end of input in the same order as the first 5 entries. Write a computer program to read the first 20 entries into one data structure and the second 5 entries into a second data structure. Compute the previous total donations and the new donations for the art center. Print the following:
   a. The list of previous donations
   b. The list of new donations
   c. An unsorted list of total donations
   d. A sorted list of total donations
   e. Total donations before the fund drive
   f. Total donations for the art center
   g. The maximum donation for the art center
5. Read in a list of ten integers from the keyboard. Place the even numbers into an array called `even`, the odd numbers into an array called `odd`, and the negatives into an array called `negative`. Print all three arrays after all numbers have been read.
6. Read in ten real numbers. Print the average of the numbers followed by all the numbers that are greater than the average.
7. Read in the names of five candidates in a class election and the number of votes received by each. Print the list of candidates, the number of votes they received, and the percentage of the total votes they received sorted into order from the winner to the person with the fewest votes. You may assume that all names are 20 characters in length.
8. In many sports events, contestants are rated by judges with an average score determined by discarding the highest and lowest scores and averaging the remaining scores. Write a program in which eight scores are entered, computing the average score for the contestant.
9. Given a list of 20 test scores (integers), print the score that is nearest to the average.
10. The game of Nim is played with three piles of stones. There are three stones in the first pile, five stones in the second, and eight stones in the third. Two players alternate taking as many stones as they like from any one pile. Play continues until someone is forced to take the last stone. The person taking the last stone loses. Write a program that permits two people to play the game of Nim using an array to keep track of the number of stones in each pile.
11. There is an effective strategy that can virtually guarantee victory in the game of Nim. Devise a strategy and modify the program in Problem 10 so that the computer plays against a person. Your program should be virtually unbeatable if the proper strategy is developed.

12. The median of a set of numbers is the value in the middle of the set if the set is arranged in order. The mode is the number listed most often. Given a list of 21 numbers, print the median and mode of the list.
13. The standard deviation is a statistic frequently used in education measurement. Write a program that, given a list of test scores, will find and print the standard deviation of the numbers. The standard deviation formula can be found in most statistics books.
14. Revise Problem 13 so that after the standard deviation is printed, you can print a list of test scores that are more than one standard deviation below the average and a list of the scores more than one standard deviation above the average.
15. The *z*-score is defined as the mean score earned on a test divided by the standard deviation. Given input data containing an unknown number of test scores (maximum of 100), print a list showing each test score (from highest to lowest) and the corresponding *z*-score.
16. Salespeople for the Wellsville Wholesale Company earn a commission based on their sales. The commission rates are as follows:

Sales	Commission (%)
$0–1000	3
$1001–5000	4.5
$5001–10,000	5.25
Over $10,000	6

In addition, any salesperson who sells above the average of all salespeople receives a $50 bonus, and the top salesperson receives an additional $75 bonus.

Given the names and amounts sold by each of ten salespeople, write a program that prints a table showing the salesperson's name, the amount sold, the commission rate, and the total amount earned. The average sales should also be printed.

17. Write a language translation program that permits the entry of a word in English, with the corresponding word of another language being printed. The dictionary words can be stored in parallel collections, with the English array being sorted into alphabetical order prior to the first entry of a word. Your program should first sort the dictionary of words.
18. Elementary and middle school students are often given the task of converting numbers from one base to another. For example, 19 in base 10 is 103 in base 4 ($1 \times 4^2 + 0 \times 4^1 + 3 \times 4^0$). Conversely, 123 in base 4 is 27 in base 10. Write an interactive program that allows the user to choose from the following:

```
<1>    Convert from base 10 to base A
<2>    Convert from base A to base 10
<3>    Quit
```

If option 1 or 2 is chosen, the user should then enter the intended base and the number to be converted. A sample run of the program would produce this output:

```
This program allows you to convert between bases. Which of the following
would you like?

    <1>    Convert from base 10 to base A
    <2>    Convert from base A to base 10
    <3>    Quit
```

continued

```
Enter your choice and press <Enter>. 1

Enter the number in base 10 and press <Enter>. 237

Enter the new base and press <Enter>. 4

The number 237 in base 4 is: 3231

Press <Enter> to continue

This program allows you to convert between bases. Which of the following
would you like?

    <1>     Convert from base 10 to base A
    <2>     Convert from base A to base 10
    <3>     Quit

Enter your choice and press <Enter>. 2

What number would you like to have converted? 2332

Converting to base 10, we get:

    2 * 1 = 2
    3 * 4 = 12
    3 * 16 = 48
    2 * 64 = 128

The base 10 value is 190

Press <Enter> to continue

This program allows you to convert between bases. Which of the following
would you like?

    <1>     Convert from base 10 to base A
    <2>     Convert from base A to base 10
    <3>     Quit

Enter your choice and press <Enter>. 3
```

19. You have been asked to write a program to grade the results of a true–false quiz and display the results in tabular form. The quiz consists of ten questions. The data file for this problem consists of (1) correct responses (answer key) on line 1, and (2) a four-digit student identification number followed by that student's ten responses on each successive line. Thus, the data file would be of the form

```
TFFTFTTFTT
0461 TTFTTFTFTT
3218 TFFTTTTFTT
.
.
```

Your program should read the key and store it in the last row of a two-dimensional array. It should then read the remaining lines, storing the student identification numbers in a one-dimensional array and the corresponding responses in rows in the two-dimensional array. Output should consist of a table with three columns: one for the student identification number, one for the number of correct responses, and one for the quiz grade. Grade assignments are A (10 correct), B (9), C (8–7), D (6–5), F (4–0). Your output should also include the quiz average for the entire class.

20. The Third Interdenominational Church has on file a list of all its benefactors (a maximum of 20 names, each up to 30 characters) along with an unknown number of amounts that each has donated to the church. You have been asked to write a program that does the following:

a. Print the name of each donor and the amount (in descending order) of any donations given by each.

b. Print the total amounts in ascending order.

c. Print the grand total of all donations.

d. Print the largest single amount donated and the name of the benefactor who made this donation.

21. Write a program to keep statistics for a basketball team consisting of 15 players. Statistics for each player should include shots attempted, shots made, and shooting percentage; free throws attempted, free throws made, and free throw percentage; offensive rebounds and defensive rebounds; assists; turnovers; and total points. Appropriate team totals should be listed as part of the output.

22. A magic square is a square array of positive integers such that the sum of each row, column, and diagonal is the same constant. For example,

16	3	2	13
5	10	11	8
9	6	7	12
4	15	14	1

is a magic square whose constant is 34. Write a program to input four lines of four positive integers from a data file. The program should determine whether or not the square is a magic square. Program efficiency should be such that computation ends as soon as two different sums have been computed.

23. Pascal's triangle can be used to recognize coefficients of a quantity raised to a power. The rules for forming this triangle of integers are such that each row must start and end with 1 and each entry in a row is the sum of the two values diagonally above the new entry. Thus, four rows of Pascal's triangle are

```
          1
       1     1
    1     2     1
 1     3     3     1
```

This triangle can be used as a convenient way to get the coefficients of a quantity of two terms raised to a power (binomial coefficients). For example,

$$(a + b)^3 = 1 \times a^3 + 3a^2b + 1 \times b^3$$

where the coefficients 1, 3, 3, and 1 come from the fourth row of Pascal's triangle.

Write a program to output Pascal's triangle for ten rows.

24. The following table shows the total sales for salespeople of the Falcon Manufacturing Company.

Salesperson	Week 1	Week 2	Week 3	Week 4
Anna, Michael	30	25	45	18
Henderson, Marge	22	30	32	35
Johnson, Fred	12	17	19	15
Striker, Nancy	32	30	33	31
Ryan, Renee	22	17	28	16

The price of the product being sold is $1985.95. Write a program that permits the input of the data in the table and displays both a replica of the table and a table showing the dollar value of sales for each individual during each week along with their total sales. Also, print the total sales for each week and the total sales for the company.

25. In the game of Penny Pitch, a two-dimensional board of numbers is laid out as follows:

```
1  1  1  1  1
1  2  2  2  1
1  2  3  2  1
1  2  2  2  1
1  1  1  1  1
```

A player tosses several pennies on the board, aiming for the number with the highest value. At the end of the game, the sum total of the tosses is returned. Develop a program that plays this game. The program should perform the following steps for a user-specified number of iterations:

a. Generate two random numbers for the row and column of the toss

b. Add the number at this position to a running total

c. Display the board, replacing the numbers with Ps where the pennies land

(*Hint:* You should use two two-dimensional arrays for this problem. The first array should contain the numbers shown above. The second array should contain Boolean values that indicate whether or not a penny has landed at a given position.)

10

Algorithm Analysis: Space and Time Considerations

Chapter Outline

Nothing puzzles me more than time and space.
Charles Lamb, 1775–1834

In this chapter, we introduce a technique for analyzing the efficiency of algorithms. We can then use this technique, known as big-O analysis, to categorize algorithms with respect to the length of time and the amount of storage they require for their execution with data sets of different sizes. In Sections 10.2 and 10.3, we will use big-O analysis to examine the time efficiency of some simple sorting algorithms. In Section 10.4, we will use big-O analysis to describe the interplay between the time and storage requirements of an algorithm. In Section 10.5, we will analyze the time efficiency of simple search algorithms. Finally, in the Case Study, we will discuss tools and strategies for developing programs to measure empirically the efficiency of an algorithm.

10.1 Designing Programs: A Look Back and a Look Ahead

Objectives

a. to develop a perspective on the study of computer science beyond the learning of a particular programming language, such as C++
b. to identify criteria by which complex software is evaluated

This chapter marks an important step in your exploration of computer science. Up to this point, it has been difficult to divorce your study of computer science from the learning of C++. You have developed problem-solving skills, but the problems we have encountered have been very focused. That is, the problems were chosen specifically to illustrate a particular feature of C++. This is the way that problem-solving skills must be developed: Start with small problems and work toward large ones.

By now, you know many of the features of the C++ programming language. You are ready to direct your attention toward larger, more complex problems that require you to integrate many of the particular skills you have developed. Now our attention will be directed more toward issues of software design and less toward describing C++. If we need a particular feature of C++ that has not yet been discussed, we will introduce it when appropriate. But our primary objective is to study more complex problems and the software design issues that arise out of them. From here on, we view C++ primarily as the vehicle to implement, test, and experiment with our solutions to problems. The techniques of software design we are about to explore will enable us to write programs that have the following characteristics:

- Large: Actually, our programs can properly be called systems because they typically involve numerous modules that interact to solve one complex problem.
- Reliable: The measure of the reliability of a system is that it can anticipate and handle all types of exceptional circumstances.
- Flexible: The system should be easily modified to handle circumstances that may change in the future.
- Expandable and reusable: If the system is successful, it will frequently spawn new computing needs. We should be able to incorporate solutions to these new needs into the original system with relative ease.
- Efficient: The system should make optimal use of time and space resources.
- Structured: The system should be divided into compact modules, each of which is responsible for a specific, well-defined task.
- User-friendly: The system should be clearly documented so that it is easy to use. Internal documentation helps programmers maintain the software, and external documentation helps users use it.

In designing software to meet these criteria, one of the key skills you must develop is the ability to choose the appropriate tools for the job. You should not have to rediscover algorithms and techniques for information storage and retrieval each time you write a new program. As a computer scientist, you must have a detailed knowledge of algorithms and data storage techniques at your fingertips and apply this knowledge when designing software to solve a variety of problems. You should look into your storehouse of algorithms and data storage strategies, choose the most appropriate methods, and then tailor them to the application at hand.

As you expand your knowledge of computer science, you will find that a given problem frequently lends itself to more than one method of solution. Hence, in addition to knowing the individual principles, you must also evaluate them comparatively. This comparative evaluation must be conducted in as systematic and quantitative a fashion as possible. That is, you must justify your choice of a method by presenting cogent arguments based on facts and figures pertinent to the problem. Given this perspective on computer science, we must turn our attention to a twofold task:

1. Stocking our algorithmic toolbox with methods that have become standards in computer science.
2. Developing criteria for knowing which tool to choose in a particular situation.

To begin this task, we reach back to the sorting and searching algorithms we first saw in Chapter 9. We also consider some new techniques for sorting and searching. We then evaluate these techniques for their efficiency in terms of execution time and use of space (memory) resources. To conduct such a time/space analysis, we introduce what has come to be known as big-O notation. In effect, big-O notation is the mathematical measuring stick by which computer scientists quantitatively evaluate algorithms. It allows us to place algorithms into categories based on their efficiency. Such categorization helps us determine whether or not a proposed solution is practical in terms of the real-world requirements and constraints dictated by the problem.

10.2 Simple Sorting Algorithms

Our discussion in this section will use an array of objects that we want to sort in ascending order according to a given attribute for each object. The attribute on which the sort is based is known as the key attribute. For instance, we may wish to arrange

Objectives

a. to develop a functional interface that can be used with a variety of sorting algorithms
b. to understand the potential difference in efficiency between the computer operations of comparing data items and interchanging them
c. to trace in detail the comparisons and interchanges of data items that occur during execution of the bubble sort algorithm
d. to trace in detail the comparisons and interchanges of data items that occur during execution of the selection sort algorithm
e. to trace in detail the comparisons and interchanges of data items that occur during execution of the insertion sort algorithm

a list of student objects in alphabetical order according to student last name or a list of inventory objects in order according to product identification numbers. To provide a suitable setting for our upcoming discussion of the sorting problem, we will make the following assumptions:

1. The objects being sorted are of type `element`. `element` is a synonym for whatever class of object we wish to place in an array.
2. If necessary, the `element` class overloads the standard C++ operators =, ==, <, and > that are used by the sort algorithms. Operator = is used for copying elements, while ==, <, and > compare two elements with respect to the key attribute.

For example, the following declarations provide a setting for sorting a simple array of integers:

```
const int MAX_LIST_SIZE = 100;
typedef int element;
typedef element ListType[MAX_LIST_SIZE];
```

We wish to write a sort function that meets the following specifications:

```
// Function: sort
// Sorts a list of elements into ascending order
//
// Inputs: a list of elements in arbitrary order and its
// current length
// Output: the list of elements arranged in ascending
// order

void sort(ListType list, int n);
```

Two aspects of these declarations are worth noting. First, the fashion in which we have made our constant and type definitions allows this function to sort an array of any size and base type provided that the definitions are appropriately altered. This method of declaration represents an attempt to make the C++ function abstract: It embodies an algorithm that can sort a variety of data types.

Second, the measure of an algorithm's run-time efficiency is in direct proportion to the number of elementary machine operations that must be performed as the algorithm is executed. With sorting algorithms, these elementary machine operations compare and interchange two data items. Depending on the amount of data in the `element` type in the preceding declarations, it is entirely possible that interchanging two data items could be considerably more costly in machine time than comparing two items. Why? An interchange of large data items will generate a loop that moves a significant number of bytes at the machine language level.

Our analysis of run-time efficiency should take this into account. It may be more important to minimize data interchanges at the expense of comparisons. This complication did not enter into our earlier discussion of sorting because, at that stage, we were concerned with sorting arrays of simple, unstructured data items only.

Bubble Sort

The *bubble sort* represents an alternative to the selection sort algorithm discussed in Section 9.4. Given a list of data objects stored in an array, a bubble sort causes a pass

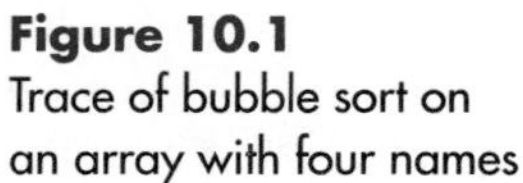

Figure 10.1 Trace of bubble sort on an array with four names

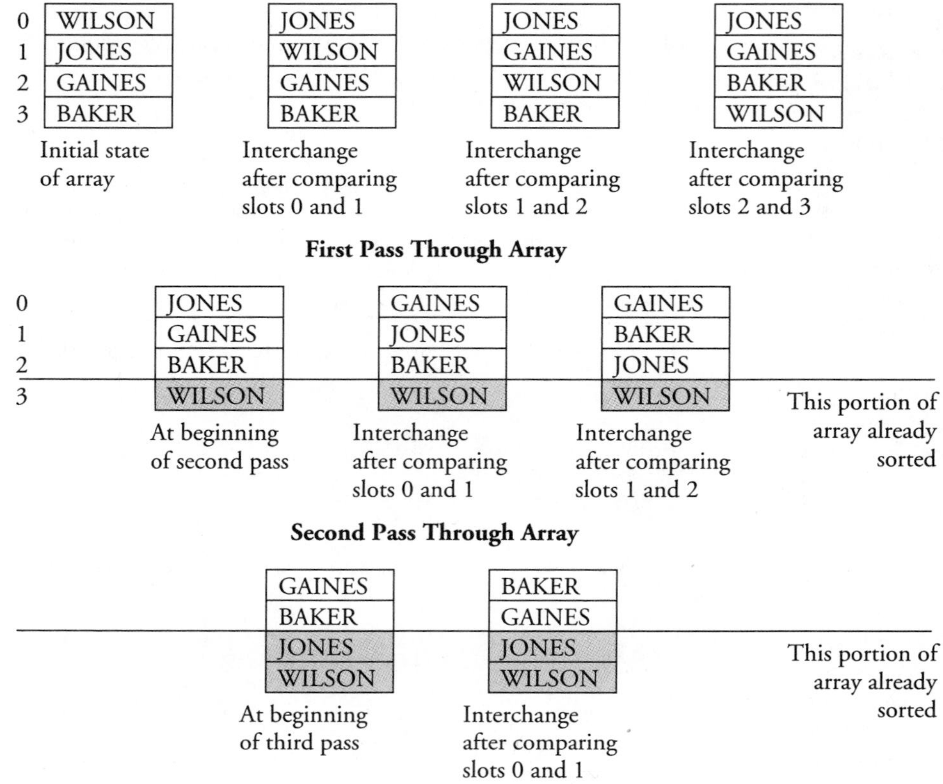

through the array to compare adjacent pairs of keys. Whenever two keys are out of order with respect to each other, the associated objects are interchanged. The effect of such a pass through a list of names is traced in Figure 10.1, where a "snapshot" of the array after each comparison is given. Notice that after such a pass, we are assured that the list will have the name that comes last in alphabetical order in the final array position. That is, the last name will "sink" to the bottom of the array, and preceding names will gradually "percolate" to the top.

If one pass through an array of n keys guarantees that the key last in order is in the appropriate position, then passing through the remaining $n-1$ entries using the same logic will guarantee that the key second to last in order is in its appropriate position. Repeating the process for a total of $n-1$ passes eventually ensures that all objects are in their appropriate positions. In general, on the kth pass through the array, $n-k$ comparisons of pairs must be made.

Thus, the bubble sort algorithm involves a nested loop structure. The outer loop controls the number of (successively smaller) passes through the array. The inner loop controls the pairs of adjacent entries being compared.

If we ever make a complete pass through the inner loop without having to make an interchange, we can declare the array sorted and avoid all future passes through the array. A top-level pseudocode development of the algorithm is

1. Initialize counter `k` to 0

2. Initialize boolean `exchangeMade` to `true`

3. While (`k < n - 1`) and `exchangeMade`
   3.1 Set exchangeMade to `false`
   3.2 Increment counter `k`
   3.3 For each `j` from 0 to `n - k`
      3.3.1 If entry in `j`th slot > entry in (`j + 1`)st slot
         3.3.1.1 Exchange these entries
         3.3.1.2 Set exchangeMade to `true`

The complete C++ function to implement this algorithm for an array of objects follows. The function assumes the existence of appropriate data declarations.

```
void bubbleSort(ListType list, int n)
{
   int j, k;
   bool exchangeMade;
   element temp;
   k = 0;
   exchangeMade = true;

   // Make up to n - 1 passes through array, exit early if no exchanges
   // are made on previous pass

   while ((k < n - 1) && exchangeMade)
   {
      exchangeMade = false;
      ++k;
      for (j = 0; j < n - k; ++j)        // Number of comparisons on kth pass
         if (list[j] > list[j + 1])
         {
            temp = list[j];              // Exchange must be made
            list[j]= list[j + 1];
            list[j + 1]= temp;
            exchangeMade = true;
         }
   }
}
```

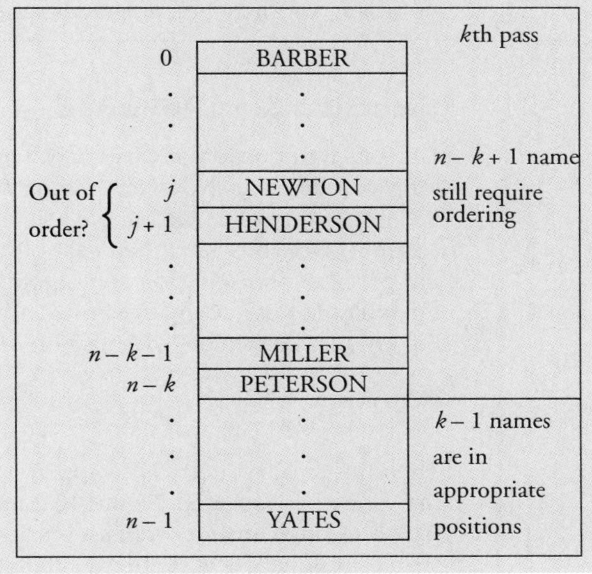

*k*th pass

0	BARBER	
.	.	
.	.	
.	.	$n - k + 1$ names still require ordering
Out of order? j	NEWTON	
$j + 1$	HENDERSON	
.	.	
.	.	
.	.	
$n - k - 1$	MILLER	
$n - k$	PETERSON	
.	.	$k - 1$ names are in appropriate positions
.	.	
.	.	
$n - 1$	YATES	

Example 10.1 Trace the action of the function `bubbleSort` if `n` is 5 and the array `list` initially contains

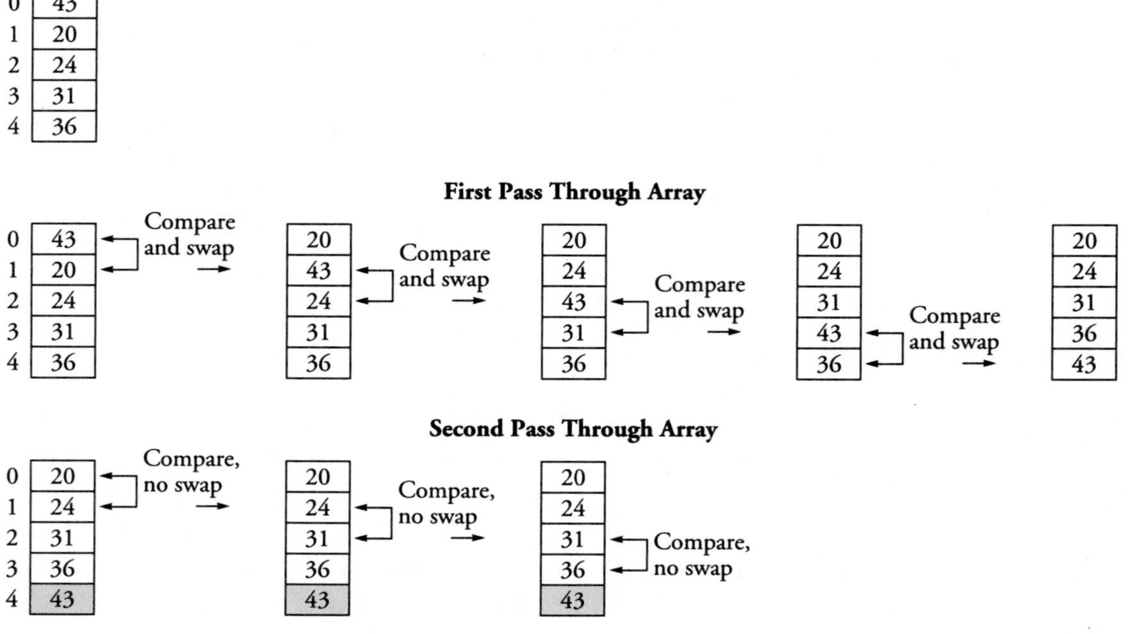

`exchangeMade` remained false throughout the inner loop, so the algorithm is done.

In the next section, we analyze in detail the run-time efficiency of the bubble sort. But we should first consider two other sorting algorithms to which the efficiency of bubble sort may be compared: *selection sort* and *insertion sort.*

Selection Sort Revisited

Since its introduction in Chapter 9, we have used the selection sort algorithm to sort arrays of elements. Now let's compare it to the bubble sort algorithm.

The strategy of the bubble sort is to place the (current) largest array value in the (current) last array slot, then seal off that slot from future consideration, and repeat the process. The selection sort algorithm has a similar plan, but it attempts to avoid the multitude of interchanges of adjacent entries. To do this, on the *k*th pass through the array, it determines the position of the smallest entry among

```
list[k], list[k + 1], ..., list[n - 1]:
```

Then this smallest entry is swapped with the *k*th entry, `k` is incremented by 1, and the process is repeated. Figure 10.2 illustrates how this algorithm works on repeated passes through an array with six entries. Asterisks are used to indicate the successively smallest (alphabetical) entries as they are correctly located in the array.

Figure 10.2
Trace of selection sort logic

Original Order of Keys	$k = 0$	$k = 1$	$k = 2$	$k = 3$	$k = 4$
DAVE	ARON*	ARON*	ARON*	ARON*	ARON*
TOM	TOM	BEV*	BEV*	BEV*	BEV*
PAM	PAM	PAM	DAVE*	DAVE*	DAVE*
ARON	DAVE	DAVE	PAM	PAM*	PAM*
BEV	BEV	TOM	TOM	TOM	SAM*
SAM	SAM	SAM	SAM	SAM	TOM*

As we see next, the C++ function for selection sort uses, as its inner loop, a simple algorithm to find the minimum entry and store its position in the variable `min-Position`. This inner loop avoids the potentially frequent interchange of array elements that is necessary in the inner loop of `bubbleSort`.

```
void selectionSort(ListType list, int n)
{
   int index;
   element temp;

   // Make n - 1 passes through successively smaller segments

   for (int k = 0; k < n - 1; ++k)
   {
      minPosition = k;
      // Find index of the smallest element
      for (int j = k + 1; j < n; ++j)
         if (list[j]< list[minPosition])
            minPosition = j;
      if (minPosition ! = k)
      {
         temp = list[minPosition];      // Exchange must be made
         list[minPosition]= list[k];
         list[k]= temp;
      }
   }
}
```

Example 10.2 Trace the action of the function `selectionSort` if `n` is 5 and the array `list` initially contains

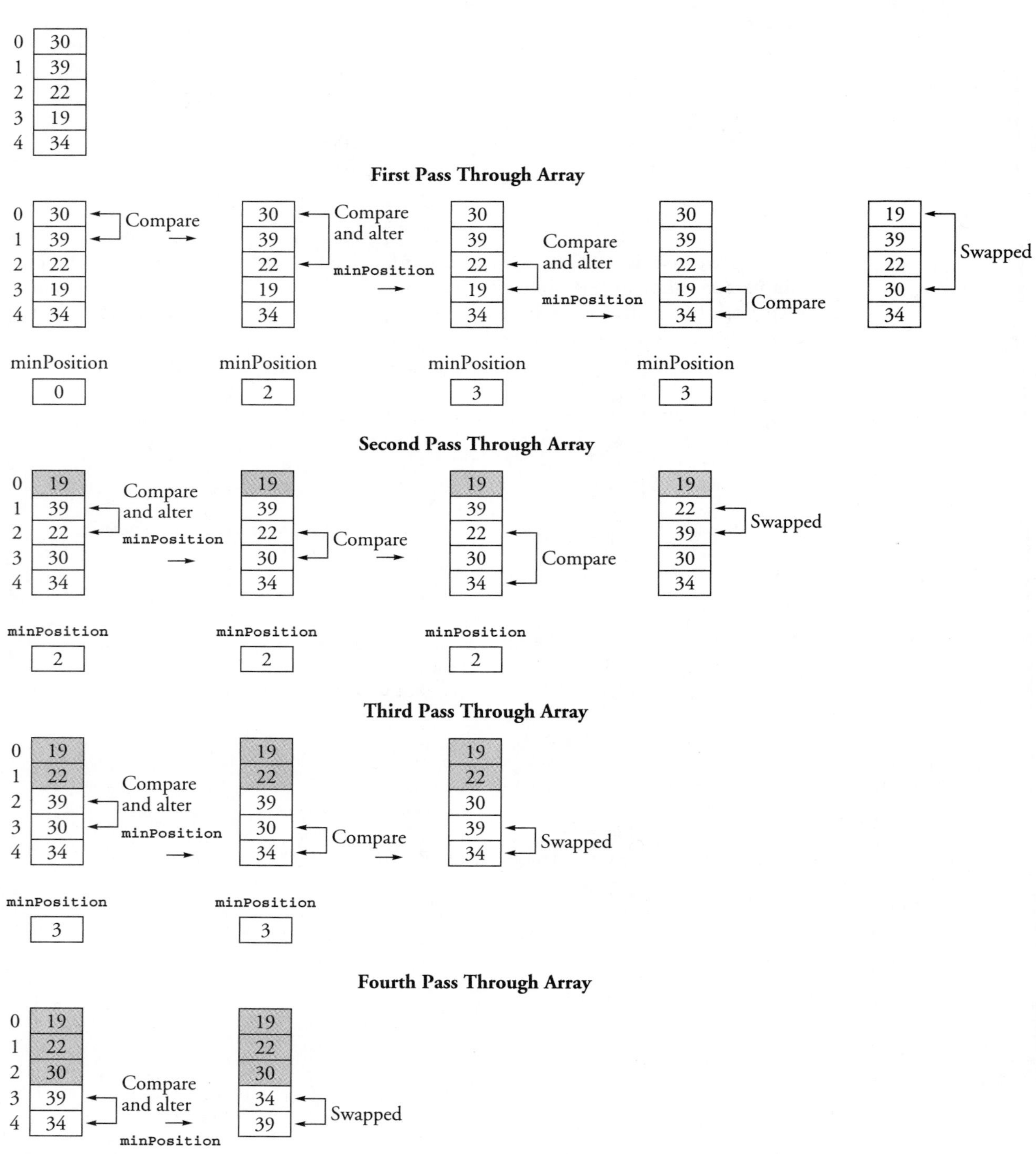

Example 10.2 indicates that the selection sort algorithm swaps no data values until exiting the inner loop. This apparently reduces the number of data interchanges and makes the selection sort more efficient than the bubble sort. Is this a significant improvement? Or have other subtle inefficiencies been introduced to offset this apparent gain? These are difficult questions to answer unless we have a better grasp of how to measure program efficiency. We'll explore efficiency in the next section; but first, let's look at one more sorting algorithm for comparison purposes.

Insertion Sort

Although it reduces the number of data interchanges, the selection sort apparently will not allow an effective—and automatic—loop exit if the array becomes ordered during an early pass. In this regard, bubble sort is more efficient than selection sort for an array that is nearly ordered from the beginning. However, even with just one entry out of order, bubble sort's early loop exit can fail to reduce the number of comparisons that are made.

The insertion sort attempts to take greater advantage of an array's partial ordering. The goal is that on the *k*th pass through, the *k*th element among

```
list[0], list[1], ..., list[k]
```

should be inserted into its rightful place among the first *k* entries in the array. Thus, after the *k*th pass (*k* starting at 1), the first *k* elements of the array should be in sorted order. This is analogous to the fashion in which many people pick up playing cards and order them in their hands. Holding the first (*k*–1) cards in order, a person will pick up the *k*th card and compare it with cards already held until its appropriate spot is found. The following steps will achieve this logic:

1. For each `k` from 1 to `n-1` (k is the index of array element to insert)
   1.1 Set `itemToInsert` to `list[k]`
   1.2 Set `j` to `k-1` (`j` starts at `k-1` and is decremented until insertion position is found)
   1.3 While (insertion position not found) and (not beginning of array)
      1.3.1 If `itemToInsert` < `list[j]`
         1.3.1.1 Move `list[j]` to index position `j` + 1
         1.3.1.2 Decrement `j` by 1
      1.3.2 Else
         1.3.2.1 The insertion position has been found
   1.4 `itemToInsert` should be positioned at index `j` + 1

In effect, for each pass, the index *j* begins at the (*k*–1)st element and moves that element to position *j* + 1 until we find the insertion point for what was originally the *k*th element.

Insertion sort for each value of `k` is traced in Figure 10.3. In each column of this diagram, the data items are sorted in alphabetical order relative to each other above the item with the asterisk; below this item, the data are not affected.

To implement the insertion sort algorithm in C++, we have the following code:

```
void insertionSort(ListType list, int n)
{
   int j, k;
   element itemToInsert;
   bool stillLooking;
```

continued

Figure 10.3
Trace of repeated passes from insertion sort

Original Order of Keys	First Pass $k = 1$	Second Pass $k = 2$	Third Pass $k = 3$	Fourth Pass $k = 4$	Fifth Pass $k = 5$
PAM	PAM	DAVE	ARON	ARON	ARON
SAM	SAM*	PAM	DAVE	DAVE	BEV
DAVE	DAVE	SAM*	PAM	PAM	DAVE
ARON	ARON	ARON	SAM*	SAM	PAM
TOM	TOM	TOM	TOM	TOM*	SAM
BEV	BEV	BEV	BEV	BEV	TOM*

```
    // On the kth pass, insert item k into its correct position among
    // the first k entries in array. }

    for (k = 1; k < n; ++k)
    {
    // Walk backwards through list, looking for slot to insert A[K]
       itemToInsert = list[k];
       j = k - 1;
       stillLooking = true;
       while ((j >= 0) && stillLooking)
          if (itemToInsert < list[j])
          {
             list[j + 1]= list[j];
             --j;
          }
          else
             stillLooking = false;
       // Upon leaving loop, j + 1 is the index
       // where itemToInsert belongs
       list[j + 1]= itemToInsert;
    }
}
```

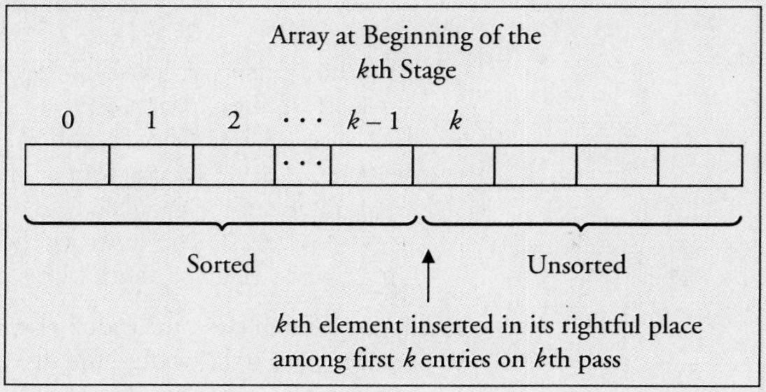

Array at Beginning of the kth Stage

0 1 2 ··· $k-1$ k

Sorted

Unsorted

kth element inserted in its rightful place among first k entries on kth pass

Example 10.3 Trace the action of the function `insertionSort` if `n` is 5 and the array `list` initially contains

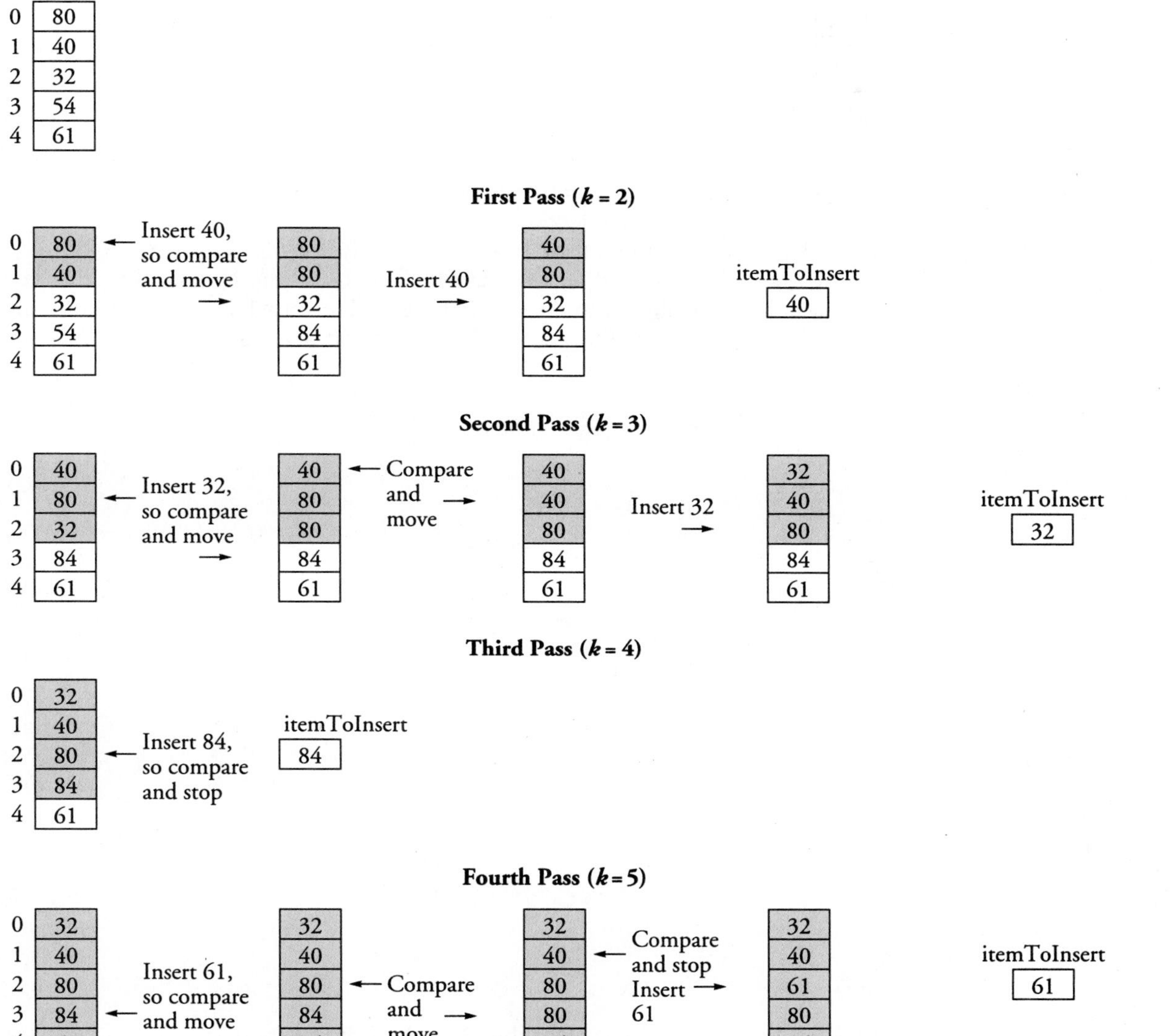

Exercises 10.2

1. Which of the sorting methods studied in this section allows a possible early exit from its inner loop? What is the potential advantage of using this early exit?
2. Which of the sorting methods studied in this section allows a possible early exit from its outer loop? What is the potential advantage of using this early exit?
3. Which of the sorting methods studied in this section does not allow for the possibility of an early exit from its inner or outer loops? What potential advantage does this method have over the other two methods that were presented?

4. Suppose that, initially, an array contains seven integer entries arranged in the following order:

0	43
1	40
2	18
3	24
4	39
5	60
6	12

Trace the order of the array entries after each successive pass of the bubble sort.

5. Repeat Exercise 4 for the selection sort.

6. Repeat Exercise 4 for the insertion sort.

7. Consider the following sort algorithm. Which of the methods studied in this section does this new algorithm most closely resemble? In what ways is it different from that method? Trace the action of this new sort algorithm on the array from Exercise 4.

```
void sort(ListType list, int n)
{
   int j, k;
   bool exchangeMade = true;
   element temp;

   k = 0;
   while ((k < n - 1) && exchangeMade)
   {
        exchangeMade = false;
        ++k;
        for (j = n - 1; j > k + 1; --j)
            if (list[j] < list[j - 1])
            {
                temp = list[j];
                list[j] = list[j - 1];
                list[j - 1] = temp;
                exchangeMade = true;
            }
   }
}
```

8. Consider the following sort algorithm. Which of the methods studied in this section does this new algorithm most closely resemble? In what ways is it different from that method? Trace the action of this new sort algorithm on the array from Exercise 4.

```
void sort(ListType list, int n)
{
   int j, k, position;
   element temp;

   for (k = 0; k < n - 1; ++k)
   {
       position = 0;
```

```
            for (j = 1; j < n - k + 1; ++j)
                if (list[j] > list[position])
                    position = j;
            temp = list[n - k + 1];
            list[n - k + 1] = list[position];
            list[position] = temp;
        }
}
```

9. Consider the following sort algorithm. Which of the methods studied in this section does this new algorithm most closely resemble? In what ways is it different from that method? Trace the action of this new sort algorithm on the array from Exercise 4.

```
void sort(ListType list, int n)
{
    int j, k;
    bool done;
    element temp;

    for (k = n - 1; k > 0; --k)
    {
            j = k;
            done = false;
            while ((j <= n - 1) && ! done)
                if (list[j] > list[j + 1])
                {
                    temp = list[j];
                    list[j] = list[j - 1];
                    list[j - 1] = temp;
                    ++j;
                }
                else
                    done = true;
    }
}
```

10. Devise sample data sets to demonstrate the *best case* and *worst case* behavior of the bubble sort, insertion sort, and selection sort. That is, for each sorting algorithm, construct data sets that illustrate the minimum and maximum number of comparisons required for that particular algorithm.

11. Construct a data set in which just one value is out of order and yet the Boolean test of the `exchangeMade` variable never allows an early exit from the outer loop of bubble sort. How does the insertion sort perform on this same data set? Better, worse, or the same? Explain why.

12. Modify the sorting algorithms of this section so that they receive an additional argument indicating whether the sort should be in ascending or descending order.

13. The inner loop of an insertion sort can be modified merely to find the appropriate position for the *k*th array entry instead of actually shifting items to make room for this entry. The shifting of items and placement of the original *k*th entry can then be achieved in a separate loop. Write a new insertion sort function that implements this modification. Intuitively, is your new version more or less efficient than the old version? Why?

14. Modify all of the sorting algorithms presented in this chapter to include counters for the number of comparisons and data interchanges that are made. Then run those sorting algorithms on a variety of data sets, maintaining a chart of the counters for each algorithm. Prepare a written statement to summarize your conclusions about the relative efficiencies of the algorithms.

10.3 Which Sort Is Best? A Big-O Analysis

Computers do their work in terms of certain fundamental operations: comparing two numbers, moving the contents of one memory word to another, and so on. It should come as no surprise to you that a simple instruction in a high-level language such as C++ may be translated (via a compiler) into many of these fundamental machine level instructions. On most modern computers, the speeds of these fundamental operations are measured in microseconds—that is, millionths of a second—although some larger supercomputers are beginning to break the nanosecond (billionth of a second) barrier.

Let's assume, for the sake of argument, that we are working with a hypothetical computer that requires 1 microsecond to perform one of its fundamental operations. With execution speeds of this kind, it makes little sense to analyze the efficiency of those portions of a program that perform only initializations and final reporting of summary results. The key to analyzing a function's efficiency is to scrutinize its loops, especially its nested loops. Consider the following two examples of nested loops intended to sum each of the rows of an $N \times N$ two-dimensional array `matrix`, storing the row sums in the one-dimensional array `rows` and the overall total in `grandTotal`.

Example 10.4

```
grandTotal = 0;
for (k = 0; k < n - 1; ++k)
{
  rows[k] = 0;
  for (j = 0; j < n - 1; ++j)
  {
         rows[k] = rows[k] + matrix[k][j];
         grandTotal = grandTotal+ matrix[k][j];
  }
}
```

Example 10.5

```
grandTotal = 0;
for (k = 0; k < n - 1; ++k)
{
   rows[k]= 0;
   for (j = 0; j < n - 1; ++j)
        rows[k] = rows[k] + matrix[k][j];
   grandTotal = grandTotal+ rows[k];
}
```

If we analyze the number of addition operations required by these two examples, it should be immediately obvious that Example 10.5 is better in this respect. Because Example 10.4 incorporates the accumulating of `grandTotal` into its inner loop, it requires $2N^2$ additions. That is, the additions `rows[k] + matrix[k][j]` and

Objectives

a. to understand the formal definition of big-O notation
b. to use big-O notation to classify the time efficiency of algorithms involving nonrecursive, iterative control constructs
c. to see the relationship between an algorithm's big-O classification and its expected run time on a computer
d. to recognize often-used big-O categories
e. to apply big-O notation in analyzing the time efficiencies of the bubble sort, selection sort, and insertion sort algorithms

`grandTotal + matrix[k][j]` are each executed N^2 times for a total of $2N^2$. Example 10.5, on the other hand, accumulates `grandTotal` after the inner loop; hence, it requires only $N^2 + N$ additions, which is less than $2N^2$ for any N beyond 1. Example 10.5 is seemingly guaranteed to execute faster than Example 10.4 for any nontrivial value of N.

But note that "faster" here may not have much significance in the real world of computing. Assume that our hypothetical computer allows us to declare an array that is 1000 by 1000. Example 10.4 would require 2 seconds to perform its additions; Example 10.5 would require just over 1 second. On a larger 100,000 by 100,000 array, Example 10.4 would crunch numbers for slightly under 6 hours, and Example 10.5 would take about 3 hours.

Although Example 10.5 is certainly better from an aesthetic perspective, it may not be good enough to be appreciably different from a user's perspective. That is, in situations where one version will respond within seconds, so will the other. Conversely, when one is annoyingly slow, the other will be also. In terms of the *order of magnitude* of run time involved, these versions should not be considered significantly different. For the 1000 by 1000 array, both versions are fast enough to allow their use in an interactive environment. For the 100,000 by 100,000 array, both versions dictate an overnight run in batch mode since an interactive user is no more willing to wait 3 hours than 6 hours for a response. The essence of the difference between the run times of these two algorithms is that, no matter what the size of the array on which they operate, the first will always be approximately twice as slow as the second. Another way of saying this is that the run times of the two algorithms are directly proportional to each other.

Because of the phenomenal execution speeds and very large amounts of available memory on modern computers, proportionally small differences between algorithms may often have little practical impact. Such considerations have led computer scientists to devise a method of algorithm classification that makes more precise the notion of order of magnitude as it applies to time and space considerations. This method of classification, typically referred to as *big-O notation* (in reference to "on the Order of"), hinges on the following definition:

Big-O notation: Suppose there exists a function $f(n)$ defined on the nonnegative integers such that the number of operations required by an algorithm for an input of size n is less than or equal to some constant C times $f(n)$ for all but finitely many n. That is, the number of operations is at worst *proportional* to $f(n)$ for all large values of n. Such an algorithm is said to be an $O[f(n)]$ algorithm relative to the number of operations it requires to execute. Similarly, we could classify an algorithm as $O[f(n)]$ relative to the number of memory locations it requires to execute.

Figure 10.4 provides a graphic aid to understanding this formal definition of big-O notation. In general, we expect an algorithm's run time to increase as it manipulates an increasing number of data items, that is, as n increases. This increasing run time is depicted by the somewhat irregular, wavy curve in Figure 10.4. Now compare the wavy curve representing actual run time to the smoother curve of $C^*f(n)$. Note that, for some small values of n, the actual number of operations for the algorithm may exceed $C^*f(n)$. However, the graph indicates that there is a point on the horizontal axis beyond which $C^*f(n)$ is always greater than the number of operations required for n data items. This is precisely the criterion that defines an algorithm's being $O[f(n)]$.

To say that an algorithm is $O[f(n)]$ thus indicates that the function $f(n)$ may be useful in characterizing how the algorithm is performing for large n. For such n, we are assured that the operations required by the algorithm will be bounded by a con-

Figure 10.4
Graphic representation of $O[f(n)]$

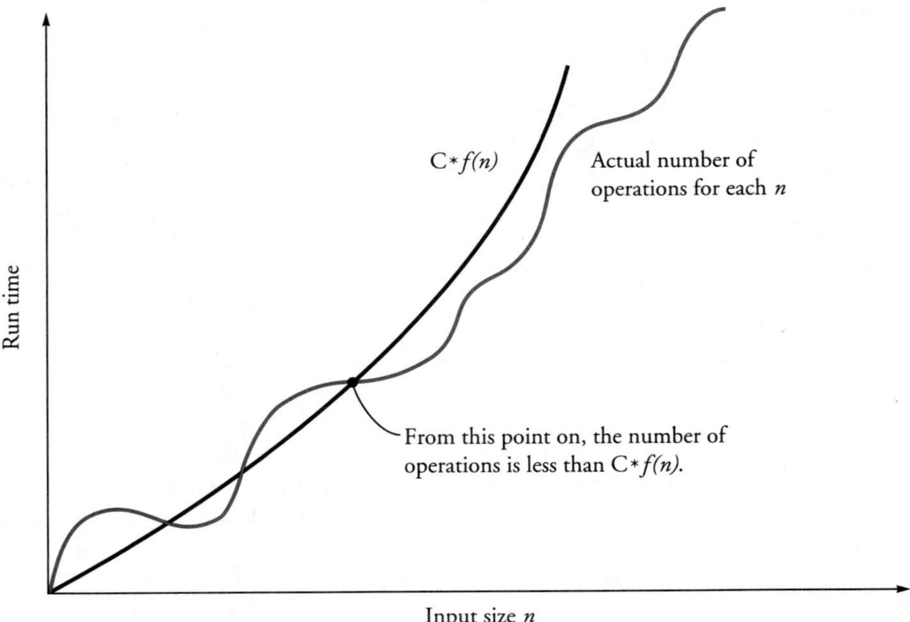

stant times $f(n)$. The phrasing "for all large values of n" in the definition highlights the fact that there is little difference in the choice of an algorithm if n is reasonably small. For example, almost any sorting algorithm would sort 100 integers instantly.

We should also note that a given algorithm may be $O[f(n)]$ for many different functions f. As Figure 10.5 depicts, any algorithm that is $O(n^2)$ will also be $O(n^3)$.

Our main interest in classifying an algorithm with big-O notation is to find a relatively simple function $f(n)$ such that $C^*f(n)$ parallels the number of operations as closely as possible. Hence, saying that an algorithm is $O(n^2)$ is considered a better characterization of its efficiency than saying it is $O(n^3)$.

The importance of the constant C, known as the constant of proportionality, lies in comparing algorithms that share the same function $f(n)$; it makes almost no difference in the comparison of algorithms for which $f(n)$ is of different magnitude. It is therefore appropriate to say that the function $f(n)$ dominates the run-time performance of an algorithm and characterizes it in its big-O analysis. The example in the following paragraph should help clarify this situation.

Consider two algorithms L_1 and L_2 with run times equal to $2n^2$ and n^2, respectively. The constants of proportionality of L_1 and L_2 are 2 and 1, respectively. The dominating function $f(n)$ for both of these algorithms is n^2, but L_2 runs twice as fast as L_1 for a data set of n values. The different sizes of the two constants of proportionality indicate that L_2 is faster than L_1. Now suppose that the function $f(n)$ for L_2 is n^3. Then, even though its constant of proportionality is half of what it is for L_1, L_2 will be frustratingly slower than L_1 for large n. This latter comparison is shown in Figure 10.6.

Example 10.6 Use big-O analysis to characterize the two code segments from Examples 10.4 and 10.5, respectively.

Because the algorithm of Example 10.4 performs $2N^2$ additions, it is characterized as $O(N^2)$ with 2 as a constant of proportionality. We previously determined that the code of Example 10.5 performs $N^2 + N$ additions. However, $N^2 + N <= 1.1N^2$ for any $N >= 10$. Hence, we can characterize Example 10.5 as an $O(N^2)$ algorithm

Figure 10.5
Any algorithm that is $O(n^2)$ is also $O(n^3)$

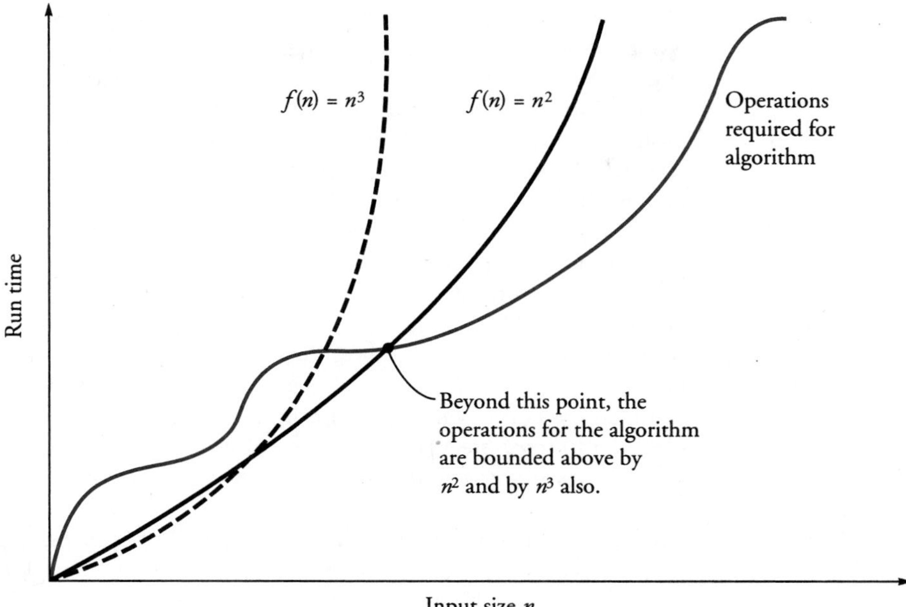

Figure 10.6
Graphic comparison of two run times

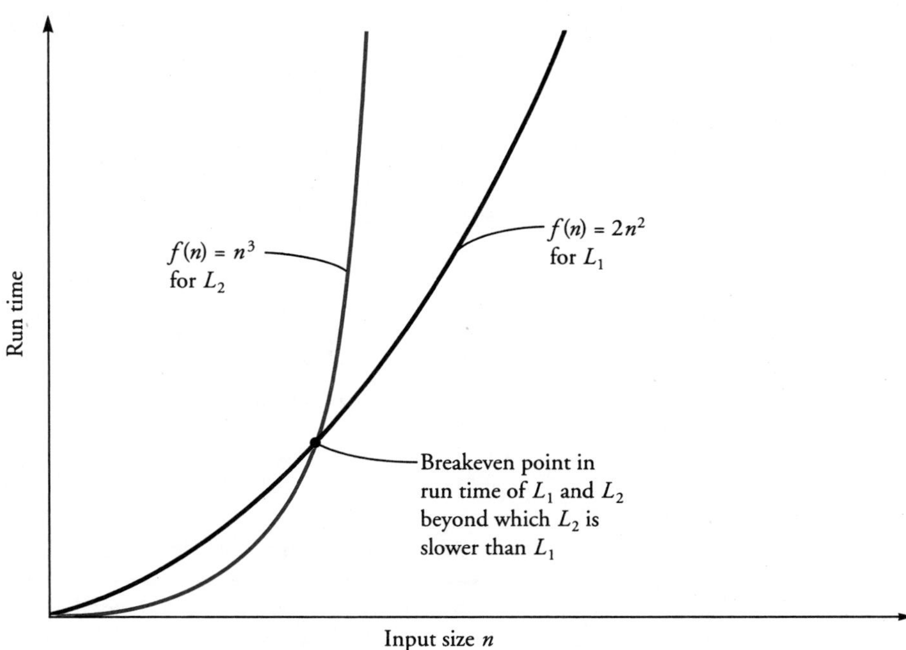

using 1.1 as a constant of proportionality. These two characterizations demonstrate that, although Example 10.5 is almost twice as fast as Example 10.4, they are in the same big-O category. Coupled with our earlier analysis of these two examples, this is an indication that algorithms in the same big-O category may be expected to have the same orders of magnitude in their run times.

How well does the big-O notation provide a way of classifying algorithms from a real-world perspective? To answer this question, consider Table 10.1. This table presents some typical $f(n)$ functions we will use to classify algorithms and their order of magnitude run times for inputs of various sizes on a hypothetical computer. From this table, we can see that an $O(n^2)$ algorithm will take hours to execute for an input of size 10^5. How many hours depends on the constant of proportionality in the definition of the big-O notation.

Regardless of the value of this constant of proportionality, a categorization of an algorithm as an $O(n^2)$ algorithm has thus achieved a very practical goal. We now know that, for an input of size 10^5, we cannot expect an immediate response for such an algorithm. Moreover, we also know that, for a reasonably small constant of proportionality, we have an algorithm for which submission as an overnight job would not be impractical. That is, unlike an $O(n^3)$ algorithm, we could expect the computer to finish executing our algorithm in a time frame that would be acceptable if scheduled not to interfere with other uses of the machine. On the other hand, an $O(n^3)$ algorithm applied to a data set of this size would be completely impractical.

How does one determine the function f(n) that categorizes a particular algorithm? We give an overview of that process here and illustrate it by doing actual analyses for our three sorting algorithms. It is generally the case that, by analyzing the loop structure of an algorithm, we can estimate the number of run-time operations (or amount of memory units) required by the algorithm as a sum of several terms, each dependent on n, the number of items being processed by the algorithm. That is, typically we are able to express the number of run-time operations (or amount of memory) as a sum of the form

$$f_1(n) + f_2(n) + \ldots + f_k(n)$$

Moreover, it is also typical for us to identify one of the terms in this expression as the *dominant term.* A dominant term is one that, for bigger values of n, becomes so large that it allows us to ignore all the other terms from a big-O perspective. For instance, suppose we had an expression involving two terms such as

$$n^2 + 50n$$

Here, the n^2 term dominates the $50n$ term since, for $n >= 50$, we have

$$n^2 + 50n <= n^2 + n^2 = 2n^2$$

Thus, $n^2 + 50n$ would lead to an $O(n^2)$ categorization because of the dominance of the n^2 term.

Table 10.1
Some Typical $f(n)$ Functions and Associated Run Times

	Assuming Proportionality Constant $K = 1$ and One Operation per Microsecond, Approximate Run Times for Input of Size		
$f(n)$	10^3	10^5	10^6
$\log_2 n$	0.000010 seconds	0.000017 seconds	0.000020 seconds
n	0.001 seconds	0.1 seconds	1 second
$n \log_2 n$	0.01 seconds	1.7 seconds	20 seconds
n^2	1 second	3 hours	12 days
n^3	17 minutes	32 centuries	3×10^4 centuries
2^n	10^{285} centuries	10^{10^4} years	10^{10^5} years

In general, the problem of big-O categorization reduces to finding the dominant term in an expression representing the number of operations or amount of memory required by an algorithm.

Example 10.7 Use big-O notation to analyze the time efficiency of the following fragment of C++ code.

```
for (k = 1; k <= n / 2; ++k)
{
   .
   .
   .
     for (j = 1; j <= n * n; ++j)
     {
         .
         .
         .
     }
}
```

Since these loops are nested, the number of times that statements within the innermost loop are executed is the product of the number of repetitions of the two individual loops. Hence, the efficiency is $n^3/2$, or $O(n^3)$ in big-O terms, with a constant of proportionality equal to 1/2.

Note that the important principle illustrated by this example is that, for two loops with $O[f_1(n)]$ and $O[f_2(n)]$ efficiencies, the efficiency of the nesting of these two loops (in any order) is $O[f_1(n) * f_2(n)]$.

Example 10.8 Use big-O notation to analyze the time efficiency of the following fragment of C++ code.

```
for (k = 1; k <= n / 2; ++k)
{
    .
    .
    .
}
for (j = 1; j <= n * n; ++j)
{
   .
   .
   .
}
```

Since one loop follows the other, the number of operations executed by both of them is the sum of the individual loop efficiencies. Hence, the efficiency is $n/2 + n^2$, or $O(n^2)$ in big-O terms.

The important principle illustrated by Example 10.8 is that, for two loops with $O[f_1(n)]$ and $O[f_2(n)]$ efficiencies, the efficiency of the sequencing of these two loops (in any order) is $O[f_D(n)]$, where $f_D(n)$ is the dominant of the functions $f_1(n)$ and $f_2(n)$.

Example 10.9 Use big-O notation to analyze the time efficiency of the following fragment of C++ code.

```
k = n;
while (k > 1)
{
    .
    .
    .
    k = k / 2;
}
```

Since the loop control variable is cut in half each time through the loop, the number of times that statements inside the loop will be executed is $\log_2 n$. Note that the halving of a loop is central to the binary search algorithm, which will be explored further in Section 10.5. The principle emerging from Example 10.9 is that an algorithm that halves the data remaining to be processed on each iteration of a loop will be an $O(\log_2 n)$ algorithm.

Table 10.2, which lists frequently occurring dominant terms, will prove helpful in our future big-O analyses of algorithms. It is worthwhile to characterize briefly some of the classes of algorithms that arise due to the dominant terms listed in Table 10.2. Algorithms whose efficiency is dominated by a $\log_a n$ term [and hence are categorized as $O(\log_a n)$] are often called *logarithmic algorithms.* Because $\log_a n$ will increase much more slowly than n itself, logarithmic algorithms are generally very efficient.

Algorithms whose efficiency can be expressed in terms of a polynomial of the form

$$a_m n^m + a_{m-1} n^{m-1} + \ldots + a_2 n^2 + a_1 n + a_0$$

are called *polynomial algorithms.* Since the highest power of n will dominate such a polynomial, such algorithms are $O(n^m)$. The only polynomial algorithms we will discuss in this book have m = 1, 2, or 3, and they are called *linear, quadratic,* or *cubic algorithms,* respectively.

Algorithms with efficiency dominated by a term of the form a^n are called *exponential algorithms.* Exponential algorithms are of more theoretical rather than practical interest because they cannot reasonably be run on typical computers for moderate values of n.

Big-O Analysis of Bubble Sort

We are now ready to carry out some real comparisons between the three sorting methods we have discussed so far—bubble, insertion, and selection. To do so, we must determine functions $f(n)$ that allow us to make statements such as, "Sorting algorithm

Table 10.2
Common Dominant Terms in Expressions for Algorithmic Efficiency, Based on the Variable n

n dominates $\log_a n$, a is often 2
$n \log_a n$ dominates n, a is often 2
n^2 dominates $n \log_a n$
n^m dominates n^k when $m > k$
a^n dominates n^m for any $a > 1$ and $m \geq 0$

A NOTE OF INTEREST

Artificial Intelligence and the Complexity of Algorithms

Perhaps no area of computer science demands as much in terms of efficient algorithms as does *artificial intelligence* (AI). Those engaged in research in this field are concerned with writing programs that have the computer mimic intelligent human behavior in limited domains such as natural language understanding, theorem proving, and game playing.

Why is efficiency so important in such programs? Typically, the strategy behind such a system is to have the computer search an enormous number of possibilities for the solution to the problem it is given. These possibilities comprise what is called the *state space* for the problem. For instance, for a computer program that plays a game such as checkers or chess, the state space would be a suitable representation of all game board configurations that could eventually be generated from the current state of the game. The computer's goal is to search through the state space, looking for a state in which it would win the game. The state space determined by the initial configuration of a chess game has been computed to be about 10^{120} different possible moves. The time required for a computer to examine each of these different moves, assuming it could examine one every microsecond, would be 10^{95} years. Even for a simpler game such as checkers, the time required for a computer to search all states in the game would require 10^{23} years.

The reason for these extraordinarily large and impractical time frames is that a "brute force" strategy of searching all states in such AI applications leads to exponential algorithms. To avoid exponential algorithms, researchers in artificial intelligence have attempted to follow the lead of human reasoning. That is, the human mind seems able to eliminate many of the possibilities in a search space without ever examining them. Similarly, AI programmers attempt to weed out large sections of the state space to be searched using what are known as *heuristics*. Heuristics are rules of thumb that enable one to rule out a vast number of possible states by doing some relatively simple computations. For instance, in checkers or chess, a heuristic might involve a mathematical formula that attached a positive or negative weight to a particular state of the game. Those states for which the heuristic value indicates a probable lack of success in future searching are simply eliminated from the state space.

Since a heuristic is the computational equivalent of an educated guess, it runs the risk of making an error. However, it is often viewed as a worthwhile risk if it can enhance the efficiency of the search algorithm to a category that is no longer exponential.

X requires $O[f(n)]$comparisons." If it turns out that all three sorts share the same $f(n)$ function, then we can conclude that the differences between them are not approaching an order of magnitude scale. Rather, they would be more subtle distinctions, which would not appear as dramatic run-time differences.

We also realize that the key to doing a big-O analysis is to focus our attention on the loops in the algorithm. We do that first for the bubble sort. Recall the loop structure of the bubble sort.

```
k = 0;                                                   ─┐
exchangeMade = true;                                      │
while ((k < n - 1) && exchangeMade)                       │
{                                                         │
     exchangeMade = false;                                │
     ++k;                                                 │
     for (j = 0; j < n - k; ++j)          ─┐              │
                                           │              │
          if (list[j] > list[j + 1])       │              │ Outer Loop
          {                                │              │
               temp = list[j];             │ Inner Loop   │
               list[j] = list[j + 1];      │              │
               list[j + 1] = temp;         │              │
               exchangeMade = true;        │              │
     }                                    ─┘              │
}                                                        ─┘
```

Let us assume that we have a worst case possible for the bubble sort, in which the `exchangeMade` variable is always set to `true` so that an early exit is never made from the outer loop. If we then consider the comparison at the top of the inner loop, we note that it will be executed first $n-1$ times, then $n-2$ times, and so on down to one time for the final execution of the inner loop. Hence, the number of comparisons will be the sum of the sequence of numbers:

$$\begin{array}{c}(n-1)\\(n-2)\\ \cdot \\ \cdot \\ \cdot \\ 1\end{array}$$

A formula from algebra will show this sum to be

$$n(n-1) / 2$$

Thus, we conclude that the bubble sort is an $O(n^2)$ algorithm in those situations for which the `exchangeMade` test does not allow an early loop exit.

Big-O Analysis of Insertion Sort

Recall that the loop structure of the insertion sort is given by

```
for (k = 1; k < n; ++k)                                    ─┐
                                                            │
{                                                           │
   itemToInsert = list[k];                                  │
   j = k - 1;                                               │
   stillLooking = true;                                     │
   while ((j >= 0) && stillLooking )      ─┐                │
         if (itemToInsert < list[j])       │                │  Outer Loop
         {                                 │                │
              list[j + 1] = list[j];       │  Inner Loop    │
              --j;                         │                │
         }                                 │                │
         else                              │                │
              stillLooking = false;       ─┘                │
   list[j + 1] =  itemToInsert;                             │
}                                                          ─┘
```

Here, if the inner loop is never short-circuited by `stillLooking`, the comparison appearing as its first statement will be executed once for the first execution of the outer loop, then twice, and so on, reaching $n-1$ executions on the final pass. We have a situation virtually identical to our preliminary analysis of the bubble sort. That is, the number of comparisons can be bounded by $n^2/2$, and the algorithm is therefore $O(n^2)$. Of course, with the insertion sort, the hope is that setting the Boolean variable `stillLooking` in the `else` clause can reduce the number of comparisons made by the inner loop. However, it is clear that we can concoct many data sets for which this will have little or no effect. So, as with bubble sort, we are forced to conclude that insertion sort cannot guarantee better than $O(n^2)$ comparisons.

Big-O Analysis of Selection Sort

The loop structure of this algorithm was given by

```
for (int k = 0; k < length - 1; ++k)
{
    minPosition = k;
    for (int j = k + 1; j < length; ++j)
          if (list[j] < list[minPosition]
                minPosition = j;
    if (minPosition != k)
    {
          temp = list[minPosition];
          list[minPosition] = list[k];
          list[k] = temp;
    }
}
```

Inner Loop

Outer Loop

A little investigation uncovers a familiar pattern to the nested loops of the selection sort. Observe that the first time the inner loop is executed, the comparison in the `if` statement will be made $n-1$ times. Then it will be made $n-2$ times, $n-3$ times, etc., and, finally, just one time. This is precisely the way the `if` statement in the bubble sort was executed in repeated passes. Thus, like the bubble and insertion sorts, the selection sort is an $O(n^2)$ algorithm in terms of number of comparisons. The area in which the selection sort potentially offers better efficiency is that the number of interchanges of data in array locations is guaranteed to be $O(n)$ because the swap in selection sort occurs in the outer loop. In both of the other sorts, the swap occurs in the inner loop but is subject to a conditional test. This means that, in their worst cases, both of the other algorithms require $O(n^2)$ swaps as well as $O(n^2)$ comparisons.

Despite the fact that selection sort will usually fare better in the number of data interchanges required to sort an array, it has a drawback not found in the other two. It is apparently impossible to short-circuit the nested loop in selection sort when it is given a list in nearly sorted order. So, for such data sets, the selection sort may be an order of magnitude worse than the other two. This is initially rather disheartening news. It seems as if it is impossible to declare any of the sorts a decisive winner. Indeed, our big-O analyses indicate that there is little to choose from the bubble, insertion, and selection algorithms.

The fact that we were able to reach such a conclusion systematically, however, is significant. It reveals the value of a big-O analysis. After all, even knowledge of a negative variety can be valuable in choosing appropriate algorithms under certain circumstances. For instance, if a particular application usually involved adding a small amount of data at the end of an already sorted list and then resorting, we now know we should avoid a selection sort. Moreover, when we study more powerful sorting techniques in the next section (and again in Chapter 16), we will see that it is indeed possible to break the $O(n^2)$ barrier limiting each of our three methods.

Exercises 10.3

1. Do a big-O analysis for those statements inside each of the following nested loop constructs.

a.
```
for (k = 1; k <= n; ++k)
  for (j = 6; j <= m; ++j)
       .
       .
       .
```

b.
```
 for (k = 1; k <= n; ++k)
{
  j = n;
  while (j > 0)
  {
       .
       .
       .
       j = j / 2;
  }
}
```

c.
```
k = 1;
do
{
  j = 1;
  do
  {
       .
       .
       .
       j = 2 * j;
  } while (j <= n);
  ++k;
} while (k <= n);
```

2. Suppose we have an algorithm that requires precisely

$$6 * \log_2 n + 34 * n^2 + 12$$

operations for an input of n data items. Indicate which of the following are valid big-O classifications of the algorithm.

a. $O(n^3)$
b. $O(n^2)$
c. $O(n)$
d. $O(n^2 * \log_2 n)$
e. $O(n * \log_2 n)$
f. $O(\log_2 n)$
g. $O(1)$

Of those that you have indicated are valid, which is the best big-O classification? Why?

3. A certain algorithm always requires 32 operations, regardless of the amount of data input. Provide a big-O classification of the algorithm that reflects the efficiency of the algorithm as accurately as possible.

4. An algorithm has an efficiency $O(|n^2\sin(n)|)$. Is it any better than $O(n^2)$ for a large integer n?

5. Suppose that each of the following expressions represents the number of logical operations in an algorithm as a function of n, the size of the list being manipulated. For each expression, determine the dominant term and then classify the algorithm in big-O terms.

a. $n^3 + n^2\log_2 n + n^3\log_2 n$
b. $n + 4n^2 + 4^n$
c. $48n^4 + 16n^2 + \log_8 n + 2^n$

6. Consider the following nested loop construct. Categorize its efficiency in terms of the variable n using big-O notation. Finally, suppose the statements indicated by the ellipses required four main memory accesses (each requiring 1 microsecond) and two disk file accesses (each requiring 1 millisecond). Express in milliseconds the amount of time this construct would require to execute if n were 1000.

```
x = 1;
do
{
    y = n;
    while (y > 0)
    {
            .
            .
            .
            —y;
    }
    x = x + x;
} while (x < n * n);
```

7. Look back at the data set you constructed for Exercise 11 in Section 10.2. Evaluate the performance of insertion sort on that data set in terms of a big-O analysis.

8. You and a friend are engaged in an argument. She claims that a certain algorithm is $O(n^2\log_2 n)$ in its efficiency. You claim that it is $O(n^2)$. Consider and answer the following questions:

a. Are there circumstances under which both of you could be correct? If so, explain them.
b. Are there circumstances under which both of you could be wrong? If so, explain them.
c. Are there circumstances under which she could be right and you could be wrong? If so, explain them.
d. Are there circumstances under which she could be wrong and you could be right? If so, explain them.

9. You and your friend are engaged in another argument. She claims that a certain algorithm is $O(n^2 + \log_2 n)$ in its efficiency. You claim that it is $O(n^2)$. Consider and answer the following questions.

a. Are there circumstances under which both of you could be correct? If so, explain them.
b. Are there circumstances under which both of you could be wrong? If so, explain them.
c. Are there circumstances under which she could be right and you could be wrong? If so, explain them.
d. Are there circumstances under which she could be wrong and you could be right? If so, explain them.

10. Is an $O(n^2)$ algorithm also an $O(n^3)$ algorithm? Justify your answer in a carefully written paragraph.

10.4 The Time/Space Trade-Off: Pointer Sort and Radix Sort

Objectives

a. to understand the concept of a pointer
b. to understand the difference between physically sorting and logically sorting
c. to apply pointers when logically sorting an array without interchanging data items
d. to understand what is meant by the time/space trade-off
e. to understand the radix sort algorithm and trace its action on appropriate data sets
f. to analyze the time and space efficiency of the radix sort algorithm
g. to understand why the radix sort algorithm is not as generally applicable as other sorting algorithms we have studied

Early in our discussion of efficiency considerations, we noted that true run-time efficiency was best measured in fundamental machine operations and that one instruction in a high-level language may actually translate into many such primitive operations. To illustrate this, suppose that the data being sorted by one of our algorithms are records, each of which requires 100 bytes of internal storage. Then, depending on your computer, it is entirely conceivable that one comparison or assignment statement in a high-level language could generate a machine language loop with 100 repetitions of such fundamental operations: one for each of the bytes that must be swapped. Those seemingly innocent portions of code, which swap two records using a temporary storage location, lead to the movement of 300 bytes inside the machine.

The first question we address in this section is whether, in such a situation, we can replace this large-scale internal transfer of entire records with the much swifter operation of swapping two integers. Although the solution we discuss does not achieve an order of magnitude speed increase in the big-O sense, it nonetheless reduces the number of actual machine-level swaps by a factor proportional to the record length involved, a factor that could produce a noticeable improvement in the function's run time.

Bubble Sort Implemented with Pointers

So far, our algorithms to sort data have implicitly assumed that the data are to be *physically sorted;* that is, the data are to be arranged in order within the array being sorted. Hence, the data in the first index of our array are the data that come first in order according to the key field, the data in the second index are second in order, and so on. However, if we are only interested in processing the data of a list in order by key field, is it really necessary that the data be arranged in physically ordered fashion in computer memory? No. It is possible to step logically through the data in order by key without physically arranging it that way in memory. To do so, we must use another array of *pointers.*

Pointer: A pointer is a memory location in which we store the location of a data item as opposed to the data item itself. In the case of an array, a pointer can be the index position of a data item in the array.

Pointers can keep track of the *logical order* of the data without requiring them to be physically moved. At the end of our sorting routine, `pointer[0]` tells us the location of the data that should come first in our alphabetical listing, `pointer[1]` contains the location of the data that should come second, and so on. The sorting algorithm itself uses the logic of the bubble sort to interchange pointers instead of interchanging data. The actual data never move; they remain precisely where they were stored on initial input. Instead of the expensive, time-consuming swapping of potentially large records, we are able to swap integer pointers quickly.

A C++ function to implement this *pointer sort* technique follows. In addition to the declarations we have already been using in this chapter, this function assumes an external declaration of the form

```
typedef int PointerArray[MAX_LIST_SIZE];
```

Besides the `list` array, the function also receives an array `pointer` of type `PointerArray`. The function initializes the pointer array to the state pictured in the "Before" snapshot of Figure 10.7. Then, via repeated swaps of integer pointers, the array is returned as shown in the "After" snapshot. As the figure indicates, the `list` array itself is never altered.

```
void pointerBubbleSort(ListType list, PointerArray pointer, int n)
{
   int j, k, temp;
   bool exchangeMade;

   // Initialize pointer array

   for (k = 0; k < n; ++k)
      pointer[k] = k;

   k = 0;
   exchangeMade = true;

   // Make up to n - 1 passes through array, exit early if no exchanges
   // are made on previous pass

   while ((k < n - 1) && exchangeMade)
   {
      exchangeMade = false;
      ++k;
      for (j = 0; j < n - k; ++j)
         // Compare via pointers
         if (list[pointer[j]] > list[pointer[j + 1]])
         {
            temp = pointer[j];          // Swap pointers
            pointer[j] = pointer[j + 1];
            pointer[j + 1] = temp;
            exchangeMade = true;
         }
   }
}
```

Figure 10.7
"Before" (left) and "After" (right) snapshots of pointer sort

	Key field of **list**	**pointer**
0	MAXWELL	0
1	BUCKNER	1
2	LANIER	2
3	AARON	3

Snapshot of **list** and **pointer** immediately after initialization

Key field of **list**	**pointer**
MAXWELL	3
BUCKNER	1
LANIER	2
AARON	0

Snapshot of **list** and **pointer** returned by **pointerBubbleSort**

Example 10.10 Given the physically ordered list of Figure 10.7, trace the action of function `pointerBubbleSort` on the array of pointers during each pass through the algorithm.

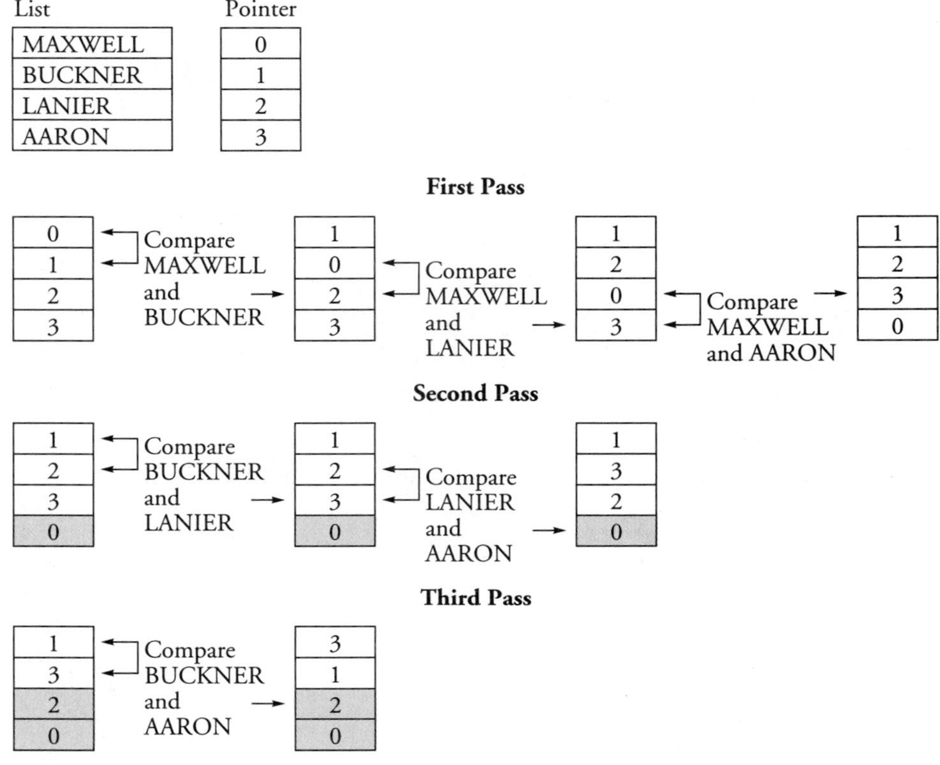

Example 10.11 Suppose that `pointerBubbleSort` was invoked from a main program or another function via the call

```
pointerBubbleSort (studentList, pointer, numberOfStudents);
```

where `numberOfStudents`, `studentList`, and `pointer` are of appropriate types. If the logical order established by the pointer array is alphabetical by student name, explain how a report that listed students alphabetically could be printed after this invocation. Assume the existence of a function `printHeading` to print column headings for the report and a function `printStudent` to receive an individual student object and print it in formatted form as one detail line of the report.

After the call to `pointerBubbleSort`, `pointer[0]` contains the position of the object that is first in alphabetical order, `pointer[1]` contains the position of the object that is second, and so on. Hence, the following loop will step through all of the entries in the desired order:

```
printHeading();
for (k = 0; k < numberOfStudents; ++k)
    printStudent(studentList[pointer[k]]);
```

A NOTE OF INTEREST

Virtual Memory and Program Performance

The more sophisticated operating systems of today often use what is known as *virtual memory.* In such systems, a programmer is able to view main memory as virtually limitless. That is, such systems give the programmer the illusion of having "infinite" main memory. How is this possible? Virtual memory is not true main memory. Rather, it is memory divided into *pages*—some of which actually reside in main memory while others reside on disk storage. When you write a program that accesses a virtual-memory page not presently in main memory, the operating system must execute a *paging algorithm.* A paging algorithm is responsible for bringing into main memory the page your program requests and deciding which page presently in main memory should be swapped out to disk storage to make room for the new page.

Virtual memory has made programmers' lives much easier. It means that we can now declare arrays in our programs that are much larger than arrays that could be declared in older systems that did not have virtual memory. Is any price paid for this convenience? Most definitely yes! Paging is the hidden price paid for the programming convenience offered by virtual memory systems. A sorting algorithm applied to an array that cannot fit in nonvirtual main memory will work correctly, but it will also cause paging to occur. Since paging represents a disk access, it will take much longer than a pure memory access, which does not generate a page swap. An operation that generates a page swap can be slower than one that doesn't by a factor as large as 1000 (milliseconds as opposed to microseconds).

The key to the efficiency of such a sorting algorithm is not only a factor of its big-O categorization but also whether the algorithm forces an excessive amount of paging to occur. Hence, even though we may know that the algorithm is $O(n^2)$ in the number of comparisons it uses, the real key to the amount of time it takes the algorithm to run is also tied to how many of those comparisons force a page swap to occur. Many a programmer has been unpleasantly surprised to find out a program that should run in seconds according to a big-O analysis of its underlying algorithm ends up requiring minutes because paging occurs.

Efficiency Analysis for Sorts Implemented with Pointers. The pointer technique illustrated here for the bubble sort may also be used with the insertion and selection algorithms. In any of these cases, the mere introduction of the pointer strategy will not reduce the big-O categorization of the sort. However, in cases where the data items being sorted use enough internal storage to slow down swapping times substantially, the pointer sort can attain a considerable savings in run time.

Is this run-time savings achieved without any sacrifice? An old saying that has been passed down by computer people since the days of the early vacuum tube machines is, "You get nothing for nothing." We have not escaped the consequences of that adage by using pointers to increase run-time efficiency. The pointers store *data about data;* this requires additional memory. If your application is not approaching the limits of memory, this cost may not be crucial. In certain situations, however, it could be the last straw for a program running short of memory. Thus, the pointer sort is essentially a trade-off; by using more memory, we get a program that runs faster.

This *time/space trade-off* continually recurs in the analysis of computer algorithms. Many sophisticated techniques to increase speed will need to store substantial data about data to do so. Those algorithms that solve a problem in a fashion that saves space *and* decreases run time are indeed worthy of special praise. We will be sure to note them.

Finally, the notion of a pointer, as defined and introduced here, plays an important role in our study of data structures beginning in Chapter 12. The time you spend exploring the details of the pointer sort technique will prove very valuable in your understanding of this topic in the future.

Radix Sort

The *radix sort* algorithm is also called the *bin sort,* a name derived from its origin as a technique used on (now obsolete) machines called card sorters. These machines would sort a deck of keypunched cards by shuffling the cards into small bins, then collecting the cards from the bins into a newly arranged deck, and repeating this shuffling–collection process until the deck was magically sorted. There was, as we shall see, a very clever algorithm behind this rapid shuffling.

For integer data, the repeated passes of a radix sort focus first on the ones digit of each number, then on the tens digit, the hundreds digit, and so on until the highest order digit of the largest number is reached. For string data, the first pass hinges on the rightmost character in each string with successive passes always shifting their attention one character position to the left. To illustrate the algorithm, we will trace it on the following list of nine integers:

```
459 254 472 534 649 239 432 654 477
```

On each pass through these data, radix sort will arrange them into ten sublists (bins)—one sublist for each of the digits 0 through 9. Hence, on the first pass, all the numbers with a ones digit equal to 0 are grouped in one sublist, all those with a ones digit equal to 1 are grouped in another sublist, and so on. The resulting sublists follow:

Digit	Sublist		
0			
1			
2	472	432	
3			
4	254	534	654
5			
6			
7	477		
8			
9	459	649	239

The sublists are then collected into one large list with the numbers in the sublist for 0 coming first, then those in the sublist for 1, and so on up to the sublist for 9. Hence, we have a newly arranged list:

```
472 432 254 534 654 477 459 649 239
```

This new list is again partitioned into sublists, this time keying on the tens digit. The result is shown below:

Digit	Sublist		
0			
1			
2			
3	432	534	239
4	649		
5	654	254	459
6			
7	472	477	
8			
9			

Note that in each sublist the data are arranged in order relative to their last two digits. The sublists would now be collected into a new master list:

```
432 534 239 649 654 254 459 472 477
```

Now, focusing on the hundreds digit, the master list is classified into ten sublists one more time. These final sublists are shown below. When the sublists are collected from this final partitioning, the data are arranged in ascending order.

Digit	Sublist			
0				
1				
2	239	254		
3				
4	432	459	472	477
5	534			
6	649	654		
7				
8				
9				

A pseudocode statement of the radix sort algorithm follows:

1. Begin with the current digit as the ones digit
2. While there is still a digit on which to classify data
    - 2.1 for each number in the master list
        - 2.1.1 add that number to the appropriate sublist, keying on the current digit
    - 2.2 for each sublist (from 0 through 9)
        - 2.2.1 append that sublist to a newly arranged master list
    - 2.3 Advance the current digit one place to the left

If the radix sort is applied to character strings instead of integers, this algorithm proceeds from the rightmost character to the leftmost character instead of from the ones digit to the highest order digit.

Efficiency of Radix Sort An analysis of the loop structure in the preceding pseudocode for radix sort indicates that, for each pass through the outer `while` loop, $O(n)$ operations must be performed. These $O(n)$ operations consist of doing the arithmetic necessary to isolate a particular digit within a number, appending that number to the proper sublist, and then collecting it again into a new master list. Since the outer `while` loop will only be executed C times—where C is the number of digits (or characters) in the integer (or string)—the radix sort is an $O(n)$ sorting algorithm.

Although the radix sort is significantly faster than the other $O(n^2)$ algorithms we have studied in this chapter, there are again trade-off factors to consider. It is potentially much less space efficient than the other sorting algorithms. This is due to the need for storing sublists for each of the possible digits in the number or characters in the string. Using arrays to store the sublists and without any prior knowledge about the distribution of the data, we would be forced to allocate an additional $10n$ storage locations when sorting an array of n integers and $27n$ storage locations when sorting n strings of letters and blanks. We shall alleviate this memory crunch somewhat when we study linked lists in Chapter 12, but even then, the radix sort will remain a space-inefficient algorithm compared to other sorting algorithms. Other criteria negating the very good time efficiency of the radix sort are its inflexibility for data of varying size and the fact that, although $O(n)$ in time, its constant of proportionality in this regard is often large enough to make it less time efficient than the more sophisticated sorting algorithms we will study in Chapter 16.

Example 10.12 Assume the existence of the following declarations and functions to perform a radix sort on an array of four-digit numbers.

```
int const MAX_LIST_SIZE = 100;

typedef int ListType[MAX_LIST_SIZE];
typedef ListType BinStructureType[10];
typedef int BinCounterType[10];

// Function: digit
// Computes the kth digit in number
//
// Inputs: integers number and k
// Output: the kth digit in number

int digit(int number, int k);

// Function: initializeCounters
// Initializes all counters to zero

void initializeCounters(BinCounterType binCounters);

// Function: addToBin
// Insert number in BinStructure indicated by place
//
// Inputs: a BinStructure, a BinCounter, a number and a place
// Outputs: a BinStructure and a BinCounter

void addToBin(BinStructureType bins,
   BinCounterType binCounters, int number, int place);

// Function: collectBins
// Append items in successive bins into one single list
//
// Inputs: a BinStructure along with a BinCounter
// Outputs: a list consisting of the (appended) items in the bins

void collectBins(ListType list, BinStructureType bins,
   BinCounterType binCounters);
```

Then the C++ code for this radix sort is:

```
void radixSort(ListType list, int n)
{
   int j, k;
   BinStructureType bins;
   BinCounterType binCounters;

   initializeCounters(binCounters);
```

```
   // For k loop controls digit used to classify data.
   for (k = 1; k <= 4; ++k)
   {
      // The inner loop iterates through all numbers, putting them into
      // bin determined by kth digit.
      for (j = 0; j < n; ++j)
         addToBin (bins, binCounters, list[j], digit(list[j], k));
      collectBins (list, bins, binCounters);
      initializeCounters(binCounters);
   }
}
```

Exercises 10.4

1. Suppose that you are given the following list of keys:

0	9438
1	3216
2	416
3	9021
4	1142
5	3316
6	94

Show what the contents of the pointer array would be after each pass through the outer loop of function `pointerBubbleSort` discussed in this section.

2. Consider again the data set given in Exercise 1. How many passes would be made through the outer loop of the radix sort algorithm for these data? Trace the contents of the array after each of these passes.

3. Consider the following list of strings:

0	CHOCOLATE
1	VANILLA
2	CARAMEL
3	PEACH
4	STRAWBERRY
5	CHERRY

How many passes would be made through the outer loop of the radix sort algorithm for these data? Trace the contents of the list after each of these passes.

4. Explain the difference between physical and logical ordering.

5. Cite an application in which the mere logical ordering of data, as achieved by the pointer sort technique, would not be sufficient; that is, give an application in which physical ordering of data is required.

6. What is the time/space trade-off? Define and discuss various contexts in which it may arise.

7. When the bubble sort was modified with an array of pointers, did it improve its $O(n^2)$ run-time efficiency in a significant sense? Under what circumstances would you call the improvement in efficiency significant? Provide your answer to this question in a short essay in which you define "significant" and then explain why the circumstance you describe would lead to a significant improvement.

8. The bubble, insertion, and selection sort algorithms are all $O(n)$ in their space requirements. That is, each algorithm requires memory proportional to n to sort the

Objectives

a. to formalize a context in which search algorithms may be applied
b. to understand the logic of the sequential search algorithm
c. to analyze the efficiency of the sequential search algorithm
d. to understand the logic of the binary search algorithm
e. to recognize situations in which a key-to-address transformation may be used as an $O(1)$ search method

items in an array of n items. From a big-O perspective, what are the space requirements of these algorithms when the pointer sort technique is incorporated into their logic?

9. Would you expect the pointer strategy to have the *least* effect on the run-time efficiency of the bubble, selection, or insertion sort? Provide a rationale for your answer in a short essay.
10. Suppose you have 1000 objects to be sorted. Would the run-time efficiency of the pointer sort increase significantly if the 1000 objects were broken into four groups, each group sorted, and then merged together as one large sorted array as compared to sorting the initial unsegmented array? Why or why not?
11. Incorporate the pointer sort technique into the selection sort algorithm.
12. Incorporate the pointer sort technique into the insertion sort algorithm.
13. Write the functions assumed to exist in the version of `radixSort` given in Example 10.12.
14. Write a radix sort function to sort an arbitrary array of integers. Analyze the space efficiency of your function.
15. Write a radix sort function to sort an array of strings. Analyze the space efficiency of your function. Be sure to state carefully the assumptions you make about strings in performing your analysis of space efficiency.
16. Describe the complications in implementing the radix sort algorithm for an array of real numbers. Discuss a strategy that could be used to overcome these complications.

10.5 Simple Search Algorithms

Many programs extensively employ algorithms that find a particular data item in a large collection of such items. Such algorithms, typically called *search algorithms,* are given the value of a key field that identifies the item being sought; they then return either all of the data associated with that particular key or a flag indicating that nothing was found. You saw a search algorithm in Section 10.4 when we described some operations that were frequently required in processing arrays. We now explore search algorithms and subject them to an efficiency analysis using the big-O notation we have developed.

The search operation will look for an object in a list that is associated with a `target` key value. Thus, rather than comparing two objects of type `element`, the search algorithm will have to compare a key value and an object of type element. We will assume that the `element` type has overloaded the standard operators for comparing a key value and an object of the `element` type. The general setup for the search algorithms we discuss in this chapter is given by the following skeletal declarations:

```
int const MAX_LIST_SIZE = 100;
typedef int element;
typedef element ListType[MAX_LIST_SIZE];

// Function: search
// Find the object associated with the target key value
//
// Inputs: a list of objects, its length, and a target key value
// Outputs: if the target key is found, return true and the object
// associated with the target key; otherwise, return false

bool search(ListType list, int n, KeyType target, element &object);
```

Figure 10.8 graphically portrays this setup.

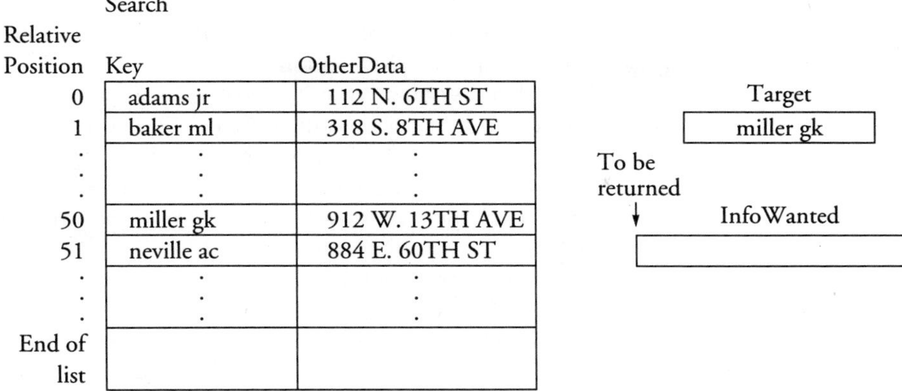

Figure 10.8
General setup for search algorithm

Sequential Search Algorithm

The task of a computer scientist working with search algorithms may be compared to that of a librarian. Just as the librarian must devise a method of storing books on shelves in a fashion that allows patrons to find the books they want easily, so must a computer scientist devise methods of organizing large collections of electronic data so that records within those data can always be found quickly. Imagine the plight of the librarian who just throws books on shelves as they are unpacked from shipping boxes, without any consideration toward organizing the chaos! Unless the library had an artificially small collection, it would take patrons an impractical length of time to find their reading material. Because of the lack of any organizational order imposed on the books, the only search strategy available would be to pull books from the shelves in some arbitrary sequence until the desired book was found.

As a programmer given a completely unordered set of data, this is the same strategy you would have to follow. The logic of such a *sequential search* strategy is extremely simple and appears in the following `sequentialSearch` function.

```
bool sequentialSearch(ListType list, int n, KeyType target, element &object)
{
   int k = 0;
   bool found = false;

   while ((k < n) && ! found)
      if (list[k] == target)
         found = true;
      else
         ++k;
   if (found)
      object = list[k];
   return found;
}
```

Efficiency of Sequential Search Unfortunately, the simplicity of the sequential search is offset by its inefficiency as a search strategy. Obviously, the average number of probes into the list before the target key is found will be $n/2$, where n is the number of records in the list. For unsuccessful invocations of the function, all n records must be checked before we can conclude failure. Thus, in terms of a big-O classification, the method is clearly $O(n)$. This may not seem bad when compared to the $O(n^2)$ efficiency of our sorting methods, but searching is conceptually a much simpler operation than sorting, and it should be significantly faster. Moreover, although $O(n)$ may seem fast enough at microsecond speeds, there are many applications where an $O(n)$ time factor can be unacceptably slow.

For instance, when a compiler processes your source program in C++, it must continually search a list of identifiers that have been previously declared. (This list is typically called a *symbol table*.) Hence, in such an application, the search operation merely represents the inner loop within a much more complex outer loop that is repeating until it reaches the end of your source file. An inner loop repeated at $O(n)$ speeds makes your compiler intolerably slow.

Another situation in which $O(n)$ is not good enough for searching occurs when the list being searched is stored in a *disk file* instead of a main memory array. Now, because accessing data on disk is a much slower operation than accessing data in main memory, each probe into the list might conceivably require approximately 1 millisecond (one-thousandth of a second) instead of 1 microsecond. Searching such a list of 1 million records at $O(n)$ speed would hence require 1000 seconds instead of just 1 second, which is too long to wait for one record and is certain to generate angry users. We conclude that, although the sequential search may be fast enough for small and infrequently accessed lists stored in main memory, we need something that is better by an order of magnitude for many practical applications.

Binary Search Algorithm

By paying what may initially seem like a small price, we can dramatically increase the efficiency of our search effort by using a *binary search* algorithm.

1. The list of objects with keys must be maintained in physically sorted order unless we are willing to use an additional list of pointers similar to that used in the `pointerBubbleSort` algorithm. (See the Exercises at the end of this section.)
2. The number of objects in the list must be maintained in a separate variable.
3. We must be able to access randomly, by relative position, objects in the list. This is the type of access you have in C++ arrays.

For instance, suppose that the list of integer keys appearing in Figure 10.9 has the access facility of the third point just cited and that we wish to locate the randomly accessible data associated with the target key 1649. The strategy of the binary search is to begin the search in the middle of the list. In the case of Figure 10.9, this means beginning the search with the key found at position 4. Since the target we are seeking is greater than the key found at position 4, we are able to conclude that the key we want will be found among positions 5 through 9—if at all.

Figure 10.9
Physically ordered random access list of keys for binary search

Position	Key
0	1119
1	1203
2	1212
3	1519
4	1604
5	1649
6	1821
7	2312
8	2409
9	3612

Number of Records $n = 10$
`target` = 1649

We will split those positions that remain viable candidates for finding the target by accessing the middle position:

$$(5 + 9) / 2 = 7$$

Since the key at position 7 is greater than `target`, we are able to conclude that the key being sought will be found in positions 5 or 6—if it is to be found at all. Notice that, after only two accesses into the list, our list of remaining viable candidates for a match has shrunk to 2. (Compare this figure to a sequential search after two accesses into the same list.) We now split the distance between positions 5 and 6, arriving (by integer arithmetic) at position 5. Here we find the key being sought after a mere three probes into the list.

Crucial to the entire binary search algorithm are two pointers, `low` and `high`, to the bottom and top, respectively, of the current list of viable candidates. We must repeatedly compute the middle index of that portion of the list between `low` and `high` and compare the data at that middle index to the target using the following logic:

```
If list[middle]equals the target
      Search is done
      Target has been found in list
Else if list[middle] < target
      Low must be set to middle + 1
Else
      High must be set to middle - 1
```

Should these pointers ever cross, that is, if `high` were to become less than `low`, we would conclude that the target does not appear in the list. The entire algorithm is formalized in the following C++ function:

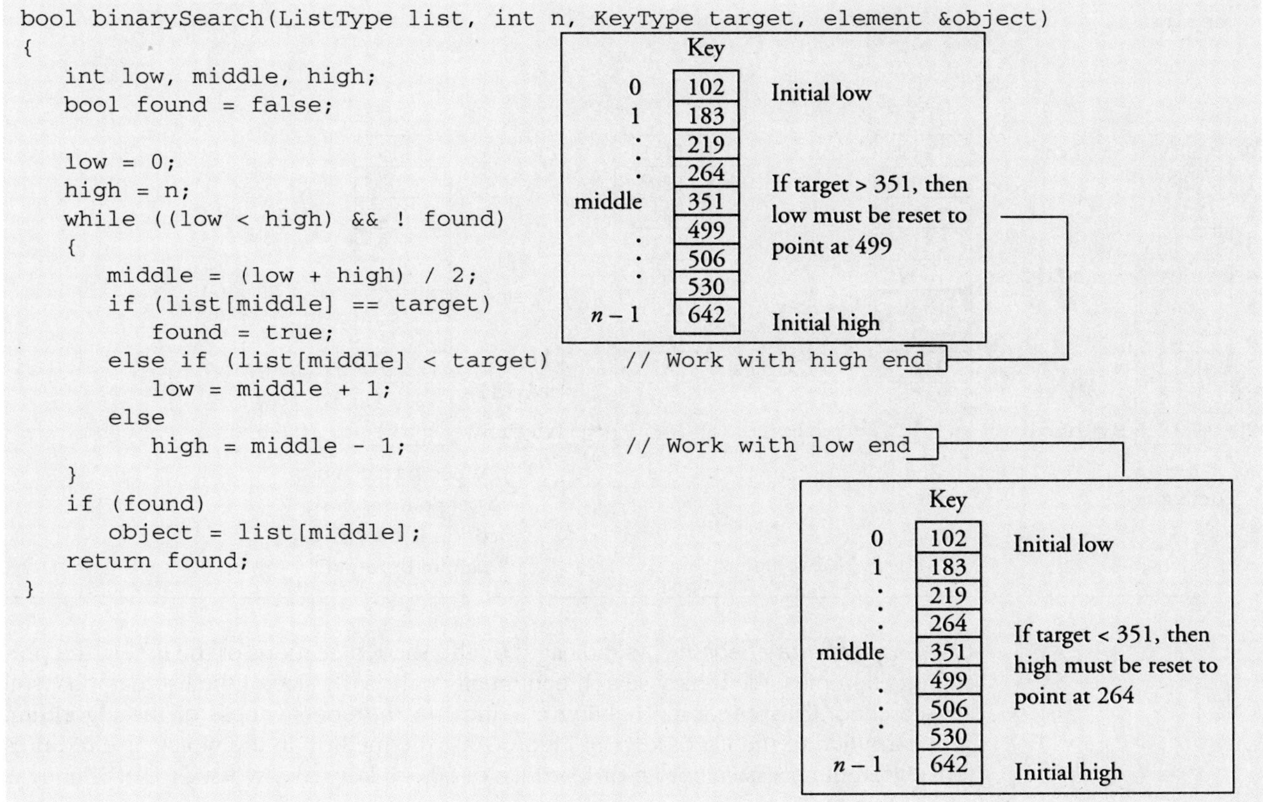

```
bool binarySearch(ListType list, int n, KeyType target, element &object)
{
   int low, middle, high;
   bool found = false;

   low = 0;
   high = n;
   while ((low < high) && ! found)
   {
      middle = (low + high) / 2;
      if (list[middle] == target)
         found = true;
      else if (list[middle] < target)      // Work with high end
         low = middle + 1;
      else
         high = middle - 1;                // Work with low end
   }
   if (found)
      object = list[middle];
   return found;
}
```

Example 10.13 Trace the action of function `binarySearch` as it locates the record associated with target 1519 in the array of Figure 10.9.

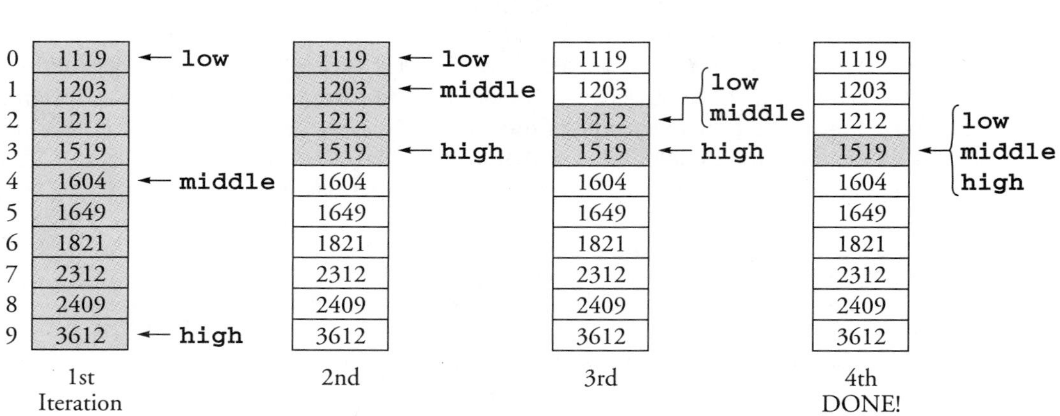

Example 10.14 Trace the action of function `binarySearch` as it reports that target 2392 cannot be found in the array of Figure 10.9.

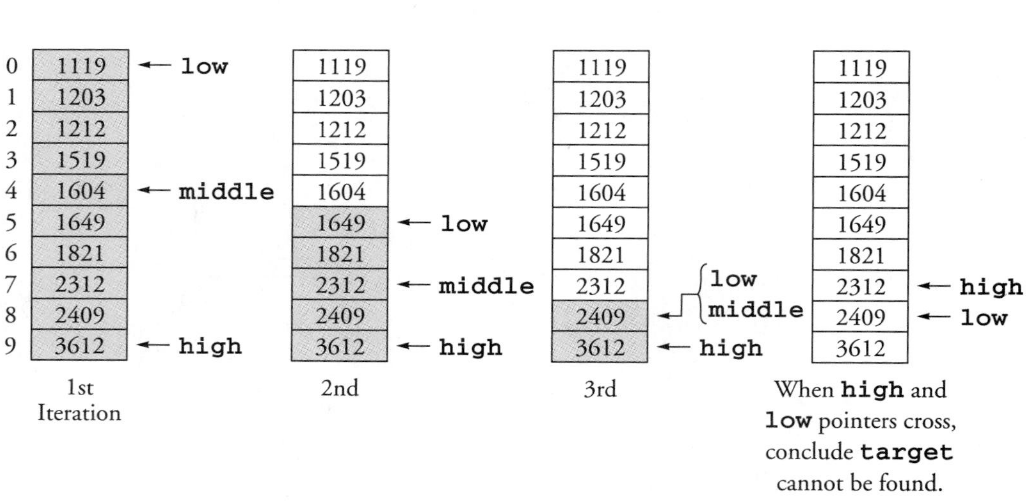

Efficiency of Binary Search As indicated by the shaded portions of the lists in the preceding examples, the binary search continually halves the size of the list that must still be searched. This continual halving is critical to the effectiveness of the algorithm. When applied to the list of keys in Figure 10.9, the method in the worst case requires four different accesses. For an ordered list of 50,000 keys, the worst case efficiency is a mere 16 different accesses. (In case you do not believe this dramatic increase in efficiency as the list gets larger, try plugging 50,000 into a hand-held calculator and count how many times you must halve the displayed number to reduce it to 1.) The same list of 1 million records stored on disk that would require approximately 1000 seconds to search sequentially will result in a virtually instantaneous response with the binary search strategy.

More formally, for a list of n items, the maximum number of times we would cut the list in half before finding the target item or declaring the search unsuccessful is

$$(\log_2 n) + 1$$

Thus, the binary search is the first $O(\log_2 n)$ algorithm we have studied (see Example 10.10). In terms of the categorizations discussed in Section 10.3, it is a logarithmic algorithm. Expressions involving a $\log_2 n$ factor will arise frequently as we analyze other algorithms. They are extremely fast compared to $O(n)$ algorithms, particularly for large values of n.

The drawback of the binary search lies not in any consideration of its processing speed but rather in a reexamination of the price that must be paid for using it. For a volatile list (that is, one undergoing frequent additions and deletions), the requirement of maintaining the list in physical order can be quite costly. For large lists, it makes the operations of adding and deleting records so inefficient that the very fast search speed is all but negated. We will analyze this problem of list maintenance in more detail in future chapters.

Key-to-Address Transformations

A search technique so simple that it is often overlooked presents itself in certain situations where a record's key value can be transformed conveniently into a position within a list by applying a function to the key value. For instance, suppose that a school assigns its students five-digit identification numbers in which the first two digits indicate the student's year of matriculation and the last three digits are simply assigned in a sequential fashion among students matriculating in a given year. Hence, the fourteenth student admitted in the class of 1999 would have the identification number

$$\underbrace{99}_{\text{year of matriculation}} \qquad \underbrace{014}_{\text{sequence number within that year}}$$

In such a situation, student records could be stored in a two-dimensional table in which rows were indexed by year of matriculation and columns indexed by sequence number within a given year. Then the integer arithmetic operations

```
key / 1000
```

and

```
key % 1000
```

yield a given student's row and column index, respectively. The address of a student's record could therefore be obtained from the student's identification number using a mere two operations.

In such situations, the search efficiency to locate a student's record is $O(1)$ in its big-O classification. The apparent restriction that must apply for this technique to work is that the transformation applied to a key to yield an address cannot yield the same address for two different students. As we shall see in Chapter 17, even this restriction can be relaxed somewhat if slightly more sophisticated search techniques are employed. Another drawback of the key-to-address transformation technique is its potentially inefficient use of space. You will perform such a space analysis for this strategy in this section's Exercises.

Exercises 10.5

1. Suppose that an array contains key values

```
18 40 46 50 52 58 63 70 77 90
```

in index locations 0 through 9. Trace the index values for the `low`, `high`, and `middle` pointers in the binary search algorithm if the `target` 43 is being sought. Repeat for `target` values 40 and 90.

2. In Exercise 10 of Section 10.2, we defined the notions of best case and worst case behavior of an algorithm. Devise sample data sets to demonstrate the best case and worst case behavior of the binary search algorithm.

3. What is a compiler symbol table? Explain why a sequential search applied to such a table is not a practical strategy.

4. Explain the difference in run-time efficiency considerations for a program that manipulates data in a main memory array versus one that accesses data stored in a disk file.

5. How many times would the `while` loop in function `binarySearch` be executed if $n = 1{,}000{,}000$?

6. Consider the following modified version of the binary search algorithm. (Modifications are indicated by a comment highlighted by asterisks.) Will this new version of the binary search algorithm work correctly for all data? If not, specify a situation in which this version will fail.

```
bool binarySearch(ListType list, int n, KeyType target, element &object)
{
   int low, middle, high;
   bool found = false;

   low = 0;
   high = n;
   while ((low < high) && ! found)
   {
       middle = (low + high) / 2;
       if (list[middle] == target)
           found = true;
       else if (list[middle] < target)
           low = middle;        // *** Modification here ***
       else
           high = middle;       // *** Modification here ***
   }
   if (found)
       object = list[middle];
   return found;
}
```

7. Consider the following modified version of the binary search algorithm. (Modifications are indicated by a comment highlighted by asterisks.) Will this new ver-

sion of the binary search algorithm work correctly for all data? If not, specify a situation in which this version will fail.

```
bool binarySearch(ListType list, int n, KeyType target, element &object)
{
   int low, middle, high;
   bool found = false;

   low = 0;
   high = n;
   do                  // *** Use do. . .while instead of while ***
   {
      middle = (low + high) / 2;
      if (list[middle] == target)
           found = true;
      else if (list[middle] < target)
           low = middle + 1;
      else
         high = middle - 1;
   } while ((low < high) && ! found); // *** Loop exit condition
   if (found)
      object = list[middle];
   return found;
}
```

8. Consider the example of a key-to-address transformation for student identification numbers given in this section. Discuss the space efficiency of this strategy. On what factor is the space efficiency dependent?
9. Devise a key-to-address transformation to locate records in a data structure for employees of the East Publishing Company. Departments in the company are identified by a one-letter code A–Z. An employee's payroll identification number consists of a department code followed by another one-letter code representing the employee's pay rate classification and a two-digit number assigned in sequential fashion to employees within a given department. Hence, the identification number DX40 is assigned to the 40th employee in department D; the X indicates the employee's pay rate category.
10. The requirement for the binary search that the data in an array be physically ordered can be circumvented by keeping track of the logical order of the data via a pointer array analogous to that used in the pointer sort. Rewrite the binary search algorithm under such an assumption. Explain why it might be advantageous to use this technique.
11. Implement the following modification to the sequential search algorithm. Temporarily insert the key for which you are searching at the end of the list. Search sequentially until you find this key; then examine the position where you found it to determine whether or not the search was successful. Note that this strategy requires your knowing the number of items in the list rather than a sentinel value stored at the end of the list. Comment on the run-time efficiency of this new strategy versus the sequential search algorithm discussed in this chapter.
12. Modify the insertion sort algorithm of Section 10.2 so that it finds the insertion point for the next array entry using an appropriate modification of the halving strategy employed by the binary search algorithm. Once this insertion point is determined, other array entries must be moved accordingly to make room for the entry being inserted. After completing this modified version of the insertion sort, perform a big-O analysis of its efficiency.

13. Imagine that you have been hired to write an information retrieval program for a company or organization. You must interview people within the organization to determine exactly their information retrieval needs. Construct questions that you could ask in such an interview to enable you to determine which search strategy would be most appropriate for the program you must write. Then, in an essay, explain how answers to these questions would dictate your choice of search strategy.

Case Study: Empirically Measuring the Efficiency of an Algorithm

We will use this chapter's Case Study to examine how we can augment a program to help us analyze its own efficiency. This technique, known as *profiling,* consists of annotating the code for the algorithm with messages sent to objects that can monitor how much work the algorithm has done to that point in its execution. One of these monitoring objects is called a *watch* and measures work in terms of time. A watch is affected by the speed of the computer on which the algorithm is running. The other monitoring object is a *counter.* A counter measures work simply by counting specific kinds of operations performed by the algorithm. As such, it is independent of the computer on which the algorithm executes.

User Request

Write a complete program to empirically demonstrate (or refute) that selection sort is a $O(n^2)$ algorithm.

Analysis

Empirically verifying the big-O category for a sorting algorithm requires a program that outputs information about its own run time. This information should take two forms: actual time as measured in seconds and implicit time as measured by the number of comparisons and exchanges performed by the algorithm. Moreover, such a program will have to randomly assign data to an array whose size is initially input by the user. The random assignment of data to the array will allow the user to gauge the average performance of the algorithm. The program should also make it convenient for the user to run multiple data sets of varying sizes through the algorithm. A run of the program should resemble the following interaction.

```
Enter the number of integers to be sorted: 40
Sorting ...
Running time = 0.062 seconds
Comparisons = 780
Exchanges = 39
Another list to sort? (Y/N) y

Enter the number of integers to be sorted: 80
Sorting ...
Running time = 0.266 seconds
Comparisons = 3160
Exchanges = 79
Another list to sort? (Y/N) y

Enter the number of integers to be sorted: 160
Sorting ...
Running time = 1.094 seconds
Comparisons = 12720
Exchanges = 159
Another list to sort? (Y/N) n
```

Design

The design of the main program should be kept rather simple, deferring complications to subordinate functions and classes. Two important subordinate functions will be (1) a function to generate a list of randomized data and (2) a function to perform selection sort, the latter of which must be annotated with messages sent to `watch` and `counter` objects that monitor the efficiency of the sort.

To generate random data, a `RandomGenerator` class will be used. The interface to members of this class is defined by the following excerpt from its header file. The protected and private data members in this header file are not shown since our profiling program will only use the `RandomGenerator` class as a client.

```
// Class declaration file: random.h

// Objects of this class generate random numbers between specified
// lower and upper bounds.

class RandomGenerator
   {

   public:

   // Class constructors

   RandomGenerator();

   // Member functions

   // Given low and high, nextNumber returns a random integer
   // between low and high inclusive
   int nextNumber(int low, int high);

   // Private and protected data members omitted
   };
```

Similarly, interfaces to the `watch` and `counter` objects that will be used to monitor the selection sort are given by:

```
// Class declaration file: watch.h

// Objects of this class behave like
// stopwatches. They can be started,
// stopped, and asked for the time passed
// in either seconds, minutes, or hours.

class watch
{

   public:

   // Class constructor

   watch();

   // Member functions
```

continued

```
    // Start the timer for the stopwatch
    void start();

    // Stop the timer for the stopwatch
    void stop();

    // Introduce a delay. During a delay the stop watch
    // continues to accumulate time, but nothing else takes
    // place. The duration of the delay is an artificial
    // measure that will have different effects on different machines.
    // Delays cause the stopwatch to artificially accumulate
    // time for monitoring an algorithm running on relatively
    // small data set. Without the delay, the granularity of the
    // stopwatch would not recognize any time as having passed
    // during the execution of the algorithm.
    void delay(int duration);

    // Return in seconds the time accumulated since the stopwatch
    // was started.
    float seconds();

    // Return in minutes the time accumulated since the stopwatch
    // was started.
    float minutes();

    // Return in hours the time accumulated since the stopwatch
    // was started.
    float hours();

    // Private and protected data members omitted
};
```

```
// Class declaration file: counter.h

// Objects of this class are used to count
// comparisons, exchanges, and one other
// operation in other algorithms.

class counter
{
   public:

   // Class constructor

   counter();

   // Member functions

   // Reset the counter for all operations to zero
   void reset();

   // Increment the counter that monitors comparisons
   void incComparisons();
```

```
    // Increment the counter that monitors data exchanges
    void incExchanges();

    // Increment the counter that monitors some other
    // operation as may optionally be needed by the
    // client program
    void incOther();

    // Return the accumulated number of comparisons
    int comparisons();

    // Return the accumulated number of data exchanges
    int exchanges();

    // Return the accumulated number of other operations
    int other();

    // Private and protected data members omitted
};
```

The main program, as a client of these classes, will iteratively have to:

1. Generate a randomized list of data
2. Reset the `counter` object
3. Start the `watch` object
4. Perform the profiled version of selection sort
5. Stop the watch
6. Output the empirical data obtained from the counter and watch objects

The two crucial functions called by the main program, the randomization function and the selection sort, have the following specifications:

Module: Get random list
Task: Determine from the user *n*, the number of values to put in the array *list*, and then fill the first *n* indices of the array with integer values between 1 and *n*
Output: the array *list* filled with randomized values

Module: Selection sort
Inputs: *n*, the number of items in the array, and *list*, the array itself
Task: Sort the array using the selection sort algorithm discussed in Section 10.2; whenever values in the array are compared or exchanged, send appropriate messages to the `watch` and `counter` objects
Output: the sorted array

Implementation

The code for the main program and the randomization and sort functions are given in their entirety here. Where a message is sent to one of the profiling `watch` and `counter` objects, a comment of the form `//Profile` has been added. The implementation of the `watch`, `counter`, and `RandomGenerator` classes is not provided here. However, if you are curious about the implementations of these classes, you will find their complete files in the source code that accompanies the book.

```
// Program file: select.cpp

// This program illustrates the gathering of data on the
// run-time performance of a sorting algorithm.

#include <iostream.h>
#include "counter.h"
#include "watch.h"
#include "list.h"

const int COMPARE_DELAY = 5000;     // Artificial duration of a comparison
const int EXCHANGE_DELAY = 5000;    // Artificial duration of an exchange

counter myCounter;  // Global counter for comparisons and exchanges
watch myWatch;      // Global watch for recording running time

void selectionSort(ListType list, int n);

int main()
{
   ListType list;
   int n;
   char again;

   do
   {
       getRandomList(list, n);
       cout << "Sorting ..." << endl;
       myCounter.reset();                                   // Profile
       myWatch.start();                                     // Profile
       selectionSort(list, n);
       myWatch.stop();                                         // Profile
       cout << "Running time = " << myWatch.seconds()
            << " seconds" << endl;
       cout << "Comparisons = " << myCounter.comparisons() << endl;
       cout << "Exchanges = " << myCounter.exchanges() << endl;
       cout << "Another list to sort? (Y/N) ";
       cin >> again;
   } while (again != 'n' && again != 'N');
   return 0;
}

void selectionSort(ListType list, int n)
{
   int minIndex;
   element temp;

   for (int k = 0; k < n - 1; ++k)
   {

      // Find index of smallest element
      minIndex = k;
      for (int j = k + 1; j < n; ++j)
      {
         myCounter.incComparisons();                          // Profile
```

```
         myWatch.delay(COMPARE_DELAY);                    // Profile
         if (list[j] < list[minIndex])
            minIndex = j;
      }
      // Exchange smallest element and element
      // at beginning of unsorted portion of list
      myCounter.incExchanges();                           // Profile
      myWatch.delay(EXCHANGE_DELAY);                         // Profile
      temp = list[minIndex];
      list[minIndex] = list[k];
      list[k] = temp;
   }
}

void getRandomList(ListType list, int &n)
{
   RandomGenerator numbers;                  // Declare a random generator

   cout << "Enter the number of integers: ";
   cin >> n;
   if (n > MAX_LIST_SIZE)
   {
      cout << "Using " << MAX_LIST_SIZE << " numbers." << endl;
      n = MAX_LIST_SIZE;
   }
   for (int i = 0; i < n; ++i)
      list[i] = numbers.nextNumber(1, n);     // Produce a random value
}
```

Discussion

The profiling program presented here represents a starting point for an experimental tool that can be used to explore empirically the run-time behavior of algorithms. Consider, for example, the results of running the program that were presented in our analysis. From these results, we see that as the size of the data set progressed from 40 to 80 to 160:

- The run time as profiled by the `watch` object increased from 0.062 to 0.266 to 1.094.
- The number of comparisons increased from 780 to 3160 to 12720.
- The number of exchanges increased from 39 to 79 to 159.

Suppose that we take the ratio of times, comparisons, and exchanges between each pair of successive runs.

Size of Data Sets in Two Runs	Ratio of Size of Data Sets	Ratio of Run Times	Ratio of Number of Comparisons	Ratio of Number of Exchanges
80 and 40	2	0.266 / 0.062 = 4.290	3160 / 780 = 4.051	79 / 39 = 2.026
160 and 80	2	1.094 / 0.266 = 4.113	12720 / 3160 = 4.025	159 / 79 = 2.013

Notice that, as the size of the data set doubles, the ratio of run times and numbers of comparisons increases by a factor of approximately 4. This is entirely consistent with an $O(n^2)$ algorithm. Why? However, the number of exchanges doesn't increase by this same factor. Why is this? Is it consistent with the algorithm's being $O(n^2)$? You will ponder these questions along with many others as you explore and expand the Case Study program in the problems at the end of the chapter.

Running, Debugging, and Testing Hints

1. When profiling a program that is also to be used as an application program above and beyond monitoring the efficiency of an algorithm, use a Boolean constant that can be set to `true` or `false` to turn profiling on or off, respectively.
2. When using integer counters in profiling a program, be careful that the number of operations executed by the algorithm does not overflow the capacity of integer storage. Most C++ implementations offer additional integer data types that can accommodate values too large for standard integers. Consult local system reference materials to find out what your version of C++ may offer in this regard.
3. A good way to keep profiling aspects of a program separate from the actual logic of algorithms in the program is to use classes specifically designed for profiling. The `counter` and `watch` classes discussed in this chapter are illustrative of such profiling tools.

Summary

Key Terms

artificial intelligence
best case
big-O analysis
big-O notation
bin sort
binary search
bubble sort
compiler symbol table
computer graphics
counter object
cubic algorithm
data about data
disk file
dominant term
exponential algorithm
heuristics
insertion sort
linear algorithm
logarithmic algorithm
logical order
$\log_2$ search algorithm
order of magnitude
paging
physically sorted
pointer sort
pointers
polynomial algorithm
profile
quadratic algorithm
radix sort
search algorithm
selection sort
sequential search
state space
symbol table
time/space trade-off
virtual memory
watch object
worst case

Key Concepts

- An integral part of designing efficient software is the selection of appropriate algorithms to perform the task at hand.
- Two of the criteria used in selecting algorithms for a given task are time and space efficiency. An algorithm's time efficiency determines how long it requires to run. An algorithm's space efficiency is a measure of how much primary and secondary memory it consumes.
- Three simple sorting algorithms are the bubble sort, insertion sort, and selection sort. The latter minimizes the number of data interchanges that must be made at the expense of not being more efficient for data that are already partially ordered.

- Pointer sort and radix sort are techniques to enhance the time efficiency of a sort at the expense of increased space requirements.
- Three simple search algorithms are the sequential search, binary search, and key-to-address transformation technique.
- Profiling is an empirical technique that can be used to measure an algorithm's efficiency when a big-O analysis is inconclusive.
- Big-O analyses of sort and search algorithms discussed in this chapter are summarized in the following table:

Algorithms	Time Efficiency	Additional Comments
Bubble sort	$O(n^2)$ comparisons and interchanges in worst case	Can be faster if input data already almost sorted.
Insertion sort	$O(n^2)$ comparisons and interchanges in worst case	Also can be faster if input data already almost sorted.
Selection sort	$O(n^2)$ comparisons and $O(n)$ interchanges in worst case	Not significantly faster if input data already almost sorted.
Pointer sort	Reflects number of comparisons of method on which it is layered	Although number of interchanges not reduced, amount of data swapped for each interchange is potentially less. Drawback is the additional memory required for pointers.
Radix sort	$O(n)$ comparisons and interchanges	Limited in the types of data on which it works, although $O(n)$ may have a large constant of proportionality, which can make the $O(n)$ rating a misleading one. For arrays, it has a large space requirement for storing sublists.
Sequential search	$O(n)$ probes into list in worst case	Most inefficient of search algorithms we will study, but still appropriate for small lists stored in main memory.
Binary search	$O(\log_2 n)$ probes in worst case	Drawbacks are that we must continually maintain a count of number of records in list and that the list must be maintained in sorted order.
Key-to-address transformation	$O(1)$ list probes	Not applicable for many types of keys. Potential space inefficiencies.

Programming Problems and Projects

1. The Case Study program in this chapter presents a wide range of opportunities for expanding the program and then using it to explore the performance of sort and search algorithms. Here are some ideas:
   a. The `getRandomList` function in the program allows a given value to appear more than once in the randomly generated array. Modify the algorithm underlying this function so that it will *guarantee* the array of n values contains each of the values $1, 2, \ldots, n$ exactly once. Make sure that your algorithm to do this is $O(n)$.
   b. Add a facility to the program that allows a user to input array values interactively or from a file as well as having them generated randomly.
   c. Add profiled versions of insertion, bubble, and radix sort to the program and allow the user to choose which sort algorithm to profile.

d. Add a facility that allows the user to save a particular data set to a file so that it can later be read using the option you programmed in part b.
e. Add profiled versions of sequential and binary search.
f. For each of the algorithms you have added to the program in parts c and e, use the profiling data accumulated from runs of the program to support (or refute) the formal big-O analysis of the algorithm that was presented in the chapter.
g. The `watch` class used to time the algorithms in the Case Study allows you to establish different times for the comparison and exchange operations. In certain contexts, it is reasonable to expect that one of these operations may take considerably longer than the other. Describe such a situation and explain why different times would arise for these two operations. Then adjust the times for comparisons and exchanges and use the data you collect from running the modified program to demonstrate which sorting algorithm performs best in that situation.
h. The Note of Interest on *Virtual Memory and Program Performance* describes how a formal big-O analysis may not be truly reflected by program performance when paging occurs. Use the Case Study program to demonstrate this. Incrementally increase the size of the array being sorted until one such increase causes an increase in time and/or number of operations that is not consistent with the increase in the size of the array. In a carefully crafted written statement, explain how the profiling data output by the program give evidence that paging has occurred.

2. In this problem, we return to the program developed in the Case Study 6.1 for Chapter 6. Recall that the central `listAllPrimes` function of this program determined all primes less than or equal to a specified positive integer called `number`.
a. Use `watches` and `counters` to profile the prime number algorithm underlying `listAllPrimes`. Based on the empirical data output by these `watches` and `counters`, provide an appropriate big-O categorization for the `listAllPrimes` function.
b. The Greek mathematician Eratosthenes devised a "sieve" technique for finding all prime numbers between 2 and `number`. The sieve of Eratosthenes can be viewed as a Boolean array indexed from 2 to `number` and initialized to `true` in all of its locations. Successive array indices are then modified in the following fashion:
   - Multiples of 2 greater than 2 are set to `false`.
   - Multiples of 3 greater than 3 are set to `false`.
   - Multiples of 4 can be ignored. Why?
   - Multiples of 5 greater than 5 are set to `false`.
   - Multiples of 6 can be ignored. Why?
   - Multiples of 7 greater than 7 are set to `false`.
   - and so on.

   The prime numbers are those array indices where a `true` value remains. Redo the `listAllPrimes` function using this sieve of Eratosthenes algorithm. Then answer the following questions:
   i. Which technique—the sieve or that used in the original function—produces the fastest runs?
   ii. Does either technique appear to be an order of magnitude better in its time efficiency? Cite results from profiling to back up your claims in this regard.
   iii. What are the time/space trade-offs involved in using these two techniques?

3. Suppose that you know the keys in a list are arranged in increasing order. How could the sequential search algorithm presented in this chapter be improved with this knowledge? Rewrite the C++ function to incorporate this improvement and then test your new function in a complete program.
4. Rewrite the binary search algorithm presented in this chapter with a splitting strategy other than halving. One possibility is to use an interpolation strategy that examines the target's distance from the current `low` and `high` pointers. This is more analogous to the way in which we look up names in a phone book. That is, for a name beginning with S, we do not open the phone book to the middle page but rather to a point approximately two-thirds of the way from the beginning of the book. Test run your program against a pure binary search and, through tracing and/or profiling the performance of each algorithm, determine whether there is any significant difference between the two techniques.
5. Repeat Problem 4, but change your algorithm so that, after the initial interpolative guess as to the location of the target, data locations are examined sequentially in an appropriate direction until the key is found or until it can be determined that the key is not in the list.
6. Consider a list of records for students at a university. The list includes fields for student name, credits taken, credits earned, and total grade points. Write a program that, based on a user's request, will sort the list of records in ascending or descending order keying on one of the four fields within the record. For instance, the user might specify that the sort should proceed in descending order according to credits earned. As much as possible, try to refrain from having to write a separate sort function for each particular ordering and field. Experiment by developing different functions based on each of the sorting strategies discussed in this chapter.
7. Consider the same list of records as in Problem 6. Now write a function to sort the records in descending order by credits earned. Records having the same number of credits earned should be arranged in descending order by total grade points. Those with the same number of credits earned and total grade points should be arranged alphabetically by name. Incorporate this function into the complete program that you wrote for Problem 6. Experiment by developing different functions based on each of the sorting strategies discussed in this chapter.
8. Rewrite the pointer sort with the pointer array as a local variable instead of as a global variable. How would this affect a higher level function that calls on the pointer sort? Illustrate by calling your new version of the pointer sort from a sample main program.
9. Merge the segmenting strategy described in Exercise 10 from Section 10.4 with the insertion sort, bubble sort, and selection sort algorithms. Empirically test how this affects the run time of the sort on a file of 1000 records. Does altering the number of segments affect the run time?
10. Implement the binary search algorithm for a disk file containing approximately 1000 records of the structure described in Problem 6.
11. Design a complete program to load information into the data base for employees of East Publishing Company described in Exercise 9 of Section 10.5. Then repeatedly call on a search function to retrieve the information associated with a given employee's identification key.

For any or all of Problems 12 through 16, design a program to answer the question posed. Then analyze the time efficiency of your program by using an appropriate combination of big-O analysis and profiling, using the `watch` and `counter` classes described in the Case Study. Run your program to try to see the relationship between big-O classification and actual run time as measured by a clock. Finally, for each program you implement, attempt to refine its run-time efficiency by making observations similar to those described in the Case Study section of this chapter.

12. In the first century A.D., the numbers were separated into "abundant" (such as 12, whose divisors have a sum greater than 12), "deficient" (such as 9, whose divisors have a sum less than 9), and "perfect" (such as 6, whose divisors add up to 6). In all cases, you do not include the number itself. For example, the only numbers that divide evenly into 6 are 1, 2, 3, and 6, and $6 = 1 + 2 + 3$. Write a program to list all numbers between 2 and *N*, classify each as abundant, deficient, or perfect, and keep track of the numbers in each class.

13. In the first century A.D., Nicomachus wrote a book entitled *Introduction Arithmetica*. In it, the question "How can the cubes be represented in terms of the natural numbers?" was answered by the statement that "Cubical numbers are always equal to the sum of successive odd numbers and can be represented this way." For example,

$$1^3 = 1 = 1$$
$$2^3 = 8 = 3 + 5$$
$$3^3 = 27 = 7 + 9 + 11$$
$$4^3 = 64 = 13 + 15 + 17 + 19$$

Write a program to find the successive odd numbers whose sum equals k^3 for k having the values from 1 to *N*.

14. A conjecture, first made by the mathematician Goldbach, whose proof has defied all attempts, is that "every even number larger than 2 can be written as the sum of two prime numbers." For example,

$$4 = 2 + 2$$
$$6 = 3 + 3$$
$$8 = 3 + 5$$
$$10 = 3 + 7$$
$$100 = 89 + 11$$

Write a program that determines for every even integer N with $2 <= N$ two prime numbers P and Q such that $N = P + Q$.

15. A pair of numbers *M* and *N* are called "friendly" (or they are referred to as an "amicable pair") if the sum of all the divisors of *M* (excluding *M*) is equal to the number *N* and the sum of all the divisors of the number *N* (excluding *N*) is equal to *M* ($M \neq N$). For example, the numbers 220 and 284 are an amicable pair because the only numbers that divide evenly into 220 (1, 2, 4, 5, 10, 11, 20, 22, 44, 55, and 110) add up to 284, and the only numbers that divide evenly into 284 (1, 2, 4, 71, and 142) add up to 220. Write a program to find at least one other pair of amicable numbers. Be prepared to let your program search for some time.

16. A consequence of a famous theorem of the mathematician Fermat is the fact that

$$2^{(P-1)} \% P = 1$$

for every odd prime number *P*. An odd positive integer *K* satisfying

$$2^{(K-1)} \% K = 1$$

is called a pseudoprime. Write a program to determine a table of pseudoprimes and primes between 2 and *N*. How many pseudoprimes occur that are not prime numbers?

17. The importance of communication skills in "selling" a program to those who will eventually use it should not be underestimated. Keeping this in mind, write a user's guide for the program you developed in Problem 5. You should assume that the user is able to log onto (or boot) the system, but beyond that has no other knowledge of how to run this or any other program. Remember that unless the user's guide is very, very clear *and* very, very concise, it will probably be thrown in a file drawer—and your program never used.

18. (For the mathematically inclined) Consider the claim that exponential algorithms will, in general, become practical on parallel processing machines. Provide a carefully constructed argument in which you show that adding more processors to a machine can never result in an exponential algorithm becoming practical for a wide variety of data sets. Your argument should explain the relationship between the number of processors used and the size of the data set that can be accommodated in reasonable time by the exponential algorithm. In essay form, justify the claim that the only real mathematical answer to solving a problem with an exponential algorithm in reasonable time is to discover a nonexponential algorithm that solves the same problem.

19. One of the drawbacks to the bubble sort algorithm is that a data set with just one item out of order can lead to worst case performance for the algorithm. First, explain how this can happen. Because of this phenomenon, a variation on the bubble sort called a *shaker sort* will, on alternative passes through the array, put the largest entry into the last index and then the smallest entry into the first index. Explain how this idea can eliminate the worst case performance of bubble sort on an array with just one item out of order. Then implement the shaker sort algorithm. Using techniques from this chapter's Case Study, profile the number of comparisons and data interchanges in both the shaker sort and the bubble sort for a variety of data sets. Keep track of the empirical results you obtain from profiling these two algorithms. Finally, in a written report, compare the performance of these two algorithms based on your empirical data. Be sure that your report addresses situations in which the shaker sort will perform worse than the plain bubble sort.

20. An interesting variation on insertion sort is to use a binary search strategy to find the index at which the insertion of the next array element should occur. Implement this change in the algorithm. From a big-O perspective, has the efficiency of the algorithm changed? Profile the new algorithm using an appropriate driver program coupled with the `watch` and `counter` classes from this chapter's Case Study. Do your profiling statistics confirm your formal big-O analysis?

11

Data Abstraction and Object-Oriented Software Engineering

Chapter Outline

I believe in Michelangelo, Velázquez, and Rembrandt; in the might of design.
George Bernard Shaw (1856–1950)

Our life is frittered away by detail . . . Simplify, simplify.
Henry David Thoreau, 1817–1862

The topics covered in the previous three chapters allow us to probe more deeply into some of the issues involved in the software development life cycle. Our study of structs and classes in Chapter 8 introduced us to the notion of encapsulating data along with operations to be performed upon those data. Then, in Chapter 9, we were introduced to arrays, which gave us the ability to manipulate larger aggregates of data than before. It is important to design algorithms that manipulate these larger data aggregates efficiently, and that led to our study of algorithm analysis and big-O notation in Chapter 10.

Now, in this chapter, we shall see how classes, arrays, and efficiency considerations fit into the software engineering process. In the first four sections, we will define four classes that can serve as useful "containers" in which client programs can conveniently store objects. These containers—the *ordered collection,* the *sorted collection,* the *one-key table,* and the *two-key table*—will all be developed following a set of guidelines that form the foundation of a key concept known as *data abstraction*. Developing classes in a "data abstract" fashion will enable us to conveniently experiment with many different ways of implementing the classes and to analyze the efficiency of each of these implementation techniques.

In the final three sections of the chapter, we shall see how these container classes fit naturally into the object-oriented software development process. By using this process, we will develop a Case Study significantly more complex than anything we have attempted previously. In future chapters, we will investigate ways in which the container classes defined in this chapter can be implemented in a more efficient fashion by using more sophisticated data structures.

11.1 The Ordered Collection Abstract Data Type

Objectives

a. to understand what is involved in defining an abstract data type (ADT)
b. to understand what is meant by data abstraction
c. to understand the process of moving from the formal definition of an ADT to the implementation of that ADT as a C++ class
d. to understand the difference between the physical size of an array and its logical size
e. to design and implement a new class that prohibits references to uninitialized data elements in an array

Motivation for the Ordered Collection

In almost any application that uses an array, the user must distinguish between the *physical size* of the array (its capacity or the number of memory locations available for data elements) and the *logical size* of the array (the number of data elements currently stored in the array). Failure to do this can cause errors when users attempt to access data locations in that portion of an array where no data values have yet been stored. For example, an array `list` might be declared to store a maximum number of five integer elements, and three integers might be currently stored in positions 0 through 2. This situation is depicted in Figure 11.1. The data at index positions 3 and 4 are still unpredictable, so the references `list[3]` and `list[4]` for these values will likely lead to unreliable results.

Users can keep track of the data within a physical array in two ways:

1. The first method stores a special sentinel value at the index position immediately following the last data element currently in the array. This method is used by C++ to recognize the boundary of a string value (the null character) within an array of characters. The cost of this method is that one location in the array must be given up to store the sentinel value. Moreover, some data elements, such as bank account objects, might not be easily represented as sentinel values.
2. The second method maintains a separate integer variable as a counter of the number of data elements currently stored in the array. We have seen this method used in many examples in Chapter 9, where a variable `length` maintains this value. When a new array is declared or reinitialized, `length` is set to 0 to reflect the fact that there are no data elements stored in the array. `length` is then passed with the array variable to any function that processes the array. Any subscript reference to a data element in an array, either for accessing or for storing a value, should use an index that satisfies the condition `0 <= index < length.` The costs of this method are that a separate variable or parameter must be maintained for the number of data elements in the array, and extra operations must be provided for adding or removing data elements.

We can use the second method to develop a new class called an *ordered collection*. As we've seen in Chapter 8, a class formalizes in C++ syntax the notion of an abstract data type (ADT).

Abstract data type (ADT): An ADT is an encapsulation of data objects that share a well-defined set of attributes and operations for processing the objects.

In providing a definition for an ADT such as an ordered collection, we must specify both the attributes and operations that all ordered collections have in common. Typically, we specify the attributes by describing the individual elements composing the ADT and the relationships among those individual elements. The operations may be specified using preconditions and postconditions.

Defining the Ordered Collection ADT

The ordered collection ADT is like an array in that it provides indexed access to data locations. However, unlike an array, the ordered collection provides indexed access just to those data locations where elements have been stored. It does this by maintaining its own logical size as a property. A user can access the logical size of an or-

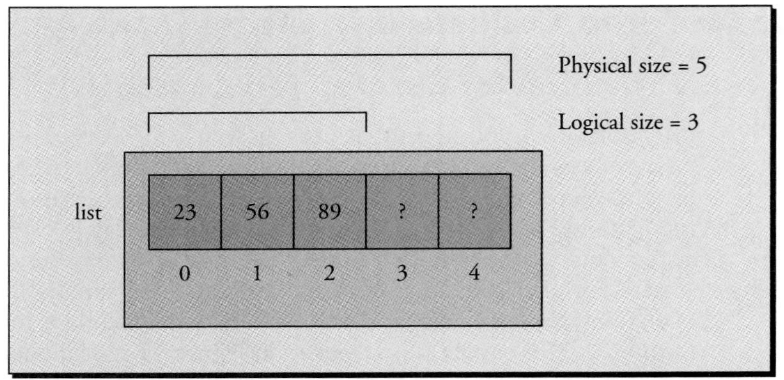

Figure 11.1
The logical size of a vector may be different from its physical size

dered collection, determine whether indexing is allowed, and if so, determine what the legitimate range of an index should be. Finally, the ordered collection class provides a set of operations for adding or removing data elements. A test driver program that illustrates the use of an ordered collection of integers follows. We will be discussing the use of such test driver programs later in this chapter as we take up the role of testing in the software engineering process.

Example 11.1 This program is merely a test driver that allows its user to exercise each of the operations provided with the ordered collection ADT. Notice from the sample run that values are initially stored in the ordered collection `list` using one of the two operations `addFirst` or `addLast`. These operations are used instead of an array index operator because a new ordered collection is always empty. The index operator for an ordered collection will not allow assignment of a value to a location unless that location has been previously initialized using the `addFirst` or `addLast` operation. When each input value is added to the collection, its logical size grows by 1. Once a value has been assigned to a location, index notation may be used to reference or modify that location. The program assumes that the ordered collection class is implemented in the library file `ordercol.h`.

```
#include <iostream.h>
#include "ordercol.h"

int main()
{
    // Create an empty ordered collection
    // of integers

    OrderedCollection<int> list;
    int choice, value, index, k;

    cout << "[1] add first" << endl << "[2] add last" << endl
         << "[3] remove first" << endl << "[4] remove last" << endl
         << "[5] remove arbitrary" << endl << "[6] inspect index" << endl
         << "[7] change index" << endl << "[8] show collection" << endl
         << "[9] quit -->" << endl;
    do {
```

```
      cout << "Which operation should be tested? ";
      cin >> choice;
      switch (choice)
      {
      case 1:
         cout << "Enter value --> ";
         cin >> value;
         list.addFirst(value);
         break;
      case 2:
         cout << "Enter value --> ";
         cin >> value;
         list.addLast(value);
         break;
      case 3:
         cout << list.removeFirst() << " has been removed" << endl;
         break;
      case 4:
         cout << list.removeLast() << " has been removed" << endl;
         break;
      case 5:
         cout << "Enter value to remove --> ";
         cin >> value;
         if (list.remove(value))
            cout << value << " has been removed" << endl;
         else
            cout << value << " was not found" << endl;
         break;
      case 6:
         cout << "Enter index --> ";
         cin >> index;
         cout << "Value at index " << index << " is " << list[index];
         break;
      case 7:
         cout << "Enter index and new value --> ";
         cin >> index >> value;
         list[index] = value;
         break;
      case 8:
         for (k = 0; k < list.length(); k++)
            cout << list[k] << " ";
         cout << endl;
         break;
      case 9:
         break;
      default:
         cout << "Invalid choice -- Please try again" << endl;
         break;
      }
   } while (choice != 9);

   return 0;
}
```

A sample run of this program is:

```
[1] add first
[2] add last
[3] remove first
[4] remove last
[5] remove arbitrary
[6] inspect index
[7] change index
[8] show collection
[9] quit
Which operation should be tested? 1
Enter value --> 20
Which operation should be tested? 1
Enter value --> 40
Which operation should be tested? 2
Enter value --> 10
Which operation should be tested? 8
40 20 10                                  Note: Entire collection shown here
Which operation should be tested? 7
Enter index and new value --> 1 50
Which operation should be tested? 8
40 50 10                                  Note: Entire collection shown here
Which operation should be tested? 5
Enter value to remove --> 50
50 has been removed
Which operation should be tested? 3
40 has been removed
Which operation should be tested? 4
10 has been removed
Which operation should be tested? 8

                                          Note: Entire collection shown here
Which operation should be tested? 9
```

To summarize the properties of an ordered collection that are illustrated by this example:

1. Range checking occurs during indexing.
2. A newly created ordered collection always has a logical length of 0. This length then grows or shrinks by 1 using appropriate operations.
3. When a data element is added to the beginning of an ordered collection, the positions of the remaining elements shift up by 1.
4. When a data element is removed from the beginning of an ordered collection, the positions of the remaining elements shift down by 1.
5. The use of ordered collections is safer than the use of arrays because references to uninitialized data elements are not allowed.

Formally Specifying the Operations for Ordered Collections

Now that we have an intuitive feel for how an ordered collection should behave, we need to provide a more specific unambiguous definition of its operations. We start by defining the attributes of an ordered collection. These attributes include:

1. Its logical length (the number of data elements currently stored)
2. Its data elements
3. The type `E` of each element in the collection

The formal specifications of the operations for an ordered collection follow:

Create Operation

Preconditions: The ordered collection is in an unpredictable state.

Postconditions: An ordered collection of length 0 is created.

Length Operation

Preconditions: The ordered collection is appropriately initialized.

Postconditions: The number of data elements in the ordered collection is returned.

Indexing Operation (for Observation or Modification of a Data Element)

Preconditions: The ordered collection is appropriately initialized.
The `index` parameter is an integer value in the range `0 <= index` `<` length of the ordered collection.

Postconditions: The location of the data element as specified by `index`, which can be used either to reference or to store a value, is returned.

Assignment Operation

Preconditions: The target is an ordered collection, appropriately initialized.
The source is an ordered collection, appropriately initialized.

Postconditions: The contents of the source object are copied into the target object, and the target's length is set to the source's length.

Add last Operation

Preconditions: The ordered collection is appropriately initialized.
The parameter is an object of type `E`.
There is memory available to store the new item in the collection.

Postconditions: The length of the ordered collection is incremented by 1, and the parameter object is placed at the end of the ordered collection.

Remove last Operation

Preconditions: The ordered collection is appropriately initialized, and the length of the ordered collection `> 0`.

Postconditions: The length of the collection is decreased by 1, and what had been the last data element in the ordered collection is returned.

Add first Operation

Preconditions: The ordered collection is appropriately initialized.
The parameter is an object of type `E`.
There is memory available to store the new element in the collection.

Postconditions: The length of the ordered collection is incremented by 1, the data elements in the ordered collection are shifted up by 1 index position, and the parameter element is placed in the first position in the ordered collection.

Remove first Operation

Preconditions: The ordered collection is appropriately initialized, and the length of the ordered collection `> 0`.

Postconditions: The length of the collection is decreased by 1, the data elements in the ordered collection that come after the first element are shifted down by 1 index position, and what had been the first element in the ordered collection is returned.

Remove Operation

Preconditions: The ordered collection object is appropriately initialized.
The parameter is the data element to be removed, the parameter must equal an element currently in the list, and the length of the ordered collection `> 0`.

Postconditions: The length of the ordered collection is decreased by 1, and the data elements in the ordered collection that come after the parameter element are shifted down by 1 index position.

Declaring the Ordered Collection Class in C++

The separation of an ADT's specification from the declarations and instructions that implement the data type in a particular language is called data abstraction. An *abstract data type* may be viewed as a formal description of data elements and relationships that is envisioned by the software engineer; it is thus a conceptual model. Ultimately, however, this model will be implemented in C++ via declarations for the elements and relationships and instructions (often in the form of function calls) for the operations. At an even deeper level, the C++ compiler will then translate the implementation of the abstract data type in C++ into a physical electronic representation on a particular computer. This hierarchy of *levels of abstraction* is illustrated in Figure 11.2.

The first step in moving toward an ADT's implementation in an object-oriented language such as C++ is to restate the operations that act on ADT objects as declarations of public member functions in a class declaration module. We shall call such a collection of function declarations the *interface for an ADT*. The class declaration module that specifies the interface for the ordered collection ADT closely adheres to the formal specifications that we presented earlier.

```
// Class definition file: ordercol.h

#ifndef ORDERCOL_H
#define ORDERCOL_H

const int MAX_ARRAY_SIZE = 50;

template <class E>
class OrderedCollection
{

public:

// Class constructors

OrderedCollection();
OrderedCollection(const OrderedCollection &oc);

// Function members

int length();

// Assignment
OrderedCollection& operator = (const OrderedCollection &oc);
```

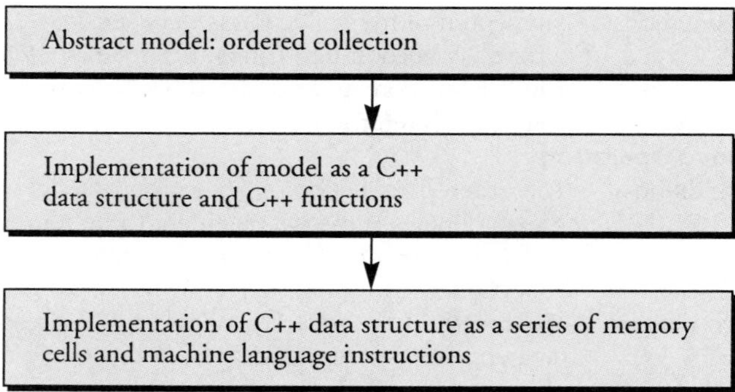

Figure 11.2 Hierarchy of levels of abstraction for implementing an ordered collection

```
// Indexing
E& operator [ ] (int index);

// Modifiers
void addLast(E e);
E removeLast();
void addFirst(E e);
E removeFirst();
bool remove(E e);

protected:

// Data members

E data [MAX_ARRAY_SIZE];
int cLength;

};

#endif
```

Note that in this implementation the data member for storing the data elements of an ordered collection is an array of physical size `MAX_ARRAY_SIZE`. The `length` function will return the value stored in `cLength`—a variable that will keep track of the logical size of the collection. We declare both data members to be `protected` so that any derived classes of `OrderedCollection` will have direct access to them, but client programs will not.

Implementing the Operations for an Ordered Collection

Default Constructor. The default constructor needs only initialize `cLength` to 0 to ensure that the `length` operation will return the correct value for an empty collection.

```
template <class E>
OrderedCollection<E>::OrderedCollection()
{
   cLength = 0;
}
```

Copy Constructor. The copy constructor assigns the array and logical length contained in the collection it is given to the corresponding members of the object being constructed.

```
template <class E>
OrderedCollection<E>::OrderedCollection(const OrderedCollection &oc)
{
   for (int j = 0; j < oc.cLength; ++j)
      data[j] = oc.data[j];
   cLength = oc.cLength;
}
```

Length Operation. As long as the implementations of other operations are consistent in updating the value of cLength, the length function need only return the value of this protected data member.

```
template <class E>
int OrderedCollection<E>::length()
{

   return cLength;
}
```

Indexing Ordered Collections. The indexing operation for an ordered collection is the same as that for an array. The only difference is that the logical size is used as an upper bound on the index value. By using assert, the indexing operation enforces the precondition that the index parameter is greater than or equal to 0 and less than the length of the collection. Put another way, this code guarantees that users can index only the data elements currently available in the collection.

```
template <class E>
E& OrderedCollection<E>::operator [ ] (int index)
{
   assert((index >= 0) && (index < cLength));
   return data[index];
}
```

Adding and Removing Elements. To add a new data element to the end of the ordered collection, we store the data element in the array location referenced by cLength and then increase cLength by 1 to reflect the new logical size of the collection. Because this implementation of an ordered collection uses an array of physical size MAX_ARRAY_SIZE, assert is used to ensure that we do not surpass this physical size. You will explore other ways of handling this error condition in the exercises.

addLast performs the necessary steps to add a data element to the end of the collection.

```
template <class E>
void OrderedCollection<E>::addLast(E e)
{
   assert(cLength < MAX_ARRAY_SIZE);
   data[cLength] = e;
   ++cLength;
}
```

To remove a data element from the end of the collection, we must perform the inverse steps:

1. Save a copy of the removed data element for return to the caller.
2. Reduce by 1 the value of cLength.

removeLast performs the necessary steps to remove a data element from the end of the collection.

```
template <class E>

E OrderedCollection<E>::removeLast()
{
   assert(cLength > 0);
   --cLength;
   E removedItem = data[cLength];
   return removedItem;
}
```

To add a new data element to the beginning of the collection, we must shift the existing data over one place to the right throughout the underlying array. The new data element can then be stored in the first position in the array. Finally, `cLength` must be increased by 1.

```
template <class E>
void OrderedCollection<E>::addFirst(E e)
{
   assert(cLength < MAX_ARRAY_SIZE);
   for (int i = cLength; i > 0; --i)
      data[i] = data[i - 1];
   data[0] = e;
   ++cLength;
}
```

Study the `for` loop in this function carefully to be sure you understand the process of shifting the data in the vector.

To remove a data element from the beginning of an ordered collection, we must store the item to be removed, shift the existing data over one place to the left throughout the array, and finally decrease `cLength` by 1.

```
template <class E>
E OrderedCollection<E>::removeFirst()
{
   assert(cLength > 0);
   E removedItem = data[0];
   --cLength;
   for (int i = 0; i < cLength; ++i)
      data[i] = data[i + 1];
   return removedItem;
}
```

The implementation of the `remove` operation is left as an exercise.

Evaluating the Implementation

In one sense, all implementations look the same to client programs because of the following two "rules" about ADTs:

ADT use rule: Algorithms that use an abstract data type should only access or modify the ADT through the operations provided in the ADT definition.

ADT implementation rule: An implementation of an abstract data type *must* provide an interface that is entirely consistent with the operations specified in the ADT's formal definition.

If users and implementors of ADTs comply fully with these rules, all high-level logic will be plug-compatible with all possible implementations of an ADT. The implementation is said to exhibit *information hiding:* It hides information about implementation details from higher level logic. This is the ideal. In some situations, the syntax of C++ will force us into compromising the ideal. We will be careful to point those situations out and hold such compromises to a minimum.

Second, if high-level logic cannot tell the difference between two implementations, then why would we ever want more than one implementation of an ADT? Part of the answer lies in the different time and space efficiencies that various implementations provide. For instance, in the implementation of the ordered collection that we have discussed here, the `addFirst`, `removeFirst`, and `remove` operations all have an $O(n)$ efficiency. (Why?) If an implementation exists that could execute these operations in $O(1)$ or $O(\log n)$ time, then a client program using that implementation would run faster even though the code in the client program would look exactly the same regardless of which implementation was used. As we study more sophisticated data structures in later chapters, we shall see that it is indeed possible to improve the efficiencies of these operations without violating the ADT implementation rule.

Another aspect to consider in evaluating the implementation of an ADT is the limitations that the implementation may impose as it attempts to model an abstraction. For instance, the array-based implementation of the ordered collection ADT that we have discussed here imposes a maximum length limitation. When we study linked lists in Chapter 12, we will provide an implementation of the ordered collection that does not have this maximum length restriction.

The availability of different implementations of an ADT—all compatible from their outward interface—gives rise to some very exciting prospects for the software design endeavor. At a high level, we design complex software by constructing a model that operates only on abstract data types. Once we have a high-level model with which we are satisfied, we can plug in the best implementation of the ADT for our particular application.

If formalized big-O analysis is inconclusive about which is the best implementation, it is relatively painless to experiment with several implementations. Different implementations can be plugged in, we can empirically profile their performance, and then choose the best. With the ADT approach, all this experimentation can be done without any modification of the high-level model.

Exercises 11.1

1. Discuss the difference between the physical size of an array and its logical size.
2. State two reasons why ordered collections are safer and more convenient to use than arrays.
3. Users complain that halting the program with an error message is too severe a price to pay for attempting to remove a data element from an empty ordered collection. They argue that a Boolean flag could be returned instead, indicating the success or failure of the operation. Discuss the relative merits of these two approaches.
4. Someone has proposed using an ordered collection rather than an array to implement a string class. She claims that the new implementation will not have to waste a storage location on the null character. Discuss the merits of this proposal.
5. Implement the remaining operations for the ordered collection class and exercise it with the test driver program presented in Example 11.1.
6. Add an operation, `indexOf`, to the ordered collection class to search the collection for a given element. If the element is found, the index position of the first instance of this element in the ordered collection should be returned. Otherwise, –1 should be returned.

7. Add an operation to the ordered collection class to sort the data elements in the collection.
8. Add an operation for output of ordered collections, overloading the << operator. Test the operation with an appropriate driver program.
9. Add an operation to concatenate two ordered collections. It should use the + operator in the same way as the `apstring` class. Discuss the limitations of this operation when using the implementation strategy presented in this section.
10. An alternate implementation strategy for an ordered collection is to store a special sentinel value at the index position immediately following the last data element currently in the array. Clearly, this approach eliminates the need to have the logical length of the collection as a protected data member. Implement each of the ordered collection operations using this strategy. Then, in a written statement, compare and contrast the efficiency and limitations of this alternate approach with the approach presented in this section.
11. If you covered the material on vectors in Section 9.6, provide an alternate implementation of the ordered collection class that uses a vector as a protected data member instead of an array. Then, in a written statement, compare and contrast the efficiency and limitations of this alternate approach with the approach presented in this section.
12. Add two operations to the `OrderedCollection` class. The first should insert an element at position *k*, making what had been the *k*th element become the element at position $k + 1$. The second operation should remove the element at position *k*. Before writing code for these operations, provide a formal definition of their pre- and postconditions.

11.2 The Sorted Collection Abstract Data Type

User Requirements for a Sorted Collection

Objectives

a. to understand the difference between an ordered collection and a sorted collection
b. to design and implement a sorted collection class

Many applications demand that data values be kept in sorted order. For example, dictionaries and telephone books are two kinds of collections of data values that must be maintained in alphabetical order. One could use the ordered collection class to represent these kinds of data as long as a sort operation is provided to alphabetize the data after each insertion into the collection. However, the sort operation can be very expensive to use with large collections. Clearly, an ordered collection that could maintain its contents in sorted form without resorting to a sort operation would be very desirable for these applications.

We can design a new class, called a *sorted collection,* to fulfill these requirements. The new class inherits many of the characteristics of an ordered collection, such as a length and index to look up a data element's value. However, to keep its data elements sorted, a sorted collection prohibits insertions at given positions in the collection. The sorted collection permits only one insertion operation, and that operation always puts a data element in its proper place in the collection. Additionally, for a data type to be stored in a sorted collection, that data type must have well-defined < and > operators.

Example 11.2 The following program provides a test driver for the sorted collection class that is similar to the driver program we used for the ordered collection class in Example 11.1. Examine the sample run following the program to gain a better understanding of the effect of the operations provided for this class.

```
// Program file: sortedcol_drv.cpp

#include <iostream.h>

#include "sortcol.h"

int main()
{
   // Create an empty ordered collection
   // of integers

   SortedCollection<int> list;
   int choice, value, index, k;

   cout << "[1] add " << endl << "[2] remove first" << endl
      << "[3] remove last" << endl << "[4] remove arbitrary" << endl
      << "[5] inspect index" << endl << "[6] show collection" << endl
      << "[7] quit " << endl;
   do {
      cout << "Which operation should be tested? ";
      cin >> choice;
      switch (choice)
      {
      case 1:
         cout << "Enter value --> ";
         cin >> value;
         list.add(value);
         break;
      case 2:
         cout << list.removeFirst() << " has been removed" << endl;
         break;
      case 3:
         cout << list.removeLast() << " has been removed" << endl;
         break;
      case 4:
         cout << "Enter value to remove --> ";
         cin >> value;
         if (list.remove(value))
            cout << value << " has been removed" << endl;
         else
            cout << value << " was not found" << endl;
         break;
      case 5:
         cout << "Enter index --> ";
         cin >> index;
         cout << "Value at index " << index << " is " << list[index];
         break;
      case 6:
         for (k = 0; k < list.length(); k++)
            cout << list[k] << " ";
         cout << endl;
         break;
      case 7:
         break;
      default:
         cout << "Invalid choice -- Please try again" << endl;
```

```
        break;
    }
} while (choice != 7);
    return 0;
}
```

A sample run of this program is:

```
[1] add
[2] remove first
[3] remove last
[4] remove arbitrary
[5] inspect index
[6] show collection
[7] quit
Which operation should be tested? 1
Enter value --> 90
Which operation should be tested? 1
Enter value --> 80
Which operation should be tested? 1
Enter value --> 70
Which operation should be tested? 6
70 80 90
Which operation should be tested? 4
Enter value to remove --> 80
80 has been removed
Which operation should be tested? 6
70 90
Which operation should be tested? 7
```

Note the use of the operation `add` to insert a data element into the sorted collection. No position is specified because the sorted collection figures this out automatically.

Formally Specifying the Operations for Sorted Collections

Because a sorted collection has so many of the attributes and behaviors of an ordered collection, it will be convenient to specify it as a derived class of an ordered collection. The situation here is similar to that of the account and savings account classes discussed in Chapter 8. Sorted collections inherit all of the attributes of ordered collections: a length, a list of data elements, and a type `E` that is the data type of each element in the collection. We also assume that all of the operations on ordered collections can be used on sorted collections, except for adding a data element to the beginning or the end of the collection and for indexing to modify a data element. We use an operation called `add` for insertions to enforce a sorted order in the collection. The formal specifications follow:

Create Operation
Preconditions: The sorted collection is in an unpredictable state.
Postconditions: A sorted collection of length 0 is created.
Length Operation
Preconditions: The sorted collection is appropriately initialized.
Postconditions: The number of data elements currently stored in the collection is returned.

Indexing Operation (for Observation of a Data Element Only)
Preconditions: The sorted collection is appropriately initialized.
The `index` parameter is an integer value in the range `0 <= index <` the length of the collection.
Postconditions: The object at the index position is returned.

Assignment Operation
Preconditions: The target is a sorted collection object, appropriately initialized.
The source is a sorted collection object, appropriately initialized.
Postconditions: The contents of the source object are copied into the target object, and the target's length is set to the source's length.

Add Operation
Preconditions: The sorted collection object is appropriately initialized, the parameter is an object of type `E`, and there is memory to store the new element in the collection.
Postconditions: The length of the collection is incremented by 1, and the parameter object is placed in its proper position in the sorted collection.

Remove last Operation
Preconditions: The sorted collection is appropriately initialized, and the length of the collection `> 0`.
Postconditions: The length of the collection is decremented by 1, and what had been the last data element in the sorted collection is returned.

Remove first Operation
Preconditions: The sorted collection is appropriately initialized, and the length of the collection `> 0`.
Postconditions: The length of the collection is decremented by 1, the data elements in the ordered collection that come after the first element are shifted down by 1 index position, and what had been the first element in the sorted collection is returned.

Remove Operation
Preconditions: The sorted collection object is appropriately initialized.
The parameter is the data element to be removed, the parameter must equal an element currently in the list, and the length of the collection `> 0`.
Postconditions: The length of the collection is decremented by 1, and the data elements in the sorted collection that come after the parameter element are shifted down by 1 index position (effectively removing the parameter element from the collection).

Declaring the Sorted Collection Class in C++

The class declaration module for the sorted collection class is

```
// Class definition file: sortcol.h

#ifndef SORTCOL_H
#define SORTCOL_H

#include "ordercol.h"

template <class E>
class SortedCollection : protected OrderedCollection<E>
{

   public:

   // Class constructors
```

```
    SortedCollection();
    SortedCollection(const SortedCollection<E> &sc);

     // Function members

     // These four are inherited from the base class
     OrderedCollection<E>::length;
     OrderedCollection<E>::removeFirst;
     OrderedCollection<E>::removeLast;
     OrderedCollection<E>::remove;

     // Assignment
     SortedCollection& operator = (const SortedCollection &sc);

     // Indexing (access only, no modification)
     const E& operator  [ ] (int index);

     // Modifier
     void add(E e);

     // All data members are defined in base class
};

#include "sortcol.cpp"

#endif
```

Note several things about this class declaration:

1. The sorted collection class inherits its attributes and behavior from the ordered collection class in `protected` mode. This means that `public` and `protected` data members and member functions from the ordered collection cannot be used by clients of the sorted collection class, unless the sorted collection class redefines them. If inheritance were specified in `public` mode, all of the `public` members of the ordered collection class, such as `addFirst`, would also be available to users of the sorted collection class as well. A derived class should be declared in `protected` mode whenever we wish to deny other users access to some of the public members of the base class.
2. Users of the sorted collection are given access to four member functions of the ordered collection class by listing them in the following form in the `public` section:

<class name>::<member name>;

   This kind of declaration is called an *access adjustment*. In general, an access adjustment broadens the scope of access no wider than the mode of access specified by the base class.
3. The remaining three member function declarations specify operations to be implemented by the sorted collection class. Note that the assignment and indexing operations are not inherited from the base class. In the case of the assignment, we must return the address of an object of a specific class (sorted collection, in this case). In the case of the index operator, we prohibit the use of the returned element as an l-value by specifying the function as constant.

Implementing the Sorted Collection Class

The constructors for the sorted collection class invoke the corresponding constructors in the base class:

```
template <class E>
SortedCollection<E>::SortedCollection()
   : OrderedCollection<E>()
{
}

template <class E>
SortedCollection<E>::SortedCollection(const SortedCollection &sc)
   : OrderedCollection<E>(sc)
{
}
```

The new operation to add a data element calls for some development. The logic of this operation faces three possibilities:

1. The collection is empty. The new data element goes at the end.
2. The new data element is greater than the last element in the collection. The new data element goes at the end.
3. The new data element is less than or equal to some data element in the collection. We search for this place, shift the data elements over to the right from there, and put the new data element in that place.

The implementation reflects these alternatives as follows:

```
template <class E>
void SortedCollection<E>::add(E e)
{
   int place = 0;

   assert(cLength < MAX_ARRAY_SIZE);
   if ((cLength == 0) || (e > data[cLength - 1]))
      data[cLength] = e;
   else
   {
      while (e > data[place])
         ++place;
      for (int index = cLength; index > place ; --index)
         data[index] = data[index - 1];
      data[place] = e;
   }
   ++cLength;
}
```

The implementations of the assignment and index operations are left as exercises.

Exercises 11.2

1. Implement the assignment and index operations for sorted collections.
2. Design and test a program that attempts to use the index operator to assign a value to a position in a sorted collection. Explain the error that occurs.
3. Explain why the index operator for ordered collections cannot be used for sorted collections. What effect will this have on client programs that use sorted collections?

4. Using big-O notation, analyze the efficiencies of each of the sorted collection operations for the implementation presented in this section.
5. Add an overloaded index operator to the sorted collection that will allow modification of the collection in the following fashion. When a new value is assigned to index `k`, if that value does not belong at location `k`, the sorted collection should store the new value at its appropriate position in the sorted order, shifting the positions of other values as needed to accomplish this. For example, if a sorted collection `s` contained 10 20 30 40 50 60 in indices 0 through 5, respectively, and a user made the assignment `s[4] = 5`, then the collection should be modified to contain 5 10 20 30 40 60. Note that 5 has replaced the 50 that was stored at index 4, but the 5 has been inserted into its correct position in the newly sorted collection. After implementing this operation, analyze the efficiency of your implementation using big-O notation.
6. Design and implement a member function `merge` for sorted collections. `merge` expects a sorted collection as a parameter. The function should build and return a sorted collection that contains the elements in the receiver collection and the parameter collection. After implementing this operation, analyze the efficiency of your implementation using big-O notation.

11.3 The One-Key Table Abstract Data Type

The ordered and sorted collections addressed one particular shortcoming of arrays: the lack of a safeguard to keep users from accessing uninitialized locations. In this section, we will examine an ADT designed to introduce another array limitation: the inability of an array to associate values with indices that are not an integer type. As the following example will indicate, there are many situations where it is more natural to associate a value with an "index" that was a string. In the context of the ADT we are about to describe, this more general type of index is called a *key*.

Example 11.3 We have been storing a person's age in a database. Each year, we must increment the person's age by 1. We also wish to add information about the person's height and weight, and remove any information about the person's waistline. The database (called person) is represented so that we can add, retrieve, or remove information (all integer values) by specifying keys (all string values). The following pseudocode algorithm describes our task:

1. Retrieve the value at the "age" key from person.
2. Add 1 to this value.
3. Store the sum at the "age" key in person.
4. Store the person's height at the "height" key in person.
5. Store the person's weight at the "weight" key in person.
6. Remove the value at the "waistline" key in person.

The states of a sample one-key table before and after this process are depicted in Figure 11.3.

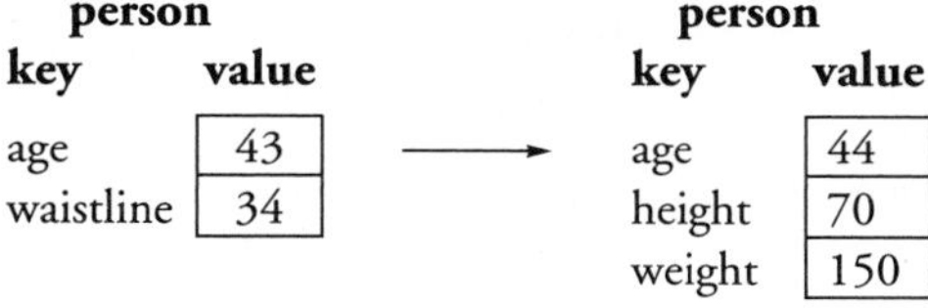

Figure 11.3 States of a one-key table before and after operations

Figure 11.4
Some typical one-key tables

person

key	value
age	44
height	70
weight	150

salaries

key	value
ortiz	55000.00
smith	45000.00
vaselli	62000.00

lineup

key	value
C	Berra
CF	Mantle
SS	Kubek

classRank

key	value
1	Steinmetz
2	O'Leary
3	Rakowski

Objectives

a. to formally define and use the one-key table ADT
b. to compare and contrast several implementations of the one-key table ADT
c. to recognize the shortcomings of each of these implementations and recognize the need for more sophisticated implementations to be studied in future chapters

The solution presented in Example 11.3 is totally independent of considerations regarding how the one-key table will be represented in C++. Instead, the high-level pseudocode takes the perspective that a one-key table consists of abstract entities manipulated by abstract operations such as *retrieve* and *store*. As we did with ordered and sorted collections, before we move to any C++ code for the one-key table, it is first necessary to pin down exactly what we mean by these abstractions. That is, we must define the notion of a one-key table precisely enough to ensure that our pseudocode algorithm is unambiguous. Moreover, this definition must be entirely conceptual: It must be free from specifics about how a one-key table will be implemented in a programming language. Such a definition will allow us to refine our algorithm without worrying about details of how a one-key table will eventually be represented.

Formally Specifying the Operations for One-Key Tables

A one-key table is a collection of objects, each of which belongs to the same class. Each object in the collection is associated with a unique key value. The set of all key values must have a well-defined ordering in the sense that, for two different key values a and b, we can determine whether $a < b$ or $a > b$. Clearly, data values such as integers, real numbers, symbols of an enumerated type, and strings meet this ordering criterion. Some examples of one-key tables are shown in Figure 11.4. Note that the objects stored in these tables are of relatively simple types; objects with a more complex internal structure may be stored in one-key tables as well.

The operations for a one-key table follow. In the specification of these operations, the term *receiver* refers to the object or the instance of the ADT being operated upon.

Create Operation
Preconditions: Receiver is an arbitrary one-key table in an unpredictable state.
Postconditions: Receiver is initialized to an empty table.

Empty Operation
Precondition: Receiver is a one-key table.
Postcondition: If receiver contains no objects, the Boolean value `true` is returned; otherwise, the Boolean value `false` is returned.

Length Operation
Precondition: Receiver is a one-key table.
Postcondition: The number of objects currently in the table is returned.

Store Operation
Preconditions: Receiver is a one-key table. *target* is a key value. *item* is an object to be inserted in receiver. If *target* is not a key already in the table, there is memory available to store *item*.
Postconditions: If an object is already associated with *target* in receiver, it is replaced by *item*. Otherwise, receiver has *item* inserted and associated with *target*.

Remove Operation
Preconditions: Receiver is a one-key table. *target* is a key value associated with an object to be removed from the table.

Postconditions:	If the object with the *target* key can be found in the table, it is removed, *item* contains the object associated with *target*, and the operation returns `true`. Otherwise, the operation returns `false`, *item*'s contents are undefined, and the table is left unchanged.
Retrieve Operation	
Preconditions:	Receiver is a one-key table, and *target* is a key value to be found in the table.
Postconditions:	If the *target* can be found in the table, then *item* contains the object associated with *target* and the operation returns `true`. Otherwise, the operation returns `false`, and *item*'s contents are undefined. In either case, the one-key table is left unchanged.

The effect of each operation is highlighted in Figure 11.5 for a one-key table in which the key is a string representing a name and the object is a real number representing a grade point average.

A C++ Interface for the One-Key Table ADT

Just as we did with ordered and sorted collections, the first step in moving toward an implementation of the one-key table ADT in an object-oriented language such as C++ is to restate the operations that act on ADT objects as declarations of public member functions in a class declaration module.

```
// Class declaration file: onetable.h

#ifndef ONETABLE_H
#define ONETABLE_H

#include "assoc.h"

// Declaration section

const int MAX_TABLE_SIZE = 50;

// Generic class for key type K and element type E

template <class K, class E> class OneKeyTable

{
```

continued

Figure 11.5
The effects of the operations on a one-key table

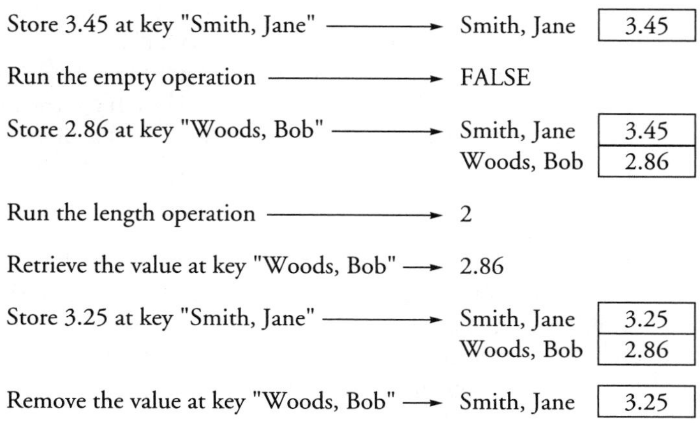

Operation		Result	
Store 3.45 at key "Smith, Jane"	→	Smith, Jane	3.45
Run the empty operation	→	FALSE	
Store 2.86 at key "Woods, Bob"	→	Smith, Jane	3.45
		Woods, Bob	2.86
Run the length operation	→	2	
Retrieve the value at key "Woods, Bob"	→	2.86	
Store 3.25 at key "Smith, Jane"	→	Smith, Jane	3.25
		Woods, Bob	2.86
Remove the value at key "Woods, Bob"	→	Smith, Jane	3.25

```
   public:

   // Class constructors

   OneKeyTable();
   OneKeyTable(const OneKeyTable<K, E> &table);

   // Function members

   int length();
   bool empty();
   void store(const K &target, const E &item);
   bool retrieve(const K &target, E &item);
   bool remove(const K &target, E &item);
   OneKeyTable<K, E>& operator = (const OneKeyTable<K, E> &table);

   protected:

   // Data members

   int tableLength;
   association<K, E> data[MAX_TABLE_SIZE];

};

#include "onetable.cpp"

#endif
```

Note several things about this class declaration module:

1. The key and element types are template parameters called `K` and `E`, respectively. We have not previously seen a class that used more than one template parameter. However, there are no surprises in this regard. Wherever the C++ compiler would expect the key type, we use `K`, and wherever the element type should appear, we use `E`.
2. The protected data members in the class declaration section also provide a clue as to how we will be representing a one-key table in C++. We will maintain the current length of a table in a data member called `tableLength`. We will use an array, called `data`, of *association* objects to store the data in the table. The association class, declared in the header file `assoc.h`, must therefore be included before the declaration of the one-key table class.
3. The use of the association class to implement a one-key table class is completely hidden from users of the one-key table. They have awareness only of using keys, elements, and one-key tables. We will return to a discussion of the role of the association class in implementing one-key tables after the following example.

Example 11.4 Here is a test driver program to exercise the various operations for the one-key table. It is similar to what we did for the ordered and sorted collection classes in Examples 11.1 and 11.2, respectively. As you examine the sample run accompanying this program, make sure you understand how the program uses a string as the key for the table and an `int` for the value associated with a given key.

A NOTE OF INTEREST

Association Lists and Dictionaries

The idea of associating data objects with key values in tables probably received its first expression in a programming language when LISP was developed in 1956. LISP, an acronym for List Processing Language, was designed to process lists of symbolic information in AI applications. These applications frequently need to associate information with a symbol. For example, a natural language processing application will have to maintain a dictionary of terms in a language. The keys for a dictionary would be symbols representing the words, and the values would be definitions or other information associated with the words. Every dialect of LISP recognizes a particular kind of list called an association list. An association list is a list consisting of key/value pairs. Once an association list has been defined, a LISP programmer can look up the value associated with a given key by using the LISP function `assoc`.

The object-oriented language Smalltalk, which is also used in many symbol processing applications, comes with a built-in hierarchy of collection classes. One subclass of the Smalltalk collection class is called a dictionary class. The dictionary class is similar to the association list in LISP. One difference is that the implementation of a dictionary in Smalltalk is geared toward very efficient retrievals, whereas a LISP association list supports only a linear search method.

Our one-key table ADT borrows much from these ideas in LISP and Smalltalk. In particular, the order of the data in the conceptual table is not specified for the user of the table, but it may be important for the efficiency of the implementation. One major difference is that we allow any key values that can be ordered, whereas LISP and Smalltalk usually allow only strings or symbols as keys. Another major difference is that all of the data values in our one-key table must be of the same type; LISP and Smalltalk allow objects of different types to be stored in the same association list or dictionary.

```
// Program file: sortedcol_drv.cpp

#include <iostream.h>
#include "apstring.h"
#include "onetable.h"

int main()
{
   // Create an empty ordered collection
   // of integers

   OneKeyTable<apstring, int> intsByStrings; // Create table
   int choice, value;
   apstring key;

   cout << "[1] length " << endl << "[2] empty" << endl
        << "[3] store " << endl << "[4] retrieve" << endl
        << "[5] remove" << endl << "[6] quit " << endl;
   do {
      cout << "Which operation should be tested? ";
      cin >> choice;
      switch (choice)
      {
      case 1:
         cout << "Table length is " << intsByStrings.length();
         break;
      case 2:
         if (intsByStrings.empty())
            cout << "Table is empty " << endl;
```

continued

```
         else
            cout << "Table is not empty " << endl;
         break;
      case 3:
         cout << "Enter key followed by associated value --> ";
         cin >> key >> value;
         intsByStrings.store(key, value);
         break;
      case 4:
         cout << "Enter key to retrieve --> ";
         cin >> key;
         if (intsByStrings.retrieve(key, value))
            cout << "Associated value is " << value << endl;
         else
            cout << key << " not in table " << endl;
         break;
      case 5:
         cout << "Enter key to remove --> ";
         cin >> key;
         if (intsByStrings.remove(key, value))
            cout << key << " and its value " << value << " removed" << endl;
         else
            cout << key << " not in table " << endl;
         break;
      case 6:
         break;
      default:
         cout << "Invalid choice -- Please try again" << endl;
         break;
      }
   } while (choice != 6);

   return 0;
}
```

A sample run of this program is:

```
[1] length
[2] empty
[3] store
[4] retrieve
[5] remove
[6] quit
Which operation should be tested? 3
Enter key followed by associated value --> foo 3
Which operation should be tested? 3
Enter key followed by associated value --> bar 7
Which operation should be tested? 3
Enter key followed by associated value --> baz 12
Which operation should be tested? 4
Enter key to retrieve --> bar
Associated value is 7
Which operation should be tested? 3
Enter key followed by associated value --> bar 1
Which operation should be tested? 4
Enter key to retrieve --> bar
```

```
Associated value is 1
Which operation should be tested? 5
Enter key to remove --> foo
foo and its value 3 removed
Which operation should be tested? 4
Enter key to retrieve --> foo
foo not in table
Which operation should be tested? 6
```

Example 11.5 This example illustrates that, *in one program,* it is possible to declare instances of one-key tables that have *different* key and element types. Here the table `intsByStrings` uses keys that are strings and elements that are `int`s, while the table `stringsByInts` reverses this by declaring `int`s to be the key type and strings to be the elements.

```
// Program file: test1key.cpp

#include <iostream.h>

#include "apstring.h"
#include "onetable.h"

void main()
{
   OneKeyTable<apstring, int> intsByStrings; // Create tables
   OneKeyTable<int, apstring> stringsByInts;

   bool success;
   int iElement;                              // Auxiliary variables
   apstring sElement;

   intsByStrings.store("age", 40);            // Store some data
   stringsByInts.store(911, "emergency");


                                              // Retrieve the data
   success = intsByStrings.retrieve("age", iElement);
   if (success)
      cout << "Age = " << iElement << endl;
   success = stringsByInts.retrieve(911, sElement);
   if (success)
      cout << "911 = " << sElement << endl;
}
```

A sample run of this program is:

```
Age = 40
911 = emergency
```

Implementations of the One-Key Table ADT

We will consider two implementations of a one-key table in this section; each will have major shortcomings from an efficiency perspective. In future chapters, we will explore more sophisticated implementations that can improve these inefficiencies. Before we examine the implementations, let us discuss the association ADT. Briefly, an association consists of two attributes: a key and a value. The only purpose of an association is to help us organize the data in a one-key table. We specify the interface for the association ADT as follows.

Create Operation
Preconditions: Receiver is an association in an unpredictable state. *key* is a key value. *item* is the object to be associated with key.
Postconditions: Receiver is initialized to associate *item* with *key*.
Get key Operation
Preconditions: Receiver is an association.
Postconditions: *key* is returned.
Get value Operation
Preconditions: Receiver is an association.
Postconditions: *value* is returned.
Set value Operation
Preconditions: Receiver is an association. *item* is an object to be inserted.
Postconditions: *item* replaces the object currently in the association.

The C++ class declaration module for the association ADT is

```
// Class declaration file: assoc.h

// Declaration section

// Generic class for key type K and element type E.

#ifndef ASSOC_H
#define ASSOC_H

template <class K, class E> class association
{
   public:

   // Class constructors

   association();
   association(const association<K, E> &a);
   association(const K &newKey, const E &newItem);

   // Member functions

   K getKey() const;
   E getValue() const;
   void setValue(const E &value);
   association& operator = (const association<K, E> &a);

   private:

   // Data members

   K theKey;
   E theValue;

};
```

```
#include "assoc.cpp"

#endif
```

Implementation 1: Physically Ordered Array with Binary Search. The strategy of this implementation is to maintain the array of associations in physical order by key. For example, the association at `data[0]` will have the smallest key, while the association at `data[tableLength - 1]` will have the largest key.

Example 11.6 This ordering for this implementation will support a binary search during the `retrieve` operation. The code for this is modeled after the algorithm we analyzed in Chapter 10:

```
template <class K, class E>
bool OneKeyTable<K, E>::retrieve(const K &target, E &item)
{
    int first, last, middle;
    K key;
    bool found = false;

    first = 0;
    last = tableLength;
    while ((first <= last) && !found)
    {
       middle = (first + last) / 2;
       key = data[middle].getKey();
       if (key == target)
          found = true;
       else if (key > target)
          last = middle - 1;
       else
          first = middle + 1;
    }
    if (found)
       item = data[middle].getValue();
    return found;
}
```

To store an object in the table in this implementation, we must do the following:

1. Search for the first association in the array that has a key greater than or equal to that of the item we are adding.
2. If the association's key is equal to our target key, just replace the item in that association with our new item and quit.
3. Otherwise, examine the current length of the table to ensure that there is room to add a new association. In this implementation, use the C++ `assert` function to halt program execution if there is no memory available. Otherwise, beginning with the current association, move all associations down one slot in the array.
4. Finally, create and insert a new association into the array slot that has been vacated and increase by 1 the length of the table.

These actions are highlighted in Figure 11.6. Carefully study this figure in conjunction with examining the code in Example 11.7.

Figure 11.6
Storing an item at a new key in a one-key table

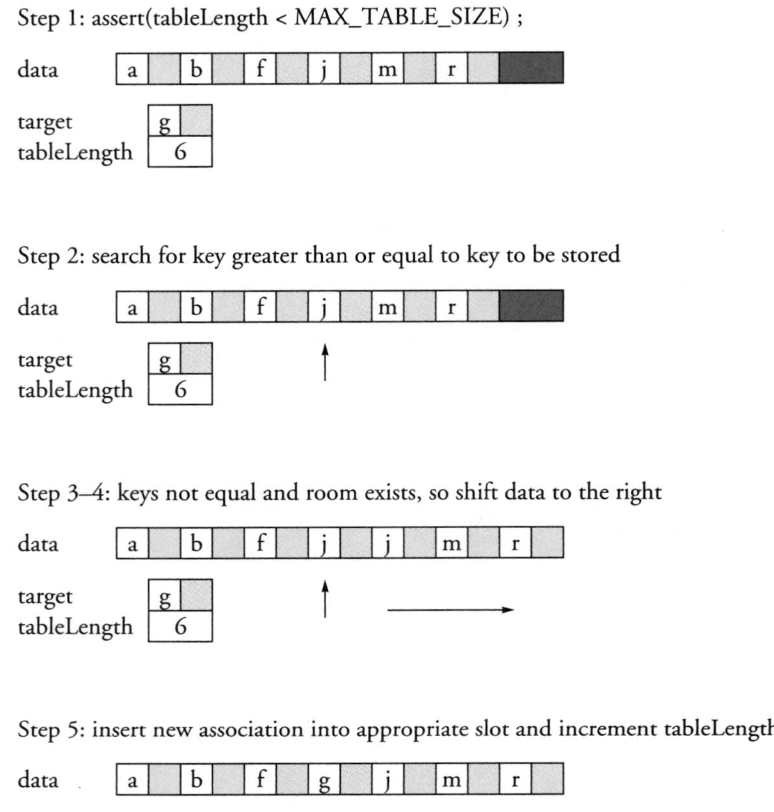

Example 11.7 Write complete C++ code for the `store` operation. This operation must maintain a correspondence between the physical order of the associations in the array and the logical order of the keys in the associations.

```
template <class K, class E>
void OneKeyTable<K, E>::store(const K &target, const E &item)
{
   int probe = 0;
   bool found = false;
   K key;

   while ((probe < tableLength) && ! found)        // Search for position
   {
     key = data[probe].getKey();
     if (key >= target)
        found = true;
     else
        ++probe;
   }
   if (found && (key == target))                   // Key already in table
      data[probe].setValue(item);
   else if (tableLength < MAX_TABLE_SIZE)          // Room available for
```

Figure 11.7
A more efficient store operation

Physical order of keys in array does not correspond to logical order in table.

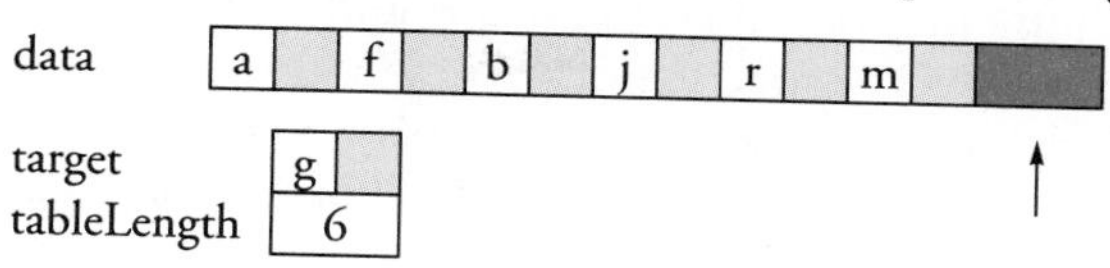

Therefore, new data are always added to the right of the last data in the table.


```
    {                                             // new association?
        for (int i = tableLength; i > probe; --i) // Yes, move them over
            data[i] = data[i - 1];
        association<K, E> a(target, item);
        data[probe]= a;
        ++tableLength;
    }
}
```

As you can see, the excellent efficiency of retrievals with this implementation is paid for by potentially expensive insertions and removals. The `create`, `remove`, `empty`, and `length` operations are left as exercises.

Implementation 2: Unordered Array with Sequential Search. Our second implementation attempts to eliminate the inefficiency involved in moving a potentially large number of objects each time a `store` is performed. The encapsulation of the one-key table ADT still includes an array of associations and a counter. However, now when an association is added, it is merely added after the last item currently stored in the array. Figure 11.7 illustrates this strategy. As you can see, the increase in efficiency of the `store` operation is being bargained for a decrease in efficiency for retrievals. The `retrieve` operation would now require a sequential search. The details of this implementation are left for you as exercises.

These trade-offs in efficiency for various operations are what make the one-key table ADT particularly interesting to study. We will return to it often in future chapters.

Exercises 11.3

1. Complete the implementation of the one-key table by developing code for the `create`, `length`, `empty`, and `remove` operations. Be sure to obey the ADT implementation rule.
2. Provide a big-O efficiency analysis of the two different implementations of the `store` operation. You should consider both the number of comparisons and data interchanges in this analysis.
3. Consider the second implementation of the `store` operation. Is there a way to take advantage of the fact that the array is sorted when looking for the target key's appropriate position? If so, write an improved version of the function and provide a big-O analysis.

4. Provide a big-O efficiency analysis of the `remove` operation. You should consider both the number of comparisons and data interchanges in this analysis.
5. Is there a way to improve the efficiency of the `remove` operation for the second implementation? If so, write a new version and provide a big-O analysis.
6. Some applications may need to process all of the objects currently in a one-key table. For example, one might wish to output all of the objects in the order of their keys. It would be useful to provide two new operations called `keys` and `values`. `keys` returns a sorted collection of the keys currently in the table, and `values` returns an unsorted ordered collection of the objects currently in the table. First specify these as ADT operations with preconditions and postconditions and then write the C++ code for them.
7. Describe the differences between the one-key table ADT and the ordered collection and sorted collection abstract data types discussed in Sections 11.1 and 11.2. Include in your discussion examples of applications for which each is most appropriate.

11.4 The Two-Key Table Abstract Data Type

Objectives

a. to understand and use the definition of the two-key table ADT
b. to consider several different implementations of the two-key table ADT
c. to recognize the shortcomings of the implementations and recognize the need for more sophisticated implementations to be studied in future chapters

Consider the problem of maintaining statistics for a baseball league. The statistics might be printed in a newspaper as follows:

	AB	HITS	2B	3B	HR	AVE
Alomar	521	192	25	6	29	.369
Brett	493	180	16	3	41	.365
Canseco	451	160	30	1	50	.354
McGwire	590	205	41	10	70	.347
Hubble	501	167	21	2	17	.333
Sosa	485	156	32	4	66	.321
Noguchi	562	180	24	2	32	.320
Perez	499	159	21	4	21	.318
Sokoloski	480	149	16	10	15	.310
Tanenbaum	490	150	14	0	23	.306

A database for storing this information should be organized so that we quickly obtain answers to queries such as, "How many home runs does Sosa have?" One way to conceptualize this organization is to imagine a table in which the desired data object is retrieved by specifying two keys: the name of the player and the category of the statistic. In the case of our example query, the answer might be obtained by running the abstract operation

retrieve the data at keys Sosa and HR

This manner of conceptualizing and using a database is so common that we will develop a new abstract data type, the two-key table, that can be used by any application. As with the one-key table, we first specify the attributes and behavior of the two-key table conceptually. Then we choose an implementation in C++. Finally, we do a big-O analysis of the behavior of our implementation and discuss the trade-offs of alternative implementations.

Two-Key Table. A two-key table is a collection of objects, each of which belongs to the same class. Each object in the collection is associated with two key values called *key1* and *key2*. Each key1 value, called a *primary key*, is unique. Each key2 value, called a *secondary key*, may be used with more than one primary key, but must indicate a unique data element when associated with a primary key. The set of all key1 values must have a well-defined ordering in the sense that, for two different key1 values a and b, we can determine whether $a < b$ or $a > b$. The same property holds for the set of all key2 values.

The operations for a two-key table follow.

Create Operation

Preconditions: Receiver is an arbitrary two-key table in an unpredictable state.

Postconditions: Receiver is initialized to an empty table.

Empty Operation

Preconditions: Receiver is a two-key table.

Postconditions: If receiver contains no objects, the Boolean value `true` is returned; otherwise, the Boolean value `false` is returned.

Store Operation

Preconditions: Receiver is a two-key table. *key1* is the primary key value. *key2* is the secondary key value. *item* is an object to be inserted in receiver. If *key1* and *key2* do not specify an object already in the table, there is memory available to store *item*.

Postconditions: If an object is already associated with *key1* and *key2* in the table, it is replaced by *item*. Otherwise, the table has *item* inserted and associated with the *key1* and *key2* values.

Remove Operation

Preconditions: Receiver is a two-key table. *key1* and *key2* are the key values associated with an object to be removed from the table.

Postconditions: If the object with the key values *key1* and *key2* can be found in the table, it is removed from the table, *item* contains the object associated with the key values *key1* and *key2*, and the operation returns `true`. Otherwise, the operation returns `false`, *item*'s contents are undefined, and the table is left unchanged.

Retrieve Operation

Preconditions: Receiver is a two-key table. *key1* and *key2* are the key values associated with an object to be found in the table.

Postconditions: If the pairing of *key1* and *key2* can be found in table, then *item* contains the object associated with *key1* and *key2* and the operation returns `true`. Otherwise, the operation returns `false`, and *item*'s contents are undefined. In either case, the table is left unchanged.

As you can see from these definitions, a two-key table is really an extension of a one-key table with an extra key. Note that we do not specify a `length` operation, however, because a two-key table is not a linear data structure.

A Class Template for the Two-Key Table ADT

In the spirit of our policy of making ADTs as general and flexible as possible, we will represent our conceptual definition of the two-key table ADT as a C++ class template. This will allow an application to specify the type of each key and the item type when a two-key table is created. For example, the table of baseball statistics discussed earlier could be declared as

```
TwoKeyTable<apstring, apstring, int> statistics;
```

where the last parameter is the type of data to be stored in the table, and the other parameters are the types of keys (first and second, respectively).

The C++ class declaration module for a two-key table class template is

```
// Class definition file: twotable.h

#ifndef TWOTABLE_H
#define TWOTABLE_H

template <class K1, class K2, class E> class TwoKeyTable
{

  public:

  // Class constructors

  TwoKeyTable();
  TwoKeyTable(const TwoKeyTable<K1, K2, E> &table);

  // Member functions

  TwoKeyTable<K1, K2, E> & operator = (const TwoKeyTable<K1, K2, E> &table);
  bool empty();
  void store(const K1 &key1, const K2 &key2, const E &item);
  bool retrieve(const K1 &key1, const K2 &key2, E &item);
  bool remove(const K1 &key1, const K2 &key2, E &item);

  protected:

  // Data members

  // Will be completed when we consider alternative implementations
};

#include "twotable.cpp"

#endif
```

Note that the interface to the class template, the function declarations, and component type parameters exactly mirrors our conceptual definition.

A Two-Dimensional Array Implementation

Since a two-key table is a two-dimensional data structure at the conceptual level, we might try to represent it as a two-dimensional array in C++. After all, we represented a one-key table as a one-dimensional array. Each row of the array would represent a `key1`, while each column would represent a `key2`. We could then choose between a direct mapping of keys to index positions along each dimension of the array (supporting efficient retrievals) or a random mapping (supporting efficient insertions).

Because there are now two keys to map to two index positions in the array, the association class must be extended to represent the association of a value with two keys. We do this by defining a derived class of association, `TwoKeyAssociation`, that contains the extra key. This approach has the effect of preserving the original association class for the use of one-key tables:

```
// Class declaration file: twoassoc.h

#ifndef TWO_ASSOC_H
#define TWO_ASSOC_H

// Declaration section

template <class K1, class K2, class E> class TwoKeyAssociation : public
      association
{
   public:
   // Class constructors

   TwoKeyAssociation();
   TwoKeyAssociation(const TwoKeyAssociation<K1, K2, E> &a);
   TwoKeyAssociation(const K1 &key1, const K2 &key2,
        const E &newItem);

   // Member functions

   K2 getKey2();
   TwoKeyAssociation<K1, K2, E>& operator =
        (const TwoKeyAssociation<K1, K2, E> &a);

   private:

   // Data members
   K2 theKey2;

};

#endif
```

Two other questions must be answered before we can write the definitions of the data members for the two-key table. First, what will be the maximum size of a two-key table? The answer to this question for one-key tables was specified by a constant, `MAX_TABLE_SIZE`, defined in the header file. For a two-dimensional array, we will need two constants, `MAX_ROW_SIZE` and `MAX_COL_SIZE`, to define the maximum sizes of the two dimensions. Application modules will again specify these values, with the understanding that `MAX_ROW_SIZE` represents the maximum number of possible `key1` values in a two-key table and `MAX_COL_SIZE` represents the maximum number of possible `key2` values.

Second, how will we maintain the current number of objects stored in a two-key table? A one-key table used an integer data member, `tableLength`, representing the next available location in the array for storing data. The situation in a two-dimensional array is more complicated. We need to know both the position of the next available row (for a new `key1`) and the next available column in each row (for a new `key2`). Therefore, we will define two data members, an integer variable and an array of integers, to represent these attributes.

The data members for the two-dimensional array can now be added to the class declaration module of the two-key table:

```
// Data members

TwoKeyAssociation<K1, K2, E> data[MAX_ROW_SIZE][MAX_COL_SIZE];
int rowLength;
int colLengths[MAX_ROW_SIZE];
```

The next example shows how we would implement the `store` operation, assuming that we simply pick the next available row and column for a new object at `key1` and `key2`.

Example 11.8 Write the implementation of the member function that stores an object in a two-key table. We assume that if the `key1` is new, we enter at a new row, and if `key2` is new, we enter at a new column.

```
template <class K1, class K2, class E>
void TwoKeyTable<K1, K2, E>::store(const K1 &key1, const K2 &key2, const E &item)
{
  int row, col;
  bool found = false;
  K1 rowKey;
  K2 colKey;

  row = 0;
  col = 0;
  while ((row < rowLength) && ! found)      // Search key1 in rows
  {
       rowKey = data[row][col].getKey();
       if (key1 == rowKey)
            found = true;
       else
            ++row;
  }
  if (found)                                // key1 already in table
  {
       found = false;                       // Search for key2 in column
       while ((col < columnLengths[row]) && ! found)
       {
            colKey = data[row][col].getKey2();
            if (key2 == colKey)
                   found = true;
            else
                   ++col;
       }
       if (found)                           // key2 also already in table
            data[row] [col].setValue(item);
       else
       {
            assert(columnLengths[row] < MAX_COL_SIZE); // Room available
                                                       // for column?
            TwoKeyAssociation<K1, K2, E> a(key1, key2, item);
            data[row][col] = a;                        // Add a new key2
            ++columnLengths[row];
```

```
        }
    }
    else
    {
        assert(rowLength < MAX_ROW_SIZE);    // Room available for row?
        TwoKeyAssociation<K1, K2, E> a(key1, key2, item);
        data[row][0] = a;                               // Add a new key1
        columnLengths[row]= 1;
        ++rowLength;

    }
}
```

By now, you will probably have surmised that there are some serious drawbacks to this implementation. The most obvious one is the length and complexity of the `store` operation. With so many alternative cases to consider and data to maintain, this code will be very difficult to read, understand, and get correct. Moreover, the `retrieve` and `remove` operations will be almost as complicated.

As far as efficiency is concerned, the current implementation introduces a new data structure, the array for maintaining the current lengths of the columns, that results in a linear growth of memory for the maximum number of secondary keys that an application needs in a table. The current version also forces us to add a data member to the association class to represent a second key. The only advantage is that binary searches for a target object might be very fast, assuming that one can get the code correct!

The choice of this implementation seems so unreasonable that we will not even leave its completion as an exercise but rather look for a simpler one.

Using One-Key Tables to Implement Two-Key Tables

Another way to think of a two-key table is as a one-key table. Each key in this table will represent a `key1` in the two-key table. At each of these keys, we store another one-key table. Each key in each of these tables will represent a `key2` in the two-key table. Thus, the data elements stored at the keys in the nested one-key tables will be the data elements stored in the two-key table.

The advantage of this representation is that it allows us to use higher level components to construct our two-key table ADT. This will allow us to use higher level operations as well. For example, the operation for retrieving a data element at `key1` and `key2` in a two-key table can now be conceptualized as follows:

1. Retrieve the element at `key1` of the top-level one-key table
2. If the retrieval is successful, then
3. From this element (also a one-key table) retrieve the element at `key2`

The advantage of this implementation over the two-dimensional array implementation is that this one's code for the search operations has already been written, so we just invoke them by name. In the two-dimensional array implementation, we are forced to reinvent the wheel by rewriting this code.

Here is a class declaration module for a two-key table that uses one-key tables to support high-level implementations of two-key operations:

```
// Class definition file: twotable.h

#ifndef TWOTABLE_H
#define TWOTABLE_H

#include "onetable.h"

template <class K1, class K2, class E> class TwoKeyTable
{

   public:

   // Class constructors

   TwoKeyTable();
   TwoKeyTable(const TwoKeyTable<K1, K2, E> &table);

   // Member functions

   TwoKeyTable<K1, K2, E> & operator = (const TwoKeyTable<K1, K2, E> &table);
   bool empty();
   void store(const K1 &key1, const K2 &key2, const E &item);
   bool retrieve(const K1 &key1, const K2 &key2, E &item);
   bool remove(const K1 &key1, const K2 &key2, E &item);

   protected:

   // Data members

   OneKeyTable<K1, OneKeyTable<K2, E> > data;

};

#include "twotable.cpp"

#endif
```

The interface of the two-key table class stays the same, but the new implementation has just one data member. This is a one-key table whose key type is `K1` and whose element type is another one-key table. The key type of this second one-key table is `K2`, and its element type is `E`. Carefully examine the line of code that defines this data member, especially the ordering of the angle brackets, so that you understand how the type parameters are passed to set up the data structure.

The next example shows how we can take advantage of the new data member definitions to implement the `retrieve` operation for two-key tables.

Example 11.9 Write the implementation of the `retrieve` operation for the two-key table class specified in the class declaration module given earlier.

```
template <class K1, class K2, class E>
bool TwoKeyTable<K1, K2, E>::retrieve(const K1 &key1, const K2 &key2, E &item)
{
   OneKeyTable<K2, E> table;
```

```
   if (data.retrieve(key1, table))
      return table.retrieve(key2, item);
   else
      return false;
}
```

After working through the code for the two-dimensional array implementation, this code must seem almost magically simple. However, it represents a straightforward use of the one-key tables in the new data representation. Using the data member `data`, we attempt to retrieve a table at `key1`. If we are successful, we use this table to attempt to retrieve an item at `key2`. If we are successful here, the item is returned and the function returns `true`. If either of the retrievals fails, the function returns `false`.

Not only is this version easy to read, understand, and get correct, but we no longer need to consider the alternatives of linear search or binary search to implement a retrieval. These considerations have been resolved at a lower level, during the implementation of the one-key table. The next example shows how to implement a `store` operation for this version. Be sure to compare it to the other version in Example 11.8.

Example 11.10 Write the implementation of the `store` operation for the one-key table implementation of the two-key table ADT.

```
template <class K1, class K2, class E>
void TwoKeyTable<K1, K2, E>::store(const K1 &key1, const K2 &key2,
   const E &item)
{
   OneKeyTable<K2, E> table;

   data.retrieve(key1, table);
   table.store(key2, item);
   data.store(key1, table);

}
```

Comparing the Two Implementations

Our intuition in choosing a two-dimensional array implementation for a two-key table seemed natural: One can think of each structure as consisting of a grid in which a data item is located by specifying a row and column. Moreover, since we were able to map a key in a one-key table to an index position in a one-dimensional array, it seemed logical to try to map two keys to the two indices of a two-dimensional array. However, when we turned to the actual data structures and algorithms for implementing this version, we quickly became lost in a welter of complexity. We found it necessary to introduce complex auxiliary data structures, such as an array of column lengths and a two-key association class, and to write pages of code for each individual operation.

By reconceiving a two-key table as a one-key table whose data items are other one-key tables, we were able to simplify both the data structures used in the implementation and the code used in the operations. The one-key table ADT handles most of the work of representing the data and implementing the operations. We no longer have to think about using auxiliary ADTs such as the association, much less about subclassing it to represent a second key. We no longer have to decide between an implementation that supports binary search (fast retrievals) or linear search (fast insertions).

On the other hand, the one-key table implementation gives us less control over the way a two-key table behaves than we might wish. If a client of the two-key table desires fast retrievals and the one-key table implements a linear search, the client is stuck with that. Moreover, clients can no longer specify separate maximum row and column sizes for two-key tables. This last factor can lead to a serious inefficiency in the use of memory, where storage would be allocated for rows or columns in the table that are not really needed by the application. We will see a way to remedy this last problem in later chapters.

The contrast between the two implementations can be viewed as a layered system versus an unlayered system. The one-key table implementation places a layer of high-level types and operations between the two-key table ADT and the underlying C++ data structures and operations. The two-dimensional array implementation represents the two-key table ADT directly in terms of the underlying C++ data structures and operations. Layered systems are generally easy to design and maintain; unlayered systems may be more efficient but are usually much more difficult to design and maintain.

These considerations lead us to formulate one more principle for the design of abstract data types:

ADT layering rule: Existing abstract data types should be used to implement new abstract data types, unless direct control over the underlying data structures and operations of the programming language is a critical factor. A well-designed implementation consists of layers of ADTs.

Exercises 11.4

1. Complete the one-key table implementation of the two-key table ADT.
2. Write a program that uses a two-key table to store and retrieve the baseball statistics described earlier in this section. Explain how you handle the data in the last column, which appear to be real numbers rather than integers.
3. A data item is located in a three-key table by specifying three keys. Write an abstract definition and an appropriate C++ class declaration module for this ADT. Remember to adhere to the ADT reuse and layering rules.
4. Example 11.4 presented a comprehensive test driver for the one-key table ADT. Write a similar test driver for the two-key table.

11.5 Revisiting the Analysis Phase of the Software Engineering Life Cycle

As early as Chapter 2, we discussed the software engineering life cycle and identified its five phases: *analysis, design, implementation, testing,* and *maintenance.* In all Case Studies since, we've developed a complete program by going through the analysis, design, and implementation phases. For large software systems, however, the process is much more complex than we've seen so far. By using data abstraction wherever possible, software engineers have been able to control and manage this complexity somewhat. The best way of understanding how data abstraction and other techniques can be used to advantage in the process is to illustrate how they are used in tackling a more substantial problem. That is what we propose to do in the rest of the chapter.

In this section, we will investigate some of the complications that can occur on the way to defining user requirements during the analysis phase. In Section 11.6, we will explore the design phase, focusing on how to progress from the user requirements document to a detailed definition of the ADTs needed by the software system.

Objectives

a. to understand more thoroughly what is done during the analysis phase of systems development
b. to define the responsibilities of a systems analyst
c. to recognize the importance of oral and written communication skills in the analysis phase

In Section 11.7, strategies for implementing and testing the system will be discussed. Finally, the Case Study will follow through on the material from the preceding sections to finish the system.

It has been said that the only simple problems in computing are those defined in textbooks. Perhaps a key to the truth of this statement is its use of the word *defined*. Once a problem has been specifically defined, the most difficult obstacle to solving it may have been surmounted. In the analysis phase, you must define in detail the problem that you are charged with solving.

It is important to remember that in trying to provide such a definition, you are typically working with a problem originally posed by someone other than yourself. We will try to emphasize this fact in the following material by introducing the problem in the form of a memorandum from computer users. This is done to emphasize that programs are written not for computer scientists but for computer users. These computer users often know virtually nothing about the computer other than a vague (and often inaccurate) notion that it can magically take care of all of their record keeping and computational needs. Bridging the gap between potentially naive users and the computer-oriented people who eventually are responsible for implementing the software system constitutes the first phase of the system life cycle.

Although many people are aware that systems analysts work with computers in some way, few know specifically what a systems analyst does. More than anything else, the systems analyst is responsible for the analysis phase of the system life cycle. A systems analyst talks to the users who initially request the system to learn exactly what they need. This is done not only by talking to users, but also by studying in detail what they do. For instance, a systems analyst working for a bank on an automated teller system would have to become an expert on the various duties and responsibilities of a teller. Having learned what the automated system is supposed to do, the systems analyst must then develop formal specifications describing the system and its requirements. The technical people who design and code the software will work from these specifications.

So, imagine yourself in the role of a systems analyst who receives the following memorandum from the registrar at the University of Hard Knocks. In it, she requests that you automate the university's recordkeeping on its students.

Memorandum
University of Hard Knocks

To: Director of Data Processing
From: Head Registrar
Date: July 29, 2000
Re: Automation of recordkeeping on students

As you know, we presently maintain our student records by manual methods. We believe the time has come to computerize this operation and request that you do so for us.

Here is what we need. Each student's record consists of her name, the total number of credits taken, the total number of credits earned, her cumulative grade point average (GPA), and a list of grades received in each course she has taken. We maintain these records by a student's last name. Of course, at numerous times, we must add new students to our records and remove those who have graduated or withdrawn from school. Students often come into our office and request to see their current record, so we must be able to find that information quickly. At the end of each semester, we print a grade report for each student. This report consists of the items cited above, although we only include the grades of courses taken in the current term. At the end of the year, the Dean of Students requests two lists of graduating seniors. One of these lists is to be printed in alphabetical order by student name. The other is printed in order by student grade point average.

Certainly, the situation described in this memo is an oversimplification of any real college registrar's office. However, even this relatively unsophisticated situation offers some interesting food for thought. For one thing, the memo demonstrates the fact that your first contact with a user requesting the system will often leave gaps in your knowledge about the system that is actually needed. The head registrar's memo leaves unanswered the following questions:

1. What is the university's definition of grade points?
2. When grade reports are printed for each student, is it important that they be printed in any particular order?
3. Since grade reports are printed at the end of each semester, do you need some means of updating a student's record at the end of a semester?
4. What is the method used to compute a student's GPA?
5. What separates seniors who graduate from those seniors who don't graduate?
6. Is the list printed in order by student GPA arranged from best student to worst student, or vice versa?
7. What naming scheme is used for courses at the university?

You need to communicate these questions to the registrar before the specifics of the system can be appropriately modeled. Suppose you do that and receive the following reply.

Memorandum
University of Hard Knocks

To: Director of Data Processing
From: Head Registrar
Date: August 2, 2000
Re: Responses to your questions

Question 1: Four grade points are assigned for a one-credit A grade, three for a B, two for a C, one for a D, and zero for an F. Courses worth more than one credit have their corresponding grade points multiplied accordingly.

Question 2: Grade reports should be printed in alphabetical order by student last name.

Question 3: At the end of each semester, faculty members turn in grades for each class they teach. We use the grades on these class rosters to update a student's academic information before printing a grade report.

Question 4: GPA is computed as the quotient of total grade points divided by credits taken.

Question 5: A graduating senior must have earned at least 120 credits.

Question 6: The list is to be printed from best student to worst student.

Question 7: Officially, our office identifies each course by a department code that is four characters or less and a course number. However, courses also have a longer descriptive title. This title should appear on the grade reports received by the student.

This process of give-and-take communication between the end users of the system and yourself as analyst continues until you conclude that you understand the registrar's operation in sufficient detail to write a formal *user requirements specification.*

User Requirements Specification
for the Registrar's System

After initially loading the student database, along with information on all of our courses, the registrar's system should present its user with a main menu that allows the following options:

- Add and delete student records from the database.
- Enter a dialogue to delete a student from the database
- Enter a dialogue to update an existing student's record with the grades from the courses that she has completed in the current semester
- Enter a dialogue to inspect the complete academic record of a student
- Enter a dialogue to produce grade reports for all students in a specified semester
- Produce end-of-year reports of graduating seniors, first in alphabetical order and then in grade-point-average order

In the dialogue to add a new student to the database, that student should be identified by her full name with last name followed by first. Initially, that student will have an empty student record stored in the database. As that student accumulates courses at the university, that student record should keep track of the total number of credits taken by the student, the total number of credits earned, the cumulative grade point average, and a list of grade records for all courses that have been taken by the student. Each grade record consists of an identification of the course taken by the student, the year and semester (fall or winter) in which it was taken, the number of credits associated with that course, and the grade the student received in the course. Officially, two keys—its department code and its course number—identify a course in our database of courses. The former is a short string of four or fewer characters; the latter is a three-digit number. Unofficially, courses are identified by a title that is much longer and more descriptive than its two-key identification. This title must often be displayed in the output triggered by other dialogues in the system.

The dialogue to delete a student from the database merely requires that the user enter the full name of the student to be deleted. If the student exists in the database, she should be removed. Otherwise, an error message should be displayed, and the user should be returned to the main menu.

The dialogue to update an existing student's record starts with entering the student's full name. Assuming the student is found in the database, the user should then enter a succession of grade records for that student. In entering these grade records, it should not be necessary to enter the number of credits for the course since, for a given course, the number of credits will always be the same. Instead, once the user identifies the course, the system should be able to determine the number of credits from the course information that is stored within the student database.

The dialogue to inspect the complete academic record of a student should again be keyed by entry of the student's full name. If that student is found in the database, the information displayed should include the total number of credits taken by the student, the total number of credits earned, the cumulative GPA, and the list of grades for all courses that have been taken by the student. In this list, the information for each course should include the department, number, credits, grade, and full descriptive title.

The dialogue to produce grade reports for all students requires that the user enter the year and the semester. The former should be entered in 19XX or 20XX format. The latter should be entered as F or W, for the fall and winter semesters, respectively. The grade reports should appear in alphabetical order by student name. The information displayed for each student should include the total number of credits taken by the student, the total number of credits earned, the cumulative GPA, and the list of grades for all courses that have been taken by the student *in the specified semester only*.

The two end-of-year reports should include for each graduating student her full name, total number of credits taken, total number of credits earned, and cumulative GPA.

The user requirements specification is the most important document emerging from the analysis phase. It provides a complete and unambiguous definition of the system's input and outputs. It must be written in language nontechnical enough to allow the end users to "sign off" on the document, that is, give their official blessing that a system delivered in the form described will indeed satisfy their needs. At the same time, it must be stated in a form that is detailed enough to allow software designers to work from it during the design phase. These software designers want a complete statement of *what* the system must do, but not *how* it should be done. This distinction between what and how is critical and is the same distinction we encountered earlier when formally defining ADTs.

Exercises 11.5

1. Write a user requirements specification to give to the designers for a software system you will use each month to maintain your checking account at a local bank.
2. Write a user requirements specification to give to the designers for a software system you will use to keep track of the musical CDs that you own.
3. Write a user requirements specification to give to the designers for a software system you will use to maintain statistics for your favorite sports team.
4. For this task, you'll work with another student. Each of you should write a memorandum to specify what you view as the information-processing needs of an administrative office at your school (or any other office environment with which you may be familiar). Your memorandum should provide information similar to that provided by the registrar at the University of Hard Knocks. Exchange your memoranda, study them, and then get together with the other person to resolve any questions you might have. Write a user requirements specification from what you have learned. Finally, have the other person critique the accuracy and completeness of your document.
5. Consider the following memorandum from the registrar at the renowned American Basket Weaving University—one of the main competitors of the University of Hard Knocks.

Memorandum
American Basket Weaving University

To: Director of Data Processing
From: Head Registrar
Date: July 29, 2001
Re: Automation of recordkeeping on students

Records for students at our school consist of a university identification number, a last name, a first name, a middle initial, a social security number, a list of courses the student has taken along with the grade received in each course, and a list of extracurricular activities in which the student has indicated an interest. A university identification number for a student consists of six-digits; the first two digits represent the year a student entered the university. The remaining four digits are simply assigned on a sequential basis as students are admitted to the school. For instance, the student with ID number 990023 is the 23rd student admitted in the class that entered ABWU in 1999.

Given this database, we frequently need to work with it in the following ways:

- Find and display all data for a particular student.
- Add and delete student records from the database.
- Print records for all students.
- Add, change, or delete the information on a course for a particular student.
- Find all students with an extracurricular interest that matches a particular target interest.

Develop a set of questions that you would ask the head registrar to resolve what you feel are ambiguities in this memo. Give your set of questions to another student. That other student, acting as the head registrar, should answer the questions you've posed. Working from the original memo and the answers to questions provided by your classmate, write a user requirements specification for this software system.

6. Write an essay in which you defend or attack the following position: To prepare for a career as a systems analyst, it is more important to develop interpersonal communication skills than it is to acquire a mass of technical knowledge about specific computer systems.

11.6 Revisiting the Design Phase of the Software Engineering Life Cycle

Objectives

a. to understand the responsibilities of the design phase of the software system life cycle
b. to see the relationship between the analysis and design phases
c. to reiterate the importance of formally defining the operations of a class before beginning to implement that class
d. to understand what is meant by the CRC design methodology
e. to see how user requirements specifications from the analysis phase may be transformed into a CRC system design

You now need to change your hat and put yourself in the place of the systems designer. You have been given the user requirements specification from the analysis phase and now must develop a model from which programmers will write the code for the system. This model should divide the system into objects with well-defined behaviors. A hallmark of engineering as a discipline is to follow recognized methodologies in building a sequence of models that ultimately evolve into a finished product. The methodology that we will describe here is called *CRC modeling*. CRC stands for Classes-Responsibilities-Collaborators. You will find that it is a natural extension of the way in which we have already approached defining classes. However, what we have done previously has typically looked at a class as an isolated entity. In designing a complete system, we must additionally specify how each class will interact with the other classes in the system.

The first step in CRC modeling is to enumerate the classes that will compose the system. A good starting point for doing this is to reread the requirements specification and identify the critical nouns in that document. Why? Objects are entities, not actions. As such, they will correspond to nouns, not verbs, in the requirements specification. Using this heuristic, we again present the beginning of the requirements specification for the registrar's system. Now, however, we have underlined the important nouns.

User Requirements Specification
for the Registrar's System

After initially loading the <u>student database</u>, along with information on all of our courses, the registrar's system should present its user with a <u>main menu</u> that allows the following options:

- Enter a dialogue to add a new student to the database
- Enter a dialogue to delete a student from the database
- Enter a dialogue to update an existing student's record with the grades from the courses that she has completed in the current semester
- Enter a dialogue to inspect the complete academic record of a student
- Enter a dialogue to produce grade reports for all students in a specified semester
- Produce end-of-year reports of graduating seniors, first in alphabetical order and then in grade-point-average order

In the dialogue to add a new student to the database, that student should be identified by her full name with last name followed by first. Initially, that student will have an empty student record stored in the database. As that student accumulates courses at the university, that <u>student record</u> should keep track of the total number of credits taken by

> the student, the total number of credits earned, the cumulative grade point average, and a list of grade records for all courses that have been taken by the student. Each grade record consists of an identification of the course taken by the student, the year and semester (fall or winter) in which it was taken, the number of credits associated with that course, and the grade the student received in the course. Officially, two keys—its department code and its course number—identify a course in our database of courses. The former is a short string of four or fewer characters; the latter is a three-digit number. Unofficially, courses are identified by a title that is much longer and more descriptive than its two-key identification. This title must often be displayed in the output triggered by other dialogues in the system.

Extracting these key nouns from the requirements specification gives us a preliminary breakdown of the system into classes. Each of these classes should then be annotated with a brief comment as to its role in the system. Table 11.1 shows the result of doing this for the registrar's system.

The first C in CRC modeling is now complete: We have defined the classes needed by the system. The next step is to define the responsibilities of each class (the R in CRC). The most essential aspect of this part of the process is one with which you are already familiar from our previous work in defining ADTs. That is, for each class, we must use pre- and postconditions to define each of the operations belonging to that class. This involves another careful reading of the requirements specification to better understand the details of the role each class will play in the system. As this is done, the good designer will not only define the operations for each class but will also:

- Recognize how preexisting ADTs may be used to help in the eventual implementation of the classes for this particular system.
- Begin to make some decisions about implementation strategies for the classes. In C++ vernacular, this means that the designer begins to make recommendations about what will ultimately become private or protected data members. Typically, these decisions will be made with an eye toward achieving a particular efficiency. The convention in CRC modeling is to use the word "knows" when making such a recommendation. The programmer who will carry out the implementation of this class should think of these recommendations as hints from the designer about effective ways to carry out the implementation.
- See how one class will have to rely on another class for help in carrying out a particular operation. The class that provides the help is called a collaborating class, and

Table 11.1
Preliminary Breakdown of Registrar's System into Classes

Class	Role
student database	this class will maintain the records of all students at the university
main menu	this class will provide the interaction with users of the system
student record	this class maintains data on each individual student
list of grade records	this class maintains all of the grades associated with each individual student
grade record	this class maintains the data on the grade a student receives in an individual course
course record	this class maintains the data on an individual course at the university
database of courses	this class maintains the collection of all course records

A NOTE OF INTEREST

Object-Oriented Design and Productivity in Software Development

In 1986, renowned software engineer Frederick Brooks published an essay called "No Silver Bullet" in *Proceedings of the IFIP Tenth World Computing Conference*, pp. 1069–1076. In it, Brooks predicted that over the 10-year span following the publication of the essay, there would be no programming technique that would lead to an order-of-magnitude improvement in the productivity of the software development process. Such a technique is what Brooks refers to as the "silver bullet." In effect, he is saying we will not discover a magical way to make easy something that is inherently hard.

In a 1995 essay called "No Silver Bullet Refired" appearing in *The Mythical Man-Month: 20th Anniversary Edition* (Reading, MA: Addison-Wesley, 1995, p. 20), Brooks takes a retrospective look at his 1986 prediction. In it, he argues that his basic predictions have held and that we have not witnessed an order-of-magnitude improvement in the productivity of software developers. However, the picture he paints is not a bleak one. In many ways, he admits that we may be getting close to something significant. Much of the reason is tied to the progress that has and will be made in object-oriented development techniques. For example, he states that, whereas he once felt that *all* programmers should see *all* the code for a system, he now has come to be a firm believer in information hiding as a way of "raising the level of software design."

Brooks contends that we have just begun to scratch the surface of the advantages inherent in object-oriented design. Two things will happen in the near future. First, the designers of classes will learn to think bigger. They will develop classes with complete functionality to solve broad ranges of problems. Examples he cites are graphical user interface classes and classes for doing finite-element analysis. Second, those who write client programs will become more adept at using these high-powered classes in new and exciting ways. The combination will still not be the silver bullet, but Brooks now does go so far as to offer the following caveat: "Object-oriented programming—will a brass bullet do?"

the designer should include notes about such collaborations in the design document that is passed on to the programmers. Doing this takes care of the second C in CRC.

Given this overview of the process, we will complete the CRC design of the registrar's system.

CRC Design Specs for Main Menu Class

Knows: the student database

Create Operation

Preconditions: Main menu is in an arbitrary state. *sd* is a student database.

Postconditions: Main menu has been initialized with information in the student database *sd*.

Start Operation

Preconditions: Main menu has been created.

Postconditions: Main menu has been displayed, allowing user choice of adding student, deleting student, inspecting student, updating student's grade, displaying grade reports, displaying end-of-year reports, or quitting.

Add Dialogue Operation

Preconditions: None

Postconditions: User has been queried for information necessary to add student to database and appropriate student record has been added.

Collaborators: Student database class

Delete Dialogue Operation

Preconditions: None

Postconditions: User has been queried for information necessary to remove student from database. Appropriate student record has been removed or user has been informed that the student cannot be found in the database.

Collaborators: Student database class

Inspect Dialogue Operation

Preconditions: None

Postconditions: User has been queried for information necessary to inspect record for particular student in the database. Appropriate student record has been displayed or user has been informed that the student cannot be found in the database.

Collaborators: Student database class

Update Dialogue Operation

Preconditions: None

Postconditions: User has been queried for student name to update. If that student is not found in the database, appropriate message is displayed. Otherwise, user is repeatedly queried for grades in each of the courses taken by the student in the current semester.

Collaborators: Student database class

Report Dialogue Operation

Preconditions: None

Postconditions: User has been queried for year and semester for which to produce grade reports. Grade reports for that semester have been printed.

Collaborators: Student database class

CRC Design Specs for Student Database Class

Knows: the course database, enabling it to access information on course titles and credits

Use Existing ADT: Extend the operations provided in the existing one-key-table class. Hence, all operations in the one-key table are available.

Create Operation

Preconditions: Student database object is in unreliable state. A stream contains information on already existing students and courses.

Postconditions: Student database has been loaded from information in stream.

Add Student Operation

Preconditions: *studentName* contains the name of the new student to be added to the database.

Postconditions: *studentName* has been added to the database along with an empty student record.

Collaborators: Student record class

Student Exists Operation

Preconditions: *studentName* contains the name of the new student to be added to the database.

Postconditions: Returns `true` if *studentName* is in the database and `false` if it is not

Delete Student Operation

Preconditions: *studentName* contains the name of the student to be removed from the database.

Postconditions: *studentName* has been removed from the database along with a returned value of `true` to indicate success or `false` to indicate *studentName* cannot be found in the database.

Inspect Student Operation

Preconditions: *studentName* contains the name of the student whose record is to be displayed.

Postconditions: The record of *studentName* has been displayed along with a returned value of `true` to indicate success or `false` to indicate *studentName* cannot be found in the database.

Collaborators: Student record class

Add Course Operation

Preconditions:	*studentName* contains the name of the student to whose list of grade records *newCourse* is to be added.
Postconditions:	The record of *studentName* has been updated to contain the grade record *newCourse* and the Boolean value `true` is returned to indicate success or `false` to indicate *studentName* cannot be found in the database.
Collaborators:	Student record class

Grade Reports Operation

Preconditions:	*year* and *semester* contain the year and semester (F for fall or W for winter) for which grade reports are to be produced.
Postconditions:	Grade reports have been printed in alphabetical order by student name.
Collaborators:	Student record class.

Graduation List by Name Operation

Preconditions:	None
Postconditions:	A list of all graduating seniors has been printed in alphabetical order.
Collaborators:	Student record class

Graduation List by GPA Operation

Preconditions:	None
Postconditions:	A list of all graduating seniors has been printed in descending order by GPA.
Collaborators:	Student record class

CRC Design Specs for Course Database Class

Use Existing ADT:	Simply use the existing two-key-table class, with department as primary key, course number as secondary key, and course record objects as the elements stored in the table. This will provide all the functionality that is needed for the course database.

CRC Design Specs for List of Grade Records Class

Use Existing ADT:	Simply use the existing ordered collection class, with grade records being the elements stored in the collection. This will provide all the functionality that is needed for the list of grade records.

CRC Design Specs for Student Record Class

Knows:	the list of grade records for the courses that have been taken by this student
Knows:	the course database (so it can look up course titles and credits)

Create Operation

Preconditions:	Student record is in an arbitrary state. *courseDatabase* references the course database.
Postconditions:	Student record has been initialized to know about *courseDatabase* with an empty list of grade records.

Get Credits Taken Operation

Preconditions:	Student record has been created and perhaps acted upon by other operations.
Postconditions:	Return the number of credits that this student has taken.

Collaborators: Course record class, grade record class, course database class, list of grade records class

Get Credits Earned Operation

Preconditions: Student record has been created and perhaps acted upon by other operations.

Postconditions: Return the number of credits that this student has earned.

Collaborators: Course record class, grade record class, course database class, list of grade records class

Get GPA Operation

Preconditions: Student record has been created and perhaps acted upon by other operations.

Postconditions: Return the student's cumulative grade point average.

Collaborators: Course record class, grade record class, course database class, list of grade records class

Add Course Operation

Preconditions: *gr* is a grade record.

Postconditions: *gr* has been added to the list of grade records for this student.

Collaborators: Grade record class, list of grade records class

Display Course History Operation (First Version)

Preconditions: None

Postconditions: Student's entire course history has been displayed.

Collaborators: Course record class, grade record class, course database class, list of grade records class

Display Course History Operation (Second Version)

Preconditions: *year* represents a year and *semester* represents a semester (F or W)

Postconditions: Student's course history for *year* and *semester* has been displayed.

Collaborators: Course record class, grade record class, course database class, list of grade records class

CRC Design Specs for Course Record Class

Knows: the course title

Knows: the number of credits for the course

Create Operation

Preconditions: Course record is in an arbitrary state. *title* is a course title and *credits* is the number of credits for the course.

Postconditions: Course record has been initialized to know about *title* and *credits.*

Get Credits Operation

Preconditions: Course record has been created.

Postconditions: Return the number of credits for this course.

Get Title Operation

Preconditions: Course record has been created.

Postconditions: Return the title for this course.

CRC Design Specs for Grade Record Class

Knows: the primary key (department) and secondary key (course number) to identify the course for which the grade was given

Knows: the year and the semester in which the course was taken

Knows: the letter grade received in the course

Create Operation

Preconditions: Grade record is in an arbitrary state. *dept, courseNum, year, semester, grade* are parameters representing the five items the record must know.

Postconditions: Grade record has been initialized to know about *dept, courseNum, year, semester, grade*.

Get Department Operation

Preconditions: Grade record has been created.

Postconditions: Return the department code (primary key) associated with the course for which grade was issued.

Get Course Number Operation

Preconditions: Grade record has been created.

Postconditions: Return the number (secondary key) associated with the course for which grade was issued.

Get Year Operation

Preconditions: Grade record has been created.

Postconditions: Return the year in which this grade was issued.

Get Semester Operation

Preconditions: Grade record has been created.

Postconditions: Return the semester (F or W) in which this grade was issued.

Get Grade Operation

Preconditions: Grade record has been created.

Postconditions: Return the letter grade that was earned in the course.

Get Grade Points Operation

Preconditions: Grade record has been created.

Postconditions: Return the number of grade points associated with letter grade for this course.

The design phase is arguably the most creative phase of the software development life cycle. Decisions made during this phase determine not only if the final system meets the needs described in the user requirements specification, but also whether those needs are met in a fashion that is efficient and easy to maintain in the future.

For example, two design decisions emerging from the preceding CRC model of the registrar's system point toward a concern with storing unnecessary and redundant information in the student database. First, we can see from the description of the "Knows" section of the student record class that we have chosen not to store as data the total number of credits taken and earned and the cumulative grade point average of a student. Rather, when requested, these values must be computed and returned through operations the class provides. Clearly, these operations will have to traverse the list of grades that is known to the student record. This traversal will require time, so here we have traded the time required to perform these computations for the space that would have been required to store the information permanently as part of the student record.

Second, we can see from the description of the grade record class that we have chosen not to store the number of credits and course title as part of each grade record. Rather, a student record is given a reference to the course database, allowing it to look up the title and number of credits in this database when needed. The potential for saving space is quite significant here. We store the title for a course only once instead of in each grade record. Imagine that a university had 500 courses, each with a course title that averaged 20 characters. In the course database, storing these titles will require 500 * 20 = 10,000 characters of storage. If the university had 10,000 students, each of whom had completed an average of 25 courses and if we had chosen to store the course title (redundantly) in each grade record, the cost of storing all these titles is 10,000 * 20 * 25 = 5,000,000 characters of storage. Thus, this decision made during the design phase of development will result in a system that is more space efficient by a factor of 50. Considerations of this kind can ultimately make or break a system in the real world.

There are many other methodologies for designing systems other than the CRC modeling technique we have described and illustrated in this section. Of course, you should not think that the treatment of CRC modeling we have provided is complete. If you are interested in more deeply exploring CRC modeling, you should read: Rebecca Wirfs-Brock, Brian Wilkerson, & Laura Wiener, *Designing Object-Oriented Software,* Upper Saddle River, NJ: Prentice Hall, 1990.

Exercises 11.6

1. In Exercise 1 of Section 11.5, you wrote a user requirements specification for a software system you will use each month to maintain your checking account at a local bank. Now follow up on this analysis by doing a complete CRC design for the system.
2. In Exercise 2 of Section 11.5, you wrote a user requirements specification for a software system you will use to keep track of the musical CDs that you own. Now follow up on this analysis by doing a complete CRC design for the system.
3. In Exercise 3 of Section 11.5, you wrote a user requirements specification for a software system that will be used to maintain statistics for your favorite sports team. Now follow up on this analysis by doing a complete CRC design for the system.
4. In Exercise 4 of Section 11.5, you wrote a user requirements specification for a software system that will be used by an administrative office at your school. Now follow up on this analysis by doing a complete CRC design for the system.
5. In Exercise 5 of Section 11.5, you wrote a user requirements specification for a system requested by the registrar at American Basket Weaving University. Now follow up on this analysis by doing a complete CRC design for the system.

11.7 Revisiting the Implementation and Testing Phases of the Software Engineering Life Cycle

In the implementation phase, you must churn out the code in C++ (or another appropriate language) necessary to put into effect the blueprint developed in the design phase. Although the terminology "churn out" may seem a bit degrading considering the amount of effort that must go into writing a program, we use it to stress the importance of the design phase. Given an appropriate set of formal specifications from the design phase, coding the programs really can be an easy task. The completeness of the design phase is the key to determining how easy coding is. Time spent in the design phase will be more than repaid by time gained in coding. This point cannot be overemphasized! The most common mistake made by many beginning programmers is jumping almost immediately into the coding phase, thereby digging themselves into holes they could have avoided by more thorough consideration of design issues.

What do the experts in software engineering see as the appropriate breakdown of time to spend in each of the phases of the software development life cycle? Frederick Brooks, in *The Mythical Man-Month: 20th Anniversary Edition,* Reading, MA: Addison-Wesley, 1995 (p. 20), recommends the following rule of thumb:

Planning (Analysis and Design)	one-third of the project development time
Coding (Implementation)	one-sixth of the project development time
Component Testing	one-fourth of the project development time
System Testing	one-fourth of the project development time

The fact that coding consumes only one-sixth of development time is consistent with our earlier statement that coding should be relatively easy if you have a good design to work from. What might be surprising in Brooks's recommendations is that half of the development time should be devoted to testing the code. The message should be

Objectives

a. to realize that writing code in a programming language represents only a small part of the overall inplementation of a system
b. to realize that we must develop well-conceived strategies for testing software if we are to ensure its reliability
c. to understand the difference between component and system testing
d. to understand the difference between white box and black box testing
e. to gain insight into developing test cases

clear: If you fail to schedule a considerable amount of time to verify the correctness of your program, your users (or instructor) will inevitably find bugs in it.

Moreover, Brooks breaks this testing down into two phases: *component testing* and *system testing*. During component testing, you are concerned with testing the individual classes in your system. When you do component testing, you will be writing short driver main programs to exercise each of the operations that a class provides, similar to what we did in Examples 11.1, 11.2, and 11.4 for the ordered collection, sorted collection, and one-key table classes, respectively. Once each component class has been thoroughly tested, you may plug the classes into the final system. System testing can begin *after* you are sure that each component in the system works in a completely reliable fashion. Often, during system testing, you will go so far as to get end users involved in testing the software. By observing their reactions as they work with the system, you can fine-tune it to be sure that it does everything they want in a satisfactory fashion.

Given the heavy emphasis placed on component testing, we need to develop effective strategies for doing it. The first point to consider as you begin to test the classes that comprise a system is the order in which they should be tested. Here's where the "collaborator" part of CRC modeling is very useful. Suppose that the operations for class X that are specified in a CRC model identify class Y as a collaborator. Then, clearly, we cannot test the operations for class X until class Y has been implemented and tested. Hence, the order in which classes should be implemented and tested may be extracted from the CRC model.

A much tougher question than establishing the order in which classes should be tested is, given a particular operation to be tested, how much should it be tested before we can conclude that it is correctly implemented? This is a critical question because it cuts to the core of the software reliability issue. As some of this chapter's Notes of Interest will attest, software reliability is not only a technical issue but also a moral and ethical one. Just as we design software, we must also systematically design the test cases to verify that software is correct. When we design test cases for a module, we must be sure to exercise all the logical possibilities the module may encounter. Be aware that such test cases consist of more than just strategically chosen input data. Each set of input data must also include its expected result (sometimes called the *test oracle*) if it is truly to convince anyone of the module's correctness.

In designing test cases, programmers begin to mix methods of science and art. Every mathematician knows that we can never actually prove anything by testing examples (that is, input data). So how can we verify a module's correctness by merely concocting examples? One proposed answer is to classify input data according to possible testing conditions. Hence, a finite set of well-chosen *equivalence classes* of test cases can be sufficient to cover an infinite number of possible inputs. Deciding what such equivalence classes should be is the point at which the process becomes more of an art than a science.

Example 11.11 To illustrate these principles, consider the fee structure at the E-Z Park parking lot. Parking fees for vehicles are based on the following rules:

The module is given two data items: a character, which may be 'C' or 'T' indicating whether the vehicle is a car or truck, and an integer number indicating the number of hours the vehicle spent in the parking lot. Cars are charged \$1.00 for each of their first 3 hours in the lot and \$0.50 for each hour after that. Trucks are charged \$2.00 for each of their first 4 hours in the lot and \$0.75 per hour thereafter.

After computing the appropriate charge, a new module (`computeParkingFee`) is to call on another new module (`prettyPrintTicket`), which appropriately formats a parking fee ticket showing the vehicle type, hours parked, and resulting fee. The `computeParkingFee` module is given here:

```
// Function: computeParkingFee
//
// Task: computes charge for parking and calls prettyPrintTicket to
//       output ticket
// Inputs: vehicle type in vehicle category and time spent in hours

void computeParkingFee (char vehicleCategory, int hours)
{
   float charge;

   switch (vehicleCategory)
   {
        case 'C': if (hours <= 3)
                          charge = hours;
                  else
                          charge = 3 + (hours - 3) * .5;
                  break;
         case 'T': if (hours <= 4)
                          charge = hours * 2;
                   else
                          charge = 8 + (hours - 4) * .75;
   }
   prettyPrintTicket(vehicleCategory, hours, charge);
}
```

An appropriate driver main program would simply allow us to repeatedly send data to the `computeParkingFee` module to check its behavior in a variety of situations. An appropriate stub for the call to `prettyPrintTicket` would merely inform us that we reached this subordinate module and print the values received so that we could be sure they had been transmitted correctly. At this stage, the stub need not concern itself with detailed, formatted output; we are at the moment interested only in testing `computeParkingFee`.

In testing this module, we can begin by identifying the following six equivalence classes:

1. A car in the lot less than 3 hours
2. A car in the lot exactly 3 hours
3. A car in the lot more than 3 hours
4. A truck in the lot less than 4 hours
5. A truck in the lot exactly 4 hours
6. A truck in the lot more than 4 hours

Choosing one test case for each equivalence class, we arrive at the following set of test cases:

Vehicle Category	Hours	Expected Results
C	2	Charge = 2.00
C	3	Charge = 3.00
C	5	Charge = 4.00
T	3	Charge = 6.00
T	4	Charge = 8.00
T	8	Charge = 11.00

The test cases for exactly 3 hours for a car and exactly 4 hours for a truck are particularly important since they represent *boundary conditions* at which a carelessly constructed conditional check could easily produce a wrong result.

This parking lot example, although illustrative of the method we wish to employ, is artificially simple. The next example presents a more complex testing situation.

Example 11.12 Consider developing a strategy to test the sorting algorithms we discussed in Chapter 10. Recall that each of these algorithms—bubble sort, insertion sort, and selection sort—received an array of physical size `MAX_LIST_SIZE` and an integer `n` to indicate the logical size of the array, that is, the number of items currently stored in the array.

Our criterion for choosing equivalence classes of test data for such a sorting algorithm is based on two factors:

1. The size of `n`, the number of items to be sorted
2. The ordering of the original data

The following table presents a partitioning of test data into equivalence classes for this example.

Size of n	Order of Original Data	Expected Results
n = 1	Not applicable	Array to be arranged in ascending order for all cases.
n = 2	Ascending	
n = 2	Descending	
n mid-size and even	Descending	
n mid-size and even	Ascending	
n mid-size and even	Randomized	
n mid-size and odd	Ascending	
n mid-size and odd	Descending	
n mid-size and odd	Randomized	
n = physical array size	Ascending	
n = physical array size	Descending	
n = physical array size	Randomized	

The module should be run for a minimum of 12 cases, one for each of the classes dictated by our table. Ideally, a few subcases should be run for each of the randomized cases. We cannot overemphasize the importance of testing seemingly trivial cases such as `n = 1` and `n = 2`. These lower boundary conditions are typical examples of data that may cause an otherwise perfectly functioning loop to be incorrectly skipped. Similarly, it is important to test the upper boundary condition in which n reaches the physical array size.

White Box/Black Box Testing

One factor that can influence the design of test cases is the knowledge you have of the design and implementation of the component being tested. If you have detailed knowledge of the design and implementation, you can engage in *white box testing*. That is, the module represents a "white box" because you are aware of the internal logic and data structure implementations in the module. In white box testing, test cases can be partitioned into equivalence classes that specifically exercise each logical path through a module. In *black box testing,* the module is approached without knowledge of its internal structure. You know what the module is supposed to do, but not how it does it.

Example 11.13 For instance, suppose that we want to test the `retrieve` operation for the one-key table class that we developed in Section 11.3. In both implementation strategies discussed for this class, we have used an array of associations in which the physical size of the array was established by the constant `MAX_TABLE_SIZE`. The physically ordered array implementation maintained the array by key so that a binary search algorithm could be used to find the data efficiently. The following table provides a set of test cases for the `retrieve` operation assuming that the physically ordered array implementation has been used.

Test Case	Number of Keys in Table (Assume That Physical Capacity Is 10)	Physical Ordering of Keys	Value to Retrieve	Expected Results	Rationale
I	10	ALLEN BAKER DAVIS GREEN HUFF MILLER NOLAN PAYTON SMITH TAYLOR	Try each key in the table.	`true` should be returned as the value of the function. The data associated with the key should be returned in the element parameter.	Can we find everything in the physically full table?
II	10	Same as test case I	Try AARON NATHAN ZEBRA	`false` returned as the value of the function.	Is `false` correctly returned when the table is physically full and the value is being sought: (1) precedes all keys in the table, (2) is interspersed with keys in the middle of the table, (3) follows all keys in the table?
III	5	ALLEN DAVIS HUFF NOLAN SMITH	Same as test case I	Same as test case I	Can we find everything in a mid-size table?
IV	5	Same as test case III	Same as test case II	Same as test case II	Same as test case II but for mid-size list
V	1	HUFF	HUFF	Same as test case I	Can we handle successful search in a table with just one key?
VI	1	HUFF	Same as test case II	Same as test case II	Can we handle successful search in a table with just one key?
VII	0		HUFF	Same as test case II	Boundary condition. Will we always return `false` when the table is empty?

A NOTE OF INTEREST

Software Reliability and Defense Systems

The issue of software testing takes on great importance as we begin to rely increasingly on the computer as an aid in the decision-making process. In the late 1980s, a nationwide debate began about the degree to which computerized weapons should be used in military and defense systems. Perhaps the most famous aspect of this debate was the notorious "Star Wars" system, envisioned as a computer-controlled multilayer defense against nuclear ballistic missiles. Experience with much smaller weapons systems in the 1990s has illustrated the pitfalls that can occur when testing such systems.

For example, during the Persian Gulf war, Peter G. Neumann reports in *Computer-Related Risks* (ACM Press, 1995) that initial early reports of the success of computerized Patriot missile systems had to be downgraded from 95% successful to 13% successful. Part of the reason was that the system had been designed and tested to work under a much less stringent environment than that in which it was used in the war. According to Neumann a clock drift error that surfaced when the Patriot systems were used for more than 100 consecutive hours resulted in tracking errors that were responsible for a Patriot missile missing a targeted Scud missile that eventually crashed into an American military barracks, killing 29 and injuring 97.

This clock drift problem resulted from something as obscure as software that used two different machine representations of the number 0.1. Because 0.1 cannot be represented with complete accuracy in the binary floating-point hardware of any computer, using two different representations resulted in two numbers being viewed as not equal when in fact they should have been equal. Although this discrepancy did not surface in the shorter usage times that were specified in the original requirements for the Patriot system, it resulted in serious clock problems when the systems were pushed beyond these requirements.

The problems in establishing the reliability of computerized military systems remain a thorny issue with serious ethical implications. According to Jeff Johnson in "The Military Impact of Information Technology," *Communications of the ACM*, Vol. 40, No. 4, Apr. 1997, pp. 20–22:

> Computers and IT [information technology] are effective mainly when the application area is ordered and predictable (i.e., when the level of chaos and entropy is fairly low). War, however, is the epitome of a chaotic, highly entropic environment. It is a breakdown of rational human behavior. In short, war and armed conflict is one of the application areas to which IT is least applicable. Put crudely, when all hell breaks loose, computers are at their worst. That computer-controlled robot drone may work fine in the lab or on the testing range, but the situations encountered in battle are by the very nature of war new and unique.

This is a white box set of test data because in test cases II and IV we make explicit use of the knowledge that the data are physically ordered. Also, in test cases I and II, we make explicit use of knowledge that there is a physical limit on the amount of data that may be stored in the table. The situation in which the table is full to its physical capacity represents a boundary condition for the algorithm; we are aware of this condition because we are testing from a white box perspective. If we were testing from a black box perspective instead, it might not be possible to exercise all such boundary conditions.

Exercises 11.7

1. Summarize what is involved in each of the phases of the system life cycle. If you were to specialize your career in one of these phases, which would it be? Why? Provide your answer in essay form.
2. What is meant by the term *boundary conditions* for an algorithm?
3. Employees at the University of Hard Knocks are paid by the following rules:

   - Employees who sign a contract for a total annual wage are paid 1/52 of that amount each week.
   - Hourly employees receive a paycheck based on the number of hours they work in a given week and their hourly rate. They are paid this hourly rate for each of the first 40 hours they work. After 40 hours, they are paid time and a half for

each additional hour of work. Moreover, work on a holiday is a special case for hourly employees. They are paid double time for all holiday work.

Write a function to compute the pay for an employee of the University of Hard Knocks and then dispatch the appropriate information to a check printing module. Completely test the function you write by integrating it with appropriate driver and stub modules and by designing a complete set of test data for the module.

4. Develop a complete set of test data for each of the operations of the ordered collection ADT. Present your answers using tables in the style of those in Examples 11.11, 11.12, and 11.13.
5. Develop a complete set of test data for each of the operations of the sorted collection ADT. Present your answers using tables in the style of those in Examples 11.11, 11.12, and 11.13.
6. Develop a complete set of test data for each of the operations of the one-key table ADT. Present your answers using tables in the style of those in Examples 11.11, 11.12, and 11.13.
7. Develop a complete set of test data for each of the operations of the two-key table ADT. Present your answers using tables in the style of those in Examples 11.11, 11.12, and 11.13.
8. This section has presented a strategy for testing that emphasized the design of equivalence classes of test cases to exercise all the logical possibilities a module may encounter. You are working on a software system with a friend who claims that such comprehensive testing is impossible. As evidence, the friend cites a module she has written with 20 `if` statements. Your friend points out that there are approximately 2^{20} logical paths through this module and that comprehensive testing of it is therefore impossible. In a written essay, describe a strategy that your friend could follow to solve this dilemma.

Case Study: Finishing the Registrar's System

In Sections 11.5 and 11.6, we made substantial progress in analyzing and designing the registrar's system. We will use the Case Study section of this chapter to finish that work.

Analysis

To complete our analysis of the registrar's system, we will show some examples of the way in which we envision users interacting with the system. Showing end users such examples before the actual implementation of the system has proceeded too far is representative of an analysis technique known as *iterative prototyping*. Using this method, analysts construct a simplified model of a system that performs just the essential functions. Implementers then get this model up and running very quickly as a prototype of the entire system. Users can react to the prototype and work with the analysts to refine the requirements for the system. Data abstraction and object-oriented design make it relatively painless to change underlying implementations of operations that require refinements without disturbing other aspects of the system.

Sample of Dialogue to Inspect a Student Record

```
[A]dd, [D]elete, [U]pdate, [I]nspect, [G]rades, [E]nd-of-year, [Q]uit -->i
Student name in form 'Last,First' --> Smart,Bea

                      Name     Taken    Earned      GPA
                 Smart,Bea        22        22     3.14
```

```
    DEPT   NUMBER                      COURSE TITLE CREDITS    GRADE
    CHEM      101        Introductory Chemistry        5          B
    MATH      200                    Calculus I        5          A
    MATH      201                   Calculus II        5          A
     ENG      200           English Composition        3          C
    CMSC      100      Introductory Programming        4          C
```

Sample of Dialogue to Add and Update Student Record

```
[A]dd, [D]elete, [U]pdate, [I]nspect, [G]rades, [E]nd-of-year, [Q]uit -->a
Student name in form 'Last,First' --> Sosa,Sammy

[A]dd, [D]elete, [U]pdate, [I]nspect, [G]rades, [E]nd-of-year, [Q]uit -->u
Student name in form 'Last,First' --> Sosa,Sammy
Enter department for course (**** to quit) --> MATH
Enter course number, year, semester (F or W), and letter grade -->202 1999 W B
Enter department for another course for this student (**** to quit) --> CMSC
Enter course number, year, semester (F or W), and letter grade -->342 1999 W C
Enter department for another course for this student (**** to quit) --> ****
```

Sample Dialogue to Produce Grade Reports

```
[A]dd, [D]elete, [U]pdate, [I]nspect, [G]rades, [E]nd-of-year, [Q]uit -->g
Enter year (19XX or 20XX) and semester (F or W) --> 1999 W
                                .
                                .
                                .
               Name   Cum. Cr. Taken   Cum. Cr. Earned    Cum. GPA
          Smart,Bea               22                22        3.14

For the semester 1999W the student's course record is:

    DEPT   NUMBER                      COURSE TITLE CREDITS    GRADE
    MATH      201                   Calculus II        5          A
    ENG       200           English Composition        3          C
    CMSC      100      Introductory Programming        4          C

               Name   Cum. Cr. Taken   Cum. Cr. Earned    Cum. GPA
         Sosa,Sammy                8                 8        2.63

For the semester 1999W the student's course record is:

    DEPT   NUMBER                      COURSE TITLE CREDITS    GRADE
    MATH      202                  Calculus III        5          B
    CMSC      342         Programming Languages        3          C
```

Sample of Dialogue to Remove a Student Record from the System

```
[A]dd, [D]elete, [U]pdate, [I]nspect, [G]rades, [E]nd-of-year, [Q]uit -->i
Student name in form 'Last,First' --> Egghead,Irma

                          Name   Taken   Earned    GPA
                  Egghead,Irma      22       22   3.77
```

continued

```
DEPT  NUMBER                    COURSE TITLE CREDITS   GRADE
 BIO    101          Introductory Biology        5       A
MATH    200                    Calculus I        5       A
MATH    201                   Calculus II        5       B
 ENG    200           English Composition        3       A
CMSC    100     Introductory Programming         4       A

[A]dd, [D]elete, [U]pdate, [I]nspect, [G]rades, [E]nd-of-year, [Q]uit -->d
Student name in form 'Last,First' --> Egghead,Irma
[A]dd, [D]elete, [U]pdate, [I]nspect, [G]rades, [E]nd-of-year, [Q]uit -->i
Student name in form 'Last,First' --> Egghead,Irma
Student Egghead,Irma not found in database
```

Production of End-of-year Reports (10 Credits Used as Graduation Cutoff)

```
[A]dd, [D]elete, [U]pdate, [I]nspect, [G]rades, [E]nd-of-year, [Q]uit -->e

                Grad list in alphabetical order
                     Name     Taken      Earned        GPA
               Average, Joe      22          19       1.50
                 Smart, Bea      22          22       3.14

                      Grad list in GPA order
                     Name     Taken      Earned        GPA
                  Smart,Bea      22          22       3.14
                Average,Joe      22          19       1.50
```

Design

The CRC design that we developed in Section 11.6 has set the stage for providing the various C++ header files needed by the system.

Main Menu Class

```
// Class declaration file: menu.h

#ifndef MENU_H
#define MENU_H

#include "apstring.h"
#include "studentDb.h"
#include "courseRec.h"
#include "gradeRec.h"
#include "studentRec.h"
#include <iostream.h>
#include <iomanip.h>

class menu
{
   public:

   // Constructors
   menu(studentDb & sd);
   menu(const menu &m);
```

```
    // Member functions
    menu& operator = (const menu &m);
    void start();

    protected:

    // Member functions
    void addDialogue();
    void deleteDialogue();
    void updateDialogue();
    void inspectDialogue();
    void reportDialogue();

    // Data members
    studentDb & studentRecords;
};

#endif
```

Student Database Class

```
// Class declaration file: studentDb.h

#ifndef STUDENTDB_H

#include <fstream.h>
#include <iostream.h>
#include <iomanip.h>
#include "apstring.h"
#include "studentRec.h"
#include "courseRec.h"
#include "onetable.h"
#include "twotable.h"

class studentDb : public OneKeyTable<apstring, studentRec>
{
    public:

   // Constructors
   studentDb();
   studentDb(const studentDb &db);

   // Member functions

   studentDb& operator = (const studentDb &table);
   void addStudent(const apstring &studentName);
   bool studentExists(const apstring &studentName);
   bool deleteStudent(const apstring &studentName);
   bool inspectStudent(const apstring &studentName);
   bool addCourse(const apstring &studentName, const gradeRec &newCourse);
   void gradeReports(int year, char semester);
   void graduationListByName();
   void graduationListByGpa();
```

continued

```
   protected:
   // Data members

   TwoKeyTable<apstring, int, courseRec> courseDb;

};

#define STUDENTDB_H
#endif
```

Course Database Class

This will just be a two-key table with primary key an `apstring` (for the department code), secondary key an `int` (for course number), and element type a `courseRec`.

List of Grade Records Class

This will just be an ordered collection, with each element of the collection a member of the `gradeRec` class.

Student Record Class

```
// Class declaration file: studentRec.h

#ifndef STUDENTREC_H
#define STUDENTREC_H

#include "apstring.h"
#include "gradeRec.h"
#include "ordercol.h"
#include "twotable.h"
#include "courseRec.h"
#include <iostream.h>
#include <iomanip.h>

// Declaration section
class studentRec
{

   public:

   // Class constructors

   studentRec();
   studentRec(TwoKeyTable<apstring, int, courseRec> * courseDatabase);
   studentRec(const studentRec &sr);

   // Function members

   studentRec& operator = (const studentRec &table);
   int getCreditsTaken();
   int getCreditsEarned();
   double getGpa();
```

```
    void addCourse(const gradeRec &gr);
    void displayCourseHistory();
    void displayCourseHistory(int year, char semester);

    protected:

    // Data members

    OrderedCollection<gradeRec> coursesTaken;
    TwoKeyTable<apstring, int, courseRec> * courseDb;

};

#endif
```

Course Record Class

```
// Class declaration file: courseRec.h

#ifndef COURSEREC_H
#define COURSEREC_H

#include "apstring.h"

// Declaration section
class courseRec
{

    public:

    // Class constructors

    courseRec();
    courseRec(const apstring &title, const int credits);
    courseRec(const courseRec &cr);

    // Function members

    courseRec& operator = (const courseRec &table);
    apstring getTitle();
    int getCredits();

    protected:

    // Data members

    apstring title;
    int credits;

};

#endif
```

A NOTE OF INTEREST

The (Lack of) Responsibility of Software Developers

If you have ever purchased software such as a word processor or spreadsheet for a microcomputer, you have probably signed a license agreement in which you agree not to copy the software except for your own backup protection. The fine print in such software licenses also typically contains disclaimers about the responsibility of the software developer should you eventually do something such as underpay your income tax because of a bug in the spreadsheet you used to keep your tax records.

For instance, the second page of the user's guide of a popular spreadsheet program provides the following disclaimer of warranties. The actual company name (designated here as X) is not given. This disclaimer is typical of that used by virtually all software companies.

> The software and user manuals are provided "as is" and without express or limited warranty of any kind by either X or anyone who has been involved in the creation, production, or distribution of the software, including, but not limited to, the implied warranties of merchantability and fitness for a particular purpose.
>
> The entire risk as to the quality and performance of the software and user manuals is with you. Should the software and user manuals prove defective, you (and not X or anyone else who has been involved in the creation, production, or distribution of the software) assume the entire cost of all necessary servicing, repair or correction.

Compare such a disclaimer to the claims that appear in the software ads that adorn all popular computing magazines and you will see a real contradiction. Products that profess to do virtually everything guarantee absolutely nothing.

Perhaps the reservations that software developers have about guaranteeing the reliability of their products should not be surprising given what we have learned about the software system life cycle. The complexity of software design and testing makes it virtually impossible to develop software that is 100% free of bugs. To customers in the software marketplace, the message is clear: *Caveat emptor* (Let the buyer beware)!

Grade Record Class

```
// Class declaration file: gradeRec.h

#ifndef GRADEREC_H
#define GRADEREC_H

#include "apstring.h"

// Declaration section
class gradeRec
{

   public:

   // Class constructors

   gradeRec();
   gradeRec(const apstring &dept, const int courseNum,
      const int year, const char semester, const char grade);
   gradeRec(const gradeRec &gr);

   // Function members

   gradeRec& operator = (const gradeRec &table);
   apstring getDept();
   int getCourseNum();
   int getYear();
```

```
   char getSemester();
   char getGrade();
   int getGradePts();

   protected:

   // Data members

   apstring dept;
   int courseNum;
   int year;
   char semester;
   char grade;

};

#endif
```

There should be no surprises in the public member functions for these classes. They are a direct reflection, in C++ syntax, of the operations we have specified in the CRC design of Section 11.6. Some of the private data members require a bit more explanation, and that will be provided in the following discussion of implementation details.

Implementation

One interesting aspect of the CRC design methodology is that it is totally object-oriented. Because of this, the main program that we are used to writing becomes almost superfluous.

```
// program file: registrar.cpp

#include "studentDb.h"
#include "menu.h"

void main()
{
   studentDb studentRecords;

   menu mainMenu(studentRecords);

   mainMenu.start();

}
```

The main program must only construct the database of student records and the main menu and then "start" the main menu. The iterative logic that continually queries a user for the next operation is embedded in the start method of the menu class.

```
void menu::start()
{
   char choice;

   do {
      cout << "[A]dd, [D]elete, [U]pdate, [I]nspect, [G]rades, "
           << "[E]nd-of-year, [Q]uit -->";
```

continued

```
      cin >> choice;
      cin.ignore(10, '\n');
      switch (choice)
      {
      case 'A':
      case 'a':
         addDialogue();
         break;
      case 'D':
      case 'd':
         deleteDialogue();
         break;
      case 'U':
      case 'u':
         updateDialogue();
         break;
      case 'I':
      case 'i':
         inspectDialogue();
         break;
      case 'G':
      case 'g':
         reportDialogue();
         break;
      case 'E':
      case 'e':
         studentRecords.graduationListByName();
         studentRecords.graduationListByGpa();
         break;
      case 'Q':
      case 'q':
         break;
      default:
         cout << "Invalid choice -- Please try again" << endl;
         break;
      }
   } while (choice != 'Q' && choice != 'q');
}
```

In the student database class, the constructor is responsible for initially loading the course data and the data for each student. These data are loaded from a text stream. The structure of that stream is documented in the following code.

```
studentDb::studentDb()
{
   apstring dept, title;
   int num, credits;
   apstring name;
   int year;
   char semester, grade;
   ifstream academicRecords;

   academicRecords.open("acad.dat");

   // First load course information. Each course's data are on four
```

```
   // lines -- department code, number, title, and credits.
   // Course information is terminated with a line containing
   // the sentinel ****
   academicRecords >> dept;
   while (dept != "*****")
   {
      academicRecords >> num;
      academicRecords.ignore(10, '\n');
      getline(academicRecords, title);
      academicRecords >> credits;
      courseRec cr(title, credits);
      courseDb.store(dept, num, cr);
      academicRecords >> dept;
   }
   academicRecords.ignore(10, '\n');

   // Now read the data for each student, terminated by
   // the sentinel ****
   getline(academicRecords, name);
   while (name != "*****")
   {
      addStudent(name);
      // For each student read grade records in form dept, number,
      // year, semester, and grade. Grade records for this student
      // are terminated with **** as a sentinel department code.
      academicRecords >> dept;
      while (dept != "*****")
      {
         academicRecords >> num;
         academicRecords >> year;
         academicRecords >> semester;
         academicRecords >> grade;
         gradeRec gr(dept, num, year, semester, grade);
         addCourse(name, gr);
         academicRecords >> dept;
      }
      academicRecords.ignore(10, '\n');
      getline(academicRecords, name);
   }
   academicRecords.close();
}
```

Most of the code that remains for implementing the student database class will be left for you to do in the problems at the end of the chapter. A member function that merits special consideration, however, is the one that produces the graduation list ordered by descending grade point average. The one-key table that the student database class is derived from uses an array of keys that is physically ordered. Here the keys are student names, so going through the table alphabetically by name presents no problem. However, to go through in grade point order, we must use the pointer sort technique described in Chapter 10.

```
void studentDb::graduationListByGpa()
{
   int pointers [MAX_TABLE_SIZE];      // Used for pointer sort
   int j, k, temp;
```

continued

```
    bool exchangeMade;
    studentRec s1(&courseDb), s2(&courseDb);

    // First we do a pointer sort on the one-key table, using
    // GPA as the basis for comparison

    // Initialize pointer array
    for (k = 0; < tableLength; k++)
       pointers[k] = k;

    k = 0;
    exchangeMade = true;

    // Next order the pointers, based on GPA
    while ((k < tableLength - 1) && exchangeMade)
    {
       exchangeMade = false;
       k++;
       for (j = 0; j < tableLength - k; j++)
       {
          s1 = data[pointers[j]].getValue();
          s2 = data[pointers[j + 1]].getValue();
          if (s1.getGpa() < s2.getGpa())
          {
             temp = pointers [j];      // Swap pointers
             pointers [j]= pointers [j + 1];
             pointers [j + 1] = temp;
             exchangeMade = true;
          }
       }
    }

    // Now follow the pointers through the data

    apstring stName;
    studentRec st(&courseDb);

    cout << setw(50) << "Grad list in GPA order" << endl;
    cout << setw(30) << "Name" << setw(10) << "Taken" << setw(10)
        << "Earned" << setw(10) << "GPA" << endl;
    cout << setiosflags(ios::fixed) << setprecision(2);
    for (int i = 0; i < tableLength; i++)
    {
       stName = data[pointers[i]].getKey();
       st = data[pointers [i]].getValue();
       if (st.getCreditsEarned() >= 120)
          cout << setw(30) << stName << setw(10) << st.getCreditsTaken()
               << setw(10) << st.getCreditsEarned() << setw(10)
               << st.getGpa() << endl;
    }

}
```

One additional consideration in implementing the registrar's system is the course database object that is a data member of the student database.

```
class studentDb : public OneKeyTable<apstring, studentRec>
{
   public:

   .
   .
   .

    // Data members

    TwoKeyTable<apstring, int, courseRec> courseDb;
};
```

Not only does the student database need to know about the course database, but each student record object in the student database must also have access to the course database. For example, the `displayCourseHistory` function in the `studentRec` class will have to traverse the ordered collection of `gradeRec` objects for that student and display the title and number of credits attached to each course for which the student received a grade.

In Section 11.6, we made the design decision not to store the course title and number of credits along with each grade to save a considerable amount of storage. Instead, as this collection is traversed, the `displayCourseHistory` function will use the course department code and number to pull the necessary information from its central repository in the course database. Now, we must consider the following question: Since each student record must know the course database, do we really want to declare such an object in each student record? The course database is likely to require quite a bit of storage, and if we allocate such an object in each student record, we are likely to pay a stiff price in the amount of space used.

There is an alternative that will give us the best of both worlds, that is, the capability for a student record to access the database without paying a large price in storage. That alternative is to give each student record a reference to the course database instead of a full-fledged copy of the course database. We can declare such a reference to an object by using a pointer. You were introduced to this notion in Section 9.6 and will continue to explore it at length in the next chapter. A pointer to an object is declared using the * *dereference operator*. Compare the declaration of the course database in the `studentRec` class to that given earlier in the `studentDb` class. Notice the dereference operator in front of `courseDbPtr` in the `studentRec` class and the lack of that operator for the corresponding declaration of `courseDb` in the `studentDb` class (see pages 547–548).

```
class studentRec
{
   public:
   .
   .
   .
   protected:

   // Data members

   OrderedCollection<gradeRec> coursesTaken;
   TwoKeyTable<apstring, int, courseRec> * courseDbPtr;

};
```

The difference between these two declarations is that the latter declares an actual instance of a course database object, whereas the former declares a pointer to such an object. Pointers store a memory address where the object can be found instead of the object itself. This concept is highlighted in Figure 11.8.

The next question that arises is: If `courseDbPtr` in the `studentRec` class is merely a reference to a course database object, what notation do we use to get at the contents of the object itself? That's where the dereference operator comes into play. The dereference operator takes a pointer to an object and returns the object referenced by that pointer. Here is another way of thinking about this notion: If `p` is a pointer to an object of type `P`, then `*p` is the object of type `P` that `p` points to.

In Figure 11.8, this means that the `courseDbPtr` member in each `studentRec` object represents the address of the `courseDb` member of the `studentDb` class. Hence, for the `studentRec` object to get at the contents of `courseDb`, it will have to use the dereferencing notation `*courseDbPtr`. For the `courseDbPtr` member in each `studentRec` object to be "aimed at" the location where `courseDb` resides, `courseDbPtr` will have to be initialized with the memory address of `courseDb`. For this type of initialization, C++ provides the ampersand (&) in its role as the "address-of" operator. Here is how you should think about the address-of operator. If `p` is declared to be a pointer to an object of type `P` and `q` is declared to be an instance of an object of type `P`, then the assignment `p = &q` will make `p` point at where `q` resides. Thereafter, `*p` can be used to refer to the contents of `q`. For instance, the following code segment will output the number 5 twice.

```
int q = 5;
int * p;

p = &q;
cout << q << endl;
cout << *p << endl;
```

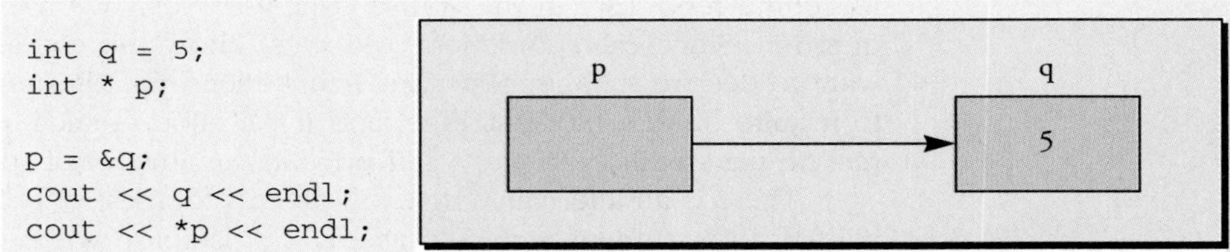

You will investigate pointers much more in the following chapter, but now we know enough to use them in the context of the registrar's system. First, consider the constructor for a `studentRec` object. Here, using an initializer list, `courseDbPtr` is initialized to the `courseDatabase` pointer that is passed to the constructor.

```
studentRec::studentRec(TwoKeyTable<apstring, int, courseRec> * courseDatabase)
   : coursesTaken(), courseDbPtr(courseDatabase)
{
}
```

In the `studentDb` class, when a new student record is added to the database, the constructor for a `studentRec` is called, passing it the address of the `courseDb` object embedded in the `studentDb` class.

```
void studentDb::addStudent(const apstring &studentName)
{
   studentRec initialEmptyRec(&courseDb);     // Construct with
                                                // address of courseDb
   store(studentName, initialEmptyRec);
}
```

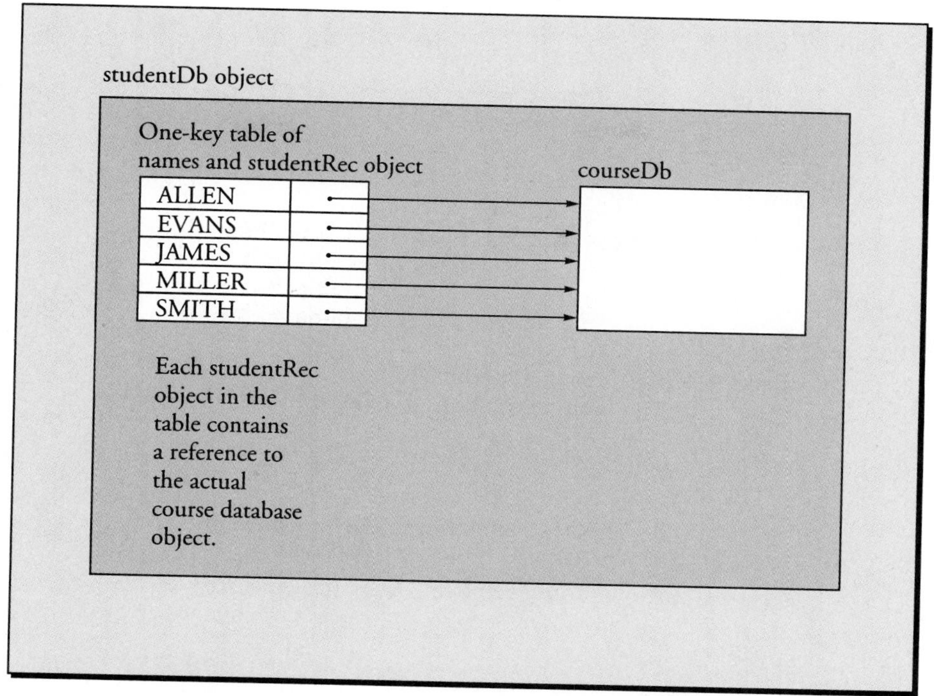

Figure 11.8 Student records in the student database each contain a pointer to the central course database

In the `studentRec` class, when we implement operations that must access the course database, the `*courseDbPtr` notation may then be used. Here, code for the `displayCourseHistory()` and `getGpa()` functions is provided to illustrate use of the notation.

```
double studentRec::getGpa()
{
   int taken = 0;
   int gradePoints = 0;
   int numCourses = coursesTaken.length();
   courseRec cr;

   for (int k = 0; k < numCourses; k++)
   {
      (*courseDbPtr).retrieve(coursesTaken[k].getDept(),
                              coursesTaken[k].getCourseNum(), cr);
      taken += cr.getCredits();
      gradePoints += cr.getCredits() * coursesTaken[k].getGradePts();
   }
   if (taken != 0)
      return ((double) gradePoints) / ((double) taken);
   else
      return 0.0;
}
```

```
void studentRec::displayCourseHistory()
{
   int numCourses = coursesTaken.length();
```

continued

```
   courseRec cr;

   cout << setw(8) << "DEPT" << setw(8) <<"NUMBER" << setw(35)
        << "COURSE TITLE" << setw(8)
        << "CREDITS" << setw(8) << "GRADE" << endl;
   for (int k = 0; k < numCourses; k++)
   {
      (*courseDbPtr).retrieve(coursesTaken[k].getDept(),
                              coursesTaken[k].getCourseNum(),cr);
      cout << setw(8) << coursesTaken[k].getDept()
           << setw(8) << coursesTaken[k].getCourseNum()
           << setw(35) << cr.getTitle()
           << setw(8) << cr.getCredits()
           << setw(8) << coursesTaken[k].getGrade() << endl;
   }
}
```

The key statement in each of these functions is:

```
(*courseDbPtr).retrieve(coursesTaken[k].getDept(),
                        coursesTaken[k].getCourseNum(), cr);
```

In this example, we want to retrieve a course record from the course database. `(*courseDbPtr).retrieve` uses the `*` dereference operator to do this and invokes the `retrieve` function for the course database two-key table. The first argument to `retrieve`, that is, `coursesTaken[k].getDept()`, provides the primary key for this retrieve operation. The second argument, `coursesTaken[k].getCourseNum()`, provides the secondary key. The third argument, `cr`, stores the `courseRec` information that is retrieved. Although this notation may seem unusual now, you will become more familiar with it as you progress through the next chapter.

Running, Debugging, and Testing Hints

1. When accessing an ADT, be sure that you only use those operations specified in the ADT definition. This is the ADT use rule. For instance, it is wrong to access an object in a one-key table by referring to its array index. This assumes that the implementor of the ADT is storing data in an array. Such an assumption is not warranted according to the definition of this ADT.
2. When writing the implementation of an ADT, be sure that the functions you develop obey the interface established by the ADT's definition. This is the ADT implementation rule. For instance, if you, as implementor, need a counter to keep track of the number of objects in a one-key table, don't add the counter as an extra parameter in function calls. Instead, encapsulate it as a private or protected data member of the implementation.
3. When providing the implementation of an ADT, be sure that each individual operation is thoroughly tested and debugged before it is used by higher level logic. Then, if errors occur when higher level modules execute, you can be assured that these errors are the result of the algorithms that use the ADT and are not in the implementation of the ADT.
4. The importance of the `create` operation for an ADT should not be underestimated. From the implementor's perspective, this is where crucial initializations

occur that will ensure the smooth functioning of other operations. From the perspective of the user of the ADT, you must be sure to call the `create` operation for each instance of a variable of that type. Failing to do so will usually lead to very bizarre program behavior.

5. When testing a large program, always test modules individually before testing the entire system.
6. When developing test cases, keep them in a file so that they can be used again easily after fixing errors.
7. Be sure to design test data that exercise the boundary conditions of a module, which is where an error is most likely to occur.

Summary

Key Terms

abstract data type (ADT)
access adjustment
ADT implementation rule
ADT layering rule
ADT use rule
analysis
association
black box testing
boundary conditions
coding phase
component testing
CRC modeling
data abstraction
dereference operator
design
driver module
equivalence classes
implementation
information hiding
interface for an ADT
iterative prototyping
key
levels of abstraction
logical size
maintenance
one-key table
ordered collection
physical size
physically ordered array implementation
pointer
primary key
prototype
secondary key
sorted collection
stub module
system testing
systems analyst
test cases
test oracle
testing
two-dimensional array implementation
two-key table
unordered array implementation
user requirements specification
white box testing

Key Concepts

- Computer scientists engage in a modeling process as they develop software to satisfy users' needs. In this respect, the way in which a computer scientist works parallels the engineering profession. Consequently, this systematic approach toward the development of successful software is often called software engineering.
- Abstract data types are defined apart from considerations of their implementation in a particular programming language. A complete definition for an abstract data type must include a description of the individual elements, the relationship between these individual elements, and the operations that can be performed on them. These operations are conveniently specified as function and function declarations.
- The ADT use rule, the ADT implementation rule, and the ADT layering rule are guidelines governing the relationship between implementations of an ADT and higher level algorithms using that implementation.
- We must often determine which of a variety of implementations is best in terms of time and space efficiency for a particular application.

- The logical size of an array is the number of data elements currently stored in it; this size may differ from the array's physical size.
- An ordered collection enables users to work with just the logical size of an array of data elements.
- A sorted collection enables users to work with an array of data elements whose alphabetical ordering is maintained automatically.
- The one-key table is an ADT characterized by operations that store, retrieve, or remove data. All of these operations are performed relative to a particular key value.
- A physically ordered array with binary search and an unordered array with pointer sort are two ways of implementing a one-key table.
- The two-key table is an ADT characterized by operations that store, retrieve, or remove data. All of these operations are performed relative to two particular key values.
- A two-dimensional array and a one-key table of one-key tables are two ways of implementing a two-key table.
- During the analysis phase of the software system life cycle, you must determine the user's requirements. Typically, this involves considerable interaction between the systems analyst and end user. A user requirements specification is one example of a document that is developed during this phase. Ultimately, the user's requirements must be described in a form suitable to pass on to the design phase.
- During the design phase, the user's requirements are examined, and the system that will ultimately meet these requirements begins to take shape. Software designers must turn out a blueprint of the eventual software system that can then be translated into program code. CRC modeling produces documents typical of those produced during the design phase.
- Testing and verification can consume up to 50% of the time spent in developing a software system. Each component should be tested as it is finished. Use drivers to feed inputs into the module and stubs to check the module's interactions with subordinate modules.
- System testing follows modular testing.
- The maintenance phase of a system follows its release to users. During this phase, adjustments must be made to the system in response to bugs and changes in user requirements.

Programming Problems and Projects

1. Complete the implementation of the registrar's system as discussed in Sections 11.5, 11.6, 11.7, and this chapter's Case Study. Be sure that you test each component individually before you proceed to a complete system test.
2. A set is a collection of unique data values in no particular order. Operations on sets include:

empty	includes (an item)
length	union (of two sets)
add (an item)	intersection (of two sets)
remove (an item)	difference (of two sets)

No other modifications or access to sets is allowed. All of the data values in a set must be of the same type. This element type must support comparisons. The union of two sets is the set of elements in both sets combined. The intersection of two sets is the set of elements they have in common. The difference of two sets is the set of elements produced by combining the elements in the two sets and then removing the elements of the second set that are not contained in the first set. No other modifications or access to a set is allowed.

Write formal specifications for a set class, declare and implement these operations in a C++ library, and test the class with an appropriate driver program. Use the + operator for union, the * operator for intersection, and the – operator for difference. (*Hint:* Use another class developed in this chapter to represent the data within a set.) When you've completed your implementation, provide a big-O analysis of the efficiency of each set operation.

3. The radix sort algorithm, presented in Section 10.4, uses the notion of bins: data repositories that contain numbers or strings in a particular category as the algorithm progresses. Formalize the concept of a bin for the radix sort algorithm by providing an ADT definition for it. Then provide an implementation for your bin ADT and use the operations provided by the bin ADT to write a high-level version of the radix sort.
4. The definition of the one-key table ADT in Section 11.3 specifies that each object in the list must have a unique key value, that is, a key value shared by no other value in the list. Consider a variation on this ADT in which we allow multiple records to share the same key value (for example, several people may have identical names). Call this ADT a one-key table with duplicate keys.
   a. Provide a complete definition for this ADT. Be very precise about what happens for each of the `store`, `remove`, and `retrieve` operations. Do you need to add any new operations because of the possibility of duplicate keys?
   b. Translate your definition from part a into a C++ interface for a one-key table with duplicate keys.
   c. Develop an implementation for this ADT. Discuss in writting any limitations of your implementation relative to the definition and interface of parts a and b.
   d. Test your implementation by plugging it into an appropriate test driver.
5. Invite the registrar of your university to your class to discuss the type of data processing operations in which the registrar's office is typically engaged. After this discussion (which should no doubt include time for questions), describe the data involved in the operations of your registrar's office in terms of abstract data types. Write a user requirements specification and develop a CRC design model for your registrar's system.
6. Consider the following data declaration and function declaration.

```
enum KindOfTriangle {SCALENE, ISOSCELES, EQUILATERAL, IMPOSSIBLE};
.
.
.
// Function: triangleType
// Task: determines the type of triangle, given the lengths of the three sides
//
// Inputs: three integers representing the lengths of the three sides of a triangle
// Output:
          // EQUILATERAL, if all sides are equal
          // ISOSCELES, if two sides are equal
          // SCALENE, if all sides are different lengths
          // IMPOSSIBLE, if the integers do not constitute valid triangle sides

KindOfTriangle triangleType (double side1, double side2, double side3);
```

For this problem, work with another student. Each of you should develop independently, first, the function just described and, second, a complete set of test data for the function. Next, jointly develop a driver program and test your functions. Have your partner use his or her test data on the function you developed. Then use your test data on your partner's function. The winner is the one whose function fails for the fewer number of test cases.

7. In Exercise 1 of Section 11.6, you designed a system for a software system you will use each month to maintain your checking account at a local bank. Implement and fully test that system.

8. In Exercise 2 of Section 11.6, you designed a system for a software system you will use to keep track of the musical CDs that you own. Implement and fully test that system.

9. In Exercise 3 of Section 11.6, you designed a system for a software system that will be used to maintain statistics for your favorite sports team. Implement and fully test that system.

10. In Exercise 4 of Section 11.6, you designed a system for a software system that will be used by an administrative office at your school. Implement and fully test that system.

11. In Exercise 5 of Section 11.6, you designed a system for a system requested by the registrar at American Basket Weaving University. Implement and fully test that system.

12. Suppose you are computer operations manager for Wing-and-a-Prayer Airlines. In that role, you receive the following important memorandum:

Memorandum
Wing-and-a-Prayer Airlines

To: Computer Operations Manager
From: Vice President in Charge of Scheduling
Date: August 28, 2001
Re: Matching flights and pilots

As you know, we presently have 1500 flights (uniquely identified by flight number) and employ 1400 pilots (uniquely identified by their last name and first initial) to fly them. However, because of factors such as type of airplane, amount of pilot experience, pilot geographic locations, and FAA regulations, each of our pilots qualifies to fly on only a relatively small percentage of flights. To help our schedulers, we frequently need to answer questions such as the following:

1. Given a flight, what are the names of the pilots qualified to fly it?
2. Given a pilot's name, what are the flight numbers that pilot is qualified to fly?
3. Given a flight's number and a pilot's name, do we have a match? In other words, is the specified pilot qualified for the particular flight?

Right now, our schedulers attempt to answer such questions by time-consuming manual methods. I'm sure that you can easily computerize this task for them. Thanks in advance for your help in this matter.

Carry out a complete analysis, design, implementation, and testing of the system requested in this memo. The document produced by your analysis should be a user requirements specification. Your design should produce a CRC model.

13. Design, implement, and test a program that takes a text file as input and displays an alphabetical list of unique words that appear in the file and their associated frequencies. The frequency of a word is the number of times that it occurs in the file. A word is any string of characters surrounded by white space characters. Case should be ignored in the spelling of words. As an added challenge, include a feature in your program that allows the user to select the sorted order for the list of words alphabetically or in descending order by frequency of occurrence. (*Hint:* Your task will be much easier if you use one of the ADTs developed in this chapter.)

12

Linked Lists

Chapter Outline

These are the ties which, though light as air, are strong as links of iron.
Edmund Burke
(1729–1797)

In the previous chapter, we discovered that an array implementation (with binary search) of a one-key table requires $O(n)$ data interchanges for the store and remove operations. Attempting to maintain in order such an array-implemented list parallels the dynamics of waiting in a long line. When someone cuts into the middle of the line, there is a dominolike effect that forces everyone behind that person to move back. When someone in the middle of the line decides to leave, the reverse effect occurs; everyone behind the departed person is able to move ahead one slot.

It is possible to draw an analogy between people waiting in a line and data items stored next to each other in computer memory. If the data items are arranged in some type of order and it becomes necessary to insert into or delete from the middle of the line, a considerable amount of data movement is involved. This data movement requires computer time and decreases program efficiency. One of the central motivations behind the linked list data structure is to eliminate the data movement associated with insertions into and deletions from such a list. Of course, by now we might suspect that efficiency in eliminating such data movement can only come by trading off other efficiency factors. One of the crucial questions to ask yourself as we study linked lists is, "What price are we paying to handle additions and deletions effectively?"

In addition to optimizing the efficiency of insertion and deletion operations, studying linked lists will also hone your skills in using dynamically allocated memory. You were first introduced to dynamic memory in Section 9.6 when we discussed vectors. In the Case Study for Chapter 11, you saw how strategically using pointers could help eliminate the need to store redundant copies of data. In the present chapter, we explore more sophisticated ways in which dynamic memory can be manipulated to our advantage.

12.1 The Need for Linked Lists

To motivate our discussion of linked lists, let us consider two problems. The first problem is the file input problem. The second problem is the data movement problem. Both problems can be solved by using data structures we have already studied. How-

Objectives

a. to understand what kinds of problems require sophisticated methods of dynamic memory manipulation
b. to understand the properties of a data structure that can solve these types of problems

ever, each problem reveals some shortcomings of those previous methods and points to the need for some new, more sophisticated techniques for dealing with dynamic memory.

The File Input Problem

The following sequence of operations is typical of many computer applications:

1. Input the data from a file into a structure in main memory.
2. Process the data.
3. Output the data back to the file.

The data in the file can be of any type, such as integers, strings, or personnel records. The processing step transforms these data in some way. For example, at the end of the year, each employee's salary might be adjusted. Because the data are written back to the same file, they must be saved in temporary locations for processing before output. Two data structures that we studied in Chapter 9 can serve as candidates for this role: a C++ array or a vector.

First, consider an approach that uses a C++ array as the temporary data structure for this problem. When the array variable is declared before the input step, the number of cells specified may be more than is needed to hold the data values from small files. This memory is consequently wasted. The number of cells may also be less than is needed to hold the data values from large files. This would cause a logic error because some data in the file would be missing from the list. Assuming an element type called `element` and an input file stream called `inFile`, the following code segment illustrates this point:

```
// Declare data for an array of 100 elements

const int MAX_LIST_SIZE = 100;
element list[MAX_LIST_SIZE];
int length = 0;
element data;

// Input no more than 100 elements from a file

inFile >> data;
while (! inFile.fail() && (length < MAX_LIST_SIZE))
{
   list[length] = data;
   ++length;
   inFile >> data;
}

// Display the consequences of the input operation

if (! inFile.fail() && (length == MAX_LIST_SIZE))
   cout << "Too bad, some data missing" << endl;
else if (length < MAX_LIST_SIZE)
   cout << "Too bad, some memory wasted" << endl;
else
   cout << "Lucky choice of size of array" << endl;
```

The vector that we studied in Section 9.6 is a better choice than an array for this problem because a vector takes advantage of dynamic memory. When the vector variable is declared, no memory is allocated for any cells. As each data value comes in from the file, the vector is resized and the data value is assigned to the last cell in the enlarged vector. At the end of the input process, no memory will have gone to waste and no data will be missing. The following code segment solves the file input problem with a vector:

```
apvector<element> list;
element data;
inFile >> data;
while (! inFile.eof())
{
   list.resize(list.length() + 1);
   list[list.length() - 1] = data;
   inFile >> data;
}
```

Each of the two solutions presented here comes with a potentially heavy price. Recall from Section 9.6 that the data elements in a vector are stored in an array data member. The process of resizing a vector for each input value requires

1. The allocation of memory for a new array almost equal to the size of the old array
2. The copying of all of the data from one array to the other array

For small files, these costs in processing time and memory are negligible. But for large files, the costs grow unreasonably. Merely adding one element to the structure is potentially an $O(n)$ operation in its time efficiency despite the fact that the added element is appended to the end of the list. This $O(n)$ categorization arises from the n separate assignments that must be made from the old array to the new array. In its space efficiency, while the copying occurs from the old array to the new array, we are charged for $2*n$ memory locations even though we only have n values that we must store. In the worst case, the computer may run out of memory when a new array is created during the input of a single data value. Or a process may not be completed on time because it took too long to copy a large number of data values from one array to the other during an input operation.

Here is a case where the overall solution of a problem is correct, but the means of getting there are too costly. When faced with such a problem, a computer scientist focuses on the cause—the way dynamic memory is manipulated—and proposes a solution—a new way of manipulating this memory. An ideal data structure for the file input problem would do these tasks:

1. Start with an empty condition.
2. Create just one cell of memory during the insertion of each input value.
3. Require the copying of just one data value—the input value—to the new memory cell.
4. Allow the processing of each data value in sequence from the beginning to the end of the data structure.

We will soon examine a new ADT called a *linked list* that uses dynamic memory to meet these requirements.

The Data Movement Problem

Another common process in computer applications is the insertion or removal of a data value from a list. When a list is represented as an array (or vector or ordered collection), the insertion or removal of a data value can result in the movement of many other data values as well. An insertion requires all of the subsequent data values to be shifted to the right. A removal requires all of the subsequent data values to be shifted to the left. In the worst case, insertion or removal at the beginning of the list, the contents of the entire list must be moved. We have seen good examples of these cases with the `addFirst` and `removeFirst` operations of the ordered collection class that we investigated in Section 11.1. Because the ordered collection was implemented with an array, both `addFirst` and `removeFirst` were $O(n)$ in their time efficiency.

A special case of this problem is that of the insertion or removal of data from a file. We must first input all of the data from the file into a list (the file input problem). Then, we add or delete data from the list. Finally, we output the contents of the list back to the file. Clearly, from an efficiency perspective, an array or a vector would be a poor choice of data structure to use in representing a list to solve this problem!

The ideal data structure for solving the data movement problem would allow insertions or removals without causing the physical movement of any other data values in the list. It turns out that the linked list ADT satisfies this requirement, as well as the others mentioned earlier. The use of dynamic memory allows a data value to be placed anywhere in a linked list with no physical movement of the other data in the list. We explore the concept of a linked list in the next section.

Exercises 12.1

1. Suppose we have n data values stored in a file, and a program reads these values into an ordered collection implemented using the array technique discussed in Section 11.1. Suppose also that, as a value is read in from the file, it is inserted at the beginning of the ordered collection; that is, the `addFirst` operation is called. Determine, using big-O notation, the running time for this program assuming that the file contains n data values.
2. Are there occasions for which we would still want to use an array or an ordered collection implemented with an array to receive file input, despite the problems we have discussed in this section? If so, discuss the reasons why.
3. Describe the case that causes the least amount of work during a data movement process in an ordered collection that is implemented with an array. Does this occur during insertion or removal, and where does it occur?
4. Suppose you sort a list of input values by reading them in one at a time and inserting them into a sorted collection object (Section 11.2). Clearly, after you have read all of the input values, you will have a sorted list. Let's call this technique the *sorted collection sort algorithm*. Using big-O notation, analyze the time efficiency of this algorithm in terms of number of comparisons and number of data interchanges. Be sure that you take into account the underlying implementation strategy that we used for the sorted collection in Section 11.2. Compare the efficiency of this algorithm to the efficiencies of the other sort algorithms we have studied—insertion, bubble, selection, and radix sort.

12.2 The Concept of a Linked List

The Characteristics and Logical Structure of a Linked List

We have just seen two applications for which a linked list is ideally suited:

1. File input into a data structure in which the data can then be processed in sequence
2. Insertions or deletions of data from a data structure with minimal physical movement of data

Objectives

a. to understand the characteristics of a linked list that make it suitable for solving some kinds of problems but not others
b. to visualize the logical structure of a linked list
c. to understand the operations on a linked list

A linked list works perfectly for these problems because it has the following characteristics:

1. It allows users to visit each data element in sequence from the first element to the last element.
2. It allows users to insert or remove a data element at a given position with no physical movement of the other data elements.
3. It uses only enough dynamic memory to store the data values inserted by the user.

To support these features, a linked list must have a special *logical structure*. Its logical structure describes the organization of data independently of how it is stored in the physical memory of a computer. The primary organizational element of this structure is called a *node*. In a linked list, a node contains two parts or *members*:

1. A data element
2. A *link* or *pointer* to the next node in the list

The sequence of data elements in a linked list is thus linked by the sequence of nodes in which the elements are contained. Figure 12.1 shows a sequence of nodes in a linked list. Note that the data elements are labeled D1 through D4. Each link is an arrow coming out of the back of a node and pointing at the next node. Note also that the link component of the last node in the list is a little box with no arrow. This designates an *empty link* or *null pointer*, indicating that there is no next node after this one in the list.

The logical structure of a linked list has four other components that support the implementation of operations on the list:

1. A first pointer to the first node in the list
2. A current pointer that can be moved to a desired node
3. A previous pointer that always points to the node before the current one
4. An integer representing the number of nodes in the list

The first three components are sometimes called *external pointers* because they are not links that hold the sequence of nodes together. Their purpose is to give users access to different nodes in the list. Figure 12.2 shows the linked list from Figure 12.1 with these additional components, after the current pointer has been moved to the second node in the list.

As we shall see shortly, this logical structure is just what we need to satisfy the requirements of a linked list mentioned earlier. Users can move through the list and visit each data element in sequence by moving the current pointer to the next node. Users can also insert or remove a data element from the list by redirecting some pointers at the appropriate nodes.

Figure 12.1
The nodes in a linked list

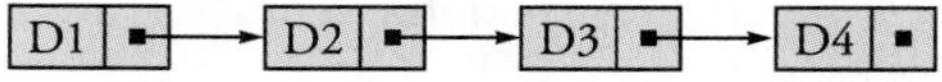

Figure 12.2
The external pointers of a linked list

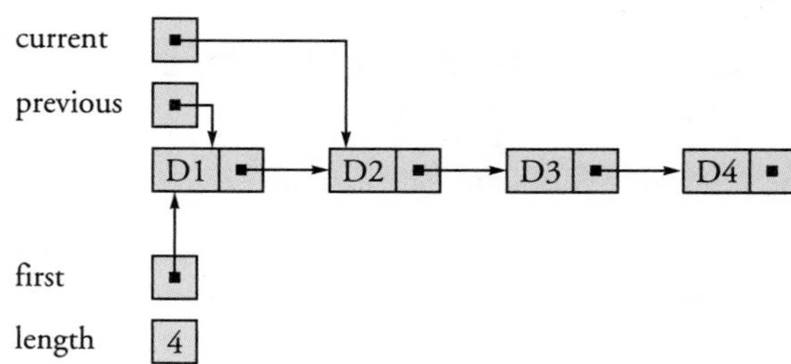

Linked List Operations

Let us now consider the abstract operations that the logical structure of a linked list makes possible. Each of these operations has a set of preconditions and postconditions. Most of these conditions concern the state of the external pointers in the linked list. In each of the following subsections, we provide an informal description of the operation, illustrate the operation with a figure, and state its preconditions and postconditions.

Creating a Linked List

When a linked list is created, it is empty and thus contains no nodes. However, the three external pointers and the length must all be initialized. Each of the pointers is set to null, as shown in Figure 12.3.

The precondition of the `create` operation is that the linked list is in an unknown state. The postconditions are that each external pointer is null, and the length is 0.

Detecting an Empty Linked List

An empty linked list looks just like the list shown in Figure 12.3. The precondition of the `empty` operation is that the list has been appropriately initialized. The postcondition is that the operation returns `true` if there are no nodes in the list and `false` otherwise.

Moving to the Next Node

The `next` operation moves the current pointer to the next node after the current one. It also moves the previous pointer ahead one node. Figure 12.4 shows the states of a linked list before and after this operation, which moves the current pointer from the first node to the second node.

Note that the previous pointer was null before the operation and points to the first node afterward.

The `next` operation has one precondition. The current pointer must point to a node in the list. This will not be the case when the list is empty or after the `next` operation is executed with the current pointer referencing the last node. The postconditions of the `next` operation are as follows:

1. The previous pointer is moved to the next node.
2. The current pointer is moved to the next node, unless this component is null. If that is the case, the current pointer becomes null.

Figure 12.5 shows the states of a linked list during a series of `next` operations to move the current pointer as far as it can go in the list.

Detecting the End of the List

To avoid running off the end of a linked list, users need a means of detecting when the current pointer can advance no further. For example, the `atEnd` operation returns `true` when a list is in the last state depicted in Figure 12.5. The operation also returns `true` when the list is empty. When neither of these conditions is true, `atEnd` returns `false`.

Figure 12.3
A newly created linked list

current	■
previous	■
first	■
length	0

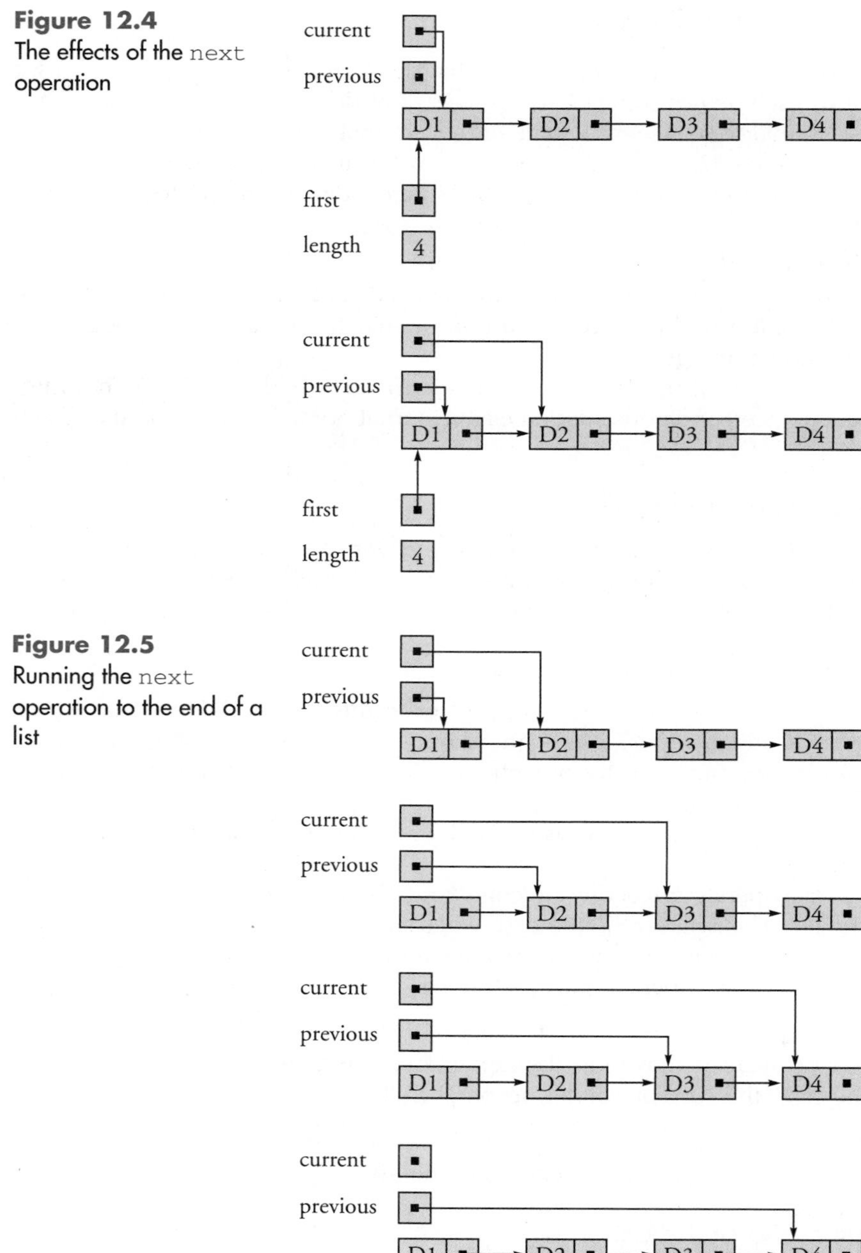

Figure 12.4
The effects of the `next` operation

Figure 12.5
Running the `next` operation to the end of a list

Accessing and Modifying the Data in the Current Node

A typical application will move the current pointer to a desired node in a linked list and then either access the data value in the node or modify it. These two operations, `access` and `modify`, assume that the current pointer is aimed at a node. In other words, `atEnd` must return `false`. `access` returns the data value in the current node. `modify` copies its parameter, a data value, into the data component of the current node. The result of an `access` operation to the contents of the last node is shown in Figure 12.6.

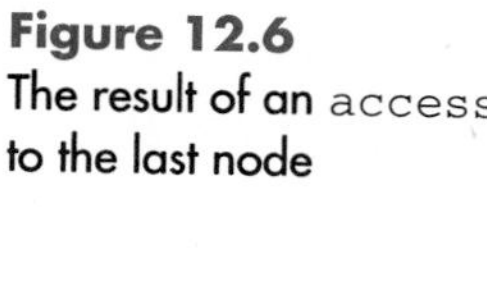

Figure 12.6
The result of an `access` to the last node

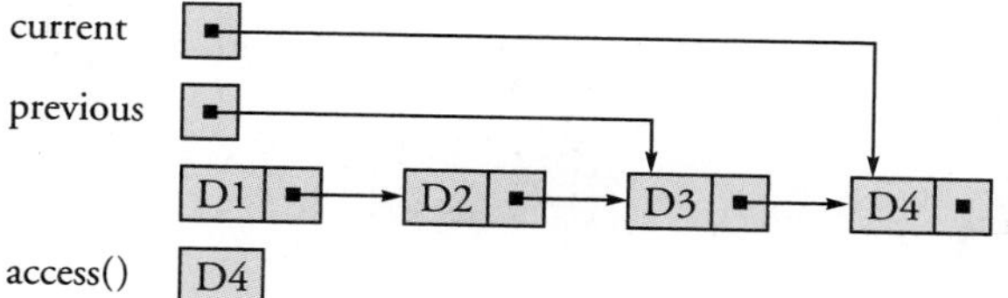

Figure 12.7
The effects of the `first` operation

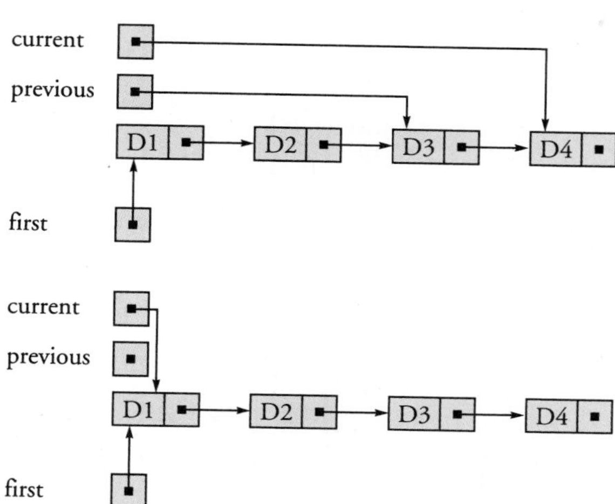

Moving to the First Node

Applications that process entire lists require an operation to move the current pointer to the first node in a list. The `first` operation assumes that the linked list has been appropriately initialized but has no other preconditions. If the list is not empty, the operation aims the current pointer at the first node and sets the previous pointer to null. If the list is empty, `first` does nothing. Figure 12.7 shows the states of a linked list before and after the `first` operation.

Adding Data to the List

To add data to a linked list, a user moves the current pointer to the node before which the data should be inserted and then invokes the `insert` operation. The only precondition of this operation is that the list has been appropriately initialized. The postcondition is that the node containing the new data element becomes the current node. The linked list handles an insertion of data in different ways, depending on the position of the current pointer.

Case 1 If the list is empty, the new data element is placed in the first node. This process is shown in Figure 12.8.

Case 2 If the current pointer points to the first node, the new data element is placed in a new node and inserted before the first node as shown in Figure 12.9. The new node becomes both the current node and the first node.

Case 3 If the current pointer points to a node after the first node, then the new data element is placed in a new node that is linked into the list between the current node and the previous node as shown in Figure 12.10. Once again, the current pointer is aimed at the node just inserted.

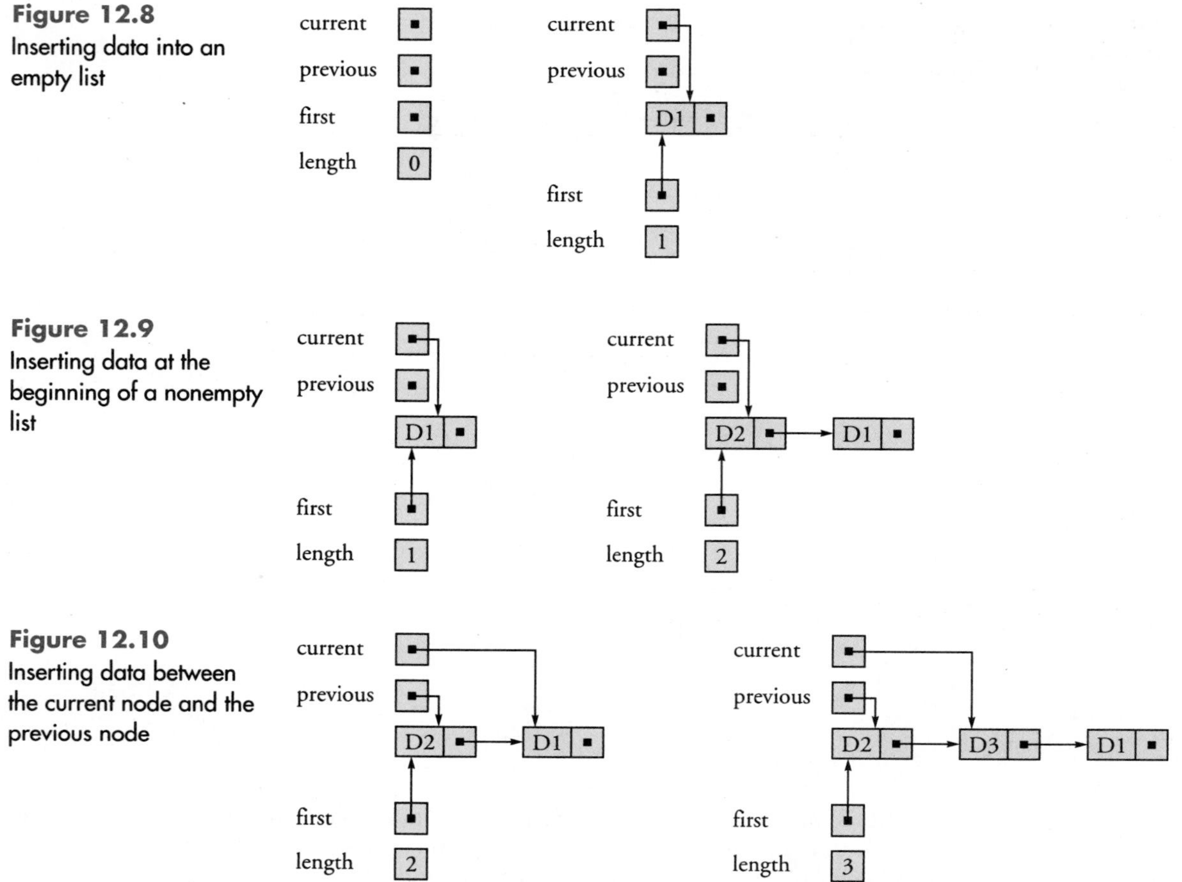

Figure 12.8 Inserting data into an empty list

Figure 12.9 Inserting data at the beginning of a nonempty list

Figure 12.10 Inserting data between the current node and the previous node

Case 4 If the current pointer has been moved past the last node in the list, the new data element is placed in a new node at the end of the list as shown in Figure 12.11.

Note that in each case the external pointers and the length are updated appropriately.

The following algorithm describes in detail the process of creating a new node and linking it into a linked list:

1. Create a new node
2. Set the data component of the new node to the new data element
3. Set the next pointer of the new node to null
4. If the list is empty or the current node is the first node,
5. Aim the first pointer at the new node

   Else
6. Aim the next pointer of the previous node at the new node
7. Set the next pointer of the new node to the current pointer
8. Aim the current pointer at the new node
9. Increment the length by 1

The steps in this process for inserting a node into the middle of a linked list are depicted in Figure 12.12. The order of steps 4 through 8 is critical. A different ordering of steps will result in the new node's not being properly linked, and the logical structure of the linked list will be corrupted. Also note that these are the only steps performed

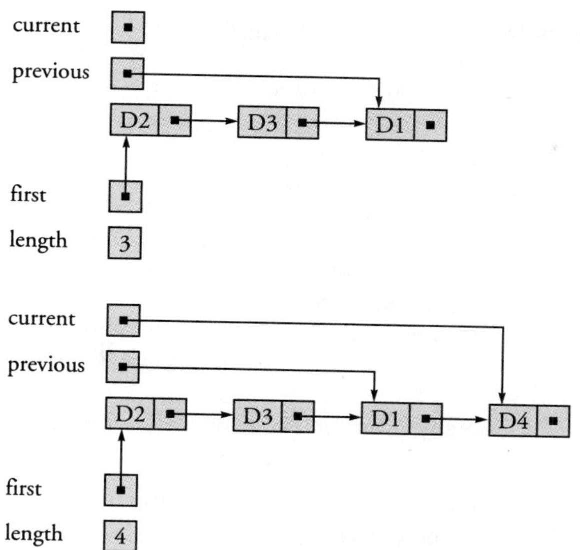

Figure 12.11
Inserting data after the last node

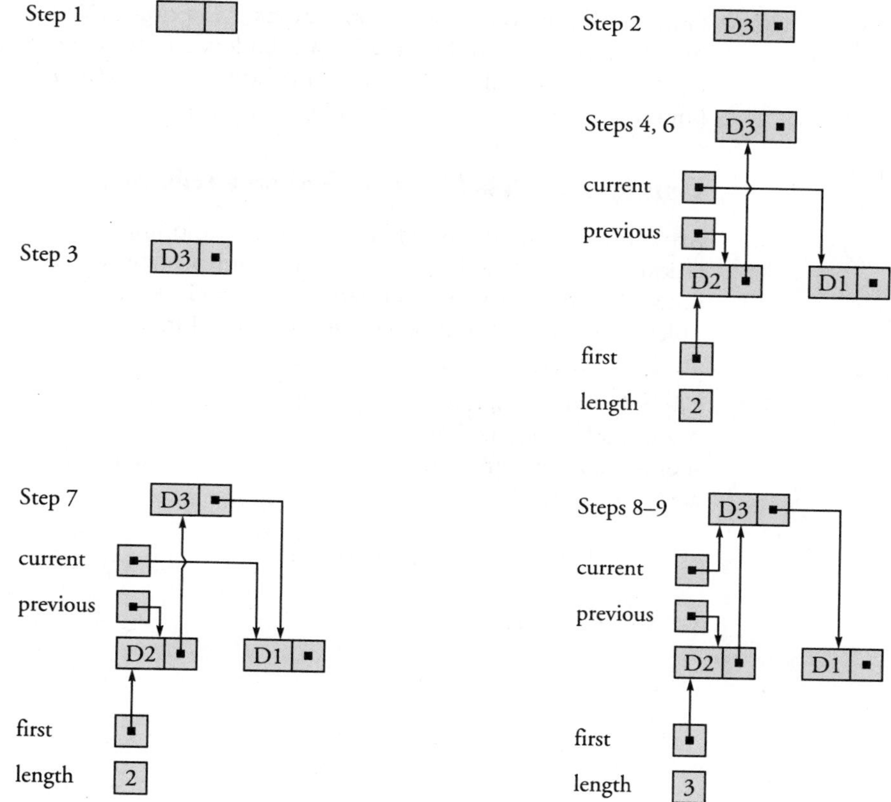

Figure 12.12
The steps in the process of inserting a node into a linked list

during an insertion, regardless of where it occurs in the list. There is no loop to adjust the positions of other data elements, as with arrays. This is why a linked list solves the data movement problem in $O(1)$ time.

Removing Data from the List

To remove data from a linked list, the user moves the current pointer to the desired node and then invokes the `remove` operation. This operation assumes that the current pointer is pointing to a node (`atEnd` returns `false`). The operation unlinks the current node, returns its memory to the system, and returns the data element to the caller. At the end of the operation, the current pointer points to the node after the node just removed. The previous pointer remains unchanged. The first pointer may be updated as well.

The following algorithm describes in detail the process of unlinking a node to remove its data element from a linked list:

1. Save the data element in a temporary variable
2. Save a pointer to the current node
3. If the current node is the first node
4.   Set the first pointer to the next pointer of the current node
   Else
5.   Set the next pointer of the previous node to the next pointer of the current node
6. Set the current pointer to the next pointer of the current node
7. Use the saved pointer to return the old node to the system
8. Decrement the length by 1
9. Return the data element to the caller

Once again, the order of the operations is important. The steps in this process for removing a node from the middle of a linked list are depicted in Figure 12.13. As with inserting a node, the operations are performed in $O(1)$ time. The operations on a linked list are summarized in Table 12.1.

Using a Linked List to Solve Problems

Armed with a linked list abstract data type and knowing nothing about its implementation, we can now look at some examples of how it is used. We assume that the linked list ADT has been defined as a C++ class template. The type parameter for the linked list class is the type of the data stored in a list.

Example 12.1 The following program is a solution to an instance of the file input problem. The program reads integers from a file named `myfile.old` into a linked list. It then increments each integer in the list. Finally, it writes the contents of the list back to the file `myfile.new`.

```
// Program file: fileprob.cpp

#include <iostream.h>
#include <fstream.h>
#include "linklist.h"

int main()
{
   ifstream inFile;
   ofstream outFile;
```

Figure 12.13 The steps in the process of removing a node from a linked list

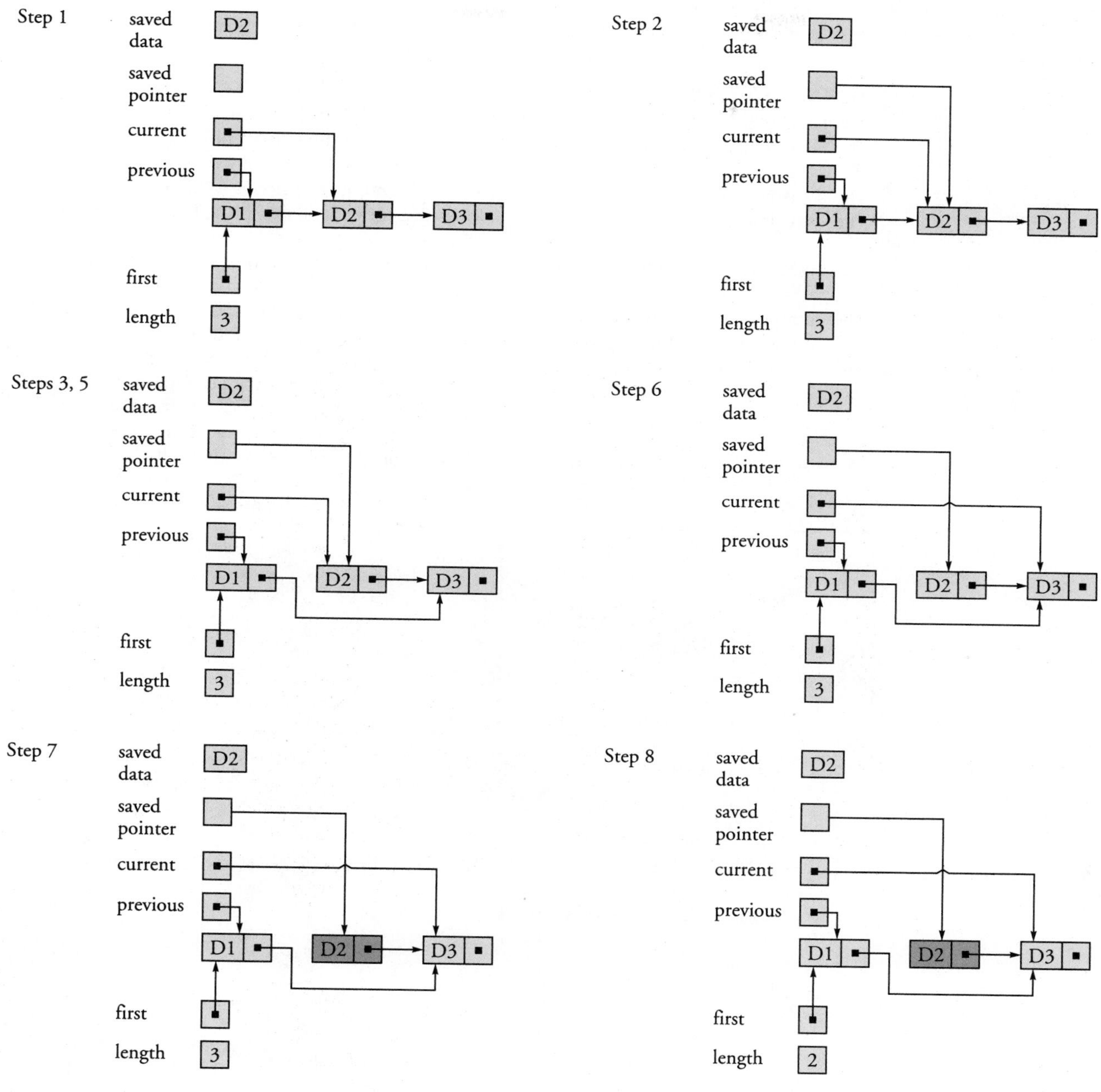


```
LinkedList<int> list;
int data;

// Input phase - insert data at end of list

inFile.open("myfile.old");
inFile >> data;
while (! inFile.fail())
```

continued

Table 12.1
The Operations on a Linked List Abstract Data Type

Operation	Preconditions	Postconditions
`create`	The list is in an unknown state.	The list is empty.
`empty`	The list is initialized.	Returns `true` if empty, `false` otherwise.
`atEnd`	The list is initialized.	Returns `true` if the current pointer has run off the end of the list, `false` otherwise.
`length`	The list is initialized.	Returns the number of nodes in the list.
`first`	The list is initialized.	Moves the current pointer to the first node in the list.
`next`	The current pointer points to a node.	Advances the current and previous pointers ahead by one node.
`access`	The current pointer points to a node.	Returns the data element stored in the current node.
`modify(newData)`	The current pointer points to a node.	Sets the data in the current node to the new data.
`insert(newData)`	The list is initialized.	If `atEnd` is true, then inserts the `newData` into a new node at the end of the list. Otherwise, inserts the `newData` into a new node before the current one. Makes the new node the current one.
`remove`	The current pointer points to a node.	Removes the current node from the list, makes the node following this node the current one, and returns the removed data to the caller.

```
   {
      list.insert(data);
      list.next();
      inFile >> data;
   }
   inFile.close();

   // Processing phase - increment all values
   //                    in the list

   list.first();
   while (! list.atEnd())
   {
      data = list.access();
      list.modify(data + 1);
      list.next();
   }

   // Output phase - write all values in the
   //                list back to the file

   outFile.open("myfile.new");
   list.first();
   while (! list.atEnd())
   {
      outFile << list.access() << endl;
      list.next();
   }
   outFile.close();
   return 0;
}
```

Let us now examine the logic of each of the three main parts of the program of Example 12.1.

Input Phase In this part of the program, the input file is opened, and we enter a standard end-of-file `while` loop. The list is assumed to be empty at the beginning of the loop. Thus, when the first data value is inserted, it goes at the end of the list automatically. After the insertion, the `next` operation is run. This has the effect of moving the current pointer beyond the last node in the list. Thus, on the next pass through the loop, the new data will continue to be inserted at the end of the list. At the end of the input phase, the data in the list will be in the same order as they were in the file and will be ready for sequential processing.

Processing Phase In this part of the program, the current pointer is moved to the first node to begin a *sequential traversal* of the list. This traversal consists of an end-of-list `while` loop. In the body of the loop, we access the data in the current node, process the data, and modify the node with the result. Then we move on to the next node, continuing the process until the end of the list is reached. Note that the control condition is tested at loop entry to guard against the cases of the empty list and the end of the list.

Output Phase This part of the program is similar to the processing phase. In this case, however, we traverse the list and simply access the data in each node for output to the file.

Example 12.2 Users would like to have a function named `reverse` that expects a linked list as a parameter and returns a new linked list with the contents of the parameter in reverse order. This is another instance of the data movement problem. The following C++ function solves this problem:

```
template <class E>
LinkedList<E> reverse(LinkedList<E> &list)
{
   LinkedList<E> result;

   list.first();
   for (int i = 1; i <= list.length(); ++i)
   {
      result.insert(list.access());
      list.next();
   }
   return result;
}
```

The function in Example 12.2 illustrates two new ideas:

1. A count-controlled `for` loop can be used to traverse a linked list. The loop assumes that the current pointer is at the first node. The loop counts from 1 to the length of the list and advances through the list by running the `next` operation.
2. The reversal of the data elements in the new list is automatically accomplished by inserting each value at the beginning of the list.

Note that the process of reversing the contents of a linked list is much more efficient than the process of reversing the contents of an ordered collection.

Exercises 12.2

1. Based on the operations for a linked list discussed in this section, describe how the linked list ADT differs from the ordered collection ADT.
2. Describe two applications for which a linked list is a suitable data structure.
3. Explain why so many linked list operations assume that the `atEnd` operation returns `false`.
4. Draw a picture of a linked list with three nodes. The current pointer should be aimed at the first node. Now draw pictures that show each step during the process of removing this node from the list.
5. Suppose that the length of a linked list is not maintained as a separate component of the data structure. How does this change affect the behavior of the `length` operation?
6. Describe the method used by a new linked list operation called `insertLast`. This operation expects a data element as a parameter and inserts it at the end of a linked list. The only precondition is that the list is initialized. Categorize the efficiency of this operation using big-O notation.
7. Describe how to overload the assignment operator for vectors so that one can assign the contents in successive nodes of a linked list to the successive indices of a vector. Why would this operation be useful?
8. Overload the + operator to define a C++ function that concatenates two linked lists and returns the result. Categorize the efficiency of this operation using big-O notation.
9. Given a linked list of `int`s, write a loop that starts at the beginning of the linked list and returns the position of the first list node with the value 0 in its data field. If no such node exists in the list, –1 should be returned.
10. Write a function to remove all of the nodes in a linked list.
11. Write a function `sum` to sum the integers in a linked list of integers.
12. Write a function called `merge` that receives two linked lists of integers arranged in ascending order. Your function should merge these two lists into a single list, also arranged in ascending order. The merged list should be returned from the function.

12.3 Defining the Linked List ADT As a C++ Class

Objectives

a. to learn how to use pointers in C++ to manipulate dynamic data
b. to learn how to create a dynamic data structure to represent a linked list

In the previous section, we examined the definition and use of a linked list as an abstract data type. We assumed the existence of a C++ class template that corresponds to that definition and showed how that class can be used to solve some problems. Now it is time to develop the code for the C++ class template for a linked list.

The first step, declaring the operations and data members for the class, results in the following file:

```
// Class declaration file: linklist.h

#ifndef LINKLIST_H
#define LINKLIST_H
template <class E> class LinkedList
{
   public:

   // constructors

   LinkedList();
   LinkedList(const LinkedList<E> &list);
```

```
    // destructor

    ~LinkedList();

    // assignment

    const LinkedList<E>& operator =
       (const LinkedList<E> &rhs);

    // accessors

    int length() const;
    bool empty() const;
    bool atEnd() const;
    E access();
    // modifiers

    void first();
    void next();
    void modify(const E &item);
    void insert(const E &item);
    E remove();

    private:

    // Data members

    struct node           // Definition of the node type
    {
       E data;
       node * next;
    };

    // External pointers to the list

    node * myFirst;
    node * myCurrent;
    node * myPrevious;

    // The number of nodes in the list

    int mySize;

    // Member functions

    node * getNode(const E &item);
};
#endif
```

The declarations of the public operations require no comment. They have been translated directly from the abstract operations listed in Table 12.1.

The data members `myFirst`, `myCurrent`, `myPrevious`, and `mySize` represent the four external components—first, current, previous, and length—of the logical structure of a linked list discussed in Section 12.2. Each of the pointer data members is of type `node *`. We now examine the definitions of this type and of the private member function `getNode`.

Defining a Pointer to a Node

As we saw in Section 12.2, each node in a linked list contains two parts: a data component and a pointer to the next node in the list. A struct is a logical choice for representing a node in C++. One component of the struct, the data element, is of type E. The other component of the struct must be a pointer to a node. As we saw in Section 9.6 and the Case Study of Chapter 11, C++ provides a special syntax for defining pointer types as follows:

<type of object pointed to> * <pointer variable name>

So if we want a member of a struct of type node to be able to point at another struct of the same type, that member must be of type node *. Such is the declaration of the next member in the struct node below.

```
struct node          // Definition of the node type
{
   E data;
   node * next;
};
```

Note in the linklist.h class declaration file, the type name node is declared as private. This means that the struct node is of use in the implementation of the linked list class only. Users of the linked list class will have no awareness of what a node is nor will they be able to access data members of a node in any way.

Declaring the getNode Function

Each time a data element is added to a linked list, three things must be done:

1. Allocate dynamic memory for a new node.
2. Set the data part of the node to the new data element.
3. Set the next pointer part of the node to null.

This threefold task is complex enough to warrant the definition of a function to perform it. Because the function will be used only within the implementation of the linked list class, we declare it as private. The function expects a data element as a parameter. It returns a pointer to a new node that contains the data element and a null pointer.

```
node * getNode(const E &item);
```

Now that we have completed the declaration of the linked list class, we can turn to its implementation.

Creating a Linked List

Recall from Section 12.2 that a new linked list is empty. Thus, its external pointers first, current, and previous should all be null, and its length should be 0. The default constructor does this:

```
template <class E>
LinkedList<E>::LinkedList()
: myFirst(0), myCurrent(0), myPrevious(0), mySize(0)
{
}
```

Note that the null pointer is represented in C++ as zero. This value looks like a number, but it is used here as a pointer value. The null value indicates that the pointer variable does not currently point to a node.

The Copy Constructor for a Linked List

The copy constructor copies all of the data from the parameter list into the receiver list. The function makes use of the temporary pointer `probe` to traverse the nodes in the parameter list. It uses `insert` and `next` to place each data value at the end of the receiver list.

```
template <class E>
LinkedList<E>::LinkedList(const LinkedList<E &list)
: myFirst(0), myCurrent(0), myPrevious(0), mySize(0)
{
    // Temporary pointer to first node in list
    node * probe = list.myFirst;

    // Loop until end of list is reached
    while (probe != 0)
    {
        // Insert data from node in list
        insert(probe->data);

        // Advance to next node of receiver
        next();

        // Move probe to next node in list
        probe = probe->next;
    }
}
```

This code is heavily commented to clarify each step. Note the following points:

1. The `probe` pointer starts at the first node of `list`.
2. The loop control condition `(probe != 0)` returns `false` as long as `probe` points at a node in `list` but returns `true` when `probe` has reached the end of `list`.
3. The expression `probe->data` accesses the `data` component in the node pointed to by `probe`. This value is passed to `insert` to add it to the end of the receiver list.
4. The assignment statement `probe = probe->next;` sets `probe` to the value of the `next` component in the node pointed to by `probe`. This has the effect of advancing `probe` to the next node in `list`.

As you saw in Section 9.6, a pointer value can be compared to zero to determine whether or not it is null. The syntax for accessing a member of a node is new. Its form is

<pointer variable>-><node member name>

The *arrow operator* directs the computer to follow the arrow from the pointer variable to the designated member in the node as shown in our box and pointer diagrams. This process is accomplished in two steps:

1. a *dereference,* in which the node is located
2. a *selection,* in which the designated member is located in the node

The same process could be accomplished by using the dereference operator (*) and the selector operator (.) introduced in Chapters 9 and 11, respectively. For example, the expressions

```
probe->next
```

and

```
(*probe).next
```

have the same effect. Obviously, the use of the arrow notation simplifies the expression, so we prefer that.

The Destructor for Linked Lists

The destructor makes use of the `first`, `empty`, and `remove` operations to return all of the nodes in the list to the system.

```
template <class E>
LinkedList<E>::~LinkedList()
{
    E item;

    first();
    while (! empty())
       item = remove();
}
```

The `first` and `next` Operations

After the `first` operation, the current pointer points to the first node and the previous pointer is null. The `first` operation thus modifies the current and previous pointers appropriately.

```
template <class E>
void LinkedList<E>::first()
{
    if (myCurrent != myFirst)
    {
       myCurrent = myFirst;
       myPrevious = 0;
    }
}
```

The `next` operation moves the current and previous pointers ahead in the list by one node each. The precondition is that the current pointer must be pointing to a node.

```
template <class E>
void LinkedList<E>::next()
{
   assert (myCurrent != 0);
   myPrevious = myCurrent;
   myCurrent = myCurrent->next;
}
```

Accessing and Modifying Data in a Node

Like the `next` operation, both the `access` and `modify` operations assume that the current pointer is pointing to a node.

```
template <class E>
E LinkedList<E>::access()
{
   assert(myCurrent != 0);
   return myCurrent->data;
}

template <class E>
void LinkedList<E>::modify(const E &item)
{
   assert(myCurrent != 0);
   myCurrent->data = item;
}
```

As you can see from the last three function implementations, it is the responsibility of the user to test for the end of the list condition before running an operation that accesses the contents of a node. The `assert` function catches any failures to do so.

Testing for the End of the List

The `atEnd` operation should return `true` if the list is empty or if the current pointer has advanced to the end of the list. Otherwise, the operation returns `false`.

```
template <class E>
bool LinkedList<E>::atEnd() const
{
   return (empty() || myCurrent == 0);
}
```

Testing for an Empty List

The current pointer is null when the list is empty, but it is also null when it is at the end of a nonempty list. Thus, the empty operation compares the length of the list to 0.

```
template <class E>
bool LinkedList<E>::empty() const
{
   return mySize == 0;
}
```

Inserting Data into a Linked List

The `insert` operation follows the algorithm presented in Section 12.2. The `getNode` function is used to create and initialize a new node with the new data element:

```
template <class E>
void LinkedList<E>::insert(const E &item)
{
   node * newNode = getNode(item);

   if (empty() || (myFirst == myCurrent))
      myFirst = newNode;
   else
      myPrevious->next = newNode;
   newNode->next = myCurrent;
   myCurrent = newNode;
   ++mySize;
}
```

Implementing `getNode`

Whenever a new node is needed for a linked list, the implementation invokes the function `getNode`. To allocate dynamic memory for the new node, `getNode` uses the `new` operator introduced in Section 9.6. In that chapter, a call to `new` took the form `new E [<number of items>]`. This expression allocates memory for an array of items and returns a pointer to the array. In the context of linked lists, we want `new` to return a pointer to a node. Thus, the form of the call to `new` should now be `new node`. The `getNode` function verifies that memory was allocated for the node by asserting that the new node pointer is not null. `getNode` then uses the pointer to initialize the contents of the new node with the new data element and the null pointer, and it returns the pointer to the caller.

```
template <class E>
LinkedList<E>::node * LinkedList<E>::getNode
   (const E &item)
{
   node * newNode = new node;

   assert(newNode != 0);
   newNode->data = item;
   newNode->next = 0;
   return newNode;
}
```

Note a slight difference in the syntax of this function's heading from the headings of the other linked list functions. The scope specifier `LinkedList<E>::` must also appear at the beginning of the heading. The reason is that the privately declared return type, `node *`, would appear to be undefined if it were not preceded by the scope specifier of the class declaration module.

Removing Data from a Linked List

The `remove` operation follows the algorithm presented in Section 12.2:

```
template <class E>
E LinkedList<E>::remove()
{
   assert (myCurrent != 0);
   E data = myCurrent->data;
   node * garbage = myCurrent;

   if (myFirst == myCurrent)
      myFirst = myCurrent->next;
   else
      myPrevious->next = myCurrent->next;
   myCurrent = myCurrent->next;
   delete garbage;
   --mySize;
   return data;
}
```

Note that the function uses the operator `delete`, introduced in Section 9.6, to return the memory for the node to the system. In Chapter 9, the form for invoking this operator was `delete [ ] <pointer to array>`. In the present context, where we want to recycle just a node, we use the form `delete <pointer to a node>`.

Exercises 12.3

1. Implement the remaining linked list member functions. Then provide a big-O efficiency analysis of each function.
2. State an algorithm for an `addFirst` operation for linked lists and write the corresponding C++ member function. Then provide a big-O analysis for your implementation of this operation.
3. State an algorithm for an `addLast` operation for linked lists and write the corresponding C++ member function. Then provide a big-O analysis for your implementation of this operation.
4. Compare the efficiencies of `addFirst` and `addLast`. Which is more expensive to run and why?
5. State an algorithm and write a function for an index operation that allows access and modification of a data value at a given position in a linked list. Overload the operator `[ ]` for the function. After you've written the function, provide a big-O analysis of its efficiency.
6. Describe the differences between the index operation defined in Exercise 5 for linked lists and the index operation for arrays.
7. Suppose we drop the `mySize` data member from the definition of a linked list. Rewrite the function `length` so that it still returns the number of nodes in a list. What was the efficiency of `length` in the original implementation? What is the efficiency of the new implementation?

12.4 Pointers and the Management of Computer Memory

Objectives

a. to understand the difference between the address of a memory location and the value stored in a memory location
b. to understand how computer memory is organized to support different data types
c. to understand how the logical structure of a linked list can be independent of its structure in memory
d. to understand the costs and benefits of using linked lists

Thus far in this chapter, we have focused on the logical structure of a linked list and paid no attention to how the list is stored in computer memory. Even when we use the operators `new` and `delete` to manipulate dynamic memory, the operations are abstract, hiding any details of how the computer performs these tasks. In this section, we explore some of the concepts underlying memory management in C++ programs. In the process, you will gain a clearer understanding of the costs and benefits of using linked lists.

Addresses and Values of Simple Variables

When we introduced the idea of a variable in Chapter 3, we illustrated the concept with little boxes and labels (Figure 12.14). As this figure shows, variables in C++ are named memory locations where values can be stored and accessed. However, the picture is abstract in that it suppresses the details of representing the memory cells and data at the machine level. When a program is loaded to run on a computer, each of the variable names is converted to a machine address, which is a binary number. The data stored in the memory cells are also represented as binary numbers. Thus, the variables in Figure 12.14 might be more accurately depicted as shown in Figure 12.15.

The binary numbers to the left of each memory cell in Figure 12.15 are called the *addresses* of the memory cells. The numbers inside of the boxes are the data or values stored there. In our hypothetical computer, note that one cell is reserved for each integer value, but two cells are needed for the real number. The whole part of the real number, 101 (5), is stored in cell 1101. The fractional part of the real number, 100 (6), is stored in the next cell. In general, the machine automatically computes the amount of memory needed for each type of data value and allocates that memory accordingly.

Addresses and Values of Array Variables

The distinction between an address and a value stored at an address is one of the most important in computer science. This distinction also applies to array variables. In Chapter 9, we visualized an array variable as a block of adjacent memory cells as

Figure 12.14
Visualizing variables and their values abstractly

```
int x = 3, y = 4;
double d = 5.6;
```

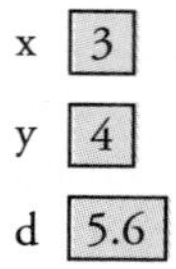

x	3
y	4
d	5.6

Figure 12.15
Visualizing variables and their values at the machine level

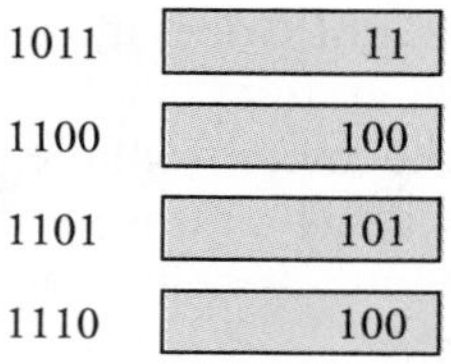

1011	11
1100	100
1101	101
1110	100

shown in Figure 12.16. Note that in the abstract view of an array, the individual cells containing the data values are labeled with index values ranging from 0 to 4. The name `list` appears to label the entire block of cells.

At the machine level, the name `list` is translated to the binary address of the first cell in the array. The address of each subsequent cell in the array is 1 greater than the previous one, as shown in Figure 12.17.

This arrangement allows the address of an array cell to be computed by adding its index value to the machine address of the first cell. (In cases where each data element requires several cells of memory, the index is first multiplied by this factor.) For example, if the machine address of `list` is 11100, the machine address of `list [2]` is 11100 + 10, or 11110 (using binary arithmetic). This method of computing the address of an array cell is the reason array indexing is so fast, no matter where the cell is in the array. In fact, an array is called a *random access data structure* because the time needed to access an array cell is independent of its position in the array. Put another way, it takes no more time to access the cell at `list[2]` than it does to access the cell at `list[0]`.

Addresses and Values of Pointer Variables

The distinction between an address and a value is even more obvious when we deal with pointer variables. A pointer variable is a special kind of memory cell capable of storing the address of another memory cell. Often a pointer variable contains either the null value (0) or a pointer to a chunk of dynamic memory (either an array or a node) returned by the `new` operator. However, as we saw in the Chapter 11 Case Study, we can use the *address-of operator* (&) to obtain the address of any C++ variable and store this value in a pointer variable. The restriction is that the variable whose address is assigned to the pointer must be of the same type as the base type of the pointer. For example, the following code segment accomplishes this for an integer variable:

Figure 12.16
Visualizing an array variable abstractly

```
int list[5];
for (int i = 0; i < 5; ++i)
     list[i] = i + 1;
```

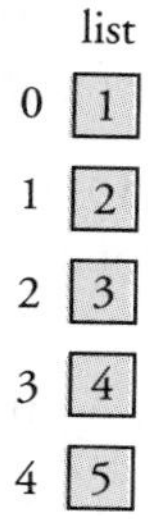

	list
0	1
1	2
2	3
3	4
4	5

Figure 12.17
Visualizing an array at the machine level

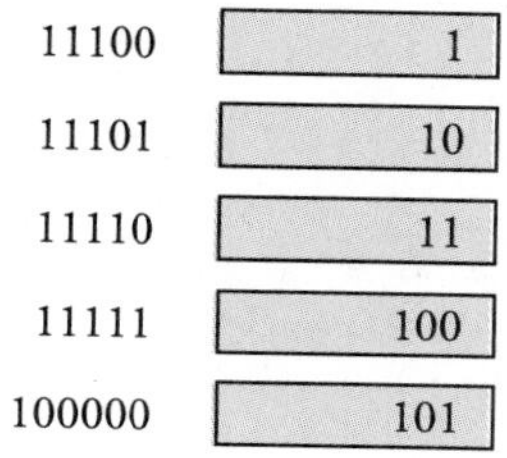

Address	Value
11100	1
11101	10
11110	11
11111	100
100000	101

```
// Declare an integer variable and set it to 2

int x = 2;

// Declare a pointer to an integer variable
// and set it to the address of x

int *intPtr = &x;
```

Figure 12.18 uses the abstract notation of boxes and arrows to distinguish the pointer and integer values stored in the variables `x` and `intPtr`. Figure 12.19 shows what the contents of the memory cells might look like at the machine level. Study the binary numbers stored in the memory cells in Figure 12.19 carefully. They both appear to be integer values. However, the value stored in cell 1001 is the address of cell 1000 and thus is a pointer value.

The dereference operator (*) is the inverse of the address-of operator. It expects a pointer value (an address) as an argument and returns the value stored at that address. Thus, the following code segment displays the machine address of `x` (in decimal) and then the value stored at that address:

```
// Declare an integer variable and set it to 2

int x = 2;

// Declare a pointer to an integer variable
// and set it to the address of x

int *intPtr = &x;

// Display the address of x

cout << intPtr << endl;

// Dereference intPtr to display the value
// stored in x

cout << *intPtr << endl;
```

Using the memory shown in Figure 12.19, when the computer evaluates the expression `*intPtr`, it goes through these steps:

1. Looks up the value in memory cell 1001
2. Uses the value from step 1, 1000, to look up the value in memory cell 1000
3. Returns the value from step 2, 10

Figure 12.18
An integer variable and a pointer to this variable

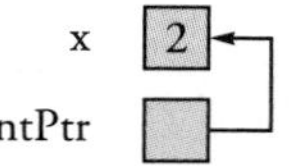

Figure 12.19
The variables of Figure 12.18 at the machine level

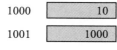

Address	Value
1000	10
1001	1000

A NOTE OF INTEREST

Garbage Collection

Programs that make frequent use of dynamic memory can be error prone. One kind of error that can occur is the failure to return pieces of dynamic memory to the heap when they are no longer needed. If this failure occurs often enough, the program will run out of memory, perhaps at a critical point in its task.

To avoid the problem of memory leakage, some programming languages have been designed so that the programmer does not have to worry about returning unused memory to the heap at all. The run-time system for these languages has a special module called a *garbage collector* that automatically recovers unused dynamic memory when it is needed.

Two such languages, Smalltalk and LISP, rely on dynamic memory for all of their data structures, so an automatic garbage collector is an essential part of their design. In Smalltalk, a pure object-oriented language, dynamic memory is used to create new objects. In LISP, which supports a linked list as a standard data structure, dynamic memory is used to add data elements to a list. When an application in either of these languages asks for a new piece of dynamic memory, the computer checks the heap to see whether the request can be satisfied. If not, the garbage collector is invoked, and all of the unused memory locations are returned to the heap. Then the request is granted if enough dynamic memory is available.

The garbage collection mechanism works roughly as follows: Every memory location is marked as either referenced by the application or not. A memory location is referenced if it is named by a variable or is part of a linked structure pointed to by such a variable. When memory is allocated for variables, it is marked as referenced. When memory becomes completely unlinked from any variable references in a program, it is marked as unreferenced. Thus, only unreferenced memory locations will be candidates for return to the heap.

Garbage collection in early versions of LISP and Smalltalk sometimes degraded the performance of a program. During a collection, an application would appear to pause for a moment while the mechanism did its work. This is one reason why Smalltalk and LISP applications have not received much play in industry, where efficiency in time-critical tasks is a priority. However, much research and development have produced very efficient garbage collection algorithms so that LISP and Smalltalk programs now perform as well as programs written in languages without any garbage collector.

Pointers and Dynamic Allocation of Memory

In all of the code examples shown thus far in this section, the computer allocates memory automatically for the variables. When this memory is no longer needed, the computer deallocates the memory by returning it to the system. Another example of this process is a function call. If the function has value parameters and locally declared variables, the computer allocates memory for these each time the function is invoked. When the function returns, the computer returns this memory to the system for other uses. Because the computer manages this memory automatically, the programmer can focus on the syntax of variable declarations and the scope rules for referencing the variables without worrying about memory management.

As we have begun to see, however, the programmer can become involved in memory management by using the `new` operator to allocate dynamic memory for data structures such as vectors and linked lists. When this memory is no longer needed, the programmer is responsible for invoking the `delete` operator to return the memory to the system.

To understand how `new` and `delete` work, we must take a more global view of the organization of memory in a computer. We can think of this memory as a giant block of cells, as shown in Figure 12.20. This block of cells resembles a giant random access data structure. In fact, that is how it is treated when the computer is asked to look up or store a value at a given memory location. That is why this memory is called *RAM* (random access memory).

Figure 12.20
Computer memory

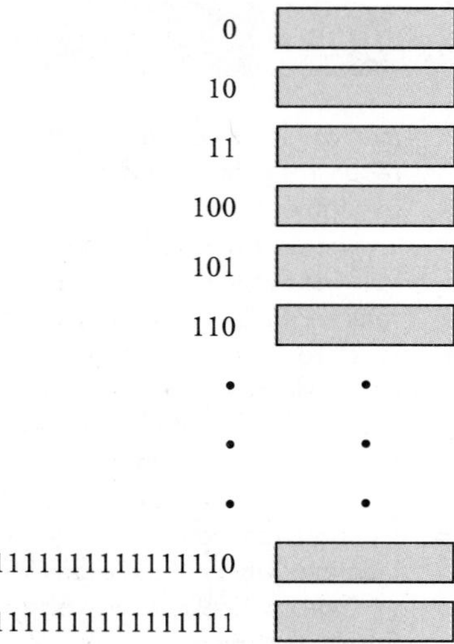

To simplify our discussion, we assume that the computer has a single user running a single C++ program. The memory of the computer at run time is divided into the following components:

1. An area of cells for the instructions and data of the computer's operating system.
2. An area of cells for the instructions of the C++ program.
3. An area of cells for the variables and data necessary for function calls, including the main program function. This area is called a *run-time stack* and is discussed further in Chapter 13.
4. An area of cells for representing dynamic data. This area is called a *heap* or *free store*.

This organization of memory is depicted in Figure 12.21.

When a programmer runs the `new` operator to request a chunk of dynamic memory, the computer attempts to obtain the desired cells from the heap. If the heap cannot provide a block of these cells, the computer returns a null pointer to the caller of `new`. Otherwise, the computer returns a pointer to the first cell of the desired chunk of memory in the heap.

For example, consider the insertion of a new node into a linked list of integers. Each node requires a block of two cells, one for the integer and one for the pointer to the next node in the list. The `getNode` function asks for this memory and initializes it by executing the statements

```
node * newNode = new node;
assert(newNode != 0);
newNode->data = item;
newNode->next = 0;
```

Assuming that `item` has the value 3, an abstract view of the memory allocated for the new node is shown in Figure 12.22.

If the address of `newNode` is 1110 in the data area of computer memory and the address of the first available block of two cells in the heap is 111111111111110, then the view of the node at the machine level is as shown in Figure 12.23.

Now suppose that the values 1 and 2 are inserted, in that order, at the beginning of an empty linked list when the program begins execution. After these operations,

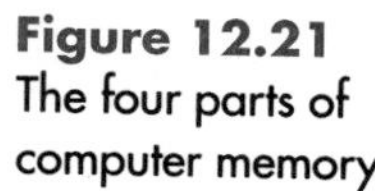

Figure 12.21
The four parts of computer memory

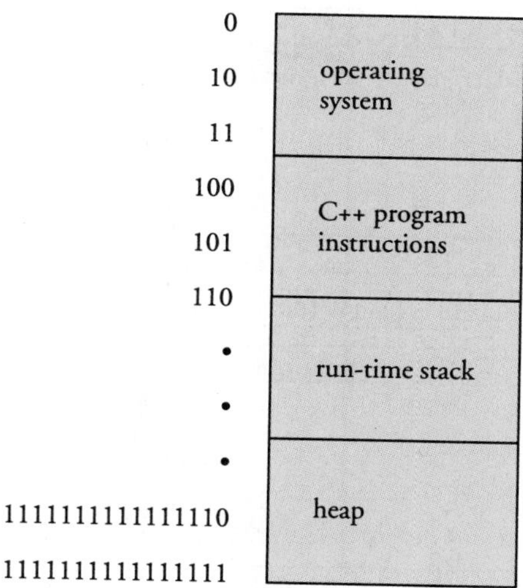

Figure 12.22
An abstract view of a pointer to a node

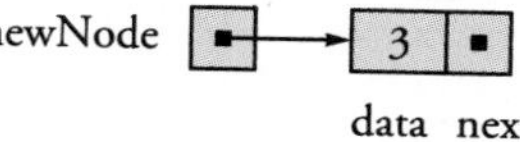

Figure 12.23
A pointer to a node at the machine level

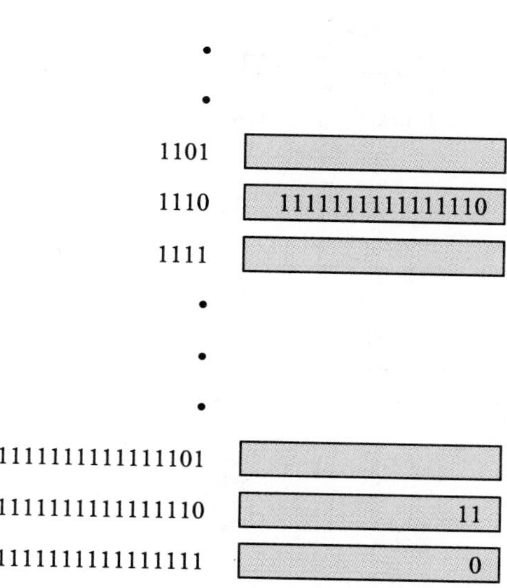

the chunks of memory for the two nodes in the heap will be adjacent to each other, as shown in Figure 12.24. Note that the positions of the two nodes in the heap are similar to the positions of two structs in an array. The positions are adjacent, and the physical order of the cells representing the nodes in memory is the same as the logical order of the nodes in the linked list. This situation might lead you to think that we could use indexing to access a data element at a given position in a linked list. However, this is true only in some cases.

Suppose the same program removed the first data element (2) from the linked list and reinserted it at the end of the list. The resulting situation is shown in Figure 12.25. The memory for the node containing the first data element is returned to the heap during the removal and reused for a new node to contain the data element during the

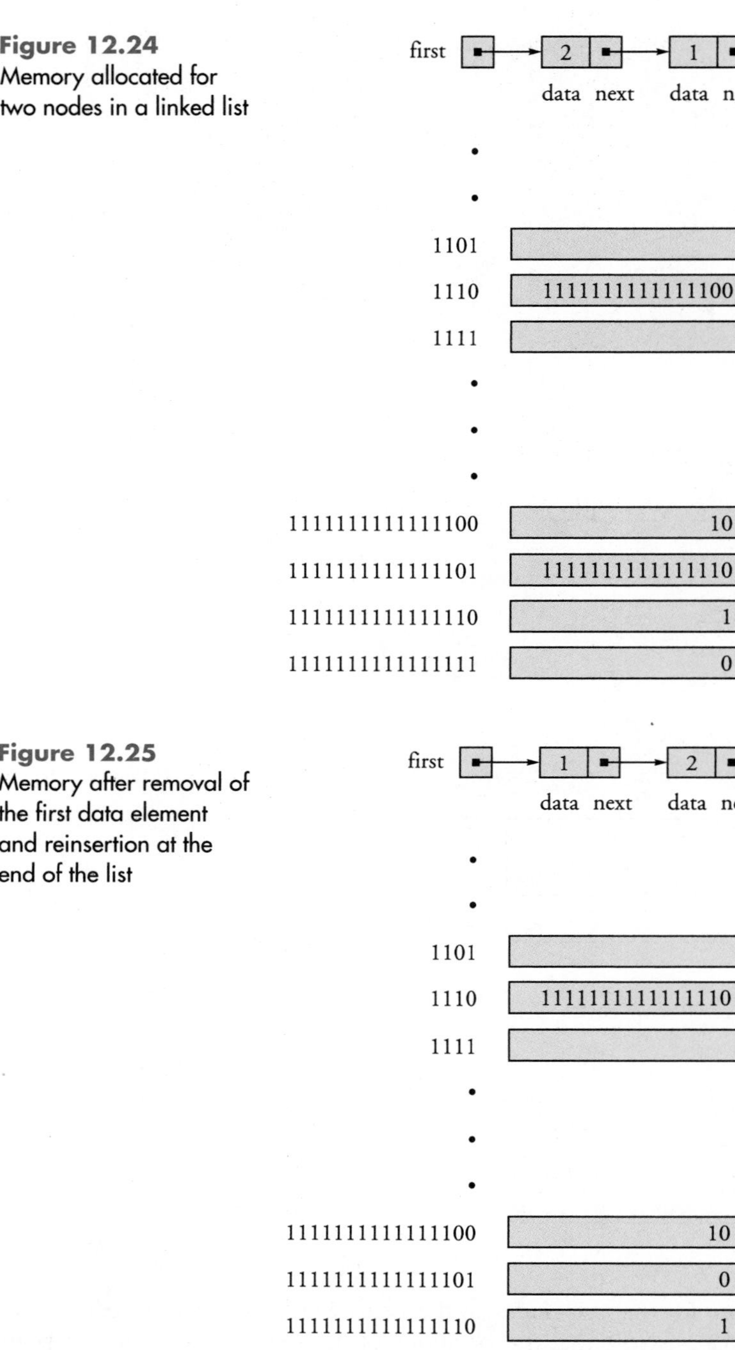

Figure 12.24
Memory allocated for two nodes in a linked list

Figure 12.25
Memory after removal of the first data element and reinsertion at the end of the list

insertion. Even though the same cells of physical memory are used for the same numbers in both cases, the logical order of the data elements in the linked list has been reversed. This is indicated by the changes in the pointer values stored in the external pointer of the linked list and in the next pointers within the nodes. The number 2 comes after 1 in the linked list from the user's perspective, but in computer memory, 2 is stored before 1. Thus, we cannot count on the physical order of cells in the heap to reflect the logical order of nodes in a linked list. That is why we must treat the logical order of the nodes in a linked list as independent of their order in computer memory.

The Costs of Using Linked Lists

Now that you understand how linked lists are represented in computer memory, you are in a position to more thoroughly assess the costs of using them. The first cost concerns the access time for a given data element in the list. Because the logical structure of a linked list is independent of its physical structure in memory, we cannot generally use random access indexing with linked lists. This is why a linked list is a *sequential access data structure*. To access a data element in this kind of data structure, we must start with a pointer to the first node and run a sequence of $n - 1$ `next` operations to reach the node at the nth position. The time of access to a given data element in a linked list depends on its position in the list. The value at the end of a linked list of 1000 elements will take about 1000 times as long to access as the value at the second position. By contrast, the access to a data element at the end of an array `a`, expressed as `a[length - 1]`, requires one or two machine instructions. The access to the last element in this array is just as fast as the access to the second data element, expressed as `a[1]`.

The low cost of random access with arrays plays a role in highly efficient search strategies, such as the binary search that was discussed in Chapter 10. The high cost of sequential access makes the linked list a poor choice of an ADT for applications that must perform many searches for given data elements or must access data elements at specified positions. Also, some operations, such as insertion at the end of the list, require $n - 1$ `next` operations for a list of length n.

Another cost associated with linked lists is the use of memory. Each node in a linked list requires memory not only for a data element but also for a pointer to the next node. The memory needed to store one pointer value is not large (probably one cell). But a linked list of 1 million nodes requires 1 million such cells. By contrast, an array of the same logical size requires 1 million fewer memory cells.

One final cost of using linked lists involves the likelihood of program errors. With dynamic data, the programmer has the entire burden of memory management. It is easy to ask for dynamic memory with the `new` operator but also easy to forget to return it with `delete` when it is no longer needed. The failure to recycle this memory is called *memory leakage*. If it is severe enough, memory leakage can lead to a condition known as *heap underflow*, in which new dynamic memory can no longer be obtained from the heap.

The Benefits of Using Linked Lists

As we saw in the first three sections of this chapter, the primary benefit of using linked lists is the low cost of inserting or removing a given data element. In each case, the process requires the rearrangement of at most three or four pointers. The number of these operations is close to the same whether the data element is at the beginning or at the end of the list. By contrast, a removal or insertion of a data element at position i in an array of n data elements requires that $n - i$ data elements be shifted (copied) by one position. When the data elements are large and positioned near the beginning of the array, insertions or removals can be very expensive.

Another benefit of using linked lists concerns the modeling of dynamic situations such as file input. In these situations, memory is allocated in a linked list for the incoming data incrementally, or node by node. By contrast, as we saw in Section 12.1, the use of arrays or ordered collections for these problems is expensive because n extra memory locations and n extra copy operations are necessary to accomplish each insertion into a list of length n.

To summarize, a linked list works very well for problems such as the file input problem or the data movement problem. In this class of problems, random access is unnecessary, but we need a data structure that can grow or shrink incrementally with the size of the data. An array works much better when random access is needed, when we can predict how many data values will be input, and when the likelihood of movement of data within the array is small.

Exercises 12.4

1. Discuss the difference between an address and the value stored at that address.
2. Draw pictures of the computer's memory, with binary addresses and data values, that show the memory cells for the following statements:
   a. `int x = 2, y = 3, z = 4;`
   b. `double a = 4.8, b = 7.6;`
   c. `char ch = 'a';`
   d. `double list[5];`
   e. `double * realPtr = 0;`
   f.
   ```
   struct
   {
         int first;
         double second;
   } aStruct;
   ```
3. Write a program to test how many nodes can be allocated for a linked list of integers until the heap has no more memory. You can accomplish this by writing a count-controlled loop whose upper bound is an input integer and which adds a new data element to the beginning of the list on each pass. Start with the input of a large integer, and if an error occurs, try another integer of half that size. If an error does not occur, repeat the input with an integer half again the size of the previous input. When your inputs can alternate between an integer that causes an error and an integer that is 1 less that does not cause an error, you will have determined how many nodes can be obtained for storing integers from the heap.
4. Simon Seeplus recommends that we use a linked list rather than an array to implement the data member of the ordered collection class (Section 11.1). He argues that the ordered collection class will then solve the data movement and file input problems very efficiently. Discuss his proposal. Does it violate any of the requirements of the ordered collection class?

Exercises 5–10 refer to the following data declaration:

```
struct node
{
      int data;
      node * next;
};
```

```
node * a;
node * b;
node * c;
```

5. Specify which of the following statements are syntactically correct. For those that are wrong, explain why they are wrong.

```
a. a = b;

b. a = a->data;

c. a = a->nodeptr;

d. delete a;

e. delete b->data;

f. delete b;
```

6. Show how the schematic below would be changed by each of the following:

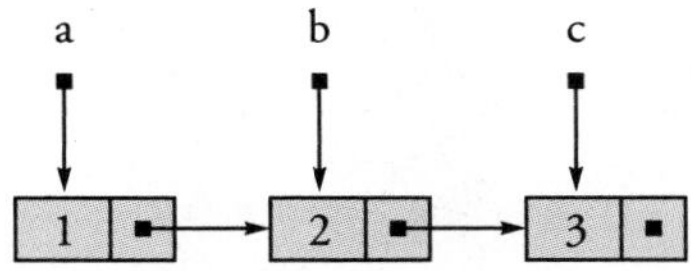


```
a. a = a->next;

b. b = a;

c. c = a->next;

d. b->data = c->data;

e. a->data = b->next->data;

f. c->next = a;
```

7. Write one statement to change

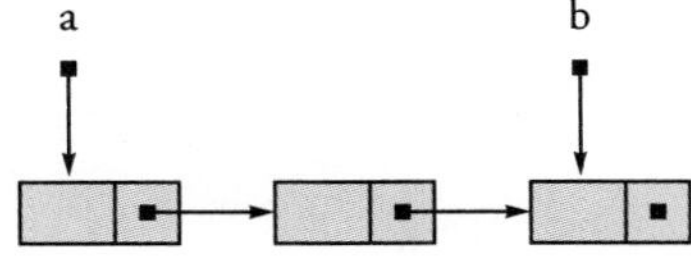

to

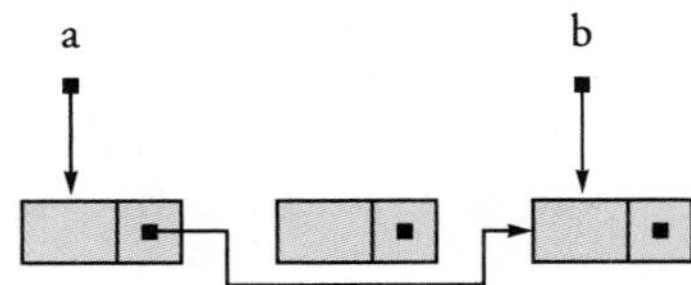

8. Consider the following list:

Write code to create a new linked list element with value 12 and insert it at the beginning of the list headed by A.

9. Consider the following list:

Write code to remove the element at the head of the list and then add this element at the end of the list.

10. Indicate the output for each of the following:

a.
```
a = new node;
b = new node;
a->data = 10;
b->data = 20;
b = a;
a->data = 5;
cout << a->data << " " << b->data << endl;
```

b.
```
c = new node;
c->data = 100;
b = new node;
b->data = c->data % 8;
a = new node;
a->data = b->data + c->data;
cout << a->data << " " << b->data << " " << c->data << endl;
```

c.
```
a = new node;
b = new node;
a->data = 10;
a->next = b;
a->next->data = 100;
cout << a->data << " " << b->data << endl;
```

For Exercises 11–13, assume that the member names of a node are `data` and `next` and that the external pointers `first`, `probe`, and `trailer` and the integer variable `number` have been declared and initialized as follows:

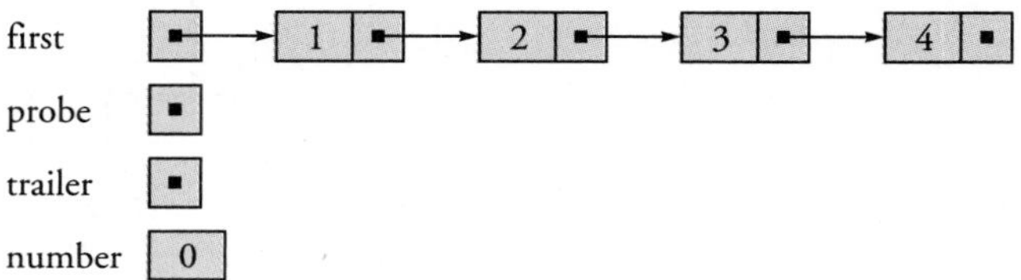

11. For the following statements labeled a through e, draw a picture of the state of these objects after the statements have been executed. Assume that the state of the objects carries over from one exercise to the next.

a.
```
probe = first;
trailer = first;
```

b.
```
while (probe != 0)
{
    trailer = probe;
    probe = probe->next;
}
```

c.
```
number = trailer->data;
```

d.
```
delete probe;
```

e.
```
trailer->next = 0;
```

12. Suppose that someone forgot to declare and implement a destructor for the linked list class. Describe a situation in which this omission is likely to cause problems.

13. Suppose that a bug has been introduced into the linked list implementation so that linked lists of the following form are created:

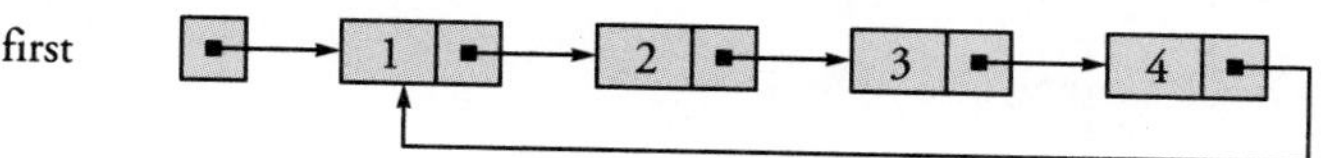

Describe the problems that this structure would cause for a sequential search for a given data element in the list.

12.5 Using a Linked List to Implement a One-Key Table

Objectives

a. to understand what is involved from a coding perspective when a linked list is used to implement a one-key table

b. to understand the efficiency trade offs that occur when a linked list, instead of an array, is used to implement a one-key table.

In Chapter 11, we analyzed the efficiency of an array-based implementation of the one-key table ADT. We discovered that the principal trade-off is that this implementation supports fast retrievals (with binary search) but slow insertions and removals. The latter operations require a linear number of copy operations, which can be very expensive for large data elements. When the data are particularly volatile, requiring frequent insertions or removals, it might be best to choose the trade-off associated with a linked list implementation. Here we get linear search times but constant insertion and removal times (in the number of copies required). An additional factor in favor of a linked implementation has gone unnoticed until now. The array implementation of a one-key table forces an application to settle for a fixed upper bound on the number of data elements that can be inserted. This constraint may cause a program to waste memory or not have enough memory to solve a problem. A linked list implementation, which provides memory for a table on an as-needed basis, uses only enough physical memory to accommodate the logical size of the table and no more.

Redefining the One-Key Table Class

We begin our new implementation of a one-key table by modifying the class declaration module from Chapter 11. We include the header file for the linked list class. The declarations of all of the public member functions (the interface to the class) remain the same. The only change in this module comes in the protected data members section. There we replace the array and the integer data members with a single data member that is a linked list:

```
// Class declaration file: onetable.h

#ifndef ONETABLE_H

#include "assoc.h"
#include "linklist.h"
```

continued

```
// Declaration section

// Generic class for key type K and element type E.

template <class K, class E> class OneKeyTable
{

   public:

   // Class constructors

   OneKeyTable();
   OneKeyTable(const OneKeyTable<K, E> &table);

   // Member functions

   int length();
   bool empty();
   void store(const K &target, const E &item);
   bool retrieve(const K &target, E &item);
   bool remove(const K &target, E &item);
   OneKeyTable<K, E>& operator = (const OneKeyTable<K, E> &table);

   protected:

   // Data members

   LinkedList<association<K, E> > list;
};

#include "onetable.cpp"

#define ONETABLE_H
#endif
```

Note that `association` will be the type of data in each node in the underlying linked list. This is specified by passing that type name to `LinkedList` as a parameter when the data member for the list is declared. Also, the `tableLength` data member is no longer needed because the length of the table is just the length of the linked list.

Reimplementing the One-Key Table Class

Another benefit that we gain from representing a one-key table as a linked list rather than an array is that our implementation becomes more abstract. You will recall our discussion of the two-key table and the layering principle in Section 11.4. There we found that it is easier to work with high-level ADT operations than with low-level data structures such as arrays that are built into C++. The same ease of use occurs in the present case. We do not have to deal with array indices or with C++ pointer manipulations; instead, we use high-level operations such as `first`, `next`, `insert`, and `remove`. A few examples will make this point clear.

Example 12.3 The simplest member functions are those that examine attributes of the one-key table. `empty` and `length` return the answers to the same questions asked of the linked list:

```
template <class K, class E>
bool OneKeyTable<K, E>::empty()
{
   return list.empty();
}

template <class K, class E>
int OneKeyTable<K, E>::length()
{
   return list.length();
}
```

Example 12.4 For retrievals, a linked list operation must do a linear search for a data item stored by its key value in the list. If we arrange the list so that the logical ordering of the keys maps directly to the ordering of the nodes in the list, then we can stop an unsuccessful search when a node's key value is greater than the target or when we have just examined the last node in the list. We begin by resetting the current pointer to the head of the list by invoking the `first` operation. We then iterate through the list, retrieve data from each node, and compare the key in the data with the target key. Then there are four cases to consider:

1. The key referenced from the list is less than the target—we must continue through the list.
2. The key referenced from the list equals the target—return `true`, along with the value associated with the key in the list.
3. The key referenced from the list is greater than the target—return `false` to signal an unsuccessful search.
4. The list's `atEnd` operation indicates we have traversed the entire list—return `false` to signal an unsuccessful search.

The C++ code reflecting this logic is:

```
template <class K, class E>
bool OneKeyTable<K, E>::retrieve(const K &target, E &item)
{

   list.first();          // Reset current pointer to head of list
   while ( (! list.atEnd()) && (list.access().getKey() < target) )
      list.next();        // Keep advancing

   // Did we go off the end of the list or advance past where
   // the target would be located if it were in the list?
   if (list.atEnd() || (list.access().getKey() > target) )
      return false;
   else                   // The key in the list must match the target
   {
      item = list.access().getValue();
      return true;
   }
}
```

Example 12.5 To store a data value in a table, we create a new association with the key and item. Then we iterate through the list, considering the same four cases as in Example 12.4, but this time taking different actions when the conditions of a particular case are satisfied.

1. The key referenced from the list is less than the target—we must continue through the list.
2. The key referenced from the list equals the target—use the list's `modify` operation to change the data associated with that key.
3. The key referenced from the list is greater than the target—use the list's `insert` operation to add the new association in front of the key that is referenced.
4. The list's `atEnd` operation indicates we have traversed the entire list—use the list's `insert` operation to add the new association at the end of the list.

The C++ code is:

```
template <class K, class E>
void OneKeyTable<K, E>::store(const K &target, const E &item)
{
   association<K, E> newData(target, item);

   list.first();          // Reset current pointer to head of list
   while ( (! list.atEnd()) && (list.access().getKey() < target) )
      list.next();        // Keep advancing

   // Did we go off the end of the list or advance past where
   // the target should have been found?
   if (list.atEnd() || (list.access().getKey() > target) )
      list.insert(newData);
   else
      list.modify(newData);
}
```

As you can see, there is a linear amount of work to do in searching for the position of the data to be inserted in the table, but the linked implementation gives us a constant amount of work involved in moving data at that position.

Exercises 12.5

1. Do a big-O analysis of each of the operations for a one-key table assuming the linked list implementation strategy is used.
2. Just as we have used a linked list instead of an array to implement a one-key table, we can also use a linked list to implement an ordered collection (Section 11.1). Assuming such an implementation, do a big-O analysis of each of the operations for an ordered collection.
3. Just as we have used a linked list instead of an array to implement a one-key table, we can also use a linked list to implement a sorted collection (Section 11.2). Assuming such an implementation, do a big-O analysis of each of the operations for a sorted collection.
4. In Section 11.4, we described an implementation of the two-key table ADT that was layered on one-key tables. Assuming a linked list implementation of the one-key tables on which the two-key table is layered, provide a big-O efficiency analysis of each of the operations for the two-key table.
5. Add `merge` and `append` operations to the interface of the one-key table and implement the operations. (Rely on the corresponding list operations developed in Exercises 12.2.)

A NOTE OF INTEREST

Storage of Disk Files and Computer Security

Operating systems typically grant their users disk storage in units called blocks. On the magnetic disk itself, a block is a contiguous area capable of storing a fixed amount of data. For example, a block in DEC's well-known OpenVMS time-sharing system is 512 bytes. As a user enters data into a disk file, the system must grant additional blocks of storage as they are needed. In such a time-sharing environment, although each block represents physically contiguous storage area on the disk, it may not be possible for the operating system to give a user blocks that are physically next to each other. Instead, when a user needs an additional storage block, the operating system may put information into the current block about where the next block is located. In effect, a link is established from the current block to the next block. By the time a naive user has completed entering a four-block file, it may be scattered over the entire disk surface.

Although this may seem like an ingenious way of extending files indefinitely, one pays in several ways for such scattered blocks. Namely, the read-write head that seeks and puts data on the disk surface is forced to move greater distances, thereby slowing system performance. To combat such inefficiencies, shrewd users can often take advantage of options that allow them to preallocate the contiguous disk storage that will be required for a file. Also, blocks may be released to users in clusters of contiguous blocks. In the event file access remains sluggish in spite of such measures, systems managers may occasionally shut down the entire system to "defragment" disks, a process that entails copying all files that are presently scattered over the disk onto a new disk in physically contiguous form.

Yet another more serious price that may be paid for storing disk files in this fashion revolves around the issue of data security and what the operating system does with blocks that are no longer needed by a user. The disk blocks used to store a file are returned to some type of available block list when a user deletes that file from his or her directory. This available list is not unlike the free store of memory that C++ maintains for you when `new` and `delete` are used to allocate and deallocate memory in a C++ program. When these "deleted" blocks are returned to that available space list, the data in them may remain intact until another user's request to extend a file results in the block's being reallocated to that new user. This means that, if clever users ("hackers") know how to access the available space list, they may be able to scavenge through data that other users once owned and then released (assuming it was not destroyed upon being released).

One of the authors was actually involved in an incident in which a clever student was able to "find" old versions of a test that a professor had processed on the computer and then discarded to this available block list. Needless to say, the professor whose tests were being explored by the student was somewhat alarmed upon discovering what had happened. As a protection against this type of scavenging, many operating systems will, by default or as an option, actually destroy data returned to the available block list.

Case Study: Optimizing Radix Sort with Linked Lists

In this chapter, we've focused on presenting the linked list as an abstraction. However, as this Case Study will show, there are situations in which delving below that layer of abstraction and writing code for special purpose linked structures can greatly enhance the efficiency of a program.

User Request

A file containing a large number of integers (one per line) must be sorted into ascending order. Assume that all the integers in the file will fit into main memory at one time. The program should be optimized for speed, sorting the integers in the fastest way possible.

Analysis

The input and output of this program will be very simple, merely calling for input of the file name that contains the integers to be sorted and the file name to which the sorted list will be output. Given the user request to optimize the sort for speed and the fact that we will only be sorting integers, our analysis of sort efficiencies and

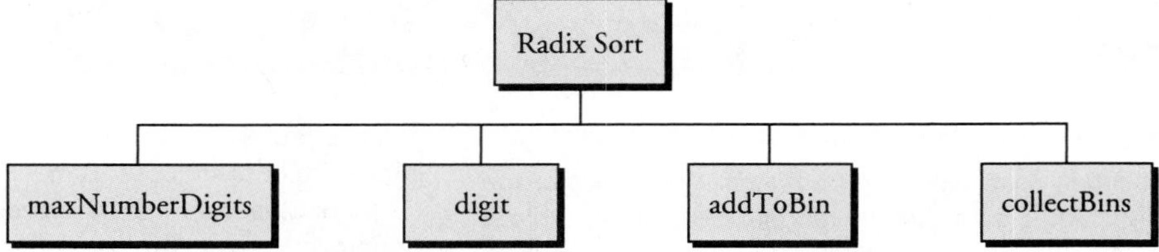

Figure 12.26
Structure chart for radix sort

limitations in Chapter 10 leads to the conclusion that radix sort is the best algorithm (among those already studied) for this program.

Design

In addition to providing a very fast sorting algorithm, if we use the linked lists to implement the bin structures of the radix sort algorithm (see Section 10.4), we can achieve a very space-efficient version. Moreover, this will be one of those rare instances in which a space-efficient version is also more time efficient. To achieve this, we will specify that the algorithm receives a linked list of integers to be sorted rather than an array. A top-level pseudocode description of radix sort is then given by:

```
Set numberOfDigits to the number of digits in largest number in the list
For each k from 1 to numberOfDigits
    While the list to sort is not empty
        Transfer the first number in the sort list to the appropriate bin, keying on
            the kth digit (k = 1 corresponding to ones digit, k = 2 to tens
            digit, and so forth).
    For each j from 0 to 9
        Append the numbers in jth bin to the list to sort
```

In our discussion of the radix sort in Section 10.4, we were somewhat shackled by approaches that employed static allocation of the bins used to classify numbers. For instance, we determined that sorting n numbers by this algorithm would require $11n$ storage locations—n for the numbers being sorted and an additional $10n$ locations for the bins associated with the ten possible digits.

Linked lists and pointer variables provide a new implementation strategy for the bins needed by radix sort. The dynamic allocation associated with these pointer variables will allow each bin to claim only the storage that it needs as the algorithm runs. We propose the following implementation for bins:

```
typedef LinkedList<int> BinStructureType[10]; // array of 10 linked lists
.
.
.
   BinStructureType bins;
```

We can now refine our high-level pseudocode for this new version of radix sort. It will require the subordinate modules indicated in the structure chart shown in Figure 12.26.

The specifications for each subordinate module are:

Module: maxNumberDigits
Input: List of integers (assumed to be nonnegative)
Output: The number of digits in the largest integer in list
Module: digit
Inputs: Nonnegative integer number `k` representing a digit position in number, with `k` = 1 corresponding to ones digit, 2 to tens digit, and so on
Output: Digit in position `k` of number

Module: addToBins
Inputs: An array of bins,
Number to put into a bin,
Index indicating which bin to transfer the number to
Outputs: Number has been put in appropriate bin
Module: collectBins
Inputs: An array of bins,
List to sort (empty when received)
Output: Sublists in bin array have been successively appended to sort list (order of appending runs from bin 0 to bin 9)

Implementation

These module specifications give rise to the following C++ functions for the radix sort algorithm. We present only the top-level sort function and the `addToBins` and `collectBins` subordinate functions. You will complete the program and further investigate improving the efficiency of radix sort in Programming Problems and Projects.

```
void radixSort(LinkedList<int> &list)
{
   int k, temp;
   BinStructureType bins;
   int numberOfDigits;

   numberOfDigits = maxNumberDigits(list);

   // For k loop controls digit used to classify data.
   for (k = 1; k <= numberOfDigits; ++k)
   {
      list.first();

      // Inner loop iterates through all numbers, putting them into
      // bin determined by kth digit.
      while (! list.empty() )
      {
         temp = list.remove();
         addToBin (bins, temp, digit(temp, k));
      }
      collectBins (list, bins);
   }
}

void addToBin(BinStructureType bins, int number, int place)
{
   bins[place].insert(number);
   bins[place].next();
}

void collectBins(LinkedList<int> &list, BinStructureType bins)
{
   int place = 0;

   for (int i = 0; i < 10; ++i)      // Loop through all bins
   {
```

continued

```
      bins[i].first();
      while ( !bins[i].empty() )     // Loop through numbers in a bin
      {
         list.insert(bins[i].remove());     // Append number from bin to list
         list.next();                 // Go to next place in list
      }
   }
}
```

Running, Debugging, and Testing Hints

1. Be careful to initialize pointer variables to the null pointer with a statement such as

   ```
   ptr = 0;
   ```

2. Be careful not to dereference a pointer that is null. Thus, if the assignment

   ```
   ptr = 0;
   ```

   is made, a reference to `*ptr` or to `ptr->data` results in an error.

3. Always test a pointer to see whether or not it is null before attempting to dereference it. Use statements of the form

   ```
   if (ptr != 0)
     process(ptr->data);
   ```

   or

   ```
   while (ptr != 0)
     ptr = ptr->next;
   ```

4. When a piece of dynamic memory is no longer needed in a program, use `delete` so that the memory can be reallocated.
5. After using `delete` with a pointer, its referenced memory is no longer available. If you use `delete ptr`, then `*ptr` and `ptr->data` are unpredictable.
6. When creating dynamic data structures, be careful to initialize properly by assigning the null pointer where appropriate and keeping track of pointers as your structures grow and shrink.
7. Operations with pointers require that they be of the same type. Thus, exercise caution when comparing or assigning them.
8. Values may be lost when pointers are inadvertently or prematurely reassigned. To avoid this, use as many auxiliary pointers as you wish. This is better than trying to use one pointer for two purposes.
9. Be sure to declare and implement a destructor operation for a class that uses dynamic memory.
10. An entry-controlled loop that tests for the end of a linked list is an important idiom in programming. It resembles an end-of-file `while` loop and describes a similar process. In both cases, we are testing for the presence of a sentinel, using the functions `atEnd` (lists) and `eof` (files). Also, in both cases, we advance to the next data value in a sequence by running the operations `next` (lists) and `>>` (files).

11. The use of the arrow operator (->) with pointers is a bit like the use of the selector (.) with structs. However, you must exercise extreme caution when attempting to access the components of a node with the arrow operator. If the pointer variable is not initialized, or if the pointer variable is null, the use of the arrow operator could cause an error at run time. Remember that a pointer variable can point to a chunk of dynamic data (a node), but it need not. To protect your programs from bad pointer references, you should follow these guidelines:
    a. Set all pointers to null when they are declared.
    b. Test a pointer for the null condition before attempting to access the contents of a node with the arrow operator.
12. You must be very careful when programming with pointers; one misplaced pointer can "lose" an entire data structure. Consequently, modular testing is more important than ever. Test the reliability of each module before releasing it for use in a large program.
13. Be sure that you consider the boundary conditions when developing linked list algorithms. Are you sure that your logic covers the empty list, the first node on the list, the last node on the list? For instance, if your insertion algorithm works for all lists but the empty list, it might as well not work at all because you'll never be able to get any data on the list.
14. Never reference the contents of the memory pointed to by `ptr` when `ptr` is a null pointer. The following loop control structure

    ```
    while ((ptr->getdata != target) && (ptr != 0))
    ```

    is asking for trouble. When `ptr` is null, the reference to `ptr->getdata` may cause a run-time error before the loop is exited. The positions of the two tests should be reversed to take advantage of short-circuit evaluation in C++.
15. Programming with pointers is programming with logical pictures of linked lists. Draw a picture of what you want to do with a pointer and then write the code to make it happen. When debugging, verify and trace your code by drawing pictures of what it does with your data. For instance, an assignment to a pointer in your code corresponds to aiming an arrow somewhere in your corresponding snapshot of the data structure.

Summary

Key Terms

address (of a memory location)
address-of operator (&)
arrow operator (->)
dereference
external pointer
free store
heap
heap underflow
link
linked list
logical structure (of a linked list)
memory leakage
node
null pointer
pointer
random access data structure
run-time stack
selection (of a member)
sequential access data structure
sequential traversal

Key Concepts

- Values are stored in memory locations; each memory location has an address.
- A pointer variable is one that contains the address of a memory location; a pointer variable can be declared by

```
int *intPtr;
```

  where the asterisk (*) is used after the predefined data type.
- Dynamic memory is memory that is referenced through a pointer variable. Dynamic memory can be used in the same context as any variable of that type. In the declaration

```
int *intPtr;
```

  the dynamic memory is available after `intPtr = new int;` is executed.
- Dynamic memory is created by

```
ptr = new BaseType;
```

  and destroyed (memory area made available for subsequent reuse) by

```
delete ptr;
```

- The success of dynamic memory allocation can be detected by examining the value returned by `new`. If it is `0`, then no more dynamic memory is available.
- Assuming the definition

```
int *ptr;
```

  the relationship between a pointer and its associated dynamic variable is illustrated by the code

```
ptr = new int;
*ptr = 21;
```

  which can be envisioned as

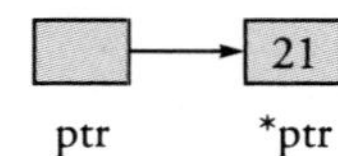

- `0` (the null pointer) can be assigned to a pointer variable; this is used in a Boolean expression to detect the end of a list.
- Dynamic data structures differ from other data structures in that space for them is allocated under program control during the execution of the program.
- A linked list is a dynamic data structure formed by having each node contain a pointer that points to the next node.
- A node is a component of a linked list. Each node contains a member for storing a data element and a member for storing a pointer to the next node.

- References to the members of a node structure use the arrow operator `->` as illustrated by

```
struct node
{
    int data;
    node *next;
};

node * ptr;

ptr = new node;
ptr->data = 45;
ptr->next = 0;
```

- When creating a linked list, the final component should have `0` assigned to its pointer member.
- Processing a linked list is accomplished by starting with the first node in the list and proceeding sequentially until the last node is reached.
- When a node is deleted from a linked list, it should be returned for subsequent use; this is done by using the standard operator `delete`.

Programming Problems and Projects

1. Complete the development of a linked list radix sort (see the Case Study) in the following stages.
   a. Write the necessary subordinate modules.
   b. Write a main program so that you can thoroughly test the algorithm.
   c. Design test data that are sure to exercise the various boundary conditions of the subordinate modules.
   d. Do a big-O analysis of the time and space requirements of this version of radix sort. If you also implemented an array version of radix sort in Chapter 10, profile both versions by counting the number of operations that each must perform (use the profiling classes from the Case Study in Chapter 10). Prepare a written report in which you compare the empirical performance of both versions.
   e. You can further enhance the efficiency of radix sort by using an implementation of linked lists in which the `collectBins` function appends successive bins to each other without removing each number from a bin and inserting it into the list to be sorted. Instead, by maintaining a pointer to the last node in the list as well as to the first, you can append one bin to another in $O(1)$ time. Figure 12.27 depicts how this efficiency can be achieved. Implement this enhanced version of radix sort along with the linked list operations it needs. After you have tested the new sort algorithm, profile it as you did for the version you wrote in part d. Compare the performance of the new algorithm to the old one.
2. One of the problems faced by businesses is how best to manage their lines of customers. One method is to have a separate line for each cashier or station. Another is to have one feeder line where all customers wait and the customer at the front of the line goes to the first open station. Write a program to help a manager decide which method to use by simulating both options. Your program should allow for customers arriving at various intervals. The manager wants to know the

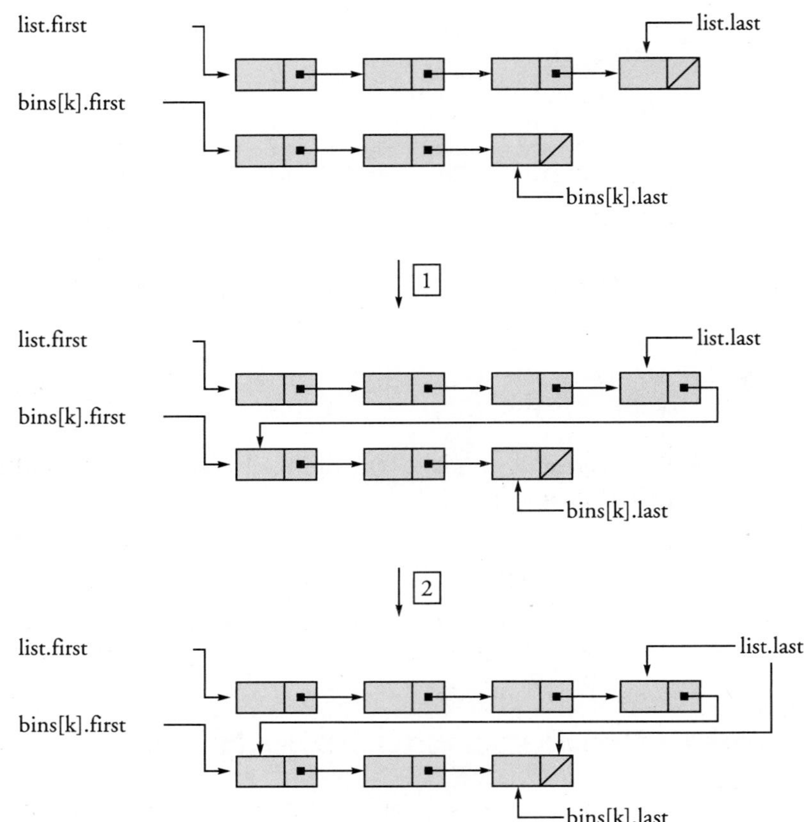

Figure 12.27 Appending one bin to another without removing and inserting items

average wait in each system, average line length in each system (because of its psychological effect on customers), and the longest wait required.

3. Write a program to keep track of computer transactions on a mainframe computer. The computer can process only one job at a time. Each line of input contains a user's identification number, a starting time, and a sequence of integers representing the duration of each job. Assume all jobs are run on a first-come, first-served basis. Output should include a list of identification numbers, starting and finishing times for each job, and average waiting time for a transaction.
4. Several previous programming problems have involved keeping structures and computing grades for students in some class. If linked lists are used for the students' structures, such a program can be used for a class of 20 students or a class of 200 students. Write a recordkeeping program that utilizes linked lists. Input is from an unsorted data file. Each student's information consists of the student's name, ten quiz scores, six program scores, and three examination scores. Output should include the following:
   a. A list, alphabetized by student name, incorporating each student's quiz, program, and examination totals; total points; percentage grade; and letter grade
   b. Overall class average
   c. A histogram depicting class averages
5. Mailing lists are frequently kept in a data file sorted alphabetically by customer name. However, when they are used to generate labels for a bulk mailing, they must be sorted by zip code. Write a program to input an alphabetically sorted file and produce a list of labels sorted by zip code. The data for each customer follow:

a. Name
b. Address, including street (plus number), city, two-letter abbreviation for the state, and zip code
c. Expiration information, including the month and year

Use a linked list to sort by zip code. Your labels should include some special symbol for all expiring subscriptions.

6. A linked list limits users to movement in one direction through the list. Sometimes it is useful to move backward to the previous node or start a process at the last node in the list. The operations `last`, `previous`, and `atBeginning` (the inverses of `first`, `next`, and `atEnd`) could be used with a doubly linked list having the following structure:

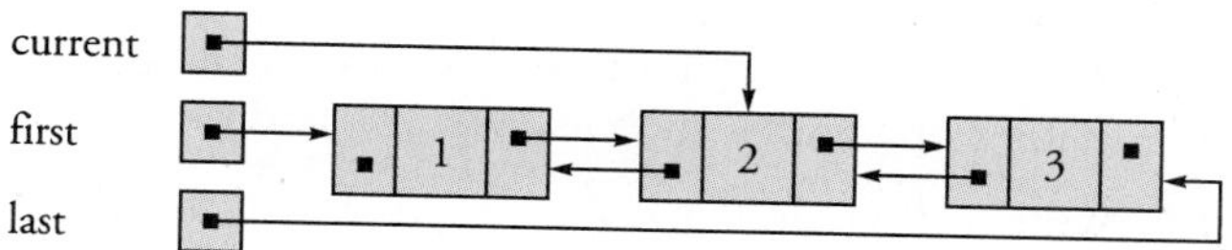

Note that a doubly linked list needs no external previous pointer. Write the specifications for the operations `last`, `previous`, and `atBeginning` and declare and implement a doubly linked list class in C++. The operations on singly linked lists should also work with doubly linked lists, but they may be implemented differently. Test the new class with an appropriate driver program.

7. Wing-and-a-Prayer Airlines maintains four scheduled flights per day, which they identify by the numbers 1, 2, 3, and 4. For each of these flights, they keep an alphabetized list of passengers. The database for the entire airline could hence be viewed as four linked lists. Write a program that sets up and maintains this database by handling commands of the following form:

Command → Add
Flight number → 3
Passenger name → BROWN
Command → Delete
From flight number → 1
Passenger name → JONES
Command → List
Flight number → 2
(List alphabetically all passengers for the specified flight.)

8. To take care of their growing business, the Fly-by-Night Credit Card Company would like to update their customer data file. Write a program in a high-level language that sets up a linked list that can support the following actions on a record:
a. Insert a record into the list in the correct place, sorted according to social security number of the customer.
b. Update a record if the customer record exists.
c. Delete a record if the customer no longer wishes to patronize the company.

In the preceding data manipulation activities, the list should always remain in order sorted by social security number.

9. As a struggling professional football team, the Bay Area Brawlers have a highly volatile player roster. Write a program that allows the team to maintain its roster as a linked list in alphabetical order by player last name. Other data items stored for each player are

Height
Weight

Age
University affiliation

As an added option, allow your program to access players in descending order of weight and age.

10. Develop a line-oriented text editor that assigns a number to each line of text and then maintains the lines in a linked list by line number order (similar to the fashion in which BASIC programs are maintained on many systems). Your program should be able to process the following commands:

    I-line number 'text' (instruction to insert text at specified line number)
    L-line1-line2 (instruction to list line1 through line2)
    D-line1-line2 (instruction to delete line1 through line2)
    If you feel really ambitious, extend your program by allowing the user to perform editing operations such as inserting and deleting characters within a given line.

11. Write a program that, given a file of text, will add to an index those words in the text that are marked by special delimiting brackets [ ]. The words in the index will be printed after the text itself has been formatted and printed. Words in this index should be listed in alphabetical order with a page number reference for each page of text on which they are delimited by the special brackets. Note that this program would be part of a word processing system an author could use when developing a book with an index of terms.
12. Write a program that allows input of an arbitrary number of polynomials as coefficient and exponent pairs. Store each polynomial as a linked list of coefficient-exponent pairs arranged in descending order by exponent. Note that the coefficient-exponent pairs need not be input in descending order; it is the responsibility of your program to put them in that order. Your program should then evaluate each of the polynomials for an arbitrary argument X and output each of the polynomials in the appropriate descending exponent order. Be sure that your program works for all "unusual" polynomials such as the zero polynomial, polynomials of degree one, and constant polynomials.
13. (Josephus Problem) Consider the following problem, often referred to as the Josephus problem. Imagine that a class of *N* students decided to choose one from among themselves to approach a curmudgeonly professor about postponing for a week an upcoming examination. They elect to arrange themselves in a circle and excuse the *M*th person around the circle—with the size of the circle being reduced by one each time a person is excused. The problem is to find out which person will be the last remaining, or more generally, to find the order in which the people are excused. For example, if $N = 9$ and $M = 5$, then the people are excused in the order 5 1 7 4 3 6 9 2. Hence the eighth person is left to face the professor. To solve the Josephus problem, write a program that inserts persons 1 through *N* into a list and then appropriately deletes them from the list until only one is left.
14. Computers can store and do arithmetic only with integers of limited size. When integers surpass that limiting value, overflow occurs and the results will either be unreliable or cause your program to die with a run-time error. However, by altering the implementation of an integer, you can develop algorithms to do virtually limitless integer arithmetic. The basis of such an implementation is to store each digit of an integer in a list. That is, represent an integer as a list of digits. Then develop algorithms to do integer arithmetic operations on a digit-by-digit basis, taking carries, borrows, and so forth into account as you do when per-

forming these operations by hand. After carefully considering which list implementation best suits the problem, develop functions to perform extended integer addition, subtraction, multiplication, and division (quotient and remainder). As one test case, add the following integers and print the sum:

```
  5643127821
+ 9276577159
```

15. By consulting reference manuals for your version of C++ and by writing a variety of experimental programs, attempt to discover the details of how your C++ compiler manages the allocation of memory in the heap. Prepare a written report in which you describe your findings.

16. Your friend offers the following criticism of linked lists: "The problem with linked lists is that they cannot be used with large databases stored in files since pointers represent locations in main memory." Explain the fallacy in your friend's criticism. Then, in a detailed statement, discuss how linked lists could be implemented for data stored in random access files.

13

Stacks and Queues

Chapter Outline

Achilles: What would happen if you took some popping-tonic without having previously pushed yourself into a picture?
Tortoise: I don't precisely know, Achilles, but I would be rather wary of horsing around with these strange pushing and popping liquids.
Douglas Hofstadter

The other line always moves faster.
Barbara Ettore

In the last chapter, we introduced the linked list as a data structure designed to handle conveniently the insertion and deletion of entries in a linearly ordered list. In this chapter, we study two special types of linearly ordered lists: the stack and the queue. These lists are special because of the restrictions imposed on the way in which entries may be inserted and removed. Both structures may be implemented by arrays or by dynamically allocated linked lists.

The restriction placed on a stack is often described as *last-in/first-out (LIFO)*. Consider, for example, the order in which a smart traveler will pack a suitcase. To minimize shuffling, the last item packed should be the first worn. Another familiar example of such a storage strategy is that of the pop-up mechanism used to store trays for a cafeteria line. The first trays loaded into the mechanism may well have a long wait before they escape to a passing diner.

A list of data items processed via a LIFO scheduling strategy is called a *stack*. As we shall see in this and later chapters, stacks are extremely useful data structures. They find extensive applications in the processing of subroutine calls, the syntactic checking and translation of programming languages by compilers, and the powerful programming technique of recursion (see Chapter 14).

In contrast to the linear order of a stack, a *queue* is a *first-in/first-out (FIFO)* list. This name comes close to completely characterizing the restricted types of adds and deletes that can be performed on a queue. Insertions are limited to one end of the list, whereas deletions may occur only at the other end. The conceptual picture that emerges from the notion of a queue is that of a waiting line; for example, jobs waiting to be serviced by a computer or cars forming a long line at a busy tollbooth.

13.1 The Stack Abstract Data Type and Its Implementation

The last-in/first-out nature of the stack implies that all additions and deletions occur at one designated end of the stack. That designated end is called the top, and the operations of adding to or deleting from the stack are referred to as *pushing* and *popping*, respectively. More formally, we define the stack ADT as follows.

Objectives

a. to define a stack as an ADT
b. to understand conceptually the role played by a stack in processing procedure and function calls
c. to implement a stack using a static array
d. to implement a stack using a dynamically allocated linked list

Stack. A stack is a restricted list in which entries are added to and removed from one designated end called the top.

The operations to be performed on a stack are specified by the following preconditions and postconditions.

Create Operation

Preconditions:	Receiver is an arbitrary stack in an unpredictable state.
Postconditions:	Receiver is initialized to the empty stack.

Empty Operation

Preconditions:	Receiver is a previously created stack.
Postconditions:	Returns `true` if receiver is empty, `false` otherwise.

Push Operation

Preconditions:	Receiver is a previously created stack. *item* is a value to be added to the top of the stack. There is memory available to store the new item in the stack.
Postconditions:	Receiver is returned with *item* added to the top of the stack.

Pop Operation

Preconditions:	Receiver is a previously created stack. The stack is not empty.
Postconditions:	The stack has its top value removed, and this value is returned.

OnTop Operation

Preconditions:	Receiver is a previously created stack. The stack is not empty.
Postconditions:	Returns the value on the top of the stack. Unlike pop, the stack is left unchanged.

Figure 13.1 depicts the critical push and pop operations for the stack ADT. Conceptually, it is easiest to develop a mental image of the `push` and `pop` operations if you picture a stack as a vertical list with the first entry at the bottom and the last at the top. Then, as indicated in Figure 13.1, adding to the stack—that is, pushing—essentially makes this stack become taller, and removing from the stack—that is, popping—results in a shorter stack.

Figure 13.1
Pushing onto and popping from the stack

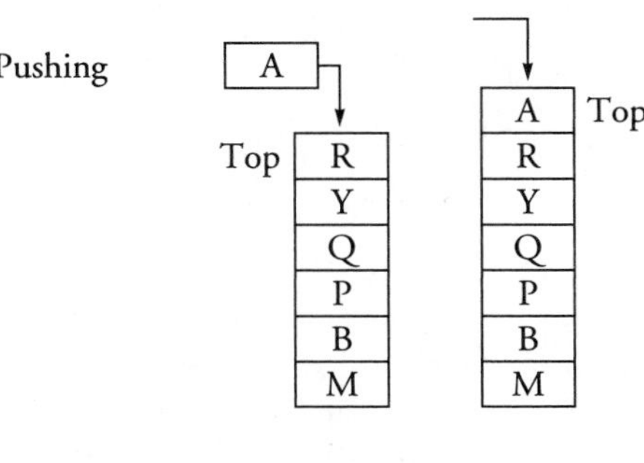

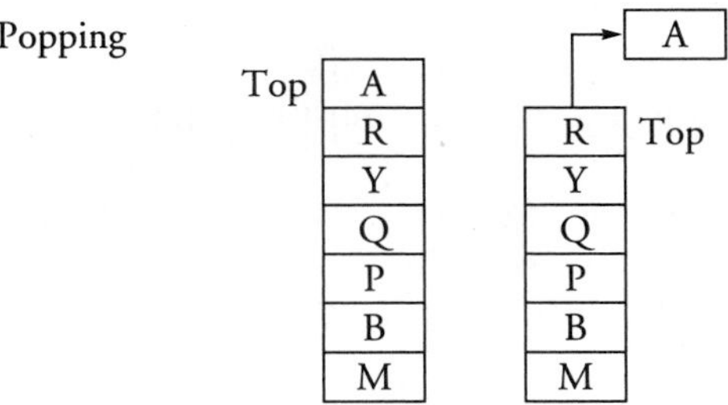

Stacks and Function Calls

Before we discuss methods of implementing a stack, we shall give some hint of their importance in the processing of function calls. Of key importance to the processing of functions in any language is that the return from a function must be to the instruction immediately following the call that originally transferred control to the function. For example, in the partial coding that follows:

```
int main()
{
   int q;
   .
   q = sub1(q);                    // Call sub1
   cout << q;
   .
}

void sub3()
{
   .
   .
   .
}

void sub2(int q)
{
   .
   sub3();                         // Call sub3
   p = p - q;
   .
}

void sub1(int b)
{
   .
   b = sub2(a);                    // Call sub2
   a = a + b;
   .
}
```

the order of operations is:

1. Leave `main` and transfer to `sub1`.
2. Leave `sub1` and transfer to `sub2`.
3. Leave `sub2` and transfer to `sub3`.
4. Return from `sub3` to the instruction `p = p - q` in `sub2`.
5. Return from `sub2` to the instruction `a = a + b` in `sub1`.
6. Return from `sub1` to the instruction `cout << q` in `main`.
7. End of `main`.

Each time a call is made, the machine must remember where to return upon completion of that function.

A stack is precisely the structure capable of storing the data necessary to handle calls and returns in this sequence. The data for each call of a function are stored in a data structure called an *activation record*. This record contains space for the return

Figure 13.2 Memory stack generated by previous partial coding

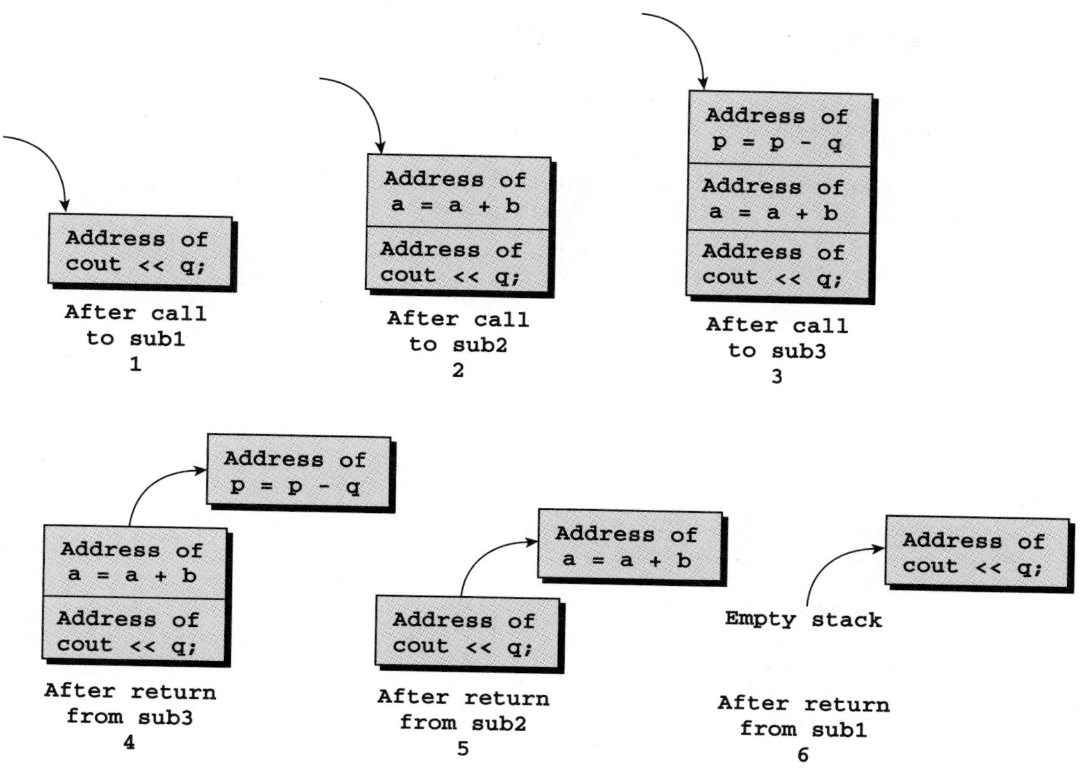

address (the address of the instruction following the call of the function) and any values or addresses of actual parameters for that call of the function. Hence, the preceding partial coding would generate a stack that develops as illustrated in Figure 13.2. (The numbers in the figure correspond to the order of operations just shown on the preceding list.) Each time a call to a function is made, a return address is placed in an activation record, and this is pushed on top of the stack. Each time a function is completed, the top record on the stack is popped to determine the memory address to which the return operation should be made. The nature of the leave–return sequence for functions makes it crucial that the first return address accessed be the last one that was remembered by the computer. Because there is only one point, the top, at which data may enter or exit a stack, it is the ideal data structure for this "last-stored, first-recalled" type of operation.

This description of the method by which a compiler actually implements function calls is just one illustration of the utility of stacks. In Chapter 14, we'll discuss a different type of function usage called recursion and examine in detail the role of the stack in handling such a recursive call.

C++ Interface for the Stack Abstract Data Type

The transition from defining a stack as an ADT to implementing this structure in a computer language requires, as usual, an interface to the ADT's operations. A C++ class declaration module for the stack ADT is:

```
// Class declaration file: stack.h

// Declaration section

#ifndef STACK_H
#define STACK_H

// We assume that the constant MAX_STACK_SIZE is
// already defined by the application in size.h

#include "size.h"

template <class E> class stack
   {

   public:

   // Class constructors

   stack();
   stack(const stack<E> &s);

   // Member functions

   bool empty();
   void push(const E &item);
   E pop();
   E onTop();
   stack<E>& operator = (const stack<E> &s);

   protected:

   // Data members

   int top;

   E data [MAX_STACK_SIZE];

   };

#include "stack.cpp"

#endif
```

We will discuss two implementations of the stack class in C++. The first uses an array and, consequently, limits the size to which a stack may grow. The second employs a linked list with pointer variables, thereby allowing the stack to become as large as the free space in the C++ heap.

Array Implementation of a Stack

Using an array to implement a stack is relatively straightforward. Because insertions and deletions occur at the same end of a stack, only one pointer will be needed. We call that pointer `top`. The array of elements will be called `data`, and its size is specified by the constant `MAX_STACK_SIZE`, defined in the application. Thus, the C++ protected data members for the stack class are

```
int top;
E data[MAX_STACK_SIZE];
```

In Figure 13.3, we trace it through the function example from Figure 13.2. As in Figure 13.2, the numbers below each array correspond to the operations performed in our previous sequence of function calls and returns. The empty stack is signaled by the condition `top = -1`. If we think of `top` as pointing to the last entry pushed, then the two instructions

```
++top;
data[top] = item;
```

will push the contents of `item` onto the stack. Popping an entry from the stack into `item` requires

```
item = data[top];
--top;
```

Complete functions for the `push` and `pop` operations follow in Example 13.1.

Example 13.1 Implement the `push` and `pop` operations for an array implementation of a stack.

```
template <class E>
void stack<E>::push(const E &item)
{
   assert(top < MAX_STACK_SIZE - 1);
   ++top;
   data[top] = item;
}

template <class E>
E stack<E>::pop()
{
   E item;
   assert(! empty());
   item = data[top];
   --top;
   return item;
}
```

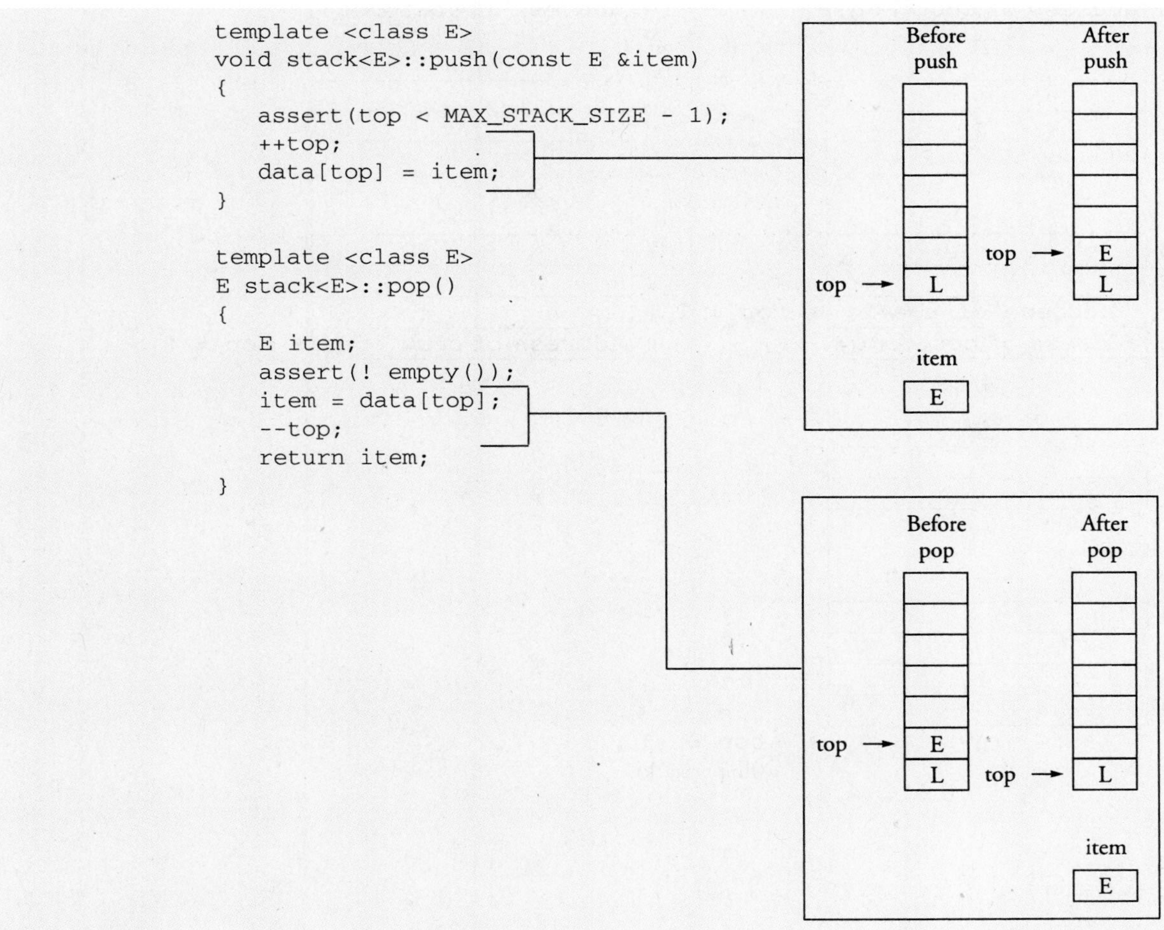

Figure 13.3 Array implementation of stack from Figure 13.2

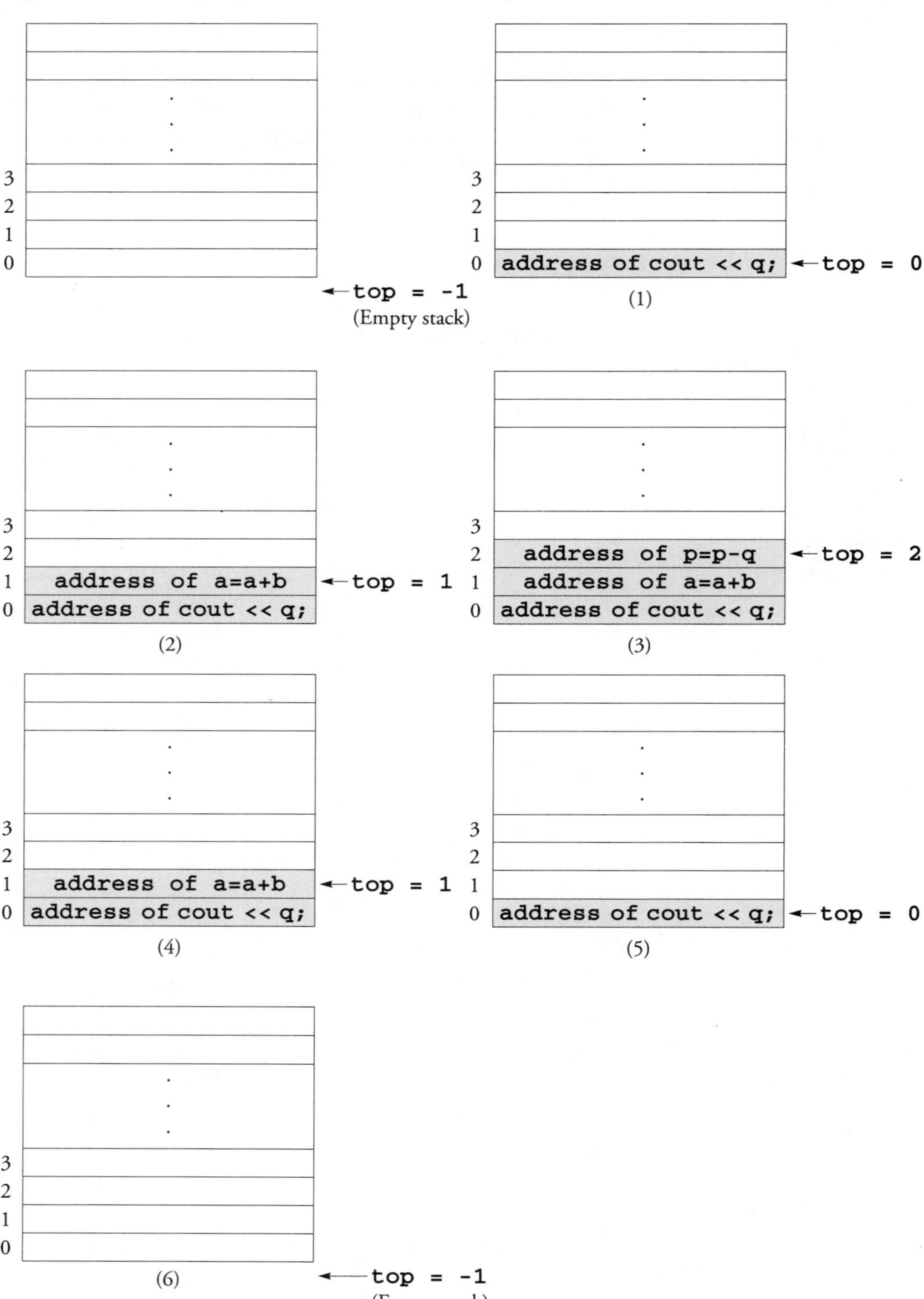

Note that the `assert` function is invoked to enforce the preconditions on each member function.

Linked List Implementation of a Stack

When we choose a linked list implementation of a stack, we are paying the price of a relatively small amount of memory space needed to maintain linking pointers for the dynamic allocation of stack space. A stack with the three integer entries 18, 40, and 31 would appear as follows:

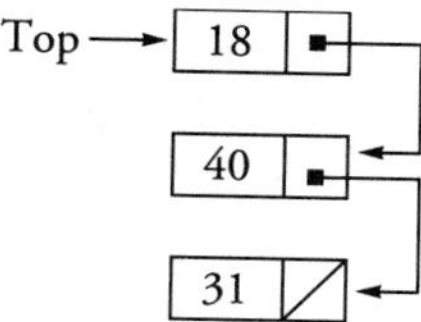

We also have the benefit of reusing a class already developed. The easiest way to use the linked list class to implement a stack class is to give the stack class a private data member that is a linked list.

```
// Class declaration file: stack.h

// Declaration section

#ifndef STACK_H
#define STACK_H

#include "linklist.h"

template <class E> class stack
   {

   public:

   // Class constructors

   stack();
   stack(const stack<E> &s);

   // Class destructor

   ~stack();

   // Member functions

   bool empty();
   void push(const E &item);
   E pop();
   E onTop();
   stack<E>& operator = (const stack<E> &s);

   private:

   // Data members
```

continued

```
   LinkedList<E> stackData;

   };

#include "stack.cpp"

#endif
```

Note that the only data member of this stack class is a linked list called `stackData`. Functions to push and pop the stack now become nothing more than insertions into and deletions from the beginning of a linked list. As such, they use high-level linked list operations already developed in Chapter 12. You will write them as exercises at the end of this section.

Example 13.2 To illustrate the use of stack operations in a program, let's consider a program that will check an arithmetic expression to make sure that parentheses are correctly matched (nested). Our program considers

```
(3 + 4 * (5 % 3))
```

to make sure that each left parenthesis is paired with a following right parenthesis in the expression.

A first-level pseudocode for this problem is

```
Get a character from the keyboard
While the character does not equal end of line
   If it is a '('
      push it onto the stack
   Else if it is a ')'
      Check for empty stack before popping previous '('
   Get a character from the keyboard
Check for empty stack
```

The growing and shrinking of the stack are illustrated in Figure 13.4. Assuming the existence of the basic stack operations, a program that examines an expression for correct use of parentheses is

```
// Program file: parens.cpp

#include <iostream.h>
#include "stack.h"

void main()
{
   stack<char> s;
   char symbol;

   cin.get(symbol);
   while (symbol != '\n')
   {
      if (symbol == '(')
         s.push(symbol);
      else if (symbol == ')')
```

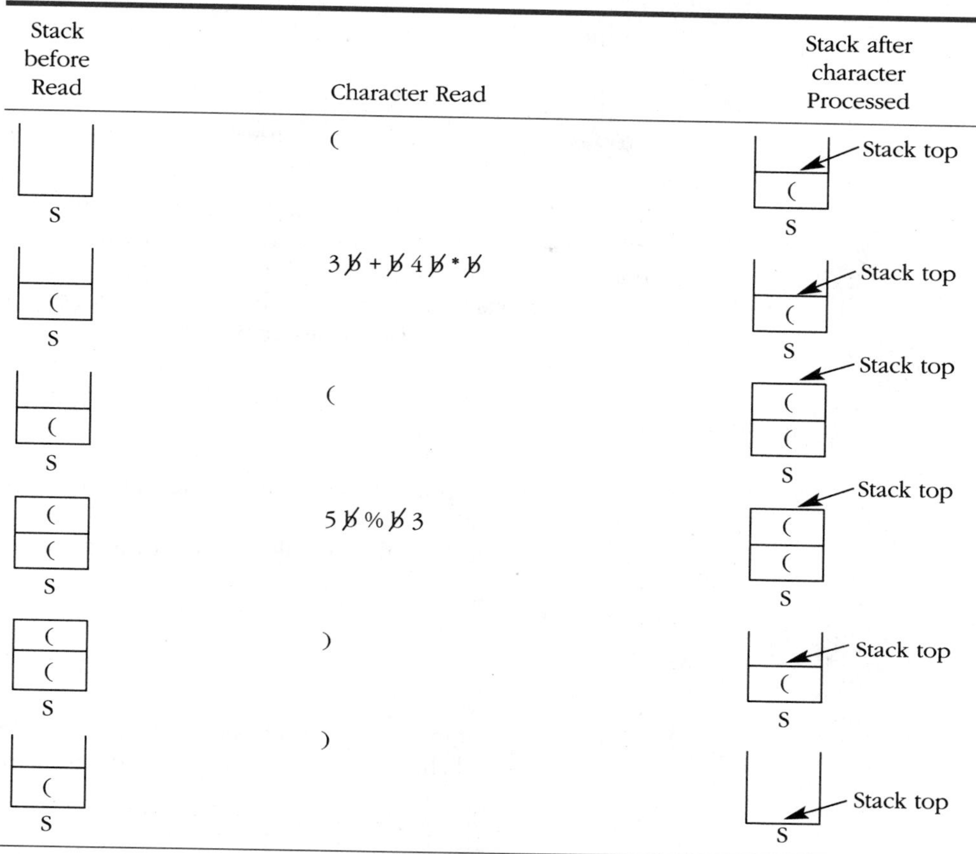

Figure 13.4 Using a stack to check for balanced parentheses

```
            if (s.empty())
                cout << "The parentheses are not correct. " << endl;
            else
                symbol = s.pop();
        cin.get(symbol);
    }
    if (! s.empty())
        cout << "The parentheses are not correct. " << endl;
}
```

This program will print an error message for an invalid expression and nothing for a valid expression. Several modifications of this short program are available and are suggested in the following exercises.

Exercises 13.1

1. Draw a picture of the stack of integers s after each of the following operations is performed:

```
stack<int> s;
s.push(4);
s.push(10);
```

continued

```
s.push(12);
item = s.pop();
s.push(3 * item);
item = s.onTop();
s.push (3 * item);
```

2. The `onTop` operation described in the definition of the stack as an abstract data type is actually unnecessary because it can be defined in terms of other stack operations. Provide such a definition of the `onTop` operation.
3. Write functions to implement each of the following operations for an array implementation of a stack. Be consistent with the operations already implemented in Example 13.1.
   a. `create` (do both the default constructor and the copy constructor)
   b. `empty`
   c. `onTop`
4. Write functions to implement each of the following stack operations for a linked list implementation of a stack.
   a. `create` (do both the default constructor and the copy constructor)
   b. `destroy`
   c. `empty`
   d. `push`
   e. `pop`
   f. `onTop`
5. Using the program for checking parentheses (Example 13.2), illustrate how the stack grows and shrinks when the following expression is examined:

```
(5 / (3 - 2 (4 + 3) - (8 / 2)))
```

6. Modify the program in Example 13.2 so that several expressions may be examined. Also provide more descriptive error messages.
7. Write a program that utilizes a stack to print a line of text in reverse order.
8. It is not necessary to use a stack to check expressions for matching parentheses. Write an algorithm that describes this task using a simple integer counter.

13.2 An Application of Stacks: Parsing and Evaluating Arithmetic Expressions

Often the logic of problems for which stacks are a suitable data structure involves the need to backtrack and return to a previous state. For instance, consider the problem of finding your way out of a maze. One approach is to probe a given path in the maze as deeply as possible. On finding a dead end, you need to backtrack to previously visited maze locations to try other paths. Such backtracking requires recalling these previous locations in the reverse order from which you visited them.

Not many of us need to find our way out of a maze. However, the designers of compilers are faced with an analogous backtracking situation in the evaluation of arithmetic expressions. As you scan the expression

$$A + B / C + D$$

in left-to-right order, it is impossible to tell upon initially encountering the plus sign whether or not you should apply the indicated addition operation to A and the im-

Objectives

a. to understand the differences between the infix, postfix, and prefix forms of algebraic expressions
b. to see why the postfix and prefix forms of expressions never need parentheses to override operator hierarchy
c. to convert infix expressions to their postfix and prefix equivalents using manual methods
d. to understand the computer algorithm that relies on a stack to convert infix expressions to their postfix equivalents
e. to be aware of the role of infix and in-stack priority functions in driving the algorithm to convert infix expressions to postfix
f. to understand the algorithm that uses a stack to evaluate a postfix expression

mediately following operand. Instead, you must probe further into the expression to determine whether an operation with a higher priority occurs. While you undertake this probing of the expression, you must stack previously encountered operation symbols until you are certain of the operands to which they can be applied.

Further compounding the backtracking problem just described are the many different ways of representing the same algebraic expression. For example, the assignment statements

$$Z = A * B/C + D;$$
$$Z = (A * B)/C + D;$$
$$Z = ((A * B)/C) + D;$$

should all result in the same order of arithmetic operations even though the expressions involved are written in distinctly different forms. The process of checking the syntax of such an expression and representing it in one unique form is called *parsing* the expression. One frequently used method of parsing relies heavily on stacks.

Infix, Postfix, and Prefix Notation

Conventional algebraic notation is often termed *infix* notation; the arithmetic operator appears between the two operands to which it is being applied. Infix notation may require parentheses to specify a desired order of operations. For example, in the expression `A / B + C`, the division will occur first. If we want the addition to occur first, the expression must be parenthesized as `A / (B + C)`.

Using *postfix* notation (also called reverse Polish notation after the nationality of its originator, the Polish logician Jan Lukasiewicz), the need for parentheses is eliminated because the operator is placed directly after the two operands to which it applies. Hence, `A / B + C` would be written as `A B / C +` in postfix form. This says:

1. Apply the division operator to `A` and `B`.
2. To that result, add `C`.

The infix expression `A / (B + C)` would be written as `A B C + /` in postfix notation. Reading this postfix expression from left to right, we are told to

1. Apply the addition operator to `B` and `C`.
2. Then divide that result into `A`.

Although relatively short expressions such as the preceding ones can be converted from infix to postfix via an intuitive process, a more systematic method is required for complicated expressions. We propose the following algorithm for humans (and will soon consider a different one for computers):

1. Completely parenthesize the infix expression to specify the order of all operations.
2. Move each operator to the space held by its corresponding right parenthesis.
3. Remove all parentheses.

Consider this three-step method as it applies to the following expression in which ^ is used to indicate exponentiation:

```
A / B ^ C + D * E - A * C
```

Completely parenthesizing this expression yields

```
(((A / (B ^ C)) + (D * E))-(A * C))
```

A NOTE OF INTEREST

Logic Programming and Backtracking

In the 1960s, J. Robinson, a mathematical logician, discovered an algorithm for automating the process of proving theorems in first-order predicate logic. This discovery made the discipline of logic programming possible. A logic program consists of a set of assertions. Some of these describe particular facts, such as "Ken is over 40 years old." Other assertions describe general facts or rules, such as "All people over 40 years old have gray hair." A program consisting of these two facts can be used to prove other facts, such as "Ken has gray hair." The proof can be executed on a computer after one enters the known facts, expressed in the syntax of a logic programming language, into a database and inputs a request for the proof of the unknown fact to the computer.

PROLOG is a logic programming language that provides a syntax for describing assertions and queries and an interpreter for user interaction and theorem proving. To return to our example, the known facts, expressed in the syntax of PROLOG, might be entered interactively at the -> prompt into the database as follows:

```
-> assert(over40(ken)).
OK

-> assert(grayhair(X) :- over40(X)).
OK
```

Queries for proofs of unknown facts might be entered as follows:

```
-> grayhair(ken).
Yes

-> over50(ken).
No
```

The PROLOG interpreter uses Robinson's algorithm to derive the unknown fact that Ken has gray hair from the fact that Ken is over 40 and the rule that if any individual is over 40, then he or she has gray hair. Here, the algorithm starts with a goal of proving `grayhair(ken)`. It finds a rule, `grayhair(X) :- over40(X)`, whose consequent, `grayhair(X)` matches the goal. The algorithm then tries to prove the rule's antecedent, `over40(X)`, with `X = ken`. A fact that matches this goal, `over40(ken)`, is found in the database, so the query or unknown fact, `grayhair(ken)`, has been proved.

Theorem proving is complicated by the fact that there may be rules that seem relevant but lead to dead ends. For example, suppose that the rules "All individuals with four children have gray hair" and "All individuals with weak backs have four children" are the other facts in the database. These rules might be expressed in PROLOG as follows:

1. `grayhair(X) :- has4children(X)`
2. `has4children(X) :- hasweakback(X)`

If the algorithm happens to try rule 1 before the one discussed earlier, it will not be able to prove that Ken has gray hair. It will try to prove that Ken has four children and fail when it discovers no assertion that Ken has a weak back.

To solve this problem, when a subgoal fails, the algorithm must backtrack to an earlier point in the process and try an alternative rule in the database. To support backtracking, the PROLOG interpreter maintains a stack of subgoals that are waiting to be proved. When a subgoal fails, the interpreter pops it off the stack and tries to prove the subgoal now at the top. In our example, the subgoals `hasweakback(ken)` and `has4children(ken)` would both be popped off the stack, and the interpreter would then try our other rule for `grayhair`. If the stack of subgoals becomes empty, then no proof of the given query can be found.

The use of a stack to implement the execution of a logic program is another example of the abstraction/implementation duality that we have emphasized throughout this book. At the abstract level, the logic programmer thinks in terms of first-order predicate logic and does not worry about how the computer proves theorems. At the implementation level, a backtracking algorithm supported by stack operations handles the real work of finding proofs.

Moving each operator to its corresponding right parenthesis, we obtain

```
(((A / (B ^ C)) + (D * E))-(A * C ))
```

Removing all parentheses, we are left with

```
A B C ^ / D E * + A C * -
```

Had we started out with

```
A / B ^ C - (D * E - A * C)
```

our three-step procedure would have resulted in

```
((A / (B ^ C)) - ((D * E) - (A * C)))
```

Removing the parentheses would then yield

```
A B C ^ / D E * A C * - -
```

In a similar way, an expression can be converted into *prefix* form, in which an operator immediately precedes its two operands. The conversion algorithm for infix to prefix specifies that, after completely parenthesizing the infix expression according to order of priority, we move each operator to its corresponding left parenthesis. Applying the method to

```
A / B ^ C + D * E - A * C
```

gives us

```
((A / (B ^ C)) + ((D * E) - (A * C)))
```

and finally the prefix form

```
+ / A ^ B C - * D E * A C
```

The importance of postfix and prefix notation in parsing arithmetic expressions is that these notations are completely free of parentheses. Consequently, an expression in postfix (or prefix) form is in unique form. In the design of compilers, this parsing of an expression into postfix form is crucial because having a unique form for an expression greatly simplifies its eventual evaluation. Thus, in handling an expression, a compiler must

1. Parse into postfix form.
2. Apply an evaluation algorithm to the postfix form.

We limit our discussion here to postfix notation. The techniques we cover are easily adaptable to the functionally equivalent prefix form.

Converting Infix Expressions to Postfix

First, consider the problem of parsing an expression from infix to postfix form. Our three-step method is not easily adaptable to machine coding. Instead, we will use an algorithm that has the following as its essential data structures:

1. A stream of characters containing the infix expression and terminated by the special delimiter, `#`
2. A stack named `opStack`, which may contain
   a. Arithmetic operators: `+`, `-`, `*`, and `/`

b. The left parenthesis, `(`. The right parenthesis, `)`, is processed by the algorithm but never stored in the stack
c. The special delimiter, `#`
3. A string named `postfix` containing the final postfix expression

To eliminate details that would only clutter the main logic of the algorithm, we will assume that the string representing the infix expression contains *tokens* (that is, incoming symbols) consisting only of the arithmetic operators `+`, `-`, `*`, and `/`; parentheses; the delimiting character, `#`; and operands that each consist of a single uppercase alphabetical character. We will also assume that these tokens may be read from a line without any intervening spaces. Later, we will consider some of the complications introduced by tokens of varying size and type and by the exponentiation operator `^`. Thus, for the present, the algorithm we discuss will convert infix expressions of the form

```
A * B + (C - D / E) #
```

into their corresponding postfix notation.

The description of the algorithm is as follows:

1. Define a function `infixPriority`, which takes an operator, parenthesis, or `#` as its argument and returns an integer as

Character	*	/	+	–	(	)	#
Returned Value	2	2	1	1	3	0	0

   This function reflects the relative position of an operator in the arithmetic hierarchy and is used with the function `stackPriority` (defined in step 2) to determine how long an operator waits in the stack before being appended to the postfix string.
2. Define another function `stackPriority`, which takes the same possibilities for an argument and returns an integer as

Character	*	/	+	–	(	)	#
Returned Value	2	2	1	1	0	Undefined	0

   This function applies to operators in the operator stack as their priority in the arithmetic hierarchy is compared to that of incoming operators from the infix string. The result of this comparison determines whether or not an operator waits in the stack or is appended to the postfix string.
3. Initialize `opStack` by pushing `#`.
4. Read the next character `ch` from the infix expression.
5. Test `ch` and
   5.1 If `ch` is an operand, append it to the postfix string.
   5.2 If `ch` is a right parenthesis, then pop entries from `opStack` and append them to `postfix` until a left parenthesis is popped. This ensures that operators within a parenthesized portion of an infix expression will be applied first, regardless of their priority in the usual arithmetic hierarchy. Discard both left and right parentheses.
   5.3 If `ch` is a `#`, pop all entries that remain on the `opStack` and append them to the `postfix` string.

5.4 Otherwise, pop from the `opStack` and append to the `postfix` string operators whose `stackPriority` is greater than or equal to the `infixPriority` of `ch`. Stop this series of popping operations when you reach a stack element whose `stackPriority` is less than the `infixPriority` of `ch`. This comparison, keying on the priority of `ch` from the infix string and operators that have previously been pushed onto the operator stack, ensures that operators are applied in the right order in the resulting postfix string. After popping these operators, push `ch`.

6. Repeat steps 4 and 5 until `ch` is the delimiter `#`.

The key to the algorithm is the use of the stack to hold operators from the infix expression that appear to the left of another given operator even though that latter operator must be applied first. The defined functions `infixPriority` and `stackPriority` are used to specify this priority of operators and the associated pushing and popping operations. This entire process is best understood by carefully tracing through an example.

Example 13.3 Parse the infix expression

$$A * B + (C - D / E) \#$$

into its equivalent postfix form. Trace the contents of the operator stack and the postfix string as each character is read.

The solution to this problem is presented in Table 13.1. In this table, the parenthesized numbers in the Commentary column refer to subcases of step 5 in the preceding algorithm.

The following C++ function implements our algorithm for converting infix expressions of the form we have specified. You should study and thoroughly understand this algorithm before moving on to this chapter's Case Study section. There, the infix-to-postfix algorithm will be the focal point for an entire program that works with expressions of a slightly more complicated form.

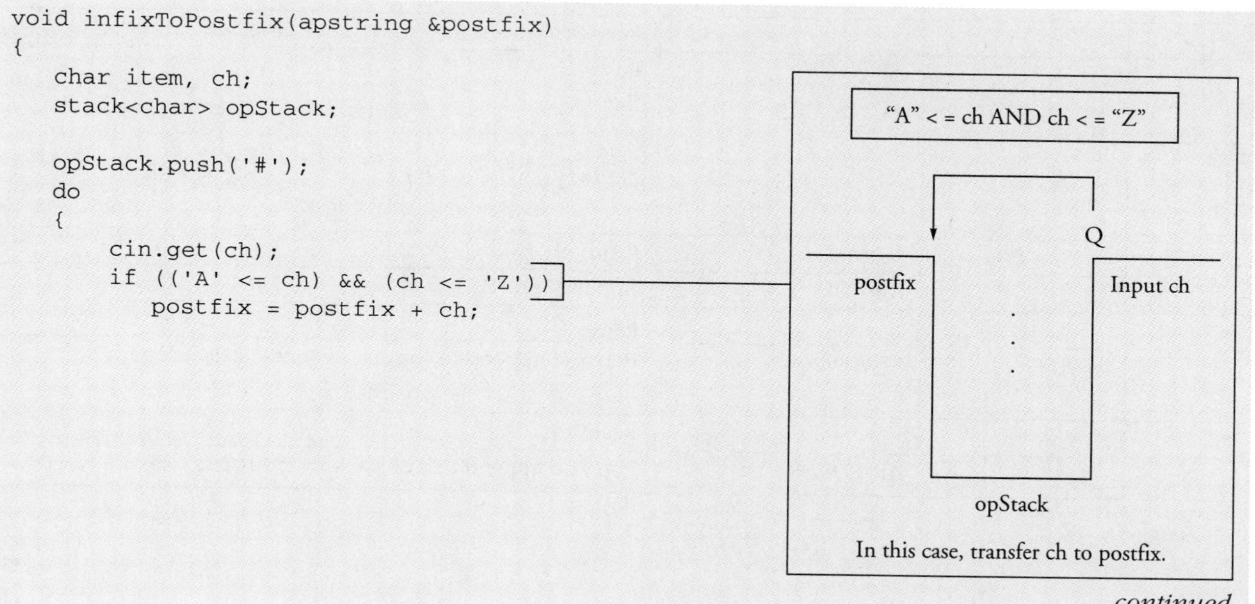

```
void infixToPostfix(apstring &postfix)
{
   char item, ch;
   stack<char> opStack;

   opStack.push('#');
   do
   {
      cin.get(ch);
      if (('A' <= ch) && (ch <= 'Z'))
         postfix = postfix + ch;
```


continued

Table 13.1
Parsing of Infix Expression $A^* B + (C - D/E)\#$

ch	opstack	postfix	Commentary
	#		Push #
A			Read ch
		A	Append ch to postfix (5.1)
*			Read ch
	* #		Push ch (5.4)
B			Read ch
		AB	Append ch to postfix (5.1)
+			Read ch
	+ #	AB*	Pop *, append * to postfix, push ch (5.4)
(			Read ch
	(+ #		Push ch (5.4)
C			Read ch
		AB*C	Append ch to postfix (5.1)
−			Read ch
	− (+ #		Push ch (5.4)
D			Read ch
		AB*CD	Append ch to postfix (5.1)
/			Read ch
	/ − (+ #		Push ch (5.4)
E			Read ch
		AB*CDE	Append ch to postfix (5.1)
)			Read ch
	+ #	AB*CDE/−	Pop and append to postfix until (is reached (5.2)
#			Read ch
		AB*CDE/− + #	Pop and append rest of stack to postfix (5.3)

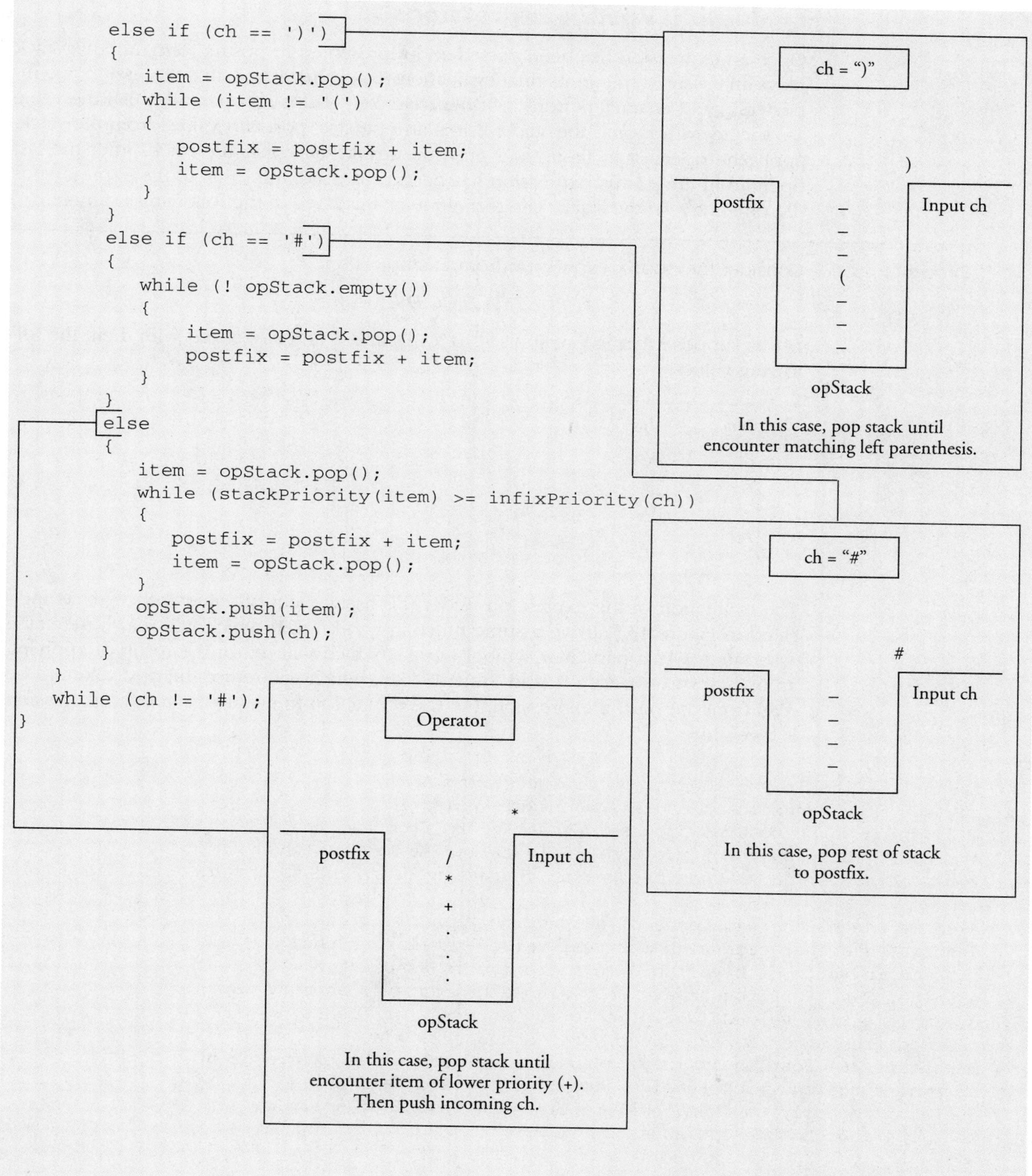

```
    else if (ch == ')')
    {
      item = opStack.pop();
      while (item != '(')
      {
         postfix = postfix + item;
         item = opStack.pop();
      }
    }
    else if (ch == '#')
    {
      while (! opStack.empty())
      {
         item = opStack.pop();
         postfix = postfix + item;
      }
    }
    else
    {
      item = opStack.pop();
      while (stackPriority(item) >= infixPriority(ch))
      {
         postfix = postfix + item;
         item = opStack.pop();
      }
      opStack.push(item);
      opStack.push(ch);
    }
  }
  while (ch != '#');
}
```

ch = ")"
)
postfix
Input ch
(
opStack
In this case, pop stack until
encounter matching left parenthesis.
ch = "#"
#
postfix
Input ch
opStack
In this case, pop rest of stack
to postfix.
Operator
*
postfix
Input ch
/
*
+
opStack
In this case, pop stack until
encounter item of lower priority (+).
Then push incoming ch.

Evaluating Postfix Expressions

Once an expression has been parsed and represented in postfix form, another stack plays an essential role in its final evaluation. To evaluate a postfix expression, we repeatedly read characters from it. If the character read is an operand, push the value associated with it onto the stack. If it is an operator, pop two values from the stack, apply the operator to them, and push the result back onto the stack. After the last operand in the postfix expression has been processed, the value of the expression is the one entry on the stack. The technique is illustrated in the following example.

Example 13.4 Consider the postfix expression from Example 13.3.

$$A\,B * C\,D\,E\,/ - + \#$$

Let us suppose that the symbols *A, B, C, D,* and *E* had associated with them the following values:

Symbol	Value
A	5
B	3
C	6
D	8
E	2

The evaluation of the expression under this assignment of values proceeds as indicated in Figure 13.5. If we assume functions `valueOf`, which will return the value associated with a particular symbol, `eval`, which will return the result of applying an operator to two values, and `nextToken`, which will return the next token to be read from the postfix expression, the C++ function to evaluate a postfix expression is given by

```
// Assume a suitable implementation of the string ADT,
// augmented by a nextToken operation. nextToken(s) is
// a function which returns successive characters from a
// string s. That is, the first time it is called it returns the
// first character in s, then the second character in s, and so forth.

// Also we assume the existence of a function valueOf which
// associates a character with its real value--similar to the
// fashion in which each variable in a program is associated with
// a value. Since our tokens are only single characters, an easy way
// of implementing valueOf would be to use an array of floats
// indexed from 0 to 25. In effect, this would create a
// miniature 26-location "memory." Finally, we assume the existence of
// an eval function which receives two real operands and the
// operator to apply to them. eval returns the result of applying
// that operator to the operands.

float evaluate(const apstring &postfix)
{
    char ch;
    float v, v1, v2;
    stack<float> valueStack;
```

Figure 13.5
Evaluation of *ABCDE/− + #***

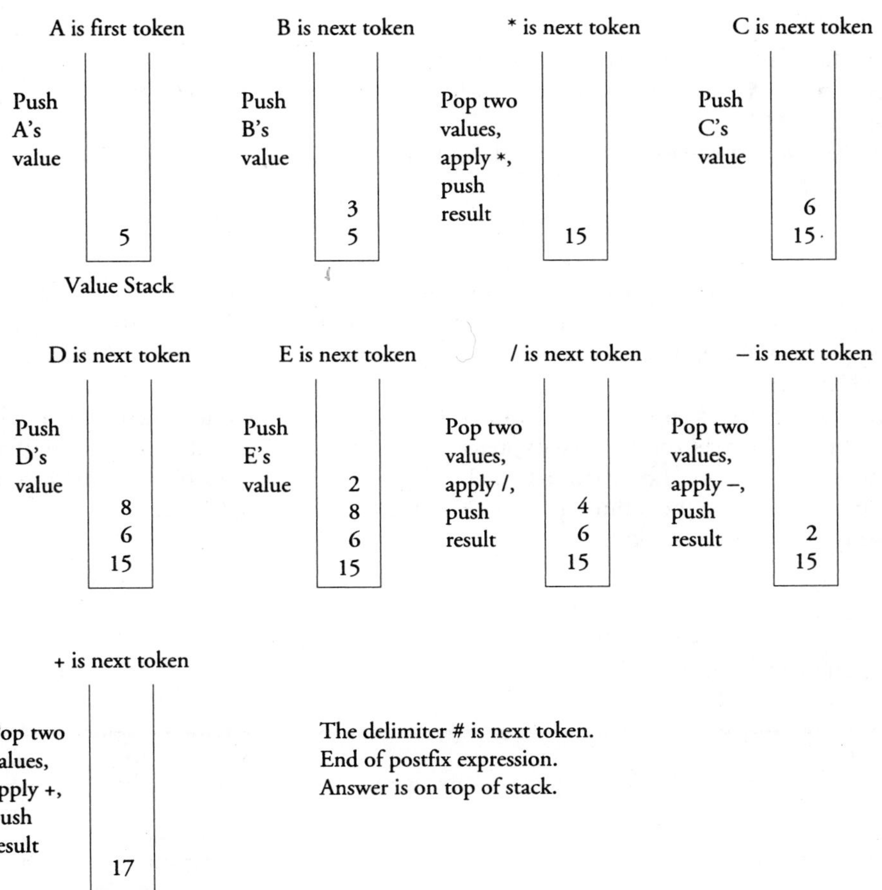


```
    ch = nextToken(postfix);
    while (ch != '#')
    {
        if (('A' <= ch) && (ch <= 'Z'))
           valueStack.push(valueOf(ch));
        else
        {
           v2 = valueStack.pop();
           v1 = valueStack.pop();
           v = eval(v1, v2, ch);
           valueStack.push(v);
        }
        ch = nextToken(postfix);
    }
    v = valueStack.onTop();
    return v;
}
```

Exercises 13.2

1. What are the infix, postfix, and prefix forms of the following expression?

$$A + B * (C - D) / (P - R)$$

2. Trace the contents of the stack as the postfix form of the expression in Exercise 1 is evaluated. Assume the following assignment of values: $A = 6$, $B = 4$, $C = 3$, $D = 1$, $P = 12$, and $R = 11$.
3. Consider the expression with the infix notation

$$P + (Q - F) / Y$$

   Using the algorithm discussed in this section to transform this into a postfix expression, trace the state of both the operator stack and postfix string as each character of the infix expression is processed. Conduct your trace following the style of Table 13.1.
4. Using the postfix expression you obtained in Exercise 3, trace the stack of real values that develop as the postfix expression is evaluated. You should indicate the numeric values on the stack as each character in the postfix expression is processed. Assume the values $F = 4$, $P = 10$, $Q = 18$, and $Y = 2$.
5. Parse the infix expression

$$P * (Q / Y) + A - B + D * Y \#$$

   using the following definitions of `infixPriority` and `stackPriority`:

Priority	*	/	+	–	(	)	#
Infix	2	2	4	4	5	0	0
Stack	1	1	3	3	0	Undefined	0

   Trace this parsing operation following the style of Table 13.1.
6. Using the postfix string you obtained in Exercise 5, trace the stack of real numeric values that develop as the postfix expression is evaluated. You should indicate the values on the stack as each character in the postfix expression is processed. Assume the values $A = 4$, $B = 3$, $D = 2$, $P = 1$, $Q = 4$, and $Y = 2$.
7. Write implementations of the `nextToken`, `valueOf`, and `eval` operations that are suitable for this section's `evaluate` function.
8. How would the functions `infixPriority` and `stackPriority` be extended to include the Boolean operators `<`, `>`, `<=`, `>=`, `==`, `!=`, `&&`, `||`, and `!`? Justify your choices of priority values for these Boolean operators.
9. Explain how the relationship between the stack priorities and infix priorities of `(`, `)`, `*`, `/`, `+`, `-`, and `#` controls the parsing of the infix expression. Then explain how you would extend the definition of the stack and infix priority functions of this section to include an exponentiation operator `^`. The exponentiation operator should be right associative; that is, in an expression such as

$$A \wedge B \wedge C$$

   the exponentiations should occur in right-to-left order.

13.3 The Queue Abstract Data Type: Its Use and Implementations

Objectives

a. to understand the definition of the queue ADT
b. to understand what is meant by a computer simulation
c. to use the queue ADT in a simulation program
d. to examine three implementations of the queue ADT: array, circular array, and linked list

The stack ADT that we have studied in the first two sections of this chapter is a last-in/first-out list. The next type of restricted list that we will examine, the queue, is a first-in/first-out list. All additions to a queue occur at one end, which we will designate as the rear of the queue. Items that enter the queue at the rear must move up to the front before they can be removed. `enqueue` is the name of the operation that adds an item to the rear of a queue, and `dequeue` is the name of the operation that removes an item from the front.

The operations on a queue thus parallel the dynamics of a waiting line. The linear order underlying a queue is determined by the length of time an item has been in it. This concept is depicted in Figure 13.6. The analogy of a waiting line makes a queue the obvious ADT to use in many applications concerned with scheduling. Before we explore such applications, however, we must formally define a queue as an ADT.

Queue. A queue is merely a restricted form of a list. In particular, the restrictions on a queue are that all additions occur at one end, the rear, and all removals occur at the other end, the front. The effect of these restrictions is to ensure that the earlier an item enters a queue, the earlier it will leave. That is, items are processed on a first-in/first-out basis.

The five basic operations on a queue are specified by the following preconditions and postconditions.

Create Operation

Preconditions:	Receiver is an arbitrary queue in unknown state.
Postconditions:	Receiver is initialized to the empty queue.

Empty Operation

Preconditions:	Receiver is a previously created queue.
Postconditions:	Returns `true` if queue is empty, `false` otherwise.

Enqueue Operation

Preconditions:	Receiver is a previously created queue. *item* is a value to be added to the rear of the queue. There is memory available to store the new item in the queue.
Postconditions:	*item* is added to the rear of the queue.

Dequeue Operation

Preconditions:	Receiver is a previously created queue. The queue is not empty.
Postconditions:	Receiver has its front value removed, and `dequeue` returns this value.

AtFront Operation

Preconditions:	Receiver is a previously created queue. The queue is not empty.
Postconditions:	`atFront` returns the value at the front of the queue. Unlike `dequeue`, the queue is left unchanged.

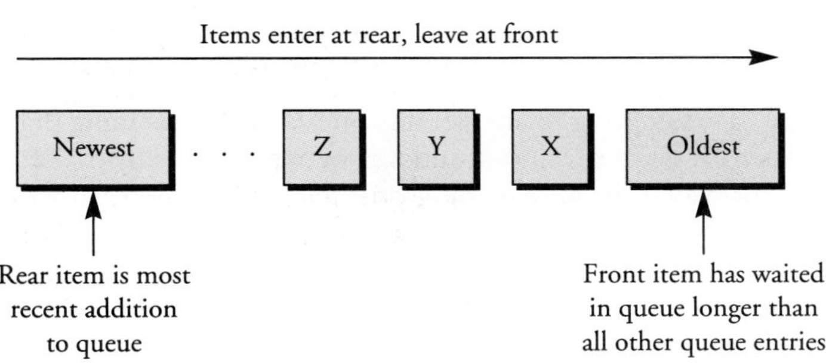

Figure 13.6
Abstract data type queue as computer embodiment of waiting line

Example 13.5 To help conceptualize queue operations, consider the following sequence of actions on a queue of integers.

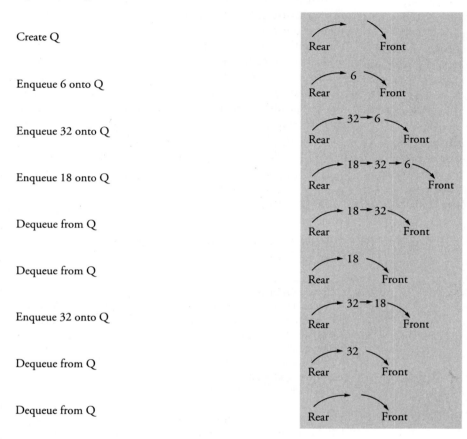

To help conceptualize queue operations, consider the following sequence of actions on a queue of integers.

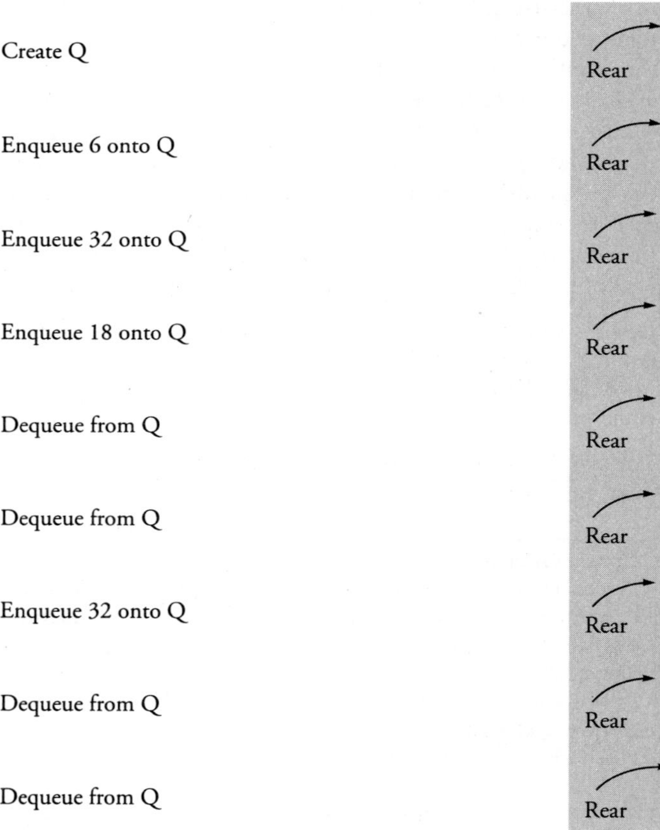

Application of a Queue in Computer Simulation

Before discussing implementations of a queue, we will examine how this ADT can be used in an application known as computer simulation. To introduce the notion of a simulation, consider the following question:

The star car-washing team at Octopus Car Wash requires precisely 4 minutes to wash a car. A car arrives on the average at Octopus every 4 minutes. In a typical 10-hour day at Octopus, how long does a car have to wait between its arrival and beginning its wash?

It's tempting to answer this question by reasoning that the combination of 4 minutes to wash a car and 4 minutes between arrivals implies that no car should wait at all. However, such reasoning does not reflect the reality that cars arrive sporadically. Such sporadic arrival patterns are what can cause dreadful waiting lines.

That cars arrive, on the average, every 4 minutes really means that, in any given minute, there is a 25% chance that a car will arrive. We wish to reflect the notion of "chance" in a program that models the operation of Octopus Car Wash during a typical day. A computer simulation is a program that models a real-life event. To incorporate chance into simulations, a special function known as a random number generator is used.

A *random number generator* is a function that returns an unpredictable numerical value each time it is called. For our purposes, the value returned from a random number generator will be a real value greater than or equal to 0 but less than 1. We will approach a random number generator as a "black box" function. That is, we will not worry about the internal logic of how such numbers are generated. (Recall that a discussion of how to generate random numbers appeared in Section 3.6.) Our only concern in using a random number generator is that if we call on the function `random` in a loop such as the following:

```
for (int k = 0; k < 100; ++k)
    cout << random() << endl;
```

then we should see 100 values that obey statistical properties of randomness. Essentially, these properties require that no pattern of values tends to recur and that values are evenly spread over the interval from 0 to 1.

How will a random number generator be used to reflect the "reality" of cars arriving at Octopus Car Wash? We will view each iteration through a loop as 1 minute in the daily operation of Octopus. On each iteration, we will call on `random` to generate a random number. If it is less than or equal to 0.25 (corresponding to the 25% chance of an arrival), our program will interpret that as a car arriving during that minute. If the random number is greater than 0.25, the program decides that no car arrived during that minute.

When a car does arrive, it will be added to the waiting queue of cars. So that we may accumulate some statistical results, the car will be time-stamped with the time that it entered the queue. This time-stamp will allow us to determine how long a car has been in the queue before it finally reaches the front. Conceptually, the queue at the core of this simulation is depicted in Figure 13.7. Pseudocode for the Octopus Car Wash simulation is

```
Initialize statistical counters
Create the queue of time-stamped cars
For each minute in the day's operation
  Call on the random number generator to determine if a new car arrived
  If a new car arrived
    Time-stamp and enqueue it onto the queue of cars
  If no car is currently being washed and the queue of waiting cars is not empty
    Dequeue a car from the queue for washing
    Use the time-stamp for the car just dequeued to determine how long it waited
    Add that wait time to the accumulating total wait time
    Record that we have just begun to wash a car
  If a car is being washed
    Reduce by 1 minute the time left before we are done washing it
```

To refine this pseudocode into a C++ main program, we must establish a formal C++ interface for the queue ADT.

Figure 13.7 Cars waiting at Octopus Car Wash, time-stamped with the minute of their arrival

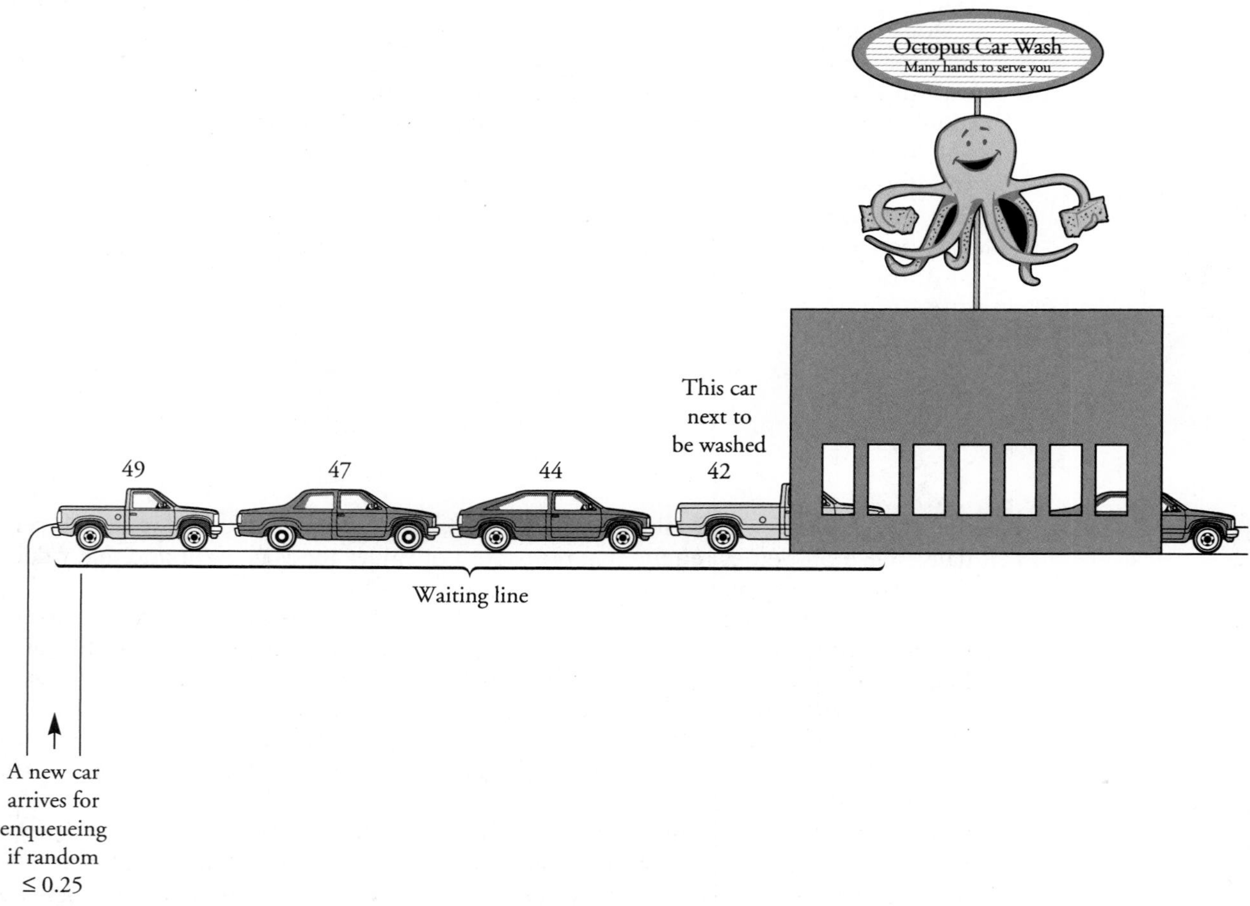

C++ Interface for the Queue ADT

```
// Class declaration file: queue.h

// Declaration section

#ifndef QUEUE_H
#define QUEUE_H

template <class E> class queue
{

   public:

   // Class constructors

   queue();
   queue(const queue<E> &q);

   // Function members
```

```
bool empty();
   void enqueue(const E &item);
   E dequeue();
   E atFront();
   queue<E>& operator = (const queue<E> &q);

   // Protected members appropriate to implementation technique
   // would be added here
};

#include "queue.cpp"

#endif
```

Example 13.6 Use the preceding C++ interface to write a main program for the Octopus Car Wash simulation. Assume the existence of a `RandomGenerator` class.

```
// Program file: octopus.cpp

// A program to simulate the operation of the Octopus Car Wash over
// 10 hours (600 minutes) of operation. The variables timeForWash
// and probOfArrival represent the time it takes to run one car through
// Octopus's star car wash team and the probability that a car
// arrives for a wash in any given minute. This program assumes the
// existence of a queue data type and a random number generator invoked
// by a call to the parameterless function random.

#include <iostream.h>
#include <iomanip.h>

#include "queue.h"
#include "random.h"

RandomGenerator generator;

float random();

void main()
{
   int timeForWash,
       minute,
       timeEnteredQueue,
       carsWashed,
       totalQueueMin,
       timeLeftOnCar;
   float probOfArrival;
   queue<int> carQueue;

   cout << "Enter time to wash one car: ";
   cin >> timeForWash;
   cout << "Enter probability of arrival in any minute: ";
```

continued

```
    cin >> probOfArrival;
    carsWashed = 0;
    totalQueueMin = 0;
    timeLeftOnCar = 0;
    for (minute = 1; minute <= 600; ++minute)
    {
        if (random() < probOfArrival)
            carQueue.enqueue(minute);
        if ((timeLeftOnCar == 0) && ! carQueue.empty())
        {
            timeEnteredQueue = carQueue.dequeue();
            totalQueueMin = totalQueueMin + (minute - timeEnteredQueue);
            ++carsWashed;
            timeLeftOnCar = timeForWash;
        }
        if (timeLeftOnCar != 0)
            --timeLeftOnCar;
    }
    cout << setw(4) << carsWashed << " cars were washed" << endl;
    cout << setiosflags(ios::fixed | ios::showpoint);
    cout << "Average wait in queue " << setw(8) << setprecision(2)
         << float(totalQueueMin) / carsWashed << endl;
}

float random()
{
    return generator.nextNumber(1, 100) / 100.0;
}
```

A sample run appears as follows:

```
Enter time to wash one car 4
Enter probability of arrival in any minute 0.25
150 cars were washed
Average wait in queue 13.53
```

The sample run of the program in Example 13.6 provides an indication of how the sporadic arrival of cars can cause a backlog of work at Octopus Car Wash. One of the great values of simulation programs is that they allow cost-free experimentation with various scenarios to see if a situation might improve or worsen. For instance, the program we have written for Octopus could be used to explore how adding help to the car wash team (and correspondingly reducing the amount of time it takes to wash a car) could affect the buildup of cars waiting for service. You will get a chance to explore further the use of queues for computer simulations in the exercises and problems in the remainder of this chapter.

Another noteworthy point about Example 13.6 is that it works with a queue even though we have no idea of how the queue of cars is actually implemented. Of course, this should not be surprising; this is the value of designing programs and data structures from an ADT perspective. However, given the high-level logic in our example, we should now turn our attention to ways in which the scheduling queue might be implemented.

Array Implementation of a Queue

From the definition of a queue, it is evident that two pointers will suffice to keep track of the data in a queue: one pointer to the front of the queue and one to the rear. This premise underlies all of the queue implementations we discuss in this section.

Let us consider computer jobs being scheduled in a batch processing environment, a good example of a queue in use. Suppose further that all job names are strings and that jobs are scheduled strictly in the order in which they arrive. Then an array and two pointers can be used to implement the scheduling queue. We will encapsulate the array and pointers in the class declaration module:

```
// Class declaration file: queue.h

#ifndef QUEUE_H
#define QUEUE_H

const int MAX_QUEUE_SIZE = 200;    // Determines maximum number of entries

template <class E> class queue
{

   public:

   // Class constructors

   queue();
   queue(const queue<E> &q);

   // Function members

   bool empty();
   void enqueue(const E &item);
   E dequeue();
   queue<E>& operator = (const queue<E> &q);

   protected:

   // Data members

   int front, rear, length;
   E data[MAX_QUEUE_SIZE];

   // Function member

   bool full();

};

#include "queue.cpp"

#endif
```

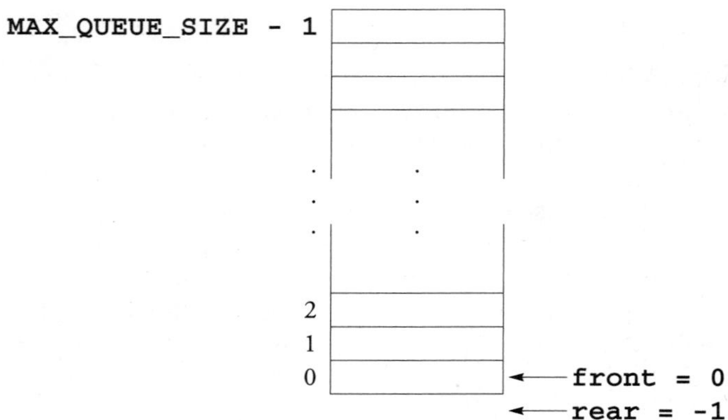

Figure 13.8
Empty quene

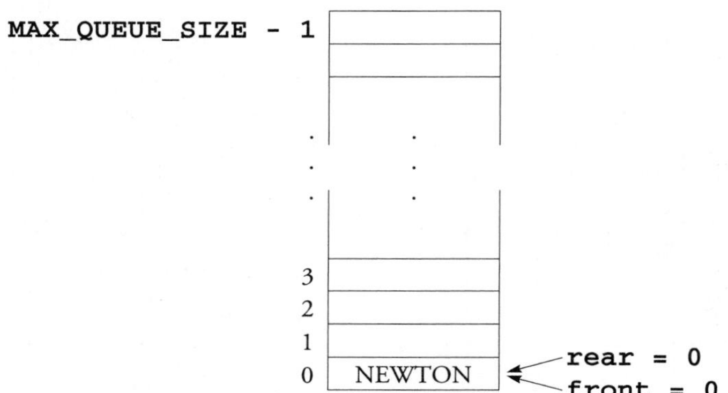

Figure 13.9
NEWTON added to the rear of the queue

If the `front` and `rear` pointers are initially set to 0 and –1, respectively, the state of the queue before any insertions or deletions appears as shown in Figure 13.8. Recalling that insertions may be made only at the rear of the queue, suppose that job NEWTON now arrives to be processed. The queue then changes to the state pictured in Figure 13.9. If job NEWTON is followed by PAYROLL, the queue's status must change to that of Figure 13.10, which shows that the addition of any item to the queue requires two steps:

```
++rear;
data[rear]= item;
```

If the system is now ready to process NEWTON, the front entry must be removed from the queue to an appropriate location designated by `item` in Figure 13.11. Here the instructions

```
item = data[front];
++front;
```

achieve the desired effect.

It should be clear that the conditions in Table 13.2 signal the associated boundary conditions for an array implementation of a queue. The conditions allow us to de-

Figure 13.10
PAYROLL added after NEWTON

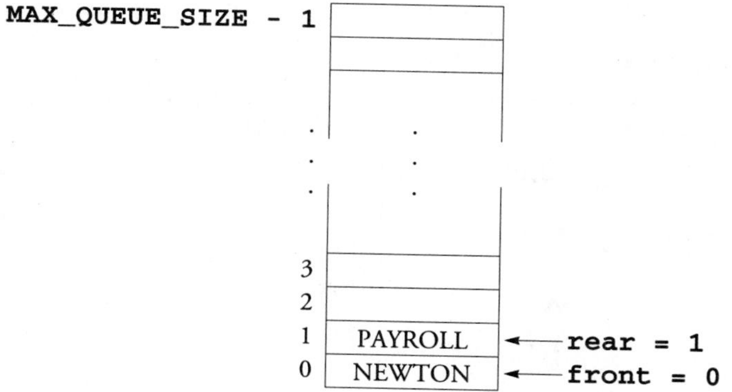

Figure 13.11
NEWTON removed from the queue

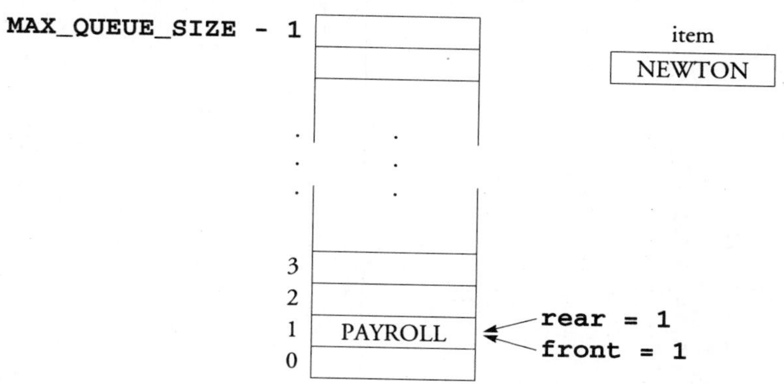

Table 13.2
Boundary Condition Checks for Array Implementation of Queue

Condition	Special Situation
`rear < front`	Empty queue
`front = rear`	One-entry queue
`rear = MAX_QUEUE_SIZE`	No more entries may be added to queue

velop our brief two-line sequences for adding to and removing from a queue into full-fledged functions. These in turn assume the existence of the Boolean-valued functions `empty` and `full` to check whether or not the `enqueue` and `dequeue` operations are possible. In the exercises, you will be asked to write the `create`, `empty`, and `full` operations.

Example 13.7 Write the `enqueue` and `dequeue` operations for an array implementation of the queue ADT.

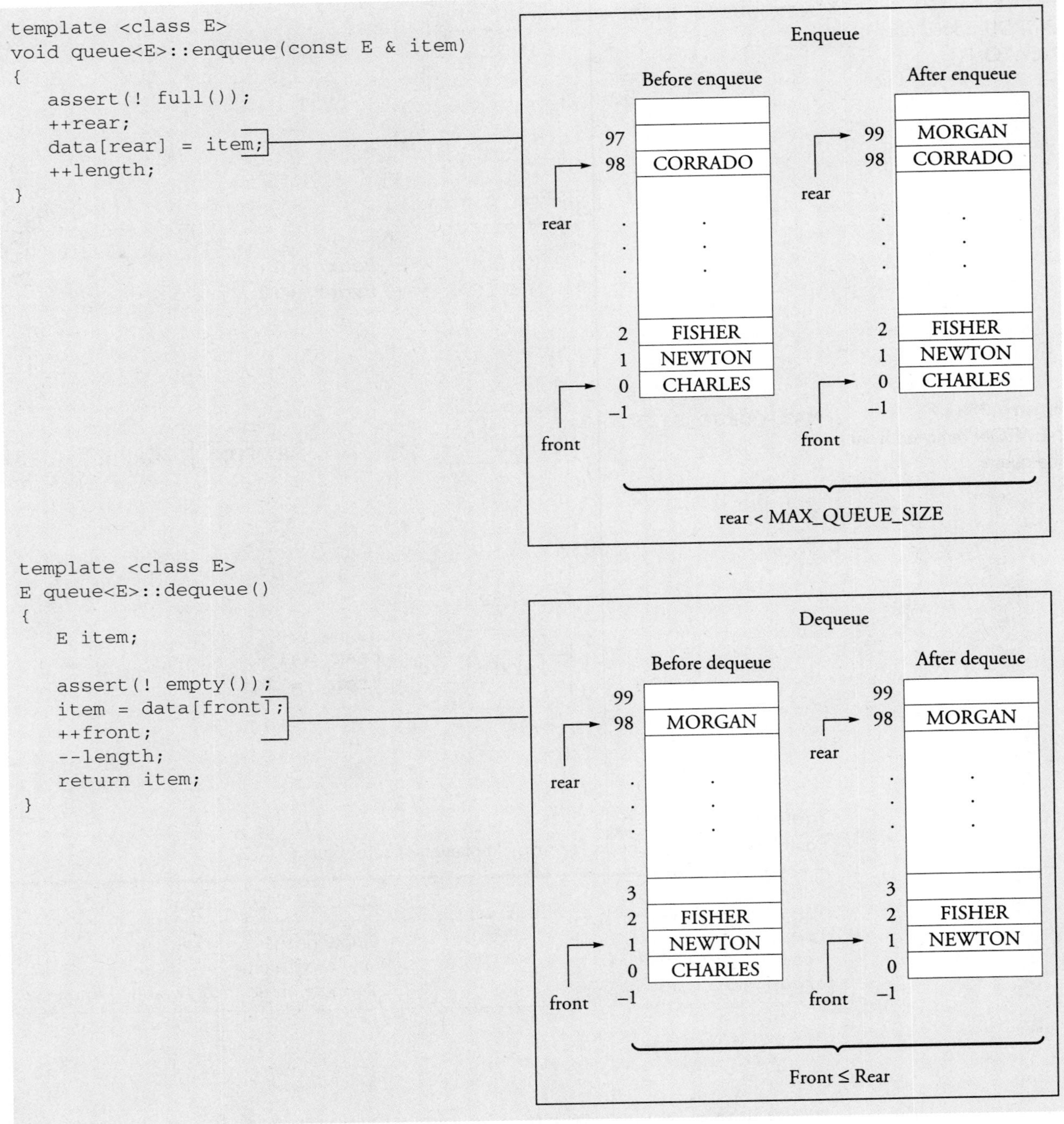

As it is now, our implementation of a queue as a scheduling structure for jobs in a batch environment functions effectively until `rear` matches `MAX_QUEUE_SIZE - 1`. Then, a call to `enqueue` fails even though only a small percentage of slots in the array may actually contain data items currently in the queue structure. In fact, given the queue pictured in Figure 13.12, we should be able to use slots 0–996 again.

This is not necessarily undesirable. For example, it may be that the mode of operation in a given batch environment is to process 1000 jobs, then print a statistical report on these 1000 jobs, and finally clear the queue to start another group of 1000

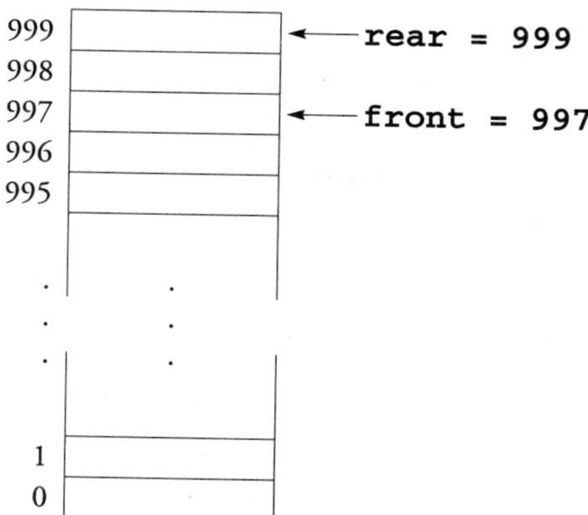

Figure 13.12
A full queue

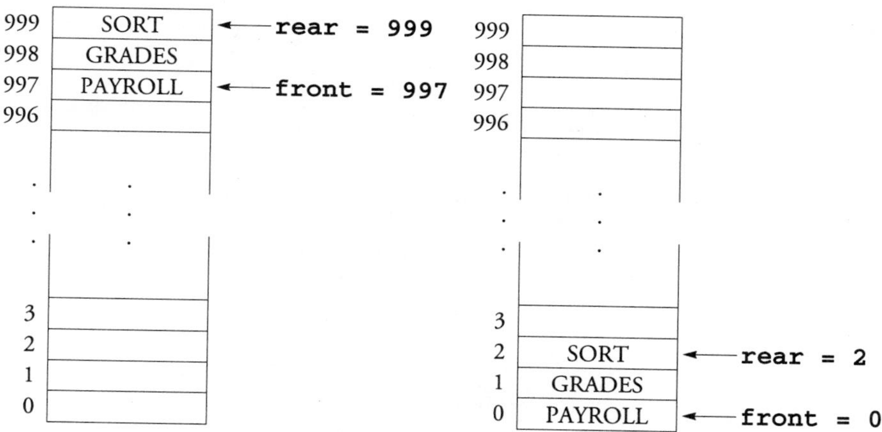

Figure 13.13
Active queue moved down

jobs. In this case, the queue in Figure 13.12 is the ideal structure because data about jobs are not lost even after they have left the queue.

However, if the goal of a computer installation is to provide continuous scheduling of batch jobs without interruption after 1000 jobs, then the queue of Figure 13.12 would not be effective. One strategy that could be employed to correct this situation is to move the active queue down the array upon reaching the condition `rear` equals `MAX_QUEUE_SIZE - 1`, as illustrated in Figure 13.13. If the queue contains a large number of items, however, this strategy is not satisfactory because it requires moving all of the individual data items. We will discuss two other strategies that allow the queue to operate in a continuous and efficient fashion: a circular implementation and a linked list implementation.

Circular Implementation of a Queue

A circular implementation of a queue essentially allows the queue to wrap around upon reaching the end of the array. This transformation is illustrated by the addition of the item UPDATE to the queue in Figure 13.14. To handle the pointer arithmetic necessary for this implementation of a queue, we must make the front and rear pointers behave in a fashion analogous to an odometer in a car that has exceeded its mileage capacity. A convenient way of doing this is to use C++'s % operator. For instance, if we replace

Figure 13.14 Queue wraps around when UPDATE is added

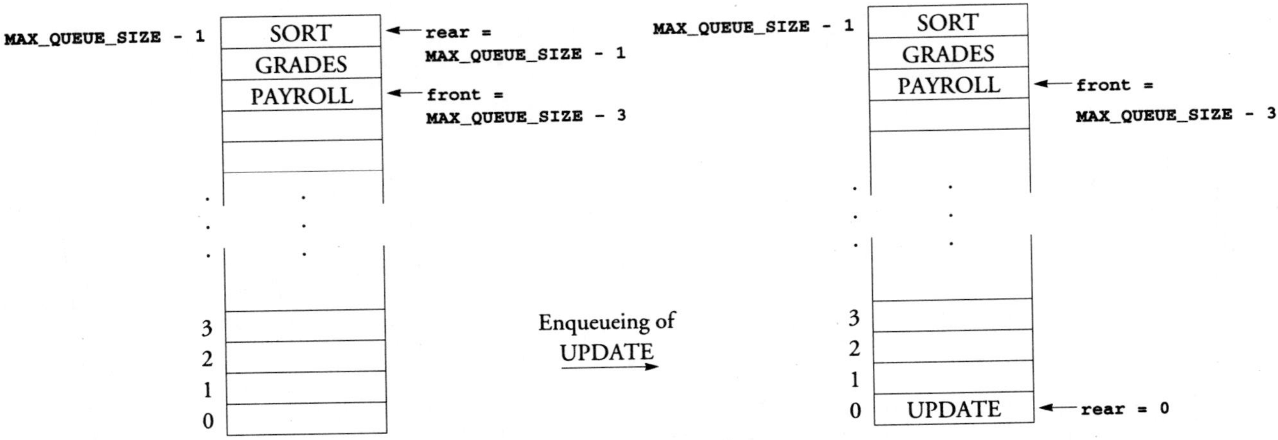


```
++front;
```

in Example 13.7 with

```
front = (front + 1) % MAX_QUEUE_SIZE;
```

and

```
++rear;
```

with

```
rear = (rear + 1) % MAX_QUEUE_SIZE;
```

we will achieve the wraparound effect depicted in Figure 13.14. Unfortunately, it is clear from Figure 13.14 that `rear < front` will no longer suffice as a condition to signal an empty queue. To derive this condition, consider what remains after we remove an item from a queue that has only a single item in it. There are two possible situations, as illustrated in Figure 13.15. An inspection of both cases reveals that after the lone entry has been removed, the relationship

```
( (rear + 1) % MAX_QUEUE_SIZE ) == front
```

holds between the pointers. There is a problem, however, with immediately adopting this as a check for an empty queue. This same relationship between pointers also exists when the queue is full.

This apparent contradiction can be avoided easily if we add a counter to our encapsulation of the queue to keep track of the number of items currently in the queue. Then, as Table 13.3 indicates, tests for empty and full conditions need merely check this counter.

The implementation of queue operations using a circular array strategy is left for you in the exercises.

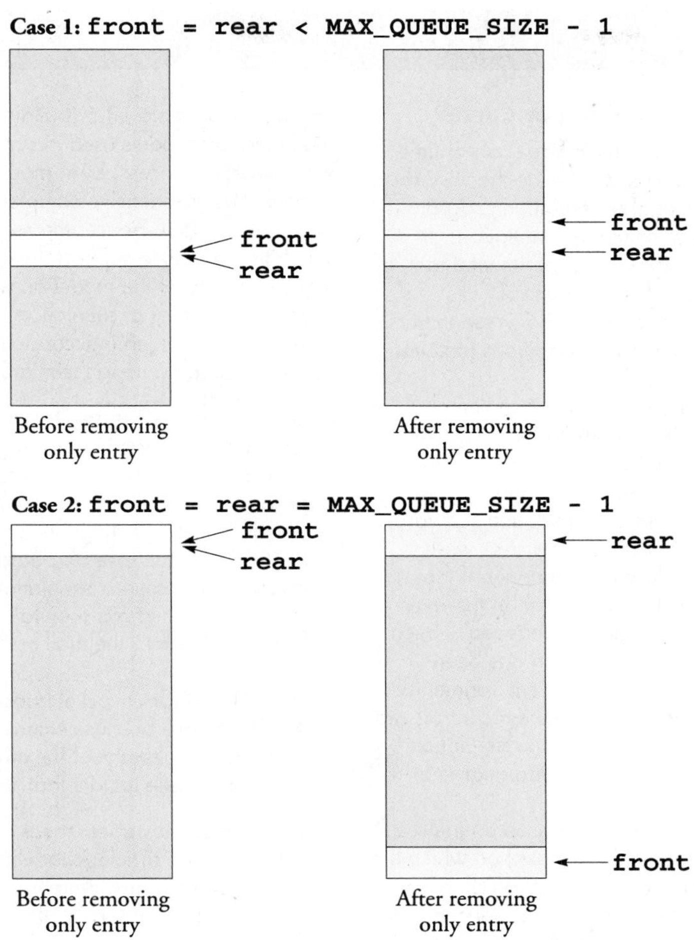

Figure 13.15
Removing from one-entry queue

Table 13.3
Boundary Condition Checks for Circular Queue with Encapsulated Counter

Condition	Special Situation
Counter is 1	One-entry queue
Counter is 0	Empty queue
Counter is `MAX_QUEUE_SIZE`	Full queue

Linked List Implementation of a Queue

The linked list method allows a queue to be completely dynamic with size restrictions imposed only by the pool of available nodes. Essentially, the queue is represented as a linked list with an additional rear pointer to the last node so that the list need not be traversed to find this node. We define a queue as a new derived class of linked list. We must be careful when we do this.

Up to this point, when we've used inheritance, the derived class has been in some sense "above and beyond" the base class. That is, the derived class provided its clients with all the operations of the base class plus new operations that were added specifically

A NOTE OF INTEREST

Computer Simulations: Blessing or Curse?

The computer's ability to condense a large span of time (such as 600 minutes in Example 13.6) into the very short time frame required for a run of a simulation program is the blessing and the curse of computer simulations. It makes the computer a very valuable experimental tool. In addition to providing a much faster means of experimentation, simulation programs allow researchers and decision makers to set up initial conditions that would be far too risky if allowed in real life.

For example, consider the area of environmental studies. Here researchers can use simulation programs to create scenarios that would be far too time consuming and dangerous if they were carried out in the environment. Researchers could use simulation software to see what might happen if pollution of a river were allowed to continue in an uncontrolled manner. If the results of the simulation indicate that all fish in the river would be gone within 10 years, nothing has really been lost. Moreover, some valuable information has been gained; those who make decisions in the environmental arena would know that some sort of pollution controls are necessary. Further experimentation with the simulation could help determine exactly what type and degree of controls should be imposed.

What can go wrong with decisions based on the result of computer simulation? Clearly, if the model on which the program is based is not an accurate reflection of the situation being simulated, results could be produced that would disastrously mislead decision makers. Additionally, we saw in Example 13.6, building the complex mathematical models used in simulation programs is a very sensitive process. Even models that seem to be relatively comprehensive can produce surprisingly inaccurate output. Hence, the real issue in using simulation results to support the decision-making process is the accuracy of the model on which the program is based. The history of simulation contains many examples of situations in which inaccurate models led to disastrous results. Included among these are:

- In 1986, erroneous results during the simulation testing of a Handley-Page Victor aircraft resulted in the conclusion that there was no tail assembly flutter problem with the aircraft. In its first real flight, the tail assembly broke, killing the crew.
- In 1986, the collapse of a Salt Lake City shopping mall involved an incorrect simulation model. The roof caved in during the first big snowfall of the season, fortunately before the mall had been opened to the public.
- In 1991, a Titan 4 rocket booster blew up at Edwards Air Force Base because extensive three-dimensional computer simulations of the motor firing dynamics did not reveal subtle factors that led to the explosion.

If you're curious about these and other simulation disasters, see the article "Modeling and Simulation" by Peter G. Neumann in *Communications of the ACM*, Vol. 36, No. 6, Jun. 1993, p. 124.

for the derived class. However, if a queue class is to inherit operations from the linked list class, we do not want client programs that use a queue to also have access to the linked list operations. Rather than extending the linked list class, the queue class is said to *adapt* the linked list class. When a derived class adapts a base class, it seals off users from operations provided by the base class and instead provides a new interface that restricts access to the base class in a form consistent with the new class.

In our present example of a queue, the derived class adds functions for inserting, removing, and examining data in the linked list. However, we must prevent clients of the queue class from using any of the operations on linked lists, such as `first` or `next`. Defining the mode of inheritance as `protected` rather than `public` will allow the queue class to inherit all of the public and protected operations from the linked list class but prevent clients of the queue class from using them.

In addition to adapting the interface of the linked list class to a form more appropriate for queues, the queue class must also maintain a rear pointer to the last node in the linked list. This will enable the `enqueue` operation to be done in $O(1)$ time. Without the rear pointer, `enqueue` is an $O(n)$ operation because we have to traverse the linked list to reach its end. Hence, the linked list implementation of the queue containing PAYROLL, GRADES, and SORT would appear as in Figure 13.16. We

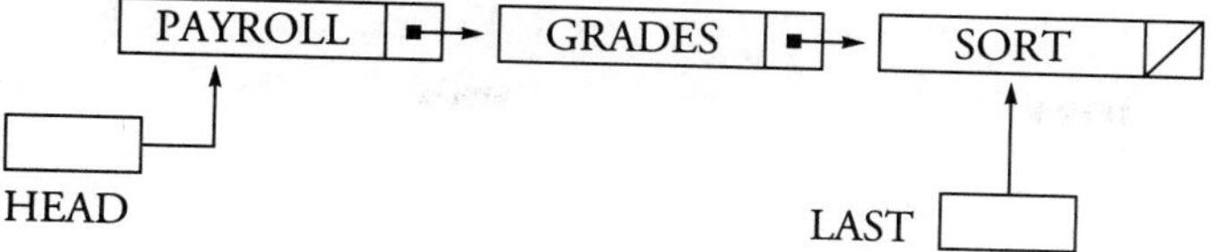

Figure 13.16 Queue with three data nodes

will follow the convention that the front pointer for the queue points at the first node, while the rear pointer points at the last node. Hence, we access the first actual item in the queue through the head pointer of the linked list and the last actual item through the last pointer.

The class declaration module for a queue as a derived class of linked list (from Chapter 12) follows. Note in particular the addition of the `node *` pointer `myLast` to achieve the $O(1)$ `enqueue` operation alluded to earlier.

```
// Class declaration file: queue.h

// Declaration section

#ifndef QUEUE_H
#define QUEUE_H

#include "linklist.h"

template <class E> class queue : protected LinkedList<E>
{
   public:

    // Class constructors

    queue();
    queue(const queue<E> &q);

    // Class destructor

    ~queue();

    // Member functions

    bool empty();
    void enqueue(const E &item);
    E dequeue();
    queue<E>& operator = (const queue<E> &q);

    protected:

    node * myLast;

};

#include "queue.cpp"

#endif
```

A NOTE OF INTEREST

Operating Systems and Scheduling Resource Use in a Time-Sharing Environment

One of the primary problems facing designers of operating systems is the allocation and scheduling of resources that must be shared by a number of users. For instance, consider a simple time-sharing system that allows multiple users, each on a video terminal, and also has one shared printer. Suppose the currently running process, called process A, makes a request to use the printer. Then, before this process completes its task on the printer, its allotted time (often called a time burst) expires, and it is replaced by process B as the currently running process. If process B requests the printer while it is running, we have a clear problem. If process B is granted to the printer, its output will be interspersed with that from process A, which did not complete its printing before its time burst expired. Obviously, we cannot let process B continue to run.

The solution developed by operating systems designers to honor both of these requests is to use multiple queues—one for processes that have cleared access to all resources they require to run and one for processes that have requested a resource currently owned by another process. The former of these queues is often called the *ready queue;* the latter is termed the *blocked queue.* Hence, the solution to the scenario described in the first paragraph involves two steps.

1. Move process A from its currently running state to the ready queue when its time burst expires (because it has all the necessary resources to start running again).
2. Move process B to the blocked queue when it requests the printer already owned by process A. Here it remains until process A is done with the printer, at which time the front entry in the blocked queue for the printer (B in this case) is moved to the ready queue.

In practice, the addition and removal of processes to and from these queues is controlled by special flags called *semaphores.* For a thorough exposition on operating system queues and semaphores, see Abraham Silberschatz & Peter B. Galvin, *Operating System Concepts,* 4th ed., Reading, MA: Addison-Wesley, 1994.

Appropriate functions for handling additions to and removals from the queue follow. Notice that from a calling module's perspective, it would make little difference whether these low-level functions used an array or a linked list to implement the queue. For each implementation, we have bundled all the information involved with the queue into a single object of class `queue`. Hence, the calling protocol for these modules is the same regardless of the implementation used. Remember the essence of data abstraction: The details of how a data structure is actually implemented are hidden as deeply as possible in the overall program structure.

Example 13.8 Code the `enqueue` and `dequeue` operations for a linked list implementation of a queue.

`enqueue` will insert data at the end of the linked list. Therefore, we move the `previous` pointer to the last node, set the `current` pointer to null, and call `insert` with the data. After returning from `insert`, the `myLast` pointer is reset to the new final node on the list.

```
template <class E>
void queue<E>::enqueue(const E & item)
{
   myPrevious = myLast;
   myCurrent = 0;
   insert(item);
   myLast = myCurrent;
}
```

`dequeue` will remove data from the beginning of the linked list. Therefore, we call `first` to position the pointers and call `remove` to delete the data from the linked list. If `remove` has deleted the one and only node from a one-node list, the `myLast` pointer must be set to null to reflect the fact that the list is now empty.

```
template <class E>
E queue<E>::dequeue()
{
   E item;

   assert(! LinkedList<E>::empty() );
   first();
   item = remove();
   if (LinkedList<E>::empty())
      myLast = 0;
   return item;
}
```

Priority Queues

So far, we have used a batch scheduling application as an example of how a queue might be used in an operating system. Typically, such batch scheduling might also give higher priorities to certain types of jobs. For instance, at a university computer center, students in introductory computer science courses may receive the highest priority for their jobs to encourage a quick turnaround. Students in upper division courses may have the next highest priority, whereas jobs related to faculty research, which require a great deal of computation, get the lowest possible priority. These jobs could be classified as types A, B, and C, respectively. Any A job is serviced before any B or C job, regardless of the time it enters the service queue. Similarly, any B job is serviced before any C job. A data structure capable of representing such a queue requires just one *front pointer* but three *rear pointers,* one for each of the A, B, and C priorities.

A queue with eight jobs waiting to be serviced might appear as shown in Figure 13.17, which tells us that STATS, PRINT, and BANK are the A jobs awaiting service; COPY and CHECK, the B jobs; and UPDATE, AVERAGE, and TEST, the C jobs. If a new A job, PROB1, were to arrive for service, it would be inserted at the end of the A queue, between BANK and COPY. Because jobs can be serviced only by leaving the front of the queue, PROB1 would be processed before any B or C jobs.

Because insertions in such a *priority queue* need not occur at the absolute rear of the queue, it is clear that an array implementation may require moving a substantial amount of data when an item is inserted at the rear of one of the higher priority queues.

Figure 13.17 Priority queue with eight jobs at three priority levels

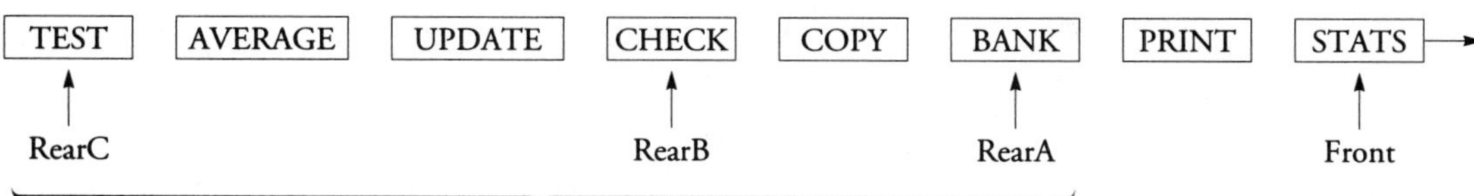

Table 13.4
Empty Conditions for a Priority Queue

Condition	Priority
`front = rear1`	For priority 1, the highest priority
`rear1 = rear2`	For priority 2
`rear (n - 1) = rear n`	For priority n

To avoid this, you can use a linked list to great advantage when implementing a priority queue. Whenever an item arrives to be inserted into a given priority level, the rear pointer for that priority gives us an immediately accessible pointer to the node after which the item is to be inserted. This avoids a costly sequential search for the insertion point. If a dummy header is included at the beginning of the list, the empty conditions for any given priority are as shown in Table 13.4. The specifics of writing a formal ADT definition of a priority queue and providing an implementation for it are included as exercises at the end of this section.

In Chapter 15, we will see that priority queues may also be implemented using the special type of tree structure known as a heap (not to be confused with the heap maintained in C++ as described in Chapter 12). Unlike the implementation we have just discussed, the heap will conveniently allow an unrestricted number of different priorities.

Exercises 13.3

1. Suppose you are given a queue that is known to contain only positive integers. Use only the fundamental queue operations to write a function

```
void replace(queue<int> &q, int oldint, int newint);
```

   which replaces all occurrences of the positive integer `oldint` in the queue with the positive integer `newint`. Other than doing this, the queue is to remain unchanged. Avoid passing through the queue more than once.
2. Suppose you are given a queue of real numbers. Using only the fundamental queue operations, write a function that returns the average value of an entry in the queue.
3. Augment the simulation program of Example 13.6 by
   a. Counting the number of minutes during the day when the Octopus Car Wash team is idle; that is, there are no cars in the queue waiting to be washed.
   b. Counting how many cars are left waiting in the queue at the end of the day. Make no assumptions about how the `carQueue` might be implemented.
4. Consider a circular array implementation of a queue in which the array is declared to have an index range 0 . . . 4. Trace the status of the array and the `front` and `rear` pointers after each of the following successive operations:

```
enqueue SMITH
enqueue JONES
enqueue GREER
dequeue
enqueue CARSON
dequeue
enqueue BAKER
enqueue CHARLES
```

```
enqueue BENSON
dequeue
enqueue MILLER
```

5. Implement the `create` and `empty` operations for a (noncircular) array implementation of a queue. Be sure that your answers are consistent with the implementation of `enqueue` and `dequeue` in Example 13.7.
6. Provide data member declarations for a circular array implementation of a queue. Then use these declarations to implement each of the basic queue operations.
7. Suppose we adopt the following conventions for the `front` and `rear` pointers associated with a queue. `front` is to point at the next item to be removed from the queue. `rear` is to point at the first available location, that is, the next location to be filled. Following these conventions, implement all queue operations for a noncircular array representation of the ADT.
8. Repeat Exercise 7 for a circular array representation.
9. In a queue used to schedule batch jobs on a computer system, it is often convenient to allow users to remove a job from the queue after submitting it. (They may, for example, realize that they accidentally submitted a job with an infinite loop.) Develop a function header for this removal operation. Be sure that you document it appropriately. Then implement it for a circular array representation of a queue.
10. Repeat Exercise 9 for a linked list representation of a queue.
11. Provide a formal ADT definition for the priority queue. Then implement the ADT under the assumption that possible priority values are drawn from a set that could be used to index an array. See if you can make your implementation of each operation $O(1)$ in its efficiency.
12. Discuss ways in which the Octopus Car Wash simulation of Example 13.6 does not reflect the way in which a car wash really operates. Then discuss ways in which the pseudocode logic behind this example should be modified to overcome these shortcomings.

Case Study: Integral Evaluation System

The application of the parsing algorithm described in Section 13.2 is not limited to compilers. Many of the programs typically used by scientists, engineers, and mathematicians can be greatly enhanced by allowing the user to enter an algebraic expression interactively as opposed to embedding the expression inside the program. Consider, for instance, the situation described in the following memorandum from the head of the physics department at the University of Hard Knocks.

User Request

Memorandum
University of Hard Knocks

To: Director of Computer Center
From: Head of Physics Department
Date: November 22, 2001
Re: Making integration program more versatile

In physics, we find frequent application to take the integral of a function $f(x)$ over the interval from a to b on the real number line. As you are aware, this essentially means that we wish to find the area under the graph of the function between endpoints a and b, as indicated in the following diagram:

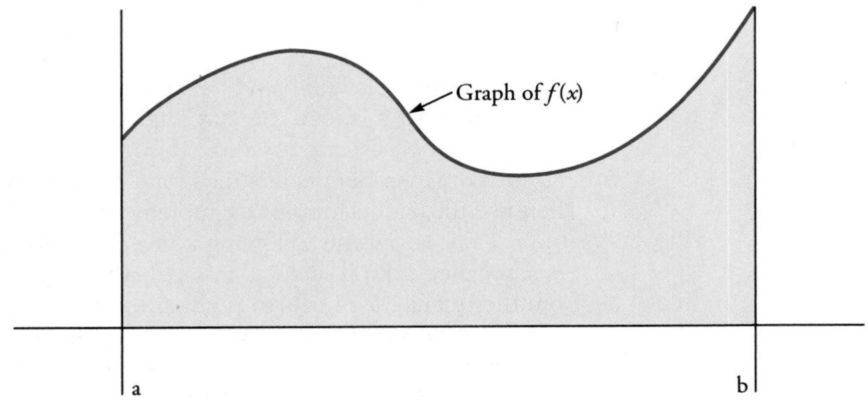

We presently have a program that obtains a good approximation of this area by adding up the areas of a large number of small rectangles, each with base along the interval from a to b and top passing through the graph of $f(x)$. This concept is highlighted in the next diagram.

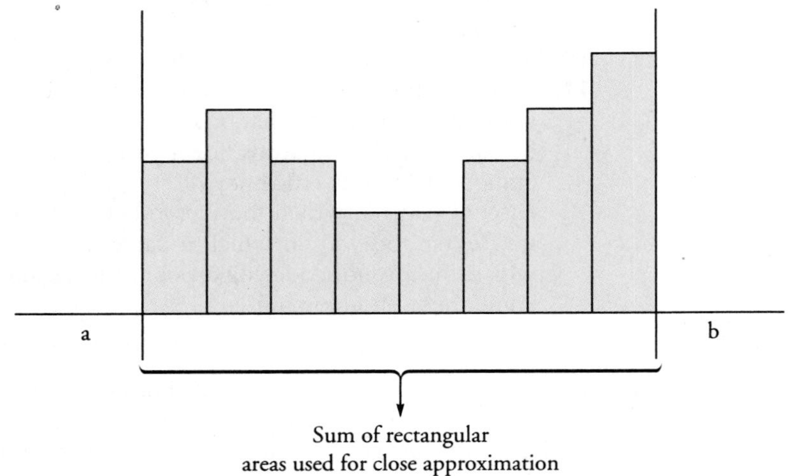

The user of our program can interactively enter the endpoints a and b and the number of rectangles. The result is a very good approximation when enough rectangles are used.

Our problem is not with the accuracy of the approximation but with the fact that, to change the function $f(x)$, the user must edit the definition of the function in the source program and then recompile. Can you help us by writing a program which will allow the user to enter the function $f(x)$ interactively? The functions we integrate in this fashion can be defined in terms of the standard arithmetic operations of addition, subtraction, multiplication, division, and exponentiation. Thanks in advance for your prompt assistance.

Analysis

The physics department head has presented us with a substantial task in the preceding memorandum. Consider some of the subordinate problems that will face us in writing this program:

- The evaluation of integrals; that is, areas under graphs of functions. Obtaining numerical answers to mathematical problems of this variety will serve to introduce us to a subject known as *numerical analysis.*
- The interactive parsing and evaluation of a function will give us an opportunity to adapt the algorithms introduced earlier.
- For the type of functions described in the memorandum, the problem of finding the next token in the expression can become complicated. Consider, for instance, a function defined by the expression

$$3.14 * X \wedge 3 + X \wedge 2 \#$$

where ^ is used to denote exponentiation. Here, from a stream of incoming characters, we must be prepared to select a token that may be a real number, the variable *X,* or an arithmetic operator. The problem of recognizing tokens in an incoming stream of characters is called *lexical analysis.* To keep our situation relatively simple, we will assume that all tokens must be separated by a space and no other operations such as trigonometric functions may be used in defining the function *f.*

Given these requirements, a reasonable way for the user to interact with the final program is the following:

```
Enter left and right endpoints (left >= right to quit)--> 0 3
Enter number of rectangles for computing area--> 10
Enter function with spaces between tokens, then <ENTER>
3 #
Approximation to area is       9.000

Enter left and right endpoints (left >= right to quit)--> 0 3
Enter number of rectangles for computing area--> 10
Enter function with spaces between tokens, then <ENTER>
X ^ 2 #
Approximation to area is       8.977

Enter left and right endpoints (left >= right to quit)--> 0 3
Enter number of rectangles for computing area--> 100
Enter function with spaces between tokens, then <ENTER>
X ^ 2 #
Approximation to area is       9.000

Enter left and right endpoints (left >= right to quit)--> 0 1
Enter number of rectangles for computing area--> 100
Enter function with spaces between tokens, then <ENTER>
( X + 2 ) ^ 3 / ( X + 1 ) #
Approximation to area is       10.526

Enter left and right endpoints (left >= right to quit)--> 0 0
```

Design

Modular Structure for the Integral Evaluation System

With these comments in mind, we turn our attention toward designing a solution to the integration problem. Recall that the first step in this design process is to develop a modular structure chart reflecting the way in which we will partition the problem

Figure 13.18 Modular structure chart for integration problem

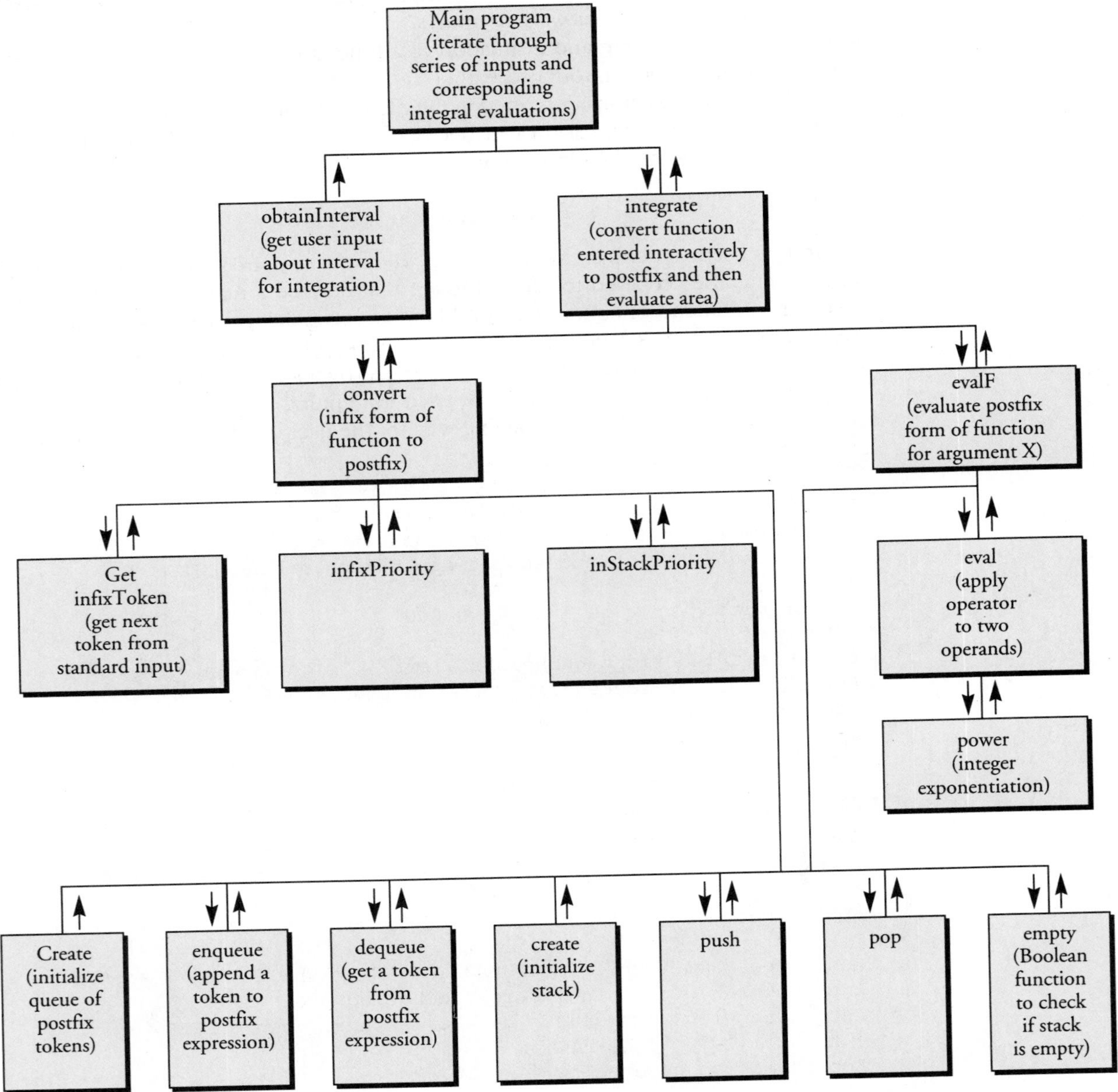

into subproblems (see Figure 13.18). Since both conversion from infix to postfix and the evaluation of a postfix expression require fundamental stack operations, we have located our stack processing modules at the deepest level of the structure chart. Here they will be accessible by both the parsing and evaluation algorithms.

Interestingly, our system will also make use of a queue. Because the tokens in the postfix expression are now more complicated objects than single characters, we need a data structure to append tokens to as they are processed by the infix-to-postfix algorithm. A queue emerges as a very nice ADT for this purpose. Hence, the structure chart also indicates the presence of fundamental queue operations at a level accessible by both the parsing and evaluation algorithms.

Data Structures for the Integral Evaluation System

We will need a queue to store the postfix expression that is built as the infix expression goes through our conversion algorithm. The data in this queue are more complex than characters, however. This is because the tokens needed from the infix string entered by the user are not necessarily individual characters. Rather, such tokens will fall into one of the following three categories:

1. *A real number:* If the token is a real number, the lexical analysis phase of our algorithm must convert it from the appropriate stream of digits and decimal point as typed by the user.
2. *The variable X:* The infix expression defines the function in terms of this general variable. When the function is evaluated, a particular value is then substituted for *X*.
3. *An operator:* We broadly include `+`, `-`, `*`, `/`, `^`, `(`, `)`, and the special delimiter `#` in this category.

The problem with a token that may be either a real number or a character is that we essentially need a data type that can assume one of several identities, depending on the current token. In the abstract, we can think of each token as having two attributes: a *code* telling us which class of token it is (real number, operator, or variable) and a *value* that the particular token assumes (a particular real number, operator, or variable name). To represent this information, we place the code attribute in a new class called *token*. Because the codes are of the same type, the code attribute will be treated as the *fixed part* of a C++ structure. Because the values can be of different types (`float` or `char`), the value attribute will be treated as the *variant part* of a C++ structure. Structure variants can be represented in C++ as *unions*. A union allows several data members of different types to be declared in a structure, but only one of them may be used at any given time. The currently used member is identified by examining the value of the fixed part of the structure. The structure definition that we will use for tokens is:

```
enum TokenCode {REAL_VALUE, VAR_X, OPERATOR};

struct TokenRecord
{
    TokenCode code;
    union
    {
        float realValue;
        char op;
        char varX;
    };
};
```

The following points concerning variant parts or unions should now be made:

1. Each variant part or union should have associated with it a *tag member* in the fixed part of the structure.
2. The tag member should be an ordinal type, such as `int`, `char`, or an enumeration. This will allow examination of the tag member's value in a `switch` statement.
3. Only one member in a union can store a value at any given time.
4. Before storing a value in a member of a union, the programmer should set the corresponding tag member to the appropriate value. In our example, the tag member

should be set to REAL_VALUE before storing a real number in the variant part or to OPERATOR or to VAR_X before storing a character there.

5. Before using the value in a member of a union, the programmer should check to see that the corresponding tag member has the appropriate value. This is typically done with a switch statement. In our example, the programmer should use the value of the realValue member only if the tag member has the value REAL_VALUE.
6. Failure to adhere to the rules just specified can cause program errors. In our example, an attempt to access the realValue member of the variant part if the tag member contains the value OPERATOR may cause an error.

Variant parts or unions are defined by a form as follows:

```
union
{
 <type 1> <member 1>;
 <type 2> <member 2>;
 .
 .
 .
 <type n> <member n>;
};
```

union is a reserved word. The members of a union are indented for readability. The member names in a union lie in the same scope as the enclosing structure member names.

Here is the class declaration module for the token class:

```
// Class declaration file: token.h

#ifndef _TOKEN_H
#define _TOKEN_H
enum TokenCode {REAL_VALUE, VAR_X, OPERATOR};

// Declaration section

class token
{

   public:

   // Class constructors:

   token(TokenCode code);
   token();
   token(const token &t);

   // Function members

   TokenCode code();
   float realValue();
   char op();
   char varX();
   void setCode(TokenCode code);
   void setRealValue(float value);
   void setOp(char op);
   void setVarX(char varX);
```

```
    token& operator = (const token &t);
    void print();

    protected:

    // Data members

    struct TokenRecord
    {
       TokenCode code;
       union
       {
          float realValue;
          char op;
          char varX;
       };
    };

   TokenRecord theToken;
};

#endif
```

In processing any given token object, we first examine the code and then use the value appropriately. Moreover, we can use the token class as an element type in other data structures such as stacks and queues. For example, the three kinds of token used in parsing can be created, pushed onto a stack of tokens, and then popped off and output:

```
token number(REAL_VALUE);
token operator(OPERATOR);
token variable(VAR_X);
stack<token> tokens;
token toOutput;
number.setRealValue(3.14);
operator.setOp('+');
variable.setVarX('X');
tokens.push(number);
tokens.push(operator);
tokens.push(variable);

while (! tokens.empty())
{
    toOutput = tokens.pop();
    switch (toOutput.code())
    {
          case REAL_VALUE:  cout << toOutput.realValue() << endl;
                            break;
          case OPERATOR:    cout << toOutput.op() << endl;
                            break;
          case VAR_X:       cout << toOutput.varx() << endl;
    }
    cout << endl;
}
```

The preceding code will produce as output:

```
X
+
3.14
```

Given this specification of a token type, an appropriate data structure for the postfix expression is a queue whose elements are of type `token`.

The final data structures needed by our program are stacks and queues. Actually, two conceptual stacks are needed: one for operator symbols during the parsing phase and one for values during the evaluation phase. However, by making `token` the class of items in the stack, we can use just one stack structure for both of the conceptual stacks that are needed. We will use a queue to store the collection of tokens that comprise the postfix expression.

The module specifications for the integral evaluation problem posed by the head of the physics department follow.

Module: Main program
Task: Repeatedly call on modules to obtain input specifications and then evaluate integral

Module: obtainInterval
Task: Issue appropriate prompts and read user input; terminate when $a >= b$
Outputs: Interval endpoints a and b, *numberOfRectangles* to use in approximating area

Module: integrate
Task: Compute width of each rectangle as $(b - a)/numberOfRectangles$; call on module *convert* to convert infix expression read from standard input to postfix notation; initialize area to 0; repeatedly evaluate f at the midpoint of the base of the current rectangle, multiply this by the width of the base, add resulting product to area accumulation
Inputs: Endpoints a and b, and *numberOfRectangles* for which area is to be accumulated
Outputs: Approximation to area under graph of function entered interactively by user

Module: infixToPostfix
Task: Follow algorithm described in Section 13.2 of text
Outputs: Postfix queue of tokens, delimited by #, corresponding to what user enters from standard input

Module: getInfixToken (*Note:* This module is responsible for lexical analysis.)
Task: Get the next token from the standard input stream
Inputs: Infix expression being read from standard input
Outputs: *fromInfix,* a token containing the next token read from standard input
Logic: (*Note:* We assume all tokens separated by one space.)

Initialize value field of fromInfix to 0 (in case token is a real number)
Do
  Let ch be next character read from standard input
  switch ch
    1. case ' ' : We are done
    2. case 'X' : Set fromInfix to ch
    3. case '+', '−', '*', '/', '^', '(', ')', '#' : Set fromInfix to ch
    4. case '.' : Set a Multiplier to 0.1 for future accumulation

5. case '0 ', '1 ', '2 ', '9': if left of decimal
   Set value to 10 * value plus ch
   else
   Set value to value + multiplier * ch
   Divide multiplier by 10 for next iteration

While ch is not a space

Module: infixPriority
Task: See Section 13.2 of text
Inputs: *t,* a token
Outputs: Infix priority rank of *t*

Module: inStackPriority
Task: See Section 13.2 of text
Inputs: *t,* a token
Outputs: In-stack priority rank of *t*

Module: evalF
Task: See evaluation algorithm in Section 13.2 of text
Inputs: Postfix queue representation of function *f* and *x,* the real number at which *f* is to be evaluated
Outputs: The real number *f*(*x*)

Module: eval
Task: Select the appropriate C++ operation based on *op*
Inputs: *v1, v2:* the values of two operands and *op:* character containing operator +, −, *, /, ^
Outputs: Numeric result of applying *op* to *v*1 and *v*2

The complete C++ program for the integral evaluation system follows, with functions named in a fashion consistent with the module specifications. Also included are graphic documentation to give you a more detailed grasp of how the program functions at particular points.

```
// Program file: integral.cpp

// Program to compute area under curve of function entered
// interactively. A stack is used to convert function expression to
// postfix notation (which is stored in a queue) and then to
// evaluate. Valid function expressions can contain the variable X,
// numeric constants, operators +, -, *, /, ^ (for
// exponentiation) and appropriate parentheses.

#include <iostream.h>
#include <iomanip.h>
#include <math.h>
#include <ctype.h>

#include "token.h"
#include "stack.h"
#include "queue.h"

const char END_TOKEN = '#';

void obtainInterval(float &a, float &b, int &numberOfRectangles);
```

continued

```
void integrate(float a, float b, int numberOfRectangles, float &area);

void infixToPostfix(queue<token> &postfix);

void getInfixToken(token &fromInfix);

int infixPriority(token t);

int instackPriority(token t);

float evalF(queue<token> postfix, float x);

float eval(float v1, float v2, char op);

bool isOp(char ch);

int main()
{
   float a, b, area;
   int numberOfRectangles;

   obtainInterval(a, b, numberOfRectangles);
   cout << setiosflags(ios::fixed | ios::showpoint) << setprecision(3);
   while (a < b)
   {
      integrate(a, b, numberOfRectangles, area);
      cout << "Approximation to area is " << setw(10) << area << endl;
      cout << endl;
      obtainInterval(a, b, numberOfRectangles);
   }

   return 0;
}

void obtainInterval(float &a, float &b, int &numberOfRectangles)
{
   cout << "Enter left and right endpoints (left >= right to quit)--> ";
   cin >> a >> b;
   if (a < b)
   {
      cout << "Enter number of rectangles for computing area--> ";
      cin >> numberOfRectangles;
   }
}

void integrate(float a, float b, int numberOfRectangles, float &area)
{
   stack<token> tokenStack;
   queue<token> postfix;
   int count;
   float width, x;

   width = (b - a) / numberOfRectangles;
   count = 0;
   x = a;
```

```
   infixToPostfix(postfix);
   area = 0.0;
   while (count < numberOfRectangles )
   {
      area = area + evalF(postfix, x + width / 2.0) * width;
      x = x + width;
      ++count;
   }

}

void infixToPostfix(queue<token> &postfix)
{
   token bottomStack(OPERATOR);
   token fromStack, fromInfix;
   stack<token> tokenStack;
   char ch;

   // Must push END_TOKEN to correspond with algorithm in Section 13.2

   bottomStack.setOp(END_TOKEN);
   tokenStack.push(bottomStack);
   cout << "Enter function with spaces between tokens, then <ENTER>" << endl;
   cin.get(ch);
   do
   {
      getInfixToken(fromInfix);
      if ((fromInfix.code() == REAL_VALUE) || (fromInfix.code() == VAR_X))
         //We have an operand -- variable or number. }
         postfix.enqueue (fromInfix);
      else if (fromInfix.op() == ')')
      {
         fromStack = tokenStack.pop();
         while (fromStack.op() != '(')
         {
            postfix.enqueue (fromStack);
            fromStack = tokenStack.pop();
         }
      }
      else if (fromInfix.op() == END_TOKEN)
         while (! tokenStack.empty())
         {
            fromStack = tokenStack.pop();
            postfix.enqueue(fromStack);
         }
      else
         // We have one of arithmetic operators +, -, *, /, ^ or )
      {
         fromStack = tokenStack.pop();
         while (inStackPriority(fromStack) >= infixPriority(fromInfix))
         {
            postfix.enqueue(fromStack);
            fromStack = tokenStack.pop();
         }
```

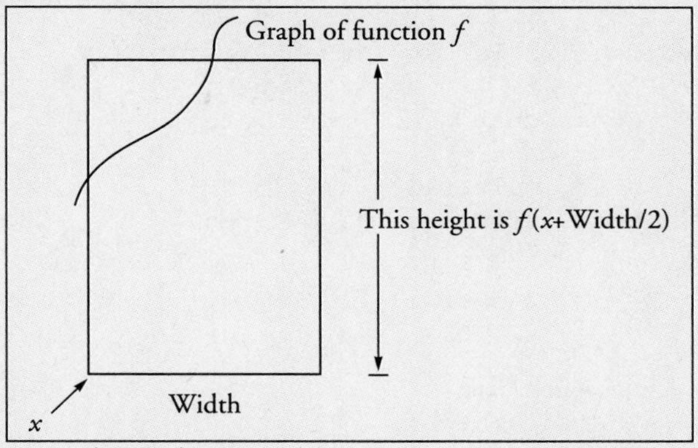

continued

```
         tokenStack.push(fromStack);
         tokenStack.push(fromInfix);
      }
   } while (! ((fromInfix.code() == OPERATOR) && (fromInfix.op() == END_TOKEN)));
}

void getInfixToken(token &fromInfix)
{
   const char SPACE = ' ';
   char ch = ' ';
   float multiplier = 0.1;
   bool leftOfDecimal = true;
   int column = 0;

   do
   {
      ++column;
      cin.get(ch);
      if (isOp(ch))
      {
         fromInfix.setCode(OPERATOR);
         fromInfix.setOp(ch);
      }
      else if (isdigit(ch))
      {
         if (column == 1)
         {
            fromInfix.setCode(REAL_VALUE);
            fromInfix.setRealValue(0);
         }
         if (leftOfDecimal)
            fromInfix.setRealValue(fromInfix.realValue() *
               10.0 + (ch - '0'));
         else
         {
            fromInfix.setRealValue(fromInfix.realValue() *
               multiplier + (ch - '0'));
            multiplier = multiplier / 10.0;
         }
      }
      else if (ch == '.')
      {
         leftOfDecimal = false;
         multiplier = 0.1;
      }
      else if (ch == 'X')
      {
         fromInfix.setCode(VAR_X);
         fromInfix.setVarX(ch);
      }
   } while ((ch != '\n') && (ch != SPACE) && (ch != END_TOKEN));
}

int infixPriority(token t)
{
```

<u>23</u>.14

For digits to left of decimal; must multiply accumulated value by 10 and add digit.

23.<u>14</u>

For digits to right of decimal; add digit scaled to appropriate decimal value by multiplier.

3.14
↑
We are currently here. Must prepare to accumulate digits to right of decimal.

```
   int priority = 0;

   switch (t.op())
   {
      case '^':        priority = 3;
                       break;
      case '*':
      case '/':        priority = 2;
                       break;
      case '+':
      case '-':        priority = 1;
                       break;
      case '(':        priority = 4;
                       break;
      case ')':
      case END_TOKEN: priority = 0;
   }
   return priority;
}

int instackPriority(token t)
{
   int priority = 0;

   switch (t.op())
   {
      case '^' :        priority = 3;
                        break;
      case '*':
      case '/' :        priority = 2;
                        break;
      case '+':
      case '-':         priority = 1;
                        break;
      case '(':
      case END_TOKEN:   priority = 0;
   }
   return priority;
}

float evalF(queue<token> postfix, float x)
{
   token result(REAL_VALUE);
   token t1, t2, t3;
   stack<token> tokenStack;

   // Because postfix is passed by value, a copy of the queue is made.
   // Hence these dequeue operations will not remove everything from
   // the queue in the calling function.
   t1 = postfix.dequeue();

   while (! ((t1.code() == OPERATOR) && (t1.op() == END_TOKEN)))
   {
      if (t1.code() != OPERATOR)
         if (t1.code() == REAL_VALUE)
```

continued

```
            tokenStack.push(t1);
         else
         {
            t1.setCode(REAL_VALUE);
            t1.setRealValue(x);
            tokenStack.push(t1);
         }
      else
      {
         t2 = tokenStack.pop();
         t3 = tokenStack.pop();
         result.setRealValue(eval(t3.realValue(), t2.realValue(), t1.op()));
         tokenStack.push(result);
      }
      t1 = postfix.dequeue();
   }
   result = tokenStack.pop();
   return result.realValue();
}

float eval(float v1, float v2, char op)
{
   float result = 1;

   switch (op)
   {
      case '+' :   result = v1 + v2;
                   break;
      case '-':    result = v1 - v2;
                   break;
      case '*':    result = v1 * v2;
                   break;
      case '/':    result = v1 / v2;
                   break;
      case '^':    result = pow(v1, v2);
                   break;
   }
   return result;
}

bool isOp(char ch)
{
   return (ch == '+') || (ch == '-') || (ch == '*') || (ch == '/') ||
      (ch == '^') || (ch == '(') || (ch == ')') || (ch == END_TOKEN);
}
```

Running, Debugging, and Testing Hints

1. In applications in which the size to which a stack or queue may grow is hard to predict, use a linked list to implement the ADT. That way, you can take advantage of C++'s dynamic memory management to avoid having to worry about a full data structure.
2. Many scientific and mathematical application programs can be enhanced by allowing users to enter function definitions at run time. This chapter's Case Study

section provides an example of how such run-time definitions of a function can be done.

3. When debugging simulations, use a random number sequence that remains the same over different runs of the program. Without such a sequence, your program will behave differently on separate runs even though you provide it with identical inputs. This is because you are getting a different pattern of random numbers. In Chapter 3, Section 6, we indicated how you can ensure a fixed sequence of random numbers from one run of the program to the next.

Summary

Key Terms

activation record
adaptor class
blocked queue
first-in/first-out (FIFO)
fixed part
front pointer
infix
infix priority
last-in/first-out (LIFO)
lexical analysis
numerical analysis
parsing
pop
postfix
prefix
priority queue
push
queue
random number generator
ready queue
rear pointer
semaphores
simulation
stack
stack priority
tag member
token
union
variant part

Key Concepts

- Conceptually, a stack is simpler than a queue because all additions and deletions are limited to one end of the structure, the top. For this reason, a stack is also known as a last-in/first-out (LIFO) list. Like a queue, a stack may be implemented using either an array or a linked list.
- The simplicity of the stack as an abstract structure belies the importance of its application. Stacks play a crucial role in the parsing done by language compilers.
- Parsing, as we have studied it in this chapter, involves the conversion of an expression from infix to postfix notation. In infix notation, an algebraic operator is located between its two operands. In postfix notation, the operator follows its two operands.
- Expressions in postfix notation do not require parentheses to override the standard hierarchy of algebraic operations.
- Stacks process function calls when a program executes.
- A queue is a first-in/first-out (FIFO) data structure used in processing data such as job scheduling in a large university computer environment. There are two basic pointers, front and rear, associated with this structure. New data items are added to the rear of the queue, and the data item that is about to be processed is removed from the front of the queue.
- The relative advantages and disadvantages of three implementations of queues—array, circular array, and linked list—are summarized in the following table:

Implementation	Advantages	Disadvantages
Array	A record of queue entries remains even after they have been removed.	Static allocation of storage limits overall queue size. Array locations cannot be reused once entries are removed from queue.
Circular array	Array locations can be reused once entries are removed from queue.	Static allocation of storage limits overall queue size.
Linked list	With C++ pointer variables, queue can grow dynamically to take full advantage of all space available in C++'s heap.	Could be less space efficient than array implementations since each node in queue must include a pointer field as well as data fields.

- Primary applications of queues are in the areas of operating systems and computer simulation of events.

Programming Problems and Projects

1. Write a program that will parse infix expressions into prefix form.
2. Write a program to call for input of a decimal number and convert it to its binary equivalent using the method described in the following flowchart. Note that this method produces the binary digits for the given number in reverse order. Use a stack to get them printed in the correct order.

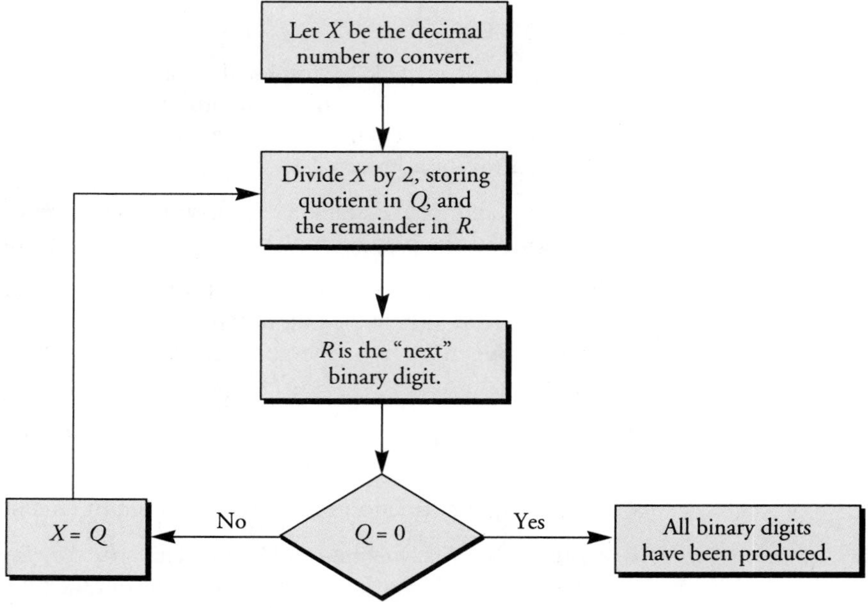

3. Earlier, you developed a passenger list processing system for the various flights of Wing-and-a-Prayer Airlines (Problem 7, Chapter 12). Wing-and-a-Prayer management would now like you to extend this system so that it processes logical combinations of flight numbers. For example, the command

```
LIST 1 OR 2
```

should list all passengers whose name appears on the flight 1 list or the flight 2 list. Your program should also accept the logical operators `AND` and `NOT` and allow parenthesized logical expressions obeying the standard logical hierarchy

```
NOT
AND
OR
```

4. A tax form may be thought of as a sequence of items, each of which is either a number or defined by an arbitrary mathematical formula involving other items in the sequence. To assist them in their tax-planning strategy, top management at the Fly-by-Night credit card company desires a program that would allow them to enter interactively numbers or formulas associated with given lines of a tax form. Once all such lines have been defined, users of the program may redefine the number or formula associated with a particular line, and all other lines dependent on that one should be appropriately updated. Note that, since formulas may be entered interactively, your program will have to use a stack to evaluate them. You will in effect have written a small-scale spreadsheet program.
5. Write a program that will accept commands of the following form:
   - `INPUT <variable name>`
   - `<variable name> = infix expression involving variable names and arithmetic operators +, -, *, /`
   - `PRINT <variable name>`
   - `GO`

   These commands are to be stored in an array of strings until the `GO` command is entered. Once the `GO` command is entered, your program should execute the previously stored commands. "Execute" here means the following:

   - **For an `INPUT` command**: Send a question mark to the terminal and allow the user to enter a real number; this real number is then stored in the variable name.
   - **For an assignment statement:** Parse the expression into postfix form and then evaluate it, storing the results in the variable name on the left of the equality sign.
   - **For a `PRINT` instruction**: Write to the terminal the numerical contents of the specified variable name.

   To make things relatively easy, you may assume a syntax that

   - Allows variable names consisting of one uppercase alphabetical character.
   - Allows only one variable name following the commands for `INPUT` or `PRINT`.
   - Allows one blank space after the commands for `INPUT` and `PRINT` and no blank spaces anywhere else.

   For an additional challenge, enable your program to handle successfully the exponentiation operator ^ within assignment statement expressions. The following example should illustrate the need for care in handling this exponentiation operator:

$$3^{2^3} = 3^8, \text{ not } 9^3$$

6. This problem is an extension of Problem 5 for a "compiler" for a primitive programming language. Write a program that will accept commands of the following form:

- `INPUT <variable name>`
- `PRINT <variable name>`
- `<variable name> = infix arithmetic expression involving variable names and arithmetic`
- `operators +, -,*, /, ^`
- `GOTO <line>` —
  - `ALWAYS, or`
  - `IF infix logical expression involving variable names and operators +, -, *, /, ^, & (for AND), | (for OR), ! (for NOT), <, >, =`
- `STOP`
- `RUN`

These commands are to be stored in an array of strings until the `RUN` command is entered. Upon encountering the `RUN` command, your program should execute the previously stored commands. "Execute" here means the following:

- **For an `INPUT` command:** Send a question mark to the terminal and allow the user to enter a real number, which is stored in the variable name.
- **For a `PRINT` command:** Write to the terminal the numerical contents of the specified variable name.
- **For an assignment command:** Parse the expression into postfix form and then evaluate it. Store the result in the variable name on the left of the equality sign.
- **For a `GOTO` command:** Branch to the line number specified when the `ALWAYS` condition follows the line number or when the infix expression that follows the `IF` evaluates to true. Here "line number" refers to the relative position of the line in the sequence of lines that were entered prior to the `RUN` command. The first line number in this sequence is "00".
- **For a `STOP` command:** Halt execution.

To make things relatively easy, you may assume a syntax that

- Specifies that one and only one blank space follows `INPUT`, `PRINT`, `GOTO`, and line number. No other blanks appear anywhere.
- Allows only one variable name to follow `INPUT` or `PRINT`.
- Allows only variable names consisting of one uppercase alphabetical character.
- Allows only line numbers consisting of two digits: 00 through 99.

The usual hierarchy for operators is assumed.

7. Modify the program in the Case Study section so that it also integrates expressions involving the functions sin, cos, tan, exp, and ln. Test your modified program by having it evaluate the following integrals:
   a. $\sin (X * 2) + \cos X / 2$ between 0 and 1
   b. $3 * (X + 4) \wedge 2 + \tan (X / 2)$ between 0 and 1
   c. $3 * (X + 4) \wedge 2 + \tan X / 2$ between 0 and 1
   d. $\exp \ln X \wedge 3$ between 1 and 3
   e. $\exp \ln (X \wedge 3)$ between 1 and 3
8. If you have access to a graphics library in your version of C++, write a program that allows a user to define interactively a function and then displays a graph of the function between two specified endpoints.

9. Develop a program to simulate the processing of batch jobs by a computer system. The scheduling of these jobs should be handled via a queue (or priority queue for more of a challenge). Examples of commands that your program should be able to process are

Command	Purpose
ADD	To add an entry to the queue.
DELETE	To take an item out of the queue.
STATUS	To report on items currently in the queue.

10. In Chapter 8, you developed a program to keep track of a bank's records. Now the bank has asked you to develop a program to simulate the arrival of customers in a waiting line at the bank. Factors to consider are the average time it takes to service one customer, the average number of customers that arrive in a given time period, and the number of service windows maintained by the bank. These factors should be provided as input to your program. Statistics such as the length of time the average customer has to spend in the waiting line could be very helpful in the bank's future planning. First write the program under the assumption each teller has a separate waiting line. Then change the model to one waiting line for all tellers. What differences do you observe?

11. Here is a problem typically encountered in text formatting applications.

Given a file of text, text that is delimited by special bracketing symbols [and] is to be considered a footnote. Footnotes, when encountered, are not to be printed as normal text but are instead stored in a footnote queue. Then, when the special symbol # is encountered, all footnotes currently in the queue are printed and the queue should be returned to an empty state.

What you learn in solving this problem will allow you to make good use of string processing techniques discussed in earlier chapters.

12. To improve their services, the Fly-by-Night credit card company (Problem 8, Chapter 12) has decided to give incentives to their customers for prompt payment. Customers who pay their bill 2 weeks before the due date receive top priority and a 5% discount. Customers who pay their bill within 1 week of the due date receive next priority and a 1% discount. Third priority is given to customers who pay their bill on or within 2 days after the due date. The customers who pay their bill thereafter are assigned the lowest priority. Write a program to set up a priority queue to access customer records accordingly.

13. The Bay Area Brawlers professional football team (Problem 9, Chapter 12) has been so successful in recent weeks that the team management is considering the addition of several new ticket windows at the team's stadium. However, before investing a sizable amount of money in such an improvement, they would like to simulate the operation of ticket sales with a variety of ticket window configurations. Develop a computer program that allows input of such data as number of ticket windows, average number of fans arriving each hour as game time approaches, and average length of time to process a ticket sale. Output from your program should include statistics such as the average waiting-line length each hour as game time approaches and the amount of time the average fan had to wait in line before having his or her ticket request processed. Use queues to represent each of the waiting lines.

14. Consider the design for an implementation of the radix sort algorithm and its associated bin (sublist) structure that was discussed in Chapter 12's Case Study section.

Note that queues could provide an alternative implementation for the bin structure needed by radix sort. What queue implementation would provide the most space-efficient bin structure for radix sort? Why? Develop a complete radix sort program that uses queues to implement the bins needed by the algorithm and then accesses these bins *only* through the defined ADT operations for a queue. Is this implementation of radix sort more or less time efficient than that described in Chapter 12's Case Study section? Justify your answer in a written memorandum.

15. As director of computer operations for Wing-and-a-Prayer Airlines, you receive the following memorandum. Design and write a simulation program according to the specifications in the memo.

> **Memorandum**
> Wing-and-a-Prayer Airlines
>
> **To:** Director of Computer Operations
> **From:** President, Wing-and-a-Prayer Airlines
> **Date:** September 30, 2000
> **Re:** Wasted Fuel and Time
>
> Wing-and-a-Prayer Airlines is becoming increasingly concerned about the amount of fuel being wasted as its planes wait to land at and take off from world-famous O'Hair Airport. Could you please help us write a program to simulate the operation of 1 day's activity at O'Hair and report on the times spent waiting to land and take off for each Wing-and-a-Prayer flight? Input data to the program should include:
>
> - Average number of Wing-and-a-Prayer arrivals each hour
> - Average number of other airline arrivals each hour
> - Average number of Wing-and-a-Prayer departures each hour
> - Average number of other airline departures each hour
> - Number of available runways
> - Average time a runway is in use for an arrival
> - Average time a runway is in use for a departure
>
> By appropriately adjusting these parameters, we hope to do some valuable "what-if" analyses regarding the time spent waiting for a runway by our arrivals and departures.

16. If an arithmetic expression is written in prefix notation, then there is no need to use parentheses to specify the order of operators. For this reason, some compilers translate infix expressions (such as 2 + 8) to prefix notation (+ 2 8) first and then evaluate the prefix string. Write a program that will read prefix expressions and then compute and display the value of the indicated arithmetic expression. Assume that the operands are single-digit positive integers separated by blanks. The operators can be +, –, *, and /, also separated by blanks, with their usual meanings of add, subtract, multiply, and divide.

17. Implement the following user-friendly enhancements for the program in this chapter's Case Study section.

a. Make the `getInfixToken` module more robust by allowing the user to separate individual tokens with an arbitrary number of zero or more spaces.

b. Make the `getInfixToken module` more robust by guarding against input of an invalid arithmetic operator.

c. Make the `getInfixToken` module more robust by guarding against an invalid character in a stream of characters intended to be a real number. When such an invalid character is detected, allow the user to recover from the point of error rather than forcing the user to retype the entire line.

18. This chapter's Note of Interest on "Computer Simulations: Blessing or Curse?" cites some issues arising out of simulation. Research and prepare a more thorough written report on computer simulation. Your report could discuss any or all of the following:

a. Examples of disciplines and industries in which simulation has been used to great advantage.
b. Limitations and inaccuracies that arise in modeling a system by computer simulation. Techniques that can be used to measure and monitor such inaccuracies.
c. The reliance of many simulation programs on the effective generation of random numbers.
d. The potential danger in relying on the results of simulation programs without examining the validity of their underlying models.

19. This chapter's Case Study section demonstrated how a computer program can be used to solve a mathematical problem in interactive fashion. In particular, the type of problem solved by this program is the evaluation of integrals. Explore other types of mathematical problems that can be solved interactively by software systems available at your school. (The *Mathematica* program from Wolfram Research is one example of such a system available at many universities.) Prepare a report on the results of your explorations. In keeping with the theme of this chapter's Case Study, be sure that your report includes a discussion of the types of mathematical expressions that can be parsed and evaluated by such systems.

14 Recursion

Chapter Outline

It's déjà vu all over again.
Lawrence Peter (Yogi) Berra

Research is the process of going up alleys to see if they are blind.
Marston Bates

In Chapter 6, we examined problems that are suited to iterative control by methods such as `while`, `do`, and `for` loops. Many of these problems can more easily be solved by designing functions that call themselves. In computer science, this form of self-reference is called *recursion*. We are now ready to embark on a detailed study of recursive problem solving.

In this chapter, we first examine the essentials of *recursive functions*. Now that we are familiar with stack operations, we will also be able to explain how recursion is implemented. The "invisible" data structure underlying recursive functions is a stack used by the system to process the call-and-return pattern of functions in a program (Section 13.1). By examining the role of this system stack more closely, you will build confidence in your ability to express algorithms recursively. In time, you will use this technique without hesitation in your problem solving.

Then we will begin to use recursion to explore problems for which nonrecursive solutions would be exceedingly difficult to fathom. We hope that you will be amazed at the ease with which recursion handles such problems. We will demonstrate that recursion is a natural and elegant way to solve many complex problems. We will also begin to explore the price paid for this elegance: The compactness of a recursive solution to a complex problem is not necessarily an accurate statement of its time or space efficiency.

We will then use recursion to develop a problem-solving methodology known as *trial-and-error*, or nondeterministic, *backtracking*. In theory, this technique can solve a large variety of problems. Unfortunately, in practice, the technique is so computationally expensive that it can only be used to solve small instances of such problems in a reasonable amount of time.

Finally, we will look at how recursive techniques can be used to specify the syntax of languages by using a formalism called a *grammar*. The advantage of defining languages in this fashion is that it leads to a very natural way of writing parsers for such languages. The resulting methodology, called *recursive descent parsing*, will be demonstrated in the Case Study.

14.1 Controlling Simple Iteration with Recursion

Objectives

a. to examine the essentials of controlling simple iteration by recursion
b. to identify and distinguish tail-recursive algorithms
c. to understand what is meant by the stack frame associated with a function or function call
d. to understand the role of the system stack in processing calls made to a recursive function, particularly a function that is not tail recursive
e. to trace the contents of the system stack during execution of recursive functions with only one embedded recursive call

Any recursive algorithm must have a well-defined stopping state, or *termination condition*. Without careful logical control by means of such conditions, recursive functions can fall prey to looping in endless circles. To illustrate this, let us suppose that we have access to an output device known as a pen plotter. Such a device is equipped with a pen held by a mechanical hand that is under control of the computer.

Typical functions to manipulate the pen could include

Function	Action
`line(n)`	Draw a line of length *n* in the current direction.
`rightTurn(d)`	Alter current direction by rotating *d* degrees in clockwise direction.

Such functions are not unlike those found in the LOGO programming language or the "turtle" graphics toolkits that accompany many popular C++ compilers. If you have access to such a compiler, you may wish to explore developing some recursive graphic figures.

If we assume that the pen is initially set to draw a line toward the north—the top of the plotting page—then the following sequence of instructions

```
line(10);
rightTurn(90);
line(10);
rightTurn(90);
line(10);
rightTurn(90);
line(10);
```

will clearly draw a square with sides of length 10. Let us now try to predict what will happen when the following recursive function `draw` is invoked by the initial call `draw(1)`.

```
void draw(int side)
{
    line(side);
    rightTurn(90);
    draw(side + 3)         // Recursive call
};
```

The initial call `draw(1)` will result in a line of length 1 in a northerly direction. We rotate the pen toward the east and, via a recursive call, generate a line of length 4. This is followed by a rotation to the south and a new invocation for a line of length 7. The emerging pattern should now be clear; the resulting right-angled spiral is shown in Figure 14.1. Unfortunately, our spiral-producing function has tumbled into a vicious circle loop of self-reference. There is currently no way to turn off the *recursive calls* made to draw. Consider what happens, however, if we provide ourselves with a *recursive termination condition* as in the following new version of `draw`:

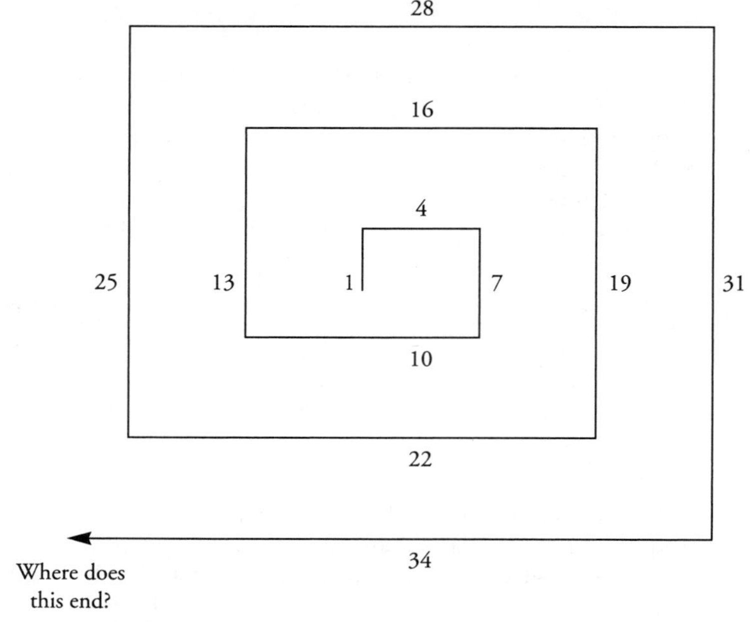

Figure 14.1
Runaway recursive spiral

```
void draw(int side)
{
  if (side <= 34)          // Recursive termination condition
  {
       line(side);
       rightTurn(90);
       draw(side + 3)      // Recursive call
   }
}
```

Now after drawing the line of length 34 in Figure 14.1, our `draw` function invokes itself once more, passing 37 for the parameter `side`. Since the recursive termination condition is now `false`, no line of length 37 will be drawn. More important, no further recursive invocation of `draw` will be made. Hence, we return immediately from the call to `draw` with `side` being 37. Moreover, that return triggers returns (in reverse order) from all the previous invocations of `draw`, eventually ending up at the instruction following our initial call; that is, `draw(1)`.

The important point to stress here is that, to use recursion appropriately, we must use a recursive termination condition to avoid an infinite series of recursive calls. If we were to view each recursive call as a descent one level deeper into an algorithm's logic, we in effect must use a recursive termination condition to allow a corresponding ascent back to the level of the first call to the function. This concept is highlighted in Figure 14.2.

Linked Lists as Recursive Data Structures

In Section 12.1, we defined the linked list ADT. We can now reformulate that definition from a recursive perspective. The key to such a perspective is the realization that the pointer leading from each linked list node references another linked list. More formally:

Figure 14.2 Unwinding from descent through recursive calls

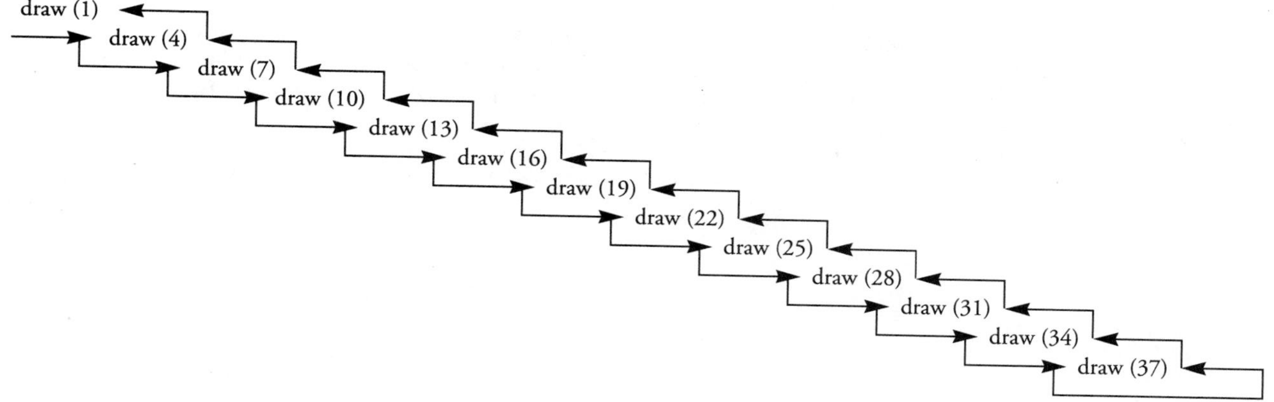

Figure 14.3 Recursive view of a linked list

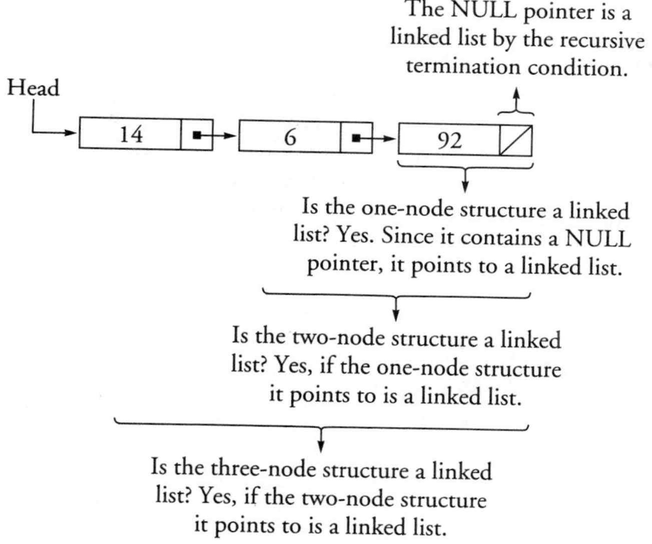

Linked list: A linked list is a pointer that is either null (the recursive termination condition signaling an empty list) or references a node designated as the head node. The head node contains a data field and a pointer that satisfies the criteria for being a linked list.

Although an English composition teacher may find fault with our defining a linked list in terms of itself, our new definition is nonetheless completely free of ambiguity. For instance, to verify that the list in Figure 14.3 is a linked list, we note the following:

1. The head node in the three-item structure contains a pointer to an embedded two-item structure, which we must verify as a linked list.
2. The head node in the two-item structure contains a pointer to an embedded one-item structure.
3. The head node in the one-node structure contains a null pointer.
4. By the recursive termination condition, a null pointer meets the criteria for being a linked list.
5. Hence, the one-node structure in step 3 contains a pointer to a linked list and meets the criteria for being a linked list.

6. Similarly, we climb up the recursive ladder to verify that the two-node and, consequently, the three-node structures in steps 1 and 2 meet the criteria for being linked lists.

Not only does our recursive definition unambiguously specify the linked list ADT, but it also provides a natural way to implement linked list operations by recursive functions. Consider the following example.

Example 14.1 A linked list of integers is implemented by C++ pointer variables in the following declarations:

```
struct node
{
  int data;
  node * next;
};
```

Develop a recursive implementation of a function that receives a pointer to the head node of the list and then traverses the list, printing the integer in each node.

The implementation of such a function literally flows from our recursive definition of the linked list structure. That is, if the list we are traversing is empty, there is nothing to do; otherwise, we must process the data in the head node and recursively traverse the linked list referenced by the `next` field in the head node. This logic is embodied in the following C++ function:

```
void traverse(node * head)
{
  if (head != 0)
  {
       cout << head->data << endl;
       traverse(head->next);
  }
}
```

A trace of the recursive function `traverse` for the list of Figure 14.3 is given in Figure 14.4. This trace shows that the function is initially called with a list pointer to the node containing 14. The data are processed, and the first recursive call then passes in a pointer to the node containing 6. Data item 6 is processed, and a pointer to the node containing 92 is recursively passed to the function. The node containing 92 is processed, and a null pointer is recursively passed to the function. Since the recursive termination condition `(head == 0)` is now met, we unwind from the series of recursive calls. As we return to each prior recursive level, there is nothing left to do since the recursive call is the last operation at that level.

A recursive function is called *tail recursive* if only one recursive call appears in the function and that recursive call is the last operation performed at that procedural level. (That is, nothing else must be done after returning from a deeper recursive level.) The `traverse` function of Example 14.1 is clearly tail recursive. Typically, such a tail-recursive function can be easily recast in the form of a nonrecursive function using a `while` or `do` control structure. We have already seen how to do this for `traverse` in Chapter 12.

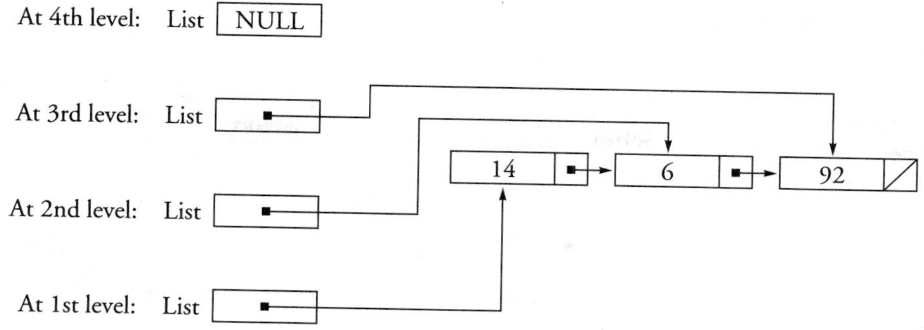

Figure 14.4
Trace of recursive function traverse on the linked list of Figure 14.3

How Is Recursion Implemented?

As we begin to examine recursive algorithms that are not tail recursive, we will also need to understand in detail how a computer language implements recursion. Here again, we encounter the abstraction/implementation duality we have emphasized throughout the book. Recursion is a powerful conceptual tool. But unless you understand details of how recursion is implemented, your use of it will be limited to an intuitive approach that often employs a trial-and-error strategy to reach a solution.

In Section 13.1, we indicated that the stack is an essential data structure in a compiler's implementation of function calls. The role of a system stack being manipulated by the function calls in your program becomes even more crucial as we use recursion. To illustrate this, let us consider a problem more computationally oriented than our previous graphics and linked list examples. N factorial, denoted $N!$, is defined by

$$N! = N \times (N-1) \times (N-2) \times \ldots \times 2 \times 1$$

That is, $N!$ is the product of the first N integers. We note that an alternative way of defining $N!$ is by means of using $(N-1)!$

$$N! = \begin{cases} 1 \text{ if } N = 1 \text{ or } N = 0 \\ N \times (N-1)! \text{ otherwise} \end{cases}$$

Notice that this alternative definition is recursive because it uses the notion of factorial to define factorial. Despite this circularity, we have a perfectly valid definition because of the recursive termination condition in the special definition of 1!.

To see how recursion works for factorial computation, think of the preceding definition as a series of clues that will eventually allow us to unravel the mystery of how to compute $N!$. That is, to compute $N!$, the recursive definition tells us to

1. Remember what N is.
2. Go compute $(N-1)!$.
3. Once we've computed $(N-1)!$, multiply that by N to get our final answer.

Of course, when we use the definition to determine how to compute $(N-1)!$, we find out that we must in turn compute $(N-2)!$. Computing $(N-2)!$ will involve finding $(N-3)!$. This downward spiral will eventually end with 1!, allowing us to begin the actual series of multiplications that will bring us to the appropriate answer. Figure 14.5 illustrates the logic of the recursive method for computing N factorial. In particular, if N were 4, the sequence of recursive invocations of the definition and resulting computations would be as shown in Figure 14.6. The program in Example 14.2 calls a recursively defined `factorial` function. The associated run indicates the behavior of the program for an input of 4.

Figure 14.5 Recursive computation of N!

Initial directive to compute N!

Remember N
Compute $(N-1)$!

Remember $N-1$
Compute $(N-2)$!

. . .

Remember 3
Compute 2!

Remember 2
Compute 1!

1! is 1

Hence, 2! = 2 × 1 = 2

Hence, 3! = 3 × 2! = 3 × 2 = 6

. . .

Hence, $(N-1)! = (N-1) \times (N-2)!$

Hence, $N! = N \times (N-1)!$

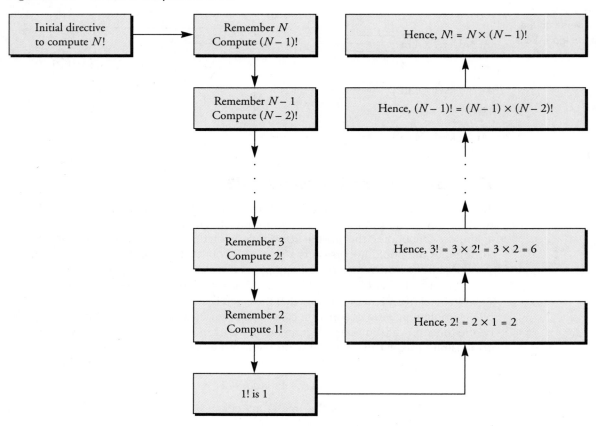

Figure 14.6 Recursive computation of 4!

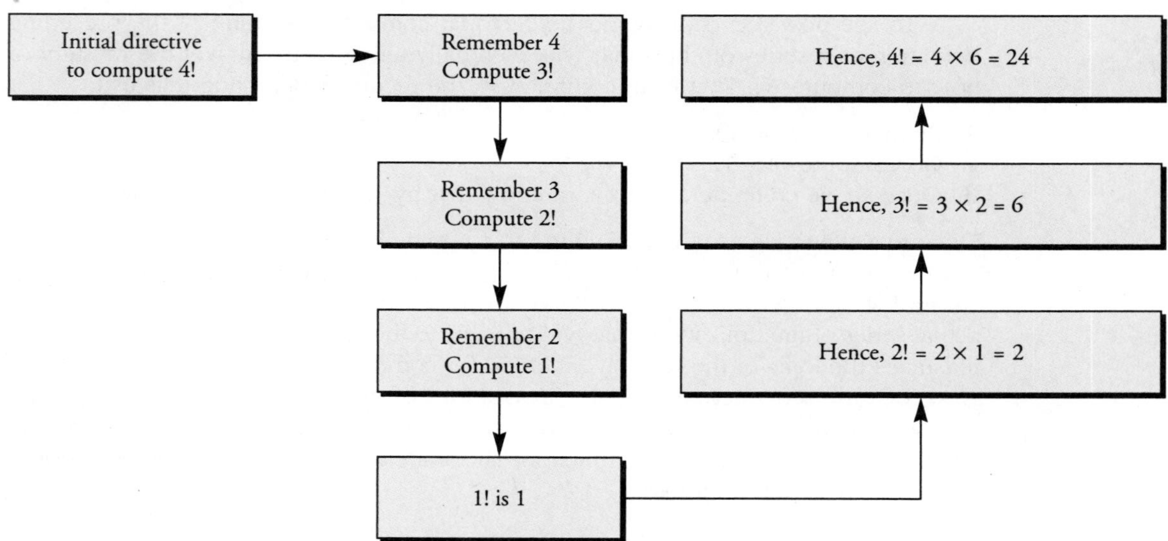

Example 14.2

```
// Program file: factor.cpp

#include <iostream.h>
#include <iomanip.h>

int indent = 0;

int factorial(int n);

int main()
{
   int m;

   cout << "ENTER NUMBER for FACTORIAL COMPUTATION--> ";
   cin >> m;
   cout << factorial(m) << endl;      // Return Point 1

   return 0;
}

int factorial(int n)
{
   int result;

   cout << setw(indent) << "" << "ENTERING FACTORIAL WITH N = " << n << endl;
   if ((n == 1) || (n == 0))
   {
      cout << setw(indent) << "" << "LEAVING FACTORIAL WITH N = " << n;
      cout << ", FACTORIAL(N) = " << 1 << endl;
      --indent;
      return 1;
   }
   else
   {
      ++indent;
                    // Return Point 2
                    ↓
      result = n * factorial(n - 1);
      cout << setw(indent) << "" << "LEAVING FACTORIAL WITH N = " << n;
      cout << ", FACTORIAL(N) = " << result << endl;
      --indent;
      return result;
   }
}
```

A sample run for the preceding code is:

```
ENTER NUMBER for FACTORIAL COMPUTATION--> 4
ENTERING FACTORIAL WITH N = 4
 ENTERING FACTORIAL WITH N = 3
  ENTERING FACTORIAL WITH N = 2
   ENTERING FACTORIAL WITH N = 1
```

continued

```
   LEAVING FACTORIAL WITH N = 1, FACTORIAL(N) = 1
  LEAVING FACTORIAL WITH N = 2, FACTORIAL(N) = 2
 LEAVING FACTORIAL WITH N = 3, FACTORIAL(N) = 6
LEAVING FACTORIAL WITH N = 4, FACTORIAL(N) = 24
24
```

The output statements used on entry to and exit from function `factorial` in Example 14.2 are not necessary but have been included to demonstrate the precise call and return sequence triggered by the initial call of `factorial(4)` in the main program. It is crucial to note that the output from `cout` statements implies that we must in some sense have multiple copies of the variable N, one copy for each descent to a recursively deeper level. As we shall see, a stack keeps track of these multiple copies of N in the appropriate fashion.

It is also important to emphasize that function `factorial` would not be tail recursive even if the output statements were removed. This is because the recursive call to `factorial` is not the last operation performed by the algorithm. After a return from the call to `factorial` $(N-1)$, we must multiply by N. This multiplication is the final operation performed. The fact that we multiply by N after returning from a recursive call indicates that, for algorithms that are not tail recursive, we must have some means of preserving the values of parameters and local variables at each level of the recursive execution of the algorithm.

The comments `// Return Point 1` and `// Return Point 2` in Example 14.2 will allow us to trace the role played by a stack as this program is run. We have already alluded to the existence of a general system stack onto which return addresses are pushed each time a function or function call is made. Let us now explain it more fully. Each time a function or function call is made, an item called a *stack frame* or *activation record* will be pushed onto the system stack. The data in this stack frame consist of the return address and a copy of each local variable and parameter for the function. Figure 14.7 illustrates how stack frames are pushed and popped from the system stack when `factorial(4)` is invoked. Return addresses have been indicated by referring to the appropriate comments in the C++ code.

Although function `factorial` of Example 14.2 provides an illustration of an algorithm that is not tail recursive, you could still validly argue that the computation of $N!$ could be achieved more easily by a nonrecursive, iterative loop structure. To sense the real power and elegance of recursion, we must begin to explore algorithms that more subtly manipulate the stack frames hidden below the surface of recursive processing. These stack frames provide us with a "free" stack data structure; that is, a structure that we need not declare formally and that we control completely by the recursive calling pattern of our algorithm.

Exercises 14.1

1. Stand between two parallel mirrors and see how recursion works for you.

2. Consider the following pair of functions to compute $N!$

```
int factorial(int n)
{
  return factHelper(n, 1);
}
int factHelper(int n, int result)
{
```

continued

Figure 14.7
Sequence of pushes and pops in computing 4!

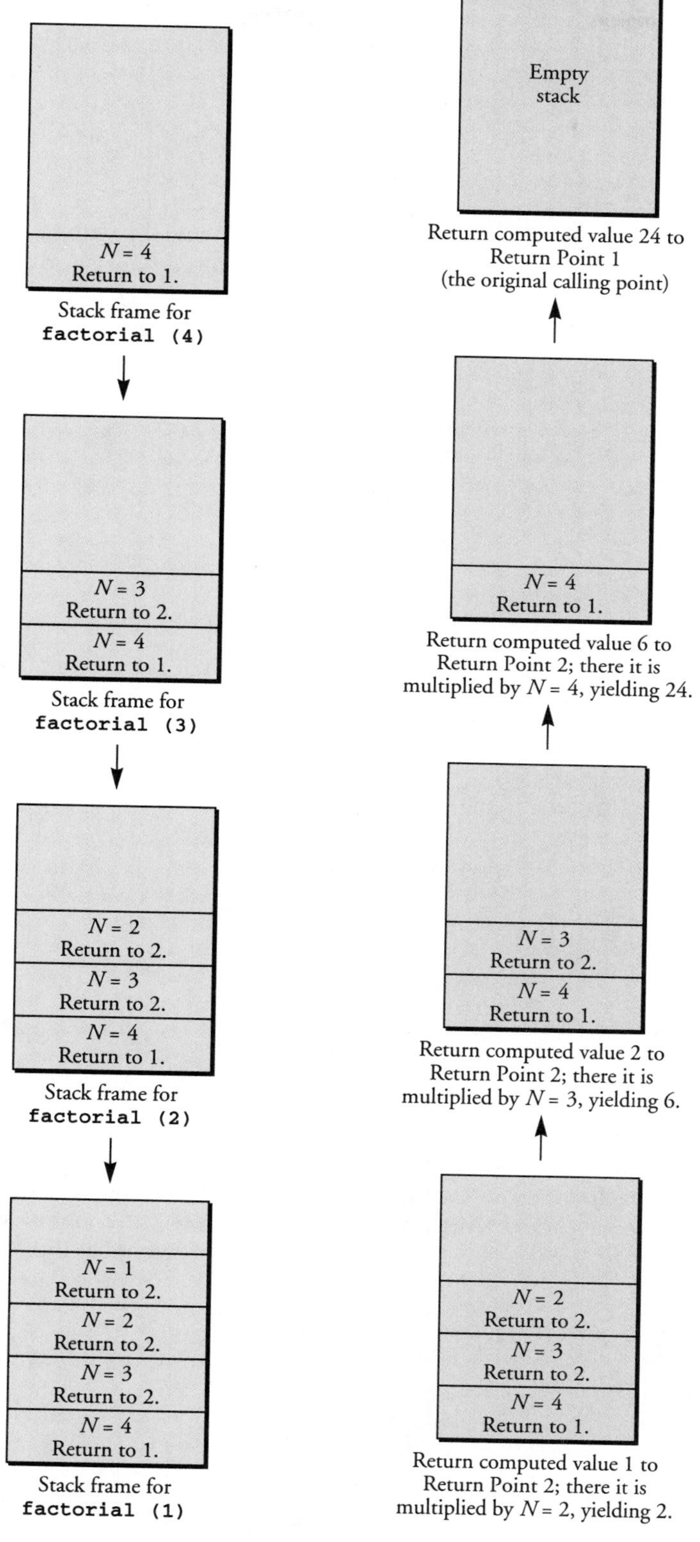

```
    if ((n ==0) || (n == 1))
         return result;
    else
         return factHelper(n - 1, n * result);
}
```

Is `factHelper` tail recursive? Will it work? Explain why or why not.

3. Each of the following functions offers a slight variation on the `traverse` function developed in Example 14.1. For each function, indicate what output would be produced if the function were called initially with the linked list of Figure 14.3. If the function would crash with a run-time error for the data of Figure 14.3 or any other test case, explain why.

a.
```
void traverse(node * head)
{
  if (head != 0)
  {
       traverse(head->next);
       cout << head->data << endl;
  }
}
```

b.
```
void traverse(node * head)
{
  cout << head->data << endl;
  if (head->next != 0)
       traverse(head->next);
}
```

c.
```
void traverse(node * head)
{
  if (head->next != 0)
  {
       cout << head->data << endl;
       traverse(head->next);
  }
}
```

4. Which of the functions in Exercise 3 are tail recursive?

5. The following programs are intended to read a string character by character, put each character on the system stack, and then print the string of characters in reverse order. Which one(s) actually achieve the intent? Which one(s) don't? Why not? What will be the output of each program for input of 'MADAM'?

a.

```
// Print out a string in reverse order to check if palindrome
#include <iostream.h>
void reverse();

int main()
{
    reverse();
```

```
    return 0;
}

// Keep recursively stacking characters until end of string.
// Then print it out in reverse by unstacking.
void reverse()
{
    char ch;      // Here ch is locally declared

    cin.get(ch);
    if (ch != '\n')
    {
           reverse();
           cout.put(ch);
    }
    else
           cout.put('\n');
}
```

b.

```
// Print out a string in reverse order to check if palindrome
#include <iostream.h>
char ch;                      // Here ch is globally declared
void reverse();

int main()
{
    reverse();
    return 0;
}

// Keep recursively stacking characters until end of string.
// Then print it out in reverse by unstacking.
void reverse()
{
    cin.get(ch);
    if (ch != '\n')
    {
           reverse();
           cout.put(ch);
    }
    else
           cout.put('\n');
}
```

6. Given the declarations for the linked list structure in Example 14.1, write a recursive function to search the list for a particular item and return a pointer to the item in the list if it is found. If the item is not found in the list, a null pointer should be returned.

7. Suppose that `NumberArray` is declared as follows:

```
typedef int NumberArray[100];
```

Study the following function and determine what it computes. (*Hint:* Try to trace it for several small instances of the array and N values.)

```
int compute(NumberArray a, int n)
{
    if (n == 0)
        return a[n];
    else if (a[n] < compute(a, n - 1))
        return a[n];
    else
        return compute(a, n - 1);
}
```

8. Write a recursive function of two integer arguments M and N, both greater than or equal to 0. The function should return M^N.
9. Write a recursive function of two integer arguments M and N, $M > 1$ and $N > 0$. The function should return the integer log of N to the base M. This is defined to be the least integer L such that $M^{L+1} > N$. (*Hint:* Although your function only receives two arguments, have it call an auxiliary function of three arguments—M, N, and L. Call on the auxiliary function initially with $L = 0$; the auxiliary function is then called recursively.)
10. Given the declaration of `NumberArray` in Exercise 7, write a recursive function `product` that receives two arguments, one of type `NumberArray` and another argument `n` that indicates the logical size of `NumberArray`. Remember that the logical size of an array is the number of indices that store well-defined data items. The recursive function `product` should return the product of the entries in the array.
11. Insert tracer output instructions at strategic points and use them to debug the following version of a function, which attempts to compute factorials recursively. After you've debugged the function, write a statement in which you explain the behavior of the function as originally coded and also why the function did not work in this original form.

```
int factorial(int n)
{
    if ((n == 0) || (n == 1))
        return 1;
    else
    {
        --n;
        return n * factorial(n);
    }
}
```

14.2 Weaving More Complex Recursive Patterns

The recursive algorithms we have examined so far share the property that, at each level of recursive execution of the algorithm, at most one recursive call will be made. The pattern of operations on the system stack for such algorithms is that a series of stack frames is pushed, a recursive termination condition is reached, and then all stack frames are successively popped until we return to the execution level of the main program. More complex recursive algorithms involve multiple recursive calls at each level

Objectives

a. to recognize problems particularly suited to recursive solutions
b. to state the solutions to such problems as a simpler instance of the same problem
c. to trace the performance of a recursive algorithm using a run-time trace diagram
d. to use an algorithm's run-time trace diagram to estimate the time and space efficiency of the algorithm
e. to see how recursive algorithms that potentially involve more than one recursive call at each level may lead to an exponential time efficiency
f. to develop an intuitive approach for developing recursive solutions to problems

of execution. Correspondingly, the pattern of operations on the system stack will not be a series of uninterrupted pushes followed by a series of uninterrupted pops. Instead, the system stack will initially grow a bit, then shrink, then grow again, then shrink, and so forth.

Towers of Hanoi Problem

An old legend has it that monks in a Hanoi monastery were given the painstaking task of moving a collection of n stone disks from one pillar, designated as pillar A, to another, designated as pillar C. Moreover, the relative ordering of the disks on pillar A had to be maintained as they were moved to pillar C. That is, as illustrated in Figure 14.8, the disks, all of different sizes, were to be stacked from largest to smallest, beginning from the bottom. Additionally, the monks were to observe the following rules in moving disks:

- Only one disk could be moved at a time.
- No larger disk could ever be placed on top of a smaller disk on any pillar.
- A third pillar B could be used as an intermediate to store one or more disks while they were being moved from their original source A to their destination C.

Consider the following recursive solution to this problem:

1. If $n = 1$, merely move the disk from A to C.
2. If $n = 2$, move the first disk from A to B. Then move the second disk from A to C. Then move the first disk from B to C.
3. If $n = 3$, call on the technique already established in step 2 to move the first two disks from A to B using C as an intermediate. Then move the third disk from A to C. Then use the technique in step 2 to move the first two disks from B to C using A as an intermediate

.
.
.

n. For general n, use the technique in the previous step to move $n - 1$ disks from A to B using C as an intermediate. Next move one disk from A to C. Then use the technique in the previous step to move $n - 1$ disks from B to C using A as an intermediate.

Notice that this technique for solving the Towers of Hanoi describes itself in terms of a simpler version of itself. That is, it describes how to solve the problem for n disks in terms of a solution for $n - 1$ disks. In general, any problem you hope to solve recursively must be approached in this fashion. This strategy is important enough to state as a principle.

Figure 14.8
Towers of Hanoi problem

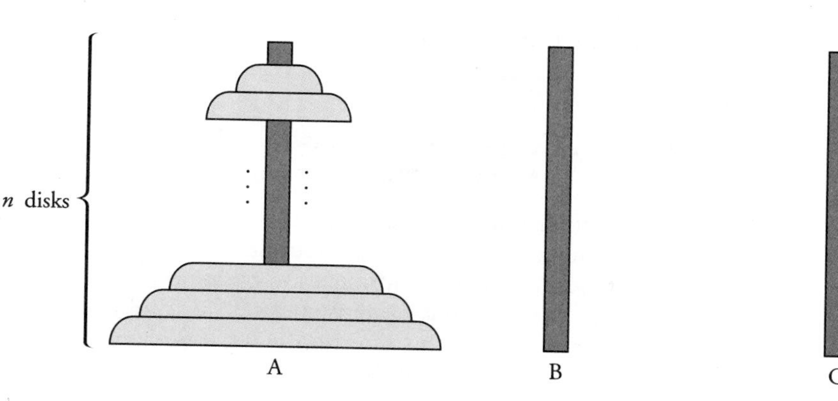

A NOTE OF INTEREST

Recursion Need Not Be Expensive

We have seen that the use of recursion has two costs: Extra time and extra memory are required to manage recursive function calls. These costs have led some to argue that recursion should never be used in programs. However, as Guy Steele has shown in "Debunking the 'Expensive Procedure Call' Myth," *Proceedings of the National Conference of the ACM*, 1977, some systems can run recursive algorithms as if they were iterative ones with no additional overhead. The key condition is to write a special kind of recursive function called a tail-recursive function. A function is tail recursive if no work is done in the function after a recursive call. For example, according to this criterion, the factorial function that we presented earlier is not tail recursive because a multiplication is performed after each recursive call. We can convert this version of the factorial function to a tail-recursive version by performing the multiplication before each recursive call. To do this, we will need an additional parameter that passes the accumulated value of the factorial down on each recursive call. In the last call of the function, this value is returned as the result:

```
int factIter(int n, int result)
{
    if (n == 1)
           return result;
    else
           return factIter(n - 1, n * result);
}
```

Note that the multiplication is performed before the recursive call of the function, when its parameters are evaluated. When the function is initially called, the value of `result` should be 1:

```
int factorial(int n)
{
    return factIter(n, 1);
}
```

Steele showed that a smart compiler can translate tail-recursive code in a high-level language to a loop in machine language. The machine code treats the function parameters as variables associated with a loop and generates an iterative process rather than a recursive one. Thus, there is no linear growth of function calls, and extra stack memory is not required to run tail-recursive functions on these systems.

The catch is that a programmer must be able to convert a recursive function to a tail-recursive function and find a compiler that generates iterative machine code from tail-recursive functions. Unfortunately, some functions, such as the one used to solve the Towers of Hanoi problem, are difficult or impossible to convert to tail-recursive versions, and the compiler optimizations are not part of the standard definitions of many languages, among them C++. If you find that your C++ compiler supports this optimization, you should try converting some functions to tail-recursive versions and see if they run faster than the original versions.

Principle of recursive problem solving: When trying to solve a problem by recursion, always ask yourself, "What could I do if I had a solution to a simpler version of the same problem?"

If you can see how to use the solution to a smaller version of the problem in solving the original problem, you have hurdled your toughest obstacle. All that remains is to determine the recursive termination conditions. This can be done by answering the question, "Under what circumstances is this problem so simple that a solution is trivial?" Your answer to this question will define parameter values that trigger an immediate return from the recursive algorithm.

Example 14.3 Implement a C++ solution to the Towers of Hanoi problem. Our earlier discussion has indicated that the problem for *n* disks can be defined in terms of $n-1$ if we switch the roles played by certain pillars. This switching can be achieved by altering the order in which parameters are passed when recursive calls are made. When a value of 1 is passed in for *n*, we have reached the recursive termination condition. The comments `// Return Point 1` and `// Return Point 2` in the following C++ code will be used in a later trace of function `hanoi`.

```
void hanoi(int n, char source, char destination, char intermediate)
{
   if (n == 1)
      cout << Move disk from << source << to << destination;
   else
   {
      // In every recursive call hanoi works with n - 1

      hanoi(n - 1, source, intermediate, destination);    // Return Point 1
```

The first recursive call transfers $n-1$ disks from **source** to **intermediate**, using **destination** for temporary storage.
$n-1$
source
intermediate
destination

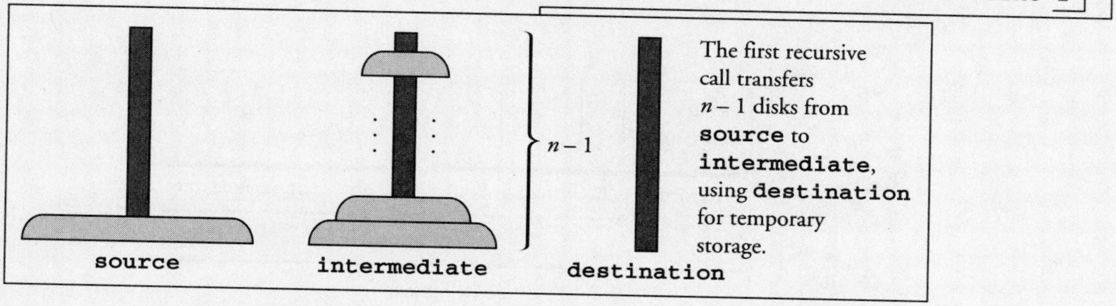

```
      cout << Move disk from << source << to << destination;
```

The single remaining disk is then transferred from **source** to **destination**.
$n-1$
source
intermediate
destination

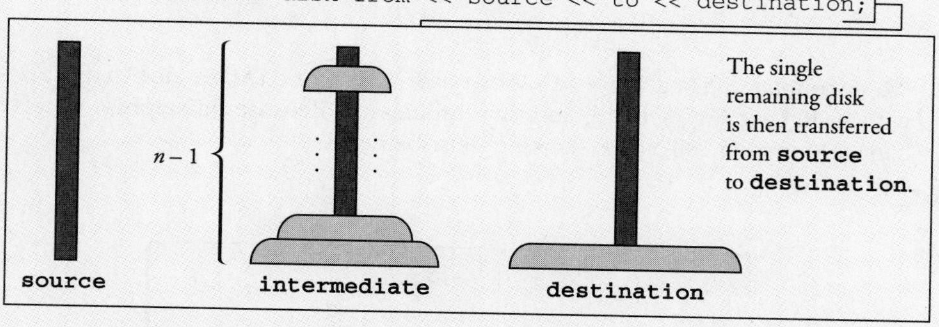

```
      hanoi(n - 1, intermediate, destination, source);    // Return Point 2
```

The second recursive call transfers $n-1$ disks from **intermediate** to **destination**, using **source** for temporary storage.
source
intermediate
destination

```
   }
}
```

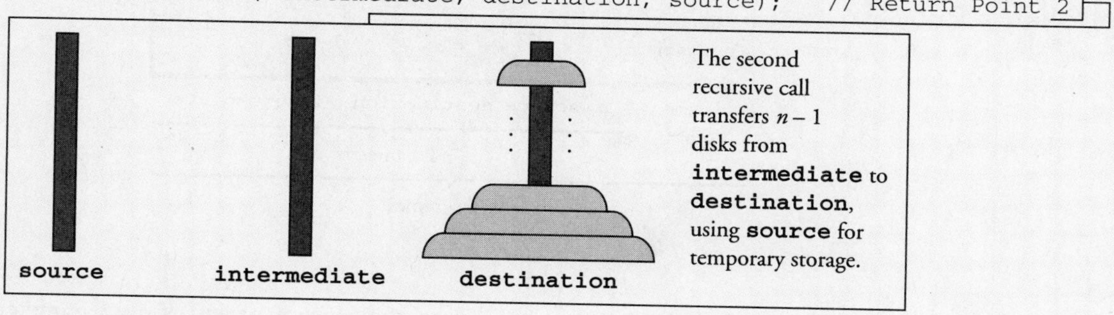

Unlike previously studied recursive algorithms in which only one recursive call was made each time the function was invoked, function `hanoi` will reinvoke itself twice each time it is called with $n > 1$. The result is a more complicated algorithm that could not be implemented easily by using mere iterative control structures. Implicitly, through its recursive calls, function `hanoi` is weaving an intricate pattern of push and pop operations on the system stack.

Example 14.4 To illustrate, we trace through the actions affecting the system stack when a call of the form

```
hanoi(3, 'A', 'C', 'B');
```

is initiated. The values in the return address portion of the stack are the documentary `// Return Point` labels in our `hanoi` function.

1. We enter `hanoi` with the following stack frame. `n` is not 1, so the condition in the `if` statement is `false`.

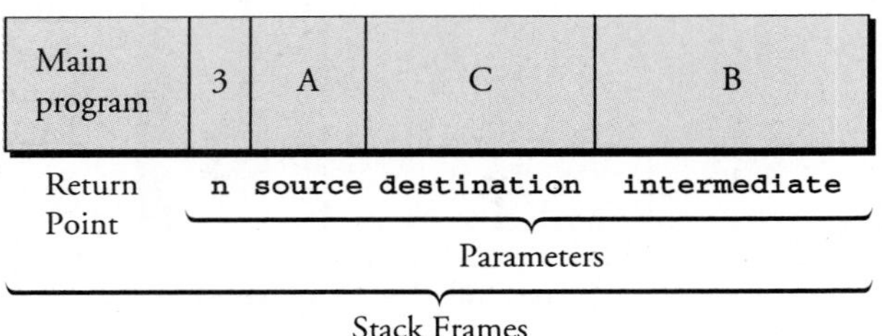

2. We encounter `hanoi(n - 1, source, intermediate, destination)` with A, B, C as first, second, and third arguments. Because this represents a (recursive) function call, some stacking must be done.

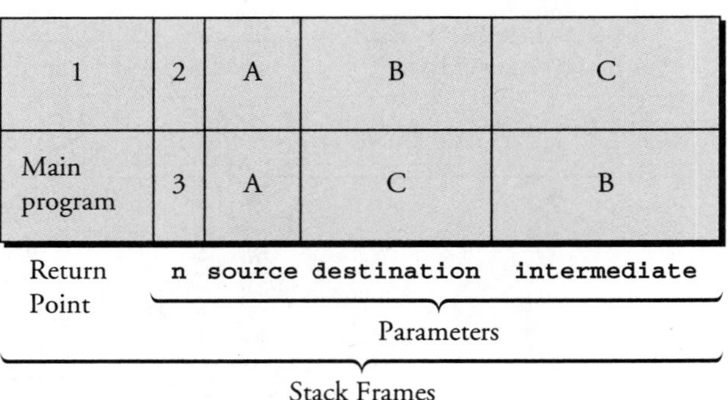

3. We reenter `hanoi`. As we enter it this time, the function's view of the parameters is `n` = 2, `source` = A, `destination` = B, and `intermediate` = C. Because `n` is not 1, the condition in the `if` statement is `false`.

4. We encounter `hanoi(n - 1, source, intermediate, destination)`. Because this is a recursive call, stacking occurs.

Return Point	n	source	destination	intermediate
1	1	A	C	B
1	2	A	B	C
Main program	3	A	C	B

Parameters

Stack Frames

5. We reenter `hanoi` with `n = 1`, `source` = A, `destination` = C, and `intermediate` = B. Because `n` = 1, the condition in the `if` statement is `true`.
6. Hence,

```
Move disk from A to C
```

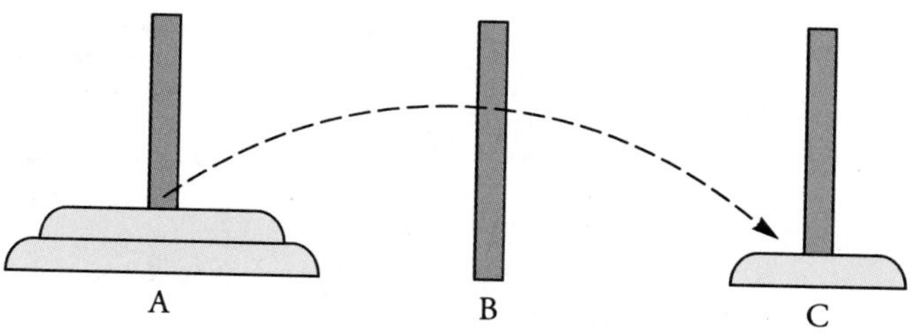

is printed and a return triggers a popping of a return address (1) and four parameters, leaving the system stack as follows:

Return Point	n	source	destination	intermediate
1	2	A	B	C
Main program	3	A	C	B

Parameters

Stack Frames

7. Because the return address popped was 1

```
Move disk from A to B
```

is printed and

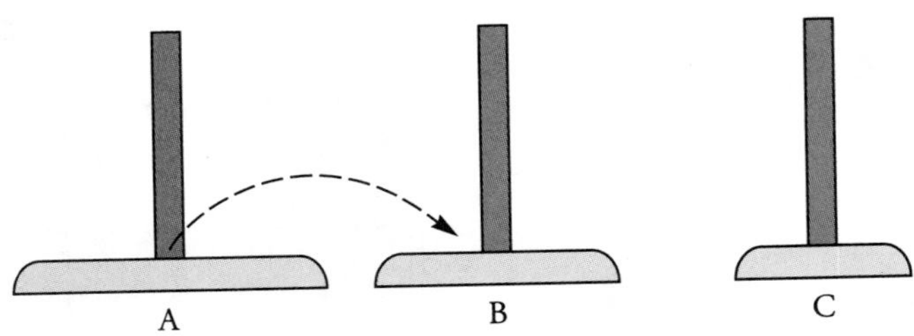


```
hanoi(n - 1, intermediate, destination, source)
```

is encountered with `n` = 2, `source` = A, `destination` = B, and `intermediate` = C.

8. The call pushes a return address and four parameters onto the system stack.

Return Point	n	source	destination	intermediate
2	1	C	B	A
1	2	A	B	C
Main program	3	A	C	B

Parameters (n, source, destination, intermediate)

Stack Frames

9. We reenter `hanoi`, this time with `n` = 1, `source` = C, `destination` = B, and `intermediate` = A.

10. Because `n` = 1, the `if` statement generates the output

```
Move disk from C to B
```

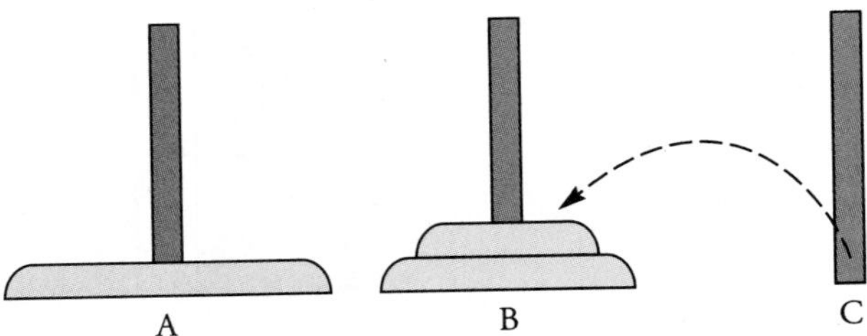

and a return.

11. The return pops a frame from the system stack and we then return to the statement labeled by 2 with `n` = 2, `source` = A, `destination` = B, and `intermediate` = C.

12. But statement 2 triggers a return itself, so a stack frame is popped again and we return to the statement labeled 1 with `n` = 3, `source` = A, `destination` = C, and `intermediate` = B.

13. Statement 1 triggers the output

```
Move disk from A to C
```

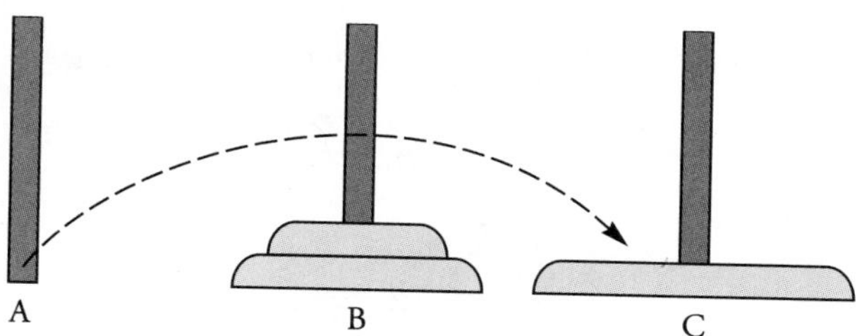

and we are immediately at another call

```
hanoi(n - 1, intermediate, destination, source)
```

Hence, the status of the system stack is changed to

Return Point	n	source	destination	intermediate
2	2	B	C	A
Main program	3	A	C	B

Parameters: n, source, destination, intermediate

Stack Frames

14. We reenter `hanoi` with `n` = 2, `source` = B, `destination` = C, and `intermediate` = A. Because `n` is not 1, another call is executed and more values are stacked.

Return Point	n	source	destination	intermediate
1	1	B	A	C
2	2	B	C	A
Main program	3	A	C	B

Parameters: n, source, destination, intermediate

Stack Frames

15. We reenter `hanoi` with `n` = 1, `source` = B, `destination` = A, and `intermediate` = C. Because `n` = 1, we print

```
Move disk from B to A
```

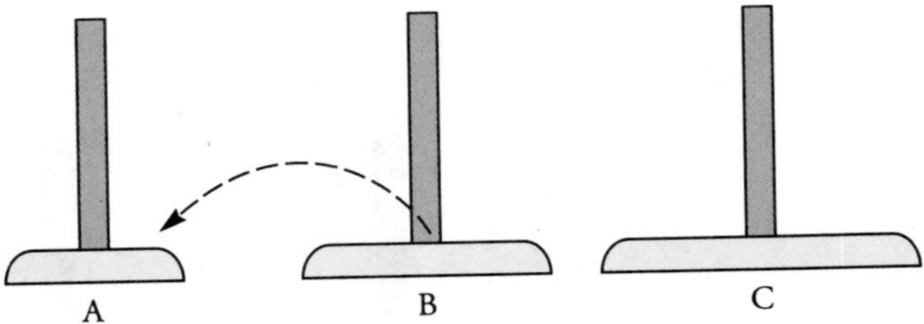

and return.

16. The return prompts the popping of the system stack. The return address popped is the statement labeled 1. Statement 1 causes output

```
Move disk from B to C
```

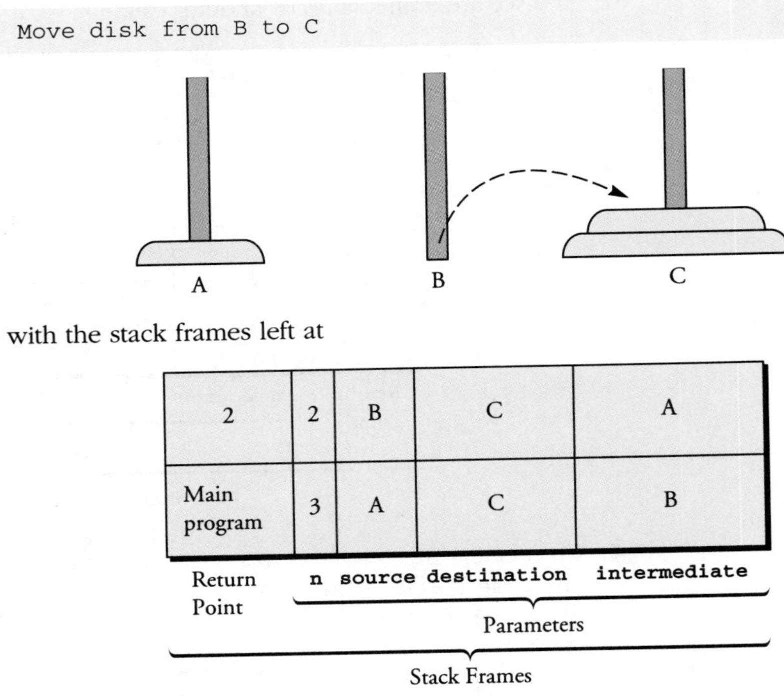

with the stack frames left at

Return Point	n	source	destination	intermediate
2	2	B	C	A
Main program	3	A	C	B

(n, source, destination, intermediate: Parameters; all columns: Stack Frames)

17. The output from statement 1 is followed by a recursive call

```
hanoi(n - 1, intermediate, destination, source)
```

Return Point	n	source	destination	intermediate
2	1	A	C	B
2	2	B	C	A
Main program	3	A	C	B

(n, source, destination, intermediate: Parameters; all columns: Stack Frames)

Hence, another frame is pushed onto the stack.

18. Finally, we reenter `hanoi` with `n` = 1, `source` = A, `destination` = C, and `intermediate` = B. Because `n` = 1, we output

```
Move disk from A to C
```

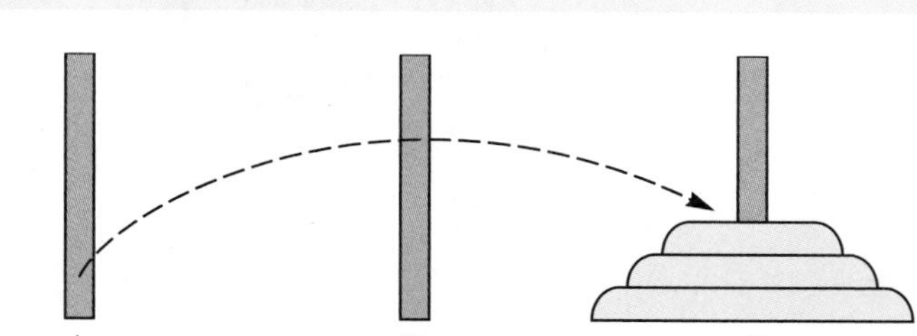

and return.

19. But now the return pops return address 2 from the stack, so return to statement 2 with the system stack given by

Return Point	n	source	destination	intermediate
2	2	B	C	A
Main program	3	A	C	B

Parameters

Stack Frames

20. Statement 2 is another return, so pop the stack again. The return address popped is 2, the same return point. But this time, the return will transfer control back to the original calling location—and we are done!

As long-winded as this example is, it is essential that you understand it. Recursive functions are crucial to many of the algorithms used in computer science, and you can acquire the necessary familiarity with recursion only by convincing yourself that it really works. If you have some doubt or are not sure you understand, we recommend that you trace through the `hanoi` function with `n` = 4 (be prepared to go through a lot of paper).

Efficiency Analysis of the Recursive Towers of Hanoi Algorithm

An analysis of the time and space efficiency of a recursive algorithm depends on two factors. First is the depth, that is, number of levels, to which recursive calls are made before reaching the recursive termination condition. Clearly, the greater the depth, the greater the number of stack frames that must be allocated and the less space efficient the algorithm becomes. It is also clear that recursive calls to a greater depth will consume more computer time and hence make the algorithm less time efficient. The second factor affecting efficiency analyses (particularly time efficiency) of recursive algorithms is the amount of resource (time or space) consumed at any given recursive level.

Figure 14.9 Generalized hierarchy of calls by recursive algorithm

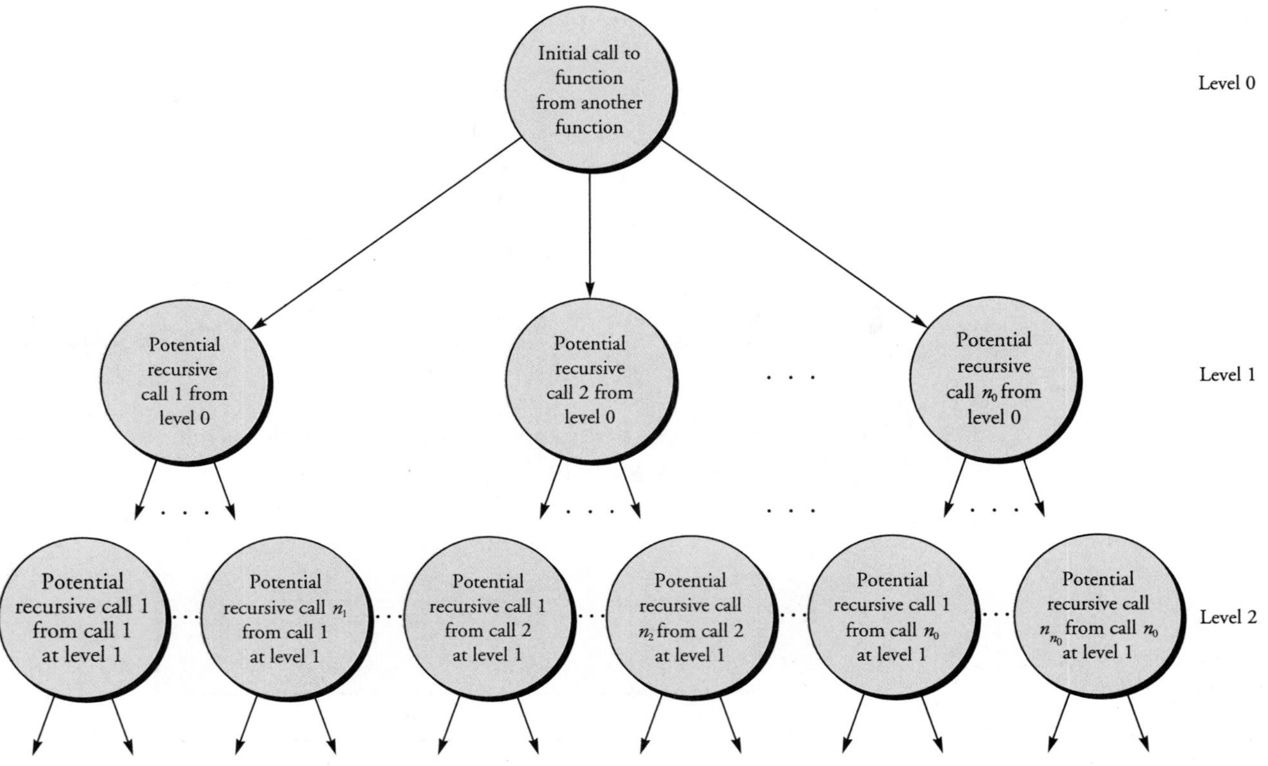

Figure 14.9 portrays this leveled view of a recursive algorithm as a hierarchy of the recursive calls that are (potentially) made as the algorithm executes. Such a hierarchy can be used as a diagrammatic model of the run-time behavior of a recursive algorithm. Consequently, we will call the hierarchy associated with the execution of a particular recursive program a *run-time trace diagram* for that algorithm. Figure 14.10 presents a run-time trace diagram for the Towers of Hanoi algorithm with `n` = 4 disks.

A run-time trace diagram can often be used in analyzing the time and space efficiency of an algorithm. We will provide two general principles for carrying out such analyses and then illustrate them in the context of the Towers of Hanoi algorithm.

Space efficiency of a recursive algorithm: Because a stack frame must be allocated at each level of recursive execution, the space efficiency of a recursive algorithm will be proportional to the deepest level at which a recursive call is made for a particular set of values, that is, the deepest level in its run-time trace diagram.

Time efficiency of a recursive algorithm: Because processing time is associated with each recursive call, the time efficiency of a recursive algorithm will be proportional to the sum, over all levels, of the times spent processing at each level.

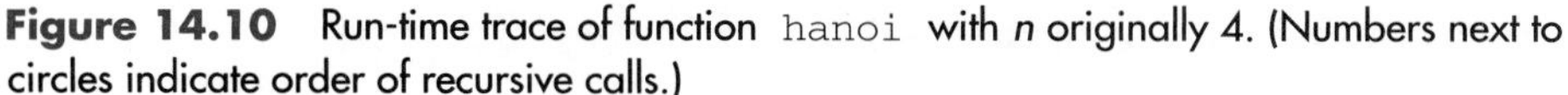

Figure 14.10 Run-time trace of function `hanoi` with *n* originally 4. (Numbers next to circles indicate order of recursive calls.)

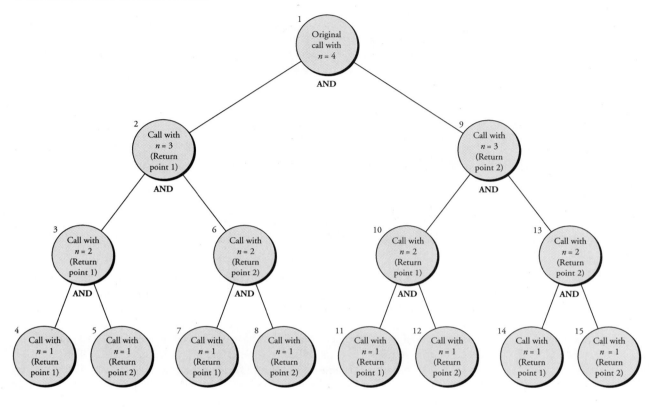

Example 14.5 Use the run-time trace diagram of function `hanoi` to analyze the time and space efficiency of the algorithm.

A graphic representation of this diagram for four disks is given in Figure 14.10. Note that the two calls descending from each call are linked by `AND`. This emphasizes that, when `n` is not 1, both potential recursive calls in the function `hanoi` will be made. The fact that both potential calls are made has a rather dramatic effect on the time efficiency of the algorithm. In particular, calling `hanoi` initially with `n` = 4 results in a total of 15 calls in the run-time trace. The numbers outside the circles in Figure 14.10 indicate the order in which these 15 calls are made. Increasing `n` to 5 in this figure adds an additional level with 16 calls to the run-time trace. In general, adding one disk adds only one level to the run-time trace diagram but doubles (plus 1) the number of calls in the diagram. This implies that the space efficiency of `hanoi` relative to the system stack is $O(n)$, but since every call in the run-time trace diagram will be made, the time efficiency is $O(2^n)$.

The analysis carried out in the preceding example demonstrates that the `hanoi` algorithm falls into the class of exponential algorithms as defined in Section 10.3. This is the first exponential algorithm we have encountered. Recall from our discussion of algorithm efficiency in Section 10.3 that such algorithms are impractical to run even for moderate values of `n`. We shall at this point complete the Hanoi legend by noting that, if the monks of Hanoi use the recursive algorithm that we have described here, the exponential efficiency of the algorithm ensures that the world will exist for many more centuries.

Recursive Implementation of the Binary Search Algorithm

Do not let our solution to the Towers of Hanoi problem mislead you into thinking that every recursive algorithm having more than one recursive call will be exponential in its efficiency. Consider, for example, a recursive formulation of the binary search algorithm. Recall the interface to this algorithm that we developed in Section 11.5:

```
// Function: binarySearch
// If data are found in list, return position of data, otherwise, return -1
//
// Inputs: A sorted list of data elements, the length of the list, and a
//           target key
// Outputs: Function returns target's position if target is found in
//           list, and -1 otherwise

int binarySearch(ListType list, int n, KeyType target);
```

The principle of recursive problem solving (stated in our discussion of the Towers of Hanoi problem) directs us to solve the binary search problem in terms of a simpler version of itself. Toward this end, we employ a perspective often used in recursive algorithms that act on an array: We view the algorithm as occurring between a certain subrange of array indices. For the binary search, that subrange is specified by `low...high`, where `low` is initially `0` and `high` is initially `n-1`. The "simpler version" of the binary search needed for a recursive statement of the algorithm is then a version that works on a smaller subrange of array indices. This subrange ultimately may become so small that it triggers the recursive termination condition for an unsuccessful search.

An intuitive recursive statement of the binary search logic then becomes:

If (recursive termination for unsuccessful search)
  Return –1 (and recursion terminated)
Else
  Compute middle index between low and high
  If (target is found at middle index)
    Search is successful (and recursion terminated by returning middle index)
  Else if (target is less than data at middle index)
      Recursively call with same low and middle –1 as high
    Else
      Recursively call with middle +1 as low and same high

According to this logic, the recursive calls result in a continual narrowing of the range to be searched until either the target is found or a recursive termination condition for an unsuccessful search is reached.

To determine what this unsuccessful recursive termination condition is, consider Figure 14.11. It portrays successive recursive calls on an array in which the target does not exist. The shaded regions of these array snapshots indicate the index subrange in which `target = 152` could possibly be found on successive recursive calls. Note that, on the fourth recursive call, no portion of the array is shaded; the condition `low > high` exists. This condition is therefore the recursive termination check for an unsuccessful search. The following example presents the code for the recursive binary search in its entirety.

Figure 14.11 Unsuccessful search for array with 15 key values

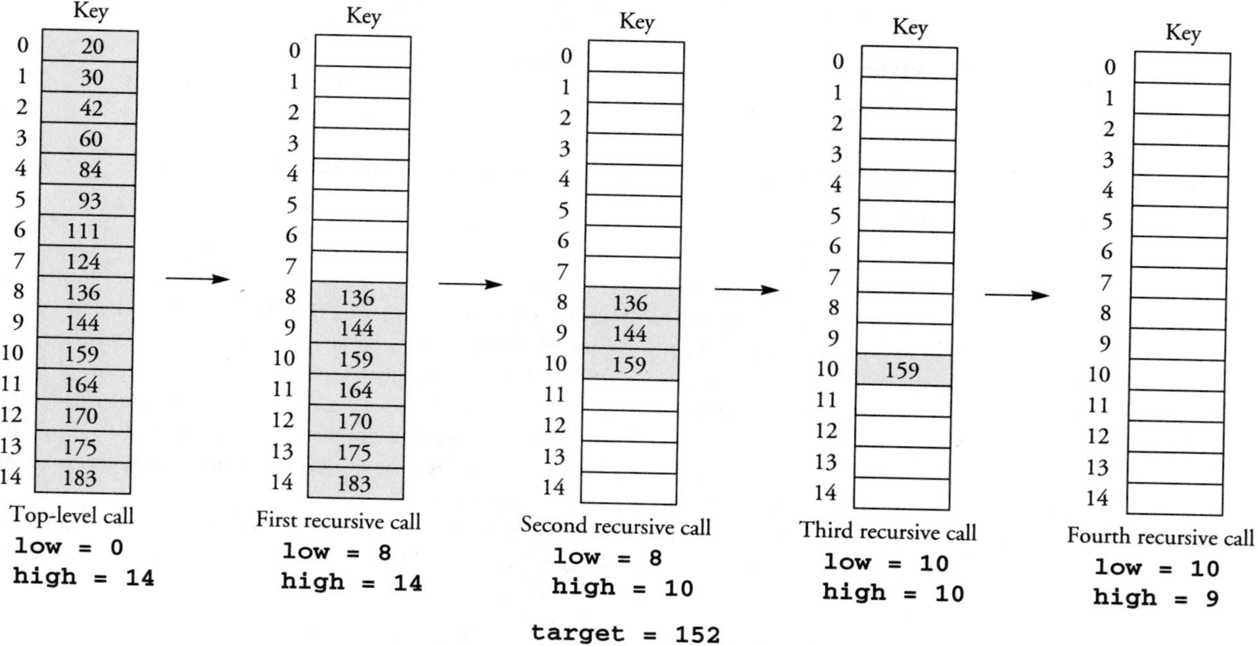

Example 14.6 Developing a recursive version of the binary search requires that we use an auxiliary function to work with the index subrange `low...high`. Using this auxiliary function will allow us to preserve the interface to function `binarySearch`. This interface should not require its user to pass in an initial low value of 0. Instead, the user need only pass in n, the number of objects in the list. From there, the front-end portion of function `binarySearch` need only call on its auxiliary function, passing in 0 for `low` and `n - 1` for `high`.

```
int binarySearch(ListType list, int n, KeyType target)
{
  return binarySearchAux(list, 0, n - 1, target);
}

int binarySearchAux(ListType list, int low, int high, KeyType target)

{
    int middle;

    if (low > high)
         return -1;
    else
    {
         middle = (low + high) / 2;
         if (list[middle] == target)
              return middle;
         else if (list[middle] > target)
              return binarySearchAux(list, low, middle - 1, target);
```

continued

```
        else
                return binarySearchAux(list, middle + 1, high, target);
    }
}
```

Efficiency Analysis of the Recursive Binary Search

As we did for the Towers of Hanoi problem, we will use a run-time trace diagram of potential recursive calls to analyze the efficiency of the recursive implementation of the binary search algorithm. This diagram appears in Figure 14.12. For the specific case of an array with 15 data items, the run-time trace stops at level 3, as indicated in Figure 14.13. The `OR`s that appear in these two figures are indicative of the fact that, at any given level, we will make at most one recursive call or the other but not both. This is important and, as we have seen, different from the `AND` pattern of recursive calls in the Towers of Hanoi problem. It implies that the work done at any given level is simply the work done at one node along that level.

In the binary search, the work done at any node is $O(1)$ since we are merely comparing the `target` item to the data at the `mid` position. Hence, the time effi-

Figure 14.12 Run-time trace diagram of potential calls for recursive binary search algorithm

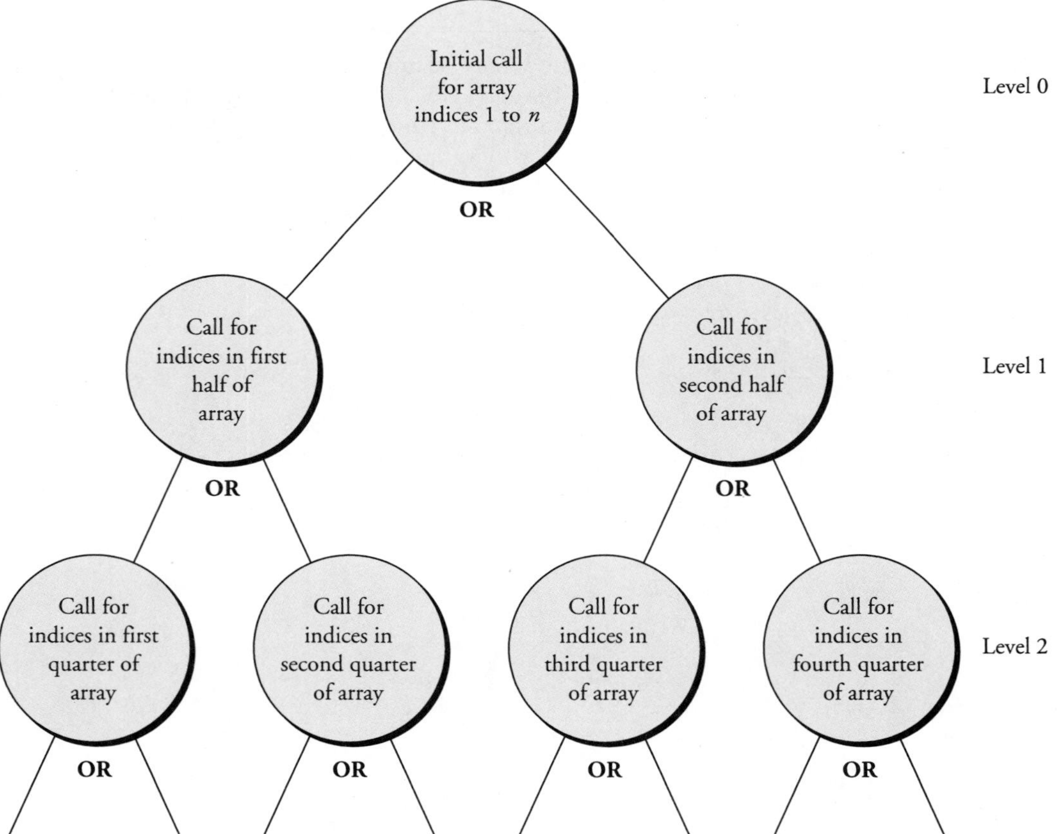

Figure 14.13 Trace of Figure 14.12 for specific case of array with 15 data items

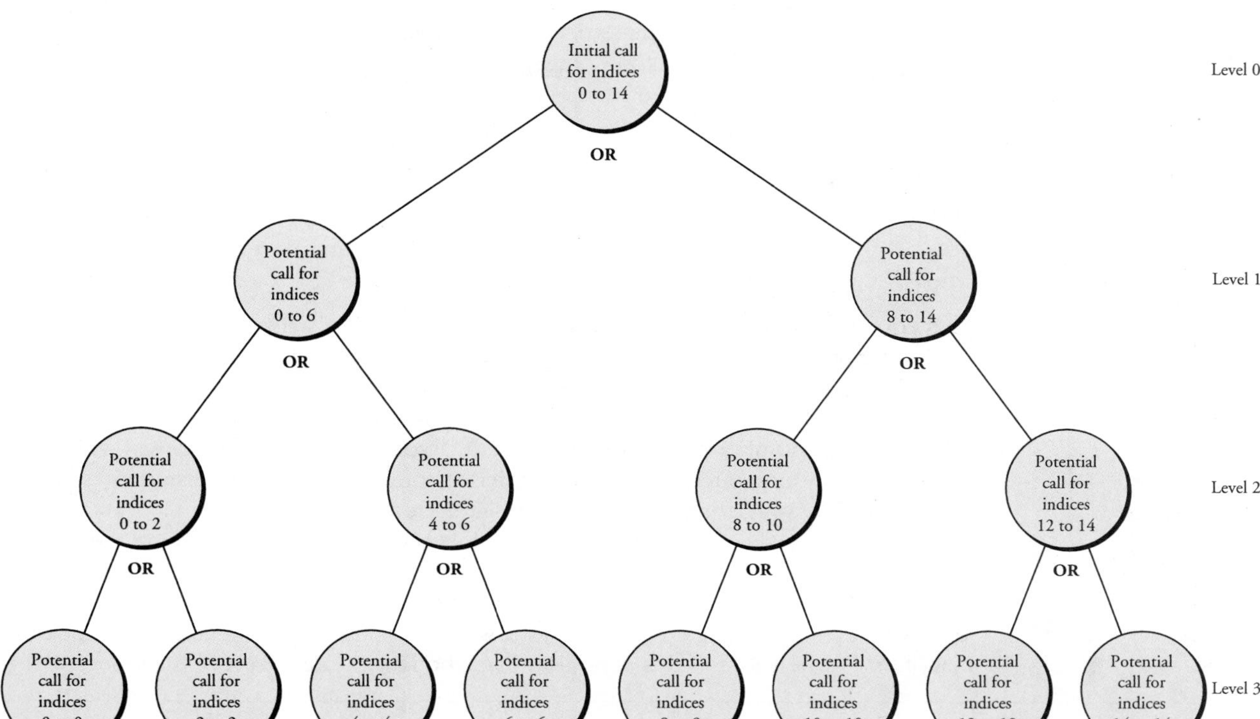

ciency of the recursive version of this algorithm will merely be proportional to the number of levels in the run-time trace for an array with n items. In Figures 14.12 and 14.13, we can see that doubling the number of items in the array will merely add one level to the run-time trace diagram. That is, the number of levels in the diagram is $\log_2 n + 1$ (truncated). With the $O(1)$ work done at each level, we can thus conclude that the time efficiency of a recursive binary search is $O(\log_2 n)$. Similarly, since a stack frame will be allocated for each recursive level, the additional space requirements of the algorithm (beyond the array itself) are $O(\log_2 n)$. Note that our earlier nonrecursive implementation of the binary search algorithm did not carry with it this additional cost in space efficiency.

Recursive Computation of "*N* Choose *K*"

The preceding discussion of the binary search algorithm has honed our ability to use the run-time trace diagram to measure the efficiency of a recursive algorithm. It did not, however, represent a solution to a problem that would be difficult to conceptualize without recursion. We close this section with an example in the latter category.

The phrase "*N* choose *K*" is often used in the combinatorics branch of mathematics to refer to the number of ways that we could choose *K* objects from among *N* different objects. For instance, "52 choose 13" represents the number of ways that you could be dealt a bridge hand (that is, 13 cards out of 52). We seek a recursive function to compute *N* choose *K* for arbitrary *N* and *K*, $K <= N$.

Our principle of recursive problem solving asks us to consider how we could use a solution to a simpler version of the same problem. For *N* choose *K*, a simpler version of the same problem could mean a solution for a smaller value of *N* or *K*. Let us designate our N objects as object #1, object #2, . . . , object #($N-1$), object #N. Figure 14.14 indicates that we can partition selections of K objects from these N as those groups of K objects that come strictly from objects #1, #2, . . . , #($N-1$) and those groups of K objects that include object #N in addition to K–1 chosen among objects #1, #2, . . . , #($N-1$). In other words,

$$\text{choose}(N, K) = \begin{cases} \text{choose}(N-1, K) & \text{(Ways of selecting } K \text{ objects from among the first } N-1\text{)} \\ +\ \text{choose}(N-1, K-1) & \text{(Ways of selecting } K-1 \text{ objects from among the first } N-1 \text{ and then including object \#}N\text{)} \end{cases}$$

This equation appears to be the recursive key we need to write our function. We need only develop recursive termination conditions to complete the puzzle. Note from the preceding equation that one of the terms being summed, `choose (N - 1, K)`, will recursively reduce N until it eventually equals K. But in such a case, we are merely asking for the number of combinations of N objects selected N at a time—and there is trivially only one such combination. Hence, our first recursive termination condition is when $N = K$, for which we immediately return the value 1.

To develop the second recursive termination condition, we examine the second term, `choose(N - 1, K - 1)`, in the sum. Since both `N` and `K` will be reduced by this recursion, K will eventually reach 0. But the number of ways of choosing 0 objects from among N is again trivially 1. Consequently, the second recursive termination condition is when $K = 0$; this condition flags the immediate return of the value of 1.

Example 14.7 Implement a recursive N choose K function based on the preceding discussion.

```
// Function: choose
// Computes N choose K, that is, the number of ways of selecting
//           K objects from N
//
// Inputs: N, the number of objects being selected from
//           and K, the number of objects being selected
// Outputs: The value of N choose K

int choose(int n, int k)
{
    if ((k == 0) || (n == k))
            return 1;
    else
            return choose(n - 1, k) + choose(n - 1, k - 1);
}
```

Figure 14.14 Formulating `choose(N, K)` in terms of `choose (N - 1, K)` and `choose(N - 1, K - 1)`

Any selection of $K-1$ objects from among these $N-1$ objects generates a selection of K objects by adding object #N to the $K-1$ selected.

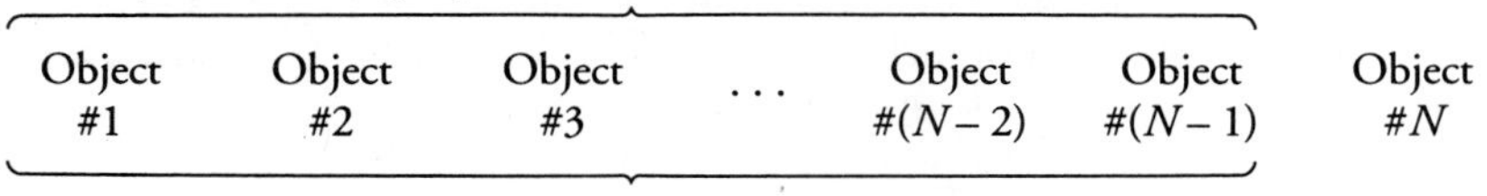

Object #1	Object #2	Object #3	. . .	Object #($N-2$)	Object #($N-1$)	Object #N

Any selection of K objects from among these $N-1$ objects is also a selection of K objects from among object #1 · · · object #N.

Figure 14.15 Run-time trace diagram for `choose(4, 2)`

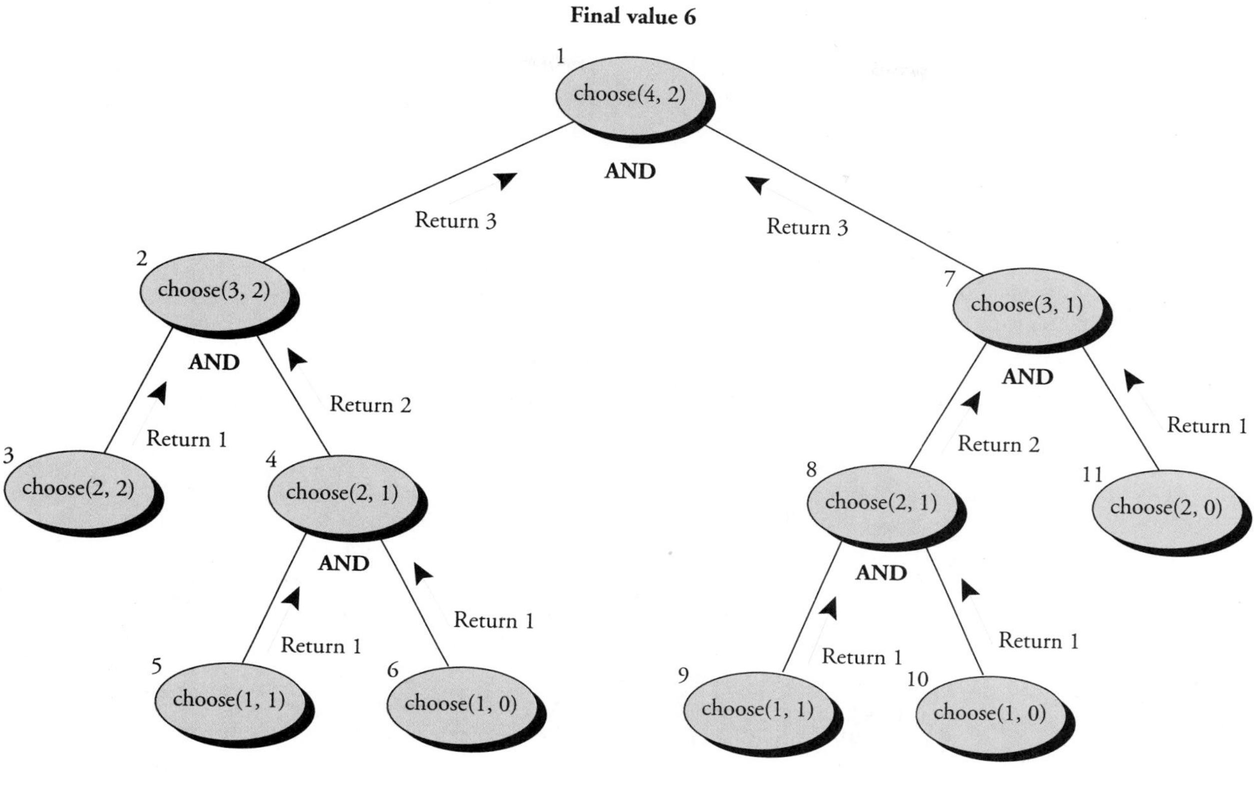

Example 14.8 Trace the `choose(n, k)` function by developing the run-time trace diagram for `choose(4, 2)`.

This diagram is provided in Figure 14.15. The numbers next to the circles indicate the order in which calls are made.

Exercises 14.2

1. Trace the stack frames that are pushed and popped from the system stack as the Towers of Hanoi algorithm executes for $n = 4$ disks.
2. Is the recursive binary search algorithm presented in this section tail recursive? Provide a written rationale for your response.
3. Construct run-time trace diagrams in the style of Example 14.8 for a variety of values of `n` and `k` in the function `choose(n, k)`. Judging from the run-time trace diagrams you construct, make conjectures about the time and space efficiency of this algorithm. Support these conjectures in a written statement.
4. Consider the following version of the function `binarySearchAux` from Example 14.6 to which a tracer output statement has been added. What output would be produced from this tracer output if we were to call on function `binarySearch` from Example 14.6 with a list of 16 integers containing these key values

```
12 34 67 89 113 125 169 180 191 201 225 237 256 270 299 304
```

and a `target` of 191?

```
int binarySearchAux(ListType list, int low, int high, KeyType target)
{
    int middle;

    cout << low << " << high << endl;         // Tracer output added here
    if (low > high)
            return -1;
    else
    {
            middle = (low + high) / 2;
            if (list[middle] == target)
                    return middle;
            else if (list[middle] < target)
                    return binarySearchAux(list, low, middle - 1, target);
            else
                    return binarySearchAux(list, middle + 1, high, target);
    }
}
```

5. Repeat Exercise 4 but this time with a `target` of 6.
6. Function `hanoi` developed in this section specified the sequence of disk moves that would have to be performed to complete the Towers of Hanoi problem for n disks. Now write a recursive function that computes the exact number of disk moves needed to solve the Towers of Hanoi problem for n disks. (*Hint:* Express the number of individual moves necessary to transfer n disks in terms of the number of moves necessary to transfer $n-1$ disks.)
7. Consider the following recursive function and associated top-level call. Comments of the form `// Return Point N` label possible return points from recursive calls. What would a stack frame for this function contain? Show by a series of stack "snapshots" how the stack would be manipulated for the calls indicated. Finally, provide the output produced by these calls.

```
#include <iostream.h>

int weird(int m, int n);

int main()
{
    cout << weird(1, 3) << endl;                   // Return Point 1
    return 0;
}

int weird(int m, int n)
{
    cout << m << " " << n << endl;
    if (m == 0)
            return n + 1;
    else if (n == 0)
            return weird(m - 1, 1);                // Return Point 2
    else
            return weird(m - 1, weird(m, n - 1));  // Return Points 3 and 4
}
```

8. Write a recursive function to determine the minimum entry in an array of n integers.

9. Write a recursive implementation of the insertion sort algorithm.
10. In essay form, discuss some of the trade-offs in terms of time and space efficiency that are made when recursion is used.
11. Suppose we have an amount of money *M* that is divisible evenly by 10 cents. Write a recursive function that computes the number of ways that *M* can be broken down into half dollars, quarters, and dimes. (*Hint:* Study Example 14.7.)
12. Both a modular structure chart and a run-time trace diagram reflect a hierarchical pattern of how functions are called in a program. In a carefully written statement, explain the differences between these two diagrammatic techniques.

14.3 Recursion, Trial-and-Error Backtracking, and Generalized Nested Loops

In the previous section, we saw examples of recursive algorithms in which the number of recursive calls at each recursive level is (potentially) more than one. In this section, we shall consider what happens when the number of recursive calls made on any given level is under the control of an iterative control structure such as a `for`, `while`, or `do` loop.

As an example of the class of problems we will study in this section, consider the notion of a permutation.

Permutation: A permutation of the integers 1, 2, . . . , *N* is an ordered arrangement of these integers in which each integer appears exactly once.

For instance, two possible permutations of the integers 1, 2, 3, 4 are 3 2 1 4 and 2 4 3 1.

The Permutation Problem

We now pose the following problem: For input of *N*, devise a program that outputs all permutations of the integers 1, 2, . . . , *N*.

Example 14.9 The following program solves this problem, but only for the special case where $N = 4$.

```
#include <iostream.h>

int main()
{
  for (int k1 = 1; k1 <= 4, k1++)
       for (int k2 = 1; k2 <= 4; k2++)
            if (k1 != k2)
                 for (int k3 = 1; k3 <= 4; k3++)
                      if ((k2 != k3) && (k1 != k3))
                           for (int k4 = 1; k4 <= 4; k4++)
                              if ((k3 != k4) && (k2 != k4) && (k1 != k4))
                                cout << setw(2) << k1 << " "
                                     << setw(2) << k2 << " "
                                     << setw(2) << k3 << " "
                                     << setw(2) << k4 << " "
                                     << endl;
  return 0;
}
```

The strategy of this program is to use a `for` loop to control a variable that runs through the four possibilities for each of the four permutation positions. Hence, four loops emerge, nested within each other. When an inner loop generates a number that matches one at a previously generated position, the `if` statement is used to reject that number.

Objectives

a. to use recursion in implementing a search strategy called trial-and-error backtracking
b. to realize that trial-and-error backtracking requires that loops be nested to arbitrarily deep levels
c. to construct a run-time trace diagram for a program that uses trial-and-error backtracking to search for solutions
d. to understand what a permutation is
e. to use trial-and-error backtracking to develop a program that produces permutations of a size not determined until run time
f. to see how trial-and-error backtracking, as studied in the context of the permutation problem, represents a strategy that can be generalized to solve a wide variety of problems

The program in Example 14.9 constitutes a simple and straightforward approach to the permutation problem. But it falls far short of solving the general problem as originally posed because it works only for the number 4, not for a general N to be input when the program runs. Note that the requirement that N be entered at run time is what causes the major complication. Certainly, the strategy of using nested loops allows us to write one program that works for $N = 2$, another that works for $N = 3$, another for $N = 4$, and so on. However, in addition to having a ridiculous number of nested `for` loops for reasonably large N, the decision as to which permutations to generate would instead be made at the time the appropriate program is compiled and not when it runs. Computer scientists typically call this a *binding time problem*. Here we would prefer to bind a value to N when our program runs instead of when it compiles. Clearly, the later the binding time, the more versatile the program. To do this, we need some means of simulating arbitrarily deep nested loops when the program runs.

To see how we can use recursion to achieve such a simulation, consider the diagram of permutation possibilities in Figure 14.16. This diagram bears a resemblance to what we called a run-time trace of recursive calls in the preceding section. Interpret the diagram by viewing any given path from the node labeled Start down to the base level of the diagram as a potential candidate for a permutation of 1, 2, . . . , N. As we progress from one level to the next along a path, we encounter the next digit in this potential permutation.

Conceptually, we must use recursion to generate all the paths that appear in the figure. As soon as we generate a path containing two equal numbers, we abandon that dead-end path and backtrack one level to continue the path along a potentially more fruitful route. If we ever complete one entire permutation along a path, we will output it, backtrack a level, and continue looking for more permutations that share the beginning of this path. At a given point in our search for a permutation, we need only store the current path. For this, a simple global array will do. Thus, the array `currentPermutation` of Figure 14.17 will store in its jth index the number in the jth position of the permutation currently being generated. The limiting factor on the size of permutations generated by our program will be the dimension of this array.

A complete program to solve our permutation problem follows. The heart of the program is the recursive function `attempt`. This function receives three parameters:

Parameter	Explanation
`n`	The number of numbers to be permuted in the current run.
`level`	The level in the tree of Figure 14.16; that is, the position in `currentPermutation` at which `attempt` is to attempt placement of a new value.
`possibility`	The new value to be placed at this level.

`attempt` initially calls on a function `addToCurrentPath` to place `possibility` at the appropriate level. Once this placement is made, there are three states in which the `currentPermutation` array could be.

1. The placement of the value `possibility` at the designated level could have completed a successful permutation. In this case, call on a function to print the permutation and then remove `possibility` from `currentPermutation` at the given `level` so that we may continue seeking additional permutations.

Figure 14.16 Candidates for permutations

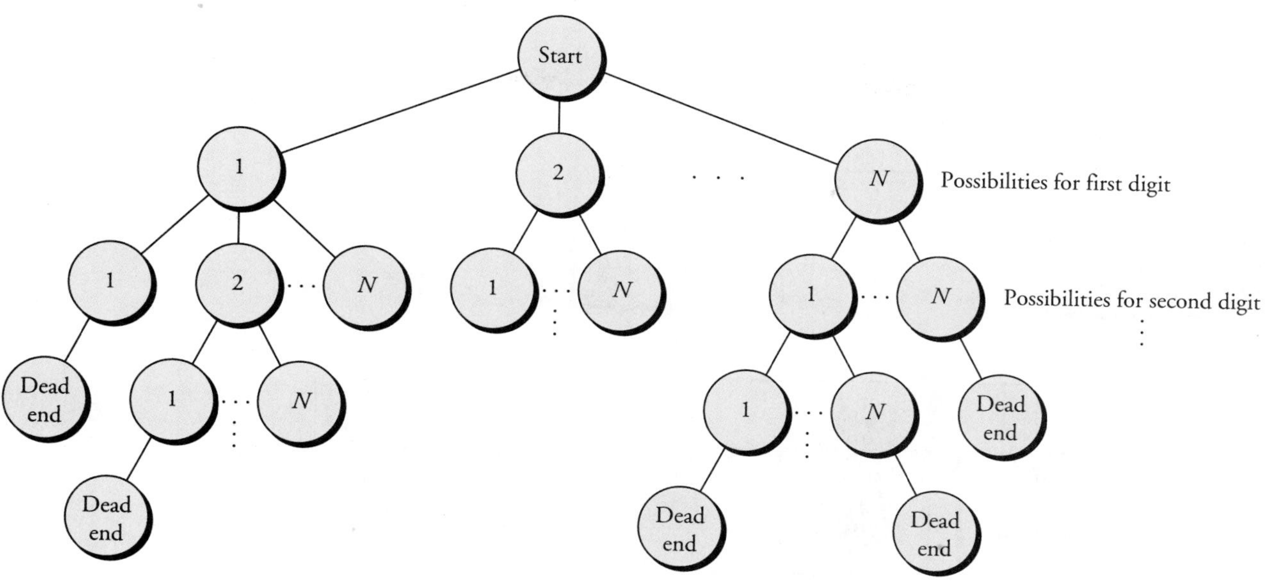

Figure 14.17 Current exploration of permutations beginning with 2 1 4

currentPermutation

1	2	3	4	5	. . .	maxPermutation Size
2	1	4	Undefined	Undefined	. . .	Undefined

2. The placement of the value `possibility` at the designated level did not complete a permutation but does represent a valid beginning of length `level` for a potential permutation. For instance, this case would occur if `n`, `level`, and `possibility` were 6, 4, and 5, respectively, and we called `attempt` with `currentPermutation` as pictured in Figure 14.17. The `currentPermutation` array would be extended to contain 2 1 4 5. Here we must test the possible candidates for a value at the next position, that is, at depth `(level + 1)`. This is done by an iterative series of recursive calls to `attempt`, passing a variety of values for `possibility` at `(level + 1)`. This iterative series of recursive calls achieves the desired simulation of nested looping. After all of these deeper level possibilities (that is, those below the beginning of the current permutation in Figure 14.16) have been explored, we return and can remove `possibility` from `currentPermutation` at position `level` since (recursively) all permutations with this beginning arrangement will have been generated.
3. The placement of the value `possibility` at `level` destroys the viability of the current path by adding a number that appeared earlier in the permutation. For instance, calling on `attempt` with `n = 6`, `level = 4`, and `possibility = 1` would cause an invalid path for the state of `currentPermutation` given in Figure 14.17. In this case, we do nothing but retract from the placement of this invalid possibility before attempting to place other possible values.

You should carefully study how these three potential cases are handled in our recursive function `attempt` in the example program. The modular structure chart presented in Figure 14.18 indicates how `attempt` invokes other functions. Following the program, we adapt the technique illustrated here to a broader class of problems.

Figure 14.18 Modular structure chart for permutations program

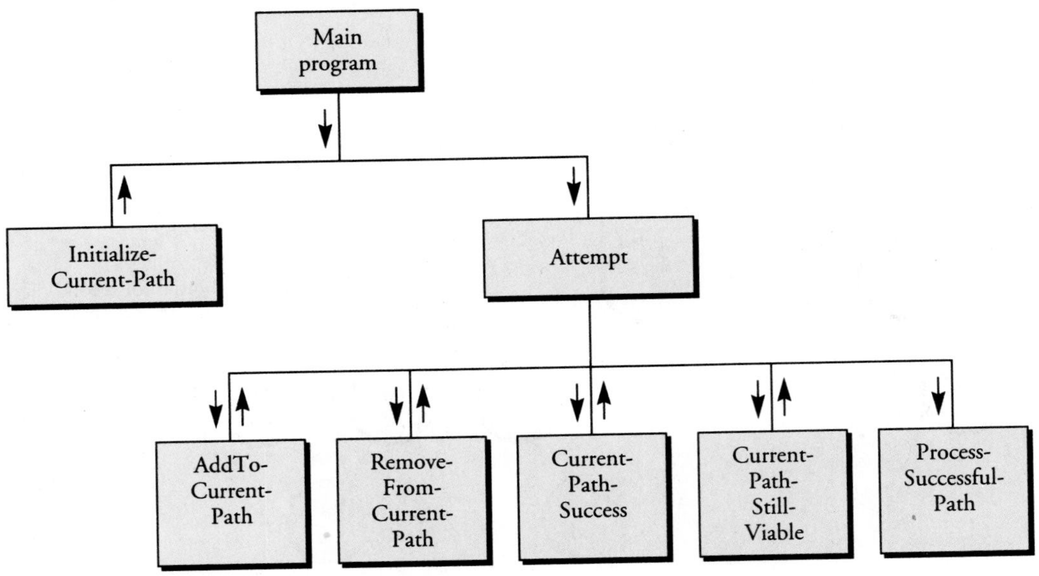


```
// Program file: permute.cpp

// Use recursion to find all permutations of 1,2, ..., N.

#include <iostream.h>
#include <iomanip.h>
#include <limits.h>

const int MAX_PERMUTATION_SIZE = 100;
const int UNDEFINED = INT_MAX;

int currentPermutation[MAX_PERMUTATION_SIZE + 1];      //index 0 not used

// Function: initializeCurrentPath
// Initializes all indices in array to the UNDEFINED flag.
//
// Inputs: The currentPermutation array in an unreliable state
// Outputs: The initialized array

void initializeCurrentPath();

// Function: attempt
// After locating possibility at specified level, check if we have a permutation.
// If so, print it. If not, check whether or not a permutation is still possible
// for this placement of possibility. If so, attempt placement at deeper level
// by recursive call.
//
// Inputs: n, the number of numbers we are attempting to permute;
//         level, the current depth of the solution path as portrayed in Figure 14.16;
//         possibility, the number we wish to place at that level
// Outputs: Relative to this level, the array is returned unaltered. However,
//          if permutation was found, contents of this array are printed.
```

```
void attempt(int n, int level, int possibility);
// Function: addToCurrentPath
// Assign possibility to this level.
//
// Inputs: level, the current depth of the solution path;
//         possibility, the number we wish to place at that level

void addToCurrentPath(int level, int possibility);

// Function: removeFromCurrentPath
// Remove value at that level.
//
// Inputs: the deepest level to which solution path has grown
// Outputs: Suitably altered array

void removeFromCurrentPath(int level);

// Function: currentPathSuccess
// Check if contents of array through index level constitute a complete
// permutation of the first n numbers.
//
// Inputs: level, the depth to which the solution path has grown,
//         n, the number of numbers we are attempting to permute.
// Outputs: true if we have a permutation, false otherwise.

bool currentPathSuccess(int n, int level);

// Function: currentPathStillViable
// Check if contents of array through index level constitute a viable
// beginning for the permutation of the first n numbers.
//
// Inputs: level, the depth to which the solution path has grown,
// Outputs: true if the current path is still viable, false otherwise.

bool currentPathStillViable(int level);

// Function: processSuccessfulPath
// Write out first n indices of the array
//
// Inputs: n, the number of numbers we are attempting to permute.

void processSuccessfulPath(int n);

int main()
{
    int n;

    initializeCurrentPath();
    cout << "Permutation of integers from 1 to ? ";
    cin >> n;
    for (int k = 1; k <= n; ++k)
       attempt(n, 1, k);
    return 0;
}
void initializeCurrentPath()
{
    for (int k = 1; k <= MAX_PERMUTATION_SIZE; ++k)
```

continued

```
      currentPermutation[k]= UNDEFINED;
}

void attempt(int n, int level, int possibility)
{
   addToCurrentPath(level, possibility);
   if (currentPathSuccess(n, level))
      processSuccessfulPath(n);
   else if (currentPathStillViable(level))
      for (int k = 1; k <= n; ++k)
         attempt(n, level + 1, k);
   removeFromCurrentPath(level);
}

void addToCurrentPath(int level, int possibility)
{
   currentPermutation[level] = possibility;
}

void removeFromCurrentPath(int level)
{
   currentPermutation[level] = UNDEFINED;
}

bool currentPathSuccess(int n, int level)
{
   bool success = true;
   int k = 1;

   if (n > level)
      success = false;
   else
      while ((k <= level - 1) && success)
      {
         success = currentPermutation[k] != currentPermutation[level];
         ++k;
      }
   return success;
}

bool currentPathStillViable(int level)
{
   bool viable = true;
   int k = 1;
   while ((k <= level - 1) && viable)
      {
         viable = currentPermutation[k]!= currentPermutation[level];
         ++k;
      }
   return viable;
}

void processSuccessfulPath(int n)
{
   for (int k = 1; k < = n; ++k)
      cout << setw(3) << currentPermutation[k];
   cout << endl;
}
```

A NOTE OF INTEREST

Fractal Geometry and Recursive Patterns

Fractal geometry as a serious mathematical endeavor began with the pioneering work of Benoit Mandelbrot, a Fellow of the Thomas J. Watson Research Center, IBM Corporation. Fractal geometry is a theory of geometric forms so complex that they defy analysis and classification by traditional Euclidean means. Yet fractal shapes occur universally in the natural world. Mandelbrot has recognized them not only in coastlines, landscapes, lungs, and turbulent water flow but also in the chaotic fluctuation of prices on the Chicago commodity exchange.

The c-curve that follows is an instance of a fractal shape. It represents a series of recursive patterns of increasing levels of complexity. When the level is zero, the c-curve is a simple line specified by the endpoints <*x*1, *y*1> and <*x*2, *y*2>. A level *N* c-curve is composed of two level $N-1$ c-curves connected at right angles.

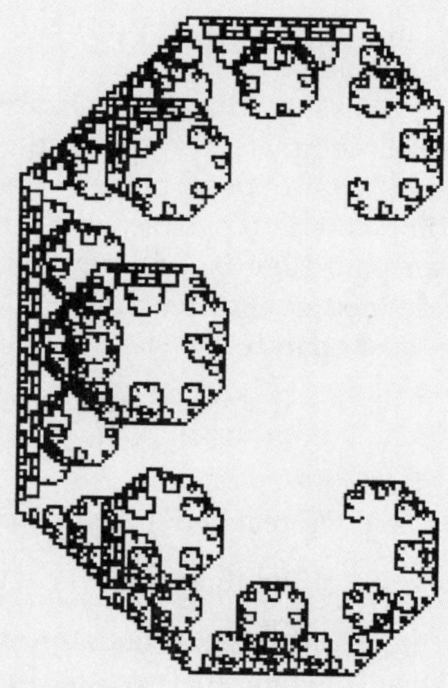

Thus, a level 1 c-curve is composed of two perpendicular lines, and a level 2 c-curve is three quarters of a square, which begins to resemble the letter C.

Our level 12 c-curve was generated on a graphics workstation by running a recursive function written in C++:

```
void cCurve(int x1, int y1, int x2, int y2, int level)
{
  int xm, ym;

  if ( level == 0)
       drawLine (x1, y1, x2, y2);
  else
  {
       xm = (x1 + x2 + y1 - y2)/2;
       ym = (x2 + y1 + y2 - x1)/2;
       cCurve(x1, y1, xm, ym, level - 1);
       cCurve(xm, ym, x2, y2, level - 1);
  }
}
```

You may have noticed that certain efficiency considerations have not been taken into account in writing the previous program. For example, the initialization of the `currentPermutation` array is unnecessary in this particular implementation. Also, the call to `removeFromCurrentPath` could have been eliminated since the undefined flag that this function assigns is quickly replaced without ever being explicitly used. Finally, additional global data could be used to keep track of information that would eliminate the necessity of using loops in the `currentPathSuccess` and `currentPathStillViable` functions. You will be asked to rewrite the program taking these economies into account in the exercises.

Our purpose in the preceding discussion has not been to present the most compact version of a permutations program, but rather to illustrate how recursion can be used to simulate generalized nested loops whose nesting depth can be established at run time. Such generalized nested loops can then be used in situations where trial-and-error backtracking is an appropriate strategy in searching for a problem's solution. In this context, we have intended the permutations program to be illustrative of a general problem-solving approach rather than a solution to a particular problem.

Consider what we must abstract from the permutations program to view it as a general template for trial-and-error backtracking instead of a mere permutation printer. Figure 14.16 presents the problem of finding permutations as a problem in finding certain types of paths through a maze. We probe deeper and deeper along a given path (that is, add new numbers to the current permutation) until we reach a predefined goal or reach a dead end. As we take a new step along the current path, we must analyze the state in which it has placed us:

1. Have we reached a goal state?
2. Have we reached a state that, although not itself a goal, is still a viable start toward that goal?
3. Have we reached a dead end?

For each of the three cases, we take appropriate action such as

1. Processing a goal state; for example, printing it out, tallying a counter, or setting a flag signaling that we are done.
2. Probing further along a viable path by recursively taking another step.
3. No action in the case of a dead end.

After taking the appropriate action, we then retract from the step that led us to the current state, possibly returning to a higher recursive level where we may find ourselves in the midst of a similar three-state analysis. The essence of this trial-and-error backtracking logic is illustrated in Figure 14.19. Upon reaching a dead end for path A,

Figure 14.19 Backtracking problem illustrated by maze solution

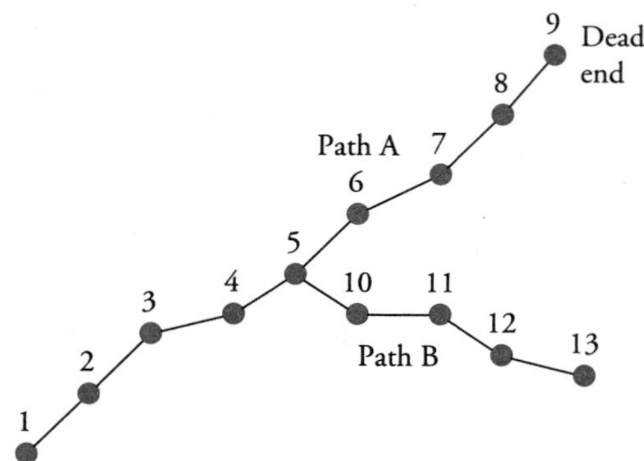

A NOTE OF INTEREST

Recursion, LISP, and the Practicality of Artificial Intelligence

Artificial intelligence, the science of implementing on computers the problem-solving methods used by human beings, is one of the most rapidly expanding fields within computer science. Research in this field includes enabling computers to play games of strategy, to understand natural languages, to prove theorems in logic and mathematics, and to mimic the reasoning of human experts in fields such as medical diagnosis. Only recently has artificial intelligence become a commercially viable area of application, capable of solving some real-life problems apart from the idealized setting of a pure research environment. More and more, we are seeing artificial intelligence systems that perform such practical functions as aiding business executives in their decision-making processes and providing a "near-English" user-interface language for database management software.

What has sparked the sudden emergence of artificial intelligence? Why wasn't it possible to produce commercially feasible programs in this field until recently? One of the primary answers to these questions is tied to the language in which most artificial intelligence programming is done. This language is called LISP (for LISt Processor). Interestingly, the control structures of LISP are based almost entirely on recursion. What a C++ programmer would view as normal iterative control structures (for example, `while`, `do`, and `for` loops) appear in various versions of LISP only as infrequently used, nonstandard extensions to the language.

One of the reasons that a recursively based language such as LISP is so ideally suited to this field is that most problem-solving methods in artificial intelligence involve searching for a particular goal state; that is, searching for a path leading to a complete problem solution. This is similar to the approaches we have taken in the permutation problem and the Eight Queens problem in this chapter.

The complexity of problems studied in artificial intelligence leads to run-time trace diagrams of enormous size. Interestingly, LISP has been available as a recursive language ideally suited to such problems for a long time. It is one of the oldest high-level programming languages, having been developed by John McCarthy in the late 1950s.

Researchers who work in artificial intelligence have realized since LISP's introduction that its ability to process general data structures recursively was, on a theoretical basis, exactly what they needed. The problem through the years has been that, because of the very high overhead associated with recursion (and some other features built into LISP), computer hardware has not been fast enough to run LISP programs in practical applications. Thus, researchers were restricted not by LISP itself but rather by the inability of computer hardware to execute LISP programs in reasonable times. One of the major reasons for the recent emergence of artificial intelligence has been the increase in speed of computing hardware and the decrease in cost of this same hardware. This has made it possible for users to have dedicated computer resources capable of meeting the demands of LISP's recursive style. As hardware continues to improve, applications in LISP and artificial intelligence will become increasingly sophisticated.

If you are curious about LISP and the important role that it plays at some of the frontiers of research in programming languages, consult the September 1991 and November 1995 issues of the *Communications of the ACM*, Vol. 34, No. 9, and Vol. 38, No. 11, respectively. Each of these issues was devoted to LISP and its application in artificial intelligence.

you must retrace steps 9 → 8 → 7 → 6 → 5 before you can attempt new path B. The retracing of states that have been visited previously is conveniently done by unwinding from recursive calls.

We shall now indicate the power of this abstract approach to trial-and-error backtracking by sketching a solution to another problem that could be solved with the same methodology. You will then complete the solution in Programming Problems and Projects.

The Eight Queens Problem

Consider what has come to be known as the Eight Queens problem, which has long intrigued chess fanatics. It requires determining the various ways in which eight queens could be configured on a chessboard so that none of them could capture any other queen. (The rules of chess allow a queen to move an arbitrary number of squares in a horizontal, vertical, or diagonal fashion.) Figure 14.20 illustrates one such configuration.

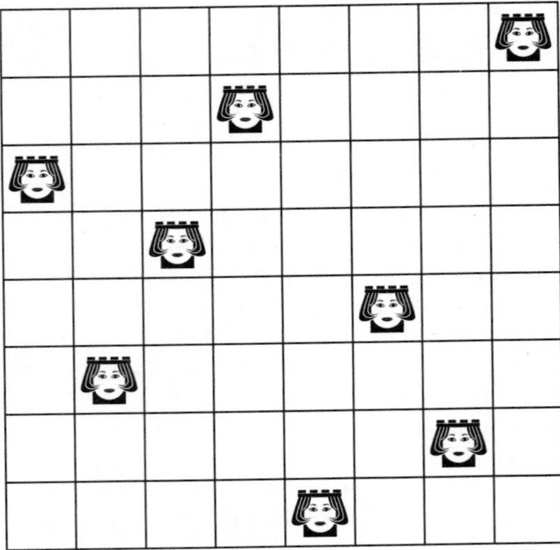

Figure 14.20 One successful Eight Queens configuration

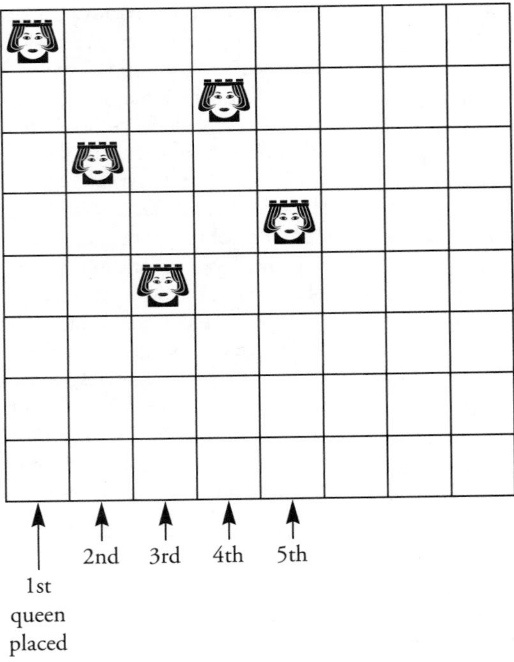

Figure 14.21 Dead end in queen placement

Applying backtracking logic to this problem, we could attempt to find a path to a configuration by successively placing a queen in each column of a chessboard until we reach a dead end: a column in which the placement of queens in prior columns makes it impossible to place the queen being moved. This situation is pictured in Figure 14.21. Here, the sixth queen cannot be placed due to the placement of the first five queens.

When we reach such a dead end, we must backtrack one column (to column 5 in Figure 14.21) and attempt to find a new placement for the queen in that column. If placement in the previous column is impossible, we must backtrack yet another column to attempt the new placement. This backtracking through previous columns continues until we finally are able to reposition a queen. At that point, we can begin a new path by again attempting to position queens on a column-by-column basis until another dead end is reached or until a fully successful configuration is developed.

The key to a program that finds all possible configurations for the eight queens is a function that attempts to place a queen in a given square and, if successful, recursively calls itself to attempt the placement of another queen in the next column. Such a function in skeletal pseudocode form follows:

```
void tryQueen (K, J)

// Place a queen in row K, column J.
// Analyze state reached by this placement.
// If appropriate, recurse to place queen in next column.

Actually put queen at position K, J
If this results in successful configuration
    Tally this configuration
Else if no queen in immediate danger
    For each L from 1 to 8
            tryQueen(L, J + 1)
Retract from position K, J
```

The similarities between this sketch of a solution to the Eight Queens problem and our complete solution to the permutation problem should convince you that, from an abstract perspective, both problems are really the same. We have intentionally left the Eight Queens problem unfinished. Still to be resolved are such issues as:

- The initial call(s) to `tryQueen`.
- How to represent the chessboard.
- How to check whether placing a queen at position `K, J` puts it in immediate danger. That is, how to determine whether there is currently another queen sharing the same row, column, or diagonal.

The resolution of these issues is left for your enjoyment in Programming Problems and Projects at the end of the chapter. Additional problems given there further illustrate the far-reaching applicability of the trial-and-error backtracking method.

Exercises 14.3

1. Consider the permutations program discussed in Section 14.3. Suppose that $N = 3$ in a particular run of this program and that we printed out the contents of the `currentPermutation` array each time the attempt function was invoked in this run. How many times would the array be printed? What would be the overall output?
2. Suppose you used the permutations function of this section to compute all permutations of 1, 2, 3, and 4. What would the complete run-time trace diagram of recursive function calls look like for such a run? Can you generalize from this diagram of function calls the efficiency of the permutations function? State your answer in big-O terms with respect to both stack size and number of stack operations. Justify your answer in a written statement.
3. Rewrite the example program for permutations in a fashion that takes into account the efficiency considerations discussed in Section 14.3. These considerations are discussed in the paragraph that follows the program.

4. What is the output from the following program?

```
#include <iostream.h>

void y(int a, int b, int c);

int main()
{
     y(16, 1, 4);
     return 0;
}

void y(int a, int b, int c)
{
     int k;

     if (b <= c)
     {
            cout << a << endl;
            for (k = b; k <= c; ++k)
                   y(k, b + 1, c);
     }
}
```

5. What is the output from the following program?

```
#include <iostream.h>

void tough(int b, int c, int d);

int main()
{
     tough(1, 4, 12);
     return 0;
}

void tough(int b, int c, int d)
{
     int k;

     if (b <= c)
     {
            cout << d << endl;
            for (k = b; k <= c; ++k)
                   tough(b + 1, c, k);
     }
}
```

6. A car's odometer may be viewed as a physical implementation of a nested loop. Suppose this odometer registers whole miles only; that is, tenths of a mile are not recorded. Each loop cycles through the digits 0 . . . 9, with the ones digit cycling the fastest, then the tens digit, and so forth. Write a function to simulate an *N*-digit odometer (*N* determined at run time) by creating a generalized nested loop structure that will run through, in sequence, all possible settings for the odometer.

14.4 Recursive Descent Parsing

Objectives

a. to understand what a context-free grammar is
b. to use context-free grammars in producing derivations of expressions
c. to understand the relationship between the derivation of an expression and a parse tree

In Section 13.3, we studied the parsing of infix algebraic expressions by the use of a stack and appropriate infix and stack priority functions. However, that parsing algorithm emphasized the conversion of the infix expression into a postfix expression and assumed that it had been given a syntactically valid infix expression. A problem equally important in parsing is the detection of syntax errors in the expression to be processed. One method of error detection, called *recursive descent parsing,* relies heavily upon recursive procedures. The inspiration for such recursive procedures comes from the linguistic concept of a context-free grammar, which provides a rigorous formalism for defining the syntax of expressions and other programming-language constructs, a formalism similar to that found in the syntax diagram of Appendix C. The scope of context-free grammars goes far beyond what we will cover in one section of this text. If your interest is aroused by the following discussion, we encourage you to consult Charles N. Fischer & Richard J. LeBlanc, *Crafting a Compiler,* Menlo Park, CA: Benjamin/Cummings, 1988.

A *context-free grammar* is composed of the following three elements.

1. A set of *terminals*. These terminals represent the tokens—characters or groups of characters that logically belong together, such as operator symbols, delimiters, keywords, variable names—that ultimately compose the expression being parsed. In the case of infix algebraic expressions, the terminals are variables, numeric constants, parentheses, and the various operators that are allowed.
2. A set of *nonterminals*. These nonterminals represent the various grammatical constructs within the language we are parsing. In particular, one nonterminal is designated as the *start symbol* for the grammar.
3. A set of *productions*. The productions are formal rules defining the syntactic composition of the nonterminals from point 2. The productions take the form:

   Nonterminal → String of terminals and/or nonterminals

   We say that the nonterminal on the left of such a production *derives* the string on the right.

An example of a context-free grammar should help clarify this three-part definition.

Example 14.10 Provide a context-free grammar for infix algebraic expressions involving addition and multiplication and show how the particular expression $A + B * C$ is derived from it.

1. Set of terminals:

   { '+', '*', '(', ')', identifier, number }

2. Set of nonterminals:

   { <expression>, <factor>, <add-factor>, <mult-factor>, <primary> }

   where < expression > is designated as the start symbol. Note that, by convention, nonterminals are enclosed in angle brackets to distinguish them from terminals.
3. Set of productions:

   a. <expression> → <factor><add-factor>
   b. <factor> → < primary>< mult-factor>
   c. <add-factor> → '+' < factor>< add-factor>
   d. <add-factor> → '–'< factor>< add-factor>
   e. <add-factor> → NULL
   f. <mult-factor> → '*' <primary><mult-factor>

g. <mult-factor> → '/' < primary ><mult-factor >
h. <mult-factor> → NULL
i. <primary> → identifier
j. <primary> → number
k. <primary> → '(' < expression > ')'

The symbol NULL is used to indicate the empty string. In effect, this implies that one defining option for < add-factor > and < mult-factor > is the empty string. We shall see why this is necessary in the derivation of $A + B * C$, which follows.

To derive a particular infix expression, we begin with the start symbol <expression>. The production that defines <expression> says that <expression> must be <factor> followed by <add-factor>. Hence, we must now try to derive these two nonterminals. This process of involving nonterminals in the definition of other nonterminals continues until we finally reach those nonterminals that are defined by the terminals in the infix expression being parsed. Thus, a formal derivation of $A + B * C$ is given by

<expression>	→ <factor> < add-factor>	By production a
	→ <primary > <mult-factor > <add-factor >	By production b
	→ A <mult-factor> <add-factor>	By production i
	→ A <add-factor>	By production h
	→ A + <factor> <add-factor>	By production c
	→ A + <primary> <mult-factor> <add-factor>	By production b
	→ A + B <mult-factor> <add-factor>	By production i
	→ A + B * <primary> <mult-factor> <add-factor>	By production f
	→ A + B * C <mult-factor> <add-factor>	By production i
	→ A + B * C	By productions e and h

Note that there is a hint of recursion in the grammar of Example 14.10 in that some of the productions defining <add-factor> and <mult-factor> use these same nonterminals in their definitional pattern on the right of the production being defined. As the next example will show, it is this recursive portion of the definition that allows us to add arbitrarily many identifiers in one expression. That is, by the recursive appearance of <add-factor> and <mult-factor> in productions c and f, respectively, we are able to keep introducing '+' and '*' into the expression being parsed.

Example 14.11 Provide a derivation of the infix expression A + B + C.

<expression> → <factor> <add-factor>
→ <primary> <mult-factor> <add-factor>
→ A <mult-factor> <add-factor>
→ A <add-factor>
→ A + <factor> <add-factor>
→ A + <primary> <mult-factor><add-factor>
→ A + B <mult-factor> <add-factor>
→ A + B <add-factor>
→ A + B + <factor><add-factor>
→ A + B + <primary> <mult-factor> <add-factor>
→ A + B + C <mult-factor> <add-factor>
→ A + B + C <add-factor>
→ A + B + C

You are encouraged to justify each step in the derivation by determining the production applied.

A NOTE OF INTEREST

Language Definition and Natural Languages

The syntax of most computer languages can be recursively defined using grammars similar to that described in this chapter. This is of tremendous importance in the writing of compilers, most of which rely heavily on stacks and recursion to parse source programs.

A broader question than the definition and parsing of programming languages is the ability of the computer to process natural languages such as English. Researchers in the field of artificial intelligence are attempting to use more general recursive techniques to define the syntax of natural languages and, consequently, program the computer to cope with this more complex type of language. To date, their work has met with success only in highly restricted domains of natural language such as that used to express word problems in algebra or interact with databases in a structured query language.

Despite these present limitations, research in language definition and the consequent processing of that language by a computer should be one of the most intensely explored fields within computer science in the future. According to researchers Kenneth Church and Lisa Rau, the vast quantity and variety of text available on the Internet and in other electronic media are "moving natural language processing along the critical path for all kinds of novel applications." If you want to read about some of these novel applications, consult Kenneth Church and Lisa Rau, "Commercial Applications of Natural Language," *Communications of the ACM*, Vol. 38, No. 11, Nov. 1995, pp. 71–79.

Just as we were able to describe recursive procedure processing with a run-time trace diagram, the formal derivation of an expression via the productions of a grammar can be represented by a diagram called a *parse tree*. (Parse trees for the derivation in Examples 14.10 and 14.11 are given in Figures 14.22 and 14.23, respectively.) Note that implicit in these parse trees is the order of operations in the algebraic expressions. That is, these parse trees are constructed, top-down, starting at each nonterminal within the tree and, from that nonterminal, descending to those nodes containing the terminals and nonterminals from the right side of the production applied in the derivation of the original nonterminal. Eventually, as we descend deeper into the tree, only terminals are left, and no nodes descend deeper from these terminals. In Figure 14.22, since the <factor> node on level 2 of the tree encompasses all of B * C below it, we have an indication that B * C must be first evaluated as a <factor> and then added to A. On the other hand, in the parse tree of Figure 14.23, the <factor> node at level 2 encompasses only the B term. Hence, B added to A, with C (below the <factor> node at Level 3) then added to that result.

In the exercises and problems, you will continue to explore the relationships between context-free grammars, derivations, parse trees, and orders of evaluation in infix expressions. In the Case Study for this chapter, we will turn our attention to the problem of transforming the formal grammar that specifies the syntax of a language into a program that determines whether or not the tokens stored in an incoming queue constitute a valid string.

Exercises 14.4

1. Using the context-free grammar of Example 14.10, provide formal derivations and parse trees for the following expressions:
   a. $A * B * C * D + E$
   b. $A + B * C * (D + E)$
   c. $((A + B) * C) * (D + E)$
2. Extend the grammar of Example 14.10 to:
   a. Allow exponentiation (^) as an algebraic operator. Be sure that your grammar yields parse trees that imply that the order of consecutive exponentiations is right to left instead of left to right (as it is with other operators).

Figure 14.22 Parse tree for $A + B * C$ reflects that $B * C$ is evaluated first.

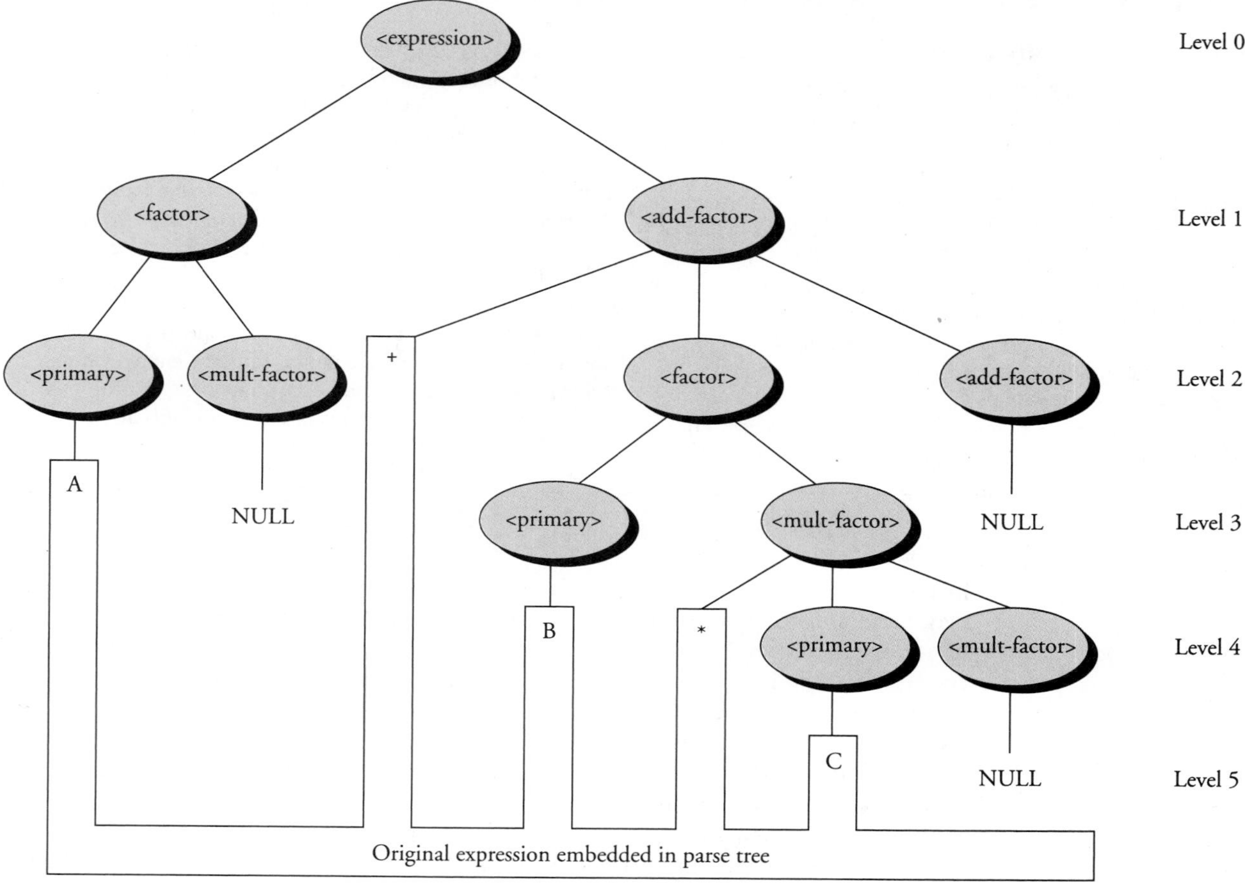

b. Allow `or (|)`, `and (&)`, and `not (!)` as logical operators so that Boolean as well as algebraic expressions are allowed by the grammar.

3. Consider the following alternative, context-free grammar for the expressions defined by the grammar of Example 14.10.

<expression> → <mult-factor>
<expression> → <mult-factor> '+' <expression>
<expression> → <mult-factor> '–' <expression>
<mult-factor> → <primary>
<mult-factor> → <primary> '*' <mult-factor>
<mult-factor> → <primary> '/' <mult-factor>
<primary> → identifier
<primary> → number
<primary> → '(' <expression> ')'

a. Does this grammar allow the same set of expressions as that in Example 14.10?
b. Provide parse trees for any of the expressions in Exercise 1 that are accepted by the grammar of this exercise.
c. What are differences in the parse trees produced by this grammar versus those produced by the grammar of Example 14.10?

Figure 14.23 Parse tree for $A + B + C$ reflects that B is added to A before addition of C

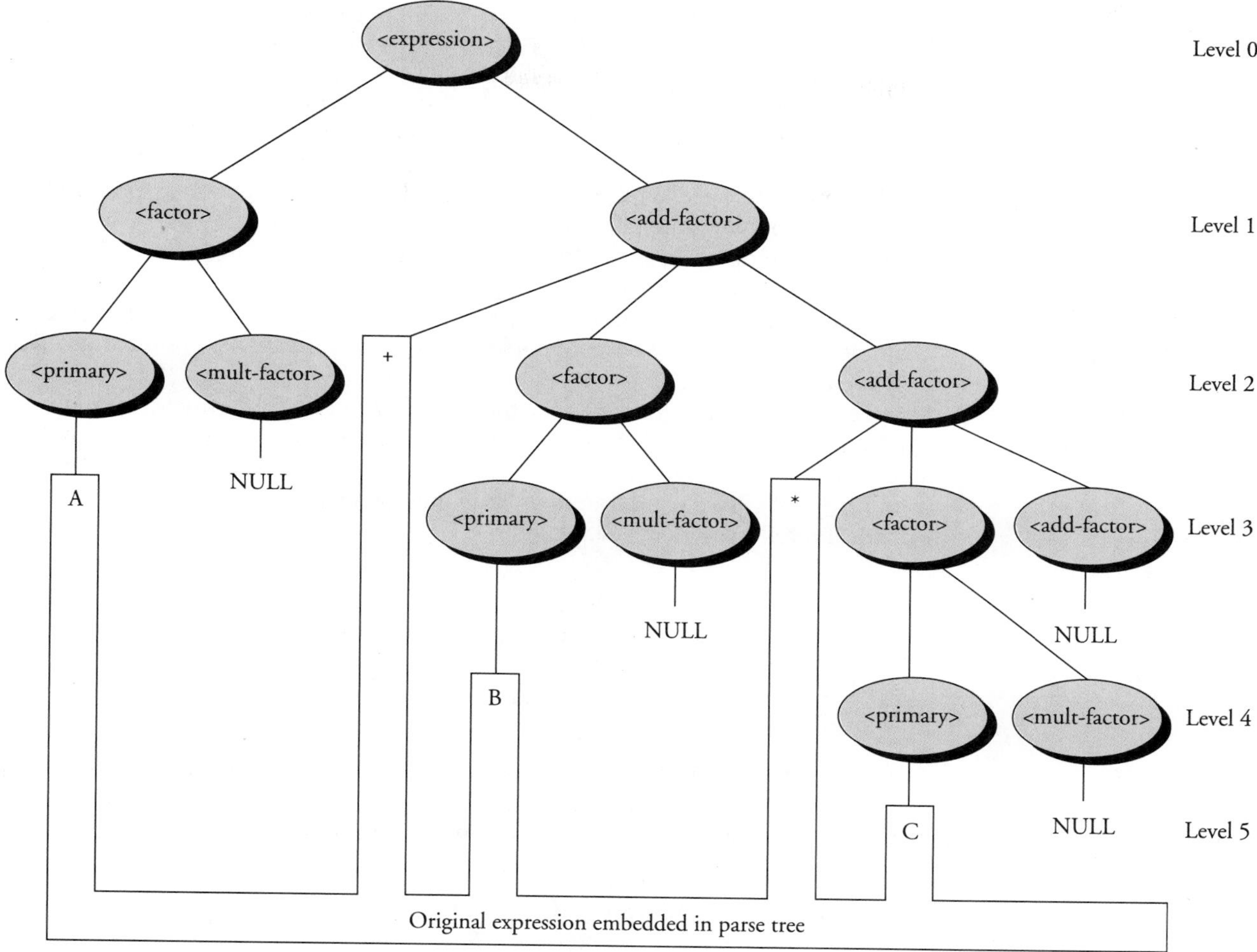

d. How would the differences you described in part c affect the order in which operators are applied?

e. Which grammar—Example 14.10 or the one defined in this exercise—more accurately reflects the order of operations in standard programming languages?

4. (Left-Recursive Grammar) Consider the following alternative, context-free grammar for the expressions defined by the grammar of Example 14.10.

<expression> → <mult-factor>
<expression> → <expression> '+' <mult-factor>
<expression> → <expression> '–' <mult-factor>
<mult-factor> → <primary>
<mult-factor> → <mult-factor> '*' <primary>
<mult-factor> → <mult-factor> '/' <primary>
<primary> → identifier
<primary> → number
<primary> → '(' <expression> ')'

This grammar is an example of a left-recursive grammar—one that admits a derivation of the form.

<a> → <a> X

where <a>is a nonterminal and X is a string of terminals and/or nonterminals. For the grammar of this exercise, productions associated with the nonterminals <expression> and <mult-factor> fit this criterion, so the grammar is left-recursive.

a. Does this grammar allow the same set of expressions as that of Example 14.10?
b. Provide parse trees for any of the expressions in Exercise 1 that are accepted by the grammar of this exercise.
c. What are differences in the parse trees produced by this grammar versus those produced by the grammars of Example 14.10 and Exercise 3?
d. How do the differences you described in part c affect the order in which operators are applied?
e. After reading the Case Study, discuss the difficulty arising when you attempt to implement a recursive descent parser that reflects directly the grammar given in this exercise.

5. Provide a context-free grammar for the `if` and `if-else` structures of a conventional programming language such as C++. Assume that the nonterminals <condition> and <statement> are suitably defined elsewhere and, hence, can be used as primitives in your grammar. How many parse trees will your grammar allow for the following C++ statement?

```
if (a < b)
   if (c < d)
      a = d;
   else
      b = c;
```

Which, if any, of your parse trees correspond to the fashion in which standard C++ interprets this statement?

6. The programming language LISP works with S-expressions. They may be defined as follows:

- NIL is a special S-expression denoting the empty S-expression.
- Any string composed of letters and/or digits with no other embedded characters is an S-expression.
- If L_1, L_2, . . . , L_k are S-expressions for $k >= 0$, then (L_1 L_2 . . . L_k) is an S-expression.

Construct a context-free grammar for S-expressions. Then provide derivations or draw parse trees for the following S-expressions:

a. ((GLARP))
b. (GLARP (GLARP) (((GLARP GLARP))) ( ))
c. (((GLARP GLARP) NIL ( )) GLARP)

Case Study: Implementing a Recursive Descent Parser from a Context-Free Grammar

In Section 14.4, we described context-free grammars as a way of recursively specifying the syntax of a language. The Case Study for this chapter will demonstrate that, by using such a rigorous definitional tool for characterizing a language, the task of writing a program to parse expressions in that language is surprisingly easy. For reasons that will become apparent, parsing programs developed using this technique are called *recursive descent parsers*.

User Request

Develop a program that will allow input of a stream of tokens corresponding to the grammar of Example 14.10. The stream should be parsed for syntactic correctness.

That is, if the stream constitutes an acceptable expression in the language, the program should so indicate. Otherwise, the program should indicate that the stream is syntactically invalid. Assume that identifiers are uppercase letters, that tokens are separated by a space when entered, and that the end token # will be used to mark the end of the input stream.

Analysis

Based upon this request, the program's interaction with a user should appear as:

```
Enter expression with spaces between tokens, then <ENTER>
( ( X + 14.3 ) / ( A * 2 ) ) #
Expression is valid

Enter expression with spaces between tokens, then <ENTER>
( ( X + 14.3 ) / A * 2 ) ) #
Expression is invalid
```

Design

At first consideration, writing this program may seem like a daunting task. However, we first note that we already have a token class from the Case Study in Chapter 13 that can be reused here. If necessary, you should reread the discussion of the token class in that Case Study to familiarize yourself with its use. In the program we are developing here, we will augment that token class with a few helper functions tied specifically to the grammar from Example 14.10.

```
// Get the next token from the input stream and return it in fromInfix
void getInfixToken(token &fromInfix);

// Read a sequence of tokens from the input stream, terminating with the
// END_TOKEN. Return this stream of tokens in a queue.
void getInfixExp(queue<token> &infix);

// Return true if tok is an "add operator", that is, a + or -.
// Otherwise return false.
bool isAddOp(token tok);

// Return true if tok is an "mult operator", that is, a * or /.
// Otherwise return false.
bool isMultOp(token tok);

// Return true if tok represents a left parenthesis.
// Otherwise return false.
bool isLeftParen(token tok);

// Return true if tok represents a right parenthesis.
// Otherwise return false.
bool isRightParen(token tok);

// Return true if tok represents the END_TOKEN #.
// Otherwise return false.
bool isEndToken(token tok);
```

Given these helper functions for tokens, the process of writing a parsing function itself is surprisingly easy. It begins with a front-end function called from the main program. This front-end function receives the queue of tokens read from the input stream and will eventually return a Boolean to indicate the success or failure of the parse.

```
// Given a queue of tokens called infix, representing an expression that is
// a candidate to satisfy the grammar of Example 14.10, return true if the
// expression is syntactically valid and false otherwise.

bool parse(queue<token> infix);
```

To do so, it performs necessary initializations and then calls on the first in a suite of "verifying" functions. The initialization that `parse` must do is to dequeue the first token from the `infix` queue and pass this along to its verifying function as the "current token." We write a separate verifying function for each nonterminal in the grammar. The responsibility of each function is simply to verify the particular grammatical construction after which it is named. To do this, it receives the `currentToken` and what remains of the `infix` queue. The verifying function strips away enough of the `infix` queue to verify its particular grammatical construction and then returns the potentially altered `currentToken` and `infix` queue to its calling function, along with a Boolean value to indicate whether or not it was successful. Formally, the specifications for these verifying functions are:

```
//----------------------------------------------------------------------------
// Function parseExpression:    verifies an expression

// Given the current token and what is left in the queue of tokens that
// originally contained the entire expression to be parsed, return true if
// an expression (according to the grammar of Example 14.10) can be
// verified and false otherwise

bool parseExpression(queue<token> &infix, token& currentToken);

//----------------------------------------------------------------------------
// Function parseFactor:     verifies a factor

// Given the current token and what is left in the queue of tokens that
// originally contained the entire expression to be parsed, return true if
// a factor (according to the grammar of Example 14.10) can be
// verified and false otherwise

bool parseFactor(queue<token> &infix, token& currentToken);

//----------------------------------------------------------------------------
// Function parseAddFactor:     verifies an addFactor

// Given the current token and what is left in the queue of tokens that
// originally contained the entire expression to be parsed, return true if
// an addFactor (according to the grammar of Example 14.10) can be
// verified and false otherwise

bool parseAddFactor(queue<token> &infix, token& currentToken);

//----------------------------------------------------------------------------
// Function parseMultFactor:    verifies a multFactor
```

```
// Given the current token and what is left in the queue of tokens that
// originally contained the entire expression to be parsed, return true if
// a multFactor (according to the grammar of Example 14.10) can be
// verified and false otherwise

bool parseMultFactor(queue<token> &infix, token& currentToken);

//-----------------------------------------------------------------------
// Function parsePrimary:    verifies a primary

// Given the current token and what is left in the queue of tokens that
// originally contained the entire expression to be parsed, return true if
// a primary (according to the grammar of Example 14.10) can be
// verified and false otherwise

bool parsePrimary(queue<token> &infix, token& currentToken);
```

Implementation

The subordinate functions called upon by a given function are dictated by the right sides of productions defining that function's associated nonterminal in the context-free grammar. Since typically many of these productions will have the terminal being defined on the left reappearing on the right, many of the associated functions will be recursive in nature. Consequently, the general algorithmic technique is termed *recursive descent parsing*. The run-time trace diagram of recursive calls will parallel the parse tree for the expression. Complete implementations of `parse` and all verifying functions follow. Study them closely; the accompanying graphic documentation will help clarify what is happening. You will get a chance to explore recursive descent parsing more deeply in the problems at the end of the chapter.

```
bool parse(queue<token> infix)
{
  token currentToken;

  if (infix.empty())
    return(false);
  else
  {
    currentToken = infix.dequeue();
    if (parseExpression(infix, currentToken))
      return(infix.empty());
    else
      return(false);
  }
}

bool parseExpression(queue<token> &infix, token& currentToken)
{
  if (parseFactor(infix, currentToken))
    return(parseAddFactor(infix, currentToken));
  else
    return(false);
}
```

<expression> → <factor><add-factor>

continued

```
bool parseFactor(queue<token> &infix, token& currentToken)
{
  if (parsePrimary(infix, currentToken))
    return(parseMultFactor(infix, currentToken));
  else
    return(false);
}
```

<factor> → <primary><mult-factor>

```
bool parseAddFactor(queue<token> &infix, token& currentToken)
{
  if (! isAddOp(currentToken))    // NULL production is satisfied
    return(true);
  else if (infix.empty())         // Something should follow add operator
    return(false);
  else
  {
     currentToken = infix.dequeue();
     if (parseFactor(infix, currentToken))
       return(parseAddFactor(infix, currentToken));
     else
       return(false);
  }
}
```

<add-factor> → '+' <factor><add-factor>

```
bool parseMultFactor(queue<token> &infix, token& currentToken)
{
  if (! isMultOp(currentToken))   // NULL production is satisfied
    return(true);
  else if (infix.empty())         // Something should follow mult operator
    return(false);
  else
  {
     currentToken = infix.dequeue();
     if (parseFactor(infix, currentToken))
       return(parseMultFactor(infix, currentToken));
     else
       return(false);
  }
}
```

<mult-factor> → '*' <factor><mult-factor>

```
bool parsePrimary(queue<token> &infix, token& currentToken)
{
  if ( currentToken.code() == VAR_X || currentToken.code() == REAL_VALUE )
  {
     if (!infix.empty())
       currentToken = infix.dequeue();
     return(true);
  }
  else
    if (! isLeftParen(currentToken))
      return(false);
    else                            // We must have parenthesized expression
      if(infix.empty())
         return(false);
      else
      {
```

<primary> → identifier
<primary> → number

```
      currentToken = infix.dequeue();
      if (parseExpression(infix, currentToken))
         if ( isRightParen(currentToken))
         {
            if (!infix.empty())
               currentToken = infix.dequeue();
            return(true);
         }
         else
            return(false);
      else
         return(false);
   }
}
```

<primary> → '(' expression ')'

The large amount of code in this suite of functions belies the ease with which each function can be written, provided that we start with a sound grammatical description of the expressions being parsed. As indicated by the graphic documentation, each verifying function merely calls on subordinate verifying functions in the order dictated by the right side of a production in the context-free grammar. For nonterminals that have more than one defining production, the `currentToken` parameter is examined to determine which production to follow.

As easy as the process seems, there are some negatives to the recursive descent parsing method. First, it applies only to context-free grammars that have their productions in a suitable form. The productions from Example 14.10 are in that form, but in Exercise 4 (Section 14.4), you explored a context-free grammar that is not appropriate for the recursive descent method. Thus, to use recursive descent parsing, you must learn to write "correct" grammars.

A second negative is the rigidity of a recursive descent parser once it has been implemented. Should you have a change of heart about the syntax rules of the language being parsed, the resulting changes in productions may lead to widespread and dramatic changes in the code for the parser itself because the code is directly tied to the productions. Hence, maintainability of the code in a recursive descent parser can be a problem. This places a real premium on getting the grammar right the first time, before you begin generating code from it. Compare this to the ease with which one can alter a parse by changing the priority functions in the parsing method discussed in Section 13.3.

Running, Debugging, and Testing Hints

1. Recursion is an elegant and powerful tool. It combines iterative control with a built-in data structure, the system stack. To properly control that iteration, be sure that you provide an appropriate recursive termination condition for your algorithms.

2. Be sure that, when you invoke a function recursively, you are in some sense passing in a smaller, simpler version of the problem being solved. Otherwise, your algorithm will infinitely recur.

3. The use of tracer output can be valuable in debugging recursive algorithms. However, you must be careful not to insert so many tracer output statements that you become lost in the copious output they produce. Remember that recursive algorithms are often exponential in efficiency and, consequently, may be exponential in the amount of output produced by tracers also. You must be careful to insert tracer output statements judiciously. Where appropriate, use a Boolean constant that can be toggled to `true` or `false` to control whether or not the tracer output is produced.

Summary

Key Terms

activation record
binding time problem
context-free grammar
generalized nested loops
grammar
LISP
nonterminals
parse tree
recursion
recursive call
recursive definition
recursive descent parser
recursive function
recursive termination condition
run-time trace diagram
stack frame
start symbol
tail recursion
terminals
termination condition
trial-and-error backtracking

Key Concepts

- Stacks process function calls when a program executes. Understanding the role of the stack in this application is essential to effective use of the programming technique known as recursion.
- A recursive function invokes itself with a simpler version of the same problem it was originally given. Ultimately, there must be a recursive termination condition to break a series of recursive function calls.
- In tail recursion, no further processing occurs at any level of recursion after a return from a recursive call is made.
- A function's stack frame contains memory locations for all parameters and local variables and the machine address of the point to return to after the function completes execution at the current level.
- A run-time trace diagram can often be used to help analyze the efficiency of a recursive algorithm. If the diagram indicates that multiple recursive calls are made at each level, there is a good chance that the algorithm is in the class of exponential algorithms.
- Recursion can be used to solve a complex class of search problems by using a trial-and-error backtracking strategy. However, often such solutions consume a tremendous amount of resources, particularly in terms of run-time efficiency.
- Do not be misled into thinking that recursion is necessarily the most efficient programming technique because the code that expresses it is often compact and lacking in any explicit loop control statements such as `while` or `do`. The very nature of a recursive call generates iteration without any need for `while` or `do`. The iteration control mechanism in recursion is the recursive termination condition that triggers a series of returns before another recursive call is made. Hence, from a time-efficiency perspective, a recursive algorithm's measure of effectiveness is closely tied to the number of times it must iterate its recursive call-and-return pattern. Moreover, with recursion, we pay a price in memory efficiency that is not present in other iterative control structures. This price is system stack space.
- The value of recursion lies in the way it enables us to express algorithms compactly and elegantly for a certain class of problems. Since we use recursion frequently throughout the rest of this text, you will learn to acquire a feel for the type of problems particularly suitable to this powerful technique. In the next chapter, we will see that recursion is an indispensable strategy for manipulating a data structure known as a tree. In later chapters, recursion will be explored as a means of sorting and searching.

Programming Problems and Projects

1. Write a program to call for input of a decimal number and convert it to its binary equivalent using the method described in the following flowchart:

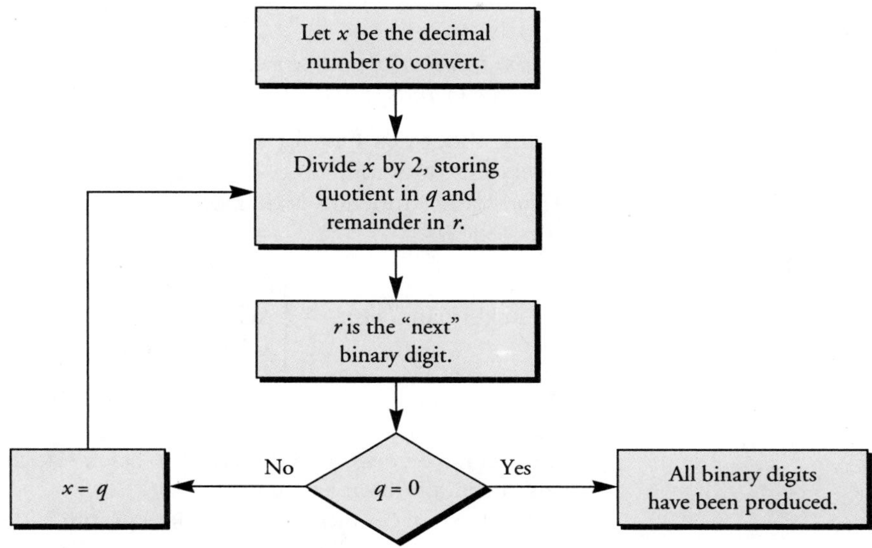

Note that this method produces the binary digits for the given number in reverse order. One strategy for printing the digits in the correct order is to store them in an array as they are produced and then print the array. However, this strategy has the drawbacks of allocating unnecessary storage for an array and then limiting the size of the binary number to the size of the array. Your program is not to employ this strategy. Rather call for input of the decimal number in your main program and then immediately transfer control to a function that in turn is called recursively, stacking the binary digits as they are produced. Once division by 2 yields 0, the succession of returns can be used to print the digits one by one as they are popped from this stack.

2. The Nth Fibonacci number is defined by

   1 if N is 1.
   1 if N is 2.
   The sum of the previous two Fibonacci numbers otherwise.

   Write a recursive function to compute the Nth Fibonacci number. Then, using a run-time trace diagram, analyze the efficiency of your function.

3. Euclid devised a clever algorithm for computing the greatest common divisor (GCD) of two integers. According to Euclid's algorithm,

$$\text{GCD}(M, N) = \begin{cases} \text{GCD}(N, M) \text{ if } N > M \\ \text{GCD}(N, M \% N) \text{ if } N > 0 \\ M \text{ if } N = 0 \end{cases}$$

   Write a recursive function to compute GCDs via Euclid's method.

4. Suppose you have N thousand dollars and can use it to buy a combination of Orange computers (which cost \$1000 each), HAL computers (which cost \$2000 each), or MAX computers (which cost \$4000 each). How many different combinations of Orange, HAL, and MAX computers could be bought with your N thousand dollars?

Write a program that receives N as input and responds with the number of possible combinations.

Hint: If N were 100, then the number of combinations is

the number of combinations totaling $100,000 and involving Orange and HAL computers only

PLUS

the number of combinations totaling $96,000 and involving potentially all three brands

Think about this hint for a while and extend it to a recursive function that answers this question.

5. Ackermann's function is defined recursively for two nonnegative integers m and n as follows:

$$\text{Ackermann}(m,n) = \begin{cases} n + 1 \text{ if } m = 0 \\ \text{Ackermann}(m-1,\ 1) \text{ if } n = 0 \\ \text{Ackermann}(m-1,\ \text{Ackermann}\ (m,\ n-1)) \text{ otherwise} \end{cases}$$

Write a recursive version of this function. Develop a run-time trace diagram for the function when $m = 2$ and $n = 3$. Attempt to deduce the big-O efficiency of the recursive version with respect to stack size and stack operations. Justify your answer in a written statement.

6. If you have access to an appropriate graphics device, write the functions `line` and `rightTurn` described in Section 14.1. Then experiment by writing recursive functions that call on these functions (and others you may develop) to produce a variety of interesting figures.

7. Write a function that receives a set of N integers and then prints all subsets of this set.

8. Write a program that completes the solution of the Eight Queens problem as sketched in Section 14.3.

9. A K-permutation of the first N positive integers, $K <= N$, is a permutation of a K-element subset of $\{1, 2, \ldots, N\}$. Write a function to generate all possible K-permutations of the first N positive integers.

10. A continued fraction is a number of the form that follows (where each a_i is an integer):

$$a_1 + \cfrac{1}{a_2 + \cfrac{1}{a_3 + \cfrac{1}{a_4 + \cfrac{\vdots}{\;\;\ddots \;\; \cfrac{1}{a_n}}}}}$$

Although a continued fraction is composed of integers a_i, it has a real value. For example, consider the following continued fraction and its indicated real value:

$$1 + \cfrac{1}{2 + \cfrac{1}{6 + \cfrac{1}{5}}} = 1 + \cfrac{1}{2 + \cfrac{1}{\frac{31}{5}}} = 1 + \cfrac{1}{2 + \frac{5}{31}} = 1 + \cfrac{1}{\frac{67}{31}} = \frac{98}{67} = 1.46$$

Provide a class declaration of your implementation of a continued fraction. Then, write a recursive function that receives a continued fraction and returns its associated real value. If you are really ambitious, write a complete suite of arithmetic operations on continued fractions.

11. There are five other teams in the same league as the Bay Area Brawlers (Problem 4, Chapter 12, and Problem 13, Chapter 13). Over a given 5-week period, the Brawlers must play each of the other teams exactly once. Using recursion, write a program to determine the ways in which such a 5-week schedule could be accomplished. For an added challenge, introduce more realistic scheduling considerations into this problem. For instance, have your program determine the ways in which a 15-game schedule could be constructed such that each of the six teams in the league plays each of the other teams exactly three times, but never consecutively.

12. Write a function that uses a random number generator to produce mazes. One way of viewing a maze is as a two-dimensional array of structures:

```
struct location
{
    bool  northBlocked,
          eastBlocked,
          southBlocked,
          westBlocked;
};
```

At each square in the array, the Boolean attributes are set to indicate whether or not we can proceed in the indicated direction. After your maze-generating function is working, develop a function that uses trial-and-error backtracking to solve the maze.

13. A transportation network such as the following can be represented as a two-dimensional integer array with rows and columns indexed by the cities in the network. The number stored at position (`K, J`) of such an array represents the distance of the link between two cities. Zero indicates that two cities are not directly linked.

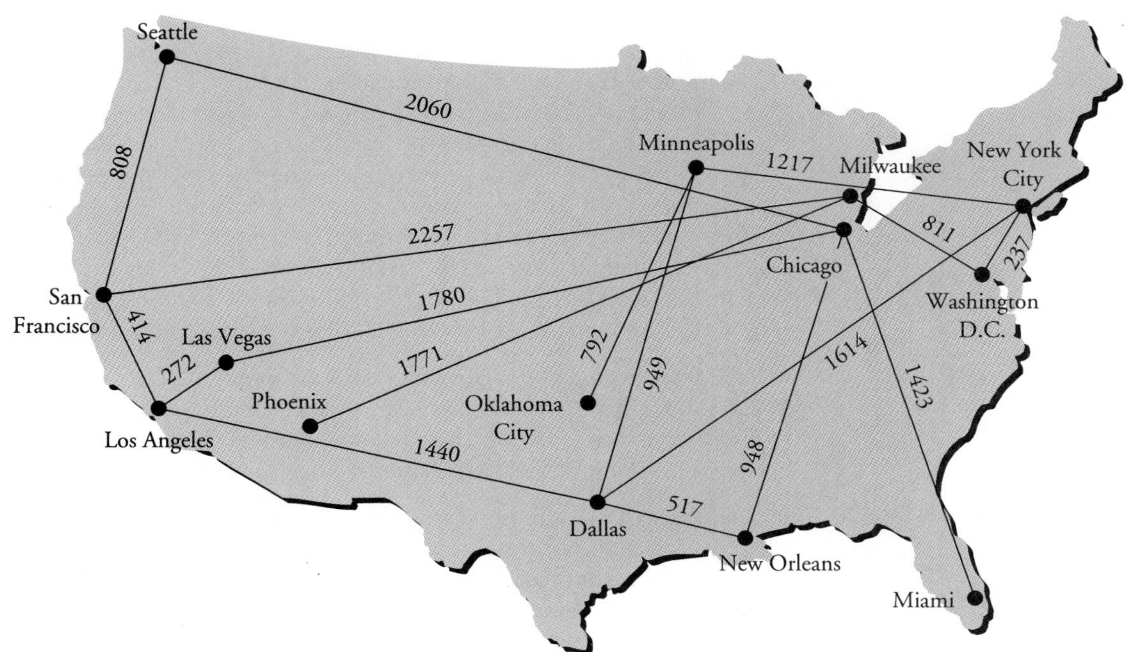

Write a program which, for input of two cities, outputs all possible paths connecting the two cities. Then modify the program so that it outputs only the shortest path linking the two cities. Use a trial-and-error backtracking strategy to do this. We will discuss a more efficient algorithm for solving this problem in the next chapter.

14. Another classic chess problem that can be solved by trial-and-error backtracking is known as the Knight's Tour. Given a chessboard with a knight initially placed at coordinates x_0, y_0, the problem is to specify a series of moves for the knight that will result in each board location being visited exactly once. From a given square on the chessboard, a knight may move to any of the eight numbered squares in the following diagram:

	3		2	
4				1
5				8
	6		7	

Write a program to find a valid Knight's Tour.

15. A famous theorem in mathematics states that four colors are enough to color any map in a fashion that allows each region on the map to be a different color from any of its adjacent neighbors. Write a program that initially allows input of a map. One way of doing this is to input each region followed by a list of its adjacent neighbors. This information can then be stored in a two-dimensional Boolean array with rows and columns indexed by region names. Store `true` at row `K`, column `J`, if region `K` and region `J` are neighbors; otherwise, store `false`. Once your program has appropriately stored the information associated with the input map, it should use trial-and-error backtracking to find a pattern for coloring the map with four colors. Note that the Four-Color theorem from mathematics guarantees that such a pattern can be found.

16. Write a program to find a solution to the following stable marriage problem (or indicate that no solution exists for the input data). According to this problem, we have *N* men and *N* women, each of whom has stated distinct preferences for their possible partners. The data regarding these preferences are the input for this problem. It can be stored in two two-dimensional arrays: one in which each woman has rated each of the men as first choice, second choice, . . . , *N*th choice and another in which each man has similarly rated each of the women. Given this input, a solution to the stable marriage problem is to find *N* couples (marriages) such that

- Each man is part of exactly one couple (marriage).
- Each woman is part of exactly one couple (marriage).
- There does not exist a man and a woman who are not married to each other but who would prefer each other to their current spouses.

If a pair as specified in the last requirement does exist, then the assignment of *N* couples is said to be unstable and should be avoided. Note that the stable marriage problem is representative of many real-life problems in which assignments have to be made according to preferences.

17. Write a program to analyze football scores by computing the point spread for any team A playing any team B. Your program should compute the point spreads as follows:

Level I analysis: Team A played B in past
Level II analysis: Average point spreads for situations such as

A played C—point spread 3
C played B—point spread 7

Total point spread 10

Level III analysis: Average point spread for situations such as

A played C—point spread 3
C played D—point spread –14 (C lost)
D played B—point spread 7

Total point spread –4

Level IV analysis: Average point spreads for situations such as

A played C—point spread 3
C played D—point spread –14
D played E—point spread 21
E played B—point spread 4

Total point spread 14

All level II point spreads are then averaged for a final level II point spread figure. Point spreads are similarly averaged for levels III and IV. Items that potentially need to be stacked (via recursion) in this program include:

- Accumulated point spread at current position
- Number of scores reflected in the accumulated point spread at current position
- Current position; that is, team A playing team B
- Path to the current position; that is, teams played to get to the current position

18. Write a solution to the Towers of Hanoi problem in which you use a nonrecursive iterative control structure and a stack. In effect, your stack will simulate the role played by the system stack in the recursive version of the algorithm. In a written statement, compare the time and space efficiency of your nonrecursive solution to the recursive solution presented in this chapter. Is your solution faster than the exponential recursive solution? If so, explain why it is. Otherwise, explain why it is still exponential in its run time.

19. Extend the recursive descent parser from the Case Study in this chapter by:
a. Providing descriptive error messages when a syntax error is encountered
b. Returning a queue of tokens representing the postfix form of the expression
c. Allowing any or all of the operators suggested in Exercise 2 of Section 14.4

20. Repeat Problem 19, but develop the recursive descent parser from the context-free grammar in Exercise 3 in Section 14.4.

21. Develop a recursive descent parser for the S-expression grammar you provided as an answer to Exercise 6 in Section 14.4.

22. If you have had a course in discrete mathematics, then you may be familiar with recurrence relations and methods for explicitly solving them. Use your knowledge of recurrence relations to analyze the time and space efficiencies of the Towers of Hanoi and recursive binary search algorithms. Your analysis should be presented as a precise mathematical argument, citing any results that you use but do not prove.

15

Binary Trees, General Trees, and Graphs

Chapter Outline

Except during the nine months before he draws his first breath, no man manages his affairs as well as a tree does.
George Bernard Shaw, 1856–1950

Human beings organize much of the world around them into *hierarchies*. For instance, an industrial body functions effectively only by defining a collection of client–server relationships among its participants. We have emphasized throughout the text that computer scientists design a software system by breaking it down into modules and defining hierarchical client–server relationships among those modules. In Chapter 14, we used hierarchical run-time trace diagrams to analyze the efficiency of recursive algorithms. In Section 14.4, we introduced the notion of a parse tree as a way of diagrammatically representing the syntax of an expression. To continue this discussion, we now introduce the idea of trees as a data structure.

The familial parent–child relationship allows a natural breakdown of a family's history into a genealogical tree. In computer science, a *tree* is a data structure that represents such hierarchical relationships between data items.

To introduce some of the terminology of tree structures, consider the record of a student at a university. In addition to the usual statistical background information such as social security number, name, and address, a typical student record contains listings for a number of courses, exams and final grades in each course, overall grade point average, and other data relating to the student's performance at the college. Figure 15.1 is a tree structure representing such a student record. As in genealogical trees, at the highest *level* (0) of a tree is its *root* (also called the *root node*). Here STUDENT is the root node. The nodes NAME, ADDRESS, SSN, COURSE, and GPA, which are directly connected to the root node, are the *child nodes* of the *parent node* STUDENT. The child nodes of a given parent constitute a set of *siblings*. Thus, NAME, ADDRESS, SSN, COURSE, and GPA are siblings. In the hierarchy represented by a tree, the child nodes of a parent are one level lower than the parent node. Thus, NAME, ADDRESS, SSN, COURSE, and GPA are at level 1 in Figure 15.1. A link between a parent and its child is called a *branch* in a tree

Figure 15.1 Tree structure representing a student record

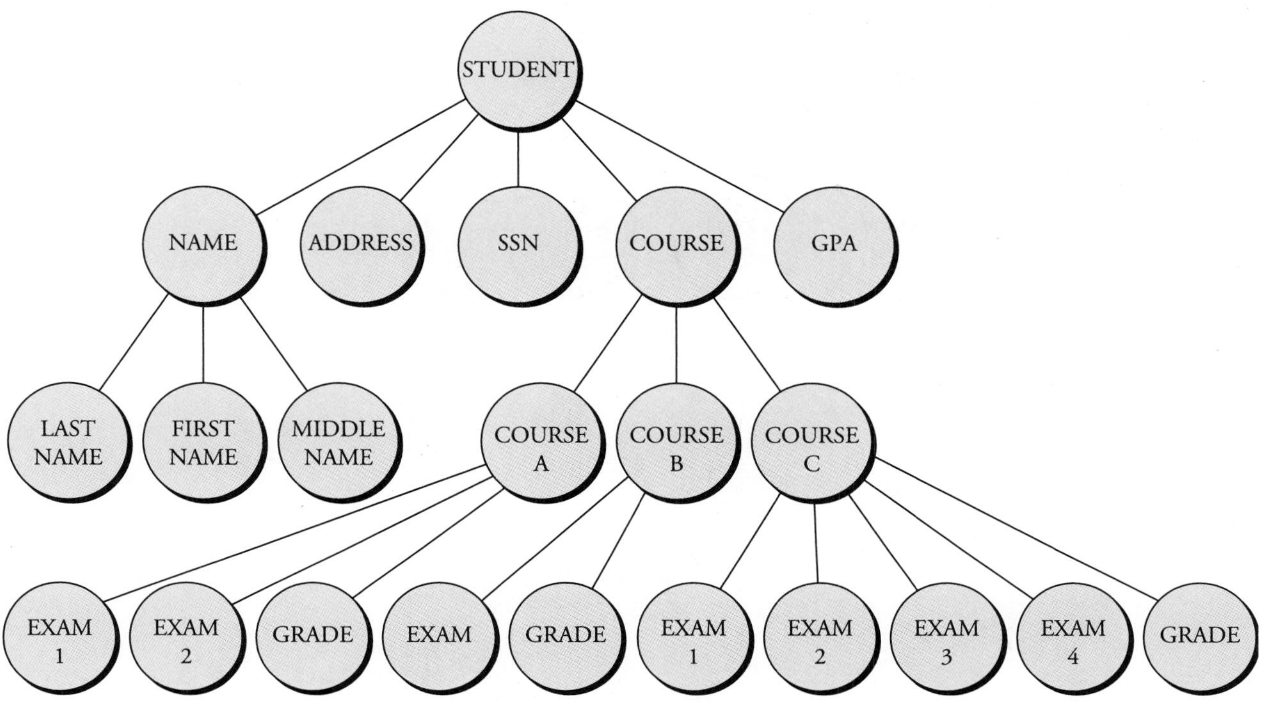

Figure 15.2
Subtree of Figure 15.1

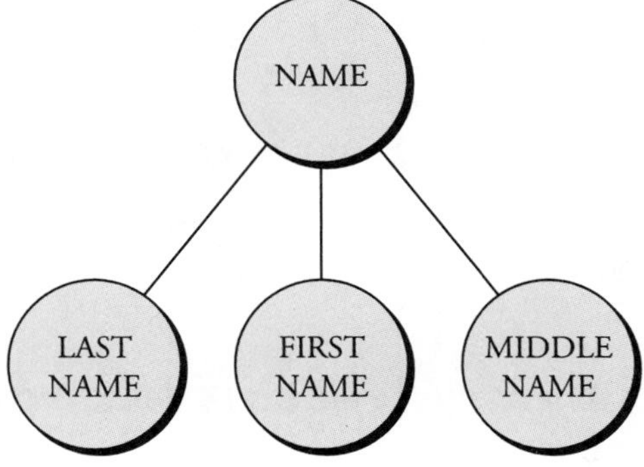

structure. Each node in a tree except the root must descend from a parent node via a branch. Thus, LAST NAME, FIRST NAME, and MIDDLE NAME descend from the parent node NAME. The root of the tree is the *ancestor* of all the nodes in the tree.

A node with no children is called a *leaf node*. In Figure 15.1, GPA is a leaf node. LAST NAME, FIRST NAME, MIDDLE NAME, EXAM 1, and EXAM 2, for instance, also are leaf nodes.

A *subtree* is a subset of a tree that is itself a tree; the tree in Figure 15.2 is a subtree of the tree in Figure 15.1. This subtree has the root node NAME. Similarly, the tree in Figure 15.3 is another subtree of the tree in Figure 15.1. Notice that the tree in Figure 15.3 is a subtree of the tree in Figure 15.1 and the tree in Figure 15.4.

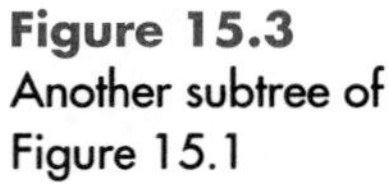

Figure 15.3 Another subtree of Figure 15.1

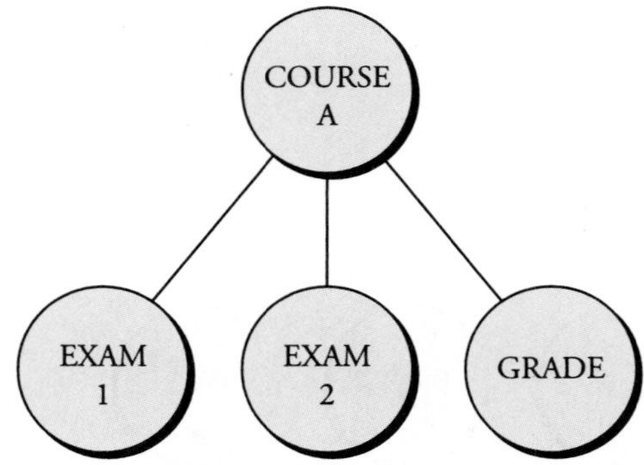

Figure 15.4 Another subtree of Figure 15.1

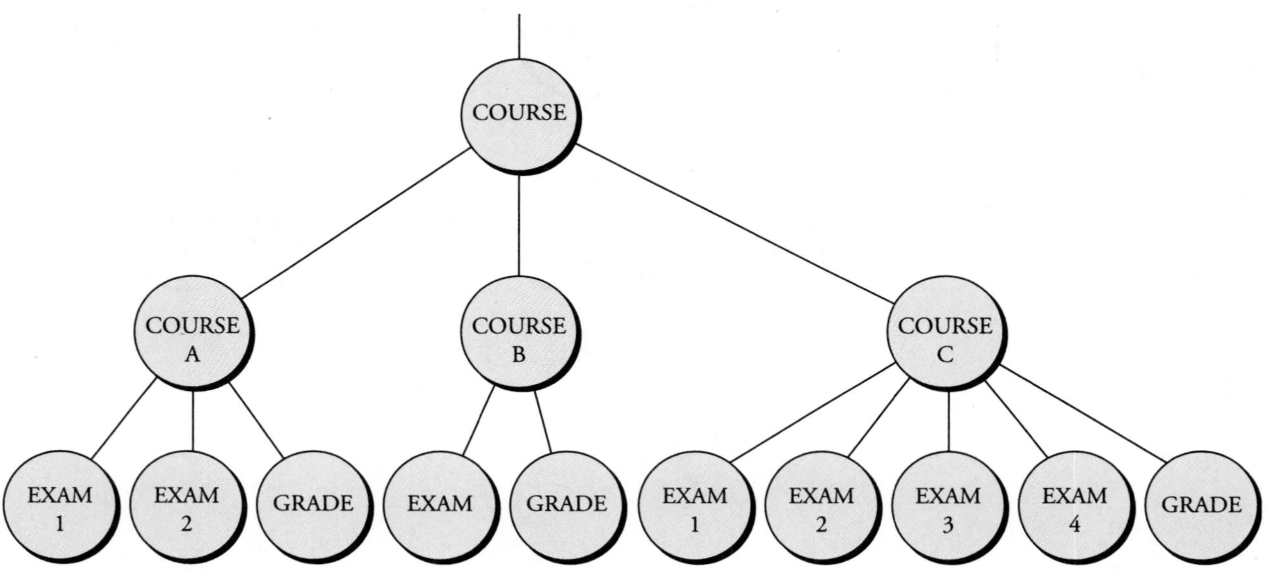

15.1 General Trees and Binary Trees as Abstract Data Types

It is evident from the preceding discussion that a tree has the following interesting property: Any given node within a tree is itself the root node of a completely analogous tree structure. That is, a tree is composed of a collection of substructures, each of which also meets the criteria for being a tree. This sounds dangerously circular, and to formally describe a tree in this fashion, we must be sure to give ourselves an escape from the recursion. This is done via the following definition of a tree as an abstract data type:

Tree: A general tree is a set of nodes that is either empty (the recursive termination condition) or has a designated node called the root from which descend zero or more subtrees. No node is an ancestor of itself, and each subtree that descends from the root also satisfies the definition of a tree.

We defer completing the definition of a general tree to Section 15.5, where we will more formally discuss the operations associated with this ADT.

Objectives

a. to define partially the general tree ADT
b. to define completely the binary tree ADT
c. to understand conceptually the effect of each of the binary tree operations
d. to become familiar with some examples of binary trees such as heaps, arithmetic expression trees, and binary search trees

Two points about this partial definition should be emphasized. First, the recursive fashion in which a tree is defined should provide a strong hint that most tree-processing algorithms will also be recursive. Second, most operations on the tree data structure are closely linked to the hierarchical relationship among nodes for that particular tree. This hierarchical relationship may vary greatly from tree to tree. To consider some examples of such relationships, which are found quite often in computer science applications, let us restrict our attention for the moment to an abstract data type called a *binary tree.*

Binary tree: A binary tree is a tree in which each node has exactly two subtrees. These two subtrees are designated as the left and right subtrees, respectively. Note that either or both of these subtrees could be empty.

We specify the following operations on a binary tree in terms of preconditions and postconditions.

Create Operation

Preconditions:	Receiver is a binary tree in an unpredictable state.
Postconditions:	Receiver is initialized to the empty binary tree.

Empty Operation

Preconditions:	Receiver is a previously created binary tree.
Postconditions:	Returns `true` if the tree is empty, `false` otherwise.

Insert Operation

Preconditions:	Receiver is a previously created binary tree based on a particular hierarchical property. `item` is a value to be inserted in the tree. There is memory available in the tree for the new item.
Postconditions:	`item` is added to the tree in a way that maintains the tree's hierarchical property.

preorderTraverse Operation

Preconditions:	Receiver is a previously created binary tree, and `process` is an algorithmic process that can be applied to each node in the tree.
Postconditions:	Each node of the tree is visited in the following order: First visit the root of the tree, then visit recursively all nodes in left subtree, then recursively all nodes in right subtree. As each node is visited, `process` is applied to it.

inorderTraverse Operation

Preconditions:	Receiver is a previously created binary tree, and `process` is an algorithmic process that can be applied to each node in the tree.
Postconditions:	Each node of the tree is visited in the following order: First visit recursively all nodes in left subtree of the tree, then visit the root of the tree, then recursively all nodes in right subtree. As each node is visited, `process` is applied to it.

postorderTraverse Operation

Preconditions:	Receiver is a previously created binary tree, and `process` is an algorithmic process that can be applied to each node in the tree.
Postconditions:	Each node of the tree is visited in the following order: First visit recursively all nodes in left subtree of the tree, then visit recursively all nodes in right subtree, then visit the root of the tree. As each node is visited, `process` is applied to it.

Several remarks are in order concerning this definition. First, the three traversal procedures require some clarification. With a linked list, there is only one obvious traversal because there was only one node that could be reached from any given node. However, with a binary tree, at any node, some choices need to be made:

- Should we apply `process` to the data field of the root before proceeding to the left and right subtrees?

- Should we apply `process` to the nodes in the left subtree and right subtree before processing the data in the root?
- Should we apply `process` to all the nodes in one of the subtrees, then to the root, and finally to all the nodes in the other subtree?

The answers to these questions determine the type of traversal. Figure 15.5 demonstrates the different orders in which nodes are visited under the three traversals.

Second, the `insert` operation specified in our ADT definition for a binary tree provides a generic tree-building operation. That is, repeated applications of the `insert` operation on an initially empty binary tree typically lead to the construction of a binary tree. However, it is virtually impossible to define or implement the `insert` operation in a way that is general enough for all applications that will use a binary tree. Each instance of a binary tree is highly dependent on the hierarchical relationship between nodes that defines that particular binary tree. Therefore, we have linked our specification of the `insert` operation to the hierarchical relationship underlying a particular binary tree.

The following three examples provide illustrations of hierarchical relationships that can be used in defining binary trees. We will often use trees based on these hierarchical properties as examples in the remainder of the chapter. However, these three properties should by no means be considered exhaustive because virtually every application that uses a binary tree will have its own essential property. The point to be emphasized now is that the `insert` operation must, in its implementation, always be tailored to the property that defines a tree.

Figure 15.5
Differences between preorder, inorder, and postorder traversals

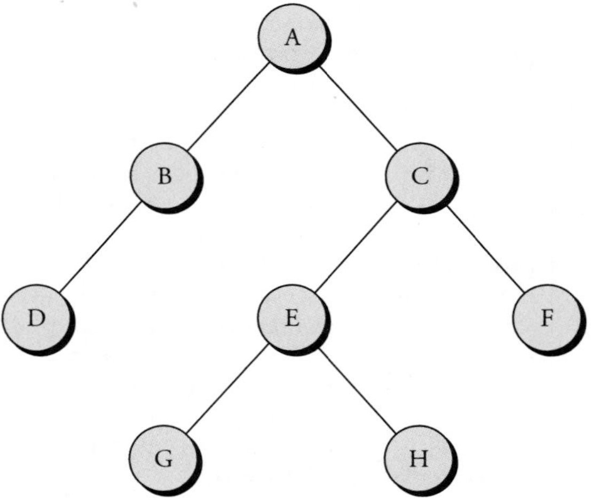

Order in which nodes are processed:

Preorder traversal		*Inorder traversal*		*Postorder traversal*	
A	root	D	left subtree	D	left subtree
B	left subtree	B		B	
D		A	root	G	right subtree
C	right subtree	G	right subtree	H	
E		E		E	
G		H		F	
H		C		C	
F		F		A	root

Example 15.1 The tree of Figure 15.6 is a binary tree. Each node of this tree has two subtrees (null or non-null) designated as the left subtree and the right subtree. The particular hierarchical relationship underlying this tree is that the data in any given node of the tree are greater than or equal to the data in its left and right subtrees. A tree with this property is said to be a *heap* and to have the *heap property*. (This notion is not to be confused with the heap maintained by C++ for allocating space to pointer variables as described in Chapter 12.) We will discuss heaps in more detail in the next section. Also, they will prove particularly important in our discussion of more powerful sorting methods in Chapter 16. The programming problems at the end of this chapter also indicate how a heap may be used to implement the priority queue abstract data type introduced in Chapter 13. The heap property is one example of a hierarchical relationship that can underlie a tree and hence must be preserved when various operations are performed on the tree.

Example 15.2 A second example of a hierarchical relationship underlying a binary tree structure is shown in Figure 15.7. This binary tree exhibits the property known as the *ordering*

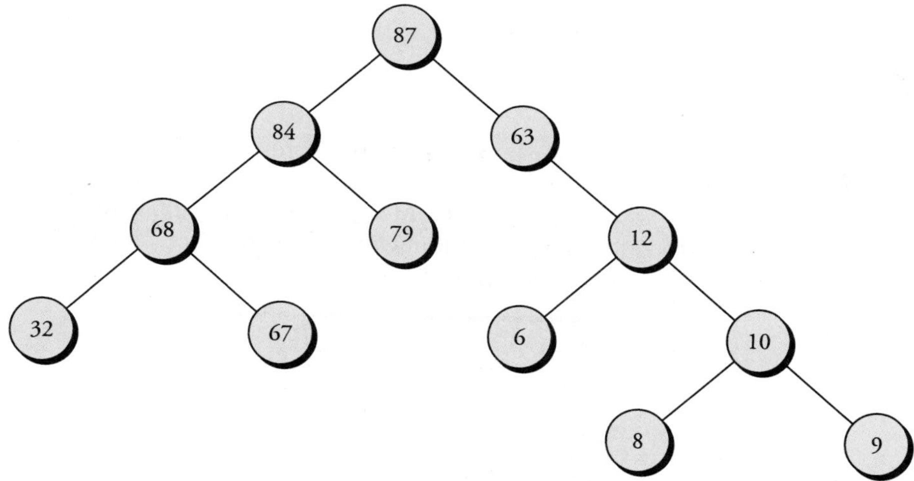

Figure 15.6
Binary tree with the heap property

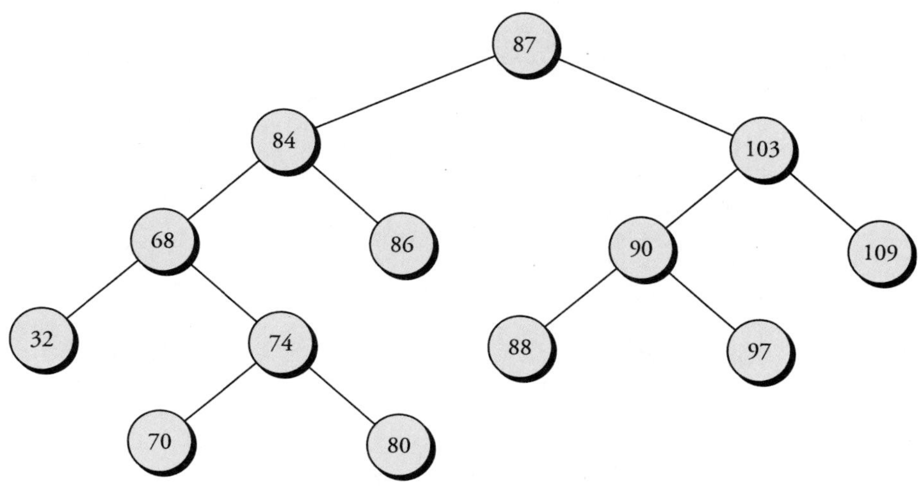

Figure 15.7
Binary search tree with the ordering property

property; the data in each node of the tree are greater than all of the data in that node's left subtree and less than or equal to all of the data in the right subtree. A binary tree with the ordering property is often called a ***binary search tree***. We shall see the importance of trees possessing this property when we explore binary trees as a means of implementing a one-key table in Section 15.3.

Example 15.3 As a final example of a hierarchical relationship that can determine the arrangement of data in a binary tree, consider Figure 15.8, in which we have a binary tree representation of the infix algebraic expression

```
(A - B) + C * (E / F)
```

Take a moment to make particular note of Figure 15.8. Since we will be referring back to it frequently throughout this chapter, you may want to clip the page or mark it with a bookmark.

The hierarchical relationship of a parent to its children in this tree is that of algebraic operator to its two operands. Note that an operand may itself be an expression (that is, a subtree) which must be evaluated before the operator in the parent node can be applied. Note also that, if the order of evaluation in the expression changes as in

```
(A - B) + C * E / F
```

then the corresponding binary expression tree must also change, as reflected in Figure 15.9. Contemporary compilers make use of tree structures in obtaining forms of an arithmetic expression for efficient evaluation. As we've seen, there are basically three forms for an arithmetic expression such as that corresponding to Figure 15.8: infix, prefix, and postfix.

Expression	Form
`(A - B) + C * (E / F)`	infix
`+ - A B * C / E F`	prefix
`A B - C E F / * +`	postfix

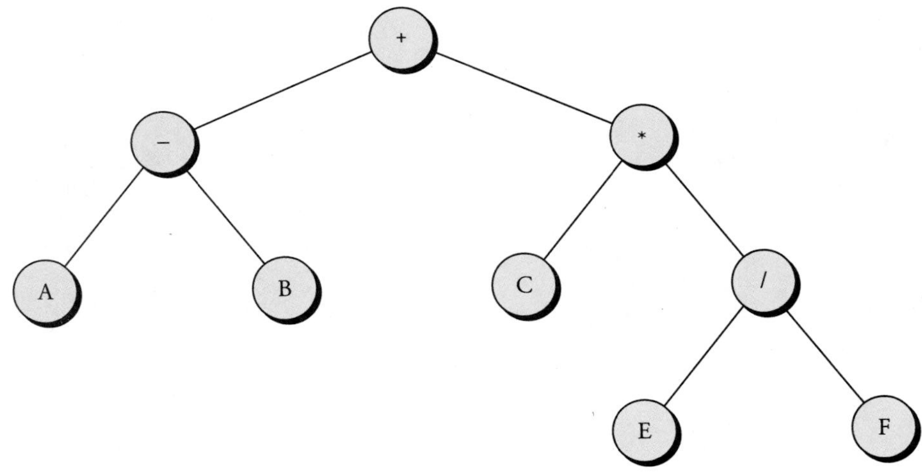

Figure 15.8
Binary expression tree for `(A - B) + C * (E/F)`

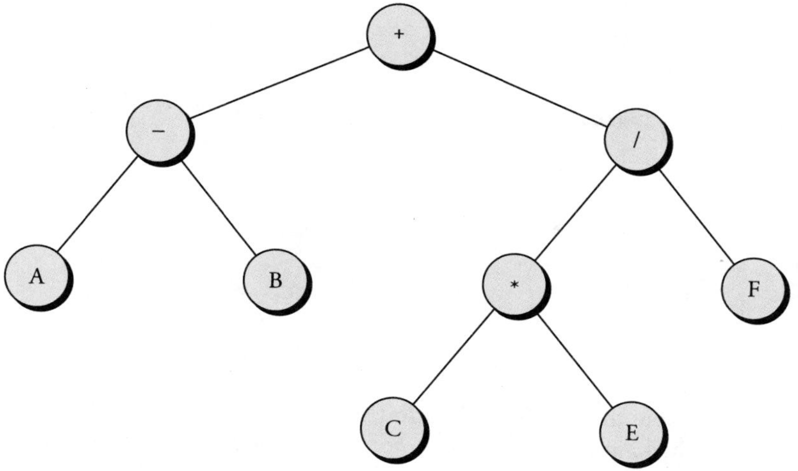

Figure 15.9
Binary expression tree for `(A - B) + C * E/F`

All three of these forms are immediately available to us if we know exactly how the corresponding tree should be traversed. The *inorder traversal* of the binary tree for an arithmetic expression gives us the expression in unparenthesized infix form. The *preorder traversal* of the same tree leads us to the prefix form of the expression, whereas the *postorder traversal* of the tree yields the postfix form of the expression. We shall study procedures for these three traversals in Section 15.2, when we discuss a method of implementing a binary tree.

We close this section with a C++ interface for the binary tree ADT. In the sections that follow, we will analyze two implementations that adhere to this interface.

C++ Interface for the Binary Tree ADT

```
// Class declaration file: bintree.h

// Declaration section

#ifndef TREE_H
#define TREE_H

template <class E> class BinaryTree
{

    public:

    // Class constructors

    BinaryTree();
    BinaryTree(const BinaryTree<E> &bt);
    // Class destructor

    ~BinaryTree();

    // Member functions

    bool empty();
    void insert(const E &item);
```

continued

```
    void preorderTraverse(void (* process) (E &item));
    void inorderTraverse(void (* process) (E &item));
    void postorderTraverse(void (* process) (E &item));
    BinaryTree<E>& operator = (const BinaryTree<E> &bt);

    protected:

    // Protected declaration dependent on implementation would go here

};

#endif
```

Note that the formal parameter list of each of the member function traverse operations has a parameter of type *pointer to function*. The syntax for declaring a parameter that is itself a (pointer to a) function is to provide the interface for any function that will be passed in this parameter slot. In the preceding traverse operations, this interface is given by `void (* process) (E &item)`, which says that any function passed in this slot must return `void` (that is, no return value) and must have one formal reference parameter of type `E`. A client program having a binary tree of integers that it wanted to display via an inorder traversal has to define the function to display one integer and then pass this function in as the actual parameter associated with `process`. The following code segment shows how this is done:

```
#include <iostream.h>

#include "bintree.h"

void print(int &x);        // Interface for the function that will
                           // display one of the ints in the tree

int main ()
{
   BinaryTree<int> my Tree;     // Tree of data

   // Here the client program would have code to load data into
   // the tree.

   ...

   myTree.inorderTraverse(print);     // Call on traversal with
                                      // function to display
   return 0;
}

void print (int &x)        // Implementation of the display function
{
   cout << x << " ";
}
```

The use of a parameter that is a pointer to a function allows the client program to decide what will be done at each node during the traversal. For instance, if the client program later wanted to display only those nodes that were even numbers during a traversal, it could define another display function:

```
void printEvens(int &x)
{
    if (x % 2 == 0)
        cout << x << " ";
}
```

and then invoke the traversal with this function

```
myTree.inorderTraverse(printEvens);
```

This method for allowing a client program to determine what a traversal will do at each node is limited to the constraints that the interface to the function allows. At times, this can be a limitation that greatly inhibits using the traversals. You will investigate ways of extending the basic binary tree class in the Case Study for this chapter.

Exercises 15.1

1. Draw a binary tree for the following expression:

```
A * B - (C + D) * (P / Q)
```

2. Represent the following information as a binary tree:

```
struct name
{
        string firstName, lastName;
);

struct year
{
       string firstSem, secondSem;
};

struct student
{
        name studentName;
        year yearOfStudy;
};
```

3. What, in an abstract sense, does a tree structure represent?

4. Indicate which of the following are binary search trees with the ordering property. Carefully explain what is wrong with those that are not.

a.

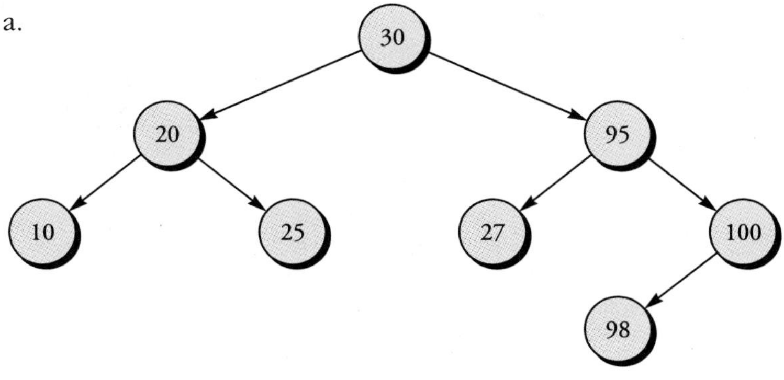

b.

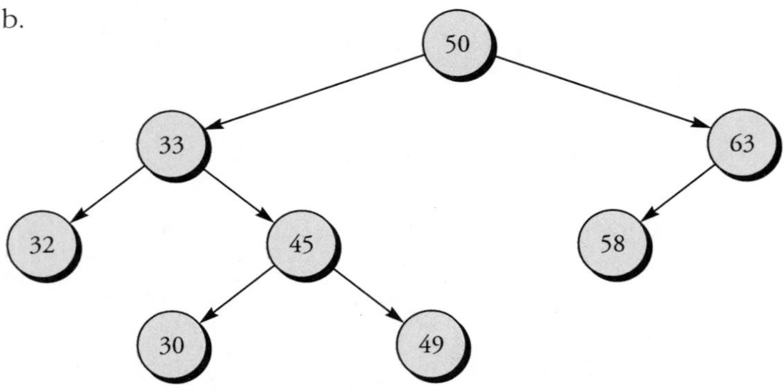

c.

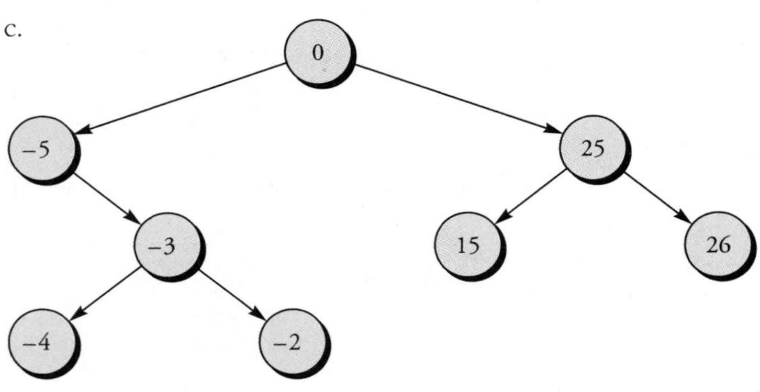

d.

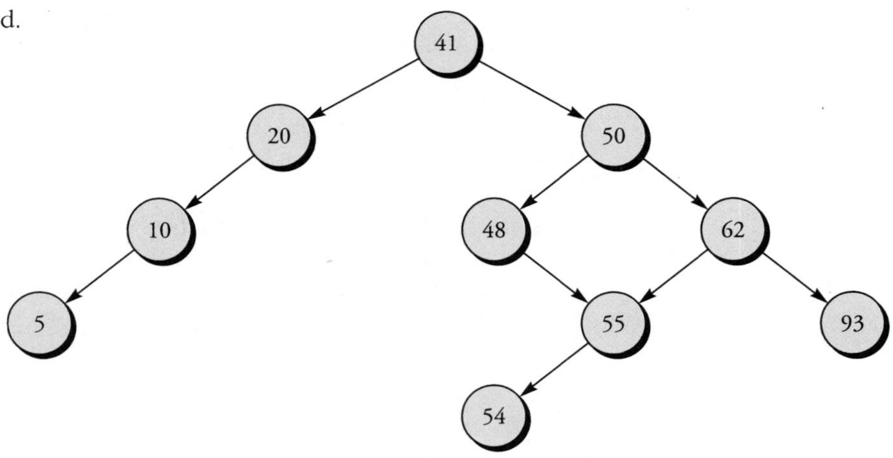

5. Indicate which of the following are binary trees with the heap property. Carefully explain what is wrong with those that are not.

a.

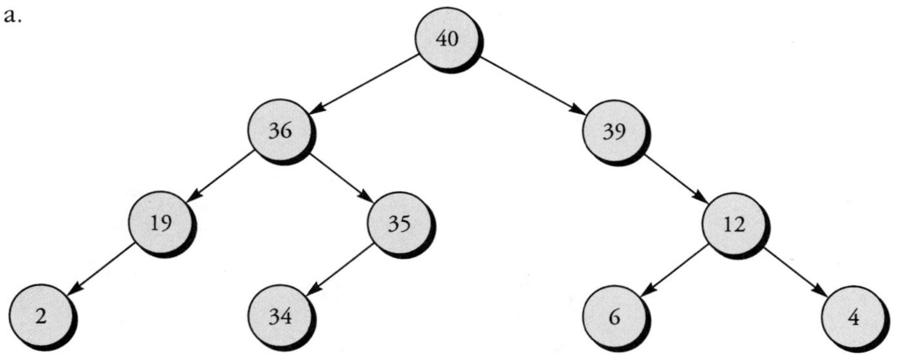

b.

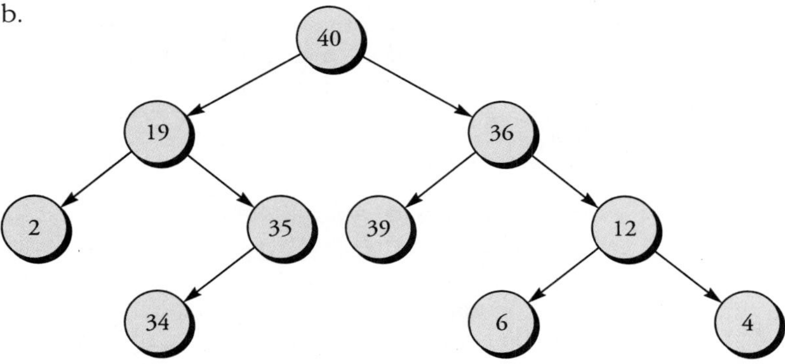

c.

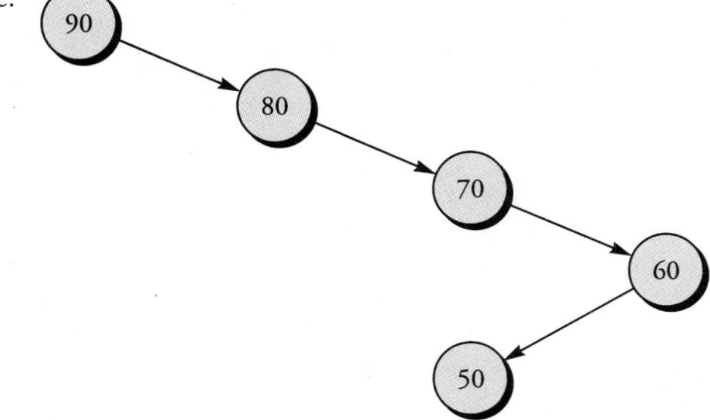

6. Given the following binary tree, indicate the order in which nodes would be processed for each of the preorder, postorder, and inorder traversals.

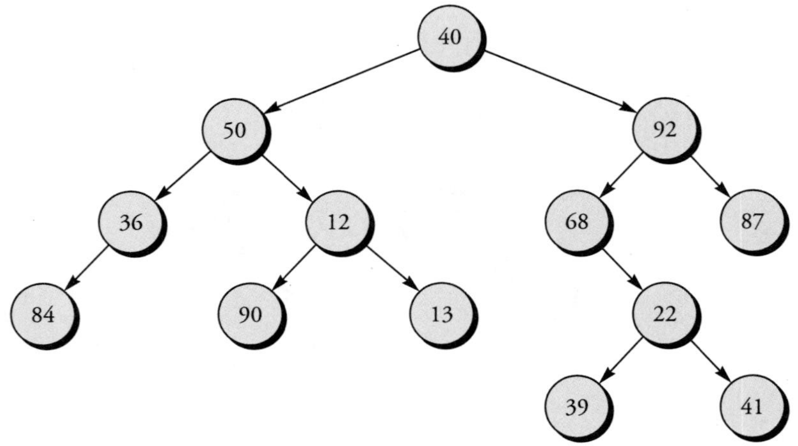

7. Construct some binary search trees with the ordering property. Then do some inorder traversals of these trees. What do you observe about the order in which nodes are processed? Be as specific as possible in stating your answer.
8. Given the following postorder and inorder traversals of a binary tree, draw the tree.

   Postorder: ABCDEFIKJGH
   Inorder: CBAEDFHIGKJ

   Attempt to deduce your answer in a systematic (and recursive) fashion, not by trial-and-error methods. After you have solved this problem, write a statement in which you describe the method you used to solve it and explain how this method could be applied to similar problems.
9. Draw binary expression trees corresponding to the algebraic expression whose:
   a. infix representation is `P / (Q + R) * X - Y`
   b. postfix representation is `X Y Z P Q R * + /- *`
   c. prefix representation is `+ * - M N P / R S`
10. In a written statement, explain how the arrangement of data in a binary expression tree reflects the order of operations in the corresponding expression.

15.2 Linked Implementation of a Binary Tree

Consistent with the way in which we have studied other data structures, we now have a very good idea of what a tree is without any consideration of how we will implement it. We now explore this latter issue.

Two common methods are available for implementing binary trees. One method, known as *linked implementation,* uses dynamic allocation of nodes and pointers to these nodes. The other, which does not require the overhead of maintaining pointers, is called *linear implementation* or array implementation. In this section and the next, we focus on the linked implementation. We will see how this implementation is particularly well suited for binary search trees and binary expression trees.

Because each node in a binary tree may have two child nodes, a node in a linked implementation has two pointer members, one for each child, and one or more members for storing data. When a node has no children, the corresponding pointer members are null. Figure 15.10 is a linked representation of the binary expression tree of Figure 15.8. The left and right members are pointers to (that is, memory addresses of) the left child node and the right child node of the current node.

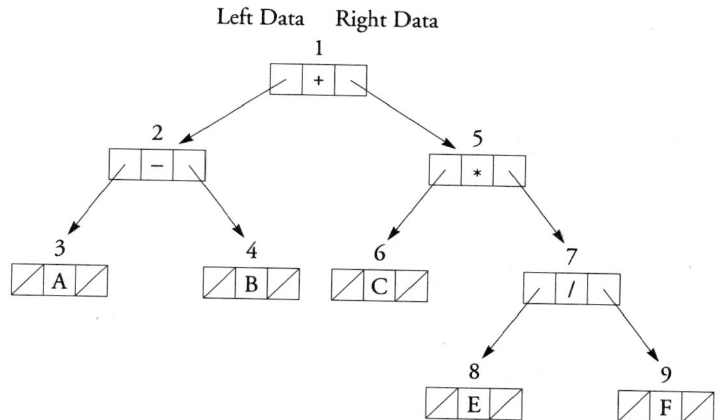

Figure 15.10
Linked representation of the binary expression tree of Figure 15.8

Objectives

a. to become familiar with the linked implementation of the binary tree ADT
b. to implement the insert operation for a binary search tree with the ordering property
c. to see how the shape of a binary search tree is dependent on the order in which data arrive for insertion into the tree
d. to develop algorithms for the three traversal operations on the linked implementation of a binary tree

For the moment, let us give a detailed description of the linked representation of the binary tree of Figure 15.8. Once the concept is thoroughly understood, we will return to using C++ pointer variables for the actual implementation of binary trees. For example, we can implement the tree of Figure 15.10 as shown in Table 15.1 by building the left subtree for each node before considering the right subtree. The numbers on top of the cells in Figure 15.10 represent the addresses given in the left and right members.

In the linked representation, insertions and deletions involve no data movement except the rearrangement of pointers. Suppose we wish to modify the tree in Figure 15.8 to that in Figure 15.11. (This change might be needed due to some recent modification in the expression represented by Figure 15.8.) The insertion of the nodes containing "–" and "P" into the tree structure can be achieved easily by simply adding the nodes "–" and "P" in the next available spaces in the array and adjusting the corresponding pointers.

For the implementation of the tree shown in Figure 15.10, the effect of this insertion is given by Table 15.2. The adjusted pointers and data fields have been circled. Notice that the change in row 1 of the right column and the additional rows 10 and 11 are all that is necessary. No data were moved.

Similarly, if we wish to shorten the tree in Figure 15.8 by deleting the nodes "*" and "C", then all we must do is rearrange the pointers to obtain the altered tree, as

Table 15.1
Implementation of Figure 15.10 Using Array of Structs

Node	Data	Left	Right
1	+	2	5
2	–	3	4
3	A	NULL	NULL
4	B	NULL	NULL
5	*	6	7
6	C	NULL	NULL
7	/	8	9
8	E	NULL	NULL
9	F	NULL	NULL

Figure 15.11
Desired modification of Figure 15.8

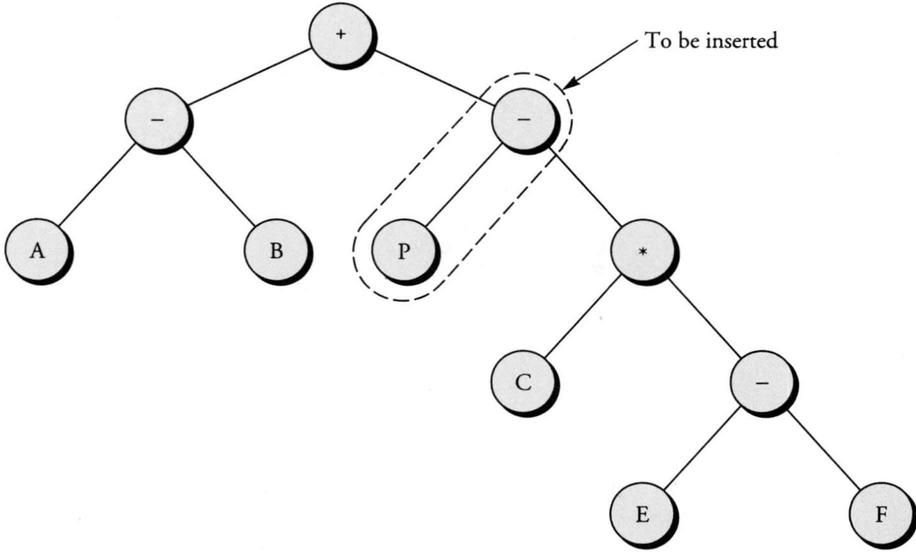

Table 15.2
Modification of Table 15.1 by Insertions into the Tree of Figure 15.8

Row	Data	Left	Right
1	+	2	10
2	–	3	4
3	A	NULL	NULL
4	B	NULL	NULL
5	*	6	7
6	C	NULL	NULL
7	/	8	9
8	E	NULL	NULL
9	F	NULL	NULL
10	–	11	5
11	P	NULL	NULL

shown in Figure 15.12. The effect of this deletion is given in Table 15.3. As before, the adjusted pointers and data fields have been circled.

A more formal statement of the algorithm underlying such insertions and deletions is dependent on the hierarchical property that forms the basis for the tree structure. We will soon examine in detail insertion and deletion algorithms for binary search trees.

Now that we have explained the linked representation of a binary tree by using pointer values that can be explicitly traced, we will use the following general structure description with C++ pointer variables to implement this structure in the remainder of this and the next sections:

```
struct node
{
   E data;
   node * left;
   node * right;
};
```

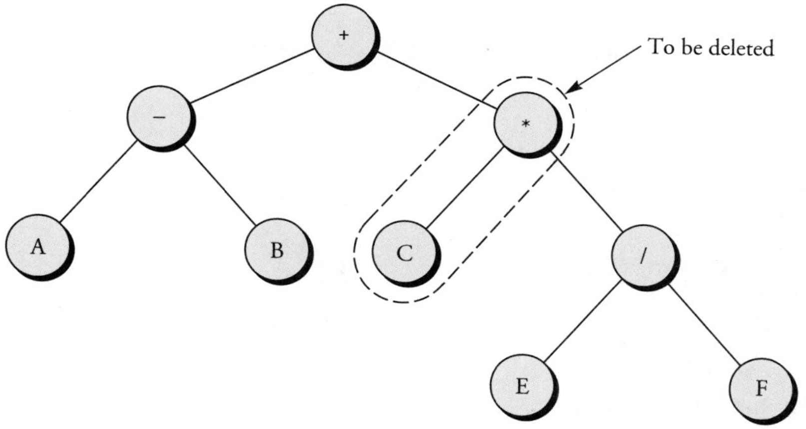

Figure 15.12
Another modification of Figure 15.8

Table 15.3
Modification of Tree of Figure 15.8

Row	Data	Left	Right	Modified Tree
1	+	2	7	
2	-	3	4	
3	A	NULL	NULL	
4	B	NULL	NULL	
5	*			Unused space after deletion of "*" and "C"
6	C			
7	/	8	9	
8	E	NULL	NULL	
9	F	NULL	NULL	

As we did for the pointer implementation of a linked list in Chapter 12, we embed this set of data definitions in the class definition for a binary tree, along with a data member for the root pointer:

```
// Class declaration file: bintree.h

// Declaration section
#ifndef TREE_H
#define TREE_H

template <class E> class BinaryTree
{

   public:

   // Class constructors
   BinaryTree();
   BinaryTree(const BinaryTree<E> &bt);

   // Class destructor
```

continued

```
    ~BinaryTree();

    // Member functions

    bool empty();
    void insert(const E &item);
    void preorderTraverse(void (* process) (E &item));
    void inorderTraverse(void (* process) (E &item));
    void postorderTraverse(void (* process) (E &item));
    BinaryTree<E>& operator = (const BinaryTree<E> &bt);

    private:

    // Individual node structure

    struct node
    {
       E data;
       node * left;
       node * right;
    };

    // Data members

    node * tree;              // root pointer

    // Member functions

    // Helper function to return pointer to a node with
    // data in it and left and right children NULL
    node * getNode(const E &data);

    // Recursive helper functions for insert and traverse operations
    void insertAux(node * &tree, const E &data);
    void preorderAux(node * tree, void (* process) (E &item));
    void inorderAux(node * tree, void (* process) (E &item));
    void postorderAux(node * tree, void (* process) (E &item));

    // Recursive helper functions for copying and destroying trees
    void copyAux(node * tree);
    void destroyAux(node * tree):
};

#include "bintree.cpp"
#endif
```

Note the comments about helper member functions. Because we will use recursion to implement many of the tree-processing algorithms, we need a way of passing the `tree` data member as a parameter to each recursive function. Since this data member is protected, it cannot be a parameter of the public functions. Therefore, each of the operations in question will consist of a public function calling a protected helper function that carries out the recursive algorithm on the tree. We will need one such function for `insert` and for each of the traversal operations.

Recall that we also defined a utility function, `getNode`, in Chapter 12 to take care of the details of creating and initializing a new node for a linked list. We can write a similar function for binary trees as well:

```
template <class E>
BinaryTree<E>::node * BinaryTree<E>::getNode(const E &data)
{
   BinaryTree<E>::node * temp = new BinaryTree<E>::node;

   assert(temp != 0);
   temp->data = data;
   temp->left = 0;
   temp->right = 0;
   return temp;
}
```

Note that `getNode` asks for new memory from the system heap and then checks for successful allocation before initializing the contents of a node. Now we have two pointers in a node to set to null. Therefore, if a pointer to a node is returned, the node is a leaf node.

Example 15.4 Using the linked representation of a binary tree, implement the `insert` operation for a binary search tree with the ordering property. The `insert` operation passes the new element and the protected data member tree to a helper function, `insertAux`:

```
template <class E>
void BinaryTree<E>::insert(const E &data)
{
   insertAux(tree, data);
}

template <class E>
void BinaryTree<E>::insertAux(BinaryTree<E>::node * &tree, const E &data)
{
   if (tree == 0)
   {
      tree = getNode(data);
      ++treeLength;
   }
   else if (data < tree->data)
      insertAux(tree->left, data);
   else
      insertAux(tree->right, data);
}
```

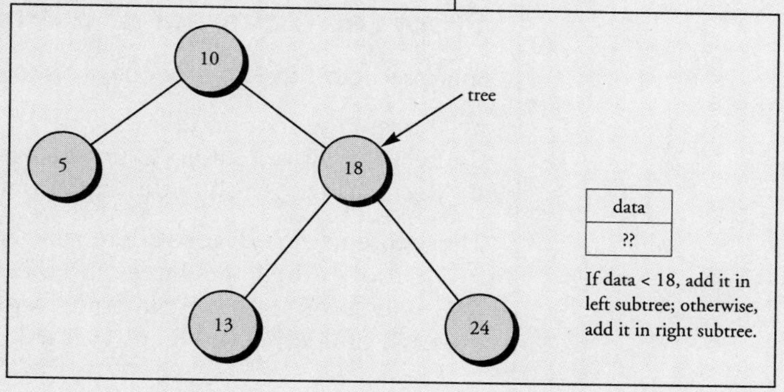

If data < 18, add it in left subtree; otherwise, add it in right subtree.

The `insertAux` function in this example implies that insertion of new nodes will always occur at the leaf nodes of a tree. As with insertion into a linked list, no data are moved; only pointers are manipulated. However, unlike the steps required by a linked list, we do not have to traverse the list sequentially to determine where the new node belongs. Instead, we use the insertion rule—if less than, go left; otherwise, go right—so that we traverse by subdividing the tree to determine the position for a new node. For example, if the `insert` function in this example is successively fed numeric items in the following order:

```
16 8 -5 20 30 101 0 10 18
```

the binary search tree that results can be traced by the sequence in Figure 15.13. Note that the shape of the binary search tree depends on the order in which data items are given to the `insert` operation. This dependence of the shape of the tree on the order in which data arrive for insertion complicates any attempt to analyze the efficiency of the `insert` function in this example. We will provide a more detailed analysis of binary search trees with the ordering property in Section 15.3.

Implementing Traversal Operations on a Binary Tree

In Section 15.1, we described conceptually three different traversal operations on a binary tree: preorder, inorder, and postorder. In Example 15.3, we established correspondences between these three traversals and the prefix, infix, and postfix forms of the algebraic formula represented by a binary expression tree. However, it is important to reiterate that the three traversals apply broadly to all binary trees, regardless of the hierarchical relationship underlying their structure.

Recall from Section 15.1 the threefold dilemma facing us at each node we visit in a traversal of a binary tree:

1. Do we process the data contained in the node at which we are currently located?
2. Do we remember the location of the current node (so that we can return to process it) and visit (and process) all nodes in its left subtree?
3. Do we remember the location of the current node (so that we can return to process it) and visit (and process) all nodes in its right subtree?

Each of the three choices is valid. The route chosen out of the three-way dilemma dictates the order in which the nodes are visited and processed.

Preorder Traversal of a Binary Tree

In a preorder traversal, the three options are combined in the following order:

1. Process the root node.
2. Recursively visit all nodes in the left subtree.
3. Recursively visit all nodes in the right subtree.

These three ordered steps are recursive. Once the root of the tree is processed, we go to the root of the left subtree, and then to the root of the left subtree of the left subtree, and so on until we can go no farther. Following these three steps, the preorder traversal of the tree of Figure 15.8 would process nodes in the order

```
+ - A B * C / E F
```

Figure 15.13 Growth of search tree when data arrive in order 16 8–5 20 30 101 0 10 18

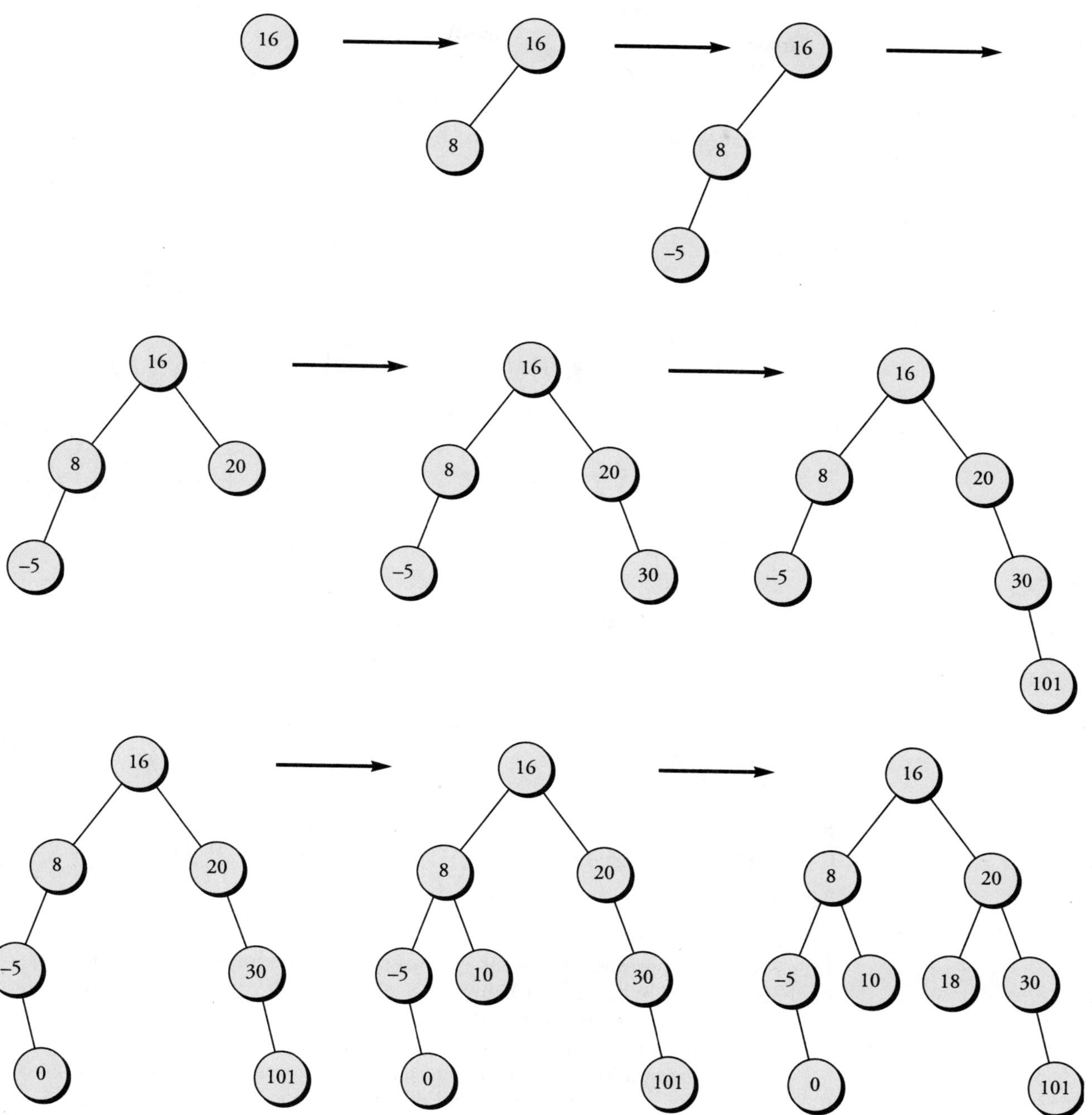

which is the prefix form of the expression

```
(A - B) + C * (E / F)
```

Hence, we conclude that if to process a node means to print it, then a preorder traversal of a binary expression tree will output the prefix form of the expression.

The preorder traversal of an existing binary tree implemented via the linked representation can be accomplished recursively using the following pair of functions, where `preorderAux` is the helper function for the public member function `preorderTraverse`:

```
template <class E>
void BinaryTree<E>::preorderTraverse(void (* process) (E &item))
{
   preorderAux(tree, process);
}

template <class E>
void BinaryTree<E>::preorderAux(BinaryTree<E>::node * tree,
                                void (* process) (E &item))
{
   if (tree != 0)
   {
      process(tree->data);
      preorderAux(tree->left, process);
      preorderAux(tree->right, process);
   }
}
```

First, process root node.
Second, traverse left subtree.
Third, traverse right subtree.

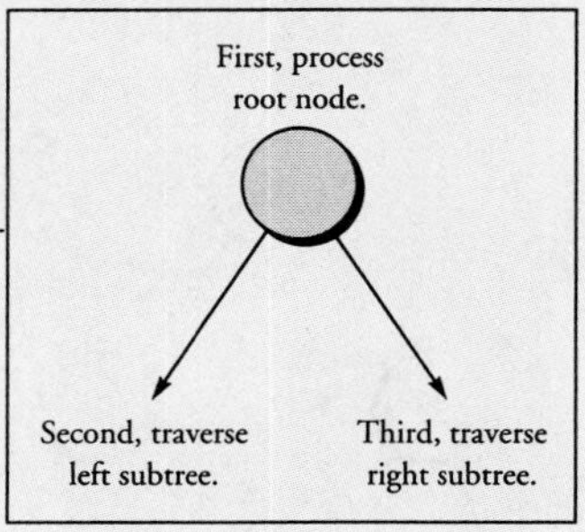

Inorder Traversal of a Binary Tree

The inorder traversal of a binary tree proceeds as outlined in the following three ordered steps:

1. Recursively visit all nodes in the left subtree.
2. Process the root node.
3. Recursively visit all nodes in the right subtree.

By carefully following these steps for the tree of Figure 15.8 and assuming "process" means "print," we obtain the readily recognizable infix expression

```
A - B + C * E / F
```

Unless we add parentheses, this infix expression is not equivalent to the order of operations reflected in the tree of Figure 15.8. The fact that prefix and postfix notations do not require parentheses to avoid such ambiguities makes them distinctly superior to infix notation for evaluation purposes.

An implementation of the recursive algorithm for an inorder traversal is given in the following pair of functions for a linked representation of a binary tree:

```
template <class E>
void BinaryTree<E>::inorderTraverse(void (* process) (E &item))
{
   inorderAux(tree, process);
}

template <class E>
void BinaryTree<E>::inorderAux(BinaryTree<E>::node * tree,
                               void (* process) (E &item))
```

```
{
    if (tree != 0)
    {
        inorderAux(tree->left, process);
        process(tree->data);
        inorderAux(tree->right, process);
    }
}
```

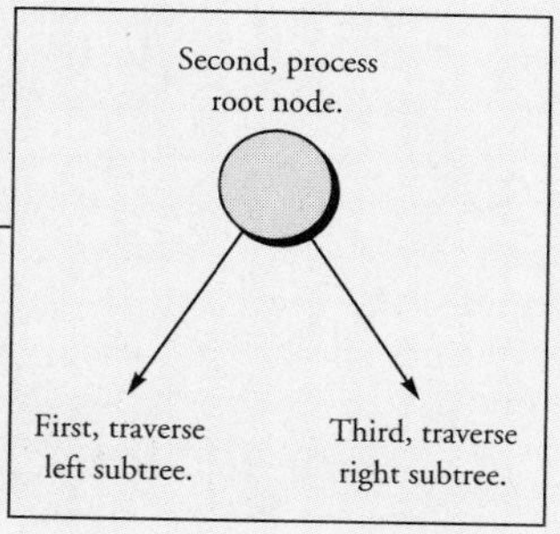

Second, process root node.

First, traverse left subtree.

Third, traverse right subtree.

Postorder Traversal of a Binary Tree

The third standard traversal of a binary tree, the postorder traversal, entails an arrangement of options that postpones processing the root node until last:

1. Recursively visit all nodes in the left subtree of the root node.
2. Recursively visit all nodes in the right subtree of the root node.
3. Process the root node.

Applying these three steps to the binary expression tree of Figure 15.8 yields the postfix form of the underlying expression:

```
A B - C E F / * +
```

The actual implementation of the postorder traversal operation is completely analogous to the inorder and preorder operations. Consequently, we will leave it as an exercise.

Although we have illustrated the three traversal algorithms using binary expression trees, we emphasize that the traversals apply in general to any binary tree. Indeed, as we shall see in the next section, the inorder traversal when used in combination with a tree exhibiting the hierarchical ordering property of a binary search tree will neatly allow us to implement a one-key table using a binary tree.

Copying and Destroying a Binary Tree

Two of the binary tree class operations that require traversals are the copy constructor and the destructor. The copy constructor should copy all of the data elements in the original (parameter) tree to the new (receiver) tree. Not only should this operation preserve the ordering of the data in the new binary tree, but the structure of the nodes should also be exactly the same as in the original tree. Thus, the root node of the new tree should contain the same data element as the root node of the original tree and so on for each subtree. To guarantee both ordering and structure, we perform a preorder traversal of the original tree. When a node in the original tree is visited, its data element is inserted into the new tree with `insert`. Then the left and right subtrees are copied in the same manner. Unfortunately, we cannot use the `preorderTraverse` operation for copying the original tree because the `process` function would have no access to the new tree. Therefore, a new helper function must be written that performs the preorder traversal directly. The code for the copy constructor and the helper function is

```
template <class E>
BinaryTree<E>::BinaryTree(const BinaryTree<E> &bt)
{
   tree = 0;
   // Pass the original tree's data member to the helper function
   copyAux(bt.tree);
}

template <class E>
void BinaryTree<E>::copyAux(BinaryTree<E>::node * tree)
{
   if (tree != 0)
   {
      // Copy from original to new (receiver) tree
      insert(tree->data);
      copyAux(tree->left);
      copyAux(tree->right);
   }
}
```

Note that the identifier `tree` in the helper function refers to the data member of the original tree, not to the receiver's `tree` data member. The receiver's `tree` data member is accessed with the same identifier within the implementation of `insert`.

Recall from Chapter 12 that any class that uses dynamic memory in its implementation should have a class destructor operation. This function returns any memory used for nodes to the system heap. The class destructor is run automatically by the computer when a variable or parameter bound to an instance of the class goes out of scope. Given these requirements, we need a traversal algorithm that visits the leaf nodes of a tree first, deletes them from the tree, and then visits the leaf nodes at the next level up. Clearly, a preorder traversal will not work because it deletes root nodes first. An inorder traversal deletes the left subtree before the root node, but the root node is lost before we visit the leaves of the right subtree. A postorder traversal is just right because it first deletes the left subtree, and then the right subtree, before deleting a root node. The recursive process guarantees that the leaf nodes at any level in the tree are deleted first. Once again, we cannot use an established traversal operation because of scope problems. So we present the code for the class destructor and a new helper operation that carries out a mass deletion in postorder fashion:

```
template <class E>
BinaryTree<E>::~BinaryTree()
{
   destroyAux(tree);
   tree = 0;
}

template <class E>
void BinaryTree<E>::destroyAux(BinaryTree<E>::node * tree)
{

   if (tree != 0)
   {
      destroyAux(tree->left);
      destroyAux(tree->right);
```

```
            delete tree;                    // Return leaf node to system heap.
        }
    }
```

Note that the identifier `tree` refers in both of these functions to the receiver's data member. After `destroyAux` has returned any nodes to the system heap, the top-level destructor operation sets the data member to null to indicate an empty binary tree.

Exercises 15.2

1. Using a preorder traversal of the tree you derived in Exercise 1 from Section 15.1, obtain the prefix form of the expression in that exercise.
2. Sketch the binary search tree that would result when the `insert` function of Example 15.4 is used for data that arrive in the following orders:
   a. 100 90 80 70 60 50 40 32 20 10
   b. 60 80 30 90 70 100 40 20 50 10
   c. 60 50 70 40 80 30 90 20 100 10
   Provide a brief written description of how the shape of the binary search tree is related to the order in which data arrive for insertion into the tree.
3. Consider the following search trees with the ordering property. For each, specify an order of arrival of data items that would result in that particular tree if the insert function of Example 15.4 is used.

a.

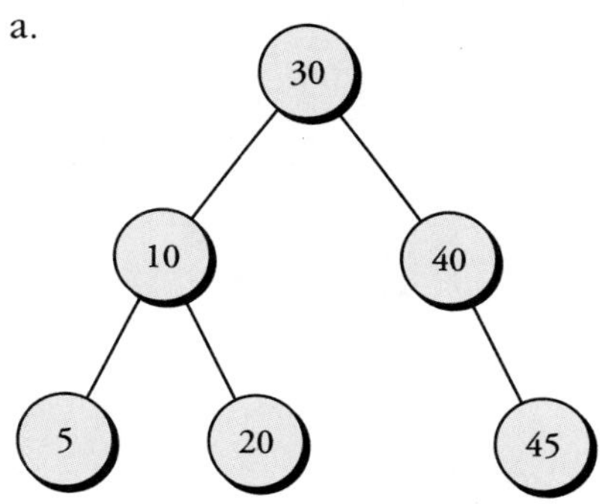

b.

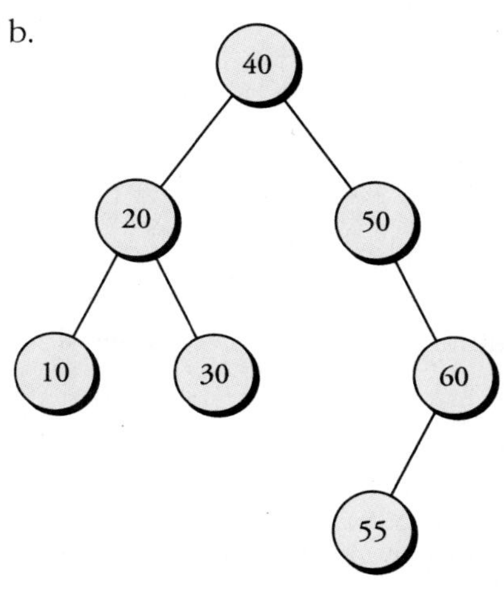

c.

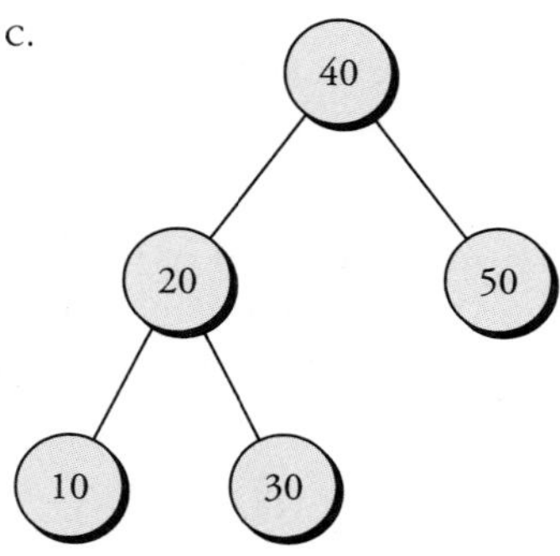

4. What is the output produced by the following function for the pictured tree?

```
void treeWalk(node * tree)
{
   if (tree == 0)
       cout << "OOPS" << endl;
   else
   {
       treeWalk(tree->right);
       treeWalk(tree->left);
       cout << tree->data << endl;
   }
}
```

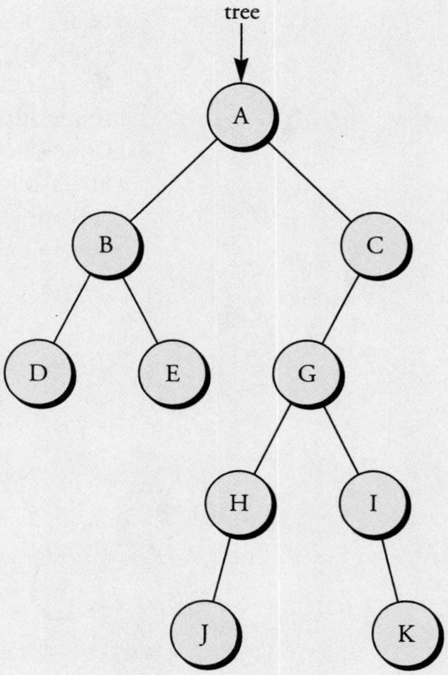

5. How does the output from Exercise 4 change if the statement

```
cout << tree->data << endl;
```

is moved ahead of the recursive calls to `treeWalk`?

6. How does the output from Exercise 4 change if the statement

```
cout << tree->data << endl;
```

is located between the recursive calls to `treeWalk`?

7. Repeat Exercises 4, 5, and 6 for the following tree:

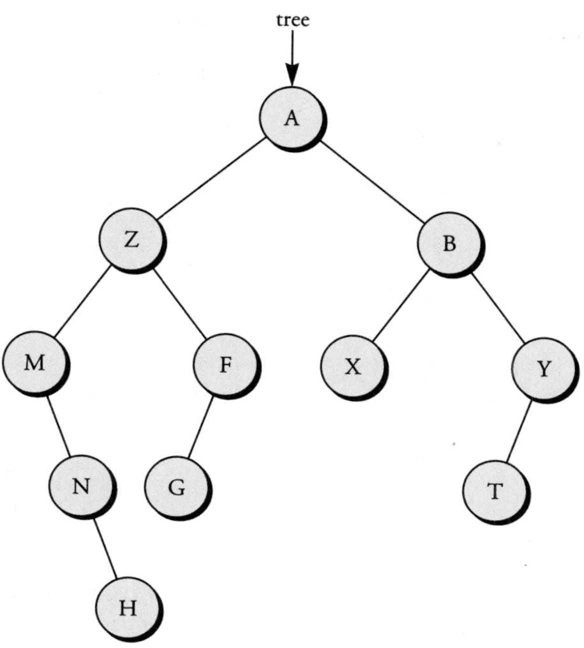

8. A *ternary tree* is one in which each node may have at most three children. A structure for a linked implementation of such a tree could thus be given by the following declarations:

```
struct node
{
   E data;
   node * left;
   node * middle;
   node * right;
};
```

What would be the output produced by the following `treeWalk` function

```
void treeWalk(node * tree)
{
  if (tree != 0)
   {
        cout << tree->data << endl;
        treeWalk(tree->right);
        treeWalk(tree->middle);
        treeWalk(tree->left);
   }
}
```

if it were initially called with the root pointer to the tree in the following diagram?

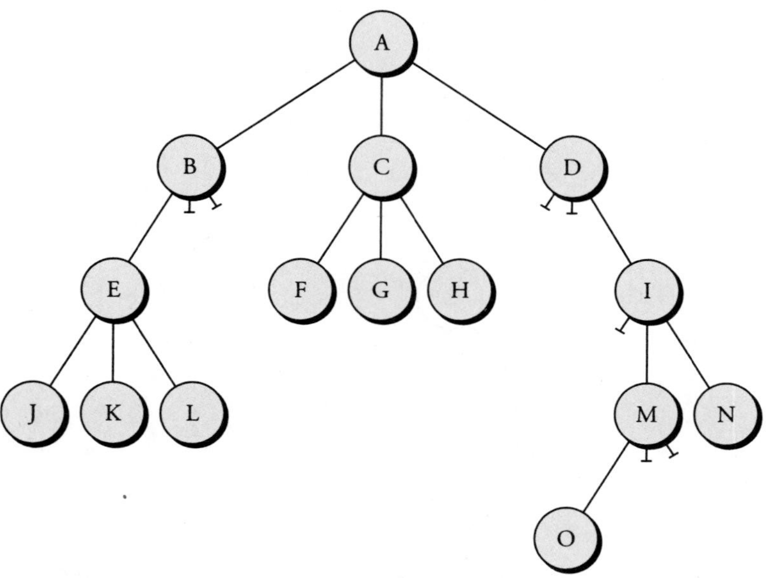

9. Write implementations of the `create` and `empty` operations for a binary search tree with the ordering property using the linked representation method.
10. Write an implementation of the postorder traversal operation for a linked representation of a binary tree.
11. Write a function that reads an algebraic expression in prefix notation and builds the binary tree corresponding to the expression (see Example 15.3). Assume that all tokens in the expression are individual characters.
12. Write a function that reads an algebraic expression in postfix notation and builds the binary tree corresponding to the expression (see Example 15.3). Assume that all tokens in the expression are individual characters.
13. Implement one of the traversal algorithms in a nonrecursive fashion by using a stack to keep track of pointers to nodes that must be visited when you finish processing the current subtree. Your stack will approximate the role played by the system stack in the recursive version of the algorithm.
14. Suppose that you have a binary tree representation of an algebraic expression consisting of the operators +, –, *, / and operands that are uppercase letters. Suppose also that you have a function value that, given an operand, will return the numeric value associated with that operand. Write a recursive function to evaluate the expression tree.
15. Write a function to solve the following puzzle. Assume that the element type stored in tree nodes is `char`. Your function receives two strings of the same length. The first represents the order in which the nodes of a tree would be visited by a preorder traversal. The second represents the order in which nodes from the same tree would be visited by an inorder traversal. Your function is to construct the tree from these two traversals.
16. Write a Boolean-valued function that receives two binary trees composed of the same type of data. The function should return `true` if the two trees are identical, that is, if they have precisely the same shape and have the same values in each node. Otherwise, it should return `false`.
17. How could the inorder traversal of a binary tree be used to sort data logically? Provide your answer in the form of a precise written statement.

15.3 Binary Search Tree Implementation of a One-Key Table

Objectives

a. to realize how a binary search tree with the ordering property can be used to provide an effective implementation of the one-key table ADT introduced in Chapter 12
b. to develop an algorithm for deleting a node from a binary search tree
c. to analyze the efficiency of this new implementation of the one-key table ADT
d. in particular, to compare the efficiency of this new one-key table implementation with the efficiencies of other implementations we have previously studied

The implementations we have considered for the one-key table have been found lacking in certain respects. The physically ordered array implementation of Chapter 11 allowed for the fast inspection of objects via the binary search algorithm but necessitated excessive data movement when objects were added to or deleted from the list. The linked list implementation suggested in Chapter 12 handled insertions and removals nicely but presented us with an undesirable $O(n)$ search efficiency due to the lack of random access.

In this section, we shall see that by implementing a one-key table using a binary tree with the ordering property, we can achieve efficiency in both searching and adding or deleting while at the same time keeping the list in order. Moreover, we do not have to pay too great a price in other trade-offs to achieve this best of both worlds. Indeed, binary trees with the ordering property are called binary search trees precisely because of their frequent application in efficiently implementing one-key tables.

A binary search tree is organized via the hierarchical ordering property discussed in Example 15.2 in Section 15.1. Recall that this ordering property stipulates:

For any given data item X in the tree, every node in the left subtree of X contains only items that are less than X with respect to a particular type of ordering. Every node in the right subtree of X contains only items that are greater than or equal to X with respect to the same ordering.

For instance, the tree of Figure 15.14 illustrates this property with respect to alphabetical ordering. You can quickly verify that an inorder traversal of this tree (in which the processing of each node consists merely of printing its contents) leads to the following alphabetized list:

ARPS	NATHAN
DIETZ	PERKINS
EGOFSKE	SELIGER
FAIRCHILD	TALBOT
GARTH	UNDERWOOD
HUSTON	VERKINS
KEITH	ZARDA
MAGILLICUDDY	

This allows us to reach the important conclusion that an inorder traversal of a binary search tree will visit nodes in ascending order. Hence, such a tree may be viewed as an ordered table. The first table element is the first item visited by the inorder traversal. More generally, the nth element visited by the inorder traversal corresponds precisely to the nth element in the table. Given this view of a binary search tree as an implementation of a one-key table, let us now consider the operations of adding, deleting, and finding (retrieving) nodes in the table.

Adding Nodes to the Binary Search Tree Implementation of a One-Key Table

Insertion of a new key into such a tree is a fairly easy process that may require significantly fewer comparisons than insertion into a linked list. The specifics of the insert operation were developed in Example 15.4. Consider, for example, the steps necessary to insert the key "SEFTON" into the tree of Figure 15.14 in such a fashion as to maintain the ordering property. We must

Figure 15.14 Ordering property with respect to alphabetical ordering

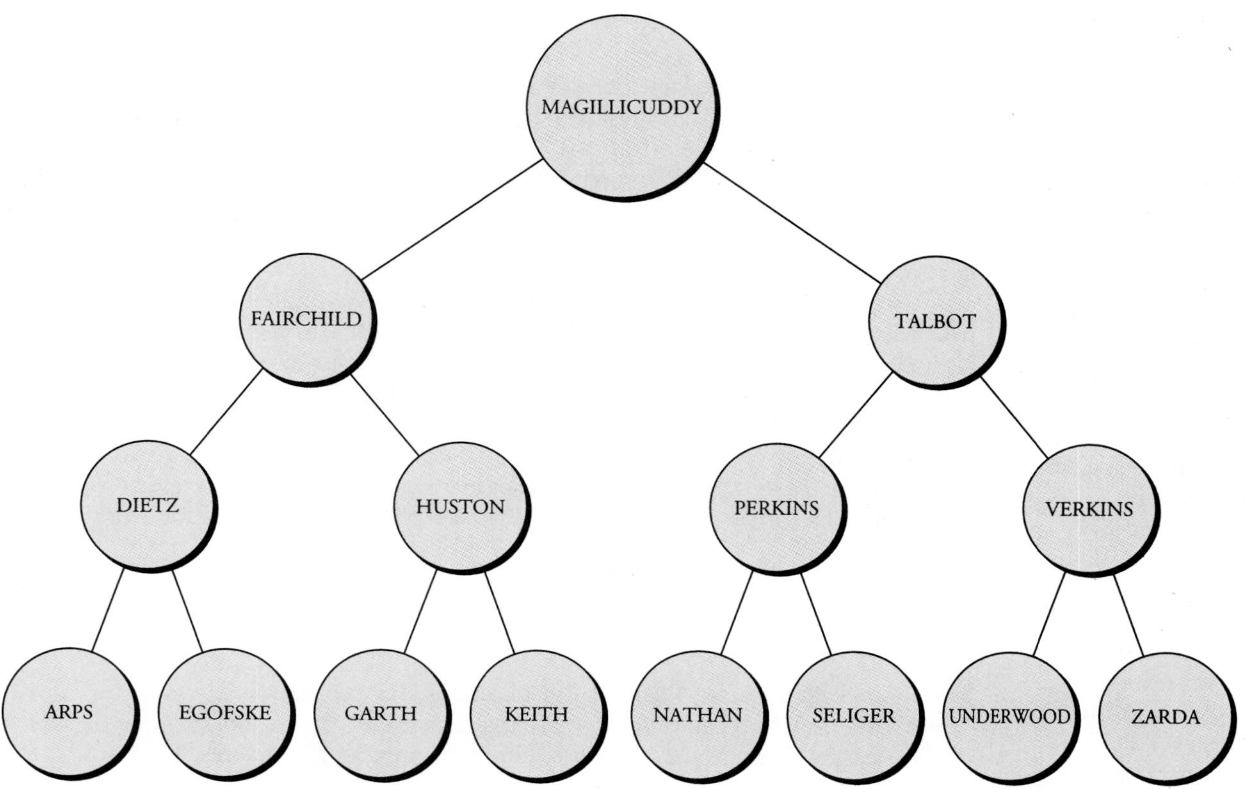

1. Compare SEFTON to MAGILLICUDDY. Because SEFTON is greater than MAGILLICUDDY, follow the right child pointer to TALBOT.
2. Compare SEFTON to TALBOT. Because SEFTON is less than TALBOT, follow the left child pointer to PERKINS.
3. SEFTON is greater than PERKINS. Hence, follow the right child pointer to SELIGER.
4. SELIGER is a leaf node, so SEFTON may be added as one of its children. The left child is chosen because SEFTON is less than SELIGER.

The resulting tree for the sample insertion is given in Figure 15.15.

Provided that the tree maintains a full shape, the number of nodes on a given branch will be at most $(\log_2 n + 1)$, where n is the total number of nodes in the tree. By full we mean that all nodes with fewer than two children must occur at level m or $m - 1$, where m is the deepest level in the tree. In other words, all nodes above level $m - 1$ must have exactly two children. Hence, adding ROBERTS to the tree of Figure 15.15 by the insertion rule would destroy its fullness.

Given this definition of full, the $(\log_2 n + 1)$ figure for the maximum number of nodes on a branch emerges immediately upon inspection or, more formally, using a proof by mathematical induction. Our purpose here, however, is not to give the details of such a proof but rather to emphasize that a binary search tree presents an alternative to a linked list structure for the type of processing involved in maintaining ordered lists. Moreover, it is a particularly attractive alternative when the tree is full because substantially fewer comparisons are needed to locate where in the structure an insertion is to be made. For instance, if n is 1024, the linked list may require as many as 1024 comparisons to make an insertion. Because $\log_2 1024$ is 10, the full binary search tree method will require at most 11 comparisons. This difference becomes even more dra-

Figure 15.15 Tree in Figure 15.14 with the insertion SEFTON

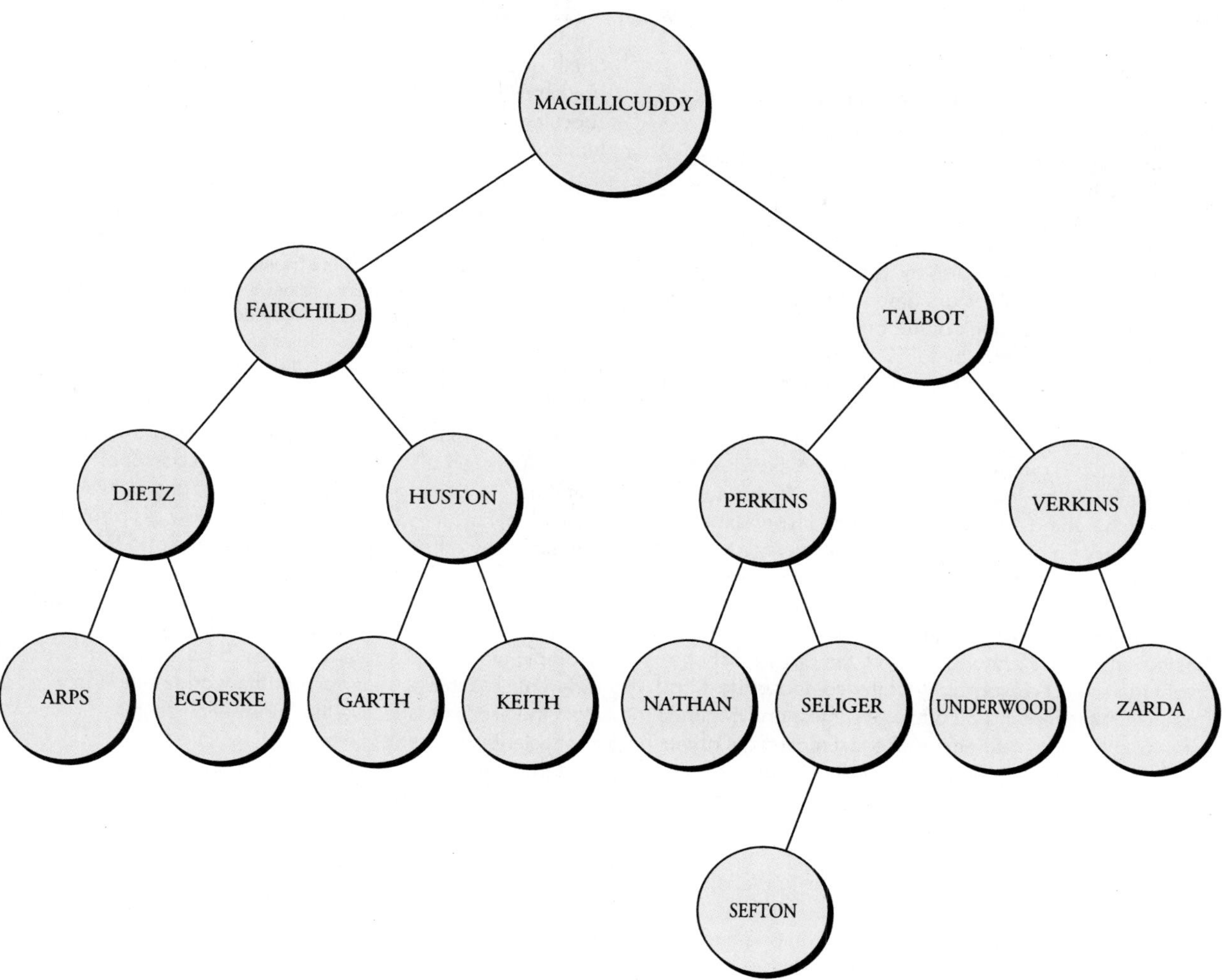

matic as n gets larger. For an ordered list with 1 million entries, a linked list may require 1 million comparisons, but the full binary search tree requires a mere 21.

What happens when the tree is not full? We will comment on that situation at the end of this section, when we discuss the overall efficiency considerations for this implementation of a one-key table. Before that, however, consider the operations of finding and deleting data in a binary search tree.

Searching for Data in a Binary Search Tree Implementation of a One-Key Table

The insertion rule also dictates the search path followed through a binary search tree when we are attempting to find a given data item. Interestingly, if we trace the nodes visited on such a search path for a full tree, we will probe exactly the same items that we would in conducting a binary search on a physically ordered array containing the same data. For instance, if we are searching for SMITH in the tree of Figure 15.14, we will have to probe MAGILLICUDDY, TALBOT, and PERKINS. These are precisely the items that are probed if the binary search algorithm is applied to the physically ordered

A NOTE OF INTEREST

Hypertext

Hypertext is a new technology that allows users to browse through any kind of information that can be stored electronically (text, images, sound, and video). Users experience hypertext associatively as a set of one-key tables. Each entry in a table is a chunk of information presented to the user by some output device. Where the output device is a visual display, the keys for locating other entries in the tables are embedded as hot spots in the currently visible chunk of information. The user retrieves a desired entry by targeting a hot spot with a mouse or cursor device. This entry in turn may have other embedded keys. Each entry also has a hot spot for returning to the entry from which its key was triggered. More structured queries for entries can be executed by entering key terms into a search engine, which returns a list of all the entries that satisfy a query. Hypertext also has the feel of a graph in that users can freely move back and forth in a nonlinear fashion among the entries or nodes.

As an example, one might begin with a query for Beethoven's Ninth Symphony. From the answer list one might then select a biography of the composer (text and images). After reading a couple of pages, one might next point at a hot spot referencing the last movement of the Ninth Symphony to listen to a few bars (sound). Returning to the biography, one might finally hit another hot spot to play a bit of *Immortal Beloved,* a film about Beethoven's life (video).

According to John B. Smith & Stephen F. Weiss, "Hypertext," *Communications of the ACM,* Vol. 31, No. 7, July 1988, this unrestricted associativity among hypertext nodes parallels the flexibility of human memory.

Smith and Weiss cite the following quotation from Vannevar Bush, a well-known electrical engineer who speculated as early as the 1940s about the way in which humans think:

> The human mind . . . operates by association. With one item in its grasp, it snaps instantly to the next that is suggested by the association of thoughts, in accordance with some intricate web of trails carried by the cells of the brain.
>
> Selection by association, rather than indexing may yet be mechanized. One cannot hope . . . to equal the speed and flexibility with which the mind follows an associative trail, but it should be possible to beat the mind decisively in regard to the permanence and clarity of the items resurrected from storage.

Early hypertext systems were implemented as a set of files residing on a single disk in the user's personal computer. With the growth of the Internet and networking technology, most hypertext systems are now distributed among many different physical sites. The World Wide Web, the best known of these systems, supports public browsing by Internet users from thousands of sites around the world. The nodes of information in the Beethoven example mentioned earlier might each be located at different sites in different parts of the world, although from the user's perspective the information seems connected in a seamless way.

If the notion of electronic hypertext intrigues you, begin by consulting the *Communications of the ACM* issue cited earlier. Then check some more recent publications such as *Communications of the ACM,* Vol. 37, No. 2, Feb. 1994, and *Communications of the ACM,* Vol. 38, No. 8, Aug. 1995, each of which have been dedicated to this revolutionary and rapidly growing field.

list associated with Figure 15.14. Our analysis of such a tree has allowed us to conclude that, as long as the binary search tree remains full, the search efficiency for this method of implementing a one-key table matches that of the physically ordered array implementation. That is, the search efficiency is $O(\log_2 n)$.

Deleting Data in a Binary Search Tree Implementation of a One-Key Table

The deletion algorithm for a binary search tree is conceptually more complex than that for a linked list. Suppose, for instance, that we wish to remove TALBOT from the list represented by the tree of Figure 15.14. Two questions arise:

1. Can such a deletion be achieved merely by manipulating pointers?
2. If so, what does the resulting tree look like?

To answer these questions, begin by recalling what is necessary to represent a one-key table with a binary search tree. That is, for each node in the tree

1. The left subtree must contain only items less than it.
2. The right subtree must contain only items greater than or equal to it.

With the preservation of this ordering property as the primary goal in processing a deletion, one acceptable way of restructuring the tree of Figure 15.14 after deleting TALBOT appears in Figure 15.16; essentially, SELIGER moves up to replace TALBOT in the tree. The choice of SELIGER to replace TALBOT is made because SELIGER represents the greatest data item in the left subtree of the node containing TALBOT. As long as we choose this greatest item in the left subtree to replace the item being deleted, we guarantee preservation of the crucial ordering property that enables the tree to represent the list accurately.

Given this general motivation for choosing a node to replace the one being deleted, let us now outline a case-by-case analysis of the deletion algorithm. Throughout this analysis, we assume that we have a pointer `p` to the item we wish to delete. The pointer `p` may be one of the following:

1. The root pointer for the entire tree.
2. The left child pointer of the parent of the node to be deleted.
3. The right child pointer of the parent of the node to be deleted.

Figure 15.17 highlights these three possibilities; the algorithm applies whether 1, 2, or 3 holds.

We now examine three cases of node deletion on a binary search tree:

1. The node to be deleted has no children.
2. The node to be deleted has a right child but no left child.
3. The node to be deleted has a left child.

Figure 15.16 Restructuring the tree in Figure 15.14 after deleting TALBOT

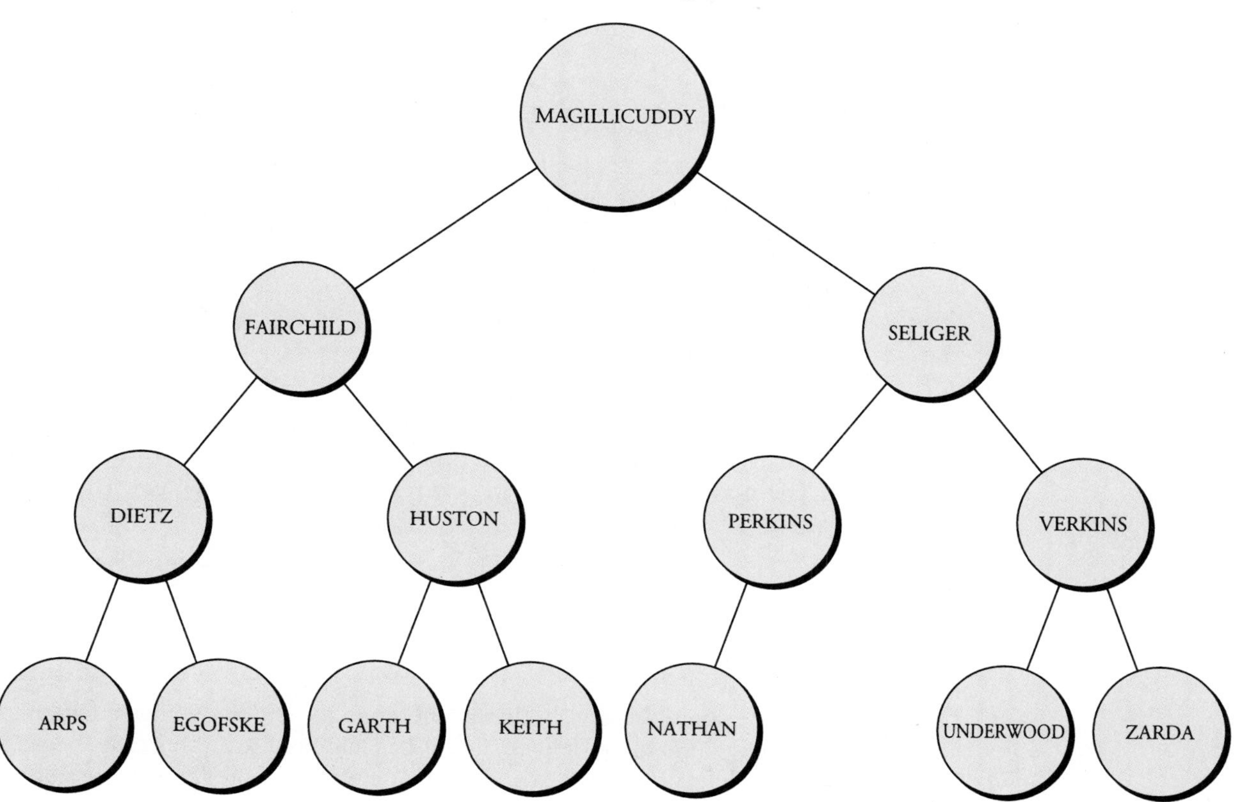

Figure 15.17 Three possibilities for the pointer `p`

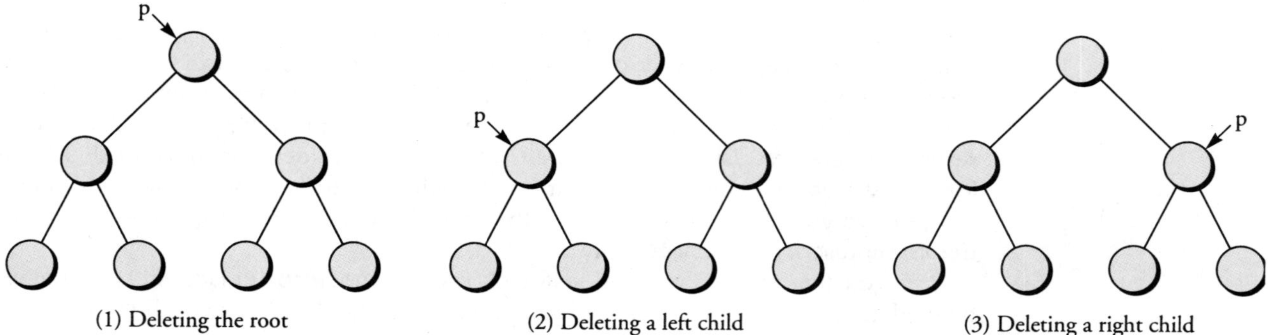

Figure 15.18
In case 2, the node pointed to by `p` has a right but no left child

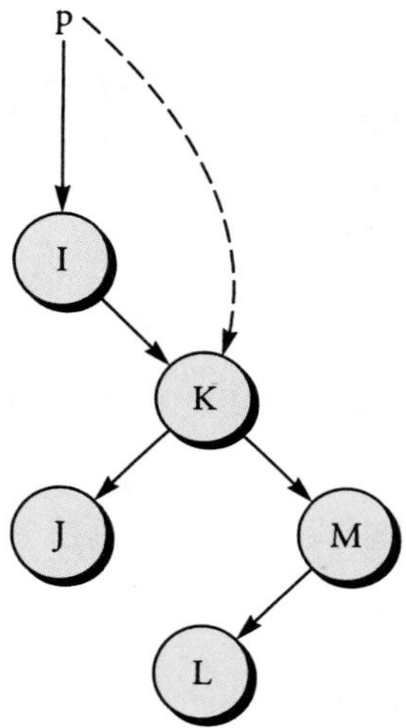

Case 1. The node pointed to by `p`, that is, the node to be deleted, has no children. This is the easiest of all the cases. It can be compactly handled

```
x = p;
p = 0;   // make the pointer null
delete x;
```

Case 2. The node pointed to by `p`, that is, the node to be deleted, has a right child but no left child. This case poses no more problems than case 1 and is described in Figure 15.18. The node to be deleted is merely replaced by its right child. The necessary C++ coding is

```
x = p;
p = x->right;
delete x;
```

Case 3. The node pointed to by `p`, that is, the node to be deleted, has a left child. In Figure 15.19, node M is to be deleted, and it has left child K. In this case, because we have a non-null left subtree of the node to be deleted, our previous discussion in-

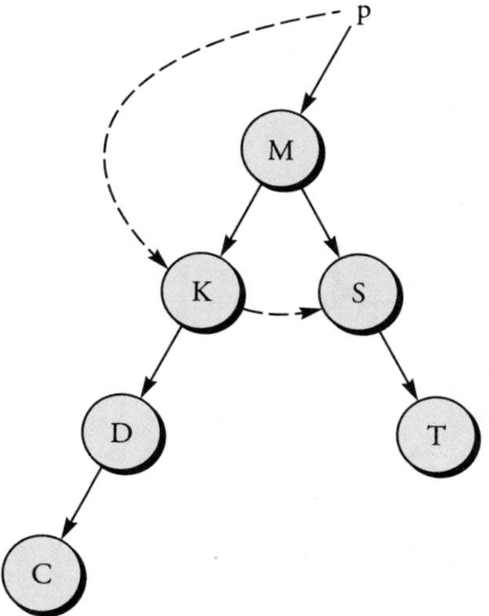

Figure 15.19
Case 3 with `p->left` (node K) having no right children

dicates that we must find the greatest node in that left subtree. If the node pointed to by `p->left` (node K in the figure) has no right child, then the greatest node in the left subtree of `p` is `p->left` itself. Figure 15.19 describes this situation; the dotted lines indicate new pointer values.

The partial coding to achieve this pointer manipulation is given by:

```
x = p;
p = x->left;
p->right = x->right;
delete x;
```

If the node pointed to by `p->left` does have a right child, then to find the greatest node in the left subtree of `p` we must follow the right branch leading from `p->left` as deeply as possible into the tree. In Figure 15.20, node R is chosen to replace the deleted node. This figure gives the schematic representation, with the pointer changes necessary to complete the deletion. The coding necessary for this slightly more complicated version of case 3 is

```
x = p;
q = x->left->right;
qParent = x->left;

// q will eventually point to node which will replace p.
// qParent will point to q's parent.
// The following loop forces q as deep as possible
// along the right branch from p->left.

while (q->left != 0)   // while not null
{
     q = q->right;
     qParent = qParent->right;
}

// Having found node q to replace p, adjust pointers
```

continued

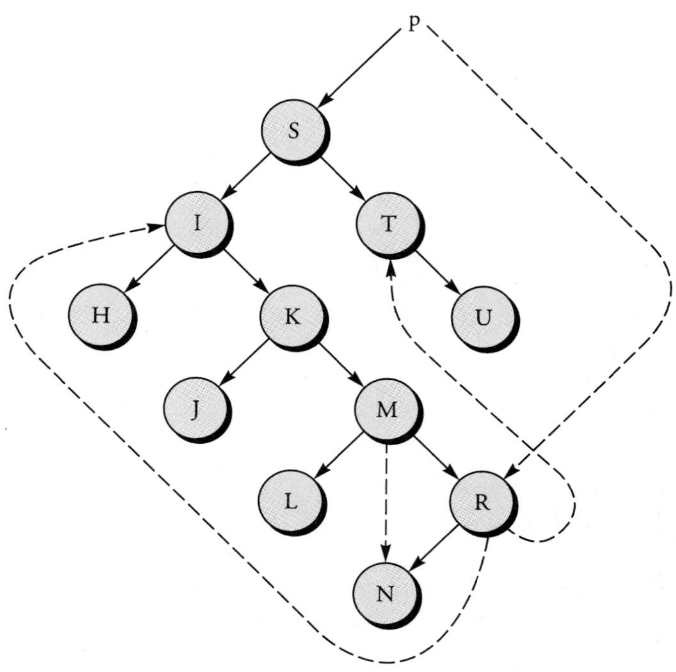

Figure 15.20
Case 3 with `p->left` having a right child

```
// to appropriately link it into the tree.

q->right = x->right;
p = q;
qParent->right = q->left;
q->left = x->left;
delete x;
```

Efficiency Considerations for Binary Search Tree Implementation of a One-Key Table

It is important to note that, in all three cases, the deletion of a node from the tree involved only pointer manipulation and no actual data movement. Hence, in a one-key table maintained with a binary search tree, we are able to process both insertions and deletions by the same pure pointer manipulation that makes linked lists so desirable. Moreover, the binary search tree approach apparently allows us to locate data for retrieval, insertion, or deletion much faster than a linked list representation does. However, there are aspects of the binary tree method that tarnish its performance in comparison to a linked list. These aspects are discussed next.

The binary search tree implementation requires more memory in two respects. First, each node has two pointers instead of the one required in a singly linked list. This proliferation of pointers is particularly wasteful because many of the pointers may be null. Second, we currently can traverse the tree in order only by using recursive techniques. A substantial amount of overhead may be needed to maintain the stack used by recursive calls.

The $O(\log_2 n)$ efficiency of the binary search tree method is only an optimal, not a guaranteed, efficiency. It is contingent on the tree remaining nearly full. The tree remaining full is in turn contingent on the order in which the data are added and deleted. In the worst possible case, data entering the tree structure in the wrong order can cause the tree to degenerate into a glorified linked list with a corresponding $O(n)$ efficiency. (The exercises at the end of this section have you explore this relationship between the order in which data arrive for insertion and the resulting search efficiency of the binary search tree.)

Both of these drawbacks can be overcome. We can avoid the overhead associated with recursion if we use a technique (known as *threading*) that puts to good use the pointers that are otherwise wasted as null.

Moreover, by using a technique known as *height balancing,* the binary search tree can be maintained in a fashion that approaches fullness at all times, regardless of the order in which data arrive for entry. This nearly full form is enough to completely guarantee the $O(\log_2 n)$ search efficiency. Originally devised by G. M. Adelson-Velskii and Y. M. Landis, the height-balancing algorithm is sufficiently complex to be beyond the scope of this book. In-depth treatments of it and the threading technique just cited are given in Ellis Horowitz & Sartaj Sahni, *Data Structures in C++*, New York: Computer Science Press, 1990, and in George J. Pothering & Thomas L. Naps, *Introduction to Data Structures and Algorithm Analysis with C++*, St. Paul, MN: West Publishing, 1995.

Overall, the binary search tree implementation of a one-key table seems the best of the three implementations we have studied for situations in which additions, deletions, and searches must all be processed efficiently. Even when steps are not taken to correct the two disadvantages we have cited, it offers the addition/deletion advantages of a linked list with a search efficiency that is bounded between $O(\log_2 n)$ and $O(n)$.

Exercises 15.3

1. Which of the following binary search trees are full?

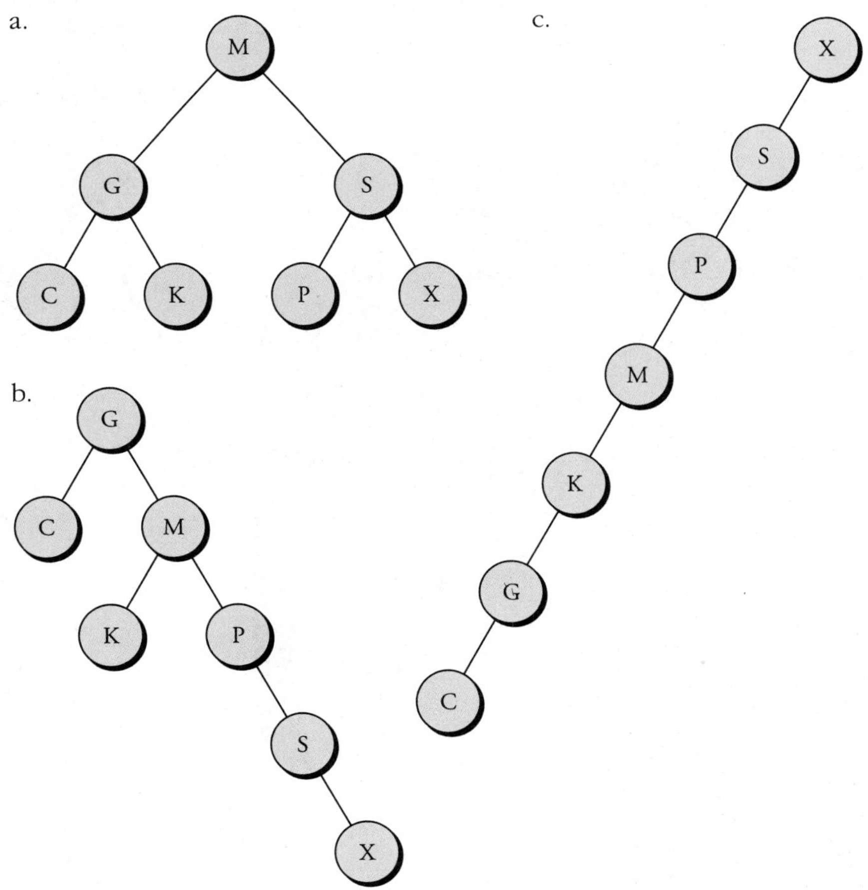

2. The key values 1 through 10 are to be inserted in a binary search tree. Specify orders of arrival for these values to create trees that correspond with each of the following shapes.

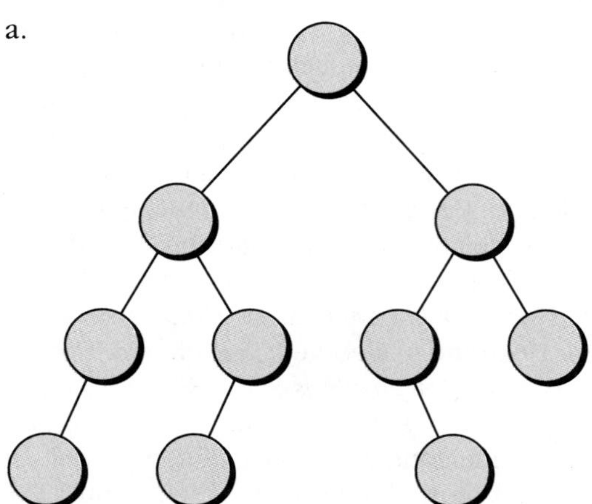

b.

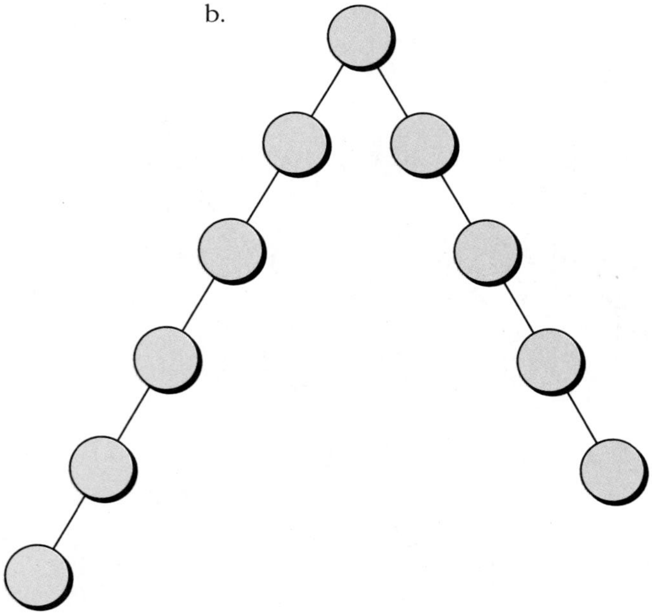

c.

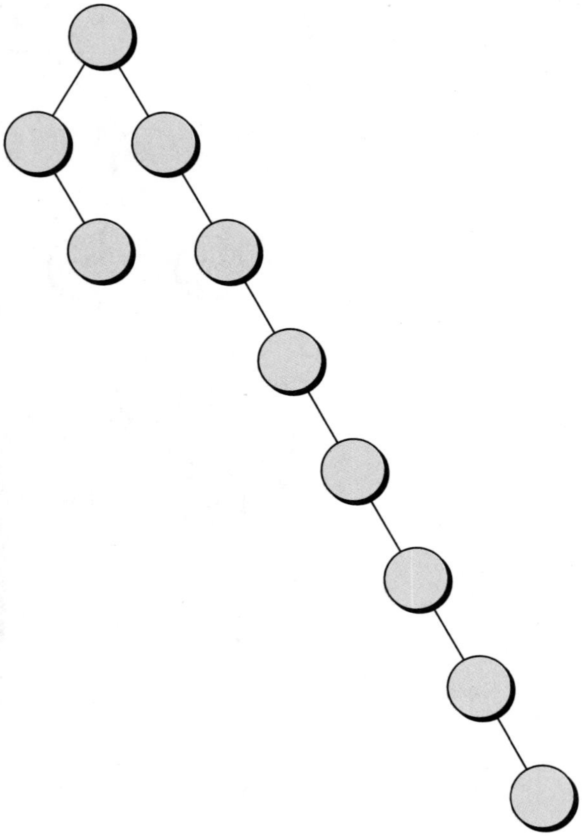

3. In an essay, discuss the relative merits of maintaining a one-key table by a binary search tree, a singly linked list, and a doubly linked list.
4. In an essay, discuss how the order in which data are entered into a binary search tree affects the fullness of the tree. Be sure to identify the best and worst possible cases. Analyze the efficiency of tree operations to add, delete, and find data for each of these cases.
5. The node containing 46 is to be deleted from each of the following binary search trees. Assuming the deletion algorithm described in this section is used, draw the tree after the deletion of 46.

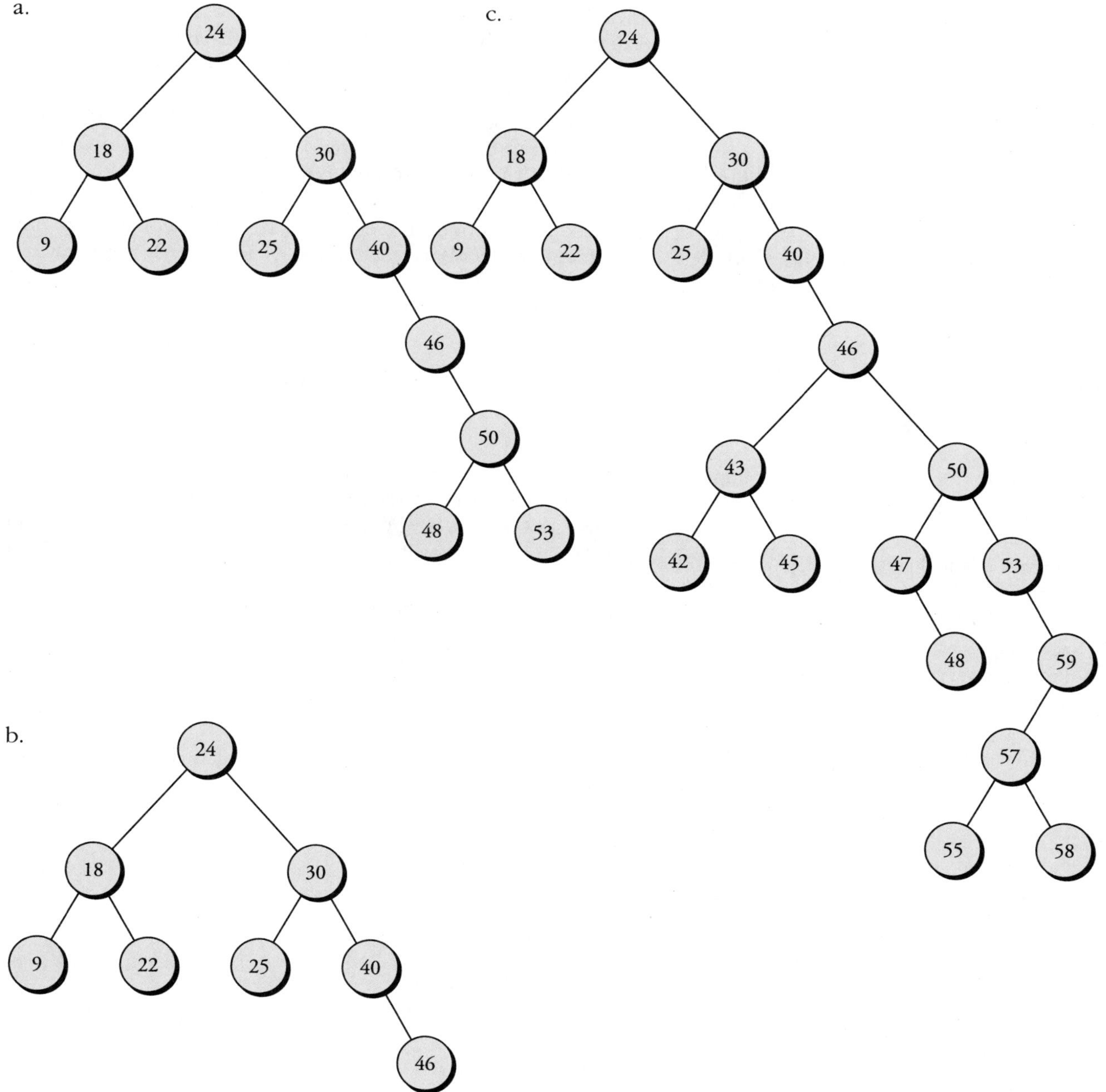

6. In Example 15.4, we provided an implementation of the `insert` operation for a binary search tree. What does the function in that example do when we try to insert a key value that already exists in the tree? Modify the function so that, when we try to insert such a key value, the tree is left unaltered.
7. The implementation of the `insert` operation for a binary search tree in Example 15.4 is recursive. Write a nonrecursive implementation of this operation.
8. Develop recursive and nonrecursive implementations of the algorithm to search for a particular data item in a binary search tree.
9. Develop a complete implementation of the algorithm to delete an item from a binary search tree. This will essentially require that you combine into one module the three cases discussed in this section. For an added challenge, try writing the function so that it handles deletion by using the "mirror image" of these three cases.
10. Look back to the definition of the one-key table ADT in Chapter 12. Provide a complete implementation of the table operations using a binary search tree as the underlying data structure. (*Hint:* You should provide comparison operations for the association class so that associations can be the objects stored in binary trees.)
11. Suppose you are given a list of data in increasing order of keys. Develop a C++ algorithm that will load this list into an optimal binary search tree.
12. A binary search tree could itself be considered an ADT that is derived from the more generic binary tree ADT defined in Section 15.1. Write a complete definition and a C++ interface for the binary search tree as an ADT. Be sure that the set of operations you describe will allow your binary search tree ADT to be used as an implementation strategy for the one-key table ADT.

15.4 Linear Implementation of the Binary Tree Abstract Data Type

Objectives

a. to become familiar with the linear implementation of the binary tree ADT
b. to recognize the advantages and disadvantages of the linear implementation versus the linked implementation
c. to see why the linear implementation is particularly well suited to representing a binary tree with the heap property
d. to analyze the efficiency of the insert operation for a linear implementation of a binary tree with the heap property

The linear implementation of a binary tree uses a one-dimensional array of size $[2^{(d+1)} - 1]$ where d is the depth of the tree, that is, the maximum level of any node in the tree. In the tree of Figure 15.8, the root + is at level 0, the nodes − and * are at level 1, and so on. The deepest level in this tree is the level of E and F, level 3. Therefore, $d = 3$ and this tree will require an array of size $2^{(3+1)} - 1 = 15$. Once the size of the array has been determined, the following method is used to represent the tree:

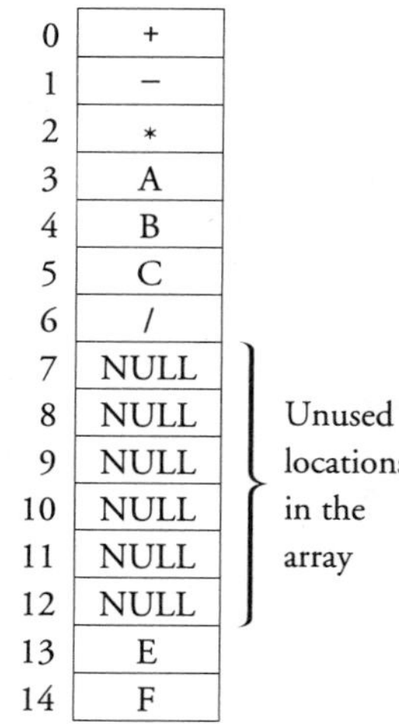

Figure 15.21
Tree of Figure 15.8 stored in a linear representation using an array

1. Store the root in the first location of the array.
2. If a node is in location n of the array, store its left child at location $(2n + 1)$ and its right child at location $(2n + 2)$.

With the aid of this scheme, the tree of Figure 15.8 is stored in the array tree of size 15 shown in Figure 15.21. Locations `tree [7]` through `tree [12]` are not used.

An encapsulated definition of the binary tree ADT for this linear representation is given by:

```
// Class declaration file: bintree.h (linear implementation)

// Declaration section

// This constant establishes the size of the underlying array
const int MAX_TREE_NODES = // To be filled in with appropriate size

template <class E> class BinaryTree
{

   public:

   // Nothing changes here

   ...

   protected:

   // Protected data members

   struct node                        // Either null or a node
   {
      bool null;
      E data;
   };

   node tree[MAX_TREE_NODES];      // Array of nodes
   int numberNodes;             // Number of nodes in tree
   // Protected function members, declared as needed

};
```

The `create` operation simply sets the `numberNodes` data member to zero and initializes the `null` member of all nodes in the array locations to `true`. The `null` flags are necessary to detect whether or not a given tree node has children. A tree node at location n has a left subtree if and only if the node at location $2n + 1$ contains a `null` flag that is `false`. A similar consideration applies to the right subtree of the tree node at location n.

Efficiency Considerations for the Linear Representation

The main advantages of this method lie in its simplicity and the fact that, given a child node, its parent node can be determined immediately. If a child node is at location n in the array, then its parent node is at location $(n - 1)/2$. In spite of its simplicity and ease of implementation, the linear representation method has all the costs that come with physically ordering items. Insertion or deletion of a node in a fashion that maintains the hierarchical relationships within the tree may cause considerable data movement up and down the array and hence use an excessive amount of processing time. Also, depending on the application, memory locations (such as locations 7 through 12 in Figure 15.21) may be wasted due to partially filled trees.

Using the Linear Implementation for a Heap

One type of binary tree for which the linear implementation of a binary tree proves to be ideal is the heap, as defined in Example 15.1. The data in a heap can be embedded in an array without ever wasting any locations. To prove this claim, we will show that, given a heap with $N - 1$ nodes embedded in an array with no gaps, we can add an Nth node and maintain the dense packing of data in the array.

To illustrate the algorithm for doing this, consider the heap with eight nodes pictured in Figure 15.22. The numbers outside the circular nodes in this figure indicate the array indices where data would be stored in the linear representation of a binary tree.

Now suppose we want to add 40 to the heap of Figure 15.22. We will begin by comparing 40 to the data in the smallest index that does not yet have two children: 20 at index 3 in Figure 15.22. Figure 15.23 shows a series of data interchanges that "walk 40 up" a path until the tree is transformed into a heap. The algorithm to achieve this "walking up" is given in the following example.

Example 15.5 Implement the `insert` operation for a linear representation of a binary tree with the heap property.

```
template <class E>
void heap<E>::insert(const E &item)
{
   int location, parent;

   assert(number_nodes < MAX_TREE_NODES);

   // Now walk the new item up the tree, starting at location

   location = number_nodes;
   parent = (location - 1) / 2;
   while ((location > 0) && (tree[parent].data < item))
   {
      tree[location] = tree[parent];
      location = parent;
      parent = (location - 1) / 2;
   }
   tree[location].data = item;
   tree[location].null = false;
   ++number_nodes;
}
```

50
30
parent
20
location
item
40
Move data at index parent to index location. Then location and parent advance up the tree until item is less than data in node referenced by parent or until location references the root of tree.

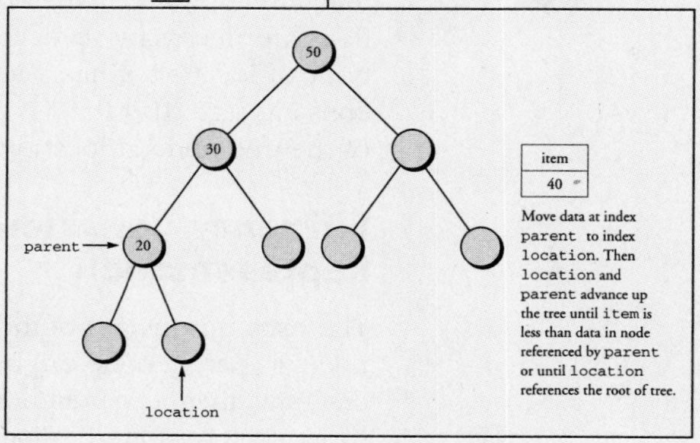

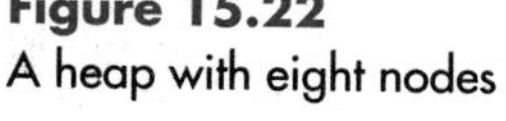

Figure 15.22
A heap with eight nodes

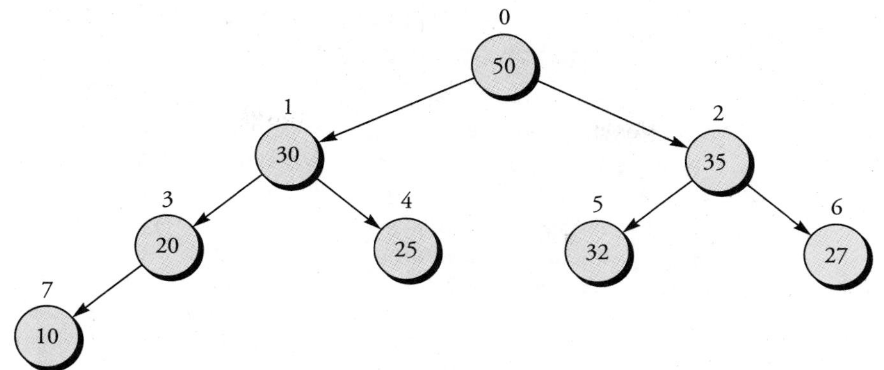

Figure 15.23 Transforming heap to accommodate insertion of 40 (numbers outside circles indicate array index positions)

Item
40

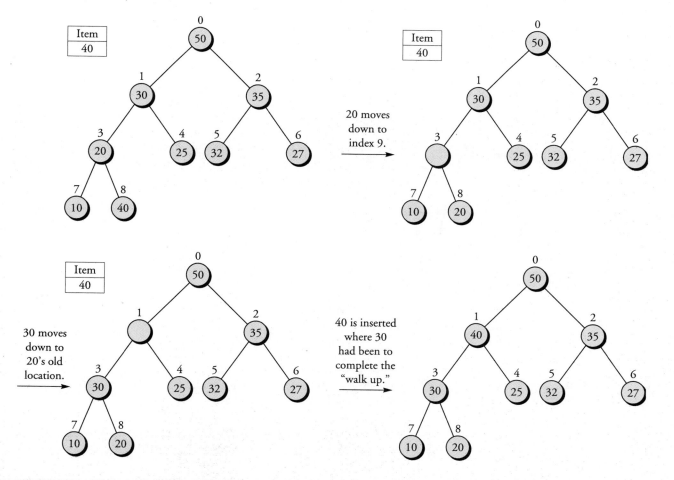

20 moves down to index 9.

Item
40

Item
40

30 moves down to 20's old location.

40 is inserted where 30 had been to complete the "walk up."

Efficiency Analysis of `insert` for Linear Representation of Heap

Clearly, the time efficiency of adding an item to the heap is directly proportional to the length of the path that the item must "walk up" as its appropriate position is determined. Because the linear representation of a heap leaves no unused gaps between values stored in the array, doubling the number of items in the heap will add only one level to the resulting binary tree. Thus, a heap with n nodes will have $\log_2 n$ levels using the linear representation. In other words, the length of the path that a new item will follow, and hence the efficiency of the `insert` operation, is $O(\log_2 n)$.

In the exercises at the end of this section, you will explore an algorithm to delete a node from a heap. That exploration will show how a heap could be used to implement the priority queue ADT defined in Chapter 13.

Example 15.6 In this example, we illustrate how the postorder traversal algorithm may be implemented for a linear array implementation of a binary tree. The algorithm is slightly more difficult for this representation since the tree is the encapsulation of an array and a count of the number of nodes. Unlike the linked implementation, there is not an explicit root pointer for the tree; instead, the root of the entire tree is understood to be at index 0. The following function, `postorderTraverse`, compensates for this by acting as a mere "front end" for a local auxiliary function, which is where the actual recursion takes place. Our front-end function `postorderTraverse` simply passes a root pointer value of 0 to the auxiliary function to start the recursion. We must also assume that a flagging null value of `true` occupies array locations that are not currently storing data in the tree. This allows the auxiliary function to detect when the equivalent of a null pointer is passed.

```
template <class E>
void BinaryTree<E>::postorderTraverse(void (* process) (E &item))
{
   if (numberNodes > 0)
      postorderAux(0, process);
}

template <class E>
void BinaryTree<E>::postorderAux(int location, void (* process) (E &item))
{
   if (location < MAX_TREE_NODES)
      if (! tree[location].null)
      {
         postorderAux(2 * location + 1, process);
         postorderAux(2 * location + 2, process);
         process(tree[location].data);
      }
}
```

Third, process root node.

First, traverse left subtree.

Second, traverse right subtree.

Exercises 15.4

1. Suppose items arrive for insertion into a heap in the following order:

```
10 20 30 40 50 60 70 80 90 100
```

Using the algorithm of Example 15.5, trace the contents of the tree array after each item is added to the heap.

2. Write implementations of the `create` and `empty` operations for a binary tree with the heap property using the linear array implementation. Be sure that your `create` operation is consistent with the postorder traversal algorithm of Example 15.6.
3. Write implementations of the preorder and inorder traversal operations for a linear array implementation of a binary tree.
4. Implement the following operation for a linear representation of a binary tree with the heap property.

```
void remove(E &item);
```

(*Hint:* When the root is removed, temporarily replace it with the tree node in the last active index of the array. Then develop an algorithm to walk this new root down a branch of the tree until the tree becomes a heap again.) In a written statement, indicate how the `insert` function of Example 15.5 and the `remove` function that you have written for this exercise could be used to implement a priority queue (Chapter 13) using a heap.

5. In a written statement, discuss the relative advantages and disadvantages of the linear array implementation of a binary tree versus the linked implementation described in Section 15.2.

15.5 General Trees

Objectives

a. to understand how a general tree may be implemented using a linked representation of a binary tree
b. given the implementation of a general tree by a binary tree, to examine which traversal operations for the underlying binary tree make sense when it is interpreted as a general tree

We began this chapter with a discussion of the many ways in which hierarchical structures are used to organize information around us. We then quickly dictated that at most two children could be used, which focused all of our attention on the seemingly restricted case of the binary tree. What about all of those applications requiring a hierarchical relationship where a parent may have an unrestricted number of children? You may have become suspicious that we are avoiding such considerations because they are too difficult.

Fortunately, we have a much more educationally sound reason. That is, we may use a binary tree to implement a *general tree*. The nice implication of this rather surprising statement is that we will not have to spend a significant amount of time discussing general trees because we have unknowingly studied them in our thorough analysis of binary trees. Moreover, the formal operations on a general tree may be viewed as operations derived from those associated with a binary tree.

The real key to using a restricted type of tree such as a binary tree to implement a more general type of tree is to adjust our perspective. For example, consider the general genealogical tree of Figure 15.24. Here BILL is the first child of the JONES family, with KATY, MIKE, and TOM as BILL's siblings. Similarly, LARRY is the first child of MARY, with PAUL and PENNY as siblings. Now, in a linked representation of a binary tree, we have two pointer fields associated with each node. We have called these pointer fields `left` and `right` because it suited our perspective at the time. However, we shall now switch that perspective in the following way. One of the pointer fields is viewed as a pointer to the leftmost child of a node in a general tree. The second pointer

Figure 15.24
Genealogical tree

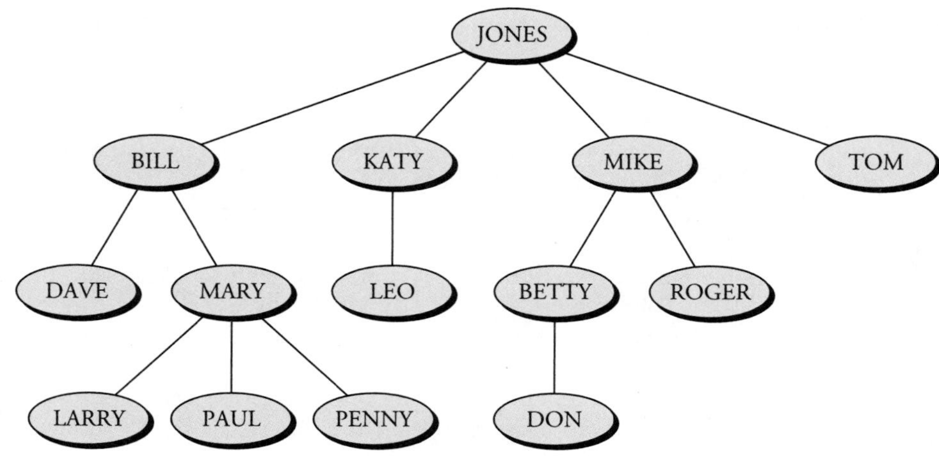

Figure 15.25 Binary tree representation of genealogical tree in Figure 15.24

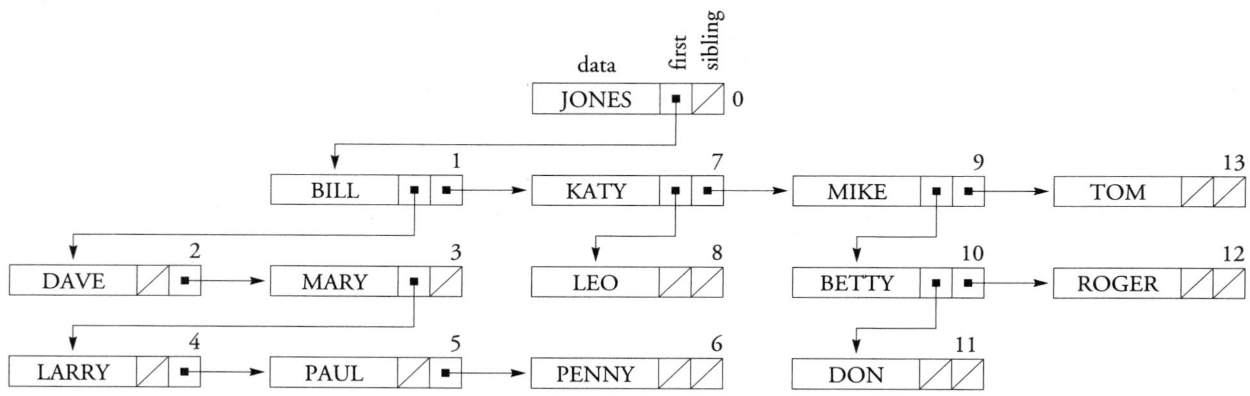

identifies the next sibling to the right of the node under consideration in the general tree. Since the children of a node taken in this context form an ordered set of nodes, we can regard the leftmost child of a node as `first` and the sibling to the right of this node as `sibling`. We will henceforth adopt this terminology for the two link fields involved with the binary tree representation of a general tree. Figure 15.25 gives the binary representation of the general genealogical tree shown in Figure 15.24.

Note that we number the pointers in the tree of Figure 15.24. This numbering is reflected in Table 15.4. You should carefully check all first and sibling values to convince yourself that the scheme used to fill this array was to store a node before any of its children and then recursively store the leftmost child.

The representation in terms of C++ pointer variables (and the representation we shall henceforth use) requires the following type declarations:

```
protected:

// Protected data members

struct node
{
    E data;
```

Table 15.4
Tree in Figure 15.24 Stored in Array of Records for Data and Pointers

Location	data	first	sibling
0	JONES	1	0
1	BILL	2	7
2	DAVE	0	3
3	MARY	4	0
4	LARRY	0	5
5	PAUL	0	6
6	PENNY	0	0
7	KATY	9	9
8	LEO	0	0
9	MIKE	10	13
10	BETTY	11	12
11	DON	0	0
12	ROGER	0	0
13	TOM	0	0

```
    node * first;
    node * sibling;
};

node * tree;                // Root pointer for entire tree
```

Traversals of a General Tree Implemented via a Binary Tree

Since this implementation scheme for a general tree is nothing more than a special interpretation of a binary tree, all of the traversals defined for a binary tree clearly exist for the general tree. A more relevant question than the mere existence of a traversal, however, is the significance of the order in which the nodes of a general tree are visited when its corresponding binary tree is traversed. Of particular interest in this regard are the preorder and postorder traversals.

You should verify that the preorder traversal algorithm for a binary tree applied to Figure 15.24 visits nodes in the following order:

```
JONES
    BILL
        DAVE
        MARY
            LARRY
            PAUL
            PENNY
    KATY
        LEO
    MIKE
        BETTY
            DON
        ROGER
    TOM
```

A NOTE OF INTEREST

Computer Security and Tree-Structured File Systems

One of the prime concerns in developing operating systems for multiuser computers is to ensure that a user cannot, in an unauthorized fashion, access system files or the files of other users. A convenient data structure to implement such a file directory system is a tree such as that pictured below.

Each interior node of the tree can be viewed as a directory containing various system information about those files or subdirectories that are its descendants. Leaf nodes in the tree are the actual files. Hence, in the diagram, files can be broken down into system files and user files. System files consist of the C++ DEVELOPMENT TOOLS, the LISP DEVELOPMENT TOOLS, and the TEXT EDITOR. User directories are called VERA, DAVID, and MARTHA. One of the very convenient features of such a system is that it allows the user to extend this tree structure as deeply as desired. For instance, in the given tree directory structure, we see that user VERA has created subdirectories for files related to PAYROLL and INVENTORY. DAVID and MARTHA could have similarly partitioned subdirectories to organize their work.

In addition to offering users the convenience of being able to group their files into appropriate subdirectories, such a file system offers a very natural solution to the problem of file security. Since each individual user is, in effect, the root of a miniature subordinate file system within the overall system, a user is given, by default, free access to every node in his or her subtree. That is, the user is viewed as the owner of every node in the subtree. To jump outside this subtree of naturally owned files and directories requires that special permissions be given the user by other users or by the operating system itself. Hence, the tree structure offers convenience as well as a means of carefully monitoring the integrity of the file system.

AT&T's UNIX operating system, developed at Bell Laboratories in the early 1970s, was one of the first to use such a tree-structured directory system. The widespread popularity of UNIX today and the adoption of this scheme by a significant number of other operating systems is evidence of the attractive way it combines user convenience with system security. However, this is not to say that such systems are completely free of security problems. Once the security of such a system is slightly compromised, the tree structure lends itself to a cascade of far-reaching security breaks. Brian Reid's "Reflections on Some Recent Widespread Computer Break-ins," *Communications of the ACM,* Vol. 30, No. 2, Feb. 1987, provides an interesting account of how such security problems surfaced at Stanford University and spread to an entire network of computers. An entertaining narrative of another security incident is presented by Clifford Stoll in *The Cuckoo's Egg,* New York: Doubleday, 1989.

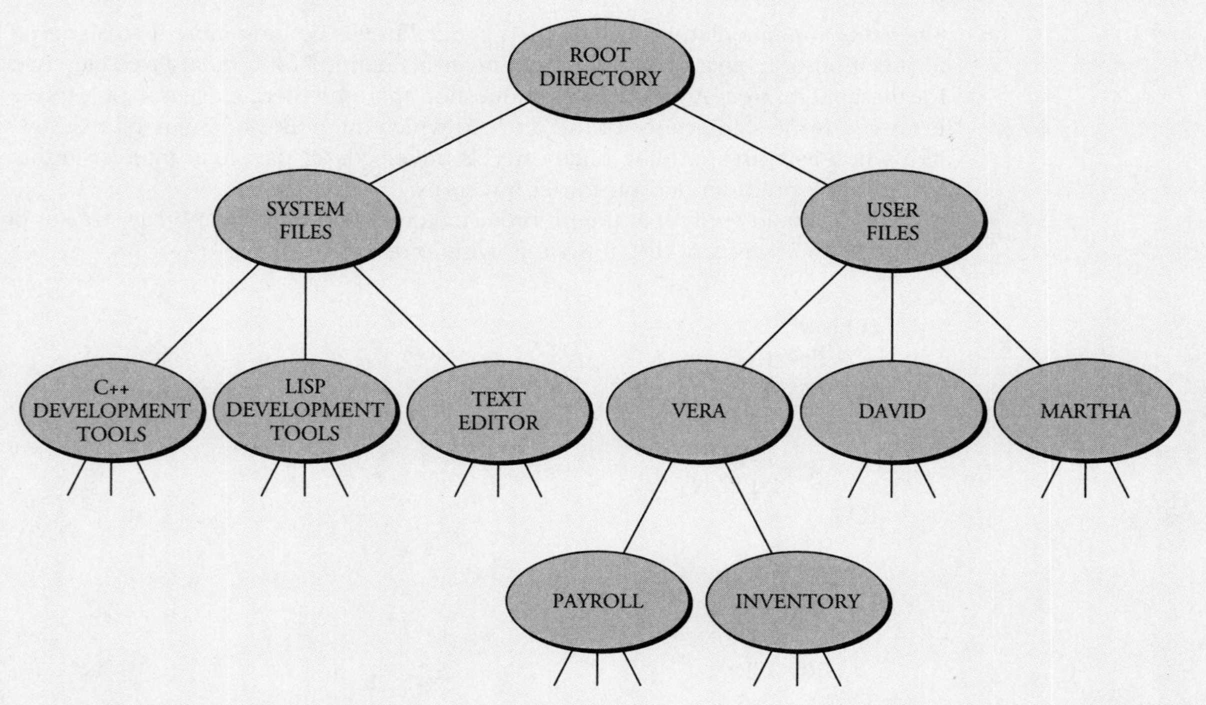

The indentation here has been added to highlight the fact that the preorder traversal will recursively process a parent node and then process the child nodes from left to right.

Relative to the general tree pictured in Figure 15.24, we see that the effect of the preorder traversal is to fix on a node at one level of the tree and then run through all of that node's children before progressing to the next node at the same level (the sibling). There is a hint here of a generalized nested loop situation which, as you will see, has some interesting applications in Programming Problems and Projects at the end of this chapter.

The other traversal of interest in a binary tree representation of a general tree is the postorder traversal. In this regard, it should first be verified that the postorder traversal applied to Figure 15.24 (and its binary tree implementation in Figure 15.25) yields the following listing:

PENNY
PAUL
LARRY
MARY
DAVE
LEO
DON
ROGER
BETTY
TOM
MIKE
KATY
BILL
JONES

In general, the postorder traversal works its way up from the leaf nodes of a tree, ensuring that no given node is processed until all nodes in the subtree below it have been processed.

Exercises 15.5

1. How would you implement a preorder traversal to print nodes in a fashion that has children indented under their parents?
2. Consider the following abstract graphic representation of a general tree:

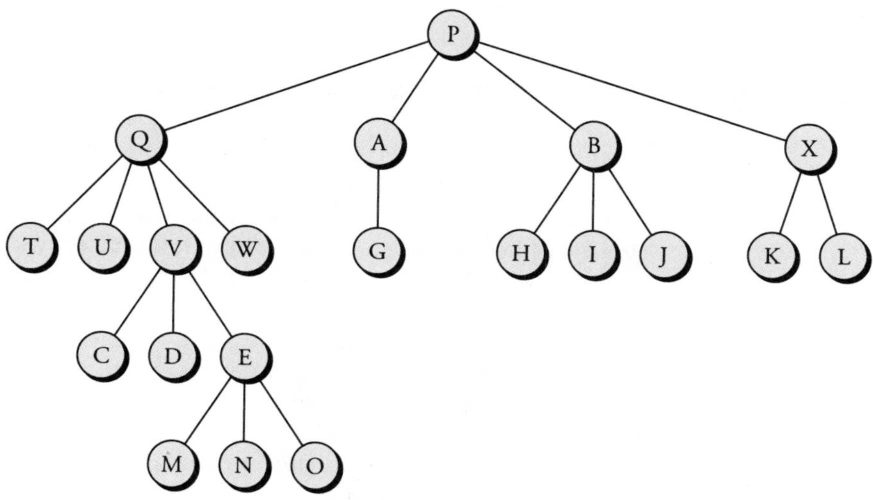

Provide a specific C++ record description for a node in this tree as you would represent it. (Do not make any assumption about maximum possible number of children.) Then draw a specific picture of how this tree would be stored using the record description you have chosen.

3. Given the tree from Exercise 2, in what order would nodes be visited by a preorder traversal? A postorder traversal?
4. For this exercise, you are to assume a linked binary tree representation of a general tree. Write a function that meets the following specification:

```
// Function: addChild
// Insert a tree st as the kth subtree of the tree receiving this message.
// If the root node of the tree already has k or more subtrees, the
// tree st becomes the kth subtree and the former kth subtree becomes
// the (k+1)st subtree.
// If the root node of the tree has fewer than k subtrees,
// then new tree st is inserted as the last subtree of the root node.

template <class E>
void generalTree<E>::addChild(node * st, int k)
```

5. Use the function you developed for Exercise 4 in another function to generate the following tree. Verify that you have generated the correct tree with a traversal function that outputs the tree in appropriate fashion.

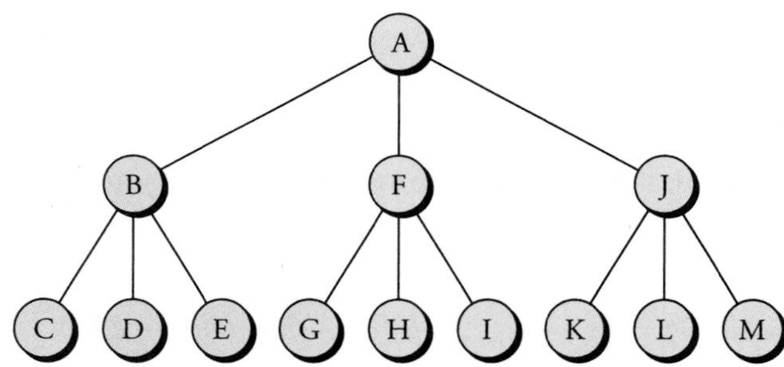

6. Is a binary tree a special case of a general tree? Provide a written rationale to justify your answer.

15.6 Graphs and Networks: Bidirectional Trees

The key defining characteristic of a tree is the hierarchical relationship between parent and child nodes. In a tree, this hierarchical relationship is one-way. That is, within the tree, there is pointer information that allows us to descend from parent to child. However, there is generally no pointer information within the tree that allows us to ascend from a child node to its parent. In many information storage applications, such a one-way relationship is not sufficient. Consider, for instance, the relationship between students and courses at a university. Each student is enrolled in several courses and could thus be viewed as a parent node with children consisting of the courses he or she is taking. Conversely, each course enrolls many students and could thus be viewed as a parent node with children consisting of the students enrolled in that particular course. The data structure that emerges from this type of bidirectional relationship is pictured in Figure 15.26.

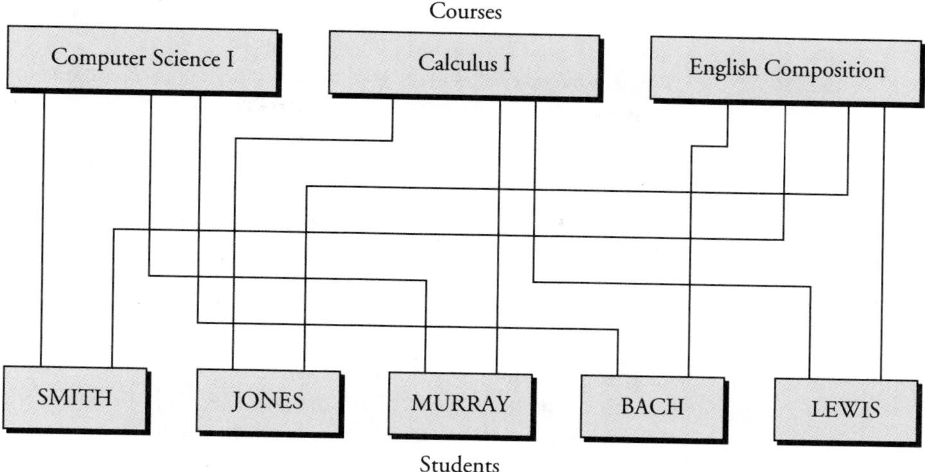

Figure 15.26
Bidirectional relationship between students and courses

Objectives

a. to understand the definition and operations for the graph ADT
b. to understand the definition and operations for the network ADT
c. to understand how a two-dimensional table may be used to implement the graph and network ADTs
d. to realize why the two-dimensional table representation of a graph or network often results in a sparse matrix
e. to understand traversal algorithms for graphs and networks
f. to understand Dijkstra's algorithm for finding the shortest path between two nodes in a network

In terms of an abstract data type, the representation of such a bidirectional relationship between nodes is called a *graph*.

Graph: A graph consists of two sets. One set is a fixed set of objects called *nodes*. The other is a set of *edges*, the contents of which vary depending on the operations that have been performed on the graph. A node is a data element of the graph, and an edge is a direct connection between two nodes. A node may also be called a *vertex* of the graph. If an edge exists between two nodes, we say that the second node is adjacent to the first node.

The operations associated with the graph ADT are specified in terms of the following preconditions and postconditions:

Create Operation

Preconditions: Receiver is a graph in an unpredictable state.

Postconditions: Graph is initialized to a state with no edges. That is, no nodes are connected to any other nodes, including themselves.

addEdge Operation

Preconditions: Receiver is an arbitrary graph that has been initialized by `create` and, potentially, affected by other operations. `node1` and `node2` are two nodes in the graph.

Postconditions: Receiver is returned with an edge from `node1` to `node2`. If an edge already existed from `node1` to `node2`, the graph is not affected.

removeEdge Operation

Preconditions: Receiver is an arbitrary graph that has been initialized by `create` and, potentially, affected by other operations. `node1` and `node2` are two nodes in the graph.

Postconditions: If there is an edge from `node1` to `node2`, it is removed. Otherwise, the graph is not affected.

edge Operation

Preconditions: Receiver is an arbitrary graph that has been initialized by `create` and, potentially, affected by other operations. `node1` and `node2` are two nodes in the graph.

Postconditions: `edge` returns `true` if there is an edge from `node1` to `node2`, `false` otherwise.

traverse Operation

Preconditions: Receiver is an arbitrary graph that has been initialized by `create` and, potentially, affected by other operations. `start` is a node at which the

	traversal is to start. `process` is an algorithmic process that can be applied to each graph node.
Postconditions:	Receiver is returned with each node that can be reached from `start` affected by `process`. A given node can be reached from `start` if the given node is the start node or if there is a sequence of edges E_0, $E_1, \ldots, E_n$ such that (1) E_0 begins at the `start` node, (2) the node at which E_{i-1} ends is the node at which E_i begins, and (3) E_n ends at the given node. In effect, the sequence of edges determines a path from `start` to the given node. The path is composed of edges between adjacent nodes. `process` is not applied to any node more than once.

Notice that, as it relates to Figure 15.26, the formal definition of a graph does not rule out the possibility of an edge connecting two courses or connecting two students. It is merely the nature of this course–student relationship that makes the existence of such a course-to-course edge or student-to-student edge impractical. In other applications, such as the transportation network pictured in Figure 15.27, it may be entirely feasible for any node in the graph to have an edge connecting it to any other node.

To illustrate how a graph grows from an initial state with no edges, suppose that we start with a set of nodes labeled A, B, C, D. Figure 15.28 traces the effect of a sequence of `addEdge` and `removeEdge` operations on a graph with these nodes. Note from this figure that the concept of an edge carries with it the notion of a direction. That is, it is possible to have an edge from `node1` to `node2` in a graph G without there being a corresponding connection in the opposite direction. Figure 15.28(8) also illustrates that it is possible to have an edge from a node to itself.

By convention, when we draw a graph without arrows on the edges, it is implicit that all edges run in both directions. Thus, in Figure 15.27, the line connecting San Francisco and Los Angeles implicitly represents two edges—one from San Francisco to Los Angeles and one from Los Angeles to San Francisco.

Figure 15.27 Transportation network as graph in which edges represent flights between cities

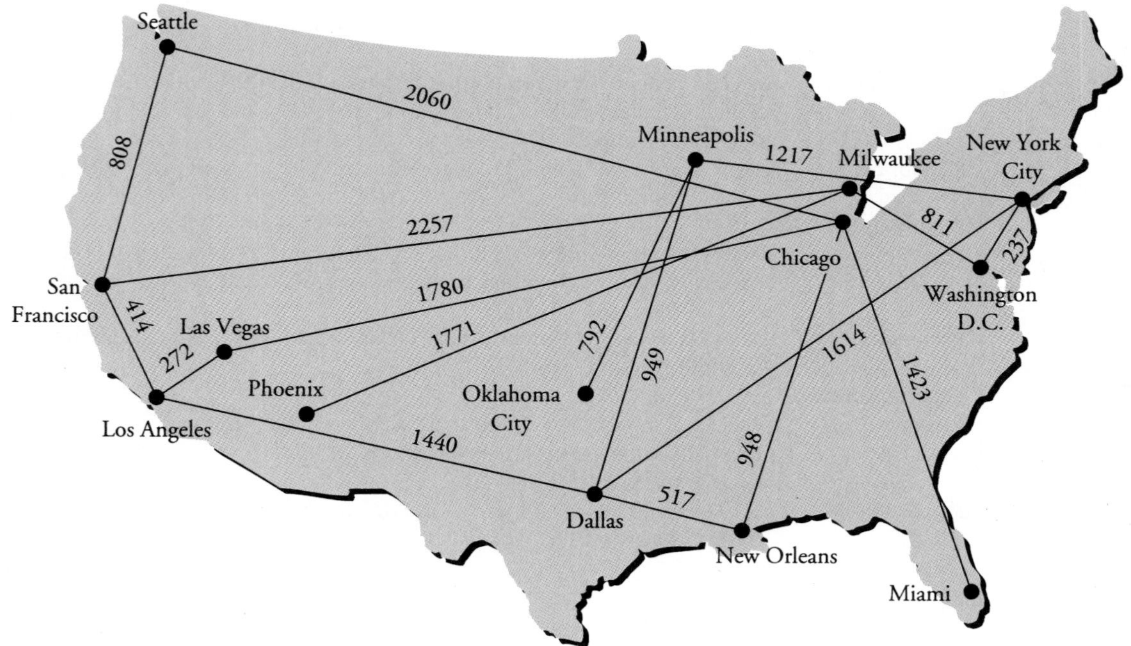

Figure 15.28 Graph affected by sequence of `addEdge` and `removeEdge` operations

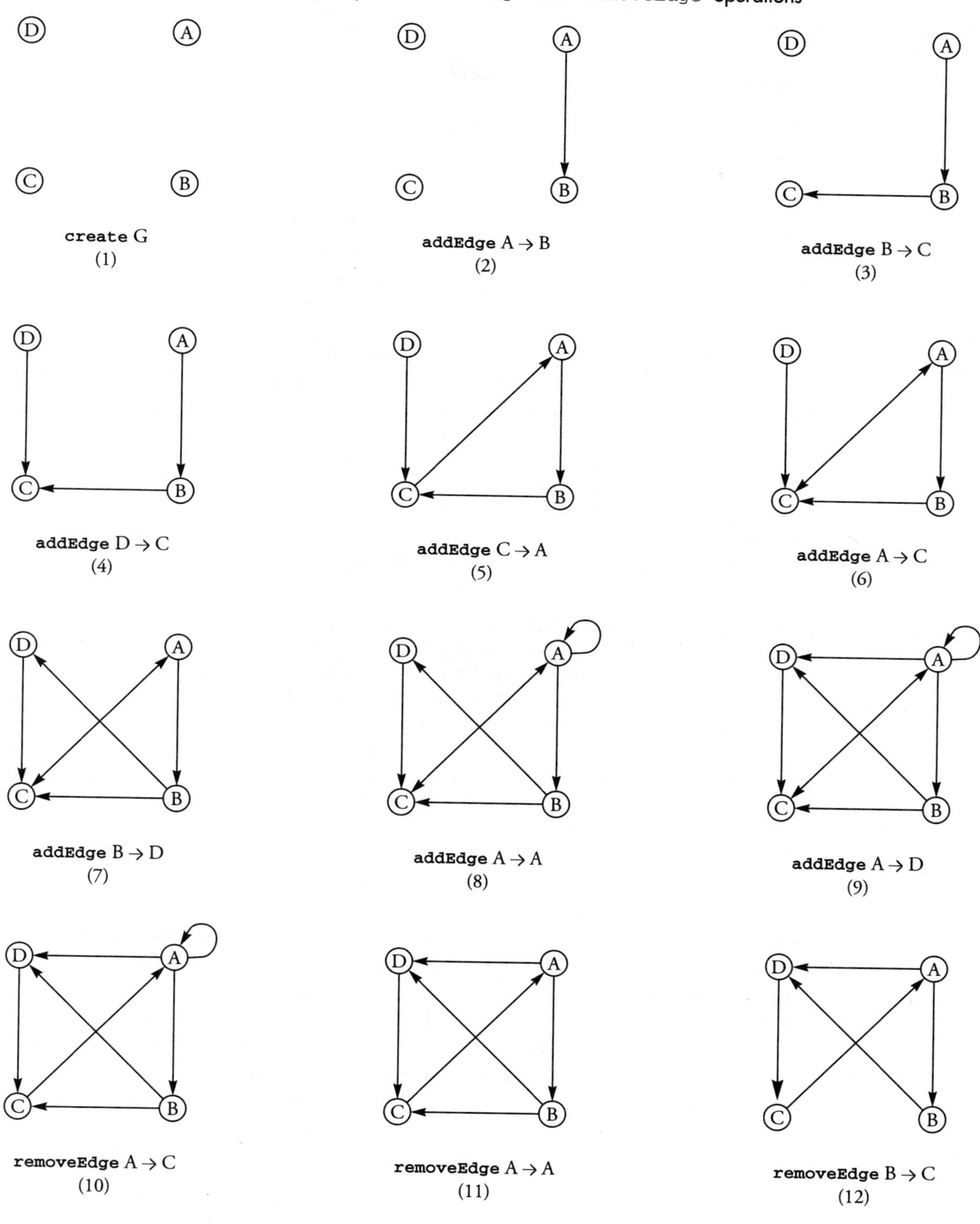

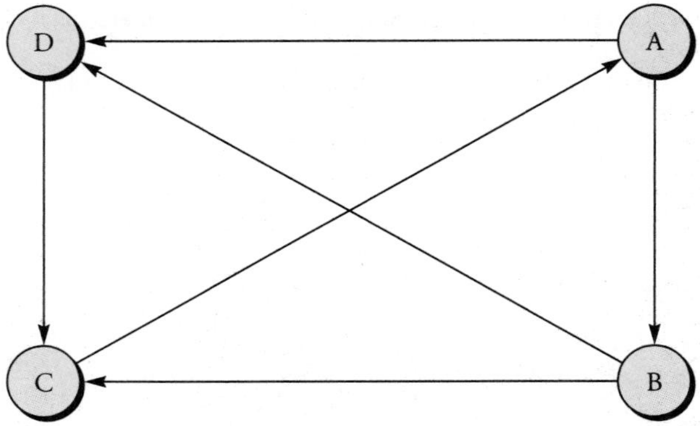

Figure 15.29
A four-node digraph

We will sometimes use the terminology *directional graph,* or *digraph,* to emphasize that a particular graph has some edges that exist only in one direction. Figure 15.29 illustrates a digraph. In a digraph, arrows specify the direction of an edge between nodes.

Before providing a C++ interface for the graph ADT, we should clarify a point of ambiguity in the definition of the traversal operation. In particular, this operation does not establish a unique order of visiting nodes that can be reached from the start node. The following examples illustrate two potential orders in which nodes can be visited starting at A in the graph of Figure 15.29.

Example 15.7 Consider a traversal from start node A in the digraph of Figure 15.29 guided by the following strategy: A given path starting at A should be explored as deeply as possible before another path is probed. If we assume that B is the first node adjacent to A, then the traversal will proceed from A to B. If we then assume that C is the first node adjacent to B, the traversal will continue from B to C. From C, it is not possible to visit any nodes that have not already been visited. Hence, we will backtrack to B and, from there, continue the traversal to D since D is adjacent to B. Hence, the overall order in which nodes are visited by a traversal under the strategy and assumptions of this example is

```
A, B, C, D
```

The strategy exemplified here is often called a *depth-first traversal* since a given path is probed as deeply as possible before we backtrack and explore another path.

Example 15.8 Indicate the order in which nodes would be visited in a traversal starting at node A in the digraph of Figure 15.29 following a strategy that does not probe one path as deeply as possible but rather "fans out" to all nodes adjacent to a given node. Hence, we would proceed from A to B and then to D because both B and D are adjacent to A. Since all nodes adjacent to A have been exhausted, we would fan out from B, the first node we visited from A. This takes us to C by the edge B → C, completing the traversal in the overall order

```
A, B, D, C
```

The fan-out strategy exemplified here is often termed a *breadth-first traversal.*

Examples 15.7 and 15.8 just begin to scratch the surface of the variety of graph traversal strategies that exist. We shall soon examine the implementation of these traversal strategies more closely. At this time, the point to emphasize is that the graph traversal operation is open to a variety of implementation techniques.

C++ Interface for the Graph ADT

Before we can develop graph algorithms in detail, we must provide a C++ interface for this ADT. This is done in the following class declaration module. The interface makes the assumption that the data in graph nodes are drawn from a range of values that can serve both as keys for tables and as values over which a `for` loop can iterate, such as `int`, `char`, or an enumerated type. Our reasons for making this assumption will become apparent when we discuss ways of implementing graphs.

```
// Class declaration file: graph.h

#ifndef GRAPH_H
#define GRAPH_H

// Definition section

template <class Node> class graph
{

   public:

   // Class constructors

   graph();
   graph(const graph<Node> &g);

   // Member functions

   void addEdge(const Node &node1, const Node & node2);
   void removeEdge(const Node &node1, const Node &node2);
   bool edge(const Node &node1, const Node &node2);
   void traverse(Node &start, void (*process) (Node &item));
   graph<Node>& operator = (const graph<Node> &g);

   // Protected data and member functions pertaining to
   // the implementation would be located here.

   };

#endif
```

The Network ADT

Graphs such as that shown in Figure 15.27 are somewhat special in that the edges have weights associated with them, here representing distances between nodes (cities). Such a graph is an example of the *network* abstract data type.

Network: A network is a graph in which each edge has a positive numeric *weight*. The operations associated with the network ADT are the same as those for the graph ADT with the exceptions that the `addEdge` operation must now specify the weight of the edge being added and we must add an operation which, given two nodes, returns the weight of the edge that may exist between them.

These two new operations are specified by the following preconditions and postconditions.

addEdge Operation

Preconditions: Receiver is an arbitrary network that has been initialized by `create` and, potentially, affected by other operations. `node1` and `node2` are two nodes in the network. `weight` is a positive number representing the weight of an edge to be added from `node1` to `node2`.

Postconditions: Receiver has an edge of weight `weight` from `node1` to `node2`. If an edge already existed from `node1` to `node2`, the weight of that edge is now `weight`.

edgeWeight Operation

Preconditions: Receiver is an arbitrary network that has been initialized by `create` and, potentially, affected by other operations. `node1` and `node2` are two nodes in the network.

Postconditions: `edgeWeight` returns 0 if there is no edge from `node1` to `node2` and the numeric value of the edge if it exists.

Graphs and networks provide excellent examples of how a theoretical area of mathematics has found very relevant application in computer science. It is beyond the scope of this text to provide a comprehensive treatment of graphs and networks. Rather, our purpose in the rest of this section is to provide you with an overview of a data structure that you will no doubt encounter again as you continue your study of computer science. More in-depth treatments of graphs and networks can be found in numerous advanced texts on data structures such as Ellis Horowitz & Sartaj Sahni, *Data Structures in C++*, New York: Computer Science Press, 1990, and George J. Pothering & Thomas L. Naps, *Introduction to Data Structures and Algorithm Analysis with C++*, St. Paul, MN: West Publishing, 1995.

Implementation of Graphs and Networks

A graph may be conveniently implemented using a two-dimensional table of Boolean values. For instance, the information in Figure 15.26 is contained in Table 15.5, a two-dimensional table. In this table, the value `true` indicates the presence of an edge between two nodes, and the value `false` indicates the absence of such an edge. In the case of a network, the two-dimensional table implementation still applies. Now, however, the data stored in the table is of a type compatible with edge weights. Such a two-dimensional table implementation of the transportation network from Figure 15.27 is given in Table 15.6. Note that the data are mirrored across the diagonal of the table because all edges are bidirectional. Table 15.6 illustrates a quality typically found in two-dimensional table implementations of large graphs and networks: the sparseness of nontrivial data. Hence, the methods we have discussed for implementing sparse two-key tables provide alternative implementation strategies for graphs and networks.

In the discussion of the two graph/network algorithms that follow, we do not tie ourselves to a particular implementation strategy for representing the underlying data structure. Rather, we discuss the algorithms in terms of the operations associated with the abstract data type involved and leave implementation considerations for the exercises at the end of this section and Programming Problems and Projects at the end of the chapter.

A NOTE OF INTEREST

Computer Networks: Their Use and Potential Abuse

It's a rare student who doesn't take advantage of electronic mail to stay in touch with friends at distant campuses. It could easily be argued that, more than any other single factor, interaction among distant users on the Internet has been responsible for making nearly everyone aware of the potential of computing. But the Internet is merely one part of the Information Superhighway. According to Haruhisa Ishida & Lawrence H. Landweber, "Internetworking," *Communications of the ACM,* Vol. 36, No. 3, Aug. 1993:

> The National Information Infrastructure (NII) and the Electronic Superhighway are two of the titles used by the Clinton/Gore administration to describe plans for an enhanced communications environment. Video conferencing and telephony, entertainment, access to libraries and information repositions, and support for medical consultations are just some of the services to be available to homes, offices, and schools. All of this has been made possible by rapid advances in communications and networking technology over the last decade.

The potential for uses of information networks is unlimited. For example, Janet Murray provides details of how the K12 Network is finding growing use in elementary and secondary education in "K12 Network: Global Education Through Telecommunications," *Communications of the ACM,* Vol. 36, No. 3, Aug. 1993. Some of the opportunities within the K12 Network include language exchanges with native speakers in French, German, Japanese, Spanish, and Russian; cooperative physics experiments, such as attempts of students in Oregon, California, Nova Scotia, and Maryland to replicate Eratosthenes's experiment in Alexandria to determine the size of the earth by measuring the length of a shadow cast by a stick; and the "MathMagic" challenge in which students post a variety of solutions to nontrivial problems.

For all of the wonders of networks, there is also a downside. As we begin to rely increasingly on networks, a variety of privacy-related problems arise. An excellent overview of these problems is presented in a series of articles under the heading "Internet Privacy: The Quest for Anonymity," *Communications of the ACM,* Vol. 42, No. 2, Feb. 1999.

Table 15.5
Two-Dimensional Table Implementation of Graph from Figure 15.26

Course	SMITH	JONES	MURRAY	BACH	LEWIS
Computer Science	TRUE	FALSE	TRUE	TRUE	FALSE
Calculus I	FALSE	TRUE	TRUE	FALSE	TRUE
English Comp.	TRUE	TRUE	FALSE	TRUE	TRUE

Examples of Graph Algorithms: Depth-First and Breadth-First Traversals

In many practical applications of graphs, there is frequently a need to visit systematically all the nodes on a graph from a designated starting node. One such application occurs when the organizers of a political campaign are interested in having their candidate visit all important political centers. The presence or absence of direct transportation routes (that is, edges) between such centers will determine the possible ways in which all the centers can be visited. At the moment, our only concern is the development of an algorithm that ensures that all possible nodes are visited. Such an algorithm will provide an implementation for the graph traversal operation. Later in the chapter, we will investigate how to determine the shortest possible distances from one node to all others.

Depth-First Traversal. This technique was illustrated in Example 15.7. The main logic of the depth-first algorithm is analogous to the preorder traversal of a tree. It is accomplished recursively as follows:

Table 15.6
Two-Dimensional Table Implementation of Network from Figure 15.27

	NY	Wash	Miam	Milw	Chi	NOrl	Mpls	OklC	Dals	LVeg	Phex	StL	SFra	LA
Ny		237		811			1217		1614					
Wash														
Miam					1423									
Milw		811									1771		2257	
Chi			1423			948				1780		2060		
NOrl					948				517					
Mpls	1217							792	949					
OklC							792							
Dals	1614					517	949							1440
LVeg					1780									272
Phex				1771										
StL					2060									808
SFra				2257								808		414
LA											272		414	

1. Designate the starting node as the search node and mark it as visited.
2. Find a node adjacent to the search node (that is, connected by an edge from the search node) that has not yet been visited. Designate this as the new search node (but remember the previous one) and mark it as visited.
3. Repeat step 2 using the new search node. If no nodes satisfying step 2 can be found, return to the previous search node and continue from there.
4. When a return to the previous search node in step 3 is impossible, the search from the originally chosen search node is complete.

This algorithm is called a depth-first traversal because the search continues progressively deeper into the graph in a recursive manner.

To illustrate this function more clearly, consider Figure 15.30; its table implementation is shown in Table 15.7. Suppose we have a function called `searchFrom`, which is invoked to begin a depth-first traversal from a given node on the graph. The steps followed by the algorithm are:

1. We begin by marking node 1 visited and invoke `searchFrom(1)`.
2. Both nodes 2 and 3 are adjacent to node 1 according to the matrix implementation of the graph, but node 2 is encountered first on a left-to-right scan of the row for 1; so the search goes to node 2. We invoke `searchFrom(2)`, and node 2 is marked as visited.
3. Since node 3 is the first unvisited node adjacent to node 2, the search now goes to node 3, `searchFrom(3)` is invoked, and node 3 is marked as visited.
4. Since there is no unvisited node adjacent to node 3, we say that this node has exhausted the search; the search goes back to its predecessor, that is, to node 2.
5. From node 2, we visit node 4.
6. From node 4, we proceed to node 5. All nodes have now been visited, and the depth-first traversal is complete.

Use Table 15.7 to verify these steps.

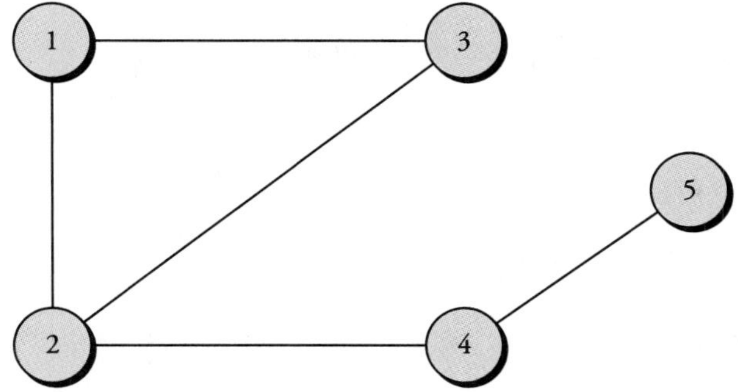

Figure 15.30
Graph to illustrate depth-first search

Table 15.7
Table Implementation of Figure 15.30

	1	2	3	4	5
1	FALSE	TRUE	TRUE	FALSE	FALSE
2	TRUE	FALSE	TRUE	TRUE	FALSE
3	TRUE	TRUE	FALSE	FALSE	FALSE
4	FALSE	TRUE	FALSE	FALSE	TRUE
5	FALSE	FALSE	FALSE	TRUE	FALSE

We note that the order in which nodes are visited in a depth-first traversal is not unique because the order depends on the manner in which adjacent nodes are chosen. That is, given two unvisited adjacent nodes, which one should be chosen to invoke the `searchFrom` function? In practice, this will usually be determined by the ordering of the data type used to implement the nodes in the graph.

Example 15.9 Implement the depth-first traversal algorithm under the assumption that the node data type is an appropriate enumeration type.

As with our implementation of the postorder traversal operation for a binary tree in Example 15.6, we use an auxiliary function as the real recursive workhorse. The traverse function is itself merely a front end, which appropriately sets the stage for the auxiliary function `searchFrom`.

We can now see the reason for the restriction placed on the node type in our C++ interface for the graph ADT. It must be a type capable of keying a table and controlling an iterative loop structure. Both of these properties are assumed in the code of this example.

```
// Assumption: Type Node represents an enumeration with a designed firstValue
//             and lastValue. This allows values of type Node to correspond to
//             indices in a bool array visited that is used to keep track of
//             graph nodes that have already had process applied to them.

template <class Node>
void graph<Node>::traverse(Node &start, void (*process) (Node &item));
{
   // Allocate an array of bool
   bool * visited = new bool [lastValue - firstValue + 1];
   Node k;
```

continued

```
    // Initially nothing is processed
    for (k = firstValue, k <= lastValue, ++k)
       visited[k - firstValue] = false;
    // Make the top-level call to searchFrom
    searchFrom(start, process, visited);
    delete [] visited;
}

template <class Node>
void graph<Node>::searchFrom(Node &start, void (*process) (Node &item), bool * visited)

{
    Node k;

    // Process the start node and mark it in the array of visited nodes
    process(start);
    visited[start - firstValue] = true;

    // Then proceed deeper into the graph
    for (k = firstValue, k <= lastValue, ++k)
       if ( (!visited[k - firstValue]) && edge(start, k))
          searchFrom(k, process, visited);
}
```

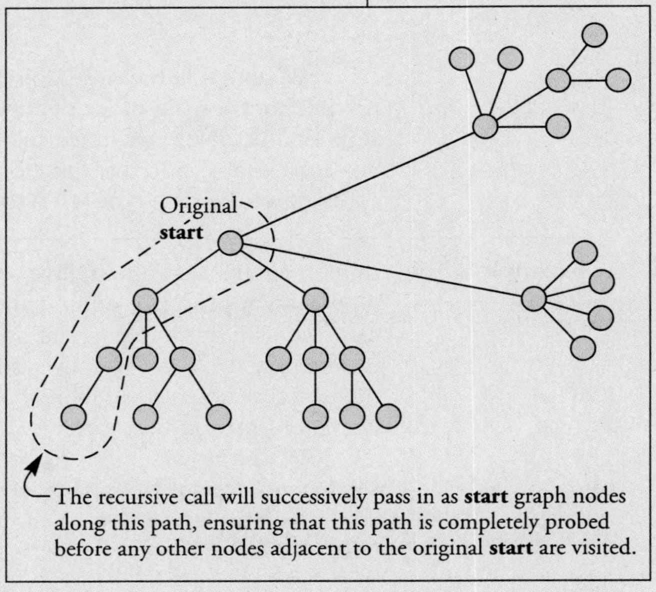

Original
start
The recursive call will successively pass in as **start** graph nodes along this path, ensuring that this path is completely probed before any other nodes adjacent to the original **start** are visited.

Breadth-First Traversal. An alternative graph traversal to the depth-first strategy is the breadth-first traversal. Instead of proceeding as deeply as possible along one path from the current node in the graph, the breadth-first traversal examines all nodes adjacent to the current node before proceeding more deeply along any given path. Hence, for the graph of Figure 15.31, implemented by Table 15.8, a breadth-first traversal starting at node 1 visits nodes in the order 1, 2, 3, 4, 5 (as opposed to the order 1, 2, 4, 5, 3 dictated by a depth-first traversal).

A NOTE OF INTEREST

The Traveling Salesperson and NP-Complete Problems

A well-known problem of classical graph theory, which is easy to state but difficult to solve, is the traveling salesperson problem. The problem essentially tries to minimize the round trip cost of visiting once and only once every city on the business route of the salesperson. This problem was first described by the Irish mathematician Sir William Rowan Hamilton (1805–1865).

The problem can be looked upon as a network such as we have discussed in Section 15.6. The cities to be visited are the nodes in the network, and the weighted edges are the distances between the cities. Unlike the shortest distance algorithm discussed in Section 15.6, the only known algorithm to solve the traveling salesperson problem is to examine *all possible* round trips that visit exactly once every city in the network.

Although this algorithm solves the traveling salesperson's problem, it is slow because of the exponential number of possible round trips. When the number of cities on the salesperson's tour is moderately large (even as large as 20), the solution is annoyingly slow, but nothing better is known which will guarantee finding a solution to the problem.

The complexity of the traveling salesperson problem places it in a class of problems known as NP-complete problems. This theoretical class of problems has the following interesting property. If we can even find for any one such problem a solution that has a polynomial time efficiency, then we will automatically have polynomial time solutions to all other problems in this class and an even larger theoretical class of problems known as NP problems. A thorough discussion of NP and NP-complete problems may be found in Thomas Cormen, Charles Leiserson, & Ronald Rivest, *Introduction to Algorithms,* New York: McGraw-Hill, 1989.

Figure 15.31
Graph to illustrate breadth-first traversal

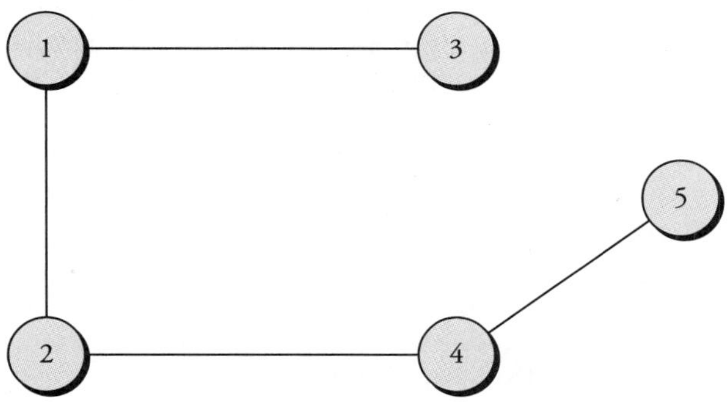

Table 15.8
Table Implementation of Figure 15.31

	1	2	3	4	5
1	FALSE	TRUE	TRUE	FALSE	FALSE
2	TRUE	FALSE	FALSE	TRUE	FALSE
3	TRUE	FALSE	FALSE	FALSE	FALSE
4	FALSE	TRUE	FALSE	FALSE	TRUE
5	FALSE	FALSE	FALSE	TRUE	FALSE

A breadth-first traversal of a graph involves the following steps:

1. Begin with the start node and mark it as visited.
2. Proceed to the next node having an edge connection to the node in step 1. Mark it as visited.
3. Come back to the node in step 1, descend along an edge toward an unvisited node, and mark the new node as visited.

4. Repeat step 3 until all nodes adjacent to the node in step 1 have been marked as visited.
5. Repeat steps 1 through 4 starting from the node visited in 2 and then starting from the nodes visited in step 3 in the order visited. Keep this up as long as possible before starting a new scan.

You will be asked to explore this strategy in Programming Problems and Projects at the end of the chapter.

Example of a Network Algorithm: Finding Shortest Paths

If the graph under consideration is a network in which edge weights represent distances, then an appropriate question is: From a given node called the `source`, what is the shortest distance to all other nodes in the network?

For instance, the network of Figure 15.32 could be thought of as showing airline routes between cities. An airline would be interested in finding the most economical route between any two given cities in the network. The numbers listed on the edges in this case represent distances between cities. Thus, the airline wishes to find the shortest paths that can be flown from node 3 to reach each of nodes 1, 2, 4, and 5.

Suppose we want to find the shortest path from node 1 to node 3. From Figure 15.32, we note that this path is $1 \rightarrow 2 \rightarrow 3$, yielding a total weight of $800 + 410 = 1210$. An algorithm to find such a path was discovered by E. W. Dijkstra. For convenience in discussing Dijkstra's algorithm, often called the shortest path algorithm, let us assume that the nodes in the network under consideration are numbered 1, 2, . . . , `numberOfNodes`. That is, the node type is the subrange of the integers given by `1 . . . numberOfNodes`.

Given such a collection of nodes, Dijkstra's algorithm requires three arrays in addition to a suitable implementation of the network M. These three arrays are identified as follows:

```
int distance[numberOfNodes + 1];
int path[numberOfNodes + 1];
boolean included[numberOfNodes + 1];
```

Identifying one node as the `source`, the algorithm proceeds to find the shortest distance from `source` to all other nodes in the network. At the conclusion of the al-

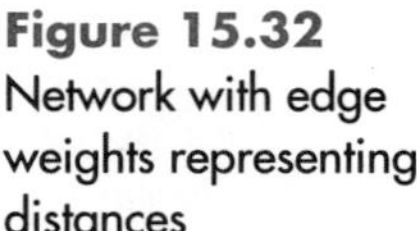

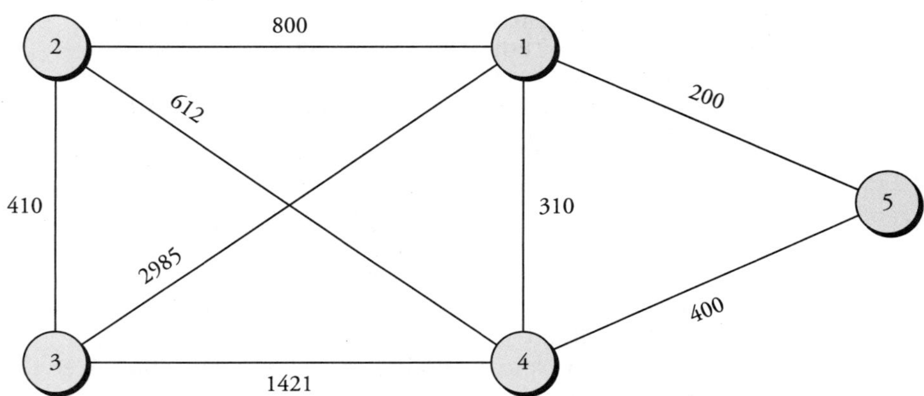

Figure 15.32 Network with edge weights representing distances

gorithm, the shortest distance from `source` to node `j` is stored in `distance[j]`, whereas `path[j]` contains the immediate predecessor of node `j` on the path determining this shortest distance. While the algorithm is in progress, `distance[j]` and `path[j]` are being continually updated until `included[j]` is switched from `false` to `true`. Once this switch occurs, it is known definitely that `distance[j]` contains the shortest distance from `source` to `j`. The algorithm progresses until all nodes have been so included. Hence, it gives us the shortest distance from `source` to every other node in the network.

Given the source node in the network M, the algorithm may be divided into two phases: an initialization phase followed by an iteration phase, in which nodes are included one by one in the set of nodes for which the shortest distance from `source` is known definitely. During the initialization phase, we must

1. Initialize included[source] to TRUE and included [j] to FALSE for all other j.
2. Initialize each index j in the distance array via the rule:

```
if j == source
   distance[j] = 0
else if M.edgeWeight(source, j) != 0
   distance[j] = M.edgeWeight(source, j)
else if j is not connected to source by a direct edge (that is, if
        M.edgeWeight(source, j) == 0)
      distance[j] = Infinity
```

3. Initialize each index j in the path array via the rule:

```
if M.edgeWeight (source, j) != 0
   path[j] = source
else
   path[j] = Undefined
```

Given this initialization, the iteration phase may be expressed in a generalized pseudocode form as follows:

```
Do
   Find the node J that has the minimal distance among those nodes not yet included
   Mark J as now included
   For each R not yet included
      If there is an edge from J to R
         If distance[J] + M.edgeWeight (J, R) < distance[R]
            distance[R] = distance[J] + M.edgeWeight (J, R)
            path[R]= J
While all nodes are not included
```

The crucial part of the algorithm occurs within the innermost `if` of the `for` loop. Figure 15.33 provides a pictorial representation of the logic involved here. The nodes included with the circle represent those nodes already included prior to a given iteration of the `do` loop. Node J in Figure 15.33 represents the node found in the first step of the `do` loop; R represents another arbitrary node, which has not yet been included. The lines emanating from `source` represent the paths corresponding to the current entries in the distance array. For nodes within the circle—that is, those already included—these paths are guaranteed to be the shortest distance paths. If J is the node having the minimal entry in distance among those not yet `included`, we will add J to the circle of included nodes and then check to see if J's connections to other nodes in the network that are not yet `included` may result in a newly found shorter path to such nodes.

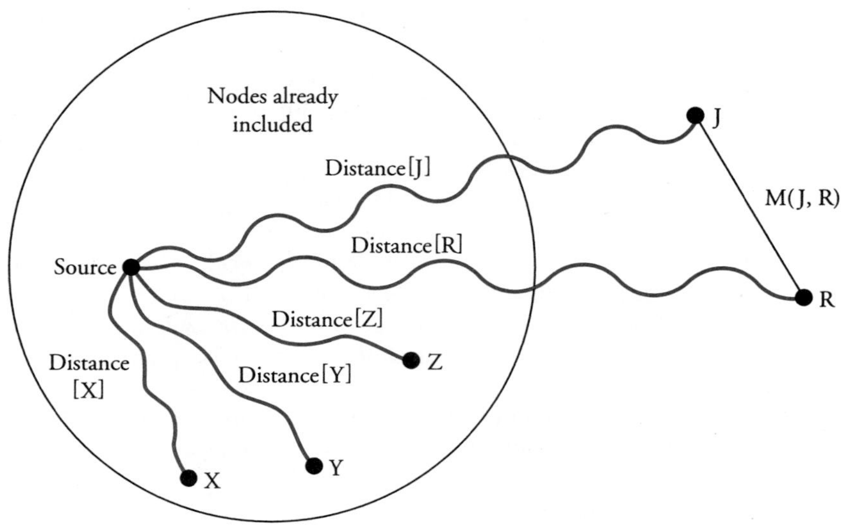

Figure 15.33 `do...while` loop logic in shortest path (Dijkstra's) algorithm

Referring to Figure 15.33 again, the sum of two sides of a triangle

```
distance[J] + M.edgeWeight(J, R)
```

may in fact be shorter than the third side,

```
distance[R]
```

This geometric contradiction is possible because these are not true straight-sided triangles, but "triangles" whose sides may be very complicated paths through a network.

It is also apparent from Figure 15.33 why Dijkstra's algorithm works. As the node J in this figure is found to have the minimal distance entry from among all those nodes not yet included, we may now include it among the nodes whose minimal distance from the source node is absolutely known. Why? Consider any other path P to J containing nodes that are not yet included at the time J is included. Let X be the first such nonincluded node on path P. Then clearly, as the first nonincluded node on the path P, X must be adjacent to an included node. However, as Figure 15.34 indicates, the criterion that dictated the choice of J as an included node ensures that

distance[J] ≤ *The total edge weight through node X on the path P*
≤ *Total edge weight of path P*

This inequality demonstrates that, once J is included, there exists no other path P to J through a nonincluded node that can yield a shorter overall distance. Hence, we have verified our claim that including a node guarantees our having found a path of shortest possible distance to that node.

Example 15.10 To be sure you understand Dijkstra's algorithm before you attempt to implement it, trace it through on the network of Figure 15.32 with `source = 1`.

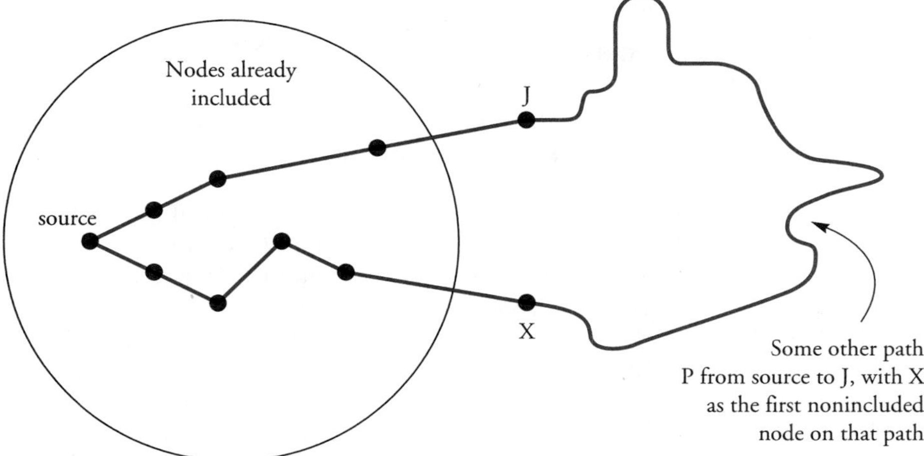

Figure 15.34
Guaranteeing the minimality of distance to J once it is included

Initially, we have

```
distance[2] = 800   path[2] = 1
distance[3] = 2985  path[3] = 1
distance[4] = 310   path[4] = 1
distance[5] = 200   path[5] = 1
```

in accordance with steps 2 and 3 of the initialization phase. According to the iteration phase of the algorithm, we then, in order, perform these steps:

1. Include node 5; no change in `distance` and `path` needed.

```
distance[2] = 800   path[2] = 1
distance[3] = 2985  path[3] = 1
distance[4] = 310   path[4] = 1
distance[5] = 200   path[5] = 1
```

2. Include node 4; update `distance` and `path` to

```
distance[2] = 800   path[2] = 1
distance[3] = 1731  path[3] = 4
distance[4] = 310   path[4] = 1
distance[5] = 200   path[5] = 1
```

(Note that it is shorter to go from node 1 to node 4 to node 3 than to follow the edge directly connecting node 1 to node 3.)

3. Include node 2; update `distance` and `path` to

```
distance[2] = 800   path[2] = 1
distance[3] = 1210  path[3] = 2
distance[4] = 310   path[4] = 1
distance[5] = 200   path[5] = 1
```

(Now we find that traveling from node 1 to node 2 to node 3 is even better than the path determined in step 2.)

4. Finally, node 3 is included with (obviously) no changes made in `distance` or `path`.

Exercises 15.6

1. Indicate the order in which nodes would be visited if a depth-first traversal of the network in Figure 15.27 were initiated from SEATTLE. Use the adjacency relationships from Table 15.6.
2. Repeat Exercise 1 but initiate the traversal from MIAMI.
3. Repeat Exercise 1 for a breadth-first traversal.
4. Repeat Exercise 2 for a breadth-first traversal.
5. Trace the contents of the `distance`, `path`, and `included` arrays as Dijkstra's shortest path algorithm is applied to the transportation network of Figure 15.27. Use PHOENIX as the `source` node.
6. Repeat Exercise 5 with MILWAUKEE as the `source` node.
7. Using a two-dimensional table, write functions to implement each of the basic operations for the graph abstract data type. Then provide a big-O time efficiency analysis of each of the operations. How is this analysis affected by a particular implementation technique that may be underlying the two-key table? Be as specific as possible in stating your answer.
8. Using a two-key table, write functions to implement each of the basic operations for the network abstract data type.
9. In a written statement, discuss the implications of eliminating the requirement that type `node` be a subrange of an ordinal type in the C++ interface for the graph ADT. Your statement should identify problems that this would cause and outline strategies for solving such problems.

Case Study: A Concordance Problem

The declarations for our binary tree class are intentionally less complete than those for other data structures we have discussed. Why? The organizational structure of a binary tree is highly dependent on the data stored in the tree and the way in which an application program wants to manipulate those data. Consequently, we have only presented a "bare bones" set of generic operations that all binary trees have in common. It is almost inevitable that any applications program using a binary tree will have to extend those operations in a fashion appropriate to its needs. Fortunately, object-oriented inheritance makes this very easy to do. We shall demonstrate such inheritance in this Case Study.

User Request

Write a program that reads a file of text representing a work of literature. Produce a *concordance* of the words in this file, that is, an alphabetical listing of the words along with a count of how many times each word appears in the work. Assume that, prior to your program reading the file, all punctuation has been stripped and all letters have been converted to lowercase. After displaying the concordance, also output the word that occurs most often, along with its frequency.

Analysis

Ideally, the program will call for input of the name of the file from which the words are read, so a sample run will appear as:

```
Name of file to read words from? tea_party.txt

a 48
about 5
```

```
above 1
accounts 1
added 5
advantage 1
...
yawning 2
year 2
yes 3
yet 3
you 50
young 1
your 4
yourself 1

Occurring most is -- the -- 159 times
```

Design

We could have solved this particular problem earlier by using an array, linked list, or sorted collection as the data structure in which to store the words (and their counts) as they are read from the file. However, all of these data structures would have led to an $O(n^2)$ efficiency, where n is the number of words in the file. With a binary search tree as the underlying data structure, there is a good chance that the processing time for each word as it is read from the file will be $O(\log_2 n)$. Hence, barring an unbalanced tree, the overall efficiency of our program will be $O(n * \log_2 n)$.

The `BinaryTree` class developed in Section 15.2 provides a good start toward solving the problem at hand. For the templated data type in each tree node, we can use a struct containing a word and the count of how many times that word appears in the file.

```
struct WordStruct
{
   apstring word;
   int count;
};
```

Once the tree is filled with words from the file, calling on the `inorderTraverse` function for the `BinaryTree`, with an appropriate display function, will produce the concordance output. Two tasks, however, will require extending the `BinaryTree` class by adding two new methods: one to take care of inserting words and their counts into the tree and another to determine the word that occurs most frequently.

The logic to insert a word into the tree is described in the following pseudocode:

```
If the tree is empty
    Insert the word along with a count of 1
Else if the word to be inserted matches the word in the root of the tree
    Increase the count for that word by 1
Else if the word to be inserted precedes the word in the root of the tree
    Recur with the left subtree
Else
    Recur with the right subtree
```

To determine the word that occurs most frequently (once the tree is built), we must use a recursive version of a standard champion–challenger algorithm:

Initialize the champion to a value, such as zero, that will be updated upon its first challenge.

If the count associated with the word at the root of the tree beats the champion
    Update the champion to this count
Recur with the champion and the left subtree
Recur with the champion and the right subtree

Implementation

The specialized insertion and maximum-finding algorithms described in the design are found in the following `WordTree` class derived from the `BinaryTree` class.

```
class WordTree : public BinaryTree<WordStruct>
{
   public:

   // Class constructor

      WordTree();

   // Member functions

      void insert(const apstring &theWord);
      WordStruct mostFrequent();

   protected:

      // Recursive helper for top-level insert
      void insertAux(BinaryTree<WordStruct>::node * &tree, const apstring &theWord);

      // Recursive helper for top-level mostFrequent
      void mostFrequentAux(BinaryTree<WordStruct>::node * &tree, WordStruct & w);
};

void WordTree::insert(const apstring &theWord)
{
   insertAux(tree, theWord);
}

void WordTree::insertAux(BinaryTree<WordStruct>::node * &tree, const apstring &theWord)
{
   WordStruct ws;

   ws.word = theWord;
   ws.count = 1;
   if (tree == 0)                            // word occurs for first time
      tree = getNode(ws);
   else if (theWord == tree->data.word)      // word appeared before
      ++(tree->data.count);
   else if (theWord < tree->data.word)
      insertAux(tree->left, theWord);
   else
      insertAux(tree->right, theWord);
}

WordStruct WordTree::mostFrequent()
{
   WordStruct w;
```

```
    w.word = "";                          // Initialize the struct
    w.count = 0;
    mostFrequentAux(tree, w);             // Call recursive helper
    return w;
}

void WordTree::mostFrequentAux(BinaryTree<WordStruct>::node * &tree, WordStruct & w)
{
    if (tree != 0)
    {
        if (tree->data.count > w.count)        // Did challenger beat champion?
        {
            w.count = tree->data.count;
            w.word = tree->data.word;
        }
        mostFrequentAux(tree->left, w);
        mostFrequentAux(tree->right, w);
    }
}
```

Running, Debugging, and Testing Hints

1. Trees are inherently recursive data structures, so learn to think recursively when devising algorithms that process trees.
2. When using the linear array representation of a binary tree, remember that all array locations must be initialized to a flagging null value if the implementations of other operations are to work correctly.
3. The use of a preorder traversal to print a tree with indentation to reflect the depth of a node is a handy tracing tool when debugging a tree program that has gone awry. Keep such a function in your library, so it is readily available when the need arises.
4. When using a binary search tree to implement a one-key table, some experimentation may be necessary to determine the efficiency of this technique for the particular data of your application.

Summary

Key Terms

ancestor
binary implementation of a one-key table
binary search tree
binary tree
binary tree implementation of general tree
branch
breadth-first traversal
child node
concordance
depth-first traversal
digraph
directional graph
edge
general tree
graph
heap
heap property
height balancing
hierarchy
inorder traversal
insertion rule
leaf node
level
linear implementation
linked implementation
network
node
ordering property
parent node
postorder traversal
preorder traversal
root
root node
siblings
subtree
ternary tree
threading
tree
tree traversal
vertex
weight

Key Concepts

- Trees are a data structure used to reflect a hierarchical relationship among data items. Indicative of this hierarchy is the parent–child terminology used to express the relationship between items on successive levels of the tree. Trees are by nature recursive structures, with each node of a tree being itself the root of a smaller embedded subtree.
- Binary trees are trees in which each parent may have at most two child nodes. Although this seems like a major restriction, binary trees find a wide range of applications. Three such applications are the representation of algebraic expressions, one-key tables, and priority queues.
- Two ways of implementing a binary tree are the linear representation and the linked representation. The former method uses an array and requires no pointers but is prone to wasting a large number of array locations. The latter uses pointers and consequently is able to take advantage of C++'s dynamic memory allocation.
- There are three standard ways of traversing a binary tree, that is, three ways of visiting all nodes exactly once. These are the preorder, postorder, and inorder traversals.
- In a preorder traversal, the current root node is processed, followed recursively by the nodes in its left subtree and then its right subtree.
- In a postorder traversal, all nodes in the left subtree of the current root are recursively processed. Then all nodes in the right subtree are processed, and the root itself is processed last.
- In an inorder traversal, the nodes in the left subtree are processed first, followed by the root node, and finally the nodes in the right subtree of the root. The inorder traversal is critical in the binary tree implementation of a one-key table because the order in which it visits nodes corresponds precisely to the ordering of items as first, second, third, . . . , within the list represented by the tree.
- The binary search tree implementation of a one-key table is the third such table implementation we have studied. The other two were the array implementation (Chapter 11) and the linked list implementation (Chapter 12). The following table summarizes the relative advantages and disadvantages of the three methods.

Method	Search	Additions/Deletions	Other Comments
Physically ordered array	$O(\log_2 n)$ with binary search	Excessive data movement	Data must be physically ordered
Linked list	Requires sequential search; hence, $O(n)$	Only pointer manipulation required	
Binary search tree	Bounded between $O(\log_2 n)$ and $O(n)$, although advanced methods can guarantee the former	Only pointer manipulation required	May necessitate the overhead associated with recursive traversals

- The binary tree may be used to implement the general tree structure. The preorder and postorder traversals emerge as the most important for this particular application.
- Graphs and networks are abstract data structures that are more complex than trees because they reflect bidirectional rather than hierarchical relationships. Depth-first and breadth-first traversals and finding the shortest path are examples of algorithms that manipulate graphs and networks.

Programming Problems and Projects

1. Discrepancies frequently arise between a user's projection of his or her computer needs and the unforeseen demands that materialize once the software system is put into use. A good systems analyst can hold those discrepancies to a minimum but not totally eliminate them. Elements of chance and probability are inherent in many algorithms.

   An example is the order of arrivals for insertion into a binary search tree. We can guarantee that search efficiency in a binary search tree will be between $O(n)$ and $O(\log_2 n)$. We can specify best and worst cases. But what happens in between? When do we cross over from response times that are acceptable to those that are not? Real-life data are rarely best case or worst case. Hence, the "in-between" question is often of vital importance. Yet it is also the one that a pure big-O analysis leaves relatively unanswered.

   Design and implement a program that can serve as a start toward further exploration of the questions just posed. The program should initially read a list of unordered integers from a file, create a binary search tree containing those integers, and then print the binary search tree using indentation to reflect the level at which various nodes occur in the tree.

   a. Use the program in its initial form to acquire a feel for the relationship between the order of input data and the shape of the binary search tree that results.
   b. Instead of reading data from a file, randomly generate the data being inserted in the tree.
   c. After a tree has been generated, add the capability to delete nodes selectively from the tree. Reprint the tree after deleting a node as verification that it has retained the critical ordering property.
   d. Use the random generation capability from part b to build some very large trees. Instead of printing out these trees after they have been generated, compute the length of the average path that must be followed to find a node in the tree. Do the results of your experiment indicate that, for random data, binary search trees yield a search efficiency that is $O(\log_2 n)$ or $O(n)$? Justify your conclusion with a written statement that is backed up by empirical data provided from your experimental runs.
   e. Extend part d by computing the maximal path length in each randomly generated tree. What percentage of randomly generated trees have a maximal path length that is $O(n)$?
   f. Depending on the availability of graphics functions in your version of C++, change the character-based tree printout into a more appealing graphic representation.
2. Use a binary tree to implement the sorted collection ADT defined in Section 2 of Chapter 11.
3. Modify the airline reservation system you developed for Wing-and-a-Prayer Airlines (Problem 2, Chapter 12) so that the alphabetized lists are maintained with binary trees instead of linked lists.

4. Write a program that sorts the records of the Fly-by-Night credit card company file (Problem 3, Chapter 12) in alphabetical order by the last name and then the first name of the customer. Use a binary tree and its inorder traversal to accomplish the sort.
5. Recall the roster maintenance system that you wrote for the Bay Area Brawlers (Problem 4, Chapter 12). The system has been so successful that the league office would like to expand the system to include all the players in the league. Again, the goal is to maintain the list of players in alphabetical order, allowing for frequent insertions and deletions as players are cut, picked up, and traded among teams. In addition to storing each player's height, weight, age, and university affiliation, each record should be expanded to include team affiliation, years in league, and annual salary. Because the database for the entire league is many times larger than that for just one team, maintain this list as a binary search tree to increase efficiency.
6. Write a program that reads an expression in its prefix form and builds the binary tree corresponding to that expression. Next write functions to print the infix and postfix forms of the expression using inorder and postorder traversals of this tree. Then see if you can extend the program to evaluate the expression represented by the tree.
7. Here is a problem you will encounter if you write statistical analysis software. Given an arbitrarily long list of unordered numbers with an arbitrary number of different values appearing in it, determine and print the marginal distribution for this list of numbers. That is, count how many times each different value appears in the list and then print each value along with its count (frequency). The final output should be arranged from smallest to largest value. This problem can be solved in elegant fashion using trees. An example of such output as produced by COSAP (Conversationally Oriented Statistical Analysis Package) of Lawrence University is:

```
Command? Marginals Judge
                    Pine County Criminal Cases

M A R G I N A L F R E Q U E N C I E S
Variable Judge            JUDGE BEFORE WHOM CASE BROUGHT (2)
Value label               Value       Absolute      Relative
                                      Frequency     Frequency

ALLEN                     1              677           80.8%
JONES                     2              88            10.5%
KELLY                     3              26            3.1%
MURCK                     5              47            5.6%

     838 Valid 0 Missing 838 Total Observations
```

Here the data file contained 838 occurrences of the values 1, 2, 3, and 5. Each value was a code number assigned to a particular judge.
8. Many compilers offer the services of a cross-referencing program to aid in debugging. Such a program will list in alphabetical order all the identifiers that appear in a program and the various lines of the program that reference them. Write such a cross-reference for your favorite language using a binary tree to maintain the list of identifiers that are encountered.
9. A relatively easy game to implement with a binary tree is to have the computer try to guess an animal about which the user is thinking by asking the user a series of questions that can be answered by yes or no. A node in the binary tree to play this game could be viewed as

Yes/No pointers leading to
1. Another question.
2. The name of the animal.
3. NULL.

If NULL, have your program surrender and then ask the user for a new question that uniquely defines the animal being thought of. Then add this new question and animal to the growing binary tree database.

10. Write a program that will differentiate expressions in the variable X. The input to this program will be a series of strings, each representing an infix expression to be differentiated. Each such expression is to be viewed as a stream of tokens. Valid tokens are integers, the variable X, the binary operators (+, −, *, /, ^), and parentheses. To make scanning for tokens easy, you may assume that each token is followed by exactly one space, with the exception of the final token, which is followed by the end-of-line character.

First, your program will have to scan the infix expression, building up an appropriate binary tree representation of it. For this, you should be able to borrow significantly on the work you did in parsing expressions in Chapters 13 and 14. The major difference here is that the end result of this parse is a binary tree instead of a postfix string.

Once the binary expression tree is built, traverse it, building up another binary expression tree, which represents the derivative of the original expression. The following differentiation rules should be used in this process:

Suppose C is a constant, and S and T are expressions in X:

```
Diff(C) = 0
Diff(X) = 1
Diff(S + T) = Diff(S) + Diff(T)
Diff(S - T) = Diff(S) - Diff(T)
Diff(S * T) = S * Diff(T) + T * Diff(S)
Diff(S / T) = ((T * Diff(S)) - (S * Diff(T)))/(T ^ 2)
Diff(S ^ C) = (C * S ^ (C - 1)) * Diff(S)    { Remember the infamous chain rule? }
```

Finally, once the binary expression tree for the derivative has been built, print the expression. Print it in completely parenthesized infix notation to avoid ambiguity.

Note that there are three distinct phases to this problem:

- Parsing of the original infix expression into a binary tree representation
- Building a binary tree representation of the derivative
- Printing the derivative in completely parenthesized infix notation

For an added challenge, simplify the expression for the derivative before printing it according to the following rules:

```
S + 0 = S
0 + S = S
S - 0 = S
S * 0 = 0
0 * S = 0
S * 1 = S
1 * S = S
0 / S = 0
S ^ 0 = 1
```

continued

```
S ^ 1 = S
S - S = 0
0 / S = 0
S / S = 1
S / 0 = DIVISION BY ZERO
0 / 0 = UNDEFINED
```

11. Wing-and-a-Prayer Airlines (Problem 3) is expanding their recordkeeping database. This database may now be pictured hierarchically as

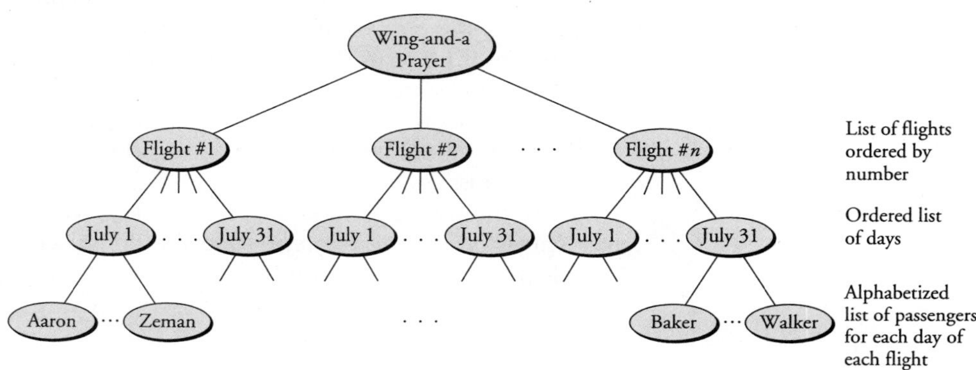

Write a program to maintain this database. Your program should process requests to add, delete, or list the following:

- Specified flight number
- Specified day of the month (for a given flight number)
- Specified passenger or all passengers (for a given flight number and day of the month)

12. Many statistical analysis packages support a "cross-tabulation" command designed to explore the relationship between statistical variables. A cross-tabulation between two variables produces a two-dimensional table containing a frequency count for each possible ordered pair of values of the two variables. However, these statistical packages typically allow this type of analysis to proceed even further than merely exploring two variables. For instance, in a legal-system database, we might be interested in cross-tabulating a defendant's age with the judge before whom the defendant stood trial. We may then wish to cross-tabulate this result with the sex of the defendant. Sex in this case is called the control variable. We would output one such cross-tabulation table for each possible value of sex. Note that this type of output is not limited to just one control variable. There may be an arbitrary number of control variables and tables to cycle through. Moreover, the variables have an arbitrary number of observations and are all in arbitrary order. Yet for each variable, the list of possible values is always printed in smallest to largest order. The general tree structure that emerges for handling cross-tabulation is

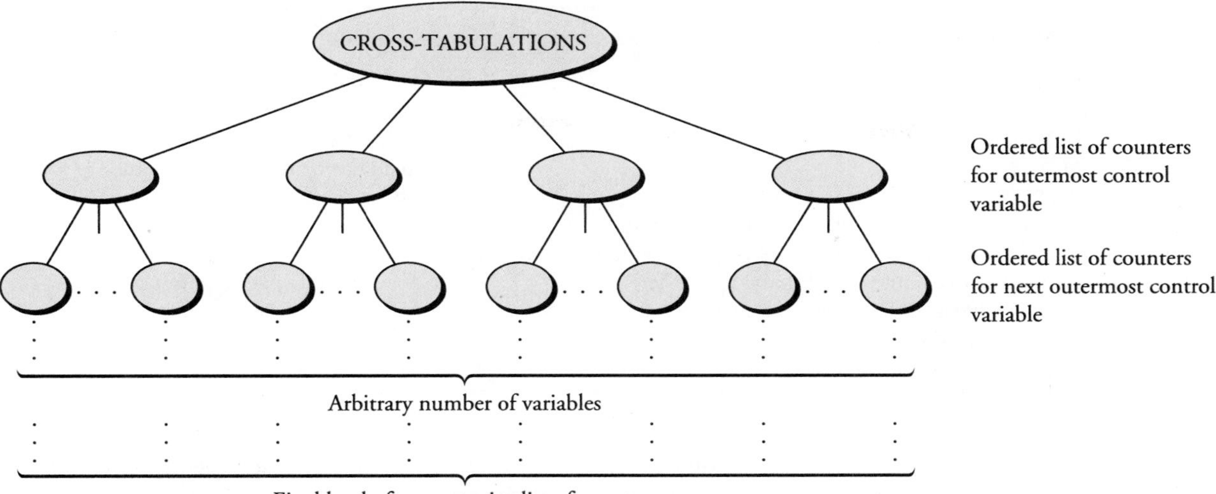

Write a program to handle the task of producing statistical cross-tabulations.

13. Write a program to print the nodes of a tree level by level; that is, all level 0 nodes, followed by all level 1 nodes, followed by all level 2 nodes, and so on. (*Hint:* This program will afford an excellent opportunity to practice using a queue in addition to a tree.)

14. Operating systems often use general trees as the data structure on which their file directory system is based. Leaf nodes in such a system represent actual files or empty directories. Interior nodes represent nonempty directories. For instance, consider the following situation:

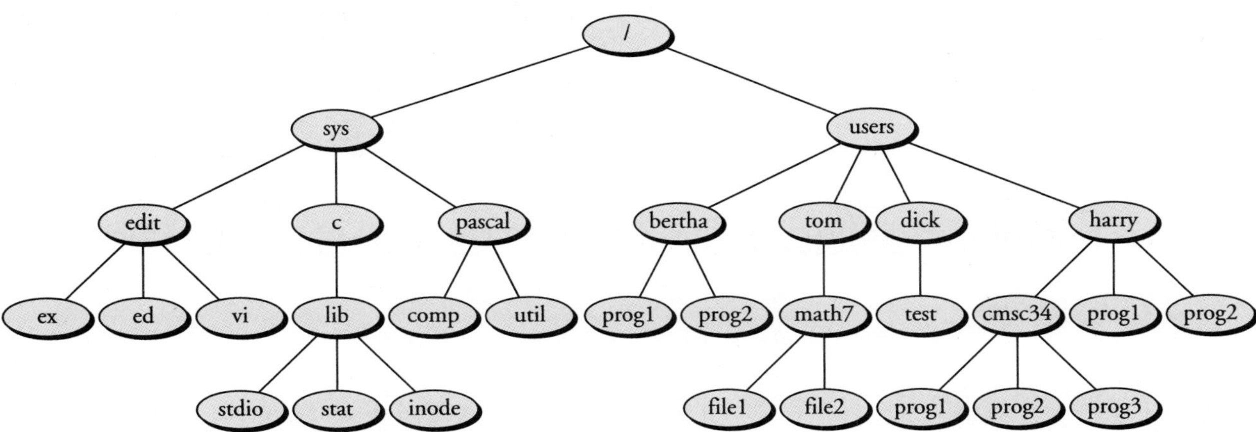

A directory entry is specified by its pathname. A pathname consists of tree node names separated by slashes. Such a pathname is absolute if it starts at the root, that is, if it starts with a slash (/). It is relative to the current directory if it does not start with a slash.

In this assignment, you are to write a command processor that will allow a user to manipulate files within such a directory structure. The commands accepted by your processor will be in the form of numbers associated with particular operations and pathnames, as shown in the following table:

Number	Operation	Pathname
1	Change directory	Absolute pathname, relative pathname, or ". ." for parent
2	Make a new directory	Absolute or relative pathname
3	Make a new file	Absolute or relative pathname
4	Remove a file	Absolute or relative pathname
5	Remove a directory, but only if it is empty	Absolute or relative pathname
6	Remove a directory and, recursively, everything below it	Absolute or relative pathname
7	Print directory entries in alphabetical order	Absolute or relative pathname
8	Recursively print directory entries in alphabetical order	Absolute or relative pathname
9	Print current directory name	Not applicable
10	Quit processing commands	Not applicable

Since even intelligent tree-walking users can easily get lost, your command processor should be prepared to trap errors of the following variety:

- Specifying a nonexistent pathname
- Specifying a pathname that is a file when it should be a directory
- Specifying a pathname that is a directory when it should be a file

Upon detecting such an error, have your command processor print an appropriate error message and then return to accept the next user command.

15. Trees have significant applications in the area of artificial intelligence and game playing. Consider, for instance, the game of Fifteen. Two players take turns selecting digits between 1 and 9 with the goal of selecting a combination of digits that adds up to 15. Once a digit is chosen, it may not be chosen again by either player. Rather than immediately considering a tree for the game of Fifteen, let us first consider a tree for the simpler game of Seven with digits chosen in the range 1 to 6. A tree that partially represents the states that may be reached in this game follows:

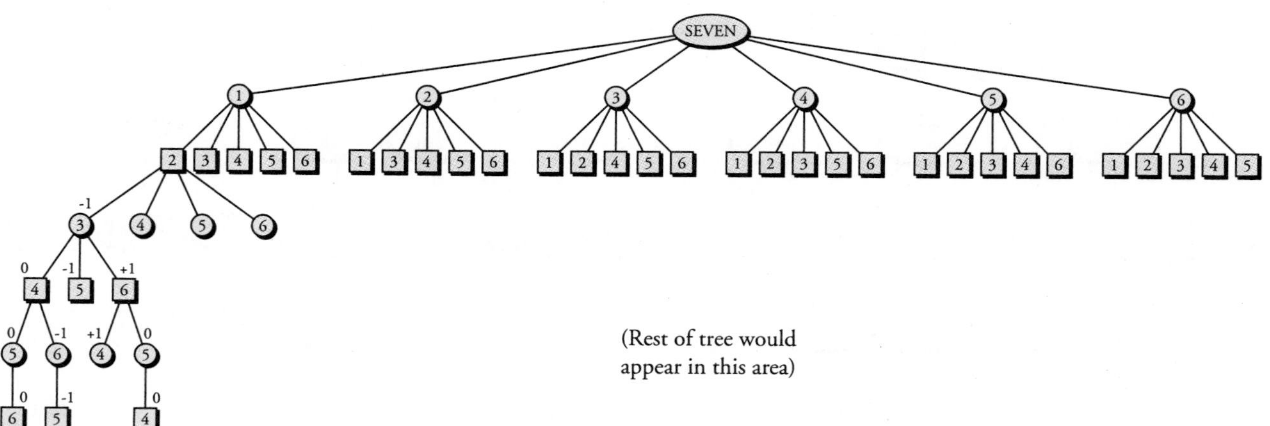

In this tree, circular nodes represent the states that may be reached by the player who moves first (the computer), and square nodes represent the states that may be reached by the player who moves second (a human opponent). The +1, 0, or −1 attached to each node represents weighting factors designed to help the computer choose the most advantageous move at any given stage of the game. The rules used to compute these weighting factors are:

If the node is a leaf node, its weight is determined by some static weighting function. In this case, the static weighting function used was to assign +1 to a leaf node representing a computer win, 0 to a leaf node representing a draw, and −1 to a leaf node representing a human win.

If the node is one in which the computer will move next (that is, a state occupied by the human opponent), then the weighting factor of the node is the maximum of the weighting factors of its children.

If the node is one in which the human opponent will move next, then the weighting factor of the node is the minimum of the weighting factors of its children.

In its turn, the computer should always choose to move to the node having the maximum possible weighting factor. The rationale behind this technique, called the minimax technique, is that the computer will move in such a way as to always maximize its chances of winning. The human opponent, if playing intelligently, will always move to a node having a minimum weighting factor. Thus, in the partial game shown, the computer would choose 4 if the human had been naive enough to select the 6 node with the weighting factor of +1.

Write a program to build a weighted game tree for the game of Fifteen and then have the computer play against a human opponent. Note that this game is really the game of tick-tack-toe if one considers the following matrix:

```
4  9  2
3  5  7
8  1  6
```

All winning tick-tack-toe paths add up to 15. Give some consideration as to the time and efficiency of your algorithm. Many games simply cannot be completely represented via a general tree because of space limitations. Consequently, a partial game tree is built in which the leaf nodes may not actually be the final moves made in the game. In such situations, the static weighting function applied to the leaf nodes in the game tree requires a bit more insight to develop.

16. Consider a priority queue (see Chapter 13, Section 13.3) in which each item is assigned a different priority. Discuss how a binary tree with the heap property could be used to maintain such a priority queue. Write functions for a heap implementation of the basic priority queue operations:

```
create
empty()
enqueue(item)
dequeue()
```

Categorize the run-time efficiency of the `dequeue` and `enqueue` operations in big-O terms. Is a linear implementation or a linked implementation of the binary tree more advantageous for this application? Explain why.

Finally, use your priority queue implementation to solve a problem such as Problem 12, Chapter 13 or to simulate the servicing of priority-rated jobs on a time-sharing computing system.

17. Implement Dijkstra's shortest path algorithm using a suitable two-key table representation scheme to store the network data. Test your program with the transportation network pictured in Figure 15.27. Note that this same problem appeared in Problem 13, Chapter 14. There you used a different algorithm for solving it. In a written statement, compare the efficiencies of the two algorithms.

18. A breadth-first traversal of a graph was discussed in Section 15.6. Implement this algorithm as a C++ function. (*Hint:* Use a queue.)

19. You are given a binary tree of integers implemented by a linked representation. Such a tree is said to be weight balanced if the sum of all the entries in the left subtree of the root equals the sum of all the entries in the right subtree of the root. Write a Boolean-valued function that receives a root pointer to such a tree and returns `true` if the tree is weight balanced and `false` otherwise. Then write a complete program to test your function. Finally, adjust your function so that it returns `true` only when every subtree of the original tree is weight balanced.

20. In the binary tree class presented in this chapter, our traversal operations have allowed the client program to pass a function as an actual parameter to the traversal. That function dictated what was to be done at each node during the traversal. This approach has limitations. In the Case Study, we demonstrated one way around these limitations—derive a new class from the generic `BinaryTree` class and then implement new specialized traversals in this subclass. There is, however, another approach that makes the `BinaryTree` class more "powerful" and often allows a client program to use the `BinaryTree` class without having to subclass from it. This approach is to provide operations that allow the client program to write a loop that iterates through all tree nodes in the order dictated by a particular traversal. Notice the difference in perspective here: The client program has iterative logic to walk through the tree nodes one at a time instead of calling a traversal algorithm that uses recursion to process all the nodes for the client program. For instance, to illustrate how a client program would proceed through tree nodes in an in-order fashion using such iterator operations, suppose we add the following two operations to our `BinaryTree` class.

```
template <class E> class BinaryTree
   {

   public:
   // Class constructors

   BinaryTree();
   BinaryTree(const BinaryTree<E> &bt);

   ...

   // Other operations appear as before

   // Return pointer to first datum in the tree that would be
   // processed by an inorder traversal
   E * inorderBegin();

   // Return pointer to next datum in the tree that would be
   // processed by an inorder traversal. If a null pointer
   // is returned, there are no additional data to be processed
   // via an inorder traversal
   E * inorderNext();

   protected:

   // Implementation-dependent declarations appear here
   };
```

Given these new `inorderBegin` and `inorderNext` functions, a client iterates through an inorder traversal of a binary tree containing integers as its data by using the following loop:

```
int * k;

for (k = tree.inorderBegin(); k != 0; k = tree.inorderNext())
   cout << *k << " ";
```

Note that this is very similar to the way we allowed a client program to iterate through a linked list. For this program, add such iterator operations to the `BinaryTree` class for each of the three traversals we studied. Test them with an appropriate driver program. (*Hint:* You will have to add a new protected node pointer for each traversal. That pointer will point at the node currently being accessed in the particular traversal. You will also find it convenient to add a "parent" pointer to each node so that you can ascend from a node to its parent as well as descend to its children.)

21. Explore some additional graph and network algorithms in one of the advanced texts cited earlier in this chapter, such as Horowitz & Sahni, *Data Structures in C++*, New York: Computer Science Press, 1990, or Pothering & Naps, *Introduction to Data Structures and Algorithm Analysis with C++*, St. Paul, MN: West Publishing, 1995. Then prepare a written or oral report in which you explain the logic behind one of the algorithms you explore.

16

More Powerful Sorting Methods

Chapter Outline

Never mistake motion for action.
Ernest Hemingway, 1889–1961

In Chapter 10, we analyzed three simple sorting algorithms: bubble sort, insertion sort, and selection sort. We also discussed a technique, called a pointer sort, which can be combined with any of these three algorithms to minimize data movement when large records are being sorted by a particular key field. The essence of the pointer sort is to maintain an array of pointers that dictates the logical order of the records in an array of records. When the sorting algorithm dictates a swap, only the pointers must be interchanged, not the actual records.

With all three of our sorting algorithms, however, we ran into a barrier. This barrier was a run-time efficiency of $O(n^2)$ comparisons. Since the pointer sort technique reduces data movement but not the number of comparisons, this barrier exists whether or not we incorporate the pointer sort idea into the sorting algorithm. Our goal in this chapter is to study sorting algorithms that break the $O(n^2)$ comparisons barrier. These new algorithms will make use of what we have learned since Chapter 10. In particular, both recursion and a conceptual understanding of trees are essential prerequisites to analyzing these more powerful methods.

The general setup for the sort algorithms of this chapter is the same as the one we used in Chapter 10:

```
const int MAX_LIST_SIZE = 100;   // Or other appropriate physical size for array
typedef int element;
typedef element ListType[MAX_LIST_SIZE];
```

We wish to write a sort function that meets the following specifications:

```
// Function: sort
// Sorts a list of elements into ascending order
//
// Inputs: a list of elements in arbitrary order and its current length
// Output: the list of elements arranged in ascending order

void sort(ListType list, int n);
```

Although our algorithms for this chapter are presented in the context of sorting arrays in ascending order, they apply more generally to any list whose elements can be directly accessed (for example, vectors or one-key tables) and they can be easily modified to sort in descending order. Moreover, some of the methods we discuss (quick sort and merge sort) do not necessarily require direct access into the list. Hence, with relatively minor modifications, these can be applied to lists that are just sequentially accessible such as sequential files and linked lists.

16.1 The Shell Sort Algorithm

Objectives

a. to understand the logic behind the shell sort algorithm
b. to see the relationship between shell sort and insertion sort
c. to develop a C++ function to perform shell sort
d. to analyze the efficiency of the shell sort algorithm

The *shell sort,* named after its inventor D. L. Shell, incorporates the logic of the insertion sort to a certain extent. However, instead of sorting the entire array at once, it first divides the array into smaller noncontiguous segments, which are then separately sorted using the insertion sort.

The advantages of doing this are twofold. First, where a comparison dictates a swap of two data items in a segment, this swap within a noncontiguous segment of the array moves an item a greater distance within the overall array than the swap of adjacent array entries in the usual insertion sort. This means that one swap is more likely to place an element closer to its final location in the array when using shell sort than when using the simple insertion sort. For instance, a large-valued entry that appears near the front of the array will more quickly move to the end of the array because each swap moves it a greater distance in the array.

The second advantage of dividing the array into segments is tied to the first; that is, because early passes tend to move elements closer to their final destination than do early passes in a straight insertion sort, the array becomes partially sorted quite rapidly. The fact that the array is likely to become partially sorted relatively early then allows the embedded insertion sort logic to make more frequent use of its check for an early exit from its inner loop. (Recall that this check is what makes the insertion sort particularly efficient for arrays that are partially sorted.) An example will help clarify this shell sort rationale.

Example 16.1 Suppose we have an array containing the following integers:

80 93 60 12 42 30 68 85 10

We first divide this into three segments of three elements each.

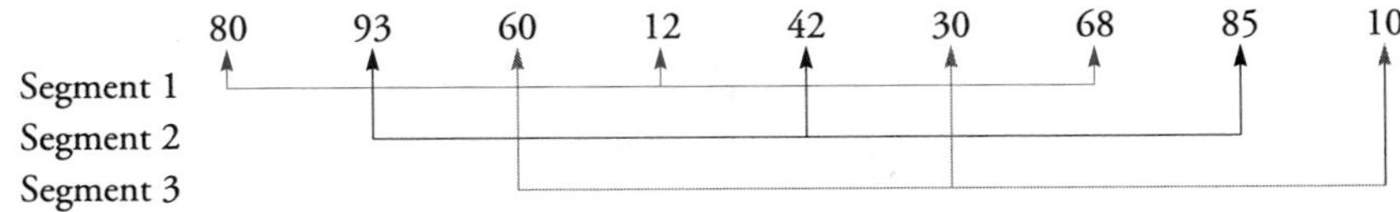

80	12	68→	Segment 1
93	42	85→	Segment 2
60	30	10→	Segment 3

and sort each of the segments:

12	68	80
42	85	93
10	30	60

The original array, partially sorted, now appears as

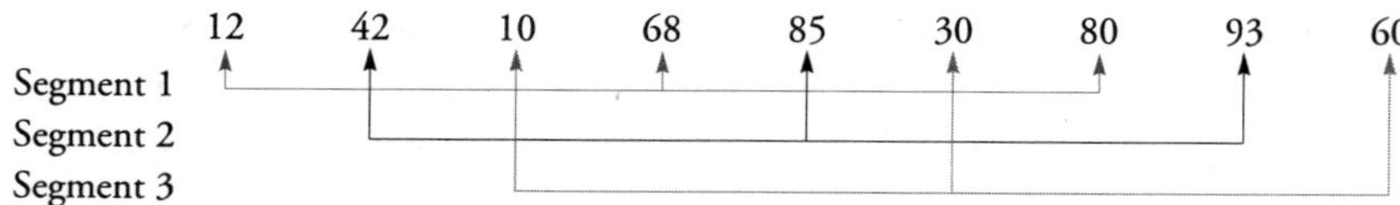

We divide this partially sorted array as

12	10	85	80	60	→ Segment 1
42	68	30	93		→ Segment 2

These segments are then sorted and the array takes the form

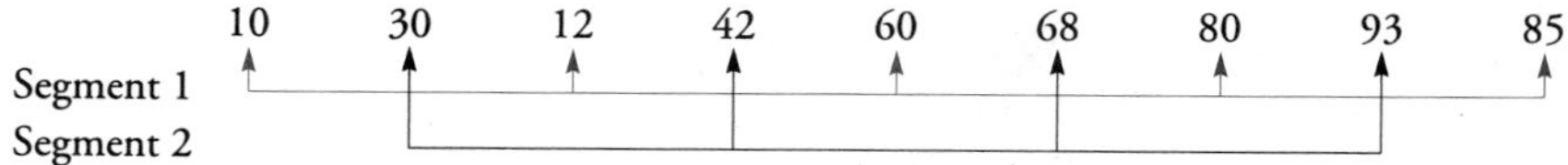

Finally, this array is sorted as one segment; 12 and 30, and 93 and 85 are swapped to give us the sorted array

10 12 30 42 60 68 80 85 93

The key to the shell sort algorithm is that the whole array is first fragmented into K segments for some number K, where K is preferably a prime number. These K segments are given by

$$a[0],\ a[K],\ a[2 * K],\ \ldots$$
$$a[1],\ a[K+1],\ a[2 * K + 1],\ \ldots$$
$$\vdots$$
$$a[K-1],\ a[2 * K - 1],\ a[3 * K - 1],\ \ldots$$

Because each segment is sorted, the whole array is partially sorted after the first pass. For the next pass, the value of K is reduced, which increases the size of each segment, hence reducing the number of segments. Preferably, the next value of K is also chosen so that it is prime relative to its previous value, or *relatively prime.* (Two integers are said to be relatively prime to each other if they have no common factor greater than 1.) The process is repeated until $K = 1$, at which point the array is sorted. The insertion sort is applied to each segment, so each successive segment is partially sorted. Consequently, the later applications of the insertion sort become very efficient, dramatically increasing the overall efficiency of the shell sort.

To emphasize the fashion in which the shell sort algorithm relies on the logic of insertion sort, we present a `segmentedInsertionSort` function, which arranges each of k segments in an n-element array into ascending order. Compare this function with the function for insertion sort that was given in Chapter 10. You will see that `segmentedInsertionSort` moves an item from position j to position $j + k$. When $k = 1$, this is precisely the original insertion sort algorithm.

```
void segmentedInsertionSort(ListType list, int n, int k)
{
    int j;
    element itemToInsert;
```

```
    bool stillLooking;

    for (int i = k; i < n; ++i)
    {
        itemToInsert = list[i];
        j = i - k;
        stillLooking = true;
        while ((j >= 0) && itemToInsert < list[j])
        {
            list[j + k] = list[j];
            j = j - k;
        }
        list[j + k] = itemToInsert;
    }
}
```

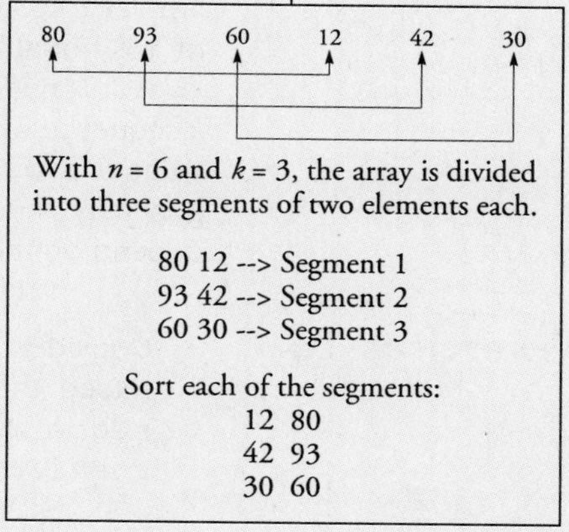

80 93 60 12 42 30

With $n = 6$ and $k = 3$, the array is divided into three segments of two elements each.

80 12 --> Segment 1
93 42 --> Segment 2
60 30 --> Segment 3

Sort each of the segments:
12 80
42 93
30 60

Given the `segmentedInsertionSort` function, we now merely call on this with values of *k* that become successively smaller. Eventually, `segmentedInsertionSort` must be called with $k = 1$ to guarantee that the array, viewed as one segment, is completely sorted.

The function `shellSort` that follows illustrates these successive calls to `segmentedInsertionSort` for values of *k* that are repeatedly halved.

```
void shellSort(ListType list, int n)
{
    int k = n / 2;

    while (k > 0)
    {
        segmentedInsertionSort(list, n, k);
        k = k / 2;
    }
}
```

Efficiency of the Shell Sort

The shell sort is also called the *diminishing increment sort* because the value of *k* (the number of segments) continually decreases. The method is more efficient if the successive values of *k* are kept relatively prime to each other, thereby helping to ensure that a pair of values previously compared to each other are not compared again. D. E. Knuth has mathematically estimated that, with relatively prime values of *k*, the shell sort will execute in an average time proportional to $O[n(\log_2 n)^2]$ (see Donald E.

Knuth, *The Art of Computer Programming, Vol. 3, Searching and Sorting,* Menlo Park, CA: Addison-Wesley, 1973). However, the sort will work for any values of *k,* as long as the last value of *k* is 1. For instance, note that in the version of `shellSort` we have given, the successive values of *k* will not often be relatively prime. When the values of *k* are not relatively prime, the efficiency of the shell sort is of the order $O(n^r)$, where $1 < r < 2$. The particular value of r makes the sort less efficient than $O[n(\log_2 n)^2]$ for large values of n, but better than the $O(n^2)$ methods of Chapter 10.

The shell sort is most efficient on arrays that are nearly sorted. In fact, the first chosen value of *k* is large to ensure that the whole array is fragmented into small individual arrays for which the insertion sort is highly effective. Each subsequent sort causes the entire array to be more nearly sorted so that the efficiency of the insertion sort as applied to larger partially sorted arrays is increased. Trace through a few examples to convince yourself that the partially ordered status of the array for one value of *k* is not affected by subsequent partial sorts for a different value of *k*.

It is not known with what value of *k* the shell sort should start, but Knuth suggests a sequence of values such as 1, 3, 7, 15, . . . , for reverse values of *k;* that is, the $(j + 1)$st value is two times the *j*th value plus 1. Knuth suggests other possible values of *k,* but generally, the initial guess at the first value of *k* is all that you need. The initial guess will depend on the size of the array and, to some extent, on the type of data being sorted.

Exercises 16.1

1. Consider the `shellSort` function given in this section. Suppose we traced the contents of the array being sorted after each call to the function `segmentedInsertionSort`. What would we see as output if we called `shellSort` with the following array?

60 12 90 30 64 8 6

2. Repeat Exercise 1 for a six-element array that initially contains

1 8 2 7 3 6

3. Where did the shell sort get its name?

4. Why is the shell sort most efficient when the original data are in almost sorted order?

5. What advantage do the relatively prime values of the increments have over other values in a shell sort? Formulate your answer in a precise written statement that explains why relatively prime values are better.

6. What property must the sequence of diminishing increments in the shell sort have to ensure that the method will work?

7. Provide examples of best case and worst case data sets for the shell sort algorithm presented in this section. Justify your data sets by explaining why they generate best case and worst case performance.

8. In Chapter 10, `pointerSort` used an index of pointers to sort data logically without rearranging them. Identify the sort algorithm that was behind the C++ `pointerSort` function. Adapt the `pointerSort` function to the shell sort algorithm.

9. The version of shell sort presented in this section uses the following sequence of diminishing increments:

$n/2$, $n/4$, . . . , 8, 4, 2, 1

Rewrite the shell sort so that the following sequence of diminishing increments is used:

k, . . . , 121, 40, 13, 4, 1

Here *k* represents the largest member of this sequence that is less than or equal to n where n is the logical size of the array being sorted.

16.2 The Quick Sort Algorithm

Objectives

a. to understand the logic behind the quick sort algorithm
b. to understand the role played by the partitioning subalgorithm in quick sort
c. to develop a C++ function to perform quick sort
d. to analyze the efficiency of the quick sort algorithm

Even though the shell sort provides a significant advantage in run time over its $O(n^2)$ predecessors, its average efficiency of $O[n(\log_2 n)^2]$ may still not be good enough for large arrays. The next group of methods, including the *quick sort,* has an average execution time of $O(n \log_2 n)$, which is the best that can be achieved. Compared to $O[n(\log_2 n)^2]$ or $O(n^r)$ for $1 < r < 2$, an $O(n \log_2 n)$ sort is often a good choice as the main vehicle for large sorting jobs.

The essence of the quick sort algorithm, originally devised in 1961 by C. A. R. Hoare, is to rely on a subordinate algorithm to *partition* the array. The process of partitioning involves moving a data item, called the *pivot,* in the correct direction just enough for it to reach its final place in the array. The partitioning process, therefore, reduces unnecessary interchanges and potentially moves the pivot a great distance in the array without forcing it to be swapped into intermediate locations. Once the pivot item is chosen, moves are made so that data items to the left of the pivot are less than (or equal to) it, whereas those to the right are greater (or equal). The pivot item is thus in its correct position. The quick sort algorithm then recursively applies the partitioning process to the two parts of the array on either side of the pivot until the entire array is sorted.

In the next example, we illustrate the mechanics of this partitioning logic by applying it to an array of numbers.

Example 16.2 Suppose the array contains integers initially arranged as

15 20 5 8 95 12 80 17 9 55

Table 16.1 shows a partitioning pass applied to this array. The following steps are involved:

1. Remove the first data item, 15, as the pivot, mark its position, and scan the array from right to left, comparing data item values with 15. When you find the first smaller value, remove it from its current position and put it in position a[0]. (This is shown in line 2.)
2. Scan line 2 from left to right beginning with position a[1], comparing data item values with 15. When you find the first value greater than 15, extract it and store it in the position marked by parentheses in line 2. (This is shown in line 3.)
3. Begin the right-to-left scan of line 3 with position a[7] looking for a value smaller than 15. When you find it, extract it and store it in the position marked by the parentheses in line 3. (This is shown in line 4.)
4. Begin scanning line 4 from left to right at position a[2]. Find a value greater than 15, remove it, mark its position, and store it inside the parentheses in line 4. (This is shown in line 5.)
5. Now, when you attempt to scan line 5 from right to left beginning at position a[4], you are immediately at a parenthesized position determined by the previous left-to-right scan. This is the location to put the pivot data item, 15. (This is shown in line 6.) At this stage, 15 is in its correct place relative to the final sorted array.

Notice that all values to the left of 15 are less than 15, and all values to the right of 15 are greater than 15. The method will still work if two values are the same. The process can now be applied recursively to the two segments of the array on the left and right of 15. Notice that these recursive calls eventually sort the entire array. The result of any one call to function `quickSort` is merely to partition a segment of the array so that the pivotal item is positioned with everything to its left being less than or equal to it and everything to its right being greater than or equal.

Table 16.1
Each Call to `quickSort` Partitions an Array Segment

Line Number	a[0]	a[1]	a[2]	a[3]	a[4]	a[5]	a[6]	a[7]	a[8]	a[9]
1	15*	20	5	8	95	12	80	17	9	← 55
2	9	→ 20	5	8	95	12	80	17	( )	55
3	9	( )	5	8	95	12	80	← 17	20	55
4	9	12	→ 5	8	95	( )	80	17	20	55
5	9	12	5	8	← ( )	95	80	17	20	55
6	9	12	5	8	15	95	80	17	20	55

*Indicates the pivot value (here 15).

The function `partition` that follows achieves one partitioning pass in the overall `quickSort` algorithm as described in Example 16.2. The indices `lo` and `hi` represent the pointers that move from the left and right, respectively, until they meet at the appropriate location for the pivot. The pivotal value is initially chosen to be `a[lo]`. We will discuss later the possible implications of choosing a different pivotal value. Note that it is crucial for `partition` to return in `pivotPoint` the position where the pivotal value was finally inserted. This information will allow the `quickSort` function that calls on `partition` to determine whether or not a recursive termination condition has been reached.

```
// Partition array between indices lo and hi.
// That is, using list[lo] as pivotal value, arrange
// entries between lo and hi indices so that all
// values to left of pivot are less than or equal
// to it and all values to right of pivot are
// greater than or equal to it.
//
// Input: array and lo and hi
// Output: Partitioned array, and pivotPoint
//         containing final location of pivot.

void partition(ListType list, int lo, int hi, int &pivotPoint)
{
   element pivot = list[lo];

   while (lo < hi)
   {
      while ((pivot < list[hi]) && (lo < hi))
         --hi;
      if (hi != lo)
      {
         list[lo] = list[hi];
         ++lo;
      }
```

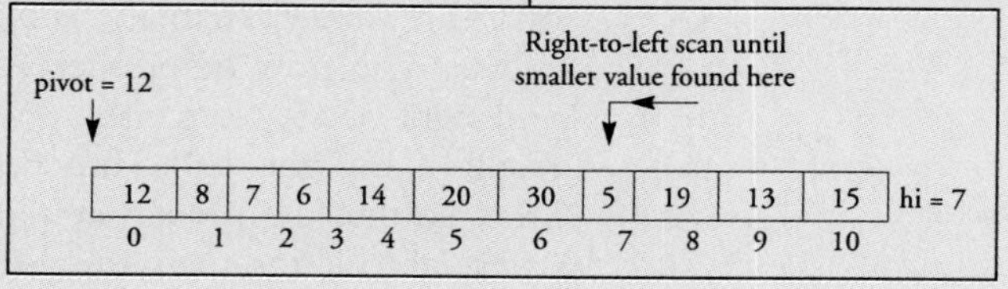

pivot = 12

Right-to-left scan until smaller value found here

12	8	7	6	14	20	30	5	19	13	15	hi = 7
0	1	2	3	4	5	6	7	8	9	10	

```
      while ((pivot > list[lo] && (lo < hi))
         ++lo;
      if (hi != lo)
      {
         list[hi] = list[lo];
         --hi;
      }
   }
   list[hi] = pivot;
   pivotPoint = hi;
}
```

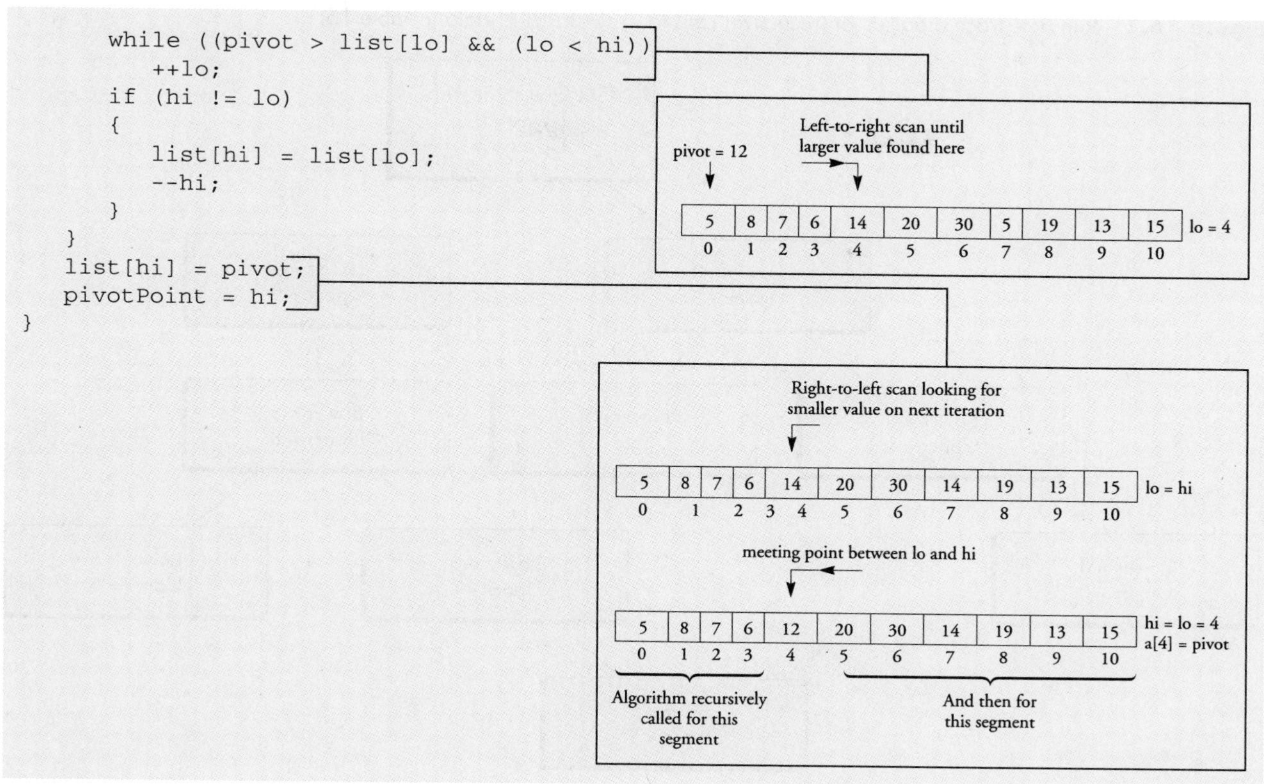

Given the previous `partition` function, `quickSort` itself must call on `partition` and then use the returned value of `pivotPoint` to decide whether or not recursive calls are necessary to perform more refined partitioning of the segments to the left and right of `pivotPoint`. The recursive logic for this decision is given in the following function `quickSort`:

```
void quickSort(ListType list, int lower, int upper)
{
   int pivotPoint;

   partition(list, lower, upper, pivotPoint);
   if (lower < pivotPoint)
      quickSort(list, lower, pivotPoint - 1);
   if (upper > pivotPoint)
      quickSort(list, pivotPoint + 1, upper);
}
```

For instance, after the first call to `quickSort` for a partitioning pass on the data in Table 16.1, we then recursively call on `quickSort` with `lower` = 0 and `upper` = 3. This triggers deeper level recursive calls from which we ultimately return, knowing that the segment of the array between indices 0 and 4 is now sorted. This return is followed by a recursive call to `quickSort` with `lower` = 5 and `upper` = 9. The run-time trace diagram of recursive calls to `quickSort` for the data of Table 16.1 is given in Figure 16.1. You should verify this call-return pattern by walking through the preceding function.

Figure 16.1 Run-time trace diagram of (recursive) calls to `quickSort` data in Table 16.1

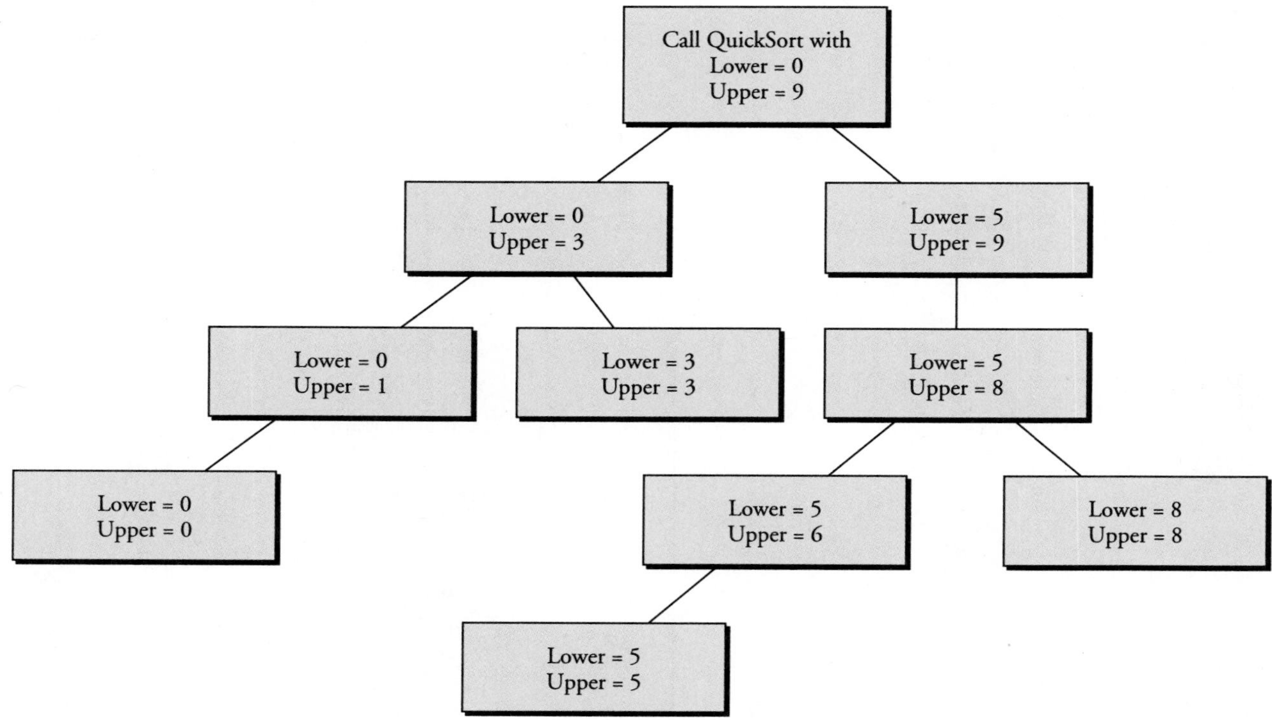

Efficiency of the Quick Sort

As mentioned earlier, the average run-time efficiency of the quick sort is $O(n \log_2 n)$, which is the best that has been achieved for a large array of size n. In the best case, it is quite easy to provide a rationale for this $O(n \log_2 n)$ figure. This best case occurs when each array segment recursively passed to `quickSort` partitions at its midpoint; that is, the appropriate location for each pivotal value in the series of recursive calls is the midpoint of the segment being partitioned. In this case, we find that:

1 call to `quickSort` (the first) is made with a segment of size n.
2 calls to `quickSort` are made with segments of size $n/2$.
4 calls to `quickSort` are made with segments of size $n/4$.
8 calls to `quickSort` are made with segments of size $n/8$.
.
.
.
n calls to `quickSort` are made with segments of size 1.

} Overall $\log_2 n$ levels

Since each call with a segment of size m requires $O(m)$ comparisons, it is clear that k calls with segments of size n/k will require $O(n)$ comparisons. Hence, the total number of comparisons resulting from the preceding sequence of calls will be $O(n \log_2 n)$.

If segments partition away from the midpoint, the efficiency of quick sort begins to deteriorate. In the worst case situation, when the array is already sorted, the efficiency of quick sort may drop down to $O(n^2)$ due to the continuous right-to-left scan all the way to the last left boundary. In the exercises at the end of the section, you will explore how the worst case situation is affected by your choice of the pivotal element.

A NOTE OF INTEREST

Privacy Issues Kill Microsoft Registration System

What are the social responsibilities that go along with state-of-the-art capabilities to sort and search through gigabytes of information? Advances in computers are making it easier to gather and piece together minutely detailed portraits of households, and marketers are gobbling these up to help choose targets for direct-mail and telephone campaigns. A recent incident involving Microsoft illustrates the importance of a social conscience in computing.

In early 1999, John Smith, a programmer and president of PharLap Software of Cambridge, Massachusetts, discovered that the Microsoft Office suite of business software was creating unique numbers identifying a user's personal computer and embedding these numbers in spreadsheet and word processing documents. Smith notified Microsoft that he believed this created a potential privacy threat. Why? This same number, related to the Ethernet adapter address of the computer, was apparently being sent to Microsoft when a user went through the on-line registration process for Microsoft Office. According to Smith, quoted in the March 7 *Milwaukee Journal,* "Microsoft never asked me if it was OK to send them this number, and they never said it was being sent. They are apparently building a database that relates Ethernet adapter addresses to personal information."

In the same article, Jason Catlett, president of a consumer privacy organization, maintains, "Microsoft is tattooing a number into each [Office] file. Think of the implications. If some whistle-blower sends a file, it can be traced back to the person himself. It's an extremely dangerous feature. Why did they do it?"

To its credit, Microsoft demonstrated belated sensitivity to the ethical issues that had been raised by the incident. Robert Bennett, Microsoft's product manager for Windows, said, "We're definitely sensitive to any privacy concerns. The software was not supposed to send this information unless the user checked a specific option." Bennett went on to say that Microsoft would alter the way that the registration software worked and also that information already collected as a result of the process would be expunged from the company's database.

Although Microsoft may have exercised poor judgment in the original policy, their decision to pull the plug after a sizable investment in the enterprise illustrates a commendable social responsibility. Such ethical dilemmas are likely to play an increasing role in the careers of many computing professionals.

You may wonder how large a stack is needed to sort an array of size n. (Remember that this stack is implicitly created even when you use recursion.) In situations where the depth of the run-time trace diagram is $O(\log_2 n)$, the maximum stack size will also be $O(\log_2 n)$. However, in the worst case, it will be $O(n)$.

Exercises 16.2

1. Consider the `quickSort` function given in this section. Suppose we inserted the following tracer output at the beginning of this function:

```
cout << lower <<   << upper << endl;
for (k = lower; k <= upper; ++k)
    cout << a[k];
cout << endl;
```

   What would we see as output from these tracers if we called on `quickSort` with the key array initially containing the following seven entries?

   60 12 90 30 64 8 6

2. Repeat Exercise 1 for a six-element array that initially contains

   1 8 2 7 3 6

3. When is a bubble sort better than a quick sort? Explain your answer in a written statement.

4. Under what circumstances would you not use a quick sort? Explain your answer in a written statement.
5. How does the choice of the pivotal value affect the efficiency of the quick sort algorithm? Suppose the middle value or the last value in a segment to be partitioned was chosen as the pivotal value. How would this alter the nature of best case and worst case data sets? Give examples to illustrate your answer.
6. Develop run-time trace diagrams of function calls to `quickSort` for a variety of test data sets (analogous to what was done in Figure 16.1). Use these diagrams to analyze the efficiency of `quickSort`. What types of data sets yield $O(n \log_2 n)$ efficiency? What types yield $O(n^2)$ efficiency?
7. In Chapter 11, `pointerSort` used an index of pointers to sort data logically without rearranging them. Adapt the pointer sort function to the quick sort algorithm.
8. Implement `quickSort` in a nonrecursive fashion by using a stack.
9. Implement a variation on the quick sort algorithm presented in this section in which the pivot is chosen to be the median of the three values:

```
a[lo], a[(lo + hi) / 2], a[hi]
```

In a carefully written statement, explain why this variation should be more efficient than the version that chooses the pivot to be `a[lo]`.

16.3 The Heap Sort Algorithm

The *heap sort* is a sorting algorithm that is roughly equivalent to the quick sort; its average efficiency is $O(n \log_2 n)$ for an array of size n. The method, originally described by R. W. Floyd, has two phases. In the first phase, the array containing the n data items is viewed as equivalent to a full binary tree. That is, the array to be sorted is viewed as the linear representation of a full binary tree containing n items (see Chapter 15). (If you want to read Floyd's description of this method, see his article, "Algorithm 245: Tree Sort 3," *Communications of the ACM,* Vol. 7, 1964, p. 701.) As an example, suppose we wish to sort the following array:

11 1 5 7 6 12 17 8 4 10 2

The tree now appears as shown in Figure 16.2.

Figure 16.2
Full binary tree corresponding to array

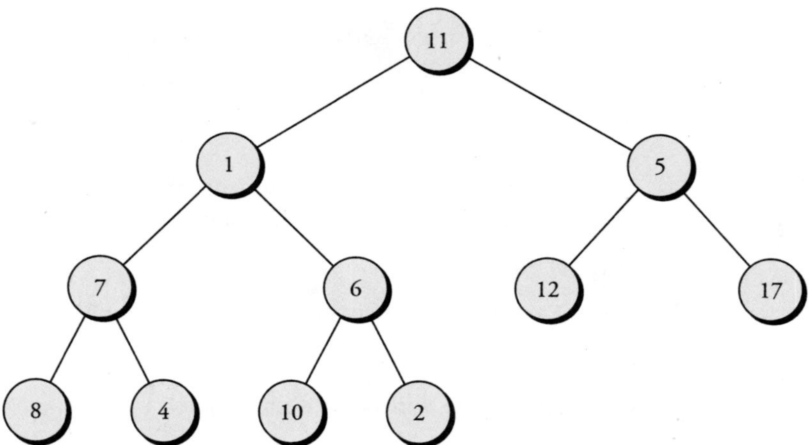

Objectives

a. to understand the logic behind the heap sort algorithm
b. to understand the relationship between heap sort and the linear representation of a binary tree in an array
c. to develop a C++ function to perform the heap sort
d. to analyze the efficiency of the heap sort

The goal of phase 1 is to sort the data elements along each path from leaf node level to the root node. If we wish to sort in ascending order, then the numbers along any path from leaf node to root should be in increasing order. Eventually, after phase 1, the tree will be a heap as described in Chapter 15. That is, the data item at each node will be greater than or equal to both of its children. To achieve this, we take the following steps:

1. Process the node that is the parent of the rightmost node on the lowest level as follows: If its value is less than the value of its largest child, swap these values; otherwise, do nothing.
2. Move left on the same level. Compare the value of the parent node with the values of the children. If the parent is smaller than the largest child, swap them.
3. When the left end of this level is reached, move up a level and, beginning with the rightmost parent node, repeat step 2. Continue swapping the original parent with the larger of its children until it is larger than its children. In effect, the original parent is being walked down the tree in a fashion that ensures all numbers will be in increasing order along the path.
4. Repeat step 3 until the root node has been processed.

Figure 16.3 shows these steps applied to Figure 16.2.

Figure 16.3 Phase 1 of heap sort applied to the binary tree in Figure 16.2

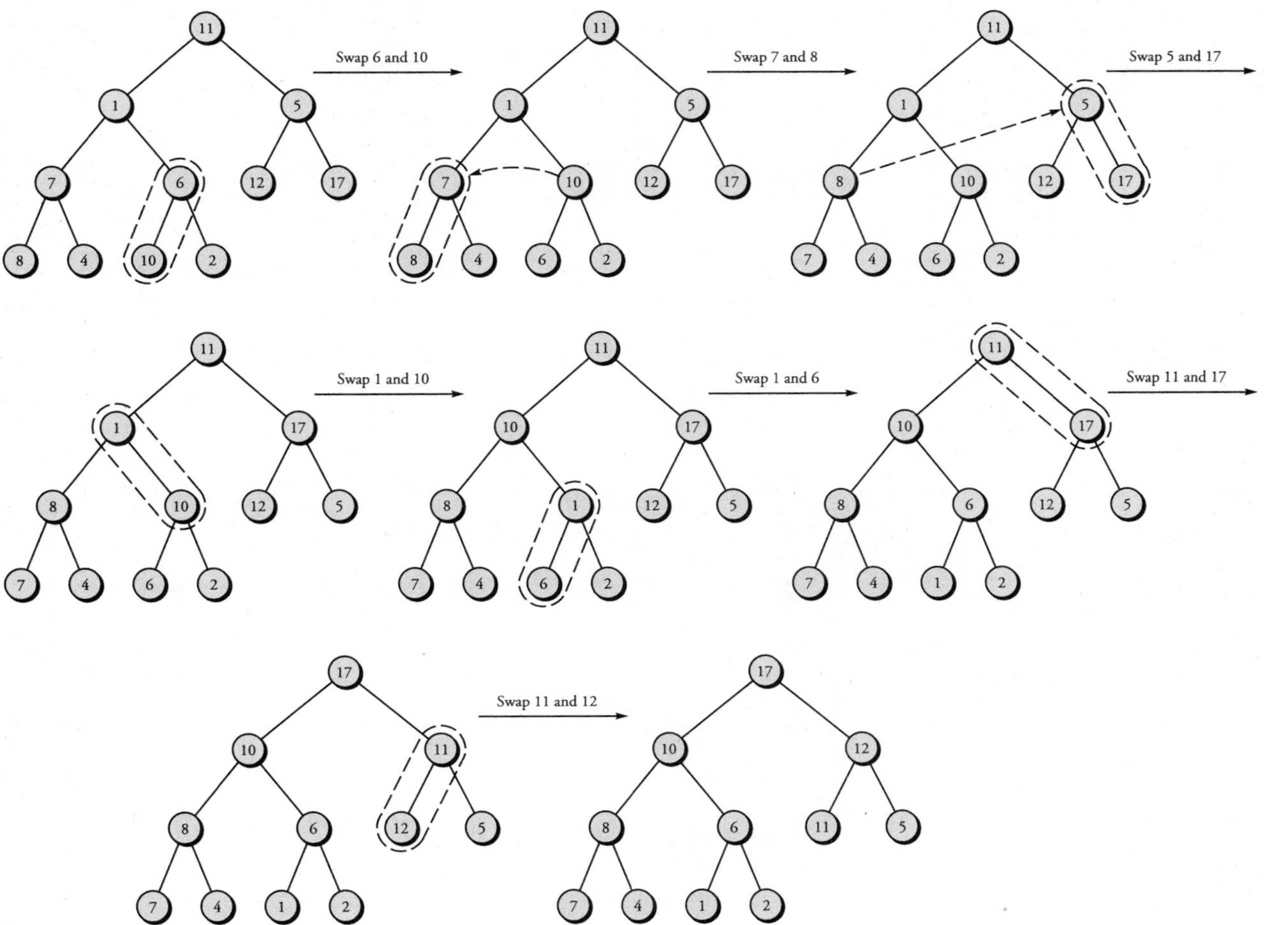

Phase 2 of the heap sort finds the node with the largest value in the tree and cuts it from the tree. This is then repeated to find the second largest value, which is also removed from the tree. The process continues until only two nodes are left in the tree; they are then exchanged if necessary. The precise steps for phase 2 are as follows:

1. Swap the root node with the bottom rightmost child and sever this new bottom rightmost child from the tree. This is the largest value.
2. Continue swapping the new root value with the larger of its children until it is not exceeded by either child. In effect, this new root value is now being walked down a path in the tree to ensure that all paths retain values arranged in ascending order from leaf node to root node. That is, the tree is being restored to a heap.
3. Repeat steps 1 and 2 until only one element is left.

Phase 2 of the heap sort begun in Figure 16.3 is shown in Figure 16.4 for the three highest values.

Both phase 1 and phase 2 use the same strategy of walking a parent down a path of the tree via a series of swaps with its children. The following function, `walkDown`, isolates this crucial subordinate algorithm. In the linear representation of a tree assumed by `walkDown`, the assignment statement `k = 2 * i` will make `k` reference the left child of the node indicated by `i`. That is, this statement will allow us to descend a level deeper into the tree.

```
// Function: walkDown
// Repeatedly exchange this parent with child of
// greatest value until the original parent is
// greater than both of its children
//
// Inputs: Array to be viewed as full binary tree.
//         n, the number of entries in the array.
//         j, the index of a parent node within the tree.
// Outputs: Tree array, as altered by this task.

void walkDown(ListType list, int j, int n)
{
   int i, k;
   element ref;
   bool foundSpot = false;

   i = j;
   ref = list[i];

   // list[i] will move along the appropriate path in the tree

   k = 2 * i + 1;

   // Initially k references left child of list[i]

   while ((k < n) && ! foundSpot)
   {
      if (k < n - 1)                    // Make k reference largest child
         if (list[k + 1] > list[k])
            ++k;
      if (list[k] > ref)                // Child must move up
      {
```

Figure 16.4 Phase 2 of heap sort for three values

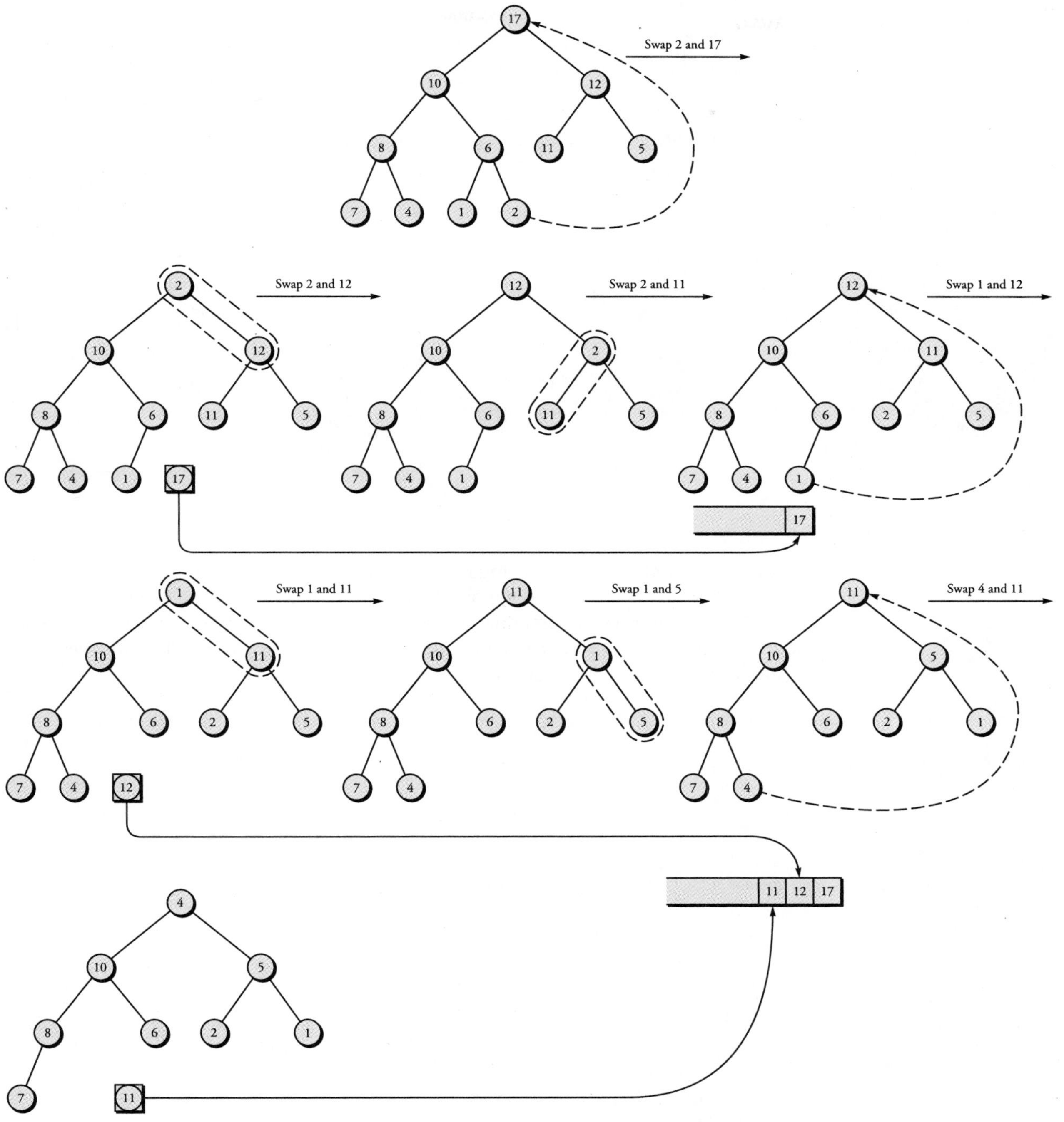

```
         list[i] = list[k];
         i = k;
         k = 2 * i + 1;
      }
      else                              // Appropriate spot has been found
         foundSpot = true;
   }
   list[i] = ref;
}
```

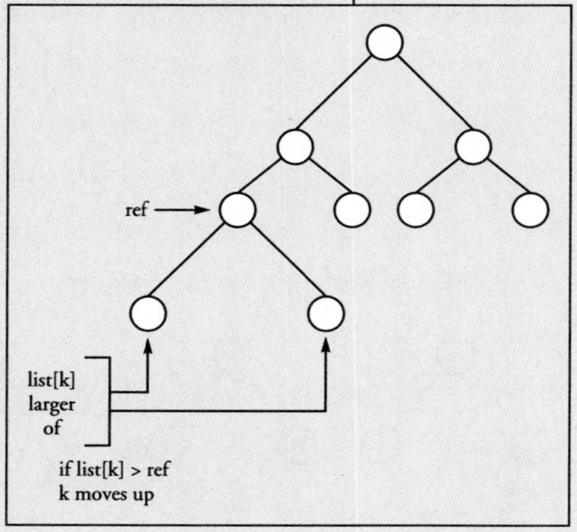

With the essential `walkDown` logic isolated in a separate function, phases 1 and 2 of `heapSort` may now be developed easily. The loop for phase 1 repeatedly calls on `walkDown` to form the tree into a heap. Then a loop for phase 2 repeatedly swaps the root of the tree with the last child and calls on `walkDown` to allow this new root to find an appropriate position in the heap.

```
void heapSort(ListType list, int n)
{
   int y;
   element temp;

   // First phase arranges the tree  into a heap

   y = n / 2 - 1;  // y starts at last node to have child
   while (y >= 0)
   {
      walkDown(list, y, n);
      --y;
   }

   // End of first phase; y is now used to point at the
   // current last array slot.

   y = n;
   while (y > 0)
   {
   // Interchange root with bottom right leaf node.
```

```
        temp = list[0];
        list[0] = list[y - 1];
        list[y - 1] = temp;
        --y;
        walkDown(list, 0, y);
    }
}
```

Swap these two and then remove leaf node from further consideration.

Efficiency of the Heap Sort

It is relatively easy to deduce that the heap sort requires $O(n \log_2 n)$ comparisons. To see this, note that the phase 1 loop in the preceding C++ function will execute $n/2$ times. Inside this loop, we call `walkDown`, which in turn has a loop that will execute at most $\log_2 n$ times (because it merely follows a path down a full binary tree). Hence, phase 1 requires at most

$$(n/2) * \log_2 n$$

iterations at its deepest level.

Phase 2 may be similarly analyzed. The phase 2 loop iterates n times. Within each iteration, `walkDown` is called, again resulting in at most $\log_2 n$ operations. Thus, phase 2 requires at most $n * \log_2 n$ iterations at its deepest level. Overall, we get

$$1.5n * \log_2 n$$

as an upper bound for the number of iterations required by the combination of phases 1 and 2.

Thus, both quick sort and heap sort yield $O(n \log_2 n)$ efficiencies. In *Searching and Sorting,* referenced in Section 16.1, Knuth has shown that, on the average, quick sort will be slightly faster since its big-O constant of proportionality will be smaller than that for heap sort. However, heap sort offers the advantage of guaranteeing an $O(n \log_2 n)$ efficiency regardless of the data being sorted. As we have already noted for quick sort, worst case data can cause its performance to deteriorate to $O(n^2)$.

Exercises 16.3

1. Consider the `heapSort` function given in this section. Note that `walkDown` is called at two points in the function: once in phase 1 and again in phase 2. Suppose we traced the contents of the array being sorted after each call to `walkDown`. What would we see as output if we called `heapSort` with an array that initially contained the following?

60 12 90 30 64 8 6

2. Repeat Exercise 1 for a six-element array that initially contains

1 8 2 7 3 6

3. Where did the heap sort get its name?

4. What is a heap sort?

5. Is a heap sort always better than a quick sort? When is it? When isn't it? Explain your answer in a written essay.

6. What is the worst case and average case efficiency of the heap sort algorithm?
7. Give examples of arrays that generate the best and worst performances, respectively, for the heap sort algorithm. Explain why these arrays generate the best and worst performances.
8. In Chapter 10, `pointerSort` used an index of pointers to sort data logically without rearranging them. Adapt the pointer sort function to the heap sort algorithm.

16.4 The Merge Sort Algorithm

Objectives

a. to understand the logic behind the merge sort algorithm
b. to understand merge sort's reliance on a subalgorithm that merges two sorted lists
c. to develop a C++ function to perform the merge sort
d. to analyze the efficiency of the merge sort

The essential idea behind *merge sort* is to make repeated use of a function that merges two lists, each already in ascending order, into a third list, also arranged in ascending order. The merge function itself only requires sequential access to the lists. Its logic is similar to the method you would use if you were merging two sorted piles of index cards into a third pile. That is, start with the first card from each pile. Compare them to see which one comes first, transfer that one over to the third pile, and advance to the next card in that pile. Repeat the comparison, transfer, and advance operations until one of the piles runs out of cards. At that point, merely move what is left of the remaining pile over to the third merged pile.

This logic is reflected in the generalized merge function that follows. For reasons that will become apparent when we incorporate it into a full sorting function, this version of merge begins with the two sorted lists stored in one array. The first list runs from subscript `lower` to `middle` of array `source`. The second runs from subscript `middle + 1` to `upper` of the same array. The merged result of the two lists is stored in a second array `destination`.

```
// Function: merge
// Merge the two ordered segments of source into
// one list arranged in ascending order.
//
// Inputs: Array source arranged in ascending order between
//         indices lower...middle and middle + 1...upper respectively.
// Outputs: The complete ordered list in destination.

void merge(ListType source, ListType destination, int lower, int middle, int upper)
{
   int s1 = lower;
   int s2 = middle + 1;
   int d = lower;

   // Repeat comparison of current item from each list.

   do
   {
      if (source[s1] < source[s2])
      {
         destination[d] = source[s1];
         ++s1;
      }
      else
      {
         destination[d] = source[s2];
         ++s2;
```

```
        }
        ++d;
    } while ((s1 <= middle) && (s2 <= upper));

    // Move what is left of remaining list.

    if (s1 > middle)
        do
        {
            destination[d] = source[s2];
            ++s2;
            ++d;
        } while (s2 <= upper);
    else
        do
        {
            destination[d] = source[s1];
            ++s1;
            ++d;
        } while (s1 <= middle);
}
```

Clearly, `merge` is an $O(n)$ algorithm where n is the number of items in the two lists to be merged. A question remains: How can `merge` be used to sort an entire array? To answer this, we need another function called `order` that will take the values in indices `lower` through `upper` of an array `source` and arrange them in ascending order in subscripts `lower` through `upper` of another array called `destination`. Notice that `order` is itself almost a sorting function except that it produces a sorted list in a second array instead of actually transforming the array it originally receives. Our use of `order` will be to obtain two sorted half-length sequences from our original array.

Then we will use the `merge` function we have already developed to merge the two sorted half-length sequences back into the original array. Of course, this merely defers our original question of how to use `merge` to sort because now we are faced with the question of how `order` will produce two sorted half-length sequences. Here is where recursion enters the picture. To produce a sorted half-length sequence, we use `order` to produce two sorted quarter-length sequences and apply `merge` to the results. Similarly, the quarter-length sequences are produced by calling on `order` to produce sorted eighth-length sequences and applying `merge` to the results. The recursive termination condition for this descent into shorter and shorter ordered sequences occurs when `order` receives a sequence of length 1.

Given the crucial `order` function, the `mergeSort` function itself is almost trivial. It need merely create a copy of the array to be sorted and then call on `order` to sort the elements of the copy into the original. Note that, because `order` continually calls on `merge` and `merge` cannot do its work within one array, the need to create a copy of the original array is unavoidable. Complete C++ versions of `mergeSort` and `order` follow:

```
void mergeSort(ListType list, int n)
{
    ListType listCopy;

    for (int k = 0; k < n; ++k)        // Make copy for call to order.
        listCopy[k] = list[k];
```

```
    order(listCopy, list, 0, n - 1);
}

// Function: order
// Transfer source in ascending order to destination,
// between indices lower...upper.
//
// Inputs: source and destination, two arrays that are
//         initially identical between indices lower...upper.
// Outputs: destination arranged in order between lower and upper.

void order(ListType source, ListType destination, int lower, int upper)
{
    int middle;

    if (lower != upper)
    {
        middle = (lower + upper) / 2;
        order(destination, source, lower, middle);
        order(destination, source, middle + 1, upper);
        merge(source, destination, lower, middle, upper);
    }
}
```

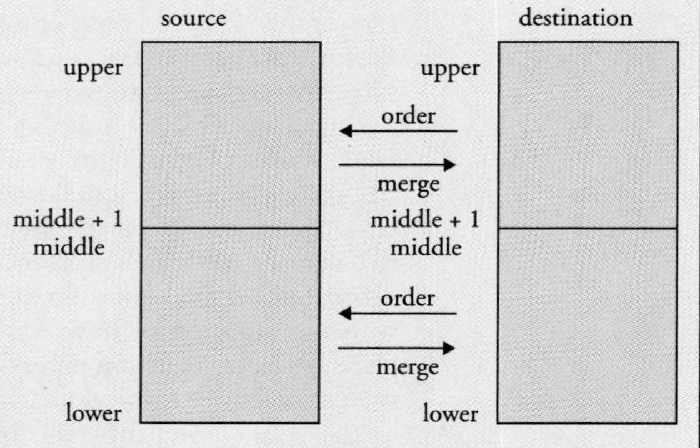

Recursively call order to get two sorted segments in source, which are then merged into destination. This requires destination originally to be a copy of source.

The run-time trace diagram of function calls in Figure 16.5 highlights the interaction between `order` and `merge` triggered by calling `mergeSort` with a sample array of size `n` = 11. The leaf nodes in this trace diagram represent the recursive termination condition reached when `lower` = `upper`.

Efficiency of the Merge Sort

From a run-time trace of function calls such as that appearing in Figure 16.5, it is quite easy to deduce that merge sort requires $O(n \log_2 n)$ comparisons. The reasoning required for this deduction is as follows. All the merge operations across any given level of the trace diagram will require $O(n)$ comparisons. There are $O(\log_2 n)$ levels to the

Figure 16.5 Run-time trace of function calls to order and `merge`

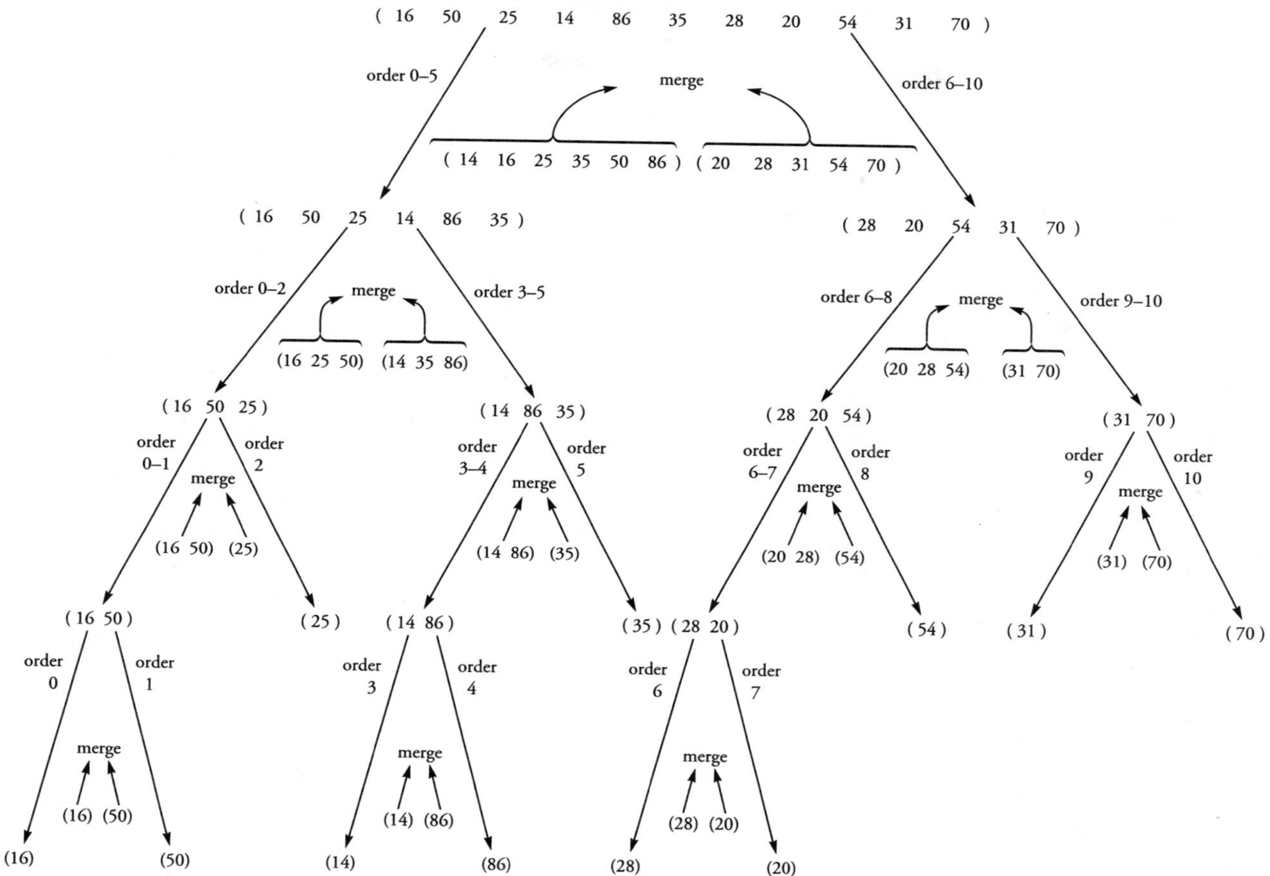

trace diagram. Hence, the overall efficiency is the product $O(n \log_2 n)$. Notice that, like the heap sort, the merge sort can guarantee this efficiency regardless of the original data. That is, there is no worst case that can cause its efficiency to deteriorate (as there is for quick sort).

The price paid for using merge sort is in the memory space it requires. Of course, there is the stack space associated with recursion. More important, however, is the need for a duplicate copy of the array being sorted. In applications where the original array barely fits in memory, this space requirement will make merge sort totally impractical.

As steep as the memory price is, there is an added benefit to merge sort that makes it the only possible choice for certain applications: Merge sort may be written in a way that necessitates only sequential access to the lists being manipulated. As we have presented it here, random access is required at only one point in the algorithm, namely, in the `merge` function to access the second list beginning at index (`middle + 1`) of `source`. The need for this could have been eliminated by having `merge` work with two separate source arrays. That is, we merge ordered arrays `source1` and `source2` into `destination`. This is very costly with arrays since it necessitates using three arrays to sort one array. However, it is less costly when the lists being manipulated are being implemented not by arrays but rather by dynamically allocated linked lists or sequential files. In both of these latter situations, the need to use sequential access makes the merge sort strategy a very effective choice.

A NOTE OF INTEREST

Public-Key Cryptography

The manner in which computers can sort through and in other ways manipulate information gives rise to concern over the security of electronic information. Cryptography is the science of encoding information to protect it from being viewed by unauthorized parties. Today, as an increasing amount of sensitive information is transmitted in electronic and magnetic form, cryptography is becoming an increasingly important field.

A conventional encryption system works much like a mailbox with a combination lock. Anyone knowing the combination can open the box to leave a message or read any of the messages in the box. In computerized information systems, the "combination" to the mailbox is a digital key, that is, a particular bit pattern that is applied to an electronic message to encode or decode it. In conventional systems, anyone knowing the digital key has access to the information in the electronic mailbox. Hence, such systems are best suited to a small number of users and not to the networking of information among many computer installations that is possible with today's technology.

An interesting development in cryptography occurred in the early 1970s with the development of a theory for public-key encryption systems. Such systems work on two different digital keys: one for writing information into the electronic mailbox and the other to read encoded information that has been left in the mailbox. As a user of such an encryption system, you could freely give out the write key to your mailbox (the public key), allowing anyone to send you an encoded letter. However, you would keep the read key (the decoding key) secret so that only you are able to make sense out of your mail.

The best-known public-key encryption scheme is known as the RSA algorithm (after Rivest, Shamir, and Adleman, the mathematicians who developed it). This algorithm is based on the difficulty of factoring large numbers that are the product of two prime numbers. For instance, the number $51 = 3 \times 17$ would satisfy this criterion except that it is not nearly large enough.

In the RSA system, the product of the two prime factors is linked to your public key. However, this public key includes only the product, not the prime factors that comprise the product. Your private key includes each of the individual prime factors. Why should such numbers be large? The answer to this question lies in the present limitations of the area of mathematics known as number theory. It turns out that, given the product of two such prime factors without being told the factors themselves, number theory provides no known way of factoring the number into its prime factors in a reasonable amount of time, even using the most advanced supercomputers. From a security perspective, this means that your code could not be broken by outside agencies, even if they were using a computer to assist them.

The role of public-key cryptography in electronic data systems will no doubt become increasingly important in the future. For an excellent description of the details underlying this technique, see Thomas Cormen, Charles Leiserson, & Ronald Rivest, *Introduction to Algorithms,* New York: McGraw-Hill, 1989. A broader overview of the entire field of cryptography and ethical issues arising out of it may be found in Bruce Schneier, *Applied Cryptography,* New York: Wiley, 1996. In a shorter article entitled "Cryptography, Security, and the Future," *Communications of the ACM,* Vol. 40, No. 1, Jan. 1997, the same Bruce Schneier forcefully presents the importance of cryptographic systems:

> Present-day computer security is a house of cards; it may stand for now, but it can't last. Many unsecure products have not yet been broken because they are still in their infancy. But when these products are widely used, they will become tempting targets for criminals. The press will publicize the attacks, undermining public confidence in these systems. Ultimately, products will win or lose in the marketplace depending on the strength of their security. (p. 138)

In the exercises at the end of the section and Programming Problems and Projects at the end of the chapter, you will be asked to adapt `mergeSort` to such sequential implementations of a list. In particular, when the list exists in a file instead of main memory, the sorting method employed is said to be an *external sort* (as opposed to the *internal sorts* we have studied in this chapter).

Exercises 16.4

1. Consider the `mergeSort` function given in this section. Note that this function contains a subordinate function called `order`. Suppose we inserted the following tracer output at the beginning of the `order` function.

```
cout << lower <<     << upper << endl;
for (int k = lower; k < upper; ++k)
    cout << source[k] << ;
cout << endl;
```

What would we see as output from these tracers if we called on `mergeSort` with an array that initially contained the following?

60 12 90 30 64 8 6

2. Repeat Exercise 1 for a six-element array that initially contains

   1 8 2 7 3 6

3. Implement `mergeSort` in a nonrecursive fashion by using a stack.
4. In Chapter 10, `pointerSort` used an index of pointers to sort data logically without rearranging them. Adapt the pointer sort function to the merge sort algorithm.
5. Identify and give an example of best case and worst case data sets for the merge sort algorithm. Explain why your data sets generate best and worst case performance.
6. A sorting method is said to be *stable* if two data items of matching value are guaranteed not to be rearranged with respect to each other as the algorithm progresses. For example, in the four-element array

   60 42_1 80 42_2

   a stable sorting method guarantees a final ordering of

   42_1 42_2 60 80

   Classify each of the sorting algorithms studied in this chapter and in Chapter 10 as to their stability. (To see why stability may be important, consider Programming Problems 5 and 6 at the end of this chapter.)
7. You are to sort an array in a program in which the following considerations are taken into account. First, the amount of data to be sorted is so large that frequent $O(n^2)$ run times will prove unsatisfactory. The amount of data will also make it impossible for your program to use a large amount of overhead data (for example, stack space) to make the sort efficient in its run time. This is because the space required by the overhead data potentially takes up space needed by the array to be sorted. Second, you are told that the array to be sorted is often nearly in order to start with. For each of the seven sorting methods indicated, specify whether or not that method is appropriate for this application and, in a brief statement, explain your answer.
   a. bubble sort
   b. insertion sort
   c. selection sort
   d. shell sort
   e. quick sort
   f. heap sort
   g. merge sort

Case Study: Efficiently Sorting a Linked List

User Request

A program has a linked list with a large number of doubles that must be sorted into ascending order. An algorithm is needed to do this. Since the list contains a large number of values, it should be an $O(n * \log_2 n)$ algorithm.

Analysis

In the Case Study for Chapter 12, we were faced with a similar problem except that the list contained integers instead of doubles. With a list of integers, we chose radix sort as the appropriate algorithm. However, radix sort will not work when the data type of the elements in the list are doubles. (Why?) Instead, for the problem now at hand, we will adapt the quick sort algorithm to linked lists.

Design

Recursively, we can specify the logic of quick sort for linked lists by the following pseudocode:

If the list L to be sorted is not empty
  Partition the list L into three components:
    (1) The PIVOT element, taken to be the first element in L
    (2) A list called SMALLS consisting of those values in L, after the first element, that are less than PIVOT
    (2) A list called BIGS consisting of those values in L, after the first element, that are greater than or equal to PIVOT
  Recursively sort the list SMALLS
  Recursively sort the list BIGS
  Now that the SMALLS and BIGS are sorted, form the sorted list by "gluing together" the values in SMALLS, followed by the PIVOT, followed by the values in BIGS

This algorithm mirrors the logic we used in Section 16.2 for quick sorting an array; that is, the pivot element is taken as the first element in the list to be sorted.

Implementation

Because we don't have direct access into a linked list, the partitioning logic used for linked lists will differ significantly from that we developed for arrays. However, because the nodes in linked lists are dynamically allocated, we have the luxury of being able to remove values from one list (the list to ultimately be sorted) and then to attach them to the lists of small and big values. In doing this, our algorithm will be manipulating three lists at each level of recursion, but we will never be charged for more space than that required for all the values in the original list. To use this approach with arrays (that is, allocate two arrays in addition to the original) would have been very wasteful. With linked lists, however, it works out beautifully! The partitioning algorithm is given by:

```
// Partition non-empty list into:
//     (1) pivot element at front of list
//     (2) the list smalls -- those values < pivot
//     (3) the list bigs -- those values >= pivot
//

void partition(LinkedList<double> &list, double & pivot,
               LinkedList<double> &smalls, LinkedList<double> &bigs)
{
   list.first();
   smalls.first();
   bigs.first();

   // Grab the pivot from the front of the list
   pivot = list.remove();
```

```
    // Rest of the list gets partitioned into smalls and bigs
    while (!list.empty())
    {
       if (list.access() < pivot)
       {
          smalls.insert(list.remove());
          smalls.next();
       }
       else
       {
          bigs.insert(list.remove());
          bigs.next();
       }
    }
}
```

Quick sort, in turn, uses `partition` as follows:

```
void quickSort(LinkedList<double> &list)
{

   LinkedList<double> smalls;
   LinkedList<double> bigs;
   double pivot;

   // if the list is empty, it's trivially sorted
   if (! list.empty())
   {
      partition(list, pivot, smalls, bigs);
      // Recursively sort smalls and bigs
      quickSort(bigs);
      quickSort(smalls);
      // Glue everything back together
      smalls.first();
      while ( !smalls.empty() )
      {
         list.insert(smalls.remove());
         list.next();
      }
      list.insert(pivot);
      list.next();
      bigs.first();
      while ( !bigs.empty() )
      {
         list.insert(bigs.remove());
         list.next();
      }
   }
}
```

Running, Debugging, and Testing Hints

1. To describe and understand the more complex sort algorithms, it is helpful to present them via subordinate algorithms and stepwise refinement. To this end, we have found it convenient initially to focus on subalgorithms (`segmentedInsertionSort` for `shellSort`, `partition` for

quickSort, walkDown for heapSort, and merge for mergeSort). Our method is illustrative of the stepwise refinement approach to problem solving: Break a complex problem down into smaller problems, solve these smaller problems, and then tie their solutions together to solve the original large problem.

2. Describing and understanding algorithms are separate issues from their actual implementation in a specific programming language on a real machine. One implication of this separation of algorithm description and algorithm implementation is the run-time cost associated with a function call. We must consider the hidden costs of making a function call and how deeply embedded the function call is in the iterative structure of the calling module.

3. Depending on the machine you are using, calling a function instead of directly inserting the code necessary may mean that your program spends more run-time handling the hidden cost of function calls than it does interchanging data items. If large data sets are being sorted and if run-time efficiency is of primary importance, then we should implement our algorithm without actually calling on a function.

4. Keep in mind the distinction between algorithm description and algorithm implementation when making decisions about whether or not to proceduralize a given sequence of instructions. What may be appropriately isolated as a trivial subalgorithm at the time when a designer is concerned with describing an algorithm may carry with it a steep price if implemented as a trivial function that is called on many times when the resulting program is put into use.

5. In making the decision whether to use functions or in-line code when implementing an algorithm, carefully weigh run-time considerations with respect to the clarity and readability of code. A useful rule of thumb is that only in exceptional circumstances should the code associated with a module exceed one printed page in length. This guideline allows in-line insertion of code for simple algorithmic units and assures that the overall software system does not become unwieldy.

Summary

Key Terms

diminishing increment sort
external sort
heap sort
internal sort
merge sort
partition
pivot
quick sort
relatively prime
shell sort

Key Concepts

- This chapter has added four sorting algorithms to those already presented in Chapter 11. This gives us a large variety of tools from which to choose when we need to perform a sorting job.
- The following comparison table summarizes the pros and cons of each sorting method we've covered.

Sorting Method	Chapter	Number of Comparisons in Terms of the Number of Data Items Being Sorted (n)	Space Requirement	Additional Comments
Binary tree	15	Between $O(n^2)$ and $O(n \log_2 n)$ depending on original data and whether tree height-balanced	Pointers for tree and possible stack space for recursive traversals	
Bubble	10	$O(n_2)$	No additional overhead	Loop check allows early exit as soon as array is ordered.
Heap	16	$O(n \log_2 n)$	No additional overhead	
Insertion	10	$O(n^2)$	No additional overhead	Loop check allows early exit as soon as item is correctly placed.
Merge	16	$O(n \log_2 n)$	Requires duplicate array and stack space for recursion	Since only requires sequential access, can be used for linked lists and sequential files.
Pointer	10	Depends on method with which it is combined	Requires list of pointers to maintain logical order	Can be combined with any method to substantially reduce size of data items being interchanged.
Quick	16	$O(n \log_2 n)$ on the average but $O(n^2)$ for worst cases	Stack space for recursion	
Radix	10, 12	$O(n)$	Space for bins	Though $O(n)$, large constant of proportionality. Not generalizable to all types of data, for example, real numbers.
Selection	10	$O(n^2)$	No additional overhead	
Shell	17	Between $O[n(\log_2 n)^2]$ and $O(n^{1.5})$ depending on increments used	No additional overhead	

Programming Problems and Projects

1. In the Case Study of Chapter 10, we presented tools and techniques for profiling sort algorithms. In particular, in that Case Study we developed a complete program that helped us empirically explore the efficiency of selection sort. Now apply the same tools and techniques to develop a profiling program for each of the sort algorithms studied in this chapter—shell, quick, heap, and merge. Write a report on the exploration that you do with your profiling program.
2. Modify your profiled version of shell sort from Problem 1 so that it uses a variety of sequences of diminishing increments. In a written report, compare the performance of the algorithm for these differing sequences. Which sequence performs the best?

3. Modify the shell sort so that it employs bubble sort logic on segments instead of insertion sort. Incorporate this change into the program you wrote for Problems 1 and 2. Compare the observed efficiency of this new version of shell sort with the original on a variety of data sets. Which performs better? Explain your answer in a carefully written statement.
4. Modify the profiled version of quick sort that you wrote for Problem 1 so that you can experiment with the selection of a pivot element or try invoking insertion sort when the size of the array segment to be partitioned becomes sufficiently small. Whatever experimentation you choose to do, write a report on your exploration. In your report, draw conclusions about the efficiencies of various strategies. Support your conclusions with empirical data obtained from your exploratory runs.
5. Given a sequential file containing an unordered list of passengers and their flight numbers for Wing-and-a-Prayer Airlines (Problem 7, Chapter 12, and Problem 12, Chapter 11), produce a listing arranged in flight-number order. Passengers on the same flight should be ordered by last name. The easy version of this program assumes that all information will fit in memory, allowing the use of an internal sort. For an added challenge, write the program using an external sort algorithm. (*Hint:* Adapt `mergeSort` along the lines discussed in the text.)
6. The Bay Area Brawlers professional football team (Problem 9, Chapter 12; Problem 5, Chapter 15) has stored the records of all the players who have played on the team during its history. One player's record consists of

   - Name
   - Total points scored
   - Number of touchdowns
   - Number of field goals
   - Number of safeties
   - Number of extra points

   Write a program that lists players in order from the most points scored in the team's history down to the fewest. Players who have scored the same number of points should then be arranged in alphabetical order.
7. Take n randomly generated integers. Now apply a bubble sort, a shell sort, a quick sort, a heap sort, and a merge sort. Observe, compare, and plot their execution time for $n = 100$; $n = 1000$; $n = 10{,}000$; $n = 100{,}000$, ...
8. Put some hypothetical data in an external file and apply a modified merge sort to them.
9. Write a C++ program to complete the following steps:

   - Artificially create a file with a large number of randomly chosen names.
   - Read into an array all names that begin with A through some letter, say, G, chosen so that all the names will fit in the array.
   - Sort this array with one of the sorting algorithms from this chapter and store this sorted array into another file.
   - Now read into the array all names from the file that begin with H through another appropriate letter.
   - Sort the array and append it to the end of the new file.

   Repeat this process until all names from the original file have been processed. The new file will be the sorted version of the original. Observe the execution time of your program. Analyze its efficiency in big-O terms.
10. Consider a list of records, each containing four fields:

   - Name
   - Month of birth

- Day of birth
- Year of birth

Write a program to sort this list in order from oldest to youngest. People with the same birth date should be arranged alphabetically. One strategy you could employ is to concatenate strategically the four fields into one and then sort just that one field. Another strategy is to sort the list four times, each time by a different field. (Think carefully about which field to sort first.) Which of the strategies requires you to choose a stable sorting algorithm? (See Exercise 6 in Section 16.4.)

11. Modify `mergeSort` so that it will sort a linked list instead of an array.

12. A variation on the merge sort is called the natural merge sort. This algorithm looks for natural "runs" of ordered data within the original array. For instance, the following array of 16 items shows eight natural runs (indicated by brackets).

```
0   [503]
1   [87 ]
2   [512]
3   [61 ]
4   [908]
5   [170]
6   [897]
7   [275]
8   [653]
9   [426]
10  [154]
11  [509]
12  [612]
13  [677]
14  [765]
15  [703]
```

These eight runs are arranged with the first run positioned at the top of a new array, the second run reversed and moved to the bottom of the array, the third run positioned after the original first run, the fourth run reversed and positioned above the original second run, and so forth. The pattern in this new array is:

```
0   [503]   ← Original first run
1   [61 ]   ← Original third run
2   [908]
3   [275]   ← Original fifth run
4   [653]
5   [154]
6   [509]
7   [612]   ← Original seventh run
8   [677]
9   [765]
10  [703]   ← Original eighth run reversed
11  [426]   ← Original sixth run reversed
12  [897]   ← Original fourth run reversed
13  [170]
14  [512]   ← Original second run reversed
15  [87 ]
```

The runs in this new array are now merged back into the original array, resulting in the following pattern of data:

Index	Value	
0	87	
1	503	← Merged data from original first and second runs
2	512	
3	275	
4	426	← Merged data from original fifth and sixth runs
5	653	
6	765	
7	703	
8	677	
9	612	← Merged data from original seventh and eighth runs
10	509	
11	154	
12	908	
13	897	
14	170	← Merged data from original third and fourth runs
15	61	

This merging pattern then cascades back and forth from between the original and new array until only one run remains. Discover this merging pattern and implement the natural merge sort. Describe circumstances under which the natural merge algorithm is likely to perform better and worse than the merge sort algorithm described in Section 16.4.

17 More Powerful Search Methods

Chapter Outline

I do not search, I find.
Pablo Picasso

In earlier chapters, we analyzed three methods of searching for items within a list: sequential search, binary search, and binary search tree. The sequential search, although easy to implement and applicable to short lists, is limited in many practical situations by its $O(n)$ search efficiency. The binary search offers a much faster $O(\log_2 n)$ search efficiency but also has limitations. Foremost among these limitations are the need to maintain the list in physically contiguous order and the need to maintain a count of the number of records in the list. Both of these limitations are particularly restrictive for volatile lists, that is, lists in which insertions and deletions are frequently made.

In Chapter 15, a binary search tree emerged as offering the best of both worlds. Insertions and deletions can be done on a binary search tree by merely manipulating pointers instead of moving data, and an $O(\log_2 n)$ search efficiency can be achieved if the tree remains close to full. Unfortunately, to guarantee that the tree remains nearly full and hence ensure the $O(\log_2 n)$ efficiency, a sophisticated technique known as height balancing (see Chapter 15) is required. The complications involved in implementing this technique frequently dictate that it not be used. Essentially, you must weigh the significant cost in development time to implement a height-balanced tree against the risk that the order in which data arrive for insertion may cause search efficiency to deteriorate from $O(\log_2 n)$ to $O(n)$. If data items arrive in a relatively random order, then taking that risk may be the prudent choice.

The efficiency of all three of these techniques depends on the number of items in the list being searched. In this chapter, we shall study another alternative, called *hashing*. Its efficiency is measurable in terms of the amount of storage you are willing to waste. In this sense, hashing can achieve phenomenally fast search times regardless of how much data you have, provided you can afford to keep a relatively large amount of unused list space available.

We shall also explore some of the special considerations that enter into searching for data stored in a disk file instead of main memory. These considerations lead to a variety of search schemes, all of which employ some variation of a data structure known as an *index*.

17.1 Density-Dependent Search Techniques

Objectives

a. To understand what is meant by a key-to-address transformation, that is, a hashing function
b. to develop techniques for constructing hashing functions
c. to understand why, for most applications, hashing functions cannot transform all possible keys to a unique address
d. to understand what the term collision means relative to hashing
e. to develop methods for processing collisions: linear probing, quadratic probing, rehashing, linked (chained) probing, and bucket hashing
f. to understand what the term clustering means relative to hashing

In an ideal data processing world, all identifying keys such as product codes, social security numbers, and so on would start at 0 and follow in sequence thereafter. Then, in any given list, we would merely store the key and its associated data at the position that matched the key. The search efficiency for any key in such a list would be one access to the list, and all data processors could live happily ever after! Unfortunately, in the real world, users (not being concerned with the happiness of data processing personnel) desire keys that consist of more meaningful characters, such as names, addresses, region codes, and so on. For instance, it may be that in a given inventory-control application, product codes are numbered in sequence beginning with 10,000 instead of 0. A moment's reflection should indicate that this is still a highly desirable situation since, given a key, we need merely locate the key at position

```
keyValue - 10000
```

in the list, and we still have a search efficiency of 1. What we have done here is to define a *key-to-address transformation,* or *hashing function.* The idea behind a hashing function is that it acts on a given key in such a way as to return the relative position in the list where we expect to find the key.

Most hashing functions are not as straightforward as the preceding one and present some additional complications that we can quickly illustrate. Suppose we use the following hashing function:

```
hash(keyValue) = keyValue % 4
```

Then the set of keys 3, 5, 8, and 10 will be scattered as illustrated here.

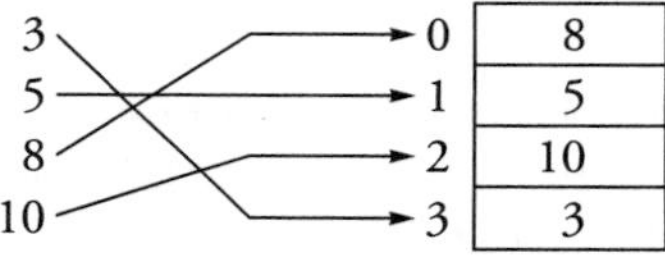

However, if we happen to have 3, 4, 8, and 10 as keys instead of 3, 5, 8, and 10, a problem arises: 4 and 8 hash to the same position. They are said to be *synonyms,* and the result is termed a *collision.* The situation—in this case, a collision at position 0—is shown in the following illustration.

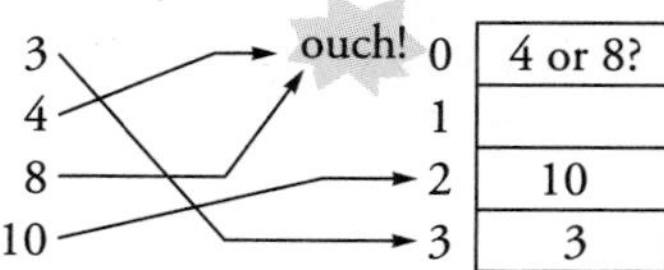

Clearly, one of the goals of the hashing functions we develop should be to reduce the number of collisions as much as possible.

The Construction of Hashing Functions

The business of developing hashing functions can be quite intriguing. The essential idea is to build a mathematical black box that will take a key value as input and issue as output the position in the list where that key value should be located. The position emitted should have a minimal probability of colliding with the position that would be produced for a different key. In addition, the black box we create must ensure that a given key will always produce the same position as output. You should begin to note a similarity between some of the properties possessed by a good hashing function and a good random number generator such as that used in our simulation Case Study in Chapter 13. Indeed, list access via a hashing function is sometimes called *randomized storage,* and the first type of hashing function we discuss makes direct use of a random number generator.

Method 1: Use of a Random Number Generator. Many high-level languages, including C++, provide a random number generator to produce random sequences of real values between 0 and 1. We have already seen such a random number generator in Chapter 3. (For readable discussions of other methods of random number generation, see William H. Press, Brian P. Flannery, Saul A. Teukolsky, & William T. Vetterling, *Numerical Recipes,* Chapter 7, Cambridge, England: Cambridge University Press, 1986.) Typically, all of these methods rely on having a global seed to start the process of generating random numbers. Computations done on this seed produce the random number. At the same time, the computations alter the value of the seed so that the next time the random number generator is called, a different random number will almost surely be produced.

In typical applications of random number generation, you need merely initialize the seed to some arbitrary value to start the random sequence. Once the seed is supplied, the random sequence is completely determined. If you have access to a system function that returns the current time, day, month, and year, this can be called to initialize the seed in a fashion that ensures there is only a very small likelihood of generating the same random sequence twice.

How does all of this relate to hashing? For a hashing application, we must slightly alter the definition of our random number generator so that the seed is supplied as a value parameter. Then we supply the values of search keys as the seeds. The nature of the random number algorithm ensures that

- Each time the same key is passed to the function, the same random value will be returned.
- It is unlikely that two different keys will yield the same random value.

The random number between 0 and 1 that is correspondingly produced can then be appropriately multiplied, truncated, and shifted to produce a hash value within the range of valid positions.

Method 2: Folding. In situations where the key to be positioned is not a pure integer, some preliminary work may be required to translate it into a usable form. Take, for instance, the case of a social security number such as

387-58-1505

Viewed as one integer, this would cause overflow on many machines. By a method known as *shift folding,* this social security number can be viewed as three separate numbers to be added

```
   387
    58
+ 1505
```

producing 1950. This result could either be regarded as the hash position itself or, more likely, as a pure integer that now could be further acted on by method 1 or 4 to produce a final hash position in the desired range.

Another common folding technique is called *boundary folding*. The idea behind boundary folding is that, at the boundaries between the numbers making up the key under consideration, every other number is reversed before being added to the accumulated total. Applying this method to our social security number example, we have

```
  387
   85
+ 1505
```

yielding 1977. Clearly, the two methods do not differ by much, and a choice between them must often be made on the basis of some experimentation to determine which will produce more scattered results for a given application.

Regardless of whether shift or boundary folding is used, one of the great advantages of the folding method is its ability to transform noninteger keys into an integer suitable for further hashing action. For keys such as names that contain alphabetical characters, the type of folding just illustrated may be done by translating characters into their ASCII (or other appropriate) codes.

Method 3: Digit or Character Extraction. In certain situations, a given key value may contain specific characters that are likely to bias any hash value arising from the key. The idea in digit or character extraction is to remove such digits or characters before using the result as a final hash value or passing it on to be further transformed by another method. For instance, a company may choose to identify the various products it manufactures by using a nine-character code that always contains either A or B in the first position and either 1 or 0 in the fourth position. The rest of the characters in the code tend to occur in less predictable fashion. Character extraction removes the biased first and fourth characters, leaving a seven-character result to pass on to further processing.

Method 4: Division-Remainder Technique. All hashing presupposes a given range of positions that can be valid outputs of the hash function. In the remainder of this section, we assume the existence of a global constant `RECORD_SPACE`, which represents the upper limit of our hashing function. That is, the function should produce values between 0 and `RECORD_SPACE - 1`. It should then be evident that

```
hash(keyValue) = keyValue % RECORD_SPACE
```

is a valid hashing function for integer `keyValue`.

To begin examining criteria for choosing an appropriate `RECORD_SPACE`, let us load the keys 41, 58, 12, 92, 50, and 91 into a list with `RECORD_SPACE` = 15. Figure 17.1 shows the results. In this array, zeros are used to denote empty positions. However, if we keep `RECORD_SPACE` the same and try to load the keys 10, 20, 30, 40, 50, 60, and 70, we have many collisions, as shown in Figure 17.2. Hence, a different set of keys can cause disastrous results even though the list seemingly has plenty of room available. On the other hand, if we choose `RECORD_SPACE` to be 11, we have a list with considerably less room but no collisions. Figure 17.3 indicates the hashing positions when the same set of keys is acted on by 11 instead of by 15.

Although these examples of the ***division-remainder technique*** are far from conclusive, they suggest that choosing a prime number for `RECORD_SPACE` may produce a more desirable hashing function. The exercises at the end of this section have you explore this question more deeply. Apart from considerations of whether or not `RECORD_SPACE` should be prime, it is clear that the nature of a particular application may dictate against the choice of certain `RECORD_SPACE` values. For instance, in a situation where the rightmost digits of key values happen to follow certain recurring patterns, it is unwise to choose a power of 10 for `RECORD_SPACE`. (Why?)

Figure 17.1
Array with `RECORD_SPACE` = 15 loaded using a division-remainder hashing function

Position	Key
0	0
1	91
2	92
3	0
4	0
5	50
6	0
7	0
8	0
9	0
10	0
11	41
12	12
13	58
14	0

Figure 17.2
Array from Figure 17.1, loaded differently, with several collisions

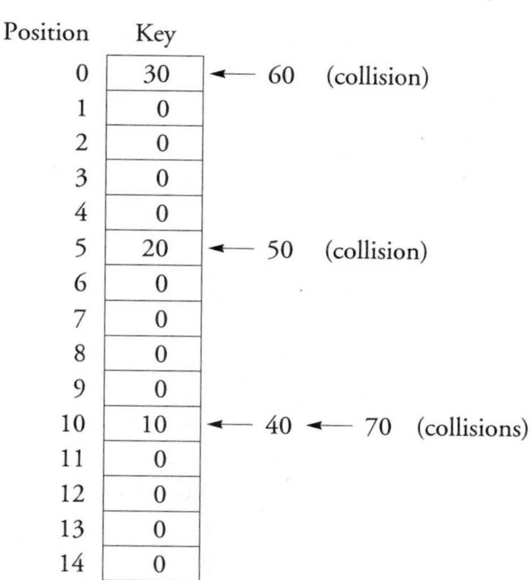

Position
Key
0 30 ← 60 (collision)
1 0
2 0
3 0
4 0
5 20 ← 50 (collision)
6 0
7 0
8 0
9 0
10 10 ← 40 ← 70 (collisions)
11 0
12 0
13 0
14 0

Figure 17.3
Array with same keys as Figure 17.2, but with `RECORD_SPACE` = 11: no collision results

Position	Key
0	0
1	0
2	0
3	0
4	70
5	60
6	50
7	40
8	30
9	20
10	10

Despite such considerations, a hashing function usually cannot rule out the possibility of collisions; it can only make them less likely. You should quickly be able to imagine a key value that will produce a collision for the hashing function used in determining the list of Figure 17.3. Notice that, as the list becomes fuller, the probability that collisions will occur increases. Hence, when using hashing as a search strategy, one must be willing to waste some positions in the list; otherwise, search efficiency will drastically deteriorate. How much space to waste is an interesting question that we will soon discuss. Further, since hashing functions generally cannot eliminate collisions, we must be prepared to handle them when they occur.

Collision Processing

The essential problem in collision processing is to develop an algorithm that will position a key in a list when the position dictated by the hashing function itself is already occupied. Ideally, this algorithm should minimize the possibility of future collisions; that is, the problem key should be located at a position that is not likely to be the hashed position of a future key.

However, the nature of hashing makes this latter criterion difficult to meet with any degree of certainty because a good hashing function does not allow prediction of where future keys are likely to be placed. We will discuss five methods of collision processing: linear, quadratic, rehashing, linked, and bucket. In all of the methods, it will be necessary to detect when a given list position is not occupied. To signify this, we use a global constant `EMPTY` to distinguish unoccupied positions. As you read, give some thought to the question of how deletions could be processed from a list accessed via one of these hashing methods. In particular, will the `EMPTY` flag suffice to denote positions that have never been occupied and positions previously occupied but now vacant? This question is explored in the exercises and in Programming Problems and Projects at the end of this chapter.

Linear Collision Processing

The linear method of resolving collisions is the simplest to implement (and unfortunately, the least efficient). *Linear collision processing* requires that, when a collision occurs, we proceed down the list in sequential order until a vacant position is found. The key causing the collision is then placed at this first vacant position. If we come to the physical end of our list in the attempt to place the problem key, we merely wrap around to the top of the list and continue looking for a vacant position. For instance, suppose we use a hashing function of

```
hash(keyValue) = keyValue % RECORD_SPACE
```

with `RECORD_SPACE` equal to 6. We then attempt to insert the keys 18, 31, 67, 36, 19, and 34. The sequence of lists in Figure 17.4 shows the results of these insertions. When a collision occurs at the third insert, it is processed by the linear method; 67 is thus loaded into position 5.

Example 17.1 Suppose an array has been loaded with data using the linear collision processing strategy illustrated in Figure 17.4. Write a C++ algorithm to seek a target key in this array.

```
// Function: linearHash
// Use linear hashing algorithm to search for target.
//
```

Figure 17.4 Insertion with linear collision processing

0	0
1	0
2	0
3	0
4	18
5	0
6	0

First insert hash(18) = 4

0	0
1	0
2	0
3	31
4	18
5	0
6	0

Second insert hash(31) = 3

0	0
1	0
2	0
3	31
4	18
5	67
6	0

Third insert hash(67) = 4

0	0
1	36
2	0
3	31
4	18
5	67
6	0

Fourth insert hash(36) = 1

0	0
1	36
2	0
3	31
4	18
5	67
6	19

Fifth insert hash(19) = 5

0	34
1	36
2	0
3	31
4	18
5	67
6	19

Sixth insert hash(34) = 6

```
// Inputs:   List of objects loaded by linear
//               hashing method.
//           target, the key of an object to be found.
// Outputs:  If key matching target is found,
//               return true and the item associated with the key;
//           otherwise return false.

bool linearHash(ListType list, KeyType target, element &item)
{
   int k = hash(target);
   int j = k;
   bool traversed = false;
   bool found = false;

   while (! list[j].empty() && ! (found || traversed))
      if (target == list[j].getKey())
      {
         item = list[j].getValue();
         found = true;
      }
      else
      {
         j = (j + 1) % RECORD_SPACE;
         traversed = (j == k);
      }
   return found;
}
```

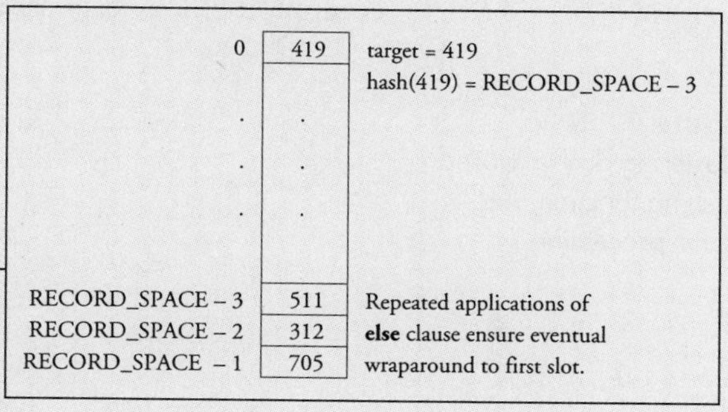

0	419	target = 419 hash(419) = RECORD_SPACE – 3
	.	
	.	
	.	
RECORD_SPACE – 3	511	Repeated applications of
RECORD_SPACE – 2	312	**else** clause ensure eventual
RECORD_SPACE – 1	705	wraparound to first slot.

Several remarks are in order concerning the function in Example 17.1. First, note that the function as it stands does not handle list processing that requires deletions to be processed. In such a situation, an additional flagging value is needed to indicate a list position that had once been occupied and is now vacant because of a deletion. Without this distinction, we do not know whether or not to exit the search loop upon encountering an empty slot. You will explore the problem of deletions from a list maintained by hashing in greater detail in the exercises and Programming Problems and Projects.

Second, note that the linear method is not without its flaws. In particular, it is prone to a problem known as *clustering*. Clustering occurs when a collision processing strategy relocates keys that have a collision at the same initial hashing position to the same region (known as a cluster) within the storage space. This usually leads to further collisions with other relocated values until everything is resolved. With linear collision processing, the clustering problem is compounded because, as one cluster expands, it can run into another cluster, immediately creating a larger cluster. This one large cluster ultimately causes collision resolutions to be drawn out longer than they would otherwise be. Hence, linear hashing is more likely to result in the clustering phenomenon pictured in Figure 17.5 than the other methods we discuss.

Efficiency Considerations for Linear Hashing. A final point to note about the linear hashing method is its search efficiency. Knuth has shown that the average number of list accesses for a successful search using the linear method is

$$(1/2)\ [1 + 1/(1 - D)]$$

where

```
D = (number of currently active records)/RECORD_SPACE
```

(See Donald E. Knuth, *The Art of Computer Programming, Vol. 3: Searching and Sorting,* Menlo Park, CA: Addison-Wesley, 1973.) An interesting fact about this search efficiency is that it is not solely dependent on the number of records in the list but rather on the density ratio of the number of records currently in the list divided by the total record space available. In other words, no matter how many records there are, a highly efficient result can be obtained if one is willing to waste enough vacant records. This is what is meant by a *density-dependent search technique.* In the case of searching for a key that cannot be found, Knuth's results indicate that the average search efficiency will be

$$(1/2)\ [1 + 1/(1 - D)^2]$$

Table 17.1 illustrates the effectiveness of linear collision resolution by showing the computed efficiencies for a few strategic values of D.

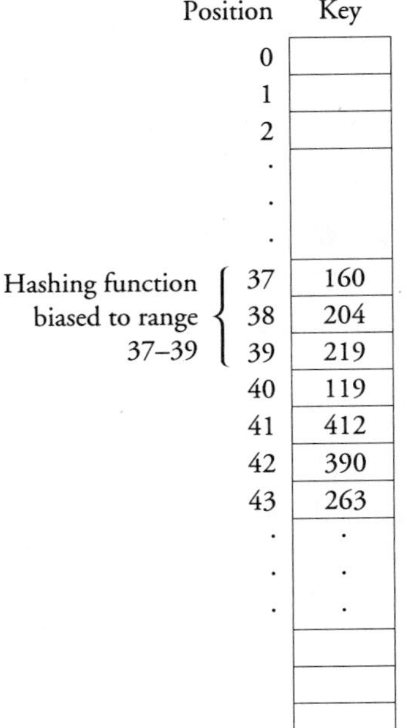

Suppose keys 160, 204, 219, 119, 412, 390, and 263 are located with

hash(160) = 37
hash(204) = 37
hash(219) = 37
hash(119) = 38
hash(412) = 38
hash(390) = 38
hash(263) = 39

If a linear method were not used, these keys would not necessarily cluster in positions 37– 43.

Figure 17.5
Clustering due to biased hashing function and linear processing

Table 17.1
Average Search Efficiency for Linear Collision Processing

D	Efficiency for Successful Search (number of accesses)	Efficiency for Unsuccessful Search (number of accesses)
0.10	1.06	1.18
0.50	1.50	2.50
0.75	2.50	8.50
0.90	5.50	50.50

Quadratic and Rehashing Methods of Collision Processing

Both the *quadratic* and *rehashing collision processing* methods attempt to correct the problem of clustering. They force the problem-causing key to immediately move a considerable distance from the initial collision. By the rehashing method, an entire sequence of hashing functions may be applied to a given key. If a collision results from the first hashing function, a second is applied, then a third, and so on until the key can be successfully placed.

The quadratic method has the advantage of not requiring numerous hashing functions for its implementation. Suppose that a key value initially hashes to position k and a collision results. Then, on its first attempt to resolve the collision, the quadratic algorithm attempts to place the key at position

$$k + 1^2$$

Then, if a second attempt is necessary to resolve the collision, position

$$k + 2^2$$

is probed. In general, the rth attempt to resolve the collision probes position

$$k + r^2$$

(with wraparound taken into account). Figure 17.6 highlights this scattering pattern. At this point, you should verify that, if the hashing function

```
hash(keyValue) = keyValue % RECORD_SPACE
```

is used with `RECORD_SPACE` equal to 7, the keys 17, 73, 32, and 80 will be located in positions 3, 4, 5, and 0, respectively.

Efficiency Considerations for the Quadratic and Rehashing Methods. Knuth's results (see *Searching and Sorting,* cited earlier in this section) demonstrate the effectiveness of the rehashing and quadratic methods versus the linear method. For the quadratic method, average search efficiencies improve to

$$1 - \log_e(1 - D) - (D/2)$$

for the successful case and

$$1/(1 - D) - D - \log_e(1 - D)$$

for an unsuccessful search, where D is density ratio as defined earlier in this section and e is the base for the natural logarithm function.

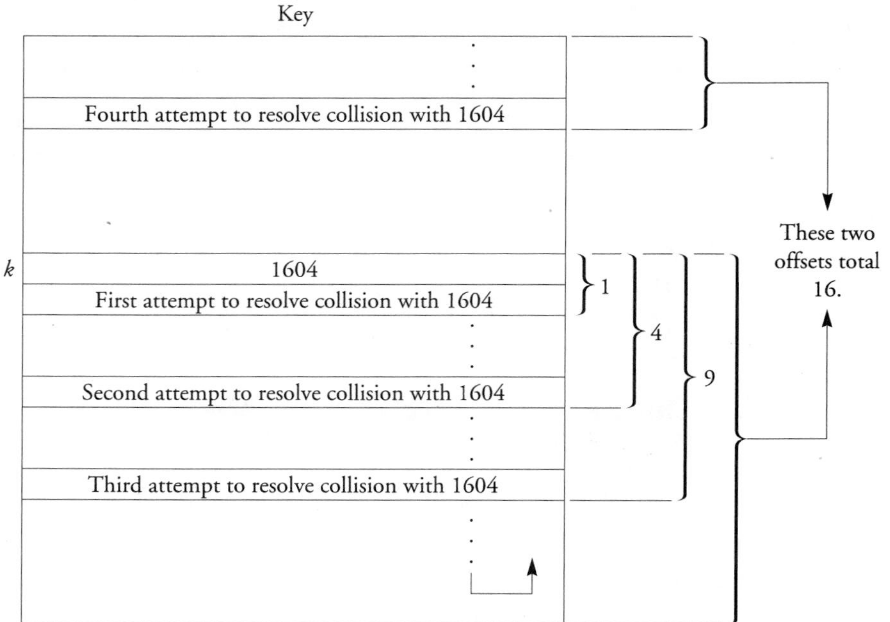

Figure 17.6 Quadratic collision processing

Rehashing with a completely random sequence of rehashing locations for each key slightly improves the efficiencies of the quadratic method to

$$-(1/D) * \log_e(1 - D)$$

for the successful case and

$$1/(1 - D)$$

for an unsuccessful search. Compare the numbers presented in Table 17.2 for quadratic collision processing and (ideal) random rehashing to those in Table 17.1 for linear collision processing.

You may have surmised that the increased efficiency of the quadratic method entails at least some drawbacks. First, the computation of a position to be probed when a collision occurs is somewhat more obscure than it was with the linear method. We leave it for you to verify that the position for the rth probe after an initial unsuccessful hash to position k is given by

```
(k + r²) % RECORD_SPACE
```

A more significant problem, however, is that the quadratic method seemingly offers no guarantee that we will try every position in the list before concluding that a given key cannot be inserted. With the linear method, as the list became relatively dense when keys and insertions were attempted, the only way that the insertion could fail is for every position in the list to be occupied. The linear nature of the search, although inefficient, ensured that every position is checked. However, with the quadratic method applied to the `RECORD_SPACE` of Figure 17.7, you can confirm that an initial hash to position 3 will lead to future probing of positions 3, 4, and 7 only; it will never check positions 0, 1, 2, 5, or 6.

A satisfactory answer to the question of what portion of a list will be probed by the quadratic algorithm was fortunately provided by Radke for values of `RECORD_SPACE` that are prime numbers which satisfy certain conditions. Radke's re-

Table 17.2
Average Search Efficiency for Quadratic and Rehashing Collision Processing

D	Efficiency for Successful Search (number of accesses)		Efficiency for Unsuccessful Search (number of accesses)	
	Quadratic	Rehashing	Quadratic	Rehashing
0.10	1.05	1.05	1.11	1.11
0.50	1.44	1.39	2.19	2.00
0.75	2.01	1.84	4.64	4.00
0.90	2.85	2.56	11.40	10.00

Figure 17.7
Quadratic probing after initial hash to 3

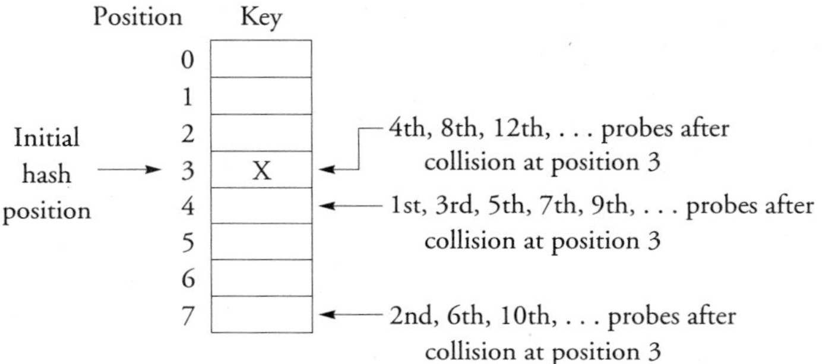

sults and their application to the quadratic algorithm are explored in the exercises at the end of the section. If you wish to read Radke's results, see C. E. Radke, "The Use of Quadratic Residue Research," *Communications of the ACM,* Vol. 13, No. 2, Feb. 1970, pp. 103–105.

Linked Method of Collision Processing

The logic of *linked collision processing* completely eliminates the possibility that one collision begets another. It requires a storage area divided into two regions: a *prime hash area* and *an overflow area*. Each record requires a link field in addition to the `key` and `otherData` fields. The global constant `RECORD_SPACE` is applicable to the prime hash area only. This storage concept is illustrated in Figure 17.8. Initially, the hashing translates function keys into the prime hashing area. If a collision occurs, the key is inserted into a linked list with its initial node in the prime area and all following nodes in the overflow area. Figure 17.9 shows how this method loads the keys 22, 31, 67, 36, 29, and 60 for `RECORD_SPACE` equal to 7 and hashing function

```
hash(keyValue) = keyValue % RECORD_SPACE
```

Example 17.2 Suppose an array has been loaded with data using the linked collision processing strategy illustrated in Figures 17.8 and 17.9. Write a C++ function to find a target key in this array.

We have made the link fields integer pointers to other array locations instead of C++ dynamic memory pointers to facilitate using the algorithm with a random access file. As written, the function assumes that all key locations in the prime area have had their corresponding key and link fields initialized to appropriate constant flags

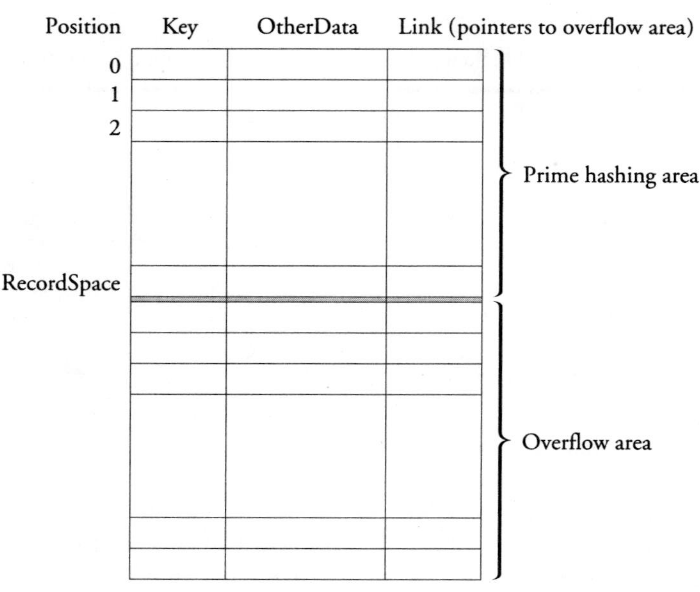

Figure 17.8
Storage allocation for linked collision processing

Figure 17.9
Loading keys with `key Value % RECORD_SPACE` and linked collision processing

Position	Key	Link
0	0	NULL
1	22	7
2	0	NULL
3	31	NULL
4	67	9
5	0	NULL
6	0	NULL
7	36	8
8	29	NULL
9	60	NULL
10	0	NULL
11	0	NULL
12	0	NULL
13	0	NULL
14	0	NULL
15	0	NULL
16	0	NULL

for `EMPTY` and `NULL`, respectively. The assumption is also made that no keys will be deleted.

```
// Function: linkedHash
// Use linked hashing algorithm to search for target.
//
// Inputs:  List of objects loaded by linked hashing method.
//          target, the value of a key to be found in list.
// Outputs: If record with key field matching target is found,
               return TRUE and object associated with target;
//          otherwise, return FALSE
```

```
bool linkedHash(ListType list, KeyType target element & item)
{
    int k = hash (target);
    bool found = false;

    do
    {
        if (target == list[k].getKey())
        {
            item = list[k].getValue();
            found = true;
        }
        else
            k = list[k].link;
    } while ((! found && (k != NULL));
    return found;
}
```

key
link
target = 419
Primary hashing area
else clause leads out of primary hashing area.
511
312
705
419
Statement k = list[k].link ; progresses along chain.

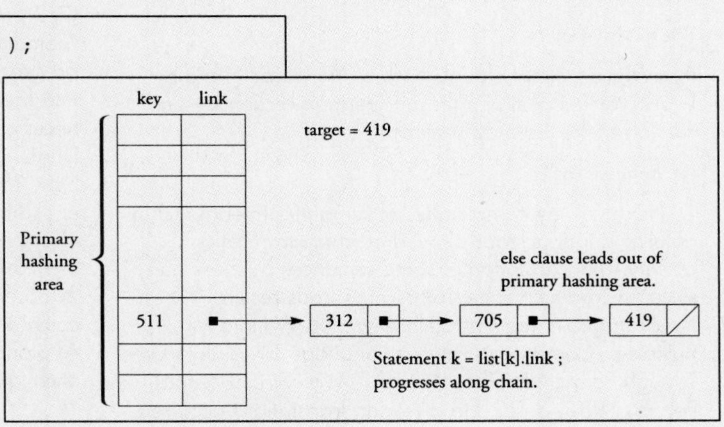

Efficiency Considerations for Linked Hashing. Knuth's efficiency results for the linked hashing method depend on a density factor *D,* which is computed using the `RECORD_SPACE` in the prime hashing area only. Hence, unlike the other hashing methods we have discussed, the linked method allows a density factor greater than 1. For example, if the `RECORD_SPACE` for the primary hash area is 200 and the overflow area contains space for 300 additional records, then 400 active records yield a density factor of 2. Given this variation, average search efficiencies for the successful and unsuccessful cases are $1 + D/2$ and *D,* respectively. Table 17.3 shows computations of this search efficiency for selected values of *D* and should be compared to the corresponding results for the linear and quadratic methods, which were presented in Tables 17.1 and 17.2, respectively.

Table 17.3
Average Search Efficiencies for the Linked Method

D	Efficiency for Successful Search (number of accesses)	Efficiency for Unsuccessful Search (number of accesses)
2	2	2
5	3.5	5
10	6	10
20	11	20

A NOTE OF INTEREST

The CYC Project: Capturing Human Knowledge in Electronic Dictionaries

When the search algorithms discussed in this chapter were first discovered, they sparked a flurry of activity in an area known as machine translation. Programs in this area attempt to translate text from one natural language to another, for example, English to German. Early attempts at machine translation tended to view the process as essentially the searching of a large dictionary. Hence, to translate the English sentence

The sun is yellow.

the program simply found each of the words in a disk-based version of an English-to-German dictionary and arrived at the German sentence

Die Sonne ist gelb.

However, the complexities of semantics (meanings) in natural language soon slowed machine translation activity. The translation of some sentences by these early systems produced some rather humorous results. According to computer folklore cited in William M. Bulkeley, "Computers Gain As Language Translators Even Though Perfect Not They Always," *Wall Street Journal,* Feb. 6, 1985, p. 25, the following translations occurred in an early English-to-Russian system:

English Phrase	Russian Translation
The spirit is willing but the flesh is weak.	The vodka is good but the meat is rotten.
Out of sight, out of mind.	Invisible maniac.

The difficulty in performing such translations is that, when humans hear a sentence such as those in the left column, they have a wealth of experiential knowledge that enables them to make the correct decisions about how to translate the sentence. This experiential knowledge was totally missing in early language processing systems and, in large part, is still missing today.

However, researchers now realize what the problem is and are taking steps to correct it. Foremost among these researchers is Douglas Lenat, founder of Cycorp. Lenat's CYC project is an attempt to construct a database of "common sense" knowledge in such a way that other programs, such as machine translation systems, can interface with it to gain the deeper understanding necessary to function as intelligent agents. The article by Daniel Lyons, "Artificial Intelligence Gets Real," in *Forbes,* Nov. 1998, summarizes Lenat's project as requiring the encoding of millions of common sense rules into an electronic data retrieval system. Lenat started the project in 1984 and figures that it won't be completed until 2035. When it is, however, we may well have what Lenat calls "a generally intelligent artifact" and what Stanford AI pioneer Edward Feigenbaum calls "The big enchilada."

Bucket Hashing

In the bucket hashing strategy of collision processing, the hashing function transforms a given key to a physically contiguous region of locations within the list to be searched. This contiguous region is called a *bucket.* Thus, instead of hashing to the *k*th location, a key hashes to the *k*th bucket of locations. The number of locations contained in this bucket depends on the bucket size. (We assume that all buckets in a given list are the same size.) Figure 17.10 illustrates this concept for a list with seven buckets and a bucket size of 3. Having hashed to a bucket, the target must then be compared in sequential order to all of the keys in that bucket. On the surface, it seems that this strategy could do no better than duplicate the efficiency of the linked hash method discussed earlier. Indeed, because a sequential search is conducted in both cases after the initial hash is made, the average number of list accesses for a successful or unsuccessful search cannot be improved by using buckets. Moreover, provisions for linking to some sort of overflow area must still be made in case a series of collisions consumes all of the space in a given bucket.

What then could be a possible advantage of using buckets? If the list to be searched resides entirely in main memory, there is no advantage. However, if the list

Figure 17.10
Storage allocation for bucket hashing

	Position	Key
	0	
Bucket #1	1	
	2	
	3	
Bucket #2	4	
	5	
	6	
Bucket #3	7	
	8	
	9	
Bucket #4	10	
	11	
	12	
Bucket #5	13	
	14	
	15	
Bucket #6	16	
	17	
	18	
Bucket #7	19	
	20	

resides in a disk file, the bucket method will allow us to take advantage of some of the physical characteristics of the storage medium itself. To see this, we must realize that a one-surface disk is divided into concentric *tracks* and pie-shaped *sectors* as indicated in Figure 17.11.

There are two ways in which the bucket hashing strategy may take advantage of the organization of the data on a disk. First, when records in a contiguous random access file are stored on a disk, they are generally located in relative record number order along one track, then along an adjacent track, and so on. The movement of the read/write head between tracks is generally the cause of the most significant delays in obtaining data from a disk. The farther the movement, the greater the delay. Hence, if our knowledge of the machine in question allows us to make a bucket coincide with a track on the disk, then hashing to the beginning of a bucket and proceeding from there using a sequential search within the bucket (that is, the track) will greatly reduce head movement. A linked hashing strategy, on the other hand, could cause considerable movement of the read/write head between tracks on the disk, thereby slowing program execution. This consideration is an excellent example of how one must examine more than just the number of list accesses when measuring the efficiency of a program involving disk files.

A second advantage of the bucket hashing algorithm when disk files are being searched is related to the way in which records are transferred between the disk and main memory. Frequently, programming languages create the illusion that each record accessed requires a separate disk access. However, records are frequently blocked (that is, positioned in contiguous regions on a track of the disk) so that a fixed number of them are brought into main memory when a record in that block is requested. Thus, if the record requested happens to be part of the block presently in main memory, a program statement that requests a record may not even require a disk access but only a different viewing window applied to the block already in main memory. Because main memory manipulations are orders of magnitude faster than the rate of data transfer to and from a disk, positioning our buckets to coincide with a disk block

Figure 17.11
One-surface disk

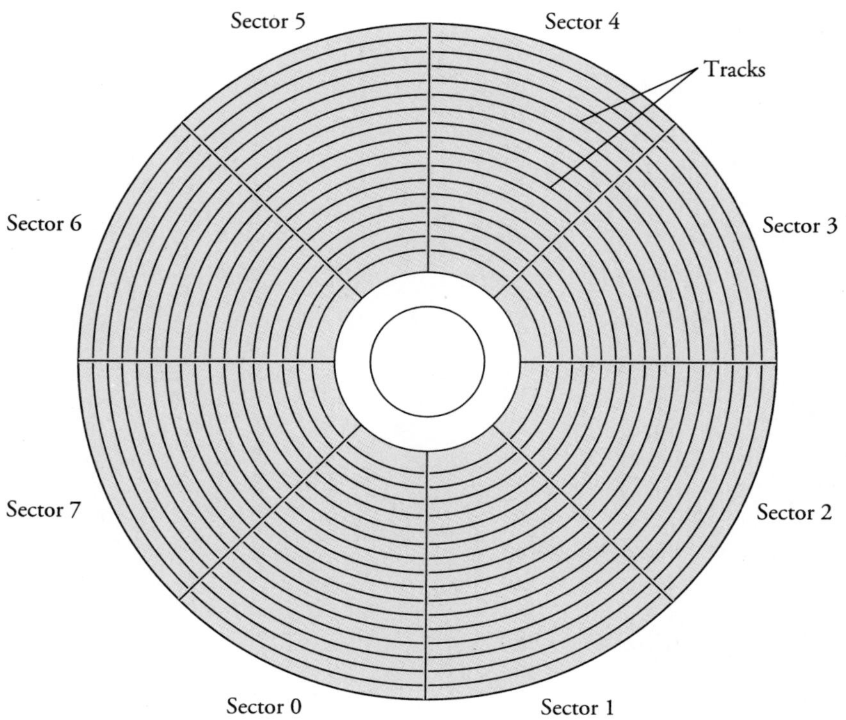

will necessitate only one disk access each time an entire bucket is sequentially searched. Here again, the more scattered nature of a purely linked hashing algorithm does not allow this disk-oriented efficiency consideration to be taken into account.

Exercises 17.1

1. Assume a hashing function has the following characteristics:

   Keys 459 and 333 hash to 0.
   Key 632 hashes to 1.
   Key 1090 hashes to 2.
   Keys 1982, 379, 238, and 3411 hash to 9.

   Assume that insertions into a hashed file are performed in the order 1982, 3411, 333, 632, 1090, 459, 379, and 238.

   a. Indicate the position of the keys if the linear method is used to resolve collisions.

Record No.	Key
0	
1	
2	
3	
4	
5	
6	
7	
8	
9	
10	

b. Indicate the position of the keys if the quadratic method is used to resolve collisions.

Record No.	Key
0	
1	
2	
3	
4	
5	
6	
7	
8	
9	
10	

c. Indicate the position of the keys and the contents of the link fields if the chaining (that is, linked) method is used to resolve collisions. Use zeros to represent NULL links and assume that the first record used in the overflow area is 11, then 12, then 13, and so on.

Record No.	Key	Link
0		
1		
2		
3		
4		
5		
6		
7		
8		
9		
10		

Prime Area

Record No.	Key	Link
11		
12		
13		
14		
15		
16		
17		
18		
19		
20		
21		

Overflow Area

2. Repeat Exercise 1 with the order of insertion of keys reversed.

3. Write functions to insert a key into a list to be searched by
   a. linear hashing
   b. quadratic hashing
   c. linked hashing
   d. bucket hashing

4. Write functions to search for a key via
   a. quadratic hashing
   b. bucket hashing

5. Devise strategies to delete keys from a list maintained by each of the four hashing strategies in Exercise 3. Write C++ versions for each of these algorithms. Given your deletion strategy, describe in detail the modifications (if any) that must be made in the various search and insertion functions of Exercises 3 and 4.

6. In Section 17.1, we mentioned a result by Radke that answered the question of how many array slots would be probed by the quadratic hashing algorithm for certain values of `RECORD_SPACE`. In particular, Radke showed that if `RECORD_SPACE` is a prime number of the form $4m + 3$ for some integer m, then half of the array slots would be probed by the sequence of probes

$k, k + 1^2, k + 2^2, k + 3^2, \ldots$

where k is the original hash position. Radke also showed that the other half would be probed by the sequence

$k - 1^2, k - 2^2, k - 3^2, \ldots$

Rewrite your insertion and search functions for the quadratic method in Exercises 4 and 5 to take into account Radke's result.

7. a. Given the arrival of integer keys in the order 67, 19, 4, 58, 38, 55, 86 and `RECORD_SPACE` = 9 with

```
hash(keyValue) = keyValue % RECORD_SPACE
```

trace the insertion steps of linearly processing collisions.

Index	keyValue
0	0
1	0
2	0
3	0
4	0
5	0
6	0
7	0
8	0

(0 indicates empty position)

b. Given the arrival of integer keys in the order 32, 62, 34, 77, 6, 46, 107 and `RECORD_SPACE` = 15 with

```
hash(keyValue) = keyValue % RECORD_SPACE
```

trace the insertion steps of quadratically processing collisions.

Index	keyValue
0	0
1	0
2	0
3	0
4	0
5	0
6	0
7	0
8	0
9	0
10	0
11	0
12	0
13	0
14	0

(0 indicates empty position)

c. Given the arrival of integer keys in the order 5, 3, 16, 27, 14, 25, 4 and `RECORD_SPACE` = 11 with initial hashing function

```
hash1(keyValue) = keyValue % RECORD_SPACE
```

trace the insertion steps of the rehashing collision processing method where the secondary hashing function is

```
hash2(keyValue) = 5 * keyValue % RECORD_SPACE
```

Assume that if the secondary hashing function is not successful in locating a position for the key, then linear collision processing is used from the address indicated by the secondary hashing function.

Index	keyValue
0	0
1	0
2	0
3	0
4	0
5	0
6	0
7	0
8	0
9	0
10	0

(0 indicates empty position)

Comment on the effectiveness of rehashing with this particular secondary hashing function. Can you think of a better one? Explain why yours is better.

8. In a written statement, explain how hashing could be used to search for keys that were not unique. For instance, you might have several people identified by the same name.

17.2 Two Abstract Data Types Revisited

Objectives

a. to discuss how hashing can be used to implement the one-key table ADT
b. to evaluate the efficiency of hashing as an implementation strategy for the one-key table ADT
c. to discuss how hashing can be used to implement the two-key table ADT

We can analyze hashing from a pragmatic perspective by considering how it might be used to implement two ADTs introduced in Chapter 11: the one-key table and the two-key table. You will then be asked to carry out these implementations in the exercises and in Programming Problems and Projects at the end of the chapter.

The One-Key Table ADT Implemented by Hashing

In this context, hashing emerges as yet another list maintenance strategy to be evaluated and compared to the strategies we have already discussed: array with binary search, linked list, and binary tree. Hence, we must examine its performance with respect to the same `insert`, `retrieve`, `remove`, and `traverse` operations that were introduced in Chapter 11 and then used to evaluate these other one-key table implementation techniques. Additionally, should an application want to extend the one-key table to allow an operation that traverses the table in ascending order by key, we will consider the efficiency of this operation when hashing is used as an implementation strategy. Assuming the existence of an appropriate hashing function to act on the key and a willingness to waste enough storage to allow for fast searching, hashing will clearly perform very well in all of these areas with the exception of ordering data. Here is where we have to pay a price for the scattered storage of records that are located via a hashing function.

Nonetheless, there are strategies that can be used to allow hashing and ordering of data to coexist. One such strategy is simply to use a pointer sort algorithm (see Chapter 10) to sort the data logically when an ordered list is needed. This strategy has the drawback of not maintaining the list in order but actually performing a potentially costly sort algorithm each time an ordering is requested. Clearly, this strategy is not wise if such an ordering is requested frequently and unpredictably.

In situations where requests for ordering come frequently enough to make maintaining the list in order (as opposed to sorting) a necessity, we could follow a strategy that combines the search speed of hashing with the ordered list advantages offered by a linked list implementation. This combination uses hashing to search for an individual record but adds link fields to each record so that a linked list for each desired ordering could be woven through the collection of hashed records. Implementing this combination of hashing and linked lists entails the following considerations with respect to the one-key table operations:

`insert`: In effect, the hashing/collision processing algorithm provides us with an available node to store data. Each linked list involved then has to be traversed to link the node into each ordering in the appropriate logical location.

`retrieve`: There is no problem here because the hash algorithm should find the desired record quickly.

`remove`: This is similar to the `retrieve` operation. Use hashing to find the record to be deleted and then adjust the link field appropriately. A doubly linked list could prove to be particularly valuable here. (Why?)

`traverseInOrder`: There is no problem here because the linked lists constantly maintain the appropriate orderings.

The Two-Key Table ADT Implemented by Hashing

We have already covered two implementation strategies for two-key tables.

1. In Section 11.4, we described a strategy that simply creates a list of the rows and columns corresponding to nontrivial values in the table. Thus, determining the value of the data at a conceptual row/column location is simply a matter of searching this list.
2. Using linked lists (Chapter 12), we could form a linked list of the nontrivial columns in each row. Here, determining the value of the data at a conceptual row/column location is reduced to the problem of sequentially searching a relatively small linked list.

At the time we explored these two strategies, the first one appeared less attractive. Because the data in the list of row/column coordinates corresponding to nontrivial values are likely to be volatile, physically ordering the data for a binary search would not be practical. Yet, without a binary search, requests to inspect the value at any given location are met with the $O(n)$ response time of a sequential search. Hashing allows us to search for a row/column coordinate in the list of the first strategy in a very efficient fashion, probably faster than the sequential search along the linked list representing a given row required by the second strategy. Moreover, since the order of the data in the list is not important for this application, the scattered nature of hashed storage does not present any obstacle at all.

The considerations we have discussed with respect to these two ADTs make it evident that hashing is a very attractive table implementation technique. It will be extremely efficient in regard to the `insert`, `retrieve`, and `remove` table operations if we are willing to pay the price of wasting enough storage to get a reasonably low density ratio. The only other drawback to hashing, in addition to this wasted storage, is the price that must be paid if various orderings of the data are frequently needed.

Exercises 17.2

1. Suppose we combine hashing with a linked list in the fashion described in this section so that all one-key table operations can be efficiently performed. Which of the variations on a linked list structure would be most effective in this context? Explain why in a carefully worded statement. (*Hint:* Think about the `retrieve` and `remove` operations.)
2. Give an example of an application where the hashing implementation of a two-key table described in this section would be less efficient (overall) than the linked list implementation. Explain why in a carefully worded statement.
3. Provide implementations of all one-key table operations using the hashing strategy described in this section. Provide alternative implementations of the traverse operations: One should invoke a pointer sort and another should combine hashing with a linked list.
4. Provide implementations of all two-key table operations defined in Chapter 11 using the hashing strategy described in this section.
5. We have covered binary search, linked lists, binary trees, and hashing as methods of implementing a one-key table ADT. Choose the method you would use to implement the data list involved for each of the following three real-world applications. In each case, you should choose the most appropriate implementation technique. "Most appropriate" refers here to efficient handling of all the required operations while not being too powerful, that is, not doing something that should be easy in an overly complicated way. Then provide a written rationale as to why yours would be the appropriate method.
   a. The list to be maintained is the card catalog of a library. Frequent additions to and deletions from this catalog are made by the library. Additionally, users are frequently searching for the data associated with a given book's key. However, the library rarely prints out an ordered list of all its holdings. Hence, ordering the list is not a high priority.
   b. You are writing a program that maintains the lists of passengers on flights for an airline company. Passengers are frequently added to these lists. Moreover, quite often passengers cancel flight plans and must be removed from a list. You are also told that the airline frequently wants alphabetized listings of the passengers on a given flight and often needs to search for a particular passenger by name when inquiries are received from individuals.
   c. You are writing a program to access a large customer database and build up counts for the numbers of customers from each of the 50 states plus the District of Columbia. To do this, you will use a list of records consisting of the two-character state abbreviation and an integer representing the count of customers from that state. For each customer you read in from the database, you must find the customer's home state in your list and increase the corresponding count field. At the end, print out the counts in order alphabetized by the two-character state abbreviation.

17.3 Indexed Search Techniques (Optional)

Objectives

a. to understand the differences between searching in main memory and in random access disk storage
b. to understand how an index may be used to advantage when searching for data in a random access file
c. to study how the indexed sequential search methodology is implemented
d. to discuss the efficiency of the indexed sequential search strategy
e. to understand how the B-tree data structure may be used to implement an index for a random access file
f. to discuss the efficiency of B-trees
g. to understand how the trie data structure may be used to implement an index for a random access file keyed by strings of variable length
h. to discuss the efficiency of tries

All of the search strategies we have studied up to this point could be applied to lists implemented in main memory or on a random access disk. However, with the exception of bucket hashing, none of the methods we have studied takes into account the physical characteristics of disk storage in an attempt to enhance their efficiency. In practice, because retrieval of data from a disk file is orders of magnitude slower than retrieval from main memory, we often cannot afford to ignore these special characteristics of disk files if we want reasonable response time for our searching efforts. The indexing schemes that we are about to discuss in this section are primarily directed toward file-oriented applications and thus will take into account the operational properties of this storage medium. We encourage you to reread the discussion of bucket hashing at the end of Section 17.1 for a summary analysis of file storage considerations.

The idea behind the use of an index is analogous to the way in which we routinely use an address book to find a person whom we are seeking. That is, if we are looking for a person, we do not knock on the doors of numerous houses until we find the one where that person lives. Instead, we apply a search strategy to an address book. There we use the name of the person as a key to find a pointer—that is, an address—to lead us swiftly to where the person can be found. Only one actual "house access" must be made, although our search strategy may require numerous accesses into the address book index.

In a computer system, records (or more precisely, blocks) could play the role of houses in the search scenario just described. When compared to main memory, data records on disk are terribly slow and awkward creatures to access. One of the reasons is that there is often so much data that must be moved from disk to main memory every time a record is accessed. Because of this, the conceptual picture for the general setup of an indexed search must be revised. The list of keys is no longer parallel to the actual data with which they are logically associated; rather, it is parallel to a list of pointers, which will lead us to the actual data. The revised picture is presented in Figure 17.12.

The general strategy of an indexed search is to use the key to search the index efficiently, find the relative record position of the associated data, and from there make only one access into the actual data. Because the parallel lists of keys and relative record positions require much less storage than the data, the entire index frequently can be loaded and permanently held in main memory, necessitating only one disk access for each record being sought. For larger indices, it still remains true that large blocks of keys and associated pointers may be manipulated in main memory, thereby greatly enhancing search efficiency.

Indexed Sequential Search Technique

The *indexed sequential search* technique is also commonly recognized by the acronym ISAM, which stands for *indexed sequential access method*. Essentially, it involves carefully weighing the disk-dependent factors of blocking and track size to build a partial index. The partial index, unlike some other index structures we will study, does not reduce to one the number of probes that must be made into the actual data.

To continue the analogy between searching for data and searching for a person, the indexed sequential strategy resembles an address book that leads us to the street on which a person lives but makes us check each house on that street. The ISAM method correspondingly leads us to an appropriate region (often a track or a cylinder

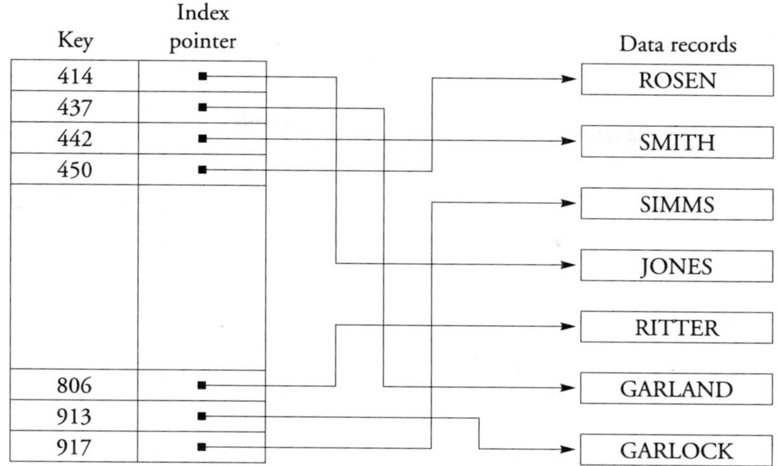

Figure 17.12
General setup for an indexed search

containing multiple tracks within a disk pack) and then leaves it to us to search sequentially within that region.

As an example, let us suppose that we can conveniently fit the partial index, or directory, pictured in Figure 17.13 into main memory and that the organization of our disk file allows six records per track. This directory is formed by choosing the highest key value in each six-record track along with a pointer indicating where that track begins. Here our pointers are simply relative record numbers; in practice, they could be a more disk-dependent locator. The strategy to conduct an indexed sequential search is:

1. Search the main memory directory for a key that is greater than or equal to the target.
2. Then follow the corresponding pointer out to the disk and there search sequentially until we find a match (success) or the key that the directory maintains as the high key within that particular region (failure).

For the data in Figure 17.13, this technique means that the 36-record file requires no more than six main memory index accesses plus six disk accesses, all of which are located in the same track.

For larger files, it may be advantageous to have more than one level of these directory structures. Consider, for instance, the two-level directory structure for a file with 216 records given in Figure 17.14. Here we might suppose that storage restrictions allow the entire primary directory to be kept in main memory, the secondary directory to be brought in from a disk file in blocks of six key-pointer pairs each, and the actual data records to be stored six per track. The primary directory divides the file into regions of 36 records each. The key in the primary directory represents the highest valued key in a given 36-record region, but the pointer leads us into the subdirectory instead of the actual file. So we search the primary directory for a key greater than or equal to the target we are seeking. Once this is done, we follow the primary directory pointer into the secondary directory. Beginning at the position indicated by the primary directory's pointer, we again search for a key greater than or equal to the target. Notice that fetching one block of six key-pointer pairs from the subdirectory has necessitated one disk access in our hypothetical situation. In return for this single disk access, we are able to subdivide the 36-record region determined by the primary directory into six 6-record regions, each of which will lie entirely on one track by the time we get out to the actual disk file. Following the subdirectory's pointer to the file,

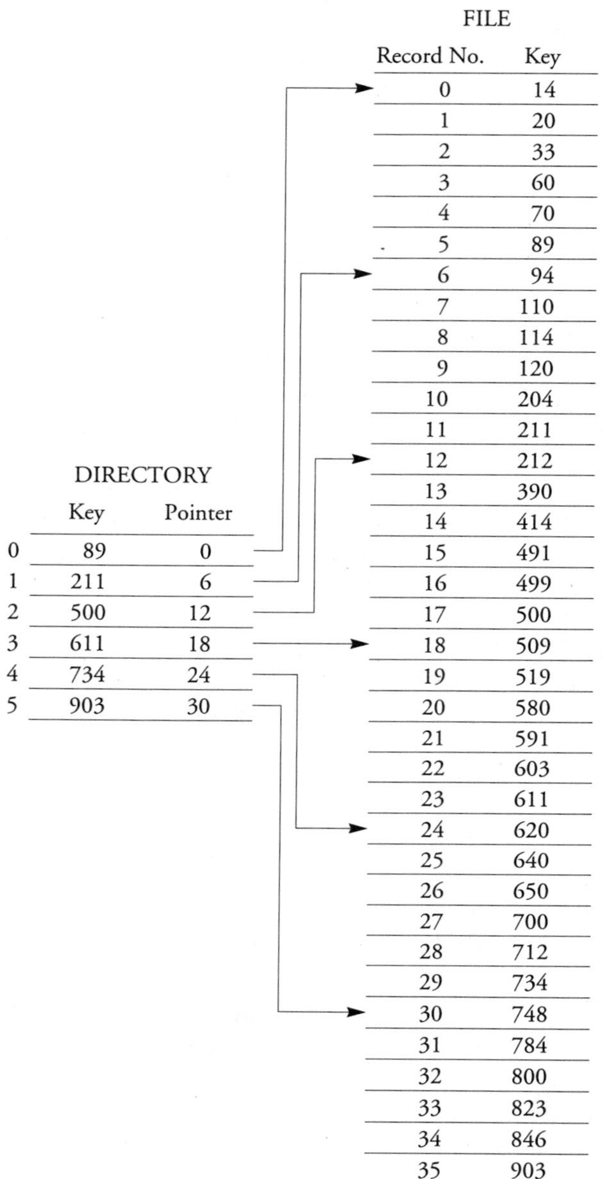

DIRECTORY

	Key	Pointer
0	89	0
1	211	6
2	500	12
3	611	18
4	734	24
5	903	30

FILE

Record No.	Key
0	14
1	20
2	33
3	60
4	70
5	89
6	94
7	110
8	114
9	120
10	204
11	211
12	212
13	390
14	414
15	491
16	499
17	500
18	509
19	519
20	580
21	591
22	603
23	611
24	620
25	640
26	650
27	700
28	712
29	734
30	748
31	784
32	800
33	823
34	846
35	903

Figure 17.13 One-level indexed sequential file

we end up with a relatively short sequential search on the storage medium itself. In this example, the maximum number of disk accesses required to find any record is seven, six of which are isolated on one track of the disk.

Efficiency Considerations for the Indexed Sequential Search. It should be clear from the preceding discussion that the search efficiency of the indexed sequential technique depends on a variety of factors. Included among them are:

- To what degree the directory structures are able to subdivide the actual file
- To what degree the directory structures are able to reside in main memory
- The relationship of data records to physical characteristics of the disk such as blocking factors, track size, cylinder size, and so on

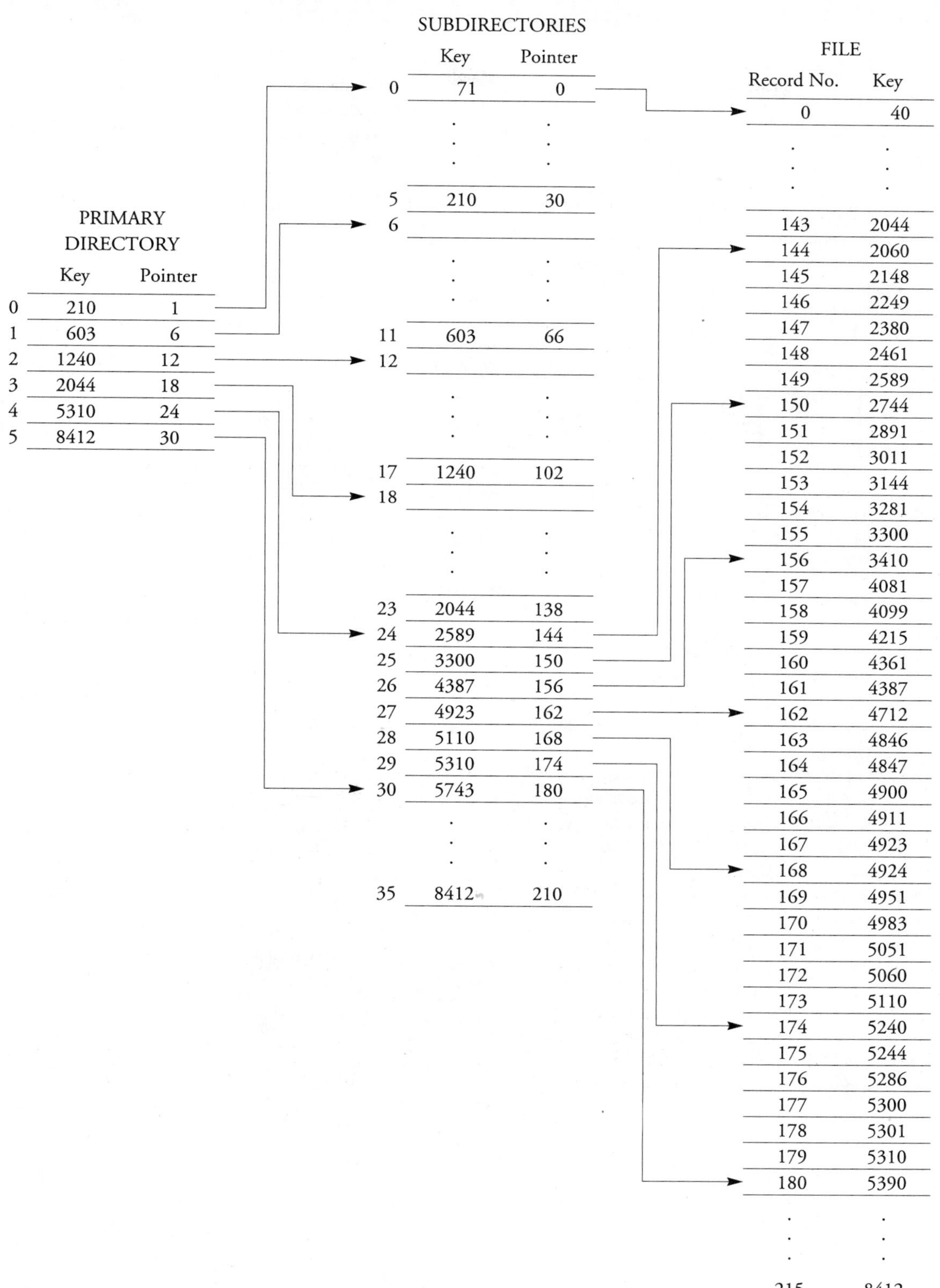

Figure 17.14 Two-level directory structure

A NOTE OF INTEREST

Data Integrity, Concurrent Updates, and Deadlock

The problems of finding and allowing a user to access a particular record in a file are complicated somewhat in a system that allows several users to access that file simultaneously. To see why, it is important to recall that when you actually manipulate a record or part of an index from a file, you really have a copy of that portion of the file in your main memory area. Now suppose two users are not only accessing the same file simultaneously but also the same record in that file simultaneously. A scenario such as the following could emerge:

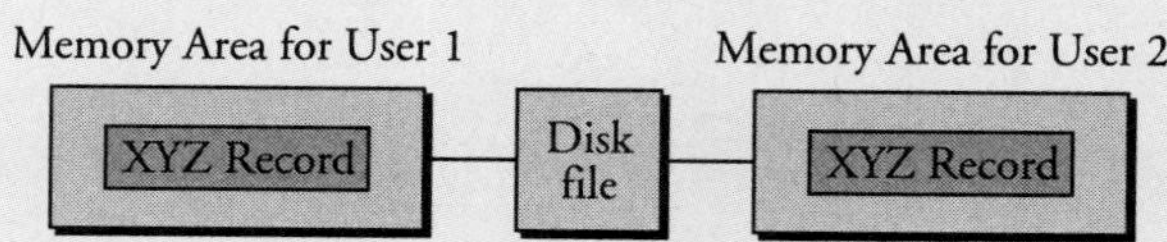

User 1 requests record associated with key XYZ.
User 2 requests record associated with key XYZ.
User 1 updates address field of that record.
User 2 updates inventory field of that record.
User 1 makes change in the file by writing that record to disk.
User 2 makes changes in the file by writing that record to disk.

What will be wrong with the new record that exists in the disk file? Clearly, the address change made by User 1 will have been destroyed when User 2's copy of the record is written back to the disk. We have what is known as a *data integrity* problem caused by the *concurrent updating* of the same record by two users. The situation can become much worse than merely losing an address change. Imagine the havoc created if one of the users deleted the record while the other was processing it or if the portion of the file being simultaneously updated by two users was not a data record but instead part of the file index.

The concurrent update problem must be avoided in any multiuser system if data integrity is to be ensured. The solution used in many systems is that of a *record lock facility.* With such a facility, the user who has a file record in main memory for updating is considered the owner of that record to the exclusion of any other users accessing that record. That lock on the record exists until the user writes the (perhaps altered) record back to the disk file. Hence, in our scenario, User 2 would not have been able to obtain the record for key XYZ immediately. Instead, that user would sit idle in a wait state until the record became available.

Although the record-locking approach guarantees data integrity, it is not without its own set of problems. For instance, consider the following scenario:

User 1 requests and gets record for key XYZ.
User 2 requests and gets record for key ABC.
To process record XYZ, User 1 needs data associated with record ABC.
Because record is owned by User 2, User 1 must wait in idle state.
To process record ABC, User 2 needs data associated with record XYZ.
Because record is owned by User 1, User 2 must wait in idle state.

Although data integrity has been maintained, we now have two users in an infinite wait state known as a *deadlock* or, more glamorously, *fatal embrace*. The avoidance and/or detection of deadlock situations in a multiuser environment is a nontrivial problem. If you are interested in exploring it more deeply, see Harvey M. Deitel, *An Introduction to Operating Systems*, 2nd ed., Reading, MA: Addison-Wesley, 1990.

Two Users in a Deadlock Situation

It should also be clear that the indexed sequential method may not be ideal for a highly volatile file. This is because, as implicitly indicated in Figures 17.13 and 17.14, the actual data records must be physically stored in increasing (or decreasing) key order. The requirement for physical ordering is obviously not conducive to frequent insertions and deletions. In practice, the solution to this problem is that each file subregion, which is ultimately the subject of a sequential search, is equipped with a pointer to an overflow area. Insertions are located in this overflow area and linked to the main sequential search area. As the overflow area builds up, the search efficiency tends to deteriorate. In some applications, this deterioration can be so severe that data processing personnel have been known to refer to ISAM as the "intrinsically slow access method."

The way to avoid deterioration is to reorganize the file periodically into a new file with no overflow. However, such reorganization cannot be done dynamically. It requires going through the file in key sequential order and copying it into a new one. Along the way, the indices must be rebuilt, of course. These types of maintenance problems involved with the ISAM structure have led to the development of several more dynamic indexing schemes.

Binary Search Tree Indexing

The concept of a binary search tree was covered in Chapter 15. The only twist added when the binary tree plays the role of an index is that each node of the tree contains a key and a pointer to the record associated with that key in some larger data aggregate. The advantages of using a binary search tree as an index structure include:

- A search efficiency potentially proportional to $\log_2 n$
- The ability to traverse the list indexed by the tree in key order
- Dynamic insertion and deletion capabilities

These qualities make the binary search tree the ideal index structure for situations in which the entire tree can fit in main memory. However, if the data collection is so large that the tree index must itself be stored on disk, the efficiency of the structure is less than optimal. This is because each node of the index may lie in a disk block separate from the other nodes and hence require a separate disk access. Using an example of 50,000 keys, a search of a binary tree index could require 16 disk accesses. To solve this problem, we would like to cluster those nodes along a given search path into one, or at least relatively few, disk blocks. The B-tree index structure is a variation on the tree index that accomplishes this goal.

B-Tree Indexing

We begin this discussion of *B-trees* by reminding you that one index entry requires nothing more than a key and a pointer. Moreover, we have assumed that both the key and the pointer are integers, and we continue to operate under this assumption during our discussion of B-trees. We emphasize this point here because, in a B-tree, a given tree node will in fact contain many such key–pointer pairs. This is because a given B-tree node will in fact coincide with one disk block. The idea behind a B-tree is that we will somehow group key–pointer pairs that are related in the search algorithm into a few strategic B-tree nodes, that is, disk blocks. At this point, we make a formal definition; later, we'll clarify this definition with some examples.

B-tree of order *n*: A B-tree of order n is a structure with the following properties:

1. Every node in the B-tree has sufficient room to store $n - 1$ key–pointer pairs.
2. Additionally, every node has room for n pointers to other nodes in the B-tree (as distinguished from the pointers within key–pointer pairs, which point to the position of a key in the file).
3. Every node except the root must have at least $(n - 1)/2$ key–pointer pairs stored in it.
4. All terminal nodes are on the same level.
5. If a nonterminal node has m key–pointer pairs stored in it, then it must contain $m + 1$ non-null pointers to other B-tree nodes.
6. For each B-tree node, we require that the key value in key–pointer pair KP_{i-1} be less than the key value in key–pointer pair KP_i, that all key–pointer pairs in the node pointed to by P_{i-1} contain keys that are less than the key in KP_i, and that all key–pointer pairs in the node pointed to by P_i contain key values that are greater than the key in KP_i.

According to property 5 of the definition, we can think of a B-tree node as a list

$$P_0, KP_1, P_1, KP_2, P_2, KP_3, \ldots, P_{m-1}, KP_m, P_m$$

where P_i represents the ith pointer to another B-tree node and KP_i represents the ith key–pointer pair. Note that a B-tree node will always contain one more pointer to another B-tree node than it does key–pointer pairs. With this picture in mind, the sixth and final property of our definition makes sense. Figure 17.15 illustrates how this rather involved definition applies to a B-tree node with three key–pointer pairs.

As a further illustration of this definition, a complete B-tree of order 6 serving as an index structure for the 36-record file of Figure 17.13 appears in Figure 17.16. (In this figure, the slash between numbers denotes a key–pointer pair; ⊦ denotes a null pointer.) Carefully verify that all six defining properties are satisfied.

Order 6 was chosen for Figure 17.16 only for the purpose of fitting the figure on a book page. In practice, the order chosen is the maximum number of B-tree pointers and key–pointer pairs that fit into one disk block. That is, the choice should be made to force a disk block to coincide with a B-tree node. It is also worth noting that B-trees of order 3 have special application as a data structure apart from indexing considerations. This application is covered in Programming Problems and Projects at the end of the chapter.

Figure 17.15 Example of a B-tree node with three key–pointer pairs

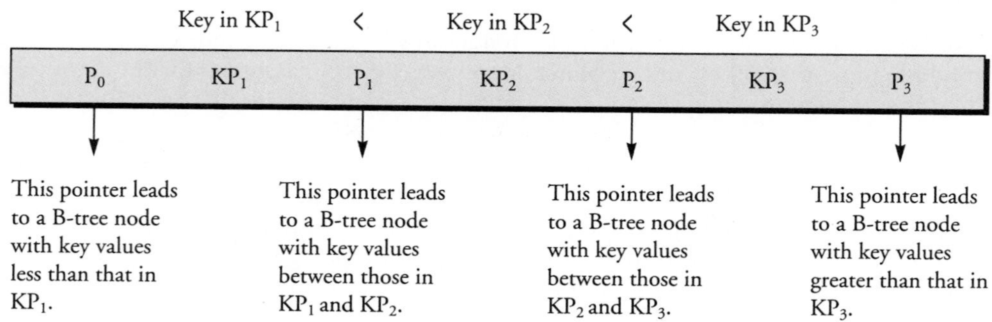

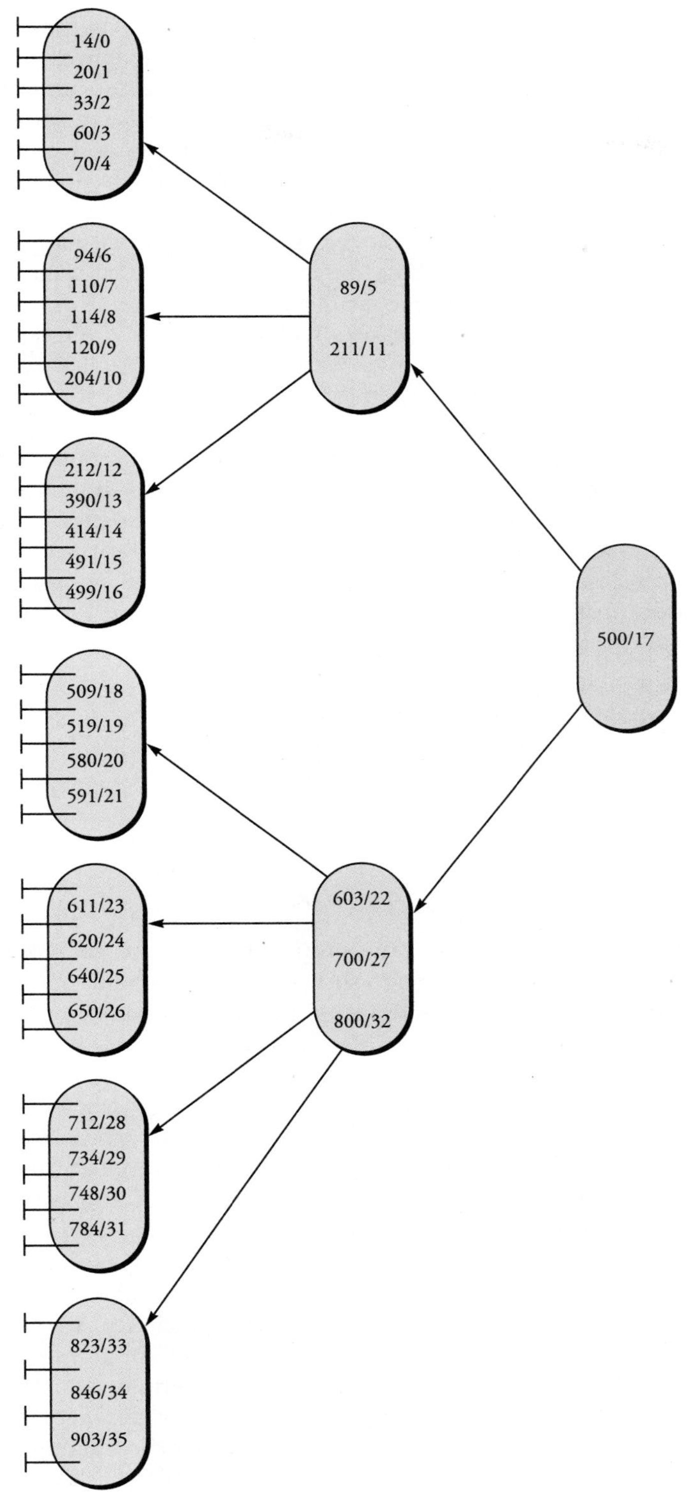

Figure 17.16
B-tree index of order 6 for file in Figure 17.13

Efficiency Considerations for B-Tree Indexing. Let us now consider what is involved in searching a B-tree for a given key. Within the current node (starting at the root), we must search sequentially through the key values in the node until we come to a match, a key value that is greater than the one being sought, or the end of the key values in that particular node. If a match is not made within a particular B-tree node, we have a pointer to follow to an appropriate follow-up node. Again, you should verify this algorithm for several of the keys appearing at various levels of Figure 17.16. The sequential search on keys within a given node may at first seem unappealing. However, the important fact to remember here is that each B-tree node is a disk block that is loaded entirely into main memory. Hence, it may be possible to search sequentially on hundreds of keys within a node in the time it takes to load one new node from disk. Our main concern is to minimize disk accesses, and here we have achieved a worst case search for our 36-entry file in three disk accesses.

What in general is the search efficiency for a B-tree index? It should be clear from the nature of the structure that the maximum number of disk accesses for any particular key will simply be the number of levels in the tree. So the efficiency question really amounts to knowing the maximum number of levels that the six defining criteria allow for a B-tree containing n key–pointer pairs. That is, this number is the worst case search efficiency, and to determine it, we use the minimum number of nodes that must be present on any given level. Let l be the smallest integer greater than or equal to $k/2$, where k is the order of the B-tree in question. Then

Level 0 contains at least 1 node.
Level 1 contains at least 2 nodes.
Level 2 contains at least $2l$ nodes.
Level 3 contains at least $2l^2$ nodes.

.
.
.

Level m contains at least $2l^{m-1}$ nodes.

An argument based on Knuth's research (see *Searching and Sorting,* cited in Section 17.1) uses this progression to show that the maximum number of levels (and thus the worst case search efficiency) for n key–pointer pairs is

$$\log_k[(n + 1)/2]$$

Thus, a B-tree search has an $O(\log_k n)$ efficiency where n is the number of records and k is the order of the B-tree. Note that this can be considerably better than an $O(\log_2 n)$ search efficiency. As an example, the index for a file of 50,000 records, which requires on the order of 16 disk accesses using a binary tree structure, can be searched with 3 disk accesses using a B-tree of order 250. Note that, given typical block sizes for files, the choice of order 250 for this example is not at all unrealistic.

Unlike ISAM, the B-tree index can dynamically handle insertions and deletions without a resulting deterioration in search efficiency. We next discuss how B-tree insertions are handled; processing deletions is left for an exercise. The essential idea behind a B-tree insertion is that we must first determine which bottom-level node should contain the key-pointer pair to be inserted. For instance, suppose we want to insert the key 742 into the B-tree of Figure 17.16. By allowing this key to walk down the B-tree from the root to the bottom level, we could quickly determine that this key belongs in the node presently containing

712/28
734/29

748/30
784/31

Since, by the definition of a B-tree of order 6, this node is not presently full, no further disk accesses are necessary to perform the insertion. We merely need to determine the next available record space in the actual data file (36 in this case) and then add the key–pointer pair 742/36 to this terminal node, resulting in

712/28
734/29
742/36
748/30
784/31

A slightly more difficult situation arises when we find that the key–pointer pair we wish to add should be inserted into a bottom-level node that is already full. For instance, this would occur if we attempted to add the key 112 to the B-tree of Figure 17.16. We would load the actual data for this key into file position 37 (given the addition already made in the preceding paragraph) and then determine that the key–pointer pair 112/37 belongs in the bottom-level node

94/6
110/7
114/8
120/9
204/10

The stipulation that any B-tree node except the root has at least $(n - 1) / 2 = 2$ key–pointer pairs allows us to split this node, creating one new node with two key–pointer pairs and one with three key–pointer pairs. We also have to move one of the key–pointer pairs up to the parent of the present node. The resulting B-tree is given in Figure 17.17.

Although it does not happen in this particular example, note that it is entirely possible that the movement of a key–pointer pair up to a parent node that is already full necessitates a split of this parent node, using the same function. Indeed, it is possible that key–pointer pairs could be passed all the way up to the root and cause a split of the root. This is in fact how a new level of the tree is introduced. A split of the root forces the creation of a new root, which has only one key–pointer pair and two pointers to other B-tree nodes. However, at the root level, this is still a sufficient number of pointers to retain the B-tree structure. Because the insertion algorithm for a B-tree requires checking whether a given node is full and potentially moving back up to a parent node, it is convenient to allow space within a node to store both of the following:

1. A count of the number of key–pointer pairs in the node
2. A back pointer to the node's parent

Trie Indexing

In all of the indexing applications we have discussed so far, the keys involved have been integers. In practice, however, we must be prepared to deal with keys of different types. Perhaps the worst case is that of keys that are variable-length character strings. *Trie indexing* has developed as a means of retrieving keys in this worst case. (The term itself is derived from the four middle letters of "retrieve," although it is usually pronounced "try.")

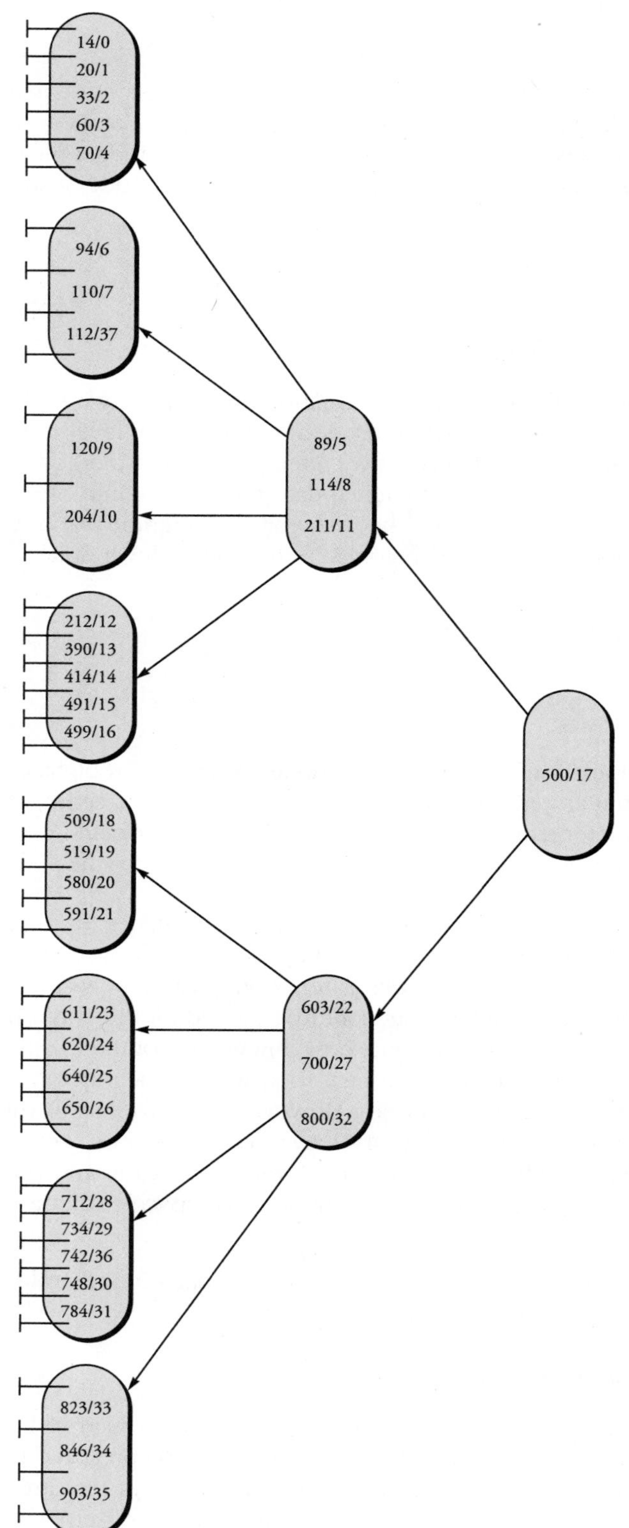

Figure 17.17
B-tree of Figure 17.16 after insertion of 112/37 and 742/36

Let us suppose that the strings in the following list represent a set of keys. Each string may be thought of as a last name followed by initials and a delimiting $.

```
ADAMS BT$
COOPER CC$
COOPER PJ$
COWANS DC$
MAGUIRE WH$
MCGUIRE AL$
MEMINGER DD$
SEFTON SD$
SPAN KD$
SPAN LA$
SPANNER DW$
ZARDA JM$
ZARDA PW$
```

An individual node in a trie structure for these keys follows:

$		A	B	C	D	E	F	G	H	I	J	K	L	M	N	O	P	Q	R	S	T	U	V	W	X	Y	Z

It is essentially a fixed-length array of 28 pointers: one for each letter of the alphabet, one for a blank, and one for the delimiter. Each pointer within one of these nodes can lead to one of two entities: either another node within the trie or the actual data record for a given key. Hence, it may be convenient to embed a Boolean flag in each pointer indicating the type of entity to which it is pointing. The trie structure for the preceding list of keys is given in Figure 17.18. In this figure, pointers to nodes labeled as data records lead us outside of the trie structure itself.

The logic behind a trie structure may best be seen by tracing through an example. This search algorithm involves examining the target key on a character-by-character basis. Let us begin by considering the easy case of finding the data record for ADAMS BT$. In this case, we look at A, the first character in the key, and follow the A pointer in the root node to its destination. From what we have previously said, we know that its destination will be either another node within the trie structure or an actual data record. If it is a node within the trie, it would be a node on the search path for all keys that begin with A. In this case, there is only one key in our list that begins with A, so the A pointer in the root node leads us directly to the actual data record for ADAMS BT$.

On the other hand, the search path to find the key COOPER CC$ in the trie is somewhat longer. We follow the C pointer from the root node down a level to a node shared by all keys starting with C. From there, the O pointer is followed to a trie node shared by all keys that start with CO. The process continues down level by level, following the O pointer to a trie node shared by all keys starting with COO, then the P pointer to a node for all keys starting with COOP, the E pointer to a node for all keys starting with COOPE, the R pointer to a node for all keys starting with COOPER, and the blank pointer to a node shared by all keys starting with COOPER followed by a blank. Notice that, as each character is read in, we must continue following these pointers from trie node to trie node (instead of from trie node to actual data record) until we finally reach a point where the next character to be read will uniquely define the key. At this point, the key in question need no longer share its pointer with other keys that match it on an initial substring. Hence, the pointer may now lead to an actual data record. This is what happens in our example when we read in the next C to form the uniquely defined substring COOPER C.

Figure 17.18 Trie index structure

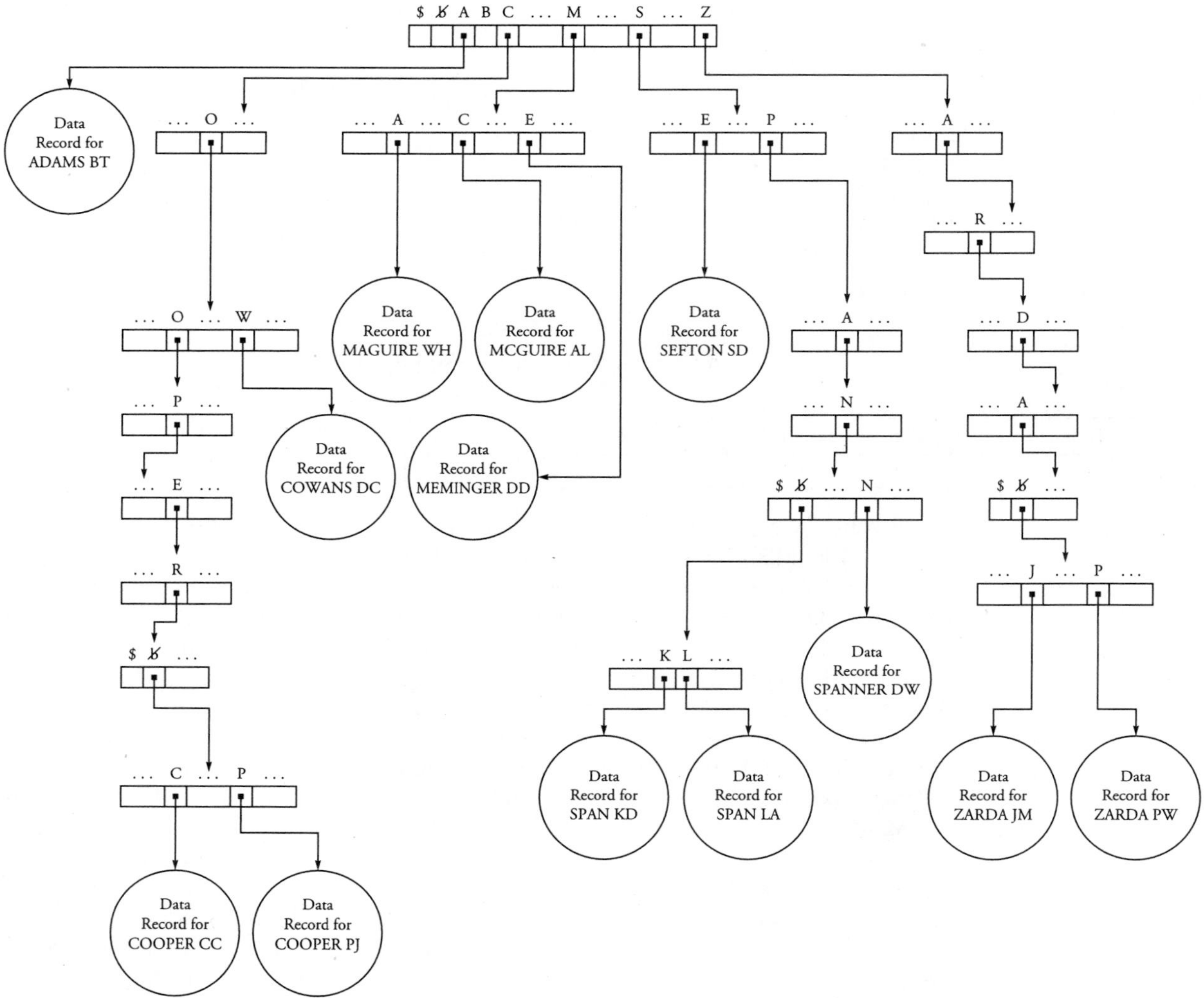

Efficiency Considerations for Trie Indexing. The search efficiency for the trie index is quite easily determined. The worst case occurs when a key is not uniquely defined until its last character is read. In this case, we may have as many disk accesses as there are characters in the key before we finally locate the actual data record. You may have observed, however, that there is another efficiency consideration to take into account when using the trie method. This is the amount of wasted storage in the trie nodes. In our example using a short list of keys, only a small percentage of the available pointers are ever used. In practice, however, a trie is only used for an extremely large file, such as the list represented by a phone book with names as keys. In such a situation, a much larger number of character combinations occurs, and the resulting trie structure is correspondingly much less sparse.

A final point to consider relative to trie indexes is their ability to handle insertions and deletions dynamically. Here we discuss insertions; deletions are left as an exercise. Insertions may be broken down into two cases. For both, we must begin by reading the key to be inserted, character by character, and following the appropriate search path in the trie until

- we come to a trie node which has a vacant pointer in the character position corresponding to the current character of the insertion key.

or

- we come to an actual data record for a key different from the one that is being inserted.

The first case is illustrated by trying to insert the key COLLINS RT$ into the trie of Figure 17.18. We follow the search path pointers until we come to the trie node shared by all keys starting with CO. At this point, the L pointer is null. The insertion is completed by merely aiming the presently null L pointer to a data record for the key COLLINS RT$. The second case is illustrated by trying to insert the key COOPER PA$ into the trie of Figure 17.18. Here, following the search path of the trie would eventually lead us to the data record for the key COOPER PJ$. The solution is to get a new trie node, aim the P pointer presently leading to the data record for COOPER PJ$ to this new trie node, and use the A and J pointers in the new trie node to lead us to data records for COOPER PA$ and COOPER PJ$, respectively. Both the COLLINS RT$ and COOPER PA$ insertions are shown with the resulting trie in Figure 17.19.

Exercises 17.3

1. a. Suppose the records associated with keys 810, 430, 602, 946, 289, 106, and 732 are stored in positions 0, 1, 2, 3, 4, 5, and 6, respectively, of a file. Draw a B-tree index of order 8 for this file.
b. Suppose the key 538 then arrives for insertion in position 8. Redraw your B-tree of order 8 after this insertion.

2. Suppose the following strings arrive for insertion into a trie index:

CARTER
HERNANDEZ
HERMAN
HERMANSKI
HERSCHEL
HALL
CARSON
CARSWELL
CARSEN

a. Draw the trie index.
b. Draw the index after CARSWELL and HERMANSKI have been deleted.

3. Discuss the key deletion strategy for B-trees. Write a function to implement your strategy.

4. Discuss a key deletion strategy for trie indexes. Write a function to implement your strategy.

5. Carefully read your system reference material concerning the specifics of how disk file records are blocked. Then explain how this knowledge would influence your decisions in the construction of
a. an ISAM index structure
b. a bucket hashing structure
c. a trie index structure
d. a B-tree index structure

6. All of the search strategies we have discussed assume a key that is uniquely valued. That is, no two records have the same value for their key field. In practice, this will not always be the case. We may have duplicate keys. For instance, a list of personnel records may contain two records for different people with the same

Figure 17.19 Trie of Figure 17.18 after inserting COLLINS RT$ and COOPER PA$

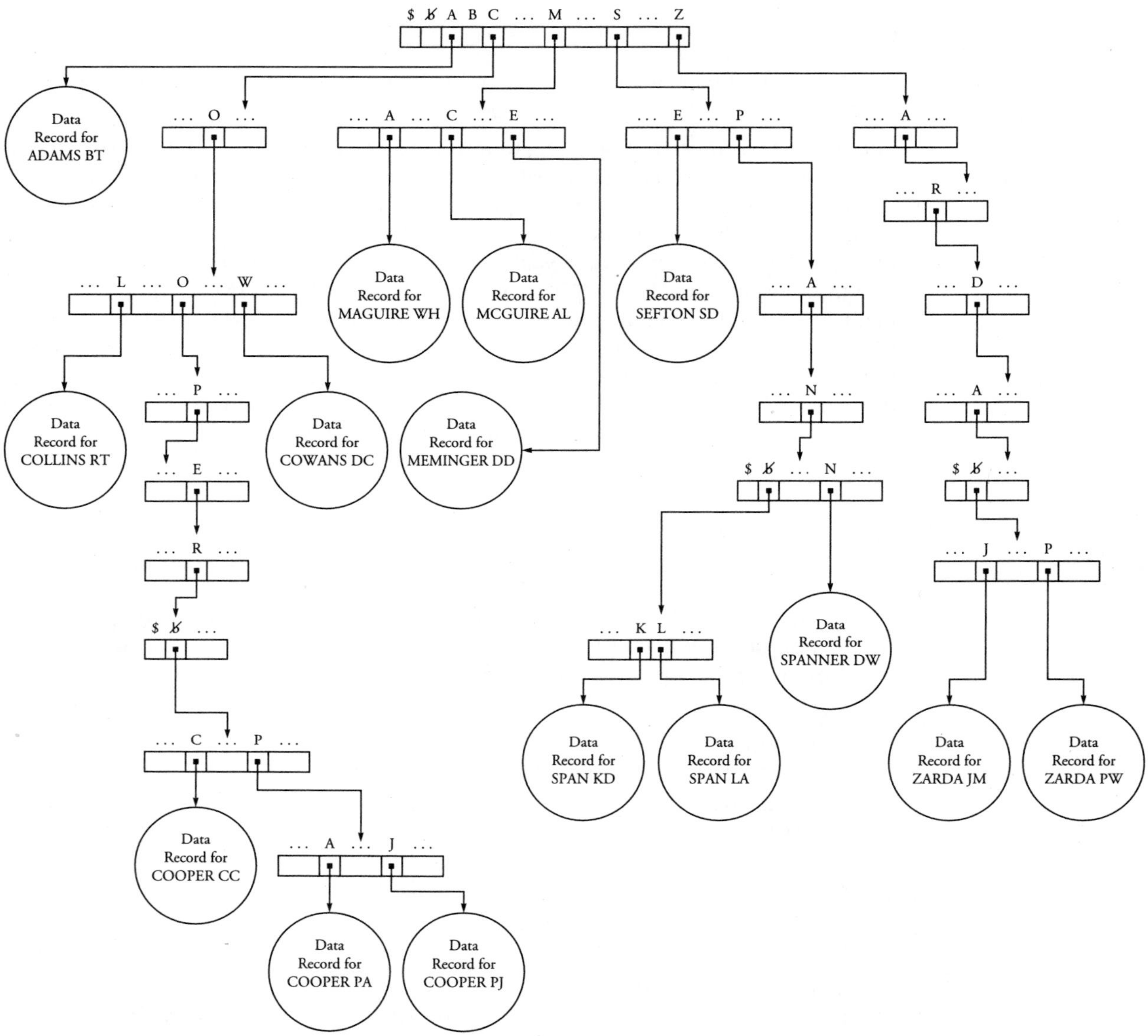

name. In a carefully worded statement, discuss how each of the search strategies we have covered would have to be modified to perform a duplicate key search. What effect would these modifications have on the performance of the algorithm?

7. Develop a function to search a list via ISAM. Initially assume just one directory. Then alter the function so that it works with one subdirectory.
8. Devise functions to handle insertions into and deletions from a list maintained by the indexed sequential method. Do the strategies reflected by these functions require any modifications in your answers to Exercise 7? If so, explain the nature of these modifications.
9. Write the algorithm to insert a key into a B-tree.
10. Write an algorithm to insert a key and its data record into a trie.

Case Study: Profiling Hash Table Operations

In the Case Study for Chapter 10, we introduced the idea of developing a program to profile an algorithm, that is, to monitor the performance of an algorithm empirically. In doing the Programming Problems and Projects in other chapters, you may have written similar programs to help you analyze the efficiency of binary search trees and more sophisticated sort algorithms. Such programs are extremely useful for algorithms whose analysis relies on somewhat random factors and hence defies purely mathematical techniques. Insertions into binary search trees and shell sort are prime examples of this type of algorithm. Certainly, the strategy of hashing, presented in Section 17.1, also falls into this category. The efficiency of hashing depends on a variety of factors: the randomness with which your hashing function scatters keys into the record space, the amount of space you are willing to sacrifice to empty storage locations, and the effectiveness of your collision-processing strategy in reducing clustering.

Because of hashing's dependence on these factors, an experimental tool for testing various hashing strategies can be very valuable in predicting how effective hashing will be for a particular application. In this section, we discuss the design of such an experimental program for situations in which we wish to study the effectiveness of hashing on keys that are strings.

User Request

Develop a profiling program to experiment with hashing strategies. The program should allow us to choose between three forms of input to the hash table:

1. A sequence of randomly generated string keys
2. A sequence of string keys that are entered interactively so that we can enter specific data sets particularly relevant to our experimentation
3. A sequence of string keys read one per line from a file

The program should also have the facility to save a particularly interesting data set in a text file form that can later be read by the program. This will allow us to fine-tune the algorithm by altering the hashing function or selecting a different collision-processing method and then testing the new program with the same set of data.

When randomly generated keys are chosen as the method for loading the table, the program should prompt to specify the size of the hash table and the number of active records contained within that record space. Once the table is loaded, the program should report the average number of probes needed for successful and unsuccessful searches. To determine the average for a successful search, the program should exercise the table's search strategy for each key occurring in the table, profiling the total number of probes made into the table as these searches are carried out. To determine the average for an unsuccessful search, the program should randomly generate a collection of keys that does not occur in the table and then profile the number of probes made as these keys are fed to the search algorithm.

Analysis

The sample runs below, annotated with italicized comments, define how the final program should interact with its user.

```
1 - Load a random table
2 - Interactively load a table
3 - Load table from a file
4 - Save table to a file
5 - Display table
6 - Test performance
7 - Quit program
```

continued

```
 Enter 1, 2, 3, 4, 5, 6, or 7 --> 1
Enter record space size: (<= 500) 40
Enter the number of records to insert: 30    { Hence table density is 75% }

 1 - Load a random table
 2 - Interactively load a table
 3 - Load table from a file
 4 - Save table to a file
 5 - Display table
 6 - Test performance
 7 - Quit program

 Enter 1, 2, 3, 4, 5, 6, or 7 --> 4

0  wSGy 11
1  Ut 21
2  tqDV 9
3  FbBU 29
4  TYG 30
5  sZ 4
6  gg 8
7  0
8  gzSA 28
9  0
10 0
11 oZd 18
... { Here the contents of table indices 0 through 39 are displayed.
    Each table entry is a random string, 2-4 characters, along with
    an integer datum. }

33 zxso 15
34 HUQ 23
35 HQS 7
36 MHv 12
37 da 17
38 sy 19
39 UD 25
Record space = 40
Active records = 30

 1 - Load a random table
 2 - Interactively load a table
 3 - Load table from a file
 4 - Save table to a file
 5 - Display table
 6 - Test performance
 7 - Quit program

 Enter 1, 2, 3, 4, 5, 6, or 7 --> 6

Average length of successful search = 2.03333
Average length of unsuccessful search = 5.2

 1 - Load a random table
 2 - Interactively load a table
 3 - Load table from a file
```

```
 4 - Save table to a file
 5 - Display table
 6 - Test performance
 7 - Quit program

 Enter 1, 2, 3, 4, 5, 6, or 7 --> 4
Enter output file name: test.dat           { Table saved for later use }
Number of active records = 30
Record space = 40

 1 - Load a random table
 2 - Interactively load a table
 3 - Load table from a file
 4 - Save table to a file
 5 - Display table
 6 - Test performance
 7 - Quit program
Enter 1, 2, 3, 4, 5, 6, or 7 --> 7
```

Now we could modify the hashing function and/or collision processing strategy and see if there is any improvement.

```
 1 - Load a random table
 2 - Interactively load a table
 3 - Load table from a file
 4 - Save table to a file
 5 - Display table
 6 - Test performance
 7 - Quit program

 Enter 1, 2, 3, 4, 5, 6, or 7 --> 3
Enter record space size: (<= 500) 40      { Load the table from last run }
Enter input file name: test.dat
30 records input from file test.dat

 1 - Load a random table
 2 - Interactively load a table
 3 - Load table from a file
 4 - Save table to a file
 5 - Display table
 6 - Test performance
 7 - Quit program

 Enter 1, 2, 3, 4, 5, 6, or 7 -> 6
Average length of successful search = 1.92481            { Notice slight improvement! }
Average length of unsuccessful search = 4.92667

 1 - Load a random table
 2 - Interactively load a table
 3 - Load table from a file
 4 - Save table to a file
 5 - Display table
 6 - Test performance
 7 - Quit program

 Enter 1, 2, 3, 4, 5, 6, or 7 --> 7
```

Figure 17.20 Structure chart for profiling program

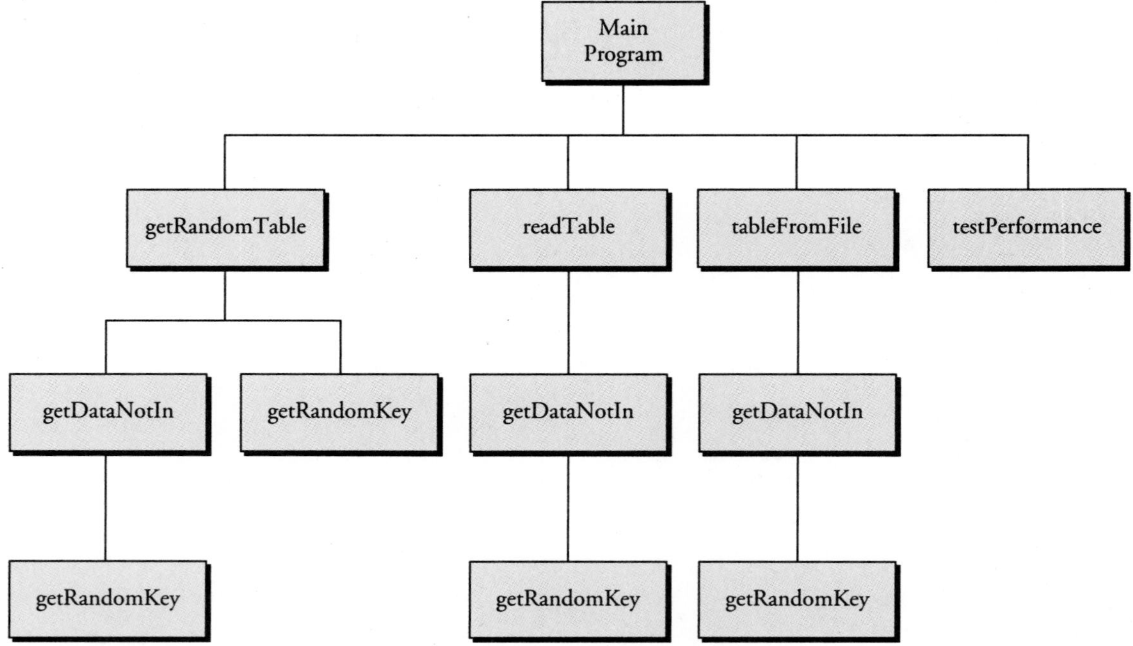

Design

A modular structure chart for the program appears in Figure 17.20. The specifications for the functions called by the main program are given as documentation accompanying the following function protocols.

```
typedef HashTable<int> IntTable;
typedef OrderedCollection<apstring> ApstringList;

// Module:  testPerformance
//
// Task: Display average number of probes for successful and unsuccessful
//       searches
// Inputs:  The hash table,
//          An ordered collection of string keys that are in the table,
//          An ordered collection of string keys that are not in the table,
//             to be used for profiling unsuccessful searches

void testPerformance(IntTable &table, ApstringList &dataIn,
                     ApstringList &dataNotIn);

// Module:  getRandomTable
//
// Task: Determine from user record space and number of active records
//       to store in hash table. Then build the hash table using random
//       string keys. Also build ordered collections of keys to be used
//       for profiling successful and unsuccessful searches
// Outputs: The hash table with appropriate number of random keys,
//          An ordered collection of string keys that are in the table,
//          An ordered collection of string keys that are not in the table,
```

```
//            to be used for profiling unsuccessful searches

void getRandomTable(IntTable &table, ApstringList &dataIn,
                ApstringList &dataNotIn);

// Module:  getRandomKey
//
// Task: Construct a random string to be used as a key for entry into hash
//       table. Size of string is at least half of and does not surpass
//       the local constant MAX_STRING_SIZE

apstring getRandomKey();

// Module:  readTable
//
// Task: Determine from user record space and number of active records
//       to store in hash table. Then build the hash table using keys
//       entered interactively. Also build ordered collections of keys
//       to be used for profiling successful and unsuccessful searches
// Outputs: The hash table with appropriate number of random keys,
//        An ordered collection of string keys that are in the table,
//        An ordered collection of string keys that are not in the table,
//           to be used for profiling unsuccessful searches

void readTable(IntTable &table, ApstringList &dataIn, ApstringList
                  &dataNotIn);

// Module:  tableFromFile
//
// Task: Determine from user record space for the hash table.
//       Then build the hash table using keys that are read from file.
//       Also build ordered collections of keys to be used for
//       profiling successful and unsuccessful searches
// Outputs: The hash table with appropriate number of random keys,
//        An ordered collection of string keys that are in the table,
//        An ordered collection of string keys that are not in the table,
//           to be used for profiling unsuccessful searches

void tableFromFile(IntTable &table, ApstringList &dataIn,
                  ApstringList &dataNotIn);

// Module:   tableToFile
//
// Task: Save the hash table to a file so it can be re-loaded in future
//       runs
// Inputs:  The hash table

void tableToFile(IntTable &table);

// Module:  getDataNotIn
//
// Task: Build the list of (random) keys not in the table to use for
//       profiling an unsuccessful search
// Inputs:  The hash table
// Outputs: The ordered collection of keys not in the table

void getDataNotIn(IntTable &table, ApstringList &dataNotIn);
```

To accumulate the statistics, the program generates two ordered collections of keys: one containing all the keys that are in the table and another containing additional random keys that are not in the table. The performance of the hash table is then exercised by sending the keys in each of these ordered collections through the search algorithm. A profiling accumulator for unsuccessful searches is maintained as these keys are processed.

The program will use a hash table class with the following declarations:

```
// Class declaration file: hashtab.h

#ifndef HASHTAB_H
#define HASHTAB_H

#include <fstream.h>
#include "assoc.h"
#include "ordercol.h"
#include "apstring.h"

const int MAX_HASH_SIZE = MAX_ARRAY_SIZE; // MAX_ARRAY_SIZE in ordered
                                          // collection class

// Class declaration for hash table with string keys and data
// elements of type E
template <class E> class HashTable
{
   public:

   HashTable();
   HashTable(const HashTable<E> &h);

   // Reset the hash table to an empty table
   void reset();

   // Return the number of active records in the hash table
   int length();

   // Display contents of table to cout
   void display();

   // Allow the user to interactively set record space to value
   // not to exceed MAX_HASH_SIZE
   void setRecordSpace();

   // Return the record space set by the user
   int recordSpace();

   // Reset probe counter used to profile performance
   void resetCounter();

   // Return the accumulated count of number of probes made
   // into the table
   int counter();

   // Insert keyValue and item into the table. If table
   // is full, return false and leave table unaltered. If
```

```
   // keyValue is already in table, use item to update its
   // associated data and return false. Return true
   // when keyValue successfully added as new value in table.
   bool add(const apstring &keyValue, const E &item);

   // Given keyValue, search the hash table for it.
   // If found, return found as true and return in index the
   // location of keyValue in the table,  If not found, return
   // found as false. When found is false, return empty as true
   // if an empty slot was found in the table while searching
   // for keyValue. index then stores the location of that empty
   // slot. If both found and empty are returned as false, it means
   // that keyValue was not found and that the table is completely
   // full. In this case, the value of index is unreliable.
   void search(const apstring &keyValue, int &index,
            bool &found, bool &empty);

   // Output the hash table to a stream
   void toFile(ofstream &outfile);

   HashTable& operator = (const HashTable<E> &h);

   private:

   // -- PRIVATE DATA MEMBERS

   // The hash table is implemented as an array of associations.
   // Each association has a string as its key and a datum of type E
   association<apstring, E> table[MAX_HASH_SIZE];

   // Record space used for profiling
   int RECORD_SPACE;

   // Number of active associations stored within RECORD_SPACE
   int tableLength;

   // Probe counter for performance measurement
   int probes;

   // -- PRIVATE MEMBER FUNCTIONS

   // The hash function
   int hash(const apstring &keyValue);

   // Given that index has produced a collision, return the next location
   // to try in the hash table
   int processCollision(int index);

   // Return true if a represents an empty association in hash table
   bool emptySlot(const association<apstring, E> &a);

};

#include "hashtab.cpp"

#endif
```

The hash table is represented as an array of associations. An empty slot in the table is detected by the presence of an empty string in an association.

Implementation

Given the specifications in our design, the main program must control the loop that was portrayed in our analysis.

```
int main()
{
   IntTable table;
   ApstringList dataIn, dataNotIn;

   char choiceOfLoad;

   do
   {
      cout << endl << endl << endl;
      cout << " 1 - Load a random table" << endl;
      cout << " 2 - Interactively load a table" << endl;
      cout << " 3 - Load table from a file" << endl;
      cout << " 4 - Save table to a file" << endl;
      cout << " 5 - Display table" << endl;
      cout << " 6 - Test performance" << endl;
      cout << " 7 - Quit program" << endl;
      cout << endl;
      cout << " Enter 1, 2, 3, 4, 5, 6, or 7 --> ";
      cin >> choiceOfLoad;
      switch (choiceOfLoad)
      {
         case '1': getRandomTable(table, dataIn, dataNotIn);
                   break;
         case '2': readTable(table, dataIn, dataNotIn);
                   break;
         case '3': tableFromFile(table, dataIn, dataNotIn);
                   break;
         case '4': tableToFile(table);
                   break;
         case '5': table.display();
                   break;
         case '6': testPerformance(table, dataIn, dataNotIn);
                   break;
         case '7': break;
         default: cout << choiceOfLoad << " is not a valid "
                       << "response - try again" << endl;
      }
   } while (choiceOfLoad! = '7');

  return 0;
}
```

Rather than show the complete implementations of all other functions in the program, we will concentrate on the four hash table functions to (1) compute the hashed position of a key, (2) add a key to the table, (3) search for a key or empty slot, and (4) process collisions. The entire implementation is available in the source code that accompanies the book, but most of your experimentation with this profiling program in Programming Problems and Projects will only require you to modify these four functions.

The `hash` function adds together the ASCII values at the beginning and the end of the key and returns the remainder of dividing this value by the record space. You may feel that this is not a good hash function. You're right! It is one of the first things you will want to change in your experimentation.

```
template <class E>
int HashTable<E>::hash(const apstring &keyValue)
{
   return (keyValue[0] + keyValue[keyValue.length() - 1])
      % RECORD_SPACE;
}
```

The `processCollision` function implements the linear method.

```
template <class E>
int HashTable<E>::processCollision(int index)
{
   return (index + 1) % RECORD_SPACE;
}
```

The `search` function calls the `hash` function to get an initial position for the key value. The function then enters a loop that stops when a matching key is found, an empty slot is found, or there are no empty slots left in the table. In the first two cases, the index position of the key's slot in the table is returned. Note that this loop advances through the table by calling `processCollision`, which in its present form either increments the position or wraps around the end of the table.

```
template <class E>
void HashTable<E>::search(const apstring &keyValue, int &index,
      bool &found, bool &empty)
{
   int initial = hash(keyValue);
   int current = initial;
   bool checkedAll = false;
   found = false;
   empty = false;

   ++probes;
   while ((! empty) && (! found) && (! checkedAll))
   {
      if  (table[current].getKey() == keyValue)
          found = true;
      else if (emptySlot(table[current]))
          empty = true;
      else
      {
          current = processCollision(current);
          checkedAll = initial == current;
          ++probes;
      }
   }
   index = current;
}
```

The add function calls search with the key. If the slot is found (a duplicate key) or is empty, the key and the associated data item are inserted at the index position. If the slot is empty, the length of the table is also incremented by 1:

```
template <class E>
bool HashTable<E>::add(const apstring &keyValue, const E &item)
{
   bool found, empty;
   int index;

   search(keyValue, index, found, empty);
   if (found || empty)
   {
      association<apstring, E> a(keyValue, item);
      table [index] = a;
      if (empty)
         ++tableLength;
   }
   else
      cout << "Table full--cannot add new item." << endl;
   return found;
}
```

Running, Debugging, and Testing Hints

1. When using hashing as a search strategy, provide yourself with a means of experimenting with your hashing function and collision-processing strategy. This will allow you to tailor your program to the particular kind of keys that are stored in the hash table.
2. Searching for data in a random access file involves different criteria than searching for data in main memory. Programs that search for data in random access files should minimize file accesses at the expense of main memory accesses. Indexed searches provide ways of doing this.
3. If a search program has to handle duplicate keys, that is, different records associated with the same key value, the search algorithm will have to be adjusted appropriately. Be sure you know and decide in advance whether this added complexity is necessary.

Summary

Key Terms

boundary folding
buckets
clustering
collision
density-dependent search techniques
digit/character extraction
division-remainder technique
folding
hashing
hashing function
index
key-to-address transformation
linear collision processing
linked collision processing
overflow area
prime hash area
quadratic collision processing
randomized storage
rehashing collision processing
sectors
shift folding
synonyms
tracks

Key Terms (Optional)

binary tree index
B-tree
concurrent updating
data integrity
deadlock
fatal embrace
indexed sequential access method (ISAM)
indexed sequential search
record lock facility
trie indexing

Key Concepts

- The following table gives a concise synopsis of the search strategies that have been discussed in this and earlier chapters. Additional comments emphasize particular strengths or weaknesses of the strategy in terms of the one-key table operations we have considered throughout the text.

Method	Efficiency (n = number of records)	Other Components Regarding One-Key Table Operations
Binary	$O(\log_2 n)$	Data must be maintained in physical order, hence making insertions and deletions inefficient.
Binary tree index	$O(\log_2 n)$ index probes, 1 file probe	Guaranteeing this efficiency requires height balancing.
B-tree index order k	Worst case requires $1 + \log_k[(n + 1)/2]$ disk accesses for index	Choose k so that index node coincides with disk block.
Indexed sequential	O(size of index) index probes, $O[n/$(size of index)] file probes	Index and file require physical ordering to maintain efficiency.
Linear hashing	Average successful: $(1/2) * [1 + 1/(1 - D)]$ Average unsuccessful: $(1/2) * [1 + 1/(1 - D)^2]$ where density $D = n/$ `RECORD_SPACE`	Data not maintained in any order.
Linked hashing	Average successful: $1 + D/2$ Average unsuccessful: D (where `RECORD_SPACE` used in computation of D is that in primary hash area)	Data not maintained in any order.
Quadratic hashing	Average successful: $1 - \log_e(1 - D) - (D/2)$ Average unsuccessful: $1/(1 - D) - D - \log_e(1 - D)$	Data not maintained in any order.
Rehashing	Average successful: $-(1/D) * \log_e(1 - D)$ Average unsuccessful: $1/(1 - D)$	Data not maintained in any order.
Sequential	$O(n)$	
Trie index	O(number of characters in target)	Specifically suited for character strings.

- In addition to hashing, other search strategies specifically oriented toward file structures include indexed sequential search, B-trees, and tries.
- As an implementation strategy for one-key tables, hashing fares very well in all of the operations except ordering. It thus represents a very viable addition to the list implementation strategies discussed in earlier chapters: array or random files with binary search, linked lists, and binary trees.

Programming Problems and Projects

1. Use the program from the Case Study as a means of conducting experiments on hashing. Be as creative as you want in your exploration, but here are some suggestions to guide you:
   a. Run the program. Enter a record space of 400 and load 300 randomly generated keys. Save the keys for later experiments. What do you observe for the average search length for successful and unsuccessful searching? Are your observations consistent with the results from Knuth cited earlier in this chapter? If not, explain why. Examine the hash function, look at the data file saved, and consider the range of ASCII codes for the letters that appear in this file.
   b. Modify the hash function so that it is not biased toward a particular region of the table. Run the program with this new hash function with the data set from part a. In a written statement, summarize the effectiveness of your modifications.
   c. Conduct a controlled experiment with four different hashing functions on five different data sets. The data sets should have the same large record space (about 400 records) but different density factors (or numbers of actual records). Use the ASCII values in the keys to develop four different hashing functions, each representing an improvement on the biased hashing function provided with the program. Record your results in a table. Also plot each hash function's successful and unsuccessful search efficiencies where the axes represent search efficiency and density factor. In a written statement, characterize the efficiencies of the four hash functions. Is one function always better? If so, why? If not, can you explain the inconsistencies in performance? Are your observed results consistent with Knuth's theoretical results presented earlier in the chapter?
   d. Determine whether minor changes in the size of the record space affect the performance of the best hash function you devised in part c. Using that function and four of the data sets from part c, run each data set with record spaces of 396, 397, 398, 399, and 400. Record the results in a table and present them in the same graphic form you used in part c. Do your results indicate that a larger record space always produces a greater efficiency than a smaller one? If not, describe the discrepancies and give a possible reason for them. Does it appear that a smaller record space could be consistently better than a larger one?
   e. Implement the rehashing method (described in Section 17.1) by using the four functions you developed in part c. If the collision is not resolved after using all four functions, then resort to linear collision processing. Run the program with the same data sets used in part c and plot its performance. Compare the performance of rehashing to that of the best hashing function developed in part c. Also address how your implementation of rehashing conforms to the theoretical results of Knuth.
2. Implement the registrar's system described in Chapter 11 using hashing as the implementation technique for the student database. Recall that this database was derived from a one-key table. Hence, the difficult part of this problem will be to implement the sorted data that the registrar wants when hashing is used as the search strategy for the one-key table.
3. Implement the Wing-and-a-Prayer flight/pilot database (Problem 12, Chapter 11) using the implementation technique described in Section 17.2 for the two-key table.
4. A B-tree of order 3 is often called a 2–3 tree since each node has two or three children. Because of its low order, a 2–3 tree is not particularly applicable as a file index. However, if we store up to two actual data records in each node instead

of up to two key–pointer pairs, then a 2–3 tree becomes an alternative to an ordered binary tree for implementing a list. Develop search, insertion, and deletion algorithms for such a 2–3 tree structure. Compare its performance characteristics with those of an ordered binary tree.

5. Implement the registrar's system of Problem 2 using a 2–3 tree representation of a list (see Problem 4).

6. Wing-and-a-Prayer Airlines has the records of all its customers stored in the following form:

- Last name
- First name
- Address
- Arbitrarily long list of flights on which reservations have been booked

Using a trie index, write a search-and-retrieval program that will allow input of a customer's last name (and if necessary, the first name and address to resolve conflicts created by matching last names) and then output all flights on which that customer has booked reservations.

7. SuperScout Inc. is a nationwide scouting service for college football talent to which the Bay Area Brawlers professional team subscribes. As the pool of college talent increases in size, SuperScout has found that its old recordkeeping system has deteriorated considerably in its ability to locate quickly the scouting record associated with a given player in its file. Rewrite their scouting record system using a trie to look up the record location of the data associated with a given player's name.

8. Using a large collection of randomly generated keys, write a series of programs that will test various hashing functions you develop. In particular, your programs should report statistics on the number of collisions generated by each hashing function. This information could be valuable in guiding future decisions about which hashing functions and techniques are most effective for your particular system.

9. Consider a student data record that consists of

- Student identification number
- Student name
- State of residence
- Sex

Choose an index structure to process a file of such records. Then write a program to maintain such a file as a one-key table.

10. Suppose data records for a phone book file consist of a key field containing both name and address and a field containing the phone number for that key. Devise an appropriate index for such a file. Then write a program which calls for input of

a. A complete key.

b. If a complete key is not available, as much of the initial portion of a key as the inquirer is able to provide.

In the case of part a, your program should output the phone number corresponding to the unique key. In the case of part b, have your program output all keys (and their phone numbers) that match the provided initial portion.

11. Consider the following problem faced in the development of a compiler. The source program contains many character-string symbols such as variable names, function names, and so on. Each of these character-string symbols has associated with it various attributes such as memory location, data type, and so on. However, it is too time consuming and awkward for a compiler to manipulate character strings. Instead, each string should be identified with an integer that is viewed as equivalent to the string for the purpose of compiler manipulation. In addition to serving as a compact equivalent form of a string symbol within the source program, this integer can also serve as a direct pointer into a table of attributes for that symbol. Devise such a transformation that associates a string with an integer, and which in turn serves as a pointer into a table of attributes. Test the structure(s) you develop by using them in a program that scans a source program written in a language such as C++. You will in effect have written the symbol table modules for a compiler.

12. Write a spell checker program. Such a program must scan a file of text, looking up each word it finds in a dictionary of correctly spelled words. When a word cannot be found in the dictionary, the spell checker should convey this fact to its user, giving the user the opportunity to take one of the following steps:

a. Skip the word.

b. Change the spelling of the word in the text file.

c. Add the word to the dictionary so it will not be reported as incorrectly spelled in the future.

Since the dictionary for such a program will be searched frequently and is likely to become quite large, an efficient search algorithm is an absolute necessity. One possibility in this regard is to use a trie index with pointers into a large string buffer instead of the pointers to data records described in Section 17.3. Test your program with a text file and dictionary large enough to handle all of the possibilities your algorithm and data structure may encounter.

13. If you solved one of the problems from Chapter 11 that involved maintaining a one-key table, redo that problem using hashing combined with linked lists as an implementation technique. When finished, write a report in which you empirically compare the performance of your two implementations.

14. If you solved one of the problems from Chapter 11 that involved maintaining a two-key table, redo that problem using hashing of row and column indices as an implementation technique. When finished, write a report in which you empirically compare the performance of your two implementations.

Appendices

APPENDIX A

Reserved Words

The following words have predefined meanings in C++ and cannot be changed. The words in boldface are discussed in the text. The other words are discussed in Stanley B. Lippman, *C++ Primer,* 3rd ed., Reading, MA: Addison-Wesley, 1998.

asm	continue	**float**	**new**	**signed**	try
auto	**default**	**for**	**operator**	sizeof	**typedef**
break	**delete**	**friend**	**private**	static	union
case	**do**	goto	**protected**	**struct**	**unsigned**
catch	**double**	**if**	**public**	**switch**	virtual
char	**else**	inline	register	template	**void**
class	**enum**	**int**	**return**	**this**	volatile
const	extern	**long**	**short**	throw	**while**

APPENDIX B

Some Useful Library Functions

Some of the most commonly used library functions in the first course in computer science come from the libraries `math`, `ctype`, and `string`. Descriptions of the most important functions in each of these libraries are presented in the following three tables.

`math`

Function Declaration	Purpose
`double abs(double x);`	Returns absolute value of x
`double acos(double x);`	Returns arc cosine for x in range -1 to $+1$
`double asin(double x);`	Returns arc sine for x in range -1 to $+1$
`double atan(double x);`	Returns arc tangent of x
`double atan2(double y, double x);`	Returns arc tangent of y/x
`double ceil(double x);`	Rounds x up to next highest integer
`double cos(double x);`	Returns cosine of x
`double cosh(double x);`	Returns hyberbolic cosine of x
`double exp(double x);`	Returns e to the xth power
`double floor(double x);`	Rounds x down to next lowest integer
`double fmod(double x, double y);`	Returns remainder of x/y
`double ldexp(double x, double exp);`	Returns x times 2 to the power of exp
`double log(double x);`	Returns natural logarithm of x
`double log10(double x);`	Returns base-10 logarithm of x
`double pow(double x, double y);`	Returns x raised to power of y
`double sin(double x);`	Returns sine of x
`double sinh(double x);`	Returns hyberbolic sine of x
`double sqrt(double x);`	Returns square root of x
`double tan(double x);`	Returns tangent of x, in radians
`double tanh(double x);`	Returns hyperbolic tangent of x

ctype

Function Declaration	Purpose
`int isalnum(int ch);`	ch is letter or digit
`int isalpha(int ch);`	ch is letter
`int iscntrl(int ch);`	ch is control character
`int isdigit(int ch);`	ch is digit (0–9)
`int isgraph(int ch);`	ch is printable but not ' '
`int islower(int ch);`	ch is lowercase letter
`int isprint(int ch);`	ch is printable
`int ispunct(int ch);`	ch is printable but not ' ' or alpha
`int isspace(int ch);`	ch is a white space character
`int isupper(int ch);`	ch is uppercase letter
`int isxdigit(int ch);`	ch is hexadecimal digit
`int tolower(int ch);`	Returns lowercase of ch
`int toupper(int ch);`	Returns uppercase of ch

string

Function Declaration	Purpose
`char *strcat(char *s1, const char *s2);`	Appends copy of s2 to end of s1
`char strcmp(const char *s1, const char *s2);`	Compares s1 and s2
`char *strcpy(char *s1, const char *s2);`	Copies s2 to s1, including '\0'
`char strlen(const char *s);`	Returns length of s, not including '\0'

APPENDIX C

Syntax Diagrams

The following syntax diagrams correspond to the syntax forms used to describe the features of C++ discussed in the text. Two points of caution are in order. First, the diagrams in this appendix by no means represent an exhaustive description of C++. Second, many of the features discussed in this text have more than one syntactically correct construction (for example, `main` can be preceded by either `int` or `void`, but the C++ programming community prefers `int`). By confining your attention to preferred ways of using a small subset of features, we hope to place your focus on concepts rather than syntax. Students wanting to learn more features of C++ or other ways of expressing them are referred to Stanley B. Lippman, *C++ Primer,* 3rd ed., Reading, MA: Addison-Wesley, 1998.

The terms enclosed in ovals in the diagrams refer to program components that literally appear in programs, such as operator symbols and reserved words. The terms enclosed in boxes refer to program components that require further definition, either by another diagram or by reference to the text. The syntax of terms for which there are no diagrams, such as `identifier`, `number`, `string`, and `character`, should be familiar to anyone who has read this text.

Main program module

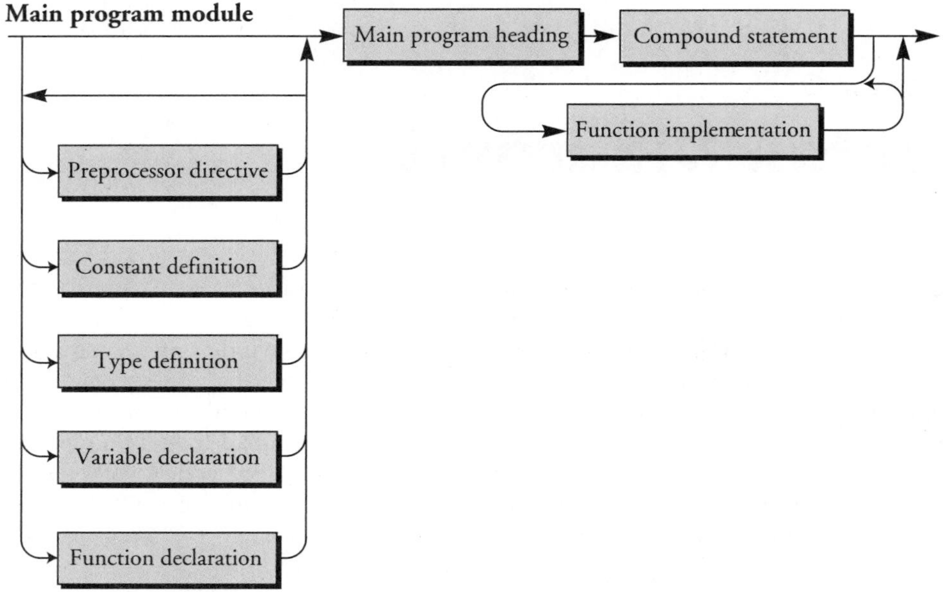

Preprocessor directive

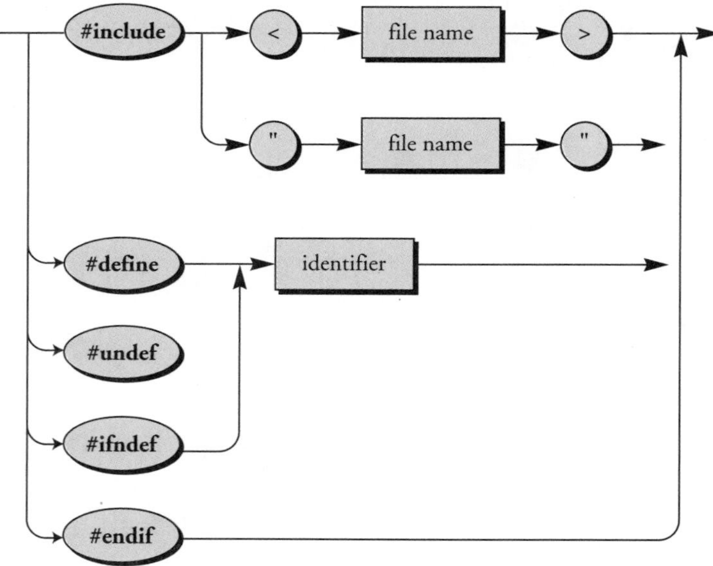

Constant definition

Type definition

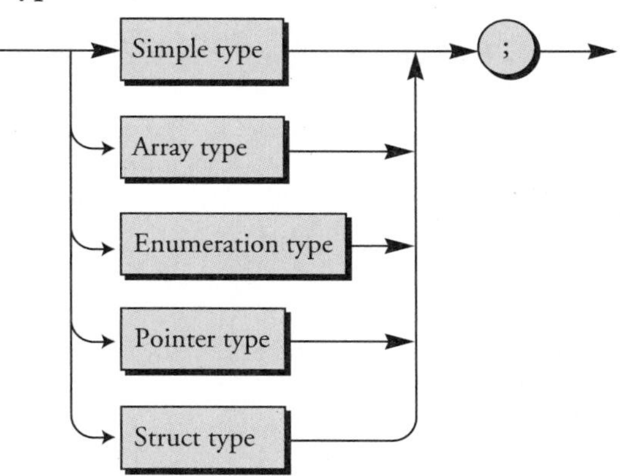

Simple type

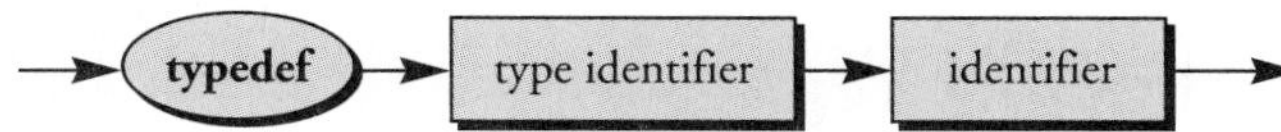

Array type

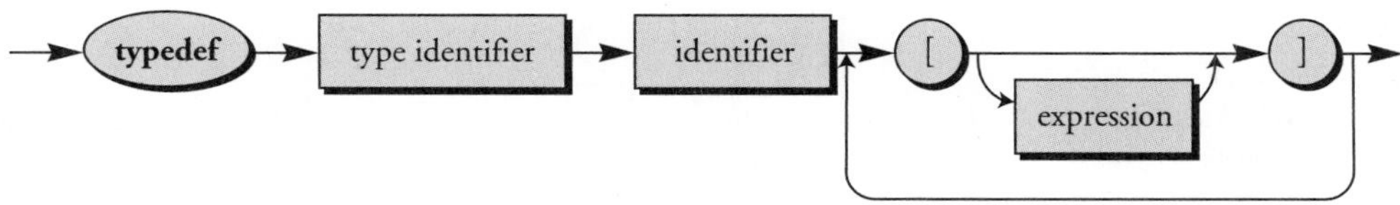

Enumeration type

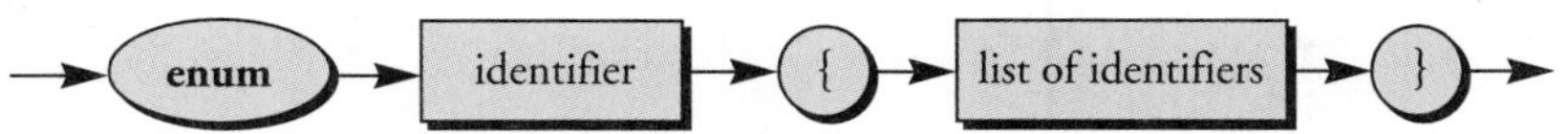

Pointer type

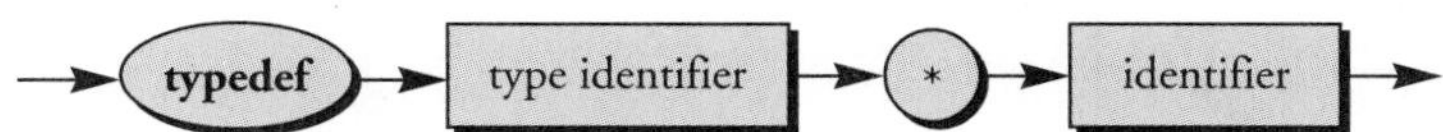

Struct type

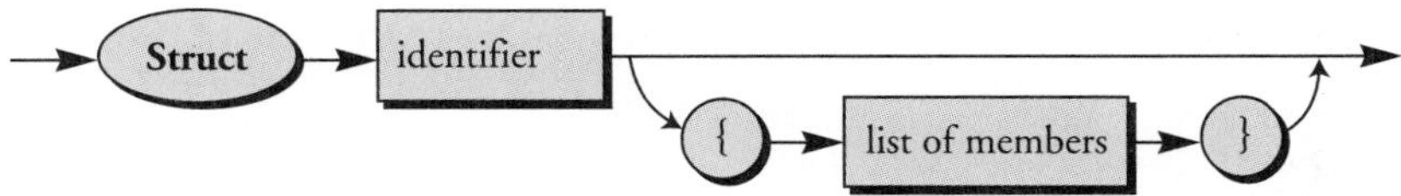

List of members

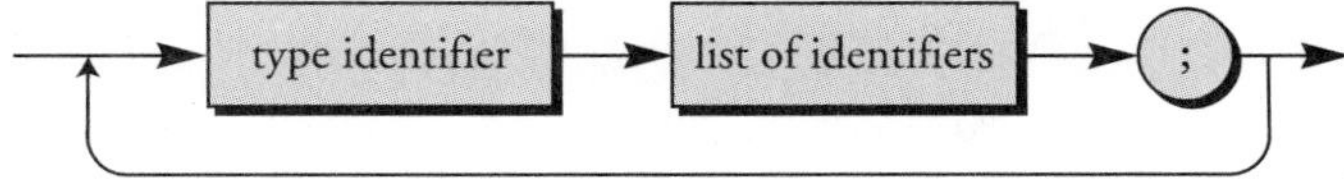

Variable declaration

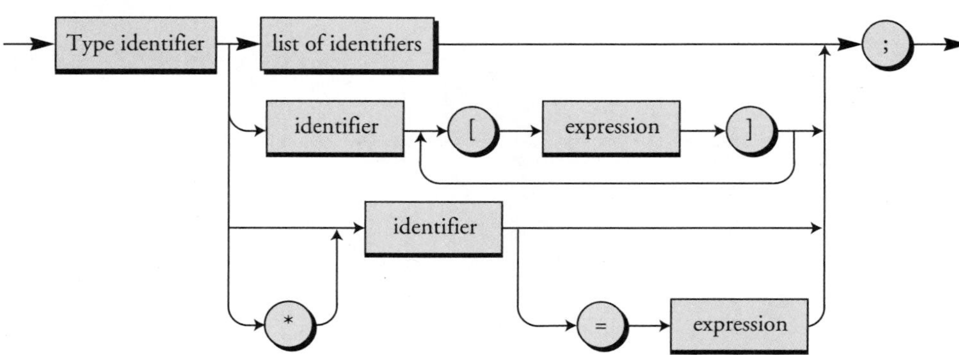

List of identifiers

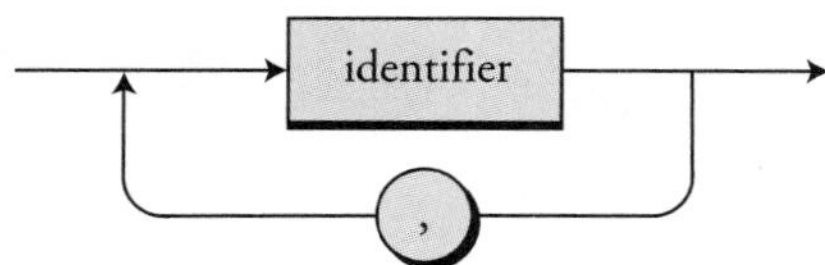

Function declaration

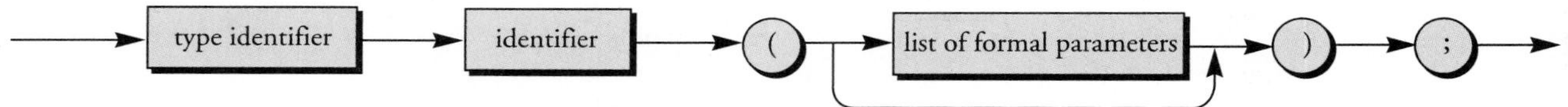

Main program heading

Compound statement

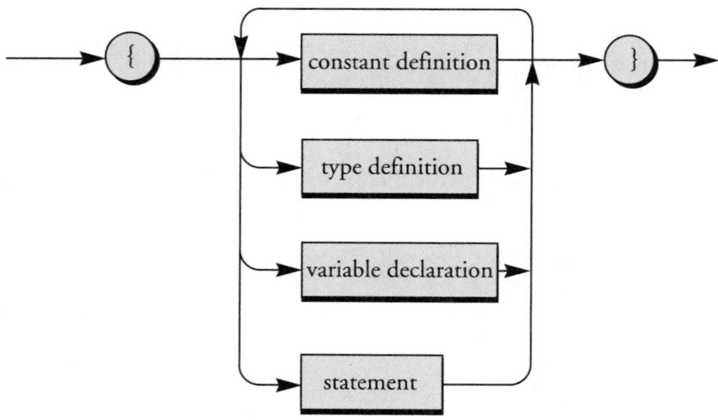

Statement

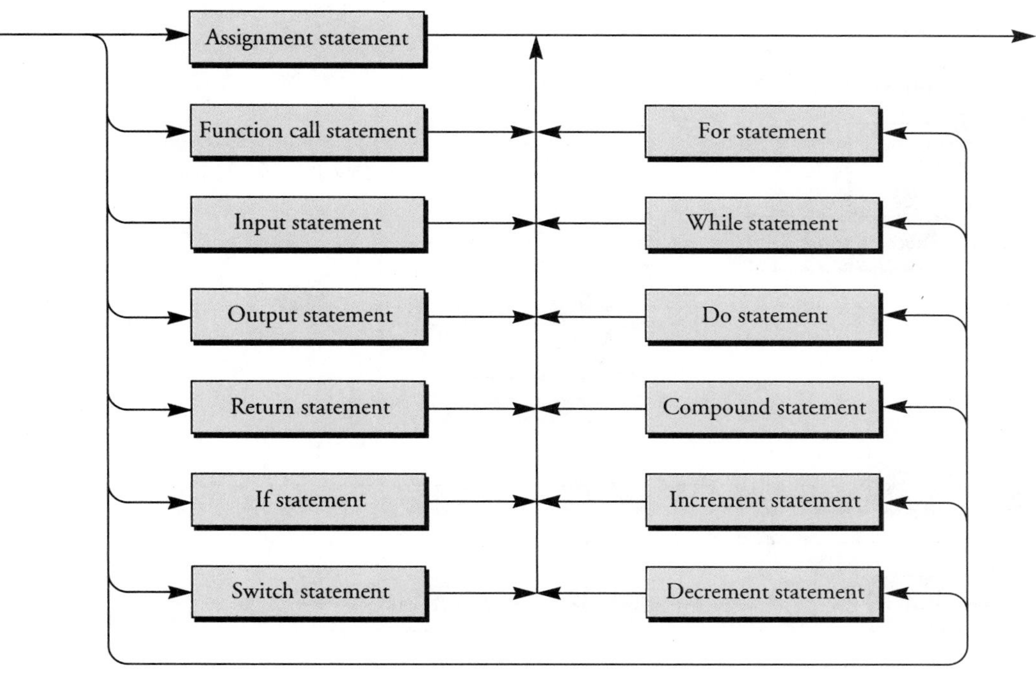

Assignment statement

Function call statement

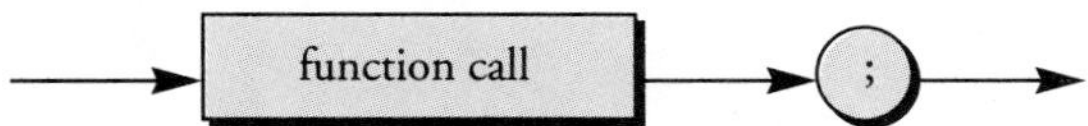

Input statement

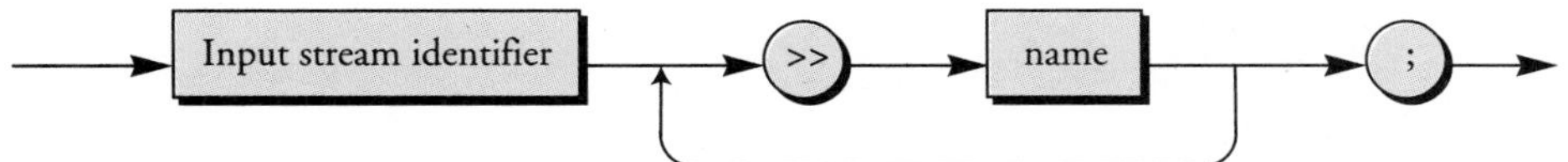

Output statement

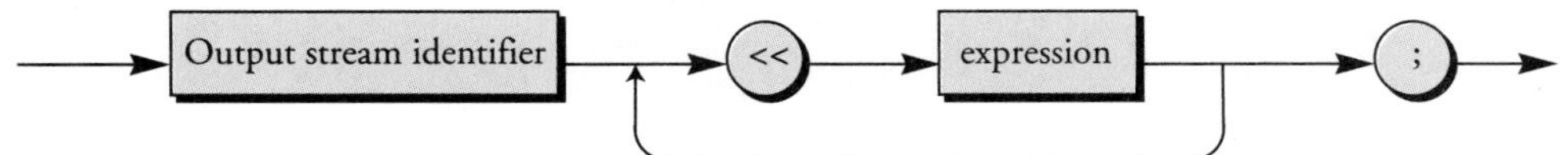

Return statement

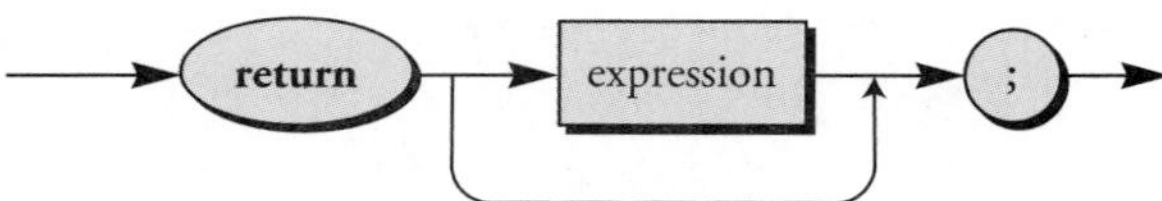

If statement

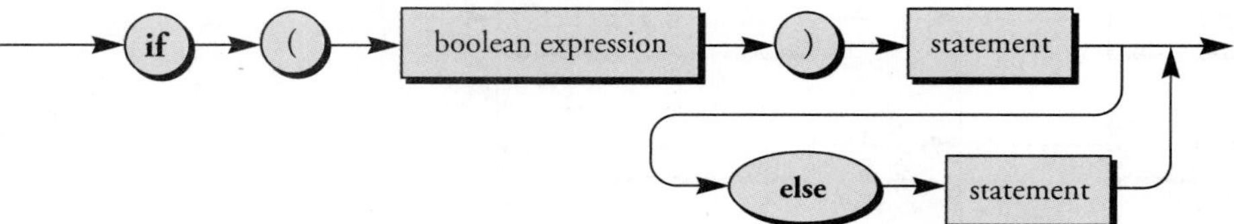

Switch statement

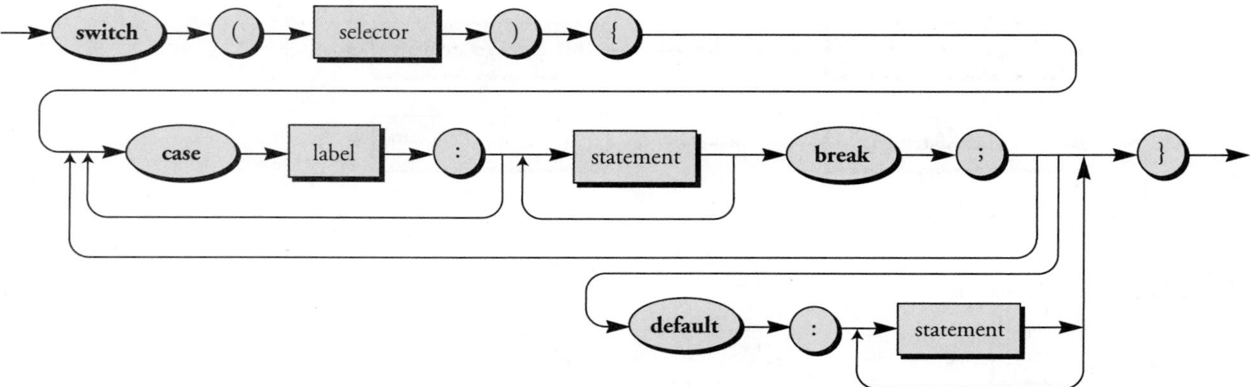

For statement

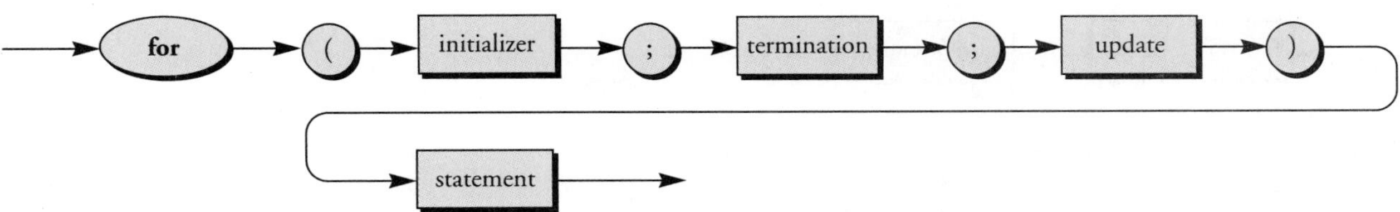

While statement

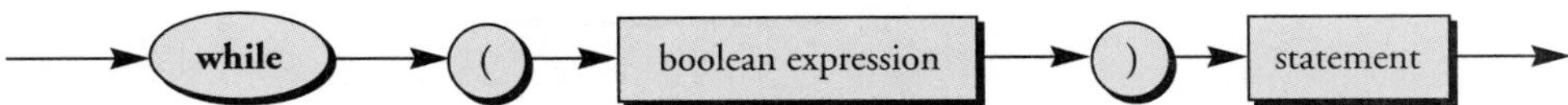

Do statement

Increment statement

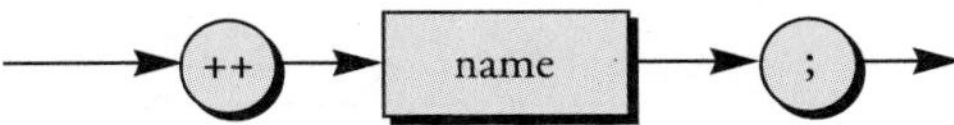

Decrement statement

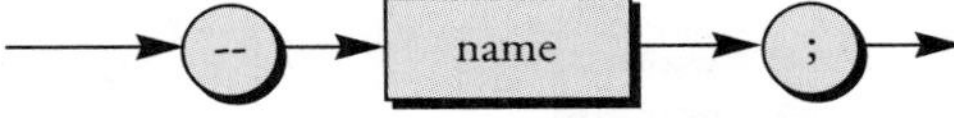

Function implementation

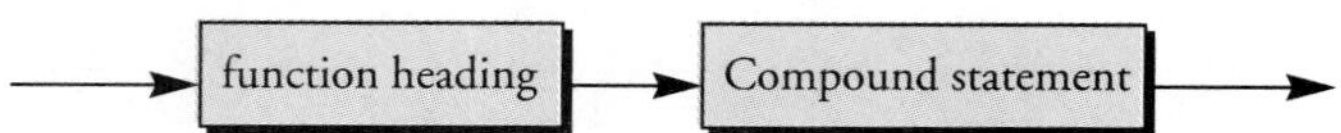

Function heading

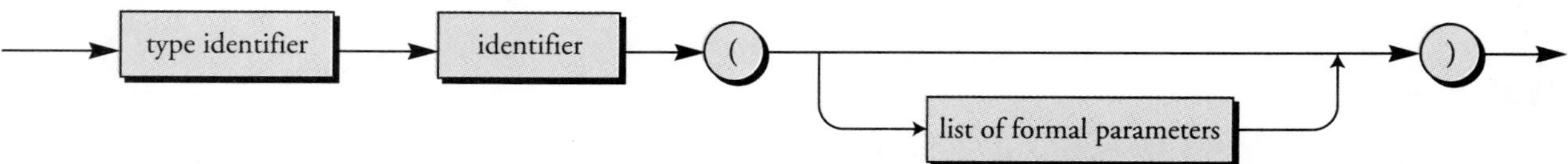

List of formal parameters

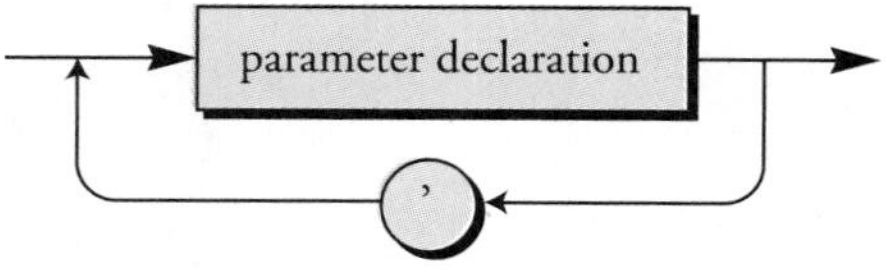

Parameter declaration

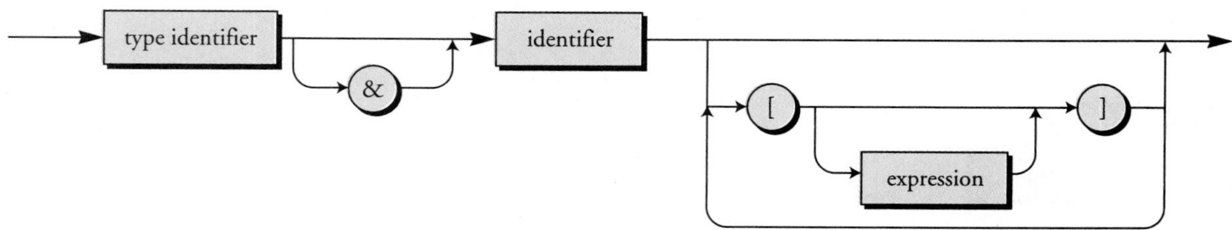

Expression

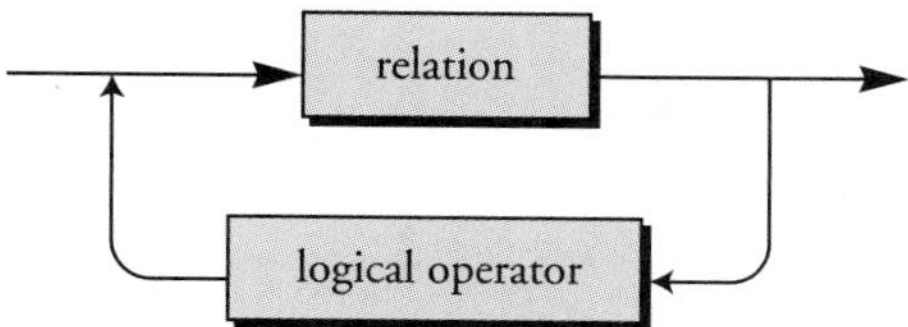

Relation

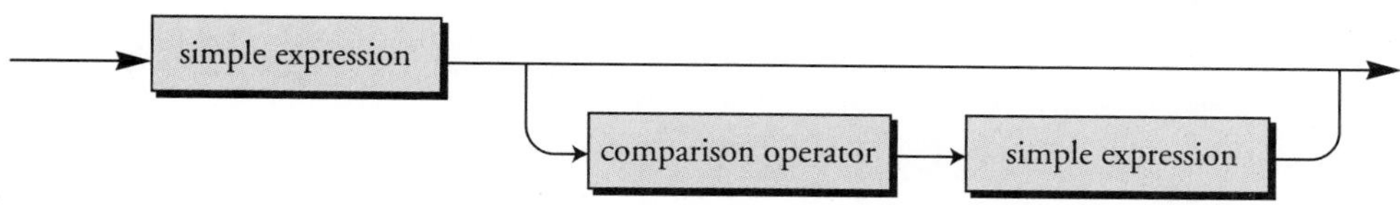

Simple expression

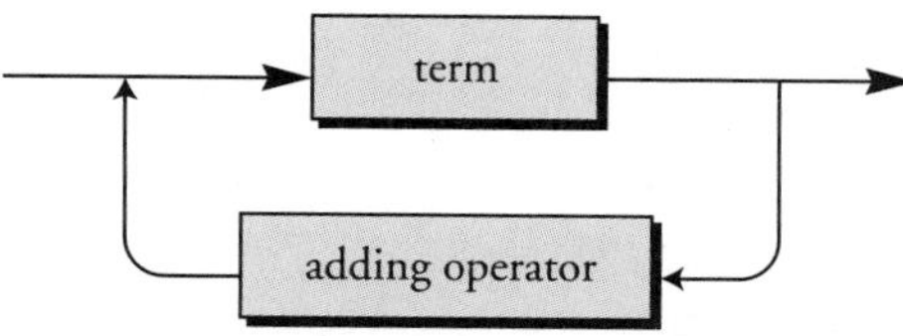

Term

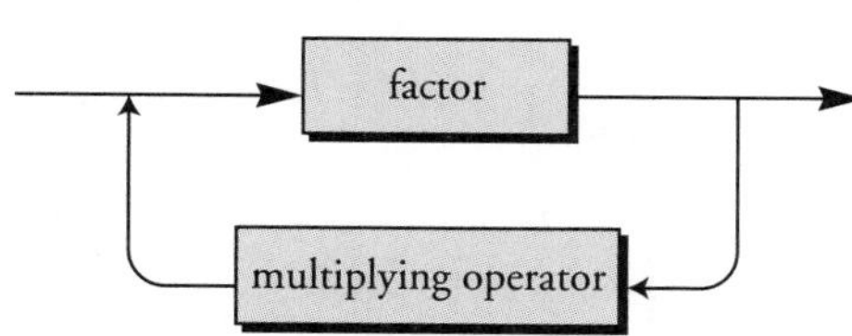

Factor

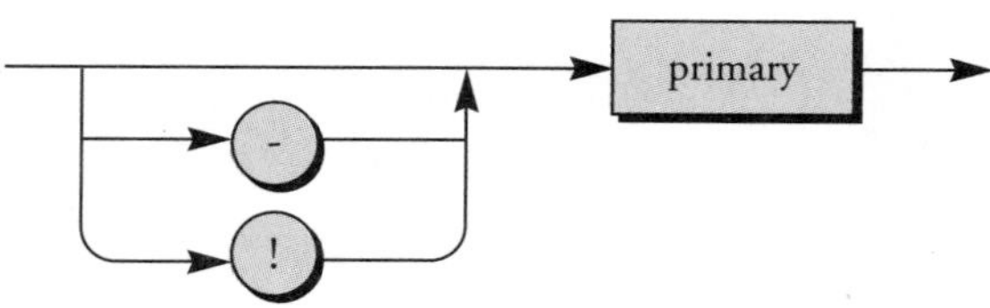

Primary

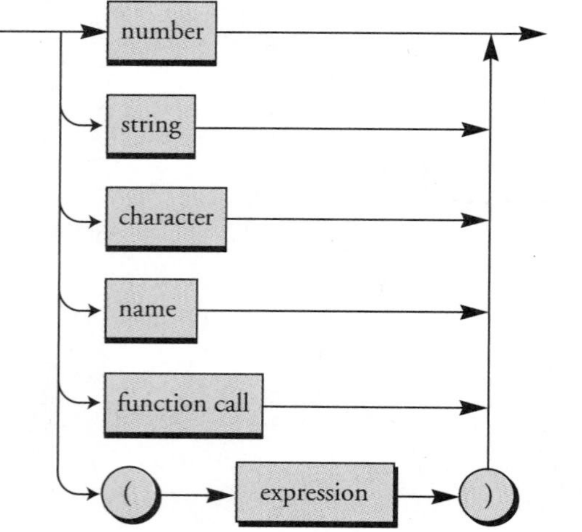

Name

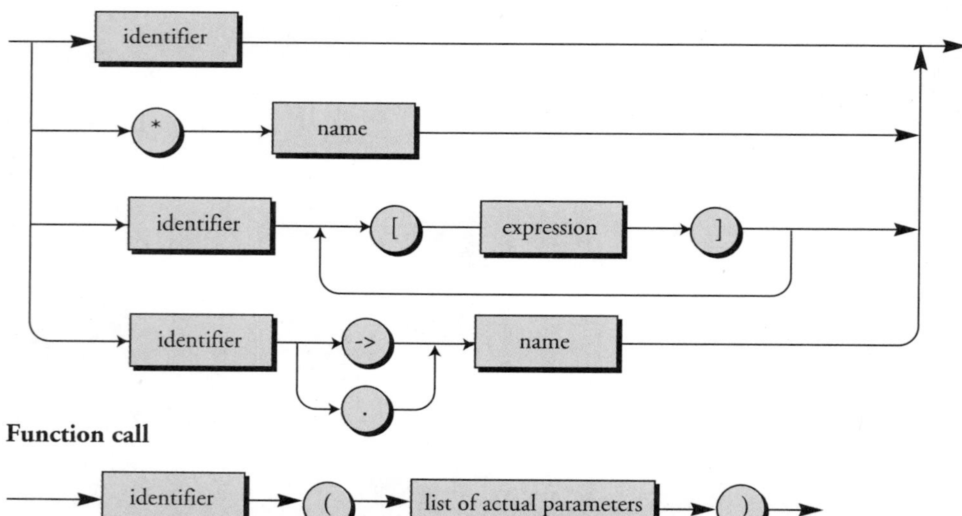

Function call

identifier (list of actual parameters)

List of actual parameters

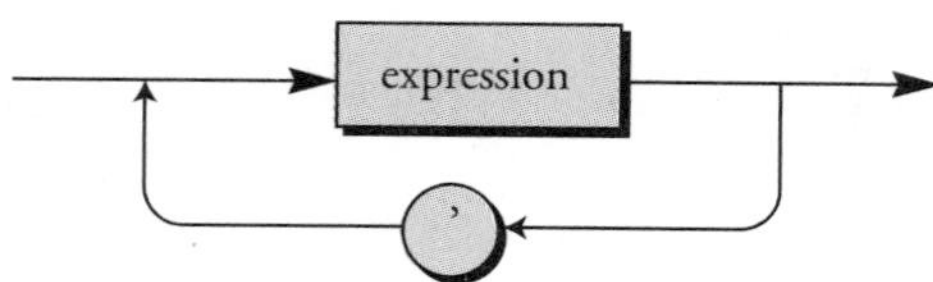

Logical operator

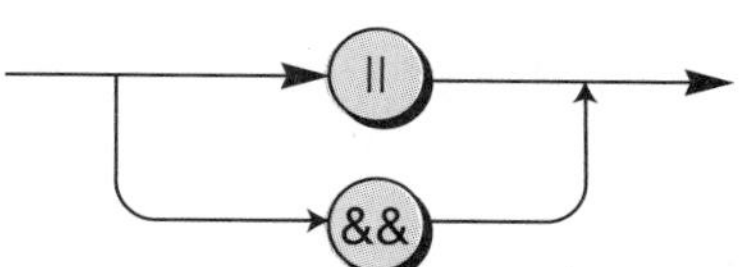

Adding operator

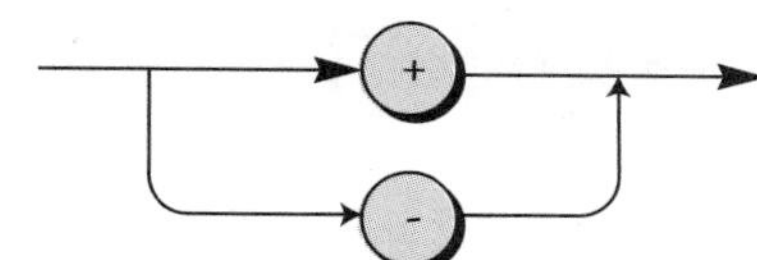

Comparison operator

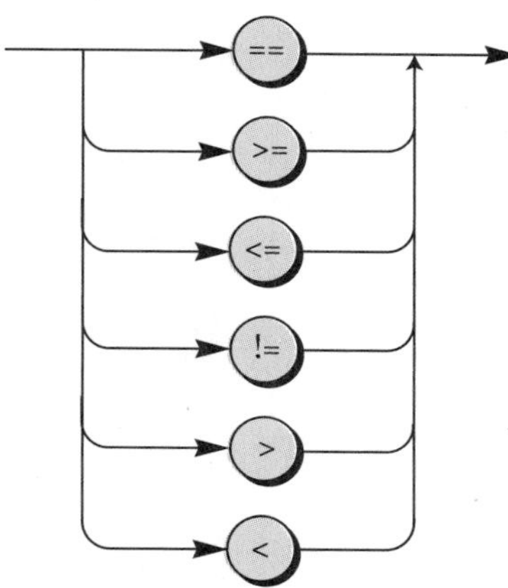

Multiplying operator

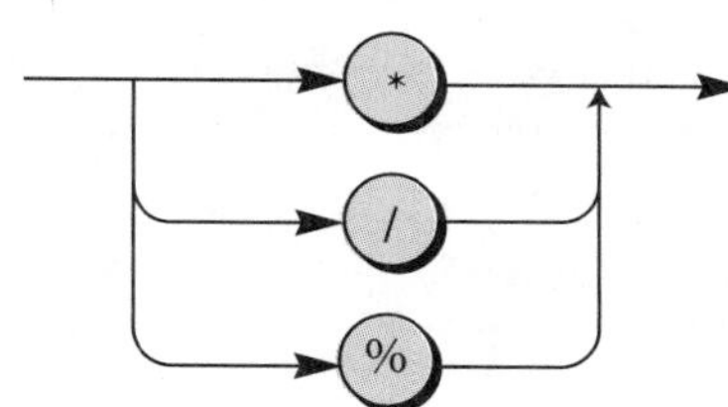

Class declaration module

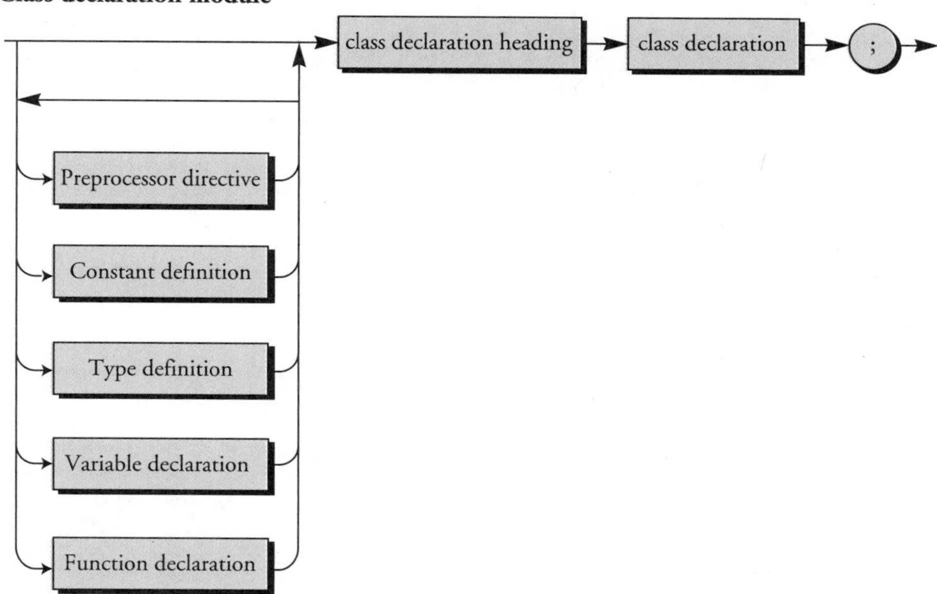

Class declaration heading

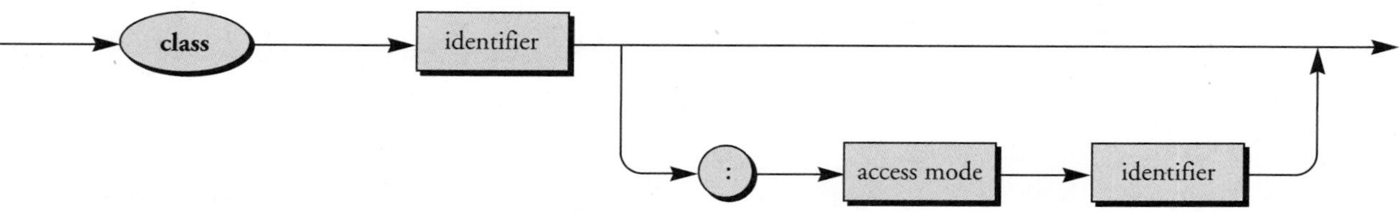

Class declaration

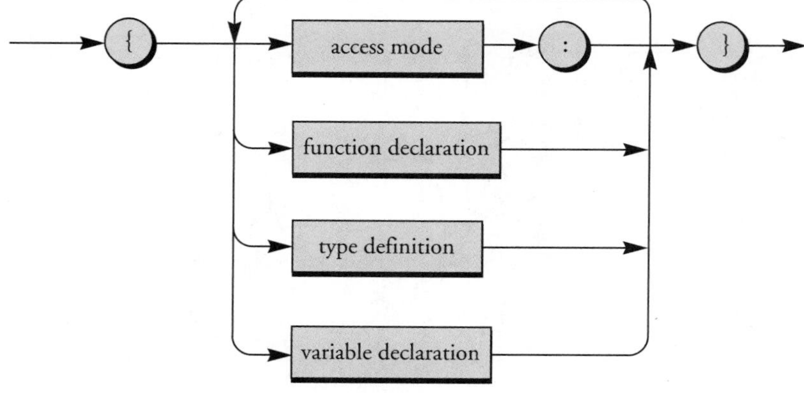

Access mode

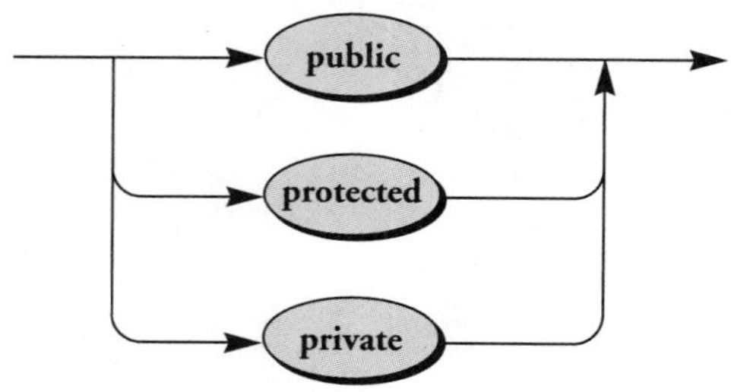

APPENDIX D

The ASCII Character Set

This table shows the ordering of the ASCII character set. The printable characters range from ASCII 33 to ASCII 126. The values from ASCII 0 to ASCII 32 and ASCII 127 are associated with white space characters, such as the horizontal tab (HT), or non-printing control characters, such as the escape key (ESC). The digits in the left column represent the leftmost digits of the ASCII code, and the digits in the top row are the rightmost digits in the ASCII code. Thus, the ASCII code of the character 'R' at row 8, column 2, is 82.

	0	1	2	3	4	5	6	7	8	9
0	NUL	SOH	STX	ETX	EOT	ENQ	ACK	BEL	BS	HT
1	LF	VT	FF	CR	SO	SI	DLE	DC1	DC2	DC3
2	DC4	NAK	SYN	ETB	CAN	EM	SUB	ESC	FS	GS
3	RS	US	SP	!	"	#	$	%	&	‘
4	(	)	*	+	,	–	.	/	0	1
5	2	3	4	5	6	7	8	9	:	;
6	<	=	>	?	@	A	B	C	D	E
7	F	G	H	I	J	K	L	M	N	O
8	P	Q	R	S	T	U	V	W	X	Y
9	Z	[	\	]	^	_	’	a	b	c
10	d	e	f	g	h	i	j	k	l	m
11	n	o	p	q	r	s	t	u	v	w
12	x	y	z	{	|	}	~	DEL		

APPENDIX E

The AP Classes

The AP classes for strings, vectors, matrices, stacks, and queues have been developed by the Advanced Placement Computer Science Ad Hoc Committee on C++ to facilitate problem solving and programming with C++ classes. The first three classes are discussed in simplified form in Chapter 9. Classes similar to the last two are discussed in Chapter 13. The following sections contain the complete listings of the class libraries for the AP classes. The AP classes are available as source code files on the Web site that accompanies the text. Documentation for the complete APCS C++ subset can be obtained on the World Wide Web at http://www.cs.duke.edu/~ola/ap/prolog.html.

apstring

```
#ifndef _APSTRING_H
#define _APSTRING_H

#include <iostream.h>
// uncomment line below if bool not built-in type
// #include "bool.h"

// ****************************************************************
//  Last Revised: 11/24/98 - corrected specification comments, dhj
//
//  8/14/98 corrected comments, dhj
//  6/29/98 - commented out the #include "bool.h", dhj
//
//  APCS string class
//
//  string class consistent with a subset of the standard C++ string class
//  as defined in the draft ANSI standard
// ****************************************************************

extern const int npos;  // used to indicate not a position in the string

class apstring
{
  public:

  // constructors/destructor

    apstring( );                          // construct empty string ""
    apstring( const char * s );           // construct from string literal
    apstring( const apstring & str );     // copy constructor
    ~apstring( );                         // destructor

  // assignment

    const apstring & operator = ( const apstring & str ); // assign str
    const apstring & operator = ( const char * s );       // assign s
    const apstring & operator = ( char ch );              // assign ch
```

```
  // accessors

    int     length( )                    const;    // number of chars
    int     find( const apstring & str ) const;    // index of first occurrence of str
    int     find( char ch )              const;    // index of first occurrence of ch
    apstring substr( int pos, int len ) const;      // substring of len chars
                                                   // starting at pos
    const char * c_str( )                const;    // explicit conversion to char *

  // indexing

    char   operator[ ]( int k )          const;    // range-checked indexing
    char & operator[ ]( int k );                   // range-checked indexing

  // modifiers

    const apstring & operator += ( const apstring & str );// append str
    const apstring & operator += ( char ch );            // append char


  private:
      int myLength;                        // length of string (# of characters)
      int myCapacity;                      // capacity of string
      char * myCstring;                    // storage for characters
};

// The following free (non-member) functions operate on strings
//
// I/O functions

ostream & operator << ( ostream & os, const apstring & str );
istream & operator >> ( istream & is, apstring & str );
istream & getline( istream & is, apstring & str );

// comparison operators:

bool operator == ( const apstring & lhs, const apstring & rhs );
bool operator != ( const apstring & lhs, const apstring & rhs );
bool operator <  ( const apstring & lhs, const apstring & rhs );
bool operator <= ( const apstring & lhs, const apstring & rhs );
bool operator >  ( const apstring & lhs, const apstring & rhs );
bool operator >= ( const apstring & lhs, const apstring & rhs );

// concatenation operator +

apstring operator + ( const apstring & lhs, const apstring & rhs );
apstring operator + ( char ch, const apstring & str );
apstring operator + ( const apstring & str, char ch );

// *******************************************************************
// Specifications for string functions
//
// Any violation of a function's precondition will result in an error
// message followed by a call to exit.
//
```

continued

```
// The apstring class assumes that '\0' is not a valid
// character in an apstring. Any attempts to place '\0'
// in an apstring will result in undefined behavior. Generally
// this means that characters that follow the '\0' will not
// be considered part of the apstring for purposes of
// comparison, output, and subsequent copying.
//
// constructors / destructor
//
// string( )
//    postcondition: string is empty
//
// string( const char * s )
//    description:   constructs a string object from a literal string
//                   such as "abcd"
//    precondition:  s is '\0'-terminated string as used in C
//    postcondition: copy of s has been constructed
//
// string( const string & str )
//    description:   copy constructor
//    postcondition: copy of str has been constructed
//
// ~string( );
//    description:   destructor
//    postcondition: string is destroyed
//
// assignment
//
// string & operator = ( const string & rhs )
//    postcondition: normal assignment via copying has been performed
//
// string & operator = ( const char * s )
//    description:   assignment from literal string such as "abcd"
//    precondition:  s is '\0'-terminated string as used in C
//    postcondition: assignment via copying of s has been performed
//
// string & operator = ( char ch )
//    description:   assignment from character as though single char string
//    postcondition: assignment of one-character string has been performed
//
// accessors
//
// int length( ) const;
//    postcondition: returns # of chars in string
//
// int find( const string & str)  const;
//    description:   find the first occurrence of the string str within this
//                   string and return the index of the first character. If
//                   str does not occur in this string, then return npos.
//    precondition:  this string represents c0, c1, ..., c(n-1)
//                   str represents s0, s1, ..., s(m-1)
//    postcondition: if s0 == ck0, s1 == ck1, ..., s(m-1) == ck(m-1) and
//                   there is no j < k0 such that s0 = cj, ...., sm == c(j+m-1),
//                   then returns k0;
//                   otherwise returns npos
//
```

```
// int find( char ch ) const;
//    description:   finds the first occurrence of the character ch within this
//                   string and returns the index. If ch does not occur in this
//                   string, then returns npos.
//    precondition:  this string represents c0, c1, ..., c(n-1)
//    postcondition: if ch == ck, and there is no j < k such that ch == cj
//                   then returns k;
//                   otherwise returns npos
//
// string substr( int pos, int len ) const;
//    description:  extract and return the substring of length len starting
//                  at index pos
//    precondition: this string represents c0, c1, ..., c(n-1)
//                         0 <= pos <= pos + len - 1 < n.
//    postcondition: returns the string that represents
//                   c(pos), c(pos+1), ..., c(pos+len-1)
//
// const char * c_str( ) const;
//    description:   convert string into a '\0'-terminated string as
//                   used in C for use with functions
//                   that have '\0'-terminated string parameters.
//    postcondition: returns the equivalent '\0'-terminated string
//
// indexing
//
// char operator [ ]( int k ) const;
//    precondition:  0 <= k < length()
//    postcondition: returns copy of the kth character
//
// char & operator [ ]( int k )
//    precondition:  0 <= k < length()
//    postcondition: returns reference to the kth character
//    note:          if this reference is used to write a '\0'
//                   subsequent results are undefined
//
// modifiers
//
// const string & operator += ( const string & str )
//    postcondition: concatenates a copy of str onto this string
//
// const string & operator += ( char ch )
//    postcondition: concatenates a copy of ch onto this string
//
//
// non-member functions
//
// ostream & operator << ( ostream & os, const string & str)
//    postcondition: str is written to output stream os
//
// istream & operator >> ( istream & is, string & str )
//    precondition:  input stream is open for reading
//    postcondition: the next string from input stream is has been read
//                   and stored in str
//
// istream & getline( istream & is, string & str )
```

continued

```
//    description:  reads a line from input stream is into the string str
//    precondition: input stream is open for reading
//    postcondition: chars from input stream is up to '\n' have been read
//                   and stored in str; the '\n' has been read but not stored
//
// string operator + ( const string & lhs, const string & rhs )
//    postcondition: returns concatenation of lhs with rhs
//
// string operator + ( char ch, const string & str )
//    postcondition: returns concatenation of ch with str
//
// string operator + ( const string & str, char ch )
//    postcondition: returns concatenation of str with ch
//
//*************************************************************
#endif
```

```
// *******************************************************************
"
//  Revised: January 13, 1998,  <= and >= redefined using ! and <
//                              operator += now takes constant
//                              amortized time for adding one char
//
//  Revised: November 19, 1998, replaced assert with exit: operator[]
//                              changed operator >> and getline
//                              so no limit on size of strings read
//
//  APCS string class  IMPLEMENTATION
//
//  see apstring.h for complete documentation of functions
//
//  string class consistent with a subset of the standard C++ string class
//  as defined in the draft ANSI standard
// *******************************************************************

#include <string.h>
#include <assert.h>
#include <stdlib.h>
#include <ctype.h>
#include "apstring.h"

const int npos = -1;

apstring::apstring()
// postcondition: string is empty
{
    myLength = 0;
    myCapacity = 1;
    myCstring = new char[myCapacity];
    myCstring[0] = '\0';           // make c-style string zero length
}

apstring::apstring(const char * s)
//description:   constructs a string object from a literal string
//               such as "abcd"
//precondition:  s is '\0'-terminated string as used in C
```

```
//postcondition: copy of s has been constructed
{
    assert (s != 0);                  // C-string not NULL?

    myLength = strlen(s);
    myCapacity = myLength + 1;        // make room for '\0'
    myCstring = new char[myCapacity];
    strcpy(myCstring,s);
}

apstring::apstring(const apstring & str)
//description:   copy constructor
//postcondition: copy of str has been constructed
{
    myLength = str.length();
    myCapacity = myLength + 1;
    myCstring = new char[myCapacity];
    strcpy(myCstring,str.myCstring);
}

apstring::~apstring()
//description:   destructor
//postcondition: string is destroyed
{
    delete[] myCstring;                  // free memory
}

const apstring& apstring::operator =(const apstring & rhs)
//postcondition: normal assignment via copying has been performed
{
    if (this != &rhs)                             // check aliasing
    {
        if (myCapacity < rhs.length() + 1)        // more memory needed?
        {
            delete[] myCstring;                   // delete old string
            myCapacity = rhs.length() + 1;        // add 1 for '\0'
            myCstring = new char[myCapacity];
        }
        myLength = rhs.length();
        strcpy(myCstring,rhs.myCstring);
    }
    return *this;
}

const apstring& apstring::operator = (const char * s)
//description:  assignment from literal string such as "abcd"
//precondition: s is '\0'-terminated string as used in C
//postcondition: assignment via copying of s has been performed
{

    int len = 0;                          // length of newly constructed string
    assert(s != 0);                       // make sure s non-NULL
    len = strlen(s); // # of characters in string

    // free old string if necessary
```

continued

```
    if (myCapacity < len + 1)
    {
   delete[] myCstring;  // delete old string
   myCapacity = len + 1;   // add 1 for '\0'
   myCstring = new char[myCapacity];
    }
    myLength = len;
    strcpy(myCstring,s);
    return *this;
}

const apstring& apstring::operator = (char ch)
//description:   assignment from character as though single char string
//postcondition: assignment of one-character string has been performed
{
    if (myCapacity < 2)
    {
        delete [] myCstring;
        myCapacity = 2;
        myCstring = new char[myCapacity];
    }
    myLength = 1;
    myCstring[0] = ch;  // make string one character long
    myCstring[1] = '\0';
    return *this;
}

int apstring::length( ) const
//postcondition: returns # of chars in string
{
    return myLength;
}

const char * apstring::c_str() const
//description:   convert string into a '\0'-terminated string as
//               used in C for use with functions
//               that have '\0'-terminated string parameters.
//postcondition: returns the equivalent '\0'-terminated string
{
    return myCstring;
}

char& apstring::operator[](int k)
// precondition:  0 <= k < length()
// postcondition: returns copy of the kth character
// note:          if this reference is used to write a '\0'
//                subsequent results are undefined
{
    if (k < 0 || myLength <= k)
    {
        cerr << "index out of range: " << k << " string: " << myCstring
            << endl;
        exit(1);
    }
    return myCstring[k];
}
```

```
char apstring::operator[](int k) const
// precondition:  0 <= k < length()
// postcondition: returns copy of the kth character
{
    if (k < 0 || myLength <= k)
    {
        cerr << "index out of range: " << k << " string: " << myCstring
            << endl;
        exit(1);
    }
    return myCstring[k];
}

ostream& operator <<(ostream & os, const apstring & str)
//postcondition: str is written to output stream os
{
    return os << str.c_str();
}

istream& operator >>(istream & is, apstring & str)
//precondition:  input stream is open for reading
//postcondition: the next string from input stream is has been read
//               and stored in str
{
    char ch;
    str = "";    // empty string, will build one char at-a-time
    is >> ch;    // whitespace skipped, first non-white char in ch

    if (! is.fail())
    {
        do
        {
            str += ch;
            is.get(ch);
        } while (! is.fail() && ! isspace(ch));

        if (isspace(ch))    // put whitespace back on the stream
        {
            is.putback(ch);
        }
    }

    return is;
}

istream & getline(istream & is, apstring & str)
//description:   reads a line from input stream is into the string str
//precondition:  input stream is open for reading
//postcondition: chars from input stream is up to '\n' have been read
{

    char ch;
    str = "";     // empty string, will build one char at-a-time

    while (is.get(ch) && ch != '\n')
```

continued

```
    {
        str += ch;
    }

    return is;
}

const apstring& apstring::operator +=(const apstring & str)
//postcondition: concatenates a copy of str onto this string
{

    apstring copystring(str);          // copy to avoid aliasing problems

    int newLength = length() + str.length(); // self + added string
    int lastLocation = length();       // index of '\0'

    // check to see if local buffer not big enough
    if (newLength >= myCapacity)
    {
        myCapacity = newLength + 1;
   if (str.length() == 1)  // special case for catenating one char
   {                       // make room for future catenations
       myCapacity *= 2;
   }
        char * newBuffer = new char[myCapacity];
        strcpy(newBuffer,myCstring); // copy into new buffer
        delete [] myCstring;        // delete old string
        myCstring = newBuffer;
    }

    // now catenate str (copystring) to end of myCstring
    strcpy(myCstring+lastLocation,copystring.c_str() );
    myLength = newLength;              // update information

    return *this;
}

const apstring & apstring::operator += ( char ch )
// postcondition: concatenates a copy of ch onto this string
{
    apstring temp;   // make string equivalent of ch
    temp = ch;
    *this += temp;
    return *this;
}

apstring operator +(const apstring & lhs, const apstring & rhs)
// postcondition: returns concatenation of lhs with rhs
{
    apstring result(lhs);  // copies lhs to result
    result += rhs;   // catenate rhs
    return result;   // returns a copy of result
}

apstring operator + ( char ch, const apstring & str )
// postcondition: returns concatenation of ch with str
```

```
{
    apstring result; // make string equivalent of ch
    result = ch;
    result += str;
    return result;
}

apstring operator + ( const apstring & str, char ch )
// postcondition: returns concatenation of str with ch
{
    apstring result(str);
    result += ch;
    return result;
}

apstring apstring::substr(int pos, int len) const
//description:   extract and return the substring of length len starting
//               at index pos
//precondition:  this string represents c0, c1, ..., c(n-1)
//               0 <pos <= pos + len - 1 < n.
//postcondition: returns the string that represents
//               c(pos), c(pos+1), ..., c(pos+len-1)
//
{
    if (pos < 0)                        // start at front when pos < 0
    {
       pos = 0;
    }

    if (pos >= myLength) return "";     // empty string

    int lastIndex = pos + len - 1;      // last char's index (to copy)
    if (lastIndex >= myLength)          // off end of string?
    {
        lastIndex = myLength-1;
    }

    apstring result(*this);               // make sure enough space allocated

    int j,k;
    for(j=0,k=pos; k <= lastIndex; j++,k++)
    {
        result.myCstring[j] = myCstring[k];
    }
    result.myCstring[j] = '\0';         // properly terminate C-string
    result.myLength = j;                // record length properly
    return result;
}

int apstring::find(const apstring & str)  const
//description:  find the first occurrence of the string str within this
//              string and return the index of the first character. If
//              str does not occur in this string, then return npos.
//precondition: this string represents c0, c1, ..., c(n-1)
//              str represents s0, s1, ..., s(m-1)
```

continued

```
//postcondition: if s0 == ck0, s1 == ck1, ..., s(m-1) == ck(m-1) and
//               there is no j < k0 such that s0 = cj, ...., sm == c(j+m-1),
//               then returns k0;
//               otherwise returns npos
{
    int len = str.length();
    int lastIndex = length() - len;
    int k;
    for(k=0; k <= lastIndex; k++)
    {
        if (strncmp(myCstring + k,str.c_str(),len) == 0) return k;
    }
    return npos;
}

int apstring::find( char ch ) const
// description:   finds the first occurrence of the character ch within this
//                string and returns the index. If ch does not occur in this
//                string, then returns npos.
// precondition:  this string represents c0, c1, ..., c(n-1)
// postcondition: if ch == ck, and there is no j < k such that ch == cj
//                then returns k;
//                otherwise returns npos
{
    int k;
    for(k=0; k < myLength; k++)
    {
        if (myCstring[k] == ch)
        {
       return k;
   }
    }
    return npos;
}

bool operator == ( const apstring & lhs, const apstring & rhs )
{
    return strcmp(lhs.c_str(), rhs.c_str()) == 0;
}

bool operator != ( const apstring & lhs, const apstring & rhs )
{
    return ! (lhs == rhs);
}

bool operator <  ( const apstring & lhs, const apstring & rhs )
{
    return strcmp(lhs.c_str(), rhs.c_str()) < 0;
}

bool operator <= ( const apstring & lhs, const apstring & rhs )
{
    return !( rhs < lhs );
}
bool operator >  ( const apstring & lhs, const apstring & rhs )
{
```

```
    return rhs < lhs;
}

bool operator >= ( const apstring & lhs, const apstring & rhs )
{
    return ! ( lhs < rhs );
}
```

apvector

```
#ifndef _APVECTOR_H
#define _APVECTOR_H

// *******************************************************************
// Last Revised: 8/14/98, abort changed to exit
//
// January 13, 1998, added explicit to int constructor
// APCS vector class template
//
// implements "safe" (range-checked) arrays
// examples are given at the end of this file
// *******************************************************************

// If your compiler supports the keyword explicit, comment out the
// #define explicit line below, leaving the #define means explicit
// is ignored, but doesn't generate an error
//
//   This will disallow a typically erroneous implicit type-conversion:
//   vector<int> v( 10 );
//   v = 0; // Oops!! Allowed because of implicit type-conversion.

#define explicit

template <class itemType>
class apvector
{
  public:

  // constructors/destructor
    apvector( );                        // default constructor (size==0)
    explicit apvector( int size );      // initial size of vector is size
    apvector( int size, const itemType & fillValue ); // all entries == fillValue
    apvector( const apvector & vec );   // copy constructor
    ~apvector( );                       // destructor

  // assignment
    const apvector & operator = ( const apvector & vec );

  // accessors
    int  length( ) const;                   // capacity of vector

  // indexing
    itemType &       operator [ ] ( int index );       // indexing with range
checking
```

continued

```
    const itemType & operator [ ] ( int index ) const; // indexing with range
checking

  // modifiers
    void resize( int newSize );                // change size dynamically;
                                               // can result in losing values
  private:

    int  mySize;                               // # elements in array
    itemType * myList;                         // array used for storage
};

// ******************************************************************
//  Specifications for vector functions
//
//  The template parameter itemType must satisfy the following two conditions:
//   (1) itemType has a 0-argument constructor
//   (2) operator = is defined for itemType
//  Any violation of these conditions may result in compilation failure.
//
//  Any violation of a function's precondition will result in an error message
//  followed by a call to exit.
//
//  constructors/destructor
//
//   apvector( )
//     postcondition: vector has a capacity of 0 items, and therefore it will
//                    need to be resized
//
//   apvector( int size )
//     precondition: size >= 0
//     postcondition: vector has a capacity of size items
//
//   apvector( int size, const itemType & fillValue )
//     precondition: size >= 0
//     postcondition: vector has a capacity of size items, all of which are set
//                    by assignment to fillValue after default construction
//
//   apvector( const apvector & vec )
//     postcondition: vector is a copy of vec
//
//   ~apvector( )
//     postcondition: vector is destroyed
//
//  assignment
//
//   const apvector & operator = ( const apvector & rhs )
//     postcondition: normal assignment via copying has been performed;
//                    if vector and rhs were different sizes, vector
//                    has been resized to  match the size of rhs
//
//  accessor
//
//   int  length( ) const
//     postcondition: returns vector's size (number of memory cells
//                    allocated for vector)
```

```
//
//  indexing
//
//   itemType &        operator [ ] ( int k )       --index into nonconst vector
//   const itemType & operator [ ] ( int k ) const--index into const vector
//     description: range-checked indexing, returning kth item
//     precondition: 0 <= k < length()
//     postcondition: returns the kth item
//
//  modifier
//
//   void resize( int newSize )
//     description: resizes the vector to newSize elements
//     precondition: the current capacity of vector is length; newSize >= 0
//
//     postcondition: the current capacity of vector is newSize; for each k
//                    such that 0 <= k <= min(length, newSize), vector[k]
//                    is a copy of the original; other elements of vector are
//                    initialized using the 0-argument itemType constructor
//                    Note: if newSize < length, elements may be lost
//
//  examples of use
//       apvector<int> v1;          // 0-element vector
//       apvector<int> v2(4);       // 4-element vector
//       apvector<int> v3(4, 22);   // 4-element vector, all elements == 22.

#include "apvector.cpp"
#endif
```

```
// *******************************************************************
//  Last Revised: 8/14/98
//                changed abort to exit
//
//  APCS vector class  IMPLEMENTATION
//
//  see vector.h for complete documentation of functions
//
//  vector class consistent with a subset of the standard C++ vector class
//  as defined in the draft ANSI standard (part of standard template library)
// *******************************************************************

#include <stdlib.h>
#include <assert.h>
#include <iostream.h>
#include "apvector.h"

template <class itemType>
apvector<itemType>::apvector()
//postcondition: vector has a capacity of 0 items, and therefore it will
//               need to be resized
    : mySize(0),
      myList(0)
{

}
```

```
template <class itemType>
apvector<itemType>::apvector(int size)
// precondition: size >= 0
// postcondition: vector has a capacity of size items
   : mySize(size),
     myList(new itemType[size])
{

}

template <class itemType>
apvector<itemType>::apvector(int size, const itemType & fillValue)
// precondition: size >= 0
// postcondition: vector has a capacity of size items, all of which are set
//                  by assignment to fillValue after default construction
    : mySize(size),
      myList(new itemType[size])
{
    int k;
    for(k = 0; k < size; k++)
    {
        myList[k] = fillValue;
    }
}

template <class itemType>
apvector<itemType>::apvector(const apvector<itemType> & vec)
// postcondition: vector is a copy of vec
    : mySize(vec.length()),
      myList(new itemType[mySize])
{
    int k;
        // copy elements
    for(k = 0; k < mySize; k++){
        myList[k] = vec.myList[k];
    }
}

template <class itemType>
apvector<itemType>::~apvector ()
// postcondition: vector is destroyed
{
    delete [] myList;
}

template <class itemType>
const apvector<itemType> &
apvector<itemType>::operator = (const apvector<itemType> & rhs)
// postcondition: normal assignment via copying has been performed;
//                if vector and rhs were different sizes, vector
//                has been resized to match the size of rhs
{
    if (this != &rhs)                          // don't assign to self!
    {
        delete [] myList;                      // get rid of old storage
        mySize = rhs.length();
```

```
        myList = new itemType [mySize];          // allocate new storage

            // copy rhs
        int k;
        for(k=0; k < mySize; k++)
        {
            myList[k] = rhs.myList[k];
        }
    }
    return *this;                                // permit a = b = c = d
}

template <class itemType>
int apvector<itemType>::length() const
// postcondition: returns vector's size (number of memory cells
//                allocated for vector)
{
    return mySize;
}

template <class itemType>
itemType & apvector<itemType>::operator [] (int k)
// description: range-checked indexing, returning kth item
// precondition: 0 <= k < length()
// postcondition: returns the kth item
{

    if (k < 0 || mySize <= k)
    {
        cerr << "Illegal vector index: " << k << " max index = ";
        cerr << (mySize-1) << endl;
        exit(1);
    }
    return myList[k];
}

template <class itemType>
const itemType & apvector<itemType>::operator [] (int k) const
// safe indexing, returning const reference to avoid modification
// precondition: 0 <= index < length
// postcondition: return index-th item
// exception: exits if index is out-of-bounds
{
    if (k < 0 || mySize <= k)
    {
        cerr << "Illegal vector index: " << k << " max index = ";
        cerr << (mySize-1) << endl;
        exit(1);
    }
    return myList[k];
}

template <class itemType>
void apvector<itemType>::resize(int newSize)
// description: resizes the vector to newSize elements
```

continued

```
// precondition: the current capacity of vector is length(); newSize >= 0
// postcondition: the current capacity of vector is newSize; for each k
//                such that 0 <= k <= min(length, newSize), vector[k]
//                is a copy of the original; other elements of vector are
//                initialized using the 0-argument itemType constructor
//                Note: if newSize < length, elements may be lost
{
    int k;
    int numToCopy = newSize < mySize ? newSize : mySize;

         // allocate new storage and copy element into new storage

    itemType * newList = new itemType[newSize];
    for(k=0; k < numToCopy; k++)
    {
        newList[k] = myList[k];
    }
    delete [] myList;                          // de-allocate old storage
    mySize = newSize;                          // assign new storage/size
    myList = newList;
}
```

apmatrix

```
#ifndef _APMATRIX_H
#define _APMATRIX_H

#include "apvector.h"

// *******************************************************************
// Last Revised: 8/14/98
//               changed abort() to exit(1), dhj
//
// APCS matrix class
//
// extends apvector.h to two dimensional "safe" (range-checked) matrices
// examples are given at the end of this file
// *******************************************************************

template <class itemType>
class apmatrix
{
  public:

  // constructors/destructor
    apmatrix( );                                      // default size 0 x 0
    apmatrix( int rows, int cols );                   // size rows x cols
    apmatrix( int rows, int cols,
            const itemType & fillValue );           // all entries == fillValue
    apmatrix( const apmatrix & mat );                   // copy constructor
    ~apmatrix( );                                     // destructor

  // assignment
    const apmatrix & operator = ( const apmatrix & rhs );
```

```
  // accessors
    int numrows( ) const;                              // number of rows
    int numcols( ) const;                              // number of columns

  // indexing
    const apvector<itemType> & operator [ ] ( int k ) const;  // range-checked
indexing
    apvector<itemType> & operator [ ] ( int k );              // range-checked
indexing

  // modifiers
    void resize( int newRows, int newCols );    // resizes matrix to newRows x newCols
                                                // (can result in losing values)
  private:

    int myRows;                               // # of rows (capacity)
    int myCols;                               // # of cols (capacity)
    apvector<apvector<itemType> > myMatrix; // the matrix of items
};


// *******************************************************************
// Specifications for matrix functions
//
// To use this class, itemType must satisfy the same constraints
// as for vector class.
//
// Any violation of a function's precondition will result in an error message
// followed by a call to exit.
//
// constructors/destructor
//
//  apmatrix( );
//     postcondition: matrix of size 0x0 is constructed, and therefore
//                    will need to be resized later
//
//  apmatrix( int rows, int cols );
//     precondition: 0 <= rows and 0 <= cols
//     postcondition: matrix of size rows x cols is constructed
//
//  apmatrix( int rows, int cols, const itemType & fillValue );
//     precondition: 0 <= rows and 0 <= cols
//     postcondition: matrix of size rows x cols is constructed
//                    all entries are set by assignment to fillValue after
//                    default construction
//
//  apmatrix( const apmatrix<itemType> & mat );
//     postcondition: matrix is a copy of mat
//
//  ~apmatrix( );
//     postcondition: matrix is destroyed
//
// assignment
//
//  const apmatrix & operator = ( const apmatrix & rhs );
```

continued

```
//     postcondition: normal assignment via copying has been performed
//                    (if matrix and rhs were different sizes, matrix has
//                    been resized to match the size of rhs)
//
// accessors
//
//  int numrows( ) const;
//     postcondition: returns number of rows
//
//  int numcols( ) const;
//     postcondition: returns number of columns
//
// indexing
//
//  const apvector<itemType> & operator [ ] ( int k ) const;
//     precondition: 0 <= k < number of rows
//     postcondition: returns k-th row
//
//  apvector<itemType> & operator [ ] ( int k );
//     precondition: 0 <= k < number of rows
//     postcondition: returns k-th row
//
// modifiers
//
//  void resize( int newRows, int newCols );
//     precondition: matrix size is rows X cols,
//                   0 <= newRows and 0 <= newCols
//     postcondition: matrix size is newRows X newCols;
//                    for each 0 <= j <= min(rows,newRows) and
//                    for each 0 <= k <= min(cols,newCols), matrix[j][k] is
//                    a copy of the original; other elements of matrix are
//                    initialized using the default constructor for itemType
//                    Note: if newRows < rows or newCols < cols,
//                          elements may be lost
//
//  Examples of use:
//
//     apmatrix<double> dmat( 100, 80 );        // 100 x 80 matrix of doubles
//     apmatrix<double> dzmat( 100, 80, 0.0 ); // initialized to 0.0
//     apmatrix<apstring> smat( 300, 1 );       // 300 strings
//     apmatrix<int> imat;                      // has room for 0 ints

#include "apmatrix.cpp"
#endif



// *******************************************************************
//  Last Revised: 8/14/98
//                abort changed to exit, dhj
//
//  September 1, 1997--APCS matrix class  IMPLEMENTATION
//
//  see matrix.h for complete documentation of functions
//
//  extends vector class to two-dimensional matrices
// *******************************************************************
```

```
#include "apmatrix.h"
#include <stdlib.h>
#include <iostream.h>

template <class itemType>
apmatrix<itemType>::apmatrix()
        : myRows(0),
          myCols(0),
          myMatrix(0)

// postcondition: matrix of size 0x0 is constructed, and therefore
//                will need to be resized later
{

}
template <class itemType>
apmatrix<itemType>::apmatrix(int rows,int cols)
        : myRows(rows),
          myCols(cols),
          myMatrix(rows)

// precondition: 0 <= rows and 0 <= cols
// postcondition: matrix of size rows x cols is constructed
{
    int k;
    for(k=0; k < rows; k++)
    {
        myMatrix[k].resize(cols);
    }
}

template <class itemType>
apmatrix<itemType>::apmatrix(int rows, int cols, const itemType & fillValue)
        : myRows(rows),
          myCols(cols),
          myMatrix(rows)

// precondition: 0 <= rows and 0 <= cols
// postcondition: matrix of size rows x cols is constructed
//                all entries are set by assignment to fillValue after
//                default construction
//
{
    int j,k;
    for(j=0; j < rows; j++)
    {
        myMatrix[j].resize(cols);
        for(k=0; k < cols; k++)
        {
            myMatrix[j][k] = fillValue;
        }
    }
}

template <class itemType>
```

continued

```
apmatrix<itemType>::apmatrix(const apmatrix<itemType> & mat)
     : myRows(mat.myRows),
       myCols(mat.myCols),
       myMatrix(mat.myRows)

// postcondition: matrix is a copy of mat
{
    int k;
    // copy elements
    for(k = 0; k < myRows; k++)
    {
        // cast to avoid const problems (const -> non-const)
        myMatrix[k] = (apvector<itemType> &) mat.myMatrix[k];
    }
}

template <class itemType>
apmatrix<itemType>::~apmatrix ()
// postcondition: matrix is destroyed
{
    // vector destructor frees everything
}

template <class itemType>
const apmatrix<itemType> &
apmatrix<itemType>::operator = (const apmatrix<itemType> & rhs)
// postcondition: normal assignment via copying has been performed
//                (if matrix and rhs were different sizes, matrix has
//                been resized to match the size of rhs)
{
    if (this != &rhs)                    // don't assign to self!
    {
        myMatrix.resize(rhs.myRows);     // resize to proper # of rows
        myRows = rhs.myRows;             // set dimensions
        myCols = rhs.myCols;

        // copy rhs
        int k;
        for(k=0; k < myRows; k++)
        {
       myMatrix[k] = rhs.myMatrix[k];
        }
    }
    return *this;
}

template <class itemType>
int apmatrix<itemType>::numrows() const
// postcondition: returns number of rows
{
    return myRows;
}

template <class itemType>
int apmatrix<itemType>::numcols() const
// postcondition: returns number of columns
```

```
{
    return myCols;
}


template <class itemType>
void apmatrix<itemType>::resize(int newRows, int newCols)
// precondition: matrix size is rows X cols,
//               0 <= newRows and 0 <= newCols
// postcondition: matrix size is newRows X newCols;
//                for each 0 <= j <= min(rows,newRows) and
//                for each 0 <= k <= min(cols,newCols), matrix[j][k] is
//                a copy of the original; other elements of matrix are
//                initialized using the default constructor for itemType
//                Note: if newRows < rows or newCols < cols,
//                      elements may be lost
//
{
    int k;
    myMatrix.resize(newRows);

    for(k=0; k < newRows; k++)
    {
        myMatrix[k].resize(newCols);
    }
    myRows = newRows;
    myCols = newCols;
}

template <class itemType>
const apvector<itemType> &
apmatrix<itemType>::operator [] (int k) const
// precondition: 0 <= k < number of rows
// postcondition: returns k-th row
{
    if (k < 0 || myRows <= k)
    {
        cerr << "Illegal matrix index: " << k << " max index = ";
        cerr << myRows-1 << endl;
        exit(1);
    }
    return myMatrix[k];
}

template <class itemType>
apvector<itemType> &
apmatrix<itemType>::operator [] (int k)
// precondition: 0 <= k < number of rows
// postcondition: returns k-th row
{
    if (k < 0 || myRows <= k)
    {
        cerr << "Illegal matrix index: " << k << " max index = ";
        cerr << myRows-1 << endl;
        exit(1);
```

continued

```
    }
    return myMatrix[k];
}
```

apstack

```
#ifndef _APSTACK_H
#define _APSTACK_H

// uncomment line below if bool not built-in type
// #include "bool.h"

// *******************************************************************
//  Last Revised: 8/14/98
//
//  - commented out the #include "bool.h", dhj
//  - abort-->> exit
//
// APCS stack class
// *******************************************************************

#include "apvector.h"                    // used for stack implementation

template <class itemType>
class apstack
{
  public:

  // constructors/destructor

    apstack( );                              // construct empty stack
    apstack( const apstack & s );            // copy constructor
    ~apstack( );                             // destructor

  // assignment

    const apstack & operator = ( const apstack & rhs );

  // accessors

    const itemType & top( )      const;   // return top element (NO pop)
    bool             isEmpty( )  const;   // return true if empty, else false
    int              length( )   const;   // return number of elements in stack

  // modifiers

    void push( const itemType & item );   // push item onto top of stack
    void pop( );                          // pop top element
    void pop( itemType & item );          // combines pop and top
    void makeEmpty( );                    // make stack empty (no elements)

  private:

    int myTop;                            // index of top element
```

```
    apvector<itemType> myElements;          // storage for stack
};

  // *******************************************************************
  //
  // Specifications for stack functions
  //
  // Any violation of a function's precondition will result in an error message
  // followed by a call to exit.
  //
  //
  // constructors/destructor
  //
  //  apstack( )
  //    postcondition: the stack is empty
  //
  //  apstack( const apstack & s )
  //    postcondition: stack is a copy of s
  //
  //  ~apstack( )
  //    postcondition: stack is destroyed
  //
  // assignment
  //
  //  const apstack & operator = ( const apstack & rhs )
  //    postcondition: normal assignment via copying has been performed
  //
  // accessors
  //
  //  const itemType & top( ) const
  //    precondition: stack is [e1, e2, ... en] with n >= 1
  //    postcondition: returns en
  //
  //  bool isEmpty( ) const
  //     postcondition: returns true if stack is empty, false otherwise
  //
  //  int length( ) const
  //     postcondition: returns # of elements currently in stack
  //
  // modifiers
  //
  //  void push( const itemType & item )
  //     precondition: stack is [e1, e2...en] with  n >= 0
  //     postcondition: stack is [e1, e2, ... en, item]
  //
  //  void pop( )
  //     precondition: stack is [e1, e2, ... en] with n >= 1
  //     postcondition: stack is [e1, e2, ... e(n-1)]
  //
  //
  //  void pop(itemType & item )
  //     precondition: stack is [e1,e2,...en] with n >= 1
  //     postcondition: stack is [e1,e2,...e(n-1)] and item == en
  //
  //  void makeEmpty( )
```

continued

```
  //     postcondition: stack is empty
  //
  //  Examples of variable definition
  //
  //    apstack<int> istack;                   // creates empty stack of integers
  //    apstack<double> dstack;                // creates empty stack of doubles
  //

#include "apstack.cpp"

#endif
```

```
// *******************************************************************
//  Last Revised: 8/18/98
//                abort() changed to exit(1)
//                comments updated
//
//  September 1, 1997--APCS stack class  IMPLEMENTATION
//
//  stack implemented using the APCS vector class
// *******************************************************************

#include "apstack.h"
#include <stdlib.h>

const int SDEFAULT_SIZE = 10;        // default initial stack size

template <class itemType>
apstack<itemType>::apstack( )
    : myTop(-1),
      myElements(SDEFAULT_SIZE)

// postcondition: the stack is empty
{

}

template <class itemType>
apstack<itemType>::apstack(const apstack<itemType> & s)
   : myTop(s.myTop),
     myElements(s.myElements)

// postcondition: stack is a copy of s
{

}

template <class itemType>
apstack<itemType>::~apstack()
// postcondition: stack is destroyed
{
    // vector destructor frees memory
}

template <class itemType>
```

```
const apstack<itemType> &
apstack<itemType>::operator = (const apstack<itemType> & rhs)
// postcondition: normal assignment via copying has been performed
{
    if (this != &rhs)
    {
        myTop = rhs.myTop;
        myElements = rhs.myElements;
    }
    return *this;
}

template <class itemType>
bool
apstack<itemType>::isEmpty() const
// postcondition: returns true if stack is empty, false otherwise
{
    return myTop == -1;
}

template <class itemType>
int
apstack<itemType>::length() const
// postcondition: returns # of elements currently in stack
{
    return myTop+1;
}

template <class itemType>
void
apstack<itemType>::push(const itemType & item)
// precondition: stack is [e1, e2...en] with  n >= 0
// postcondition: stack is [e1, e2, ... en, item]
{
    if( myTop + 1 >= myElements.length() )   // grow vector if necessary
    {
        myElements.resize(myElements.length() * 2);
    }
    myTop++;                                // new top most element
    myElements[myTop ] = item;
}

template <class itemType>
void
apstack<itemType>::pop()
// precondition: stack is [e1,e2,...en] with n >= 1
// postcondition: stack is [e1,e2,...e(n-1)]
{
    if (isEmpty())
    {
        cerr << "error, popping an empty stack" << endl;
        exit(1);
    }
    myTop--;
}
```

continued

```
template <class itemType>
void
apstack<itemType>::pop(itemType & item)
// precondition: stack is [e1,e2,...en] with n >= 1
// postcondition: stack is [e1,e2,...e(n-1)] and item == en
{
    if (isEmpty())
    {
        cerr << "error, popping an empty stack" << endl;
        exit(1);
    }
    item = myElements[myTop];
    myTop--;
}

template <class itemType>
const itemType &
apstack<itemType>::top() const
// precondition: stack is [e1, e2, ... en] with n >= 1
// postcondition: returns en
{
    if (isEmpty())
    {
        cerr << "error, popping an empty stack" << endl;
        exit(1);
    }
    return myElements[myTop];
}

template <class itemType>
void
apstack<itemType>::makeEmpty()
// postcondition: stack is empty
{
    myTop = -1;
}
```

apqueue

```
#ifndef _APQUEUE_H
#define _APQUEUE_H

// uncomment line below if bool not built-in type
// #include "bool.h"

// *******************************************************************
// Last Revised: 8-14-98
//
//  - commented out the #include "bool.h", dhj
//  - updated comments for constructor/destructor, dhj
//
// APCS queue class
// *******************************************************************
```

```
#include "apvector.h"                        // used to implement queue

template <class itemType>
class apqueue
{
  public:

  // constructors/destructor

    apqueue( );                              // construct empty queue
    apqueue( const apqueue & q );             // copy constructor
    ~apqueue( );                             // destructor

  // assignment

    const apqueue & operator = ( const apqueue & rhs );

  // accessors

    const itemType & front( )   const;      // return front (no dequeue)
    bool             isEmpty( ) const;      // return true if empty else false
    int              length( )  const;      // return number of elements in queue

  // modifiers

    void enqueue( const itemType & item );  // insert item (at rear)
    void dequeue( );                        // remove first element
    void dequeue( itemType & item );        // combine front and dequeue
    void makeEmpty( );                      // make queue empty

   private:

    int mySize;                    // # of elts currently in queue
    int myFront;                   // index of first element
    int myBack;                    // index of last element
    apvector<itemType> myElements; // internal storage for elements

        // private helper functions
    void DoubleQueue();              // double storage for myElements
    void Increment(int & val) const; // add one with wraparound
};

// **********************************************************************
// Specifications for queue functions
//
// Any violation of a function's precondition will result in an error message
// followed by a call to exit.
//
// constructors/destructor
//
//  apqueue( )
//     postcondition: the queue is empty
//
//  apqueue( const apqueue & q )
//     postcondition: queue is a copy of q
```

continued

```
//
//  ~apqueue( )
//     postcondition: queue is destroyed
//
// assignment
//
//  const apqueue & operator = ( const apqueue & rhs )
//     postcondition: normal assignment via copying has been performed
//
// accessors
//
//  const itemType & front( ) const
//     precondition: queue is [e1, e2, ..., en] with n >= 1
//     postcondition: returns e1
//
//  bool isEmpty( ) const
//     postcondition: returns true if queue is empty, false otherwise
//
//  int length( ) const
//     precondition: queue is [e1, e2, ..., en] with n >= 0
//     postcondition: returns n
//
// modifiers:
//
//  void enqueue( const itemType & item )
//     precondition: queue is [e1, e2, ..., en] with n >= 0
//     postcondition: queue is [e1, e2, ..., en, item]
//
//  void dequeue( )
//     precondition: queue is [e1, e2, ..., en] with n >= 1
//     postcondition: queue is [e2, ..., en]
//
//  void dequeue( itemType & item )
//     precondition: queue is [e1, e2, ..., en] with n >= 1
//     postcondition: queue is [e2, ..., en] and item == e1
//
//  void makeEmpty( )
//     postcondition: queue is empty
//
// Examples for use:
//
//    apqueue<int> iqueue;          // creates empty queue of integers
//    apqueue<double> dqueue        // creates empty queue of doubles

#include "apqueue.cpp"

#endif
```

```
// *******************************************************************
//  Last Revised: 8/14/98
//
//  APCS queue class  IMPLEMENTATION
//
//  queue implemented using the APCS vector class
```

```
//  based on queue class in Mark Weiss' : Algorithms, Data Structures,
//                                         and Problem Solving with C++
// ****************************************************************

#include "apqueue.h"
#include <stdlib.h>

const int QDEFAULT_SIZE = 10;        // default initial queue size

template <class itemType>
apqueue<itemType>::apqueue()
   : mySize(0),
     myFront(0),
     myBack( -1 ),
     myElements(QDEFAULT_SIZE)

// postcondition: the queue is empty
{

}

template <class itemType>
apqueue<itemType>::apqueue(const apqueue<itemType> & q)
    : mySize(q.mySize),
      myFront(q.myFront),
      myBack(q.myBack),
      myElements(q.myElements)

// postcondition: queue is a copy of q
{

}

template <class itemType>
apqueue<itemType>::~apqueue()
// postcondition: queue is destroyed
{
   // vector destructor takes care of memory
}

template <class itemType>
const apqueue<itemType> &
apqueue<itemType>::operator=(const apqueue<itemType> & rhs)
// postcondition: normal assignment via copying has been performed
{
    if( this != &rhs)
    {
        mySize = rhs.mySize;                    // copy all fields of rhs
        myElements.resize(rhs.myElements.length());  // resize storage
        myFront = 0;
        myBack = mySize - 1;                    // index from 0 .. mySize - 1

        int k;
        int rhsk = rhs.myFront;
```

continued

```
        for(k=0; k < mySize; k++)
        {
            myElements[k] = rhs.myElements[rhsk];
            Increment(rhsk);
        }
    }
    return *this;
}

template <class itemType>
const itemType &
apqueue<itemType>::front() const
// precondition: queue is [e1, e2, ..., en] with n >= 1
// postcondition: returns e1
{
    return myElements[myFront];
}

template <class itemType>
bool
apqueue<itemType>::isEmpty() const
// postcondition: returns true if queue is empty, false otherwise
{
    return mySize == 0;
}

template <class itemType>
int
apqueue<itemType>::length() const
// precondition: queue is [e1, e2, ..., en] with n >= 0
// postcondition: returns n
{
    return mySize;
}

template <class itemType>
void
apqueue<itemType>::enqueue(const itemType & item)
// precondition: queue is [e1, e2, ..., en] with n >= 0
// postcondition: queue is [e1, e2, ..., en, item]
{
    if (mySize >= myElements.length()) // grow if necessary to add element
    {
        DoubleQueue();
    }

    Increment(myBack);                  // add element at back of queue
    myElements[myBack] = item;
    mySize++;
}

template <class itemType>
void
apqueue<itemType>::dequeue()
// precondition: queue is [e1, e2, ..., en] with n >= 1
// postcondition: queue is [e2, ..., en] and item == e1
```

```
{
    if (isEmpty())
    {
        cerr << "dequeue from empty queue" << endl;
        exit(1);
    }

    mySize--;                           // one fewer element
    Increment(myFront);
}

template <class itemType>
void
apqueue<itemType>::dequeue(itemType & item)
// precondition: queue is [e1, e2, ..., en] with n >= 1
// postcondition: queue is [e2, ..., en] and item == e1
{
    if (isEmpty())
    {
        cerr << "dequeue from empty queue" << endl;
        exit(1);
    }
    item = myElements[myFront];
    mySize--;                           // one fewer element
    Increment(myFront);
}

template <class itemType>
void
apqueue<itemType>::makeEmpty()
// postcondition: queue is empty
{
    mySize = 0;
    myFront = 0;
    myBack = -1;
}

template <class itemType>
void
apqueue<itemType>::Increment( int & val ) const
// postcondition: val increased by one relative to size of myElements
//                i.e., wraps to 0 after reaching capacity of vector storage
{
    val++;
    if (val >= myElements.length() )
    {       val = 0;
    }
}

template <class itemType>
void
apqueue<itemType>::DoubleQueue()
// precondition: queue = e1, e2, ..., en, size = n, capacity = m
// postcondition: queue = e1, e2, ..., en, size = n, capacity = 2*m
{
```

continued

```
    // this could be made more efficient by doing the copy
    // in place (without the temporary vector temp)

    apvector<itemType> temp(myElements.length()*2);    // new storage
    int j,k=myFront;                                    // copy to 0..
    for(j=0; j < mySize; j++)
    {
        temp[j] = myElements[k];
        Increment(k);
    }
    myElements = temp;      // reset private vars to mirror new storage
    myFront = 0;
    myBack = mySize-1;
}
```

Glossary

abstract data type (ADT) A form of abstraction that arises from the use of defined types. An ADT consists of a class of objects, a defined set of properties of those objects, and a set of operations for processing the objects.

abstraction The description of data structures at a conceptual level, apart from their implementation using a particular technique and language.

abstract syntax tree See *parse tree.*

access adjustment A method of changing the access mode of an inherited member from within a derived class. For example, a derived class may inherit all members from a base class in protected mode and then make some members public by means of access adjustments. See also *access mode, base class, derived class,* and *inheritance.*

access mode A symbol (public, protected, or private) that specifies the kind of access that clients have to a server's data members and member functions. See also *private member, protected member,* and *public member.*

accumulator A variable for summing successive values of some other variable.

actual parameter A variable or expression contained in a function call and passed to that function. See also *formal parameter.*

address An integer value that the computer can use to reference a location. Often called *address of a memory location.* See also *value.*

ADT See *abstract data type.*

ADT generality rule An abstract data type should not be limited by the types of its components. Wherever possible, users should be able to specify the component types of a generic abstract data type.

ADT implementation rule An implementation of an ADT must provide an interface that is entirely consistent with the operations specified in the ADT's definition.

ADT layering rule Existing abstract data types should be used to implement new abstract data types, unless direct control over the underlying data structures and operations of the programming language is a critical factor. A well-designed implementation consists of layers of ADTs.

ADT use rule An algorithm that uses an ADT should access variables of that abstract data type only through the operations provided in the ADT definition.

algorithm A finite sequence of effective statements that, when applied to the problem, will solve it.

alias A situation in which two or more identifiers in a program come to refer to the same memory location. An alias can become the cause of subtle side effects.

analysis phase The first phase of the software system life cycle in which the systems analyst determines the user's needs and develops formal specifications describing the proposed system and its requirements.

ancestor A tree node that is hierarchically related to another tree node at a lower level in the tree.

application software Programs designed for a specific use.

argument A value or expression passed in a function call.

arithmetic/logic unit (ALU) The part of the central processing unit (CPU) that performs arithmetic operations and evaluates expressions.

array A data structure whose elements are accessed by means of index positions.

array index The relative position of the components of an array.

artificial intelligence (AI) The field of computer science in which the goal is to program the computer to mimic intelligent human behavior.

ASCII collating sequence The American Standard Code for Information Interchange ordering for a character set.

assembly language A computer language that allows words and symbols to be used in an unsophisticated manner to accomplish simple tasks.

assertion Special comments used with selection and repetition that state what you expect to happen and when certain conditions will hold.

assignment statement A method of putting values into memory locations.

association A data structure whose two parts are a key and a value.

association list A data structure consisting of a set of associations. See also *association*.

attribute A property that a computational object models, such as the balance in a bank account.

automatic program synthesis A process whereby one computer program can be given the specifications for another computer program, generate the code to satisfy those specifications, and then prove the correctness of that code.

Backus-Naur grammar A standard form for defining the formal syntax of a language.

base class The class from which a derived class inherits attributes and behavior. See also *derived class* and *inheritance*.

behavior The set of actions that a class of objects supports.

best case The arrangement of data items prior to the start of a sort function to finish in the least amount of time for that particular set of items. See also *worst case*.

big-O analysis A technique for estimating the time and space requirements of an algorithm in terms of order of magnitude.

big-O notation Saying that an algorithm is $O(f(n))$ indicates that the function $f(n)$ may be useful in characterizing how efficiently the algorithm performs for large n. For such n, we are assured that the operations required by the algorithm will be bounded by the product of a constant and $f(n)$.

bin sort See *radix sort*.

binary digit A digit, either 0 or 1, in the binary number system. Program instructions are stored in memory using a sequence of binary digits. Binary digits are called *bits*.

binary search The process of examining a middle value of a sorted array to see which half contains the value in question and halving until the value is located.

binary search tree A binary tree with the ordering property.

binary tree A tree such that each node can point to at most two children.

binary tree search A search algorithm driven by the hierarchical relationships of data items in a tree with the ordering property.

binding time The time at which a program variable is bound to a particular value. This can occur either at compile time or at run time.

bit See *binary digit*.

black box testing The method of testing a module whereby the tester is aware of only what the module is supposed to do, not the method of implementation or the internal logic. See also *white box testing*.

block The area of program text within a compound statement containing statements and optional data declarations.

blocked queue In an operating system, the queue of processes that have requested a resource currently owned by another process.

Boolean expression An expression whose value is either true or false. See also *compound Boolean expression* and *simple Boolean expression*.

bottom-up testing The independent testing of modules.

boundary conditions Values that separate two logical possibilities. These are important cases to check when testing a module.

boundary folding A variation on shift folding: In boundary folding, the digits of every other numeric section are reversed before the addition is performed. See also *shift folding*.

branch In a tree, a link between a parent and its child node.

breadth-first traversal A visiting of all nodes in a graph; it proceeds from each node by first visiting all nodes adjacent to that node.

B-tree An efficient, flexible index structure often used in database management systems.

bubble sort A sort that rearranges elements of an array until they are in either ascending or descending order. Consecutive elements are compared to move (bubble) the elements to the top or bottom accordingly on each pass. See also *heap sort, insertion sort, merge sort, quick sort, radix sort, selection sort,* and *shell sort*.

bucket In bucket hashing, a contiguous region of storage locations.

bucket hashing A method of handling collisions whereby the hashing function sends the key to a bucket of locations rather than a single location. The key is then placed by performing a sequential search within the bucket.

bus A group of wires imprinted on a circuit board to facilitate communication between components of a computer.

byte A sequence of bits used to encode a character in memory. See also *word*.

call Any reference to a subprogram by an executable statement. Also referred to as *invoke*.

central processing unit (CPU) A major hardware component that consists of the arithmetic/logic unit (ALU) and the control unit.

character set The list of characters available for data and program statements. See also *collating sequence.*

child node A node that descends from another node in a tree.

children The nodes pointed to by a node in a tree.

circular linked list A linked list whose last node points to the first or head node in the list.

class A description of the attributes and behavior of a set of computational objects.

class constructor A member function used to create and initialize an instance of a class.

class declaration module An area of a program used to declare the data members and member functions of a class.

class destructor A member function defined by the programmer and automatically used by the computer to return dynamic memory used by an object to the heap when the program exits the scope of the object. See also *dynamic memory.*

class implementation module An area of a program used to implement the member functions of a class.

class template A special kind of class definition that allows clients to specify the component types of objects of that class.

client A computational object that receives a service from another computational object.

clustering A hashing function's bias toward the placement of keys in a given region of the storage space.

code (writing) The process of writing executable statements that are part of a program to solve a problem.

cohesive subprogram A subprogram designed to accomplish a single task.

collating sequence The particular order sequence for a character set used by a machine. See also *ASCII collating sequence.*

collision A condition in which more than one key hashes to the same position with a given hashing function.

column-major order A means of traversing a two-dimensional array whereby all of the data in one column are accessed before the data in the next column. See also *row-major order.*

comment A nonexecutable statement used to make a program more readable.

compatible type Expressions that have the same base type. A parameter and its argument must be of compatible type, and the operands of an assignment statement must be of compatible type.

compilation error An error detected when the program is being compiled. See also *design error, logic error, run-time error,* and *syntax error.*

compiler A computer program that automatically converts instructions in a high-level language to machine language.

compound Boolean expression The complete expression when logical connectives and negation are used to generate Boolean values. See also *Boolean expression* and *simple Boolean expression.*

compound statement Uses the symbols { and } to make several simple statements into a single compound statement.

conditional statement See *selection statement.*

constant A symbol whose value cannot be changed in the body of the program.

constant definition section The section where program constants are defined for subsequent use.

constant parameter A method of declaring a formal array parameter so that the value of an actual array parameter will not change in a function.

constant reference A method of declaring a formal parameter so that the actual parameter is passed by reference but will not change in a function.

control structure A structure that controls the flow of execution of program statements.

control unit The part of the central processing unit that controls the operation of the rest of the computer.

copy constructor A member function defined by the programmer and automatically used by the computer to copy the values of objects when they are passed by value to functions.

counter A variable used to count the number of times some process is completed.

coupling The amount of interaction between a pair of modules.

cubic algorithm A polynomial algorithm in which the highest nonzero term is n^3.

data The particular characters that are used to represent information in a form suitable for storage, processing, and communication.

data abstraction The separation between the conceptual definition of a data structure and its eventual implementation.

data flow diagram A graphic tool used by systems analysts to represent data flow and transformations as a conceptual process. Also referred to as a *bubble diagram.*

data member A data object declared within a class declaration module.

data type A formal description of the set of values that a variable can have.

data validation The process of examining data prior to their use in a program.

deadlock An infinite wait state in which two processes each own and will not release system resources the other needs until they have obtained the remaining resources they need. Also referred to as *fatal embrace.*

debugging The process of eliminating errors or "bugs" from a program.

declaration sections The sections used to declare (name) symbolic constants, data types, variables, and subprograms that are necessary to the program.

decrement To decrease the value of a variable.

density The number of storage locations used divided by the total number of storage locations available.

density-dependent search technique A search technique whose efficiency is determined solely by the density of the data.

depth-first traversal A visiting of all nodes in a graph, proceeding from each node by probing as deeply as possible along one path leading from that node.

dereference The operation by which a program uses a pointer to access the contents of dynamic memory. See also *dynamic memory* and *pointer variable.*

derived class A class that inherits attributes and behavior from other classes. See also *base class* and *inheritance.*

design error An error such that a program runs, but unexpected results are produced. Also referred to as a logic error. See also *compilation error, run-time error,* and *syntax error.*

design phase The second phase of the software system life cycle. In this phase, a relatively detailed design plan is created from the formal specifications of the system produced in the analysis phase.

dictionary A data structure consisting of a set of associations. See also *association.*

digit/character extraction In creating a hashing function, the process of removing from a key those digits of characters that may bias the results of the function.

digraph A graph having some edges that point in only one direction.

diminishing increment sort A sort in which the number of segments in any one pass decreases with each successive pass. See also *shell sort.*

directional graph See *digraph.*

divide-and-conquer algorithms A class of algorithms that solves problems by repeatedly dividing them into simpler problems. See also *recursion.*

division-remainder technique A hashing technique that ensures that the result will be a valid output. It uses the modulus operation to scale the value into the proper range.

dominant term The highest power of *n* in a polynomial. For large *n,* the behavior of the entire polynomial will approach the behavior of a polynomial that contains only that term.

doubly linked list A linked list in which each node has two pointers instead of one. One of these points to the previous node in the list and the other points to the next node in the list.

do . . . while loop A posttest loop examining a Boolean expression after causing a statement to be executed. See also *for loop, loops,* and *while loop.*

dynamic memory Memory allocated under program control from the heap and accessed by means of pointers. See also *heap* and *pointer variable.*

dynamic structure A data structure that may expand or contract during execution of a program. See also *dynamic memory.*

echo checking A debugging technique in which values of variables and input data are displayed during program execution.

edge A direct connection between two nodes in a graph.

effective statement A clear, unambiguous instruction that can be carried out.

empty statement A semicolon used to indicate that no action is to be taken. Also referred to as a *null statement.*

encapsulation The process of hiding implementation details of a data structure.

end-of-file marker A special marker inserted by the machine to indicate the end of the data file.

end-of-line character A special character ('\0') used to indicate the end of a line of characters in a string or a file stream.

entrance-controlled loop See *pretest loop.*

equivalence classes A partitioning of all the logical possibilities that can be checked when testing a module. All test cases within a single equivalence class are identical from the standpoint of the logic of the module.

error See *compilation error, design error, logic error, run-time error,* and *syntax error.*

executable section The statements that cause the computer to do something.

executable statement The basic unit of grammar in C++ consisting of valid identifiers, standard identifiers, reserved words, numbers, and/or characters, together with appropriate punctuation.

execute To carry out the instructions of a program.

exit-controlled loop See *posttest* loop.

expert system A program able to reason as an expert in a limited domain.

exponential algorithm An algorithm whose efficiency is dominated by a term of the form *kn*.

exponential form See *floating point*.

extended if statement Nested selection where additional if . . . else statements are used in the else option. See also *nested if statement*.

factorial The product of the first *N* positive integers (denoted as *N*!).

fatal embrace See *deadlock*.

field width The phrase used to describe the number of columns used for various output. See also *formatting*.

FIFO See *queue*.

file stream A data structure that consists of a sequence of components that are accessed by input or output operations.

finite state algorithms Algorithms driven by a table indexed by the possible states that can exist and the possible categories of input symbols.

finite state automata Machines that run finite state algorithms.

first-in, first-out (FIFO) See *queue*.

fixed point A method of writing decimal numbers in which the decimal is placed where it belongs in the number. See also *floating point*.

fixed-repetition loop A loop used when it is known in advance the number of times a segment of code needs to be repeated.

floating point A method for writing numbers in scientific notation to accommodate numbers that may have very large or very small values. See also *fixed point*.

folding A method of hashing in cases where the key is not an integer value. The nonnumeric characters are removed and the remaining digits are combined to produce an integer value.

for loop A structured loop consisting of an initializer expression, a termination expression, an update expression, and a statement.

formal parameter A name, declared and used in a function declaration, that is replaced by an actual parameter when the function is called.

formal verification The use of logic to produce a proof of the correctness of an algorithm.

formatting Designating the desired field width when printing integers, reals, and character strings. See also *field width*.

free store See *heap*.

front pointer The pointer to the front of a queue.

function See *library function* and *user-defined function*.

function member A function declared within a class declaration module.

functional abstraction The process of considering only what a function is to do rather than details of the function.

general list A collection of data items that are related by their relative position in the collection.

general tree A set of nodes that is either empty or has a designated node (called the *root*) from which descend zero or more subtrees.

generalized nested loops Loops whose nesting depth is determined at run time using recursive logic.

generic abstract data type An abstract data type whose component types are specified as parameters. For example, a generic stack ADT could be used to create stacks of integers as well as stacks of characters.

global identifier An identifier that can be used by the main program and all subprograms in a program.

global variable See *global identifier*.

graph A set of data elements called *nodes* and the paths between them called *edges*.

halting problem A problem concerned with determining whether or not a given program will terminate or loop indefinitely when provided with a given set of input data.

hardware The actual computing machine and its support devices.

has-a relation The property of one class having an object of another class as a data member. See also *is-a relation*.

hashing A density-dependent search technique whereby the key for a given data item is transformed using a function to produce the address where that item is stored in memory.

head pointer A pointer to the first item in a list.

header file A C++ file that provides data and function declarations in a library to client modules.

heap An area of computer memory where storage for dynamic data is available.

heap A binary tree with the heap property.

heap property A binary tree in which the data at any given node are greater or equal to the data in its left and right subtrees.

heap sort A sort in which the array is treated like an array implementation of a binary tree. The items are repeatedly manipulated to create a heap from which the root is removed and added to the sorted portion of the array. See also *bubble sort, insertion sort, merge sort, quick sort, radix sort, selection sort,* and *shell sort.*

height balancing A technique for ensuring that an ordered binary tree remains as full as possible in form.

heuristics Rules of thumb that cut down on the number of possible choices to examine. They often lead to quick solutions but do not guarantee a solution the way an algorithm does. See also *algorithm.*

hierarchy A relation between nodes whereby one is viewed as above or prior to another.

high-level language Any programming language that uses words and symbols to make it relatively easy to read and write a program. See also *assembly language* and *machine language.*

identifiers Words that must be created according to a well-defined set of rules but can have any meaning subject to these rules. See also *library identifiers.*

implementation file A C++ file that provides the implementations of data and functions declared in a header file.

index See *array index* and *loop index.*

index sort Sorting an array by ordering the indices of the components rather than exchanging the components.

indexed sequential access method (ISAM) The most common method of indexed sequential search.

indexed sequential search The use of a partial index based on disk-dependent factors to find the proper portion of the disk for sequential searching for a key.

inductive assertion A method of formally proving the correctness of an algorithm by using an inductive proof.

infinite loop A loop in which the controlling condition is not changed in such a manner as to allow the loop to terminate.

infix Algebraic notation in which the operator appears between the two operands to which it will be applied.

infix priority A function that ranks the algebraic operators in terms of their precedence.

information hiding The process of suppressing the implementation details of a function or data structure so as to simplify its use in programming.

inheritance The process by which a derived class can reuse attributes and behavior defined in a base class. See also *base class* and *derived class.*

inorder predecessor The node preceding a given node in an inorder traversal.

inorder successor The node following a given node in an inorder traversal.

inorder threads Pointers to the inorder predecessor and successor of a node.

inorder traversal A binary tree traversal in which a node's left subtree is visited first, then that node is processed, and finally the node's right subtree is visited.

input Data obtained by a program during its execution.

input assertion A precondition for a loop.

input device A device that provides information to the computer. Typical devices are keyboards, disk drives, card readers, and tape drives. See also *I/O device* and *output device.*

insertion rule For binary trees, a rule whereby a new item is placed in the left subtree of an item greater than it or in the right subtree of an item less than it.

insertion sort Sorts an array of elements that starts with an empty array and inserts elements one at a time in their proper order. See also *bubble sort, heap sort, merge sort, quick sort, radix sort, selection sort,* and *shell sort.*

instance A computational object bearing the attributes and behavior specified by a class.

integer arithmetic operations Operations allowed on data of type int. This includes the operations of addition, subtraction, multiplication, division, and modulus to produce integer answers.

interface A formal statement of how communication occurs between subprograms, the main driver, and other subprograms.

invariant expression An assertion that is true before the loop and after each iteration of the loop.

invoke See *call.*

I/O device Any device that allows information to be transmitted to or from a computer. See also *input device* and *output device.*

is-a relation The property of one class being a derived class of another class. See also *has-a relation, derived class,* and *base class.*

iteration See *loops.*

key A field in a data structure that is used to access an element in that structure.

key-to-address transformation A transformation in which the key of a data item maps to the address at which the data are stored.

keywords Either reserved words or library identifiers.

last-in, first-out (LIFO) See *stack.*

leaf In a tree, a node that has no children.

level All nodes in a tree with a path of the same length from the root node.

lexical analysis The task of recognizing valid words or tokens in an input stream of characters.

l-value A computational object capable of being the target of an assignment statement.

library constant A constant with a standard meaning, such as *NULL* or *INT_MAX,* available in most versions of C++.

library function A function available in most versions of C++. A list of useful C++ library functions appears in Appendix B.

library identifiers The words defined in standard C++ libraries. See also *identifiers.*

LIFO See *stack.*

linear algorithm A polynomial algorithm in which the highest nonzero term is n.

linear collision processing A method of handling a collision in which the storage space is searched sequentially from the location of the collision for an available location where the new key can be placed.

linear ordering Any ordering of data in which there is an identifiable first element, second element, and so forth.

linear representation (of binary tree) An implementation of a binary tree in an array. For a given node stored at index position K, that node's left child is at position $2K$, and the right child is at position $2K + 1$.

linear search See *sequential search.*

linked collision processing A method of handling a collision in which the second key is stored in a linked list located in an overflow area.

linked list A list of data items where each item is linked to the next one by means of a pointer.

linked representation An implementation of a binary tree in which pointer fields are used to reference the right and left child of a node in the tree (as opposed to the linear representation of a binary tree).

LISP (LISt Processor) A highly recursive computer programming language used heavily in artificial intelligence (AI).

list traversal The process of sequentially visiting each node in a list.

local identifier An identifier that is restricted to use within a subblock of a program.

local variable See *local identifier.*

logarithmic algorithm An algorithm whose efficiency is dominated by a term of the form $\log n$.

logic error See *design error.*

logical operator Either logical connective (&, |) or negation (!).

logical order An ordering of data items according to some defined criterion such as alphabetic, increasing numeric, and so forth. That logical order of the data may or may not be the physical order of the data as stored in the computer.

logical size The number of data items actually available in a data structure at a given time. See also *physical size.*

logically sorted Data for which pointers to the data themselves been sorted, even though the data themselves have not been touched. Hence, items that the sort places consecutively need not be physically adjacent.

$\log_2 n$ search algorithm A search algorithm whose efficiency is dominated by a term of the form $\log_2 n$.

loop index A variable used for control values in a loop.

loop invariant An assertion that expresses a relationship between variables that remains constant throughout all iterations of the loop.

loop variant An assertion whose truth changes between the first and final execution of the loop.

loop verification The process of guaranteeing that a loop performs its intended task.

loops Program statements that cause a process to be repeated. See also *for loop, do . . . while loop,* and *while loop.*

low-level language See *assembly language.*

machine language The language used directly by the computer in all its calculations and processing.

main block The main part of a program.

main driver The main program when subprograms are used to accomplish specific tasks. See also *executable section.*

main (primary) memory Memory contained in the computer. See also *memory* and *secondary memory.*

main unit A computer's main unit contains the central processing unit (CPU) and the main (primary) memory; it is hooked to an input device and an output device.

mainframe Large computers typically used by major companies and universities. See also *microcomputer* and *minicomputer.*

maintenance phase The fifth phase of the software system life cycle. In this phase, changes must be made in the original program either to fix errors discovered by program users or to meet new user needs.

manifest interface The property of a function such that, when the function is called, the reader of the code can tell clearly what information is being transmitted to it and what information is being returned from it.

mapping function A function that transforms row–column array coordinates to the linear address of that array entry.

memory The ordered sequence of storage cells that can be accessed by address. Instructions and variables of an executing program are temporarily held here. See also *main memory* and *secondary memory*.

memory location A storage cell that can be accessed by address. See also *memory*.

merge The process of combining lists. Typically refers to files or arrays.

merge sort A sort in which the array is repeatedly split in half and then these pieces are merged together. See also *bubble sort, heap sort, insertion sort, quick sort, radix sort, selection sort,* and *shell sort*.

message In object-oriented programming, a signal to perform an operation on an object.

message-passing In object-oriented programming, one object's telling another object to perform an operation that is part of its encapsulation.

method of inductive assertions A method of formally verifying the correctness of an algorithm by identifying the input assertions, output assertions, and loop invariants of the algorithm and constructing a verification proof by mathematical induction.

microcomputer A computer capable of fitting on a laptop or desktop, generally used by one person at a time. See also *mainframe* and *minicomputer*.

minicomputer A small version of a mainframe computer. It is usually used by several people at once. See also *mainframe* and *microcomputer*.

mixed-mode Expressions containing data of different types; the values of these expressions will be of either type, depending on the rules for evaluating them.

modular development The process of developing an algorithm using modules. See also *module*.

modularity The property possessed by a program that is written using modules.

module An independent unit that is part of a larger development. It can be a function or a class (set of functions and related data). See also *modular development*.

module specifications In the case of a function, a description of data received, information returned, and task performed by a module. In the case of a class, a description of the attributes and behavior.

modular structure chart A graphic tool used by software designers to display the hierarchical relationships among the modules of the software system.

modular testing A method of testing in which each module is tested immediately after it has been completed rather than when the entire system has been completed.

multilinked list A linked list in which each node has two or more link fields.

natural language A language by which humans normally communicate (such as English), as opposed to a formal programming language (such as C++).

negation The use of the logical operator ! to negate the Boolean value of an expression.

nested if statement A selection statement used within another selection statement. See also *extended if statement*.

nested loop A loop as one of the statements in the body of another loop.

nested selection Any combination of selection statements within selection statements. See also *selection statement*.

network A graph in which the edges have weight values associated with them.

node An object containing a data item and a link to another node in a linked structure.

null character The special character ('\0') used to mark the end of a string in C++.

null statement See *empty statement*.

numerical analysis A field concerned with obtaining numerical answers to mathematical problems which involve much computation.

object code See *object program*.

object-oriented programming A programming paradigm in which a data object is viewed as the owner of operations, as opposed to procedural programming in which an operation is passed data objects as actual parameters. Object-oriented programming emphasizes the ADT approach and allows the users of an ADT to extend the operations of an ADT library in a convenient and efficient fashion.

object program The machine code version of the source program.

one-key table A set of values each of which is accessed by specifying a unique key value, where the key values are ordered.

opened for reading The positioning of an input stream pointer at the beginning of a file for the purpose of reading from the file.

opened for writing Positions an output stream pointer at the beginning of a file for the purpose of writing to the file.

opening a file Positions a pointer at the beginning of a file. See also *opened for reading* and *opened for writing.*

operating system A large program that allows the user to communicate with the hardware and performs various management tasks.

order of magnitude Power of ten. Two numbers have the same order of magnitude if their representations in scientific notation have identical exponents to designate the power of ten.

ordered collection A linear data structure that orders data items by position and supports indexing for retrieval or change of items, the detection of the logical size of the structure, and addition or removal of data items from the logical end of the structure.

ordering A means of arranging the elements in a list.

ordering property In a binary tree, the data in each node of the tree are greater than or equal to all of the data in that node's left subtree and less than or equal to all of the data in its right subtree.

ordinal data type A data type ordered in some association with the integers; each integer is the ordinal of its associated character.

output Information that is produced by a program.

output assertion A postcondition for a loop.

output device A device that allows you to see the results of a program. Typically it is a monitor or printer. See also *input device* and *I/O device.*

overflow In arithmetic operations, a value may be too large for the computer's memory location. A meaningless value may be assigned or an error message may result. See also *underflow.*

overloading The process of using the same operator symbol or identifier to refer to many different functions. See also *polymorphism.*

parallel arrays Arrays of the same length but with different component data types.

parallel processing The use of more than one processor to execute parts of a program concurrently. The effect is that these parts are completed in parallel rather than in sequence.

parameter See *argument.*

parameter list A list of parameters. An actual parameter list is contained in the function call. A formal parameter list is contained in the function declaration and heading.

parent In a tree, the node that is pointing to its children.

parse tree A tree representation of the syntactic structure of a source program produced by a compiler. Also referred to as *abstract syntax tree.*

parser A program that checks the syntax of an expression and represents that expression in a unique form.

parser generator A program that can take the input grammar for a language and produce the parser for that language.

parsing The procedure of checking the syntax of an expression and representing it in one unique form.

partition In quick sort, the process of moving the pivot to the location where it belongs in the sorted array and arranging the remaining data items to the left of the pivot if they are less than or equal to the pivot and to the right if they are greater than the pivot.

passed by reference When the address of the actual parameter is passed to a subprogram.

passed by value When a copy of the value of the actual parameter is passed to a subprogram.

path A sequence of edges which connect two nodes in a graph or network.

peripheral memory See *memory* and *secondary memory.*

permutation An ordered arrangement of the first *n* positive integers in which each integer appears exactly once.

physical size The number of memory units available for storing data items in a data structure. See also *logical size.*

pivot An item used to direct the partitioning in quick sort.

pointer A memory location containing the location of another data item.

pointer sort A sort in which pointers to the data are manipulated rather than the data themselves.

pointer variable Frequently designated as `ptr`, a pointer variable is a variable that contains the address of a memory location. See also *address* and *dynamic memory.*

polymorphism The property of one operator symbol or function identifier having many meanings. See also *overloading.*

polynomial algorithm An algorithm whose efficiency can be expressed in terms of a polynomial.

postcondition An assertion written after a segment of code.

postfix Unambiguous algebraic notation in which the arithmetic operator appears after the two operands upon which it is to be applied.

postorder traversal A binary tree traversal in which at any node, that node's left subtree is visited first, then that node's right subtree is visited, and finally that node is processed.

posttest loop A loop where the control condition is tested after the loop is executed. do . . . while loop is a posttest loop. Also referred to as an *exit-controlled loop.*

precondition An assertion written before a particular statement.

prefix Unambiguous algebraic notation in which the arithmetic operator appears before the two operands upon which it is to be applied.

preorder traversal A binary tree traversal in which at any node, that node is first processed, then that node's left subtree is visited, and finally that node's right subtree is visited.

pretest condition A condition that controls whether the body of the loop is executed before going through the loop.

pretest loop A loop where the control condition is tested before the loop is executed. A while loop is a pretest loop. Also referred to as an *entrance-controlled loop.*

primary memory See *main memory* and *memory.*

prime hash area In linked collision processing, the main storage area in which keys are placed if no collision occurs.

priority queue A queue in which the entries on the queue are ranked into groups according to priority. Such a queue requires a rear pointer for each different possible priority value.

private member A data member or member function that is accessible only within the scope of a class declaration.

profile an algorithm A means of empirically measuring the execution of an algorithm by inserting counters to keep track of the number of times certain instructions are executed during a run of the program.

program A set of instructions that tells the machine (the hardware) what to do.

program heading The heading of the main block of any C++ program; it must contain the identifier `main`.

program proof An analysis of a program that attempts to verify the correctness of program results.

program protection A method of using selection statements to guard against unexpected results.

program walk-through The process of carefully following, using pencil and paper, steps the computer uses to solve the problem given in a program. Also referred to as a *trace.*

programming language Formal language that computer scientists use to give instructions to the computer.

prompt A message or marker on the terminal screen that requests input data.

proportional The term applied to two algebraic functions whose quotient is a constant.

protected member A data member or member function that is accessible only within the scope of a class declaration or within the class declaration of a derived class.

protection See *program protection.*

pseudocode A stylized half-English, half-code language written in English but suggesting C++ code.

public member A data member or member function that is accessible to any program component that uses the class.

quadratic algorithm A polynomial algorithm in which the highest nonzero term is n^2.

quadratic collision processing A method of handling a collision in which the storage space is searched in the k^2 place, for successive integer values of k starting at the location of the collision, until an available spot is found.

queue A dynamic data structure where elements are entered at one end and removed from the other end. Referred to as a FIFO (first-in/first-out) structure.

quick sort A relatively fast sorting technique that uses recursion. See also *bubble sort, heap sort, insertion sort, merge sort, radix sort, selection sort,* and *shell sort.*

r-value A computational object capable of being assigned to a variable.

radix sort Sorts integer data by repeatedly placing the items into bins and then collecting the bins, starting with the least significant digit for the first pass and finishing with the most significant digit. Also referred to as *bin sort.* See also *bubble sort, heap sort, insertion sort, merge sort, quick sort, selection sort,* and *shell sort.*

random access The ability to access any elements in a list without first accessing all preceding elements.

random access file A file whose components can be accessed using random access.

random number generator A function that returns a number in a given range each time it is called. The numbers it returns are statistically random in that, after repeated calls to the function, the sequence of numbers returned is evenly distributed over the interval yet each one is completely unpredictable.

randomized storage A name given to list access via a hashing function.

range bound error The situation that occurs when an attempt is made to use an array index value that is less than 0 or greater than or equal to the size of the array.

reading from a file Retrieving data from a file.

ready queue In an operating system, the queue of processes with cleared access to all the resources the processes require to run.

real arithmetic operations The operations allowed on data of type float. These include addition, subtraction, multiplication, and division.

rear pointer The pointer to the rear of a queue.

receiver object A computational object to which a request is sent for a service.

recursion The process of a subprogram calling itself. A clearly defined stopping state must exist. Any recursive subprogram can be rewritten using iteration.

recursive step A step in a recursive process that solves a similar problem of smaller size and eventually leads to a termination of the process.

recursive subprogram See *recursion*.

reference parameter A formal parameter that requires the address of the actual parameter to be passed to a subprogram. The value of the actual parameter can be changed within the subprogram.

rehashing A method of handling a collision in which a sequence of new hashing functions is applied to the key that caused the collision until an available location for that key is found.

rehashing collision processing Resolving a collision by invoking a sequence of hashing functions on a key.

relational operator An operator used for comparison of data items of the same type.

relative ordering Ordering imposed on the entries in a list by their relative positions in that list.

relatively prime Two numbers are relatively prime if and only if their only common factor is 1.

repetition See *loops*.

reserved words Words that have predefined meanings that cannot be changed. A list of C++ reserved words is given in Appendix A.

return type The type of value returned by a function.

robust The state in which a program is protected against most possible crashes from bad data and unexpected values.

root The first or top node in a tree.

row-major order A means of traversing a two-dimensional array whereby all of the data in one row are accessed before the data in the next row. See also *column-major order*.

run-time error The error detected when, after compilation is completed, an error message results instead of the correct output. See also *compilation error*, *design error*, *logic error*, and *syntax error*.

scope of identifier The largest block in which the identifier is available.

secondary memory An auxiliary device for memory, usually a disk or magnetic tape. See also *main memory* and *memory*.

sector A particular portion of a magnetic disk used at the machine language level in addressing information stored on the disk.

selection sort A sorting algorithm that sorts the components of an array in either ascending or descending order. This process puts the smallest or largest element in the top position and repeats the process on the remaining array components. See also *bubble sort*, *heap sort*, *insertion sort*, *merge sort*, *quick sort*, *radix sort*, and *shell sort*.

selection statement A control statement that selects some particular logical path based on the value of an expression. Also referred to as a *conditional statement*.

self-documenting code Code that is written using descriptive identifiers.

semantics The semantics of an algorithmic statement is the action dictated by that statement.

semaphore In an operating system, special flags that regulate the addition and removal of processes to and from the blocked and ready queues.

sender A computational object that requests a service from another computational object.

sentinel value A special value that indicates the end of a set of data or of a process.

sequential access The requirement that elements of a list must be accessed according to the list's ordering so that before a particular element can be accessed, all preceding elements must be accessed first.

sequential access file A file whose components must be accessed using sequential access.

sequential algorithm See *straight-line algorithm*.

sequential search The process of searching a list by examining the first component and then examining successive components in the order in which they occur. Also referred to as *linear search*.

server A computational object that provides a service to another computational object.

shaker sort A variation on the bubble sort in which each pass through the data positions the (current) largest element in the (current) last array index and the (current) smallest element in the (current) first array index.

shell sort A sort that works by dividing the array into smaller, noncontiguous segments. These segments are separately sorted using the insertion sort algorithm. The number of these segments is repeatedly reduced on each successive pass until the entire array has been sorted. See also *bubble sort, heap sort, insertion sort, merge sort, quick sort, radix sort,* and *selection sort.*

shift folding A variation on folding in which each numeric part of the key is treated as a separate number, and these numbers are added to form an integer value. See also *boundary folding.*

short-circuit evaluation The process whereby a compound Boolean expression halts evaluation and returns the value of the first subexpression that evaluates to TRUE, in the case of `||`, or FALSE, in the case of &&.

siblings The child nodes of a given node.

side effect A change in a variable, which is the result of some action taken in a program, usually from within a function.

sieve of Eratosthenes A technique devised by the Greek mathematician Eratosthenes for finding all prime numbers greater than 2 and less than or equal to a given number.

simple Boolean expression An expression where two numbers or variable values are compared using a single relational operator. See also *Boolean expression* and *compound Boolean expression.*

simulation A computer model of a real-life situation.

simulation of system stack A technique used to eliminate recursion by making a program explicitly perform the duties of the system stack.

software Programs that make the machine (the hardware) do something, such as word processing, database management, or games.

software engineering The process of developing and maintaining large software systems.

software reuse The process of building and maintaining software systems out of existing software components.

software system life cycle The process of development, maintenance, and demise of a software system. Phases include analysis, design, coding, testing/verification, maintenance, and obsolescence.

sort-merge The process of repeatedly subdividing a long list, sorting shorter lists, and then merging to obtain a single sorted list.

sorted collection A derived class of ordered collection, in which the data items are maintained in ascending or descending order. See also *ordered collection.*

source program A program written by a programmer. See also *system program.*

sparse table A table in which a high percentage of data storage locations will be of one uniform value.

stack A dynamic data structure where access can be made from only one end. Referred to as a LIFO (last-in/first-out) structure.

stack priority A function to rank algebraic operators hierarchically in order of precedence.

standard simple types Predefined data types such as `int`, `double`, and `char`.

state space The space of all possible states which can be generated in the solution to a given problem.

state-transition diagram A diagram used to model the logic of a finite state machine.

stepwise refinement The process of repeatedly subdividing tasks into subtasks until each subtask is easily accomplished. See also *structured programming* and *top-down design.*

stopping state The well-defined termination of a recursive process.

straight-line algorithm An algorithm that consists of a sequence of simple tasks. Also called a *sequential algorithm.*

string An abbreviated name for a string literal.

string data type A data type that permits a sequence of characters. In C++, this can be implemented using an array of characters.

string literal One or more characters, enclosed in double quotes, used as a constant in a program.

structure chart A graphic method of indicating the relationship between modules when designing the solution to a problem.

structured design A method of designing software by specifying modules and the flow of data among them.

structured programming Programming that parallels a solution to a problem achieved by top-down design. See also *stepwise refinement* and *top-down design.*

stub programming The process of using incomplete functions to test data transmission among them.

subblock A block structure for a subprogram. See also *block.*

subprogram A program within a program. Functions are subprograms. See also *program.*

subscript See *array index.*

subtree A subset of a tree that is itself a tree.

symbol table list of identifiers maintained by a compiler as it parses a source program.

synonyms Two keys that hash to the same position and therefore cause a collision.

syntax The formal rules governing the construction of valid statements.

syntax diagramming A method to formally describe the legal syntax of language structures; syntax diagrams appear in Appendix C.

syntax error An error in spelling, punctuation, or placement of certain key symbols in a program. See also *compilation error, design error, logic error,* and *run-time error.*

system software The programs that allow users to write and execute other programs, including operating systems such as DOS.

system testing Exercising the interfaces between modules instead of the logic of a particular module.

systems analyst The person responsible for analyzing the needs of the users and then formally specifying the system and its requirements to meet those needs.

tail-recursive The property that a recursive algorithm has of performing no work after each recursive step. See also *recursion.*

test cases Collection of sets of test data that will exercise all the logical possibilities the module will encounter. See also *test oracle.*

test oracle The expected result for a particular test case when a module is being tested.

test program A short program written to provide an answer to a specific question.

testing phase The fourth phase of the software system life cycle. In this phase, the program code is thoroughly tested in an effort to discover errors both in the design of the program and in the code itself.

thread A pointer contained in a tree node which leads to the predecessor or successor of the node relative to a specified traversal.

threaded tree A tree in which threading is used.

threading A technique of avoiding recursion in tree traversal algorithms whereby the pointers unused in tree formation are turned into pointers to the inorder predecessor and inorder successor of that node.

time/space trade-off The maxim that an attempt to make a program more efficient in terms of time will only come as a result of a corresponding decrease in efficiency in terms of space, and vice versa.

token A language symbol comprised of one or more characters in an incoming stream of characters. The basic unit in lexical analysis.

top-down design A design methodology for solving a problem whereby you first state the problem and then proceed to subdivide the main task into major subtasks. Each subtask is then subdivided into smaller subtasks. This process is repeated until each remaining subtask is easily solved. See also *stepwise refinement* and *structured programming.*

trace See *program walk-through.*

track A particular portion of a magnetic disk used at the machine language level in addressing information stored on the disk.

tree See *general tree.*

tree traversal A means of processing every node in the tree.

trial-and-error backtracking Recursion in which more recursive calls may be made after the first return operation occurs.

trie index A type of indexing used when the keys are variable-length character strings. Although taken from the word retrieve, trie is pronounced "try."

Turing machine A hypothetical computing machine which consists of input and output units, and infinite memory in the form of a sequentially organized tape to store characters from a finite alphabet, a finite collection of states in which the machine could exist at any given time, and a control unit capable of checking and potentially modifying the contents of any memory cell.

two-dimensional array An array in which each element is accessed by a reference to a pair of indices.

two-key table A set of values each of which is accessed by two keys, where the set of primary keys is ordered and the set of secondary keys for each primary key is also ordered.

two-way merge The process of merging two sorted lists.

type See *data type.*

undecidable proposition A statement within an axiomatic system such that neither that statement nor its negation can be proven by reasoning within the system itself.

underflow If a value is too small to be represented by a computer, the value is automatically replaced by zero. See also *overflow.*

user-defined data type A new data type introduced and defined by the programmer.

user-defined function A new function introduced and defined by the programmer.

user-friendly A phrase that describes an interactive program with clear, easy-to-follow messages for the user.

value The value of the contents of a memory location. Often called *value of a memory location*. See also *address*.

value parameter A formal parameter that is local to a subprogram. Values of these parameters are not returned to the calling program.

variable A memory location, referenced by an identifier, whose value can be changed during a program.

variable condition loop A repetition statement in which the loop control condition changes within the body of the loop.

variable declaration section The section of the declaration section where program variables are declared for subsequent use.

vertex A data object (or node) in a graph.

volatile list A list that undergoes frequent insertions and deletions.

weight The numeric value associated with an edge in a network.

while loop A pretest loop examining a Boolean expression before causing a statement to be executed.

white box testing The method of testing a module in which the tester is aware of the method of implementation and internal logic of that module. See also *black box testing*.

word A unit of memory consisting of one or more bytes. Words can be addressed.

worst case The arrangement of data items prior to the beginning of the sort procedure which causes that procedure to take the longest amount of time for that particular set of items. See also *best case*.

writing to a file The process of entering data to a file.

Answers to Selected Exercises

This section contains answers to selected exercises from the exercise sets at the end of each section. In general, answers to odd-numbered problems are given.

CHAPTER 2

Section 2.1

1. **a** and **c** are effective statements.
b is not effective because you cannot determine when to perform the action.
d is not effective because there is no smallest positive fraction.
e is not effective because you cannot determine in advance which stocks will increase in value.

3. **a.** 1. Select a topic
2. Research the topic
3. Outline the paper
4. Refine the outline
5. Write the rough draft
6. Read and revise the rough draft
7. Write the final paper

c. 1. Get a list of colleges
2. Examine criteria (programs, distance, money, and so on)
3. Screen to a manageable number
4. Obtain further information
5. Make a decision

5. **a.** First-level development:
1. Get information for first employee
2. Perform computations for first employee
3. Print results for first employee
4.
5. } Repeat for second employee
6.

Second-level development:
1. Get information for first employee
   1.1 get hourly wage
   1.2 get number of hours worked
2. Perform computations for first employee
   2.1 compute gross pay
   2.2 compute deductions
   2.3 compute net pay
3. Print results for first employee
   3.1 print input data
   3.2 print gross pay
   3.3 print deductions
   3.4 print net pay
4.
5. } Repeat for second employee
6.

Third-level development:
1. Get information for first employee
   1.1 get hourly wage
   1.2 get number of hours worked
2. Perform computations for first employee
   2.1 compute gross pay
   2.2 compute deductions
      2.2.1 federal withholding
      2.2.2 state withholding
      2.2.3 social security
      2.2.4 union dues
      2.2.5 compute total deductions
   2.3 compute net pay
      2.3.1 subtract total deductions from gross
3. Print results for first employee
   3.1 print input data
      3.1.1 print hours worked
      3.1.2 print hourly wage
   3.2 print gross pay
   3.3 print deductions
      3.3.1 print federal withholding
      3.3.2 print state withholding
      3.3.3 print social security
      3.3.4 print union dues
      3.3.5 print total deductions
   3.4 print net pay
4.
5. } Repeat for second employee
6.

7. There are several ways to solve this problem, one of which is:
1. Get the numbers as input
2. Put them in order—-small, large
3. Check for a divisor
   3.1 if small is a divisor of large
      3.1.1 gcd is small
      else
      3.1.2 Decrease small until a common divisor is found
4. Print the results
   3.1.2 can be further refined as
   3.1.2 Decrease small until a common divisor is found
   3.1.2.2 do
   if gcdCandidate is a common divisor
   gcd is gcdcandidate
   else
   Decrease gcdcandidate by 1 while a common divisor is not found

Section 2.2

3. **a** is valid.
b is a Pascal program heading.
c is missing a return type and should omit parameters.
d is missing a return type and should use lowercase letters.

5. **a.** const char GENDER = 'F';
   b. const int AGE = 18;
   c. const double PI = 3.1416;

Section 2.3

1. **a, e,** and **g** are valid.
   b has a decimal.
   c has a comma.
   d has an illegal octal digit.
   f is probably larger than INT_MAX.
3. **a.** 1.73E2
   b. 7.43927E11
   c. −2.3E–8
   d. 1.4768E1
   e. −5.2E0
5. **a** and **d** are integers.
   b, c, and **g** are doubles.
   e and **f** are string literals.
7. **a.**

```
cout << setw(14) << "Score" << endl << endl;
cout << setw(13) << 86 << endl;
cout << setw(13) << 82 << endl;
cout << setw(13) << 79 << endl;
```

CHAPTER 3

Section 3.1

1. **a.** 11
   b. −49
   c. 3
   d. 24
   e. 120
   f. 63
   g. −64
   h. 108
   i. −2
   j. 7
3. **a, b, f, i,** and **j** are valid, type int.
   c, e, g, and **h** are valid, type double.
   d is invalid.
5. Output will vary according to local implementation.

Section 3.2

1. **a, b, c, e, f, g,** and **h** are valid assignment statements. **d** is invalid. An operand cannot be on the left of an assignment statement.
3. **a.** [3] A [−5] B
   b. [26] A [31] B
   c. [−3] A [−5] B
   d. [9] A [9] B

5.

```
Gender      M
Age         23
Height      73 inches
Weight      186.5 lbs
```

7. column 11

```
*******************************
*                             *
*    Name       Age     Sex   *
*    ----       ---     ---   *
*    Jones       21       M   *
*                             *
*******************************
```

9. column 10

```
This reviews string formatting.
When a letter A is used,
    Oops! I forgot to format.
    When a letter A is used,
    it is a string of length one.
```

Section 3.3

1. cin is the name of the standard input stream. This stream is connected to the keyboard and allows data to be input from the user. cout is the name of the standard output stream. This stream is connected to the terminal screen and allows data to be output to the user.

Section 3.4

1. **a.**

```
cout << first << " " << second;
```

   b.

```
apstring third = first + " " + second;
```

   c.

```
first = "";
second = "";
```

   d. prompt the user for new strings to be entered into the variables and input them

```
cout << "Enter the first string: ";
cin >> first;
cout << "Enter the second string: ";
cin >> second;
```

3. **a.** word1 is "567", word2 and number are undefined.
   b. word1 is "567 is a small number", word2 and number are undefined.
   c. number is 567, word1 and word2 are undefined.
   d. number is 567, word1 is "is", and word2 is undefined.
   e. number is 567, word1 is "", and word2 is undefined.
   f. number is 567, word1 is "", and word2 is " is a small number".

5. **a, b,** and **e** are valid. **c** is invalid because an `int` cannot be concatenated to a string. **d** is invalid because no string is an operand.

Section 3.5

3.
```
const double PI = 3.1416;
const double CELSIUS_TO_FAHR = 32;
const int RIGHT_ANGLE = 90;
const char LAST_LOW_LET = 'z', LAST_UP_LET = 'Z';
```

CHAPTER 4

Section 4.2

1. **c** and **d** are valid.
a has no return type.
b has no types for the parameters.

Section 4.3

1. **a.** Both parameters should be declared as reference parameters rather than value parameters.
b. `width` should be declared as a value parameter rather than a reference parameter.
c. `radius` should be declared as a value parameter rather than a reference parameter.

Section 4.5

7. Identifiers for this program are represented schematically by the figure to the right.

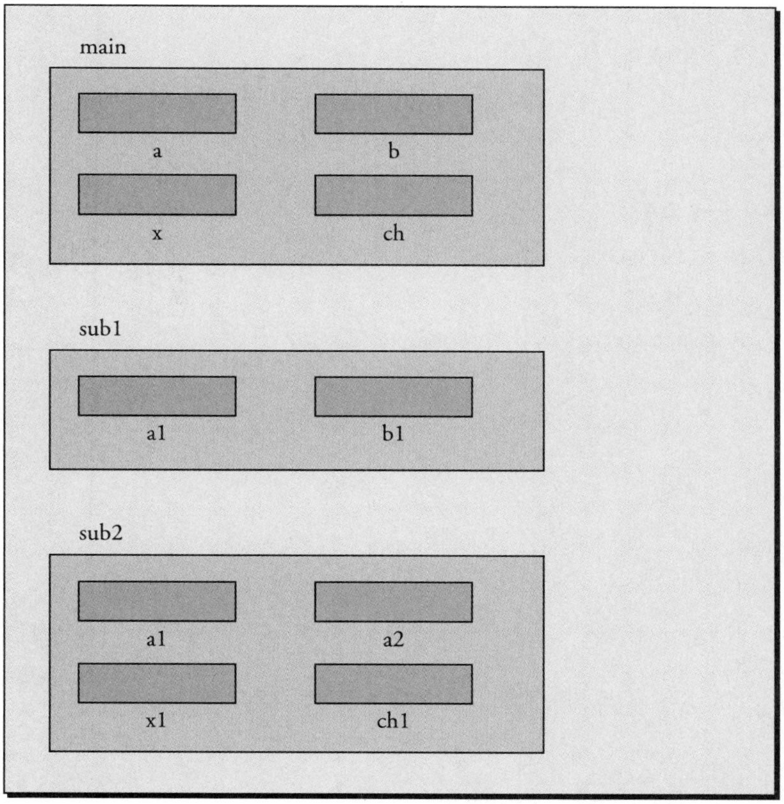

9. 10
20
10

11. There are several syntax errors. `x1` is not visible in the main program block. `x` cannot be used as an actual parameter for function `sub1` because `x` is a `double` and `sub1` expects an `int` as a parameter. `x` and `y` are not visible in the block of `sub1`.

CHAPTER 5

Section 5.1

1. 1 1 0
0

3. **a, b,** and **c** are `true`.
d and **e** are `false`.

Section 5.2

1. **a.** 10 5
b. no output
c. 5 Since `b` has no value, the result will vary.
d. 10 5
e. 15 4
15 4
f. 10 5

3. **a.** no error
b. `3 < x < 10` cannot be evaluated. This should be `(3 < x) && (x < 10)`.

c. The two statements following the condition should be enclosed in braces:

```
if (a > 0)
{
   count = count + 1;
   sum = sum + a;
}
```

5. yes.

9.

```
{
cin >> num1 >> num2 >> num3;
total = total + num1 + num2 + num3;
cout << num1 <<    << num2 << " "  << num3 << endl;
cout << total << endl;
}
```

11.

```
cin >> ch1 >> ch2 >> ch3;
if (ch1 <= ch2) && (ch2 <= ch3)
   cout << ch1 << ch2 << ch3 << endl;
```

Section 5.3

1. **a.** −14
b. 5025
175
c. 105
50

Section 5.4

1. **a.** 38.15 763.0
b. −21.0 21.0
c. 600.0 1200.0
d. 3000.0 9000.0

3. **a.**

```
if (ch == 'M')
if (sum > 1000)
   x = x + 1;
else
   x = x + 2;
else if (ch == 'F')
if (sum > 1000)
   x = x + 3;
else
   x = x + 5;
```

b.

```
cin >> num;
if (num > 0)
    if (num <= 10000)
    {
       count = count + 1;
       sum = sum + num;
    }
    else
       cout << setw(27) << "Value out of range" << endl;
```

c.
```
if (a > 0)
    if (b > 0)
       cout << setw(22) << "Both positive" << endl;
    else
       cout << setw(22) << "Some negative" << endl;
```

d.
```
if (c < 0)
    if (a > 0)
       if (b > 0))
          cout << setw(19) << "Option one" << endl;
       else
          cout <<setw(19) << "Option two" << endl;
    else
       cout << setw(19) << "Option two" << endl;
else
    cout << setw(19) << "Option one" << endl;
```

7. 8 13 104
a b c

Section 5.5

3. **a.** has a semicolon rather than a colon after third label and a list of values as last label.
b. has no colon after first label, a semicolon after third label, and a list of values as last label.
c. has a list of values as first label.
d. reserved word `case` is missing from all labels.
e. cases for 2 and 1 are missing statements.

CHAPTER 6

Section 6.2

1. **a.**
```
*
 *
  *
   *
    *
     *
```

b.
```
 1 :  9
 2 :  8
 3 :  7
 4 :  6
 5 :  5
 6 :  4
 7 :  3
 8 :  2
 9 :  1
10 :  0
```

c.
```
 2
 3
 4
 5
 6
 7
 8
 9
10
11
12
13
14
15
16
17
18
19
20
```

d.
```
1
2
3
4
5
6
7
8
9
10
11
12
13
14
15
16
17
18
19
20
21
```

3. **a.**
```
for (int j = 1; j <= 4; ++j)
   cout <<  "*" << endl;
```

b.
```
for (int j = 1; j <= 4; ++j)
   cout << setw(j + 3) << "***" << endl;
```

c.
```
cout << setw(6) << "*" << endl;
for (int j = 1; j <= 3; ++j)
   cout << setw(6 - j) << "*" setw(2 * j) << * << endl;
cout << **** **** << endl;
for (int j = 1; j <= 2; ++j)
   cout << setw(7) << "* *" << endl;
cout << setw(7) << "***" << endl;
```

d. This is a "look ahead" problem that can be solved by a loop within a loop. This idea is developed in Section 5.6.

```
for (int j = 5; j >= 1; --j)
{
   cout << setw(6 - j) << ;                     // Indent a line
   for (int k = 1; k <= 2 * j - 1; ++k)       // Print a line
      cout << *;
   cout << endl;
}
```

5. a.
```
for (int j = 1; j <= 5; ++j)
   cout << setw(3) << j;
for (int j = 5; j >= 1; --j;
   cout << setw(3) << 6 - j;
```

b.
```
for (int j = 1; j <= 5; ++j)
   cout << setw(j) << '*' << endl
for (int j = 5; j >= 1; --j)
   cout << setw(6 - j) << '*' << endl;
```

7.
```
for (j = 2; j <= 10; ++j)
   cout << setw(j) << j << endl;
```

Section 6.3

3. a.
```
 1
 2
 3
 4
 5
 6
 7
 8
 9
10
```

b.
```
1  0
2  1
3  2
4  1
5  2
```

c. 54 50

d.
```
The partial sum is  1
The partial sum is  3
The partial sum is  6
The partial sum is 10
The partial sum is 15
The count is 5
```

e. 96.00 2.00

5. a.

```
while (num > 0)
{
   cout << setw(10) << num << endl
   num = num - .5;
}
```

Section 6.4

1. A pretest loop tests the Boolean expression before executing the loop. A posttest loop tests the Boolean expression after the loop has been executed.

3. a. This loop is infinite because the value of j is never changed within the loop.

b. This loop terminates.

c. This loop is infinite because the value of a will always be a power of 2 and thus never equal 20.

d. This loop terminates.

Section 6.6

1. a.

```
for (int k = 1; k <= 5; ++k)
{
   cout << setw(k) << ' ';
   for (int j = k; j <= 5; ++j)
      cout << '*';
   cout << endl
}
```

c.

```
for (int k = 1; k <= 7; ++k)
   if (k < 5)
   {
      for (int j = 1; j <= 3; ++j)
         cout << '*';
      cout << endl;
   }
   else
   {
      for (int j = 1; j <= 5; ++j
         cout << '*';
      cout << endl;
   }
```

3.

```
4 5 6 7
4 5 6 7
4 5 6 7
4 5 6 7

5 6 7
5 6 7
5 6 7

6 7
6 7
```

Section 6.7

1. a. This is an infinite loop.

b. The loop control variable, k, is unassigned once the for loop is exited. Thus, the attempt to use k in the expression k % 3 == 0 may result in an error.

CHAPTER 7

Section 7.1

1. a. The first two input statements read the two data values from the file, and they are displayed by the first two output statements. The third input statement also reads the second data value because the end of file has been reached. Thus, the third output statement displays the second data value also.

b. The first data value is read before the loop starts. It is output on the first pass through the loop because the end-of-file condition is not yet true. Then the second data value is read at the bottom of the loop. The end-of-file condition is not yet true, so the loop is entered once more, where the second data value is output. At the bottom of the loop, the second data value is read once more, and the end-of-file condition becomes true, forcing an exit from the top of the loop.

c. Because the >> operator must be run three times before the end-of-file condition becomes true, three outputs will occur. Thus, the second data value in the file is output twice to the screen.

3. We use the apstring library for strings. Note that all input can be received as strings.

```
// Program file: person.cpp

#include <iostream.h>
#include <fstream.h>
#include <assert.h>
#include "apstring.h"

int main()
{
   apstring  stringVar;
   ifstream infile;

   infile.open("myfile");
   assert(! infile.fail());
   infile >> stringVar;
   cout << "Name: " << stringVar << endl;
   infile >> stringVar;
   cout << "Address: " << stringVar << endl;
   infile >> stringVar;
   cout << "Age: " << stringVar << endl;
   infile.close();
   assert(! infile.fail());
   return 0;
}
```

5. Note that the data for the person's name are received from a priming input and are also received at the bottom of the loop.

```
// Program file: persons.cpp

#include <iostream.h>
#include <fstream.h>
#include <assert.h>
#include "apstring.h"

int main()
{
   string stringVar;
   ifstream infile;

   infile.open("myfile");
   assert(! infile.fail());
   infile >> stringVar;
   while (! infile.fail())
   {
      cout << "Name: " << stringVar << endl;
      infile >> stringVar;
      cout << "Address: " << stringVar << endl;
      infile >> stringVar;
      cout << "Age: " << stringvar << endl;
      infile >> stringVar;
   {
   infile.close();
   assert(! infile.fail());
   return 0;
}
```

CHAPTER 8

Section 8.1

1. Explain the differences between strings and structs as structured data types.

2. Use a `struct` to define a new type called `book`. This type should contain the components for a title, author, publication date, and price.

Section 8.2

1. Describe the differences between a class and a data structure, such as an array or a struct. Pay particular attention to the concepts of an abstract data type and data encapsulation.

3. Describe the differences between a default constructor, a constructor with user-specified initial values, and a copy constructor.

5. We assume that a private data member `password` has been added to the class declaration and that appropriate modifications have been made to the declarations of member functions `deposit`, `withdraw`, and `getbalance`. The implementations are updated as follows:

```
double account::deposit(double amount, string yourName, string yourPassword)
{

    if ((yourName == name) && (yourPassword == password))
    {
            balance = balance + amount;
            return balance;
    }
    else
            return 0;
}

double account::withdraw(double amount, string yourName, string yourPassword)
{
```

```
    if ((yourName == name) && (yourPassword == password))
            if (amount > balance)
                   return -1;
            else
            {
                   balance = balance - amount;
                   return balance;
            }
    else
            return 0;
}

double account::getBalance(string yourName, string yourPassword)
{
    if ((yourName == name) && (yourPassword == password))
            return balance;
    else
            return 0;
}
```

Section 8.4

3. Total number of operations = $M \times N$.

5. The following implementations cover all of the possibilities. If the rational number is already in lowest terms, then the implementations can be simplified and made more efficient.

```
bool rational::wholenumber()
{
   return (denominator == 1) || (numerator % denominator == 0);
}

int rational::makeint()
{
   if (denominator == 1)
      return numerator;
   else
      return numerator / denominator;
}
```

Section 8.5

1. Define a password in the base class. Its access mode should be protected.

5. A derived class of the checking account class, with attributes and behavior for maintaining interest, allows much of the software to be reused.

CHAPTER 9

Section 9.1

4. a.

```
const int MAX_SCORES = 35;
typedef int scoreList[MAX_SCORES];
scoreList scores;
```

b.

```
const int MAX_PRICES = 20;
typedef double priceList[MAX_PRICES];
priceList prices;
```

c.

```
const int MAX_ANSWERS = 50;
typedef boolean answerList[MAX_ANSWERS];
answerList answers;
```

d.
```
const int MAXGRADES = 4;
typedef char gradeList[MAX_GRADES];
gradeList grades;
```

3. **a, b, d, e, f, h,** and **l** are valid.
c will run but display the address of the array.
g uses three indices, but the array expects one.
i attempts to input a value into the address of the array.
j `list[100]` is a range error.
k Type names cannot be indexed.

5. `waistSizes`

Value	Index
34	0
36	1
32	2
30	3
33	4

7.
```
for (int i = 0; i < 10; ++i)
    list[i] = 0.0;
```

Section 9.2

1. a. `list`

Value	Index
0	0
0	1
0	2
1	3
1	4

b. `list`

Value	Index
4	0
5	1
6	2
7	3
8	4

`scores`

Value	Index
1	0
1	1
2	2
2	3
2	4

c. `answers`

Value	Index
TRUE	0
FALSE	1
TRUE	2
FALSE	3
TRUE	4
FALSE	5
TRUE	6
FALSE	7
TRUE	8
FALSE	9

d. `initials`

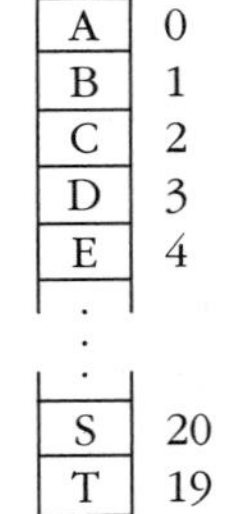

3. The code counts the number of scores that are greater than 90.

5.
```
const int MAX_CHARS = 20;
typedef char nameType[MAX_CHARS];
nameType name;
int length = 0;
char ch;

cin >> ch;
while (ch != •\n•)
{
    name[length] = ch;
    ++length;
    cin >> ch;
}
```

7.
```
for (int i = 0; i < 100; ++i)
    a[i] = 0;
```

9.
```
cout << •Test scores• << endl;
cout << ----------- << endl;
for (int i = 0; i < 50; ++i)
   cout << setw(2) << i << •.• << setw(3) << testScores[i] << endl;
```

Section 9.3

1. **a** is valid.
b is invalid because arrays are declared as reference parameters.
c is valid.
d is invalid because arrays are declared as reference parameters.
e is invalid because a type name is used to declare a parameter name.
f is valid.
g is invalid because name has not been defined as a type.
h is valid.
i is invalid because name has not been defined as a type.
j is invalid because arrays are declared as reference parameters.

3. a.
```
void inputScores(int scores[20]);
inputScores(scores);
```

b.
```
int charCount(char name[50], char ch);
number = charCount(name, •A•);
```

c.
```
void scoreData(int scores[], int &length, int &count90);
scoreData(scores, length, count90);
```

5.
```
void arrayData(int data[MAX_ARRAY_SIZE], int &max,
               int &min, int &negValues)
{
 max = INT_MIN;                     // Initial maximum value.
 min = INT_MAX;                     // Initial minimum value.
 negValues = 0;                     // Initial count negative values.
 for (int i = 0; i < MAX_ARRAY_SIZE; ++i)
    if (data[i] > max)
       max = data[i];
    if (data[i] < min)
       min = data[i];
    if (data[i] < 0)
       ++negvalues;
}
```

Section 9.4

1. `First pass` `Second pass`

First pass		Second pass	
–20	0	–20	0
10	1	–2	1
0	2	0	2
10	3	10	3
8	4	8	4
30	5	30	5
–2	6	10	6

3. We use a new function, `findMaximum`, that locates the largest value in the unsorted portion of the array. On each pass, the largest remaining value will be placed at the end of the sorted portion of the array. Thus, at the end of the process, the array will be sorted from high to low.

```
void sort(int a[ ], int length)
{
   int maxIndex = 0;

   for (int j = 0; j < length - 1; ++j)
   {
      maxIndex = findMaximum(a, j, length);
      if (maxIndex != j)
         swap(a[j],  a[maxIndex]);
   }
}
```

5.

```
void sort(int a[ ], int length, int &count)
{
   int minIndex = 0.
   count = 0;
   for (int j = 0; j < length - 1; ++j)
   {
      minIndex = findMinimum(a, j, length);
      if (minIndex != j)
      {
         swap(a[j],  a[minIndex]);
         ++count;
      }
   }
}
```

7. The sort of the test scores will have no effect on the order of the names. If the test scores are all the same, then there will be no change in the meaning of the table. Otherwise, the names will no longer always be correlated with their test scores.

Section 9.5

1.

```
const int MAX_STORES = 5;
const int MAX_PRICES = 4;
typedef double[MAX_STORES][MAX_PRICES] tableType;
tableType table;
```

3.

```
const int MAX_STUDENTS = 30;
const int MAX_SCORES = 12;
typedef int[MAX_STUDENTS][MAX_SCORES] tableType;
tableType table;
```

Section 9.6

1. **a.** `apvector<int> intVector(20);`
   b. `apvector<char> charVector(100, 'a');`
   c. `apvector<person> personVector(50);`
   d. `apvector<apvector<int> > twentyByTwenty(20);`
3. One indexing operation is a `const` member function that returns the value stored at the index position. The other indexing operation returns a constant reference to the value stored at the index position. Because the second operation returns a constant reference or the address of a cell in the vector, the caller can modify the contents of the cell. Thus, the second operation cannot be used in functions to which vectors are passed by value or constant reference. The first operation can be used in such functions, but for access only.

Section 9.7

3. A string object is an instance of a class. This means that users are restricted to the operations defined by the string class. A C-style string is an array of characters. In general, string objects are safer and more convenient to use than C-style strings.

5. The following function makes use of the `ctype` library function `toupper`:

```
apstring makeUppercase(const apstring &str)
{
   apstring result(str);
   int len = str.length();
   for (int i = 0; i < len; ++i)
      result[i] = toupper(result[i]);
   return result;
}
```

Section 9.8

3. Both index values are checked after the subscript operations for the underlying vectors are invoked.
5. The following function returns the sum of the numbers in a matrix:

```
double sum(const apmatrix<double> &m)
{
   double result = 0;
   for (int row = 0; row < m.numrows(); ++row)
      for (int col = 0; col < m.numcols(); ++col)
         sum = sum + m[row] [col];
   return result;
}
```

CHAPTER 10

Section 10.2

1. Insertion sort provides for a possible early exit from its inner loop. This early exit can potentially reduce the number of comparisons necessary, especially for data that are "almost" in order.
3. Selection sort does not provide for an early exit from either the outer or the inner loop; however, it does guarantee that only n data exchanges will be made—fewer than either insertion or selection sort can guarantee (both require n^2 data exchanges on average).
5.

Original	k=1	k=2	k=3	k=4	k=5	k=6
43	12	12	12	12	12	12
40	40	18	18	18	18	18
18	18	40	24	24	24	24
24	24	24	40	39	39	39
39	39	39	39	40	40	40
60	60	60	60	60	60	43
12	43	43	43	43	43	60

7. This sort algorithm resembles a bubble sort but is different in that small array entries "bubble up" instead of having large array entries "bubble down" on each successive pass. That is, in the bubble sort, we can guarantee that after the kth pass, the *largest* k array entries are in their rightful place, whereas in this sort algorithm, we can guarantee that after the kth pass, the *smallest* k entries are in their rightful place.

Original	k=1	k=2	k=3	k=4	k=5	k=6
43	12	12	12	12	12	12
40	43	18	18	18	18	18
18	40	43	24	24	24	24
24	18	40	43	39	39	39
39	24	24	40	43	40	40
60	39	39	39	40	43	43
12	60	60	60	60	60	60

9. This sort algorithm resembles insertion sort in that it, too, positions the kth element in its rightful place among $k - 1$ entries already in order. The difference between the two sorts lies in the section of the array each has sorted with

each successive iteration. In insertion sort, the *first* $k + 1$ entries are in order after the kth pass; in this sort, the *last* k entries are in order after the kth pass.

Original	k=1	k=2	k=3	k=4	k=5	k=6
43	43	43	43	43	43	12
40	40	40	40	40	12	18
18	18	18	18	12	18	24
24	24	24	12	18	24	39
39	39	12	24	24	39	40
60	12	39	39	39	40	43
12	60	60	60	60	60	60

11. The integers

20
30
40
50
10

or any such arithmetically or alphabetically ordered data cause the bubble sort to make comparisons, but no data are interchanged until the 10 is "bubbled up" to the top. For the insertion sort, the inner loop is shut off after a single comparison, until the final 10 is reached. Then the 10 is inserted at the top.

13.
```
// Same inputs, outputs, and task as insertion sort.
// New logic: move element only after all comparisons
// per loop are finished.
void modifiedInsertionSort(ListType list, int n)
{
int i, j, k, remember;
bool done;

for (k = 1; k < n; ++k)
{
    j = k;
    remember = j;
    done = false;
    while ((j >= 1) && ! done)
          if (list[remember].getKey() <
              list[j - 1].getKey())
              --j;
          else
              done = true;
    if (j != remember)
    {
          for (k = remember; k >= j + 1; --k)
              list[k] = list[k - 1];
          list[j] = list[remember];
    }
}
}
```

Section 10.3

1. a. Inner loop: $m - 6$ repetitions. Outer loop: n repetitions. For each outer loop repetition, the inner loop is traversed $m - 6$ times. Therefore, $(m - 6) \times n$ overall repetitions are performed. This is $O(mn)$.

b. The inner loop will be executed $\log_2 n$ times and the outer loop will be executed n times. Thus, the loops are $O(n\log_2 n)$.

c. The inner `do...while` is executed $n/2$ times for each execution of the outer loop. The outer `do...while` is executed n times. Thus, there are $n \times (n/2)$ repetitions. Thus, the loops are $O(n^2)$.

3. The efficiency of the algorithm in question is constant—32 operations—for all input. Remembering that in big-O analysis we are concerned primarily with the order of magnitude of the algorithm's efficiency, we write this algorithm's efficiency as $O(1) * 32$. And recalling that constants bear no importance except in comparing algorithms with the same big-O, we drop the constant 32 to arrive at the big-O that most accurately characterizes the algorithm—$O(1)$.

5. **a.** The $n^3\log_2 n$ term dominates and this is $O(n^3\log_2 n)$.
b. The 4^n exponential term will (eventually) dominate any polynomial terms. Thus, this is $O(4^n)$.
c. The 2^n exponential term will (eventually) dominate any polynomial terms. Thus, this is $O(2^n)$.

7. For this small set of integers, the trace of the insertion sort is

20	20	20	20	10
30	30*	30	30	20
40	40	40*	40	30
50	50	50	50*	40
10	10	10	10	50

The inner loop of the insertion sort is "shut off" after one comparison for each value of K, until the "bottom" 10 is reached. At that point, four swaps are required to move it into the "top" position. For these almost ordered data, the insertion sort is $O(n)$.

9. Since n^2 dominates $n^2 + \log_2 n$, $O(n^2 + \log_2 n)$ is the same as $O(n^2)$. Hence, we have the following answers for a–d:
a. You are both correct for any algorithm whose performance is dominated by a term such as n^k for $k > 2$ or a^n for any base $a > 1$.
b. You are both wrong for any linear or logarithmic algorithm.
c. no
d. no

Section 10.4

1.

Original	K=1 J=0	K=1 J=1	K=1 J=2	K=1 J=3	K=1 J=4	K=1 J=5
0	1	1	1	1	1	1
1	0	2	2	2	2	2
2	2	0	3	3	3	3
3	3	3	0	4	4	4
4	4	4	4	0	5	5
5	5	5	5	5	0	6
6	6	6	6	6	6	0

K=2 J=0	K=2 J=1	K=2 J=2	K=2 J=3	K=2 J=4
2	2	2	2	2
1	1	1	1	1
3	3	4	4	4
4	4	3	5	5
5	5	5	3	6
6	6	6	6	3
0	0	0	0	0

K=3 J=0	K=3 J=1	K=3 J=2	K=3 J=3
2	2	2	2
1	4	4	4
4	1	1	1
5	5	5	6
6	6	6	5
3	3	3	3
0	0	0	0

K=4 J=0	K=4 J=1	K=4 J=2
2	2	2
4	4	4
1	1	6
6	6	1
5	5	5
3	3	3
0	0	0

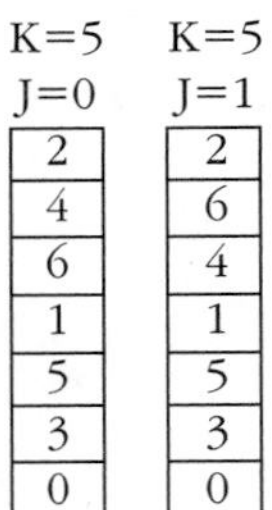

K=5 J=0	K=5 J=1
2	2
4	6
6	4
1	1
5	5
3	3
0	0

K=6 J=0
6
2
4
1
5
3
0

3. Ten passes would be made through the outer `while` loop of the radix sort algorithm because the length of the longest data item is ten characters. It is assumed that strings are padded with space beyond their last alphabetical character.

Pass 0:
List: CHOCOLATE VANILLA CARAMEL PEACH STRAWBERRY CHERRY

Pass 1:
Bins:
  Space: CHOCOLATE VANILLA CARAMEL PEACH CHERRY
  Y: STRAWBERRY
List: CHOCOLATE VANILLA CARAMEL PEACH CHERRY STRAWBERRY

Pass 2:
Bins:
  Space: VANILLA CARAMEL PEACH CHERRY
  E: CHOCOLATE
  R: STRAWBERRY
List: VANILLA CARAMEL PEACH CHERRY CHOCOLATE STRAWBERRY

Pass 3:
Bins:
  Space: VANILLA CARAMEL PEACH CHERRY
  R: STRAWBERRY
  T: CHOCOLATE
List: VANILLA CARAMEL PEACH CHERRY STRAWBERRY CHOCOLATE

Pass 4:
Bins:
Space: PEACH CHERRY
A: VANILLA CHOCOLATE
E: STRAWBERRY
L: CARAMEL
List: PEACH CHERRY VANILLA CHOCOLATE STRAWBERRY CARAMEL

Pass 5:
Bins:
Space: PEACH
B: STRAWBERRY
E: CARAMEL
L: VANILLA CHOCOLATE
Y: CHERRY
List: PEACH STRAWBERRY CARAMEL VANILLA CHOCOLATE CHERRY

Pass 6:
Bins:
H: PEACH
L: VANILLA
M: CARAMEL
O: CHOCOLATE
R: CHERRY
W: STRAWBERRY
List: PEACH VANILLA CARAMEL CHOCOLATE CHERRY STRAWBERRY

Pass 7:
Bins:
A: CARAMEL STRAWBERRY
C: PEACH CHOCOLATE
I: VANILLA
R: CHERRY
List: CARAMEL STRAWBERRY PEACH CHOCOLATE VANILLA CHERRY

Pass 8:
Bins:
A: PEACH
E: CHERRY
N: VANILLA
O: CHOCOLATE
R: CARAMEL STRAWBERRY
List: PEACH CHERRY VANILLA CHOCOLATE CARAMEL STRAWBERRY

Pass 9:
Bins:
A: VANILLA CARAMEL
E: PEACH
H: CHERRY CHOCOLATE
T: STRAWBERRY
List: VANILLA CARAMEL PEACH CHERRY CHOCOLATE STRAWBERRY

Pass 10:
Bins:
C: CARAMEL CHERRY CHOCOLATE
P: PEACH

S: STRAWBERRY
V: VANILLA
List: CARAMEL CHERRY CHOCOLATE PEACH STRAWBERRY VANILLA

5. An application in which the array of data items consumed all available memory does not have the space necessary to store the array of pointers.

7. Although the introduction of pointers into the bubble sort routine will not improve its $O(n^2)$ nature, there will most likely be an increase in run-time efficiency. This is because physical swapping of data is drastically reduced. If the data to be swapped were records with numerous fields of records themselves, many machine operations are involved. But with pointers, only integers need be swapped, involving many fewer machine operations.

9. The pointer strategy has the least effect on selection sort because it guarantees a fewer number of data exchanges (only one per outer loop iteration) than either of the other sorts. Since the pointer sort affects the efficiency of data exchanges and since fewer swaps are made with selection sort, less overall time is saved with selection sort than with the other two sorting algorithms; these sorting algorithms swap more often and therefore benefit more significantly from improved swapping efficiency.

11.

```
// Function: pointerSelectionSort
// Selection sort logic using pointers
//
// Inputs: a list of data values, a list of pointers,
//          and n, the logical size of the list
// Output: the list of pointers pointing to sorted data
void pointerSelectionSort(ListType  list,
   IntArray pointers, int n)
{
int minPosition, temp;
for (int k = 0; k < n - 2; ++k)
{
   minPosition = pointer[k];
   for (int j = k + 1; j < n - 1; ++j)
       if (list[pointer[j]].getKey( ) <
           list[minPosition].getKey( ))
           minPosition = pointer[j];
   temp = pointer[k];
   pointer[k] = pointer[minPosition];
   pointer[midPosition] = temp;
}
}
```

13.

```
// Function: digit
// Determine the kth digit of a number
//
// Inputs: integers number and k
// Output: the kth digit of number
int digit(int number, int k)
{
   int p = pow(10, k);
   int q = pow(10, k - 1);
   return (number - p * (number / p)) / q;
}
```

Section 10.5

1. Initial array with `low, high,` and `middle = (high + low) / 2.` `target` is 43. `found` is `false` to begin.

Low ↓				Mid ↓					High ↓
0	1	2	3	4	5	6	7	8	9
18	40	46	50	52	58	63	70	77	90

Since 43 < 52, high points to 3.

Low Mid High

0	1	2	3	4	5	6	7	8	9
18	40	46	50	52	58	63	70	77	90

Since 43 > 40, low points to 2.

Mid
Low High

0	1	2	3	4	5	6	7	8	9
18	40	46	50	52	58	63	70	77	90

Since 43 < 46, high points to 1 and the search ends with `found = false`.

3. A symbol table is a list of the identifiers that have been declared in a program and which the compiler continually searches as the program is compiled. Since the sequential search is $O(n)$, the continual searching of the symbol table uses up too much time to be practical.
5. 21 or fewer times
7. This version of the binary search will work correctly provided the variable n never comes in as 0 (indicating an empty list). In this situation, `middle` will be computed to be 0, which will generate an array index out-of-range error.
11. Although still $O(n)$ in its efficiency, the code for this version of the algorithm can reduce the number of comparisons by a factor of 2. This is because we need not test for the sentinel and the target data each time through the loop.

CHAPTER 11

Section 11.1

1. The physical size of an array is the number of cells of memory allocated for storing data in it. The logical size of the array is the number of data values currently stored in it that have meaning for a program.
3. The addition of a Boolean flag to the removal operation places a slight burden on the implementer and makes the operation's interface more complex. However, removals will be more efficient in that only one search will be necessary to determine that the target is in the collection and to remove it.
9. The following free function concatenates two ordered collections:

```
template <class E>
orderedCollection<E> operator +
    (const orderedCollection<E> &lhs,
    const orderedCollection<E> &rhs)
{
    orderedCollection<E> result(lhs);     // Copy lhs
    for (int i = 0; i < rhs.length(); ++i)    // Copy rhs
       result.add_last(rhs[i]);
    return result;
}
```

Section 11.2

1.

```
template <class E>
sortedCollection<E>& sortedCollection<E>::operator = (const
             sortedCollection<E> &sc)
{
   for (int i = 0; i < sc.cLength; ++i)
      data[i] = sc.data[i];
   cLength = sc.cLength;
   return *this;
}
```

continued

```
template <class E>
const E& sortedCollection<E>::operator [ ] (int index)
{
   assert((index >= 0) && (index < cLength));
   return data[index];
}
```

3. The index operator for ordered collections allows references to elements as l-values or as r-values. A sorted collection object should not allow references to elements as l-values because clients could then store elements that might violate the ordering of the elements in the collection.

Section 11.3

3. Because the keys are physically ordered in the array, we can do a binary search for the position where we should insert the new key. The search process will thus be logarithmic. However, the data movement required to make room for the new value in the array will still be linear, so the overall behavior of the algorithm will still be linear.
5. The answer to this problem is the same as the answer to Exercise 3.
7. The ordered and sorted collection ADTs allow data to be accessed by key values that are numeric index positions. However, data can be added to or removed from the beginning or end of an ordered collection, or can simply be added to a sorted collection, without specifying a key.

Section 11.4

3. The abstract specification of operations on a three-key table is:

Create Operation

Preconditions:	Receiver is an arbitrary three-key table in an unpredictable state.
Postconditions:	Receiver is initialized to an empty table.

Empty Operation

Preconditions:	Receiver is a three-key table.
Postconditions:	If receiver contains no objects, the Boolean value `true` is returned; otherwise, the Boolean value `false` is returned.

Store Operation

Preconditions:	Receiver is a three-key table. `key1` is the key1 value. `key2` is the key2 value. `key3` is the key3 value. `item` is an object to be inserted in receiver. If `key1`, `key2`, and `key3` do not specify an item already in the table, there is memory available to store item.
Postconditions:	If an object is already associated with `key1`, `key2`, and `key3` in the table, it is replaced by item. Otherwise, the table has `item` inserted and associated with the `key1`, `key2`, and `key3` values.

Remove Operation

Preconditions:	Receiver is a two-key table. `key1`, `key2`, and `key3` are the key values associated with an object to be removed from the table.
Postconditions:	If the object with the key values `key1`, `key2`, and `key3` can be found in the table, it is removed from the table, `item` contains the object associated with the key values `key1`, `key2`, and `key3`, and the operation returns `true`. Otherwise, the operation returns `false`, *item*'s contents are undefined, and the table is left unchanged.

Retrieve Operation

Preconditions:	Receiver is a two-key table. `key1`, `key2`, and `key3` are the key values associated with an object to be found in the table.
Postconditions:	If the pairing of `key1`, `key2`, and `key3` can be found in the table, then *item* contains the object associated with `key1`, `key2`, and `key3`, and the operation returns `true`. Otherwise, the operation returns `false`, and `item`'s contents are undefined. In either case, the table is left unchanged.

Section 11.5

3. A sample of a user requirements specification for a baseball team might appear as follows:
   The baseball recordkeeping system should present its user with a main menu that allows the following options:

- Add a new player to the team.
- After a game, enter the player's statistics for that game. For pitchers, these statistics are number of innings pitched, runs allowed, strikeouts, and whether a win or loss was recorded. For nonpitchers, these statistics are number of at-bats, hits, home runs, and runs batted in.
- At periodic intervals during the baseball season, allow the user to print out a report showing the cumulative statistics for each player on the team.

Section 11.6

3. Examples of classes that might emerge from the user requirements specification in Exercise 3 of Section 11.5 are:

Class	Role
team	This class will store the records of all players on the team.
pitcher	This class will store the data for an individual pitcher.
batter	This class will store the data for an individual nonpitcher.

The CRC design specifications for the team class are:

Knows: the list of all players on the team

Create Operation
Preconditions: Team is in an arbitrary state.
Postconditions: Team is initialized to a team with no players.

Add Pitcher Operation
Preconditions: Team has been created; *p* is a pitcher.
Postconditions: *p* has been added to the team.

Add Batter Operation
Preconditions: Team has been created; *b* is a batter.
Postconditions: *b* has been added to the team.

Report Operation
Preconditions: Team has been created.
Postconditions: Cumulative statistics for all players on team have been displayed.

The CRC design specifications for the pitcher class are:

Knows: total innings pitched, total runs allowed, total strikeouts, total wins, total losses

Create Operation
Preconditions: Pitcher is in an arbitrary state.
Postconditions: Pitcher is initialized with zeroes for all cumulative statistics.

Enter Game Data Operation
Preconditions: Pitcher has been created.
Postconditions: User has been able to enter the statistics for one game for the pitcher.

Display Operation
Preconditions: Pitcher has been created.
Postconditions: Cumulative statistics for the pitcher have been displayed.

The CRC design specifications for the batter class is analogous to those for the pitcher class.

Section 11.7

3. Test data for the function to compute an employee's pay are:

Test Case	Employee Type	Annual or Hourly Wage	Hours Worked (if hourly worker)	Holiday Hours (if hourly worker)	Expected Results	Rationale
I	Annual	$52,000	N/A	N/A	$1,000	Only test case needed for annual employee
II	Hourly	$10.00	30	0	$ 300	Normal hours only—no overtime and no holiday pay
III	Hourly	$10.00	40	0	$ 400	Boundary case in which no overtime should be given
IV	Hourly	$10.00	45	0	$ 475	Overtime but no holiday pay
V	Hourly	$10.00	30	10	$ 500	Holiday pay but no overtime
VI	Hourly	$10.00	50	10	$ 700	Holiday pay and overtime
VII	Hourly	$10.00	0	10	$ 200	Only holiday pay

CHAPTER 12

Section 12.1

1. The total number of times values in the array underlying the ordered collection will have to be copied is $1 + 2 + 3 + \ldots + n$, or $1/2\ n^2 + 1/2\ n$. Hence, $O(n^2)$ is the appropriate big-O categorization.

3. Removal of a given data value requires the most work in that a linear search for the value must be performed. Otherwise, $O(n)$ copies must be performed for all insertions and removals.

Section 12.2

1. Ordered collections and linked lists both represent linear sequences of data values. Ordered collections allow access to data elements in constant time. Linked lists allow access to data elements in linear time. Ordered collections are resized in linear time. Linked lists are resized in constant time.

3. The `atEnd` operation returns `false` when the current pointer is referencing a node in the list. Only in this case is it safe to access, modify, remove, or move to the next node.

5. The length of the list has to be computed by counting the number of nodes, thus resulting in a linear process each time the length is requested.

7. One could redefine the assignment operator for a vector so that a linked list is the parameter and the contents of the list are copied to the end of the vector. This operation usefully transfers data after input from a file to a structure more suitable for fast access times during processing.

9.

```
// Note: This logic uses zero to indicate first position in the list
int positionOfFirstZero(LinkedList<int> &list)
{
 int data, position;
 bool found = false;

 if (list.empty())
     return -1;
 else
 {
     list.first();
     position = 0;
     while (! found && (position < list.length()))
     {
         if (list.access() == 0)
             found = TRUE;
         else
         {
```

```
                ++position;
                list.next();
            }
        }
        if (found)
            return position;
        else
            return -1;
    }
}
```

11.
```
int sum(LinkedList<int> list)
{
 int total, data;
 total = 0;
 list.first();
 while  (! list.atEnd())
 {
      total = total + list.access();
      list.next();
 }
 return total;
}
```

Section 12.3

3. An algorithm for an operation to add a data value to the end of a linked list is:
   While not at the end of the list
      Move to the next node
   Run the insert operation
   The worst case efficiency for this operation is $O(n)$.
5. An algorithm for an index operation for a linked list is:
   Assert that 0 <= index < length of list
   Move to the first node
   While index > 0
      Move to the next node
      Decrement index by 1
   Return the data value in the current node
   Note that the operation should return a constant reference to the data value so that users can target the data cell for assignment. This operation will be $O(n)$ in its efficiency.

Section 12.4

1. An address is the label of a cell in memory. The value stored at an address is contained in the cell labeled by the address.
5. **a, d,** and **f** are syntactically correct.
   b is incorrect—cannot assign an integer to a pointer variable.
   c is incorrect—cannot use a type name to refer to a member of a structure.
   e is incorrect—cannot delete an integer.
7. The statement:

```
a->next->next = b;
```

affects the deletion of the second node.

9.
```
a->next->next->next->next = a;
a = a->next;
a->next->next->next->next = NULL;
```

Section 12.5

1. Create operation—$O(1)$
   Empty operation—$O(1)$
   Length operation—$O(1)$
   Store operation—$O(n)$
   Remove operation—$O(n)$
   Retrieve operation—$O(n)$
3. Create operation—$O(1)$
   Length operation—$O(1)$
   Indexing operation (for observation of a data element only)—$O(n)$
   Assignment operation—$O(n)$
   Add operation—$O(n)$
   Remove last operation (provided you maintain a pointer to the last node)—$O(1)$
   Remove first operation—$O(1)$
   Remove operation—$O(n)$

CHAPTER 13

Section 13.1

1.

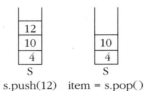

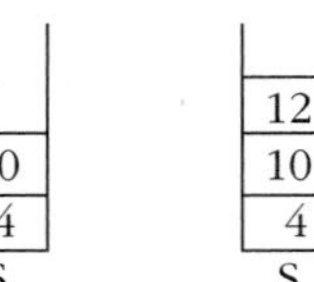

5. The stack grows and shrinks as follows:

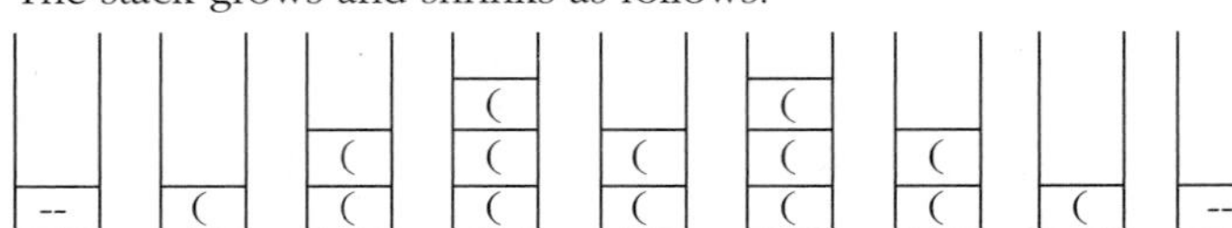

7. As each character is read, push it onto a stack. Once the end of the line is reached, pop and print each character on the stack.

Section 13.2

1. Infix: A + B * C − D/P − R
   Postfix: ABCD − PR −/* +
   Prefix: + A * B/ − CD − PD

3.

Ch	OpStack	Postfix	Commentary
#			Push #
P			Read Ch
		P	Append Ch to Postfix
+			Read Ch
	+ #		Push Ch
(			Read Ch
	+ (#		Push Ch
Q			Read Ch
		PQ	Append Ch to Postfix
–			Read Ch
	– (+ #		Push Ch
F			Read Ch
		PQF	Append Ch
)		Read Ch	
	+ #	PQF–	Pop and Append
/			Read Ch
	/ + #		Push Ch
Y			Read Ch
		PQF–Y	Append Ch
#			Read Ch
		PQF–Y/+#	Pop and Append rest of stack

9. If operand A has a stack priority that is greater than or equal to the infix priority of operand B, then A has equal or greater operator precedence; therefore, it is appended to the postfix string before B and will be applied before B. Such precedence, however, can be overridden by parentheses, which force the operators between them to be unconditionally appended to the postfix string, regardless of their stack priority. In summary, the order in which operators are appended to the postfix string is dictated by stack priority relative to infix priority; equal or greater stack priority indicates either higher operator precedence (if the two operators being compared are different) or left-associativity (if the two operators being compared are the same). Hence, if we want to make the ^ operator right-associative, we merely make its infix priority greater than its stack priority. Our infix and stack priority functions then appear as follows:

Priority	*	/	+	–	(	)	^	#
Infix	2	2	1	1	5	0	4	0
Stack	2	2	1	1	0	undefined	3	0

The adjusted infix and stack priorities reflect both the fact that exponentiation has the highest operator precedence and the fact that all operators except exponentiation are left-associative.

Section 13.3

3. **a.** Introduce an integer variable `minutesIdle`, which is initialized to 0 before entering the `for` loop. We then add the following `else` clause to the `if ((timeLeftOnCar == 0) && carQueue.empty())` clause:

```
else if ((timeLeftOnCar == 0) && carQueue.empty())
  //This minute is idle
  ++minutesIdle;
```

b. To make this count, we merely dequeue the queue of cars until it is empty after we have exited the `for` loop. In C++, this amounts to introducing an integer variable `carsRemaining`, which we initialize to zero before dequeuing begins:

```
int carsRemaining = 0;
```

Now we are prepared to execute a `while` loop:

```
while (! carQueue.empty())
{
  minute = carQueue.dequeue();
  ++carsRemaining;
}
```

CHAPTER 14

Section 14.1

3. **a.** 92
6
14

b. 14
6
92

Note, however, that because this function neglects to test `head` for being the null pointer before referencing it, the program may behave mysteriously at run time.

c. 14
6

Note that because this function neglects to test `head` for being the null pointer before it references `head->next`, the program may behave mysteriously at run time when the empty list is passed in for `head`.

5. Program a will achieve the original intent presented. Its output is

```
MADAM
```

Program b will fail because it globally declares the characters being read, so the recursive calls do not result in copies of the characters being pushed onto the system stack. Consequently, only the last character read is remembered and written when the recursion unwinds. Its output is

```
MMMMM
```

7. This function computes the smallest value in the `NumberArray` within the index range 0 . . . *n*, where *n* is the value originally passed in.

Section 14.2

5. The output is:

```
1 16
9 16
9 11
9 16
```

7. The stack frames for this function should contain three pieces of information: the current value of M, the current value of N, and the point in the program to which to return.

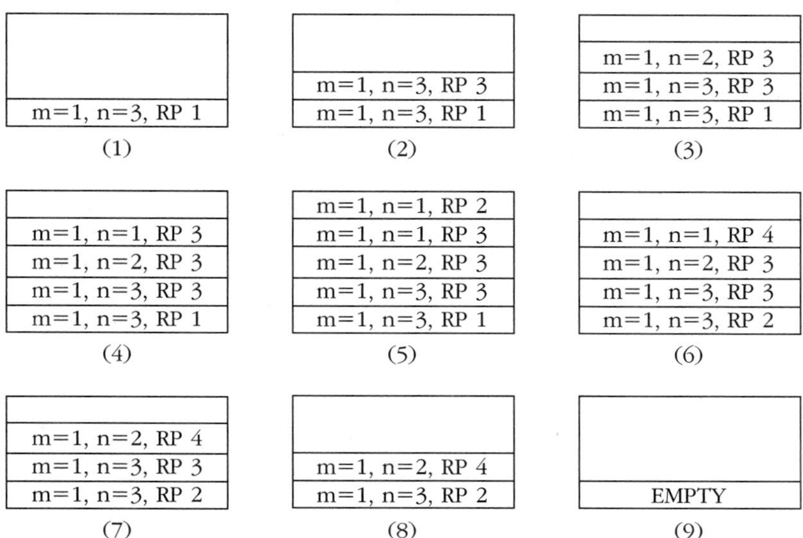

The output is:

```
1 3
1 2
1 1
1 0
0 1
0 2
0 3
0 4
5
```

11. *Hint:* Consider the number of ways that M can be broken down into quarters and dimes plus the number of ways that (M = 50 cents) can be broken down into half dollars, quarters, and dimes. The total of these two provide the answer in terms of quantities that are (recursively) easier to compute.

Section 14.3

5. The output is:

```
12 1 2 3 4 3 3 4
 4 3 4 2 2 3 4 3
 3 4 4 3 4 3 2 3
 4 3 3 4 4 3 4 4
 2 3 4 3 3 4 4 3
 4
```

Section 14.4

1. a.

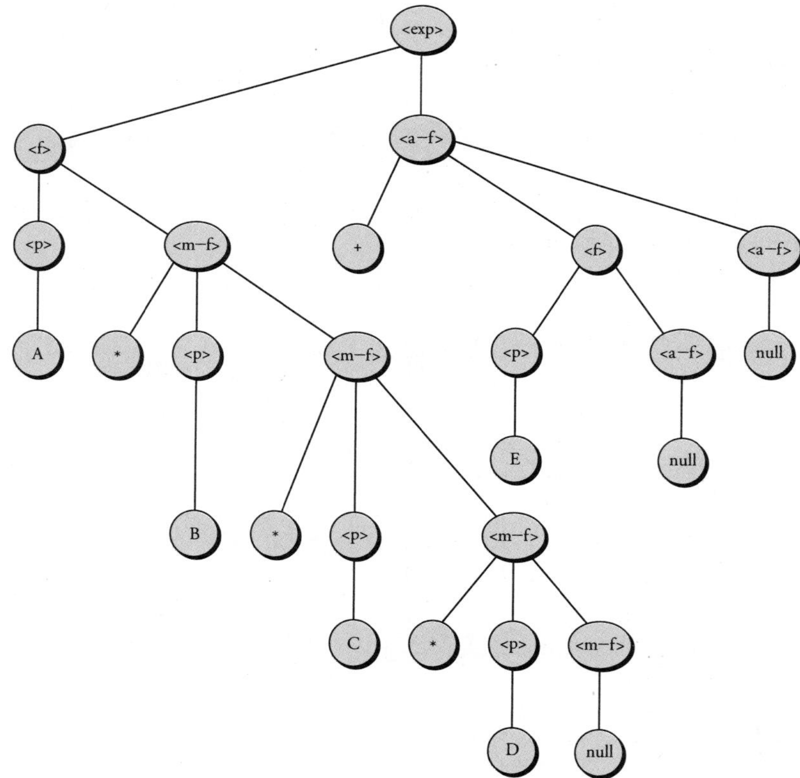

3. a. yes

b. Here is the parse tree for the expression from Exercise 1a:

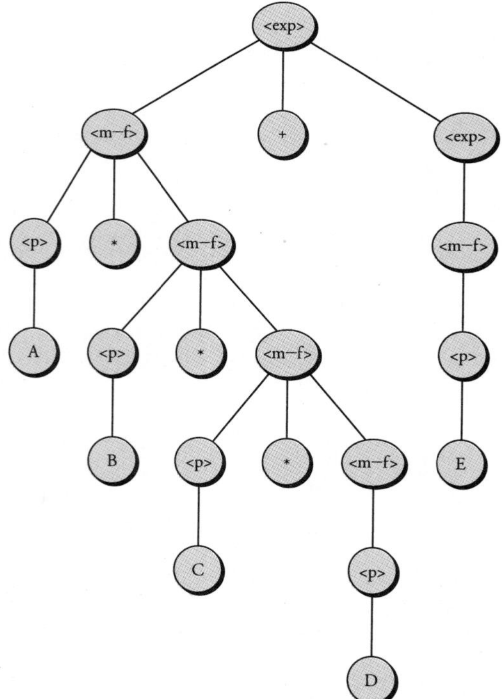

d. The grammar of this exercise has right-to-left associativity for the operators + and *, whereas the grammar of 14.10 has left-to-right associativity for these two operators.

5. `<if-statement>` → `if <condition> then <statement>`
→ `if <condition> then <statement> else <statement>`

We assume `<statement>` is also defined.

Two different parse trees may be derived from this grammar. Hence, this grammar is ambiguous. In the two diagrams below, let `<s>` correspond to `<statement>`, `<c>` correspond to `<condition>`, and `<ifs>` correspond to `<if-statement>`. The interpretation C++ uses for `if-then-else` corresponds to the first parse tree.

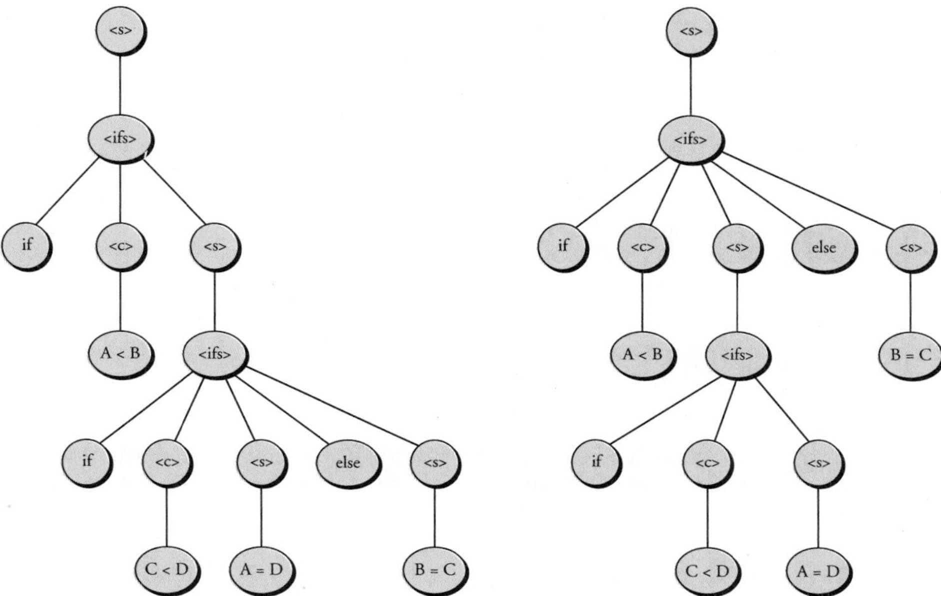

CHAPTER 15

Section 15.1

1.

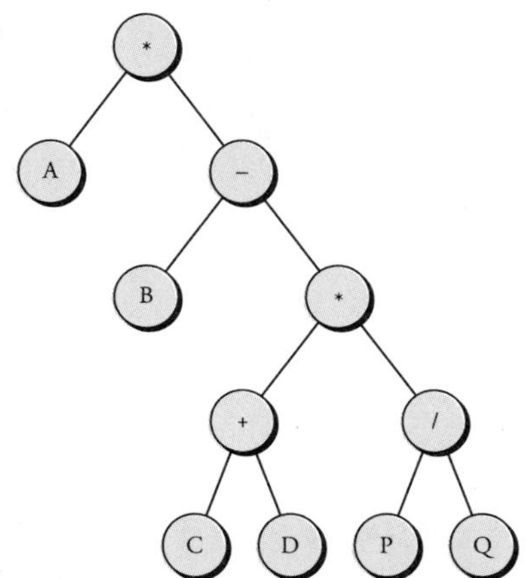

3. A tree is a hierarchically ordered data structure consisting of nodes and links to nodes. A tree is accessed by a node called the root.

5. **a** and **c** are binary trees with the heap property.
b is not because the node containing 35 is a subtree of the node containing 19. The situation is similar for the node containing 39.

9. a.

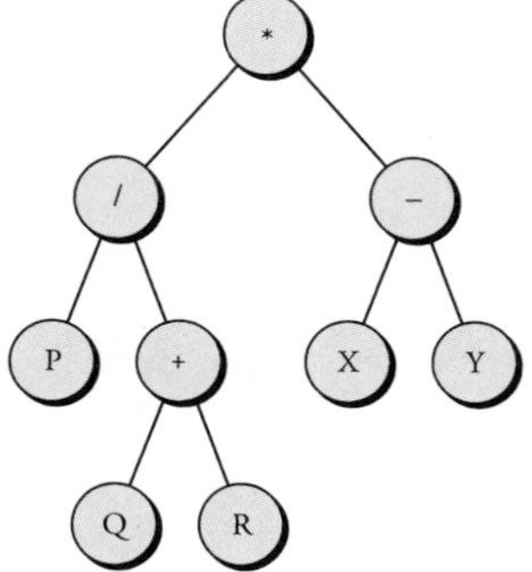

c.

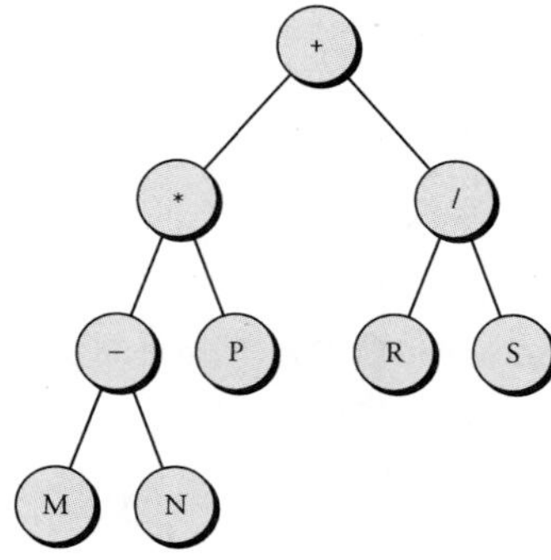

Section 15.2

1. * A − B * + C D / P Q

3. Note that the orders of arrival are not unique for each problem. Some variation is possible between the left and right subtree arrival order. There are several possible answers for each of these exercises.

a. 30 10 5 40 45 20 or 30 40 10 20 5 45

b. 40 50 20 10 60 55 30

c. 40 50 20 10 30

5. A C G I K H J B E D

7. With output after recursive calls: T Y X B G F H N M Z A
With output before recursive calls: A B Y T X Z F G M N H
With output between recursive calls: Y T B X A F G Z H N M

17. As each node is visited during the traversal, its data contents are placed at the logical end of the structure (an array or file, perhaps) or device (output on a terminal screen, perhaps). At the end of the traversal, the data will appear in sorted order in the destination structure or on the destination device.

Section 15.3

1. **a** is full.
b and **c** are not full.

5. **b** is full.

Section 15.4

1.

Item	1	2	3	4	5	6	7	8	9	10
10	10									

Item	1	2	3	4	5	6	7	8	9	10
20	20	10								

Item	1	2	3	4	5	6	7	8	9	10
30	30	10	20							

Item	1	2	3	4	5	6	7	8	9	10
40	40	30	20	10						

Item	1	2	3	4	5	6	7	8	9	10
50	50	40	20	10	30					

Item	1	2	3	4	5	6	7	8	9	10
60	60	40	50	10	30	20				

Item	1	2	3	4	5	6	7	8	9	10
70	70	40	60	10	30	20	50			

Item	1	2	3	4	5	6	7	8	9	10
80	80	70	60	40	30	20	50	10		

Item	1	2	3	4	5	6	7	8	9	10
90	90	80	60	70	30	20	50	10	40	

Item	1	2	3	4	5	6	7	8	9	10
100	100	90	60	70	80	20	50	10	40	30

Section 15.5

1. The indentation can be obtained by increasing the indentation before traversing the left (child) subtree and decreasing the indentation again before traversing the right (sibling) subtree.
3. Preorder traversal

```
P Q T U V C D E M N O W A G B H I J X K L
```

Section 15.6

1. The order of the nodes is Seattle, Chicago, Miami, New Orleans, Dallas, New York City, Washington, Milwaukee, Phoenix, San Francisco, Los Angeles, Las Vegas, Minneapolis, Oklahoma City.
3. One way the cities could be visited is Seattle, Chicago, San Francisco, Miami, New Orleans, Las Vegas, Milwaukee, Los Angeles, Dallas, Washington, Phoenix, Minneapolis, New York City, Oklahoma City.
9. Eliminating the requirement that the node be a subrange of an ordinal type means that there is not a convenient way to index the nodes in the graph, making the normal operations more difficult to perform. One strategy to overcome that problem is to build an indexing scheme that makes use of a two-key table.

CHAPTER 16

Section 16.1

1.
```
60  12  90  20  64   8   6  8  12   6  20  64  90  60  6  12
8  20  60  90  64  6   8  12  20  60  64  90
```

3. The shell sort is named after its inventor D. L. Shell.
5. Relatively prime values of the increments are better because they ensure distinct increments that will not divide evenly into each other so that data that have been compared to each other are less likely to be compared again.
7. The best case for the shell sort algorithm presented in this section is a data set with the data already in order: Each segment is in order and no data need to be swapped. The worst case is a data set arranged in descending order because every data element is out of order and there are a maximum number of data swaps.

Section 16.2

1. The output is:

```
1  7
60 12 90 30 64 8 6

1  4
6 12 8 30

2 4
12 8 30

2 2
8

4 4
30

6 7
64 90

7 7
90
```

3. The bubble sort is better than the quick sort when the data are already in order. The bubble sort can safely conclude that the data are in order after the first pass through the data; the quick sort must perform the entire sort even if the data are already in order.
5. The choice of the pivotal point will not change the overall efficiency of the quick sort; however, it does dramatically change the best and worst data sets.

9. Change the instruction

```
pivot = key[low];
```

to

```
// Assume that medianOf3 gives the index of the median of three values
// located at indices low, high, (low+high)/2 in array key.
pivotIndex = medianOf3(key, low, high);
temp = key[lo];
key[lo] = key[pivotIndex];
key[pivotIndex] = key[lo];
```

This should be more efficient because the pivot value is more likely to split the array being sorted more evenly. Quick sort is most efficient when the array is split at the midpoint.

Section 16.3

1.

```
60 12 90 30 64  8  6
60 12 90 30 64  8  6
60 64 90 30 12  8  6
 6 64 60 30 12  8 90
 8 30 60  6 12 64 90
12 30  8  6 60 64 90
 6 12  8 30 60 64 90
 8  6 12 30 60 64 90
 6  8 12 30 60 64 90
```

3. The sort derives its name from the heap structure that it uses in sorting the data.

5. The heap sort is not always as efficient as the quick sort. On average, the quick sort is slightly better than the heap sort because its big-O constant of proportionality will be smaller. However, the heap sort handles data already sorted much faster than the quick sort.

Section 16.4

1. The output for merge sort is:

```
1  7
60 12 90 30 64 8 6
1  4
60 12 90 30
1  2
60 12
1 1
60
2  2
60 12
2  2
60 12
```

and so on.

CHAPTER 17

Section 17.1

1. a. The keys have the following positions:

Record No.	Key
0	333
1	632
2	1090
3	459
4	379
5	238
6	
7	
8	
9	1982
10	3411

c. With the chaining method, the keys and links are:

Record No.	Key	Link
0	333	13
1	632	0
2	1090	0
3		
4		
5		
6		
7		
8		
9	1982	12
10		
11	3411	13
12	459	0
13	379	14
14	238	0
15		
16		
17		
18		
19		
20		
21		

Section 17.2

1. As suggested in the text, the doubly linked list is the best choice for implementing linked lists with hashing. When the order of the list is disturbed during a change of a key field or during a deletion of an item in the list, the linked list must be rebuilt. If a doubly linked list is not used, the list has to be traversed to find the predecessor node in the linked list. The doubly linked list makes rebuilding lists more efficient.

5. a. The best method to implement the card catalog in this situation is hashing. Hashing allows for very quick searches and is fairly good at handling additions and deletions. Since the library rarely prints out an ordered list of books, the time it takes to sort the list doesn't really matter.

c. The best method to implement the database is the binary search. The states are kept in order by a two-letter code. All the program need do is access the record quickly, increment a field, and print the list out in order. All these are handled very well by a binary search.

Section 17.3

1. a.

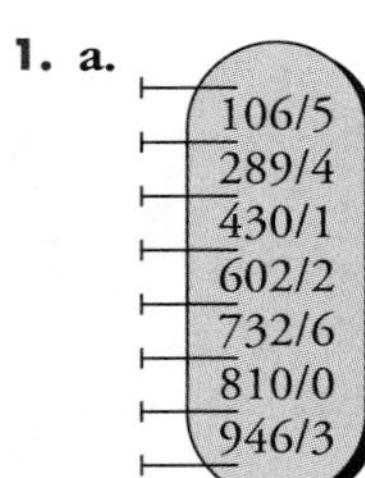

5. a. For the ISAM index, this knowledge will enable us to set the index so that the subsequent search on the disk will be more efficient.

c. The trie is constructed the same no matter what the disk structure may be.

Index

A

B

K

L

Credits

This page constitutes an extension of the copyright page. We have made every effort to trace the ownership of all copyrighted material and to secure permission for copyright holders. In the event of any question arising as to the use of any material, we will be pleased to make the necessary corrections in future printings. Thanks are due to the following authors, publishers, and agents for permission to use the material indicated.

Photos

Pages 10-11, Figures 1.4, 1.5a, 1.5b, 1.5c, and 1.6b: Courtesy of IBM Corporation.

Pages 10-11, Figures 1.5d and 1.6a: Courtesy of Apple Computer, Inc.

Page 11, Figure 1.8: Robert Barclay.

Notes of Interest

Page 23: Software Verification

From Ivars Peterson, "Finding Fault: The Formidable Task of Eradicating Software Bugs," *Science News,* February 16, 1991, Vol. 139. Reprinted with permission from *Science News.* Copyright 1991 by Science Services, Inc. Photo courtesy of Ontario Hydro.

Page 56: Herman Hollerith

Reprinted by permission from *Introduction to Computers with BASIC,* pp. 27-28, by Fred G. Harold. Copyright 1984 by West Publishing Company. All rights reserved.

Page 78: *Defined Constants and Space Shuttle Computing Communications of the ACM 27,* No. 9 (September 1984); 880. Copyright 1984, Association for Computing Machinery, Inc. Reprinted by permission of Association for Computing Machinery, Inc.

Page 117: Computer Ethics: Hacking and Other Intrusions

Reprinted by permission from *Computers Under Attack: Intruders, Worms, and Viruses,* pp. 150-155, edited by Peter J. Denning, Article 7, "The West German Hacker Incident and Other Intrusions," by Mel Mandell. Copyright 1990, Association for Computing Machinery, Inc.

Page 162: George Boole

Adapted from William Dunham, *Journey Through Genius: The Great Theorems of Mathematics,* John Wiley & Sons, 1990. Photo: Corbis/The Bettmann Archive.

Page 176: Artificial Intelligence

Reprinted by permission from *The Mind Tool,* Fifth ed., pp. 394-398, by Neill Graham. Copyright 1989 by West Publishing Company. All rights reserved.

Page 199: A Software Glitch

From Ivars Peterson, "Finding Fault: The Formidable Task of Eradicating Software Bugs," *Science News,* February 16, 1991, Vol. 139. Reprinted with permission from *Science News.* Copyright 1991 by Science Services, Inc.

Page 234: Charles Babbage

Reprinted by permission from *Introduction to Computers with BASIC,* pp. 24-26, by Fred G. Harold. Copyright 1984 by West Publishing Company. All rights reserved.

Page 243: Ada Augusta Byron

Reprinted by permission from *Introduction to Computers with BASIC,* pp. 26-27, by Fred G. Harold. Copyright 1984 by West Publishing Company. All rights reserved. Photo: Corbis/The Bettmann Archive.

Page 262: A Digital Matter of Life and Death

From Ivars Peterson, "A Digital Matter of Life and Death," *Science News,* March 12, 1988, Vol. 133. Reprinted with permission from *Science News.* Copyright 1988 by Science Services, Inc.